Microsoft

Microsoft®
SQL Server™ 2000

Resource Kit

PUBLISHED BY
Microsoft Press
A Division of Microsoft Corporation
One Microsoft Way
Redmond, Washington 98052-6399

Library of Congress Cataloging-in-Publication Data
Microsoft SQL Server 2000 Resource Kit / Microsoft Corporation.
      p. cm.
   ISBN 0-7356-1266-8
   Includes index.
    1. SQL server.   2. Client/server computing.   I. Microsoft Corporation.
 QA76.9.C55 M5325   2001
 005.75'6--dc21   00-069442

Printed and bound in the United States of America.

3 4 5 6 7 8 9   QWT   7 6 5 4 3 2

Distributed in Canada by H.B. Fenn and Company Ltd.

A CIP catalogue record for this book is available from the British Library.

Microsoft Press books are available through booksellers and distributors worldwide. For further information about international editions, contact your local Microsoft Corporation office or contact Microsoft Press International directly at fax (425) 936-7329. Visit our Web site at mspress.microsoft.com. Send comments to *rkinput@microsoft.com*.

Acquisitions Editor: Juliana Aldous
Project Editor: Maureen Williams Zimmerman

Part No. X08-04962

Contributors to this book include the following:

User Education Group Manager
Ann Beebe

Project Manager
Kathy Harding

CD-ROM Manager
Dave Browning

Production Manager
Maura Dunn

Technical Architects
Charlie Kindschi, Dave Browning

Technical Editing Lead
Cynthia Givens

Production Lead
Dave Oxley

Contributing Writers
Tom Barclay, Alan Brewer, Dave Browning, Jim Carroll, Cathan Cook, Kevin Cox, Gail Erickson, Andrea Fox, David Gaynes, Allan Hirt, Ninia Ingram, Dennis Kennedy, Christian Kleinerman, Lubor Kollar, Michelle Larez, Diane Larsen, Kami LeMonds, Henry Lau, Jamie MacLennan, John Mikesell, John H. Miller, Joy Mundy, John Peltonen, Anna Rembecki, Jeff Ressler, Heidi Steen, LeRoy Tuttle, Jr., Ranjit Varkey, Richard Waymire, Wei Xiao

Technical Editors
James Dunn, Beth Inghram, Elaine Leyda, Ken Sánchez

Technical Contributors
Sameet Agarwal, Ari Auvinen, Craig Avis, Steven Barker, David Bauer, Thomas Davidson, Sasha (Alexander) Berger, Jeff Bernhardt, Marin Bezić, Yuri Budilov, Rick Byham, Peter Byrne, Tomas Byström, David Campbell, David Chesnut, Britt Cluff, Patrick Conlan, Eduardo Dardet, Jeff East, Michael Entin, Tamer Farag, Peter Fenton, Maurice Franklin, Mark Fussell, Euan Garden, Scott Gaskins, Sudhir Gajre, Brian Goldstein, Cindy Gross, Rick Gutierrez, Steve Hale, Simon Harris, Dax Hawkins, Simon Hay, Chris Hays, Al Hilwa, Steve Hoberecht, Jim Hong, Stephen Howard, MacLennan Jamie, Rahul Kapoor, Christian Kleinerman, Amit Kripalani, Doug Laudenschlager, Wendy Lehman, Bob Leithiser, Jean Francois LeSaux, Charles Levine, George Li, Randy Loeschner, Cesare Margaria, Tom Mathews, Scott Mauvais, Frank McBath, Mark McLoughlin, Dan Meacham, Reyna Meenk, John Mikesell, Steve Murchie, Julian Murren, William Ngoh, Gisli Olafsson, Mosha Pasumansky, Seth Paul, John Peltonen, Jing-Song Peng, Daniel Pham, Dave Poole, Bill Ramos, Michael Rys, Sujay Sahni, Greg Smith, Steven Snyder, Mark Souza, Maria Stergiou, Mirek Sztajno, Keven Tag, Yu-Tien Tang, Javier Tobio, Waldek Trafidlo, Kimberly Tripp-Simonnet, Don Vilen, Jason Ward, Richard Waymire, David Whitney, Benjamin Wilk, Roger Wolter, Shih Shen Wong, Steven Wright, Len Wyatt, Wei Xia, Howard Yin, Rodwell Chikomba Zvarayi, Michael Zwilling

Production
Bryan Franz, Brenda Yen

Graphic Designer
Steven Fulgham

Copyeditors
Keith Gipson, Steve Mohundro

Indexer
Julie Hatley

Contents

CHAPTER 9 Storage Engine Enhancements **233**

CHAPTER 10 Implementing Security **255**

PART 1

Introducing SQL Server 2000 and This Resource Kit

CHAPTER 1

Introducing the SQL Server 2000 Resource Kit

Welcome to the Microsoft® SQL Server™ 2000 Resource Kit. This resource kit is designed for people who are already users of SQL Server and who want some helpful tips, advanced techniques, and useful tools or samples to enhance their work with SQL Server 2000.

If you are responsible for administering or designing SQL Server databases, or developing applications that work with SQL Server, this resource kit is for you. This resource kit was written by members of the SQL Server product team and Microsoft Consulting Services, with the intention of extending the information provided in SQL Server Books Online (the online documentation included with SQL Server 2000). The information in this resource kit addresses specific questions from customers, and includes helpful tips for using SQL Server that were not available at the time SQL Server 2000 was released.

In addition to the information in this resource kit, the enclosed *Microsoft SQL Server 2000 Resource Kit* CD-ROM contains various SQL Server tools, utilities, and code samples. It also contains an online version of the SQL Server 2000 Resource Kit, and selected topics from SQL Server Books Online in eBook format for Microsoft Windows® CE devices.

Inside the Resource Kit

Chapter 2: New Features in SQL Server 2000

Taken directly from SQL Server Books Online, this chapter describes the new product features that were introduced in SQL Server 2000, including Analysis Services and English Query.

Chapter 3: Choosing an Edition of SQL Server 2000

This chapter provides an overview of the editions of SQL Server, and helps you choose the edition or editions best suited to your environment and application. Specialized usage of SQL Server in development, mobile, and evaluation scenarios is discussed. Information about obtaining the editions of SQL Server 2000 is also provided.

Chapter 4: Choosing how to License SQL Server

This chapter describes what type of SQL Server licensing to implement. SQL Server has introduced a processor-based license designed for e-business customers building business-to-business, business-to-consumer, and business-to-employee scenarios. These licenses can be used where traditional measures of users or connecting devices are impossible to track. Separate server licenses and per seat CALs (Client Access Licenses) will continue to be offered to customers using SQL Server. This method of licensing may appeal to a non-Web based business with a limited number of users.

Chapter 5: Migrating Access 2000 Databases to SQL Server 2000

This chapter is intended for Microsoft Access developers and managers who are interested in migrating their Access databases to SQL Server 2000. It discusses some of the benefits this migration will provide, and focuses on moving data and queries from Access to SQL Server. Application design considerations are also discussed.

Chapter 6: Migrating Sybase Databases to SQL Server 2000

This chapter is intended for Sybase database administrators and managers who are planning a database application migration to SQL Server 2000. It outlines the steps involved in migrating a Sybase database to SQL Server and helps application developers anticipate issues, based on experience with other customers. The chapter focuses on the differences between Sybase Transact-SQL and Microsoft Transact-SQL statements, as well as administrative differences.

Chapter 7: Migrating Oracle Databases to SQL Server 2000

This chapter is for developers of Oracle applications who want to convert their applications to Microsoft SQL Server. The tools, processes, and techniques required for a successful conversion are described. The essential design points that allow the creation of high-performance, high-concurrency SQL Server-based applications are also discussed.

Chapter 8: Managing Database Change

This chapter describes the best practices for handling database changes from the earliest development stage, through the quality assurance stage, and finally to implementation in the production environment. It provides practical advice for database administrators about handling development issues that arise when supporting a 24 x 7 operation where database implementations must not be a point of failure. This chapter covers management of the development environment and the quality assurance environment. The chapter also addresses issues such as documentation and version control.

Chapter 9: Storage Engine Enhancements

This chapter provides insight into the inner workings of SQL Server architecture. It covers storage engine enhancements and provides tips for using them.

Chapter 10: Implementing Security

This chapter introduces SQL Server administrators and developers to the new security features of SQL Server 2000. New features are outlined, and a detailed discussion is provided about how to best implement security in a Microsoft Windows 2000 domain environment. Source code examples are included for developers who want to implement the security model immediately.

Chapter 11: Using BLOBs

This chapter discusses the basic principles involved when working with binary large objects (BLOBs) in SQL Server. Applying knowledge gathered from the design and implementation of the Microsoft TerraServer database, this chapter enumerates issues to consider when designing tables with BLOB data. Using the **Northwind** database, this chapter explains the creation of a table with **text**, **ntext**, or **image** columns; and explains the insertion and modification of BLOB data, both on the server and the client.

Chapter 12: Failover Clustering

This chapter presents SQL Server 2000 failover clustering as one option to create high availability for a Web site or application to increase overall system uptime. It describes the components and processes involved in failover clustering, and describes best practices, design considerations, and tips for troubleshooting.

Chapter 13: Log Shipping

This chapter introduces SQL Server 2000 log shipping as a method to create a standby server in the event of a primary server failure.

Chapter 14: Data Center Availability: Facilities, Staffing, and Operations

Data center operations are critical to meeting the high availability standards required for many enterprise and e-commerce applications. This chapter provides guidelines for data center facilities, lists the staff required to run SQL Server in a data center, and suggests standards for data center and SQL Server operations to ensure system availability and recoverability.

Chapter 15: High Availability Options

This chapter discusses the high availability options in SQL Server 2000. It covers failover clustering, log shipping, replication, SANs, and other alternatives. It also covers the importance of people, processes, policies, and procedures.

Chapter 16: Five Nines: The Ultimate in High Availability

In the world of the Internet, e-commerce, and mission critical applications, it is imperative to design highly available backend systems. This chapter gives real world examples of how to design, implement, and support a highly available server running SQL Server 2000.

Chapter 17: Data Warehouse Design Considerations

This chapter addresses issues, choices, and approaches to be considered when designing and implementing a data warehouse. Differences between data warehouses and online transaction processing (OLTP) systems, data warehouse tools such as online analytical processing (OLAP) and data mining, and the purpose of data warehousing must all be considered when designing a data warehouse. A number of considerations that occur in the design of dimensional models, slowly and rapidly changing dimensions, fact tables, and other elements of a data warehouse are discussed. The chapter also provides suggested approaches and alternate techniques.

Chapter 18: Using Partitions in a SQL Server 2000 Data Warehouse

This chapter describes how to use partitions to improve the manageability, query performance, and load speed of data warehouses in SQL Server 2000 Enterprise Edition. Horizontal partitioning of dimensional schema, both in the relational database and in Analysis Services cubes, is addressed.

Chapter 19: Data Extraction, Transformation, and Loading Techniques

This chapter addresses various design considerations and deployment issues involved in developing the ongoing processes that extract, transform, and load data in data warehousing. Topics include data staging database design, as well as techniques for using tools such as Transact-SQL, and Data Transformation Services (DTS) in data extraction, transformation, and loading (ETL) processes. The development, maintenance, and use of ETL meta data is also addressed.

Chapter 20: RDBMS Performance Tuning Guide for Data Warehousing

This chapter covers tools and techniques that can be used to tune any RDBMS, and discusses considerations when tuning an RDBMS that is used for data warehousing.

Chapter 21: Monitoring the DTS Multiphase Data Pump in Visual Basic

This chapter illustrates a technique for monitoring the phases of the DTS data pump process from an out-of-process application in real time. A sample solution presented uses a COM+ event class to communicate to a Microsoft Visual Basic® application, which graphically depicts phase activity and allows you to set phase break points during the execution of a DTS package that contains a Transform Data task or a Data Driven Query task. This may help both in the understanding of multiphase data pump behavior and in troubleshooting.

Chapter 22: Cubes in the Real World

Analysis Services provides a wide variety of features for developing OLAP solutions, but practical application of such features can be challenging. This chapter provides details and guidance for leveraging all of the features of Analysis Services, addressing dimension and cube design, dimension varieties and characteristics, cube varieties and characteristics, and processing dimensions and cubes.

Chapter 23: Business Case Solutions Using MDX

This chapter gives direct and informative answers to a wide variety of common questions involving the Multidimensional Expressions (MDX) query language, grouped according to business usage. As a query language, MDX is designed to support the specific requirements of accessing multidimensional data, including a rich library of functions. The use of MDX is key to the efficient performance of multidimensional queries, and some business questions can be complex to answer with MDX. This chapter addresses some of the more commonly asked business questions, such as how to perform basic basket analysis using MDX, and technical questions, such as how to skip levels when drilling down on multidimensional data.

Each question is explained with an example illustrating the problem, the issues involved in resolving the question, and the MDX solutions used to resolve them. Full details and practical application notes are provided for each MDX solution.

Chapter 24: Effective Strategies for Data Mining

Data mining is not just a set of powerful Analysis Services tools, but also a set of strategies used to discover meaningful business information from large amounts of historical data. This chapter provides guidance in developing data mining solutions, including a discussion on of model-driven and data-driven data mining, an overview of the process used to construct and use data mining models, and practical examples of training and prediction analysis using data mining models. Common issues are addressed at every step discussed in the data mining process, and examples are provided to illustrate the use of MDX for predictive analysis in operational and closed loop data mining.

Chapter 25: Getting Data to the Client

This chapter provides a review of, and usage guidelines for, client-side technologies that can be used to retrieve and process data and meta data stored in the Analysis Services engine. Analysis Services provides access to data and meta data through PivotTable® Service, its implementation of the OLE DB for OLAP specification. Data on the analysis server can be accessed by using PivotTable Service in conjunction with OLE DB, Microsoft ActiveX® Data Objects (ADO), or ActiveX Data Objects (Multidimensional) (ADO MD). Meta data can be accessed by using Decision Support Objects (DSO), and by using PivotTable Service with OLE DB, ADO, or ADO MD.

Brief explanations of sample applications (Meta Data Explorer, Meta Data Scripter, Schema Rowset Explorer) included in the SQL Server 2000 Resource Kit suggest possible uses of the technologies discussed. The Meta Data Scripter, for example, allows you to script the meta data of any object, including dependent objects, that can be selected in Analysis Manager; the accompanying add-in generates a Visual Basic Scripting Edition (VBScript) file that uses DSO to recreate the scripted objects.

Chapter 26: Performance Tuning Analysis Services

This chapter provides detailed technical information about performance tuning Analysis Services, including tuning Analysis Services for overall performance and tuning specifically for query and processing performance. Discussions on Analysis Services architecture, hardware management, memory and storage management, partition strategy, aggregation design, and performance evaluation techniques are all included, with data and examples provided directly from case studies.

Chapter 27: Creating an Interactive Digital Dashboard

This chapter uses a hands-on approach to explain how to deploy a SQL Server-based digital dashboard that contains interactive parts. A digital dashboard is a framework for building portals. SQL Server is one of several platforms that can be used to deploy a dashboard. Although you can build dashboards that contain stand-alone components, a more promising use of the technology is to build lightweight applications that are composed of functionally related parts. In this chapter, you can find out how to set up the tools for digital dashboard development. You also learn how to build a dashboard that displays **Northwind** customer data in one component and aggregated order information in a second component. The two components are related through an event-driven script that causes summarized order data to appear in response to a customer name selection.

Chapter 28: A Digital Dashboard Browser for Analysis Services Meta Data

This chapter steps through creating a digital dashboard browser to view Analysis Services meta data. Using interactive digital dashboard concepts, the components are created using VBScript and DSO. The completed dashboard allows the user to connect to a selected analysis server, choose a database, and view the cubes, dimensions, roles, and other objects made available by the DSO object model.

Chapter 29: Common Questions in Replication

This chapter provides answers to common replication questions. Subjects covered include types of replication, subscriptions, replication options, and replication implementation.

Chapter 30: Creating Merge Replication Custom Conflict Resolvers Using Visual Basic

This chapter describes how to create a Visual Basic application for merge replication conflict resolution. This chapter documents programmability that enables developers to gather information from the Publisher and Subscriber sites and use that information to resolve data conflicts and propagate the final data to both locations.

Chapter 31: Exposing SQL Server Data to the Web with XML

This chapter offers an introduction to the native XML features of SQL Server 2000. It demonstrates how to configure Internet Information Services (IIS) for SQL XML support and how to retrieve data in various XML formats from Transact-SQL queries in a URL and from XML Template files.

Chapter 32: English Query Best Practices

English Query provides an interface for querying SQL Server in English, which gives those without Transact-SQL knowledge a way to submit ad hoc queries to a database. This chapter provides best practices for starting, expanding, and deploying an English Query application using the tools provided with SQL Server.

Chapter 33: The Data Tier: An Approach to Database Optimization

This chapter outlines the process for optimizing a database in the most effective manner. It covers application/database testing, through performance tuning, and hardware configuration. The chapter follows an example-oriented approach, demonstrating how to focus database administration and design efforts.

Chapter 34: Identifying Common Administrative Issues

This chapter contains two sections. The first section describes a set of stored procedures used to identify some common configuration problems with SQL Server. These stored procedures can be packaged and distributed to DBAs across an enterprise to help maintain a consistent configuration of SQL Server. The second section explains a stored procedure that can help a DBA troubleshoot blocking problems.

Chapter 35: Using Visual Basic to Remotely Manage SQL Server 2000

This chapter provides an overview of the implementation of SQL Distributed Management Objects (SQL-DMO) and SQL Namespace (SQL-NS) objects from within Visual Basic. SQL-DMO and SQL-NS provide a COM interface for database management tasks usually available only within SQL Server itself. The chapter also includes complete Visual Basic code samples and a working application that illustrates the use of the COM interface.

Chapter 36: Using Views with a View on Performance

This chapter explains indexed views, describes specific scenarios that they enhance performance in, and provides guidelines for designing effective indexed views.

Chapter 37: Extending Triggers with INSTEAD OF

New with SQL Server 2000, the INSTEAD OF trigger increases the capabilities of views by allowing updating of multiple tables and enhanced event handling. In this chapter, design guidelines for INSTEAD OF triggers are provided along with several best-practice recommendations and sample code.

Chapter 38: Scaling Out on SQL Server

This chapter covers the process that goes into determining what type of scale-out solution might be best for your application. It also discusses the federated SQL Server configurations, and provides insight about how this technology works.

Chapter 39: Tools, Samples, eBooks, and More

This chapter describes the tools, utilities, and code samples included on the *Microsoft SQL Server 2000 Resource Kit* CD-ROM. The tools and utilities will help you manage and troubleshoot your SQL Server 2000 installations and databases, and the code samples will help you develop your own applications to use with SQL Server 2000.

Additional Sources of Information

SQL Server 2000 Product Documentation

SQL Server Books Online contains comprehensive documentation for SQL Server 2000. SQL Server Books Online is available from the following sources:

- SQL Server 2000
- MSDN Library, at http://www.msdn.microsoft.com/library/
- MSDN download site, at http://www.msdn.microsoft.com/downloads/

SQL Server 2000 Reference Library, published by Microsoft Press, is a condensed, printed version of carefully selected sections of SQL Server Books Online. It contains the following volumes:

- SQL Server 2000 Architecture and XML/Internet Support
- Database Creation, Warehousing, and Optimization
- Analysis Services (OLAP)
- Replication and English Query
- Transact-SQL Language Reference
- Transact-SQL Stored Procedures and Tables

The SQL Server Reference Library is available from retail bookstores. ISBN# 0-7356-1280-3

SQL Server 2000 Internet Sites

- Microsoft SQL Server product Web site, at http://www.microsoft.com/sql/.

- Microsoft SQL Server 2000 Analysis Services Web site, at http://www.microsoft.com/sql/techinfo/olap.htm.

- Microsoft SQL Server English Query Web site, at http://www.microsoft.com/sql/productinfo/eqmain.htm.

- Microsoft SQL Server Developer Center, at http://www.msdn.microsoft.com/sqlserver/.

- Microsoft XML Developer Center, at http://www.msdn.microsoft.com/xml/.

- Professional Association for SQL Server (PASS), at http://www.sqlpass.org.

- SQL Server Magazine, at http://www.sqlmag.com/.

- SQL Server Newsgroups, at news://msnews.microsoft.com/.

Conventions Used in This Resource Kit

The following conventions are used to distinguish elements of text.

Convention	Used for
UPPERCASE	Transact-SQL keywords and SQL elements
Initial Capitals	Paths and file names
Bold	Database names, table names, column names, stored procedures, command-prompt utilities, menus, commands, dialog-box options, programming elements, and text that must be typed exactly as shown
Italic	User-supplied variables, relationships, and phrasings
Monospace	Code samples, examples, display text, and error messages

Resource Kit Support Policy

Microsoft does not support the software supplied in the *SQL Server 2000 Resource Kit*. Microsoft does not guarantee the performance of the tools, response times for answering questions, or bug fixes for the tools. However, Microsoft does provide a way for customers who purchase the *SQL Server 2000 Resource Kit* to report any problems with the software and receive feedback for such issues. To report any issues or problems, send e-mail to rkinput@microsoft.com. This e-mail address is used only for issues related to the *SQL Server 2000 Resource Kit*. For issues related to the SQL Server 2000 product, see the support information included with the product.

New Features in SQL Server 2000

Microsoft® SQL Server™ 2000 extends the performance, reliability, quality, and ease-of-use of Microsoft SQL Server version 7.0. Microsoft SQL Server 2000 includes several new features that make it an excellent database platform for large-scale online transactional processing (OLTP), data warehousing, and e-commerce applications.

The OLAP Services feature available in SQL Server 7.0 is now called SQL Server 2000 Analysis Services. The term OLAP Services has been replaced with the term Analysis Services. Analysis Services also includes a new data mining component. For more information, see "Analysis Services Enhancements" in this chapter.

The Repository component available in SQL Server 7.0 is now called Microsoft SQL Server 2000 Meta Data Services. References to the component now use the term Meta Data Services. The term repository is used only in reference to the repository engine within Meta Data Services. For more information, see "Meta Data Services Enhancements" in this chapter.

This chapter contains brief overviews of the new features and provides cross-references to related chapters in this book as well as to their specific topics in SQL Server Books Online.

Relational Database Enhancements

Microsoft SQL Server 2000 introduces several server improvements and new features:

XML Support

The relational database engine can return data as Extensible Markup Language (XML) documents. Additionally, XML can also be used to insert, update, and delete values in the database. For more information, see Chapter 31, "Exposing SQL Server Data to the Web with XML," and the topics "SQL Server and XML Support" and "XML and Internet Support Overview" in SQL Server Books Online.

Federated Database Servers

SQL Server 2000 supports enhancements to distributed partitioned views that allow you to partition tables horizontally across multiple servers. This allows you to scale out one database server to a group of database servers that cooperate to provide the same performance levels as a cluster of database servers. This group, or federation, of database servers can support the data storage requirements of the largest Web sites and enterprise data processing systems. For more information, see Chapter 38, "Scaling Out on SQL Server," and "Federated SQL Server 2000 Servers" in SQL Server Books Online.

SQL Server 2000 introduces Net-Library support for Virtual Interface Architecture (VIA) system-area networks that provide high-speed connectivity between servers, such as between application servers and database servers. For more information, see "Communication Components" in SQL Server Books Online.

User-Defined Functions

Creating your own Transact-SQL functions can extend Transact-SQL programmability. A user-defined function can return either a scalar value or a table. For more information, see "SQL User-Defined Functions" in SQL Server Books Online.

Indexed Views

Indexed views can significantly improve the performance of an application in which queries frequently perform certain joins or aggregations. An indexed view allows indexes to be created on views, where the result set of the view is stored and indexed in the database. Existing applications do not need to be modified to take advantage of the performance improvements with indexed views. For more information, see "SQL Views" in SQL Server Books Online.

New Data Types

SQL Server 2000 introduces three new data types:

- **bigint** is an 8-byte integer type.

- **sql_variant** is a type that allows the storage of data values of different data types.

- **table** is a type that allows applications to store results temporarily for later use. It is supported for variables, and as the return type for user-defined functions.

For more information, see "Data Types and Table Structures" in SQL Server Books Online.

INSTEAD OF and AFTER Triggers

INSTEAD OF triggers are executed instead of the triggering action (for example, an INSERT, UPDATE, or DELETE statement). They can also be defined on views, in which case they greatly extend the types of updates a view can support. AFTER triggers fire after the triggering action. SQL Server 2000 introduces the ability to specify which AFTER triggers fire first and last. For more information, see Chapter 37, "Extending Triggers with INSTEAD OF," and "Triggers" in SQL Server Books Online.

Cascading Referential Integrity Constraints

You can control the actions SQL Server 2000 takes when you attempt to update or delete a key to which existing foreign keys point. To control these actions, you can use the new ON DELETE and ON UPDATE clauses in the REFERENCES clause of the CREATE TABLE and ALTER TABLE statements. For more information, see "Constraints" in SQL Server Books Online.

Collation Enhancements

SQL Server 2000 replaces code pages and sort orders with collations. SQL Server 2000 includes support for most collations supported in earlier versions of SQL Server, and introduces a new set of collations based on Microsoft Windows® collations. You can now specify collations at the database level or at the column level. In earlier versions of SQL Server, code pages and sort orders could be specified only at the server level and applied to all databases on a server. For more information, see "Collations" in SQL Server Books Online.

Collations support code page translations. Operations with **char** and **varchar** operands having different code pages are now supported. Code page translations are not supported for **text** operands. You can use ALTER DATABASE to change the default collation of a database. For more information, see the topics "SQL Server Collation Fundamentals" and "ALTER DATABASE" in SQL Server Books Online.

Full-Text Search Enhancements

Full-text search now includes change tracking and image filtering. Change tracking maintains a log of all changes to the full-text indexed data. You can update the full-text index with these changes, by flushing the log manually, on a schedule, or as they occur, using the background update index option. Image filtering allows you to index and query documents stored in **image** columns. The user provides the document type in a column containing the file name extension the document would have had if it were stored as a file in the file system. Using this information, full-text search is able to load the appropriate document filter to extract textual information for indexing. For more information, see "Microsoft Search Service" in SQL Server Books Online.

Multiple Instances of SQL Server

SQL Server 2000 supports running multiple instances of the relational database engine on the same computer. Each computer can run one instance of the relational database engine from SQL Server 6.5 or SQL Server 7.0, along with one or more instances of the database engine from SQL Server 2000. Each instance has its own set of system and user databases. Applications can connect to each instance on a computer similar to the way they connect to instances of SQL Servers running on different computers. The SQL Server 2000 utilities and administration tools have been enhanced to work with multiple instances. For more information, see "Multiple Instances of SQL Server" in SQL Server Books Online.

Index Enhancements

You can now create indexes on computed columns. You can specify whether indexes are built in ascending or descending order, and if the database engine should use parallel scanning and sorting during index creation. For more information, see the topics "Table Indexes" and "Parallel Operations Creating Indexes" in SQL Server Books Online.

The CREATE INDEX statement can now use the **tempdb** database as a work area for the sorts required to build an index. This results in improved disk read and write patterns for the index creation step, and makes it more likely that index pages will be allocated in contiguous strips. In addition, the complete process of creating an index is eligible for parallel operations, not only the initial table scan. For more information, see the topics "tempdb and Index Creation," "Parallel Operations Creating Indexes," and "CREATE INDEX" in SQL Server Books Online.

Failover Clustering Enhancements

The administration of failover clusters has been greatly improved to make it very easy to install, configure, and maintain a Microsoft SQL Server 2000 failover cluster. Additional enhancements include the ability to failover and failback to or from any node in a SQL Server 2000 cluster, the ability to add or remove a node from the cluster through SQL Server 2000 Setup, and the ability to reinstall or rebuild a cluster instance on any node in the cluster without affecting the other cluster node instances. The SQL Server 2000 utilities and administration tools have been enhanced to work with failover clusters. For more information, see Chapter 12, "Failover Clustering," and Chapter 15, "High Availability Options," and "Failover Clustering Architecture" in SQL Server Books Online.

Net-Library Enhancements

The SQL Server 2000 Net-Libraries have been rewritten to virtually eliminate the need to administer Net-Library configurations on client computers when connecting SQL Server 2000 clients to instances of SQL Server 2000. The new Net-Libraries also support connections to multiple instances of SQL Server on the same computer, and support Secure Sockets Layer encryption over all Net-Libraries. SQL Server 2000 introduces Net-Library support for Virtual Interface Architecture (VIA) system-area networks that provide high-speed connectivity between servers, such as between application servers and database servers. For more information, see "Communication Components" in SQL Server Books Online.

64-GB Memory Support

Microsoft SQL Server 2000 Enterprise Edition can use the Microsoft Windows 2000 Advanced Windows Extension (AWE) API to support up to 64 GB of physical memory (RAM) on a computer. For more information, see "Using AWE Memory on Windows 2000" in SQL Server Books Online.

Distributed Query Enhancements

SQL Server 2000 introduces the OPENROWSET function, which you can use to specify ad hoc connection information in a distributed query. SQL Server 2000 also specifies methods that OLE DB providers can use to report the level of SQL syntax supported by the provider and statistics on the distribution of key values in the data source. The distributed query optimizer can then use this information to reduce the amount of data that has to be sent from the OLE DB data source. SQL Server 2000 delegates more SQL operations to OLE DB data sources than earlier versions of SQL Server. Distributed queries also support the other functions introduced in SQL Server 2000, such as multiple instances, mixing columns with different collations in result sets, and the new **bigint** and **sql_variant** data types. For more information, see "Distributed Query Architecture" in SQL Server Books Online.

SQL Server 2000 distributed queries add support for the OLE DB Provider for Exchange and the Microsoft OLE DB Provider for Microsoft Directory Services. For more information, see the topics "OLE DB Provider for Microsoft Directory Services" and "OLE DB Provider for Exchange" in SQL Server Books Online.

Updatable Distributed Partitioned Views

SQL Server 2000 introduces enhancements to distributed partitioned views. You can partition tables horizontally across several servers, and define a distributed partitioned view on each member server that makes it appear as if a full copy of the original table is stored on each server. Groups of servers running SQL Server that cooperate in this type of partitioning are called federations of servers. A database federation built using SQL Server 2000 databases is capable of supporting the processing requirements of the largest Web sites or enterprise-level databases. For more information, see Chapter 38, "Scaling Out on SQL Server," and "Creating a Partitioned View" in SQL Server Books Online.

Kerberos and Security Delegation

SQL Server 2000 uses Kerberos to support mutual authentication between the client and the server, as well as the ability to pass the security credentials of a client between computers, so work on a remote server can proceed using the credentials of the impersonated client. With Microsoft Windows 2000, SQL Server 2000 uses Kerberos and delegation to support both integrated authentication as well as SQL Server logins. For more information, see Chapter 10, "Implementing Security," and "Security Account Delegation" in SQL Server Books Online.

Backup and Restore Enhancements

SQL Server 2000 introduces a new, more easily understood model for specifying backup and restore options. The new model makes it clearer that you are balancing increased or decreased exposure to losing work against the performance and log space requirements of different plans. SQL Server 2000 introduces support for recovery to specific points of work using named log marks in the transaction log, and the ability to do partial database restores. For more information, see "Backup/Restore Architecture" in SQL Server Books Online.

Users can define passwords for backup sets and media sets that prevent unauthorized users from accessing SQL Server backups. For more information, see "BACKUP" in SQL Server Books Online.

Scalability Enhancements for Utility Operations

SQL Server 2000 enhancements for utility operations include faster differential backups, parallel Database Console Command (DBCC), and parallel scanning. Differential backups can now be completed in a time that is proportional to the amount of data changed since the last full backup. DBCC can be run without taking shared table locks while scanning tables, thereby enabling them to be run concurrently with update activity on tables. Additionally, DBCC now takes advantage of multiple processors, enabling near-linear gain in performance in relation to the number of CPUs (provided that I/O is not a bottleneck). For more information, see the topics "Data Integrity Validation" and "Differential Backup and Restore" in SQL Server Books Online.

Text in Row Data

SQL Server 2000 supports a new **text in row** table option that specifies that small **text**, **ntext**, and **image** values be placed directly in the data row instead of in a separate page. This reduces the amount of space used to store small **text**, **ntext**, and **image** data values, and reduces the amount of disk I/O needed to process these values. For more information, see Chapter 11, "Using BLOBs," and "**text**, **ntext**, and **image** Data" in SQL Server Books Online.

XML Integration of Relational Data

The Microsoft SQL Server 2000 relational database engine natively supports Extensible Markup Language (XML).

You can access SQL Server 2000 over HTTP using a Universal Resource Locator (URL). You can define a virtual root on a Microsoft Internet Information Services (IIS) server, which provides HTTP access to the data and XML functionality of SQL Server 2000. For more information, see Chapter 31, "Exposing SQL Server Data to the Web with XML."

HTTP, Microsoft ActiveX® Data Objects (ADO), or OLE DB can be used to work with the XML functionality of SQL Server 2000:

- XML views of SQL Server 2000 databases can be defined by annotating XML-Data Reduced (XDR) schemas to map the tables, views, and columns that are associated with the elements and attributes of the schema. The XML views can then be referenced in XPath queries, which retrieve results from the database and return them as XML documents.

- The results of SELECT statements can be returned as XML documents. The SQL Server 2000 Transact-SQL SELECT statement supports the FOR XML clause, which specifies that the statement results be returned in the form of an XML document instead of a relational result set. Complex queries, or queries that you want to make secure, can be stored as templates in an IIS virtual root, and executed by referencing the template name.

- Data from an XML document can be exposed as a relational rowset using the new OPENXML rowset function. OPENXML can be used everywhere a rowset function can be used in a Transact-SQL statement, such as in place of a table or view reference in a FROM clause. This allows you to use the data in XML documents to insert, update, or delete data in the tables of the database, including modifying multiple rows in multiple tables in a single operation.

Graphical Administration Enhancements

Microsoft SQL Server 2000 introduces the following graphical administration improvements and new features:

Log Shipping

Log shipping allows the transaction logs from a source database to be continually backed up and loaded into a target database on another server. This is useful for maintaining a warm standby server, or for offloading query processing from the source server to a read-only destination server. For more information, see Chapter 13, "Log Shipping," and "Log Shipping" in SQL Server Books Online.

SQL Profiler Enhancements

SQL Profiler supports size-based and time-based traces, and includes new events for Data File Auto Grow, Data File Auto Shrink, Log File Auto Grow, Log File Auto Shrink, Show Plan All, Show Plan Statistics, and Show Plan Text.

SQL Profiler has been enhanced to provide auditing of SQL Server activities, up to the auditing levels required by the C2 level of security defined by the U.S. government. For more information, see the topics "Auditing SQL Server Activity" and "Monitoring with SQL Profiler" in SQL Server Books Online.

SQL Query Analyzer Enhancements

SQL Query Analyzer now includes Object Browser, which allows you to navigate through and get information (such as parameters and dependencies) about database objects, including user and system tables, views, stored procedures, extended stored procedures, and functions. The Object Browser also supports generating scripts to either execute or create objects. Other enhancements include server tracing and client statistics that show information about the server-side and client-side impact of a given query.

SQL Query Analyzer includes a stored procedure debugger. SQL Query Analyzer also includes templates that can be used as the starting points for creating objects such as databases, tables, views, and stored procedures. For more information, see the topics "SQL Query Analyzer" and "Overview of SQL Query Analyzer" in SQL Server Books Online.

Copy Database Wizard

Users can run the Copy Database Wizard to upgrade SQL Server 7.0 databases to SQL Server 2000 databases. It can also be used to copy complete databases between instances of SQL Server 2000. For more information, see "Copying Databases to Other Servers" in SQL Server Books Online.

Replication Enhancements

Microsoft SQL Server 2000 introduces the following replication improvements and new features:

Implementing Replication

SQL Server 2000 enhances snapshot replication, transactional replication, and merge replication by adding:

- Alternate snapshot locations, which provide easier and more flexible methods for applying the initial snapshot to Subscribers. You can save (and compress) the snapshot files to a network location or removable media, which can then be transferred to Subscribers without using the network.

- Attachable subscription databases, which allow you to transfer a database with replicated data and one or more subscriptions from one Subscriber to another SQL Server. After the database is attached to the new Subscriber, the subscription database at the new Subscriber will automatically receive its own pull subscriptions to the publications at the specified Publishers.

- Schema changes on publication databases, which allow you to add or drop columns on the publishing table and propagate those changes to Subscribers.

- On demand script execution, which allows you to post a general SQL script that will be executed at all Subscribers.

- Pre- and post-snapshot scripts, which allow you to run scripts before or after a snapshot is applied at the Subscriber.

- Remote agent activation, which allows you to reduce the amount of processing on the Distributor or Subscriber by running the Distribution Agent or Merge Agent on one computer while activating that agent from another computer. You can use remote agent activation with push or pull subscriptions.

- Support of new SQL Server features, which includes user-defined functions, indexed views, new data types, and multiple instances of SQL Server.

- The ActiveX Snapshot Control, which makes programmatic generation of snapshots easier.

- More snapshot scripting options, which support transfer of indexes, extended properties, and constraints to Subscribers.

Merge Replication

Merge replication is the process of distributing data from Publisher to Subscribers, allowing the Publisher and Subscribers to make updates while connected or disconnected, and then merging the changes between sites when they are connected. Enhancements to merge replication include:

- Greater parallelism of the Merge Agent for improved server-to-server performance.

- Optimizations for determining data changes relevant to a partition at a Subscriber.

- Dynamic snapshots, which provide more efficient application of the initial snapshot when using dynamic filters.

- Vertical filters for merge publications.

- More powerful dynamic filtering with user-defined functions.

- The ability to use alternate synchronization partners when synchronizing data. Using alternate synchronization partners, a Subscriber to a merge publication can synchronize with any specified server that has the same data as the original Publisher.

- Automated management of identity ranges. In merge replication topologies where a publication contains an identity column, and where new rows can be inserted at Subscribers, automated management of identity ranges at the Subscriber ensures the same identity values are not assigned to rows inserted at different subscription databases, and that primary key constraint violations do not occur. This feature is also available when queued updating is used with snapshot replication or transactional replication.

- Support for **timestamp** columns in published tables.

- Improved management of merge tracking data growth.

- Several new merge replication conflict resolvers including interactive resolvers that provide a user interface for immediate, manual conflict resolution, priority based on a column value, minimum/maximum value wins, first/last change wins, additive/average value, and merge by appending different text values.

- New options to validate permissions for a Subscriber to upload changes to a Publisher (*check_permissions*) and security enhancements including code signing of conflict resolvers included with Microsoft SQL Server 2000.

- New COM interfaces that support heterogeneous data sources as Publishers within a SQL Server replication topology.

- Validation of replicated data per subscription or on a publication-wide basis. Validation is also available through SQL Server Enterprise Manager.

- Reinitialization to allow uploading of changes from the Subscriber before the application of a new snapshot.

For more information, see the topics "Merge Replication" and "Replication Options" in SQL Server Books Online.

Transactional Replication

With transactional replication, an initial snapshot of data is applied at Subscribers, and then when data modifications are made at the Publisher, the individual transactions are captured and propagated to Subscribers. Enhancements to transactional replication include:

- Concurrent snapshot processing so that data modifications can continue on publishing tables while the initial snapshot is generated.

- Improved error handling and the ability to skip specified errors and continue replication.

- Validation of replicated data at the Subscriber, including validation on vertical partitions. Validation is also available through SQL Server Enterprise Manager.

- Publishing indexed views as tables.

- The option to store data modifications made at the Subscriber in a queue (queued updating).

- The option to transform data as it is published to Subscribers (transforming published data).

- The ability to restore transactional replication databases without reinitializing subscriptions or disabling and reconfiguring publishing and distribution. You can also set up transactional replication to work with log shipping, enabling you to fail over to a warm standby server without reconfiguring replication. For more information, see the "Strategies for Restoring Snapshot or Transactional Replication" topic in SQL Server Books Online.

For more information, see "Transactional Replication" in SQL Server Books Online.

Queued Updating

Queued updating allows snapshot replication and transactional replication Subscribers to modify published data without requiring an active network connection to the Publisher.

When you create a publication with the queued updating option enabled and a Subscriber performs INSERT, UPDATE, or DELETE statements on published data, the changes are stored in a queue. The queued transactions are applied asynchronously at the Publisher when network connectivity is restored.

Because the updates are propagated asynchronously to the Publisher, the same data may have been updated by the Publisher or by another Subscriber and conflicts can occur when applying the updates. Conflicts are detected automatically and several options for resolving conflicts are offered.

For more information, see "Queued Updating" in SQL Server Books Online.

Transforming Published Data

Transformable subscriptions (available with snapshot replication or transactional replication) leverage the data movement, transformation mapping, and filtering capabilities of Data Transformation Services (DTS).

Using transformable subscriptions in your replication topology allows you to customize and send published data based on the requirements of individual Subscribers, including performing data type mappings, column manipulations, string manipulations, and using functions as data is published.

For more information, see "Transforming Published Data" in SQL Server Books Online.

Replication Usability

There have been several improvements in SQL Server Enterprise Manager that provide for easier implementation, monitoring, and administration of replication. Enhancements to replication usability include:

- A centralized Replication folder in the SQL Server Enterprise Manager tree, which organizes all subscriptions and publications on the server being administered.

- The ability to browse for and subscribe to publications (when permission is allowed) using Microsoft Active Directory™ in Windows 2000.

- The ability to see multiple Distributors in a single monitoring node in SQL Server Enterprise Manager.

- Standard and advanced replication options separated in the Create Publication, Create Push Subscription, and Create Pull Subscription Wizards. You can choose to show advanced options in these wizards on the Welcome page of each wizard.

- New wizards for creating jobs that create dynamic snapshots for merge publications that use dynamic filters (Create Dynamic Snapshot Job Wizard), and for transforming published data in snapshot replication or transactional replication (Transform Published Data Wizard).

Data Transformation Services Enhancements

Microsoft SQL Server 2000 introduces the following Data Transformation Services (DTS) improvements and new features:

New Custom Tasks

The SQL Server 2000 DTS Designer and the DTS object model introduce new custom tasks that allow you to create packages that perform tasks or set variables based on properties of the run-time environment. These include:

- Importing data from and sending data and completed packages to Internet and FTP sites.
- Running packages asynchronously.
- Building packages that send messages to each other.
- Building packages that execute other packages.
- Joining multiple package executions as part of a transaction.

For more information, see "Building a DTS Custom Task" in SQL Server Books Online.

Saving DTS Packages to Visual Basic Files

Saving a DTS package to a Microsoft Visual Basic® file allows a package created by the DTS Import Wizard, the DTS Export Wizard, or DTS Designer to be incorporated into Visual Basic programs or to be used as prototypes by Visual Basic developers who need to reference the components of the DTS object model. For more information, see "Saving a DTS Package" in SQL Server Books Online.

Multiphase Data Pump

DTS includes a new multiphase data pump that allows advanced users to customize the operation of the data pump at various stages of its operation. Advanced users can monitor the activity of the Multiphase Data Pump from outside of a DTS package using the techniques described in Chapter 21, "Monitoring the DTS Multiphase Data Pump in Visual Basic." Global variables can now be used as input and output parameters for queries. DTS also introduces new package-logging capabilities. For more information, see the topics "Multiphase Data Pump Functionality," "Using Parameterized Queries in DTS," and "Using DTS Package Logs" in SQL Server Books Online.

Analysis Services Enhancements

Microsoft SQL Server 2000 extends and renames the former OLAP Services component, now called Analysis Services. Many new and improved features significantly enhance the analysis capabilities of OLAP Services introduced in SQL Server 7.0. In this release, Analysis Services introduces data mining, which can be used to discover information in OLAP cubes and relational databases.

Feature	Description
Cube enhancements	New cube types and enhanced cube functionality substantially extend the scalability and functionality of Analysis Services.
Dimension enhancements	New dimension and hierarchy types, features, and improvements extend the analysis capabilities of cubes.
Data mining enhancements	Data mining is integrated into online analysis and can be used to discover information in OLAP cubes and relational databases.
Security enhancements	Security enhancements include using roles on cube cells and dimension members, additional authentication methods, and improved enforcement.
Client connectivity enhancements in PivotTable® Service	Client applications can use many new features and enhancements such as data mining, HTTP or HTTPS connections, additional dimension types, and cell allocation for writeback.
Other enhancements	Other enhancements provide a variety of new features including multiuser administration, MDX Builder, additional Multidimensional Expressions (MDX) functions, Virtual Cube Editor, support for Active Directory™, and more.

Cube Enhancements

Microsoft SQL Server 2000 Analysis Services substantially extends the scalability and functionality of OLAP cubes. You can distribute cube data across multiple servers to provide more storage capacity, create linked cubes to distribute end-user access to information without duplicating cube data, create cubes that are updated in real time as data changes, and use a number of other new features to create cubes that address your specific business needs.

Distributed Partitioned Cubes

You can create distributed partitioned cubes by using remote partitions that distribute a cube's data among multiple Analysis servers. A distributed partitioned cube is administered on a central Analysis server. For more information, see "Remote Partitions" in SQL Server Books Online.

Real-Time OLAP

Real-time OLAP provides a multidimensional OLAP view of data that is continually updated as the underlying data changes. Real-time cubes implement real-time OLAP by using ROLAP storage for partitions and dimensions, new SQL Server 2000 indexed views for aggregations, and automatic notification by the SQL Server 2000 relational engine when data changes. Real-time cubes provide the capability to develop new categories of OLAP solutions such as call-center management, stock market analysis, or campaign management. For more information, see "Real-Time Cubes" in SQL Server Books Online.

Linked Cubes

A cube can be stored on a single Analysis server and then defined as a linked cube on other Analysis servers. End users connected to any of these Analysis servers can then access the cube. This arrangement avoids the more costly alternative of storing and maintaining copies of a cube on multiple Analysis servers. Linked cubes can be connected using TCP/IP or HTTP. To end users, a linked cube looks like a regular cube. For more information, see "Linked Cubes" in SQL Server Books Online.

Indexed Views for Aggregations

Indexed views for increased performance and flexibility are used instead of aggregation tables for ROLAP partitions if the partition's source data is stored in SQL Server 2000 and if certain criteria are met. For more information, see "Indexed Views for ROLAP Partitions" in SQL Server Books Online.

Cube Processing

You can use lazy aggregations to make cube data available to end users while aggregations are being calculated. When processing cubes for which the underlying data contains dimension key errors, you can elect to stop processing on key errors, stop processing after a specified number of errors, or ignore all key errors. You can have errors logged to a file for later review. For more information, see "Processing Cubes" in SQL Server Books Online.

Calculated Cells

You can specify formulas that apply to individual cells or to sets of cells in a cube. These formulas can contain conditional calculations that compute a new value for a cell or set of cells based on values in the cell or cells, or on values in other cells in the cube. Calculated cells use Multidimensional Expressions (MDX) expressions and you can specify calculations to be performed in multiple passes. Calculated cells can be used in complex financial modeling and budgeting applications; for example, you can specify a default value such as a percentage of a parent cell if the cell value is zero, or to use the actual value if it is not zero. For more information, see "Calculated Cells" in SQL Server Books Online.

Drillthrough

Client applications that support drillthrough can now allow end users to select a cube cell and retrieve a result set from the source data for that cell. You can use roles to control user access to the drillthrough functionality. For more information, see "Specifying Drillthrough Options" in SQL Server Books Online.

Actions

Actions enable end users to act upon the outcomes of their analyses. An action is a predefined operation that an end user can initiate upon a selected cube or portion of a cube. The operation can launch an application with the selected item as a parameter or retrieve information about the selected item. A wizard is provided to help you create actions. For more information, see "Actions" in SQL Server Books Online.

DistinctCount Function

You can use the new **DistinctCount** aggregate function to analyze the number of unique occurrences of events or transactions in your data, such as unique users visiting a Web site. For more information, see "DistinctCount" in SQL Server Books Online.

Hidden Cube Elements

You can hide complete cubes, dimensions, levels, measures, or member properties from end users who browse cubes with client applications. The visibility of these objects is controlled by the **Visible** property. For more information, see the topics "Properties Pane (Cube Editor Data View)" and "Properties Pane (Dimension Editor Data View)" in SQL Server Books Online.

Named Sets

You can create, name, and save sets of dimension members or set expressions in a cube. Client applications can use a named set like a dimension by placing the named set on an axis. For more information, see "Named Sets" in SQL Server Books Online.

Default Measures

Default measures can be specified for each cube and varied by role to control default views of cubes for end users. For more information, see the topics "Properties Pane (Cube Editor Data View)" and "Custom Rules in Dimension Security" in SQL Server Books Online.

Virtual Cube Editor

This new editor for virtual cubes is similar in function to Cube Editor. Virtual Cube Editor replaces and expands the functionality provided by the Calculated Member Manager Add-in for SQL Server 7.0 OLAP Services. For more information, see "Virtual Cube Editor" in SQL Server Books Online.

Dimension Enhancements

This release of Microsoft SQL Server 2000 Analysis Services adds significant functionality to OLAP analysis with a number of new dimension types, features, and improvements.

Parent-Child Dimensions

A new parent-child dimension type supports hierarchies based on parent-child links between members in columns in a source table. Such hierarchies represent structures that include organizational charts and part assemblies. Data members can be used to provide data for nonleaf members, such as the direct commission amount for a sales department manager or the individual salaries for all members in an organizational chart. For more information, see "Parent-Child Dimensions" in SQL Server Books Online.

ROLAP Dimensions

Extremely large dimensions can now be accommodated using the ROLAP storage mode. The dimension data remains in the database table and is not subject to the size limitations of MOLAP. For more information, see "Dimension Storage Modes" in SQL Server Books Online.

Write-Enabled Dimensions

The members of write-enabled dimensions can be updated through Analysis Manager and client applications that support dimension writeback. Roles are used to control dimension write access by client applications. For more information, see "Write-Enabled Dimensions" in SQL Server Books Online.

Changing Dimensions

The new changing dimension type permits dimension members to be deleted, moved, added, or renamed without requiring the cube to be fully processed after changes. This increases the availability of cubes to client applications. For more information, see "Changing Dimensions" in SQL Server Books Online.

Dependent Dimensions

Dependent dimensions permit improved aggregation design optimization by using knowledge of nonintersecting member combinations to reduce storage requirement estimation in the design algorithm. For more information, see "Dependent Dimensions" in SQL Server Books Online.

Ragged Dimensions

Ragged dimensions have at least one member whose logical parent is not in the level immediately above the member, such as is the case of countries/regions that do not have a state or province level between the country/region and city levels. For more information, see "Ragged Dimension Support" in SQL Server Books Online.

Enhanced Virtual Dimensions

Virtual dimensions have better performance and greater flexibility than in earlier versions. They can be based directly on columns in another dimension's table and include multiple levels. Virtual dimensions are no longer limited to 760 members. For more information, see the topics "Virtual Dimensions" and "Virtual Dimensions Created in Version 7.0" in SQL Server Books Online.

Custom Rollup Formulas and Custom Member Formulas

Cube cell values associated with members can be calculated according to custom expressions rather than the aggregate functions of measures. The expressions can be applied to all the members in a level or individual members. For more information, see "Custom Rollup Formulas and Custom Member Formulas" in SQL Server Books Online.

Automatic Member Grouping

System-generated member groups can be used to accommodate members that have more than 64,000 children. This feature can also be used to provide an intermediate level for drilldown between a level with few members and one with numerous members. For more information, see "Member Groups" in SQL Server Books Online.

Default Members

Default members can be specified for each dimension and varied by role. They control end users' default views of cubes that include the dimension. For more information, see the topics "Set Default Member Dialog Box" and "Custom Rules in Dimension Security" in SQL Server Books Online.

Dimension Filters

A filter (WHERE clause expression) can be used to limit the dimension table rows that are included in the dimension. The filter is specified in the **Source Table Filter** property of the dimension. For more information, see "Properties Pane (Dimension Editor Data View)" in SQL Server Books Online.

Data Mining Enhancements

Data mining technology analyzes data in relational databases and OLAP cubes to discover information of interest. The data mining features of Microsoft SQL Server 2000 Analysis Services are incorporated in an open and extensible implementation of the new OLE DB for Data Mining specification. SQL Server 2000 includes data mining algorithms developed by Microsoft Research.

Relational and OLAP Data Mining

Analysis Services has incorporated data mining technology so you can use it to discover information in relational databases and in OLAP cubes in Analysis Services. You can use the results of data mining to create a dimension that you can add to a cube to further analyze your data. For more information, see "Data Mining Models" in SQL Server Books Online.

Microsoft Decision Trees

The Microsoft Decision Trees algorithm uses classification techniques to analyze data. It then constructs one or more decision trees that can be used to predict attributes or values for new data. For example, you can use this algorithm to analyze credit history data and predict the credit risk of new applicants. For more information, see "Microsoft Decision Trees" in SQL Server Books Online.

Microsoft Clustering

The Microsoft Clustering algorithm uses a nearest neighbor method to group records into clusters that share similar characteristics. Often, these characteristics may be hidden or not intuitive. For more information, see "Microsoft Clustering" in SQL Server Books Online.

Data Mining User Interface

Analysis Services provides new user interface wizards, dialog boxes, and editors to help you quickly perform data mining administrative tasks such as building data mining models and incorporating the results in OLAP cubes. You can browse a single decision tree model or the dependency network model of multiple trees produced when multiple attributes are predicted. For more information, see "Building and Using Data Mining Models" in SQL Server Books Online.

MDX Extensions for Data Mining

Multidimensional Expressions (MDX) syntax has been extended to provide data mining capabilities in connection with OLAP cubes. For more information, see "MDX" in SQL Server Books Online.

DTS Tasks for Data Mining

The Analysis Services Processing task has been enhanced to allow processing mining models, and a new Data Transformation Services (DTS) task is provided that you can use to create predictions from mining models. For more information, see "Automating and Scheduling Administrative Tasks" in SQL Server Books Online.

Data Mining in Client Applications

Client applications for Analysis Services can use data mining algorithms to discover information in OLAP cubes by creating data mining models and virtual cubes. For more information, see "What's New in PivotTable Service" in SQL Server Books Online.

Security Enhancements

This release of Microsoft SQL Server 2000 Analysis Services includes features that provide more flexibility in controlling access to cube data, additional methods for authentication of users, and enhanced enforcement of roles.

Dimension Security

You can use roles to control end-user access to dimensions. For each role, you can limit access to individual dimensions, levels, and members, and you can set various read and read/write permissions. For more information, see "Dimension Security" in SQL Server Books Online.

Enhanced Cell Security

Analysis Manager now includes dialog boxes that enable you to define cell security by setting role options to control end user access to cube cells. You can limit a role's access to any combination of a cube's cells and you can vary the read and read/write permission of the role. For more information, see "Cell Security" in SQL Server Books Online.

Additional Authentication Methods

You can use HTTP authentication methods for client connections to Analysis servers. Analysis Services also supports Windows 2000 negotiated protocol authentication. For more information, see "Server Security and Authentication" in SQL Server Books Online.

Enhanced Role Enforcement

Role specifications are enforced on Analysis servers installed on either file allocation table (FAT) or NTFS file systems.

Client Connectivity Enhancements in PivotTable Service

Enhancements to PivotTable Service provide new connection options and support new cube and security features introduced in this release of Microsoft SQL Server 2000 Analysis Services. Additional new functionality in PivotTable Service can be used by client applications when connected to an Analysis server or when working offline. For more information, see "What's New in PivotTable Service" in SQL Server Books Online.

Connecting to the Analysis Server

Client applications can communicate with the Analysis server through Microsoft Internet Information Services (IIS) using HTTP or HTTPS. Third-party security providers can also be used.

Allocated Writeback

You can write data to aggregation cells in a cube and, using one of four different allocation formulas, automatically distribute the data to the lowest-level members. For more information, see "Using Writebacks" in SQL Server Books Online.

Managing Local Cubes

Many of the new features for server cubes, such as new dimension types, custom rollups, and calculated members, can also be used in local cubes.

Data Mining

PivotTable Service supports the advanced data mining and analysis techniques that are available in SQL Server 2000 Analysis Services. You can create and use data mining models to analyze data in server cubes or local databases.

Other Enhancements

This release of Microsoft SQL Server 2000 Analysis Services incorporates various enhancements to improve usability, processing performance, and MDX functionality.

Multiuser Administration

Multiple users can administer an Analysis server using Analysis Manager. Locking is applied only to the objects being edited and their dependent objects. For more information, see "Analysis Manager" in SQL Server Books Online.

Integration of Add-ins

The Archive and Restore Databases Add-in and the Copy and Paste Objects Add-in originally created for SQL Server 7.0 OLAP Services are upgraded, installed, and fully integrated in this release. You can now use Analysis Manager to archive and restore SQL Server 2000 Analysis Services databases and to copy and paste objects in the Analysis Manager tree pane. For more information, see the topics "Archiving and Restoring Databases" and "Copying and Pasting Objects" in SQL Server Books Online.

MDX Enhancements

A number of new functions have been added to the Multidimensional Expressions (MDX) syntax that you can use for calculated members and increased analytical evaluation. For more information, see "MDX" in SQL Server Books Online.

MDX Builder

A new MDX Builder tool helps you create MDX expressions using drag-and-drop techniques. The MDX editing text box has been enhanced to provide color coding of keywords and functions, indication of parentheses balance, and smart tips that show function syntax. For more information, see "MDX Builder" in SQL Server Books Online.

Table Aliases

In Cube Editor and Dimension Editor you can specify table aliases. For more information, see the topics "Schema Tab (Cubes Editor Schema View)" and "Schema Tab (Dimension Editor Schema View) in SQL Server Books Online.

Active Directory Support

Analysis Services supports Active Directory, the directory service that is included with Microsoft Windows 2000. You can enable an Analysis server so that it publishes Active Directory entries when the server starts, and updates the entries when the server status changes. For more information, see "Using Active Directory with Analysis Services" in SQL Server Books Online.

Performance Monitor Counters

A number of performance counters are now available for Analysis server that can be used with Performance Monitor in Microsoft Windows NT® 4.0 or System Monitor in Windows 2000. For more information, see "Monitoring Analysis Services Performance" in SQL Server Books Online.

Meta Data Services Enhancements

Microsoft SQL Server 2000 Meta Data Services extends and renames the former repository component known as Microsoft Repository. Meta Data Services extends repository technology by introducing a new browser for viewing data in a repository database, new Extensible Markup Language (XML) interchange support, and new repository engine features.

Feature	Description
Meta Data Browser enhancement	Meta Data Browser is a new tool you can use to browse a repository database.
XML Encoding enhancements	XML Encoding supports a new implementation of meta data interchange in Meta Data Coalition (MDC) Open Information Model (OIM) XML.
Repository engine programming enhancements	Programming enhancements detail new and better ways for programming against an installed information model.
Repository engine modeling enhancements	Modeling enhancements support new definitions that you can include in an information model.

Meta Data Browser Enhancement

Meta Data Browser is a new tool you can use to browse the contents of a repository database. This tool is introduced in Microsoft SQL Server 2000 Meta Data Services. You can run Meta Data Browser when you select Meta Data Services. Meta Data Services is available for each copy of SQL Server you install. For more information, see "Using Meta Data Browser" in SQL Server Books Online.

XML Encoding Enhancements

Microsoft SQL Server 2000 Meta Data Services now uses Extensible Markup Language (XML) encoding in native mode. You can import, export, and publish repository meta data in a format that more closely matches your information model.

XML encoding supersedes the XML Interchange Format (XIF) that was part of previous versions of the software. For more information, see the topics "XML in Meta Data Services" and "Using XML Encoding" in SQL Server Books Online.

New COM Interfaces

XML IExport Interface

XML IImport Interface

For more information, see the specific interface topics in SQL Server Books Online.

Repository Engine Programming Enhancements

Repository engine version 3.0 is backward compatible with version 2.0 functionality and interfaces. You can use version 3.0 with no change to the databases. In this case, only the version 2.0 features will work. You can upgrade the database version 2.0 to the database version 3.0 format by passing the REPOS_CONN_UPGRADE flag when you open the repository database. Another way to upgrade a repository database is through Meta Data Browser, during repository database registration. Upgrading allows you to use all the features of version 3.0. After you upgrade; however, you cannot open the upgraded database using a version 2.0 engine.

Microsoft SQL Server 2000 Meta Data Services introduces the following new repository engine features in version 3.0. These features extend the ability to program against an information model that resides in a repository database.

View Generation

View generation provides a way to automatically generate relational views based on classes, interfaces, and relationships in an information model. You can use the relational views that you define to simplify repository database queries. To generate views, four new interfaces have been exposed to the repository engine. For more information, see "Generating Views" in SQL Server Books Online.

New COM Interfaces

IViewClassDef Interface

IViewInterfaceDef Interface

IViewPropertyDef Interface

IViewRelationshipDef Interface

For more information, see the specific interface topics in SQL Server Books Online.

Performance Hints

New performance hints described in SQL Server Books Online can be used to optimize engine performance. In addition to the existing list of optimization techniques, you can adjust cache aging to vary aging for different row types, enable atomicity of operations, and preload object collections for each repository object. The new performance enhancements can be implemented through **IReposOptions**. For adjustable cache aging, set one or more of the AGEOUT options. For atomicity of operations, set OPT_ATOMICMODE. For preloading object collections, set OPT_EXPORT_MODE or OPT_PRELOAD_COL_MODE to specify the maximum number of objects in each collection.

New COM Interfaces

IReposOptions Interface

For more information, see the specific interface topic in SQL Server Books Online.

Property Extensions for BLOBs and Large Text Fields

Property extensions have been exposed to the repository engine to handle large properties or binary large objects (BLOBs) and give access to the meta data about the object. For more information, see "Programming BLOBs and Large Text Fields" in SQL Server Books Online.

New COM Interfaces

IReposProperty2 Interface

IReposPropertyLarge Interface

IRepositoryObject2 Interface

For more information, see the specific interface topics in SQL Server Books Online.

Collection Filters

Collection filters now support SQL selection criteria through the repository API. In this version of the repository engine, you can specify selection criteria for any target object at run time to precisely select objects of interest. To set criteria, use the **GetCollection** method of the **IReposQuery** interface.

New COM Interfaces

IReposQuery Interface

For more information, see the specific interface topic in SQL Server Books Online.

Integration with MS DTC

The repository engine is integrated with Microsoft Distributed Transaction Coordinator (MS DTC), so that an application that is using the repository engine can execute a transaction that spans multiple database systems. For more information, see "Integration with Distributed Transaction Coordinator" in SQL Server Books Online.

New COM Interfaces

IRepositoryTransaction2 Interface

For more information, see the specific interface topic in SQL Server Books Online.

Version Propagation

Version propagation behavior has been extended to relationships through two new flags. You can set COLLECTION_NEWDESTVERSIONADD to specify that an origin object always link to the latest version of a destination object. This eliminates manual versioning of an origin object in response to a new versioned destination object. The second new flag, COLLECTION_NEWDESTVERSIONPROPAGATE, has the opposite effect. It can be set to expand propagation behavior deeper into a chain of relationships. In cases where an object is both an origin and a destination, setting this flag creates a reverse-cascade versioning effect. A new destination object version causes the creation of a new origin object version, repeating this behavior until the engine reaches an unfrozen object. Setting this flag automates a task that developers previously had to handle in application code. For more information, see the topics "Propagating Versions" and "CollectionDefFlags Enumeration" in SQL Server Books Online.

Repository Engine Modeling Enhancements

Microsoft SQL Server 2000 Meta Data Services introduces the following new repository engine features in version 3.0 of the engine. These features extend the ability to create an information model that can take advantage of new features added to this version of the repository engine.

Scripting Support

Scripting support provides the ability to validate properties and implement methods through ActiveX scripts. Model creators can assign scripts to methods that are defined in an information model. With scripting support, you no longer need to use aggregation to validate properties and implement methods. For more information, see "Defining Script Objects" in SQL Server Books Online.

New COM Interfaces

IClassDef2 Interface

IInterfaceMember2 Interface

IInterfaceDef2 Interface

IScriptDef Interface

For more information, see the specific interface topics in SQL Server Books Online.

Interface Implication

Interface implication enables a client to define an implication between two interfaces in an information model. Using **IInterfaceDef2**, you can simulate some of the functionality of multiple inheritance, which is not allowed in COM. For more information, see "Interface Implication" in SQL Server Books Online.

New COM Interfaces

IInterfaceDef2 Interface

For more information, see the specific interface topic in SQL Server Books Online.

Member Delegation

Member delegation extends the engine to support the delegation of derived members on one interface to base members on another interface. This delegation can be used to support relationship inheritance. Two interfaces support this new mapping capability: **IInterfaceMember2** and **IInterfaceDef2**. For more information, see "Member Delegation" in SQL Server Books Online.

New COM Interfaces

IInterfaceMember2 Interface

IInterfaceDef2 Interface

For more information, see the specific interface topics in SQL Server Books Online.

Sharing Model Information

Model dependency allows model developers to define dependencies between information models, to support the creation of more modular, integrated models. To support model dependency, use the new **DependsOn** collection of **IReposTypeLib2**. For more information, see "Define Dependencies Between Type Libraries" in SQL Server Books Online.

New COM Interfaces

IReposTypeLib2 Interface

For more information, see the specific interface topic in SQL Server Books Online.

Naming Semantics for Objects

Object naming semantics have been extended to support more consistent naming. In this version of repository engine, you can set the COLLECTION_OBJECTNAMING flag of **CollectionDefFlag** to specify an object name automatically when creating names for subsequent collections and relationships. For more information, see "CollectionDefFlags Enumeration" in SQL Server Books Online.

Parameter Support

Parameters can now be defined in models. Version 3.0 supports method parameter definitions so model creation can include complete object descriptions. You can now use the Meta Data Services Software Development Kit (SDK) to generate fully descriptive Interface Definition Language (IDL) files from an information model. For more information, see "Defining a Parameter" in SQL Server Books Online.

New COM Interfaces

IMethodDef Interface

IParameterDef Interface

For more information, see the specific interface topics in SQL Server Books Online.

Enumeration Definition

Repository enumeration definition allows you to specify a property as an enumeration that has a fixed set of constant strings or integer values that correspond to real-world concepts. To use this feature, specify an **EnumerationDef** object and associated **EnumerationValue** objects and associate these with **PropertyDef** objects. For more information, see "Repository Enumeration Definition" in SQL Server Books Online.

New COM Interfaces

IEnumerationDef Interface

IEnumerationValueDef Interface

IPropertyDef2 Interface

For more information, see the specific interface topics in SQL Server Books Online.

Type Information Aliasing

Classes, interfaces, and relationships can be referred to by a second name (a synonym). You can implement type information aliasing through new interfaces.

New COM Interfaces

IReposTypeInfo Interface

IReposTypeInfo2 Interface

IInterfaceMember2 Interface

For more information, see the specific interface topics in SQL Server Books Online.

Version Labeling

Version labeling allows users to set or retrieve the version comments properties. Use **IVersionAdminInfo2** to implement version labeling.

New COM Interfaces

IVersionAdminInfo2 Interface

For more information, see the specific interface topic in SQL Server Books Online.

Virtual Members

Virtual member support enables you to define nonpersistent members by setting the VIRTUAL_MEMBER flag on the **InterfaceMemberFlags** property. If this flag is set and the member is a property, the engine does not allocate a column for it in the interface's table. For more information, see the topics "Virtual Members" and "**IInterfaceMember Flags** Property" in SQL Server Books Online.

English Query Enhancements

English Query contains the following new features:

- Microsoft® Visual Studio® Integration
- Graphical Authoring
- SQL Project Wizard
- Analysis Services Integration (formerly OLAP Services) and OLAP Project Wizard
- Semantic Modeling Format (SMF) and Authoring Object Model

- New Regression Features

- Full-Text Query Support

For more information, see Chapter 32, "English Query Best Practices."

Visual Studio Integration

The English Query authoring tool is now integrated into the familiar Visual Studio version 6.0 development environment.

Graphical Authoring

A diagramming tool is provided that displays the entities and relationships in the English Query model you are creating. You can also drag entities onto one another to automatically create relationships between them.

SQL Project Wizard

You can use the SQL Project Wizard to automatically create entities and relationships for all tables in the database. For each entity, it automatically builds name and trait relationships, plus other relationships, resulting in automatic creation of the majority of the entities and relationships needed in a model.

Analysis Services Integration (formerly OLAP Services) and OLAP Project Wizard

The OLAP Project Wizard provides an even higher percentage of automatic entity and relationship creation for OLAP databases. When connected to Microsoft SQL Server 2000 Analysis Services and a model authored for an OLAP cube, Multidimensional Expressions (MDX), rather than SQL, are generated.

Semantic Modeling Format (SMF) and Authoring Object Model

SMF is an XML-based language that is used for persisting English Query model information (entities and relationships and their ties to the database). Combined with SMF, the Authoring object model provides programmatic authoring of English Query models.

New Regression Features

Regression test output can now be promoted to serve as the new regression text file. Structured results output can be used as input to other tools.

Full-Text Query Support

This version integrates the SQL Server full-text feature, which allows the searching of both structured and unstructured textual data within English Query applications.

Two-Click Deployment

You can deploy an English Query application to the Web and to Analysis Services simply by clicking twice and selecting several commands from the **Project** menu.

Enhanced Authoring by Example

During the testing process, you can see suggested entities and phrasings that need to be defined to answer questions. The new version provides multiple suggestions and simplifies the clarification process by providing a single form in which you can work.

Oracle Database Support

English Query can generate SQL for Oracle.

Graphical Question Builder

A querying interface is now provided for the end user of English Query applications. Question Builder uses the English Query model behind the application to provide easy question building and quick answers from the database. End users can drag entities onto other entities to display all available relationships.

Documentation Enhancements

The following enhancements have been made to the documentation for Microsoft SQL Server 2000:

F1 Help Integrated with SQL Server Books Online

The F1 Help for SQL Server 2000 has been integrated with SQL Server Books Online. When you select F1 Help, a related topic in SQL Server Books Online is displayed.

SQL Server Books Online Supports Subsets

SQL Server Books Online allows you to define subsets of the entire SQL Server Books Online, against which you can perform a search. You can define your own subsets; however, a set of default subsets is also provided. The subsets are targeted at specific audiences, and each subset covers multiple topics. Subsets make it easier to search for information related to your activities by minimizing the number of search hits.

Thumbnail Art

Some diagrams in SQL Server Books Online now appear as thumbnail diagrams. The full diagram can be viewed by clicking **Enlarge diagram**. The full diagram appears when the topic is printed.

Glossary Improvements

Glossary terms appear as colored, underlined text. When a term is clicked, a pop-up window appears with the term definition.

Easier to Access Related Topics

Many topics have a list of related topics, called "See Also," at the end. SQL Server Books Online adds a See Also icon that displays the list of related topics when you click it.

PART 2

Planning

Choosing an Edition of SQL Server 2000

Introduction

Microsoft® SQL Server™ 2000 is more than a relational database management system; it is a complete database and analysis product that meets the scalability and reliability requirements of the most demanding enterprises. It is appropriate for a broad range of solution types, including e-commerce, data warehousing, and line-of-business applications.

Of course, SQL Server 2000 contains many features that help businesses manage and analyze data, but one "feature" that might not be so obvious is the selection of SQL Server 2000 editions. There are seven different editions to choose from. That might seem like a lot of different products to worry about, but understanding the differences and appropriate uses for these various editions is actually quite simple.

The different editions are designed to accommodate the unique performance, runtime, and price requirements of organizations and individuals. For example, your organization may require not only that its database and analysis solution run on the largest, most powerful computers in your company's data center, but also that this solution be able to "scale down" to desktops, laptops, and even devices like the Pocket PC. SQL Server 2000 achieves this goal while maintaining maximum application compatibility across platforms. Understanding these options allows organizations to make the most cost-effective and technically appropriate choice for their particular needs.

In this chapter, you'll learn more specifically about the differences among the various editions of SQL Server 2000, and how you can save time and money by choosing the right one for the job.

SQL Server 2000 Server Editions Explained

We will begin by making a statement that will go a long way toward helping you understand the different offerings in the SQL Server 2000 family:

SQL Server 2000 Enterprise Edition and SQL Server 2000 Standard Edition are the only editions of SQL Server 2000 that can be installed and used in live (deployed) server environments.

What does this mean? Simply, if you are building a database or analysis application that accesses SQL Server 2000, you must use SQL Server 2000 Standard or Enterprise editions. Other editions cannot be used in deployed, server solutions, due to technical and licensing restrictions. The terms "deployed" and "live" are intended to differentiate such a solution from one that is "under development" or "in testing." It is also worth noting that the Enterprise and Standard editions can only be installed on server operating systems, namely Microsoft Windows® 2000 Server, Windows 2000 Advanced Server, Windows 2000 Datacenter Server, Windows NT® Server 4.0, or Windows NT Server 4.0 Enterprise Edition (for more information, see http://www.microsoft.com/sql/).

So, the central choice most organizations must make is between two editions: Enterprise or Standard.

SQL Server 2000 Enterprise Edition

This edition is comprehensive: it includes the complete set of SQL Server database and analysis features and is uniquely characterized by several features that make it the most scalable and available edition of SQL Server 2000. It scales to the performance levels required to support the largest Web sites and enterprise online transaction processing (OLTP) and data warehousing systems. Its support for failover clustering also makes it ideal for any mission critical line-of-business application. Additionally, this edition includes several advanced analysis features that are not included in SQL Server 2000 Standard Edition.

There are four main areas in which the additional features of SQL Server 2000 Enterprise Edition are most evident:

- Scalability
- Availability/uptime
- Performance
- Advanced analysis

For each of these areas, the following guidelines will help you decide whether to choose the Enterprise Edition or Standard edition. And, for a detailed list of features included in the various editions of SQL Server 2000, please see "Features Supported by the Editions of SQL Server 2000" in SQL Server 2000 Books Online.

Scalability Requirements

Whether for data warehousing or for a transactional system, Enterprise Edition scales best. It supports more memory (up to 64 gigabytes [GB]) and processors (up to 32) than Standard Edition. Use Enterprise Edition for improved scalability if you:

- Need more than four CPUs in the database server. For more information, see "Maximum Capacity Specification" in SQL Server Books Online.

- Need more than 2 GB of physical memory (RAM) in the database server.

- Will be dividing database workload across independent servers (that is, "scaling out").

- Are using System Area Networking (SAN) connection technologies between servers (for example, Compaq ServerNet II or Giganet cLAN).

Availability/Uptime

Enterprise Edition includes features that ensure the highest levels of availability for mission critical applications. Use Enterprise Edition for improved availability/uptime if you:

- Are installing a system that will use failover clustering to ensure that your applications stay up and running even when disaster strikes.

- Rely on log shipping to maintain a warm standby server.

Performance

Other enhancements ensure that the performance of Enterprise Edition exceeds that of other editions. Because these features are optimizations for common operations, many—if not most—applications will realize performance improvements running atop SQL Server 2000 Enterprise Edition. Use Enterprise Edition for improved performance if you:

- Need to speed up an application by taking full advantage of symmetric multiprocessor (SMP) computers (that is, enhanced parallelism).

- Need to improve performance of applications that frequently use queries that perform particular types of joins or aggregations, as in reporting applications (using indexed views).

- Need to speed up transactional applications that do many database reads and full table scans.

Advanced Analysis

In the area of data warehousing and OLAP, Enterprise Edition offers a variety of unique features including allowing OLAP cubes with very large dimensions to be created, stored, and analyzed. Use Enterprise Edition for your data warehousing and analysis tasks if you:

- Need to define OLAP partitions.

- Will be creating and updating large cubes with very large dimensions.

- Have extremely large dimensions that require relational OLAP (ROLAP) storage.

- Need to update cubes quickly, in real time.

- Need to link cubes or provide cube access over the Web.

SQL Server 2000 Standard Edition

This is a more affordable option for small- and medium-sized organizations that do not require the advanced scalability, availability, performance, or analysis features of SQL Server 2000 Enterprise Edition. Standard Edition can be used on symmetric multiprocessing systems with up to 4 CPUs and 2 GB of RAM.

Standard Edition includes the core functionality needed for non-mission-critical e-commerce, data warehousing, and line-of-business solutions. For instance, all of the XML features present in Enterprise Edition are also included in Standard Edition. And while a handful of advanced OLAP features are reserved for Enterprise Edition, all data mining features and the core OLAP functionality are included in SQL Server 2000 Analysis Services in Standard Edition. Similarly, components that other database vendors charge for as separate add-on products for their highest-end editions are included in Standard Edition:

- Data Transformation Services

- Replication (snapshot, transactional, and merge)

- Full-Text Search

- English Query

- Stored procedure development and debugging tools

- SQL Profiling and performance analysis tools

Before choosing Standard Edition, make sure you review "Features Supported by the Editions of SQL Server 2000" in SQL Server Books Online.

SQL Server 2000 Editions for Special Uses

Besides the two server editions of SQL Server 2000, five editions exist for special uses. These are:

- SQL Server 2000 Personal Edition
- SQL Server 2000 Developer Edition
- SQL Server 2000 Evaluation Edition (also known as SQL Server 2000 Enterprise Evaluation Edition)
- SQL Server 2000 Windows CE Edition
- SQL Server 2000 Desktop Engine

SQL Server 2000 Personal Edition

SQL Server 2000 Personal Edition is ideal for mobile users who spend some of their time disconnected from the network but run applications that require SQL Server data storage, and for stand-alone applications that require local SQL Server data storage on a client computer.

This edition is functionally equivalent to the Standard Edition, with the following exceptions:

- It includes a concurrent workload governor that limits its scalability; performance degrades when more than five Transact-SQL batches are executed concurrently.
- It can use a maximum of two processors in an SMP computer (only one processor if running Windows 98 or Windows Millennium Edition).
- It cannot act as a transactional replication publisher (subscriber only).

In addition to running on the server operating systems of the Microsoft Windows NT 4.0 and Windows 2000 operating system families, Personal Edition runs on non-server operating systems including Windows 2000 Professional, Windows NT Workstation 4.0, Windows Millennium Edition, and Windows 98. Full-Text Search and SQL Server 2000 Analysis Services (including OLAP, data mining, and data warehousing features) are included in Personal Edition but cannot be installed on Windows 98 or Windows Millennium Edition.

SQL Server 2000 Developer Edition

This edition allows developers to build any type of application on top of SQL Server. It includes all of the functionality of Enterprise Edition but with a special development and test end-user license agreement (EULA) that prohibits production deployment (for complete details, see the SQL Server 2000 Developer Edition EULA at http://www.microsoft.com/sql/). For maximum flexibility during development, it will install to the aforementioned server operating systems as well as Windows 2000 Professional and Windows NT Workstation 4.0.

SQL Server 2000 Developer Edition is the only edition of SQL Server 2000 that gives the licensee the right to download and install SQL Server 2000 Windows CE Edition (SQL Server CE) from http://www.microsoft.com/sql. The Developer Edition licensee also has the right to redistribute SQL Server CE-based applications to an unlimited number of devices at no additional cost beyond the purchase price of SQL Server 2000 Developer Edition. Devices running SQL Server CE that access or otherwise use the resources of a SQL Server must be properly licensed. For more information, see http://www.microsoft.com/sql/.

SQL Server 2000 Developer Edition is the ideal choice for Independent Software Vendors (ISVs), consultants, system integrators, solution providers, and corporate developers developing and testing applications because it is cost effective, runs on a variety of platforms, and can be upgraded for production use to SQL Server 2000 Enterprise Edition.

SQL Server 2000 Evaluation Edition

SQL Server 2000 Evaluation Edition (also known as SQL Server 2000 Enterprise Evaluation Edition) is a time-limited version of SQL Server 2000 Enterprise Edition that is licensed for demonstration, testing, examination, and evaluation for a period of 120 days. This means that Evaluation Edition is not for production use; solutions must be deployed on SQL Server 2000 Enterprise or Standard Edition. Evaluation Edition will not function after the 120-day limit has been reached. The only cost for this edition is a minimal shipping and handling fee. The advantage of the Evaluation Edition is that you can evaluate the complete set of features in SQL Server 2000, which can be useful whether you are already familiar with SQL Server or are completely new to the product.

Like Developer Edition, Evaluation Edition will install to the aforementioned server operating systems as well as Windows 2000 Professional and Windows NT Workstation 4.0. This gives developers and database administrators additional flexibility in evaluating the product, as it can easily be installed on laptops or desktop systems running these non-server operating systems.

For more information about the Evaluation Edition, please go to http://www.microsoft.com/sql/.

SQL Server 2000 Windows CE Edition

Microsoft SQL Server 2000 Windows CE Edition (SQL Server CE) is the compact database for rapidly developing applications that extend enterprise data management capabilities to devices. SQL Server CE is a full-fledged member of the SQL Server 2000 family, with tools, application programming interfaces (APIs), and SQL grammar that developers and database administrators with existing SQL Server skills will recognize. SQL Server CE is the only edition of SQL Server 2000 that provides relational database management capabilities on Windows CE-based devices.

The SQL Server CE engine provides an essential set of relational database features—including an optimizing query processor and support for transactions and assorted data types—while it maintains a compact footprint that preserves system resources. Remote data access and merge replication, which work over Hypertext Transfer Protocol (HTTP) and support encryption, ensure that data from enterprise SQL Server databases is reliably delivered and that this data can be manipulated offline and synchronized later to the server. This makes SQL Server CE ideal for mobile and wireless scenarios.

SQL Server CE runs on devices that use Windows CE version 2.11 or later, including the Handheld PC Pro (H/PC Pro), Palm-size PC (P/PC), and Pocket PC. SQL Server CE can access SQL Server data in SQL Server version 6.5 or later, but can act as a merge replication subscriber only with SQL Server 2000 databases. SQL Server CE has a device footprint of approximately 1 megabyte (MB). Database size is currently limited to 2 GB. For more information on SQL Server CE (or to download SQL Server CE if you are a licensed SQL Server 2000 Developer Edition user) please see http://www.microsoft.com/sql/.

SQL Server 2000 Desktop Engine

SQL Server 2000 Desktop Engine is the successor to Microsoft Data Engine (MSDE) 1.0, which was based on SQL Server version 7.0. As such, SQL Server 2000 Desktop Engine is often referred to as MSDE 2000. The SQL Server 2000 Desktop Engine is not related to SQL Server 7.0 Desktop Edition.

Probably the most significant characteristic of the Desktop Engine is that it is a redistributable version of the SQL Server relational database engine. Third-party software developers can include it in their applications that use SQL Server to store data. The SQL Server 2000 Desktop Engine is made available as a set of Windows Installer merge modules that can be included in the application setup. The Desktop Engine is an ideal embedded or offline data store, because it is easy to install and has the smallest footprint of any edition of SQL Server 2000.

The SQL Server 2000 Desktop Engine does not include graphical management tools; the application distributing the engine is usually coded to perform any needed database administration. You can manage instances of the Desktop Engine from the SQL Server 2000 graphical tools if installed with another edition of SQL Server. Other items not included in the Desktop Engine include analysis capabilities (such as OLAP, data mining, and data warehousing features) and SQL Server Books Online. Desktop Engine also limits database size to 2 GB and employs the same concurrent workload throttle described above for Personal Edition.

Like all of the editions of SQL Server 2000 described so far in this chapter, the Desktop Engine supports multiple instance installations, lessening the likelihood that an instance installed by an application of one vendor will conflict with subsequent MSDE-based applications installed by applications by other vendors. Additionally, all of the APIs and most of the functionality of the other editions of SQL Server 2000 are supported. Desktop Engine includes the SQLServerAgent service for managing scheduled tasks. Although the Desktop Engine does not include the management tools or wizards, applications can fully administer an instance of the Desktop Engine using the SQL Server administration APIs, such as SQL-DMO, the DTS and Replication programming objects, or the general database APIs (such as ADO, OLE DB, and ODBC). Applications can use the general database APIs to access data in the Desktop Engine, and the Desktop Engine can participate alongside other editions of SQL Server 2000 in DTS transformations and replication plans (except operating as a transactional replication publisher).

Redistribution rights exist for the Desktop Engine and can be found in the EULAs for the products that include it (see "Obtaining SQL Server 2000" later in this chapter). If the Desktop Engine is not used in a purely standalone manner—that is, if the Desktop Engine is connecting to or otherwise utilizing the resources of a SQL Server (even if this use occurs through middleware, across multiple computers, or through multiplexing, where no direct connection is present)—then it is acting as a client to a SQL Server server and must be properly licensed. In such a case, customers using the Processor licensing model on the server enjoy unlimited connections to the server, and thus require no further action for the Desktop Engine or any other clients. However, customers using the Server/Client Access License (CAL) licensing model in this scenario must have a CAL dedicated to any device using the Desktop Engine. For more information, see Chapter 4, "Choosing How to License SQL Server." You can also visit http://www.microsoft.com/sql/.

Obtaining SQL Server 2000

SQL Server 2000 Enterprise Edition and SQL Server 2000 Standard Edition are available through a variety of channels. Competitive and version upgrades to SQL Server 2000 may lower your cost considerably. Additionally, small business, enterprise, government, and academic discounts are available. For complete information on how to obtain SQL Server 2000, please visit http://www.microsoft.com/sql/.

SQL Server 2000 Personal Edition is not a separate product but rather a client component of SQL Server 2000 (included as part of Enterprise and Standard Editions), designed to bring SQL Server functionality to non-server hardware, including workstations and laptops. SQL Server Personal Edition can be installed on any client device to be used in conjunction with the server software. Licensing is governed by the same rules as Enterprise and Standard Edition licensing.

SQL Server 2000 Developer Edition can be ordered online directly from Microsoft at http://shop.microsoft.com or from an authorized reseller (http://www.microsoft.com/shop/reseller.htm). SQL Server 2000 Developer Edition is also included in the MSDN Universal subscription (http://msdn.microsoft.com/subscriptions/).

SQL Server 2000 Evaluation Edition can be ordered for a minimal fee from http://shop.microsoft.com/devtools/.

SQL Server 2000 Windows CE Edition is available for free download to licensed SQL Server 2000 Developer Edition users. Please see http://www.microsoft.com/sql/ for more information.

SQL Server 2000 Desktop Engine is included in a directory called "MSDE" at the root of the SQL Server 2000 Enterprise, Standard, and Developer Edition CD-ROMs. SQL Server 2000 Desktop Engine will also be included in upcoming Microsoft products, just as MSDE 1.0 shipped in products like Microsoft Visual Studio® 6.0 Enterprise Edition and Microsoft Office 2000 Developer.

Conclusion

Whether you are a developer, IT professional, or a database administrator, whether you are just developing and testing or are ready to deploy in production, there is a SQL Server 2000 edition for you and your organization. The variety of SQL Server 2000 editions ensures that you pay a fair price for the functionality you need. You will likely find that you use several editions of SQL Server 2000 on a single project: development and testing on Developer Edition, deployment to servers on Enterprise Edition, with replication subscriptions managed by Personal Edition running on laptops. And in the future, maybe you will extend your solution to devices, relying on SQL Server 2000 Windows CE Edition for reliable, high performance database management. The important thing is to consider up front what edition will work best for your organization; by making the right choice you will end up saving time and money.

You have also learned how to obtain the various editions of SQL Server, but you may have one lingering question: "What should I run SQL Server 2000 on?" To answer this question, you must consider both the hardware and the operating system. Your hardware vendor can help you pick an appropriate server computer for your solution, and may even have sizing tools available for download from its Web site. For the operating system, keep in mind several things. The deployable server edition of SQL Server 2000 requires a server operating system, and it is optimized for Windows 2000. Several features in SQL Server 2000 are dependent on features in the operating system and thus are unavailable when SQL Server 2000 is run atop Windows NT Server 4.0. For example, Microsoft Active Directory™ integration requires Windows 2000 Server or greater. Such issues need to be considered when you plan your SQL Server 2000 deployments.

CHAPTER 4

Choosing How to License SQL Server

If your organization is evaluating deployment of Microsoft® SQL Server™, you will find there are a number of different options for licensing this database technology, and some changes have recently been made to the licensing model at Microsoft. This chapter helps you determine the type of SQL Server licensing to implement. Based on extensive input from customers, partners, and analysts, Microsoft has introduced a processor-based licensing model for the .NET Enterprise Server products (including SQL Server). This new licensing model was designed for today's e-business customers who are building business-to-business, business-to-consumer, and business-to-employee Web-based applications. Such hardware-based models have become standard in a Web-based world where traditional measures of users or connecting devices are impossible to track.

For customers using SQL Server in non-Web-based scenarios, per-seat licensing is still available.

Licensing Model Changes

Microsoft is standardizing processor-based licensing with the .NET Enterprise servers to improve consistency and to simplify how customers license certain software products. Under this new model, a customer acquires a Processor License for each processor running their server software. A Processor License includes access for an unlimited number of users/devices to connect from either inside the corporate LAN or WAN, or outside the firewall. Customers do not need to purchase additional Server Licenses, Client Access Licenses (CALs) or Internet Connector Licenses.

This kind of license can be used in any Internet, extranet, or intranet scenario, and is designed especially for e-business customers. These licenses are appropriate when traditional measures of users or connecting devices are impossible to track.

Separate server licenses and per seat CALs (Client Access Licenses) will continue to be offered to customers using SQL Server. The Server Licenses allow access for a single device (for example, a personal computer, pager, or cell phone). SQL Server 2000 CALs can only be used in the per-seat mode. One CAL is required for each device that will be accessing the server software. This method of licensing may be most cost-effective to non-Web-based businesses with a limited number of users that are easy to track.

What is a Processor License?

A Processor License gives you the right to install one copy of the server software on a single server, as long as you have purchased Processor Licenses for all of the processors on that server. For example, if you have a server with a single processor, one Processor License is all you need to install and use the server software on that computer. If you have a server with four processors, you will need to purchase four Processor Licenses in order to install and use the server software on that server.

A Processor License for SQL Server 2000 Enterprise Edition gives you the right to install any number of copies of the server software on any processor that has a license.

In addition to the installation rights to the actual server software, Processor Licenses also grant any number of users the rights to access and use the server software running on those processors. These access rights are available to all users, regardless of whether they are inside the organization (for example, in an intranet scenario) or outside the organization (in an extranet scenario).

The Processor License is all you will need. With this license, you do not need to purchase separate Server, Client Access, or Internet Connector Licenses.

You must have a separate Processor License for each processor on a server, even if some processors are not intended for running server software. This is because all processors on a given server will be used to run server software in the vast majority of scenarios. There are, however, larger, multi-processor servers that give you the ability to partition groups of processors within a single computer, allowing you to run the server software on a subset of the total processors. For this case, an exception in licensing is made for servers with sixteen or more processors. For those servers, Processor Licenses are required only for those processors actually running the server software.

Upgrades

Existing SQL Server customers can upgrade to SQL Server 2000 at approximately 50 percent of the full license price.

- Customers with Upgrade Advantage licenses for servers running SQL Server and CALs are entitled to upgrades to those licenses at no additional charge.

- BackOffice CAL Upgrade Advantage customers are entitled to access SQL Server 2000 servers with those CALs.

Internet Connector Upgrade Advantage customers are eligible to receive SQL Server Processor Licenses as upgrades, either in SQL Server 2000 Enterprise or Standard editions, depending on what edition of the server software the Internet Connectors use. To determine how to upgrade from previous versions of SQL Server, use the upgrade calculator found at:
http://www.microsoft.com/sql/productinfo/HowToUpgradeCalculator.xls.

Choosing a Licensing Model

What licensing model to chose depends on your specific business requirements. Here are some general guidelines to follow:

- Per Processor is generally the best choice for all externally focused server applications.

  - This includes servers used in Internet and extranet situations. Typically, counting seats in these scenarios is very difficult, so hardware-based pricing for the server is useful.

  - In addition, for servers that will be accessed from both inside and outside the firewall of an organization, Per Processor licensing is usually best. This is because Processor Licenses are likely to be needed for external users, licensing Per Processor means you will not need to purchase access separately for internal users through CALs.

  - In environments inside the firewall, where client-to-server processor ratios are high, the Per Processor model will likely be more cost effective.

  An advantage to the Per Processor model is it eliminates the need to count seats, which many customers find difficult to manage on an ongoing basis.

- The Per Seat CAL model is likely the most cost effective choice in environments inside the firewall where client-to-server ratios are low.

The listing below indicates the number of seats you would need, to make buying Processor License(s) less expensive than buying Server Licenses. Therefore, if you have more seats than shown in the list, you should buy the Processor Licenses.

- SQL Server 2000 Enterprise Edition — purchase Processor License if:

  - 1 processor computer: with more than 80 seats

  - 2 processor computer: with more than 198 seats

  - 4 processor computer: with more than 435 seats

  - 8 processor computer: with more than 909 seats

- SQL Server 2000 Standard Edition — purchase Processor License if:

  - 1 processor computer: with more than 24 seats

  - 2 processor computer: with more than 53 seats

  - 4 processor computer: with more than 112 seats

  - 8 processor computer: with more than 229 seats

Mixed License Environments

There are no restrictions prohibiting you from having a mixed-license environment. There may be scenarios when this is the best solution for your business. For example, if the Internet servers for your organization are segregated from the servers used to support internal users, you could license the Internet servers with Processor Licenses and purchase separate Server Licenses for internal customers, and CALs for each internal user's devices. However, you should not purchase CALs to allow users to access a server already licensed through Processor License, since those Processor Licenses allow access to that server for all users. In addition, you should never purchase Processor Licenses for a server that will be accessed exclusively by users for whom CALs have already been purchased.

Licensing for a Failover Cluster Configuration

If your organization uses SQL Server 2000 in a failover cluster configuration, this means servers are clustered together to pick up each others' processing if one computer fails, in this situation, you have special licensing considerations. This option is only available in SQL Server 2000 Enterprise Edition.

Failover clustering support can be configured two ways:

- Active/Active. This option allows all servers in the failover cluster to regularly process information. When a server fails, one server or more takes on the additional workload of the failed server.

- Active/Passive. This option is characterized by at least one server in the cluster that do not regularly process information, but waits to pick up the workload when an Active server fails.

All Active servers in a cluster must be fully licensed, with either Processor Licenses or Server Licenses. However, if a server is strictly Passive, and works only when an Active server has failed, no additional licenses are needed for that Passive server. The exception to this is if the failover cluster is licensed under Processor License, and the number of processors on the Passive server exceeds the number of processors on the Active server. In this case, additional Processor licenses must be purchased for the additional processors on the Passive computer.

For more information about failover clustering, see SQL Server Books Online.

Licensing for a Multi-Instance Configuration

SQL Server 2000 includes the ability to run multiple instances of the server software on a single server. Multiple instances are used by organizations that have several applications running on a server, but want them to run in isolation. Running them in isolation protects each from a failure on another instance. SQL Server 2000 Enterprise Edition Processor Licenses and Server Licenses allow you to install multiple instances of SQL Server on the same computer without requiring additional licenses. SQL Server 2000 Standard Edition supports multiple instances, but you must have a separate license for each instance.

For more information about multiple instances of SQL Server, see SQL Server Books Online.

Licensing in Multi-Tier Environments (Including Multiplexing or Pooling)

Sometimes organizations develop network solutions that use various forms of hardware and/or software to reduce the number of devices that directly access or use the software on a particular server. This particular solution is often called multiplexing or pooling hardware or software. It is particularly common in multi-tier environments. For example, say a client computer is using a server application that calls Component Services, available with Microsoft Windows 2000 Server, on one server, which in turn pulls data from a SQL Server database on another server. In this case, the only direct connection to SQL Server is coming from the server running Component Services. The client computer has a direct connection to the server running Component Services, but the client computer also has an indirect connection to SQL Server because it is ultimately retrieving and using the SQL Server data through Component Services. Use of multiplexing or pooling hardware and/or software does not reduce the number of CALs required to access or use SQL Server. A CAL is required for each distinct input to the multiplexing or pooling software or hardware front end. If, in the above example, 50 client computers were connected to the server running Component Services, 50 SQL Server CALs would be required. This is true no matter how many tiers of hardware or software exist between the SQL Server and the client devices that ultimately use its data, services, or functionality.

SQL Server 2000 Personal Edition Licensing

SQL Server 2000 Personal Edition is not a separate product, but rather a client component of SQL Server (included as part of Enterprise and Standard editions) that is designed to bring SQL Server functionality to non-server hardware, including workstations and laptops. SQL Server 2000 Personal Edition can be installed on any client device running the Microsoft Windows operating system within an organization, and is to be used in conjunction with the server software. Licensing is governed by the same rules as licensing for the Enterprise and Standard editions.

SQL Server 2000 Desktop Engine Licensing

SQL Server 2000 Desktop Engine is fully compatible with other editions of SQL Server and is available through various Microsoft products beyond SQL Server 2000 Enterprise, Standard, and Developer editions. These include MSDN® Universal and Microsoft Office Developer Edition 10. The Desktop Edition, sometimes referred to as MSDE 2000, is intended to be a stand-alone desktop device and does not require any CALs when used on a purely stand-alone basis. Some Microsoft products grant MSDE redistribution rights to the licensee; please see the End User License Agreement for the software package that included MSDE 1.0 or MSDE 2000 to determine your eligibility to redistribute these versions of MSDE.

Customers using the Processor licensing model have unlimited connections to the server running the licensed SQL Server. Customers using the Server/CAL (versus Per-Processor) licensing model must have a CAL dedicated to any device using the Desktop Engine—either in stand-alone form, or as part of one of the products mentioned above.

Switching Licenses

It is possible to switch from SQL Server CALs to Processor Licenses, or from Processor Licenses to CALs. To do so, you must purchase the appropriate new licenses. Generally, the most logical time to do this is when you upgrade to a new version of SQL Server; however, switching from a combination of Server Licenses and CALs to Processor Licenses may make sense when you need to allow Web usage (either Internet or extranet), or when the number of users is expected to grow significantly. Moving to Processor Licensing could offer financial benefits in this case.

For more information about SQL Server licensing, answers to commonly asked questions can be found at http://www.microsoft.com/catalog/ or at http://www.Microsoft.com/sql/productinfo/licensing.htm.

CHAPTER 5

Migrating Access 2000 Databases to SQL Server 2000

As your business grows and demands more high-level performance from your database system, you may have to move from the file-server environment of the Microsoft® Access 2000 Jet engine to the client/server environment of Microsoft SQL Server™ 2000. You may be considering migrating (upsizing) your database to SQL Server because:

- The number of database users is increasing.

  As the number of users increases, the file-sharing mechanism of a Microsoft Access database may result in a slower performance and increased network traffic. The client/server environment of Microsoft SQL Server is designed for a large number of users and minimizing network traffic.

- The size of your database is growing.

  Microsoft SQL Server 2000 can support databases of up to 2 terabytes in size.

- You must access your database over the Internet.

  SQL Server 2000 is an XML-enabled database server that allows you to access the server through a URL, and to write and retrieve data as XML documents.

- You require increased security.

  Integration of Microsoft SQL Server's security with the security of a Microsoft Windows NT® or Microsoft Windows® 2000 network allows easier administration of complex network security settings.

- You want higher availability.

  SQL Server can be backed up and restored dynamically while the database is in use. Users do not have to close the database while the daily backup is performed. In addition, the process of transaction logging makes it possible to restore the database up to the point of failure.

Migration Options

The process of migrating an Access database to SQL Server 2000 moves some or all data and data definitions to the server. After the data is safely transferred to SQL Server, you still must decide how to interact with the server-based data. The following options are possible solutions:

- Create a two-tier application.

  You can link server-based tables to local tables in Access and use the other existing database objects (queries, forms, reports, modules, and macros) as before. This creates a two-tier application, in which the server running SQL Server stores data, and copies of the interface are stored in Access on the users' computers. Queries are run on the client tier. Locally stored forms, reports, modules, and macros provide the remaining elements of the user interface. The design of server-based tables cannot be modified from Access. The advantage of this method is a low transition cost because no modifications are needed to the front-end database objects. Users continue to interact with a familiar interface, and the SQL Server provides centralized data storage, backup and recovery options, a multiuser environment, an integrated security model, and other advantages. The main disadvantages of this method are that queries are still processed locally, and a large amount of network traffic is generated.

- Create a client/server application.

  Microsoft Access 2000 introduces Microsoft Access Project, a new type of Access file (.adp) designed as a client/server application. Communication between the client and the server takes place through OLE DB component architecture, which was specifically designed for efficient client/server communication. All tables and data definition objects such as views, stored procedures, and database diagrams are stored on the server. The client stores only code-based or HTML-based objects such as forms, reports, modules, and macros. Most data processing takes place on the server, and only filtered data is sent to the client, thus minimizing network traffic.

- Upsize data without making any modifications to the Access application.

  If you are going to create a new application in Microsoft Visual Basic®, Active Server Pages (ASPs), or another environment, you may not want to migrate the application-specific logic and user interface.

Before You Migrate

Several issues should be considered before you begin migrating your database:

- Confirm the integrity of the original database. The best way to protect your database is to create a complete backup and safely store it away from the computers involved in migrating. Consider this step as the single most critical step of the entire operation.

- Ensure that you have adequate permissions on both the Access database and the instance of SQL Server to which you are migrating. You will need at least Read Design permission on all objects that will be migrated and on all objects that act as data source for migrated objects. For example, to properly migrate a query you must have Read Design permissions on the query itself as well as the table or tables that the query uses as the data source.

- If you are upsizing an MDE file, make sure that you have access to a copy of the original Access database. In an MDE file all source code for Microsoft Visual Basic for Applications is removed and replaced with a compiled, binary format. This creates a more efficient database but also prevents access to the design of forms, reports, and modules, making migration of these objects impossible. Tables, queries, macros, and data access pages are not affected and can be migrated.

- You will need a password to any Visual Basic for Applications projects within your database.

Migration Tools

You have two main methods to upsize your database:

- The Upsizing Wizard available with Microsoft Access

- SQL Server Tools such as Data Transformation Services (DTS), SQL Server Enterprise Manager, SQL Query Analyzer, and SQL Profiler

The actual process of moving a database to SQL Server will most likely be a combination of these methods. The Upsizing Wizard can be used to quickly move your database, and the SQL Server Tools can be used in the process of fine-tuning your queries and indexes.

Upsizing Wizard

The Upsizing Wizard moves a Microsoft Access database to a new or existing Microsoft SQL Server database or to a new Microsoft Access Project. The wizard moves data and data definitions to the server and migrates database objects. The wizard re-creates primary keys, table relationships, and any existing rules and defaults.

To use the Upsizing Wizard, you must run the Access 2000 and SQL Server 2000 Readiness Update. This update is available on the *SQL Server 2000 Resource Kit* CD-ROM in \ToolsAndSamples\AccessUpsizing.

Before you use the Upsizing Wizard:

1. Create the database and log devices on SQL Server.

2. Gather data on table relationships with the Access database.

3. Ensure that the names in the .mdb file comply with SQL Server rules.

4. Make note of all default values in the database. You will want to confirm the defaults were set correctly after you migrate.

5. Make a backup of your database.

When you use the Upsizing Wizard:

1. Use Declarative Referential Integrity (DRI), not triggers, to enforce table relationships.

2. Unless you want timestamps, do not allow the wizard to decide where to put them. You can always add these exactly where you want them later.

3. After running the wizard, check the log to ensure that the migration went smoothly.

4. In SQL Server, update foreign keys to support cascading deletes and updates where desired.

SQL Server Tools Used in Migrations

SQL Server 2000 provides several tools that you can use to migrate your Access data and applications. Using these tools provides more control over the migrating process, but may be time-consuming because they require more manual input.

SQL Server Enterprise Manager

Using SQL Server Enterprise Manager, you can configure and manage SQL Server and SQL Server objects throughout your enterprise. SQL Server Enterprise Manager provides access to a powerful scheduling engine, administrative alert capabilities, and a built-in replication management interface. You can also use SQL Server Enterprise Manager to:

- Manage logins and user permissions.

- Create scripts.

- Manage backup of SQL Server objects.

- Back up databases and transaction logs.

- Manage tables, views, stored procedures, triggers, indexes, rules, defaults, and user-defined data types.

- Create full-text indexes, database diagrams, and database maintenance plans.

- Import and export data.

- Transform data.

- Perform various Web administration tasks.

Data Transformation Services (DTS)

DTS enables importing and exporting data between SQL Server and any OLE DB or ODBC data source, including Microsoft Access, and to transfer databases and database objects (for example, indexes and stored procedures) between multiple computers running

SQL Server 2000. Both SQL Server and Microsoft Data Engine (MSDE) include the DTS Import/Export Wizard, which enable creating and running DTS packages interactively.

You can use the DTS Import/Export Wizard to automatically create tables on SQL Server, and then to copy data from Access to the new SQL Server or MSDE tables. DTS can move data at a faster rate than the Microsoft Access Upsizing Wizard, but DTS does not provide all of the features of the Access Upsizing Wizard. The following is a list of actions that the Access Upsizing Wizard can perform, but which the DTS Import/Export Wizard cannot perform:

- The Access Upsizing Wizard automatically migrates all rules and defaults that exist in a table to SQL Server; DTS does not.

- DTS does not upsize any Access queries.

SQL Query Analyzer

SQL Query Analyzer is a graphical query tool that allows visually analyzing the plan of a query, executing multiple queries simultaneously, viewing data, and obtaining index recommendations. SQL Query Analyzer shows graphical query plan information, which is used to report data retrieval and sorting methods chosen by the SQL Server query optimizer. SQL Query Analyzer can be used to test Transact-SQL statements against development databases or to run Transact-SQL statements that perform queries, data manipulation (INSERT, UPDATE, or DELETE), or data definition (CREATE TABLE).

SQL Profiler

SQL Profiler captures a continuous record of server activity in real time. SQL Profiler allows monitoring events produced through SQL Server, filtering events based on user-specified criteria, and directing the trace output to the screen, a file, or a table. Using SQL Profiler, you can replay previously captured traces. Application developers can use this tool to identify transactions that might be deteriorating the performance of an application.

Optimizing performance in the client/server environment is the last step in migrating an Access database to SQL Server. At this stage, you are likely to use the output generated by SQL Profiler and the Index Tuning Wizard to optimize queries and indexes.

Moving Data

Before you use DTS Import/Export Wizard, you must decide into which database to import the Access database. You can use either an existing database or create a new database on the server. For more information about creating a new database, see SQL Server Books Online.

To transfer Access tables to SQL Server

1. Open SQL Server Enterprise Manager, expand the server, and click the Databases folder.

2. On the **Tools** menu, point to **Data Transformation Services**, and then click **Import Data**.

3. In the **Choose a Data Source** dialog box, select **Microsoft Access** as the Data Source, and then type the path and file name of your Access database (.mdb), or use the browser to browse for the file.

4. In the **Choose a Destination** dialog box, select **Microsoft OLE DB Provider for SQL Server**, and then select the database server and the required authentication mode. In the **Database** dialog box, select the target database on the server.

5. In the **Specify Table Copy or Query** dialog box, click **Copy tables and views from the source database**.

6. In the **Select Source Tables and Views** dialog box, select the tables and queries to import.

7. In the **Save, Schedule, and Replicate Package** dialog box, select **Run Immediately**.

8. Click **Finish**.

Migrating Access Queries

Microsoft Access queries must be converted into one of the following SQL Server formats:

- Stored procedures

  Stored procedures are optimized and precompiled Transact-SQL statements that are stored as one unit. Stored procedures can be called from other programs, call other stored procedures themselves, and accept input variables. Stored procedures are best suited for queries that undertake some sort of action, such as inserting or updating data.

- Views

  Views are used as virtual tables that expose specific rows and columns from one or more tables. Views enable you to create queries without directly implementing the complex joins that underlie the query. Views do not support the use of parameters. Views that join more than one table cannot be modified using INSERT, UPDATE, or DELETE statements. Views are called from Transact-SQL statements and can also be used in scripts that are run in SQL Query Analyzer. SQL Server views and the SQL-92 standard do not support ORDER BY clauses in views.

- User-defined functions

  User-defined functions are subroutines of encapsulated Transact-SQL logic that can be called from other bits of Transact-SQL code. Thus, they provide an excellent way to store logic that will be accessed repeatedly. Earlier versions of SQL Server include built-in functions such as GETDATE(),REPLACE() and POWER(). User-defined functions allow for this same easy functionality, but with your own logic.

  User-defined functions can return either a scalar value or a table. The scalar data types allowed in user-defined functions include any scalar data type in SQL Server 2000, except **table**, **text**, **ntext**, **image**, **cursor**, and **timestamp**. User-defined functions that return tables can consist of one or multiple Transact-SQL statements and can be accessed directly in the FROM clause of a Transact-SQL statement. However, the dataset in the returned table cannot be modified.

- Indexed views

  With an indexed view, the result set of a query is stored and indexed on disk. Furthermore, the indexed view is dynamically updated when any of the source data changes. Therefore, the overhead saved by storing this data on disk can be lost if the underlying data is changed frequently.

- Transact-SQL scripts

  Transact-SQL scripts are text files that contain Transact-SQL statements. Transact-SQL scripts can be executed directly from SQL Query Analyzer or be used as input in the **isql** and **osql** utilities. You can also use them as permanent copies of Transact-SQL syntax kept separate from any database.

There are several benefits to using stored procedures, views, or user-defined functions instead of Transact-SQL scripts:

- All three run faster than SQL scripts because they are optimized at the time when they are created. After a stored procedure is executed, a copy of it remains in the memory and executes even faster when it is called again.

- Stored procedures and views can be used to implement security mechanisms. Users can be granted permission to execute a procedure that returns data in a restricted and standardized manner.

- They add modular structure to your programs. The same stored procedure, view, or user-defined function can be called from various parts of the program and modified independently from the program code.

- Most Transact-SQL statements that originate from Access queries (select, insert, update, and delete) can be moved into a stored procedures view or user-defined function.

For more information about Transact-SQL scripts, stored procedures, and views, see SQL Server Books Online.

Limitations in Upsizing Queries

The following queries cannot be upsized by the upsizing tools and must be re-created manually:

- Action queries containing nested queries
- Action queries with parameters
- Crosstab queries
- SQL Data Definition Language (DDL) queries
- SQL pass-through queries
- Queries that reference values on a form
- Union queries

For more information about running upsized make-table and append queries, search for the Microsoft Knowledge Base article "Q229681-ACC2000: Cannot Use Upsized Append and Make-Table Queries in an Access Project" at http://support.microsoft.com/.

For more information about parameters and setting table properties, see SQL Server Books Online.

The following table provides a summary of migration options for several of the Access query types.

Access query type	SQL Server migration options and comments
Select	Select statements are best suited to SQL Server views. Views are used to expose certain subsets or supersets of data to users without necessarily giving them access to the underlying tables.
Crosstab	Crosstabs are often used for summary reports. An Access crosstab query can be implemented as a Transact-SQL SELECT statement in an SQL script, a stored procedure, or a view. The data join is executed each time a query is issued, ensuring that the latest data is always used. Depending on the application, it might be appropriate to store data from the crosstab as a temporary table (see make-table in the next row). The temporary table requires fewer resources, but offers only a snapshot of the data at the time the temporary table is created.

Make-table	An Access make-table query can be implemented as a Transact-SQL CREATE TABLE statement in a Transact-SQL script or stored procedure. The syntax is:
	<pre>SELECT [ALL | DISTINCT]
	[{TOP integer | TOP integer PERCENT} [WITH TIES]]
	<select_list>
	[INTO new_table]
	[FROM {<table_source>} [,…n]]
	[WHERE <search_condition>]
	[GROUP BY [ALL] group_by_expression [,…n]
	[WITH { CUBE | ROLLUP }]
	 CREATE TABLE mytable (low int, high int)</pre>

Update	An update query can be stored in a Transact-SQL script; however, the recommended way to implement an update statement is to create a stored procedure.
Append	An append query can be stored in a Transact-SQL script; however, the recommended way to implement an append query is to create a stored procedure.
Delete	A delete query can be stored in a Transact-SQL script; however, the recommended way to implement a delete query is to create a stored procedure.
Pass-through	If you have the appropriate OLE DB provider, you can use a linked server configuration in SQL Server to allow for the executing of queries directly against a remote data source.

Migrating Access Queries into User-Defined Functions

User-defined functions can accept parameters and return either a scalar value or a table. Unlike stored procedures, their result sets can be accessed directly from another query. For example, the following user-defined function returns all the employees from the **employees** table for a given state in the **Northwind** sample database in SQL Server:

```
CREATE FUNCTION dbo.udfEmpByCity(@City varchar(15))
RETURNS TABLE
AS
RETURN (
        SELECT EmployeeID, LastName, FirstName
        FROM dbo.Employees
        WHERE (City = @City)
)
```

To access the result set of this function, simply use:

```
SELECT * FROM udfEmpByCity('Seattle')
```

For more information about user-defined functions, see SQL Server Books Online.

Migrating Access Queries into Stored Procedures and Views

Each Access query must be placed into one of the following statements:

- To create a stored procedure, use:

```
CREATE PROCEDURE <NAME_HERE> AS
< SELECT, UPDATE, DELETE, INSERT, CREATE TABLE statement from Microsoft Access >
GO
```

- To create a view, use:

```
CREATE VIEW <NAME_HERE> AS
<Place (SELECT only, with no parameters) Microsoft Access Query>
GO
```

To migrate each Access query

1. Start Microsoft Access and open the database to export.

2. In the Database window, click the **Queries** tab, select the query to export, and then click **Design**.

3. On the **View** menu, click **SQL**. Select and copy the entire SQL query.

4. In SQL Server Enterprise Manager, on the **Tools** menu, click **SQL Query Analyzer**.

5. Paste the entire query into SQL Query Analyzer.

6. On the **Query** menu, click **Parse**. This verifies that the SQL syntax is compliant with Transact-SQL.

7. On the **Query** menu, click **Run**. This creates a new view or procedure. To confirm that a new object was created, right-click **Views** or **Stored Procedures**, and select **Refresh**.

Converting Make-Table and Crosstab Queries

The Access make-table and crosstab queries can be converted into views, temporary tables, or indexed views.

- View

    This creates virtual, temporary tables with current data. Views are dynamic structures that allow the user to change the underlying tables. A view does not save any I/O time because it requires rejoining the data tables each time the query is executed.

- Temporary table

    A temporary table creates a static snapshot of data for a connected user's session. You can create local and global temporary tables. Local temporary tables are visible only in the current session. Global temporary tables are visible to all sessions. Prefix local temporary table names with one number sign (**#table_name**), and prefix global temporary table names with two number signs (**##table_name**). Queries run quickly against temporary tables because they generally use only one table rather than dynamically joining together several tables to obtain a result set. Using Data Transformation Services (DTS) in SQL Server 2000, you can standardize, automate, and schedule the creation of temporary tables by creating packages. Temporary tables are not dynamically updated. Therefore, if the underlying tables are updated without rebuilding the temporary table, the data in the temporary table can be inaccurate.

- Indexed view

    Like a temporary table, an indexed view stores its result set on disk, and like a view, an indexed view dynamically reflects changes that occur against the underlying tables. Thus, with indexed views, you can avoid the overhead of a regular view and the limited availability of a temporary table. The benefits of using an indexed view can be negated, however, if the data in the base tables is updated frequently.

For more information about views, temporary tables, indexed views, and DTS, see SQL Server Books Online.

Migrating Access Queries into Transact-SQL Scripts

Most Access queries should be translated into stored procedures, views, and user-defined functions. Nevertheless, some statements that are run infrequently by an application developer can be stored as Transact-SQL scripts.

If you plan to transfer some of your Access queries to .sql files, consider grouping the Transact-SQL statements into logical scripts. Distinct scripts can be created for statements that are run with the same frequency, that are run only under certain conditions, or that must be run in a specific order.

To move a Jet-SQL statement from Access to a Transact-SQL file

1. Start Microsoft Access and open the database to export.

2. In the Database window, click the **Queries** tab, select the query to export, and then click **Design**.

3. On the **View** menu, click **SQL**. Select and copy the entire SQL query

4. In SQL Server Enterprise Manager, on the **Tools** menu, click **SQL Query Analyzer**.

5. Paste the entire query into SQL Query Analyzer.

6. On the **Query** menu, click **Parse** (or press CTRL+F5).

7. Execute the statement if appropriate.

8. Save the Transact-SQL syntax as an .sql file

Additional Design Considerations for Queries

Often there is more than one way to migrate the logic within an Access query to SQL Server. The following section provides some additional considerations for migrating that logic.

Parameter Queries

Some Access queries require the user to enter parameter values. In SQL Server, parameters cannot be part of a view definition, but can be used in stored procedures and user-defined functions. In the following example, the Access query queries the **Northwind** sample database for the total number of orders by each company from a country specified by the user. This nested query uses the ORDER BY clause to sort the results by the **CompanyName** column.

```
SELECT [CompanyName], [City], Region,
(SELECT Count(*)
FROM Orders
```

```
WHERE Orders.CustomerID = Customers.CustomerID)
AS Number_of_Orders
FROM Customers
WHERE [Customers].[Country]=[Enter Country]
ORDER BY Customers.CompanyName;
```

In SQL Server, the query can become either a view and a stored procedure or a single user-defined function. The result set of these solutions cannot be updated. The view has a derived column in it and the result sets of user-defined functions are not updatable.

View and stored procedure	User-defined function

<pre>DROP VIEW "No_of_Orders"
GO
CREATE VIEW "No_of_Orders"
AS
SELECT CompanyName, City, Region,
Country,
(SELECT Count(*)
FROM Orders
WHERE Orders.CustomerID =
Customers.CustomerID)
AS Number_of_Orders
FROM Customers
GO
 	
DROP PROCEDURE OBC
GO
CREATE PROCEDURE "OBC" @CountryName
Char(15)
AS
SELECT * FROM No_of_Orders
WHERE No_of_Orders.Country = @CountryName
ORDER BY CompanyName
GO</pre>
	<pre>CREATE FUNCTION udfCompOrders(@CountryName
	varchar(30))
	RETURNS @tCompOrders TABLE
	(
	    companyname varchar(80),
	    city varchar(30),
	    region varchar(30),
	    country varchar(30),
	    number_of_orders int
	)
	AS
	BEGIN
	    INSERT @tCompOrders
	    SELECT companyname, city, region,
	country, (select count(*) FROM orders
	WHERE orders.customerid =
	customers.customerid) AS number_of_orders
	    FROM customers
	    WHERE country = @CountryName
	    ORDER BY companyname asc
	RETURN
	END
	GO</pre>

In the first column of the preceding table, the stored procedure queries the view, filters the results according to the **CountryName** parameter, and then sorts the output according to the ORDER BY clause. All of this logic can be encapsulated into one user-defined function, including the parameter and the order by clause, as shown in the second column.

When making your decision, you should determine whether there are individual units of logic in the query that might be needed by other queries. If this is the case, you might consider breaking your query up into multiple views, stored procedures, and user-defined functions so that your logic can be reused.

Nested Queries

Nested queries are one of more queries contained within another query. The nested query often acts as a data source for the nesting query. Nested queries can be migrated to SQL Server as user-defined functions or nested views. In some queries the nested query contains parameters, and the nesting one does not. In this case, you must use a user-defined function because views cannot take parameters.

Make-Table Queries

In earlier versions of SQL Server, select into and bulk copy operations were not logged, leading to an inconsistent transaction log. SQL Server 2000 can be configured to log these operations to maintain point-in-time recovery by setting the recovery model of the database to FULL. For more information about setting SQL Server recovery models, see the SQL Server Books Online.

Append Queries

The upsizing tools convert the AutoNumber field to an integer column that uses the IDENTITY property in the upsized table. The combination of an integer column with the IDENTITY property can act the same way as the AutoNumber data type in Access. For an insert statement to explicitly name the IDENTITY column, the IDENTITY_INSERT property must be set to ON. By default, a new table will have the property set to OFF, and a newly upsized append query will fail.

To set the IDENTITY_INSERT property, use this Transact SQL statement:

```
SET IDENTITY_INSERT {TableName} {ON|OFF}
```

> **Note**   Only one table per session can have the IDENTITY_INSERT property set to ON at any given time.

Verifying SQL Server–Compliant Syntax

In SQL Query Analyzer, you can use the **Parse** command on the **Query** menu to verify whether a view or stored procedure functions in SQL Server. As shown in the following illustration, the ORDER BY clause is used in a view. Views do not support the ORDER BY clause without the TOP clause to limit the number of rows returned in the result set. The lower pane of the SQL Query Analyzer lists all detected errors, their locations, and a short message to assist in correcting the syntax.

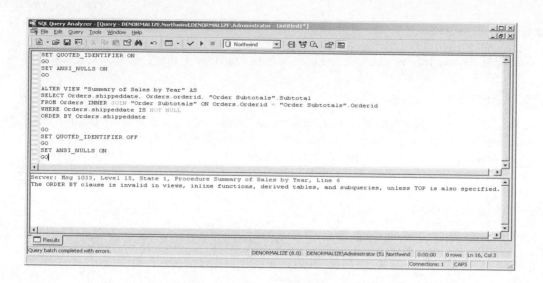

Access and SQL Server Syntax

The following table compares Access and SQL Server syntax.

Access syntax	SQL Server syntax
String concatenation with "&"	String concatenation with "+"
Supported clauses/operators	
DISTINCTROW	If the query is a multi-table join, then DISTINCT. If the query uses DISTINCTROW against a single table, it will have to be recoded.
FROM	FROM
GROUP BY	GROUP BY
HAVING	HAVING
INTO	INTO
Not supported	COMPUTE FOR BROWSE OPTION
ORDER BY	*Not supported in views*
SELECT	SELECT

continued on next page

Access syntax	SQL Server syntax
SELECT TOP N [PERCENT]	SELECT TOP N [PERCENT]
UNION (ALL)	UNION (ALL)
WHERE	WHERE
WITH OWNER ACCESS	*Not supported*
Aggregate functions	
Not supported	GROUPING (column_name)
AVG	AVG ([ALL | DISTINCT] expression)
COUNT(*)	COUNT(*)
COUNT(column)	COUNT ([ALL | DISTINCT] expression)
FIRST, LAST	*Not supported*
MAKE TABLE, ALTER TABLE	CREATE TABLE, ALTER TABLE
MAX	MAX(*expression*)
MIN	MIN(*expression*)
PIVOT	*Not supported*
STDEV, STDEVP	STDEV, STDEVP
SUM	SUM ([ALL | DISTINCT] expression)
TRANSFORM (SELECT statement)	WITH ROLLUP, WITH CUBE on SELECT statements
VAR, VARP	VAR, VARP
Other supported clauses	
ADD COLUMN	ADD COLUMN
CONSTRAINT	CONSTRAINT
DROP COLUMN	DROP COLUMN
Not supported	GRANT, LOCK
DROP INDEX	DROP INDEX
String concatenation with "&"	String concatenation with "+"

Visual Basic Functions

The following tables show the Visual Basic conversion and date functions used in Access and the corresponding Transact-SQL functions used in SQL Server.

Visual Basic conversion function	Transact-SQL function
Cint(x)	CONVERT(smallint,x)
CLng(x)	CONVERT (int,x)
CSng(x)	CONVERT (real,x)
CDbl(x)	CONVERT (float,x)
CStr(x)	CONVERT (varchar,x)
Ccur(x)	CONVERT (money,x)
CVdate(x)	CONVERT (datetime,x)

Visual Basic date function	Transact-SQL function
DATEADD()	DATEADD
DATEDIFF()	DATEDIFF
FORMAT()	DATENAME
DATEPART()	DATEPART
NOW(), DATE()	GETDATE

Not all Visual Basic for Applications functions are supported by Transact-SQL equivalents. The following table shows functions that must be converted to a different syntax in Transact-SQL.

Visual Basic function	Transact-SQL function
ASC()	ASCII()
INSTR()	CHARINDEX
STRING()	REPLICATE
STRREVERSE()	REVERSE
STR()	STR

Access and SQL Server Data Types

Data types in Microsoft Access and Microsoft SQL Server are not identical. When you convert from Access to SQL Server data types, use the following table as a guideline.

Access data type	SQL Server data type
Autonumber (Long Integer)	**int** (Identity)
Binary	**varbinary**
Byte	**Smallint**
Currency	**Money**
Date/time	**Datetime**
Double	**Float**
Hyperlink	**ntext** (link functionality lost)[*]
Integer	**Smallint**
Long Integer	**Int**
Memo	**Ntext**
Memo	**Text**
Number	**Decimal**
Number	**Float**
Number	**Int**
Number	**Decimal**
Number	**Real**
Number	**Smallint**
Number	**Tinyint**
Number	**uniqueidentifier**
OLE Object	**Image**
Replication ID	**varbinary**
Single	**Real**
Text	**Nvarchar**
Text	**Varchar**
Yes/No	**Bit**

[*] Access hyperlinks can store additional information such as Screen Tips, Sub Address, and Display Text. This information is not visible in Access, but will become visible once converted to SQL Server.

For more information about converting data types between Access and SQL Server, search for the Microsoft Knowledge Base article "Q224529 ACC2000: Data Types Change Importing from ADP to MDB and Back" at http://support.microsoft.com/.

Migrating Your Applications

The process of migrating your Access applications to SQL Server 2000 is a three-step procedure:

1. Create a working version of the application for SQL Server.

2. Optimize the application for the client/server environment.

3. Optimize SQL Server-based data structure.

Creating a Client/Server Application

Access provides the user-interface functionality that SQL Server does not. Often, when an Access application is migrated, the user interface is migrated as well to Visual Basic, Active Server Pages, or another environment. Here are some things to think about when moving the front-end of an Access application.

Converting Code

Regardless of which method of data migration you use, your application code remains unaffected. Currently, there are two data access object models you are likely to encounter:

- For versions of Access prior to Access 2000, Data Access Objects (DAO) is the most common object model. DAO version 3.6 is currently available in Access 2000 and can still be used with Jet-SQL 4.0. DAO cannot expose a number of features of SQL Server; therefore, DAO-based code must be modified for the application to work in the client/server environment.

    DAO code that works with strictly Access objects, such as forms or reports, continues to work in a front end application. However, any code that works with server-based objects (for example, tables and queries) must be manually converted to ADO.

- With the release of Access 2000, Microsoft ActiveX® Data Objects (ADO) is the new object model. ADO is a high-speed, low-memory/disk footprint data access object model that is optimized for Internet and intranet access, and very well suited for the client/server environment. ADO manipulates SQL Server data using the Microsoft OLE DB Provider for SQL Server.

For more information about ADO and DAO, see SQL Server Books Online, or see http://www.microsoft.com/data/ado/.

Forms

Forms and Reports in Access derive their data from queries or SELECT statements bound to the **RecordSource** property. In the client/server environment, the **RecordSource** property is based on a server-based view or on a stored procedure that is expected to return the same data as the original Access query. When you convert the record source, the same rules apply as for queries (see "Migrating Access Queries" earlier in this chapter).

If your form or report contains bound controls, you may receive errors when you view them after upsizing. Most likely the error is caused by one of the following conditions:

- The query or a SELECT statement does not refer to field names using their table names, for example, [TableName].[FieldName]. Instead, the query or statement uses only [FieldName], which works perfectly well in Access, but causes errors in SQL Server.

- The control refers to a parameter query.

- The WHERE statement in a query or a SELECT statement refers to a form or a report-based control.

Optimizing the Application for the Client/Server Environment

The next step in migrating your database to SQL Server is to optimize the application for the client/server environment. Here are some considerations and guidelines:

- If you linked local tables to SQL Server-based data, use pass-through queries wherever possible. Pass-through queries are not processed locally but, instead, are passed unmodified to the server. For example, instead of running multiple code loops to local tables, you can run a single pass-through query with the appropriate Transact-SQL syntax.

- Use as few queries as possible. If your forms contain subforms, they will send at least two queries to the server. If you base your form on a single query, you can modify that number to one.

- If a form is used only to display data (not to enter or update information), change the **RecordsetType** property to Snapshot. This will retrieve a faster, static object.

- Consider using local tables as record sources for combo boxes and list boxes where information never changes. For example, the list of countries, U.S. states, planets, or poisonous snakes in Arizona can be kept locally. In Access project you cannot create local tables, but you can store the information in a text file. For more information, see the Microsoft Access documentation.

- Request less data. If most users use only a small set of fields on a form, you can make only those most frequently accessed fields available when the form opens. Any additional fields can be triggered with another query fired with a command button.

- Monitor the growth of your database. Solutions that work with smaller databases may become awkward and inefficient as the amount of data grows. A user interface that retrieves 50 records can be still useful, but one that retrieves 5000 records requires another approach.

Optimizing Data Structure

The last step in the migrating process is to optimize the data structure. SQL Server provides the graphical tools that can help you in optimize your database:

- SQL Profiler

  Use this to record a number of statistics about the operation of the entire database, such as warnings, errors, objects created and dropped, stored procedure operation, Transact SQL and RPC statistics, I/O and CPU stats, and more. This tool records server activity in a trace (.trc) file that can be used by other programs to optimize your database.

- SQL Query Analyzer

  Use this to create and test Transact-SQL statements, manage indexes, and display details of query execution plans.

- Index Tuning Wizard

  Using the information in the trace file and the structure of the database, the Index Tuning Wizard makes suggestions and implements the most efficient index structure for your database and its average workload.

For more information about optimizing indexes, the SQL Profiler, SQL Query Analyzer, and the Index Tuning Wizard, see SQL Server Books Online.

Migrating Sybase Databases to SQL Server 2000

Microsoft® SQL Server™ and the Sybase relational database systems were developed together until their respective 4.2 versions. This commonality provides for a unique, low-cost opportunity for Sybase customers to migrate their databases to SQL Server and, therefore, to benefit from the new functionality of SQL Server 2000.

This chapter outlines the steps to follow in migrating Sybase databases to SQL Server 2000 and presents information to help database application developers anticipate migration issues. The information in this chapter is intended for Sybase database administrators (DBAs) and managers who are planning to migrate a database application to SQL Server 2000. It assumes the reader is familiar with Sybase databases (SQL Server or Adaptive Server Enterprise).

This chapter also describes the differences between Sybase T-SQL and SQL Server Transact-SQL statements, and differences in administrative procedures. Issues regarding conversion from CT-Library applications or the porting of ODBC applications from Sybase to SQL Server databases are not addressed.

Why Migrate to SQL Server 2000?

Reasons why you should consider migrating your Sybase application to SQL Server 2000 are:

- Performance-ready for the enterprise edition
- Scalability and performance of very large databases
- Dynamic self-management
- Ease of use
- Integration with Microsoft Windows® 2000, Microsoft Office, and Microsoft .NET Enterprise Servers
- Accessible business intelligence
- Single, scalable code base

Performance-Ready for the Enterprise Edition

SQL Server 2000 provides outstanding performance on the Microsoft Windows 2000 operating system and has delivered record-setting results on industry standard benchmarks. In November 2000, SQL Server 2000, running on Windows 2000, set a new world record for overall performance in the TPC-C benchmarks with an overall rate of 505,302 tpm/C and a cost of $19.80/tpmC. At that time, this overall level of performance was approximately 15% higher than the best results posted using IBM's DB2 and over twice as high as any results posted using Oracle.

Companies running on systems with 32 CPUs or fewer can enjoy the benefits of SQL Server 2000, a database that offers top performance and can be very cost-effective.

Scalability and Performance of Very Large Databases

SQL Server 2000 is the foundation for the Microsoft TerraServer Web site. TerraServer accesses 1 terabyte of satellite images of the world. Currently, the site has received more than 1 billion hits, with peak loads of more than 29 million hits and almost 18 million database queries in a day.

The following statistics from the first 21 days of operation demonstrate that SQL Server 2000 is capable of providing huge database capacity and outstanding transaction throughput:

- Total number of hits: 317,670,000
- Average hits per day: 15,130,000
- Peak hits per day: 28,940,000
- Average database queries per day: 8,810,000
- Peak database queries per day: 17,760,000

Dynamic Self-Management

A common task for a DBA is to monitor the use of memory and disk space. In some scenarios, such as mobile applications, remote users cannot ask a DBA to tune and monitor the application. Other databases require you to monitor the use of the system carefully to ensure that the application has the amount of memory and disk space it requires. By providing dynamic self-management, SQL Server 2000 helps to reduce both serious errors and the amount of errors caused by disk and memory allocation.

Ease of Use

SQL Server 2000 is easy to use. SQL Server 2000 provides graphical tools, task pads, and more than 30 wizards to help DBAs automate and schedule routine tasks. For example, the Index Tuning Wizard helps to determine how to best tune an application, and the graphical SQL Query Analyzer can provide graphical execution plans for database statements, helping in identifying performance bottlenecks.

Sybase does not offer the same tools found in SQL Server 2000 for automating and scheduling tasks, and proactively alerting DBAs if there is any problem.

An increasing number of applications run on laptops (mobile applications). Mobile knowledge workers often do not even know what a database is, let alone how to tune a database. Additionally, DBAs must be available during critical periods, such as the close of the fiscal year. Memory and disk-space management should not occupy their valuable time.

Integration with Microsoft Windows 2000, Microsoft Office, and Microsoft .NET Enterprise Servers

With SQL Server 2000 and Microsoft Excel 2000, Microsoft offers desktop analysis, enabling Excel users for the first time to analyze gigabytes and terabytes of data with Microsoft SQL Server 2000 Analysis Services. SQL Server 2000 integrates with Microsoft Windows NT® security and systems management to provide greater productivity and ease of use for users. A single security model offers single-user login when accessing a database. Management tools such as Microsoft Windows NT Event Viewer offer automated alerts; for example, the server can send a page or e-mail if there are any database issues. Microsoft Transaction Server, part of Windows NT Server, allows easy building of multitier applications. SQL Server also integrates closely with Microsoft Exchange Server, Microsoft Systems Management Server, and Microsoft SNA Server. All of these features provide ease of use to the administrator.

Users can be more productive if they can use their favorite data analysis tool as the interface for data warehouses.

Accessible Business Intelligence

SQL Server 2000 includes comprehensive data warehousing capabilities, such as integrated Data Transformation Services (DTS), SQL Server 2000 Analysis Services, and even graphical tools that help model your data warehouse. SQL Server 2000 enables easy, cost-effective development of data warehouses, and Microsoft Office 2000 provides easy-to-use capabilities for exploring and analyzing data. By using complementary products from members of the Microsoft Data Warehousing Alliance, you can integrate even more advanced data warehousing tools that will work seamlessly with a SQL Server-based application. The capabilities of SQL Server 2000 can benefit users with data lineage. When data is coming in from many sources (manufacturing databases, sales databases, channel databases), the lineage feature helps identify the origin of the data.

Creating a data warehouse can be a very complex process, and integrated tools make the process of developing your data warehouse more intuitive and efficient.

Single, Scalable Code Base

Sybase offers different database engines in different editions of the program. This means that code written for to one edition may not run the same way on another edition. In contrast, SQL Server 2000 is developed from a single code base that scales from a laptop running on Microsoft Windows 95 or Microsoft Windows 98 operating systems to multiprocessor clusters running on Microsoft Windows 2000 Server, Enterprise Edition. This offers 100 percent application compatibility. Microsoft Data Engine (MSDE) is a new, SQL Server 2000-compatible data engine that ships with Microsoft Office 2000. With Office 2000, applications can be developed, accessed, and managed using the Microsoft Access 2000 as the interface and MSDE as the storage engine.

Only one version of an application, which runs on different hardware environments, would have to be developed and supported. This is especially important if you want to create mobile applications that run the same, whether they are on a laptop, desktop, server, or clustered server.

Understanding the Migration Process

These areas must be considered for migrating databases from Sybase Adaptive Server Enterprise to SQL Server 2000:

- Data and object definitions
- Changes to Transact-SQL and system stored procedures
- Administrative changes

The steps to follow for the migration process are:

1. Review the architectural differences between SQL Server 2000 and the Sybase server that require changes to administrative procedures.

2. Migrate data and objects using DTS.

3. Review Sybase stored procedures, triggers, SQL scripts, and applications for necessary language changes.

4. Make the necessary changes to client code. Sybase SQL statements issued by applications must reflect changes to object names forced by keyword conflicts. The Sybase application SQL must reflect any changes required to comply with SQL Server Transact-SQL syntax.

5. Test the client code.

6. Make required changes to administrative procedures of the customer.

7. Review the new features available in SQL Server 2000 and make changes to take advantage of these features.

Reviewing Architectural Differences

To start a successful migration, you should understand the basic architecture and terminology associated with SQL Server 2000. Furthermore, you should be familiar with the architectural differences between the database servers.

Client Configuration and Net-Libraries

Although it is easier to use Microsoft DB-Library to migrate Sybase applications that use CT-Library, to take advantage of SQL Server 2000 functionality, it is recommended that SQL Server-based clients use either an OLE DB provider or an ODBC driver to connect with the server. Microsoft supplies two components, Ntwdblib.dll (DB-Library) and Sqlsrv32.dll (ODBC driver), to replace the Sybase client components.

SQL Server-based clients should use the appropriate Microsoft SQL Server Network Library components shown in this table.

Net-Library	Win32® DLL
TCP/IP Windows Sockets	Dbnetlib.dll
Named Pipes	Dbnmpntw.dll
Multiprotocol	Dbmsrpcn.dll
Novell IPX/SPX	Dbnetlib.dll
Banyan VINES	Dbmsvinn.dll
AppleTalk	Dbmsadsn.dll
VIA (Giganet)	Dbmsgnet.dll
VIA (Servernet II)	Dbmsgnet.dll

The SQL Server Client Network Utility is a client-side component, installed in the SQL Server program group that is used to manage the client-side Net-Libraries.

On the **Alias** tab of the SQL Server Client Network Utility, you can alias a server multiple times with different network libraries or connection parameters specified:

Server alias
> The label by which the entry will be referenced at connect time. For example, if an advanced entry is created with SERVER=XYZ, the server **XYZ** will be used for the connection when the **osql** utility is run with a **/Sxyz** switch.

Network library
> The SQL Server Net-Library used by the client to connect to the aliased server. Select the check box that corresponds with the appropriate Net-Library.

Connection parameters

The network address of the server. For example, if it is a Windows Sockets entry, specify the port and socket address of the server. If it is a Named Pipes or Multiprotocol entry, specify the network name of the server.

Sybase and SQL Server servers are compatible with the client software of the other, provided the software is limited to the features in SQL Server 4.2. SQL Server servers can host Sybase clients, and Sybase servers can host SQL Server clients. Since the release of SQL Server 4.2, the servers diverge by introducing new data types, new Transact-SQL statements, new ANSI SQL statements, and new administrative procedures. Sybase customers migrating to SQL Server 2000 should convert the client software to use OLE DB providers or ODBC drivers. This software is included with SQL Server 2000 or can be downloaded from http://www.microsoft.com/data/.

For more information about SQL Server Net-Libraries, see SQL Server Books Online.

System Databases

The following table provides a quick overview of the implementation of Sybase Adaptive Server Enterprise and SQL Server 2000 system databases.

Database item	Sybase Adaptive Server Enterprise (SQL Server 10+)	SQL Server 2000	Comments
System stored procedures	Stored in the **sybsystemprocs** database	Stored in the **master** database	Change references from **sybsystemprocs** to **master**
Memory management	Beginning with System 11, user-defined data caches allow each user to create an area of data cache that can be reserved for specific objects	Dynamic memory management techniques eliminate the need for administrative configuration of memory	
Information about the oldest open transaction	The **syslogshold** table records the oldest open transaction	The DBCC OPENTRAN statement returns the oldest open transaction.	Replace all references to **syslogshold** with DBCC OPENTRAN logic.

For a complete explanation of the Microsoft SQL Server system database structure, see "System Databases and Data" in SQL Server Books Online.

Database Size

Sybase Adaptive Server Enterprise for Windows NT supports up to 128 disk devices per database. Each device can be up to 8 gigabytes (GB). This means that a database cannot grow larger than 1 terabyte. Instead of devices, SQL Server 2000 uses files, which can be configured to grow dynamically and can be grouped into filegroups. For more information about files and filegroups, see "Physical Database Files and Filegroups" in SQL Server Books Online.

Furthermore, SQL Server 2000 supports databases up to 1,048,416 terabytes in size. SQL Server 2000 Enterprise Edition supports distributed partitioned views, which allow groups of database servers and an enterprise application to distribute workload. For more information about Partitioned Views, see "Designing Partitions" in SQL Server Books Online.

Data Types

For a comprehensive list of system-defined data types, see "Data Types" in SQL Server Books Online.

Keyword Conflicts

Before you transfer your entire Sybase production system to SQL Server 2000, migrate your Sybase database to a test SQL Server 2000 database, and then fully test your applications and administrative procedures against this test database, including stress testing.

Review your Sybase T-SQL statements and the names of database objects for keyword conflicts before transferring your objects and data to SQL Server 2000.

The following tables list Sybase System 11 keywords that do not function in SQL Server 2000 and keywords that are reserved by SQL Server 2000. If your Sybase T-SQL statements use any of the listed keywords, replace them with other words before you migrate your Sybase database to SQL Server. For a comprehensive list of reserved keywords, see "Reserved Keywords" in SQL Server Books Online.

Sybase System 11 keywords

ARITH_OVERFLOW	NOHOLDLOCK	SHARED
AT	NUMERIC_TRANSACTION	STRIPE
CHAR_CONVERT	ONLINE	SYB_IDENTITY
ENDTRAN	PARTITION	SYB_RESTREE
ERRORDATA	REPLACE	UNPARTITION
MAX_ROWS_PER_PAGE	ROLE	USER_OPTION
NATIONAL	ROWS	USING

SQL Server 2000 reserved keywords

CASE	IDENTITY	RESTRICT
COALESCE	IDENTITYCOL	RIGHT
COMMITTED	INNER	SCROLL
CROSS	INSENSITIVE	SERIALIZABLE
CURRENT_DATE	JOIN	SESSION_USER
CURRENT_TIME	LEFT	SYSTEM_USER
CURRENT_TIMESTAMP	NOCHECK	TAPE
CURRENT_USER	NULLIF	THEN
DISTRIBUTED	OUTER	UNCOMMITTED
DROP	PIPE	UPDATETEXT
FLOPPY	REPEATABLE	WHEN
FULL	REPLICATION	

Migrating Tables and Data

DTS enables importing and exporting data between multiple heterogeneous sources that use an OLE DB-based architecture (such as Microsoft Excel spreadsheets and flat text files) and transferring databases and database objects (for example, indexes and stored procedures) between multiple computers running SQL Server 2000. You can also use DTS to transform data so it can be used more easily to build data warehouses and data marts from an online transaction processing (OLTP) system.

Using the DTS Import/Export Wizard, you can interactively create DTS packages that use OLE DB and ODBC to import, export, validate, and transform heterogeneous data. Using the wizards, you can also copy schema and data between relational databases. To use the this wizard, you must have an ODBC or OLE DB driver for your Sybase server on the computer on which you are running DTS

To transfer your Sybase data into SQL Server using the DTS Import/Export Wizard

1. Create an ODBC data source for the Sybase database.

2. Start SQL Server Enterprise Manager, on the **Tools** menu, point to **Data Transformation Services**, and then click **Import Data**.

3. In the **Choose a Data Source** dialog box, select **Other (ODBC Data Source)** as the Source, and then select the DSN that corresponds to your Sybase data source.

4. In the **Choose a Destination** dialog box, select **Microsoft SQL Server OLEDB Provider**, select the database server, and then select the required authentication mode for the selected database server.

5. In the **Specify Table Copy or Query** dialog box, select **Copy table(s) and view(s) from the source database**.

6. In the **Select Source Tables** dialog box, click **Select All**. Click the gray box found in the **Transform** column of the **Select Source Tables** dialog box to change column names, data types, nullability, size, and precision, and even to write code to make unique transformations to your data before importing data into SQL Server.

7. Run the data migration package immediately or at a later time. The DTS Import/Export Wizard will show you the progress and status of the data migration, step by step.

Reviewing the Differences Between Sybase T-SQL and Transact-SQL

Some differences between Sybase T-SQL and Transact-SQL and system stored procedures must be addressed to ensure a successful migration. The following issues affect Transact-SQL in scripts, applications, triggers, and stored procedures.

Transaction Management

Both Sybase and SQL Server 2000 support explicit transactions managed with the BEGIN TRANSACTION, SAVE, COMMIT TRANSACTION, and ROLLBACK TRANSACTION statements.

ROLLBACK Triggers

The Sybase ROLLBACK TRIGGER statement rolls back only the work performed by the statement that fired the trigger.

In SQL Server 2000, you must replace the ROLLBACK TRIGGER statements with paired SAVE TRANSACTION (tr1)…ROLLBACK TRANSACTION (tr1) statements to roll back a single Transact-SQL statement without affecting the rest of the transaction. Sybase applications that currently use ROLLBACK TRIGGER should be changed to issue SAVE TRANSACTION (tr1), fire the trigger, and then issue the ROLLBACK TRANSACTION (tr1) statement if needed before executing any other Transact-SQL statements.

Chained Transactions

In Sybase System 10, chained transactions were introduced. Chained transactions are transactions that have implicit starting points but must be explicitly committed. A connection can put itself into or out of a chained transaction state with the SET statement:

```
SET CHAINED [ON | OFF]
```

In SQL Server version 6.5, implicit transactions were introduced. Implicit transactions function in the same way as Sybase chained transactions. SQL Server implicit transactions are also controlled by the SET statement:

```
SET IMPLICIT_TRANSACTIONS [ON | OFF]
```

Change the SET CHAINED statements in Sybase applications to SET IMPLICIT_TRANSACTION statements for SQL Server.

Sybase stored procedures are tagged with the transaction mode (chained or unchained) with which they were created, and SQL Server procedures operate in the transaction mode that exists when they are executed. Therefore, Sybase procedures can have COMMIT TRANSACTIONS that are not matched with a BEGIN TRANSACTION statement; this is not allowed in SQL Server procedures. Scan all Sybase procedures created in chained mode for COMMIT TRANSACTION statements that do not have matched BEGIN TRANSACTION statements. Either remove the COMMIT TRANSACTION from, or add a BEGIN TRANSACTION to the procedure before it is migrated to SQL Server.

The Sybase @@**tranchained** global variable, indicating the current transaction mode (0 = unchained, 1 = chained), has no SQL Server equivalent. The 2 bits in the SQL Server variable @@OPTIONS report the mode of **implicit_transactions**:

```
IF (@@options & 2) > 0
    PRINT 'Implicit_transactions on'
ELSE
    PRINT 'Implicit_transactions off'
```

The Sybase @@**transtate** global variable, indicating whether a transaction is in progress, successful, or canceled, has no SQL Server equivalent. Replace @@**transtate** logic with either @@ERROR checking or SET XACT_ABORT ON to enable SQL Server to roll back a transaction automatically when an error occurs.

The Sybase **sp_procxmode** system stored procedure, used to control the transaction modes of stored procedures, has no SQL Server equivalent. Sybase procedures must have COMMIT statements matched with BEGIN TRANSACTION statements or be removed from the stored procedures before migrating to SQL Server.

Transaction Isolation Levels

Sybase identifies its transaction isolation levels with numbers, and SQL Server identifies the levels with character tags. Scan for SET TRANSACTION ISOLATION LEVEL statements and change the Sybase level specifications to SQL Server 2000 specifications.

Sybase	SQL Server 2000
0	READ UNCOMMITTED
1	READ COMMITTED
2	REPEATABLE READ
3	SERIALIZABLE

Cursors

SQL Server 2000 supports the Sybase cursor statements except for a minor difference in syntax for the DEALLOCATE CURSOR:

```
DEALLOCATE CURSOR cursor_name
```

The keyword CURSOR is not used by SQL Server with the DEALLOCATE cursor statement:

```
DEALLOCATE cursor_name
```

For more information about cursors, see "Cursors" in SQL Server Books Online.

Cursor Error Checking

Sybase and SQL Server 2000 implement error checking differently. Sybase cursors report errors through @@**sqlstatus**, and SQL Server 2000 reports errors through @@FETCH_STATUS. As shown in the table, Sybase and SQL Server report different values.

@@sqlstatus	@@FETCH_STATUS
	-2 = Row deleted from result set
	-1 = End of result set
0 = Success	0 = Success
1 = Type mismatch	
2 = End of result set	

Sybase allows different stored procedures to open cursors with identical names. Each cursor with the same name gets a separate result set. SQL Server considers the scope of a cursor name to be the current session. The server does not allow different stored procedures that are executed by the same connection to open cursors with duplicate names.

SQL Server cursors default to optimistic concurrency control, which does not place shared locks on tables. Sybase cursors generally default to pessimistic concurrency control, which places shared locks on the underlying tables. The pessimistic concurrency can reduce performance in high-use environments.

Index Optimizer Hints

Optimizer hints are important in Sybase implementations because Sybase does not update index statistics automatically. The Sybase query optimizer is not always reliable because it often will be optimizing based on outdated statistics.

SQL Server 2000 updates statistics automatically, so the SQL Server query optimizer is more likely than the Sybase query optimizer to make the best choice of index use. In addition, SQL Query Analyzer can help programmers and DBAs determine the system I/O bottlenecks. The automatically updated statistics, the accurate query optimizer, and the ability to troubleshoot using SQL Query Analyzer are all reasons to delete Sybase optimizer hints from the statements, not simply replace them. For more information about implementing optimizer hints, see SQL Server Books Online.

Optimizer Hints for Locking

A range of table-level locking hints can be specified by using the SELECT, INSERT, UPDATE, and DELETE statements to direct SQL Server to the type of locks to be used. Table-level locking hints can be used when you need a finer control of the types of locks acquired on an object. These locking hints override the current transaction isolation level for the session.

The SQL Server query optimizer automatically makes the correct determination. It is recommended that table-level locking hints be used to change the default locking behavior only when absolutely necessary. Disallowing a locking level can adversely affect concurrency.

To implement optimizer hints for locking manually, you must remove the System 11 hints PREFETCH, LRU, or MRU because SQL Server does not support them. SQL Server automatically uses READ AHEAD (RA) processing when it is appropriate. This behavior can be tailored with new RA options on **sp_configure** (see "System Stored Procedures" in this chapter). For more information about locking hints, see "Locking Hints" in SQL Server Books Online.

Server Roles

SQL Server 2000 does not support the Sybase server roles of **sa_role**, **sso_role**, and **oper.** The GRANT and REVOKE statements referencing these roles must be removed.

In SQL Server, the **sysadmin** fixed server role has functions equivalent to the Sybase **sa_role** and **sso_role**. By using the GRANT statement, you can give individual users permissions to perform the operator actions of dumping databases and transactions, but you cannot give them permissions to load databases and transactions.

The Sybase **proc_name** function, which validates a username, is not supported by SQL Server and must be removed.

The following table describes the fixed server roles in SQL Server 2000.

Fixed server role	Permission
sysadmin	Can perform any activity in SQL Server
serveradmin	Can set server-wide configuration options and shut down the server
setupadmin	Can manage linked servers and startup procedures
securityadmin	Can manage logins and CREATE DATABASE permissions and read error logs
processadmin	Can manage processes running in SQL Server
dbcreator	Can create and alter databases
diskadmin	Can manage disk files
bulkadmin	Can perform bulk insert operations

You can get a list of the fixed server roles by executing **sp_helpsrvrole**, and you can get the specific permissions for each role by executing **sp_srvrolepermission**.

Each database has a set of fixed database roles. Although roles with the same names exist in each database, the scope of an individual role is only within a specific database. For example, if **Database1** and **Database2** both have user IDs named **UserX**, adding **UserX** in **Database1** to the **db_owner** fixed database role for **Database1** has no effect on whether **UserX** in **Database2** is a member of the **db_owner** role for **Database2**.

The following table describes the fixed database roles in SQL Server 2000.

Fixed database role	Permission
db_owner	Has all permissions in the database
db_accessadmin	Can add or remove user Ids
db_securityadmin	Can manage all permissions, object ownerships, roles, and role memberships
db_ddladmin	Can issue ALL DDL, but cannot issue GRANT, REVOKE, or DENY statements
db_backupoperator	Can issue DBCC, CHECKPOINT, and BACKUP statements
db_datareader	Can select all data from any user table in the database
db_datawriter	Can modify any data in any user table in the database
db_denydatareader	Can deny or revoke SELECT permissions on any object
db_denydatawriter	Can deny or revoke INSERT, UPDATE, and DELETE permissions on any object

Raising Errors

The Sybase version of RAISERROR allows argument substitution in any order, but the arguments must be of data type **varchar** or **char**.

The SQL Server RAISERROR statement requires positional argument substitution, like **printf** in the C language, but supports integer and string substitution: %d, %i, %s. This RAISERROR statement also supports the specification of a severity level (range 1 through 25).

The SQL Server RAISERROR statement includes a WITH LOG parameter so the server will enter the message in the error log. Messages raised with severities from 19 through 25 require the WITH LOG parameter.

PRINT

The Sybase version of PRINT allows argument substitution; the SQL Server version does not. The most straightforward solution is to change any Sybase PRINT that uses argument substitution to a RAISERROR with a severity of 10 or lower. Another solution is to print a string built of substrings in SQL Server:

```
DECLARE @msg VARCHAR(255)
SELECT @msg = 'The object ' + @tablename + 'does not allow duplicate keys.\n'
PRINT @msg
```

Partitioned Tables vs. Row Locking

In Sybase 11 or later, partitions are supported only on user tables that do not have clustered indexes. This System 11 feature helps to reduce the blocking caused by the lack of row-level locking.

SQL Server 2000 supports row-level locking on all table types, and does not support the keyword PARTITION on the ALTER TABLE statement. SQL Server 2000 Enterprise Edition allows for updatable distributed partitioned views. These views allow you to spread a table across multiple servers and access the full table data from any one of the servers.

For more information about locking, see "Locking Architecture" in SQL Server Books Online.

Setting ANSI NULL Behavior

Both Sybase version 11 and later and SQL Server version 6.5 and later support SQL-92-compliant NULL behavior; however, the syntax in the two systems is different.

Sybase	SQL Server 2000
SET ANSINULL {ON|OFF}	SET ANSI_NULLS {ON|OFF}
	SET ANSI_WARNINGS {ON|OFF}

SQL Server supports setting options that define whether columns in CREATE TABLE statements take the ANSI NULL defaults:

```
SET ANSI_NULL_DFLT_ON {ON|OFF}
SET ANSI_NULL_DFLT_OFF {ON|OFF}
```

IDENTITY Columns

SQL Server 2000 and Sybase use the same syntax for defining identity columns. The SQL Server default name for an identity column is IDENTITYCOL; the Sybase default name is SYB_IDENTITY. All references to SYB_IDENTITY must be changed to IDENTITYCOL.

SET Statement

Since their respective 4.2 versions, the SET statement options implemented by Sybase and SQL Server have diverged. Although the new options may have the same or similar names, their defined characteristics can be slightly different. For example, the full effect of the Sybase ANSINULLS option combines behavior defined by the SQL Server ANSI_NULLS and ANSI_WARNINGS options.

The following table lists the Sybase-specific options that do not have exact SQL Server equivalents, and lists the SQL Server options that most closely match the desired Sybase behavior. To understand the differences between the Sybase statement and the alternative offered, review SQL Server Book Online carefully. The table does not list the options that Sybase and SQL Server share.

Sybase option	SQL Server 2000 option
ANSINULLS	ANSI_NULLS, ANSI_WARNINGS
ANSI_PERMISSIONS	No equivalent.
ARITHABORT can take overflow or truncated options.	ARITHABORT does not support options.
ARITHIGNORE can take overflow option.	ARITHIGNORE does not support options.
CHAINED	IMPLICIT_TRANSACTION
CLOSE ON ENDTRAN	CURSOR_CLOSE_ON_COMMIT
CHAR_CONVERT	Set with either ODBC or DB-Library connect options.
CURSOR ROWS	No equivalent.
DUP_IN_SUBQUERY (System 10 only)	No equivalent.
FIPSFLAGGER takes ON/OFF.	FIPSFLAGGER takes a FIPS level identifier.

continued on next page

Sybase option	SQL Server 2000 option
FLUSHMESSAGE	No equivalent.
PREFETCH	See READ AHEAD processing.
ROLE	No equivalent.
SELF_RECURSION	No equivalent.
STATISTICS SUBQUERYCACHE	No equivalent (STATS TIME and I/O supported).
STRING_RTRUNCATION	No equivalent.
TABLE COUNT	No equivalent.
TRANSACTION ISOLATION LEVEL {0|1|3}	Levels specified with strings (like READ COMMITTED).

Join Syntax

Sybase joins use an old style syntax in which the join takes place in the WHERE statement. This syntax is supported in SQL Server 2000 for backward compatibility only. It will not be supported in future releases. When migrating your database from Sybase to SQL Server 2000, you should update the joins to an SQL-92 compliant syntax.

Sybase	SQL Server 2000
| ```
SELECT a.col1, b.col1
FROM table1 a, table2 b
WHERE a.col1 *= b.col2
``` | ```
SELECT a.col1, b.col1
FROM table1 a
LEFT OUTER JOIN table2 b
ON a.col1 = b.col2
``` |

These two queries can return different results because the FROM clause is evaluated before the WHERE clause. For example, if a search condition were added to the WHERE clause, it would be evaluated at different times in the query. In the Sybase syntax, it would be evaluated along with the join. In the SQL-92–standard syntax, it would be evaluated after the join and reduce the result set.

For more information, see "Specifying Joins in FROM or WHERE Clauses" in SQL Server Books Online.

Subquery Behavior

Sybase SQL Server 4.9.2 and Microsoft SQL Server 4.2x subqueries are not SQL-92–standard; subqueries can return duplicate rows.

Sybase System 10 defaults to SQL-92–standard behavior, but the earlier subquery behavior can be set to ON to ease migration. Sybase 10 is backward compatible to the non–SQL-92I behavior if the SET DUP_IN_SUBQUERY option is set to ON. Sybase 11 and SQL Server 2000 only support SQL-92 subquery behavior. If you are migrating an application from Sybase 10 and the system uses

SET DUP_IN_SUBQUERY ON, you must review the Sybase queries so they do not cause errors. If you are migrating from a Sybase version earlier than version 10, you also must review queries that have subqueries.

Grouping Results

SQL Server 2000 requires that all nonaggregate columns in the select list be named in the GROUP BY clause if it is used. Sybase allows the nonstandard method of not explicitly naming all columns in the group by statement. The same functionality can be achieved using derived tables in SQL Server 2000.

Sybase	SQL Server 2000
`SELECT au_lname, city, count(*) FROM authors GROUP BY city`	`SELECT au_lname, city, (select count(*) FROM authors WHERE city = a.city) FROM authors a`

System Stored Procedures

The SQL Server 2000 and Sybase implementations of the **sp_addmessage**, **sp_dboption**, and **sp_configure** system stored procedures are not the same.

sp_addmessage

In Sybase systems, the range for user-defined message numbers starts at 20,000. In SQL Server 2000, the range starts at 50,000 and also requires a severity to be specified (range is from 1 through 25) to support alerts.

SQL Server 2000 stores user messages in **master.dbo.sysmessages**, and Sybase stores them in **master.dbo.sysusermessages**.

sp_dboption

The following table shows the parameters for **sp_dboption** that are different for Sybase and SQL Server 2000 implementations.

Sybase	SQL Server 2000
ABORT TRAN ON LOG FULL	No equivalent.
ALLOW NULLS BY DEFAULT	ANSI NULL DEFAULT
AUTO IDENTITY	No equivalent.
DDL IN TRAN	SQL Server 2000 allows DDL in transactions.
IDENTITY IN NONUNIQUE INDEX	No equivalent.

Sybase requires a checkpoint in the affected database after **sp_dboption** completes, and SQL Server 2000 automatically check points the affected database. Also, SQL Server 2000 allows DDL in transactions without requiring the system administrator to set any server or database options.

sp_configure

You can manage and optimize SQL Server 2000 resources through configuration options by using SQL Server Enterprise Manager or the **sp_configure** system stored procedure. The most commonly used server configuration options are available through SQL Server Enterprise Manager; all configuration options are accessible through **sp_configure**.

SQL Server 2000 has internal features for self-tuning and reconfiguring. These features reduce the need to set server configuration options manually. You should consider the effects on your system carefully before setting these options.

The options for **sp_configure** are quite different in Sybase and SQL Server 2000. Detailing all of the differences is beyond the scope of this chapter. For more information about the options for **sp_configure**, see SQL Server Books Online.

sp_configure allows members of the **sysadmin** fixed server role to set defaults for user options, such as SQL-92 options, although individual connections can change the settings later. The current state of a connection's settings are made visible to it through the @@OPTIONS. @@OPTIONS returns a numeric value that records the current option settings. For more information about a stored procedure that returns a character list of the options recorded by @@OPTIONS, search for the Microsoft Knowledge Base Article "Q156498" at http://support.microsoft.com/.

DUMP/LOAD

The DUMP statement is included in SQL Server 2000 for backward compatibility. It is recommended that the BACKUP statement be used instead of the DUMP statement. In future versions of SQL Server, DUMP will not be supported. For more information about database back up and restore operations, see "Backing Up and Restoring Databases" in SQL Server Books Online.

Use DTS to perform imports and exports on a regular basis with SQL Server 2000.

DUMP/LOAD statements	Sybase Adaptive Server Enterprise	SQL Server 2000
Dump devices	FILE	DISK
Listing	LISTONLY	Not supported in the same way; closest statement is HEADERONLY.
	HEADERONLY only lists the first dump.	HEADERONLY lists information about all dumps in a device.

continued on next page

DUMP/LOAD statements	Sybase Adaptive Server Enterprise	SQL Server 2000
Striping	STRIPE=n	Remove the STRIPE=n parameter from the Sybase DUMP and LOAD statements and set the **sp_configure backup threads** parameter to n.

Replace all logic that uses the Sybase **syslogshold** table to determine the oldest outstanding transaction with logic that uses the SQL Server DBCC OPENTRAN statement.

Understanding Database Administration Differences

Microsoft SQL Server 2000 offers several tools for database administration.

Graphical Administration

SQL Server Enterprise Manager allows for easy enterprise-wide configuration and management of SQL Server and SQL Server objects. SQL Server Enterprise Manager provides a powerful scheduling engine, administrator alert capability, and a built-in replication management interface. You can also use SQL Server Enterprise Manager to:

- Manage logins, permissions, and users.

- Create scripts.

- Manage backup devices and databases.

- Back up databases and transaction logs.

- Manage tables, views, stored procedures, triggers, indexes, rules, defaults, and user-defined data types.

- Create full-text indexes, database diagrams, and database maintenance plans.

- Import and export data.

- Transform data.

- Perform various Web administration tasks.

By default, SQL Server Enterprise Manager is installed by SQL Server Setup as part of the server software on computers running Windows 2000 or Windows NT 4.0, and as part of the client software on computers running Windows 2000, Windows NT 4.0, Windows 95, or Windows 98. Because SQL Server Enterprise Manager is a 32-bit application, it cannot be installed on computers running 16-bit operating systems.

Auditing

SQL Profiler is a graphical tool that enables system administrators to monitor engine events in SQL Server 2000. SQL Profiler captures a continuous record of server activity in real time. SQL Profiler enables you to monitor events produced through SQL Server, filter events based on user-specified criteria, and direct the trace output to the screen, a file, or a table. Using SQL Profiler, you can replay previously captured traces. This tool helps identify transactions that may be deteriorating the performance of an application. This can be very useful when migrating an application from a file-based architecture to a client/server architecture, because the last step involves optimizing the application for its new client/server environment.

Examples of engine events include:

- Login connects, fails, and disconnects.

- Transact-SQL SELECT, INSERT, UPDATE, and DELETE statements.

- Remote procedure call (RPC) batch status.

- The start or end of a stored procedure.

- The start or end of statements within stored procedures.

- The start or end of a Transact-SQL batch.

- Errors written to the SQL Server error log.

- Locks acquired or released on a database object.

- Open cursors.

Data about each event can be captured and saved to a file or a SQL Server table for later analysis.

Threshold Manager

SQL Server 2000 uses two tools to manage transaction logs in a manner equivalent to the Sybase Threshold Manager:

- SQL Server Enterprise Manager enables you to set up a system of periodic, scheduled backups.

- SQL Server Agent monitors System Monitor, available in Windows 2000, counters. You must set up an alert to execute a backup of the transaction log when the appropriate threshold is exceeded.

Rebuilding master

In Sybase 4.x, the **master** databases were rebuilt by the **bldmstr** utility. In later versions of Sybase, the **sybinit** utility is used to rebuild the **master** database.

SQL Server 2000 has a Rebuild Master utility that provides the same functionality.

Graphical Query Analysis

SQL Query Analyzer is a graphical query tool that enables you to visually analyze the plan of a query, execute multiple queries simultaneously, view data, and obtain index recommendations. SQL Query Analyzer provides the graphical diagram of the showplan information, which is used to report data retrieval methods chosen by the query optimizer.

Migration Checklist

You must make the following changes to your Sybase database and applications before migrating to SQL Server 2000.

1. Change references to chained transaction mode to either unchained transactions or SQL Server 2000 implicit transactions. Change @@**trainchain** references to @@OPTIONS. Change @@**transtate** references to @@ERROR logic.

2. Convert ROLLBACK TRIGGER to savepoints.

3. Change transaction isolation levels from Sybase numeric-level identifiers to SQL Server 2000 string-based identifiers.

4. Move user-supplied stored procedures from **sybsystemprocs** to **master**.

5. Delete (preferably) or change index and locking optimizer hints to SQL Server 2000 format.

6. Change permanent temporary tables to global tables.

7. Change range and add severity to user-defined messages.

8. Remove:

   - Arguments from the PRINT statement.

   - Sybase server roles.

   - User-defined data cache references.

   - Thresholds.

   - Table partitioning.

9. Make required syntax changes:

   - DUMP and LOAD statements change to BACKUP and RESTORE statements

   - Cursor processing (change @@**sqlstatus** to @@FETCH_STATUS)

   - Identity column default name changes to IDENTITYCOL

   - SET TRANSACTION ISOLATION LEVEL

- SELECT statement optimizer hints

- **sp_addmessage** (message range and severity)

- Reserved SQL Server 2000 keywords

- DBCC

- RAISERROR

10. Change message ranges to >= 50,000.

11. Change argument substitution such as C **printf**.

Optionally, you can choose to make the following changes to your Sybase database and applications before migrating to SQL Server 2000:

- Change tuning options for read ahead.

- Change scrollable server cursors.

- Encrypt stored procedures in **syscomments**.

- Replace nested IF statements with the CASE statement.

- Use RPCs with result sets in INSERTS.

- Schedule automatic maintenance tasks, alerts, and replication.

- Use extended stored procedures for mail notification, paging, and scheduling.

- Log user messages to the Windows application log and/or the SQL Server error log by using **xp_logevent**.

- Change trusted connections and *NT_username*.

- Start up stored procedures automatically.

- Change EXECUTE strings.

- Use the SQL Server Agent autostart functionality.

- Change the SELECT statement to use SQL-92–style joins (INNER JOIN, CROSS JOIN, LEFT OUTER JOIN, RIGHT OUTER JOIN, FULL OUTER JOIN).

Migrating Oracle Databases to SQL Server 2000

This chapter is for developers of Oracle applications who want to convert their applications to Microsoft® SQL Server™ 2000. The tools, processes, and techniques required for a successful conversion are described. Also highlighted are the essential design points that allow you to create high-performance, high-concurrency SQL Server–based applications.

Target Audience

The target audience can be new to SQL Server and its operation, but should have a solid foundation in the Oracle RDBMS and general database concepts. The target audience should have:

- A strong background in Oracle RDBMS fundamentals.

- General database management knowledge.

- Familiarity with the Oracle SQL and PL/SQL languages.

- Membership in the **sysadmin** fixed server role.

For clarity and ease of presentation, the reference development and application platform is assumed to be the Microsoft Windows® 2000 operating system and SQL Server 2000. The Visigenic Software ODBC driver is used with Oracle, and the SQL Server ODBC driver is used with SQL Server 2000. SQL Server 2000 includes an OLE DB driver for Oracle, but that driver is not discussed extensively in this chapter.

Overview

The application migration process can appear complicated. There are many architectural differences between each RDBMS. The words and terminology used to describe Oracle architecture often have completely different meanings in Microsoft SQL Server. Additionally, both Oracle and SQL Server have made many proprietary extensions to the SQL-92 standard.

From an application developer's perspective, Oracle and SQL Server manage data in similar ways. The internal differences between Oracle and SQL Server are significant, but if managed properly, have minimal impact on a migrated application.

SQL Language Extensions

The most significant migration issue that confronts the developer is the implementation of the SQL-92 SQL language standard and the extensions that each RDBMS has to offer. Some developers use only standard SQL language statements, preferring to keep their program code as generic as possible. Generally, this means restricting program code to the entry-level SQL-92 standard, which is implemented consistently across many database products, including Oracle and SQL Server.

This approach can produce unneeded complexity in the program code and can substantially affect program performance. For example, Oracle's DECODE function is a nonstandard SQL extension specific to Oracle. The CASE expression in SQL Server is a SQL-92 extension beyond entry level and is not implemented in all database products.

Both the Oracle DECODE and the SQL Server CASE expressions can perform sophisticated conditional evaluation from within a query. The alternative to not using these functions is to perform the function programmatically, which might require that substantially more data be retrieved from the RDBMS.

Also, procedural extensions to the SQL language can cause difficulties. The Oracle PL/SQL and SQL Server Transact-SQL languages are similar in function, but different in syntax. There is no exact symmetry between each RDBMS and its procedural extensions. Consequently, you might decide not to use stored programs such as procedures and triggers. This is unfortunate because they can offer substantial performance and security benefits that cannot be duplicated in any other way.

The use of proprietary development interfaces introduces additional issues. The conversion of a program using the Oracle OCI (Oracle Call Interface) often requires a significant investment in resources. When developing an application that may use multiple RDBMSs, consider using the Open Database Connectivity (ODBC) interface.

ODBC

ODBC is designed to work with numerous database management systems. ODBC provides a consistent application programming interface (API) that works with different databases through the services of a database-specific driver.

A consistent API means that the functions a program calls to make a connection, execute a command, and retrieve results are identical whether the program is talking to Oracle or SQL Server.

ODBC also defines a standardized call-level interface and uses standard escape sequences to specify SQL functions that perform common tasks but have different syntax in different databases. The ODBC drivers can automatically convert this ODBC syntax to either Oracle-native or SQL Server–native SQL syntax without requiring the revision of any program code. In some situations, the best approach is to write one program and allow ODBC to perform the conversion process at run time.

ODBC by itself does not provide complete database independence, full functionality, and high performance from all databases. Different databases and third-party vendors offer varying levels of ODBC support. Some drivers implement only core API functions mapped on top of other interface libraries. Other drivers, such as the SQL Server ODBC driver, offer full Level 2 support in a native, high-performance driver.

If a program uses only the core ODBC API, it will likely forego features and performance capabilities with some databases. Furthermore, not all native SQL extensions can be represented in ODBC escape sequences (such as Oracle DECODE and SQL Server CASE expressions).

Additionally, it is common practice to write SQL statements to take advantage of the database's optimizer. The techniques and methods that enhance performance within Oracle are not necessarily optimal within SQL Server 2000. The ODBC interface cannot translate techniques from one RDBMS to another.

ODBC does not prevent an application from using database-specific features and tuning for performance, but the application needs some database-specific sections of code. ODBC makes it easy to keep the program structure and the majority of the program code consistent across multiple databases.

OLE DB

SQL Server 2000 takes advantage of OLE DB within the components of SQL Server itself. Additionally, application developers should consider OLE DB for new development with SQL Server 2000. Microsoft includes an OLE DB provider for Oracle 8 with SQL Server 2000.

OLE DB is an open specification designed to build on the features of ODBC. ODBC was created to access relational databases, and OLE DB is designed to access relational and nonrelational information sources, such as mainframe ISAM/VSAM and hierarchical databases, e-mail and file system stores, text, graphical and geographical data, and custom business objects.

OLE DB defines a collection of COM interfaces that encapsulate various database management system services and allows the creation of software components that implement such services. OLE DB components consist of data providers (that contain and expose data), data consumers (that use data), and service components (that process and transport data, for example, query processors and cursor engines).

OLE DB interfaces are designed to help components integrate smoothly so that OLE DB component vendors can bring high quality OLE DB components to the market quickly. In addition, OLE DB includes a bridge to ODBC to allow continued support for the broad range of ODBC relational database drivers available today.

Organization of This Chapter

To assist you in implementing a systematic migration from Oracle to SQL Server, each section includes an overview of the relevant differences between Oracle databases and Microsoft SQL Server 2000. The chapter also includes conversion considerations, SQL Server 2000 advantages, and multiple examples.

Where appropriate, the chapter provides references to external sources that describe the topic in more detail.

Architecture and Terminology

To start a successful migration, you should understand the basic architecture and terminology associated with SQL Server 2000.

Definition of Database

In Oracle, a database refers to the entire Oracle RDBMS environment and includes these components:

- Oracle database processes and buffers (instance).
- SYSTEM tablespace containing one centralized system catalog, which is made up of one or more datafiles.
- Other tablespaces as defined by the DBA (optional), each made up of one or more datafiles.
- Two or more online Redo Logs.
- Archived Redo Logs (optional).
- Miscellaneous other files (control file, Init.ora, config.ora, etc.).

A SQL Server database provides a logical separation of data, applications, and security mechanisms. A SQL Server installation (an instance) can support multiple databases. Applications built using SQL Server can use databases to logically divide business functionality. There can be multiple instances of SQL Server on a single computer. Each instance of SQL Server can have multiple databases.

Each SQL Server database can support filegroups, which provide the ability to distribute the placement of the data physically. A SQL Server filegroup categorizes the operating-system files containing data from a single SQL Server database to simplify database administration tasks, such as backing up. A filegroup is a property of a SQL Server database and cannot contain the operating-system files of more than one database, although a single database can contain more than one filegroup. After a database is created, filegroups can be added to the database.

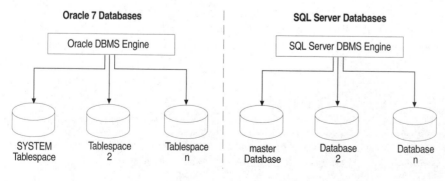

SQL Server also installs the following databases by default:

- The **model** database is a template for all newly created user databases.
- The **tempdb** database is similar to an Oracle temporary tablespace in that it is used for temporary working storage and sort operations. Unlike the Oracle temporary tablespace, SQL Server users can create temporary tables that are automatically dropped when the user logs off.
- The **msdb** database supports the SQL Server Agent and its scheduled jobs, alerts, and replication information.
- The **pubs** and **Northwind** databases are provided as sample databases for training.

For more information about the default databases, see SQL Server Books Online.

Database System Catalogs

Each Oracle database runs on one centralized system catalog, or data dictionary, which resides in the SYSTEM tablespace. Each SQL Server 2000 database maintains its own system catalog, which contains information about:

- Database objects (tables, indexes, stored procedures, views, triggers, and so on).
- Constraints.
- Users and permissions.
- User-defined data types.
- Replication definitions.
- Files used by the database.

SQL Server also contains a centralized system catalog in the **master** database, which contains system catalogs as well as some information about the individual databases:

- Database names and the primary file location for each database.
- SQL Server login accounts.
- System messages.
- Database configuration values.
- Remote and/or linked servers.
- Current activity information.
- System stored procedures.

Similar to the SYSTEM tablespace in Oracle, the SQL Server **master** database must be available to access any other database. It is important to protect against failures by backing up the **master** database after any significant changes are made in the database. Database administrators can also mirror the files that make up the **master** database.

For information about a list of the system tables contained in the **master** and all other databases, see "System Tables" in SQL Server Books Online.

Physical and Logical Storage Structures

The Oracle RDBMS is comprised of tablespaces, which in turn are comprised of datafiles. Tablespace datafiles are formatted into internal units termed *blocks*. The block size is set by the DBA when the Oracle database is first created. When an object is created in an Oracle tablespace, the user can specify its space in units called *extents* (initial extent, next extent, min extents, and max extents). If an extent size is not defined explicitly, a default extent is created. An Oracle extent varies in size and must contain a chain of at least five contiguous blocks.

SQL Server uses filegroups at the database level to control the physical placement of tables and indexes. Filegroups are logical containers of one or more files, and data contained within a filegroup is proportionally filled across all files belonging to the filegroup.

If filegroups are not defined and used, database objects are placed in a default filegroup that is implicitly defined during the creation of a database. Filegroups allow you to:

- Distribute large tables across multiple files to improve I/O throughput.
- Store indexes on different files than their respective tables, again to improve I/O throughput and disk concurrency.
- Store **text**, **ntext**, and **image** columns (large objects) on separate files from the table.
- Place database objects on specific disk spindles.
- Back up and restore individual tables or sets of tables within a filegroup.

SQL Server formats files into internal units called *pages*. The page size is fixed at 8192 bytes (8 KB). Pages are organized into extents that are fixed in size at 8 contiguous pages (64 KB). When a table or index is created in a SQL Server database, it is automatically allocated one page within an extent. As the table or index grows, it is automatically allocated space by SQL Server. This allows for more efficient storage of smaller tables and indexes when compared to allocating an entire extent as in Oracle. For more information, see "Physical Database Architecture" in SQL Server Books Online.

Striping Data

Oracle-type segments are not needed for most SQL Server installations. Instead, SQL Server can distribute, or stripe, data more efficiently with hardware-based RAID or with software–based RAID available through the Windows Disk Management utility or from third parties. With RAID, you can set up striped volumes (stripe sets in Windows NT 4.0) consisting of multiple disk drives that appear as one logical drive. If database files are created on this striped volume, the disk subsystem assumes responsibility for distributing I/O load across multiple disks. It is recommended that administrators spread out the data over multiple physical disks using RAID.

The recommended RAID configuration for SQL Server is RAID 1 (mirroring) or RAID 5 (stripe sets with an extra parity drive, for redundancy). RAID 10 (mirroring of striped sets with parity) is also recommended, but is much more expensive than the first two options. Stripe sets work very well to spread out the usually random I/O done on database files.

If RAID is not an option, filegroups are an attractive alternative and provide some of the same benefits available with RAID. Additionally, for very large databases that might span multiple physical RAID arrays, filegroups may be an attractive way to further distribute your I/O across multiple RAID arrays in a controlled fashion.

Transaction log files must be optimized for sequential I/O and must be secured against a single point of failure. Accordingly, RAID 1 (mirroring) is recommended for transaction logs. When migrating, the size of this drive should be at least as large as the sum of the size of the Oracle online redo logs and the Oracle rollback segment tablespace(s). Create one or more log files that take up all the space defined on the logical drive. Unlike data stored in filegroups, transaction log entries are always written sequentially and are not proportionally filled.

For more information about RAID, see SQL Server Books Online, your Microsoft Windows 2000 documentation, and the *Microsoft Windows 2000 Resource Kit*.

Transaction Logs and Automatic Recovery

The Oracle RDBMS performs automatic recovery each time it is started. It verifies that the contents of the tablespace files are coordinated with the contents of the online redo log files. If they are not, Oracle applies the contents of the online redo log files to the tablespace files (roll forward), and then removes any uncommitted transactions that are found in the rollback segments (roll back). If Oracle cannot obtain the information it requires from the online redo log files, it consults the archived redo log files.

SQL Server 2000 also performs automatic data recovery by checking each database in the system each time it is started. It first checks the **master** database and then launches threads to recover all of the other databases in the system. For each SQL Server database, the automatic recovery mechanism checks the transaction log. If the transaction log contains any uncommitted transactions, the transactions are rolled back. The recovery mechanism then checks the transaction log for committed transactions that have not yet been written out to the database. If it finds any, it performs those transactions again, rolling forward.

Each SQL Server transaction log has the combined functionality of an Oracle rollback segment and an Oracle online redo log. Each database has its own transaction log that records all changes to the database and is shared by all users of that database. When a transaction begins and a data modification occurs, a BEGIN TRANSACTION event (as well as the modification event) is recorded in the log. This event is used during automatic recovery to determine the starting point of a transaction. As each data modification statement is received, the changes are written to the transaction log prior to being written to the database itself. For more information, see "Transactions, Locking, and Concurrency" in this chapter.

SQL Server has an automatic checkpoint mechanism that ensures completed transactions are regularly written from the SQL Server disk cache to the transaction log file. A checkpoint writes any cached page that has been modified since the last checkpoint to the database. Checkpointing these cached pages, known as dirty pages, onto the database, ensures that all completed transactions are written out to disk. This process shortens the time that it takes to recover from a system failure, such as a power outage. This setting can be changed by modifying the recovery interval setting by using SQL Server Enterprise Manager or with Transact-SQL (**sp_configure** system stored procedure).

Backing Up and Restoring Data

Microsoft SQL Server offers several options for backing up data:

Full database backup

> A database backup makes a copy of the full database. Not all pages are copied to the backup set, only those actually containing data. Both data pages and transaction log pages are copied to the backup set.
>
> A database backup set is used to re-create the database as it was at the time the BACKUP statement completed. If only database backups exist for a database, it can be recovered only to the time of the last database backup taken before the failure of the server or database. To make a full database backup, use the BACKUP DATABASE statement or the Create Database Backup Wizard.

Differential backup

> After a full database backup, regularly back up just the changed data and index pages using the BACKUP DATABASE WITH DIFFERENTIAL statement or the Create Database Backup Wizard.

Transaction log backup

> Transaction logs in Microsoft SQL Server are associated with individual databases. The transaction log fills until it is backed up or truncated. The default configuration of SQL Server 2000 is that the transaction log grows automatically until it uses all available disk space or it meets its maximum configured size. When a transaction log gets too full, it can create an error and prevent further data modifications until it is backed up or truncated. Other databases are not affected. Transaction logs can be backed up using the BACKUP LOG statement or the Create Database Backup Wizard.

File backup, filegroup backup

> A file or filegroup backup copies one or more files of a specified database, allowing a database to be backed up in smaller units: at the file or filegroup level. For more information, see SQL Server Books Online.

Backups can be performed while the database is in use, allowing backups to be made of systems that must run continually. The backup processing and internal data structures of SQL Server maximize their rate of data transfer with minimal effect on transaction throughput.

Both Oracle and SQL Server require a specific format for log files. In SQL Server, these files, called backup devices, are created using SQL Server Enterprise Manager, the Transact-SQL **sp_addumpdevice** stored procedure, or the equivalent SQL-DMO command.

Although backups can be performed manually, it is recommended that you use SQL Server Enterprise Manager and/or the Database Maintenance Plan Wizard to schedule periodic backups, or backups based on database activity.

A database can be restored to a certain point in time by applying transaction log backups and/or differential backups to a full database backup (device). A database restore overwrites the data with the information contained in the backups. Restores can be performed using SQL Server Enterprise Manager, Transact-SQL (RESTORE DATABASE), or SQL-DMO.

Just as you can turn off the Oracle archiver to override automatic backups, in Microsoft SQL Server, members of the **db_owner** fixed database role can force the transaction log to erase its contents every time a checkpoint occurs. This can be accomplished by using SQL Server Enterprise Manager (set the recovery model to **Simple**), Transact-SQL (ALTER DATABASE), or SQL-DMO.

Networks

Oracle SQL*Net supports networked connections between Oracle database servers and their clients. It communicates with the Transparent Network Substrate (TNS) data stream protocol, and allows users to run many different network protocols without writing specialized code.

With SQL Server, Net-Libraries (network libraries) support the networked connections between the clients and the server by using the Tabular Data Stream (TDS) protocol. They enable simultaneous connections from clients running Named Pipes, TCP/IP Sockets, or other Inter-Process Communication (IPC) mechanisms. The SQL Server 2000 CD-ROM includes all client Net-Libraries so that there is no need to acquire them separately.

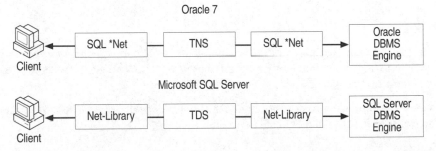

SQL Server Net-Library options can be changed after installation. The Client Network utility configures the default Net-Library and server connection information for a client running the Windows 2000, Windows NT 4.0, Windows 95, Windows 98, or Windows Millennium (WinMe) operating systems. All ODBC client applications use the same default Net-Library and server connection information, unless it is changed during ODBC data source setup or explicitly coded in the ODBC connection string. For more information about Net-Libraries, see SQL Server Books Online.

Database Security and Roles

To migrate your Oracle applications to SQL Server 2000 adequately, you must understand how SQL Server implements database security and roles.

Database File Encryption

Microsoft Windows 2000 allows users to encrypt files using the Encrypting File System (EFS). SQL Server 2000 can use EFS. The database files can be encrypted, preventing other users from moving, copying, or viewing their contents. This encryption is done on the operating-system level, not the logical database level. After SQL Server opens the encrypted file, the data within the file appears as unencrypted.

Network Security

SQL Server 2000 supports the use of the Secure Sockets Layer (SSL) to encrypt network communications between itself and clients. This encryption applies to all inter-computer protocols supported by SQL Server 2000, and is either 40- or 128-bit depending on the version of the Windows operating system on which SQL Server is running. For more information, see "Net-Library Encryption" in SQL Server Books Online.

Login Accounts

A login account allows a user to access SQL Server data or administrative options. The **guest** login account allows users to log in to SQL Server and only view databases that allow **guest** access. (The **guest** account is not set up by default and must be created.)

A login account allows a user to administer or access data in an instance of SQL Server 2000. SQL Server 2000 uses two different methods to authenticate logins:

- Windows Authentication
  A DBA specifies which Windows login accounts can be used to connect to an instance of SQL Server 2000. Users logged in to Windows using these accounts can connect to SQL Server 2000 without having to specify a separate database login and password. When using Windows Authentication, SQL Server 2000 uses the security mechanisms of Windows NT 4.0 or Windows 2000 to validate login connections, and relies on a user's Windows security credentials. Users do not need to enter login IDs or passwords for SQL Server 2000 because their login information is taken directly from the trusted network connection. This functions like the IDENTIFIED EXTERNALLY option associated with Oracle user accounts.

- SQL Server Authentication
  A DBA defines a separate database login account. A user must specify this login account and its password when they attempt to connect to SQL Server 2000. The database login is not related to the user's Windows login. This functions like the IDENTIFIED BY PASSWORD option associated with Oracle user accounts.

Each instance of SQL Server 2000 is run in one of two authentication modes:

- Windows Authentication Mode (known as integrated security in earlier versions of SQL Server). In this mode, SQL Server 2000 allows only connections that use Windows Authentication.

- Mixed Mode. In this mode, connections can be made using either Windows Authentication or SQL Server Authentication.

For more information about these security mechanisms, see SQL Server Books Online.

Groups, Roles, and Permissions

SQL Server and Oracle use permissions to enforce database security. SQL Server statement-level permissions are used to restrict the ability to create new database objects (similar to the Oracle system-level permissions).

SQL Server also offers object-level permissions. As in Oracle, object-level ownership is assigned to the creator of the object and cannot be transferred. Object-level permissions must be granted to other database users before they can access the object. Members of the **sysadmin** fixed server role, **db_owner** fixed database role, or **db_securityadmin** fixed database role can also grant permissions on one user's objects to other users.

SQL Server statement- and object-level permissions can be granted directly to database user accounts. However, it is often easier to administer permissions to database roles. SQL Server roles are used for granting and revoking privileges to groups of database users (much like Oracle roles). Roles are database objects associated with a specific database. There are a few specific fixed server roles associated with each installation, which work across databases. An example of a fixed server role is **sysadmin**. Windows groups can also be added as SQL Server logins, as well as database users. Permissions can be granted to a Windows group or a Windows user.

A database can have any number of roles or Windows groups. The default role **public** is always found in every database and cannot be removed. The **public** role functions much like the PUBLIC account in Oracle. Each database user is always a member of the **public** role. A database user can be a member of any number of roles in addition to the **public** role. A Windows user or group can also be a member of any number of roles, and is also always in the **public** role.

Database Users and the guest Account

In Microsoft SQL Server, a user login account must be authorized to use a database and its objects. One of the following methods can be used by a login account to access a database:

- The login account can be specified as a database user.

- The login account can use a guest account in the database.

- A Windows group login can be mapped to a database role. Individual Windows accounts that are members of that group can then connect to the database.

Members of the **db_owner** or **db_accessadmin** roles, or the **sysadmin** fixed server role, create the database user account roles. An account can include several parameters: the SQL Server login ID, database user name (optional), and up to one role name (optional). The database user name does not have to be the same as the user's login ID. If a database user name is not provided, the user's login ID and database user name are identical. If a role name is not provided, the database user is only a member of the **public** role. After creating the database user, the user can be assigned to as many roles as necessary.

Members of the **db_owner** or **db_accessadmin** roles can also create a **guest** account. The **guest** account allows any valid SQL Server login account to access a database even without a database user account. By default, the **guest** account inherits any privileges that have been assigned to the **public** role; however, these privileges can be changed to be greater or less than that of the **public** role.

A Windows user account or group account can be granted access to a database, just as a SQL Server login can. When a Windows user who is a member in a group connects to the database, the user receives the permissions assigned to the Windows group. If a member of more than one Windows group that has been granted access to the database connects to the database, the user receives the combined rights of all of the groups to which he or she belongs.

sysadmin Role

Members of the SQL Server **sysadmin** fixed server role have similar permissions to that of an Oracle DBA. In SQL Server, the **sa** SQL Server Authentication login account is a member of this role by default, as are members of the local **Administrators** group if SQL Server is installed on a computer running Windows 2000. A member of the **sysadmin** role can add or remove Windows users and groups, as well as SQL Server logins. Members of this role typically have the following responsibilities:

- Installing SQL Server.
- Configuring servers and clients.
- Creating databases.*
- Establishing login rights and user permissions.*
- Transferring data in and out of SQL Server databases.*
- Backing up and restoring databases.*
- Implementing and maintaining replication.
- Scheduling unattended operations.*
- Monitoring and tuning SQL Server performance.*
- Diagnosing system problems.

*These items can be delegated to other security roles or users.

A member of the **sysadmin** fixed server role can access any database and all of the objects (including data) on a particular instance of SQL Server. Similar to an Oracle DBA, there are several commands and system procedures that only members of the **sysadmin** role can issue.

db_owner Role

Although a SQL Server database is similar to an Oracle tablespace in use, it is administered differently. Each SQL Server database is a self-contained administrative domain. Each database is assigned a database owner (**dbo**). This user is always a member of the **db_owner** fixed database role. Other users can also be members of the **db_owner** role. Any user who is a member of this role has the ability to manage the administrative tasks related to her database (unlike Oracle, in which one DBA manages the administrative tasks for all tablespaces). These tasks include:

- Managing database access.

- Changing database options (read-only, single user, and so on).

- Backing up and restoring the database contents.

- Granting and revoking database permissions.

- Creating and dropping database objects.

Members of the **db_owner** role have permissions to do anything within their database. Most rights assigned to this role are separated into several fixed database roles, or can be granted to database users. It is not necessary to have **sysadmin** server-wide privileges to have **db_owner** privileges in a database.

Defining Database Objects

Oracle database objects (tables, views, and indexes) can be migrated to SQL Server easily because each RDBMS closely follows the SQL-92 standard that regards object definitions.

For more information, see "Logical Database Components" in SQL Server Books Online.

Converting Oracle SQL table, index, and view definitions to SQL Server table, index, and view definitions requires relatively simple syntax changes. This table shows some differences in database objects between Oracle and SQL Server.

Category	Microsoft SQL Server	Oracle
Number of columns	1,024	1,000
Row size	8,060 bytes, including 16 bytes to point to each text or image column	Unlimited (only one long or long raw allowed per row)
Maximum number of rows	Unlimited	Unlimited

continued on next page

Category	Microsoft SQL Server	Oracle
Blob type storage	16-byte pointer stored with row. Data stored on other data pages	One long or long raw per table, must be at end of row, data stored on same block(s) with row
Clustered table indexes	1 per table	1 per table (index-organized tables)
Nonclustered table indexes	249 per table	Unlimited
Maximum number of columns in single index	16	32
Maximum length of column values within of an index	900 bytes	40% of block
Table naming convention	[[[Server.]database.]owner.] table_name	[schema.]table_name
View naming convention	[[[Server.]database.]owner.] table_name	[schema.]table_name
Index naming convention	[[[Server.]database.]owner.] table_name	[schema.]table_name

It is assumed that you are starting with an Oracle SQL script or program that is used to create your database objects. Copy this script or program and make the following modifications. Each change is discussed throughout the rest of this section.

1. Ensure database object identifiers comply to Microsoft SQL Server naming conventions. You may need to change only the names of indexes.

2. Consider the data storage parameters your SQL Server database will require. If you are using RAID, no storage parameters are required.

3. Modify Oracle constraint definitions to work in SQL Server. If tables cross databases, use triggers to enforce foreign key relationships.

4. Modify the CREATE INDEX statements to take advantage of clustered indexes.

5. Use Data Transformation Services (DTS) to create new CREATE TABLE statements. Review the statements, taking note of how Oracle data types are mapped to SQL Server data types.

6. Remove any CREATE SEQUENCE statements. Replace the use of sequences with IDENTITY or **uniqueidentifier** columns in CREATE TABLE or ALTER TABLE statements.

7. Modify CREATE VIEW statements if necessary.

8. Remove any reference to synonyms.

9. Evaluate the use of SQL Server temporary tables and their usefulness in your application.

10. Change any Oracle CREATE TABLE...AS SELECT commands to SQL Server SELECT...INTO statements.

11. Evaluate the potential use of user-defined rules, data types, and defaults.

Database Object Identifiers

The following table compares how Oracle and SQL Server handle object identifiers. In most cases, you do not need to change the names of objects when migrating to SQL Server.

Oracle	Microsoft SQL Server
1-30 characters in length. Database names: up to 8 characters long Database link names: up to 128 characters long	1-128 Unicode characters in length Temporary table names: up to 116 characters
Identifier names must begin with an alphabetic character and contain alphanumeric characters, or the characters _, $, and #.	Identifier names can begin with an alphanumeric character, or an _, and can contain virtually any character. If the identifier begins with a space, or contains characters other than _, @, #, or $, you must use [ ] (delimiters) around the identifier name. If an object begins with: @ it is a local variable. # it is a local temporary object. ## it is a global temporary object.
Tablespace names must be unique.	Database names must be unique.
Identifier names must be unique within user accounts (schemas).	Identifier names must be unique within database user accounts.
Column names must be unique within tables and views.	Column names must be unique within tables and views.
Index names must be unique within a user's schema.	Index names must be unique within database table names.

Qualifying Table Names

When accessing tables that exist in your Oracle user account, the table can be selected simply by its unqualified name. Accessing tables in other Oracle schemas requires that the schema name be prefixed to the table name with a single period (.). Oracle synonyms can provide additional location transparency.

SQL Server uses a different convention when it references tables. Because one SQL Server login account can create a table by the same name in multiple databases, the following convention is used to access tables and views: [[*database_name.*]*owner_name.*]*table_name.*

Accessing a table in...	Oracle	Microsoft SQL Server
Your user account	SELECT * FROM **STUDENT**	SELECT * FROM **USER_DB.STUDENT_ ADMIN.STUDENT**
Other schema	SELECT * FROM **STUDENT_ADMIN.STU DENT**	SELECT * FROM **OTHER_DB.STUDENT_ ADMIN.STUDENT**

Here are guidelines for naming SQL Server tables and views:

- Using the database name and user name is optional. When a table is referenced only by name (for example, **STUDENT**), SQL Server searches for that table in the current user's account in the current database. If it does not find one, it looks for an object of the same name owned by the reserved user name of **dbo** in the database. Table names must be unique within a user's account within a database.

- The same SQL Server login account can own tables with the same name in multiple databases. For example, the **ENDUSER1** account owns the following database objects: **USER_DB.ENDUSER1.STUDENT** and **OTHER_DB.ENDUSER1.STUDENT**. The qualifier is the database username, not the SQL Server login name, because they do not have to be the same.

- At the same time, other users in these databases may own objects by the same name:

  - **USER_DB.DBO.STUDENT**

  - **USER_DB.DEPT_ADMIN.STUDENT**

  - **USER_DB.STUDENT_ADMIN.STUDENT**

  - **OTHER_DB.DBO.STUDENT**

Therefore, it is recommended that you include the owner name as part of the reference to a database object. If the application has multiple databases, it is recommended that the database name also is included as part of the reference. If the query spans multiple servers, include the server name.

- Every connection to SQL Server has a current database context, set at login time with the USE statement. For example, assume the following scenario:

  A user, using the **ENDUSER1** account, is logged in to the **USER_DB** database. The user requests the **STUDENT** table. SQL Server searches for the table **ENDUSER1.STUDENT**. If the table is found, SQL Server performs the requested database operation on **USER_DB.ENDUSER1.STUDENT**. If the table is not found in the **ENDUSER1** database account, SQL Server searches for **USER_DB.DBO.STUDENT** in the **dbo** account for that database. If the table is still not found, SQL Server returns an error message indicating the table does not exist.

- If another user, for example **DEPT_ADMIN**, owns the table, the table name must be prefixed with the database user's name (**DEPT_ADMIN.STUDENT**). Otherwise, the database name defaults to the database that is currently in context.

- If the referenced table exists in another database, the database name must be used as part of the reference. For example, to access the **STUDENT** table owned by **ENDUSER1** in the **OTHERDB** database, use **OTHER_DB.ENDUSER1.STUDENT**.

The object's owner can be omitted by separating the database and table name by two periods. For example, if an application references **STUDENT_DB..STUDENT**, SQL Server searches as follows:

1. STUDENT_DB.current_user.STUDENT

2. STUDENT_DB.DBO.STUDENT

If the application uses only a single database at a time, omitting the database name from an object reference makes it easy to use the application with another database. All object references implicitly access the database that is currently being used. This is useful when you want to maintain a test database and a production database on the same server.

Creating Tables

Because Oracle and SQL Server support SQL-92 entry-level conventions for identifying RDBMS objects, the CREATE TABLE syntax is similar.

Oracle	Microsoft SQL Server
CREATE TABLE [*schema.*]*table_name* ({*col_name column_properties* [*default_expression*] [*constraint* [*constraint* [...*constraint*]]]| [[,] *constraint*]} [[,] {*next_col_name* | *next_constraint*}...]) [Oracle Specific Data Storage Parameters]	CREATE TABLE [*server.*][*database.*][*owner.*] table_name ({*col_name column_properties*[*constraint* [*constraint* [...*constraint*]]]| [[,] *constraint*]} [[,] {*next_col_name* | *next_constraint*}...]) [ON *file group_name*]

Oracle database object names are not case-sensitive. In SQL Server, database object names can be case-sensitive, depending on the installation options selected.

When SQL Server is first set up, the default sort order is dictionary order, case-insensitive. (This can be configured differently using SQL Server Setup.) Because Oracle object names are always unique, you should not have any problems migrating the database objects to SQL Server. It is recommended that all table and column names in both Oracle and SQL Server be uppercase to avoid problems if a user installs on a case-sensitive SQL Server.

Table and Index Storage Parameters

With Microsoft SQL Server, using RAID usually simplifies the placement of database objects. A SQL Server clustered index is integrated into the structure of the table, like an Oracle index-organized table.

Oracle	Microsoft SQL Server

CREATE TABLE DEPT_ADMIN.DEPT(
DEPT   VARCHAR(4) NOT NULL,
DNAME   VARCHAR(30) NOT NULL,
CONSTRAINT dept_pk PRIMARY KEY (dept) ,
CONSTRAINT dept_dname_unique
UNIQUE(dname)
)
ORGANIZATION INDEX
	CREATE TABLE
	USER_DB.DEPT_ADMIN.DEPT (
	DEPT VARCHAR(4) NOT NULL,
	DNAME VARCHAR(30) NOT NULL,
	CONSTRAINT DEPT_DEPT_PK
	          PRIMARY KEY CLUSTERED
	(DEPT),
	CONSTRAINT DEPT_DNAME_UNIQUE
	          UNIQUE NONCLUSTERED
	(DNAME)
	)

Creating Tables With SELECT Statements

Using Oracle, a table can be created with any valid SELECT command. Microsoft SQL Server provides the same functionality with different syntax.

Oracle	Microsoft SQL Server
CREATE TABLE STUDENTBACKUP AS SELECT * FROM STUDENT	SELECT * INTO STUDENTBACKUP FROM STUDENT

The SELECT …INTO statement creates a new table and populates it with the results of the SELECT statement. Referential integrity definitions are not transferred to the new table. If the database recovery mode is set to FULL, then the SELECT …INTO statement is logged in the transaction log and a point-in-time recovery can take place.

For more information on database recovery models see "Selecting a Recovery Model" in SQL Server Books Online.

Views

The syntax used to create views in SQL Server is similar to that of Oracle.

Oracle	Microsoft SQL Server
CREATE [OR REPLACE] [FORCE | NOFORCE] VIEW [*schema.*]*view_name* [(*column_name* [, *column_name*]...)] AS *select_statement* [WITH CHECK OPTION [CONSTRAINT *name*]] [WITH READ ONLY]	CREATE VIEW [*owner.*]*view_name* [(*column_name* [, *column_name*]...)] [WITH ENCRYPTION] AS *select_statement* [WITH CHECK OPTION]

SQL Server views require that the tables exist and that the view owner has privileges to access the requested tables(s) specified in the SELECT statement (similar to the Oracle FORCE option).

By default, data modification statements on views are not checked to determine whether the rows affected are within the scope of the view. To check all modifications, use the WITH CHECK OPTION. The primary difference between the WITH CHECK OPTION is that Oracle defines it as a constraint, and SQL Server does not. Otherwise, it functions the same in both.

Oracle provides a WITH READ ONLY option when defining views. SQL Server–based applications can achieve the same result by granting only SELECT permission to the users of the view.

Both SQL Server and Oracle views support derived columns, using arithmetic expressions, functions, and constant expressions. Some of the specific SQL Server differences are:

- Data modification statements (INSERT or UPDATE) are allowed on multitable views if the data modification statement affects only one base table. Data modification statements cannot be used on more than one table in a single statement.

- READTEXT or WRITETEXT cannot be used on **text** or **image** columns in views.

- ORDER BY, COMPUTE, FOR BROWSE, or COMPUTE BY clauses cannot be used.

- The INTO keyword cannot be used in a view.

When a view is defined with an outer join and is queried with a qualification on a column from the inner table of the outer join, the results from SQL Server and Oracle can differ. In most cases, Oracle views are easily translated into SQL Server views.

Oracle	Microsoft SQL Server

CREATE VIEW
STUDENT_ADMIN.STUDENT_GPA
(SSN, GPA)
AS SELECT SSN, ROUND(AVG(**DECODE(grade**
                   ,'A', 4
                   ,'A+', 4.3
                   ,'A-', 3.7
                   ,'B', 3
                   ,'B+', 3.3
                   ,'B-', 2.7
                   ,'C', 2
                   ,'C+', 2.3
                   ,'C-', 1.7
                   ,'D', 1
                   ,'D+', 1.3
                   ,'D-', 0.7
                   ,0)),2)
FROM STUDENT_ADMIN.GRADE
GROUP BY SSN
	CREATE VIEW
	STUDENT_ADMIN.STUDENT_GPA
	(SSN, GPA)
	AS SELECT SSN, ROUND(AVG(**CASE grade**
	                 WHEN 'A' THEN 4
	                 WHEN 'A+' THEN 4.3
	                 WHEN 'A-' THEN 3.7
	                 WHEN 'B' THEN 3
	                 WHEN 'B+' THEN 3.3
	                 WHEN 'B-' THEN 2.7
	                 WHEN 'C' THEN 2
	                 WHEN 'C+' THEN 2.3
	                 WHEN 'C-' THEN 1.7
	                 WHEN 'D' THEN 1
	                 WHEN 'D+' THEN 1.3
	                 WHEN 'D-' THEN 0.7
	                 ELSE 0
	                 END),2)
	FROM STUDENT_ADMIN.GRADE
	GROUP BY SSN

Indexed Views

Microsoft SQL Server 2000 introduces indexed views. Like Oracle's materialized views, indexed views are views that physically store their indexed result set on disk. Indexed views are automatically updated when their base data is updated. Indexed views are capable of providing a large boost to performance in decision-support systems in which large amounts of data must be aggregated, or in online transaction processing (OLTP) systems in which many joins are used to aggregate slowly changing data.

SQL Server indexed views cannot reference objects in remote databases. SQL Server has multiple internal replication schemes including both Snapshot and Transactional replication that provide more functionality in terms of moving data among servers.

In SQL Server, for a view to be eligible for indexing, it must be defined with the SCHEMABINDING option that locks the underlying table schemas that the view references. The view also cannot reference only nondeterministic functions. The first index created against the view must be a clustered unique index. This is required so SQL Server can quickly locate rows when the data in the base schema is modified.

For more information, see "Designing an Indexed View" in SQL Server Books Online.

Indexes

Microsoft SQL Server offers clustered and nonclustered index structures. These indexes are made up of pages that form a branching structure known as a B-tree (similar to the Oracle B-tree index structure). The starting page (root level) specifies ranges of values within the table. Each range on the root-level page points to another page (decision node), which contains a more limited range of values for the table. In turn, these decision nodes can point to other decision nodes, further narrowing the search range. The final level in the branching structure is called the leaf level.

B-Tree Architecture

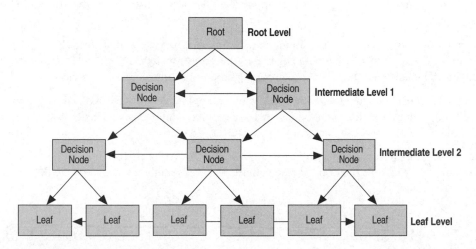

Clustered Indexes

Clustered indexes are implemented in Oracle as index-organized tables. A clustered index is an index that has been physically merged with a table. The table and index share the same storage area. The clustered index physically rearranges the rows of data in indexed order, forming the intermediate decision nodes. The leaf pages of the index contain the actual table data. This architecture permits only one clustered index per table. Microsoft SQL Server automatically creates a clustered index for the table whenever a PRIMARY KEY or UNIQUE constraint is placed on the table. Clustered indexes are useful for:

- Primary keys.

- Columns that are not updated.

- Queries that return a range of values, using operators such as BETWEEN, >, >=, <, and <=, for example:

```
SELECT * FROM STUDENT WHERE GRAD_DATE
BETWEEN '1/1/97' AND '12/31/97'
```

- Queries that return large result sets, such as:

```
SELECT * FROM STUDENT WHERE LNAME = 'SMITH'
```

- Columns that are used in sort operations (ORDER BY, GROUP BY).

  For example, on the **STUDENT** table, it might be helpful to include a nonclustered index on the primary key of **ssn**, and a clustered index could be created on **lname**, **fname**, (last name, first name), because this is the way students are often grouped.

- Distributing update activity in a table to avoid *hot spots*. Hot spots are often caused by multiple users inserting into a table with an ascending key. This application scenario is usually addressed by row-level locking.

Dropping and re-creating a clustered index is a common technique for reorganizing a table in SQL Server. It is an easy way to ensure that data pages are contiguous on disk, and to reestablish some free space in the table. This is similar to exporting, dropping, and importing a table in Oracle.

A SQL Server clustered index is not at all like an Oracle cluster. An Oracle cluster is a physical grouping of two or more tables that share the same data blocks and use common columns as a cluster key. SQL Server does not have a structure similar to an Oracle cluster.

As a general rule, defining a clustered index on a table improves SQL Server performance and space management. If you do not know the query or update patterns for a given table, you can create the clustered index on the primary key.

Oracle	Microsoft SQL Server

CREATE TABLE STUDENT_ADMIN.GRADE (
SSN   CHAR(9) NOT NULL,
CCODE   VARCHAR2(4) NOT NULL,
GRADE   VARCHAR2(2) NULL,
CONSTRAINT GRADE_SSN_CCODE_PK
   PRIMARY KEY (SSN, CCODE)
CONSTRAINT GRADE_SSN_FK
   FOREIGN KEY (SSN) REFERENCES
   STUDENT_ADMIN.STUDENT (SSN),
CONSTRAINT GRADE_CCODE_FK
   FOREIGN KEY (CCODE) REFERENCES
   DEPT_ADMIN.CLASS (CCODE)
)
 	
ORGANIZATION INDEX
	CREATE TABLE STUDENT_ADMIN.GRADE
	(
	SSN CHAR(9) NOT NULL,
	CCODE VARCHAR(4) NOT NULL,
	GRADE VARCHAR(2) NULL,
	CONSTRAINT GRADE_SSN_CCODE_PK
	   PRIMARY KEY **CLUSTERED** (SSN,
	   CCODE),
	CONSTRAINT GRADE_SSN_FK
	   FOREIGN KEY (SSN) REFERENCES
	   STUDENT_ADMIN.STUDENT (SSN),
	CONSTRAINT GRADE_CCODE_FK
	   FOREIGN KEY (CCODE) REFERENCES
	   DEPT_ADMIN.CLASS (CCODE)
	)

Nonclustered Indexes

In nonclustered indexes, the index data and the table data are physically separate, and the rows in the table are not stored in the order of the index. You can move Oracle index definitions to Microsoft SQL Server nonclustered index definitions (as shown in the following example). For performance reasons, however, you might want to choose one of the indexes of a given table and create it as a clustered index.

Oracle	Microsoft SQL Server
CREATE INDEX **STUDENT_ADMIN**.STUDENT_MAJOR_IDX ON STUDENT_ADMIN.STUDENT (MAJOR) TABLESPACE USER_DATA **PCTFREE 0** **STORAGE (INITIAL 10K NEXT 10K** **MINEXTENTS 1 MAXEXTENTS** **UNLIMITED)**	CREATE **NONCLUSTERED** INDEX STUDENT_MAJOR_IDX ON **USER_DB**.STUDENT_ADMIN.STUDENT (MAJOR)

Index Syntax and Naming

In Oracle, an index name is unique within a user account. In SQL Server, an index name must be unique within a table name, but it does not have to be unique within a user account or database. Therefore, when creating or dropping an index in SQL Server, you must specify both the table name and the index name. Additionally, the SQL Server DROP INDEX statement can drop multiple indexes at one time.

Oracle	Microsoft SQL Server
CREATE [UNIQUE] INDEX [*schema*].*index_name* ON [*schema.*]*table_name* (*column_name* [, column_name*]...) [INITRANS n] [MAXTRANS n] [TABLESPACE *tablespace_name*] [STORAGE *storage_parameters*] [PCTFREE n] [NOSORT] DROP INDEX ABC;	CREATE [UNIQUE] [CLUSTERED | NONCLUSTERED] INDEX *index_name* ON table (*column* [,...*n*]) [WITH [PAD_INDEX] [[,] FILLFACTOR = *fillfactor*] [[,] IGNORE_DUP_KEY] [[,] DROP_EXISTING] [[,] STATISTICS_NORECOMPUTE]] [ON file group] DROP INDEX USER_DB.STUDENT.DEMO_IDX, USER_DB.GRADE.DEMO_IDX

Index Data Storage Parameters

The FILLFACTOR option in SQL Server functions in much the same way as the PCTFREE variable does in Oracle. As tables grow in size, index pages split to accommodate new data. The index must reorganize itself to accommodate new data values. The fill factor percentage is used only when the index is created, and it is not maintained afterwards.

The FILLFACTOR option (values are 0 through 100) controls how much space is left on an index page when the index is initially created. The default fill factor of 0 is used if none is specified—this will completely fill index leaf pages and leave space on each decision node page for at least one entry (two for nonunique clustered indexes).

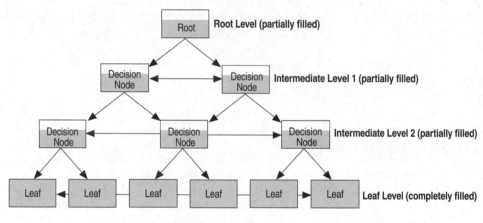

Fill Factor of 0

A lower fill factor value initially reduces the splitting of index pages and increases the number of levels in the B-tree index structure. A higher fill factor value uses index page space more efficiently, requires fewer disk I/Os to access index data, and reduces the number of levels in the B-tree index structure.

The PAD_INDEX option specifies that the fill factor setting be applied to the decision node pages as well as to the data pages in the index.

Although it may be necessary to adjust the PCTFREE parameter for optimal performance in Oracle, it is seldom necessary to include the FILLFACTOR option in a CREATE INDEX statement. The fill factor is provided for fine-tuning performance. It is useful only when creating a new index on a table with existing data, and then it is useful only when you can accurately predict future changes in that data.

If you have set PCTFREE to 0 for your Oracle indexes, consider using a fill factor of 100. This is used when there will be no inserts or updates occurring in the table (a read-only table). When fill factor is set to 100, SQL Server creates indexes with each page 100 percent full.

Ignoring Duplicate Keys

With both Oracle and SQL Server, users cannot insert duplicate values for a uniquely indexed column or columns. An attempt to do so generates an error message. Nevertheless, SQL Server lets the developer choose how the INSERT or UPDATE statement will respond to the error.

If IGNORE_DUP_KEY was specified in the CREATE INDEX statement, and an INSERT or UPDATE statement that creates a duplicate key is executed, SQL Server issues a warning message and ignores (does not insert) the duplicate row. If IGNORE_DUP_KEY was not specified for the index, SQL Server issues an error message and rolls back the entire INSERT statement. For more information about these options, see SQL Server Books Online.

Indexes on Computed Columns

Oracle allows you to place an index directly on a function. Microsoft SQL Server allows for indexes to be placed on computed columns within a table. Within SQL Server, a table can consist of multiple computed columns but must have at least one noncomputed column. Computed columns can consist either of SQL Server functions or user-defined functions, but the functions must be deterministic in nature. That is, the function must return the same value each time it is called with identical parameters. For example, the SQL Server GETDATE() function is nondeterministic because it is always called with the same parameters and returns a different value each time.

For more information, see "Creating Indexes on Computed Columns" in SQL Server Books Online.

Using Temporary Tables

An Oracle application might have to create tables that exist for short periods. The application must ensure that all tables created for this purpose are dropped at some point. If the application fails to do this, tablespaces can quickly become cluttered and unmanageable.

Microsoft SQL Server provides temporary table database objects, which are created for just such a purpose. These tables are always created in the **tempdb** database. The table name determines how long they reside within the **tempdb** database.

Table name	Description
#table_name	This local temporary table only exists for the duration of a user session or the procedure that created it. It is automatically dropped when the user logs off or the procedure that created the table completes. These tables cannot be shared between multiple users. No other database users can access this table. Permissions cannot be granted or revoked on this table.
##table_name	This global temporary table also typically exists for the duration of a user session or procedure that created it. This table can be shared among multiple users. It is automatically dropped when the last user session referencing it disconnects. All other database users can access this table. Permissions cannot be granted or revoked on this table.

Indexes can be defined for temporary tables. Views can be defined only on tables explicitly created in **tempdb** without the # or ## prefix. The following example shows the creation of a temporary table and its associated index. When the user exits, the table and index are automatically dropped.

```
SELECT SUM(ISNULL(TUITION_PAID,0)) SUM_PAID, MAJOR INTO #SUM_STUDENT
FROM USER_DB.STUDENT_ADMIN.STUDENT GROUP BY MAJOR

CREATE UNIQUE INDEX SUM STUDENT IDX ON #SUM STUDENT (MAJOR)
```

You may find that the benefits associated with using temporary tables justify a revision in your program code.

Data Types

Although some data type conversions from Oracle to SQL Server are straightforward, other data type conversions will require evaluating a few options. It is recommended that you use the DTS Import/Export Wizard to automate the creation of the new CREATE TABLE statements. These statements will provide you with the recommended conversion of the data types. You can then modify these statements as necessary.

Oracle	Microsoft SQL Server
CHAR	**char** is recommended. **char** type columns are accessed somewhat faster than **varchar** columns because they use a fixed storage length.
VARCHAR2 and LONG	**varchar** or **text**. (If the length of the data values in your Oracle column is 8000 bytes or less, use **varchar**; otherwise, you must use **text**.)
RAW and LONG RAW	**varbinary** or **image**. (If the length of the data values in your Oracle column is 8000 bytes or less, use **varbinary**; otherwise, you must use **image**.)

continued on next page

Oracle	Microsoft SQL Server
NUMBER	If integer between 1 and 255, use **tinyint**. If integer between -32768 and 32767, use **smallint**. If integer between -2,147,483,648 and 2,147,483,647 use **int**.
	If integer between -2^{63} and 2^{63} use **bigint**. If you require a float type number, use **numeric** (has precision and scale). **Note**: Do not use **float** or **real**, because rounding may occur (Oracle NUMBER and SQL Server numeric do not round). If you are not sure, use **numeric**; it most closely resembles Oracle NUMBER data type.
DATE	**datetime**.
ROWID	Use the **identity** column type or the **uniqueidentifier** data type and the NEWID function.
CURRVAL, NEXTVAL	Use the **identity** column type, and @@IDENTITY global variable, IDENT_SEED() and IDENT_INCR() functions.
SYSDATE	GETDATE()
USER	USER

Using Unicode Data

The Unicode specification defines a single encoding scheme for practically all characters widely used in businesses around the world. All computers consistently translate the bit patterns in Unicode data into characters using the single Unicode specification. This ensures that the same bit pattern is always converted to the same character on all computers. Data can be freely transferred from one database or computer to another without concern that the receiving system will correctly translate the bit patterns into characters.

One problem with data types that use 1 byte to encode each character is that the data type can represent only 256 different characters. This forces multiple encoding specifications (or code pages) for different alphabets. It is also impossible to handle systems such as the Japanese Kanji or Korean Hangul alphabets that have thousands of characters.

Microsoft SQL Server translates the bit patterns in **char**, **varchar**, and **text** columns to characters using the definitions in the code page installed with SQL Server. Client computers use the code page installed with the operating system to interpret character bit patterns. There are many different code pages. Some characters appear on some code pages, but not on others. Some characters are defined with one bit pattern on some code pages, and with a different bit pattern on other code pages. When you build international systems that must handle different languages, it becomes difficult to pick code pages for all the computers that meet the language requirements of multiple countries. It is also difficult to ensure that every computer performs the correct translations when interfacing with a system that uses a different code page.

The Unicode specification addresses this problem by using 2 bytes to encode each character. There are enough different patterns (65,536) in 2 bytes for a single specification covering the most common business languages. Because all Unicode systems consistently use the same bit patterns to represent all characters, there is no problem with characters being converted incorrectly when moving from one system to another.

In SQL Server, **nchar**, **nvarchar**, and **ntext** data types support Unicode data. For more information about SQL Server data types, see SQL Server Books Online.

User-Defined Data Types

User-defined data types can be created for the **model** database or for a single-user database. If the user-defined data type is defined for **model**, that data type is available to all new user databases created from that point forward. The user-defined data type is defined with the **sp_addtype** system stored procedure. For more information, see SQL Server Books Online.

You can use a user-defined data type in the CREATE TABLE and ALTER TABLE statements, and bind defaults and rules to it. If nullability is explicitly defined when the user-defined data type is used during table creation, it takes precedence over the nullability defined when the data type was created.

This example shows how to create a user-defined data type. The arguments are the user-type name, data type, and nullability:

```
sp_addtype gender_type, 'varchar(1)', 'not null'
go
```

This capability might initially appear to solve the problem of migrating Oracle table creation scripts to SQL Server. For example, it is quite easy to add the Oracle DATE data type:

```
sp_addtype date, datetime
```

This does not work with data types that require variable sizes, such as the Oracle data type NUMBER. An error message is returned indicating that a length must also be specified:

```
sp_addtype varchar2, varchar
Go
Msg 15091, Level 16, State 1
You must specify a length with this physical type.
```

SQL Server timestamp Columns

The **timestamp** columns enable BROWSE-mode updates and make cursor update operations more efficient. The **timestamp** is a data type that is automatically updated every time a row containing a **timestamp** column is inserted or updated.

Values in **timestamp** columns are not stored as an actual date or time, but are stored as **binary(8)** or **varbinary(8)**, which indicates the sequence of events on rows in the table. A table can have only one **timestamp** column.

For more information, see SQL Server Books Online.

Object-Level Permissions

Microsoft SQL Server object privileges can be granted to, denied from, and revoked from other database users, database groups, and the **public** role. SQL Server does not allow an object owner to grant ALTER TABLE and CREATE INDEX privileges for the object as Oracle does. Those privileges must remain with the object owner.

The GRANT statement creates an entry in the security system that allows a user in the current database to work with data in the current database or to execute specific Transact-SQL statements. The syntax of the GRANT statement is identical in Oracle and SQL Server.

The Transact-SQL DENY statement creates an entry in the security system that denies a permission from a security account in the current database and prevents the security account from inheriting the permission through its group or role memberships. Oracle does not have a DENY statement.

The Transact-SQL REVOKE statement removes a previously granted or denied permission from a user in the current database.

Oracle	Microsoft SQL Server
GRANT {ALL [PRIVILEGES][*column_list*] | *permission_list* [*column_list*]} ON {*table_name* [(*column_list*)] | *view_name* [(*column_list*)] | *stored_procedure_name*} TO {PUBLIC | *name_list* } [WITH GRANT OPTION]	GRANT {ALL [PRIVILEGES] | *permission*[,...*n*]} { [(*column*[,...*n*])] ON {*table* | *view*} | ON {*table* | *view*}[(*column*[,...*n*])] | ON {*stored_procedure* | *extended_procedure*} } TO *security_account*[,...*n*] [WITH GRANT OPTION] [AS {group | role}] REVOKE [GRANT OPTION FOR] {ALL [PRIVILEGES] | *permission*[,...*n*]} { [(*column*[,...*n*])] ON {*table* | *view*} | ON {*table* | *view*}[(*column*[,...*n*])] | {*stored_procedure* | *extended_procedure*} }

continued on next page

Oracle	Microsoft SQL Server
	{TO | FROM}
	security_account[,...*n*]
	[CASCADE]
	[AS {*group* | *role*}]
	DENY
	{ALL [PRIVILEGES] | *permission*[,...*n*]}
	{
	[(*column*[,...*n*])] ON {*table* | *view*}
	| ON {*table* | *view*}[(*column*[,...*n*])]
	| ON {*stored_procedure* |
	extended_procedure}
	}
	TO *security_account*[,...*n*]
	[CASCADE]

For more information on object-level permissions, see SQL Server Books Online.

In Oracle, the REFERENCES privilege can be granted only to a user. SQL Server allows the REFERENCES privilege to be granted to both database users and database groups. The INSERT, UPDATE, DELETE, and SELECT privileges are granted in the same way in both Oracle and SQL Server.

Enforcing Data Integrity and Business Rules

Enforcing data integrity ensures the quality of the data in the database. Two important steps when planning tables are identifying valid values for a column and deciding how to enforce the integrity of the data in the column. Data integrity falls into four categories, and is enforced in various ways.

Integrity Type	How Enforced
Entity integrity	PRIMARY KEY constraint
	UNIQUE constraint
	IDENTITY property
Domain integrity	Domain DEFAULT definition
	FOREIGN KEY constraint
	CHECK constraint
	Nullability

continued on next page

Integrity Type	How Enforced
Referential integrity	FOREIGN KEY constraint CHECK constraint
User-defined integrity	All column- and table-level constraints in CREATE TABLE Stored procedures Triggers

Entity Integrity

Entity integrity defines a row as a unique entity for a particular table. Entity integrity enforces the integrity of the identifier column(s) or the primary key of a table through indexes, UNIQUE constraints, PRIMARY KEY constraints, or IDENTITY properties.

Naming Constraints

You should always name your constraints explicitly. If you do not, Oracle and Microsoft SQL Server will use different naming conventions to name the constraint implicitly. These differences in naming can complicate your migration process unnecessarily. The discrepancy appears when dropping or disabling constraints, because constraints must be dropped by name. The syntax for explicitly naming constraints is the same for Oracle and SQL Server:

```
CONSTRAINT constraint_name
```

Primary Keys and Unique Columns

The SQL-92 standard requires that all values in a primary key be unique and that the column not allow null values. Both Oracle and Microsoft SQL Server enforce uniqueness by automatically creating unique indexes whenever a PRIMARY KEY or UNIQUE constraint is defined. Additionally, primary key columns are automatically defined as NOT NULL. Only one primary key is allowed per table.

A SQL Server clustered index is created by default for a primary key, though a nonclustered index can be requested. The Oracle index on primary keys can be removed by either dropping or disabling the constraint, whereas the SQL Server index can be removed only by dropping the constraint.

In either RDBMS, alternate keys can be defined with a UNIQUE constraint. Multiple UNIQUE constraints can be defined on any table. UNIQUE constraint columns are nullable. In SQL Server, a nonclustered index is created by default, unless otherwise specified.

When migrating your application, it is important to note that SQL Server allows only one row to contain the value NULL for the complete unique key (single or multiple column index), and Oracle allows any number of rows to contain the value NULL for the complete unique key.

Oracle	Microsoft SQL Server

CREATE TABLE DEPT_ADMIN.DEPT
(DEPT **VARCHAR2**(4) NOT NULL,
DNAME **VARCHAR2**(30) NOT NULL,
CONSTRAINT DEPT_DEPT_PK
   PRIMARY KEY (DEPT)
   USING INDEX TABLESPACE USER_DATA
   PCTFREE 0 STORAGE (
   INITIAL 10K NEXT 10K
   MINEXTENTS 1 MAXEXTENTS
UNLIMITED),
CONSTRAINT DEPT_DNAME_UNIQUE
   UNIQUE (DNAME)
   USING INDEX TABLESPACE USER_DATA
   PCTFREE 0 STORAGE (
   INITIAL 10K NEXT 10K
   MINEXTENTS 1 MAXEXTENTS
UNLIMITED)
)
	CREATE TABLE
	USER_DB.DEPT_ADMIN.DEPT
	(DEPT **VARCHAR**(4) NOT NULL,
	DNAME **VARCHAR**(30) NOT NULL,
	CONSTRAINT DEPT_DEPT_PK
	   PRIMARY KEY CLUSTERED (DEPT),
	CONSTRAINT DEPT_DNAME_UNIQUE
	   UNIQUE NONCLUSTERED (DNAME)
	)

Adding and Removing Constraints

Disabling constraints can improve database performance and streamline the data replication process. For example, when you rebuild or replicate table data at a remote site, you do not have to repeat constraint checks, because the integrity of the data was checked when it was originally entered into the table. You can program an Oracle application to disable and enable constraints (except for PRIMARY KEYand UNIQUE). It is recommended that you use the NOT FOR REPLICATION clause to suspend column-level, foreign key, and CHECK constraints during replication.

In cases where you are not replicating data, and need to remove a constraint, you can accomplish this in Microsoft SQL Server using the CHECK and WITH NOCHECK options with the ALTER TABLE statement.

This illustration shows a comparison of this process.

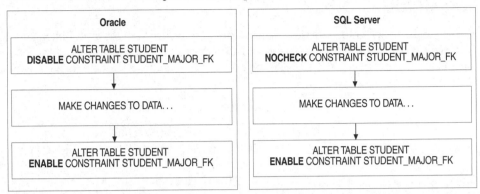

With SQL Server, you can defer all of the table constraints by using the ALL keyword with the NOCHECK clause.

If your Oracle application uses the CASCADE option to disable or drop PRIMARY KEY or UNIQUE constraints, you may need to rewrite some code because the CASCADE option disables or drops both the parent and any related child integrity constraints.

This is an example of the syntax:

```
DROP CONSTRAINT DEPT_DEPT_PK CASCADE
```

The SQL Server–based application must be modified to first drop the child constraints and then the parent constraints. For example, in order to drop the PRIMARY KEY constraint on the **DEPT** table, the foreign keys for the columns **STUDENT.MAJOR** and **CLASS.DEPT** must be dropped. This is an example of the syntax:

```
ALTER TABLE STUDENT
DROP CONSTRAINT STUDENT_MAJOR_FK
ALTER TABLE CLASS
DROP CONSTRAINT CLASS_DEPT_FK
ALTER TABLE DEPT
DROP CONSTRAINT DEPT_DEPT_PK
```

The ALTER TABLE syntax that adds and drops constraints is almost identical for Oracle and SQL Server.

Generating Unique Values

A SQL Server table can have one column defined as an identity column, which is an auto-incrementing integer field. SQL Server automatically tracks inserts and adds the value for the identity column to the record. If your application uses Oracle SEQUENCE to generate unique integers for a column, then you can replace it with the identity field.

Category	Microsoft SQL Server IDENTITY
Syntax	CREATE TABLE new_employees (Empid int IDENTITY (1,1), Employee_Name varchar(60), CONSTRAINT Emp_PK PRIMARY KEY (Empid)) If increment interval is 5: CREATE TABLE new_employees (Empid int IDENTITY (1,5), Employee_Name varchar(60), CONSTRAINT Emp_PK PRIMARY KEY (Empid))
Identity columns per table	One
Null values allowed	No
Use of default constraints, values	Cannot be used.
Enforcing uniqueness	Yes
Querying for maximum current identity number after an INSERT, SELECT INTO, or bulk copy statement completes	@@IDENTITY (function)
Returns the seed value specified during the creation of an identity column	IDENT_SEED('*table_name*')
Returns the increment value specified during the creation of an identity column	IDENT_INCR('*table_name*')
SELECT syntax	The keyword IDENTITYCOL can be used in place of a column name when you reference a column that has the IDENTITY property, in SELECT, INSERT, UPDATE, and DELETE statements.

Although the IDENTITY property automates row numbering within one table, separate tables, each with its own identifier column, can generate the same values. This is because the IDENTITY property is guaranteed to be unique only for the table on which it is used. If an application must generate an identifier column that is unique across the entire database, or every database on every networked computer in the world, use the ROWGUIDCOL property, the **uniqueidentifier** data type, and the NEWID function. SQL Server uses globally unique identifier columns for merge replication to ensure that rows are uniquely identified across multiple copies of the table.

If your application uses an Oracle SEQUENCE to generate a unique value that is then concatenated with another value to produce a unique string, you will have to create some custom code, either in a trigger or stored procedure that will generate the concatenated string for you.

For more information about creating and modifying **uniqueidentifier** columns, see SQL Server Books Online.

Domain Integrity

Domain integrity enforces valid entries for a given column. Domain integrity is enforced by restricting the type (through data types), the format (through CHECK constraints), or the range of possible values (through REFERENCE and CHECK constraints).

DEFAULT and CHECK Constraints

Oracle treats a default as a column property, and Microsoft SQL Server treats a default as a constraint. The SQL Server DEFAULT constraint can contain constant values, built-in functions that do not take arguments (niladic functions), or NULL.

To easily migrate the Oracle DEFAULT column property, you should define DEFAULT constraints at the column level in SQL Server without applying constraint names. SQL Server generates a unique name for each DEFAULT constraint.

The syntax used to define CHECK constraints is the same in Oracle and SQL Server. The search condition must evaluate to a Boolean expression and cannot contain subqueries. A column-level CHECK constraint can reference only the constrained column, and a table-level check constraint can reference only columns of the constrained table. Multiple CHECK constraints can be defined for a table. SQL Server syntax allows only one column-level CHECK constraint to be created on a column in a CREATE TABLE statement, and the constraint can have multiple conditions.

The best way to test your modified CREATE TABLE statements is to use the SQL Query Analyzer in SQL Server, and parse only the syntax. The Results pane indicates any errors. For more information about constraint syntax, see SQL Server Books Online.

Oracle	Microsoft SQL Server

CREATE TABLE STUDENT_ADMIN.STUDENT (
SSN CHAR(9) NOT NULL,
FNAME VARCHAR2(12) NULL,
LNAME VARCHAR2(20) NOT NULL,
GENDER CHAR(1) NOT NULL
   CONSTRAINT STUDENT_GENDER_CK
   CHECK (GENDER IN ('M','F')),
MAJOR VARCHAR2(4)
   DEFAULT 'Undc' NOT NULL,
BIRTH_DATE DATE NULL,
TUITION_PAID NUMBER(12,2) NULL,
TUITION_TOTAL NUMBER(12,2) NULL,
START_DATE DATE NULL,
GRAD_DATE DATE NULL,
LOAN_AMOUNT NUMBER(12,2) NULL,
DEGREE_PROGRAM CHAR(1)
   DEFAULT 'U' NOT NULL
   CONSTRAINT STUDENT_DEGREE_CK
CHECK
   (DEGREE_PROGRAM IN ('U', 'M', 'P', 'D')),
...
	CREATE TABLE USER_DB.STUDENT
	   _ADMIN.STUDENT (
	SSN CHAR(9) NOT NULL,
	FNAME VARCHAR(12) NULL,
	LNAME VARCHAR(20) NOT NULL,
	GENDER CHAR(1) NOT NULL
	   CONSTRAINT STUDENT_GENDER_CK
	   CHECK (GENDER IN ('M','F')),
	MAJOR VARCHAR(4)
	   DEFAULT 'Undc' NOT NULL,
	BIRTH_DATE DATETIME NULL,
	TUITION_PAID NUMERIC(12,2) NULL,
	TUITION_TOTAL NUMERIC(12,2) NULL,
	START_DATE DATETIME NULL,
	GRAD_DATE DATETIME NULL,
	LOAN_AMOUNT NUMERIC(12,2) NULL,
	DEGREE_PROGRAM CHAR(1)
	   DEFAULT 'U' NOT NULL
	   CONSTRAINT STUDENT_DEGREE_CK
	   CHECK
	   (DEGREE_PROGRAM IN ('U', 'M', 'P',
	'D')),
	...

Note The syntax for Microsoft SQL Server rules and defaults remains for backward compatibility purposes, but CHECK constraints and DEFAULT constraints are recommended for new application development. For more information, see SQL Server Books Online.

Nullability

Microsoft SQL Server and Oracle create column constraints to enforce nullability. An Oracle column defaults to NULL, unless NOT NULL is specified in the CREATE TABLE or ALTER TABLE statements. In Microsoft SQL Server, database and session settings can override the nullability of the data type used in a column definition.

All of your SQL scripts (whether Oracle or SQL Server) should explicitly define both NULL and NOT NULL for each column. When not explicitly specified, column nullability follows these rules.

Null Setting	Description
Column is defined with a user-defined data type	SQL Server uses the nullability specified when the data type was created. Use the **sp_help** system stored procedure to get the data type's default nullability.

Column is defined with a system-supplied data type	If the system-supplied data type has only one option, it takes precedence. Currently, the **bit** data type can be defined only as NOT NULL.
	If any session settings are ON (set with the SET), then:
	    If ANSI_NULL_DFLT_ON is ON, NULL is assigned.
	    If ANSI_NULL_DFLT_OFF is ON, NOT NULL is assigned.
	If any database settings are configured (changed with the ALTER DATABASE statement), then:
	    If ANSI NULL DEFAULT is TRUE, NULL is assigned.
	    If ANSI NULL DEFAULT is FALSE, NOT NULL is assigned.

NULL/NOT NULL Not defined	When not explicitly defined (neither of the ANSI_NULL_DFLT options are set), the session has not been changed and the database is set to the default (ANSI NULL DEFAULT is FALSE), then SQL Server assigns it NOT NULL.

Referential Integrity

The table provides a comparison of the syntax used to define referential integrity constraints.

Constraint	Oracle	Microsoft SQL Server
PRIMARY KEY	[CONSTRAINT *constraint_name*] PRIMARY KEY (*col_name* [, *col_name2* [..., *col_name16*]]) [USING INDEX *storage_parameters*]	[CONSTRAINT *constraint_name*] PRIMARY KEY [CLUSTERED | NONCLUSTERED] (*col_name* [, *col_name2* [..., *col_name16*]]) [ON *segment_name*] [NOT FOR REPLICATION]
UNIQUE	[CONSTRAINT *constraint_name*] UNIQUE (*col_name* [, *col_name2* [..., *col_name16*]]) [USING INDEX *storage_parameters*]	[CONSTRAINT *constraint_name*] UNIQUE [CLUSTERED | NONCLUSTERED](*col_name* [, *col_name2* [..., *col_name16*]]) [ON *segment_name*] [NOT FOR REPLICATION]

continued on next page

141

Constraint	Oracle	Microsoft SQL Server
FOREIGN KEY	[CONSTRAINT *constraint_name*] [FOREIGN KEY (*col_name* [, *col_name2* [..., *col_name16*]])] REFERENCES [*owner.*]*ref_table* [(*ref_col* [, *ref_col2* [..., *ref_col16*]])] [ON DELETE CASCADE]	[CONSTRAINT *constraint_name*] [FOREIGN KEY (*col_name* [, *col_name2* [..., *col_name16*]])] REFERENCES [*owner.*]*ref_table* [(*ref_col* [, *ref_col2* [..., *ref_col16*]])] [ON DELETE CASCADE	No Action] [ON UPDATE CASCADE	No Action] [NOT FOR REPLICATION]
DEFAULT	Column property, not a constraint DEFAULT (*constant_expression*)	[CONSTRAINT *constraint_name*] DEFAULT {*constant_expression*	*niladic-function*	NULL} [FOR *col_name*] [NOT FOR REPLICATION]
CHECK	[CONSTRAINT *constraint_name*] CHECK (*expression*)	[CONSTRAINT *constraint_name*] CHECK [NOT FOR REPLICATION] (*expression*)

The NOT FOR REPLICATION clause is used to suspend column-level, FOREIGN KEY, and CHECK constraints during replication.

Foreign Keys

The rules for defining foreign keys are similar in each RDBMS. The number of columns and data type of each column specified in the foreign key clause must match the REFERENCES clause. A nonnull value entered in this column(s) must exist in the table and column(s) defined in the REFERENCES clause, and the referenced table's columns must have a PRIMARY KEY or UNIQUE constraint.

Microsoft SQL Server constraints provide the ability to reference tables within the same database. To implement referential integrity across databases, use table-based triggers.

Both Oracle and SQL Server support self-referenced tables, tables in which a reference (foreign key) can be placed against one or more columns on the same table. For example, the column **prereq** in the **CLASS** table can reference the column **ccode** in the **CLASS** table to ensure that a valid course code is entered as a course prerequisite.

In SQL Server 2000, foreign keys have an ON DELETE clause that is used to define what action should be taken if a candidate key to which the foreign key is pointing is deleted. The NO ACTION option causes the delete to fail with an error. The CASCADE option cascades the delete to any rows that reference the data within the FOREIGN KEY constraint.

User-Defined Integrity

User-defined integrity allows you to define specific business rules that do not fall into one of the other integrity categories.

Stored Procedures

Microsoft SQL Server stored procedures use the CREATE PROCEDURE statement to accept and return user-supplied parameters. With the exception of temporary stored procedures, stored procedures are created in the current database. The table shows the syntax for Oracle and SQL Server.

Oracle	Microsoft SQL Server
CREATE OR REPLACE PROCEDURE [*user.*]*procedure* [(*argument* [IN | OUT] *datatype* [, *argument* [IN | OUT] *datatype*] {IS | AS} block	CREATE PROC[EDURE] *procedure_name* [*;number*] [{ @*parameter data_type*} [VARYING] [= *default*] [OUTPUT]] [*,...n]* [WITH { RECOMPILE | ENCRYPTION | RECOMPILE, ENCRYPTION}] [FOR REPLICATION] AS *sql_statement* [*...n*]

In SQL Server, temporary procedures are created in the **tempdb** database by prefacing *procedure_name* with a single number sign (#*procedure_name*) for local temporary procedures and with a double number sign (##*procedure_name*) for global temporary procedures.

A local temporary procedure can be used only by the user who created it. Permission to execute a local temporary procedure cannot be granted to other users. Local temporary procedures are automatically dropped at the end of the user session.

A global temporary procedure is available to all SQL Server users. If a global temporary procedure is created, all users can access it, and permissions cannot be explicitly revoked. Global temporary procedures are dropped at the end of the last user session using the procedure.

SQL Server stored procedures can be nested up to 32 levels. The nesting level is incremented when the called procedure starts execution, and it is decremented when the called procedure finishes execution.

The following example shows how a Transact-SQL stored procedure can be used to replace an Oracle PL/SQL packaged function. In this example, the Transact-SQL version is much simpler because of the ability of SQL Server to return result sets directly from SELECT statements in a stored procedure, without using a cursor.

Oracle	Microsoft SQL Server

```
CREATE OR REPLACE PACKAGE
STUDENT_ADMIN.P1 AS
    ROWCOUNT NUMBER :=0;
    CURSOR C1 RETURN
STUDENT%ROWTYPE;
    FUNCTION
SHOW_RELUCTANT_STUDENTS
        (WORKVAR OUT VARCHAR2) RETURN
NUMBER;
END P1;
/

CREATE OR REPLACE PACKAGE BODY
STUDENT_ADMIN.P1 AS
    CURSOR C1 RETURN STUDENT%ROWTYPE
IS
        SELECT * FROM
STUDENT_ADMIN.STUDENT
                WHERE NOT EXISTS
        (SELECT 'X' FROM
STUDENT_ADMIN.GRADE
        WHERE GRADE.SSN=STUDENT.SSN)
ORDER BY SSN;

FUNCTION SHOW_RELUCTANT_STUDENTS
    (WORKVAR OUT VARCHAR2) RETURN
NUMBER IS
    WORKREC STUDENT%ROWTYPE;
    BEGIN
        IF NOT C1%ISOPEN THEN OPEN C1;
        ROWCOUNT :=0;
        ENDIF;
        FETCH C1 INTO WORKREC;
        IF (C1%NOTFOUND) THEN
            CLOSE C1;
            ROWCOUNT :=0;
        ELSE
            WORKVAR := WORKREC.FNAME||'
```

```
CREATE PROCEDURE
STUDENT_ADMIN.SHOW_RELUCTANT_S
TUDENTS
AS SELECT FNAME+" +LNAME+', social
security
    number'+ SSN+' is not enrolled in any
classes!'
FROM STUDENT_ADMIN.STUDENT S
WHERE NOT EXISTS
    (SELECT 'X' FROM
STUDENT_ADMIN.GRADE G
        WHERE G.SSN=S.SSN)
ORDER BY SSN
RETURN@@ROWCOUNT
GO
```

continued on next page

Oracle	Microsoft SQL Server

```
'||WORKREC.LNAME||
        ', social security number
'||WORKREC.SSN||' is not enrolled


            in any classes!';
        ROWCOUNT := ROWCOUNT + 1;
    ENDIF;
RETURN(ROWCOUNT);

EXCEPTION
    WHEN OTHERS THEN
        IF C1%ISOPEN THEN CLOSE C1;
            ROWCOUNT :=0;
        ENDIF;
        RAISE_APPLICATION_ERROR(-
20001,SQLERRM);
END SHOW_RELUCTANT_STUDENTS;
END P1;
/
```

SQL Server does not support constructs similar to Oracle packages, and does not support the CREATE OR REPLACE option for creating stored procedures. Instead, SQL Server supports either the CREATE or ALTER statements to create or modify stored procedures.

Delaying the Execution of a Stored Procedure

Microsoft SQL Server provides WAITFOR, which allows developers to specify a time, time interval, or event that triggers the execution of a statement block, stored procedure, or transaction. This is the Transact-SQL equivalent to the Oracle dbms_lock.sleep.

WAITFOR {DELAY *'time'* | TIME *'time'*}

where

DELAY:
   Instructs Microsoft SQL Server to wait until the specified amount of time has passed, up to a maximum of 24 hours.

'time'
   The amount of time to wait. *time* can be specified in one of the acceptable formats for **datetime** data, or it can be specified as a local variable. Dates cannot be specified; therefore, the data portion of the **datetime** value is not allowed.

TIME:
    Instructs SQL Server to wait until the specified time.

For example:

```
BEGIN
    WAITFOR TIME '22:20'
    EXECUTE update_all_stats
END
```

Specifying Parameters in a Stored Procedure

To specify a parameter within a stored procedure, use this syntax.

Oracle	Microsoft SQL Server
Varname datatype DEFAULT <value>;	{ *@parameter data_type* } [VARYING] [= *default*] [OUTPUT]

Triggers

Both Oracle and Microsoft SQL Server have triggers, which have some differences in their implementations.

Description	Oracle	Microsoft SQL Server
Number of triggers per table	Unlimited	Unlimited
Triggers executed before INSERT, UPDATE, DELETE	Yes	Yes. This functionality can be created with the INSTEAD OF option.
Triggers executed after INSERT, UPDATE, DELETE	Yes	Yes
Statement Level Triggers	Yes	Yes
Row Level Triggers	Yes	No
Constraints checked prior to execution	Yes, unless trigger is disabled.	Yes. In addition, this is an option in Data Transformation Services.
Referring to old or previous values in an UPDATE or DELETE trigger	:old	DELETED.column

continued on next page

Description	Oracle	Microsoft SQL Server
Referring to new values in an INSERT trigger	:new	INSERTED.column
Disabling Triggers	ALTER TRIGGER	Option in Data Transformation Services

Triggers can be created to execute either after (AFTER trigger) the INSERT, UPDATE or DELETE statement or INSTEAD OF the statement. If you need the functionality of a BEFORE trigger from Oracle, you will have to add the INSERT, UPDATE or DELETE statement to the logic within the INSTEAD OF trigger.

The **deleted** and **inserted** tables are logical (conceptual) tables created by SQL Server for trigger statements. They are structurally similar to the table on which the trigger is defined and hold the old values or new values of the rows that might be changed by the user action. The tables track row-level changes in Transact-SQL. These tables provide the same functionality as Oracle row-level triggers. When an INSERT, UPDATE, or DELETE statement is executed in SQL Server, rows are added to the trigger table and to the **inserted** and **deleted** table(s) simultaneously.

The **inserted** and **deleted** tables are identical to the trigger table. They have the same column names and the same data types. For example, if a trigger is placed on the **GRADE** table, the **inserted** and **deleted** tables have this structure.

GRADE	inserted	deleted
SSN CHAR(9)	SSN CHAR(9)	SSN CHAR(9)
CCODE VARCHAR(4)	CCODE VARCHAR(4)	CCODE VARCHAR(4)
GRADE VARCHAR(2)	GRADE VARCHAR(2)	GRADE VARCHAR(2)

The **inserted** and **deleted** tables can be examined by the trigger to determine what types of trigger actions should be carried out. The **inserted** table is used with the INSERT and UPDATE statements. The **deleted** table is used with DELETE and UPDATE statements.

The UPDATE statement uses both the **inserted** and **deleted** tables because SQL Server always deletes the old row and inserts a new row whenever an UPDATE operation is performed. Consequently, when an UPDATE is performed, the rows in the **inserted** table are always duplicates of the rows in the **deleted** table.

The following example uses the **inserted** and **deleted** tables to replace a PL/SQL row-level trigger. A full outer join is used to query all rows from either table.

Oracle	Microsoft SQL Server

CREATE TRIGGER
    STUDENT_ADMIN.TRACK_GRADES
AFTER
INSERT OR UPDATE OR DELETE
ON STUDENT_ADMIN.GRADE
FOR EACH ROW
BEGIN
INSERT INTO GRADE_HISTORY(
    TABLE_USER, ACTION_DATE,
    OLD_SSN, OLD_CCODE, OLD_GRADE,
    NEW_SSN, NEW_CCODE, NEW_GRADE)
VALUES (USER, SYSDATE,
    :OLD.SSN, :OLD.CCODE, :OLD.GRADE,
    :NEW.SSN, :NEW.CCODE, :NEW.GRADE),
END;
	CREATE TRIGGER
	STUDENT_ADMIN.TRACK_GRADES
	ON STUDENT_ADMIN.GRADE
	FORAFTER INSERT, UPDATE, DELETE
	AS
	INSERT INTO GRADE_HISTORY(
	    TABLE_USER, ACTION_DATE,
	    OLD_SSN, OLD_CCODE, OLD_GRADE
	    NEW_SSN, NEW_CCODE, NEW_GRADE)
	SELECT USER, GETDATE(),
	    OLD.SSN, OLD.CCODE, OLD.GRADE,
	    NEW.SSN, NEW.CCODE, NEW.GRADE
	FROM INSERTED NEW FULL OUTER JOIN
	    DELETED OLD ON NEW.SSN =
	OLD.SSN

You can create a trigger only in the current database, though you can reference objects outside the current database. If you use an owner name to qualify a trigger, qualify the table name the same way.

There can be multiple AFTER triggers defined for each data modification event for a table. However, there can be only one INSTEAD OF trigger defined for a table.

Triggers can be nested 32 levels deep. If a trigger changes a table on which there is another trigger, the second trigger is activated and can then call a third trigger, and so on. If any trigger in the chain sets off an infinite loop, the nesting level is exceeded and the trigger is canceled. Additionally, if an update trigger on one column of a table results in an update to another column, the update trigger is activated only once. SQL Server declarative referential integrity (DRI) does not provide cross-database referential integrity. If cross-database referential integrity is required, use triggers. The following statements are not allowed in a Transact-SQL trigger:

- CREATE statements (DATABASE, TABLE, INDEX, PROCEDURE, DEFAULT, RULE, TRIGGER, SCHEMA, and VIEW)

- DROP statements (TRIGGER, INDEX, TABLE, PROCEDURE, DATABASE, VIEW, DEFAULT, RULE)

- ALTER statements (DATABASE, TABLE, VIEW, PROCEDURE, TRIGGER)

- TRUNCATE TABLE

- GRANT, REVOKE, DENY

- UPDATE STATISTICS

- RECONFIGURE

- UPDATE STATISTICS

- RESTORE DATABASE, RESTORE LOG
- LOAD LOG, DATABASE
- DISK statements
- SELECT INTO (because it creates a table)

For more information about triggers, see SQL Server Books Online.

Transactions, Locking, and Concurrency

This section explains how transactions are executed in both Oracle and Microsoft SQL Server and presents the differences between the locking processes and concurrency issues in both database types.

Transactions

In Oracle, a transaction is started automatically when an insert, update, or delete operation is performed. An application must issue a COMMIT command to save changes to the database. If a COMMIT is not performed, all changes are rolled back or undone automatically.

By default, SQL Server automatically performs a COMMIT statement after every insert, update, or delete operation. Because the data is automatically saved, you are unable to roll back any changes.

You can start transactions in SQL Server as explicit, autocommit, or implicit transactions. Autocommit is the default behavior; you can use implicit or explicit transaction modes to change this default behavior.

Autocommit transactions
    This is the default mode for SQL Server. Each individual Transact-SQL statement is committed when it completes. You do not have to specify any statements to control transactions.

Implicit transactions
    As in Oracle, an implicit transaction is started whenever an INSERT, UPDATE, DELETE, or other data manipulating function is performed. To allow implicit transactions, use the SET IMPLICIT_TRANSACTIONS ON statement.

    If this option is ON and there are no outstanding transactions, every SQL statement automatically starts a transaction. If there is an open transaction, no new transaction is started. The open transaction must be committed by the user explicitly with the COMMIT TRANSACTION statement for the changes to take effect and for all locks to be released.

Explicit transactions
    An explicit transaction is a grouping of SQL statements surrounded by the following transaction delimiters. Note that BEGIN TRANSACTION and COMMIT TRANSACTION are required:

- BEGIN TRANSACTION [*transaction_name*]
- COMMIT TRANSACTION [*transaction_name*]

- ROLLBACK TRANSACTION [transaction_name | savepoint_name]
- SAVE TRANSACTION {savepoint_name | @savepoint_variable}

The SAVE TRANSACTION statement functions in the same way as the Oracle SAVEPOINT command, setting a savepoint in the transaction that allows partial rollbacks.

In the following example, the English department is changed to the Literature department. Note the use of the BEGIN TRANSACTION and COMMIT TRANSACTION statements.

Oracle	Microsoft SQL Server
INSERT INTO DEPT_ADMIN.DEPT (DEPT, DNAME) VALUES ('LIT', 'Literature') / UPDATE DEPT_ADMIN.CLASS SET MAJOR = 'LIT' WHERE MAJOR = 'ENG' / UPDATE STUDENT_ADMIN.STUDENT SET MAJOR = 'LIT' WHERE MAJOR = 'ENG' / DELETE FROM DEPT_ADMIN.DEPT WHERE DEPT = 'ENG' / **COMMIT** /	**BEGIN TRANSACTION** INSERT INTO DEPT_ADMIN.DEPT (DEPT, DNAME) VALUES ('LIT', 'Literature') UPDATE DEPT_ADMIN.CLASS SET DEPT = 'LIT' WHERE DEPT = 'ENG' UPDATE STUDENT_ADMIN.STUDENT SET MAJOR = 'LIT' WHERE MAJOR = 'ENG' DELETE FROM DEPT_ADMIN.DEPT WHERE DEPT = 'ENG' **COMMIT TRANSACTION GO**

Transactions can be nested one within another. If this occurs, the outermost pair creates and commits the transaction, and the inner pairs track the nesting level. When a nested transaction is encountered, the @@TRANCOUNT function is incremented. Usually, this apparent transaction nesting occurs as stored procedures or triggers with BEGIN...COMMIT pairs calling each other. Although transactions can be nested, they have little effect on the behavior of ROLLBACK TRANSACTION statements.

In stored procedures and triggers, the number of BEGIN TRANSACTION statements must match the number of COMMIT TRANSACTION statements. A stored procedure or trigger that contains unpaired BEGIN TRANSACTION and COMMIT TRANSACTION statements produces an error message when executed. The syntax allows stored procedures and triggers to be called from within transactions if they contain BEGIN TRANSACTION and COMMIT TRANSACTION statements.

Wherever possible, break large transactions into smaller transactions. Make sure each transaction is well defined within a single batch. To minimize possible concurrency conflicts, transactions should not span multiple batches nor wait for user input. Grouping many Transact-SQL statements into one long-running transaction can negatively affect recovery time and cause concurrency problems.

When programming with ODBC, you can select either the implicit or explicit transaction mode by using the **SQLSetConnectOption** function. An ODBC program's selection of one or the other depends on the AUTOCOMMIT connect option. If AUTOCOMMIT is ON (the default), you are in explicit mode. If AUTOCOMMIT is OFF, you are in implicit mode.

If you are issuing a script through SQL Query Analyzer or other query tools, you can either include the explicit BEGIN TRANSACTION statement shown previously, or start the script with the SET IMPLICIT_TRANSACTIONS ON statement. The BEGIN TRANSACTION approach is more flexible, and the implicit approach is more compatible with Oracle.

Locking and Transaction Isolation

One of the key functions of a database management system (DBMS) is to ensure that multiple users can read and write records in the database without reading inconsistent sets of records due to in-progress changes and without overwriting each other's changes inadvertently. Oracle and SQL Server approach this task with different locking and isolation strategies. You must consider these differences when you convert an application from Oracle to SQL Server or the resulting application may scale poorly to high numbers of users.

Oracle uses a multiversion consistency model for all SQL statements that read data, either explicitly or implicitly. In this model, data readers, by default, neither acquire locks nor wait for other locks to be released before reading rows of data. When a reader requests data that has been changed but not yet committed by other writers, Oracle re-creates the old data by using its rollback segments to reconstruct a snapshot of rows.

Data writers in Oracle request locks on data that is updated, deleted, or inserted. These locks are held until the end of a transaction, and they prevent other users from overwriting uncommitted changes.

SQL Server, in contrast, uses shared locks to ensure that data readers only see committed data. These readers take and release shared locks as they read data. These shared locks do not affect other readers. A reader waits for a writer to commit the changes before reading a record. A reader holding shared locks also blocks a writer trying to update the same data.

Releasing locks quickly for applications that support high numbers of users is more important in SQL Server than in Oracle. Releasing locks quickly is usually a matter of keeping transactions short. If possible, a transaction should neither span multiple round-trips to the server nor wait for the user to respond. You also need to code your application to fetch data as quickly as possible because unfetched data scans can hold share locks at the server and thus block updaters.

Dynamic Locking

SQL Server uses a dynamic locking strategy to determine the most cost-effective locks. SQL Server automatically determines what locks are most appropriate when the query is executed, based on the characteristics of the schema and query. For example, to reduce the overhead of locking, the optimizer may choose page-level locks in an index when performing an index scan. Dynamic locking has the following advantages:

- Simplified database administration, because database administrators no longer have to be concerned with adjusting lock escalation thresholds.

- Increased performance, because SQL Server minimizes system overhead by using locks appropriate to the task.

- Application developers can concentrate on development, because SQL Server automatically adjusts locking.

Oracle's inability to escalate row-level locks can cause problems in queries that include the FOR UPDATE clause and in UPDATE statements that request many rows. For example, assume that the **STUDENT** table has 100,000 rows, and an Oracle user issues the following statement (note that 100,000 rows are affected):

```
UPDATE STUDENT set (col) = (value);
```

The Oracle RDBMS locks every row in the **STUDENT** table, one row at a time; this can take quite a while, and can require many system resources. Oracle does not escalate the request to lock the entire table.

The same statement in SQL Server will cause the (default) row-level locks to escalate to a table-level lock, which is both efficient and fast.

Changing Default Locking Behavior

Both Microsoft SQL Server and Oracle use the same default transaction isolation level: READ COMMITTED. Both databases also allow the developer to request nondefault locking and isolation behavior. In Oracle, the most common mechanisms for this are the FOR UPDATE clause on a SELECT command, the SET TRANSACTION READ ONLY command, and the explicit LOCK TABLE command.

Because their locking and isolation strategies are so different, it is difficult to map these locking options directly between Oracle and SQL Server. To obtain a better understanding of this process, it is important to understand the options that SQL Server provides for changing its default locking behavior.

In SQL Server, the most common mechanisms for changing default locking behavior are the SET TRANSACTION ISOLATION LEVEL statement and the locking hints that are supported in the SELECT and UPDATE statements. The SET TRANSACTION ISOLATION LEVEL statement sets transaction isolation levels for the duration of a user's session. This becomes the default behavior for the session unless a locking hint is specified at the table level in the FROM clause of an SQL statement. The transaction isolation is set like this:

```
SET TRANSACTION ISOLATION LEVEL
    {
        READ COMMITTED
        | READ UNCOMMITTED
        | REPEATABLE READ
        | SERIALIZABLE
    }
```

READ COMMITTED

This option is the SQL Server default. Shared locks are held while the data is being read to avoid dirty reads, but the data can be changed before the end of the transaction, resulting in nonrepeatable reads or phantom data.

READ UNCOMMITTED

Implements dirty read, or isolation level 0 locking, which means that no shared locks are issued and no exclusive locks are honored. When this option is set, it is possible to read uncommitted or dirty data; values in the data can be changed and rows can appear or disappear in the data set before the end of the transaction. This option has the same effect as setting NOLOCK on all tables in all SELECT statements in a transaction. This is the least restrictive of the four isolation levels.

REPEATABLE READ

Locks are placed on all data that is used in a query, preventing other users from updating the data, but new phantom rows can be inserted into the data set by another user and are included in later reads in the current transaction. Because concurrency is lower than the default isolation level, use this option only when necessary.

SERIALIZABLE

A range lock is placed on the data set preventing other users from updating or inserting rows into the data set until the transaction is complete. This is the most restrictive of the four isolation levels. Because concurrency is lower, use this option only when necessary. This option has the same effect as setting HOLDLOCK on all tables in all SELECT statements in a transaction.

SQL Server implements all four SQL-92 standard transaction isolation levels; Oracle only implements READ COMMITTED (the default) and SERIALIZABLE.

SQL Server does not directly support the non–SQL-92 standard READ ONLY transaction isolation level offered by Oracle. If a transaction in an application requires repeatable read behavior, you may need to use the SERIALIZABLE isolation level offered by SQL Server. If all of the database access is read only, you can improve performance by setting the SQL Server database option to READ ONLY.

SELECT...FOR UPDATE

The SELECT...FOR UPDATE statement in Oracle is used when an application needs to issue a positioned update or delete on a cursor using the WHERE CURRENT OF syntax. In this case, optionally remove the FOR UPDATE clause; SQL Server cursors are updatable by default.

SQL Server cursors usually do not hold locks under the fetched row. Rather, they use an optimistic concurrency strategy to prevent updates from overwriting each other. If one user attempts to update or delete a row that has been changed since it was read into the cursor, SQL Server detects the problem and issues an error message. The application can trap this error message and retry the update or delete as appropriate.

The optimistic technique supports higher concurrency in the normal case where conflicts between updaters are rare. If your application really needs to ensure that a row cannot be changed after it is fetched, you can use the UPDLOCK hint in your SELECT statement to achieve this effect.

This hint does not block other readers, but it prevents any other potential writers from also obtaining an update lock on the data. When using ODBC, you can also achieve a similar effect using SQLSETSTMTOPTION (...,SQL_CONCURRENCY)= SQL_CONCUR_LOCK. Either of these options reduces concurrency.

Explicitly Requesting Table-Level Locks

Microsoft SQL Server can provide the same table-locking functionality as Oracle.

Functionality	Oracle	Microsoft SQL Server
Lock an entire table—allows others to read a table, but prevent them from updating it. By default, the lock is held until the end of the statement.	LOCK TABLE...IN SHARE MODE	SELECT...*table_name* (TABLOCK)
Lock the table until the end of the transaction		SELECT...*table_name* (TABLOCK REPEATABLEREAD)

continued on next page

Functionality	Oracle	Microsoft SQL Server
Exclusive lock -prevent others from reading or updating the table and is held until the end of the command or transaction	LOCK TABLE...IN EXCLUSIVE MODE	SELECT...*table_name* (TABLOCKX)
Specify the number of milliseconds a statement waits for a lock to be released.	NOWAIT works like "LOCK_TIMEOUT 0"	LOCK_TIMEOUT

Handling Deadlocks

A deadlock occurs when one process locks a resource needed by another process, and the second process locks a page the first process needs. SQL Server automatically detects and resolves deadlocks. If a deadlock is found, the server terminates the user process that has completed the deadly embrace.

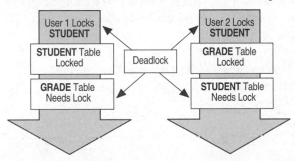

After every data modification, your program code should check for message number 1205, which indicates a deadlock. If this message number is returned, a deadlock has occurred and the transaction was rolled back. In this situation, your application must restart the transaction.

Deadlocks can usually be avoided by using a few simple techniques:

- Access tables in the same order in all parts of your application.

- Use a clustered index on every table to force an explicit row ordering.

- Keep transactions short.

For more information, search for the Microsoft Knowledge Base article "Detecting and Avoiding Deadlocks in Microsoft SQL Server" at http://support.microsoft.com/.

Remote Transactions

To perform remote transactions in Oracle, you must have access to a remote database node with a database link. In SQL Server, you must have access to a *remote server*. A remote server is a server running SQL Server on the network that users can access by using their local server. When a server is set up as a remote server, users can use the system procedures and the stored procedures on it without explicitly logging in to it.

Remote servers are set up in pairs. You must configure both servers to recognize each other as remote servers. The name of each server must be added to its partner with the **sp_addlinkedserver** system stored procedure or SQL Server Enterprise Manager.

After you set up a remote server, use the **sp_addremotelogin** system stored procedure or SQL Server Enterprise Manager to set up remote login IDs for the users who must access that remote server. After this step is completed, you must grant permissions to execute the stored procedures.

The EXECUTE statement is then used to run procedures on the remote server. This example executes the **validate_student** stored procedure on the remote server **STUDSVR1** and stores the return status indicating success or failure in **@retvalue1**:

```
DECLARE @retvalue1 int
EXECUTE @retvalue = STUDSVR1.student_db.student_admin.validate_student '111111111'
```

For more information, see SQL Server Books Online.

Distributed Transactions

Oracle automatically initiates a distributed transaction if changes are made to tables in two or more networked database nodes. SQL Server distributed transactions use the two-phase commit services of the Microsoft Distributed Transaction Coordinator (MS DTC) included with SQL Server.

By default, SQL Server must be instructed to participate in a distributed transaction. SQL Server participation in an MS DTC transaction can be started by either of the following:

- The BEGIN DISTRIBUTED TRANSACTION statement. This statement begins a new MS DTC transaction.

- A client application calling MS DTC transaction interfaces directly.

In the example, notice the distributed update to both the local table **GRADE** and the remote table **CLASS** (using a **class_name** procedure):

```
BEGIN DISTRIBUTED TRANSACTION
UPDATE STUDENT_ADMIN.GRADE
   SET GRADE = 'B+' WHERE SSN = '111111111' AND CCODE = '1234'
```

```
DECLARE @retvalue1 int
EXECUTE @retvalue1 = CLASS_SVR1.dept_db.dept_admin.class_name '1234',    'Basketweaving'
COMMIT TRANSACTION
GO
```

If the application cannot complete the transaction, the application program cancels it by using the ROLLBACK TRANSACTION statement. If the application fails or a participating resource manager fails, MS DTC cancels the transaction. MS DTC does not support distributed savepoints or the SAVE TRANSACTION statement. If an MS DTC transaction is terminated or rolled back, the entire transaction is rolled back to the beginning of the distributed transaction, regardless of any savepoints.

Two-Phase Commit Processing

The Oracle and MS DTC two-phase commit mechanisms are similar in operation. In the first phase of a SQL Server two-phase commit, the transaction manager requests each enlisted resource manager to prepare to commit. If any resource manager cannot prepare, the transaction manager broadcasts an abort decision to everyone involved in the transaction.

If all resource managers can successfully prepare, the transaction manager broadcasts the commit decision. This is the second phase of the commit process. While a resource manager is prepared, it is in doubt about whether the transaction is committed or terminated. MS DTC keeps a sequential log so that its commit or terminate decisions are durable. If a resource manager or transaction manager fails, they reconcile in-doubt transactions when they reconnect.

SQL Language Support

This section outlines the similarities and differences between Transact-SQL and PL/SQL language syntax and presents conversion strategies.

SELECT and Data Manipulation Statements

Use the following guidelines when migrating your Oracle DML statements and PL/SQL programs to SQL Server.

1. Verify that the syntax of all SELECT, INSERT, UPDATE, and DELETE statements is valid. Make any required modifications.

2. Change all outer joins to SQL-92 standard outer join syntax.

3. Replace Oracle functions with the appropriate SQL Server functions.

4. Check all comparison operators.

5. Replace the "||" string concatenation operator with the "+" string concatenation operator.

6. Replace PL/SQL programs with Transact-SQL programs.

7. Change all PL/SQL cursors to either noncursor SELECT statements or Transact-SQL cursors.

8. Replace PL/SQL procedures, functions, and packages with Transact-SQL procedures.

9. Convert PL/SQL triggers to Transact-SQL triggers.

10. Use the SET SHOWPLAN statement to tune your queries for performance.

SELECT Statements

The SELECT statement syntax used by Oracle and Microsoft SQL Server is similar.

Oracle	Microsoft SQL Server

SELECT [/*+ optimizer_hints*/]
 [ALL
	DISTINCT] *select_list*
	 [FROM
	 {*table_name*
		view_name	*select_statement*}]
			 [WHERE clause]
			 [GROUP BY *group_by_expression*]
			 [HAVING *search_condition*]
			 [START WITH ... CONNECT BY]
			 [{UNION
				UNION ALL	INTERSECT	
						   MINUS} SELECT ...]
						 [ORDER BY clause]
						 [FOR UPDATE]
							SELECT select_list
							 [INTO new_table_]
							 FROM *table_source*
							 [WHERE *search_condition*]
							 [GROUP BY [ALL] *group_by_expression* [,...*n*]
							    [WITH { CUBE
								ROLLUP }]]
								 [HAVING *search_condition*]
								 [ORDER BY *order_expression* [ASC
									DESC]]
									
									 In addition:
									
									 UNION operator
									 COMPUTE clause
									 FOR BROWSE clause
									 OPTION clause

Oracle-specific cost-based optimizer hints are not supported by SQL Server, and must be removed. The recommended technique is to use SQL Server cost-based optimization. For more information, see "Tuning SQL Statements" in this chapter.

SQL Server does not support the Oracle START WITH...CONNECT BY clause. You can replace this in SQL Server by creating a stored procedure that performs the same task. For more information, see "Expanding Hierarchies" in SQL Server Books Online, or search the Microsoft Knowledge Base for relevant articles at http://support.microsoft.com/

The Oracle INTERSECT and MINUS set operators are not supported by SQL Server. The SQL Server EXISTS and NOT EXISTS clauses can be used to accomplish the same result.

The following example uses the INTERSECT operator to find the course code and course name for all classes that have students. Notice how the EXISTS operator replaces the use of the INTERSECT operator. The data that is returned is identical.

Oracle	Microsoft SQL Server
SELECT CCODE, CNAME FROM DEPT_ADMIN.CLASS **INTERSECT** **SELECT C.CCODE, C.CNAME** **FROM STUDENT_ADMIN.GRADE G,** **DEPT_ADMIN.CLASS C** **WHERE C.CCODE = G.CCODE**	SELECT CCODE, CNAME FROM DEPT_ADMIN.CLASS C **WHERE EXISTS** **(SELECT 'X' FROM** **STUDENT_ADMIN.GRADE G** **WHERE C.CCODE = G.CCODE)**

This example uses the MINUS operator to find those classes that do not have any students.

Oracle	Microsoft SQL Server
SELECT CCODE, CNAME FROM DEPT_ADMIN.CLASS **MINUS** **SELECT C.CCODE, C.CNAME** **FROM STUDENT_ADMIN.GRADE G,** **DEPT_ADMIN.CLASS C** **WHERE C.CCODE = G.CCODE**	SELECT CCODE, CNAME FROM DEPT_ADMIN.CLASSC **WHERE NOT EXISTS** **(SELECT 'X' FROM** **STUDENT_ADMIN.GRADE G** **WHERE C.CCODE = G.CCODE)**

INSERT Statements

The INSERT statement syntax used by Oracle and Microsoft SQL Server is similar.

Oracle	Microsoft SQL Server

INSERT INTO
{table_name
	view_name	*select_statement*}
		[*(column_list)*]
		{*values_list*
			select_statement}	INSERT [INTO]
				{
				    table_name [[AS] *table_alias*] WITH (
				<table_hint_limited> [...n])
				
					view_name [[AS] *table_alias*]
					
						rowset_function_limited
						}
						
						{ [*(column_list)*]
						    { VALUES ({ DEFAULT
						                | NULL
						                | *expression*
						            }[,...*n*]
						        )

continued on next page

Oracle	Microsoft SQL Server
		derived_table | *execute_statement* } } | DEFAULT VALUES

The Transact-SQL language supports inserts into tables and views, but does not support insert operations into SELECT statements. If your Oracle application code performs inserts into SELECT statements, this must be changed.

Oracle	Microsoft SQL Server
INSERT INTO **(SELECT SSN, CCODE, GRADE FROM GRADE)** VALUES ('111111111', '1111',NULL)	INSERT INTO **GRADE (SSN, CCODE, GRADE)** VALUES ('111111111', '1111',NULL)

The Transact-SQL *values_list* parameter offers the SQL-92 standard keyword DEFAULT, which is not supported by Oracle. This keyword specifies that the default value for the column be used when an insert is performed. If a default value does not exist for the specified column, a NULL is inserted. If the column does not allow NULLs, an error message is returned. If the column is defined as a **timestamp** data type, the next sequential value is inserted.

The DEFAULT keyword cannot be used with an identity column. To generate the next sequential number, columns with the IDENTITY property must not be listed in the *column_list* or *values_clause*. You do not have to use the DEFAULT keyword to obtain the default value for a column. As in Oracle, if the column is not referenced in the *column_list* and it has a default value, the default value is placed in the column. This is the most compatible approach to use when performing the migration.

One useful Transact-SQL option (EXECute *procedure_name*) is to execute a procedure and pipe its output into a target table or view. Oracle does not allow this.

UPDATE Statements

Because Transact-SQL supports most of the syntax used by the Oracle UPDATE command, minimal revision is required.

Oracle	Microsoft SQL Server

UPDATE
{*table_name* | *view_name* | **select_statement**}
SET [*column_name(s)* = {*constant_value* |
expression | *select_statement* | *column_list* |
variable_list]
{*where_statement*}
	UPDATE
	{
	    table_name [[AS] *table_alias*] WITH (
	    <table_hint_limited> [...n])
	    | *view_name* [[AS] *table_alias*]
	
	continued on next page

Oracle	Microsoft SQL Server
	| *rowset_function_limited* } SET {*column_name* = {*expression* | DEFAULT | NULL} | @*variable* = *expression* | @*variable* = *column* = *expression* } [,...*n*] {{[FROM {<table_source>} [, ...*n*]] [WHERE <search_condition>] } | [WHERE CURRENT OF { { [GLOBAL] *cursor_name* } | *cursor_variable_name*}] } [OPTION (<query_hint> [,...*n*])]

The Transact-SQL UPDATE statement does not support update operations against SELECT statements. If your Oracle application code performs updates against SELECT statements, you can turn the SELECT statement into a view, and then use the view name in the SQL Server UPDATE statement. See the example shown previously in "INSERT Statements."

The Oracle UPDATE command can use only program variables from within a PL/SQL block. The Transact-SQL language does not require the use of blocks to use variables.

Oracle	Microsoft SQL Server

DECLARE
 VAR1 NUMBER(10,2);
 BEGIN
    VAR1 := 2500;
    UPDATE STUDENT_ADMIN.STUDENT
    SET TUITION_TOTAL = **VAR1;**
 END;
	DECLARE
	 @VAR1 NUMERIC(10,2)
	 SELECT @VAR1 = 2500
	 UPDATE STUDENT_ADMIN.STUDENT
	 SET TUITION_TOTAL=**@VAR1**

The keyword DEFAULT can be used to set a column to its default value in SQL Server. You cannot set a column to a default value with the Oracle UPDATE command.

Transact-SQL and Oracle SQL support the use of subqueries in an UPDATE statement. However, the Transact-SQL FROM clause can be used to create an UPDATE based on a join. This capability makes your UPDATE syntax more readable and in some cases can improve performance.

Oracle	Microsoft SQL Server

UPDATE STUDENT_ADMIN.STUDENT S
SET TUITION_TOTAL = 1500
WHERE SSN IN (SELECT SSN
    FROM GRADE G
        WHERE G.SSN = S.SSN
        AND G.CCODE = '1234')
	Subquery:
	
	UPDATE STUDENT_ADMIN.STUDENT S
	SET TUITION_TOTAL = 1500
	WHERE SSN IN (SELECT SSN
	    FROM GRADE G
	        WHERE G.SSN = S.SSN
	        AND G.CCODE = '1234')
	
	FROM clause:
	
	UPDATE STUDENT_ADMIN.STUDENT S
	SET TUITION_TOTAL = 1500
	FROM GRADE G
	WHERE S.SSN = G.SSN
	    AND G.CCODE = '1234'

DELETE Statements

In most cases, you do not need to modify DELETE statements. If you perform deletes against SELECT statements in Oracle, you must modify the syntax for SQL Server, because Transact-SQL does not support this functionality.

Transact-SQL supports the use of subqueries in the WHERE clause, as well as joins in the FROM clause. The latter can produce more efficient statements. See the example shown previously in "UPDATE Statements."

Oracle	Microsoft SQL Server

DELETE [FROM]
{*table_name* | *view_name* | ***select_statement***}
[WHERE clause]
	DELETE
	  [FROM]
	    {
	      table_name [[AS] *table_alias*] WITH (
	<table_hint_limited> [...*n*])
	      | *view_name* [[AS] *table_alias*]
	      | *rowset_function_limited*
	    }
	
	  [FROM {<table_source>} [, ...*n*]]

continued on next page

Oracle	Microsoft SQL Server
	[WHERE
	{ <search_condition>
	| { [CURRENT OF
	{
	{ [GLOBAL] *cursor_name* }
	| *cursor_variable_name*
	}
	]
	}
	]
	[OPTION (<query_hint> [,...*n*])]

TRUNCATE TABLE Statement

The TRUNCATE TABLE syntax used by Oracle and Microsoft SQL Server is similar. TRUNCATE TABLE is used to remove all of the rows from a table. The table structure and all of its indexes continue to exist. Unlike the DELETE statement, which explicitly deletes each record of a table, TRUNCATE TABLE removes the data from the table by deallocating the data pages of the table and logging these deallocations in the transaction log. Because the rows are not explicitly deleted, DELETE triggers are not executed. If a table is referenced by a FOREIGN KEY constraint, it cannot be truncated.

Oracle	Microsoft SQL Server
TRUNCATE TABLE *table_name* **[{DROP | REUSE} STORAGE]**	TRUNCATE TABLE *table_name*

In SQL Server, only the table owner can issue this statement. In Oracle, this command can be issued if you are the table owner or have the DELETE TABLE system privilege.

The Oracle TRUNCATE TABLE command can optionally release the storage space occupied by the rows in the table. The SQL Server TRUNCATE TABLE statement always reclaims space occupied by the table data and its associated indexes.

Manipulating Data in Identity and timestamp Columns

Oracle sequences are database objects that are not directly related to any given table or column. The relationship between a column and a sequence is implemented in the application, by assigning the sequence value to a column programmatically. Therefore, Oracle does not enforce any rules when it works with sequences. However, in Microsoft SQL Server identity columns, values cannot be updated and the DEFAULT keyword cannot be used.

By default, data cannot be inserted directly into an identity column. The identity column automatically generates a unique, sequential number for each new row inserted in the table. This default can be overridden using the following SET statement:

```
SET IDENTITY_INSERT table_name ON
```

With IDENTITY_INSERT set to ON, the user can insert any value into the identity column of a new row. To prevent the entry of duplicate numbers, a unique index must be created against the column. The purpose of this statement is to allow a user to re-create a value for a row that has been deleted accidentally. The @@IDENTITY function can be used to obtain the last identity value.

The TRUNCATE TABLE statement resets an identity column to its original SEED value. If you do not want to reset the identity value for a column, use the DELETE statement without a WHERE clause instead of the TRUNCATE TABLE statement. You will have to evaluate how this affects your Oracle migration, because ORACLE SEQUENCES are not reset following the TRUNCATE TABLE command.

You can perform only inserts or deletes when working with **timestamp** columns. If you attempt to update a **timestamp** column, you receive this error message:

```
Msg 272, Level 16, State 1 Can't update a TIMESTAMP column.
```

Locking Requested Rows

Oracle uses the FOR UPDATE clause to lock rows specified in the SELECT command. You do not need to use the equivalent clause in Microsoft SQL Server because this is the default behavior.

Row Aggregates and the Compute Clause

The SQL Server COMPUTE clause is used to generate row aggregate functions (SUM, AVG, MIN, MAX, and COUNT), which appear as additional rows in the query results. The COMPUTE clause allows you to see detail and summary rows in one set of results. You can calculate summary values for subgroups, and you can calculate more than one aggregate function for the same group.

The Oracle SELECT command syntax does not support the COMPUTE clause. Nevertheless, the SQL Server COMPUTE clause works just like the COMPUTE command found in the Oracle SQL*Plus query tool.

Join Clauses

Microsoft SQL Server 2000 allows up to 256 tables to be joined in a join clause, including both temporary and permanent tables. There is no join limit in Oracle.

When using outer joins in Oracle, the outer join operator (+) is placed typically next to the child (foreign key) column in the join. The (+) identifies the column with fewer unique values. This always occurs unless the foreign key allows null values, in which case (+) can be placed on the parent (PRIMARY KEY or UNIQUE constraint) column. You cannot place the (+) on both sides of the equal sign (=).

With SQL Server, you can use the *= and =* outer join operators. The * is used to identify the column that has more unique values. If the child (foreign key) column does not allow null values, the * is placed on the parent (PRIMARY KEY or UNIQUE constraint) column side of the equal sign. The placement of the * is essentially reversed in Oracle. You cannot place the * on both sides of the equal sign (=).

The *= and =* are considered legacy join operators. SQL Server also supports the SQL-92 standard join operators listed below. It is recommended that you use this syntax. The SQL-92 standard syntax is more powerful and has fewer restrictions than the * operators.

Join operation	Description
CROSS JOIN	This is the cross product of two tables. It returns the same rows as if no WHERE clause was specified in an old-style join. This type of join is called a Cartesian-join in Oracle.
INNER	This join specifies that all inner rows be returned. Any unmatched rows are discarded. This is identical to a standard Oracle table join.
LEFT [OUTER]	This type of join specifies that all of the left table outer rows be returned, even if no column matches are found. This operates just like an Oracle outer join (+).
RIGHT [OUTER]	This type of join specifies that all of the right table outer rows be returned, even if no column matches are found. This operates just like an Oracle outer join (+).
FULL [OUTER]	If a row from either table does not match the selection criteria, this specifies the row be included in the result set and its output columns that correspond to the other table be set to NULL. This would be the same as placing the Oracle outer join operator on both sides of the "=" sign (col1(+) = col2(+)), which is not allowed.

The following code examples return lists of classes taken by all students. Outer joins are defined between the student and grade tables that allow all students to appear, even those who are not enrolled in any classes. Outer joins are also added to the class table in order to return the class names. If outer joins are not added to the class tables, those students who are not enrolled in any classes are not returned because they have null course codes (**CCODE**).

Oracle	Microsoft SQL Server
SELECT S.SSN AS SSN, FNAME, LNAME **FROM STUDENT_ADMIN.STUDENT S,** **DEPT_ADMIN.CLASS C,** **STUDENT_ADMIN.GRADE G** **WHERE S.SSN = G.SSN(+)** **AND G.CCODE = C.CCODE(+)**	SELECT S.SSN AS SSN, FNAME, LNAME **FROM STUDENT_ADMIN.GRADE G** **RIGHT OUTER JOIN** **STUDENT_ADMIN.STUDENT S** **ON G.SSN = S.SSN** **LEFT OUTER JOIN** **DEPT_ADMIN.CLASS C** **ON G.CCODE = C.CCODE**

Using SELECT Statements as Table Names

Microsoft SQL Server and Oracle support the use of SELECT statements as the source of tables when performing queries. SQL Server requires an alias; the use of an alias is optional with Oracle.

Oracle	Microsoft SQL Server
SELECT SSN, LNAME, FNAME, TUITION_PAID, SUM_PAID FROM STUDENT_ADMIN.STUDENT, **(SELECT SUM(TUITION_PAID) SUM_PAID FROM STUDENT_ADMIN.STUDENT)**	SELECT SSN, LNAME, FNAME, TUITION_PAID, SUM_PAID FROM STUDENT_ADMIN.STUDENT, **(SELECT SUM(TUITION_PAID) SUM_PAID FROM STUDENT_ADMIN.STUDENT) SUM_STUDENT**

Reading and Modifying BLOBs

Microsoft SQL Server implements binary large objects (BLOBs) with **text** and **image** columns. Oracle implements BLOBs with LONG and LONG RAW columns. In Oracle, a SELECT command can query the values in LONG and LONG RAW columns.

In SQL Server, you can use a standard Transact-SQL statement or the specialized READTEXT statement to read data in **text** and **image** columns. The READTEXT statement allows you to read partial sections of a **text** or **image** column. Oracle does not provide an equivalent statement for working with LONG and LONG RAW columns.

The READTEXT statement makes use of a *text_pointer*, which can be obtained using the TEXTPTR function. The TEXTPTR function returns a pointer to the **text** or **image** column in the specified row or to the **text** or **image** column in the last row returned by the query if more than one row is returned. Because the TEXTPTR function returns a 16-byte binary string, it is best to declare a local variable to hold the text pointer, and then use the variable with READTEXT.

The READTEXT statement specifies how many bytes to return. The value in the @@TEXTSIZE function, which is the limit on the number of characters or bytes to be returned, supersedes the size specified by the READTEXT statement if it is less than the specified size for READTEXT.

The SET statement can be used with the TEXTSIZE parameter to specify the size, in bytes, of text data to be returned with a SELECT statement. If you specify a TEXTSIZE of 0, the size is reset to the default (4 KB). Setting the TEXTSIZE parameter affects the @@TEXTSIZE function. The SQL Server ODBC driver automatically sets the TEXTSIZE parameter when the SQL_MAX_LENGTH statement option is changed.

In Oracle, UPDATE and INSERT commands are used to change values in LONG and LONG RAW columns. In SQL Server, you can use standard UPDATE and INSERT statements, or you can use the UPDATETEXT and WRITETEXT statements. Both UPDATETEXT and WRITETEXT allow a nonlogged option, and UPDATETEXT allows for partial updating of a **text** or **image** column.

The UPDATETEXT statement can be used to replace existing data, delete existing data, or insert new data. Newly inserted data can be a constant value, table name, column name, or text pointer.

The WRITETEXT statement completely overwrites any existing data in the column it affects. Use WRITETEXT to replace text data and UPDATETEXT to modify text data. The UPDATETEXT statement is more flexible because it changes only a portion of a text of image value rather than the entire value.

For more information, see SQL Server Books Online.

Functions

The tables in this section show the relationship between Oracle and SQL Server scalar-valued and aggregate functions. Although the names appear to be the same, the functions vary in numbers and types of arguments. Also, functions that are supplied only by Microsoft SQL Server are not mentioned in this list because this chapter is limited to easing migration from existing Oracle applications. Examples of functions not supported by Oracle are: degrees (DEGREES), PI (PI), and random number (RAND).

Number/Mathematical Functions

The following are number/mathematical functions supported by Oracle and their Microsoft SQL Server equivalents.

Function	Oracle	Microsoft SQL Server
Absolute value	ABS	Same
Arc cosine	ACOS	Same
Arc sine	ASIN	Same
Arc tangent of n	ATAN	Same
Arc tangent of n and m	ATAN2	ATN2
Smallest integer >= value	CEIL	CEILING
Cosine	COS	Same
Hyperbolic cosine	COSH	COT
Exponential value	EXP	Same
Largest integer <= value	FLOOR	Same
Natural logarithm	LN	LOG
Logarithm, any base	LOG(N)	N/A
Logarithm, base 10	LOG(10)	LOG10

continued on next page

Function	Oracle	Microsoft SQL Server
Modulus (remainder)	MOD	USE MODULO (%) OPERATOR
Power	POWER	Same
Random number	N/A	RAND
Round	ROUND	Same
Sign of number	SIGN	Same
Sine	SIN	Same
Hyperbolic sine	SINH	N/A
Square root	SQRT	Same
Tangent	TAN	Same
Hyperbolic tangent	TANH	N/A
Truncate	TRUNC	N/A
Largest number in list	GREATEST	N/A
Smallest number in list	LEAST	N/A
Convert number if NULL	NVL	ISNULL

Character Functions

The following are character functions supported by Oracle and their Microsoft SQL Server equivalents.

Function	Oracle	Microsoft SQL Server
Convert character to ASCII	ASCII	Same
String concatenate	CONCAT	(expression + expression)
Convert ASCII to character	CHR	CHAR
Return starting point of character in character string (from left)	INSTR	CHARINDEX
Convert characters to lowercase (LOWER)	LOWER	Same
Convert characters to uppercase (UPPER)	UPPER	Same
Pad left side of character string	LPAD	N/A

continued on next page

Function	Oracle	Microsoft SQL Server
Remove leading blanks	LTRIM	Same
Remove trailing blanks	RTRIM	Same
Starting point of pattern in character string	INSTR	PATINDEX
Repeat character string multiple times	RPAD	REPLICATE
Phonetic representation of character string	SOUNDEX	Same
String of repeated spaces	RPAD	SPACE
Character data converted from numeric data	TO_CHAR	STR
Substring	SUBSTR	SUBSTRING
Replace characters	REPLACE	STUFF
Capitalize first letter of each word in string	INITCAP	N/A
Translate character string	TRANSLATE	N/A
Length of character string	LENGTH	DATALENGTH or LEN
Greatest character string in list	GREATEST	N/A
Least character string in list	LEAST	N/A
Convert string if NULL	NVL	ISNULL

Date Functions

The following are date functions supported by Oracle and their Microsoft SQL Server equivalents.

Function	Oracle	Microsoft SQL Server
Date addition	(date column +/- value) or ADD_MONTHS	DATEADD
Difference between dates	(date column +/- value) or MONTHS_BETWEEN	DATEDIFF
Current date and time	SYSDATE	GETDATE()
Last day of month	LAST_DAY	N/A
Time zone conversion	NEW_TIME	N/A

continued on next page

Function	Oracle	Microsoft SQL Server
First weekday after date	NEXT_DAY	N/A
Character string representation of date	TO_CHAR	DATENAME
Integer representation of date	TO_NUMBER(TO_CHAR))	DATEPART
Date round	ROUND	CONVERT
Date truncate	TRUNC	CONVERT
Character string to date	TO_DATE	CONVERT
Convert date if NULL	NVL	ISNULL

Conversion Functions

The following are conversion functions supported by Oracle and their Microsoft SQL Server equivalents.

Function	Oracle	Microsoft SQL Server
Number to character	TO_CHAR	CONVERT
Character to number	TO_NUMBER	CONVERT
Date to character	TO_CHAR	CONVERT
Character to date	TO_DATE	CONVERT
Hex to binary	HEX_TO_RAW	CONVERT
Binary to hex	RAW_TO_HEX	CONVERT

Other Row-Level Functions

The following are other row-level functions supported by Oracle and their Microsoft SQL Server equivalents.

Function	Oracle	Microsoft SQL Server
Return first non-null expression	DECODE	COALESCE
Current sequence value	CURRVAL	N/A

continued on next page

Function	Oracle	Microsoft SQL Server
Next sequence value	NEXTVAL	N/A
If exp1 = exp2, return null	DECODE	NULLIF
User's login ID number	UID	SUSER_ID
User's login name	USER	SUSER_NAME
User's database ID number	UID	USER_ID
User's database name	USER	USER_NAME
Current User	CURRENT_USER	Same
User environment (audit trail)	USERENV	N/A
Level in CONNECT BY clause	LEVEL	N/A

Aggregate Functions

The following are aggregate functions supported by Oracle and their SQL Server equivalents.

Function	Oracle	Microsoft SQL Server
Average	AVG	Same
Count	COUNT	Same
Maximum	MAX	Same
Minimum	MIN	Same
Standard deviation	STDDEV	STDEV or STDEVP
Summation	SUM	Same
Variance	VARIANCE	VAR or VARP

Conditional Tests

Both the Oracle DECODE statement and the Microsoft SQL Server CASE expression perform conditional tests. When the value in *test_value* matches any following expression, the related value is returned. If no match is found, the *default_value* is returned. If no *default_value* is specified, both DECODE and CASE return NULL if there is no match. The table shows the syntax as well as an example of a converted DECODE command.

Oracle	Microsoft SQL Server
DECODE (test_value, *expression1, value1* [[,*expression2, value2*] [...]] [,*default_value*])	**CASE** *test_value* **WHEN** *expression1* **THEN** *value1* [[**WHEN** *expression2* **THEN** *value2*] [...]] [**ELSE** *default_value*] **END**
CREATE VIEW STUDENT_ADMIN.STUDENT_GPA (SSN, GPA) AS SELECT SSN, ROUND(AVG(**DECODE(grade** **,'A', 4** **,'A+', 4.3** **,'A-', 3.7** **,'B', 3** **,'B+', 3.3** **,'B-', 2.7** **,'C', 2** **,'C+', 2.3** **,'C-', 1.7** **,'D', 1** **,'D+', 1.3** **,'D-', 0.7** **,0)),2)** FROM STUDENT_ADMIN.GRADE GROUP BY SSN	CREATE VIEW STUDENT_ADMIN.STUDENT_GPA (SSN, GPA) AS SELECT SSN, ROUND(AVG(**CASE grade** **WHEN 'A' THEN 4** **WHEN 'A+' THEN 4.3** **WHEN 'A-' THEN 3.7** **WHEN 'B' THEN 3** **WHEN 'B+' THEN 3.3** **WHEN 'B-' THEN 2.7** **WHEN 'C' THEN 2** **WHEN 'C+' THEN 2.3** **WHEN 'C-' THEN 1.7** **WHEN 'D' THEN 1** **WHEN 'D+' THEN 1.3** **WHEN 'D-' THEN 0.7** **ELSE 0** **END),2)** FROM STUDENT_ADMIN.GRADE GROUP BY SSN

The CASE expression can support the use of SELECT statements for performing Boolean tests, something the DECODE command does not allow. For more information about the CASE expression, see SQL Server Books Online.

Converting Values to Different Data Types

The Microsoft SQL Server CONVERT and CAST functions are multiple purpose conversion functions. They provide similar functionality, converting an expression of one data type to another data type, and supporting a variety of special date formats:

CAST (*expression* AS *data_type*)

CONVERT (*data type*[(*length*)], *expression* [, *style*])

CAST is a SQL-92 standard function. These functions perform the same operations as the Oracle TO_CHAR, TO_NUMBER, TO_DATE, HEXTORAW, and RAWTOHEX functions.

The data type is any system data type into which the expression is to be converted. User-defined data types cannot be used. The *length* parameter is optional and is used with **char**, **varchar**, **binary**, and **varbinary** data types. The maximum allowable length is 8000.

Conversion	Oracle	Microsoft SQL Server
Character to number	TO_NUMBER('10')	CONVERT(**numeric**, '10')
Number to character	TO_CHAR(10)	CONVERT(**char**, 10)
Character to date	TO_DATE('04-JUL-97') TO_DATE('04-JUL-1997', 'dd-mon-yyyy') TO_DATE('July 4, 1997', 'Month dd, yyyy')	CONVERT(**datetime**, '04-JUL-97') CONVERT (**datetime**, '04-JUL-1997') CONVERT (**datetime**, 'July 4, 1997')
Date to character	TO_CHAR(sysdate) TO_CHAR(sysdate, 'dd mon yyyy') TO_CHAR(sysdate, 'mm/dd/yyyy')	CONVERT(**char**, GETDATE()) CONVERT(**char**, GETDATE (), 106) CONVERT(**char**, GETDATE (), 101)
Hex to binary	HEXTORAW('1F')	CONVERT(**binary**, '1F')
Binary to hex	RAWTOHEX(binary_column)	CONVERT(**char**,*binary_column*)

Notice how character strings are converted to dates. In Oracle, the default date format model is "DD-MON-YY." If you use any other format, you must provide an appropriate date format model. The CONVERT function automatically converts standard date formats without the need for a format model.

When you convert from a date to a character string, the default output for the CONVERT function is "dd mon yyyy hh:mm:ss:mmm(24h)". A numeric style code is used to format the output to other types of date format models. For more information about the CONVERT function, see SQL Server Books Online.

The following table shows the default output for Microsoft SQL Server dates.

Without century	With century	Standard	Output
-	0 or 100 (*)	Default	mon dd yyyy hh:miAM (or PM)
1	101	USA	mm/dd/yy
2	102	ANSI	yy.mm.dd
3	103	British/French	dd/mm/yy
4	104	German	dd.mm.yy

continued on next page

Without century	With century	Standard	Output
5	105	Italian	dd-mm-yy
6	106	-	dd mon yy
7	107	-	mon dd, yy
8	108	-	hh:mm:ss
-	9 or 109 (*)	Default milliseconds	mon dd yyyy hh:mi:ss:mmm (AM or PM)
10	110	USA	mm-dd-yy
11	111	JAPAN	yy/mm/dd
12	112	ISO	yymmdd
-	13 or 113 (*)	Europe default	dd mon yyyy hh:mm:ss:mmm(24h)
14	114	-	hh:mi:ss:mmm(24h)

User-Defined Functions

The syntax to create a user-defined function that returns a scalar data type is similar between Oracle and SQL Server 2000.

Oracle	Microsoft SQL Server
SELECT ssn, fname, lname, tuition_paid, tuition_paid/get_sum_major(major) as percent_major FROM student_admin.student	SELECT ssn, fname, lname, tuition_paid, tuition_paid/sum_major as percent_major FROM student_admin.student, (SELECT major, sum(tuition_paid) sum_major FROM student_admin.student GROUP BY major) sum_student WHERE student.major = sum_student.major
CREATE OR REPLACE FUNCTION get_sum_major (inmajor varchar2) RETURN NUMBER AS sum_paid number; BEGIN SELECT sum(tuition_paid) into sum_paid FROM student_admin.student WHERE major = inmajor; RETURN(sum_paid); END get_sum_major;	CREATE FUNCTION get_sum_major (@inmajor varchar(40)) RETURNS money AS BEGIN DECLARE @sum_paid money SELECT @sum_paid = sum(tuition_paid) FROM student_admin.student WHERE major = @inmajor RETURN @sum_paid END

SQL Server user-defined functions also can return a table data type. These functions can be either in-line functions, consisting of a simple SELECT statement or multistatement functions, consisting of many statements used to build a table. Both of these functions can accept parameters and can be accessed in the FROM clause of a Transact-SQL statement. These functions can provide a powerful alternative both to using stored procedures, because their result set can be accessed directly within a Transact-SQL statement, and to using views because they can accept parameters to narrow down a result set.

Here is the syntax to create the user-defined function types that return tables.

Syntax for an inline-table function

CREATE FUNCTION [*owner_name.*] *function_name*
   ([{ @*parameter_name* [AS] *scalar_parameter_data_type* [= *default*] } [,...*n*]])

RETURNS TABLE

[WITH <function_option > [[,] ...*n*]]

[AS]

RETURN [( ] *select-stmt* [ )]

Syntax for a multistatement table function

CREATE FUNCTION [*owner_name.*] *function_name*
   ([{ @*parameter_name* [AS] *scalar_parameter_data_type* [= *default*] } [,...*n*]])

RETURNS @*return_variable* TABLE < table_type_definition >

[WITH < function_option > [[,] ...*n*]]

[AS]

BEGIN
   function_body
  RETURN
END

Comparison Operators

Oracle and Microsoft SQL Server comparison operators are nearly identical.

Operator	Oracle	Microsoft SQL Server
Equal to	(=)	Same
Greater than	(>)	Same
Less than	(<)	Same
Greater than or equal to	(>=)	Same

continued on next page

Operator	Oracle	Microsoft SQL Server
Less than or equal to	(<=)	Same
Not equal to	(!=, <>,^=)	Same
Not greater than, not less than	N/A	!> , !<
In any member in set	IN	Same
Not in any member in set	NOT IN	Same
Any value in set	ANY, SOME	Same
Referring to all values in set.	!= ALL, <> ALL, < ALL, > ALL, <= ALL, >= ALL	Same
Like pattern	LIKE	Same
Not like pattern	NOT LIKE	Same
Value between x and y	BETWEEN x AND y	Same
Value not between	NOT BETWEEN	Same
Value exists	EXISTS	Same
Value does not exist	NOT EXISTS	Same
Value {is | is not} NULL	IS NULL, IS NOT NULL	Same. Also supports = NULL, != NULL for backward compatibility (not recommended).

Pattern Matches

The SQL Server LIKE keyword offers useful wildcard search options that are not supported by Oracle. In addition to supporting the % and _ wildcard characters common to both RDBMSs, the [ ] and [^] characters are also supported by SQL Server.

The [ ] character set is used to search for any single character within a specified range. For example, if you search for the characters a through f in a single character position, you can specify this with LIKE '[a-f]' or LIKE '[abcdef]'. The usefulness of these additional wildcard characters is shown in this table.

Oracle	Microsoft SQL Server

SELECT * FROM STUDENT_ADMIN.STUDENT WHERE LNAME LIKE **'A%'**
    OR LNAME LIKE 'B%'
    OR LNAME LIKE 'C%'
	SELECT * FROM STUDENT_ADMIN.STUDENT WHERE LNAME LIKE **'[ABC]%'**

The [^] wildcard character set is used to specify characters NOT in the specified range. For example, if any character except a through f is acceptable, you use LIKE '[^a - f]' or LIKE '[^abcdef]'.

For more information about the LIKE keyword, see SQL Server Books Online.

Using NULL in Comparisons

Although Microsoft SQL Server traditionally has supported the SQL-92–standard as well as some nonstandard NULL behaviors, it supports the use of NULL in Oracle.

SET ANSI_NULLS should be set to ON for executing distributed queries.

The SQL Server ODBC driver and OLE DB Provider for SQL Server automatically SET ANSI_NULLS to ON when connecting. This setting can be configured in ODBC data sources, in ODBC connection attributes, or in OLE DB connection properties that are set in the application before connecting to SQL Server. SET ANSI_NULLS defaults to OFF for connections from DB-Library applications.

When SET ANSI_DEFAULTS is ON, SET ANSI_NULLS is enabled.

For more information about the use of NULL, see SQL Server Books Online.

String Concatenation

Oracle uses two pipe symbols (||) as the string concatenation operator, and SQL Server uses the plus sign (+). This difference requires minor revision in your application program code.

Oracle	Microsoft SQL Server
SELECT FNAME||' '||LNAME AS NAME FROM STUDENT_ADMIN.STUDENT	SELECT FNAME +' '+ LNAME AS NAME FROM STUDENT_ADMIN.STUDENT

Control-of-Flow Language

The control-of-flow language controls the flow of execution of SQL statements, statement blocks, and stored procedures. PL/SQL and Transact-SQL provide many of the same constructs, although there are some syntax differences.

Keywords

These are the keywords supported by each RDBMS.

Statement	Oracle PL/SQL	Microsoft SQL Server Transact-SQL
Declare variables	DECLARE	DECLARE
Statement block	BEGIN...END;	BEGIN...END
Conditional processing	IF...THEN, ELSIF...THEN, ELSE ENDIF;	IF...[BEGIN...END] ELSE <condition> [BEGIN...END] ELSE IF <condition> CASE expression
Unconditional exit	RETURN	RETURN
Unconditional exit to the statement following the end of the current program block	EXIT	BREAK
Restarts a WHILE loop	N/A	CONTINUE
Wait for a specified interval	N/A (dbms_lock.sleep)	WAITFOR
Loop control	WHILE LOOP...END LOOP; LABEL...GOTO LABEL; FOR...END LOOP; LOOP...END LOOP;	WHILE <condition> BEGIN... END LABEL...GOTO LABEL
Program comments	/* ... */, --	/* ... */, --
Print output	RDBMS_OUTPUT.PUT_LINE	PRINT
Raise program error	RAISE_APPLICATION_ERROR	RAISERROR
Execute program	EXECUTE	EXECUTE
Statement terminator	Semicolon (;)	N/A

Declaring Variables

Transact-SQL and PL/SQL variables are created with the DECLARE keyword. Transact-SQL variables are identified with @) and, like PL/SQL variables, are initialized to a null value when they are first created.

Oracle	Microsoft SQL Server
DECLARE	DECLARE
VSSN CHAR(9);	@VSSN CHAR(9),
VFNAME VARCHAR2(12);	@VFNAME VARCHAR2(12),
VLNAME VARCHAR2(20);	@VLNAME VARCHAR2(20),
VBIRTH_DATE DATE;	@VBIRTH_DATE DATETIME,
VLOAN_AMOUNT NUMBER(12,2);	@VLOAN_AMOUNT NUMERIC(12,2)

Transact-SQL does not support the %TYPE and %ROWTYPE variable data type definitions. A Transact-SQL variable cannot be initialized in the DECLARE command. The Oracle NOT NULL and CONSTANT keywords cannot be used in Microsoft SQL Server data type definitions.

Like Oracle LONG and LONG RAW data types, **text** and **image** data types cannot be used for variable declarations. Additionally, the PL/SQL style record and table definitions are not supported.

Assigning Variables

Oracle and Microsoft SQL Server offer these ways to assign values to local variables.

Oracle	Microsoft SQL Server
Assignment operator (:=)	SET @*local_variable* = value
SELECT...INTO syntax for selecting column values from a single row	SELECT @local_varialbe = *expression* [FROM...] for assigning a literal value, an expression involving other local variables, or a column value from a single row
FETCH...INTO syntax	FETCH...INTO syntax

Here are some syntax examples.

Oracle	Microsoft SQL Server

DECLARE VSSN CHAR(9);
 VFNAME VARCHAR2(12);
 VLNAME VARCHAR2(20);
 BEGIN
 VSSN := '123448887';
 SELECT **FNAME, LNAME INTO VFNAME,**
 VLNAME FROM STUDENTS WHERE
 SSN=VSSN;
 END;
	DECLARE @VSSN CHAR(9),
	 @VFNAME VARCHAR(12),
	 @VLNAME VARCHAR(20)
	 SET **@VSSN = '12355887'**
	 SELECT
	 @VFNAME=FNAME,
	 @VLNAME=LNAME FROM
	 STUDENTS WHERE SSN =
	 @VSSN

Statement Blocks

Oracle PL/SQL and Microsoft SQL Server Transact-SQL support the use of BEGIN…END terminology to specify statement blocks. Transact-SQL does not require the use of a statement block following the DECLARE statement. The BEGIN…END statement blocks are required in Microsoft SQL Server for IF statements and WHILE loops if more than one statement is executed.

Oracle	Microsoft SQL Server

DECLARE
     DECLARE VARIABLES ...
 BEGIN -- THIS IS REQUIRED SYNTAX
     PROGRAM_STATEMENTS ...
     IF ...THEN
         STATEMENT1;
         STATEMENT2;
         STATEMENTN;
 END IF;
 WHILE ... **LOOP**
         STATEMENT1;
         STATEMENT2;
         STATEMENTN;
     END LOOP;
 END; -- THIS IS REQUIRED SYNTAX
	DECLARE
	     DECLARE VARIABLES ...
	 BEGIN -- THIS IS OPTIONAL SYNTAX
	     PROGRAM_STATEMENTS ...
	     IF ...
	     BEGIN
	         STATEMENT1
	         STATEMENT2
	         STATEMENTN
	     END
	 WHILE ...
	     BEGIN
	         STATEMENT1
	         STATEMENT2
	         STATEMENTN
	     END
	 END -- THIS IS REQUIRED SYNTAX

Conditional Processing

The Microsoft SQL Server Transact-SQL conditional statement includes IF and ELSE rather than the ELSIF statement in Oracle PL/SQL. Multiple IF statements can be nested to achieve the same effect. For extensive conditional tests, the CASE expression may be easier to read.

Oracle	Microsoft SQL Server

```
DECLARE                                    DECLARE
VDEGREE_PROGRAM CHAR(1);                    @VDEGREE_PROGRAM CHAR(1),
VDEGREE_PROGRAM_NAME VARCHAR2(20);         @VDEGREE_PROGRAM_NAME
BEGIN                                       VARCHAR(20)
    VDEGREE_PROGRAM := 'U';                SELECT @VDEGREE_PROGRAM = 'U'
    IF VDEGREE_PROGRAM = 'U' THEN          SELECT @VDEGREE_PROGRAM_NAME =
        VDEGREE_PROGRAM_NAME :=                CASE @VDEGREE_PROGRAM
            'Undergraduate';                      WHEN 'U' THEN 'Undergraduate'
    ELSIF VDEGREE_PROGRAM = 'M' THEN              WHEN 'M' THEN 'Masters'
        VDEGREE_PROGRAM_NAME :=                   WHEN 'P' THEN 'PhD'.
            'Masters';                            ELSE 'Unknown'
    ELSIF VDEGREE_PROGRAM = 'P' THEN       END
        VDEGREE_PROGRAM_NAME := 'PhD';
    ELSE VDEGREE_PROGRAM_NAME :=
        'Unknown';
    END IF;
END;
```

Repeated Statement Execution (Looping)

Oracle PL/SQL provides the unconditional LOOP and FOR LOOP. Transact-SQL offers the WHILE loop and the GOTO statement for looping purposes.

```
WHILE Boolean_expression
    {sql_statement | statement_block}
    [BREAK] [CONTINUE]
```

The WHILE loop tests a Boolean expression for the repeated execution of one or more statements. The statement(s) are executed repeatedly as long as the specified expression evaluates to TRUE. If multiple statements are to be executed, they must be placed within a BEGIN...END block.

Oracle	Microsoft SQL Server

DECLARE
COUNTER NUMBER;
BEGIN
   COUNTER := 0
   WHILE (COUNTER <5) LOOP
      COUNTER := COUNTER + 1;
   END LOOP;
END;
	DECLARE
	@COUNTER NUMERIC
	SELECT @COUNTER = 1
	WHILE (@COUNTER <5)
	BEGIN
	   SELECT @COUNTER = @COUNTER +1
	END

Statement execution can be controlled from inside the loop with the BREAK and CONTINUE keywords. The BREAK keyword causes an unconditional exit from the WHILE loop, and the CONTINUE keyword causes the WHILE loop to restart, skipping any statements that follow. The BREAK keyword is equivalent to the Oracle PL/SQL EXIT keyword. Oracle does not have an equivalent to CONTINUE.

GOTO Statement

Both Oracle and Microsoft SQL Server have GOTO statements, with different syntax. The GOTO statement causes the execution of a Transact-SQL batch to jump to a label. None of the statements between the GOTO statement and the label are executed.

Oracle	Microsoft SQL Server
GOTO label; <<label name here>>	GOTO *label* :label

PRINT Statement

The Transact-SQL PRINT statement performs the same operation as the PL/SQL RDBMS_OUTPUT.*put_line* procedure. It is used for printing user-specified messages.

The message limit for the PRINT statement is 8,000 characters. Variables that are defined using the **char** or **varchar** data type can be embedded in the printed statement. If any other data type is used, the CONVERT or CAST function must be used. Local variables, global variables, and text can be printed. Both single and double quotation marks can be used to enclose text.

Returning from Stored Procedures

Both Microsoft SQL Server and Oracle have RETURN statements. RETURN lets your program exit unconditionally from a query or procedure. RETURN is immediate and complete and can be used at any point to exit from a procedure, batch, or statement block. Statements following RETURN are not executed.

Oracle	Microsoft SQL Server
RETURN *expression*:	RETURN i*nteger_expression*

Raising Program Errors

The Transact-SQL RAISERROR statement returns a user-defined error message and sets a system flag to record that an error has occurred. It is similar in function to the PL/SQL *raise_application_error* exception handler.

The RAISERROR statement allows the client to retrieve an entry from the **sysmessages** table or build a message dynamically with user-specified severity and state information. When defined, this message is sent back to the client as a server error message.

```
RAISERROR ({msg_id | msg_str}, severity, state
   [, argument1 [, argument2]])
   [WITH options]
```

When converting your PL/SQL programs, it may not be necessary to use the RAISERROR statement. In the following code example, the PL/SQL program uses the *raise_application_error* exception handler, and the Transact-SQL program uses nothing. The *raise_application_error* exception handler has been included to prevent the PL/SQL program from possibly returning an ambiguous *unhandled exception* error message. Instead, it always returns the Oracle error message (SQLERRM) when an unanticipated problem occurs.

When a Transact-SQL program fails, it always returns a detailed error message to the client program. Therefore, unless some specialized error handling is required, the RAISERROR statement is not always needed.

Oracle	Microsoft SQL Server
CREATE OR REPLACE FUNCTION DEPT_ADMIN.DELETE_DEPT (VDEPT IN VARCHAR2) RETURN NUMBER AS BEGIN DELETE FROM DEPT_ADMIN.DEPT WHERE DEPT = VDEPT; RETURN(SQL%ROWCOUNT); EXCEPTION WHEN OTHER THEN RAISE_APPLICATION_ERROR (-20001,SQLERRM); END DELETE_DEPT; /	CREATE PROCEDURE DEPT_ADMIN.DELETE_DEPT @VDEPT VARCHAR(4) AS DELETE FROM DEPT_DB.DBO.DEPT WHERE DEPT = @VDEPT RETURN @@ROWCOUNT GO

Implementing Cursors

Oracle always requires that cursors be used with SELECT statements, regardless of the number of rows requested from the database. In Microsoft SQL Server, a SELECT statement that is not enclosed within a cursor returns rows to the client as a default result set. This is an efficient way to return data to a client application.

SQL Server provides two interfaces for cursor functions. When cursors are used in Transact-SQL batches or stored procedures, SQL statements can be used to declare, open, and fetch from cursors as well as positioned updates and deletes. When cursors from a DB-Library, ODBC, or OLE DB program are used, the SQL Server client libraries transparently call built-in server functions to handle cursors more efficiently.

When porting a PL/SQL procedure from Oracle, first determine whether cursors are needed to do the same function in Transact-SQL. If the cursor returns only a set of rows to the client application, use a noncursor SELECT statement in Transact-SQL to return a default result set. If the cursor is used to load data a row at a time into local procedure variables, you must use cursors in Transact-SQL.

Cursor Syntax

The table shows the syntax for using cursors.

Operation	Oracle	Microsoft SQL Server
Declaring a cursor	**CURSOR** *cursor_name* [*(cursor_parameter(s))*] **IS** *select_statement*;	**DECLARE** *cursor_name* **CURSOR** **[LOCAL	GLOBAL]** **[FORWARD_ONLY	SCROLL]** **[STATIC	KEYSET	DYNAMIC	FAST_FORWARD]** **[READ_ONLY	SCROLL_LOCKS	OPTIMISTIC]** **[TYPE_WARNING]** **FOR** *select_statement* **[FOR UPDATE [OF** *column_name* [*,...n*]]]
Opening a cursor	OPEN *cursor_name* [*(cursor_parameter(s))*];	OPEN *cursor_name*

Continued on next page

Operation	Oracle	Microsoft SQL Server
Fetching from cursor	**FETCH** *cursor_name* **INTO** *variable(s)*	**FETCH [[NEXT | PRIOR | FIRST | LAST | ABSOLUTE {*n* | @nvar} | RELATIVE {*n* | @nvar}] FROM]** *cursor_name* **[INTO @variable(s)]**
Update fetched row	UPDATE *table_name* SET *statement(s)...* WHERE CURRENT OF *cursor_name*;	UPDATE *table_name* SET *statement(s)...* WHERE CURRENT OF *cursor_name*
Delete fetched row	DELETE FROM *table_name* WHERE CURRENT OF *cursor_name*;	DELETE FROM *table_name* WHERE CURRENT OF *cursor_name*
Closing cursor	CLOSE *cursor_name*;	CLOSE *cursor_name*
Remove cursor data structures	**N/A**	**DEALLOCATE** *cursor_name*

Declaring a Cursor

Although the Transact-SQL DECLARE CURSOR statement does not support the use of cursor arguments, it does support local variables. The values of these local variables are used in the cursor when it is opened. Microsoft SQL Server offers many additional capabilities in its DECLARE CURSOR statement.

The INSENSITIVE option is used to define a cursor that makes a temporary copy of the data to be used by that cursor. All of the requests to the cursor are answered by this temporary table. Consequently, modifications made to base tables are not reflected in the data returned by fetches made to this cursor. Data accessed by this type of cursor cannot be modified.

Applications can request a cursor type and then execute a Transact-SQL statement that is not supported by server cursors of the type requested. SQL Server returns an error that indicates the cursor type has changed, or given a set of factors, implicitly converts a cursor. For a complete list of factors that trigger SQL Server 2000 to implicitly convert a cursor from one type to another, see SQL Server Books Online.

The SCROLL option allows backward, absolute, and relative fetches in addition to forward fetches. A scroll cursor uses a keyset cursor model in which committed deletes and updates made to the underlying tables by any user are reflected in subsequent fetches. This is true only if the cursor is not declared with the INSENSITIVE option.

If the READ ONLY option is chosen, updates are prevented from occurring against any row within the cursor. This option overrides the default capability of a cursor to be updated.

The UPDATE [OF *column_list*] statement is used to define updatable columns within the cursor. If [OF *column_list*] is supplied, only the columns listed allow modifications. If no list is supplied, all of the columns can be updated unless the cursor has been defined as READ ONLY.

It is important to note that the name scope for a SQL Server cursor is the connection itself. This is different from the name scope of a local variable. A second cursor with the same name as an existing cursor on the same user connection cannot be declared until the first cursor is deallocated.

Opening a Cursor

Transact-SQL does not support the passing of arguments to a cursor when it is opened, unlike PL/SQL. When a Transact-SQL cursor is opened, the result set membership and ordering are fixed. Updates and deletes that have been committed against the base tables of the cursor by other users are reflected in fetches made against all cursors defined without the INSENSITIVE option. In the case of an INSENSITIVE cursor, a temporary table is generated.

Fetching Data

Oracle cursors can move in a forward direction only—there is no backward or relative scrolling capability. SQL Server cursors can scroll forward and backward with the fetch options shown in the following table. These fetch options can be used only when the cursor is declared with the SCROLL option.

Scroll option	Description
NEXT	Returns the first row of the result set if this is the first fetch against the cursor; otherwise, it moves the cursor one row within the result set. NEXT is the primary method used to move through a result set. NEXT is the default cursor fetch.
PRIOR	Returns the previous row within the result set.
FIRST	Moves the cursor to the first row within the result set and returns the first row.
LAST	Moves the cursor to the last row within the result set and returns the last row.
ABSOLUTE n	Returns the nth row within the result set. If n is a negative value, the returned row is the nth row counting backward from the last row of the result set.
RELATIVE n	Returns the nth row after the currently fetched row. If n is a negative value, the returned row is the nth row counting backward from the relative position of the cursor.

The Transact-SQL FETCH statement does not require the INTO clause. If return variables are not specified, the row is automatically returned to the client as a single-row result set. However, if your procedure must get the rows to the client, a noncursor SELECT statement is much more efficient.

The @@FETCH_STATUS function is updated following each FETCH. It is similar in use to the CURSOR_NAME%FOUND and CURSOR_NAME%NOTFOUND variables used in PL/SQL. The @@FETCH_STATUS function is set to the value of 0 following a successful fetch. If the fetch tries to read beyond the end of the cursor, a value of –1 is returned. If the requested row has been deleted from the table after the cursor was opened, the @@FETCH_STATUS function returns –2. The value of –2 usually occurs only in a cursor declared with the SCROLL option. This variable must be checked following each fetch to ensure the validity of the data.

SQL Server does not support Oracle's cursor FOR loop syntax.

CURRENT OF Clause

The CURRENT OF clause syntax and function for updates and deletes is the same in both PL/SQL and Transact-SQL. A positioned UPDATE or DELETE is performed against the current row within the specified cursor.

Closing a Cursor

The Transact-SQL CLOSE CURSOR statement closes the cursor but leaves the data structures accessible for reopening. The PL/SQL CLOSE CURSOR statement closes and releases all data structures.

Transact-SQL requires the use of the DEALLOCATE CURSOR statement to remove the cursor data structures. The DEALLOCATE CURSOR statement is different from CLOSE CURSOR in that a closed cursor can be reopened. The DEALLOCATE CURSOR statement releases all data structures associated with the cursor and removes the definition of the cursor.

Cursor Example

The example below shows equivalent cursor statements in PL/SQL and Transact-SQL.

Oracle	Microsoft SQL Server
DECLARE	DECLARE
VSSN CHAR(9);	@VSSN CHAR(9),
VFNAME VARCHAR(12);	@VFNAME VARCHAR(12),
VLNAME VARCHAR(20);	@VLNAME VARCHAR(20)
CURSOR CUR1 IS	DECLARE cur1 CURSOR FOR
SELECT SSN, FNAME, LNAME	SELECT SSN, FNAME, LNAME
FROM STUDENT ORDER BY LNAME;	FROM STUDENT ORDER BY SSN
BEGIN	OPEN CUR1
OPEN CUR1;	FETCH NEXT FROM CUR1
FETCH CUR1 INTO VSSN, VFNAME,	INTO @VSSN, @VFNAME, @VLNAME
VLNAME;	WHILE (@@FETCH_STATUS <> -1)

continued on next page

Oracle	Microsoft SQL Server

WHILE (CUR1%FOUND) LOOP
    FETCH CUR1 INTO VSSN, VFNAME,
VLNAME;
END LOOP;
CLOSE CUR1;
END;
	BEGIN
	    FETCH NEXT FROM CUR1
	    INTO @VSSN, @VFNAME,
	@VLNAME
	    END
	CLOSE CUR1
	DEALLOCATE CUR1

For more information about cursors, see "Cursors" in SQL Server Books Online.

Tuning Transact-SQL Statements

This section provides information about several SQL Server tools you can use to tune Transact-SQL statements.

Microsoft SQL Server 2000 is a largely auto-configuring and self-tuning database server, dramatically reducing the burden of server configuration on the database administrator. In most cases, SQL Server runs best when these autotuning parameters are left at their default settings and when administrators allow SQL Server to handle the performance tuning. For the latest information about tuning your SQL Server database, see http://msdn.microsoft.com/sqlserver/.

SQL Query Analyzer

You can use the graphical showplan feature of SQL Query Analyzer to learn more about how the optimizer will process your statement.

SQL Profiler

This graphical tool captures a continuous record of server activity in real-time. SQL Profiler monitors many different server events and event categories, filters these events with user-specified criteria, and outputs a trace to the screen, a file, or another server running SQL Server.

SQL Profiler can be used to:

- Monitor the performance of SQL Server.

- Debug Transact-SQL statements and stored procedures.

- Identify slow-executing queries.

- Troubleshoot problems in SQL Server by capturing all the events that lead up to a particular problem, and then replaying the events on a test system to replicate and isolate the problem.

- Test SQL statements and stored procedures in the development phase of a project by single-stepping through statements, one line at a time, to confirm that the code works as expected.

- Capture events on a production system and replay those captured events on a test system, thereby re-creating what happened in the production environment for testing or debugging purposes. Replaying captured events on a separate system allows the users to continue using the production system without interference.

SQL Profiler provides a graphical user interface to a set of extended stored procedures. You can also use these extended stored procedures directly. Therefore, it is possible to create your own application that uses the SQL Profiler extended stored procedures to monitor SQL Server.

SET Statement

The SET statement can set SQL Server query-processing options for the duration of your work session, or for the duration of a running trigger or a stored procedure.

The SET FORCEPLAN ON statement forces the optimizer to process joins in the same order as the tables appear in the FROM clause, similar to the ORDERED hint used with the Oracle optimizer.

The SET SHOWPLAN_ALL and SET SHOWPLAN_TEXT statements return only query or statement execution plan information and do not execute the query or statement. To execute the query or statement, set the appropriate showplan statement OFF. The query or statement will then execute. The SHOWPLAN option provides results similar to the Oracle EXPLAIN PLAN tool.

With SET STATISTICS PROFILE ON, each executed query returns its regular result set, followed by an additional result set that shows a profile of the query execution. Other options include SET STATISTICS IO and SET STATISTICS TIME.

Transact-SQL statement processing consists of two phases, compilation and execution. The NOEXEC option compiles each query but does not execute it. After NOEXEC is set ON, no subsequent statements are executed (including other SET statements) until NOEXEC is set OFF.

```
SET SHOWPLAN ON
SET NOEXEC ON
go
SELECT * FROM DEPT_ADMIN.DEPT,
    STUDENT_ADMIN.STUDENT
WHERE MAJOR = DEPT
go
STEP 1
The type of query is SETON
STEP 1
The type of query is SETON
STEP 1
The type of query is SELECT
```

```
FROM TABLE
DEPT_ADMIN.DEPT
Nested iteration
Table Scan
FROM TABLE
STUDENT_ADMIN.STUDENT
Nested iteration
Table Scan
```

Query Optimization

Oracle requires the use of hints to influence the operation and performance of its cost-based optimizer. The SQL Server cost-based optimizer does not require the use of hints to assist in its query evaluation process. They are offered; however, as some situations do warrant their use.

The INDEX = {*index_name* | *index_id*} hint specifies the index name or ID to use for that table. An *index_id* of 0 forces a table scan, while an *index_id* of 1 forces the use of a clustered index, if it exists. This is similar to the index hints used in Oracle.

The SQL Server FASTFIRSTROW hint directs the optimizer to use a nonclustered index if its column order matches the ORDER BY clause. This hint operates in a similar fashion to the Oracle FIRST_ROWS hint.

Using XML

Microsoft SQL Server 2000 introduces new features to support XML functionality. Using XML, you can:

- SELECT, INSERT and UPDATE a SQL Server database.
- Use Xpath queries against XDR (XML Data Reduced schemas).
- Format the results of Transact-SQL statements in XML using FOR XML.

For more information about SQL Server XML support, see Chapter 31, "Exposing SQL Server Data to the Web with XML" in this book and "XML and Internet Support Overview" in SQL Server Books Online. You can also search the MSDN® Library for the articles "Duwamish Online SQL Server XML Catalog Browsing" and "SQL Server XML and Web Application Architecture" at http://msdn.microsoft.com/xml/.

Using ODBC

This section provides information about the ways Oracle and SQL Server use ODBC and information about developing or migrating applications with ODBC.

Recommended Conversion Strategy

Use the following process when you convert your application code from Oracle to SQL Server:

1. Consider converting your application to ODBC if it is written using Oracle Pro*C or the Oracle Call Interface (OCI).

2. Understand SQL Server default result sets and cursor options, and choose the fetching strategy that is most efficient for your application.

3. Remap Oracle ODBC SQL data types to SQL Server ODBC SQL data types where appropriate.

4. Use the ODBC Extended SQL extensions to create generic SQL statements.

5. Determine if manual commit mode is required for the SQL Server–based application.

6. Test the performance of your application(s) and modify the program(s) as necessary.

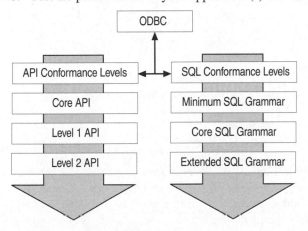

ODBC Architecture

Microsoft provides both 16-bit and 32-bit versions of its ODBC SQL Server driver. The 32-bit ODBC SQL Server driver is thread-safe. The driver serializes shared access by multiple threads to shared statement handles (hstmt), connection handles (hdbc), and environment handles (henv). However, the ODBC program is still responsible for keeping operations within statements and connection spaces in the proper sequence, even when the program uses multiple threads.

Because the ODBC driver for Oracle can be supplied by one of many possible vendors, there are many possible scenarios regarding architecture and operation. You must contact the vendor to ensure that the ODBC driver meets your application's requirements.

In most cases, the ODBC driver for Oracle uses SQL*Net to connect to the Oracle RDBMS. SQL*Net may not be used, however, when connecting to Personal Oracle.

The illustration shows the application/driver architecture for 32-bit environments.

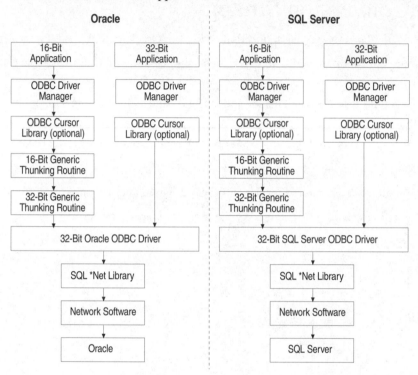

The term *thunking* means intercepting a function call, doing a special processing to translate between 16-bit and 32-bit code, and then transferring control to a target function. The ODBC Cursor Library optionally resides between the driver manager and its driver. This library provides scrollable cursor services on top of drivers that support only forward-only cursors.

Forward-Only Cursors

Oracle and SQL Server treat result sets and cursors differently. Understanding these differences is essential for successfully moving a client application from Oracle to SQL Server and having it perform optimally.

In Oracle, any result set from a SELECT command is treated as a forward-only cursor when fetched in the client application. This is true whether you are using ODBC, OCI, or Embedded SQL as your development tool.

By default, each Oracle FETCH command issued by the client program (for example, **SQLFetch** in ODBC) causes a round-trip across the network to the server to return one row. If a client application wants to fetch more than one row at a time across the network, it must set up an array in its program and perform an array fetch.

Between fetches, no locks are held at the server for a read-only cursor because of Oracle's multiversioning concurrency model. When the program specifies an updatable cursor with the FOR UPDATE clause, all of the requested rows in the SELECT command are locked when the statement is opened. These row-level locks remain in place until the program issues a COMMIT or ROLLBACK request.

In SQL Server, a SELECT statement is not always associated with a cursor at the server. By default, SQL Server simply streams all the result set rows from a SELECT statement back to the client. This streaming starts as soon as the SELECT is executed. Result set streams can also be returned by SELECT statements within stored procedures. Additionally, a single stored procedure or batch of commands can stream back multiple result sets in response to a single EXECUTE statement.

The SQL Server client is responsible for fetching these default result sets as soon as they are available. For default result sets, fetches at the client do not result in round-trips to the server. Instead, fetches from a default result set pull data from local network buffers into program variables. This default result set model creates an efficient mechanism to return multiple rows of data to the client in a single round-trip across this network. Minimizing network round-trips is usually the most important factor in client/server application performance.

Compared to Oracle's cursors, default result sets put some additional responsibilities on the SQL Server client application. The SQL Server client application must immediately fetch all the result set rows returned by an EXECUTE statement. If the application needs to present rows incrementally to other parts of the program, it must buffer the rows to an internal array. If it fails to fetch all result set rows, the connection to SQL Server remains busy.

If this occurs, no other work (such as UPDATE statements) can be executed on that connection until the entire result set rows are fetched or the client cancels the request. Moreover, the server continues to hold share locks on table data pages until the fetch has completed. The fact that these share locks are held until a fetch is complete make it mandatory that you fetch all rows as quickly as possible. This technique is in direct contrast to the incremental style of fetch that is commonly found in Oracle applications.

Server Cursors

Microsoft SQL Server offers *server cursors* to address the need for incremental fetching of result sets across the network. Server cursors can be requested in an application by simply calling **SQLSetStmtOption** to set the SQL_CURSOR_TYPE option.

When a SELECT statement is executed as a server cursor, only a cursor identifier is returned by the EXECUTE statement. Subsequent fetch requests pass the cursor identifier back to the server along with a parameter specifying the number of rows to fetch at once. The server returns the number of rows requested.

Between fetch requests, the connection remains free to issue other commands, including other cursor OPEN or FETCH requests. In ODBC terms, this means that server cursors allow the SQL Server driver to support multiple active statements on a single connection.

Furthermore, server cursors do not usually hold locks between fetch requests, so you are free to pause between fetches for user input without affecting other users. Server cursors can be updated in place using either optimistic conflict detection or pessimistic scroll locking concurrency options.

Although these features make programming with server cursors more familiar to Oracle developers than using default result sets, they are not free. Compared to default result sets:

- Server cursors are more expensive in terms of server resources, because temporary storage space is used to maintain cursor state information at the server.

- Server cursors are more expensive to retrieve a given result set of data with, because the EXECUTE statement and each fetch request in a server cursor requires a separate round-trip to the server.

- Server cursors are less flexible in terms of the kind of batches and stored procedures they support. This is because a server cursor can execute only one SELECT statement at a time, whereas default result sets can be used for batches and stored procedures that return multiple result sets or include statements other than SELECT statements.

For these reasons, it is recommended that you limit the use of server cursors to those parts of your application that need their features.

Scrollable Cursors

The Oracle RDBMS supports only forward-scrolling cursors. Each row is fetched to the application in the order that it was specified in the query. Oracle does not accept requests to move backward to a previously fetched row. The only way to move backward is to close the cursor and reopen it. Unfortunately, you are repositioned back to the first row in the active query set.

Because SQL Server supports scrollable cursors, you can position a SQL Server cursor at any row location. You can scroll both forward and backward. For many applications involving a user interface, scrollability is a useful feature. With scrollable cursors, your application can fetch a screen full of rows at a time, and only fetch additional rows as the user asks for them.

Although Oracle does not directly support scrollable cursors, this limitation can be minimized by using one of several ODBC options. For example, some Oracle ODBC drivers, such as the one that ships with the Microsoft Developer Studio® visual development system, offer client-based scrollable cursors in the driver itself.

Alternatively, the ODBC Cursor Library supports block scrollable cursors for any ODBC driver that complies with the Level One conformance level. Both of these client cursor options support scrolling by using the RDBMS for forward-only fetching, and by caching result set data in memory or on disk. When data is requested, the driver retrieves it from the RDBMS or its local cache as needed.

Client-based cursors also support positioned UPDATE and DELETE statements for the result sets generated by SELECT statements. The cursor library constructs an UPDATE or DELETE statement with a WHERE clause that specifies the cached value for each column in a row.

If you need scrollable cursors and are trying to maintain the same source code for both Oracle and SQL Server implementations, the ODBC Cursor Library is a useful option. For more information about the ODBC Cursor Library, see your ODBC documentation.

Strategies for Using SQL Server Default Result Sets and Server Cursors

With all of the options that SQL Server offers for fetching data, it is sometimes difficult to decide what to use and when. Here are some useful guidelines:

- Default result sets are always the fastest way to get an entire set of data from SQL Server to the client. Look for opportunities in your application where you can use this to your advantage. Batch report generation, for example, generally processes an entire result set to completion, with no user interaction and no updates in the middle of processing.

- If your program requires updatable cursors, use server cursors. Default result sets are never updatable when using positioned UPDATE or DELETE statements. Additionally, server cursors are better at updating than client-based cursors, which have to simulate a positioned UPDATE or DELETE by constructing an equivalent searched UPDATE or DELETE statement.

- If your program needs scrollable, read-only cursors, both the ODBC Cursor Library and server cursors are good choices. The ODBC Cursor Library gives you compatible behavior across SQL Server and Oracle, and server cursors give you more flexibility as to how much data to fetch across the network at one time.

- When you use default result sets or ODBC Cursor Library cursors built on top of default result sets, be sure to fetch to the end of a result set as quickly as possible to avoid holding share locks at the server.

- When you use server cursors, be sure to use **SQLExtendedFetch** to fetch in blocks of rows rather than a single row at a time. This is the same as array-type fetching in Oracle applications. Every fetch request on a server cursor requires a round-trip from the application to the RDBMS on the network.

- Shopping provides an analogy. Assume you purchase several bags of goods, load one bag into your car, drive home, drop it off, and return for the next bag. This is an unlikely scenario, but this is what you do to SQL Server and your program by making single-row fetches from a server cursor.

- If your program requires only forward-only, read-only cursors but depends on multiple open cursors on the same connection, use default result sets when you know you can fetch the entire result set immediately into program variables. Use server cursors when you do not know if you can fetch all of the rows immediately.

This strategy is not as difficult as it sounds. Most programmers know when they are issuing a singleton select that can return a maximum of one row. For singleton fetches, using a default result set is more efficient than using a server cursor.

For more information about cursor implementations, see SQL Server Books Online.

Multiple Active Statements (hstmt) per Connection

The ODBC driver uses a statement handle (hstmt) to track each active SQL statement within the program. The statement handle is always associated with a RDBMS connection handle (hdbc). The ODBC driver manager uses the connection handle to send the requested SQL statement to the specified RDBMS. Most ODBC drivers for Oracle allow multiple statement handles per connection. However, the SQL Server ODBC driver allows only one active statement handle per connection when using default result sets. The **SQLGetInfo** function of this SQL Server driver returns the value 1 when queried with the SQL_ACTIVE_STATEMENTS option. When statement options are set in a way that uses server cursors, multiple active statements per connection handle are supported.

For more information about setting statement options to request server cursors, see SQL Server Books Online.

Data Type Mappings

The SQL Server ODBC driver offers a richer set of data type mappings than most available Oracle ODBC drivers.

Microsoft SQL Server data type	ODBC SQL data type
binary	SQL_BINARY
bit	SQL_BIT
char, character	SQL_CHAR
datetime	SQL_TIMESTAMP
decimal, dec	SQL_DECIMAL
float, double precision, float(n) for n = 8-15	SQL_FLOAT
image	SQL_LONGVARBINARY
int, integer	SQL_INTEGER

continued on next page

Microsoft SQL Server data type	ODBC SQL data type
money	SQL_DECIMAL
nchar	SQL_WCHAR
ntext	SQL_WLONGVARCHAR
numeric	SQL_NUMERIC
nvarchar	SQL_WVARCHAR
real, float(n) for n = 1-7	SQL_REAL
smalldatetime	SQL_TIMESTAMP
smallint	SQL_SMALLINT
smallmoney	SQL_DECIMAL
sysname	SQL_VARCHAR
text	SQL_LONGVARCHAR
timestamp	SQL_BINARY
tinyint	SQL_TINYINT
uniqueidentifier	SQL_GUID
varbinary	SQL_VARBINARY
varchar	SQL_VARCHAR

The **timestamp** data type is converted to the SQL_BINARY data type. This is because the values in **timestamp** columns are not **datetime** data, but rather **binary(8)** data. They are used to indicate the sequence of SQL Server activity on the row.

The Oracle data type mappings for the SQL Server ODBC driver for Oracle are shown in this table.

Oracle data type	ODBC SQL data type
CHAR	SQL_CHAR
DATE	SQL_TIMESTAMP
LONG	SQL_LONGVARCHAR
LONG RAW	SQL_LONGVARBINARY
NUMBER	SQL_FLOAT
NUMBER(P)	SQL_DECIMAL

continued on next page

Oracle data type	ODBC SQL data type
NUMBER(P,S)	SQL_DECIMAL
RAW	SQL_BINARY
VARCHAR2	SQL_VARCHAR

Oracle ODBC drivers from other vendors can have alternative data type mappings.

ODBC Extended SQL

The ODBC Extended SQL standard provides SQL extensions to ODBC that support the advanced nonstandard SQL feature set offered in both Oracle and SQL Server. This standard allows the ODBC driver to convert generic SQL statements to Oracle- and SQL Server–native SQL syntax.

This standard addresses outer joins, such as predicate escape characters, scalar functions, date/time/timestamp values, and stored programs. This syntax is used to identify these extensions:

```
--(*vendor(Microsoft), product(ODBC) extension *)--
OR
{extension}
```

The conversion takes place at run time and does not require the revision of any program code. In most application development scenarios, the best approach is to write one program and allow ODBC to perform the RDBMS conversion process when the program is run.

Outer Joins

Oracle and SQL Server do not have compatible outer join syntax. This can be resolved by using the ODBC extended SQL outer join syntax. The Microsoft SQL Server syntax is the same as the ODBC Extended SQL/SQL-92 syntax. The only difference is the {oj   } container.

ODBC Extended SQL and SQL-92	Oracle	Microsoft SQL Server
SELECT STUDENT.SSN, FNAME, LNAME, CCODE, GRADE FROM {oj STUDENT LEFT OUTER JOIN GRADE ON STUDENT.SSN = GRADE.SSN}	SELECT STUDENT.SSN, FNAME, LNAME, CCODE, GRADE FROM STUDENT, GRADE WHERE STUDENT.SSN = GRADE.SSN(+)	SELECT STUDENT.SSN, FNAME, LNAME, CCODE, GRADE FROM STUDENT LEFT OUTER JOIN GRADE ON STUDENT.SSN = GRADE.SSN

Date, Time, and Timestamp Values

ODBC provides three escape clauses for date, time, and timestamp values.

Category	Shorthand syntax	Format
Date	{d 'value'}	"yyyy-mm-dd"
Time	{t 'value'}	"hh:mm:ss"
Timestamp	{Ts 'value'}	"yyyy-mm-dd hh:mm:ss[.f…]"

The format of dates has more of an impact on Oracle applications than on SQL Server–based applications. Oracle expects the date format to be "DD-MON-YY". In any other case, the TO_CHAR or TO_DATE functions are used with a date format model to perform a format conversion.

Microsoft SQL Server automatically converts most common date formats, and also provides the CONVERT function when an automatic conversion cannot be performed.

As shown in the table, ODBC Extended SQL works with both databases. SQL Server does not require a conversion function. Nevertheless, the ODBC shorthand syntax can be generically applied to both Oracle and SQL Server.

ODBC Extended SQL	Oracle	Microsoft SQL Server
SELECT SSN, FNAME, LNAME, BIRTH_DATE FROM STUDENT WHERE BIRTH_DATE < {D '1970-07-04'}	SELECT SSN, FNAME, LNAME, BIRTH_DATE FROM STUDENT WHERE BIRTH_DATE < **TO_DATE**('1970-07-04', **'YYYY-MM-DD'**)	SELECT SSN, FNAME, LNAME, BIRTH_DATE FROM STUDENT WHERE BIRTH_DATE < '1970-07-04'

Calling Stored Procedures

The ODBC shorthand syntax for calling stored programs supports Microsoft SQL Server stored procedures, and Oracle stored procedures, functions, and packages. The optional "?=" captures the return value for an Oracle function or a SQL Server procedure. The parameter syntax is used to pass and return values to and from the called program. In most situations, the same syntax can be generically applied to Oracle- and SQL Server–based applications.

In the following example, the SHOW_RELUCTANT_STUDENTS function is part of the Oracle package P1. This function must exist in a package because it returns multiple rows from a PL/SQL cursor. When you call a function or procedure that exists in a package, the package name must be placed in front of the program name.

The SHOW_RELUCTANT_STUDENTS function in the package P1 uses a package cursor to retrieve multiple rows of data. Each row must be requested with a call to this function. If there are no more rows to retrieve, the function returns the value of 0, indicating that there are no more rows to retrieve. The resulting performance of this sample Oracle package and its function might be less than satisfactory. In this example, the SQL Server procedure is more efficient.

Generic ODBC Extended SQL	Oracle	Microsoft SQL Server
{?=} call *procedure_name*[(*parameter(s)*)]} SQLExecDirect(hstmt1,(SQLCHAR *)"{? = call *owner.procedure*(?)}", SQL_NTS);	SQLExecDirect(hstmt1, (SQLCHAR*)"{? = call **STUDENT_ADMIN.P1. SHOW_RELUCTANT _STUDENTS(?)}"**, SQL_NTS);	SQLExecDirect(hstmt1, (SQLCHAR*)"{? = call **STUDENT_ADMIN. SHOW_RELUCTANT _STUDENTS}"**, SQL_NTS);

Native SQL Translation

Because of the variety of ODBC drivers for both Oracle and SQL Server, you may not always get the same conversion string for the extended SQL functions. To assist with application debugging issues, you might want to consider using the **SQLNativeSql** function. This function returns the SQL string as translated by the driver.

The following are possible results for the following input SQL string that contains the scalar function CONVERT. The column **SSN** is defined as the type CHAR(9), and is converted to a numeric value.

Original statement	Converted Oracle statement	Converted SQL Server statement
SELECT (**fn CONVERT (SSN, SQL_INTEGER))** FROM STUDENT	SELECT **TO_NUMBER(SSN)** FROM STUDENT	SELECT **CONVERT(INT,SSN)** FROM STUDENT

Manual Commit Mode

Oracle automatically enters the transaction mode whenever a user modifies data. This must be followed by an explicit COMMIT to write the changes to the database. If a user wants to undo the changes, the user can issue the ROLLBACK statement.

By default, SQL Server automatically commits each change as it occurs. This is called autocommit mode in ODBC. If you do not want this to occur, you can use the BEGIN TRANSACTION statement to signal the start of a block of statements comprising a transaction. After this statement is issued, it is followed by an explicit COMMIT TRANSACTION or ROLLBACK TRANSACTION statement.

To ensure compatibility with your Oracle application, it is recommended that you use the **SQLConnectOption** function to place your SQL Server–based application in implicit transaction mode.

The SQL_AUTOCOMMIT option must be set to SQL_AUTOCOMMIT_OFF in order to accomplish this. This code excerpt demonstrates this concept:

```
SQLSetConnectOption(hdbc1, SQL_AUTOCOMMIT,-sql_AUTOCOMMIT_OFF);
```

The SQL_AUTOCOMMIT_OFF option instructs the driver to use implicit transactions. The default option SQL_AUTOCOMMIT_ON instructs the driver to use autocommit mode, in which each statement is committed immediately after it is executed. Changing from manual commit mode to autocommit mode commits any open transactions on the connection.

If the SQL_AUTOCOMMIT_OFF option is set, the application must commit or roll back transactions explicitly with the **SQLTransact** function. This function requests a commit or rollback operation for all active operations on all statement handles associated with a connection handle. It can also request that a commit or rollback operation be performed for all connections associated with the environment handle.

```
SQLTransact(henv1, hdbc1, SQL_ROLLBACK);
(SQLTransact(henv1, hdbc1, SQL_COMMIT);
```

When autocommit mode is off, the driver issues SET IMPLICIT_TRANSACTIONS ON statement to the server. Starting with SQL Server 6.5, DDL statements are supported in this mode.

To commit or roll back a transaction in manual commit mode, the application must call **SQLTransact**. The SQL Server driver sends a COMMIT TRANSACTION statement to commit a transaction, and a ROLLBACK TRANSACTION statement to roll back a transaction.

Be aware that manual commit mode can adversely affect the performance of your SQL Server–based application. Every commit request requires a separate round-trip to the server to send the COMMIT TRANSACTION string.

If you have single atomic transactions (a single INSERT, UPDATE, or DELETE immediately followed by a COMMIT), use the autocommit mode.

Developing and Administering Database Replication

This section explains the differences between Oracle and Microsoft SQL Server replication support.

Oracle	Microsoft SQL Server
Read-Only Snapshot Replication	Snapshot with immediate updating subscribers
Multimaster Replication, Updatable snapshot	Transactional replication with immediate updating subscribers—better for well-connected subscribers who are online when updating.
	Merge Replication—better for mobile disconnected. This supports default and custom conflict resolution.

As its name implies, SQL Server snapshot replication takes a picture, or snapshot, of the published data in the database at a moment in time. Snapshot replication requires less constant processor overhead than transactional replication because it does not require continuous monitoring of data changes on source servers. Instead of copying INSERT, UPDATE, and DELETE statements (characteristic of transactional replication), or data modifications (characteristic of merge replication), Subscribers are updated by a total refresh of the data set. Hence, snapshot replication sends all the data to the Subscriber instead of sending only the changes.

SQL Server also offers transactional replication, a type of replication that marks selected transactions in the Publisher's database transaction log for replication and then distributes them asynchronously to Subscribers as incremental changes, while maintaining transactional consistency.

SQL Server merge replication allows sites to make autonomous changes to replicated data, and at a later time, merge changes made at all sites. Like Oracle, merge replication supports both column-level and row-level conflict detection. That is, you can define a conflict to be any change to the same row at two locations, or only when changes to the same column(s) at two locations.

SQL Server offers heterogeneous replication, which is the simplest way to publish data to a heterogeneous Subscriber by using ODBC or OLE/DB and creating a push subscription from the Publisher to the ODBC Subscriber. As an alternative, however, you can create a publication and then create an application with an embedded distribution control. The embedded control implements the pull subscription from the Subscriber to the Publisher. For ODBC Subscribers, the subscribing database has no administrative capabilities regarding the replication being performed.

The table compares conflict-resolution mechanisms for Oracle and SQL Server:

Oracle	Microsoft SQL Server
Site priority or priority value resolvers programmed using PL/SQL	Priority-based resolution using COM or Transact-SQL.
Conflict resolution for column groups	Supported through custom resolvers.
Column-level and row-level conflict resolution	Support for both.

ODBC, OLE/DB, and Replication

With Microsoft SQL Server, a distribution server connects to all subscription servers as an ODBC or OLE/DB client. Replication requires that the ODBC 32-bit driver be installed on all distribution servers. The SQL Server Setup program automatically installs the necessary driver on Windows 2000–based computers.

You do not have to preconfigure ODBC Data Sources for SQL Server subscription servers because the distribution process simply uses the subscriber's network name to establish the connection.

SQL Server also includes an ODBC driver that supports Oracle subscriptions to SQL Server. The driver exists only for Intel-based computers. To replicate to Oracle ODBC subscribers, you must also obtain the appropriate Oracle SQL*Net driver from Oracle or from your software vendor.

If a password is provided in the Windows registry, the Oracle ODBC driver connects to Oracle without requesting a password. If a password is not provided in the Windows registry, you must enter a username and a password for the Oracle ODBC data source when specifying the DSN in the **New ODBC Subscriber** dialog box of SQL Server Enterprise Manager.

The following restrictions apply when replicating to an Oracle ODBC subscriber:

- The **datetime** data type is mapped to DATE. The range for the Oracle DATE data type is between 4712 B.C. and 4712 A.D. If you are replicating to Oracle, verify that SQL Server **datetime** entries in a replicated column are within this range.

- A replicated table can have only one **text** or **image** column.

- The **datetime** data type is mapped to the Oracle CHAR data type .

- The SQL Server ranges for **float** and **real** data types are different from the Oracle ranges.

Drivers for other ODBC subscriber types must conform to the SQL Server replication requirements for generic ODBC subscribers. The ODBC driver:

- Must be ODBC Level 1 compliant.

- Must be 32-bit and thread-safe for the processor architecture that the distribution process runs on.

- Must be transaction capable.

- Must support the data definition language (DDL).

- Cannot be read-only.

Migrating Your Data and Applications

This section presents various methods for migrating data from an Oracle database to a Microsoft SQL Server database.

Data Migration Using DTS

The simplest method of migrating between Oracle and SQL Server is to use the Data Transformation Services (DTS) feature in Microsoft SQL Server 2000. The DTS Import/Export Wizard guides you through moving the data to SQL Server.

Oracle Call Interface (OCI)

If you have applications that were written by using the Oracle Call Interface (OCI), you may want to consider rewriting them by using ODBC. The OCI is specific to the Oracle RDBMS and cannot be used with Microsoft SQL Server or any other database.

In most cases, you can replace OCI functions with the appropriate ODBC functions, followed by relevant changes to the supporting program code. The remaining non-OCI program code should require minimal modification. The example shows a comparison of the OCI and ODBC statements required for establishing a connection to an Oracle database.

Oracle Call Interface	Oracle ODBC
rcl = olog(&logon_data_area, &host_data_area, user_name, -1, (text*) 0, -1, (text) 0, -1, OCI_LM_DEF);	rcl = SQLConnect(hdbc1, (SQLCHAR*) ODBC_dsn, (SQLSMALLINT) SQL_NTS, (SQLCHAR*) user_name, (SQLSMALLINT) SQL_NTS, (SQLCHAR*) user_password, (SQLSMALLINT) SQL_NTS);

The table suggests conversions between Oracle OCI function calls and ODBC functions. These suggested conversions are approximate. There may not be an exact match in the conversion process. Your program code might require additional revision to obtain similar functionality.

OCI function	ODBC function
Obindps	**SQLBindParameter**
Obndra	**SQLBindParameter**
Obndrn	**SQLBindParameter**
Obndrv	**SQLBindParameter**
Obreak	**SQLCancel**
Ocan	**SQLCancel, SQLFreeStmt**
Oclose	**SQLFreeStmt**
Ocof	**SQLSetConnectOption**
Ocom	**SQLTransact**
Ocon	**SQLSetConnectOption**
Odefin	**SQLBindCol**

continued on next page

OCI function	ODBC function
Odefinps	**SQLBindCol**
Odescr	**SQLDescribeCol**
Oerhms	**SQLError**
Oexec	**SQLExecute, SQLExecDirect**
Oexfet	**SQLExecute, SQLExecDirect, and SQLFetch**
Oexn	**SQLExecute, SQLExecDirect**
Ofen	**SQLExtendedFetch**
Ofetch	**SQLFetch**
Oflng	**SQLGetData**
Ogetpi	**SQLGetData**
Olog	**SQLConnect**
Ologof	**SQLDisconnect**
Oopen	**SQLExecute, SQLExecDirect**
Oparse	**SQLPrepare**
Orol	**SQLTransact**

Embedded SQL

Many applications are written using the Oracle Programmatic Interfaces (Pro*C, Pro*Cobol, and so on). These interfaces support the use of SQL-92 standard embedded SQL. They also include nonstandard Oracle programmatic extensions.

Oracle embedded SQL applications can be migrated to SQL Server by using the Microsoft Embedded SQL (ESQL) for C development environment. This environment provides adequate, but less than optimal, control over the performance and the use of SQL Server features compared to an ODBC application.

Some of the Oracle Pro*C features are not supported in Microsoft's ESQL precompiler. If your Oracle application makes extensive use of these features, a rewrite to ODBC is probably a better migration choice. These features include:

- Host array variables.

- VAR and TYPE statements for data type equivalencing.

- Support for embedded SQL in Microsoft Visual C++® modules.

- Support for embedded PL/SQL or Transact-SQL blocks.

- Cursor variables.

- Multithreaded application support.

- Support for the Oracle Communication Area (ORACA).

If your Oracle application has been developed in Cobol, it can be moved to Embedded SQL for Cobol from Micro Focus. You may run into some of the same limitations in Cobol as with the Microsoft ESQL for C precompiler.

You can convert your Oracle embedded SQL application to the ODBC environment. This migration process is quite easy and offers many advantages. ODBC does not require the use of a precompiler, as does embedded SQL. Consequently, much of the overhead associated with program development is eliminated.

The table shows the approximate relationship between Embedded SQL statements and ODBC functions.

Embedded SQL statement	ODBC function
CONNECT	SQLConnect
PREPARE	SQLPrepare
EXECUTE	SQLExecute
DECLARE CURSOR and OPEN CURSOR	SQLExecute
EXECUTE IMMEDIATE	SQLExecDirect
DESCRIBE SELECT LIST	SQLNumResultCols, SQLColAttributes, SQLDescribeCol
FETCH	SQLFetch
SQLCA.SQLERRD[2]	SQLRowCount
CLOSE	SQLFreeStmt
COMMIT WORK, ROLLBACK WORK	SQLTransact
COMMIT WORK RELEASE, ROLLBACK WORK RELEASE	SQLDisconnect
SQLCA, SQLSTATE	SQLError
ALTER, CREATE, DROP, GRANT, REVOKE	SQLExecute, SQLExecDirect

The most significant change, when converting embedded SQL programs to ODBC, involves the handling of SQL statement errors. The MODE = ORACLE option is often used when developing embedded SQL programs. When this option is used, the SQL Communications Area (SQLCA) is typically used for error handling operations.

The SQLCA structure provides:

- Oracle error codes.

- Oracle error messages.

- Warning flags.

- Information regarding program events.

- The number of rows processed by the most recent SQL statement.

In most cases, you should check the value in the **sqlca.sqlcode** variable following the execution of each SQL statement. If the value is less than zero, an error has occurred. If the value is greater than zero, the requested statement executed with warnings. The Oracle error message text can be retrieved from the **sqlca.sqlerrm.sqlerrmc** variable.

In ODBC, a function returns a numeric status code that indicates its success or failure following the requested operation. The status codes are defined as string literals, and include SQL_SUCCESS, SQL_SUCCESS_WITH_INFO, SQL_NEED_DATA, SQL_ERROR, and others. It is your responsibility to check these return values following each function call.

An associated SQLSTATE value can be obtained by calling the **SQLError** function. This function returns the SQLSTATE error code, the native error code (specific to the data source), and the error message text.

An application typically calls this function when a previous call to an ODBC function returns SQL_ERROR or SQL_SUCCESS_WITH_INFO. However, any ODBC function can post zero or more errors each time it is called, so an application may call **SQLError** after every ODBC function call.

Here are examples of error handling for each environment.

Oracle Pro*C and EMBEDDED SQL	Oracle ODBC
EXEC SQL DECLARE CURSOR C1 CURSOR FOR SELECT SSN, FNAME, LNAME FROM STUDENT ORDER BY SSN; EXEC SQL OPEN C1; if (sqlca.sqlcode) != 0 { /* handle error condition, look at sqlca.sqlerrm.sqlerrmc for error description...*/}	if (SQLExecDirect(hstmtl, (SQLCHAR*)"SELECT SSN, FNAME, LNAME FROM STUDENT ORDER BY SSN", SQL_NTS) != SQL_SUCCESS) { /* handle error condition, use SQLError for SQLSTATE details regarding error...*/}

Developer 2000 and Third-Party Applications

If you have developed an application using Oracle Developer 2000 and want to use it with SQL Server, consider converting it to Microsoft Visual Basic®. Visual Basic is a powerful development system that works well with both databases. You might also consider other development tools in the Microsoft Visual Studio® development system, or PowerBuilder, SQL Windows, and others.

If you are unable to immediately migrate from Developer 2000, consider the Oracle Gateway to SQL Server. It can be used as an intermediate step when migrating from Oracle to SQL Server. This gateway allows the Oracle RDBMS to connect to SQL Server. All requests for SQL Server data are automatically translated by the gateway. From the perspective of the Developer 2000 application, this connection is transparent. SQL Server data appears as Oracle data. Very few changes need to be made to the application program code.

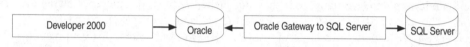

Another intermediate step is to use the Developer 2000 application directly with SQL Server. Developer 2000 can directly access SQL Server using the Oracle Open Client Adapter (OCA). The OCA is ODBC Level 1 compliant and has limited support for ODBC Level 2 functions.

The OCA establishes a connection with the SQL Server ODBC driver. When connecting the Developer 2000 tools to SQL Server, you must specify an ODBC data source name as part of the database connection string. When you exit the Developer 2000 application, the OCA connection to the ODBC data source is disconnected.

The syntax for the logon connect string is demonstrated in the following example. In this example, the user logs on to the SQL Server **STUDENT_ADMIN** account. The name of the SQL Server ODBC data source is **STUDENT_DATA**:

```
STUDENT_ADMIN/STUDENT_ADMIN@ODBC:STUDENT_DATA
```

Using an ODBC driver does not ensure that a Developer 2000 application will work correctly with SQL Server. The application program code must be modified to work with a non-Oracle data source. For example, the column security property is Oracle-specific and does not work with SQL Server.

You must change the key mode that is used to identify each row of data. When using Oracle as the data source, a ROWID is used to identify each row. When using SQL Server, you must work with unique primary key values to ensure unique row values.

The locking mode also must be changed. When using Oracle, Developer 2000 attempts to lock a row of data immediately following any change to that row. When using SQL Server, the locking mode should be set to delayed so that the record is locked only when it is written to the database.

They are many other issues that must be resolved, including the potential for a deadlock situation if multiple inserts on a table access the same page of data in a PL/SQL program block. For more information, see "Transactions, Locking, and Concurrency" earlier in this chapter.

Internet Applications

Microsoft SQL Server includes the Web Assistant Wizard, which generates standard HTML files from SQL Server data. The wizard can configure your Web page so that it is static, updated periodically, or updated when the data is updated. A wizard walks you through the process of creating the Web page.

Database Administration

Managing Database Change

Describing best practices for handling database changes from the earliest development stage, through the quality assurance (QA) check stage, and finally to implementation in the production environment, this chapter gives practical advice for Database Administrators (DBAs) on handling issues that arise when supporting a 24 x 7 operation where database implementations must not be a point of failure.

Preparing for a Changing Environment

Although many companies already have processes in place that deal with information systems change management, some frequently have uncontrolled development environments, little or no QA formalities, and impromptu production implementations. In the development environment, the need for a controlled process is evident in situations where the constant changing of objects or code disrupts ongoing work. In the QA environment, the need becomes evident when testers are uncertain what version of the code they have and whether it has changed since they began testing. In the operations environment, the lack of a controlled change process is perhaps the highest risk of all, because when a disruption of production service occurs, the result may be financial loss for the company.

So how does your information systems environment measure up? Can you tell what changes were made last month, or what changes were made on a certain project? Can you provide information on when and why a change was made, and who authorized it, tested it, or implemented it?

As your company grows, you will likely need more formal processes for dealing with changes, especially in regard to changes made to the database. The management process described in this chapter will help you gain control over the process of change to the database servers, and ultimately this will benefit both you and your company.

Conflicting Goals

The development cycle begins with planning in the development group and ends with the support of the finished system by the operations group. The development group has different goals and priorities than the operations group. When changes are planned for the database server, the Database Administrator essentially has to mediate between these two groups, balancing the needs of all parties involved.

Operations Goals

Among the primary goals of the operations group is stability and availability. Its responsibility is to resist changes that may have a negative impact. This includes any new system, or change to a current system, which would represent an unknown process, or which could be identified as raising known issues in the production environment. Without the ability to identify exactly what changed when and for what purpose, operations staff face repeated "fire-fighting" issues. Accomplishing the goal of stability requires control, measurement, and up-to-date support information for all systems. Appropriate operations staff should have input into system design and must be informed of any system changes in a timely manner.

Development Goals

The main goal of most development groups is to provide flexibility and constant improvement in response to user needs. This is an area of rapid design and change. The developers need freedom to work, yet they also require a stable environment and some isolation from other ongoing development. They should be able to verify the effect other development projects may have on their work, to identify potential design problems before they reach production.

Database Administrator Goals

The goal of the DBA is to be responsive to both environments, balancing fast action with cautious evaluation. How can this be done most effectively? While there is certainly more than one approach, the guidelines presented here may help answer this question.

It is important to decide on a level of control that is both supportable by your group and required by your business, in relation to the size of your Information Systems (IS) department, the number of ongoing development projects, and the number of production systems that must be maintained. While the need for control tends to be driven by the operations group, the need for a stable process tends to come from the developers as their numbers grow. The process must actually begin at the source of change: So, for a development project, it must begin with the development group.

In many ways, contributing to change control is part of the responsibility of the DBA. The primary role of the DBA is to protect the integrity of the data, both as an asset in itself and as private information accessible only to authorized personnel. A stable, successful production database environment exists only with appropriate change management, characterized by controlled, tested, and documented releases.

Managing the Development Environment

In an ideal environment, all databases would be designed and implemented by a cohesive team of DBAs with impressive development skills and years of production support experience. In the real business environment, this work is usually done by a disparate group of people with a wide variety of project priorities, skill levels, and personal development styles. The logistics of coordinating development of database objects by a large disjointed group can become enormously challenging to the DBA, who is responsible for supporting the resulting database in production. But when the operations group makes a call because of a problem on the database server, it will be the DBA's phone, not the one belonging to the developer, that rings. Therefore, this should become a priority: to understand and control (document, test, protect) all database changes, whether they are made to the stored procedure or function code, the physical database structures, the data, or the storage components upon which everything rests.

As you take steps toward conforming to a change control process, you will need to make decisions and develop standards based on the following considerations:

- How will you duplicate and refresh data in the development environment?

- What is the best development environment you can provide?

- How will you track changes made in association with various development projects?

- How will you review and test the changes?

- How will you implement the changes?

- How will the new system or change be supported in production?

Development Database Process

Often by the time a DBA is included in project meetings, the project team is no longer considering actual design, but simply how to implement the solution they came up with. This is unfortunate, because for the development DBA, understanding why the design is set in a certain way can reveal alternate, better solutions. Occasionally, you will also discover that a team is trying to reinvent a process that is already in place and available to them. It is also important during the design phase to involve a representative from operations, who may have important information on standards or requirements from an infrastructure standpoint. Clearly, open communication is key.

A database is only as good as the code written against it, and it is the responsibility of the DBA to facilitate that process. Ongoing communication between team members is vital to success, and can be encouraged by the following means:

- Daily or regularly recurring brief triage meetings within each role group, or within all roles working on a specific system, that give updates on key or time-critical system and business issues and the action needed

- Regular status reports in a format that is easy to distribute and read (e-mail, for example), delivered to IT management and the business community on key performance indicators for operations (for example, metrics against service level agreement, help desk log statistics, progress toward division goals, and so on)

As database technology progresses, it is becoming more focused on work that was once considered design or development related. One good way to foster skills in the new areas of Microsoft® SQL Server™ 2000 is to become more involved in development projects.

Control: Helping or Hindering?

An effective development environment requires a significant amount of control and monitoring of the development database. This is not to say that you should restrict the developers from being able to do their work, but that you are protecting the integrity of the database design while providing a safe environment for all the developers to work together. When you first implement a controlled change process in the development environment, it is a good idea to meet with the developers and explain the advantages of the new system, while reassuring them that they will still be able to do their job in the most effective (if not the absolute fastest) manner possible.

Keep in mind that in order to help the development teams be successful, you must be able to quickly support their requests, regardless of ongoing production problems. This will almost certainly require consistent or rotating allocation of one or more DBAs to the role of development support.

The amount of autonomy you give the developers will naturally be inversely proportional to the amount of time you can devote to supporting the development environment. Do not attempt to lock down the development environment too far if you do not have the resources or the skill sets within your team to support the influx of requests you will get. Also, be sure you have the agreement of upper management before you begin the process of implementing the ideas presented here.

Managing Development

Assuming we are dealing with a standardized database where all production objects are owned by **dbo**, then these objects should be changed only by a DBA. No developers should have db_owner or db_ddladmin permissions. Instead, each of them should be given individual permissions to create procedures, functions, and, at your discretion, views. But, again, the original **dbo** objects will remain in place until you make the change.

In this scenario, the developers each have their own schema, their own work area for code, even though they are all working in the same database. Each owner name is a different schema. Everyone can have a different copy of the same stored procedure, and multiple test copies without causing anyone else problems. Their changes to their own copy of an object will not affect everyone else on the development system until they are finished with it. They will still be able to share their work, by granting permissions on the objects they are finished with.

This layer of security isolates and protects each developer's work from the others. It also has a few advantages that become clear in the process of development. The first advantage is control over structural changes. When the developers require table changes, you will be involved immediately. This will give you input into the foundation of the database, the tables which drive the code. In designing any new tables or table changes, you will also be alert to modeling standardization requirements the developers may overlook. Another advantage here is that if you are the only one making table changes, you will already be aware of the changes if a second developer requests additional changes to the same object. A simple e-mail at this point can avert a design clash.

The second advantage is the opportunity to review and optimize the code before it causes a production problem. At some point the developers are going to ask you to create their objects as **dbo**. Take the time to look through their code and make sure it follows standards of documentation, proper formatting, good usage, and design. If you see a problem, fix it, but also send a note to the developer explaining the reason for the change. The developers will begin to adjust to the new standards and will produce better code, shortening the review process over time. The respectful exchange of information and the mutual desire for high quality design and code will foster a superior development environment.

Also take the time during the code review process to make sure that adequate comments are provided in the database code. At minimum, you want to have a sample syntax line, a statement of purpose, a notation on who wrote the code and for what system, and a list of modifications and associated Service Request numbers. The sample syntax line, which should be valid for testing using SQL Query Analyzer, is the single most useful part of this. It will allow you to simply highlight that line and run the code, so you can check the execution plan, resources consumed, and so on.

An additional hidden benefit of this strategy is creating a unit test environment. This gives you the opportunity to create your implementation scripts, and test them by implementing them to the **dbo** schema of the database. Be sure to make notes at this time regarding what server and database the object belongs to, and whether any changes will be required at implementation time, such as re-pointing code to the production version of a linked server. When you are finished, the developer can then run their code in this environment. All **dbo** objects are part of the unit test environment (although, the data is not unless you protect it). Developers quickly become accustomed to requesting that their objects be promoted to **dbo** ownership, at which point they can update their code and conduct unit tests before having a very public test in front of the QA team.

Action	Permissions
Creation of **dbo** objects	Restricted to DBA use only
Code for stored procedures and functions	Created by developers with their own user name. For example, **dbo**.usp_sample would be copied to new procedure **sample**.usp_sample for all changes.
Standard views	You may choose to treat this as a stored procedure, or you may wish to exercise more control over the creation and use of views.
Trigger code	Because the use of triggers should be carefully examined, DBAs should create and control this code.
Table and materialized views	DBAs make changes to tables after reviewing the design.
Indexes	Indexes should be created by experienced DBAs. Although they are fluid, indexes should be controlled even in development.

How Control Can Become a Hindrance

Despite the various advantages in the development environment discussed above, please note that it is possible to take the idea of control too far. Although you may find individual projects where the lack of sufficient time or skill on the part of the development team will cause the development DBA to do all of the database coding, do not encourage this as a standard solution. While any good DBA should have the appropriate skills to code difficult stored procedures, this service should be an exception to the rule, when there is a requirement for advanced database knowledge.

Under no circumstances should you set up a database group whose purpose is to keep such control over the development environment that only DBAs have permissions to write all the database code. This system of development has several faults. First, it turns into a game of keep away with the data, which limits the amount of creativity that can be employed to find the best design. Secondly, it will discourage developers from learning better database coding techniques. This is not beneficial for the company, the developers, or the database group.

It is best to fix the problem at its source: train the developers. A good guideline is to employ the minimum level of control that is required. Control should serve a useful purpose and contribute to the manageability of the environment rather than just add complexity.

Duplication of the Production Database

Regardless of the size of your development team, you will need to create a development database to avoid endangering the production database with untested code. If this is not a new system, you will have to copy the production database to the development server. The easiest way to do this is to restore a backup to the development server.

However, in most cases the development server is smaller than the production server, and you will not usually need the entire production image. If you need a subset of the data, you will not be able to restore the database from a production backup. Instead, you will have to script the production database and develop a set of processes to transfer the data (preferably from a standby image). This can be done using either a saved Data Transformation Services (DTS) package or a set of Transact-SQL scripts. If you use a source control application, you can generate the scripts from that application, but you will still need a data transfer process. Make sure to design this process so it permits restoration of tables either individually or in related groups. Taking the time to simplify this process now will make it easier for you to respond quickly to developer requests for fresh or repaired data.

If you have secure data on your production server, such as credit card, financial, or other private information, you should skew this data by some secret algorithm. For example, all credit cards could be set to the same fake number; or if you want to show different numbers for each one, start at a particular number and increment by one. If you load the data using a DTS package or a Transact-SQL script, you

can make these data transformations during the transfer process. These steps will keep your sensitive production data secure.

In some scenarios, the developers or testers create test case data, and this must also be preserved. Make an effort to check if your developers or testers have data they wish to keep, so they will not have to waste time recreating it every time you refresh the tables. To make this easier, the test data restore should be a separate process that runs after the regular data refresh.

Security

Logins will have to be created both for the developers and for a set of test users. Each developer and test user should have an individual login, and should be required to use it rather than sharing one login with a group. This makes administration simpler, and can save you some valuable time when you need to find out who is running a particularly resource-intensive query or when you want to run SQL Profiler to gauge the performance of the queries involved.

The test user accounts should each represent a unique permissions profile or role in the production database. You can create these as test scenario logins, or your developers and testers may choose real users who characterize the permissions. Isolating permissions like this to imitate the production environment will allow the developers to do more thorough unit testing. It is not a good practice to just duplicate all the production logins on the development (or QA) server.

If you have restored the database from production, you may find that the Security Identifiers (SIDs) for your database logins no longer match the server logins. The most noticeable symptom of this is that your user will be able to login, but unable to connect to the database; the error message will either state that the server user is not a valid user in the database or, if the database in question is the default database of the user, that SQL Server cannot open the user default database. You can re-link the SIDs between syslogins and sysusers databases by using sp_change_users_login. This approach lends itself to generating a script to automatically synchronize the users as part of the data load.

Using Command Line Scripts for Implementation

Although almost all implementations to a database can be performed using SQL Server Enterprise Manager, the best practice is to use command line scripts. Scripts have several advantages in database change implementations. First, they provide you with a permanent, verifiable record of exactly what you did to the database. Not what you think you did in the GUI, but what you actually did. Secondly, a script gives you peace of mind and objectivity. If you follow this entire formalized plan, you will have tested your implementation scripts twice before running them in production, and while there is always a chance something unexpected may occur, it is reduced to a very small percentage. This means that if your implementation window is at 4 A.M., and you have another server that needs attention at the same moment, you will still be able to walk through the scripts without worrying that you missed something. As an added bonus, if you are unavailable for any reason, a stand-in can do the implementation.

When the development process is complete and the code is ready for unit testing, create the implementation scripts and store them in a secure area. Resist the urge to use sp_change_object_owner to change the owner to **dbo** on objects delivered for unit test. This is very fast, but if you do this, you have missed out on your only opportunity to pretest your implementation scripts, and your first opportunity to test those scripts before the production implementation. Take a few extra minutes to script each object with the fully defined production implementation method, and implement the changes to the unit test environment of the development server as a trial run. The unit test area of the development server is simply the **dbo** schema in the development database. For the purpose of keeping your database clean, it is usually a good idea to remove the copies of the objects belonging to the developers once you have implemented them as **dbo** objects. This is a good opportunity to ensure that all of your implementation scripts are complete and in order.

Its important that you create and run the implementation scripts, even if development and QA team members have to wait for you to finish. You may not get another chance to test your implementation scripts.

On rare occasions, or when you first begin to apply control to your environment, you may find that the development group has no record of what changes were made. There are a variety of reasons this can occur, none of them good. However, you are left with the task of identifying a few small changes in the vastness of the database. It is possible to do an item-by-item compare between two databases during off-hours.

The first rule of using scripts for database implementations is to script everything; ideally, nothing should be done through the graphical interface (and if you must do that, be sure to document that very carefully). The second is to provide supporting documentation. Your scripts should contain comments regarding what is happening in the next section, and any observations you made when you last ran it (that is, how long it took, how many rows were affected, and so on). Adding application roles? Changing database files? Linking servers? Updating rows? Script it all, so you can easily reproduce your steps.

To make this simpler, you can save the change scripts created in the Diagram pane in SQL Server Enterprise Manager. Rather than saving your changes to the Diagram, use the change script it creates. Take care to review these automatically generated scripts first and make appropriate changes. For example, if you add a column into the middle of a table, the change script will copy the data into a temp table, drop the original table, create the new one, populate the data and then rebuild the indexes. This might be a minor action on a small table, but if it is a table with millions of rows and many indexes, you could be unpleasantly surprised if you did not review the code first.

The third rule is to protect the scripts. Because they will be used for the implementation, the scripts should be treated like production objects. Keep them in a secured directory, or even better in a version control project that is accessible only to your group. Because of the obvious differences between a standard script and a change script (for example, the difference between a `CREATE TABLE` and `ALTER TABLE` script), you should maintain a separate folder for implementation scripts.

Organization is the key to managing scripts. Do not create a separate script file for each action, but instead for each logical step in the implementation. For example, if you number your script files, your script storage area might have a structure like this:

```
Northwind_App
    Release_Mar2001
        RelatedDocuments
        1_ReadThisFirst.sql
        2_add_roles and users.sql
        3_AlterTableSample.sql
        4_AddViewSampleVu.sql
        5_usp_Sample_ins.prc.sql
        5_usp_Sample_sel.prc.sql
```

Although you do not really need the Readme script, this is a simple way to explain what the implementation was for, and store any other notes that might be necessary to remind, educate, or reassure the person running the scripts. Storing it as a SQL file makes it easily visible from SQL Query Analyzer, and also makes it clear that it relates to the other script files, rather than being a document or e-mail that relates to the project but not to the act of implementing it. Numbering the scripts organizes them into the order or hierarchy required during production implementation.

If you are doing a very large implementation, you may consider creating a batch script that executes numerous procedures by looping through them in **osql**. If you would like to try this, remember that it is important to build error handling into a batch process, so if the process encounters a problem during implementation, you will know which changes completed before the error occurred.

Source Storage Methods

The easiest way to start storing code is to put it in a protected folder, and use a simple directory structure. Another popular alternative is to use version control software. This has some immediate advantages over directory storage, but it requires a little more administration. It also allows you to easily grant read access to developers in a way already familiar to them, so they can feel reassured that they have the latest version of the code.

Version control software, however, is not integrated with SQL Server, and it can be time-consuming to maintain for a database, especially in regard to change scripts. You will need to be sure that everyone in your group understands how it works, and is committed to using. After all, the main weakness of any storage system for database scripts is that you have to manually update it.

Version control programs have features that allow you to label a set of scripts as part of one release, making it easy to get the most recent copy of all changes. You will need to define and rigidly uphold agreements on how to comment objects to be identified in a certain grouping for a release. You must also maintain change scripts separately from version scripts, since they are fundamentally different.

To step up to this level of source control, choose one target application at a time, and incorporate your archived scripts from your simple file directory as you go.

You can search the directories by going to the Windows taskbar, clicking **Start**, and then clicking **Search**. You can search either by filename or by keyword. Version control software will also allow you search code text or comments.

One way to organize your code is by application, like this:

📁 ApplicationName
   📁 Server Information
   📁 Related Documents
   📁 Database Objects
      📁 Tables and Views
      📁 Procedures and Functions
      📁 Rules Defaults and Datatypes
      📁 Other (DTS, Tasks, Linked Servers, UDLs, DSNs)
      📁 Roles and Permissions
   📁 Implementations
      📁 January2001
      📁 April2001
         📁 SR A2957182
         📁 SR B8389840

Another way is to use the same basic structure to store information on your servers, if your company does not maintain a configuration management database. For example:

📁 ServerName
   📁 Configuration
   📁 File Layout
   📁 Dependencies and Contacts

It is also useful to store related documents for applications, implementations, or server configurations. Store e-mails outlining varying opinions, any design documents, approvals from the QA person, or anything else. In six months when someone asks you what happened to the **AddressLine7** where they were storing their customer comments, you will be able to give them an accurate answer. If it later becomes apparent that the design could have been better, you will have adequate documentation on any alternate designs that were suggested, and reasons (if any) that they were discarded.

First Trial

The first opportunity to test your production implementation scripts occurs when you create them to change the database for the development environment. As soon as you have a stored procedure to implement to the "unit test" area of the development server, you should create the implementation script and save it to the related directory. Your script should contain code comments indicating the eventual target production server and database.

Expecting the Unexpected During Implementation

Even at this early date, you should be thinking ahead to what could go wrong during this implementation. This risk analysis is vital to the success of your process, and may change what is implemented or how it is done.

At minimum, you should make a list of what you think is likely to be a problem, and what would be good alternative actions in the event that things go awry. You must also make sure that when you have implementation problems of a non-fatal nature, you alter the implementation scripts as you use them, adding documentation or code that will help you during a later investigation into the problem. This provides two advantages: it allows you to be more prepared to discuss what went wrong, and it allows your group to learn from the implementation experience.

Contingency Plans

If you can predict problems by thinking through the possibilities, or based on problems you have encountered in the past, make a chart showing these risks and what you could do to correct the problem. Also list any risks that will prevent the implementation from being completed. No matter what kind of risks you identify, even if you cannot identify any, you must have a rollback strategy for your production implementation.

Rollback Strategies

You should never plan a system change without also planning how to undo it. Your rollback strategy is simply a script for how to undo every change you have made, and put everything back the way it was before you started. Even if you have planned everything out correctly, the need for a rollback can still occur. If a call comes to roll the implementation, you may have a very short amount of time to undo all the changes.

If your database is small enough, you might simply elect to use a restore of the database as your method. If this is an option, you should consider using a marked transaction to coordinate rolling back to the first change in your implementation. However, in a larger database, or an implementation that includes changes to elements outside the table or code objects, you will need a more detailed plan, and possibly even the prewritten code to undo the change. These scripts may be tested during the first unit test or QA implementation.

Managing the QA Environment

The QA environment operates under different principles and priorities than the development environment. The goal of the QA person is to test the code in a controlled environment where there is no chance for interference from either development or operations staff. Without this isolation, the test is considered to be invalid, and must be redone. The QA person has final approval of all implementations, and often moderates cases in which the weighing of necessity versus risk is the deciding factor in going forward with an implementation.

It is in your best interests to develop a sense of teamwork with some people in the QA team. In fact, this is of mutual advantage. When they find a problem with a system, they may come to you for supporting documentation to explain why a system change should not be implemented. If you find that a development change that you consider to be risky is being pushed through to the QA team, you can accompany the QA implementation with an objective document outlining your concerns, the risks, and recommended mitigating action.

Another important function of the QA team is to perform milestone testing. All too often, testing is left to the last part of the project. At this point, the sum of all the changes must be tested simultaneously. Because it is all tested together, if one piece fails, the entire implementation must wait until the next release date. The reason for this is the same as the reason for the controlled environment: The concern of the QA team is that if one part of the code is removed from a set of changes, this may also have unexpected effects due to dependencies in other code.It is a good practice to have the QA representative involved in the unit tests and project milestone tests to identify any potential problems early, when implementation dependencies are still fluid.

Implementing in QA

Second Trial

When you transfer the changes to the QA environment, you have another chance to test your implementation scripts. If you do not have a controlled development environment, this will be your one and only chance to test and refine your scripts before implementing to production.

Always do a backup of the QA database before you start, and keep the backup until the production implementation is complete. This is a firm record of what was in QA before the test process began, and may become an essential part of testing if things do not go as planned. Keep in mind that if the testing fails, you will have to roll the changes out of QA. Make sure your rollback scripts are ready in advance, and view this as a chance to test your rollback scenario with a timer running.

Handing Off to QA

Another rule when running QA servers is that after you have implemented your change scripts, and you have informed the QA representatives that testing can begin, do not make even the smallest change without asking a QA representative for approval. Altering the implementation, even in the smallest detail, can invalidate the test. You should always consult the QA staff before working with their servers. It is a good practice to limit developer access to a QA server. The reason for this is that they are the experts on the system. To hand it off, they should have supplied documentation in sufficient detail so the QA team can handle the system without intervention. Any omissions found can then be addressed in this environment rather than in production.

Implementation the QA process described here is not difficult work, but it is meticulous. Indeed, the closer you get to the production environment, the more attention you should give to the details. Add notes into your scripts and related files regarding the time it took to load a change, or any unusual conditions. Make sure that you have verified the scripts to include, and the order in which they should be run.

QA Administration

The QA database servers are owned by the QA team and should be treated like a production environment. It is critical that you never make any changes to QA servers without getting approval from all involved QA personnel. Make sure that the QA environment emulates production as closely as possible. Any and all deviations from production should be carefully and completely documented, and communicated to the team.

Part of maintaining a QA environment includes keeping appropriate operations personnel informed as to the state of the project. Operations staff may raise issues now that will ease the transition to production support later.

Sterile Lab

QA generally does not require as fast a response time as either development or production, unless the QA team is in the middle of a testing phase. Generally, you do not need to run regular backups in QA either, unless restoring from production would be time-consuming or awkward to do on short notice. However, you should do as many backups as necessary to be able to restore to a point before each implementation. You may face some challenges regarding differences in server names, allowable logins, or hardware constraints. Enlist the help of representatives from QA and development to determine what variations are acceptable, and what negotiated fixes are affordable and supportable. You cannot, for example, agree to change the database name in every database code object, nor would QA personnel be happy with such a resolution. However, you might need to alter linked server code to reference a server that has a different name.

 A single point of contact in each group should be in charge of change requests in QA, and everyone should know which people to ask before making a change. Everything should be documented, and this information should be available to the entire group. This information can be distributed by way of e-mail or a collaborative Web site. The key is accuracy, completeness, and accessibility.

Significance of the QA Phase

The QA phase is your chance to prove that you have performed due diligence for an implementation. Does it work? Does it scale? Does it affect any other system? Document all of this, record your concerns, and communicate all of these to everyone involved in the project, including Operations, Development, QA, Project Management, and, of course, Database Administration. The stability, accountability, and learning inherent in the process is the key to success.

Managing Production Implementations

Production implementations are usually viewed as a risky but necessary operation: change to the database. Care must be taken to make sure that system disruption is minimal, and that the corporate data is preserved at all costs. Failure on either of these counts will incur an immediate and tangible loss for the company.

Owning the Change: Production vs. DBA

Who should change the production database? This can be a topic of debate in a group of DBAs. The development DBA is closer to the change, and understands all the related parts; but ultimately the production DBA is responsible for the system.

In the end, it is a question of ownership. The person doing the change should have a good understanding both of the system in question and the change being performed. They must have the authority to take drastic corrective action if necessary without undue delay, and they must possess all the appropriate contacts among those in operations who can help them with related issues outside the DBA realm.

Determining an Implementation Window

If this is a 24 x 7 system, your project team will have to negotiate an implementation window that is acceptable to all groups affected by the change. In a truly mission critical system, even the shortest downtime may be unacceptable, so you may need to provide a read-only database as an alternative to access. In this case, the team should try to identify a small number of key users and re-point their database connections to a different server through ODBC.

To do this effectively, you will need to have a list of the IT contacts involved, and the user contacts both at management level and staff level. It is essential for the IT department to maintain credibility with the users by clearly communicating to them the nature of service interruption and the expected duration; any change to this situation must also be communicated. In addition, if you are supplying alternative access, interim support of the read-only system must also be provided, and the users and help desk personnel should be kept informed.

Planning the Implementation, Twice

You should compile an implementation plan and distribute it to everyone in IS who will be involved in or affected by the implementation. The plan is simply a list of the steps, who is responsible for each, the times that everything is expected to occur, and who to contact in order to initiate the next step. Be sure to include cell phone and pager numbers for everyone on site or on call during that timeframe.

You should make a secondary plan that accommodates these variables. Experience with your application and infrastructure will help you gauge the level of detail required. Note any showstoppers that would cancel the entire implementation and invoke the rollback plan.

7As a group, the implementation team should create a backup plan. This is a little different than a simple rollback strategy for the database. If anyone's section fails, the group should have an overall plan for evaluating the situation, making a decision, and then proceeding or canceling the implementation.

When a Good Plan Comes Together

The beginning of the ownership of the system by operations begins with a release readiness review, also called a "go/no go" meeting, which determines whether this system or change to a system is ready for implementation. Although operations staff should be involved throughout the project, this will be the first meeting that is run by them, rather than by the development or QA teams.

The purpose of this meeting is to allow members from each team to indicate their final approval (or disapproval) and any issues they wish to raise. This is the last chance to alter the implementation schedule short of an all-out crisis. All groups should be prepared for the deployment. It is important that operations staff members indicate that they are sufficiently knowledgeable and prepared to take on operational support of the product or system.

Any votes of a no-go should be seriously considered; if no resolution can be reached by those present, the meeting should be adjourned with a no-go status until resolution is reached or the objection is overridden by senior IT staff. In any case, the objection, the reasons for it, and any risks that are brought up should be recorded for future reference.

The agenda for this meeting should include:

- The readiness of the release itself.

- Alterations to the physical environment.

- The preparedness of the operations staff and processes.

- The installation plan.

- The contingency plan.

- Potential impacts on other systems.

If you have a formal change control process that requires registration for implementation, be sure you have followed their procedures. It may be your responsibility to file a change request for the database server. If there is no formal change process in your operations department, you will need to send an e-mail announcement to people in operations who may be affected by the change or any difficulties encountered during or after the implementation. This would include, at minimum, the support staff, the help desk technicians, and network and security administration. There should not be anyone who can reasonably claim they should have been informed and were not.

Coordinating Application Changes

The first step of your implementation should always be a backup of the current system. Once this is complete and verified, you are ready to begin. But the DBA group is rarely the lead on the implementation. Normally, this person is going to be someone from the project team who has responsibility for deployment. You should call your contact person and inform them that backups are complete and the database team is ready, and then await their signal to begin changing the system.

Support During Implementation

Except in the very smallest of shops, there should always be a second DBA on standby for an implementation. In a large implementation, you may have several DBAs involved in the deployment of the system, but you should still have a standby in the event that someone becomes ill, or in case of related or unrelated system failures. Remember, even if another production server goes down during an implementation, the deployment must continue as planned. Every reasonable effort should be made to uphold the DBA end of the contract.

In addition to supporting an implementation, you should also be sure that people are in place to support you. Be sure you have handy the contact numbers of the on-call server room technicians, network administrators, or security administrators whose help you may need during the implementation.

Contingencies

Sometimes, in spite of all your plans, something truly unforeseen will occur during a production implementation. If you are lucky it will be something minor. But, regardless of what it is, you should make a note of it in your implementation script. Whatever code you had to run, whatever action you had to perform: everything must be recorded. Do not wait until the crisis has passed to start making notes. The sequence of events and steps taken may later be significant, either for support calls you end up making, for later analysis, or for similar future implementations. Remember that meticulous accuracy is more important than anything else at this stage. Due diligence requires that even if you make a mistake, you record that too. Your thoroughness now might save someone else making the same mistake later on, and will help the group learn as a whole. Not just about technical issues, but about teamwork as well. Good teamwork is a vital part of the success of an implementation team, which crosses many departments in IT, and it relies on the irreproachable accuracy of the information provided by team members.

Remember that Rollback Plan?

In the event of all out failure of the deployment, you will have to put your rollback plan into action. This rarely happens, but just like paying for insurance, you will appreciate the value of a good rollback plan the first time you have to use it. While you are running your rollback scripts or your database restore, make some notes in an e-mail explaining what caused the implementation to be called off. It might have had nothing to do with the database at all, but this should still be noted and the appropriate people informed as a matter of responsibility. Remember to inform all of the people in IS who were originally notified that the deployment would occur. Unless you have a direct link of communications with the user community, leave that contact up to the project managers or to the change control group.

Sounding the All Clear

After you have completed your portion of the implementation, immediately notify your contact person, so the next part of the implementation can proceed. Your task now is to stand by in case the group needs something, most notably a rollback. If the implementation completes successfully, the testers test the application in the production environment to be sure that everything is indeed working, and the users are informed that they can resume working in the system. You should make sure that the contact person has an action item to call you to inform you that you can stand down. It is a good idea to know what time they plan to be finished, and to make it generally known what time you will give up waiting for your phone call.

Business As Usual: Implementation Review

After implementation, a meeting should take place to evaluate the success (or failure) of the project. Everything including the project plan, the design, the arguments, the solutions, the crises, and the final outcome will be examined. The point of this process is to learn from the events that occurred; if you have things to add, take your documentation with you to share. And remember to share your positive remarks, not just the negative ones.

Once this is complete, the development cycle for that application begins again in the visioning of the next release.

Conclusion

The processes described here should give you a good foundation to begin structuring your own environment for better manageability. In addition to the development cycle and basic operations covering change control, several broad concepts are touched on here that you should further research before implementing on a grand scale: source and version control, data modeling, and the Microsoft Solution Frameworks (MSF) and Microsoft Operations Frameworks (MOF) guidelines. If you want to incorporate all of these ideas into your mode of operations, keep in mind that this will be a gradual process requiring sponsorship by your management. The end result is well worth the effort.

Further Reading

Microsoft Operations Framework: http://www.microsoft.com/mof/

Planning, Deploying, and Managing Highly Available Solutions at Microsoft TechNet: http://www.microsoft.com/technet/sql/default.asp

Microsoft Solutions Framework: http://www.microsoft.com/msf/

IT Infrastructure Library, best practices: http://www.itil.co.uk/

Microsoft SQL Server 2000 Administrator's Companion, Chapter 3 "Roles and Responsibilities of the Microsoft SQL Server DBA"

For samples that may help in managing database change, see the *SQL Server 2000 Resource Kit* CD-ROM in the folder, \ToolsAndSamples\DBManagement.

Storage Engine Enhancements

This chapter describes the new storage engine features in Microsoft® SQL Server™ 2000 and offers tips for using them, along with some insight into how the storage engine works. Developing a basic understanding of the inner workings of the storage engine can help you get the most out of SQL Server.

In a world that is focused on highly scalable applications, databases are now designed and implemented on short schedules, and they remain in a constant state of evolution as development requirements change and production usage grows. Scalability, availability, and ease-of-use requirements demand a responsive and flexible data storage engine. Different editions of SQL Server 2000 support a wide variety of systems, ranging in size from a tiny mobile system for a Pocket PC all the way up to a high availability multiple-terabyte transaction processing or decision support system running clustered Windows® 2000 Datacenter Servers. All of these systems maintain the flexibility, security, and reliability mission-critical business systems demand.

You can deploy SQL Server 2000 applications for projects of varying purposes and sizes, as a result of intelligent, automated storage engine operations. A highly sophisticated architecture improves performance, availability, and scalability.

Availability

Reliability and concurrency are enhanced with new algorithms for physical file interaction. These algorithms eliminate the need to run database console commands (DBCCs) as part of regular maintenance. However, DBCC is still available, and the new DBCC CHECK commands can be run without inhibiting online processing.

Scalability

The storage subsystem, which consists of the physical database files and their layout on disk, supports scaling from very small to very large databases. Data can be stored according to usage across files and filegroups that span many physical disks. SQL Server can now support up to 64 GB of physical memory and up to 32 processors.

Ease of Use

Enhanced administration capabilities help the Database Administrator (DBA) to automate and centralize server management. This also allows easy maintenance of remote servers and applications without the necessity of having a DBA at every site. Server configuration, managed by a sophisticated algorithm, is dynamically responsive to server usage patterns, freeing the DBA to work on database management and optimization tasks.

Storage Engine Enhancements

The relational database server of SQL Server 2000 has two main parts: the relational engine and the storage engine. The two engines work independently, interacting with each other through native data access components such as OLE DB. The relational engine provides an interface into the storage engine, which is composed of services to interact with the underlying database storage components and features.

The primary responsibilities of the storage engine include:

- Providing features to improve ease of use for managing storage components.
- Managing the data buffers and all I/O to the physical files.
- Controlling concurrency, managing transactions, locking, and logging.
- Managing the files and physical pages used to store data.
- Recovering from system faults.

The SQL Server 2000 storage engine offers new features that add conceptual simplicity and physical flexibility, while reducing the need for meticulous capacity planning and performance tuning. SQL Server 2000 reacts to its own environment and dynamically adapts to changes in database usage accurately and quickly. This breakthrough in technology has elevated the focus of database administration to the facilitation of data as a service. SQL Server 2000 DBAs can focus on designing a system that is responsive to data flow and usage, rather than spending time tuning individual parameters.

The changes in SQL Server 2000 are built on architectural enhancements, introduced in SQL Server 7.0, that provide a foundation for continuing future improvement and innovation. The primary goal of this release was to reduce the amount of time and effort spent tuning the server on a regular basis. Because most tuning parameter settings could be based on database usage, the engine was designed to dynamically adjust to situations in the database environment according to an adaptive algorithm. This automated flexibility has been implemented for tuning parameters that required constant adjustment and experimentation in earlier versions. You can still manually adjust tuning features, but SQL Server 2000 does more of the work for you.

The following table summarizes the key enhancements made to the SQL Server 2000 storage engine. They are described in greater detail later in this chapter.

Feature	Description and benefits
Application lock manager	If you need to control concurrent access to application-defined resources, such as forms, new stored procedures now allow you to lock these resources using the SQL Server application lock manager.

Continued on next page

Feature	Description and benefits
Database console commands (DBCCs)	The DBCC CHECK commands can now run during online processing, without blocking updates. New enhancements allow verifying consistency of physical pages to detect hardware-induced errors. In SQL Server 2000 Enterprise Edition, DBCC now runs in parallel across multiple processors.
Database options	All database options can now be modified using ALTER DATABASE. This ability simplifies administration.
Differential backups	Differential backups are quicker in SQL Server 2000, due to an enhancement that tracks database changes at the extent level.
Dynamic tuning	Using dynamic adaptive algorithms, the server automatically adjusts previously static configuration settings. Administrative control is still available to manage system-wide resources, but you will not usually need to use it. Manually set parameters adapt dynamically within their constrained boundaries.
In-row text	In tables that include a small, frequently used text column, smaller text values can be stored in the same page with the standard data row, rather than on a page of text values. In tables where this text data is accessed frequently, this feature can eliminate a large amount of disk I/O.
Index builds in parallel	In Enterprise Edition, index builds automatically make use of all processors configured for parallel processing, reducing the time it takes to build an index by as much as a factor of six on an 8-processor server. Index builds also take advantage of available resources in memory and **tempdb**.
Index read ahead	Index reads have been enhanced to increase performance on index scans.
Index reorganization	Improvements made to DBCC SHOWCONTIG provide more detailed information regarding index fragmentation. A new DBCC command, INDEXDEFRAG, reorganizes index pages online without disrupting database service or incurring any risk to database consistency or recovery.
Descending order key columns on indexes	Individual keys columns in an index can be specified as ascending or descending order.

Continued on next page

Feature	Description and benefits
KILL command	This command now reports completion progress. If this command is waiting on another process, such as a rollback, you can view how much of the command has been executed. This command has been enhanced to allow stopping of Microsoft Distributed Transaction Coordinator (MS DTC) transactions, which are not associated with a specific session.
Large memory support	Windows 2000 technology improves the performance of Enterprise Edition systems that use a large amount of memory. Using the AWE extensions of Windows 2000, SQL Server 2000 can support up to 64 GB of physical memory.
Locking	The lock manager has been enhanced to detect deadlocks across additional resources such as threads and memory. Concurrency improvements reduce deadlocks. This further enhances scalability in SQL Server 2000.
Logical log marks	Transact-SQL commands can create a bookmark in the log to permit restoration of the database to the point in time indicated by the bookmark. This feature also synchronizes restoration of multiple databases used for the same application.
Online index reorganization	Improvements made to DBCC SHOWCONTIG provide more detailed information regarding index fragmentation. A new DBCC command, INDEXDEFRAG, reorganizes index pages online without disrupting database service or incurring any risk to database consistency or recovery.
Optimized I/O read-ahead	SQL Server 2000 issues multiple serial read-ahead reads at once for each file involved in the scan. The query optimizer uses serial, read-ahead I/O when scanning tables and indexes for improved performance.
Passwords on backups	Backup media and individual backup can be password-protected. This prevents an unauthorized user restoring a backup and gaining access to a database.
Recovery models	Using recovery models, you can select the level of logging in the database. This allows greater flexibility of transaction log management. The recovery model can be altered online to complement varying usage of the database throughout the day.
Shared table scans	In Enterprise Edition, multiple scans of a table can now take advantage of other ongoing scans of that table, reducing physical I/O to the disk.

Continued on next page

Feature	Description and benefits
Shrinking the log	The command to shrink the log runs immediately in more situations. When the log cannot be shrunk immediately, SQL Server will provide constructive feedback on what must be done before continuing with or completing the shrink operation.
Snapshot backups	Support for snapshot backups by third-party vendors has been enhanced. Snapshot backups take advantage of storage technologies to backup or restore an entire database in seconds. These backups can now be combined with conventional transaction log and differential backups to provide complete protection for OLTP databases. This is especially beneficial for moderate to very large databases in which availability is extremely important.
Space-efficient empty tables and indexes	No disk pages are allocated for empty tables and indexes in SQL Server 2000. SQL Server 7.0 allocated as many as three pages for empty tables and indexes.
Top n sort	This new feature optimizes retrieval of top n values (for example, `SELECT TOP 5 * FROM tablename`).
Xlock	SQL Server 2000 provides this new Transact-SQL locking hint. It can be used to explicitly invoke an exclusive transaction-level page or table lock.

SQL Server 2000 has been enriched with features that allow more efficient interaction with the data and more flexibility from an administrative perspective. The following sections give more details on these enhancements and some tips on how to use them.

Interacting with Data

In SQL Server 2000, the storage engine has been enhanced to provide even more scalability and performance when interacting with the data. Understanding these enhancements can help you use SQL Server more effectively.

The exchange of data begins with a query, whether it originates from a user interface or from an automated task. The data request is passed into the relational engine, which interacts with the storage engine to get the data and pass it back to the user. From the perspective of the user, and even the DBA, the functioning of the storage and relational engines are indistinguishable.

Reading Data More Effectively

Data flows between the server and the user through a series of transactions. The application or user initiates the work, and the database passes it to the query processor for completion and then returns the end results. The query processor does the work by accepting, interpreting, and executing SQL statements.

For example, when a user session issues a SELECT statement, the following steps occur:

1. The relational engine compiles and optimizes the statement into an execution plan (which is a series of steps required to get the data). The relational engine then runs the execution plan. The execution steps involve accessing tables and indexes through the storage engine.

2. The relational engine interprets the execution plan, making calls into the storage engine to gather the necessary data.

3. The relational engine combines all the data returned by the storage engine into the final result set and then sends it back to the user.

A couple of improvements have been made to boost performance in this process. In SQL Server 2000, the relational engine relays qualifying query predicates to the storage engine so they can be applied earlier in the process, resulting in more efficient exchange between the storage and relational engine. This can provide a significant performance gain for qualifying queries.

Top *n* Enhanced

Another improvement is in the way the storage engine handles selection of the top *n* records from a result set. In SQL Server 2000, a new top *n* engine analyzes the best path of operation for statements like this one:

```
SELECT top 5 * from orders order by date_ordered desc
```

For this example, if the whole table must be searched, the engine analyzes the data and tracks only the top *n* values in the cache. This is a tremendous performance boost for this type of SELECT statement, because only the values in the top *n* will be sorted, rather than the whole table.

Shared Scans

In Enterprise Edition, two or more queries can share ongoing table scans, which can improve performance in very large SQL Server 2000 enterprises. For example, when a query searches a really large table using an unordered scan, the pages flow through the cache to make room for the data flowing in. If another query is started, a second scan of the same table would incur disk I/O to retrieve those pages again. In an environment where there are frequent table scans, this can cause disk thrashing as both queries search the same data pages.

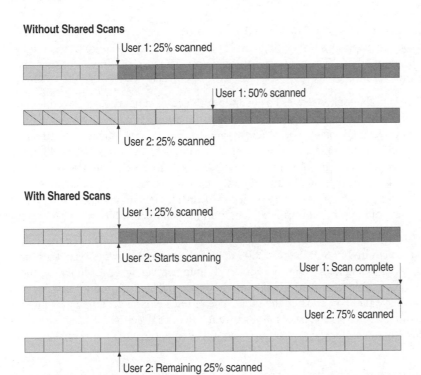

Without Shared Scans

User 1: 25% scanned

User 1: 50% scanned

User 2: 25% scanned

With Shared Scans

User 1: 25% scanned

User 2: Starts scanning

User 1: Scan complete

User 2: 75% scanned

User 2: Remaining 25% scanned

An optimizing process reduces the amount of disk I/O produced by this type of data access pattern. The first unordered scan of a table will read the data from the disk; instead of having to read the disk again, subsequent unordered scans of the same table can build on the information already in memory. During multiple simultaneous scans of the same table, this synchronization process may boost performance as much as eightfold. This improvement is even more noticeable in large decision support queries, where the total table size is much larger than the size of the cache.

Shared scans are a feature invoked by the storage engine to assist with queries that have no better available execution plan. The intent of this feature is to assist in frequent reads of very large tables. When the query processor determines that the best execution plan includes a table scan, this feature is invoked. However, while it is possible to use query or index tuning to force shared scans, no performance gain is achieved by forcing a table scan where a well-maintained index would do the job as well or better.

Concurrency

In order to maintain transactional consistency while many users are interacting with the data, the storage engine locks resources to manage dependencies on rows, pages, keys, key ranges, indexes, tables, and databases. By locking resources while they are being altered, the engine prevents more than one user from altering the same data at the same time. SQL Server locks are dynamically applied at various levels of granularity, in order to select the least restrictive lock required for the transaction.

In SQL Server 2000, concurrency improvements further reduce deadlocks and avoidable locking of resources. For example, the lock manager has been enhanced to be aware of other resources that might be in contention, such as threads and memory. This new ability can help a database administrator identify a wider variety of design or hardware limitations.

A new Transact-SQL interface into the lock manager has been introduced to support customized locking logic within programming code. Locks necessary for business logic can be initiated by invoking **sp_getapplock** within your Transact-SQL batch, which allows you to specify an application-defined resource to be locked (for example, a lock on an application resource like a form, instead of a lock on a data row), the mode of locking to use, the timeout value, and whether the scope of the lock should be the transaction or the session. After locks have been initiated with the new application lock manager, they participate in the normal lock management of SQL Server, just as if the storage engine had initiated them, so you do not have to worry that your application-initiated lock will remain open if the calling transaction is terminated.

The process by which locks are acquired in SQL Server 2000 takes into account whether or not all the data on the page is committed. For example, if you run a SELECT statement against a table whose data has not changed recently, such as a table in the **pubs** database, the process does not produce any locks because no active transactions have recently updated the table. The storage engine accomplishes this by comparing the log sequence number on the data page to the current active transactions. In databases where most of the data is older than the oldest active transaction, this can reduce locking significantly, enhancing performance.

While locks protect data during transactions, another process, latching, controls access to physical pages. Latches are very lightweight, short-term synchronization objects protecting actions that do not need to be locked for the life of a transaction. When the engine scans a page, it latches the page, reads the row, gives it back to the relational engine, and then unlatches the page again so another process can reach the same data. Through a process called lazy latching, the storage engine optimizes access to the data pages by releasing latches only when a page is also requested by another ongoing process. If no ongoing process requests the same data page, a single latch remains valid for the entire operation on that page.

For improving concurrency in your system, you should focus on the design of the database system and the code objects that touch it. SQL Server 2000 is designed to support multiple terabytes of data and to scale upwards for virtually limitless performance. The role of the DBA is to manage the database life cycle, a cycle of design and optimization of all database components from code to data storage on disk, to ensure that the design continues to meet the service level agreement.

Tables and Indexes

Enhancements have also been made to the physical data structures, to allow more flexibility of design and maintenance.

As a table or index grows, SQL Server allocates new data pages in sets of eight; these are called extents. A row of data cannot cross pages, so it can hold only 8 KB of data, although associated **text**, **ntext**, or **image** columns can be stored on different pages. Tables that have clustered indexes are physically stored in key order on disk. Heaps, which are tables that do not have clustered indexes, are not sorted. The records are stored in the order in which they were inserted.

SQL Server 2000 supports indexes on views. (Indexed views are called materialized views in some other database products.) This is because when you create a clustered index on a view, the view is no longer a derived object, but becomes a base object and is stored in the database with the same structure as a table with a clustered index. An indexed view is useful for storing precalculated values, or the result of a complex join, in cases where the maintenance cost does not outweigh the performance gain. In Enterprise Edition, the query processor automatically uses an indexed view whenever this would optimize a query plan. Indexed views can improve query speed on data that is rarely changed but is frequently part of a complex join or calculation query.

In-Row Text

In-row text allows you to store small text data in the primary page. For example, if you have a table that has a text column, but the text values are frequently small enough to fit on a normal page with the rest of the row, you can set a threshold on the text column. The threshold determines the size below which data is stored on the primary page rather than a separate text page. This results in much faster performance if the majority of the data will fit on the page, and only a small percentage of the data is actually large enough to justify the creation of a text page.

To determine when to use this new feature, balance the storage density or how many rows are stored on each data page versus the I/O improvement. For example, you have a text column for comments. In the table, you observe that 20 percent of the text values are large, but the other 80 percent are less than 100 bytes. This may seem like a logical candidate for the in-row text solution; however, you should only use in-row text if the data in that column is accessed frequently. If your users access this table frequently, but they do not look at the comments column unless they are doing special research, using in-row text might not be the best answer. The storage density is reduced, because fewer rows per page are stored, but table scan response times are increased, because the table contains more pages. The best case for implementing in-row text is when you have a frequently accessed text column that also happens to have many small values that could be stored in the row.

New Data Types

SQL Server 2000 introduces three new data types. **bigint** is an 8-byte integer type. **sql_variant** allows the storage of data values of different data types. The third data type, **table**, is useful for optimizing performance. Table variables make more efficient use of **tempdb**, and are faster than temporary tables. They are scoped to the batch where they were declared. As long as the data stored in them does not fill the data cache, these temporary tables are much faster. As a general rule, always consider the resources of your server when you use either table variables or temporary tables.

Indexes

Access to the data is optimized through the use of indexes. Correct indexing is vital to performance. Incorrect indexing is one of the most common causes of slowness in a database. Indexing is based on usage, which usually changes over time. Therefore, in addition to performing standard index maintenance, you should periodically check current indexing and adjust it to current system usage by dropping or adding indexes as appropriate.

Several new features in SQL Server 2000 make index maintenance more efficient and easier for administration. These enhancements decrease disk I/O, increasing the performance of index scans. This is especially useful where there is a secondary index available for a range scan.

Building Indexes

When you build an index, the storage engine samples the rows and calculates the most efficient way to utilize server resources to build the index. Options allow you to control how indexes are built, so you can choose to control how system resources are allocated. You can use these options to balance resources in a process that is important to performance of the system as a whole, in accordance with your knowledge of the particular database system, so the index build will have the lowest possible impact on transaction processing.

Resource	Command	Option	Description
Memory	`sp_configure` (advanced)	`index create memory`	Specifies the amount of memory used by any index build
TempDB	`create index`	`Sort_in_tempdb`	Causes disk space used for sorting during the index build to be allocated from **tempdb**. This can result in more I/O bandwidth if **tempdb** is on separate disks and can result in a possible more physically contiguous layout of index pages if the database is low on contiguous space.
CPU	`sp_configure` (advanced)	`max degree of parallelism`	Limits the number of processors (CPU) used in parallel operations (server wide).

For more information about these options, see SQL Server Books Online.

Another scalability feature for large systems is the parallel index build, which is available in Enterprise Edition. This process is invoked automatically when you issue a single CREATE INDEX statement. The storage engine calculates the requirements for the data and then creates separate threads, each of which builds a section of the index.

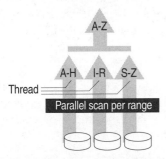

An index build can also make use of a shared table scan, to further optimize the process.

Defragmenting Indexes

SQL Server 2000 supports online reorganization of indexes, a tremendous advancement from earlier versions. Online index reorganization has minimal impact on transaction throughput and can be stopped and restarted at any time without loss of work. The reorganization is accomplished in small increments and is fully recoverable.

As information is inserted, deleted, and updated in a table, the clustered and nonclustered index pages can eventually become fragmented, decreasing the efficiency of range queries against that data. Therefore, it can be beneficial to defragment your indexes periodically. You can use DBCC SHOWCONTIG, which has been improved in SQL Server 2000, to analyze and report fragmentation. For more information, see SQL Server Books Online.

If you determine that an index is fragmented, use DBCC INDEXDEFRAG to reorganize it. It reorders the pages in logical key order, compacting free space and moving rows within the established extents to conform to the fill factor setting. This enhances read performance by densely populating the pages so less of them must be read during a scan of the data. Running DBCC INDEXDEFRAG has far less impact on online performance than rebuilding the index does, provided the index has been regularly maintained and is not completely fragmented.

DBCC INDEXDEFRAG is one of a number of long-running online administrative operations that use small transactions internally. These small transactions maximize concurrency within the server, allow the operation to be stopped without loss of work, and are fully logged to prevent having to redo them in case of a failure.

Logging and Recovery

The transaction log is a stream of records that records changes to the database from the point the database was created until the current point in time. Every logged operation creates a log record. The log records generated by a transaction are written to disk when the transaction commits. In contrast, the data pages modified by the transaction are not immediately written to disk, but are retained in the SQL Server buffer cache and written to disk some time later. Delaying writes of the data to disk maximizes the efficiency of multiple accesses to the data pages and avoids disrupting scans. Forcing the log to disk on commit guarantees that no committed work is lost if the server goes down.

Recovery ensures that a database is transactionally consistent prior to bringing it online. If a database is transactionally consistent, all committed work is present and any uncommitted work has been undone. The log always defines the correct view of the database. Simply put, recovery is the process of making the data consistent with the transaction log at a given point in time.

Recovery is performed automatically when SQL Server starts, when a database is attached, or as the final step in restoring a database from backups. Recovery performed by SQL Server when it starts is called *startup recovery*. Recovery from backups is typically due to disk failure. This type of recovery is called *media recovery*.

Startup recovery occurs automatically each time an instance of SQL Server is started and consists of rolling back any transactions that were incomplete when the instance was last shut down. In the case of recovery from backups, the DBA may choose to recover to an earlier point in time. This is subject to restrictions. For more information, see SQL Server Books Online. In both cases, recovery operates based on this target point in time.

Recovery consists of two phases:

1. Redo all changes until the target point in time is encountered in the transaction log.

2. Undo all work performed by transactions that were active at the point where redo stopped.

SQL Server uses *checkpoints* to limit the amount of time required for startup recovey. A checkpoint forces all modified data pages currently in the buffer cache to disk. This creates a starting point for the redo portion of recovery. Checkpoints can be expensive, so SQL Server automatically manages checkpoints to maximize performance while minimizing restart time.

The logging and recovery technology used in SQL Server requires that writes that complete successfully be stored durably on disk. If you use write-caching disk storage, work with your storage vendor to ensure that the cache is fault tolerant. Fault tolerance means that the cache is immune to power failures or operator actions. If your cache is not fault tolerant, it should be disabled.

Logical Log Marks

In SQL Server 7.0, it was possible to recover to any specified point in time. In the case of hardware failure, the restore process was fairly straightforward. However, another threat to a database is the possibility that invalid data may be entered or that valid data may be destroyed by a user's action. In this case, you need to determine when the problem transaction began. In SQL Server 7.0, the only way to do this was to restore logs to a copy of the database until the problem recurred; then you could run your restore to the production image up to a point in time just prior to the discovered time of error.

In SQL Server 2000, you can mark transactions in the log. Later, if you need to restore, you can reference the mark that was used at the time of execution, rather than using wall-clock time. To do this, use a named BEGIN TRANSACTION statement and the WITH MARK [*description*] clause. The marks are stored in **msdb**. Recovery can include or stop right before a transaction that contains the mark. For example, if you have a process that runs in batch and changes many records, you can use this feature to ensure that you can roll the data back to the point in time that the command was executed.

Mark names do not need to be unique. To indicate which transaction you need, specify a **datetime** value. The syntax for this is:

```
RESTORE LOG WITH [ STOPBEFOREMARK|STOPAFTERMARK ] = @TaggedTransaction AFTER @datetime
```

You can also use marks in a distributed transaction, known as distributed marks, to support recovery of multiple related databases to a transactionally consistent state. These related databases might reside on the same or different instances of SQL Server. You can set distributed marks across a set of databases periodically (for example, once every five minutes). If the transaction log of one of the databases is damaged, you must recover the set of databases to an earlier point in time. The distributed mark provides this point. Using distributed marks negates the worry of coordinating precise timing of backups for multiple related databases. For more information, see "Recovering to a Named Transaction" in SQL Server Books Online.

Shrinking the Transaction Log

Log shrink operations were not executed immediately in SQL Server 7.0. They were deferred until the transaction log was next backed up or truncated. This confused many SQL Server 7.0 customers. SQL Server 2000 shrinks the log as much as possible and then indicates if further shrinking will be possible after a log backup. In this case, run the shrink command again after the log backup has completed. For more information, see "Shrinking the Transaction Log" in SQL Server Books Online.

The size of the log will be based on your current recovery model and your application design. If you find that you need to shrink to log periodically, look beyond the symptom to the cause; You should further investigate what is causing the log to fill up, rather than focus on constant maintenance with the shrink command.

Recovery Models

Recovery models were added to SQL Server 2000 to facilitate data protection planning. They clarify tradeoffs between performance, log space requirements, and protection from media (disk) failure. There are three models: Simple Recovery, Full Recovery, and Bulk-Logged.

The choice of recovery model is based on database usage and availability requirements and helps determine appropriate backup and restore procedures. Recovery models only apply to media recovery, that is, recovery from backups. Startup recovery recovers all committed work. For more information, see "Selecting a Recovery Model" in SQL Server Books Online.

You can easily transition between recovery models. For example, on a very large database, you can use full or bulk logged, or both. You can use full during the day and bulk_logged at night, during a data load process that consists of bulk insert and rebuilding indexes. You can also switch to bulk logging while you run a data load and switch back to full mode, run a transaction log backup, and be able to restore to that point in time without having to run a full database backup. This feature allows you to do the bulk processing more efficiently; all you need to do is make a transaction log backup afterwards.

To change recovery models, use the following syntax:

```
ALTER DATABASE SET RECOVERY RecoveryModel
```

For more information, see "Switching Recovery Models" in SQL Server Books Online.

Simple Recovery Model

The Simple Recovery model typically requires less log space, but it incurs the greatest potential work loss if data or log files are damaged. Only events needed for basic recovery are logged. Using the Simple Recovery Model, only full database and differential database backups are available. In the event of a failure, all committed work since the last backup must be redone. This model is the simplest to administer, but it is not a good choice for a mission-critical application where loss of committed work cannot be tolerated.

This model is similar to the **truncate log on checkpoint** option in SQL Server 7.0 and earlier versions.

Full Recovery Model

In the Full Recovery model, everything is logged. Full Recovery model provides complete protection against work loss from a damaged data file. If the transaction log is damaged, work committed since the most recent log backup is lost and must be redone manually.

Even when you use the Full Recovery model, it is important to use fault-tolerant disks for the transaction log to prevent data loss. The Full Recovery model also allows recovery to any specific point in time.

Bulk-Logged Recovery Model

The Bulk-Logged Recovery model provides the highest performance for bulk operations. These operations also consume less log space than they do under the Full Recovery model. For example, the allocation of a new page is logged, but the data inserted onto the page is not. In SQL Server 2000, bulk operations consist of bulk load (BCP and BULK INSERT, including when they run within a DTS package), SELECT INTO, CREATE INDEX, WRITETEXT, and UPDATETEXT.

Compared with the Full Recovery model, the Bulk-Logged Recovery model minimizes logging for bulk operations. Keep in mind that in the event that recovery becomes necessary, if the log is damaged or if bulk operations have occurred since the most recent log backup, changes made in the database since the last log backup are lost.

This model does not support recovery to a specific point in time, but it will allow recovery to the end of a transaction log backup containing bulk changes. Transaction log backups made using the Bulk-Logged Recovery model contain the extents modified by bulk operations. This feature improves support for log shipping, because you no longer need to worry that a bulk operation will invalidate your backups. SQL Server maintains a bitmap to track the data extents modified, which optimizes the process by which SQL Server identifies changes.

Improved Backup Functionality

In addition to the introduction of recovery models to simplify data protection in general, SQL Server 2000 has improved manageability: snapshot technology, differential backups, and security have been enhanced.

- The transaction log backup chain is never broken. In SQL Server 7.0, certain operations, such as adding a file to a database, broke the log chain and required a subsequent full database backup.

- Backup operations do not conflict with applications or other administrative actions. For example, backups can occur concurrently with bulk operations such as create index and bulk load.

- Log and file backups can occur concurrently.

Unattended backup operations, regardless of system activity, are also better supported in SQL Server 2000.

SQL Server supports snapshot backup and restore technologies in conjunction with independent hardware and software vendors. Snapshot backups minimize or eliminate the use of server resources to accomplish the backup. This is especially beneficial for moderate to very large databases in which availability is extremely important. The primary benefits of this technology are:

- A backup can be created in a very short time, usually measured in seconds, with little or no impact on the server.

- A disk backup can be used to restore a database just as quickly.

- Another host can create a backup with no impact on the production system.

- A copy of a production database can be created instantly for reporting or testing.

Snapshot backups and restores are accomplished in cooperation with third-party hardware and/or software vendors who use features of SQL Server 2000 designed for this purpose. The backup technology creates an instantaneous copy of the data being backed up, usually by splitting a mirrored set of disks. At restore time, the original is immediately available. The underlying disks are synchronized in the background, resulting in almost instantaneous restores.

Differential database backups can be completed in a time that is proportional to the amount of data changed since the last full backup. The less your data has changed, the quicker the backup. SQL Server 2000 uses a bitmap to track data extents modified since the most recent database or file backup to enable them to be located efficiently. In addition, SQL Server 2000 supports file differential backups.

Backups still accumulate changes made to the database since the most recent full backup, functioning the same way in the event of recovery. They are significantly faster, however, because they only record the small amount of information that has changed, especially for very large databases that contain only a small amount of changed data.

For added security, you can implement password protection for your backup media and backup sets. This helps prevent unauthorized users from adding to your backups or restoring to your database.

Administrative Improvements

Several administrative features of the storage engine have been altered and enhanced in SQL Server 2000.

Database Verification

The DBCCs provide a variety of administrative capabilities, including the CHECK commands for verifying database consistency

Experience with SQL Server 7.0 and SQL Server 2000 has shown that database inconsistency is caused by hardware problems that may or may not be detected by the database engine or applications during normal operation. This is particularly applicable to data that is accessed infrequently. In response to this need, SQL Server 2000 introduces a checking mode, Physical_Only, that is designed to detect most hardware-caused problems. It is very fast, approximately disk scan speed, and is not resource intensive.

Due to fundamental architectural improvements in the SQL Server storage engine, which started with SQL Server 7.0, it is not necessary to run database verification as part of normal maintenance. However, Microsoft remains committed to database verification tools as an important part of managing mission critical data. Microsoft recommends that you:

- Run the Physical_Only check occasionally, depending on your confidence in underlying hardware, particularly the disk subsystems.
- Run a complete database check at critical times, such as a hardware or software upgrade, or whenever a problem is suspected regardless of cause.

Microsoft does not recommend running a complete check as part of regular maintenance.

SQL Server 2000 also includes important enhancements to database verification:

- By default, checking is fully online. Online checking has low impact on the transaction workload. This impact will vary depending on the system load, hardware configuration, and speed of **tempdb**. Microsoft has measured this impact at 15 to 20 percent with a medium OLTP workload (50 percent CPU). The TABLOCK option is provided to force the check to take shared table locks, which enables it to run faster but will prevent updates.
- Checking is done in parallel on symmetric multiprocessing (SMP) computers, limited by the maximum degree of parallelism you have set for the instance of SQL Server.

SQL Server 2000 check commands continue to support the repair functionality introduced in SQL Server 7.0. Repair can provide an alternative to a restore from backups in some situations. The database must be offline during repair.

Database State Control

SQL Server 2000 includes enhancements to the ALTER DATABASE statement that allow more control of database states through Transact-SQL. All database options can now be modified with greater control through the ALTER DATABASE command; **sp_dboption** and **databaseproperty**() will no longer be updated in future releases. The Transact-SQL commands **sp_helpdb** and **DatabasePropertyEx**() provide information about the state of your database.

The following table lists database state options.

Option type	Available settings
User access	SINGLE_USER
	RESTRICTED_USER
	MULTI_USER
Availability	ONLINE
	OFFLINE
Updatability	READ_ONLY
	READ_WRITE

SQL Server also sets the following states in reaction to conditions within the database: restoring, recovering, and suspect. The database options can be set by using the SET clause of the ALTER DATABASE statement, the **sp_dboption** system stored procedure, or, in some cases, SQL Server Enterprise Manager.

When the database state is changed, the session making changes to the database state remains connected, while sessions inconsistent with the new state can be terminated and their transactions rolled back. Session termination options include the following:

- Terminate immediately

- Terminate after a specified time

- Allow the ongoing processes to complete normally

- Check for activity and disregard the state change if active user sessions are found

Here are two examples of the syntax:

```
alter database accting set read_only with rollback immediate
alter database accting set single_user with rollback after 60 seconds
```

For more information, see "Setting Database Options" in SQL Server Books Online.

System Process IDs and Units of Work

An additional administrative enhancement helps when you need to stop a process. The KILL command has been enhanced with status feedback. So, if you want to learn the status of an outstanding KILL command, run the following:

```
KILL SPID WITH STATUSONLY
```

If you try to stop a system process ID (SPID) that is being stopped by another KILL command, the system returns the same status information.

In SQL Server 2000, Microsoft Distributed Transaction Coordinator (MS DTC) transactions can exist without an associated connection or SPID. Therefore, a connection can be used for other processes while waiting for a transaction or unit of work to complete. When the MS DTC transaction manager sends a message that it has completed the task, you can either commit or roll back the transaction.

The term for this is a unit of work (UOW), which is the transaction identifier used by MS DTC for the transaction. A UOW does not have a SPID. For more information, see SQL Server Books Online.

Dynamic Tuning

In SQL Server 2000, usage-based performance tuning is managed dynamically, without required or recommended manual adjustments. The static parameters have been eliminated, but administrative control has been retained for certain resources (for example, setting an upper limit on the amount of memory SQL Server can use). This method is far more accurate and responsive than a manually calculated system based on averages and estimates. This allows you to concentrate on the design aspects of database management.

Traditional database systems require a great deal of manual management and tuning. For example, to tune the system in response to usage, the DBA would be required to monitor the system, recording a vast amount of statistics over time, in order to select a static setting that seems to provide the optimal advantage for the system. Then the DBA would re-evaluate the system to judge what effect the new setting has, and the tuning process would begin again.

SQL Server 2000 introduces a dynamic algorithm into the storage engine, which actively monitors usage of the server and adjusts the settings internally. Dynamic feedback and analysis in SQL Server 2000 keeps the setting within 10 percent of the absolute optimal value. The result is a better-tuned and highly adaptive system.

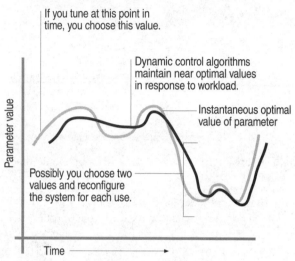

Data Storage Components

SQL Server 2000 balances across all available processors in coordination with the Windows 2000 operating system. If you are running a dedicated instance of SQL Server, and no other applications share the same resources, leave the processor related settings at their default to take full advantage of all the processors. SQL Server can take advantage of parallel processing across multiple processors for queries, index builds, and DBCCs across available processors. SQL Server 2000 Standard Edition can support up to four processors and 2 GB of physical memory (RAM). Enterprise Edition can scale upwards to new levels, to support up to 32 processors and 64 GB of physical memory.

The main source of memory for an instance of SQL Server is called its memory pool. Almost all data structures that use memory in an instance of SQL Server are allocated from the memory pool. Examples of objects allocated from the memory pool include the buffer cache, where recently read data pages are stored, and the procedure cache, which holds recent execution plans.

The assignments within the memory pool are highly dynamic. To optimize performance, SQL Server constantly adjusts the amounts of the memory pool assigned to the various areas. In situations where the number of stored execution plans is lower, the memory pool is adjusted to make optimal use of the resources by making more memory available for the data cache.

SQL Server 2000 is designed to use memory to minimize disk I/O as much as possible. To accomplish this, SQL Server uses the buffer cache to hold recently referenced data, in physical memory, where it can be reused. One potential way to reduce disk I/O and speed up your database system would be to add to the physical memory available to SQL Server.

Normally, memory settings do not require any adjustment. However, they can be controlled in certain situations. For example, memory requires special attention where you are running multiple instances of SQL Server on the same server, especially if you use failover clustering. You also need to monitor memory usage if you are running applications in addition to SQL Server on the same server.

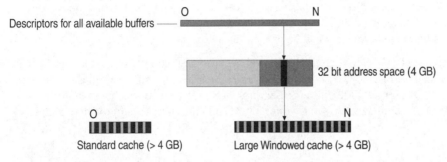

Use of physical memory beyond 3 GB is vastly improved in SQL Server 2000 because it is built on functionality in the Windows 2000 operating system. SQL Server 2000 Enterprise Edition can use as much memory as Windows 2000 Advanced Server or Windows 2000 Datacenter Server allows.

For more information on large memory support in SQL Server 2000, see "Managing AWE Memory" in SQL Server Books Online.

Files, Filegroups, and Disks

SQL Server stores data and the log on disk files. In a basic installation, and as a default, data and log files are created in the default location specified in the server configuration. However, to maximize performance, you can apply a few basic principles:

- Spread data over as many disks, channels, and controllers as possible.

  In general, the more disks you have (regardless of their individual size), the faster the storage engine can read and write data. The larger your system becomes, the more important it is to store the data files and log files on separate physical drives. Also, because the use of **tempdb** has changed, you should now store **tempdb** on a large number of disks, for example, with the data files or on a separate set of disks.

- Use filegroups to scale your enterprise database.

  Every database begins with one default filegroup. Because SQL Server 2000 can work effectively without additional filegroups, many systems will not need to add user-defined filegroups. However, as a system grows, the use of additional filegroups supports scalability by allowing you to increase performance by distributing I/O appropriately for your system.

  In SQL Server 2000, if you set a particular filegroup within a database to read-only, the data on that filegroup cannot be altered, but catalog information such as permissions can still be managed.

To successfully implement an optimized database design, carefully consider the configuration of the database storage components, including the layout of physical and logical disks, the correct sizing of hardware, and the arrangement of the physical database files across disks.

For more information about SQL Server architecture and the storage engine, see SQL Server Books Online and Kalen Delaney's *Inside Microsoft SQL Server 2000*. For more information about hardware and SQL Server, see "SQL Server 2000 on Large Servers" in SQL Server Books Online. For more information about database optimization, see Chapter 33, "The Data Tier: An Approach to Database Optimization."

Innovation and Evolution

For DBAs, increased flexibility and control over performance provides the freedom to focus their database technology skills and experience on managing the database code, design, and storage components as a unified approach to database system management. The storage engine for SQL Server 2000 was designed to help meet these needs.

Implementing Security

Introduction

This chapter introduces Microsoft® SQL Server™ administrators and developers to the new security features of SQL Server 2000. New features are outlined, and a detailed discussion is provided about how to best implement security in a Microsoft Windows® 2000 domain environment. Source code examples are included for developers who want to implement the security model immediately.

For those who will be upgrading servers from SQL Server version 7.0 and earlier, this chapter explains the security part of the upgrade, and provides notes for those who know how security was performed in SQL Server 6.5 and earlier.

This chapter does not cover security in Microsoft English Query, SQL Server 2000 Meta Data Services, or SQL Server 2000 Analysis Services. For more information about those components, see SQL Server Books Online.

New Security Features

This section examines the new security features of SQL Server 2000, and gives an overview of how security has been enhanced in this release.

Secure Setup

SQL Server 2000 Setup is secure out of the box. When you run SQL Server Setup in any edition (except Microsoft SQL Server Desktop Engine), you can now select Windows Authentication Mode, which is the default. For more information about authentication modes, see "Authentication Modes" in this chapter.

Windows Authentication Mode is more secure than Mixed Mode authentication. If you select Mixed Mode, you will need to set a password for the system administrator (**sa**) login to SQL Server. Optionally, you can set a blank password, but this is not recommended because your system will be vulnerable to attack.

When installing SQL Server on a Microsoft Windows NT® 4.0 or Windows 2000 operating system using the NTFS file system, SQL Server Setup limits access to the directories into which SQL Server installs. Only the service account(s) selected for SQL Server services and the built-in Administrators group can access those directories during setup. By default, the directory is C:\Program Files\Microsoft SQL Server\MSSQL. Access to the SQL Server registry keys (starting at HKLM\Software\Microsoft\ MSSQLServer, or HKLM\Software\Microsoft\Microsoft SQL Server\MSSQL$InstanceName for a named instance) is also restricted to the service account(s) selected during SQL Server Setup.

SQL Server 2000 Desktop Engine Setup

The Microsoft SQL Server 2000 Desktop Engine Setup program installs on Windows NT 4.0 and Windows 2000 operating systems in Windows Authentication Mode by default. On Microsoft Windows 98 or Microsoft Windows Millennium (Windows Me) operating systems, Windows Authentication is not available, so Mixed Mode is selected. To change the installation default to Mixed Mode, specify the **SECURITYMODE=SQL** option at the command prompt for Setup (or in the .ini file). For more information, see SQL Server Books Online.

As noted in the Readme.txt file for SQL Server 2000 and in SQL Server Books Online, two parameters, USEDEFAULTSAPWD and SAPASSWORD, are ignored by the final version of Desktop Engine Setup. The **sa** login password used when the Desktop Engine is set up with Mixed Mode authentication will always be blank, and it should be changed immediately after installation.

C2 Security Evaluation Completed

SQL Server 2000 meets the C2 security certification for the evaluated configuration from the US government. C2 auditing is necessary if you are running a C2-certified system. A C2-certified system meets a government standard that defines the security level. To have a C2-certified installation of SQL Server, you must configure SQL Server in the evaluated C2 configuration. For more information about the configuration for a C2-compliant system, see http://www.microsoft.com/technet/sql/. For an announcement about the C2 certification, see the Trusted Product Evaluation Program at http://www.radium.ncsc.mil.

Kerberos and Delegation in Windows 2000 Environments

Kerberos is the primary authentication mechanism on Windows 2000 networks. Delegation is the ability to pass security credentials across multiple computers and applications. As users access different computers and applications, the security credentials of users are preserved. SQL Server 2000 fully supports Kerberos, including the ability to accept delegated Kerberos tickets and delegate these tickets further (when running on the Windows 2000 operating system) with Windows 2000 domain controllers and Active Directory™. This affects remote stored procedures as well as distributed queries. For more information about Kerberos and Windows 2000 security, see http://www.microsoft.com/windows2000/.

To configure delegation, all servers that you are connecting to must be running Windows 2000 with Kerberos support enabled, and you must use Active Directory. The following must be set in Active Directory for delegation to work:

- **Account is sensitive and cannot be delegated.** This option must not be selected for the user requesting delegation.
- **Account is trusted for delegation.** This option must be selected for the service account of SQL Server.
- **Computer is trusted for delegation.** This option must be selected for the server running an instance of SQL Server.

To use security account delegation, SQL Server must have a Service Principal Name (SPN) assigned by the Windows 2000 account domain administrator. The SPN must be assigned to the service account of the SQL Server service on that particular computer. Delegation enforces mutual authentication. The SPN is necessary to prove that SQL Server is verified on the particular server, at the particular socket address by the Windows 2000 account domain administrator. Your domain administrator can establish an SPN for SQL Server. For more information about the **setspn** utility, see the Windows 2000 Resource Kit.

To create an SPN for SQL Server 2000

- Run the following command:

```
setspn -A MSSQLSvc/Host:port serviceaccount
```

For example:

```
setspn -A MSSQLSvc/server1.redmond.microsoft.com sqlaccount
```

You must use the TCP/IP Sockets Network Library for delegation to work. You cannot use Named Pipes because the SPN targets a particular TCP/IP socket. If you are using multiple ports, you must have a SPN for each port.

You can also enable delegation by running under the **LocalSystem** account. SQL Server 2000 self-registers at service startup and automatically registers the SPN. This option is easier than enabling delegation using a domain user account; however, when SQL Server 2000 shuts down, the SPNs will be unregistered for the **LocalSystem** account.

Security Auditing

One of the requirements for the US government C2 certification is a security auditing capability. SQL Server 2000 has a fully functional audit mechanism built into the product. This audit mechanism has several components, each of which is described here. When put together, these components allow you to track any permissions usage of any kind within SQL Server 2000.

SQL Trace

SQL Trace is the name given to the server-side components of the auditing mechanism. Auditing has been added to the same mechanism used in SQL Server 7.0 to provide performance information about SQL Server. Performance information is still returned, as well as audit information, but the interface has been completely redesigned in SQL Server 2000. All SQL Server 7.0 extended stored procedures have been replaced. For information about the new stored procedures used for security auditing, see SQL Server Books Online.

Each time an auditable security event occurs inside the SQL Server relational or storage engine, the event engine (SQL Trace) is notified. If a trace is currently enabled and running that would capture the event that was generated, the event is written to the appropriate trace file.

For information about how to enable traces both for ordinary security audits and C2-specific auditing, see SQL Server Books Online.

SQL Profiler

SQL Profiler is the graphical utility that allows you to view audit trace files and perform selected actions on them. You can search through the files, save the files out to a table, and create and configure trace definitions. SQL Profiler is a client to SQL Trace, and you do not need to have SQL Profiler running to perform a security audit.

C2-Mode Auditing

SQL Server 2000 has been certified as C2 compliant. One of the requirements of being in the C2-evaluated configuration is that C2-style auditing is enabled. C2 auditing has predetermined selections that determine which events are audited (all security events), which data columns are captured (all that might have information from these events), and other fixed settings. Each setting is documented in the Trusted Facilities Manual for SQL Server 2000, available at http://www.microsoft.com/Downloads/.

Elimination of the SQLAgentCmdExec Proxy Account

SQL Server 2000 has eliminated the creation of the **SQLAgentCmdExec** account. In SQL Server version 7.0 and earlier, SQL Server Agent jobs that were owned by logins without system administrator permissions could access Windows resources, but they did so using a proxy account known as **SQLAgentCmdExec**. This was a Windows NT 4.0 and Windows 2000 user account created locally on the computer on which SQL Server was installed during setup.

By default, the ability of non-system administrators to access resources outside of SQL Server has been disabled. However, when enabling a proxy account with SQL Server 2000, you can now specify a domain user account. This allows users who are not system administrators to access network resources instead of resources local to the computer on which you installed SQL Server.

Server Role Enhancements

SQL Server 2000 includes minor enhancements to fixed server roles. For information about using fixed server roles, see "Predefined Roles" in this chapter.

bulkadmin

bulkadmin is a new role in SQL Server 2000. Membership in this role allows a login to run the BULK INSERT command. Users who are members of this group can load data from any file on the network and from any computer the server is running on, as long as the SQL Server service account has access to the data. Membership should be considered carefully. Members of this role still must have the INSERT permission on any table they want as the target of the BULK INSERT command. Membership in **bulkadmin** only grants permission to execute the BULK INSERT command and the right to access files during the execution of this command.

securityadmin

Members of the **securityadmin** role can change the passwords of SQL Server Authentication mode logins. The exception to this is that the passwords of **sysadmin** fixed-server role members cannot be reset. For example, people who work in internal technical support, who do not need full system administrator access to SQL Server, might be members of this role.

serveradmin

The **serveradmin** role has been modified in the area of server-wide messages. Membership in this role now allows a login to execute **sp_addmessage**, **sp_dropmessage**, and **sp_altermessage**.

Encryption

Network Encryption Using SSL/TLS

SQL Server 2000 now automatically supports encryption of data and other network traffic as it travels between the client and server systems on a network. The encryption strength depends on the encryption capabilities authorized by the certificate installed for SQL Server and the cryptographic capabilities of the client and the server.

The certificate selected for SQL Server must be assigned to the name of the server, in the form of the fully qualified Domain Name System (DNS) server name (for example, SQLServer.Redmond.corp.Microsoft.com). The certificate must be valid for server authentication. Log in to SQL Server as the SQL Server service account, obtain the certificate (from either an internal certificate authority or a trusted third-party provider), and then install it on the server in the location suggested when you import the certificate.

Login Packet Encryption

During any login attempt, if a certificate is present on the server and is usable (that is, it is valid for server authentication and has the DNS name of the computer as the subject name in the certificate) all login-related packets will be encrypted. This happens automatically, and as long as the certificate is installed, no additional server configuration is required.

Client-Requested Encryption

The client can request encryption of all data traffic to SQL Server. This option is set using the Client Network Utility (using the **Force Protocol Encryption** option), and it applies to all outbound connections from that computer. The **Client-Requested Encryption** option also prevents access to SQL Server 7.0 and earlier, as well as any SQL Server 2000 server that does not have a valid certificate.

You can also set this option programmatically with the **Encrypt=yes** option in the connection string of your OLE DB or ODBC connection to a database server.

Server-Requested Encryption

Encryption can be required on the server if the database administrator requests it. This option is set using the Server Network Utility (using the **Force Protocol Encryption** option). Setting the **Server-Requested Encryption** option guarantees that all network traffic to SQL Server will be encrypted. If a client is unable to negotiate encryption with SQL Server, the connection will be terminated.

Encrypted File System Support on Windows 2000

SQL Server 2000 works on Windows 2000 if you use Encrypting File System (EFS), which is part of Windows 2000, to protect data files.

You must encrypt the files using the service account of SQL Server, and if you change to service account, you must re-encrypt the files using the new account. (To do this, unencrypt the files, change the service account for SQL Server services, and then re-encrypt the files with the new service account.) If you do not update the encryption when you change the service account, SQL Server may not be able to start, because it will not be able to decrypt the files that were encrypted with the previous service account's credentials.

Server-Based Encryption Enhanced

All server-based encrypted data (passwords, encrypted stored procedures, and so on) now use CryptoAPI. This ensures more robust and secure storage of protected items within SQL Server.

DTS Package Encryption

Data Transformation Services (DTS) packages are now encrypted using CryptoAPI. All packages are encrypted, regardless of whether or not a password is supplied.

Password Protection

Backups and Backup Media Sets

SQL Server 2000 allows you to specify a password either for an individual backup or for a backup media set. Without this password, you will be unable to restore the backup. This allows you to protect your backups from unauthorized restores.

The data is not encrypted, so a program not using the Microsoft Tape Format can ignore the password and give you access to the data within the backup. All SQL Server restore mechanisms use the password.

SQL Server Enterprise Manager

In SQL Server 2000, passwords for authenticated logins are always encrypted using CryptoAPI.

Service Account Changes Using SQL Server Enterprise Manager

When you change the service account for SQL Server services (SQL Server or SQL Server Agent) using SQL Server Enterprise Manager, the utility resets File and Directory permissions (when data is stored in NTFS). The utility also resets the registry key permissions. The new permissions are added, and the previous service account remains, as well as the built-in administrators group. The password is reset in the services database as if you reset the account information in Control Panel in Services, and then the appropriate Windows NT 4.0 or Windows 2000 security permissions are granted to the newly selected service account. Finally, the new service account is made a **sysadmin** fixed server role member in SQL Server.

SUID Column

The **SUID** column has been removed in SQL Server 2000. In SQL Server 7.0, it was superseded by the **SID** column, but it was preserved for backward compatibility. The **sysalternates** table has also been removed, because it contained only relationships between SUIDs.

The **SUID** column was present in the following system tables in earlier releases:

- **sysdatabases**
- **syslogins**

- **sysremotelogins**
- **sysusers**
- **sysprocesses**
- **sysalternates**

Security Model

To implement security in the most practical ways on SQL Server 2000, it is important to understand how the design team expected the users to implement the security model. The design team saw two basic ways to implement security in SQL Server 2000, both taking advantage of the power of users and groups in

Windows 2000. The first uses local groups, and the second uses roles. (Universal groups in Windows 2000 are also supported.)

The local group-based method follows this general outline:

1. Users in each domain are assigned to Windows global groups.

2. The Windows global groups from the various domains are placed into a Windows local group.

3. The Windows local group is granted rights to log in to SQL Server 2000.

4. The Windows local group is granted access rights to the appropriate databases. This Windows local group may not be the same one as was used for granting login rights in Step 3. Therefore, Steps 1 and 2 are often repeated to group the users by their required access permissions.

5. The Windows local group is assigned permissions on the specific database objects.

Roles reduce the requirements of grouping users within Windows, by grouping the users within SQL Server 2000. The role-based approach is similar to the local group-based approach, except that multiple Windows global and local groups would probably not be created in this scenario. Also, when roles are used to assign object permissions, individuals must still be granted permissions on the server and the database by following the steps outlined here.

1. Users in each domain are assigned to Windows global groups.

2. The Windows global groups from the various domains are placed into a Windows local group.

3. The Windows local group is granted rights to log in to SQL Server 2000.

4. The Windows local group is granted access rights to the appropriate databases. This Windows local group may not be the same one as was used for granting login rights in Step 3. Therefore, Steps 1 and 2 are often repeated to group the users by access permissions required.

5. Individual Windows accounts and Windows groups are assigned to a role.

6. Object permissions are assigned to the roles.

Authentication Modes

SQL Server 2000 provides two authentication modes for securing access to the server: Windows Authentication Mode and Mixed Mode.

Windows Authentication Mode

Windows Authentication Mode is the default authentication mode in SQL Server 2000. In Windows Authentication Mode, SQL Server 2000 relies solely on Windows to authenticate users. Windows users or groups are then granted access to SQL Server.

Windows Authentication Mode allows SQL Server 2000 to rely on Windows to authenticate users. Connections made to the server using this mode are known as trusted connections.

When Windows Authentication Mode is used, the database administrator allows users to access the computer running SQL Server by granting them the right to log in to SQL Server 2000. Windows security identifiers (SIDs) are used to track Windows authenticated logins. As Windows SIDs are used, the database administrator can grant login access directly to Windows users or groups.

Mixed Mode

In Mixed Mode, users can be authenticated by Windows Authentication or by SQL Server Authentication. Users who are authenticated by SQL Server have their username and password pairs maintained within SQL Server. (The username and password pairs are stored in the **sysxlogins** system table of the **master** database.)

In SQL Server 2000, Mixed Mode relies on Windows to authenticate users when the client and server are capable of using NTLM (standard Windows NT 4.0 or Windows 2000 logon using challenge/response) or Kerberos logon authentication protocols. If the client is unable to use a standard Windows logon, SQL Server requires a username and password pair, and compares this pair against those stored in its system tables. Connections that rely on username and password pairs are called non-trusted connections.

Mixed mode is supplied for backward compatibility and when SQL Server 2000 is installed on the Windows 98 or Windows Me operating systems. Trusted connections are not supported if the server is running on Windows 98 or Windows Me.

Using SIDs Internally

SQL Server 2000 uses SIDs internally. Windows users and groups can be granted access to databases or specific database objects directly. For example, Jane is a member of the SALES and MARKETING groups in Windows. The SALES group has been granted permission to log in to SQL Server and access the **pubs** database. An administrator could grant access to the **authors** table for Jane by her Windows name, REDMOND\Jane (the Windows account must be referenced by domain and username). In this case, Jane's SID would be stored in the system tables of the **pubs** database.

SQL Server 2000 does not support User Principal Names (UPNs). For example, if Jane's login is domain SALES, user SOMEONE, the login to SQL Server would be SALES\SOMEONE. A login in the form of SOMEONE@microsoft.com, as supported by Windows 2000 Active Directory, would not work.

Roles

Roles are used in SQL Server 2000 the way groups are used in Windows. Roles allow users to be collected into a single unit against which permissions can be applied. Permissions granted, denied, or revoked from a role apply to members of the role. For example, roles can be used to represent a job performed by a class of workers in an organization. Permissions can then be granted to that role. As workers rotate into the job, they are made members of the role; as they rotate out of the job, they are removed. This removes the requirement to repeatedly grant, deny, and revoke permissions to or from individuals as they accept or leave a job. For more information, see SQL Server Books Online.

Several concepts are important to understand when you are working with roles in SQL Server. First, with the exception of fixed server roles, roles are implemented within a database. This means that the database administrator does not rely on the Windows administrator for the grouping of users. Second, roles can be nested. This nesting is not limited by levels, but for obvious reasons does not allow circular nesting. Third, unlike groups in SQL Server 6.5 and earlier, a database user can be a member of more than one role simultaneously.

Public Role

The **public** role exists in every database, including the **master**, **msdb**, **tempdb**, and **model** system databases. The **public** role provides the default permissions for users in a database. Functionally, it is similar to the Everyone group in the Windows environment. Every database user is a member of this role automatically; users cannot be added or removed from this role, and it cannot be deleted.

Predefined Roles

SQL Server 2000 includes several predefined roles. These roles have predefined implied permissions, which cannot be granted to other user accounts. There are two types of predefined roles: fixed server roles and fixed database roles.

Fixed Server Roles

Fixed server roles are server-wide in their scope. They exist outside of the databases. Each member of a fixed server role is able to add other logins to that same role.

> **Note** All members of the Windows BUILTIN\Administrators group (the local administrator's group) are members of the **sysadmin** role by default.

Fixed server roles found in SQL Server 2000

Fixed server role	Members can
Sysadmin	Perform any activity in SQL Server.
Serveradmin	Configure server-wide configuration options and shut down the server.
Setupadmin	Manage linked servers and startup procedures
Securityadmin	Manage server-wide security settings, including linked servers, and CREATE DATABASE permissions. Reset passwords for SQL Server authentication logins.
Processadmin	Terminate processes running in SQL Server.
Dbcreator	Create, alter, drop, and restore any database.
Diskadmin	Manage disk files.
Bulkadmin	Run the Bulk Insert command without having to be a member of the **sysadmin** role.

To add users to the fixed server roles, use the following Transact-SQL statement:

```
/* Add Bob to the sysadmin server role */
exec sp_addsrvrolemember "REDMOND\Bob", "sysadmin"
```

Windows users and groups can be added to server roles.

To add a user to a server role using SQL Distributed Management Objects (SQL-DMO)

```
' Declare variables.
Dim oServer As SQLDMO.SQLServer

' Create a server object and connect.
Set oServer = CreateObject("SQLDMO.SQLServer")
oServer.Connect ("SERVERNAME")

' Add Bob to the sysadmin server role.
oServer.ServerRoles("sysadmin").AddMember ("REDMOND\Bob")
```

For more information about fixed server roles, see SQL Server Books Online.

Fixed Database Roles

Fixed database roles are defined at the database level, and they exist in each database. Members of the **db_owner** and **db_security** roles can manage fixed database role membership; however, only members of the **db_owner** role can add others to the **db_owner** role.

The following table lists the fixed database roles in SQL Server 2000. Most fixed database roles enable members to perform certain actions; however, some exist to explicitly prevent members from performing certain actions.

SQL Server 2000 fixed database roles

Fixed database roles	Members
db_owner	Can perform all maintenance and configuration activities in the database.
db_accessadmin	Can add or remove access for Windows users, groups, and SQL Server logins.
db_datareader	Can read all data from all user tables.
db_datawriter	Can add, delete, or change data in all user tables.
db_ddladmin	Can run any data definition language (DDL) command in a database.
db_securityadmin	Can modify role membership and manages permissions.
db_backupoperator	Can back up the database.
db_denydatareader	Cannot read any data in user tables within a database.
db_denydatawriter	Cannot add, modify, or delete data in any user tables or views.

For more information about the use of fixed database roles, see SQL Server Books Online.

User-Defined Roles

User-defined roles provide an easy way to manage permissions in a database when a group of users performs a specified set of activities in SQL Server 2000 and there is no applicable Windows group, or if the database administrator does not have sufficient permissions to manage the Windows user accounts. In these situations, user-defined roles provide the database administrator the same flexibility as Windows groups.

User-defined roles apply only at the database level, and are local to the database in which they were created.

Application Roles

Application roles allow the database administrator to restrict user access to data based on the application that the user is using. Application roles allow the application to take over the responsibility of user authentication.

When an application makes a connection to SQL Server 2000, it executes the **sp_setapprole** stored procedure, which takes two parameters: **username** and **password**. These parameters can be encrypted. The **password** can always be encrypted before being sent to SQL Server. If the Multiprotocol Net-Library is used, the packet containing the **password** can also be encrypted. Registry keys are the best place to store the **username** and **password** in an application. The key should be encrypted, and only the application should have the key to unencrypt it. The existing permissions assigned to the user are dropped, and the security context of the application role is assumed.

After application roles are activated, they cannot be deactivated. The only way to return to the original security context of the user is to disconnect from and then reconnect to SQL Server.

Application roles work with both authentication modes, and contain no members. Users cannot be associated with application roles, because the application requests the application role's security context using the **sp_setapprole** stored procedure.

Like user-defined roles, application roles exist only within a database. If an application (in the security context of an application role) connects to one database and then attempts to access a second database, access to the other database is granted (using permissions) through the **guest** account in that database. If the **guest** account has not been specifically granted access to the data, or if it does not exist, the application cannot access the objects.

Another key concept in the use of application roles is that the user who is running the application is audited within SQL Server 2000. In other words, application roles provide the security context within which the database object permissions are checked, but the identity of the actual user is not lost.

Here is an example of an implementation using application roles. If Jane is a member of the ACCOUNTING group, and the ACCOUNTING group members are given access to the data in SQL Server only through the accounting software package, an application role could be created for the accounting software. The **ACCOUNTING** application role would be granted access to the data, while the ACCOUNTING group in Windows would be denied access to the data. Thus, when Jane attempts to access the data using SQL Query Analyzer, she will be denied access; but when Jane uses the accounting software, she will be able to access the data.

To use application roles

1. Create an application role.

2. Assign permissions to the application role.

3. Ensure that the client application connects to SQL Server 2000.

4. Ensure that the client application activates the application role.

The first two steps of this process are usually separated from the last two steps. Therefore, two code fragments will follow for Transact-SQL and Microsoft Visual Basic® respectively.

The Transact-SQL script is as follows:

```
/* Create the application role. */
EXEC sp_addapprole "AccAppRole", "ABC"

/* Grant permissions to SELECT. */
GRANT SELECT
ON authors
TO AccAppRole
GO
```

Here is the code to activate the role:

```
/* Activate the role. */
EXEC sp_setapprole "AccAppRole", {ENCRYPT N "ABC"}
```

The encryption of the password is optional, but encryption ensures greater security when the password has to pass through a wide area network (WAN).

Here is the Visual Basic code to create the role:

```
' Declare variables.
Dim oServer As SQLDMO.SQLServer
Dim oDbRole As SQLDMO.DatabaseRole

' Create a server object and connect.
Set oServer = CreateObject("SQLDMO.SQLServer")
oServer.Connect ("SERVERNAME")

' Create the Role object.
Set oDbRole = CreateObject("SQLDMO.DatabaseRole")

' Set the appropriate properties.
oDbRole.Name = "AccAppRole"
oDbRole.AppRole = True
oDbRole.Password = "ABC"

' Add the Role object to the server's Role collection.
oServer.Databases("pubs").DatabaseRoles.Add oDbRole
```

Here is the Visual Basic code to use the role:

```
' Declare variables.
Dim oConnection As ADODB.Connection

' Create the connection object and connect.
Set oConnection = CreateObject("ADODB.Connection")
oConnection.Provider = "sqloledb"
oConnection.Open "Server=SERVERNAME;Database=pubs;Trusted_Connection=yes"

' Activate the application role. There is no error handling for this sample.
oConnection.Execute "EXEC sp_setapprole 'AccAppRole', {ENCRYPT N 'ABC'}, 'ODBC'"
```

The encryption style (the last parameter) must be set for OLE DB and ODBC data sources. Other data sources cannot explicitly encrypt the password. In these cases, you must use an encrypted communications protocol with the server.

Application roles are implemented per session. If your application opens multiple sessions and all sessions are required to use the same role, each session must first activate the role.

Application roles can be used to provide much more granular security than ever before. For example, a client application could use the user's security context on some connections, while using an application role on another.

When using application roles, executing SELECT USER returns the name of the application role currently being used. If the identity of the logged-on user is required, use the following SQL statement: SELECT SYSTEM_USER.

Securing Access to the Server

Access to the server is controlled differently by the two authentication modes in SQL Server 2000. However, after a user gains access to the server, the authentication modes are identical. SQL Server 2000 security defaults to Windows Authentication when it is installed.

Windows Level

When securing access at the Windows level, administrators should create a login account for each user who will be accessing SQL Server (if the user does not already have an account).

In each user account's domain, global groups should be created to group users by job requirements. The users should then be placed into the appropriate global groups in their domain.

On the computer running SQL Server 2000, local groups should be created according to the various job requirements for which access to SQL Server needs to be granted. The appropriate global groups from the various trusted domains should then be placed into the respective local groups on the computer running SQL Server.

It may seem time-consuming to follow the procedures outlined earlier for a small single-domain network, but experience has shown great value in doing this.

The base requirement is to get all the users with the same security requirements grouped into one unit, which can then be used by the database administrator to grant access to SQL Server 2000. Granting access to SQL Server by group does not eliminate the ability to identify the individual user from within a database. (This is largely the same action as securing a file on NTFS by giving access to members of the SALES group only. If Bob, a member of the SALES group, tries to access the file, the audit log will contain an entry for Bob, not SALES.)

Although the recommendations are strong, they enable the database administrator to assign permissions to objects for Windows universal groups, global groups, local groups, and individual user accounts.

Note Programmatically creating user accounts and groups in the Windows environment is beyond the scope of this chapter. This can be achieved by using the ADSI object model from Visual Basic, or by interacting directly with the Win32® API from Microsoft Visual C++®.

SQL Server Level

At the SQL Server 2000 level, permissions must be granted for the created Windows local groups to log in to SQL Server. Permission to log in to SQL Server can also be granted to users directly, but is not as practical to administer except for the smallest of environments.

Permissions to log in to the server can be granted through the user interface or implemented programmatically using Visual Basic or Transact-SQL.

Note The following definitions are within the context of this document: Visual Basic refers to writing an application using the Visual Basic environment with the SQL-DMO library or using any Visual Basic for Applications environment with the SQL-DMO library. Transact-SQL is the Microsoft implementation of the SQL standard.

New stored procedures have been written to grant access for Windows users and groups. These security-related stored procedures are listed here.

sp_addalias
sp_addapprole
sp_addgroup
sp_addlinkedsrvlogin
sp_addlogin
sp_addremotelogin
sp_addrole
sp_addrolemember
sp_addserver
sp_addsrvrolemember
sp_adduser
sp_approlepassword
sp_change_users_login
sp_changedbowner
sp_changegroup
sp_changeobjectowner
sp_dbfixedrolepermission
sp_defaultdb
sp_defaultlanguage
sp_denylogin
sp_dropalias
sp_dropapprole
sp_dropgroup
sp_droplinkedsrvlogin
sp_droplogin
sp_dropremotelogin

sp_droprole
sp_droprolemember
sp_dropserver
sp_dropsrvrolemember
sp_dropuser
sp_grantdbaccess
sp_grantlogin
sp_helpdbfixedrole
sp_helpgroup
sp_helplinkedsrvlogin
sp_helplogins
sp_helpntgroup
sp_helpremotelogin
sp_helprole
sp_helprolemember
sp_helpprotect
sp_helpsrvrole
sp_helpsrvrolemember
sp_helpuser
sp_password
sp_remoteoption
sp_revokedbaccess
sp_revokelogin
sp_setapprole
sp_srvrolepermission
sp_validatelogins

The following Transact-SQL statement grants login rights to the SALESLG local group:

```
/* Grant login. */
exec sp_grantlogin 'REDMOND\SALESLG'
```

Alternatively, login rights can be granted with the following Visual Basic code:

```
' Declare variables.
Dim oServer As SQLDMO.SQLServer
Dim oLogin As SQLDMO.Login

' Create a server object and connect.
Set oServer = CreateObject("SQLDMO.SQLServer")
oServer.Connect ("SERVERNAME")

' Create the Login object.
Set oLogin = CreateObject("SQLDMO.Login")

' Set the appropriate properties.
oLogin.Name = "REDMOND\SALESLG"
oLogin.Type = SQLDMOLogin_NTGroup

' Add the Login object to the server's Logins collection.
oServer.Logins.Add oLogin
```

To allow a user access to SQL Server 2000 using non-trusted connections, user accounts must be created on SQL Server.

> **Note** When SQL Server 2000 is installed on Windows and configured to use Mixed Mode, capable clients can still make trusted connections.

The following Transact-SQL script creates a login for a non-trusted connection:

```
/* Add a login. */
exec sp_addlogin 'Bob', 'password', 'pubs'
```

This statement adds a user called Bob and sets the password to **password**. The default database becomes **pubs**. The default database is the database to which the user is switched when attempting to log in. A user must still create a user account in the default database for this to work; **sp_addlogin** does not add a user account in the referenced database.

The following example illustrates the same procedure using Visual Basic:

```
' Declare variables.
Dim oServer As SQLDMO.SQLServer
Dim oLogin As SQLDMO.Login
```

```
' Create a server object and connect.
Set oServer = CreateObject("SQLDMO.SQLServer")
oServer.Connect ("SERVERNAME")

' Create the Login object.
Set oLogin = CreateObject("SQLDMO.Login")

' Set the appropriate properties.
oLogin.Name = "Bob"
oLogin.Type = SQLDMOLogin_Standard
oLogin.SetPassword "","password"

' Add the Login object to the server's Logins collection.
oServer.Logins.Add oLogin
```

Securing Access to the Database

A successful login does not automatically allow a user access to all databases on SQL Server 2000. Permissions must be granted to allow users to access a database.

In this section, no differentiation is made between non-trusted users, Windows users, and Windows groups. Comments about Windows users or groups also apply to users or global groups in trusted domains, or domains within the same tree or forest.

Within each database, a user is created and is linked to a SQL Server login, a Windows user, or a Windows group.

SQL Server Enterprise Manager does not allow the creation of users who do not have specific login permissions. Microsoft Management Console (MMC), which hosts SQL Server Enterprise Manager, creates a list of all accounts that have been granted the permission to log in to the server, and a selection needs to be made from this list. The same applies to the SQL-DMO object model.

With Transact-SQL, any valid SQL Server login, Windows user, or Windows group can be granted the right to access the database, whether or not a specific login exists in the **sysxlogins** table in the **master** database.

> **Note** Although not a technical requirement, if you are using trusted connections, it is strongly recommended that you create users with the same username in each database as the login name.

Some examples for the Transact-SQL statements required to grant permission to use a database are listed here:

```
/* Grant access to Bob. */
exec sp_grantdbaccess 'REDMOND\Bob'

/* Grant access to Wendy, referring to her by first name within this database. */
exec sp_grantdbaccess 'REDMOND\WendyH', 'Wendy'
```

Only one modification would be required to make this example work with non-trusted clients. Instead of the domain username, use the username that SQL Server 2000 uses to authenticate the user.

Using SQL-DMO, the equivalent functionality would be achieved by the following code:

```
' Declare variables.
Dim oServer As SQLDMO.SQLServer
Dim oUser As SQLDMO.User

' Create a server object and connect.
Set oServer = CreateObject("SQLDMO.SQLServer")
oServer.Connect ("SERVERNAME")

' Create the User object.
Set oUser = CreateObject("SQLDMO.User")

' Set the appropriate properties.
oUser.Name = "Bob"
oUser.Login = "REDMOND\Bob"

' Add the User object to the server's Users collection.
oServer.Databases("pubs").Users.Add oUser
```

Securing Access to the Database Objects

Permissions can be granted to roles and users, and they can be assigned to allow users to execute certain statements and to access certain database objects. Statement permissions restrict who can execute statements such as CREATE DATABASE, CREATE TABLE, or CREATE FUNCTION. Object permissions restrict access to objects such as tables, views, user-defined functions, or stored procedures. Object permissions depend on the object being referenced. For example, object permission for tables include the SELECT, INSERT, UPDATE, DELETE, and REFERENCES permissions, while the object permissions on a stored procedure include EXECUTE permissions.

User-Defined Database Roles

In an ideal environment, roles would not be necessary. In such an environment, all users would be running SQL Server 2000 on Windows NT 4.0 or Windows 2000 in Windows Authentication Mode. The database administrator could ask the Windows administrator to place all the users with a specific data access requirement (or role) into one Windows group, and the database administrator would then grant permissions to that Windows group as required.

However, as this is not the case in most environments, creating Windows groups is not always possible. For example, when SQL Server 2000 is installed on the Windows 98 operating system, Windows groups are not technically possible. In this case, roles can be used to group users by their permission requirements.

Any Windows user or group can be assigned to a role, which can then be assigned permissions to database objects the same way as database users are assigned permissions.

Note   User-defined roles can be created only in a database. Fixed server roles and fixed database roles are predefined and cannot be modified.

Roles can be created with the following Transact-SQL code:

```
/* Add role for Telephone Operators. */
exec sp_addrole "TelephoneOperators"
```

Alternatively, roles can be created with the following Visual Basic code:

```
' Declare variables.
Dim oServer As SQLDMO.SQLServer
Dim oDbRole As SQLDMO.DatabaseRole

' Create a server object and connect.
Set oServer = CreateObject("SQLDMO.SQLServer")
oServer.Connect ("SERVERNAME")

' Create the Database Role object.
Set oDbRole = CreateObject("SQLDMO.DatabaseRole")

' Set the appropriate properties.
oDbRole.Name = "TelephoneOperators"

' Add the Role object to the server's Roles collection.
oServer.Databases("pubs").DatabaseRoles.Add oDbRole
```

After a user-defined database role is created, users, groups, or other roles are added to it. Roles can be nested, although not in a circular manner, as this would not be productive.

This sample Transact-SQL code adds a Windows user, a Windows group, and a database role to the newly created role:

```
/* Add a Windows user to the TelephoneOperators role. */
exec sp_addrolemember "TelephoneOperators", "REDMOND\Bob"

/* Add a Windows group to the TelephoneOperators role. */
exec sp_addrolemember "TelephoneOperators", "REDMOND\Sales"

/* Add HelpDeskOperators role to TelephoneOperators role. */
exec sp_addrolemember "TelephoneOperators", "HelpDeskOperators"
```

Here is an example of the same operation using SQL-DMO:

```
' Declare variables.
Dim oServer As SQLDMO.SQLServer

' Create a server object and connect.
Set oServer = CreateObject("SQLDMO.SQLServer")
oServer.Connect ("MSNZBENTHOM")

' Use with statement for code legibility.
With oServer.Databases("pubs").DatabaseRoles("TelephoneOperators")

' Add the Windows user to the TelephoneOperators role collection.
.AddMember ("REDMOND\Bob")

   ' Add the Windows group to the TelephoneOperators role collection.
.AddMember ("REDMOND\Sales")

' Add the HelpDeskOperators role to the TelephoneOperators role collection.
.AddMember ("HelpDeskOperators")

End With
```

Permissions System

The permission system in SQL Server 2000 is based on the same additive model that forms the basis of Windows permissions. If a user is a member of the **sales**, **marketing**, and **research** roles (multiple group memberships are now possible), the user gets the sum of the respective permissions of each role. For example, if **sales** has SELECT permissions on a table, **marketing** has INSERT permissions, and **research** has UPDATE permissions, the user would be able to use SELECT, INSERT, and UPDATE. However, as with Windows, if a particular role of which the user is a member has been denied a specific object permission (such as SELECT), the user is unable to exercise that permission. The most restrictive permission, DENY, takes precedence.

Granting and Denying Permissions to Users and Roles

Permissions within a database are always granted to database users, roles, and Windows users or groups, but never to SQL Server 2000 logins. The methods used to set the appropriate permissions for users or roles within a database are: granting permissions, denying permissions, and revoking permissions.

The DENY permission allows an administrator to deny an object or statement permission to a user or role. As with Windows permissions, DENY takes precedence over all other permissions.

For example, if some database users are frivolously changing data, it would not make sense to remove permissions for all users, because the majority of the users are using the data responsibly. It is possible to create a new role with a name like **trouble_makers**, and then use DENY to prevent INSERT, UPDATE, and DELETE operations on all tables for this role. Users can be added to the **trouble_makers** role without regard for their other personal, group, or role permissions.

Revoking permissions is not the same as denying permissions. The REVOKE permission deletes a previous GRANT or DENY; the DENY permission prevents access even when access permissions have been granted.

In this section, each of these methods will be applied in a Visual Basic example and in a Transact-SQL example. The following Transact-SQL code grants Bob and Jane permissions to select from the **authors** table, and grants Jane permissions to insert into the **titles** table:

```
/* Grant permissions to use SELECT. */
GRANT SELECT
ON authors
TO Bob, [REDMOND\Jane]
GO

/* Grant permissions to use INSERT. */
GRANT INSERT
ON titles
TO [REDMOND\Jane]
GO
```

The previous example shows how the GRANT statement works when permissions are granted to explicit users of the database (Bob) and when permissions are granted to a Windows user (Jane).

Here is the same example in Visual Basic:

```
' Declare variables.
Dim oServer As SQLDMO.SQLServer

' Create a server object and connect.
Set oServer = CreateObject("SQLDMO.SQLServer")
oServer.Connect ("SERVERNAME")

' Grant Jane and Bob permissions to select from the authors table.
oServer.Databases("pubs").Tables("authors").Grant SQLDMOPriv_Select, "Bob"
oServer.Databases("pubs").Tables("authors").Grant SQLDMOPriv_Select, _
"[REDMOND\Jane]
' Grant Jane permissions to insert from the titles table.
oServer.Databases("pubs").Tables("titles").Grant SQLDMOPriv_Insert, _
"[REDMOND\Jane]"
```

In the previous examples, granting access to a user by fully qualifying their domain name is much like granting access to a user who already has permissions to access the database directly. Due to these similarities, the following examples show only the code for existing database users.

The following Transact-SQL statement shows how a user can be denied SELECT permissions:

```
/* Deny permissions to use SELECT. */
DENY SELECT
ON authors
TO Bob
GO
```

Here is the same action using Visual Basic:

```
' Declare variables.
Dim oServer As SQLDMO.SQLServer

' Create a server object and connect.
Set oServer = CreateObject("SQLDMO.SQLServer")
oServer.Connect ("SERVERNAME")

' Deny Bob permissions to select from authors table.
oServer.Databases("pubs").Tables("authors").Deny SQLDMOPriv_Select, "Bob"
```

Here is a Transact-SQL example that shows how to revoke permissions from a user:

```
/* Revoke permissions to use SELECT. */
REVOKE SELECT
ON authors
FROM Bob
GO
```

Here is the Visual Basic code:

```
' Declare variables.
Dim oServer As SQLDMO.SQLServer

' Create a server object and connect.
Set oServer = CreateObject("SQLDMO.SQLServer")
oServer.Connect ("SERVERNAME")

' Revoke Bob's permissions to select from the authors table.
oServer.Databases("pubs").Tables("authors").Revoke SQLDMOPriv_Select, "Bob"
```

Ownership Chains

A thorough understanding of ownership chains is crucial for the development of a secure SQL Server 2000 environment. The concept of ownership chains is established when permissions on an object are checked. For example, when a user accesses a view, the permissions on the view should be checked, but what about the permissions on the underlying table?

SQL Server 2000 always checks the permissions on objects when there is a broken ownership chain. A broken ownership chain occurs when an object does not have the same owner as its underlying objects. For example, if Bob creates a table, and Mary creates a view based on that table, this creates a broken ownership chain.

In relation to security, broken ownership chains specify where permissions should be checked over and above the original object accessed. This makes for a very practical model.

The concepts of ownership chains are best explained with a detailed example. Assume that Bob owns a table. He secures access to it by granting SELECT permissions on the table to only Mary. Mary creates a view of Bob's table that suits her needs. One day Sue sees Mary using this view, and exclaims how brilliant it is. Mary agrees to give Sue access to the view. It was not Bob's original intention that Sue should see the data in his table. Fortunately, there is a broken ownership chain, as Bob owns the table and Mary owns the view. The owner of the view does not own the underlying objects. In this case, when Sue tries to use the view, SQL Server checks the permissions on the view to ensure that Sue has been granted access. Following this, the permissions on Bob's table are also checked. If Sue has not been granted access to the table, she cannot use the view because of the broken ownership chain. Effectively, a broken ownership chain guards against a user gaining unwanted access to data.

Conversely, if Bob decided to create the view and to deny Sue access to his table, but grant her access to the view, Sue would be able to access the view. This is because the permissions are checked only when Sue accesses the view. There is no broken ownership chain, so permissions for the underlying table are not checked. Because Bob has created both objects, he should understand that giving access to the view requires implicit access to the underlying objects.

SQL Server 2000 also uses the power of ownership chains in the implementation of passwords. Users cannot update system tables directly, especially not those found in the **master** database. In Mixed Mode authentication, username and password combinations are stored in the **sysxlogins** system table. Users should be given the opportunity to change their passwords on a regular basis; SQL Server 2000 achieves this by implementing a stored procedure to change the password, which any user can execute. Access to the **sysxlogins** table is denied, but permission to execute the **sp_password** stored procedure is granted to all users. Because the **sp_password** stored procedure and **sysxlogins** system table have the same owner, there is no broken ownership chain, and permissions are checked only on the stored procedure.

Ownership chains allow SQL Server 2000 to implement a security system that allows the owner of the original data to control all access to it. At the same time, performance is increased because permissions do not require checking as long as the ownership chain is not broken.

Implementation of Server-Level Security

Use of SIDs

SQL Server 2000 checks whether the user's SID or group membership SIDs have been specifically denied access to the server. If the user is not specifically denied access, the server checks whether the user has been granted access directly or by virtue of a group membership. If access has been granted through one of these methods, the connection to SQL Server 2000 is maintained. The user then proceeds to the appropriate default database (to which the user must also have been granted access). Whenever the user attempts to access an object, the user's access rights are checked. If access has not been granted for a particular set of login credentials, the connection to the server is terminated.

When a Windows NT 4.0 or Windows 2000 user or group is either granted or denied access to SQL Server 2000, this information is stored in the **sysxlogins** system table. Permissions on a registry key no longer control access to the server. SQL Server 2000 identifies users connecting through a trusted connection by their SID and group membership SIDs.

Elimination of SUIDs

The **SUID** column no longer exists in SQL Server 2000.

In SQL Server 6.5 and earlier, security was tracked using the server user identification number (SUID) value in the **sysxlogins** system table in the **master** database. This column also existed in SQL Server 7.0 in several system tables.

The **<name>** column was dropped from the following system tables:

- **sysdatabases**
- **syslogins**
- **sysremotelogins**
- **sysusers**
- **sysprocesses**

The **sysalternates** view has been completely removed. The SUSER_ID() and SUSER_NAME() functions have been deprecated. They will always return NULL. For more information, see "SUID Column" in this chapter.

Generation of GUIDs for Non-Trusted Users

Windows SIDS are not available for non-trusted connections, such as connections to and from SQL Server 2000 installed on a Windows 98 operating system. In this case, SQL Server 2000 generates a 16-byte globally unique identifier (GUID). The generated GUID is then used internally in the same way as Windows SIDs are used for Windows users and groups. In this way, security can function identically in a trusted and non-trusted environment.

Renaming Windows User or Group Accounts

If a Windows user or group is renamed using the User Manager for Domains tool in Windows NT 4.0 or the Active Directory utility in Windows 2000, SQL Server 2000 is not aware of the change. SQL Server 2000 maintains the user or group's fully qualified name in the **sysxlogins** table for performance reasons, because it can be very slow to query the domain controller for this information. This is true when many name lookups are done or the domain controller is connected over a slow WAN link.

The fact that the names of users and groups may be different from SQL Server 2000 to Windows does not cause security problems. The permissions set for the user or the group continue to function correctly, because SQL Server relies only on the SIDs internally.

When the SUSER_SNAME() and SUSER_SID() functions are used to return the username and user's SID respectively, they attempt to resolve these values by first querying the **sysxlogins** table. The Windows Local Security Authority (LSA) is queried only if the **sysxlogins** table does not contain the username or SID. For more information, see the Windows documentation.

Another effect of using these functions is that the usernames in system messages may not report an up-to-date name.

sysxlogins System Table

The **sysxlogins** system table contains the login permission (or lack of such) for users. In SQL Server version 6.5 and earlier, this information was stored in the **syslogins** system table. For backward compatibility, the **syslogins** system table can still be queried as it is a view over the **sysxlogins** table. This view should not be necessary because system tables should not be accessed directly. System tables can change at any time. The **sysxlogins** system table exists only in the **master** database.

SQL Server 2000 includes three views that depend on the **sysxlogins** table.

- The **syslogins** view provides backward compatibility; at the same time it interprets the **status** column so that the column can be understood more readily.

- The **sysremotelogins** view provides backward compatibility, and allows information regarding remote logins to be accessed more readily.

- The **sysoledbusers** view provides information about remote logins.

xstatus Column

The **xstatus** column provides a number of status settings, including the server role memberships. The various status values are listed in the following table.

Status settings

Purpose	Bit*	Notes
denylogin	1	None
hasaccess	2	None
Isntname	3	Not "ISN'T" but "IS WINDOWS"
Isntgroup	3	Only if status bit 4 is not set
Isntuser	4	Must also have status bit 3 set
Sysadmin	5	Server role
securityadmin	6	Server role
serveradmin	7	Server role
setupadmin	8	Server role
processadmin	9	Server role
diskadmin	10	Server role
dbcreator	11	Server role
bulkadmin	12	Server role

*Bit: counting status bits from right to left.

dbid and language Columns

These columns provide default database and default language settings for users. When a user connects to SQL Server 2000, the server looks for a row containing the user's specific SID (or GUID in the case of non-trusted connections) in the **sysxlogins** table. If that row is found, the server takes the default database and default language settings from it. If that row is not found, the server looks for SIDs for the groups of which this user is a member. The default database and language settings from the first group that is found are used.

If the first group found contains a default language, but the default database is NULL, SQL Server continues to the next group the user is a member of and tries to ascertain the default database from there. For example, if Bob is a member of the SALES and MARKETING groups, and he does not have a default database and default language configured specifically for his account, the system looks for the default settings applied to the SALES and MARKETING groups. The first settings returned are used. Thus, if a user is a member of more than one group, and does not have default database and default language settings assigned, the defaults chosen based on membership in any specific group are not guaranteed if another group's defaults are returned first.

It is possible to assign default database and language settings specifically to a user without granting specific login rights to that user. The user can be granted access to SQL Server based on group memberships, but receive the default settings based on the defaults recorded in the **sysxlogins** system table specifically for that user. In this case, the **hasaccess** flag of the **sysxlogins** table would be set to zero for this user's specific entry in the **sysxlogins** table.

hasaccess Status

The **hasaccess** status in the **sysxlogins** system table allows configuration of default settings for a specific user without implicitly granting that user access. Typically, the **sysxlogins** table is used to grant login rights to particular users or groups. If the **hasaccess** status is zero, the user is not granted login access explicitly. However, when the user logs on through a group membership, the defaults are established.

The **hasaccess** status is also crucial for another reason, which is best explained by an example. Bob is a member of the REDMOND\SALES group, and he has not been specifically granted permission to log in to SQL Server 2000. The **sysxlogins** table has no entries for Bob. However, the REDMOND\SALES group has been granted login permissions, so Bob is able to log in. When Bob becomes a member of a fixed server role, he should not automatically gain permission to access the server directly; his access should still be through the SALES group. In this case, a new row is added to **sysxlogins** for Bob, but the **hasaccess** flag is set to zero so that the relevant server role memberships can be granted without implicitly granting access to the server.

If the **denylogin** flag is set, the **sysxlogins** table can contain entries that do not specifically grant access to a user or group.

denylogin Status

The **denylogin** status is used to mark a user or group as being explicitly denied access to SQL Server 2000. For example, to prevent access to SQL Server for a specific user (or group), the following Transact-SQL statement can be executed:

```
Exec sp_denylogin 'REDMOND\Bob'
```

This is not the same as the following statement:

```
Exec sp_revokelogin 'REDMOND\Bob'
```

The difference between the two statements is that the first statement denies access to SQL Server and the second revokes access for that particular account only. If Bob is a member of the MARKETING group, which does have access, the second statement would allow him to continue to access the server by virtue of membership in the MARKETING group. The first statement would deny access irrespective of any group memberships that may grant access.

Note On Windows operating systems, one DENY is all that is required to lock a user out of a resource.

sysremotelogins View

The **sysremotelogins** view is provided for backward compatibility. In SQL Server 6.5 and earlier, a table with the name **sysremotelogins** provided the mapping used for remote logins.

sysoledbuser View

When a user wants to run a query on a remote server, the local server must log in to the linked server on behalf of the user.

The **sp_addlinkedsrvlogin** stored procedure adds new linked accounts to remote servers. This information is stored in the **sysxlogins** table. The stored procedure requires the remote server name, the local username, the remote username, and the remote password as parameters.

Implementation of Object-Level Security

How Permissions Are Checked

SQL Server 2000 uses SIDs to identify Windows users and groups. However, due to the length of SIDs (which can be up to 85 bytes), SQL Server 2000 maps the SIDs to user IDs inside each database. The SIDs are mapped to user IDs in the **sysusers** table. The user ID is then used in the **sysobjects** table to denote the owner of a table. It is also used in the **syspermissions** table to set permissions on objects, and in the **systypes** table to denote the owner of a user-defined type.

When a user connects to SQL Server 2000, the server creates a process status structure (PSS) (referred to in several error messages produced by SQL Server 7.0) in memory, which contains the user's SID, group SIDs, and other security and state information. This structure is a snapshot taken when the user connects, and the snapshot is not refreshed. This structure exists per session connecting to the server; a single user establishing multiple sessions with SQL Server 2000 will have multiple PSSs.

When the user accesses a database, SQL Server checks the **sysusers** table to determine whether the user has been denied access directly or by virtue of being a member of a group that has been denied access. If the user is denied access, this is enforced. If not, the **sysusers** table is checked again, but this time all user IDs the user qualifies for are collected. After it is established that the user has been granted access to the database, the **sysmembers** table is scanned to establish all the role memberships of the user. For example, the user may be a member of a role, a member of a Windows group, or aliased to another user. User IDs of all the applicable memberships are established so that the appropriate permissions for this user can be applied. Unlike the PSSs, this information is not stored permanently.

When the user starts accessing objects in the database, the applicable permissions are determined by checking the **syspermissions** table for entries with matching user IDs (as identified earlier). The system checks DENY permissions first. If DENY permissions are found, the user cannot access the object. However, if no DENY permissions are found, and entries that give the user the required access exist, access is granted. The effective access permissions are then cached, so that permissions do not have to be checked every time the user attempts to access the object.

Cost of Changing Permissions

Checking permissions can be expensive. For this reason, SQL Server 2000 caches the object permissions on a per-session basis (as stated earlier). Unlike the PSS, which does not change the security information after it is created, the permissions cache is always up-to-date. This is implemented by the versioning method.

When the initial checking of permissions takes place, a version number is established.SQL Server 2000 increases the version counter when the permissions on an object are changed. Whenever an object is accessed, the version of the permission counter is checked, and if it differs from the cached counter, the content of the cache is discarded and the effective permissions are re-established.

The cached security is used whenever an object is accessed, as long as the version counter has not changed. If the counter has changed, a small overhead is incurred for that operation.

Changes to Windows User or Group Account Names

In SQL Server 2000, it is possible to grant Windows users and groups access to objects in the database directly. In that case, the SID and Windows user or group names are stored in the **sysusers** table. For information about this issue with login names, see "Renaming Windows User or Group Accounts" in this chapter.

When the Windows administrator renames the Windows group or user, the name change is not propagated to SQL Server 2000. This avoids breaking existing stored procedures, views, and so on that use the group or user name. For example, Susie Jones is a user who creates a table in the database. Susie's login name is SUSIEJ, and her table is named **SUSIEJ.SALESDEMO**. Susie grants permissions for others to access her table, and several of her colleagues create views and stored procedures based on her table. When Susie marries Bob Taylor, her username is changed to SUSIET. If SQL Server 2000 were to pick up the change, Susie's table would suddenly be **SUSIET.SALESDEMO**, which is a completely different object. Any views, stored procedures, and any code written to access this table would no longer work.

In the interest of stability, SQL Server 2000 does not automatically rename user accounts when the real account in the Windows User Directory is renamed.

sysprocedures System Table Removed

In SQL Server 6.5 and earlier, when a stored procedure was created, the query text was stored in the **syscomments** system table, and a normalized query tree was saved in the **sysprocedures** system table. The normalization process parsed the SQL statements into more efficient formats and resolved all referenced objects into their internal representations. When the procedure was subsequently executed, the tree was retrieved from the **sysprocedures** table and used as the basis for an optimized execution plan, which was then stored in the procedure cache. (This approach was also used for views, defaults, rules, triggers, check constraints, and default constraints.)

At first, it may appear that there is no link between the process outlined earlier and security. However, there is a connection: In an attempt to protect their source code, some software developers deleted the original SQL text from **syscomments**, particularly if they were working with versions earlier than SQL Server 6.0. In most cases, the original SQL text was not used again until the server was upgraded with a later version of SQL Server, or when a service pack was applied. Microsoft provided a better mechanism for hiding the original SQL text from anyone who should not have access with the introduction of the WITH ENCRYPTION option in SQL Server version 6.0. This option encrypted the original SQL text upon the creation of the stored procedure.

If the appropriate entries from the **syscomments** table are deleted in SQL Server 7.0 and SQL Server 2000, the stored procedure no longer executes. This is because the **sysprocedures** table has been removed. The SQL text is now obtained directly from the **syscomments** table prior to execution.

WITH GRANT OPTION

The WITH GRANT OPTION is optional syntax that can be used with the GRANT statement. This option applies only to object permissions, and allows the recipient of the GRANT statement to pass on any permissions the statement grants.

For example, if Jane grants Bob SELECT permissions and uses the WITH GRANT OPTION, Bob can grant SELECT permissions. (If Jane revokes SELECT permissions from Bob, she can use the CASCADE option to revoke the SELECT permissions from users to whom Bob granted SELECT permissions.)

sysusers System Table

In some ways, the **sysusers** table is to the database what the **sysxlogins** table is to the server. The **sysusers** table exists in each database, and contains information about who is granted or denied access to the database.

hasdbaccess Column

The **hasdbaccess** column is similar to the **hasaccess** column in the **sysxlogins** table. In **hasdbaccess**, entries with this flag set to zero are created when a user has not been granted rights to access the database explicitly but creates objects, is explicitly granted permissions, or is added explicitly to a role. Objects created by a user are always owned by the user, not by the group through which the user was granted database access. The only exception is a member of a role or Windows group who explicitly qualifies the role or group as the object's owner when the object is created. The following syntax should be used: **CREATE TABLE [BUILTIN\administrators].test_table(acolumn VARCHAR(2))**. In this situation, an entry for the user must exist in the **sysusers** table so that the object can have the appropriate owner. The entry is created automatically, but the user is not granted explicit access to the database automatically, because the **hasaccess** flag is set to zero.

The **hasdbaccess** column is set to zero for roles, which are also listed in the **sysusers** table.

sysmembers System Table

The **sysmembers** system table records the membership of users in database roles. It contains one row for each member of a database role.

SQL Server 2000 improves the performance related to roles by placing a user's first membership of a role into the **gid** column of the **sysusers** table. Thus, when SQL Server 2000 tries to identify all the roles to which a user belongs, it does not have to query the **sysmembers** table if the **gid** column of the **sysusers** table contains zero. If the entry in that column is not zero, the entry specifies one of the roles, and the **sysmembers** table must be queried for a complete list of all the roles to which the user belongs.

syspermissions System Table

The **syspermissions** system table, which exists in every database, was introduced in SQL Server 7.0. It tracks permissions that have been granted or denied to users. For more information about backward compatibility with the **sysprotects** table, see "sysprotects System Table" in this chapter.

The **syspermissions** system table contains very few columns. The **id** column references the object ID for which the permissions are being granted or denied. For statement permissions, this column is set to zero.

The **grantee** and **grantor** columns are self-explanatory. They contain the ID of the role, Windows user, or Windows group as it is found in the **sysusers** table.

The **actadd** column refers the positive permission (or permissions granted) on all columns (in the case of a table) of the object, while the **actmod** column refers to the negative (or permissions denied) permissions on all columns (in the case of a table) of the object.

The remaining columns are used only when column-level permissions are implemented. The **seladd** column is a bitmap of the columns that have been granted SELECT permissions. Because column IDs are never reused, the bitmap approach works very well. The **selmod** column is for SELECT permissions denied.

sysprotects System Table

The implementation of the **sysprotects** system table has changed from earlier releases. In SQL Server 6.5 and earlier, the **sysprotects** table stored the object permissions. In SQL Server 7.0 and SQL Server 2000, this information is stored in the **syspermissions** table.

Named Pipes and Multiprotocol Permissions

When discussing the internal security of SQL Server 2000, it is important to point out a key concept that is often overlooked. This is not new for SQL Server 2000, but is mentioned here for completeness.

The Named Pipes Net-Library is an interprocess communication (IPC) mechanism, which is implemented over the IPC$ share on Windows. Thus, when a client connects to SQL Server using the Named Pipes Net-Library, the connection is made to the IPC$ share, at which point authentication takes place. After Windows has authenticated the client (in the same way as it would for access to any other resource), the Named Pipes session is established over the IPC$ share. This takes place before any attempt is made to pass the connection to SQL Server.

All users who will be connecting to SQL Server 2000 using the Named Pipes Net-Library must have a Windows account and have permissions in Windows to access the IPC$ share. If you do not want this authentication to take place, switch to another network library such as TCP/IP Sockets or Multiprotocol; these connections are not validated against the Windows NT 4.0 IPC$ share. TCP/IP Sockets is the default network library in SQL Server 2000.

With the Multiprotocol Net-Library, Windows authentication also takes place before SQL Server 2000 passes the connection. This is because the remote procedure call (RPC) run-time services authenticate the client when the connection is requested. Like the Named Pipes Net-Library, the Multiprotocol Net-Library requires a valid Windows account.

The Multiprotocol Net-Library does not work to connect to named instances of SQL Server 2000. It is no longer required, because all network libraries support encryption.

Enabling the Windows **guest** account is one way of dealing with users who do not have a Windows account, but who want to connect using the Named Pipes or Multiprotocol Net-Libraries. When these users request a session, they can connect to Windows using the **guest** user account, and then attempt to log in to SQL Server. Because enabling the **guest** account makes your entire Windows environment less secure, this option is not usually recommended. It is mentioned here only as a workaround of last resort.

Upgrading from SQL Server 7.0

There are no architectural changes in security from SQL Server 7.0 to SQL Server 2000. For information about new security features in SQL Server 2000, see "New Security Features in SQL Server 2000" in this chapter.

Upgrading from SQL Server 6.5

The security model for SQL Server 6.5 is different from that of SQL Server 2000. These changes were necessary to provide a practical working environment for SQL Server. Because of this change, permissions need to be carefully considered when performing an upgrade.

Upgrade Considerations

The information covered in this section applies only to upgrading from SQL Server 6.5 Integrated Mode or Mixed Mode. If the upgrade is performed from a computer running SQL Server 6.5 that is configured in standard mode, no security problems will be encountered. However, it is recommended that the new security functionality available as part of Windows Authentication Mode be used in the upgraded environment. The best method of ensuring that the security settings of SQL Server 6.5 are upgraded in the most constructive way possible is to plan the upgrade thoroughly and prepare the security environment.

Upgrade Process

The upgrade can be performed either on one computer or remotely from one computer to another. Logically, a single computer upgrade is the same as a two-computer upgrade where the source and target computers are the same. The two computers will be referred to in this document as source and target servers. The source server is expected to have SQL Server 6.5 installed, and the target server must have SQL Server 2000 installed.

During the version upgrade process, a program opens the SQL Server 6.5 integrated registry key on the source computer, and reads the SIDs of all accounts that have integrated logins granted to them. The accounts that have integrated security configured on the source server may be Windows global groups, Windows local groups, or Windows users. In the case of the global groups and users, these accounts can be from a local domain (if SQL Server 2000 is running on a member server) or a trusted domain. If SQL Server 2000 is installed on a domain controller, the local groups are the local groups from the domain controller's domain; otherwise, the local groups are the local groups of the member server.

Accounts that were given administrative permissions on the source server are ignored in the drilldown and account-mapping processes.

> **Note** The **sp_grantlogin** statement is executed on the computer running SQL Server 2000 for each Windows account that was configured to use integrated security on SQL Server 6.5.

Analyzing the Upgrade Output

Most of the security-related upgrade difficulties occur because in SQL Server 6.5, integrated security was implemented by securing a key in the registry, and only users who had access to that key could gain access to the server. The permissions on the registry key were linked to user login accounts, which were stored in the **syslogins** table.

SQL Server 2000 does not use this method for securing access to the server. Instead, it allows access to the server to be granted based on Windows user or group SIDs. Therefore, the upgrade process is sometimes unable to identify the original security requirements. This is usually because the SQL Server security environment was not up-to-date, or because the upgrade is going into a different environment.

The following table shows how logins appear in SQL Server Enterprise Manager after an upgrade. The contents of this table are explained in the sections that follow.

SQL Server Enterprise Manager logins

Name	Type	Server access	Default database	User	Line
user1	Standard	Permit	Master		1
a#user2	Standard	Permit	Master		2
BUILTIN\Administrators	Windows group	Permit	Master	**dbo**	3
DOM3\SQLUsers	Windows group	Permit	Master		4
DOM3_user#3	Standard	Permit	Master		5
DOM3_Administrator	Standard	Permit	Master		6
REDMOND\a user4	Windows user	Through group	Master		7
REDMOND\user5	Windows user	Through group	Master		8

User Has Been Deleted

Lines 1 and 2 in the previous table are produced when the users are not found in the Windows User Directory. Specifically, if the **xp_logininfo** system stored procedure does not return the username, it is converted as a standard login as in these two lines. The number sign (#) character in Line 2 is used to represent the space, because SQL Server 6.5 and earlier did not support special characters.

Administrator Account

The BUILTIN\Administrators local group in Line 3 of the previous table has been aliased to the **dbo** user of the **master** database.

Users of a Trusted Domain

Line 4 in the table refers to the DOM3\SQLUsers group, a global group on a trusted domain. The members of this group have been granted login rights. The members of this group have also been granted login rights with standard security using their username, as they would have appeared in SQL Server 6.5 and earlier. This provides backward compatibility for standard mode security.

Notice the entry for the Administrator account in Line 6; the Windows administrator account of the DOM3 domain was granted user login rights prior to the upgrade. These rights have been preserved. All user-level login access is processed in this way.

Users of the Current Default Domain

Users of the current default domain (as configured in SQL Server 6.x prior to the upgrade) are upgraded as per Lines 7 and 8. Notice the type of the account and the existence of the space in Line 7. SQL Server 2000 supports special characters in the account names.

Preparing the SQL Server 6.5 Security Environment

It is strongly recommended that all security settings be cleaned up thoroughly prior to the upgrade. SQL Security Manager should be run to ensure that all Windows accounts are synchronized with SQL Server. If the environment is in order, the upgrade process is more likely to proceed seamlessly.

Step Through the Upgrade

It is relatively easy to monitor the upgrade process and identify how the upgrading of user accounts and groups is likely to go. A SQL Server Upgrade Wizard option allows the process to be stopped after every step. If this is selected, the user can analyze the output created by the early stages of the security upgrade. The specific files to analyze are Loginmap.sid and Loginmap.txt. If the content does not appear correctly, these text files can be edited before the upgrade continues.

> **Note** Microsoft does not support the editing of Loginmap.sid and Loginmap.txt files during the upgrade process.

Upgrading to a New Domain

When upgrading from SQL Server 6.x using the tape method, do not back up the database in one domain and then upgrade it into another domain. When the **xp_logininfo** stored procedure is executed, it will probably not find any of the accounts that existed in the original domain (and if it does, they are probably not the correct accounts, but are just identical in name). The login rights will be treated as if the accounts have been deleted. For more information, see "User Has Been Deleted" in this chapter.

Character Mapping

Character mapping is not required; SQL Server 2000 can handle spaces and backslashes (\) in account names.

In SQL Server 6.5 and earlier, character mapping had to be configured to deal with Windows NT account names, which contained special characters such as the backslash character. Therefore, SQL Server 6.5 and earlier provided three mapping characters: the number sign (#), underscore (_), and dollar sign ($).

sa Account

In SQL Server 6.5 and earlier, administrators logged in to SQL Server using the **sa** account to perform most administrative tasks. This often required a large number of people to have administrative access.

All Windows NT 4.0 and Windows 2000 users who are given **sa**-type rights on SQL Server 2000 should be assigned to the **sysadmin** fixed server role.

For more information, see "sa Account" in this chapter.

Aliasing

It is recommended that you use roles instead of aliasing. Although SQL Server 2000 supports aliasing of user accounts within a database for backward compatibility, using aliasing for this purpose is no longer recommended. Roles are more powerful, and they provide similar functionality to aliasing. For more information, see "User-Defined Roles" in this chapter.

Setting Up a Secure SQL Server 2000 Installation

The information discussed in this section applies to SQL Server 2000 installed on Windows NT 4.0 or Windows 2000 only. The Windows 98 and Windows Me environments do not provide the security features discussed.

This section assumes that SQL Server 2000 has been configured with Windows Authentication Mode to provide the highest level of security.

sa Account

It is recommended that all administrators of SQL Server be granted access to SQL Server through Windows group membership, and that this same group be made a member of the **sysadmin** server role. This approach has one minor drawback: Windows administrators can give anyone **sysadmin** permissions on SQL Server 2000, as they are able to add any user to the appropriate Windows group.

If a site does not want to give Windows administrators the ability to give others (or themselves) **sysadmin** access to SQL Server, only individual Windows accounts should be assigned to the role of **sysadmin**.

In each case, it is strongly recommended that the **sa** account not be used for day-to-day administration. Instead, a password should be assigned that is hard to break, and it should be locked in a safe for emergency access only.

If you are running SQL Server 2000 with Windows Authentication Mode (as recommended in this chapter), you cannot log in using the **sa** account. Only trusted connections are allowed.

> **Note** Even thought the **sa** account cannot be used to log in to SQL Server 2000 when it is running in mixed Authentication Mode, it is still important to assign an **sa** password. This is because a small change in the registry (`HKLM\Software\Microsoft\MSSQLServer\LoginMode`: a value of 0 indicates Mixed Mode and a value of 1 indicates Windows Authentication Mode) can change the security mode from Authentication Mode to Mixed Mode. If the **sa** password is blank (this is the default at installation), an intruder or the Windows administrator can to gain access to the server. For information about ways to reduce the chance of such an attack, see "Registry" in this chapter.

Service Accounts

SQL Server 2000 runs as four Windows services:

- MSSQLServer (or MSSQL$InstanceName for a named instance). Provides the core relational functionality of SQL Server.

- SQLServerAgent (or SQLAgent$InstanceName for a named instance). Provides the capability to schedule regular commands, schedule replication, supply a method for dealing with errors, contact SQL Server operators when errors occur, as well as other support functions.

- Microsoft Search service. Provides the full-text search capability. This service must always be configured to use the local system account.

- MSSQLServerOLAPService. The Analysis Services engine, which provides the OLAP and data mining functionality for SQL Server.

SQL Server and SQL Server Agent services can be configured to use one of the following types of Windows accounts:

- Local service account

- Local user account

- Domain user account

The selection depends on the functionality that is required for SQL Server 2000. Both services can be configured to use the same Windows user account.

If the service account needs to be changed after the server has been installed, SQL Server Enterprise Manager should be used. While it is also possible to change the service account for the SQL Server and SQL Server Agent services in Control Panel, this is not recommended because the configuration details for the Microsoft Search service are not synchronized.

The changes to account information take effect the next time the service is started. The SQL Server and SQL Server Agent services can be configured to use different Windows user accounts, although this is not usually recommended. When the service account is changed, the changes must be made to both services, because they are configured separately.

One consideration that can reduce administrative overhead in a multiple-server environment is the use of one domain user account for all SQL Server 2000 servers in the enterprise.

Local System Account

SQL Server 2000 can be run using the local system account if SQL Server is not configured for replication and does not require access to network resources.

The following permissions must be set for the local system account for SQL Server 2000 to perform its tasks correctly (Setup assigns these permissions automatically):

- Full control on the SQL Server directory (by default C:\Program Files\Microsoft SQL Server\MSSQL)

- Full control on all .mdf, .ndf, and .ldf database files

- For installations other than named instances, full control on the registry keys at and under:

    - `HKEY_LOCAL_MACHINE\SOFTWARE\Microsoft\MSSQLServer`

    - `HKEY_LOCAL_MACHINE\SYSTEM\CurrentControlset\Services\MSSQLServer`

- For named instances, full control on the registry keys at and under the following:

    - `HKEY_LOCAL_MACHINE\SOFTWARE\Microsoft\Microsoft SQL Server\InstanceName`

    - `HKEY_LOCAL_MACHINE\SYSTEM\CurrentControlset\Services\MSSQL$InstanceName`

Local User Account

If SQL Server 2000 is configured to use a Windows local user account, the same restrictions apply as for a local system, with the following addition (Setup grants this by default):

- The user account must be granted Log On As A Service permission.

Domain User Account

Configuring SQL Server 2000 with a domain user account provides the greatest level of flexibility. Some examples of functionality available only when a domain user account is used, include:

- Replication
- Backing up to and restoring from network drives
- Performing heterogeneous joins that involve remote data sources
- SQL Server Agent mail features and SQL Mail

For SQL Server 2000 to perform its tasks, the domain user account must be configured like the local user account discussed earlier. However, some extended functionality is available only if further permissions are considered. This is best outlined in the following table.

Configuring local user accounts

Service	Permission	Functionality
SQL Server	Network write permissions	Ability to read/write to remote backups, data loads, and so on
SQL Server	Act as part of the operating system and replace process level token	Run **xp_cmdshell** for a user other than a SQL Server administrator
SQL Server Agent	Member of the Administrators local group	Create **CmdExec** and **ActiveScript** jobs belonging to someone other than a SQL Server administrator
SQL Server Agent	Member of the Administrators local group	Use the autorestart feature
SQL Server Agent	Member of the Administrators local group	User run-when-idle jobs

To provide maximum functionality to SQL Server 2000, it is recommended that the domain user account be a member of the Administrators local group.

File System

Windows provides an excellent security framework for securing operating system objects such as files. It is recommended that NTFS file permission be applied to the data and log files of all databases. The user account that SQL Server 2000 is configured to use must be given full control permissions on the database files.

All SQL Server 2000 files, including executables and DLLs, should be configured so that users cannot manipulate them. Permissions on these files should be set to allow the user account that SQL Server uses, the Administrators group, and local system accounts full control permissions. No other permissions should be set.

SQL Server 2000 Setup automatically grants the service account(s) full control permissions to SQL Server-related files, as well as full control to the local administrators group.

Registry

To secure SQL Server 2000 installation from security attacks by users who have login rights on the physical server, it is prudent to set Windows permissions on the registry keys that are used to configure SQL Server 2000.

Specifically, all the keys under the following should be secured:

- `HKEY_LOCAL_MACHINE\SOFTWARE\Microsoft\MSSQLServer` (for a default instance) or

- `HKEY_LOCAL_MACHINE\SOFTWARE\Microsoft\Microsoft SQL Server\InstanceName` (for a named instance)

The Everyone group permissions on this key should be removed, and full control permissions added for the Administrators group, the local system account, or the SQL Server service account. Setup does this automatically for the service accounts selected during the setup process.

Setting permissions on the registry keys is particularly important if SQL Server administrators want to stop the Windows administrators from accessing SQL Server. In this case, SQL Server administrators should also take ownership of the registry key and remove permissions from the Administrators group. In this case, the SQL Server service account must have full control permissions. Although this does not prevent Windows administrators from gaining access, it allows SQL Server administrators to know when the Windows administrators have compromised security. Administrators can always take ownership, but they cannot give it. For more information about Windows administrators gaining access to SQL Server, see "sa Account" in this chapter.

Auditing

SQL Server 2000 provides auditing as a way to trace and record activity that has happened on each instance of SQL Server. This allows audits of logins to the server in the Windows event log. The audit level can be configured using SQL Server Enterprise Manager, or by using the **sp_loginconfig** stored procedure.

Possible auditing settings are:

- **None.** Logs no auditing information.

- **Success.** Causes only successful logins to be logged.

- **Failure.** Causes only failed logins to be logged.

- **All.** Causes successful and failed logins to be logged.

The auditing information is written to the SQL Server 2000 error log.

Profiling for Auditing

SQL Server 2000 provides a powerful profiler, SQL Profiler, which allows analysis of many internal events within SQL Server, including full security auditing capabilities.

SQL Profiler works by capturing and analyzing all the actions performed on SQL Server. The capture can be viewed real-time on the screen, saved to a text file, or inserted into a SQL Server table.

SQL Profiler allows the capture of virtually all events that take place within SQL Server, including:

- End user activity, including all SQL commands, logout/login, and enabling of application roles

- Database administrator activity, including DDL, other than GRANT, REVOKE, and DENY; security events, and configuration (database or server)

- Security events, including GRANT, REVOKE, and DENY; login user/role, and add/remove/configure

- Utility events, including back up, restore, bulk insert, bcp, and database consistency checker (DBCC) commands

- Server events, including shutdown, pause, and start

- Audit events, including add audit, modify audit, and stop audit

This information can help establish who did what, and when. For more information about how to enable auditing, including how to create an audit stored procedure that runs when SQL Server starts, see SQL Server Books Online.

Another mode of auditing is known as C2 audit mode. C2 audit mode captures all audit-related events and all data columns for those events. This can produce a very large amount of data in a short amount of time, so it is not recommended unless you are setting up SQL Server 2000 in a C2 configuration. For more information, see SQL Server Books Online.

Backup and Restore

Security of Backup Files and Media

The most secure method for backups is to use SQL Server 2000 to back up to data files and then to use the Windows NT 4.0 or Windows 2000 backup program to back up the data files to backup media using the password feature. This ensures that only users who know the password can restore the files. In SQL Server 2000, you can set a password directly on a backup set.

The backup data files should be on an NTFS partition with directory permissions set to prevent the ordinary user from gaining access to the files.

If backup media can be physically secured, the standard SQL Server 2000 backups will not pose any security risks. However, even when the media has a password, the data itself is not encrypted and can be read if the media has no physical protection.

Restoring to Another Server

Three specific scenarios come up when restoring the database to another server. The first scenario applies where the old server (where the database originated from) and the new server (where the database is going) are using Mixed Mode for authentication.

The second and third scenarios apply where Windows Authentication Mode is used; the difference between these is that the second scenario addresses where a database is restored to a server in the same domain, while the third applies to a database being restored to a server in another domain.

Mixed Mode

When a database is restored to a server using Mixed Mode authentication for security, the database security breaks. This is because the logins are maintained in the **sysxlogins** table in the **master** database, and the user's rights to access a database are stored in the **sysusers** table of the respective database; a logical link is maintained between the user's entry in the **sysxlogins** table and the user's entry in the **sysusers** table. This link is a generated 16-byte GUID. For more information, see "Generation of GUIDs for Non-Trusted Users" in this chapter.

The net effect of the GUID implementation for Mixed Mode authentication is that when a database is restored to a computer running SQL Server 2000, other than the one where the database access was granted, the link between the **sysxlogins** table and the **sysusers** table breaks, thereby effectively granting access to the database to no one. Members of the **sysadmin** group are an exception to this. All role memberships and user permissions would have to be re-created.

Windows Authentication (Same Domain)

If the database is restored to another computer running SQL Server 2000 in the same domain, the permissions in the database remain intact. The only consideration here is whether users are granted permission to log in to the server. The permission to log in to the server is implemented at each instance of SQL Server.

For example, Bob is a member of the SALES group, and the SALES group is granted login permissions at SQLSERVER1. Bob is granted database access rights to the **sales** database. When the **sales** database is restored to SQLSERVER2, Bob's permissions still exist in the **sales** database. However, because the SALES group is not granted login rights to the server, Bob cannot use the database. If the administrator grants the Everyone group login rights to the server, Bob can use the database. This is because the only restriction stopping Bob from using the **sales** database was logging in to the server.

When restoring a database to another server in the same domain, the permissions within the database remain intact, but the permissions to log in to this specific server may need to be granted.

Windows Authentication (Different Domain)

When a database is being restored to another domain, some scenarios should be considered. These scenarios apply to users who want to access the database.

Users from a Trusted Domain

If a Windows trust relationship has been established between the old and the new domain, such that the new domain trusts the old domain, the users from the old domain may use the database with all permissions intact, if they have been granted the right to log in to SQL Server.

Users from other trusted domains would not have rights to access the database, much like the users from the new domain.

Users from the New Domain

No users from the new domain will have access, because their SIDs do not exist in the **sysusers** table of the database.

The only exception to this are the BUILTIN accounts of Windows. Because these accounts always have the same SIDs on all servers, any permissions granted to a BUILTIN account, such as the local Administrators group, remain intact. This assumes that the BUILTIN accounts have login rights, and that SQL Server is installed on a domain controller.

Users from Any Domain with Same Username and Password

In most Windows security implementations, when access is required to a resource that is not in the user's own domain, the user is able to access the resource providing that a user account exists with the same username and password combination. This behavior is transparent.

If the user is using named pipes to connect to the server, this method will work if the user establishes a connection to a file share first. This method also works if a user wants to use an account of another name, providing that the user is running Windows as the operating system. If a user is denied access when connecting to a file resource from a computer running Windows NT 4.0 or Windows 2000 (and the user is not currently using any other credentials on the computer being connected to), the opportunity is given to provide a username and password for login purposes.

Attaching and Detaching Database Files

The issues associated with attaching and detaching database files are identical to those discussed in "Restoring to Another Server" in this chapter. An exception is the requirement to create the database before restoring the data.

General Windows Security Configurations

SQL Server 2000 relies on the Windows security architecture; therefore, all security principles that apply to Windows also apply in some way to Windows-based servers running SQL Server 2000.

Disable Windows Guest Account

When running SQL Server 2000 in Windows Authentication Mode, the server relies on Windows to authenticate all clients. This brings with it the security framework that applies to Windows. To ensure the strength of your security, it is strongly recommended that the **Guest** account be disabled, if this has not already been done.

Restrict Physical Access

As with any Windows-based server, it is recommended to restrict physical access wherever possible. One of the risks of unauthorized physical access is the ability of an intruder to start the server from a floppy disk and gain access to the Windows file system. Your mission-critical production database servers should be physically secured.

Additional Resources

For more information about SQL Server security, see the following:

Books

Inside Microsoft SQL Server 2000 by Kalen Delaney. Copyright 2000, Microsoft Press. ISBN: 0-7356-0998-5.

Sams Teach Yourself Microsoft SQL Server 2000 in 21 Days by Richard Waymire and Rick Sawtell. Copyright 2000, Sams Publishing. ISBN: 0-672-31969-1.

SQL Server Books Online (installed as part of SQL Server 2000)

Web Sites

http://www.microsoft.com/sql/ – SQL Server home page

http://support.microsoft.com/support/sql/ – SQL Server support home pages

http://www.microsoft.com/technet/ – TechNet resource site

http://www.msdn.microsoft.com/sqlserver/– MSDN® resource site

http://www.microsoft.com/security/ – Microsoft's central site for security information

White Papers

http://msdn.microsoft.com/sqlserver/ – SQL Server Developer Center, contains recent technical white papers and downloads

Using BLOBs

This chapter discusses the basic principles involved when working with BLOBs (binary large objects) in Microsoft® SQL Server™ 2000. Applying lessons learned from the design and implementation of the Microsoft TerraServer database, this chapter discusses issues to consider when designing tables with BLOB data. Using the **Northwind** database in SQL Server 2000, this chapter shows how to create a table with **text**, **ntext**, or **image** columns, and how to insert and modify BLOB data on the server and on the client.

In this chapter and in SQL Server Books Online, BLOB is a generic term that refers to **text**, **ntext**, and **image** data. In the 1999 SQL ANSI standard (SQL-99), BLOB refers to large binary-valued **image** data. CLOB refers to large **text** data, and NCLOB refers to large **ntext** data.

The code examples in this chapter are also available on the *SQL Server 2000 Resource Kit* CD-ROM in the file \Docs\ChapterCode\Ch11Code.txt. For more information, see Chapter 39, "Tools, Samples, eBooks, and More."

This chapter contains the following sections:

- **Designing BLOBs**

  BLOB Storage in SQL Server. Discusses ways that SQL Server can store BLOB data, and discusses the **text in row** option and the text pointer functionality.

  Learning from the Microsoft TerraServer Design and Implementation. Discusses the options database designers have when creating tables with **text**, **ntext**, or **image** columns.

  BLOBs in Special Operations. Identifies information needed when BLOBs are part of operations such as backing up and restoring a database.

- **Implementing BLOBs**

  BLOBs on the Server. Discusses ways to use Transact-SQL to manipulate BLOB data on the server when data is stored outside the data row (out-row text, out-row BLOB) and when it is stored inside the row (in-row text, in-row BLOB).

  BLOBs on the Client. Discusses ways to work with BLOB data on the client, and how to use the application programming interfaces (API) ADO, OLE DB, and ODBC.

- **Working with BLOBs**

  Summarizes considerations when working with BLOBs in SQL Server.

Designing BLOBs

This topic covers issues to consider before programming the database application with **text**, **ntext**, and **image** data:

- How BLOB data is stored in SQL Server
- How to learn from applications that have used BLOBS successfully in SQL Server
- Information about using BLOBs when they are part of operations such as backing up a database

BLOB Storage in SQL Server

BLOBs are very large variable binary or character data, typically documents (.txt, .doc) and pictures (.jpeg, .gif, .bmp), which can be stored in a database. In SQL Server, BLOBs can be **text**, **ntext**, or **image** data type:

text

Variable-length non-Unicode data, stored in the code page of the server, with a maximum length of 2^{31} - 1 (2,147,483,647) characters.

ntext

Variable-length Unicode data with a maximum length of 2^{30} - 1 (1,073,741,823) characters. Storage size, in bytes, is two times the number of characters entered. The SQL-92 synonym for **ntext** is **national text**.

image

Variable-length binary data from 0 through 2^{31} - 1 (2,147,483,647) bytes.

SQL Server handles these data types the same: SQL Server stores **image** data in the same way it stores **text** or **ntext** data, under the same conditions. It is common for **text**, **ntext**, and **image** data to be called generally as text data.

Each **text**, **ntext**, and **image** column in a table can contain up to 2 gigabytes (GB) of BLOB data. The BLOB data is stored in a collection of 8-kilobyte (KB) data pages that are separate from the data pages that store the other data in the same table. These data pages are arranged in a B-tree structure.

SQL Server 2000 introduced an option in which small-sized BLOBs can be stored in the **text**, **ntext**, and **image** columns in the same data row as other columns of a table. This option, called **text in row** because the BLOB data is stored in the data row, must be enabled explicitly. Until the release of SQL Server 2000, all text data was stored outside the data row (out row). Only 16-byte pointers to the root of the BLOB B-tree structure were stored in the **text**, **ntext**, or **image** columns of a table (BLOB root pointer).

Out-Row BLOBs

Unless the **text in row** option is enabled for a table, and therefore belongs in a SQL Server 2000 database, you do not need to know whether SQL Server 7.0 or SQL Server 2000 is running to determine how the BLOB data is stored; both versions of SQL Server store BLOBs outside the row. Only BLOB root pointers are stored in the **text**, **ntext**, or **image** columns in the table. The BLOB root pointers point to the root of the B-tree structure that actually stores the BLOB data. When the size of the BLOB data is less than or equal to 64 bytes, the root structure holds the data. When the BLOB size is longer than 64 bytes, the root structure holds the links that map the path to the data, which are stored in the leaf nodes of the B-tree.

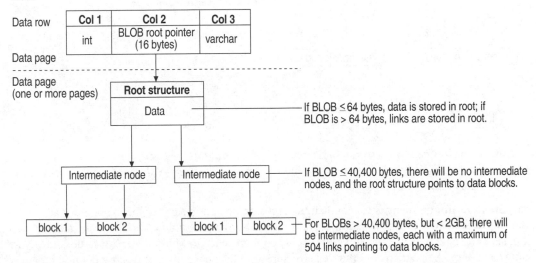

In-Row BLOBs

The **text in row** option allows small-sized **text**, **ntext**, and **image** data to be stored inside a table row. When the **text in row** option is enabled, SQL Server stores the BLOB data in the data row if the size is less than or equal to the in-row limit, and if there is enough space in the row to hold the BLOB data. The **text in row** limit applies to each BLOB column in the row. Thus, if the in-row limit is 256 bytes, each BLOB column in the row can store up to 256 bytes of data as long as the total bytes for the row does not exceed 8,060 bytes.

When the **text**, **ntext**, or **image** data is stored in the data row, SQL Server does not have to access a separate page or set of pages to read or modify the data. Reading and writing the in-row **text**, **ntext**, or **image** data becomes as fast as reading or writing **varchar**, **nvarchar**, or **varbinary** data.

When the BLOB string is too long for the data row and is stored in a separate BLOB page, with the **text in row** option enabled, SQL Server continues to access the data faster. With in-row BLOB, the root structure is stored in the data row when the BLOB data itself is too large. Thus, the path by which SQL Server accesses the BLOB data is shorter. This is different from regular out-row BLOBs where the data row never holds the BLOB data, and where the root structure that holds pointers to the BLOB data is in a separate page.

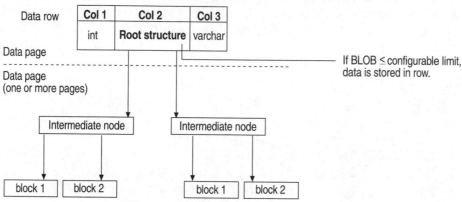

The **text**, **ntext**, or **image** strings stored in the data row are stored in the same way as other variable-length data is stored. SQL Server uses only the number of bytes needed to store the BLOB string even if the specified **text in row** limit is longer.

If a **text**, **ntext**, or **image** string is longer than the **text in row** option limit or the available space in the row, the BLOB root structure is stored in the row. The root structure holds pointers to the text fragments stored in separate data pages. SQL Server uses only enough space to hold the root structure; however, the row must have enough space to hold the root structure, and the space needed to store the root structure should be shorter than the **text in row** option limit. If the row data, including the BLOB root structure, is larger than 8,060 bytes, the insert action will fail.

If a table has several **text**, **ntext**, or **image** columns, and you attempt to insert multiple **text**, **ntext**, or **image** strings, SQL Server assigns space to the strings one at a time, based on the order of the column ID.

For example, **TableS** contains six columns; four are BLOB columns. The **text in row** option is enabled and the **text in row** limit is 1,000 bytes. If you insert into **TableS** a row that includes a total of 5,060 bytes for the non-BLOB columns and 900 bytes for each of the four BLOB columns, SQL Server:

1. Inserts the 5,060 bytes to the non-BLOB column.

2. Reads the column IDs of the BLOB columns and identifies the order.

3. Inserts 900 bytes to the first three BLOB columns, based on the column IDs.

4. Places a root structure in the fourth BLOB column and stores the 900-byte BLOB in a separate data page.

The **sp_tableoption** stored procedure is used to manage the **text in row** option on tables that have **text**, **ntext**, or **image** columns. Use **sp_tableoption** to set **text in row** on or off, and to set the option limits. The **text in row** option limit defaults to 256 bytes, but can be set from 24 bytes through 7,000 bytes.

For more information about **sp_tableoption**, see SQL Server Books Online.

These examples show ways to use **sp_tableoption** to change **text in row** option settings on the **Employees** table of the **Northwind** database.

Code Example 11.1

```
--Turns option ON and sets in-row limit to default, 256 bytes.
sp_tableoption 'Employees', 'text in row', 'on'

--Sets in-row limit to 5,000 bytes.
sp_tableoption 'Employees', 'text in row', '5000'

--Turns option OFF.
sp_tableoption 'Employees', 'text in row', 'off'

--Results in error; parameter is below the allowed range.
sp_tableoption 'Employees', 'text in row', '20'

--Results in error; parameter is above allowable range.
sp_tableoption 'Employees', 'text in row', '7003'
```

Considerations When Enabling or Changing text in row Option Values

When you enable the **text in row** option in a table or change the **text in row** option settings of a table, consider the following:

- When the **text in row** option is enabled for the first time, SQL Server does not convert the existing **text**, **ntext**, or **image** data to in-row text immediately; it makes the conversion when the text is updated. Any **text**, **ntext**, or **image** data inserted after the **text in row** option has been enabled is inserted as an in-row text.

- When the **text in row** option limit is increased, SQL Server does not convert the existing **text**, **ntext**, or **image** data to adhere to the new limit immediately; it makes the conversion when the data is updated. Any **text**, **ntext**, or **image** data inserted after the limit is increased adheres to the new limit.

- Turning off the **text in row** option can be a long-running, logged operation. SQL Server locks the table and converts all in-row **text**, **ntext**, and **image** data to regular **text**, **ntext**, and **image** strings. The length of time the procedure must run, and the amount of data modified depends on how much **text**, **ntext**, and **image** data must be converted from in-row to out-row text.

- Reducing the **text in row** option limit can be a long-running, logged operation. SQL Server locks the table and changes all in-row **text**, **ntext**, and **image** columns, which have current in-row data longer than the new limit, to adhere to the new limit.

Out-Row and In-Row BLOB Functionality Differences

When BLOB data is stored outside the data row, the data stored in the BLOB column depends on whether or not **text in row** is enabled. If **text in row** is enabled, and the BLOB data is too large for the row, the root structure is stored in the row. The root structure contains pointers to the text fragments stored in separate data pages. If **text in row** is not enabled, BLOB data is never stored in the row, and the BLOB root pointer is stored in the row. The BLOB root pointer points to the root structure that contains pointers to the text fragments.

The text pointers are 16-byte handles with which text fragments are accessed. Whether or not the **text in row** option is on, you obtain the text pointer value by using the TEXTPTR function. For more information, see SQL Server Books Online.

The text pointers for in-row text differ from text pointers for out-row text. The following table summarizes the functionality differences. For more information, see "Managing ntext, text, and image Data" in SQL Server Books Online.

Functionality	Out-Row Text	In-Row Text
Lifetime	Valid while the row exists.	Valid only within a transaction.
	Actions that invalidate text pointers:	Actions that invalidate in-row text pointers:
	• Deletion of a row	• Termination of a session, even if a transaction is still active
		• Deletion of a row (DELETE)
		• Schema changes to a table through DDL statements (ALTER TABLE, CREATE [CLUSTERED] INDEX, DROP [CLUSTERED] INDEX, DROP TABLE, TRUNCATE TABLE)
		• **sp_indexoption**
		• **sp_tableoption** with **text in row** option
		It is recommended that text pointers are invalidated explicitly after they are needed through the **sp_invalidate_textptr** stored procedure.

continued on next page

Functionality	Out-Row Text	In-Row Text
Locking	Data row is not locked. The only way to lock the data row is to raise the isolation level to Repeatable Read or higher.	Data row is locked in Shared (S) mode while text pointer is valid, when the transaction is Read Committed isolation level or higher. When the transaction ends, the text pointer becomes invalid and the lock is released. No locks are needed and none are placed on the data row if the isolation level of the transaction is Read Uncommitted or the database is in read-only mode.
Number Limit	Allows an unlimited number of text pointers.	Allows 1,024 text pointers for each database in a transaction. If a transaction is operating on more than one database, each database in that transaction can have a maximum of 1,024 transactions.
Null Values	You cannot obtain a text pointer when you insert NULL text. To obtain a text pointer, you must use the UPDATE statement to set the text to NULL. At that time, SQL Server allocates an 84-byte root structure for the NULL value.	You can obtain a text pointer on NULL text. When you update a text value to NULL, SQL Server does not allocate any root space.

SQL Server 2000 introduced the **sp_invalidate_textptr** stored procedure as a tool for explicitly invalidating in-row text pointers. If the optional text pointer value is specified, the stored procedure invalidates that text pointer; otherwise, **sp_invalidate_textptr** invalidates all text pointers in the transaction. This stored procedure can be used only when the **text in row** option is enabled.

Due to the limited number of text pointers allowed and their use of system resources, text pointers should be invalidated explicitly when they are not needed. Invalidating text pointers through **sp_invalidate_textptr** is an efficient and quick process that will not affect performance.

For more information about **sp_invalidate_textptr**, see SQL Server Books Online.

The following code samples illustrate the interaction among transaction levels, locking, and text pointers.

Code Example 11.2

```
--Use the example table, Tbl, and turn text in row ON.
DROP TABLE Tbl
GO
```

```
CREATE TABLE Tbl (EmployeeID int, LastName nvarchar(40), Notes ntext)

EXEC sp_tableoption 'Tbl', 'text in row', 'on'

INSERT INTO Tbl VALUES(1, 'Davolio', 'This field holds information on a specific
employee.')
INSERT INTO Tbl VALUES(2, 'Fuller', 'This field holds information on a specific
employee.')

SELECT * FROM Tbl

--Here is the result set.
1  Davolio  This field holds information on a specific employee.
2  Fuller   This field holds information on a specific employee.


--Although the transaction isolation level is READ UNCOMMITTED, this code will succeed
because READTEXT is only reading the data.

SET TRANSACTION ISOLATION LEVEL READ UNCOMMITTED
GO
BEGIN TRAN
DECLARE @ptr VARBINARY(16)
SELECT @ptr=TEXTPTR(Notes)
FROM Tbl
WHERE EmployeeID=2
READTEXT Tbl.Notes @ptr 17 26
COMMIT TRAN
GO


--Because the transaction isolation level is READ UNCOMMITTED and WRITETEXT is updating
an existing ntext column, this code will fail.

SET TRANSACTION ISOLATION LEVEL READ UNCOMMITTED
GO
BEGIN TRAN
DECLARE @ptr VARBINARY(16)
SELECT @ptr=TEXTPTR(Notes)
FROM Tbl
WHERE EmployeeID=2
WRITETEXT Tbl.Notes @ptr 'This is the changed text information on the employee.'
COMMIT TRAN
GO


--This is the error message:
You cannot update a blob with a read-only text pointer. The statement has been
terminated.
```

```
--When the transaction isolation level is raised to READ COMMITTED, the same transaction
will succeed.

SET TRANSACTION ISOLATION LEVEL READ COMMITTED
GO
BEGIN TRAN
DECLARE @ptr VARBINARY(16)
SELECT @ptr=TEXTPTR(Notes)
FROM Tbl
WHERE EmployeeID=2
WRITETEXT Tbl.Notes @ptr 'This is the changed text information on the employee.'
COMMIT TRAN
GO

SELECT Notes
FROM Tbl
WHERE EmployeeID=2
--The result shows the changed text.
```

The following code confirms that each database in a transaction is limited to 1,024 valid text pointers.

Code Example 11.3

```
DROP TABLE Tbl
GO
CREATE TABLE Tbl (EmployeeID int, LastName nvarchar(40), Notes ntext)
EXEC sp_tableoption 'Tbl', 'text in row', 'on'

BEGIN TRAN
DECLARE @ptrval VARBINARY(16)
DECLARE @ivar INTEGER
SET @ivar = 1
WHILE @ivar <= 1025 BEGIN
    INSERT Tbl VALUES ( 1,'', 'mnopqrstuvwxyz')
    SET @ivar = @ivar + 1
END
SELECT COUNT(*) FROM Tbl
SET @ivar = 1
WHILE @ivar <= 1024 BEGIN
    SELECT @ptrval = TEXTPTR(Notes) FROM Tbl WHERE EmployeeID=@ivar
    SET @ivar = @ivar + 1
END
PRINT 'You will get an error here. You can have up to 1,024 text pointers per database
per transaction.'
SELECT @ptrval = TEXTPTR(Notes) FROM Tbl WHERE EmployeeID = 1025
DELETE Tbl WHERE EmployeeID = 1
PRINT 'Now, you can read the data. The DELETE explicitly invalidated one text pointer,
so there are only 1,024 text pointers.'
```

```
SELECT @ptrval = TEXTPTR(Notes) FROM Tbl WHERE EmployeeID = 1025
READTEXT Tbl.Notes @ptrval 0 1
COMMIT
GO
```

Learning from the TerraServer Design and Implementation

BLOBs are data types that can be very large and can place heavy demands on disk, memory, and network resources. When designing tables containing **text**, **ntext**, and **image** data types, the database designer needs to be aware of the choices available for BLOB data storage and the implications of each choice.

This topic discusses when to use, and how to design the use of, BLOBs in SQL Server applications. These guidelines are based on techniques developed by the SQL Server team in creating Microsoft TerraServer, a very large database application that provides free public access to maps and aerial photographs of the United States over the Internet. TerraServer contains more than 250 million .jpeg and .gif files stored in BLOB fields, which demonstrates the ability of SQL Server 7.0 and SQL Server 2000 to scale to very large databases. For more information about TerraServer, see http://www.terraserver.microsoft.com/.

Based on the SQL Server TerraServer implementation, these choices must be considered when designing tables with BLOBs:

- Use a BLOB data type, or a **varchar** or **varbinary** data type.

- Store BLOBs either in a database or in a file system.

- Store each large object in one field, or divide the object into several BLOB fields.

BLOB Data Type vs. varchar or varbinary Data Type

Binary large objects do not need to be stored as **text**, **ntext**, or **image** data; they can be stored in tables as **varchar** or **varbinary** data types. The choice of data type depends on the predominant size of the BLOBs to be stored. If the data will never exceed 8 KB, use **varbinary** or **varchar** data types. If the size of these large objects will exceed 8 KB, use **text**, **ntext**, or **image** data types.

Database or File System

Web applications often have graphics associated with tabular data. For example, real estate Web sites typically include photographs of homes for sale. On company intranet sites, client databases can contain image files of client products. For such applications, a common design question involves whether the images should be stored in the database or in a file system. In most cases, the best choice is to store the images in the database together with the other data.

Storing the images in a database is the better choice if the application in which the images will be used count on the benefits of a database system. The benefits of storing the images in the database include:

- Manageability. When BLOBs are stored in the database with the other data:

    - BLOB and tabular data are backed up and recovered together. This reduces the chances of having the table data out of synchronization with the BLOB data, and lowers the risk of other users deleting the path to the location of the BLOB data in the file system.

    - INSERT, UPDATE, and DELETE of BLOB and other data occur in the same transaction. This ensures data consistency and consistency between files and the databases.

    - Separate security for files in the file system will not need to be set up.

- Scalability. Although file systems are designed to handle a large number of objects of varying sizes, file systems usually are not optimized for a huge number (tens of millions) of small files. Database systems are optimized for such cases.

- Availability. SQL Server has availability features that extend beyond those provided by the file system.

    - SQL Server replication is a set of solutions that allow you to copy, distribute, and potentially modify data in a distributed environment.

    - Log shipping provides a way of keeping a stand-by copy of a database in case the primary system fails.

Storing images in a file system would be a better choice if:

- The application in which the images will be used requires streaming performance, such as real-time video playback.

- BLOBs require frequentaccess by applications, such as Microsoft PhotoDraw® or Adobe Photoshop, which only know how to access files.

- You want to use some specific feature in the NTFS file system such as Remote Storage.

As with most guidelines though, these points can assist in decision making only after a thorough research of the specific use, environment, and purpose of the application.

Storing BLOBs

A database may follow good entity modeling and have a logical design, but if the application and users cannot access and manipulate the BLOB data stored in it efficiently, the database is not effective. BLOBs are large and can put a great deal of stress on the underlying memory, disk, and network hardware. More than any other data type, BLOBs require database designers to understand how the application will access and use the BLOBs in practice. Spend time designing how the BLOB objects will be represented in the database. Analyze how the BLOB data is going to be used, and by whom. How you lay out the large objects within the database affects both the response time and throughput of the application. This topic uses the TerraServer implementation to illustrate the choices available for storing BLOBS, and their impact on performance.

Users around the world access TerraServer using a Web browser. In the TerraServer Web site users choose if a single TerraServer Web page contains a 400 x 200 pixel image, a 600 x 400 pixel image, or an 800 x 600 pixel image. Buttons on the Web page give users the ability to move an image to the north, south, east, or west, and zoom in or zoom out on an image. Depending on their Internet connection, users could choose a large or small image size. (The TerraServer application assumed that users might be accessing the Internet using a slow-speed modem, and might have a small computer monitor.)

A set of Web servers running Microsoft Internet Information Services (IIS) host the TerraServer application logic and generate HTML Web pages that are sent back to the Web browsers of users. The Web servers execute SQL queries to retrieve the meta data and image data stored in database tables. As of the last quarter of 2000, TerraServer contained 157,000 images produced by the United States Geological Survey (USGS). The average size of a black and white image was 45 MB, and the average single-color infrared image is 151 MB. The average image was 6,200 by 7,700 pixels.

Given this scenario, the choices for BLOB handling became evident.

- Store each image file as a single BLOB. This choice may be an obvious one, but it is not practical. The average black and white image is 45 MB, which could take hours to download over the Internet to a Web browser.

- Process the BLOB using the middle-tier system. For TerraServer, the middle-tier arrangement means the Web servers extract the appropriate number of pixels from a 45-MB BLOB, compress the extracted pixels in a format supported by the browser, and then send the compressed format to the user. From a database system perspective, this is the simplest design. From the perspective of TerraServer, it could have been a major mistake. TerraServer averages 46,000 visitors per day accessing 1 million Web pages containing images. At times, 3,000 or more simultaneous users are connected to TerraServer. Such a design would have taxed the disk, memory, and network components of the SQL Server database and Web servers.

- Divide and store image files in tiles. Terra Server implemented this choice because the design strategy supports the TerraServer application optimally. TerraServer is designed so an image starts to appear on the Web browser immediately, regardless of the connection speed to the Internet. In the current design, each image tile is stored in the TerraServer database as a single 200 pixel by 200 pixel BLOB compressed to 9.5 KB in either .jpeg or .gif format. The smallest TerraServer image page contains two 200 x 200 pixel image tiles. The TerraServer Web page is a 25-KB HTML document containing references (IMG SRC tags) to the BLOBs in the database; therefore, it takes only a few seconds on a slow modem to transfer 34.5 KB of data.

For an example of how a console application can load image data in the **image** data type field of a database, run the Bii utility. Bii detects when an image field is the destination in the database and the input is a file name that can be located in the file system. The Bii.exe (Bii) utility is available on the *SQL Server 2000 Resource Kit* CD-ROM in the folder \ToolsAndSamples\Bii.

BLOBs in Special Operations

When you store BLOBs in a database, certain operations may be affected.

- Backup and restore operations

When designing your database backup strategy, consider that SQL Server 2000 can perform text and image operations with considerably less transaction log usage, depending on the recovery model selected for the database. Selecting a recovery model involves tradeoffs in performance and risks of transaction loss. For information about guidelines for selecting a recovery model, see "Selecting a Recovery Model" in SQL Server Books Online.

For more information, see "Backup and Restore Operations" and "Using Recovery Models" in SQL Server Books Online.

- Copy and logged operations

If your database application sends or receives large amounts of BLOB data, consider changing the packet size of the chunks of data that transfer requests and results between clients and servers. To change or set the packet size, use the **network packet size** option in **Configuration Options**. A packet size larger than the 4,096-byte default may improve efficiency by lowering the network reads and writes. A packet size of 8,080 bytes is best for performance in SQL Server 2000 and SQL Server 7.0.

- Full-text index and search operations

You can index and search certain types of data stored in BLOB columns. When a database designer decides that a table will contain a BLOB column and the column will participate in a full-text index, the designer must create, in the same table, a separate character-based data column that will hold the file extension of the file in the corresponding BLOB field. During the full-text indexing operation, the full-text service looks at the extensions listed in the character-based column, applies the corresponding filter to interpret the binary data, and extracts the textual information needed for indexing and querying.

When a field in a BLOB column contains documents with one of the following file extensions, the full-text search service uses a filter to interpret the binary data and extract the textual information.

- .doc

- .txt

- .xls

- .ppt

- .htm

The extracted text is indexed and becomes available for querying.

In addition, after it has been full-text indexed, text data stored in BLOB columns can be queried using the CONTAINS or FREETEXT predicates. For example, this query searches the **Description** column in the **Categories** table for the phrase "bean curd". **Description** is an **ntext** column.

Code Example 11.4

```
USE Northwind
GO
SELECT Description
FROM Categories
WHERE CONTAINS(Description, ' "bean curd" ' )
```

For more information, see "Full-text Search" and "Full-text Indexes" in SQL Server Books Online.

Implementing BLOBs

BLOB data types are similar to other data types. SQL statements can insert, modify, and retrieve them from tables, and SQL functions can compute the length of BLOB strings.

However, BLOB data types are opaque; they cannot be compared. Because BLOBs can be very large, and moving them around can be resource intensive, applications may not want to cache their values.

On the server, when programming tables with BLOB data, you can use **text**, **ntext**, and **image** data types in SELECT, INSERT, UPDATE, and DELETE statements, but you cannot use them with most aggregate functions as well as clauses and expressions that perform comparisons (GROUP BY, HAVING, COMPUTE, and ORDER BY).

In addition, you can use the text pointer, which is a programming element defined to provide chunked manipulation of BLOB data. As discussed in previous sections in this chapter, there are two kinds of text pointers, the out-row text pointer and the in-row text pointer.

This table summarizes the Transact-SQL statements, functions, and stored procedures to use in programming BLOBs on the server. These Transact-SQL elements are used for **text**, **ntext**, and **image** data types, unless otherwise specified. In addition, many of these Transact-SQL elements are not specific for BLOBs, but also are used for other data types.

Transact-SQL	Description
@@TEXTSIZE	Returns the current value of the TEXTSIZE option in the SET TEXTSIZE statement
	When used for **ntext** data, the value returned is @@TEXTSIZE/2 characters.
CREATE TABLE	Creates tables that can contain **text**, **ntext**, or **image** columns
DATALENGTH	Returns the number of bytes used to represent the expression
DELETE	Removes rows from tables
INSERT	Adds new rows to tables
PATINDEX	Used only for **text** data types (not **image** or **ntext**)
	Returns the starting position of the first occurrence of a pattern in a specified expression on valid **text** data types
READTEXT	Reads **text**, **ntext**, or **image** values from **text**, **ntext**, or **image** columns, starting from a specified offset and reading the specified number of bytes
SELECT	Retrieves all or specified row data from tables
SET TEXTSIZE	Specifies the size of **text**, **ntext**, and **image** data returned with a SELECT statement
	When used for **ntext** data, the value is size/2 characters.
sp_invalidate_textptr	Invalidates text pointers
sp_tableoption	Sets the **text in row** option on or off, and specifies option limits
SUBSTRING	Retrieves a block of data starting at a specific offset from the start of a column
TEXTPTR	Returns the value, in varbinary format, of the text pointer that corresponds to a **text**, **ntext**, or **image** column
TEXTVALID	Checks if a specified text pointer is valid
UPDATE	Changes existing data in tables
UPDATETEXT	Changes a portion of existing **text**, **ntext**, or **image** field
WRITETEXT	Replaces data in existing **text**, **ntext**, or **image** field

BLOBs on the Server

This topic discusses the process of creating tables with BLOB columns, inserting and modifying BLOB data, retrieving this data, and getting information about the BLOB data and columns using Transact-SQL. For more information about specific Transact-SQL statements and functions, see SQL Server Books Online.

1. Creating tables with BLOB columns

    A table with BLOB columns is created using the CREATE TABLE statement (the same way as tables without BLOB columns).

    Code Example 11.5

    ```
    CREATE TABLE Tbl (EmployeeID int, LastName nvarchar(40), Notes ntext)
    ```

    SQL Server can store the BLOB columns of the table on filegroups separate from the filegroup that stores the rest of the table by using the TEXTIMAGE_ON keyword. By default, SQL Server stores the BLOB columns in the same filegroup as the table.

    Code Example 11.6

    ```
    DROP TABLE Tbl
    GO
    CREATE TABLE Tbl (EmployeeID int, LastName nvarchar(40), Notes ntext)
    TEXTIMAGE_ON [DEFAULT]
    ```

    Designing database schema carefully becomes even more important when your tables contain BLOB columns. You cannot use ALTER COLUMN in the ALTER TABLE statement if the column you are changing is **text**, **ntext**, or **image**. (A **timestamp** column also cannot be altered.)

    Code Example 11.7

    ```
    --This statement will generate an error.
    ALTER TABLE Tbl
    ALTER COLUMN Notes text

    --This is the error.
    Cannot alter column 'Notes' because it is 'ntext'.
    ```

    All BLOB data that you insert into the table will not be stored in the data row. Instead, an out-row BLOB root pointer that points to the root structure of a data tree is stored in the row. To store BLOB data in row, execute the **sp_tableoption** stored procedure with the **text in row** option.

Code Example 11.8

```
--This command turns on text in row with the default in-row limit of 256 bytes.
USE Northwind
GO
EXEC sp_tableoption 'Employees', 'text in row', 'on'
```

You can enable the **text in row** option at any time, but changing from out-row to in-row BLOB storage or from in-row to out-row BLOB storage can be long-running operations when the table already has **text** data, which has to be converted. For more information, see "Considerations When Enabling or Changing text in row Option Values" in this chapter.

2. Modifying BLOB values

   Transact-SQL provides several ways with which you can modify BLOB fields in a table.

   - Insert the actual data using the INSERT statement.

   ### Code Example 11.9

   ```
   DROP TABLE Tbl
   GO
   CREATE TABLE Tbl (EmployeeID int, LastName nvarchar(40), Notes ntext)
   INSERT Tbl VALUES(1, 'Davolio', 'This field holds information on a specific
   employee.')
   INSERT Tbl VALUES(2, 'Fuller', 'This field holds information on a specific
   employee.')
   ```

   If the table does not have in-row text and you insert a null value into a **text**, **ntext**, or **image** column, SQL Server saves space by not creating a text pointer and not allocating an 8-KB text page for the NULL value.

   - Modify a text column using the UPDATE statement.

   ### Code Example 11.10

   ```
   --This example updates the Notes for Employee 2.
   UPDATE Tbl
   SET Notes = 'This (just updated) field holds information on a specific employee.'
   WHERE EmployeeID=2
   ```

   When you use an UPDATE statement to modify a **text**, **ntext**, or **image** column, the UPDATE initializes the column. This means a valid text pointer is assigned to the column, and at least one data page is allocated for the column.

UPDATE actions are logged operations. Thus, when **text**, **ntext**, or **image** data is written to the database using the UPDATE statement, the operation can fill the transaction log with the large amount of data that typically comprise BLOB data types. To avoid this, use the WRITETEXT or UPDATETEXT statements to replace large blocks of **text**, **ntext**, or **image** data. By default, these statements are not logged.

You do not obtain text pointers automatically when the BLOB data you insert in a table with **text in row** enabled is too large. You must use the TEXTPTR function to obtain the text pointer.

- Change the whole block of text data using the WRITETEXT statement.

The WRITETEXT statement rewrites, or replaces, the entire data value for the **text**, **ntext**, or **image** field. A WRITETEXT operation is not logged if the database recovery model is simple or bulk-logged. For WRITETEXT to work properly, the column must already contain a valid text pointer.

Code Example 11.11

```
BEGIN TRAN
    DECLARE @ptrval varbinary(16)
    SELECT @ptrval = TEXTPTR(Notes)
    FROM Tbl
    WHERE EmployeeID = 1
    WRITETEXT Tbl.Notes @ptrval 'The original text in this field is delimited by
brackets [This field holds information on a specific employee.]. '
COMMIT
```

- Change part of the data using the UPDATETEXT statement.

To change a portion of a **text**, **ntext**, or **image** field rather than the entire field, use the UPDATETEXT statement.

This example uses UPDATETEXT to update an employee's academic degree in the Employees table.

Code Example 11.12

```
USE Northwind
GO
BEGIN TRAN
    DECLARE @ptrval varbinary(16)
    SELECT @ptrval = TEXTPTR(Notes)
    FROM Employees
    WHERE EmployeeID = 9
    UPDATETEXT Employees.Notes @ptrval 11 20 'Master''s degree in Medieval
Literature'
COMMIT
```

3. Retrieve BLOB values

The SELECT statement, on its own and using functions, is the main way in which BLOB values or information about BLOB values is retrieved. Use the SELECT statement for the following tasks:

- To reference a BLOB column.

    For example, this query retrieves **Photo** and **Notes**, which are **image** and **text** columns, from the **Employees** table of the **Northwind** database

    Code Example 11.13

    ```
    SELECT Photo, Notes
    FROM Employees
    ```

    You cannot use **ntext**, **text** or **image** columns in the select list of subqueries.

- To retrieve the binary value of image files stored in **image** columns, or the text value of data stored in **text** or **ntext** columns.

    Code Example 11.14

    ```
    SELECT Photo, Notes
    FROM Employees
    WHERE EmployeeID='1'
    ```

    The default limit of the length of the text data returned by a SELECT statement is 4,000 bytes. The default length of **text** or **ntext** columns included in the select list is set by the smallest of the actual size of the text, the default TEXTSIZE session setting, or the hard-coded application limit.

    The current TEXTSIZE setting is reported by the @@TEXTSIZE function. The full amount of data is returned if the length is less than TEXTSIZE. (The Microsoft OLE DB Provider for SQL Server and the SQL Server ODBC driver automatically set @@TEXTSIZE to its maximum of 2 GB, 2,147,483,647 bytes.) TEXTSIZE is set at execute time and not at parse time.

    For example, to determine the current TEXTSIZE setting, execute this query.

    Code Example 11.15

    ```
    SELECT @@TEXTSIZE
    --Returns 64512
    ```

    To specify or change the length of the returned text for the session use the SET TEXTSIZE statement, which specifies the size of **text** and **ntext** data returned with a SELECT statement. The maximum setting for SET TEXTSIZE is 2 GB, as specified in bytes. Setting the TEXTSIZE to 0 resets it to the default of 4 KB, 4,096 bytes.

Code Example 11.16

```
SET TEXTSIZE 0

SELECT @@TEXTSIZE  --Shows that the TEXTSIZE has changed to 4,096.
```

To determine the number of bytes used to represent a BLOB data, use the DATALENGTH function, which is useful for data types that store variable-length data. (When the value of the data field is NULL, the DATALENGTH is NULL.)

- To retrieve blocks of **text**, **ntext**, or **image** data.

Use the SUBSTRING function with the SELECT statement to retrieve blocks of BLOB data. The READTEXT statement also can be used to retrieve blocks of data. You use this statement after obtaining the text pointer value from a BLOB field by using the TEXTPTR function with the SELECT statement.

To retrieve blocks of BLOB data up to 8 KB, use SUBSTRING; to retrieve larger blocks of BLOB data, use READTEXT.

Use the SUBSTRING function to retrieve parts of **text**, **ntext**, or **image** data starting from a specific offset from the start of the column. When used with BLOB data, offsets, which are the start and length of the data, must be specified in bytes. The returned string when the expression is a BLOB is as follows:

Given expression	Return type
Text	**Varchar**
Ntext	**Nvarchar**
Image	**Varbinary**

Use the READTEXT statement to read blocks of **ntext**, **text**, or **image** data. READTEXT reads the specified number of bytes in a BLOB column starting from a given point or offset. Execute the TEXTPTR function to obtain the text pointer value to be used in the *text_ptr* argument of the READTEXT statement. The text pointer value also can be used in WRITETEXT and UPDATETEXT statements.

Code Example 11.17

```
SELECT TEXTPTR(Notes)
FROM Employees
```

Because the *text_ptr* argument and the TEXTPTR function work with 16-byte binary strings, declare a local variable to hold the text pointer and use that variable with READTEXT.

Code Example 11.18

```
DECLARE @ptr varbinary(16)
SELECT @ptr=TEXTPTR(Notes)
FROM Employees
WHERE LastName = 'Callahan'
READTEXT Employees.Notes @ptr 23 44
```

When the value of the *size* argument in READTEXT is more than the value of the @@TEXTSIZE function, SQL Server uses the value of the @@TEXTSIZE function.

For tables with in-row text, TEXTPTR returns a handle for the text to be processed. You can obtain a valid text pointer even if the text value is null.

If the table does not have in-row text, and if a **text**, **ntext**, or **image** column has not been initialized by an UPDATETEXT statement, TEXTPTR returns a null pointer.

You cannot use UPDATETEXT, WRITETEXT, or READTEXT without a valid text pointer. To check whether or not a text pointer exists and is valid, use the TEXTVALID function. This function returns 1 if the pointer is valid and 0 if the pointer is invalid. The identifier for the text column must include the table name.

Code Example 11.19

```
--This example reports whether or not a valid text pointer exists for each value
in the Notes column of the Employees table.

SELECT EmployeeID, 'Valid (if 1) Text data'
   = TEXTVALID ('Employees.Notes', TEXTPTR(Notes))
FROM Employees
ORDER BY EmployeeID
GO
```

For BLOBs that are text data type, use the PATINDEX function to retrieve offset information on particular patterns of bytes. PATINDEX returns the starting position of the first occurrence of a pattern in a specified expression. If SQL Server does not find the pattern, the function returns zeros. Values returned by PATINDEX can be used in a SUBSTRING function or a READTEXT statement.

This SELECT statement uses the SUBSTRING and PATINDEX functions to retrieve any part of a **text** value that is between a start tag and an end tag:

Code Example 11.20

```
USE Northwind
GO
CREATE TABLE TextParts (ColA INT PRIMARY KEY, ColB TEXT)
GO
```

```
INSERT INTO TextParts
   VALUES( 1,
          'Sample string START TAG What I want END TAG Trailing text.')
GO
SELECT SUBSTRING(   ColB,
                    /* Calculate start as start of tag + tag length. */
                    (PATINDEX('%START TAG%', ColB) + 10),
                    /* Calculate SUBSTRING length as end - start. */
                    (
                      PATINDEX('%END TAG%', ColB) -
                      ( PATINDEX('%START TAG%', ColB) + 10 )
                    )
                )
FROM TextParts
GO
```

Here is the result set:

```
------------------------
What I want

(1 row(s) affected)
```

Tables cannot be joined directly on **ntext**, **text**, or **image** columns; however, tables can be joined indirectly on **ntext**, **text**, or **image** columns by using SUBSTRING. For example, SELECT * FROM t1 JOIN t2 ON SUBSTRING(t1.*textcolumn*, 1, 20) = SUBSTRING(t2.*textcolumn*, 1, 20) performs a two-table inner join on the first 20 characters of each text column in tables **t1** and **t2**. In addition, another possibility for comparing **ntext** or **text** columns from two tables is to compare the lengths of the columns with a WHERE clause.

```
WHERE DATALENGTH(p1.pr_info) = DATALENGTH(p2.pr_info)
```

The **text in row** option affects the way you read and access data in row. You still can use the SELECT statement to read entire BLOB strings, and use the SUBSTRING function to read parts of the string.

- With in-row text pointers, you can use READTEXT, UPDATETEXT, or WRITETEXT statements to read or modify parts of the BLOB values stored in row.

Code Example 11.21

```
DROP TABLE Tbl
GO
CREATE TABLE Tbl (EmployeeID int, LastName nvarchar(40), Notes ntext)
GO
INSERT INTO Tbl VALUES(1, 'Davolio', 'This field holds information on a specific
employee.')
```

```
INSERT INTO Tbl VALUES(2, 'Fuller', 'This field holds information on a specific
employee.')
DECLARE @ptrval varbinary(16)
SELECT @ptrval = TEXTPTR(Notes)
FROM Tbl
WHERE EmployeeID = 1
READTEXT Tbl.Notes @ptrval 34 17
```

- All INSERT and UPDATE statements referencing the table must specify complete strings and cannot modify only parts of the BLOB strings.

BLOBs and Cursors

The existence of BLOB columns in tables accessed by cursors can affect cursor functionality and performance. If your cursors access tables with **text**, **ntext**, or **image** data, consider these points.

- When BLOB columns are referenced in SELECT statements, SQL Server converts fast-forward cursors to:

  - Dynamic cursors, if the OLE DB Provider for SQL Server or the SQL Server ODBC driver is used.

  - Keyset-driven cursors, if a TOP clause is also used in the SELECT statement.

- On tables with **text in row** enabled, you cannot have a cursor over in-row text pointers, but you can have a cursor over in-row text.

BLOBs on the Client

The database APIs follow a common pattern in handling BLOBs:

Reading BLOB columns
To read a long column, the application includes the **text**, **ntext**, or **image** column in a select list, and then binds the column to a program variable large enough to hold a reasonable block of the data. The application then executes the statement and uses an API function or method to retrieve the data into the bound variable one block at a time.

Writing BLOB columns
To write a long column, the application executes an INSERT or UPDATE statement with a parameter marker (?) in the place of the value to be placed in the **text**, **ntext**, or **image** column. The parameter marker (or parameter, in the case of ADO) is bound to a program variable large enough to hold the blocks of data. The application goes into a loop where it first moves the next set of data into the bound variable, and then calls an API function or method to write that block of data. This is repeated until the entire data value has been sent.

This is a summary of the ways the database APIs handle **text**, **ntext**, and **image** data:

- **ADO**

  ADO can map **text**, **ntext**, or **image** columns or parameters to a **Field** or **Parameter** object. Use the **GetChunk** method to retrieve the data one block at a time and the **AppendChunk** method to write data one block at a time.

  GetChunk and **AppendChunk** are sequential in nature. For example, when **GetChunk** is first called, the method starts reading the value of the BLOB column and keeps a pointer to the next byte that will be read. Subsequent calls keep reading from this stream. Because the API manages the process, reading and writing to any other field resets the internal pointer, consequently resetting calls to **GetChunk** for a specific column as well.

- **OLE DB**

  OLE DB uses the **ISequentialStream** interface to support **text**, **ntext**, and **image** data types. The **ISequentialStream::Read** method reads the long data one block at a time, and **ISequentialStream::Write** writes the long data to the database one block at a time.

- **ODBC**

  ODBC has a data-at-execution feature that handles the ODBC data types for long data: SQL_LONGVARCHAR (**text**), SQL_WLONGVARCHAR (**ntext**), and SQL_LONGVARBINARY (**image**). These data types are bound to a program variable. **SQLGetData** is then called to retrieve the long data one block at a time, and **SQLPutData** is called to send long data one block at a time. The ODBC **SQLPutData** function is faster and uses less dynamic memory than the Transact-SQL WRITETEXT statement. These functions can insert up to 2 GB of **text**, **ntext**, or **image** data.

  The **text in row** option does not affect the operation of the OLE DB Provider for SQL Server or the SQL Server ODBC driver, other than to speed access to the **text**, **ntext**, and **image** data.

ADO: Storing and Retrieving Files Using the Stream Object

One way of handling BLOBs from client-side applications is by using the ADO stream object. ADO is included as part of the MDAC (Microsoft Data Access Components) stack, which is included with SQL Server 2000. The following samples illustrate how to store files in SQL Server BLOB columns and how to store a BLOB column to a file. Unless otherwise specified, all samples use the **Northwind** database, and following are the variables declared:

```
Dim cn As ADODB.Connection
Dim rs As ADODB.Recordset
Dim st As ADODB.Stream
```

The ADOBlob.bas (ADOBlob) sample is available on the *SQL Server 2000 Resource Kit* CD-ROM in the folder \ToolsAndSamples\BLOB\ADO.

Saving a BLOB Column to a File

This sample saves the contents of the **Notes** field of Employee 9 in the **Employees** table to a file.

1. Establish a connection to SQL Server.

```
'Create a new connection object
Set cn = New ADODB.Connection

'Specify connection information
cn.ConnectionString = "Provider=SQLOLEDB; Data Source=(local); Integrated
Security=SSPI; Initial Catalog=Northwind"

'Establish the connection
cn.Open
```

2. Open an updatable recordset containing the row to be updated.

```
'Execute the command and retrieve the returned recordset
Set rs = New ADODB.Recordset
rs.Open "select Notes from employees where EmployeeID=9", cn, adOpenForwardOnly,
adLockReadOnly
```

3. Ensure files with the same name do not exist.

```
'Clear any existing file of the same name
If Dir("c:\Emp9.txt") <> "" Then
    Kill "c:\Emp9.txt"
End If
```

4. Set up the stream object specifying type (text or binary).

```
'Initialize the stream object used to persist to a file
Set st = New ADODB.stream
st.Type = adTypeText
st.Open
```

5. Load the file to be stored, and update the recordset with the contents of the stream.

```
'Write the value of the field to the stream
st.WriteText rs.fields("Notes").Value

'Save the content of the stream to a file
st.SaveToFile("c:\Emp9.txt")

'Close the stream
st.close
```

6. Close the connection and free resources.

```
'Close recordset and connection
rs.Close
cn.Close

'Free resources
Set rs = Nothing
Set st = Nothing
Set cn = Nothing
```

Saving a File in a BLOB Column

This sample updates the **Notes** field of Employee 9 in the **Employees** table with the contents of a file. This example uses the same text file as the previous example. To make the update operation more obvious, edit the text file and change the content.

1. Establish the connection, as in the previous sample. Retrieve the desired column and row.

```
'Execute the command and retrieve the returned recordset.
Set rs = New ADODB.Recordset
rs.Open = "select Notes from employees where EmployeeID = 9", cn, adOpenKeyset,
adLockOptimistic
```

2. Set up the stream object. The object has to be created and its type defined (text or binary); it has to be opened, and the value of the file written to the stream.

```
'Initialize the stream object used to load the file.
Set st = New ADODB.stream
st.Type = adTypeText
st.Open
st.LoadFromFile ("c:\Emp9.txt")

'Write the value of the field to the stream.
rs.Fields("Notes").Value = st.ReadText
```

3. Save the contents of the stream to the field.

```
rs.Update
```

4. Close the connection and free resources, as in the previous sample.

OLE DB: Reading BLOBs from a Database and Saving BLOBs in a File System

The following sample excerpts show how to use the SQL Server OLE DB Provider (SQLOLEDB) to connect to a SQL Server database, execute a SELECT statement retrieving a photo from **EmployeeID** 9 in the **Employees** table, and save the photo in the file "Employee9Photo.jpg".

The OLEDBLOBS.cpp (OLEDBLOBS) sample is available on the *SQL Server 2000 Resource Kit* CD-ROM in the folder \ToolsAndSamples\BLOB\OLEDB.

1. Call **CoInitialize** to initialize the OLE and OLE DB libraries.

```
//Initialize OLE environment.
CoInitialize(NULL);
```

2. Create an instance of the SQL OLE DB provider. An **IDBInitialize** interface is obtained and will be used to set connection information and connect to a server.

```
//Create an instance of the SQL Server OLEDB Provider.
CoCreateInstance(CLSID_SQLOLEDB, NULL, CLSCTX_INPROC_SERVER, IID_IDBInitialize,
(void**)&pIDBInitialize);
```

Properties defined as part of a property set with information to connect to the data source are: Servername, database, userid, and password.

```
//Initialize the property values needed to establish the connection.
for(i = 0; i < nProps; i++)
VariantInit(&InitProperties[i].vValue);

//Server name.
InitProperties[0].dwPropertyID  = DBPROP_INIT_DATASOURCE;
InitProperties[0].vValue.vt     = VT_BSTR;
InitProperties[0].vValue.bstrVal= SysAllocString(DATA_SOURCE);
InitProperties[0].dwOptions     = DBPROPOPTIONS_REQUIRED;
InitProperties[0].colid         = DB_NULLID;

//Database.
InitProperties[1].dwPropertyID  = DBPROP_INIT_CATALOG;
InitProperties[1].vValue.vt     = VT_BSTR;
InitProperties[1].vValue.bstrVal= SysAllocString(DATABASE);
InitProperties[1].dwOptions     = DBPROPOPTIONS_REQUIRED;
InitProperties[1].colid         = DB_NULLID;

//Username (login).
InitProperties[2].dwPropertyID  = DBPROP_AUTH_USERID;
InitProperties[2].vValue.vt     = VT_BSTR;
InitProperties[2].vValue.bstrVal= SysAllocString(USERNAME);
InitProperties[2].dwOptions     = DBPROPOPTIONS_REQUIRED;
InitProperties[2].colid         = DB_NULLID;

//Password.
InitProperties[3].dwPropertyID  = DBPROP_AUTH_PASSWORD;
InitProperties[3].vValue.vt     = VT_BSTR;
InitProperties[3].vValue.bstrVal= SysAllocString(PASSWORD);
InitProperties[3].dwOptions     = DBPROPOPTIONS_REQUIRED;
```

```
InitProperties[3].colid          = DB_NULLID;

/*
Construct the DBPROPSET structure(rgInitPropSet). The
DBPROPSET structure is used to pass an array of DBPROP
structures (InitProperties) to the SetProperties method.
*/
rgInitPropSet[0].guidPropertySet = DBPROPSET_DBINIT;
rgInitPropSet[0].cProperties     = nProps;
rgInitPropSet[0].rgProperties    = InitProperties;
```

3. Set the properties, obtain an **IDBProperties** interface, and then call the **SetProperties** method.

```
//Set initialization properties.
hr = pIDBInitialize->QueryInterface(IID_IDBProperties, (void **)&pIDBProperties);
hr = pIDBProperties->SetProperties(1, rgInitPropSet);
```

4. After the connection properties are set, call the **Initialize()** method on **IDBInitialize** to establish the connection:

```
//Establish the connection to the data source.
pIDBInitialize->Initialize();
```

5. After there is a connection to the server, create a session by obtaining an **IDBCreateSession** and calling **CreateSession()** on it. With this last call, retrieve a reference to an **IDBCreateCommand** interface that will allow creation of new commands that can be sent to the server.

```
if (FAILED(pIDBInitialize->QueryInterface(IID_IDBCreateSession,(void**)
&pIDBCreateSession)))
...
// The next session created receives the SQL Server connection of
// the data source object.
if (FAILED(pIDBCreateSession->CreateSession(NULL,IID_IDBCreateCommand, (IUnknown**)
&pIDBCreateCommand)))
```

6. On the **IDBCreateCommand** interface, call the **CreateCommand()** method to create a new command and obtain a reference to an **ICommandText** interface. This is the interface to use for sending SQL batches to the server to be executed.

```
if (FAILED(pIDBCreateCommand->CreateCommand(NULL, IID_ICommandText, (IUnknown**)
&pICommandText)))
```

For example, to retrieve the record from the **Photo** column of **EmployeeID** 10 in the **Employees** table, set the text of the command this way:

```
if (FAILED(pICommandText->SetCommandText(DBGUID_DBSQL,OLESTR("select Photo from
employees where EmployeeId=9"))))
```

The command can be executed to obtain **IRowset** to bind, fetch rows, and read the columns of each row.

```
if (FAILED(pICommandText->Execute(NULL, IID_IRowset, NULL, &cRowsAffected,
(IUnknown**) &pIRowset)))
```

7. To retrieve the BLOB column (**Photo**) in chunks, bind **ISequentialStream** to the only column in the rowset. To do this, create an accessor specifying the bindings required.

```
//Retrieve data from a rowset.
//Set up the DBOBJECT structure to bind as IsequentialStream.
dbobject.dwFlags = STGM_READ;
dbobject.iid = IID_ISequentialStream;

//Create the DBBINDING, requesting a storage-object pointer.
dbbinding.iOrdinal = 1; //First and single column
dbbinding.obValue = 0;
dbbinding.obStatus = sizeof(IUnknown*);
dbbinding.obLength = 0;
dbbinding.pTypeInfo = NULL;
dbbinding.pObject = &dbobject;
dbbinding.pBindExt = NULL;
dbbinding.dwPart = DBPART_VALUE | DBPART_STATUS;
dbbinding.dwMemOwner = DBMEMOWNER_CLIENTOWNED;
dbbinding.eParamIO = DBPARAMIO_NOTPARAM;
dbbinding.cbMaxLen = 0;
dbbinding.dwFlags = 0;
dbbinding.wType = DBTYPE_IUNKNOWN;
dbbinding.bPrecision = 0;
dbbinding.bScale = 0;

if (FAILED(hr = pIRowset->QueryInterface(IID_IAccessor, (void**) &pIAccessor)))
...
if (FAILED(hr = pIAccessor->CreateAccessor(DBACCESSOR_ROWDATA, 1, &dbbinding, 0,
&haccessor, &ulbindstatus)))
```

8. Memory must be allocated for the data being retrieved from each row. Because you are binding as **IsequentialStream**, only enough memory to receive the interface pointer and a status field needs to be allocated.

```
//Allocate memory for the returned pointer and the status
//field. The first sizeof(IUnknown*) bytes are for the pointer
//to the object; the next sizeof(ULONG) bytes are for the status.
pData=new BYTE[sizeof(IUnknown*)+sizeof(ULONG)];
```

9. Call **GetNextRows** on **IRowset** to return the next row; and then call **GetData** for each returned row.

```
if (FAILED(pIRowset->GetNextRows(NULL, 0, 1, &cRows, &pRows)))
...
if (SUCCEEDED(pIRowset->GetData(*pRows, haccessor, pData)))
```

To separate the pieces of information of the returned buffer:

```
dwStatus = (ULONG)((BYTE*)pData)[dbbinding.obStatus];
pISequentialStream = *((ISequentialStream**) pData);
```

10. Use the Win32 API **CreateFile** to open the destination file.

```
lstrcpy(FileName,L"Employee9Photo.jpg");
HANDLE hfile=CreateFile(FileName,GENERIC_READ | GENERIC_WRITE, FILE_SHARE_READ,
NULL,CREATE_ALWAYS,FILE_ATTRIBUTE_NORMAL,NULL);
```

11. Use the returned **ISequentialStream** interface to read chunks of CHUNK_SIZE bytes and save them in the file.

```
do
{
    //Read each chunk of CHUNK_SIZE bytes.
    if (SUCCEEDED(hr =pISequentialStream->Read(Picture,CHUNK_SIZE, &cbRead)))
    {
    WriteFile(hfile, Picture, cbRead, &BytesWritten,NULL);
    }
}
while (SUCCEEDED(hr) && cbRead >= CHUNK_SIZE);
```

12. Close the file, disconnect from the server, and then release all interfaces.

```
//Close the file.
CloseHandle(hfile);

pISequentialStream->Release();
pIAccessor->ReleaseAccessor(haccessor, NULL);
pIAccessor->Release();
pIRowset->Release();
pIDBInitialize->Release();
```

13. Uninitialize the OLE libraries.

```
//Uninitialize OLE libraries.
CoUninitialize();
```

ODBC: Handling BLOBs in a Database

The samples in this section save the photo field for each record of the **Employees** table into a separate file named "EmpNo" + EmployeeId and update the photo field of Employee 9 with the contents of a file named "Employee9Photo.jpg".

1. Saving BLOBs to FileAllocate an environment handle and specify an ODBC version 3.0 application using **SQLAllocHandle** and **SQLSetEnvAttr**.

   ```
   retcode = SQLAllocHandle (SQL_HANDLE_ENV, NULL, &henv);
   retcode = SQLSetEnvAttr(henv, SQL_ATTR_ODBC_VERSION, (SQLPOINTER)SQL_OV_ODBC3,
   SQL_IS_INTEGER);
   ```

2. Allocate the connection handle and connect using the specified data source, username, and password using **SQLAllocHandle** and **SQLConnect**.

   ```
   retcode = SQLAllocHandle(SQL_HANDLE_DBC, henv, &hdbc1);
   retcode = SQLConnect(hdbc1, szDSN, (SWORD)strlen((const char *)szDSN),szUID,
   (SWORD)strlen((const char *)szUID),szAuthStr, (SWORD)strlen((const char
   *)szAuthStr));
   ```

3. Allocate a statement handle and execute it with the SELECT statement using **SQLAllocHandle** and **SQLExecDirect**.

   ```
   SQLAllocHandle(SQL_HANDLE_STMT, hdbc1, &hstmt1);
   SQLExecDirect(hstmt1, (SQLTCHAR*)"SELECT EmployeeID, Photo FROM Employees", SQL_NTS);
   ```

   Columns in ODBC may be retrieved by binding program variables to columns or by using **SQLGetData** to read from a column into a variable or buffer. Binding requires reading a whole column in a single call, and **SQLGetData** allows reading a column in multiple sequential chunks.

   This section of the code retrieves the **EmployeeId** and **Photo** columns. **EmployeeId** will be used to make part of the output file name and **Photo** is the actual binary chunk. **EmployeeId** will be read as a bound variable into a character array (to be concatenated as part of the file name) and **Photo** will be read using **SQLGetData** in chunks of 8,000 bytes.

4. Bind the first column before starting to fetch the result set.

   ```
   SQLBindCol(hstmt1, 1, SQL_C_CHAR, (SQLPOINTER) &sEmpID, CHUNK_SIZE, &pIndicators[0]);
   ```

5. Fetch each row of the resulting rowset.

   ```
   while (SQLFetch(hstmt1) == SQL_SUCCESS)
   ```

6. Call **SQLGetData** for the first time with a buffer size of 0 to find out the total size, in bytes, of the column.

```
retcode=SQLGetData(hstmt1, 2, SQL_C_BINARY, Picture, 0, &pIndicators[1]);
```

7. Open the destination file using the Win32® **CreateFile** API.

```
lstrcpy(FileName,"EmpNo");
lstrcat(FileName, (LPCTSTR) sEmpID);
HANDLE hfile=CreateFile(FileName,GENERIC_READ | GENERIC_WRITE, FILE_SHARE_READ,
NULL,CREATE_ALWAYS,FILE_ATTRIBUTE_NORMAL,NULL);
```

8. Call **SQLGetData** in a loop, and then write to the opened file.

```
while (SQLGetData(hstmt1, 2, SQL_C_BINARY, Picture, CHUNK_SIZE,
&pIndicators[1])!=SQL_NO_DATA)
{
    if (pIndicators[1]>CHUNK_SIZE)
        WriteFile(hfile, Picture, CHUNK_SIZE, &BytesWritten,NULL);
    else
        WriteFile(hfile, Picture, pIndicators[1], &BytesWritten,NULL);
}
```

9. Close the file using **CloseHandle**, disconnect from SQL Server, and then release the statements, connection, and environment handles.

```
CloseHandle(hfile);
}
    else
    {
        SQLGetDiagRec(SQL_HANDLE_STMT, hstmt1,1, State, &NativeError, Message,
BuffLen, &TextLen);
        printf("%s",Message);
    }
}
SQLFreeHandle(SQL_HANDLE_STMT, hstmt1);
SQLDisconnect(hdbc1);
SQLFreeHandle(SQL_HANDLE_DBC, hdbc1);
SQLFreeHandle(SQL_HANDLE_ENV, henv);
```

The ODBCSaveToFile.cpp (ODBCSaveToFile) sample is available on the *SQL Server 2000 Resource Kit* CD-ROM in the folder \ToolsAndSamples\BLOB\ODBCSave.

Loading an Image File to a BLOB Column

Allocation of an environment handle and connection is the same as in the previous sample.

1. When a statement handle is allocated, open the source file and retrieve its byte length.

```
HANDLE hfile=CreateFile(FileName,GENERIC_READ, FILE_SHARE_READ,
NULL,OPEN_EXISTING,FILE_ATTRIBUTE_NORMAL,NULL);
FileSize=GetFileSize(hfile,NULL);
```

2. Bind a parameter to the statement indicating that the data for the parameter will be supplied at execution.

```
cbTextSize=SQL_LEN_DATA_AT_EXEC(FileSize);
retcode = SQLBindParameter(hstmt1, 1, SQL_PARAM_INPUT, SQL_C_BINARY,
SQL_LONGVARBINARY, FileSize, 0,(VOID *)NULL, 0, &cbTextSize);
```

3. Execute an UPDATE statement with a parameter marker (?) for the **Photo** value.

```
SQLExecDirect(hstmt1, (SQLTCHAR*)"UPDATE Employees set Photo = ? where EmployeeId=9",
SQL_NTS);
```

4. Call **SQLParamData** to return information about whether or not a parameter needs data, and to fill a passed-in parameter indicating data for which parameter data is being requested. All subsequent **SQLPutData** calls will be mapped to the current bound parameter. To move to the next parameter (if that were the case) or to indicate the end of the data for the parameter, **SQLParamData** is called again.

```
retcode = SQLParamData(hstmt1, &pParmID);
```

5. Iterate reading from the file and calling **SQLPutData**.

```
while (BytesWritten < FileSize)
{
    if (FileSize-BytesWritten>CHUNK_SIZE)
        lChunkSize=CHUNK_SIZE;
    else
        lChunkSize=FileSize-BytesWritten;
ReadFile(hfile,Picture,lChunkSize, &BytesRead, NULL);
SQLPutData(hstmt1, Picture, lChunkSize);
BytesWritten+=BytesRead;
}
```

6. Complete the statement execution calling **SQLParamData**. The row is updated.

```
SQLParamData(hstmt1, &pParmID);
```

7. Closing the source file and freeing ODBC resources are the same as in the previous sample.

The ODBCLOBS.cpp (ODBCLOBS) sample is available on the *SQL Server 2000 Resource Kit* CD-ROM in the folder \ToolsAndSamples\BLOB\ODBCLoad.

For more information, see "Managing text and image Columns" in SQL Server Books Online.

Working with BLOBs in SQL Server

In summary, the BLOB data types—**text**, **ntext**, and **image** data—are similar to other data types in SQL Server. They can be inserted, modified, and retrieved from tables. BLOBs, however, are unique in that they can be very large.

Consequently, when working with BLOBs, you might address similar issues as when working with other kinds of data. You also must be aware of and understand the effects and demands of BLOB data on systems, applications, and performance. Knowing the features and tools in SQL Server 2000 will help you implement and manipulate BLOB data in your applications efficiently.

Considerations when planning BLOB storage include:

- In SQL Server, **text**, **ntext**, and **image** data are stored the same way. BLOB data is stored in separate data pages from other table data. Small-sized BLOBs can be stored in the data row in SQL Server 2000, if the **text in row** option is enabled explicitly. Text pointers for BLOB data stored in the table row are different from text pointers for BLOBs stored outside the table.

- BLOBs do not need to be stored as **text**, **ntext**, and **image** data types, they do not need to be stored in one piece, and they do not need to be stored in a database. Binary large objects can be stored as **varchar** or **varbinary** data types. BLOB data can be stored in file systems, and BLOB data can be chunked or tiled.

- The presence of BLOB data may require different procedures, options, or settings for operations such as backing up a database, copying, and full-text search.

When programming BLOBs:

- You can use the same Transact-SQL statements—such as SELECT, INSERT, UPDATE, DELETE—used for other kinds of data. At the same time, some Transact-SQL elements work only with BLOB data and text pointers.

- When BLOB columns are referenced in SELECT statements, SQL Server converts fast-forward cursors to either dynamic or keyset-driven cursors, depending on conditions.

- On the client, a simple way of storing and retrieving BLOBs is by using the ADO stream object. You also can use SQL OLE DB and ODBC to read and save BLOBs.

Availability

Failover Clustering

Continuous uptime in a production environment, whether it is a database powering a mission-critical client/server application or an e-commerce Web site, is becoming a common businesses requirement. This chapter describes Microsoft® SQL Server™ 2000 failover clustering, one method of creating high availability. Failover clustering is available only in SQL Server 2000 Enterprise Edition.

Failover clustering is a process in which the operating system and application software work together to provide continuous availability in the event of an application failure, hardware failure, or operating-system error. Failover clustering provides hardware redundancy through a configuration in which other servers essentially act as clones of the main production system. Failover clustering also allows system maintenance to be performed on a computer while another node does the work. This benefit can also ensure that system downtime due to normal maintenance is minimized.

Failover clustering can be part of an overall scale-up and scale-out solution that takes into account backups, redundancy, and performance. However, failover clustering does not protect against viruses, denial of services, database corruption, logical corruption, or failed software installations, and is also not a load balancing solution. Failover clustering should be used for redundancy, not for increasing performance. If software and/or hardware problems occur, failover clustering combined with other high availability methods (such as SQL Server 2000 log shipping) can enable a production environment to be up and running in a short amount of time. For more information about high availability and achieving five nines, see Chapter 16, "Five Nines: The Ultimate in High Availability."

Enhancements to Failover Clustering

SQL Server 2000 failover clustering offers improvements over the clustering functionality provided in SQL Server version 7.0, Enterprise Edition. Some of the enhancements in SQL Server 2000 failover clustering include:

- Failover clustering is now part of the SQL Server 2000 setup process. This provides the following functionality:

  - SQL Server 2000 is tightly integrated with the Microsoft Windows® 2000 Advanced Server and Microsoft Windows 2000 Datacenter Server operating systems, thereby taking advantage of the Windows Clustering application programming interfaces (APIs).

- To uninstall clustering, run SQL Server 2000 Setup to uninstall SQL Server. You do not need to run a separate failover cluster wizard to remove failover clustering, as you did in SQL Server 7.0.

- SQL Server 2000 is built on multiple instances , which allows SQL Server to simultaneously support up to 16 instances of SQL Server.

- Because you create a failover cluster through SQL Server Setup, to remove failover clustering you must uninstall SQL Server 2000.

- SQL Server 2000 has extensive support for recovering from a failure of a node in the cluster. If a node fails it can be removed, reinstalled, and rejoined to the cluster. It is then a simple operation with SQL Server 2000 Setup to add the new server back into the virtual server definition.

- SQL Server 2000 supports a one-node cluster. This enhancement best serves a two-node cluster— when one node is lost completely, the cluster will still function properly. A one-node cluster, however, can be used for testing purposes in a development environment to simulate a cluster environment without having two or more computers. Another potential use is if clustering is going to be done later, it may be easier to set up a one-node cluster right from the start, and then add nodes later.

- SQL Server 2000 running on Windows 2000 Datacenter Server supports up to four nodes in a cluster .

- All nodes now have local copies of the SQL Server tools as well as the executables. In SQL Server 7.0, the binaries were on the shared disk, and only the primary node had shortcuts to the tools and proper COM components registered. This meant that administration had to be performed from a client computer in the event of a failover.

- SQL Server 2000 failover clustering supports Microsoft Search Services.

- SQL Server 2000 cluster configurations can be updated by rerunning the setup program. This is true even when applying a service pack. You only need to rerun the setup program.SQL Server 2000 supports multiple network addresses. This enables SQL Server 2000 to use different networks for internal and external communications. It does not completely remove a single point of failure, because the clustered SQL Server resource is dependent upon the IP address, and the SQL Server resource can fail while the IP address may be alive. It does provide some fault tolerance and, potentially, extra bandwidth so one network connection will not be overworked, but if there is a hardware failure (for example, a router) external to the cluster, Windows Clustering will still function properly although external clients may not be able to access the cluster.

- Database administrators can now use SQL Server Service Manager or SQL Server Enterprise Manager to start and stop SQL Server without having to use Cluster Administrator to start and stop SQL Server services.

Windows Clustering

SQL Server 2000 failover clustering is built on top of Windows Clustering. There are two main types of clusters in a Windows environment:

- Server cluster

  SQL Server 2000 clustering is built on top of a server cluster. A server cluster provides high availability, scalability, and manageability for resources and applications by clustering as many as four servers to maintain client access to applications and server resources during unplanned outages due to hardware failures, natural and man-made disasters, software failure, and so on. Unlike the behavior of a Network Load Balancing cluster, when a server, resource, or cluster-aware application within the cluster becomes unavailable, it will be transferred to another server that is available.

- Network Load Balancing cluster

  A Network Load Balancing cluster provides high availability and scalability for TCP/IP-based services, including Web servers, FTP servers, other mission-critical servers, and COM+ applications. In an Network Load Balancing scenario, multiple servers run independently, and do not share any resources. Client requests are distributed among the servers, and in the event of a server failure, a Network Load Balancing cluster detects the problem and the load is distributed to another server. SQL Server 2000 clustering does not fall into this category, but it can be part of an overall architecture where a Web farm using a Network Load Balancing cluster connects to a backend SQL Server that may be part of a server cluster. Because you employ a Network Load Balancing cluster due to an application requirement, you need to consider Network Load Balancing during the application planning and configuration stage.

For more information about the architecture, technology, and terminology of a Windows cluster, see "Windows Clustering Technologies: Cluster Service Architecture" at http://www.microsoft.com/windows2000/library/.

Microsoft Cluster Service Components

Windows Clustering is the collective name for the operating-system components that comprise Windows-level clustering. This section describes the various components involved.

Hardware

The following is a list of hardware components used with Windows Clustering, available with Windows 2000, and Microsoft Cluster Service (MSCS), available with Windows NT 4.0:

- Cluster Nodes

  A node is a server within the cluster. Windows NT Server 4.0, Enterprise Edition and Windows 2000 Advanced Server both support two-node clustering, and Windows 2000 Datacenter Server supports up to four-node clustering.

- Heartbeat

  The heartbeat is a private network set up between the nodes of the cluster that checks to see if a server is up and running. This occurs at regular intervals known as time slices. If the heartbeat is not functioning, a failover is initiated and another node in the cluster will take over the services.

- External Networking

  Besides the heartbeat private network, at least one public network needs to be enabled so that external connections can be made to the cluster.

- Shared Disk Array

  The shared disk array is a collection of physical disks (SCSI RAID or Fibre Channel) that will be accessed by the cluster. Windows Clustering supports shared nothing disk arrays. A shared nothing disk array is a setup in which only one node can own a given resource at any given moment. All other nodes are denied access until they own the resource. This protects the data from being overwritten data if two computers have access to the same drives concurrently.

- Quorum Drive

  The Quorum Drive is a logical drive designated on the shared disk array for Windows Clustering. This drive contains information about the state of the cluster. If this drive becomes corrupt or damaged, the cluster installation will also become corrupt or damaged.

Operating System

The following is a list of components that are exposed at the operating-system level:

- Cluster Name

  This is the name that all Windows NT or Windows 2000 external connections will use to refer to the cluster; the individual nodes will never be referenced.

- Cluster IP Address

  This is the IP address that all external connections will use to reach the failover cluster. SQL Server 2000 allows multiple IP addresses to be associated with a SQL Server virtual server.

- Cluster Administrator Account

  This account is used to administer and own the failover cluster. A Cluster Administrator account must be created at the domain level.

- Cluster Resource Types

  Cluster resources include any services, software or hardware that can be configured within a cluster. These include: DHCP, File Share, Generic Application, Generic Service, Internet Protocol, Network Name, Physical Disk, Print Spooler, and WINS.

- Cluster Group

  A Cluster Group is a collection of logically grouped cluster resources, and may also contain cluster-aware application services such as SQL Server 2000. Conceptually, think of a cluster group as a folder on your hard drive that contains related information.

For more information about Windows NT Server 4.0, Enterprise Edition, see http://www.microsoft.com/ntserver/, and for more information about Windows 2000 Advanced and Datacenter Servers, see http://www.microsoft.com/windows2000/.

Virtual Server

Understanding the concept of a virtual server is a key to understanding clustering. To a client or application, a virtual server is the server name or IP address(es) that is used for access. The connection from the client to the virtual server does not need to know which node within a cluster is currently hosting the virtual server. An instance of a clustered SQL Server is known as a SQL Server virtual server.

SQL Server 2000

SQL Server 2000 is built on top of the existing operating-system clustering, because it is a cluster-aware application. The SQL Server 2000 virtual server sits on top of the existing Windows Clustering installation, as shown in the following illustration.

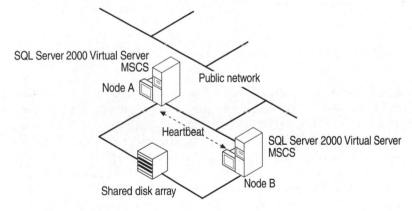

Components

- SQL Server Virtual Server Name

  This is the name that all applications and clients will use to refer to the SQL Server instance; the individual nodes will never be referenced.

- SQL Server Virtual Server IP Address(es)

  There are one or more IP addresses that all external connections will use to reach the SQL Server instance.

- SQL Server Virtual Server Administrator Account

  This is the SQL Server service account. This account must be a domain administrator. For more information about creating this account, see "Setting up Windows Services Accounts" in SQL Server Books Online.

Instances of SQL Server

An instance is an installation of SQL Server that is completely separate from any other, with a few underlying shared components that affect how SQL Server 2000 works in a clustered environment.

The following components are the underlying shared components:

- Full-text search

  Although each instance gets its own clustered full text search resource, which relies on the underlying Microsoft Search service that is shared by all instances and, potentially, by other applications.

- Microsoft Distributed Transaction Coordinator (MS DTC)

  There is only one MS DTC resource per cluster.

- Microsoft Message Queuing (MSMQ)

  Any application using MSMQ has the same limitation as with MS DTC; all instances share one resource.

SQL Server 2000 supports multiple instances per server—one default instance, and up to 15 named instances. SQL Server can either be installed as a default instance or a named instance. If a SQL Server 7.0 installation exists, and SQL Server 2000 is installed, the SQL Server 7.0 instance will become the default instance, or it can be upgraded to SQL Server 2000. Only one SQL Server 7.0 instance can be running, but multiple SQL Server 2000 named instances can be running in conjunction with the single SQL 7.0 instance. In a clustered environment, SQL Server 6.5 and SQL Server 7.0 clustering is not supported on the same computer on which an instance of SQL Server 2000 exists, whether it is clustered or not. A SQL Server 2000 virtual server can also have local named instances or a local SQL Server 7.0 default instance, but these will not appear visible to Windows Clustering. These are instances local to the particular server in which they are installed.

With instances, come two new concepts for failover clustering: single instance, which replaces an active/passive cluster, and multiple-instances, which replaces an active/active cluster.

Single-Instance Cluster

A single-instance cluster has only one active instance of SQL Server owned by a single node, and all other nodes of the cluster are in a wait state. Another node would be enabled in the event of a failure on the active node, or during a manual failover for maintenance. The following illustration shows a single-instance cluster.

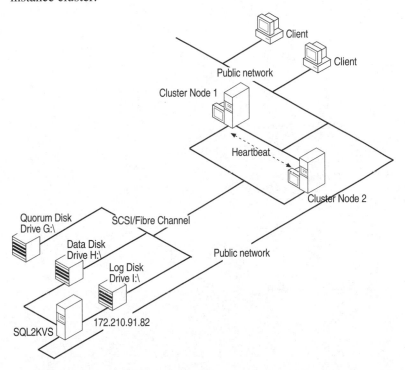

Multiple-Instance Cluster

A multiple-instance cluster has up to four nodes, and although SQL Server can support up to the 16-instance limit, having more than four (which is a 1:1 ratio for virtual servers to nodes) is not recommended. Each virtual server requires individual shared disk resources. The physical disks may be in the same, shared disk array, but the logical names must be unique to the instance. SQL Server in a clustered environment also behaves differently from a stand-alone named instance when it comes to IP ports. The default behavior for a stand-alone named instance is that it picks a dynamic port when it is first started, and then keeps that port number. In a cluster, multiple instances can share the same port because it listens only on the IP address assigned to the SQL Server virtual server, and is not limited to a 1:1 ratio as is the case on a single computer. It is recommended, however, that each SQL Server virtual server be assigned to its own unique port to ensure that no potential problems may occur during setup, when the SQL Server services are started and then clustered. It also ensures that each virtual server is completely unique. The following illustration shows a multiple-instance cluster.

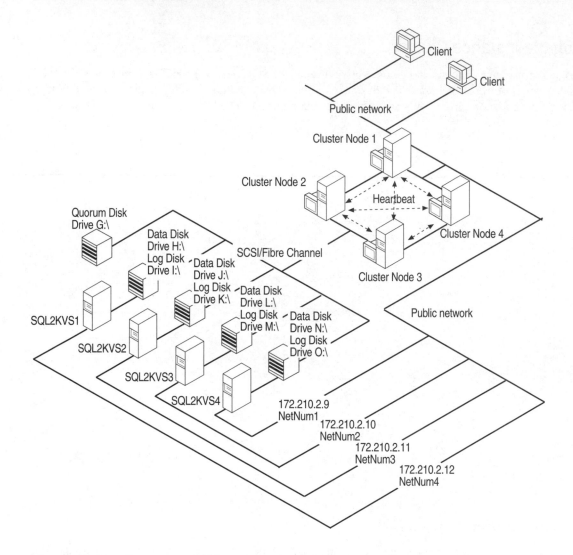

How SQL Server 2000 Failover Clustering Works

The clustered nodes check over the heartbeat to see whether each node is alive, both at an operating-system and SQL Server–level. The operating system issues a protocol whereby all nodes in the cluster compete for the resources of the cluster. The primary node reserves the resource every 3 seconds, and the challenger every 5. The process lasts for 25 seconds. If something happened, for example, at second 19, the challenger will detect it at the 20 second mark, and if it is determined that the primary node no longer has control, the challenger will take over the resource.

From a SQL Server perspective, the node hosting the SQL Server resource does a looks alive check every 5 seconds. This is a lightweight check to see whether the service is running and may succeed even if the SQL instance is not fully operational. The is-alive check is more thorough, and involves running a SELECT @@VERSIONSQL query against the server to determine whether it is operational. If this query fails, it will retry five times and then attempt to reconnect to the instance of SQL Server. Should all five retries fail, the SQL Server resource will fail. Depending on the failover threshold configuration of the SQL Server resource, it will either attempt to restart the resource on the same node or fail over to another available node. The execution of the query will tolerate a few errors, such as licensing issues or having a paused SQL Server, but will ultimately fail if its threshold is exceeded.

During the failover from one node to another, the SQL Server service on the other node will start, and go through the recovery process to start the databases. This means that any completed transactions in the transaction log will be rolled forward, and any incomplete transactions will be rolled back. In most cases, a failover will usually not take longer than 30 seconds to one minute

End users and applications access a SQL Server virtual server with its name or IP address. The user or application does not need to worry about which node owns the resources. During the failover process, any active connections are broken. For Web browser users, a simple refresh of the Web page should create a new database connection. In a more traditional client/server application, or one that relies heavily on a middle tier, application designers may want to consider checking to see if the connection exists, and if not, reconnect. Therefore, whatever the user was working on when the server went down may not be completed unless the transaction completes before the server goes down or the transaction is handled within the application.

For more information about failover clustering, see SQL Server Books Online.

Configuring SQL Server 2000 Failover Cluster Servers

Perhaps the most important aspect of a successful SQL Server 2000 failover cluster installation is ensuring that the right hardware and software are correctly deployed for the application designed to run on the failover cluster. The hardware should be highly performing, and scale along with the specific needs of the application(s) accessing SQL Server.

Software Requirements

SQL Server 2000 failover clustering requires SQL Server 2000 Enterprise Edition and one the following operating systems:

- Windows NT Server 4.0, Enterprise Edition (with a minimum of Service Pack 5)
- Windows 2000 Advanced Server

- Windows 2000 Datacenter Server

  Note Windows 2000 Datacenter Server is part of the Windows Datacenter Program (WDP). For more information, see http://www.microsoft.com/windows2000/.

Hardware Requirements

A SQL Server 2000 virtual server should be a highly performing server, and one that takes into account high availability. There are two main factors that go into determining what hardware is needed:

- What is the application or Web site's current workload, and what is the projected workload in six months, a year, or even two years from now?

  This is the information that most people do not have prior to implementing a solution. Having benchmarks on how an application or website performs is critical in determining which operating system and what hardware to buy. The best way to benchmark an application prior to production is in a lab environment. Using tools such as System Monitor (Performance Monitor in Windows NT 4.0) can also establish performance trends. Without a baseline, or some sort of performance documentation, it will be difficult to determine exactly what is needed. Also, any application issues affecting performance, either in current production versions or updates being planned, should be taken into account. SQL Server and its underlying hardware platform will only perform as well as the code that was written to access it.

- How much money is budgeted to the project?

  A good rule of thumb is to plan for at least six months worth of capacity, but also take into account some amount of time (whether it is a year, two years, or more) in which the server being configured will still be employed and expected to perform. Underestimating the power you will need in the future and incomplete planning will result in poor performance or system downtime, reducing how highly available the solution is.

  Important All nodes in a cluster should be configured the same or potentially greater (if the node will own more than one instance) in all aspects to ensure proper application performance in a failover.

For more information about creating a highly available server, see Chapter 16, "Five Nines: The Ultimate in High Availability."

Memory

Depending on which operating system is employed, SQL Server can take advantage of different amounts of maximum memory. An installation of SQL Server 2000 Enterprise Edition supports up to 32 gigabytes (GB) of memory on Windows 2000 Datacenter Server (without AWE enabled). The table shows the maximum amount of memory available to SQL Server per operating system.

Operating system	Maximum
Windows NT 4.0, Enterprise Edition	3 GB
Windows 2000 Advanced Server	8 GB (with AWE enabled)
Windows 2000 Datacenter Server	64 GB (with AWE enabled)

Address Windowing Extensions Memory

With Address Windowing Extensions (AWE), a memory-intensive application can now run much more efficiently under SQL Server 2000 to increase performance. Windows 2000 servers introduced the enhanced AWE API. AWE allows applications to access large amounts of physical memory. Due to limitations of 32-bit memory addressing, only up to 4 GB of physical memory can be used by Windows NT 4.0 and Windows 2000. By default, 2 GB of memory is dedicated to the operating system and 2 GB of memory to the application. With a /3GB switch in the BOOT.INI used by the operating system, the application can access up to 3 GB of memory, and the operating system is reduced to 1 GB of memory. As a result, even if a server were configured with 8 GB of memory, anything past 4 GB would have been virtually unusable. This problem limited the amount of scalability of an application. AWE is the support built into the operating system as a way of exposing extended memory to Win32-based applications.

AWE requires an application, like SQL Server 2000, to be coded specifically for AWE. AWE support within SQL Server 2000 must be configured using the **sp_configure** option **awe enabled**. This is set per instance. By default, **awe enabled** is set to 0, or off. Enabling AWE support in SQL Server 2000 also requires some additional operating-system configuration. For more information, see SQL Server Books Online.

Note If you are enabling AWE memory, it is highly recommended that the configuration be tested prior to bringing the server(s) online in a production capacity.

There are considerations to take into account when you implement AWE memory:

- The instance of SQL Server does not dynamically manage the size of the memory address space used.

    When AWE is enabled with SQL Server 2000, if the **max server memory** configuration parameter is not set, it will grab the total memory available (except 128 MB to allow the base operating system to function), potentially depriving the operating system and any other processes that would be running on the same server.

- Once initialized, AWE memory holds all the memory acquired at startup until it is shut down.

    If AWE is enabled and is taking too much memory, SQL Server would need to be shut down to reconfigure it, causing downtime (which makes a high availability option like failover clustering less available).

Because the memory pages used by the SQL Server instance are taken from the nonpageable pool of Windows memory, none of the memory can be exchanged. This means that if the physical memory is filled up, it cannot use the page file set up on a physical disk to account for the surplus in memory usage.

For more information about configuring AWE memory on your server, see "Using AWE Memory on Windows 2000" in SQL Server Books Online.

Disk Configuration and File Placement

The main component of any database system is its storage—it contains the valuable data used and inserted by an application. For high availability, disks should be part of an external array and should be fault tolerant. The disks should be high speed for performance and support a large capacity.

The disks can be configured either with a small computer system interface (SCSI) or Fibre Channel. Fibre Channel is the typical method of implementing. Fibre Channel was specifically designed for high bandwidth and capacity. Storage Area Networks (SANs) are disk arrays that use networking protocols over fibre to do all I/O. Use of SANs may be supported for use in conjunction with failover clustering as a Cluster/Multi-Cluster Device. SCSI is not supported for Windows 2000 Datacenter, so this consideration should be taken into account when deciding on hardware and the operating system.

Note SCSI is not supported in a Windows Datacenter Server cluster. Fibre Channel must be used.

Data and log devices, as well as **tempdb**, should be placed on separate disks. If possible, put them all on different channels. If your system is very large, or has hotspots, you may decide to use filegroups as a method of splitting up the disk I/O. Further segmenting this by putting filegroups on different disks, on different channels, can result in a performance boost. It is important to keep the file placement in mind when you are analyzing your high-availability design. Performance issues caused by bottlenecks can be incorrectly viewed as availability problems.

Data should be configured with RAID 0+1 for high availability and performance, but RAID 5 is also acceptable (however, RAID 5 may result in slower restore times). Logs should be placed on RAID 1.

For more information on RAID levels and high availability, see Chapter 16, "Five Nines: The Ultimate in High Availability," in this book.

Quorum Disk

It is recommended that you do not install SQL Server database files on the quorum disk, and that you do not put SQL Server or any other applications in the same group as the quorum disk. Furthermore, SQL Server 2000 Setup will never use the quorum disk by default unless there are no other disks available.

Controller Configuration

Choose a card with enough channels to split the logical grouping of disks (for example, data and logs) to reduce I/O contention. If the Fibre Channel/RAID controller is internal to the node, and not in the shared disk array, writeback caching should be disabled. The reason for this is that even with battery backup, once the resources fail over to another node, there could be items in the cache. If the services are failed back over to the node, corruption could occur because it will attempt to overwrite things on the disk. It would also cause data loss in a failover if transactions were in the cache but not yet processed.

Using more than one RAID controller will also increase performance and reduce I/O contention.

Making Sure Logical Disks are Seen by the Virtual Server

A common problem in failover clusters occurs when it is improperly configured to allow the virtual server to see the Physical Disk resource. This could be caused by one of two things:

- The proper disk drivers might not be installed.

  Make sure that they are installed. In some cases, for example, an operating-system upgrade from Windows NT 4.0, Enterprise Edition to Windows 2000 Advanced Server, there may be specific drivers for Windows 2000, but the old drivers may still be on the system.

- The drive might not be a dependency of the SQL Server 2000 virtual server.

To check whether the drive is a dependency of the virtual server

1. Start Cluster Administrator, right-click the SQL Server 2000 virtual server, and then click **Properties**.

2. On the **SQL Server (nodename) Properties** dialog box, click the **Dependencies** tab, and then click **Modify**.

3. On the **Modify Dependencies** dialog box, the available resources for the cluster appear in the **Available** resources list. Select the drive to add, click the arrow to move the resource to the **Dependencies** list, and then click **OK**.

4. To verify that the resource is now a dependency, on the **SQL Server (nodename) Properties** dialog box, click the **Dependencies** tab.

Networking

SQL Server 2000 supports multiple IP addresses and network cards. For configuration information, see "Best Practices" in this chapter. If larger bandwidth is required, SQL Server 2000 has support for higher bandwidth networking with Giganet or Compaq's Servernet II technology on Compaq hardware. If these technologies are used, they will create higher performance between multiple SQL Servers. Giganet support is built-in, and the update to enable Servernet II is located at http://www.microsoft.com/sql/.

Location

In Windows Clustering, server nodes must be physically located near each other. That means that, in a data center, when there is an event such as a power failure, no one will be able to connect to the cluster. There are two approaches to solving this issue:

- Configure log shipping to a server in a different location.

  A log-shipped server is one in which the transaction logs from the primary server are applied to a secondary server. This server may not be clustered, but it will at least allow SQL connectivity for users. A disaster recovery plan will need to be in place.

Hardware Compatibility List

Before deciding on all final hardware, consult the Microsoft Hardware Compatibility List. All hardware must appear on the HCL, or the cluster configuration will not be supported. There are specific cluster categories, including "Cluster," which contains complete server configurations. The HCL can be found at http://www.microsoft.com/hcl/.

Configuration Worksheets

A SQL Server 2000 failover cluster configuration requires certain resources. At a minimum, you need a domain-level administrator account for the cluster installation (this account may be an existing administrator in the domain and does not need to be a specific account). Some environments have a main cluster administrator account, and one for the SQL Server services; this is recommended to conceptually make the cluster's relationship with the domain easier to understand and troubleshoot. Some combine both. Also needed are specific static IP addresses for the following: MS DTC, any SQL Server virtual server, and the cluster itself.

Two worksheets are provided below that can be copied and placed in a Run Book (for more information about a Run Book, see Chapter 16, "Five Nines: The Ultimate in High Availability") or a configuration document. These worksheets are designed for you to enter the values used in your environment for the configuration of failover clustering. Using these worksheets will not only help you reconfigure your clustering solution if servers must be rebuilt, but can serve as an excellent resource for anyone who wants to know how your SQL Server environment is configured.

Cluster Configuration Worksheet

Parameter	Value
Cluster Domain Administration Account	
Cluster Domain Administration Password	
SQL Server Domain Administration Account	
SQL Server Domain Administration Password	
Cluster Name	
Cluster IP Address	
Number Of Nodes In Cluster	
Disk Array Configuration (RAID Level, size, logical disk names, number of disks per each drive, channels, cache setting, and so on)	

SQL Server Virtual Server Configuration Worksheet

There can be up to 16 instances of SQL Server per failover cluster. If more than 4 instances are used, copy the following chart with new virtual server numbers.

Parameter	SQL VS1	SQL VS2	SQL VS 3	SQL VS4
Instance Name				
IP Address(es)				
IP Port(s)				
Network Name(s)				
Allocated drives				

Implementing SQL Server 2000 Failover Clustering

This section describes the implementation considerations when configuring your failover cluster. For complete installation instructions, see "Installing Failover Clustering" in SQL Server Books Online. To ensure a successful installation, restarting the server is recommended to allow locked resources to be released and any pending file renames to be completed.

Prerequisites

Prior to installing SQL Server 2000, verify that only the services necessary for the operating system are running. Any other services should be stopped because they may interfere with the installation process. These services include SNMP, the World Wide Web Publishing service, and vendor specific programs. The easiest way to start and stop multiple services is to create two batch files, one that contains multiple **net stop** commands, and one that contains the corresponding **net start** commands.

Below is a list of services that should be left running:

Windows NT 4.0 Server, Enterprise Edition

- Alerter
- Cluster Service
- Computer Browser
- Event Log
- License Logging Service
- Messenger
- Net Logon
- Windows NT LM Security Support Provider
- Plug And Play
- Remote Procedure Call (RPC) Locator
- Remote Procedure Call (RPC) Service
- Server
- Spooler
- TCP/IP NetBIOS Helper
- Time Service
- Workstation

Windows 2000 Advanced Server and Windows 2000 Datacenter Server

- Alerter
- Cluster Service
- Computer Browser
- Distributed File System
- Distributed Link Tracking Client
- Distributed Link Tracking Server
- DNS Client
- Event Log
- IPSEC Policy Agent
- License Logging Service
- Logical Disk Manager
- Messenger
- Net Logon
- Windows NT LM Security Support Provider
- Plug and Play
- Process Control
- Remote Procedure Call (RPC) Locator
- Remote Procedure Call (RPC) Service
- Remote Registry Service
- Removable Storage
- Security Accounts Manager
- Server
- Spooler
- TCP/IP NetBIOS Helper
- Windows Management Instrumentation Driver Extensions
- Windows Time Service
- Workstation

Installation Order

This section provides the installation order for your specific operating system and SQL Server 2000.

Windows NT 4.0 Server, Enterprise Edition

- Install Windows NT 4.0 Server, Enterprise Edition (do not install Internet Information Service).
- Create domain users.
- Install Windows NT 4.0 Service Pack 3.
- Install Microsoft Internet Explorer 5.
- Disable NetBIOS on internal private networks.
- Install Microsoft Cluster Server (MSCS) on both nodes.
- Manually create MS DTC Cluster Resources, see "Creating the MS DTC Resources (Windows NT 4.0, Enterprise Edition Only)" in this chapter.
- Install Windows NT 4.0 Option Pack if you want, but do not install MSMQ.
- Install Windows NT Service Pack 5 or later.
- Stop unnecessary services.
- Install SQL Server 2000.

Windows 2000 Advanced/Datacenter Servers

- Install Windows 2000 Advanced/Datacenter Server.
- Install Microsoft Internet Explorer 5 Update (if necessary).
- Create domain users.
- Disable NetBIOS on internal private networks.
- Install MSCS on all nodes.
- Create MS DTC Cluster Resource (for installation instructions, see "Failover Clustering Dependencies" in SQL Server Books Online).
- Stop unnecessary services.
- Install SQL Server 2000.

Creating the MS DTC Resources (Windows NT 4.0, Enterprise Edition Only)

This section provides the instructions for configuring the MS DTC resources for servers running Windows NT 4.0, Enterprise Edition, which requires a more complex setup procedure than that for Windows 2000 servers.

IP Address

To configure the MS DTC IP address for the cluster

1. In Cluster Administrator, select the disk group that contains the Quorum disk resource. Right-click the disk group, and then rename it.

2. Select the disk group you want, and on the **File** menu, click **New**, and then click **Resource**. In the **New Resource** dialog box, in the **Name** box, enter **MSDTC IP Address**; in the **Resource Type** box, select **IP Address**; and in the **Group** box, select the group you want. Click **Next** to continue.

3. Both nodes of the cluster should appear as possible owners. If not, add the node(s), and select **Next**.

4. In the **Dependencies** dialog box, select the disk resource in the group you selected from the **Available Resources** box, and then click **Add**. The disk resource appears in the **Resource Dependencies** box. Click **Next** to continue.

5. In the **TCP/IP Address Parameters** dialog box enter the TCP/IP information. In the **Address** box, enter the static IP address (for example, 10.1.14.131); in the **Subnet mask** box, enter the IP subnet (for example, 255.255.255.0); and in the **Network to use** box, select the cluster network you want. Click **Finish** to continue.

6. A message appears confirming that the IP address is successfully configured.

7. In the Cluster Administrator window, the newly created resource appears in the right pane. To start the resource (which is currently offline), right-click the resource, and click **Bring Online**.

Network Name

To configure the MS DTC network name for the cluster running on Windows NT 4.0, Enterprise Edition

1. In Cluster Administrator, on the **File** menu, point to **New**, and then click **Resource**.

2. In the **New Resource** dialog box, in the **Name** box, enter **MSDTC Network Name**; in the **Resource type** box, select **Network Name**; and in the **Group** box, select the group you want. Click **Next** to continue.

3. In the **Possible Owner** dialog box, both nodes of the cluster should appear as possible owners. If not, add the node(s), and click **Next**.

4. In the **Dependencies** dialog box, the MSDTC IP address resource you configured previously appears in the **Available resources** box. Select the resource, and then click **Add**. The resource appears in the **Resource dependencies** box. Click **Next** to continue.

5. In the **Network Name Parameters** dialog box, enter **MSDTC**, and then click **Finish**.

6. A message appears confirming that the IP address is successfully configured.

7. In the Cluster Administrator window, the newly created resource appears in the right pane. To start the resource (which is currently offline), right-click the resource, and then click **Bring Online**.

Best Practices

In addition to understanding the fundamentals of failover clustering, you may find it useful to keep the following tips and best practices in mind.

Using More IP Addresses

When configuring a network card for use within a cluster, you should consider the options available based on how many types you must support, given the number of network cards available. For example, you could maximize the use of your network cards by configuring one card for all communications including:

- All external client connections and inter-node traffic.

- Internal cluster (private network between the cluster nodes only).

- Client access only (public network to allow client connectivity).

Even though only one network card in a cluster can handle all cluster network communications, this creates a single point of failure. The optimum configuration is to have a separate network card to handle each type of connectivity.

Ideally, three IP addresses and three network cards should be associated with any instance of SQL Server:

- Heartbeat

  This could be configured as "internal cluster communications only" or "all communications". If configured as "all communications", although it serves a dual purpose, it will only decrease potential bandwidth on the internal side. Choose "internal cluster communications only" for higher availability.

- Client Connectivity

  This should be configured to "client access only". This, too, could also be configured as "all communications", but the intra-cluster communications will affect the client connectivity pipe.

- Separate Private Network

  This is different than the Heartbeat, and should be configured as "client access only". It should be configured so that only the servers in the cluster will be able to access this particular IP address. It will enable files to be transferred, or optimally, allow log shipping to be configured in a way that it will not affect the Heartbeat or Client network traffic.

All three IP addresses cannot be on the same subnet. Connectivity problems may be encountered if the same subnet is used for more than one IP address, even if it is not currently being used in the cluster. For example, the following server configuration will not work:

Network Card 1: 172.22.10.1

Network Card 2 (configured as Public Network): 172.22.10.2

Network Card 3 (configured as Private Network): 172.23.7.3

Network Card 4 (configured as Heartbeat): 172.24.2.5

Also, there are network cards that support multiple IP addresses being bound to them. Although this would allow a failover cluster to talk over more than one network, it still creates a single point of failure, which is something that must be avoided in a high availability solution.

Configuring Node Failover Preferences

When you use more than two nodes in a cluster, it is important to consider in the event of a failover, which node should own the SQL Server processes? With up to four nodes available, there should be an order that makes logical sense for the production environment. The failover preferences should be set for the group containing all the resources for the instance of SQL Server (not only on the virtual server) to ensure that all resources properly fail over to the same node.

To configure the nodes available for failover and the preferred order

1. Start Cluster Administrator. Right-click the group containing the SQL Server 2000 virtual server, and then click **Properties**.

2. On the **General** tab, the **Preferred** owners list box displays all cluster nodes that can potentially own the processes in that group, and the current order in which they would fail over. To change these, click **Modify**.

3. In the **Modify Preferred Owners** dialog box, make any changes to which nodes can own the processes. All available nodes (if not already selected) will appear in the left pane, and all nodes currently configured as potential owners will appear in the right pane in the order of failover preference. For example, there are four nodes in a cluster: **DENNIS**, **TOMMY**, **ANN**, and **CHUCK**. All four nodes of the cluster can be potential owners, and the order of failover if **DENNIS** goes down is set to be **ANN** then **TOMMY**, and finally **CHUCK** if both **ANN** or **TOMMY** are unavailable.

Memory Configuration

This section presents the considerations for memory usage in a failover cluster.

Single Instance Failover Cluster

In a single-instance SQL Server 2000 failover cluster, the failover scenario is simple: If the primary node fails, all processes go to the designated secondary node configured (see "Configuring Node Failover Preferences" in this chapter). The secondary node should always be configured exactly the same as Node A in terms of hardware. If not, problems may occur if the failover node does not have the same capacity as the primary node, especially in terms of memory, as evidenced in Example Two. Keep in mind any other processes that may be running on the server node, as well as overhead for the operating system.

Example One: Two Nodes, Exact Configuration

There are two nodes in the cluster, A and B. Both are configured exactly the same with 4 GB of memory, and SQL Server is configured to use 3 GB. Because it is a single-instance failover cluster, at least one node is waiting to have services failed over to it.

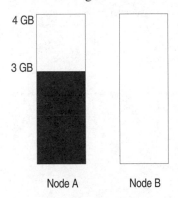

MSCS detects failure on Node A, and fails over to Node B.

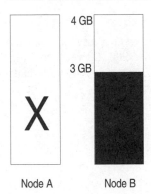

All services fail over successfully, and there is no memory contention on Node B.

Example Two: Nonexact Configuration

There are two nodes in the failover cluster, A and B. Node A is configured with 4 GB of memory, of which SQL Server uses 3 GB. Node B is configured with 2 GB of memory.

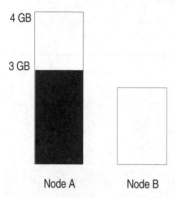

Node A has some sort of failure detected by Windows Clustering, and fails over to Node B.

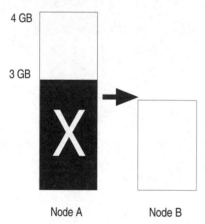

Node B does not have the physical memory to support the instance of SQL Server from Node A. In the failover process, the server node will immediately start paging to disk because SQL Server is looking for more memory than is physically available. The server will now be short of resources, potentially causing the node to become unresponsive and stop responding.

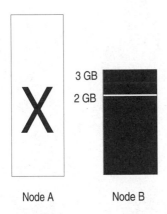

Node A   Node B

Multiple-Instance Failover Cluster

In a multiple-instance SQL Server 2000 failover cluster, the scenario becomes more complex. With up to 16 instances that could be active at a time on one node, how does one effectively manage memory? First and foremost, ensure that all servers have the same amount of memory, and that it is enough to handle the instances that could potentially fail to that node. Another important thing is to cap memory usage of the instance of SQL Server with **max server memory**, as with the previously described AWE. Especially if AWE memory is enabled, **max server memory** must be set in a multiple-instance cluster to prevent starving the server node, as shown in Example Two that follows. Consider any other processes that may be running on the server, as well as overhead for the operating system.

Example One: Two Instances of SQL Server, Noncapped Memory

Nodes A and Node B both have the same configuration, with 4 GB of physical memory, and each has a SQL Server virtual server using 3 GB of memory.

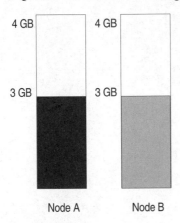

Node A   Node B

There is a failure on Node B, requiring the failover process to change the SQL Server resources to Node A.

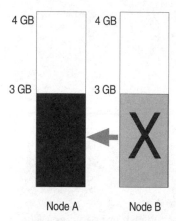

Because there is not enough memory on Node A, Node A cannot properly handle both instances of SQL Server.

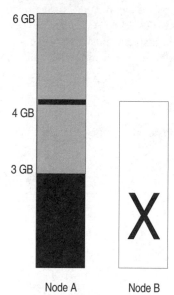

Example Two: Two Instances of SQL Server, Capped Memory

In this example, there are two Nodes, A and B. Both are configured with 8 GB of AWE memory and are each running an instance of SQL Server with **max server memory** capped to 3 GB.

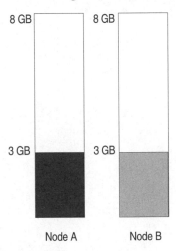

There is a failure on Node B, requiring the failover process to change the SQL Server resources to Node A.

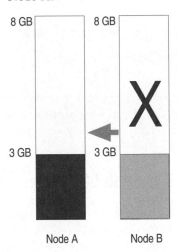

Because the system is configured properly, both instances of 3 GB fit comfortably under the 8 GB of physical memory on the server, and there is still 2 GB of memory left for the operating system and any other processes running.

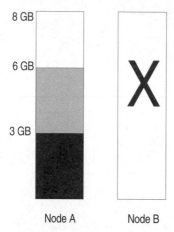

Using More Than Two Nodes

When using more than two nodes on a SQL Server 2000 failover cluster, consider the following:

- How much memory should be configured for each instance?

- What nodes are the failover cluster nodes for the particular instance? What is the preferred order?

- Is there enough disk space and memory to support every instance configured to fail over to a particular node?

Because SQL Server 2000 can use four nodes when supported by the operating system (the number of virtual servers is only limited by the choice of operating system and the capacity of your hardware), and have up to 16 instances, these considerations become more important as mission-critical systems become larger.

Scenario One: Four-Node Multiple-Instance SQL Server 2000 Failover Cluster, Three Active Nodes, One Standby (N+1)

With four-node support, Windows 2000 Datacenter Server provides more flexibility in terms of a cluster configuration. The recommended way of using a four-node Windows 2000 Datacenter Server cluster in a SQL Server environment is to have three of the nodes each owning an instance SQL Server, and have the fourth be the warm standby, not unlike a log shipping scenario, or a single-instance failover cluster where at least one node is waiting for work. This scenario is known as N+1. Because a failure should be considered unlikely to happen, the fourth node should be configured as the primary failover. This would reduce the issue of having too many instances starving the resources of one node. AWE memory should be enabled in this scenario to allow each instance of SQL Server to not have to be capped at or under 1 GB of memory. This would also enable a highly scalable solution as well. The following illustration shows an example of an N+1 cluster.

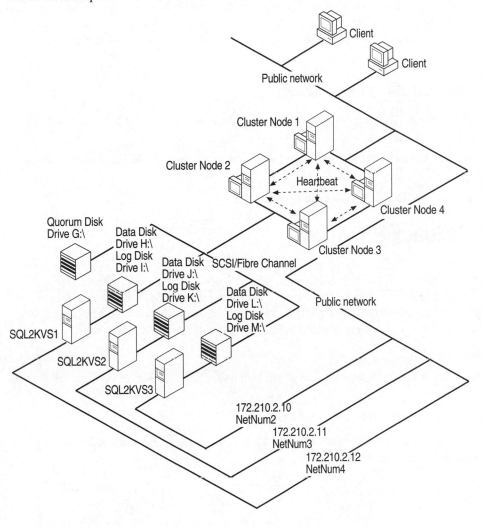

Scenario Two: Four Node Multi-Instance SQL Server 2000 Failover Cluster, All Four Nodes Active

Running four instances of SQL Server on four nodes requires planning, so that another instance will not starve resources due to memory and processor consumption in the event of a failover. Memory is not as much of a problem as processor resources. For example, if the workload on the production OLTP system regularly pegs 8 processors at 50-percent utilization and all four active SQL Servers demonstrate similar behavior, memory can only compensate for processor so much. More processors would have to be added (if possible).

Miscellaneous Configuration Issues

- If encryption is used in a clustered SQL Server environment, all nodes must have the certificate applied.

- It is not recommended to have both Microsoft Exchange 2000 and SQL Server 2000 on the same cluster.

For additional considerations, see SQL Server Books Online.

Failover/Failback Strategies

An overall cluster failback/failover policy should be implemented. Failovers can be controlled in terms of a threshold, meaning that after a certain point, a resource will not be failed over. In the event of a failover, the cluster can be configured to failback to the primary node when and if it becomes available again. By default, this option is turned off because usually there is no problem with continuing on the secondary node, and it will allow you a chance to analyze and repair the problem on the failed node.

To configure automatic failback

1. Start Cluster Administrator. Right-click the group containing the SQL Server 2000 virtual server, and click **Properties**.

2. In the **Properties** dialog box, click the **Failback** tab.

3. To prevent an automatic failback, select **Prevent Failback**. To allow automatic failback, select **Allow Failback**, and then one of these options:

- **Immediately**

  This means that the second MSCS detects that the preferred cluster node is online, and it will fail back any resources. This is not advisable because it could disrupt clients and applications, especially at peak times in a business day.

- **Failback between *n* and *n1* hours**

  This option allows a controlled failback to a preferred node (if it is online) during a certain time period. The hours are set using numbers from 0 through 23.

To configure failover thresholds

1. Start Cluster Administrator. Right-click the group containing the SQL Server 2000 virtual server, and click **Properties**.

2. In the **Properties** dialog box, click the **Failover** tab.

3. To configure the failover policy, in the **Threshold** box, enter the number of times the group is allowed to failover within a set span of hours. In the **Period** box, enter the set span of hours.

   For example, if **Threshold** is set to 10 and **Period** is set to 6, the Cluster service will fail the group over at most 10 times in a six-hour period. At the eleventh failover in that six-hour period, MSCS will leave the group offline. This affects only resources that were failed over; therefore, if the SQL Server resource failed 11 times, it would be left offline, but the IP could be left online.

Maintaining a SQL Server 2000 Failover Cluster

Maintaining a failover cluster can be challenging. For example, how do you create an environment that is seamless, and works no matter what node owns the SQL Server processes? There are some unique considerations to take into account in a clustered environment.

Backing Up and Restoring

Because a SQL Server 2000 failover cluster is a single-server instance, normal best practices around backing up and restoring the databases on that server will apply, including:

- Frequent backups.

- Offline and tape (or other media) rotation to offsite storage of backups.

- Testing restore of backups on another server to ensure that data can successfully and reliably be recovered in the event of an emergency.

Backing Up to Disk

If a network drive other than part of the cluster were selected, all nodes would need to have this drive mapped. Or, if the node were defined with a *\\servername\sharename* convention, it would have access to the drive. Another consideration is that if the shared disk array is going to be used as a backup medium, it could be considered a single point of failure in the event of a drive failure or disk corruption unless allowances are made for another backup medium. Besides mirroring the disks with RAID, a third-party disk mirroring solution (possibly even a distance cluster) would solve the single point of failure problem.

Another way would be to provide two steps in the backup task. Set up two backup drives: (either two network or one local and one network). Set up your maintenance plan, and then alter the backup task. If the first backup succeeds, exit with success code, and if it fails (for any reason), the second step is invoked. The second step would be the backup to the alternate target. The second task should send an e-mail notification that there was a failure of the primary backup area.

To make this even more secure, part of the backup task should include making a copy of the new backup file to a secondary storage area. Ideally, you want a local backup to restore from, a secondary backup on another server, and a tertiary backup on a tape. This would be in addition to any standby or clustering solution. Because clustering is a high availability solution that focuses on the hardware portion of the design, you should call a lot of attention to your disaster recovery plan. There is little point in spending the money on the cluster if you do not adequately backup your data and provide the fastest and most secure methods allowable.

Backing Up to Tape

Using tape as a backup solution presents a larger challenge. The device would need to be shared between all nodes of the cluster, or an identical device configured in exactly the same way would need to exist on each node of the cluster. A better solution is backing up the databases to either a share or a remote mirror, and then back up the files to tape from that location, simplifying the process.

Snapshot Backups

One way to backup and restore a clustered SQL Server is to use a snapshot backup. SQL Server 2000 supports snapshot backups, which involves the mirroring of your disks, and then breaking a complete set of disks off the mirror and using them as a backup. This requires specialized hardware, but is fully supported within SQL Server. Snapshot backups may create higher availability.

Backing Up an Entire Clustered System

One challenge to any environment is backing up the entire system (all files, operating system, databases, and so on). The biggest obstacle is that Windows locks files when they are in use. Third-party backup solutions exist that allow hot backups. In a clustered configuration, the problem is compounded because the backup solution must be cluster aware and work on each node. The previous considerations for backing up to disk and tape still apply: Ensure that there are no single points of failure and all nodes have access to the same devices in the same way.

Ensuring a Virtual Server Will Not Fail Due to Other Service Failures

To prevent the failure of specific services from causing the SQL Server group to fail over, configure those services using Cluster Administrator in Windows NT 4.0 or Windows 2000. For example, to prevent the failure of the Full-Text Search service from causing a failover of SQL Server, clear the **Affect the Group** check box on the **Advanced** tab of the Full Text **Properties** dialog box. If SQL Server causes a failover, however, the full-text search service will restart.

Adding, Changing, or Updating a TCP/IP Address

In earlier versions of SQL Server 2000 failover clustering, changing the TCP/IP address required SQL Server to be unclustered. Now, you can change the TCP/IP address by running the setup program again. Also, due to the new multiple network card/IP address support built into SQL Server 2000, additional TCP/IP addresses can be configured for the instance. For example, if you have internal and external customers accessing the instance, you can assign SQL Server two separate IP addresses to maximize network utilization and to more easily track the use of your instance of SQL Server.

To add, change, or update a TCP/IP address

1. Insert the SQL Server 2000 Enterprise Edition compact disc in your CD-ROM drive. Select **Install SQL Server 2000 Components**.

2. Click Install SQL Server 2000 Components, click Install Database Server, and then click Next.

3. On the **Computer Name** dialog box, select **Virtual Server**, and enter the name of an existing clustered instance of SQL Server 2000.

4. On the **Installation Selection** dialog box, select **Advanced options**, and then click **Next**.

5. On the Advanced Options dialog box, select the Maintain a Virtual Server for Failover Clustering, and then click Next.

6. On the **Failover Clustering** dialog box, a TCP/IP address can be added to or removed from the selected instance of SQL Server 2000.

   To remove a TCP/IP address, select the address, and click **Remove**.

   Note An instance of SQL Server 2000 in a failover cluster requires a TCP/IP address to function. Only remove a TCP/IP address if more than one exists and if this will not affect users or applications accessing SQL Server.

To add a TCP/IP address, enter the new TCP/IP address in the **IP Address** box, select the network to use, and then click **Add**. The new IP address appears after the existing IP address.

7. Click **Next**.

8. On the **Remote Information** dialog box, enter the user name and password for the domain administrator account used for the clustered instance of SQL Server 2000, and then click **Next**.

9. When the process is complete, click **Finish**.

Adding or Removing a Cluster Node from the Virtual Server Definition

Another new feature of SQL Server 2000 failover clustering is the ability to add or remove a cluster node from a SQL Server virtual server definition. Adding nodes to the existing SQL Server virtual server definition performs all the necessary operations on the new nodes (including installing binaries, system components, and creating services) and performs the necessary modifications to the cluster configuration.

To add or remove a node

1. Insert the SQL Server 2000 Enterprise Edition compact disc in your CD-ROM drive. Select **Install SQL Server 2000 Components**.

2. Click Install SQL Server 2000 Components, click Install Database Server, and then click **Next**.

3. On the **Computer Name** dialog box, select **Virtual Server**, and enter the name of an existing clustered instance of SQL Server 2000.

4. On the **Installation Selection** dialog box, select **Advanced options**, and then click **Next**.

5. On the Advanced Options dialog box, select the **Maintain a Virtual Server for Failover Clustering**, and then click **Next**.

6. On the **Failover Clustering** dialog box, a TCP/IP address can be added to or removed from the selected instance of SQL Server 2000.

   To remove a TCP/IP address, select the address, and click **Remove**.

   Note An instance of SQL Server 2000 in a failover cluster requires a TCP/IP address to function. Only remove a TCP/IP address if more than one exists and if this will not affect users or applications accessing SQL Server.

   To add a TCP/IP address, enter the new TCP/IP address in the **IP Address** box, select the network to use, and then click **Add**. The new IP address appears after the existing IP address.

7. Click **Next**.

8. Select the appropriate nodes to add or remove from the cluster, and then click **Next** when you are finished.

Troubleshooting SQL Server 2000 Failover Clusters

This section presents some of the common issues encountered when implementing failover clustering, and how to solve them. For more tips and tricks, see "Failover Cluster Troubleshooting" in SQL Server Books Online.

Q *When the installation process attempts to install the SQL Server binaries on the other node(s), it fails (possibly with a failed logon request error). Why?*

A If you are installing from a network share, make sure that both nodes have connectivity to the share without specifying a network password to connect (for example, you should be able to view *\\sharecomputer\sharepath* without specifying credentials). If installing from CD-ROM drive on Node A, make sure the cluster nodes are configured to communicate properly, including making sure the proper accounts exist on each node, and that the other nodes are set up for Windows authentication. Mapping a drive letter, even if it is the same on all nodes, will not work because the installation process accesses the UNC path of the share.

Q *After installing and rebooting the server, the SQL Server install doesn't seem to complete. Why?*

A Sometimes file renames are blocked due to locks on startup (for example, MDAC); therefore, if the file remains read only, it never completes.

Q *How do I troubleshoot my cluster in the event of a failure?*

A The best place to look from a SQL Server perspective is in the directory that is set for the variable *%clusterlog%* (generally \\winnt\cluster). These are the files:

- Sqlstp*n*.log – log for the SQL Server setup, where *n* is the number of the setup attempts

- Sqlclstr.log – log for the clustered SQL Server(s)

- Cluster.log – the main cluster log file

- Sqlstp.log – the log from the user interface part of Setup

Follow clustering guidelines for enabling cluster logging. Here are some sample settings:

```
set ClusterLog=D:\WINNT\cluster\cluster.log
set ClusterLogLevel-3
set ClusterLogSize=10 (this number is in MB)
```

Q *MSCS lost connectivity to my SQL Server virtual server. Why?*

A This may be because the **BUILTIN\Administrators** user was removed. This user is used to run the IsAlive process.

Q *Problems ensue when changing the network name of SQL Server after the install. How can this be fixed?*

A SQL Server binds itself to the network name used at install time, and if, for some reason, it is changed, in certain occurrences, it may require a complete reinstall.

Q *After an installation of a new SQL Server virtual server, clients cannot connect to the server, especially using graphical user interface (GUI) tools. Why?*

A Sometimes a successful manual connection using a command line tool (for example, the **bcp** or **osql** utilities) must be initiated first.

Q *Microsoft Exchange 2000 and SQL Server 2000 are both installed on my cluster; however, the full-text service in SQL Server seems to be failing. Why?*

A If both must exist on the same cluster, install Exchange 2000 first, and then install SQL Server 2000.

Q *I am encountering problems with full-text setup in my failover clustering. What might be wrong?*

A In some cases, Setup may fail because the full-text resource type does not exist. The resource is called Microsoft Search Service. If this is the case, you may have to manually create the type to get the installation to complete next time. To create the resource, execute the following from a command prompt:

```
cd %windir%\cluster
regsvr32 gathercl.dll
```

It would be a good idea to register this file on all nodes. You can then re-run Setup and everything should work fine.

Finding More Information

For more information about SQL Server 2000 failover clustering, see the following resources:

- Microsoft SQL Server home page at http://www.microsoft.com/sql/.

- MSDN® developer program at http://msdn.microsoft.com/.

- Microsoft Support Services Web site (contains technical articles and downloadable updates) at http://support.microsoft.com/.

- High Availability Operations Guide for Windows NT Server 4.0 at http://www.microsoft.com/NTServer/nts/.

Log Shipping

It is 2 PM on a record business day. The Microsoft® SQL Server™ 2000 server housing your mission-critical customer database experiences a disk failure. What do you do? When was the last known good backup? Is there another server available to restore the backup onto? Is SQL Server even on that server? One way to protect your database from a potentially prolonged outage is to utilize a feature new to SQL Server 2000 Enterprise Edition: log shipping.

Log shipping is a process that takes transaction logs from a primary SQL Server and applies them sequentially on a scheduled basis to another SQL Server. In the event of a failure, an application could be redirected to this other server, which would be only slightly out of sync with the primary server or potentially up to date with it, depending on when the last transactions were applied. Log shipping is a means of protecting organizations in the event of a logical or physical system failure.

For the first time with SQL Server 2000, log shipping is built into the product, and is no longer a custom implementation. The feature is robust, and it is easy to configure flexible deployments and monitor them in SQL Server Enterprise Manager. Log shipping complements other technologies in SQL Server, such as replication and SQL Server 2000 failover clustering. Its foundation is built on the standard SQL Server backup and restore commands, and is augmented by additional tables and stored procedures.

How Log Shipping Works

To understand how to use the log shipping feature in SQL Server, you must first become familiar with the components involved in the process.

Components

The SQL Server 2000 implementation of log shipping is comprised of the following elements:

- Primary server

  This is the production box that contains the source database to be log shipped.

- One or more secondary servers

  This server will receive the transaction logs and apply them to the proper database. This server is also known as a "warm standby."

- Monitor Server

  This server will display the status of the log shipping processes configured. This is known as the Log Shipping Monitor, and can be found under the Management folder in SQL Server Enterprise Manager.

The combination of a primary server, with the database to log ship, and a secondary server, with the database to which to apply the transaction logs, is known as a log shipping pair.

Note You cannot implement log shipping between two instances of SQL Server 2000 if one part of the log shipping pair is not an Enterprise Edition installation. Log shipping can be set up between SQL Server version 7.0 with Service Pack 2 installed and SQL Server 2000 (see "Log Shipping Interoperability Between SQL Server 7.0 and SQL Server 2000" later in this chapter).

Database Tables

In addition to the basic components involved in log shipping, a number of tables designed to support log shipping are included in SQL Server 2000. They are:

- **log_shipping_database**

  This table contains a list of all databases configured to be log shipped, as well as the maintenance plan ID associated with it. Only the primary server uses this table.

- **log_shipping_monitor**

  This table stores the name of the monitor server, and how to connect to it. All primary and secondary log shipping servers use this table.

- **log_shipping_plan_databases**

  This table stores the relevant parameters involved in the log shipping process: the maintenance plan, the source and destination databases, the last file copied and loaded, and other configuration parameters. This is populated only on the warm standby server.

- **log_shipping_plan_history**

  This table stores the history information for the log shipping plans: the maintenance plan name, the file name to be shipped, the source and destination databases, whether or not the process was a success, how long it took, and what error occurred if it was unsuccessful. This is populated only on the warm standby server.

- **log_shipping_plans**

  This table stores the information associated with each log shipping maintenance plan, namely the server and path names involved, and any jobs associated with the log shipping maintenance plan. This is populated only on the warm standby server.

- **log_shipping_primaries**

  This table stores the information associated with each log shipping maintenance plan on the primary server only, including the server name, plan name, database name, thresholds, and the name of the last transaction log backup file.

- **log_shipping_secondaries**

  This table stores the information associated with each log shipping maintenance plan on the secondary server, including the server name, plan name, database name, thresholds, and the name of the last transaction log backup file copied and loaded. This is populated only on the primary server.

- **sysdbmaintplans**

  This is a system table that stores the complete information about the maintenance plans associated with log shipping.

- **sysjobs**

  This is a system table that stores the complete information about the jobs associated with log shipping.

- **syslogins**

  This is a system table that stores the logins for each SQL Server database.

Stored Procedures

Listed below are all of the stored procedures used in log shipping:

- **sp_add_log_shipping_database**
- **sp_add_log_shipping_plan**
- **sp_add_log_shipping_plan_database**
- **sp_add_log_shipping_primary**
- **sp_add_log_shipping_secondary**
- **sp_change_monitor_role**
- **sp_change_primary_role**

- **sp_change_secondary_role**
- **sp_create_log_shipping_monitor_account**
- **sp_define_log_shipping_monitor**
- **sp_delete_log_shipping_database**
- **sp_delete_log_shipping_monitor_info**
- **sp_delete_log_shipping_plan**
- **sp_delete_log_shipping_plan_database**
- **sp_delete_log_shipping_primary**
- **sp_delete_log_shipping_secondary**
- **sp_get_log_shipping_monitor_info**
- **sp_remove_log_shipping_monitor**
- **sp_resolve_logins**
- **sp_update_log_shipping_monitor_info**
- **sp_update_log_shipping_plan**
- **sp_update_log_shipping_plan_database**

For complete details on the stored procedures, including the specific parameters associated with each one, see SQL Server Books Online.

log_shipping_monitor_probe User

It is recommended that you use integrated security with your SQL Server installation. However, if integrated security is not used, and mixed mode is, the installation of log shipping creates the user **log_shipping_monitor_probe**. This account is used by the primary and secondary servers to update the **log_shipping_primaries** and **log_shipping_secondaries** tables when a transaction log backup, copy, or restore operation occurs.

Log Shipping Process

First, make a full backup of the database to be log shipped. This backup is then applied to any secondary server that will receive the transaction logs. When you want to restore the database, choose among the following restore options: WITH STANDBY (making it read-only, but able to restore transaction logs), WITH NORECOVERY (making it available to restore transaction logs only), and, depending on the configuration, KEEP_REPLICATION (preserving replication settings on a particular database when log shipping is employed).

Once the backup is applied, the transaction log shipping may commence. Transaction logs are backed up on the primary server at a specified interval, generally 1 to 15 minutes apart. That file is then copied across the network to the secondary server and applied. This process would continue indefinitely unless manually shut down, or there is a primary server failure. The transaction log filename is **databasename_tlog_YYYYMODDHHMI.TRN**, where YYYY is the four-digit year, MO is the month, DD is the day, HH is the hour, and MI is the minute. When the transaction log is applied, SQL Server needs exclusive access to the database on the secondary server. No users can be in the database, active or inactive, and a process to terminate the users automatically can be configured. Otherwise, it will need to be done manually.

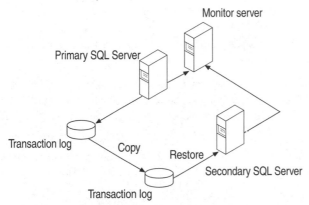

After configuration, the log shipping process is implemented by using a database maintenance plan (for each database log shipped). Use this plan with corresponding SQL Server Agent jobs that all invoke the command line utility **sqlmaint** through the extended stored procedure xp_sqlmaint:

1. Back up the transaction log. The job is located on the primary server; if the secondary server is configured as a potential primary server, the job also exists on the secondary server as well. It is named "Transaction Log Backup Job for DB Maintenance Plan '*Configured Plan Name*' ".

2. Copy the transaction log file. This job is located on the secondary server, and is named "Log Shipping Copy for PRIMARYSERVER.*databasename*_logshipping". Currently, the transaction log is copied to the secondary server using a standard filesystem copy, and no compression is used.

3. Restore the transaction log file. This job is located on the secondary server, and is named "Log Shipping Restore for PRIMARYSERVER.*databasename*_logshipping".

Two additional SQL Server Agent jobs are configured on the primary server: an alert job for the backup process reported in the log shipping monitor, and an alert job for the restore process as well.

Bringing a Secondary Server Online as a Primary

The need to create a redundant copy of your data exists for one main purpose: In the event that the primary server goes down, either planned or unplanned, you want to have access to the data and continue to be up and running. This is why it is vital to understand how to bring the designated secondary database online.

A major part of the switch process is to ensure that all logins from the primary exist on the secondary. A Data Transformation Services (DTS) package needs to be created on the primary server to copy the logins from the primary to the secondary. A SQL Server Agent job should back up the **syslogins** table, and copy this backup file to a location accessible by the secondary. Once this is done, the DTS package should be executed. If the primary server is completely unavailable, and the logins were never transferred, the warm standby cannot be brought online.

It is now time to initiate the role change to make the secondary server the new primary server. This is achieved by executing four stored procedures that should be configured as individual steps in a SQL Server Agent job, ensuring that there will be no human error when entering syntax and if the need arises to bring the secondary online.

For complete details on creating the DTS package to copy logins and on how to change server roles, see "How to set up and perform a log shipping role change (Transact-SQL)" in SQL Server Books Online.

The final step is to repoint any applications, direct end users, and other things, such as middle-tier servers like Component Services, available in Microsoft Windows® 2000, and ODBC Datasource Names (DSNs), to the "new" primary server. This is potentially the most time consuming part of the process. Utilizing a Network Load Balanced may help; consider evaluating this for your production environment.

Configuring Log Shipping

Now that you have an understanding of how log shipping works, it is time to implement it. This section will list some of the important considerations to take into account when configuring your solution. For complete installation instructions, see "How to configure log shipping (Enterprise Manager)" in SQL Server Books Online.

Keeping the Data in Sync

This is the most important aspect of configuring log shipping. How close should the secondary server be behind the primary? Or, from a business standpoint, how many transactions can we afford to lose? A few factors go into making this decision:

- How many transactions are generated per hour? This number should be measured in some way before implementing log shipping. One possible way is to load test the application in a lab situation.

- How big is the transaction log file generated, and how long does it take to copy and apply to the secondary server?

By default, transaction logs are backed up every 15 minutes. You can set this interval to be as frequent as every 1 minute, or as infrequent as, say, every 30 or 60 minutes. Each environment and use will be different. On a highly utilized OLTP database, such as one that would power an e-commerce site, transactions are more important, so the backup frequency may drop to every 5 minutes to ensure a smaller file size.

In conjunction with determining the frequency of transaction log file backups, devise a plan as to how often the files will be copied to the secondary server(s), and if there will be any delay in applying them. If the load delay is set to 0, which is the default, the transaction log file will be applied as soon as it is copied. For more information, see the "Best Practices" section later in this chapter.

Servers

This section will detail where to place your servers for log shipping, and some tips on connectivity.

Location

The location of the log shipped servers is crucial to a successful implementation. If the primary and secondary are located next to each other in the same data center, and a failure occurs, you may have lost both your main and backup servers. So the point of having redundancy is negated.

Log shipping allows you to place servers in any geographic location. This is the recommended practice. For example, a company has data centers in Boston, New York, Tokyo, London, and Sydney. The primary HR server is located in New York, but is log shipped to servers in each location. If it is not possible to spread the primary and secondary servers to different locations, then other precautions should be met: The primary and secondary should be, at a minimum, on different power grids, and other similar high availability principles should be applied. For more information, see Chapter 16, "Five Nines: The Ultimate in High Availability."

The log shipping pair should never exist on the same server. Even though this is possible due to the multiple instances support of SQL Server 2000, the reason for not having them on the same box is that the server becomes a single point of failure.

Connectivity

The log shipping pair must be able to communicate with each other. This may mean that both servers are part of the same domain, or that proper login credentials are provided so the servers have the proper access. Ensure that all secondary servers also have connectivity to the public network so all users and applications can connect to it in the event of a switch.

Basic connectivity is not the only thing to take into consideration. Since log shipping does not utilize any form of compression on the transaction log files or the initial backup made by the Database Maintenance Plan Wizard, the files copied over the network have the potential of being large. As these files grow, they may take longer to copy, and slow down the log shipping process. So having a properly designed network with low latency is important. You can compensate for the size of the files and the corresponding latency if the load delay is altered.

To alleviate this potential problem without having to alter load delay after log shipping is implemented, do one or both of the following:

- Configure a private LAN between the log shipping pair servers to create a direct pipe into each server, instead of sharing network bandwidth over the public network, and potentially over the same network card used for all SQL Server connections.

- Use higher bandwidth network cards (provided your network infrastructure can handle it). SQL Server 2000 supports Giganet as a built-in feature, and Compaq's Servernet II technology on Compaq hardware is supported by using an update located online at:

  http://www.microsoft.com/sql/downloads/servrnet.htm

Keeping Old Transaction Log Files

Even though the transaction logs are being copied and applied, it is important to back them up in case a manual restore becomes necessary. SQL Server can be configured to automatically delete the older transaction log files after a certain period of time to conserve disk space. Every environment is different, but backing up transaction logs to an offline tape once a week may be a reasonable timeframe for archiving and freeing up disk space.

Thresholds

The DBA maintaining the SQL Server environment needs to know if log shipping becomes too far out of sync and/or may be failing. The two parameters to configure are: backup alert threshold and out of sync alert threshold. The alerts are triggered by error messages 14420 and 14421, respectively, and can be changed. After log shipping is installed, access the parameters by selecting the properties of the log shipping pair listed under the Log Shipping Monitor.

Installation Considerations

- If the option **Back up the database as part of the maintenance plan** is checked on the **Specify the Database Backup Plan** dialog box, it will create a SQL Server Agent job named "DB Backup Job for DB Maintenance Plan '*Configured Plan Name*' ". Selecting this option may not be necessary if a backup plan already exists for the database.

- Configuring the directory to backup and store the transaction logs is done first on the **Specify Transaction Log Backup Disk Directory** dialog box and, immediately following, on the **Specify the Transaction Log Share** dialog box. It is extremely important to ensure that the values specified for each of these are the same location, and that they are a valid universal naming convention (UNC) share (for example, \\servername\dirname) that is accessible by the log shipping pair. If they are not, the file copies will not occur, and subsequently, the transaction logs will not be applied to the warm standby.

- A database that is being log shipped cannot have more than one log shipping database maintenance plan. To add additional secondaries, modify the existing database maintenance plan.

- If a load delay is set, adjust the Out of sync threshold to compensate for this so the Log Shipping Monitor will not display a false error.

- When running the Database Maintenance Plan Wizard to configure log shipping, only one database can be selected. If more than one is selected, the wizard will disable the log shipping check box.

- Make sure the default local backup directory on the primary has enough room. This is important because when log shipping copies a file, it is copied from where the backup was made to the default directory, and then to the secondary. If there is not enough room, or a backup file exists with the same filename (for example, if a full database backup was done and the wizard also attempts to do one), errors will occur.

- Backup, copy, and restore the database to the secondary prior to running the Database Maintenance Plan Wizard. While the Database Maintenance Plan Wizard can do the initial backup, copy, and restore of the selected database if you choose, it is not the recommended practice due to the following reasons:

  - The backup, copy, and restore process can encounter errors. For example, if **Perform a full database backup now** is selected, it uses the default backup directory, so if there is either not enough room on the hard drive, or a backup file exists with the same filename (if a previous backup was done), log shipping will encounter errors and not be configured—thereby forcing a manual backup, copy, and restore.

  - Similarly, if "Use most recent backup file" is selected, a variation on the previous bullet point happens: Although the backup file exists and may be on another drive, it utilizes the default backup directory for the instance during the copy process. Should this fail, a manual backup, copy, and restore will be necessary.

- If using the wizard to do the database backup, make sure either the **Leave database non-operational but able to restore additional transaction logs** or **Leave database read-only and able to restore additional transaction logs** option is selected on the **Options** screen for restoring a database. If doing it through Transact-SQL, use the WITH STANDBY or WITH NORECOVERY options.

- If a backup file is created for use with the wizard, place it in a separate directory different from the one being used as the share for log shipping to prevent a possible configuration failure.

Preparation Worksheet

Below is a worksheet that can be copied and placed in a Run Book (for more information on a Run Book, see Chapter 16, "Five Nines: The Ultimate in High Availability") or a configuration document. It is done in the order of the Database Maintenance Plan Wizard. This worksheet is designed for you to enter the values used in your environment for the configuration of log shipping. It will not only enable log shipping to be able to be easily reconfigured if servers need to be rebuilt, but can also serve as an excellent resource for anyone who needs to know how your SQL Server environment is configured.

Parameter	Server	Value
Primary Server Name		
Secondary Server Name(s)		
Database to Log Ship (on Primary)	Primary server	
Directory to Store the Backup File (should be a valid UNC name)	One accessible by primary and secondary	
Create a subdirectory under the UNC for each database	N/A – UNC file path	Yes/No
Delete transaction log files older than a certain time period	N/A – UNC file path	
Backup File Extension (default is TRN)	N/A	
Network Share Name for Backup directory	One accessible by primary and secondary	Same as directory to store Backup File
Transaction Log Destination Directory (should be valid UNC on secondary server)	Secondary server	

continued on next page

Parameter	Server	Value
Create and Initialize New Database	Secondary server	Yes/No If No, name of existing database: If Yes: Name of database: Data path: Log path:
Database Load State	Secondary server	No recovery/Standby
Terminate User Connections in Database	Secondary server	Yes
Allow Database to Assume Primary Role	Secondary server	Yes/No If Yes: Transaction log backup directory: (should be the same as directory to store backup file)
Perform a Full Backup (if not using an existing DB)	Primary	Yes/No
Use Most Recent Backup File (if not using an existing DB)	Primary	Yes/No If Yes, what file:
Transaction Log Backup Schedule (default is every 15 minutes)	Primary	
Copy/Load Frequency (default is 15 minutes)	Primary/Secondary	
Load Delay (default is 0 minutes)	Secondary	
File Retention Period (default is 24 hours)		
Backup alert threshold		
Out of sync alert threshold		
Log Shipping Monitor server	N/A	

continued on next page

Parameter	Server	Value
Authentication mode for Monitor Server	Monitor server	Windows/SQL Server
Generate a Report	Primary	Yes/No
		If yes: Directory:
		Delete files after:
		E-mail report to:
Limit number of history entries in the **sysdbmaintplan_history** table		Yes/No
		If Yes: Number of rows:

Log Shipping Tips and Best Practices

In addition to understanding the fundamentals of log shipping, configuration, and installation issues, you may find it useful to keep these tips and best practices in mind.

Secondary Server Capacity

The secondary server ought to have the same capacity as the primary server. This ensures that the application will perform as expected. However, it is not mandatory the secondary server be exactly the same as the primary server. In some cases, the secondary server may need more capacity. It is acceptable to have multiple databases log shipped to a single secondary server. Before configuring multiple databases to one secondary, consider the following: What if the different applications share a user, with different rights? Does the application require a specific service pack level (either SQL Server or operating system) that the secondary server may not have? Do you have enough server processor and memory capacity to run all the databases? What if the application eats up disk space too quickly and affects the others? What if the application has a memory leak?

Generating Database Backups from the Secondary

Since the log shipped database is only a small increment of time out of sync with the primary database, it is a good idea to use it to generate the full database backups. This would keep the primary production server free of the potential overhead and contention incurred by a daily (or scheduled) backup.

It is also important to backup the **msdb** database on all servers involved with log shipping, including the log shipping monitor. This database contains all the configuration and status information for log shipping.

Keeping Logins in Sync

The DTS package that is created to copy the logins for the database from the primary to the secondary needs to be created for each secondary server that is part of the log shipping plan. This package should be scheduled to run on a regular basis. Another SQL Server Agent job should be created for the backing up of the **syslogins** table, and have the job copy the file to the secondary. As with the DTS package, this job must either have multiple job steps to copy the file to all secondary servers, or have multiple jobs.

When log shipping is first configured, these jobs should be run to ensure that the secondary is in sync with the primary; then it can be run manually or scheduled at a regular interval (scheduled is the recommended way). If the primary server is completely unavailable, and the logins were never transferred, the warm standby cannot be brought online. If the logins were scheduled to be applied, the worst-case scenario is that the secondary would be a bit out of sync if users are added on a regular basis and some would need to be added manually.

Monitoring Log Shipping

After log shipping is configured, check its status from time to time to ensure that it is functioning properly. The status can be viewed in the Log Shipping Monitor. You can view the history of the transaction log backups, the history of the copy and restore process, and various configuration properties for the log shipping pair.

Modifying or Removing Log Shipping

Sometimes it may be necessary to modify your log shipping configuration, or to completely remove it. For more information, see "Modifying Log Shipping" and "How to remove log shipping (Enterprise Manager)" in SQL Server Books Online.

Log Shipping Interoperability Between SQL Server 7.0 and SQL Server 2000

SQL Server allows transaction logs to be manually shipped from a SQL Server 7.0 installation with Service Pack 2 (SP2). However, you cannot send transaction logs from SQL Server 2000 to SQL Server 7.0. For log shipping to work, the option **pending upgrade** must be set to TRUE on the SQL Server 7.0 SP2 server. A backup of a database from SQL Server 7.0 cannot be restored in SQL Server 2000. Therefore, an alternative method, such as bulk copy (**bcp**) or Data Transformation Services (DTS), will need to be used for creating the initial database to be log shipped to SQL Server 2000. Log shipping between SQL Server 7.0 and SQL Server 2000 will not be tracked by the monitor server. A custom solution needs to be implemented to track the status. Some uses for log shipping from SQL Server 7.0 to SQL Server 2000 are:

- Using it to upgrade to SQL Server 2000 by phasing out the SQL Server 7.0 installation.

- In a development or test environment, keeping data concurrent when SQL Server 7.0 is the current development/production platform, and SQL Server 2000 is the future platform for the application.

    Note When log shipping from a SQL Server 7.0 SP2 server, the **pending upgrade** option should always be set to FALSE for any SQL Server 7.0 system that is not interoperating with SQL Server 2000. If **pending upgrade** is set, users cannot create indexes or statistics in the database. Attempts to create indexes or statistics will generate an error message. .

For more information, see SQL Server Books Online.

Using the Log Shipped Database to Check the Health of the Production Database

A benefit of having a secondary server, or multiple secondaries, is that—depending on how the copy and load delays are set—routine maintenance tasks, such as DBCCs, can be run against the log shipped database. As with the backup processes, it alleviates overhead and reduces potential downtime on the primary. Some recommended consistency checks are: DBCC CHECKALLOC, DBCC CHECKDB or DBCC CHECKTABLE (depending on what your environment dictates; doing a check table by table may be the only option on a log shipped server if the tables are large), and DBCC SHOWCONTIG.

Using the Log Shipped Database for Reporting

Since the secondary database is read-only, it can be used for reporting, such as in a DSS environment. With log shipping, by default, the secondary database is not available for reporting unless you restore with the STANDBY option and even then the database may only be available for intermittent read-only access. One limitation to be aware of is that SQL Server needs exclusive use of the database to apply the transaction logs. The secondary database can be made available for continuous read-only access only if you apply log backups when you do not need to run queries; if you do this, however, the data being queried will become more and more out of sync with the primary. This will potentially lower your high availability if there are large amounts of transactions.

Combining Log Shipping and Snapshot Backups

Log shipping can be employed in conjunction with a third party snapshot backup solution, which mirrors disks in a remote location that are attached to another server. In this scenario, the primary would log ship to the secondary, and the snapshot backup would mirror the secondary server, providing extra redundancy.

Terminating User Connections in the Secondary Database

SQL Server requires exclusive use of the database to apply the transaction log file, so both active and inactive connections must be terminated for log shipping to complete its process. Two scenarios are outlined below:

- Terminate user connections in database selected

  Bob is using the log shipped database to do his accounting reports. He knows that every 15 minutes the system needs exclusive use of the database; otherwise it will be out of sync. However, Bob forgets to close the reporting tool with a connection into the database before he goes to lunch. Since log shipping was configured to terminate the user connections, Bob's connection will be terminated at the next interval.

- Terminate user connections in database deselected

  During configuration, the option to terminate user connections was not selected. Log shipping is set to apply a transaction log every 15 minutes, and delete any transaction log files older than two hours. If Bob is running end of quarter reports all day, he winds up tying up the database for eight hours. Since the older transaction log files are deleted after two hours, not only will the database be out of sync, but also it could not be synchronized any other way besides a full database backup since the transaction log files no longer exist.

Warm Standby Role Change

It is critical when a high availability method is employed as part of a disaster recovery scenario that you contemplate and document how to respond in the event of a failure.

- Determine the amount of time to wait before deciding to fail over to the warm standby server.

- Do you have to switch ODBC Datasource Names (DSNs) to another server for your application or Web server? Or do you repoint a DNS and change a TCP/IP address on the secondary server? These must be determined before implementing log shipping.

- If the last transaction log did not get applied from the production server due to a failure, and the system is still alive from an operating system perspective, copy over and apply that final transaction log before bringing up the warm standby as your new primary. If the primary server is completely unavailable, check the log shipping monitor to see what the last backup applied was.

- Make sure new users are added and applied before bringing the warm standby online. For more information, see "How to set up and perform a log shipping role change (Transact-SQL)" in SQL Server Books Online.

- Tests should be conducted at semi-regular intervals to determine if a failover scenario to a warm standby server is successful.

- Failovers can be planned to perform typical system maintenance on the primary. If the secondary node is configured to become the primary, transaction logs can be built up, and then applied to the original primary to bring it back in sync when it comes online.

For more information on disaster recovery, see Chapter 16, "Five Nines: The Ultimate in High Availability."

Failback to Primary

After bringing a secondary server online as the primary, devise a strategy to bring the original primary server back online if it is necessary. Keep in mind that if the secondary server is equal from a hardware and capacity standpoint, there may be no need to switch back to the primary. This should be a decision determined by the business prior to implementing log shipping. After the failover to the secondary, it is recommended that you diagnose the problem on the primary to ensure that the failure does not occur again in your environment.

Here are two examples:

Example One

1. Make sure the original primary is online and functional.

2. Bring the application/Web server down.

3. Apply any transaction logs that were generated by the current primary database.

4. Switch the log shipping role back to the original primary, ensuring all new logins are applied to the server.

Example Two

1. Make sure the original primary is online and functional.

2. Bring the application/Web server down.

3. Stop log shipping on the current primary server.

4. Make a full backup of the database, and restore it on the original primary.

5. Make the original primary the "live" database by switching the log shipping role, and restart log shipping.

Network Load Balancing and Log Shipping

When Network Load Balancing (NLB) and log shipping are used together, both servers are set to inactive at startup. This requires the use of a private network between the log shipping pair, and works well in a Web-based environment. The primary node is started manually. When NLB is used for read-only SQL Servers (for example, reporting or catalog usage), all servers can be set in auto-start mode. In dual-homed configurations, the network cards must be non-routable to each other. And although direct IP communication can be achieved, the preferred method is to use a WINS server entry (LMHosts is another good alternative). Manual intervention is required to ensure client connectivity, but the problem is that clients cannot depend on one SQL Server name. A potential remedy is to have the IIS server point directly to the SQL Server instead of having the clients access the SQL Server directly.

Log Shipping and Replication

Both transactional and merge replication work with log shipping. The main reason for using log shipping with replication is to provide protection in the event of a Publisher failure. Make sure to use the KEEP_REPLICATION option on the restore of the last transaction log as part of the failover process that involves recovering the secondary database. KEEP_REPLICATION tells the recovery process to keep replication settings intact, since these are normally cleaned up as part of the restore process. As mentioned earlier, **msdb** is important to backup for log shipping, but it is equally important to back up for replication. For more information, see the topics "Strategies for Backing Up and Restoring Merge Replication," "Transactional Replication and Log Shipping," and "Strategies for Backing Up and Restoring Transactional Replication" in SQL Server Books Online.

Log Shipping and Application Code

Do not hard code a server name into an application when using log shipping. If the primary server fails, the application would not be able to utilize the secondary server, and would therefore render log shipping impossible.

Log Shipping and Failover Clustering

Many businesses use log shipping in conjunction with another feature of SQL Server 2000 Enterprise Edition—failover clustering. This is a solution that offers extreme high availability. Cost may be a consideration, though, since additional servers to ensure that the application could run with the acceptable level of performance could be expensive. The hardware requirements for log shipping are not as stringent as they are for failover clustering.

Note All hardware employed in a Windows environment should be on the Hardware Compatibility List to ensure complete compatibility and supportability. To see the Hardware Compatibility List, go to http://www.microsoft.com/hcl/.

For more information on failover clustering, see Chapter 12, "Failover Clustering." For more information on high availability, including a more detailed comparison of methods such as failover clustering and log shipping, see Chapter 16, "Five Nines: The Ultimate in High Availability."

Monitor Server

While the primary or the secondary can be configured as the log shipping monitor server, this is not recommended due to the fact that it stores the state of the log shipping process, and should the primary or secondary be lost, so will the history. This becomes important especially if a reporting tool is used to generate status documents for external people to read.

Using Full-Text Search with a Log Shipped Database

The full-text search feature will fail when the primary system fails. Another copy of the search indexes must also exist on the secondary server. As soon as the search service is restarted on the second computer, clients can use it again. While this can be automated, it is not an instantaneous failover, and should be part of the failover plan if full-text is used.

Troubleshooting

Sometimes errors may occur after log shipping has been configured or during the configuration process. Below are some of the common problems, and how to attempt to solve them. For more information, refer to "Installation Considerations" in this chapter.

Q *Log shipping does not seem to be working or I cannot get it configured. Where do I start to look?*

A First and foremost, make sure that SQL Server Agent is started on all SQL Server instances, especially the secondary. If log shipping is configured, SQL Server Agent should be set to start automatically. Also make sure that the servers are set up as linked servers.

Q *Log shipping seems to be set up correctly, but no files get copied or applied. I just see* first_file_000000000000.trn *when I bring up the log shipping pair properties.*

A If different file locations were specified in setup (see "Installation Considerations" in this chapter), this is a common result when the secondary cannot access the file share.

Q *I see an error message similar to the one below when a transaction log is applied:*

```
[Microsoft SQL-DMO (ODBC SQLState: 42000)]
Error 4305: [Microsoft][ODBC SQL Server Driver][SQL Server]The log in this backup set
begins at LSN 7000000026200001, which is too late to apply to the database. An earlier
log backup that includes LSN 6000000015100001 can be restored.
[Microsoft][ODBC SQL Server Driver][SQL Server]RESTORE LOG is terminating abnormally.
```

A When the full database backup was restored, one that was too old was restored. The transaction logs must be applied sequentially, so if the full backup is out of date, log shipping will fail.

Data Center Availability: Facilities, Staffing, and Operations

The Internet is having a major impact on information systems departments. With online shopping, business-to-business commerce, customer service, and employee communications, companies of all sizes are experiencing significant growth in their information systems. Many small- to medium-sized companies are now faced with managing more data and more systems to provide information when and where it is needed.

Companies with worldwide operations also face the demands of providing an around-the-clock enterprise network, with around-the-clock access to information. If employees around the world need access to a customer database, the database must be available at times that used to be "off-hours."

Enterprise networks and the Internet place high demands on information systems, while providing little opportunity for maintenance. As system size and system availability requirements increase, facilities and staffing become more important for optimal system performance.

The purpose of this chapter is to provide facility and staffing recommendations for high availability, and to suggest operational guidelines specific to data centers and Microsoft® SQL Server™. The chapter ends with a brief discussion of Application Service Providers, an alternative to running your own data center.

Data Centers

You have data—lots of it. How do you store, secure, move, and manage that data? You definitely need the hardware, software, and network infrastructure to physically host and move the data. You also need staff to manage the systems and data. And, you need facilities to keep the systems (and staff) secure and operational. Data, systems, staff, and facilities comprise a data center.

There is no one type of data center. Depending on business size, budget, and data availability requirements, data center operations can vary dramatically. The volume of servers and other hardware, the required support services, and the number of employees determines the type of data center required:

- Small data centers may be located in a small room in a building. The room often has only enough room for equipment, may or may not be secure, and provides limited protection for systems in an emergency. These small data centers are sometimes referred to as "data closets."

- Mid-sized data centers are often located in the same building as other business operations, but have separate security systems to restrict access to the data. Inside the data center may be mainframes, servers, automated backup equipment, offices, and climate control systems. Support services, such as power and telecommunications, are often redundant so the data center can be operational when a service is lost.

- Large data centers may occupy entire buildings. Data security and redundant systems are provided throughout such buildings. Emergency backup systems allow the data center to be operational in case of a major disaster, such as a large earthquake or long-term power outage. This is especially important to businesses such as banks and insurance companies that need systems to be operational during such emergencies.

The term "data center" can mean these medium to large facilities.

Facility and Equipment Requirements

A data center must provide reliable access to data. Several factors determine the availability of data: Facilities must support availability requirements; equipment must be high quality and designed to meet availability and performance requirements; and communication between components must support those requirements.

The Data Center Facility

A data center facility is designed to ensure system availability and protect against data loss. During a fire, power loss, or equipment failure, the redundant systems of a well-planned data center can mean the difference between data availability and data disaster. Here are some facility recommendations.

- Raised Floors

    All medium to large data centers should consider raised floors. A raised floor provides space for the massive amounts of cable required in a data center, and can simplify the process of adding and moving equipment. Another benefit of a raised floor is cooling: cool air can be pushed under raised floors and directed at servers and other heat-sensitive equipment.

- Fire Suppression

    Good smoke detectors and fire extinguishers are crucial. Gas (such as FM200) and water systems are commonly used for fire suppression. Smoke detectors and temperature sensors should be located throughout the data center so conditions can be monitored and controlled in zones. Make sure the fire suppression system can be started and stopped manually.

- Temperature and Humidity Control

  Computer equipment reliability is better in cool conditions — 68 degrees Fahrenheit (20 C) is reasonable for both equipment and people. While desktop computers and individual servers use fans to keep the CPU cool, fans do not provide enough cooling for a data center.

  Small data centers often rely on the air conditioning in their building. Larger data centers have more equipment, producing more heat, and need a dedicated, redundant cooling system. Make sure emergency generators can power the cooling systems.

  Humidity is also a concern for data centers. High humidity can lead to condensation on equipment. Very low humidity can lead to excess static electricity. Large fluctuations in humidity can cause circuit boards to expand and contract, damaging circuitry. A good target is 40–45 percent relative humidity.

- Redundant Power

  Power outages can be either widespread or very local. Preparing for both possibilities will reduce the odds that power loss will cause a significant service interruption.

  Bad weather is not the only cause of a widespread power outage. Other common reasons for power outages include blown transformers, construction, and accidents. When an event like this occurs and power to the data center is lost, a battery backup system can supply enough power for an orderly shutdown. If systems must be operational, install redundant backup generators to power critical equipment.

  Within the data center, blown circuits or damaged wiring can cause an outage to a rack or to individual components. Redundant power supplies to each rack of equipment can prevent a blown circuit from causing downtime; if a main circuit loses power, a redundant power supply automatically switches the rack to a second power supply. For incidental electrical problems, make sure to stock spare parts on site.

- Data Connectivity

  To provide communications with people outside the data center, the facility needs voice and high-speed data connections. Like power systems, communication systems should be redundant. If one carrier loses service or must take their system down for maintenance, having a second carrier will allow users to keep accessing the information they need.

  To prevent damage to multiple lines during construction or maintenance, the redundant lines should enter the data center at different locations. Also, for optimal service and cost effectiveness, the facility should be near an Internet hub.

- Backup Systems and Off-Site Storage

  Databases and file systems must be backed up frequently according to a defined schedule. Small data centers might manually back up data, while larger data centers typically need automated backup devices, such as tape libraries that mechanically insert and remove tapes.

  Store backups off site. If backups are stored on site, a disaster at the data center might destroy both production and the backups.

- Security

  Stolen data is a big concern for most companies. Intruders can access data in person by physically entering the data center, or can obtain virtual access through a network connection.

  To stop intruders from entering the data center, require staff and visitors to provide credentials on entry. Security cameras are also helpful. To stop virtual intruders, enforce security on each server, secure the network using a firewall, and require employees to use strong passwords that change frequently. The best defense against network attacks is a well-trained staff that stays current with "hacking" trends.

- Space

  A data center should provide enough room for equipment to be organized, room for growth, and room for staff. Relocating equipment often causes downtime. Adequate room for employees is important for employee productivity.

Data Center Hardware

Once the data center facility is ready, you will need to bring in the servers and network infrastructure to support your systems. SQL Server Books Online provides absolute minimum hardware configurations for SQL Server 2000. Necessary hardware configurations depend on the performance and availability requirements.

Hardware requirements are often system specific. Individual hardware and application vendors often provide system requirements or white papers that include hardware, configuration, and tuning guidelines. Follow vendor guidelines for hardware selection, as well as other system requirements.

How a database is used also affects hardware selection. Large databases with higher transaction throughput require lots of memory and a robust disk subsystem. In any database that sustains heavy read or write activity, separate the system files, data files, and log files on multiple disks and controllers to improve performance by load-balancing disk reads and writes. For very large or busy databases, further performance improvements are possible by spreading the data files across multiple drives.

Finally, availability requirements also affect hardware selection. For some applications, downtime is very expensive, so a backup system must be available at all times. Availability solutions such as SQL Server 2000 failover clustering, log shipping, and replication require multiple servers.

For more information on SQL Server hardware configurations, see Chapter 33, "The Data Tier: An Approach to Database Optimization."

Data Communication Within the Data Center

Within a data center, communication rates between components impact system performance. For example, if you have a group of servers that store data on an array of disks, the communication rate between the servers and the storage array affects system response time. If communication between system components occurs over a shared network, any network congestion will slow system performance.

High-speed interconnects, often referred to as SANs, can improve performance within a data center. Note that the acronym SAN has multiple meanings:

- A storage area network is an interconnect between multiple servers and a shared resource, such as a storage subsystem. Fibre Channel is typical for this type of interconnect.

- A system area network is an interconnect between servers, and is often used for communication within a cluster or federation of servers. An example of this type of interconnect is Giganet's cLAN.

A new standard for interconnects is called the Virtual Interface Architecture (VIA). The standard, created by Compaq, Intel, Microsoft, and other companies, defines a protocol for a high-speed messaging interface that reduces communication latency between connected devices. This latency reduction is accomplished by using hardware to create virtual connections between devices, bypassing slower network protocols such as TCP/IP.

SQL Server 2000 Enterprise Edition supports the Giganet VIA SAN implementation. Because system area networks are intended to support fast communications between servers, SQL Server 2000 supports the VIA Net-Libraries only on Microsoft Windows NT® Server and the Windows® 2000 Server, Advanced Server, and Datacenter Server operating systems. You can download updated tools and libraries at http://www.microsoft.com/sql/.

Staffing Recommendations

Running a data center requires a highly trained staff that can plan and implement complex systems, and can respond quickly when problems arise. Microsoft Consulting Services (MCS) works with organizations to develop systems and recommend system support procedures, and has defined several roles for implementing and supporting SQL Server in a data center.

Note that these roles do not necessarily map to individual employees. In smaller organizations, a team of two or three people might cover all the roles. In a larger organization, the number of servers, databases, and tasks may require multiple people to fill one role. Also, in your organization you may use different names. For example, your organization may have a Database Administrator (DBA) that fills the roles of the Deployment Specialist and SQL Developer.

Deployment Specialist

The Deployment Specialist is responsible for the installation, configuration, and operation of SQL Server. To meet the requirements of this role, the Deployment Specialist performs the following tasks:

- Works with the staff to determine the requirements for SQL Server installations.

- Installs and configures SQL Server on test machines.

- Creates setup scripts for quick installation on other servers and for server recovery.

- Documents all SQL Server installations before moving them to production, and documents all changes made to SQL Server in production.

- Deploys SQL Server to production.

- Maintains SQL Server installations.

In high-availability configurations, the Deployment Specialist also configures and manages failover clustering, linked servers, and replication.

Security Specialist

The Security Specialist develops and implements security plans for each server. A security plan ensures that the server and databases are secure, and that users can access the data they need. The Security Specialist typically performs the following tasks:

- Determines which SQL Server security mode to implement on each instance of SQL Server.

- Administers server login accounts for individuals and groups.

- Administers database user accounts and roles.

- Creates scripts for restoring security settings.

- Manages permissions of applications within SQL Server.

If the environment supports the passing of security credentials between servers (delegation), the Security Specialist configures delegation.

Disaster Recovery Specialist

The Disaster Recovery Specialist develops and implements database backup and recovery strategies. This role is crucial for availability of each database. The Disaster Recovery Specialist typically performs the following tasks:

- Works with Application Specialist and SQL Developer to create a reliable backup and recovery plan according to application usage.

- Documents the backup and recovery plan for each database.

- Creates automated jobs and alerts to implement backups.
- Creates jobs for on-demand backup and recovery.
- Tests backups to ensure they will recover the databases.
- Works with Deployment Specialist to develop server recovery procedures.

The Disaster Recovery Specialist owns the backup and recovery plans, and must update the plans as necessary. This requires knowledge of the entire system, and input from other staff members.

SQL Developer

The SQL Developer designs and creates databases. In some organizations, this role is performed by a DBA. The SQL Developer typically performs the following tasks:

- Designs databases according to customer and application specifications.
- Implements database schemas, files, and indexes.
- Tunes databases for performance.
- Trains support specialists on the design and function of each database.
- Documents the schema and functions of each database for support specialists and future developers.
- Works with the Disaster Recovery Specialist to create a recovery plan for each database.
- Provides SQL scripts for rebuilding each database.

Once a system is in production, the role of the SQL Developer in that database is reduced. The developer may be involved with implementing significant changes and performing some maintenance.

Application Specialist

The role of the Application Specialist is to know third party and custom applications, and to work with other staff members to integrate and troubleshoot the applications. The Application Specialist typically performs the following tasks:

- Learns how to use the database applications, and how the applications use the databases.
- Works with the System Continuity Specialist to identify key application monitors.
- Works with the SQL Developer and Deployment Specialists to ensure applications are making optimal use of SQL Server.
- Provides documentation for application support and recovery.

For Web applications, knowledge of Web technologies such as XML and scripting is important as well.

System Continuity Specialist

The System Continuity Specialist develops and implements the monitoring strategy for servers, databases, and applications. The System Continuity Specialist typically performs the following tasks:

- Determines which tools to use to monitor hardware, software, and applications.

- Picks the counters and conditions to monitor.

- Creates monitoring templates for tools like SQL Profiler and System Monitor.

- Creates the baseline reports used to compare system performance over time and after significant system changes.

- Defines the monitoring schedule and creates automated jobs for common monitoring tasks.

- Documents the monitoring strategy.

- Works with other staff members to troubleshoot poor performance.

Monitoring Specialist

The Monitoring Specialist performs day-to-day monitoring tasks, working closely with the System Continuity Specialist and Trend Analysis Specialist. The Monitoring Specialist typically performs the following tasks:

- Works with the System Continuity Specialist to create the monitoring strategy.

- Ensures monitoring jobs are running.

- Responds to system alerts and provides problem details to other staff.

- Consistently documents system performance and creates reports for the Trend Analysis Specialist.

  Note Monitors should always be running, so starting and stopping monitoring jobs should not be a common task.

Trend Analysis Specialist

The Trend Analysis Specialist looks at system performance over time and after significant system changes, and determines when to take measures to improve performance. The Trend Analysis Specialist typically performs the following tasks:

- Analyzes monitoring reports and looks for performance trends.

- Works with the staff to determine the causes of performance degradation.

- Works with the staff to find permanent solutions to performance degradation.

Quality Assurance Specialist

The Quality Assurance Specialist ensures all servers, databases, and applications are fully tested and comply with all operational guidelines before being released to production. The Quality Assurance Specialist typically performs the following tasks:

- Defines quality assurance guidelines, which define minimum standards for production systems.

- Ensures all production systems pass quality assurance guidelines.

- Creates the change control process, which is a procedure used for implementing changes on production systems.

- Owns or manages the use of a test lab where all new or modified systems are tested.

Hardware Specialist

The Hardware Specialist is responsible for the selection, configuration, and operation of data center hardware. The Hardware Specialist typically performs the following tasks:

- Recommends server, storage, and network components.

- Installs and configures hardware.

- Works with the Trend Analysis Specialist and other staff to determine when hardware upgrades and additions are necessary.

The hardware specialist is also responsible for hardware during disaster recovery, and needs to make sure adequate supplies of hardware are available for emergencies.

Support Specialist

The Support Specialist provides customer support, and is the primary customer contact. The Support Specialist typically performs the following tasks:

- Learns customer applications and how the applications integrate into data center systems.

- Takes support calls from customers and helps them troubleshoot basic problems.

- Creates a support escalation procedure.

- Works with the rest of the team to define a troubleshooting procedure.

- Documents customer concerns and system bugs.

Operational Guidelines

Facilities and staffing are critical to data center operations. In addition, establishing a set of guidelines and tasks for the daily operations of a data center will help the data center run smoothly and be prepared for emergencies.

General Operations

Each system in a data center has its own operational guidelines. But the data center itself must have operational guidelines to ensure quality, to control changes to production, and to prepare for emergencies.

Quality Assurance

Quality Assurance is the process of determining if a system meets predefined measures of quality. In a data center, a quality assurance process ensures that new or changed systems work as specified, integrate well with other systems, and are documented so they can be maintained and recovered. For example, here is a high-level process for new systems:

- Determine a set of standards that must be met by the application. For example, the application needs to run in a test lab for two weeks without failure.

- Configure the test lab for integration testing, and test the new system:

  - Determine if application integration standards are met.

  - Simulate a variety of server loads to evaluate system performance.

  - Test how the system responds to errors.

- Evaluate performance against an actual baseline.

- Determine if additional hardware is necessary. If it is, configure the additional hardware and re-test the system.

- Ensure documentation exists, as well as scripts for installation and recovery.

Once the system passes the quality assurance process and is released on the production servers, create a new performance baseline, and then continue to monitor the system.

Change Control

A data center is not a stable environment. Equipment, operating systems, and applications change frequently to improve or maintain performance. In such a complex environment, a change on one system can cause unexpected problems. To reduce the possibility of problems, changes must be thoroughly planned. Change control is the process of ensuring that changes are planned and tested before being moved to production, and that changes to production are scheduled and documented.

Each data center needs to develop a change control procedure to meet the needs of the staff, management, and systems. However, most change control processes follow a similar process, such as the following:

1. In a document created from a change control template, a customer or a staff member proposes a change to production.

2. A small committee reviews the proposal, and either agrees to implement a test system or denies the proposal.

3. If the staff agrees to pursue the change, the staff implements the changes in the test lab. Much of the staff may be involved in this process, especially if hardware and security changes are necessary.

4. The Quality Assurance Specialist leads the testing effort, making sure the new or changed system is performing as expected, and that other systems are not negatively impacted.

5. If the system performs well in the lab, the Deployment Specialist makes the final decision on implementing the changes in production.

6. The Quality Assurance Specialist makes sure all quality assurance guidelines are met before approving the system for production, the System Continuity Specialist develops a monitoring plan, and the Disaster Recovery Specialist develops a backup and recovery plan.

7. The Deployment Specialist, along with any other necessary staff, implements the changes in production during a change control window, and according to change control guidelines.

8. The Monitoring Specialist monitors the new system, watching for unexpected impacts.

The change control process can differ significantly based on the complexity of the change. A simple change, such as adding an alert to a database, may have an expedited change control process. A complex change, such as installing an application, requires more decisions and a more substantial process.

Here are some change control suggestions:

-   Justify all changes before modifying a production system.

-   Ensure that all changes run successfully in a test lab before implementing in production. And make sure to document all changes.

-   Use Sunday evening, or another low-impact time, to update production. A set change-control time window will reduce the impact on production, and will help enforce change control guidelines.

Emergency Preparedness

During an emergency or system failure, you need to have a recovery plan with which everyone is familiar and comfortable. Here are some recommendations for emergency preparedness:

-   Provide up-to-date contact information for everyone in the data center, and everyone you may need to contact in an emergency. Include home and work phone numbers, pager numbers, and backup contacts.

- Have recovery instructions for all equipment. Do not store the recovery instructions online in a system that may itself need to be recovered.

- Stock spare parts, especially disk drives.

- Practice. Run fire drills. Recover test systems from production data.

SQL Server Operations

The following guidelines provide a starting point for SQL Server operations. Organizations need to customize their SQL Server operations to their systems and availability requirements.

Security

Before any system is placed in production, the Security Specialist must work with the Deployment Specialist, Application Specialist, and SQL Developer to make sure the system is secure. The following is a short list of security recommendations:

- Do not use the **sa** password, which is provided in SQL Server 2000 for backward compatibility only. Instead, use the default mode for SQL Server 2000, which is to disable the **sa** password. If you enable the **sa** password during installation, set a password immediately.

- For user and group logins, Windows Authentication is more secure and easier to administer than SQL Server Authentication. In this mode, administrators grant SQL Server access to Windows users and groups, and SQL Server relies solely on the Windows authentication of the user. User passwords are not stored in SQL Server; however, applications and Web sites often need to use SQL Server Authentication to establish a connection with a database. If you need to use SQL Server Authentication for some purposes, and can use Windows Authentication for some users, use Mixed Mode security.

- If a server uses SQL Server Authentication, create scripts for the recovery of security information. When a database is moved from one server to another, database users are transferred, but server logins are not, which can cause a mismatch between logins and users. The script needs to establish all necessary logins on the new server, and then run **sp_change_users_login** to match logins with users.

- Restrict or disable the **guest** user accounts. If a person has a SQL Server login account, but does not have explicit access to a database, that person has **guest** permissions on every database with a **guest** user account. Also, application roles can gain access to other databases through the **guest** user account.

- Create set procedures for adding and removing accounts.

For more information see Chapter 10, "Implementing Security."

Monitoring

Monitoring is the only good way to know how systems are performing. Without monitoring, you may not be aware when downtime occurs.

For SQL Server, the primary areas to monitor are disk usage, memory usage, CPU performance, and SQL Server performance. Two tools commonly used to monitor performance are System Monitor and SQL Profiler. For a complete list of SQL Server tools, see "Choosing a Monitoring Tool" in SQL Server Books Online.

System Monitor

System Monitor is a Windows 2000 tool used to collect and view real-time data about system performance. Use System Monitor to establish a performance baseline, and to constantly monitor system performance. To analyze performance trends, compare current performance against the baseline.

The following lists of counters and events provide a starting point for monitoring SQL Server. System Continuity Specialists should create a custom monitoring system for individual servers, databases, and applications. For a complete list of applicable counters, see "Monitoring with System Monitor" in SQL Server Books Online.

Disk usage counters:

- **Logical Disk: % Free Space** — Make sure you have adequate free space for data and log file growth. Set an alert when the percentage of free space is low, typically between 10 and 30 percent, depending on database size and growth rate.

- **Physical Disk: Avg Disk Queue Length** — The average disk queue length indicates the number of disk requests that are on hold because the disk cannot keep up with requests. If this number is greater than two on any disk, consider adjusting the disk configuration or rearranging data. This counter is also available for logical disks.

- **Physical Disk: % Disk Time** — This counter indicates how often the disk is busy servicing reads or writes. If this number is greater than 90 percent on any disk, consider adjusting the disk configuration or rearranging data. You can also compare the Disk Write Bytes/sec, Disk Writes/sec, Disk Read Bytes/sec, and Disk Reads/sec counters to find out what type of activity is causing high usage rates. These counters are also available for logical disks.

Memory counters:

- **Process: Page Faults/sec: sqlservr** — This counter indicates the number of times the **sqlservr** process could not find data in memory and had to go to disk to find the data. This number should be at or near 0 during normal operations. Two other counters, **Memory: Pages/sec** and **Memory:Page Faults/sec**, can help you analyze total system memory. If these counters are high, such as over 20, another process may be using too much memory, or the server needs additional memory.

- **SQL Server: Buffer Manager: Buffer Cache Hit Ratio** — This counter indicates the percentage of requested data that exists in memory. The counter should be 90 percent or greater. If the hit ratio is too low, add more memory to the server.

Processor counters:

- **System: Processor Queue Length** — This counter indicates how many threads are waiting for the processor. If this number is greater than two per CPU, tune your databases or provide more processing power. Slow performance, a queue of 0, and low CPU usage may indicate a performance bottleneck elsewhere, such as the disk subsystem.

- **Processor: % Processor Time** — If the server is running SQL Server only, and the processor active time is greater than 90 percent, you probably need to adjust how applications are using the database, tune the database, or increase processing power.

- **Process: % Processor Time: sqlservr** — This counter indicates the percentage of time that all threads of the **sqlservr** process are using to execute instructions. Compare this to **% Processor Time**. If other processes are consuming too much time, terminate nonessential processes or move them to other servers.

SQL Server and database counters:

- **SQL Server: General Statistics: User Connections** — Once you set user connections to the maximum expected number of concurrent users, use this counter to track the number of user connections. Set an alert to notify when the number of current user connections reaches the maximum.

- **SQL Server Locks: Number of Deadlocks/sec** — This counter should be 0. When two threads, each having a lock on one piece of data, attempt to acquire a lock on the other's piece of data, the threads are deadlocked. SQL Server does break deadlocks, but it is best to find the source of deadlocks and fix the problem, or deal with deadlocks in the application.

- **SQL Server: Databases: Transactions/sec** — This counter shows how many transactions per second the specified database is supporting. This information is important for trend analysis.

- **SQL Server: Databases: Percent Log Used** — This counter indicates how full the transaction log is for the specified database. Create a log backup job that is triggered whenever the log is almost full, such as when it reaches 80 percent capacity. Send a notification when the job runs successfully, and send an alert when the job fails.

- **SQL Server: Databases: Data File(s) Size (KB)** — This counter indicates the combined size of all the data files that make up the specified database, including any automatic growth. To minimize autogrow operations, which generate a lot of I/O, make sure this counter is large enough to hold the data that will be stored in the database. This is especially true with the **tempdb** database. The **tempdb** database is recreated each time SQL Server starts. If the size specified for the **tempdb** data files is too small, then overall performance may be impacted by numerous **tempdb** autogrow operations. Compare the size reported for **tempdb** by this counter to the space allocation reported when you use SQL Server Enterprise Manager to display the properties of **tempdb**. If the counter is reporting a much higher size, increase the space allocation defined for **tempdb** in SQL Server Enterprise Manager.

- **SQL Server: Databases: Backup/Restore Throughput/sec** — Use this counter to monitor data throughput during backup and restore operations. You can test multiple configurations to find out which configuration is more efficient.

Many more counters are available for SQL Server. For example, the **SQL Server: Access Methods** object provides several counters to monitor how the logical pages within a database are accessed, including index usage. For more information about choosing counters to monitor for performance, see *Inside Microsoft SQL Server 2000* by Kalen Delaney.

SQL Profiler

If System Monitor counters do not indicate performance issues, but a server has periodic poor performance, use SQL Profiler to analyze SQL Server activity. Monitoring tools such as SQL Profiler use system resources, so limit the number and complexity of traces. Here are some examples of how to use SQL Profiler:

- List all long-running queries.

- Count all table scans, which are an indication that indexes are not being used.

- Analyze the queries that are creating deadlocks.

- Analyze the activity of a specific database user.

- Create a complete sample of database activity for the Index Tuning Wizard.

SQL Profiler provides templates for many common analysis scenarios. You also can create your own templates for custom scenarios. For more information about SQL Profiler, see "Monitoring with SQL Profiler" in SQL Server Books Online.

Backup and Recovery

A backup and recovery plan is critical to the availability of a data center, and requires more than simply backing up data on a regular schedule. For large databases, backing up the entire database can take more time than is available. And, if backup is slow, recovery will likely be slow as well. Consider the following when creating a backup and recovery plan:

- Create backup schedules for each database based on size, tolerance for data loss, and the time available for backups and recovery. Here are three scenarios and possible solutions:

  - For a small database that has few updates, or when the owner will tolerate some data loss, use a simple plan. For example, back up the entire database nightly, and truncate the log after the backup. Any updates since the last backup are lost.

  - For medium-to-large databases in which data cannot be lost, use a combination of database, differential, and log backups. For example, back up the entire database nightly, perform a differential backup hourly, and back up the transaction log every 20 minutes.

  - For very large databases, use files and filegroups to speed backup and recovery time. If data is grouped in files according to how often the data changes, some files can be backed up less frequently. For example, back up the entire database each weekend. Stagger the backup of active files, backing up data as frequently as necessary, but not all at the same time. Back up log files frequently, as log files are not backed up with file backups.

- Create a step-by-step system recovery plan and keep it up-to-date.

- Create recovery scripts for configuration settings, databases, logins, and users.

- Store backups in a secure, off site location.

- Test your recovery plan using real backups.

- Create an alert to notify the Disaster Recovery Specialist when the log is 80 percent full (or less, if necessary).

Maintenance

Although SQL Server is a self-tuning system that requires little maintenance, you do need to maintain databases and indexes and watch system performance. The following tasks will help maintain database performance.

- Maintain indexes. Creating indexes can greatly improve performance, but index fragmentation and changes in usage patterns can make indexes less useful to queries. Analyze index performance, and defragment or rebuild indexes as necessary. The Index Tuning Wizard is very useful for this task.

- Update statistics. SQL Server uses distribution statistics to improve its use of indexes. If you have turned off the automatic updating of statistics for performance reasons, you need to frequently update statistics. This is especially important with significant changes to data or changes to the distribution of data.

- Maintain load balance. As a database grows, the balance of data and activity across disks can change. If one disk becomes more active than others, redistribute files to rebalance the load.

- Stock spare disk drives, cables, installation disks, and other critical components.

- Document the amount of downtime you experience in the data center. This will help measure how well the data center is operating.

For easy maintenance, automate as many maintenance tasks as you can. For example, let SQL Server statistics update automatically, or create a job that updates statistics.

Application Service Providers

Some companies may not want to invest in the equipment and skills necessary to run a data center. For these companies, Application Service Providers (ASPs) provide another option. ASPs offer various levels of application and system hosting, such as:

- Customers simply leasing rack space for their own servers.

- Customers leasing space on a server, and managing their own applications and data.

- Customers receiving comprehensive services, including system development, hosting, and maintenance.

Internet Service Providers (ISPs), a similar business model, focus on providing Internet access, Web site hosting, and Web site development. ISPs typically do not provide the same range of services as ASPs.

Using an ASP

ASPs provide valuable services, but when does using an ASP make the most sense? This decision is often based on several factors, including the company size, the reason for outsourcing, and the company's comfort with the ASP model. Here are some reasons companies use ASPs:

- Small companies can benefit from economies of scale—the large ASPs may provide service at a lower cost, especially if the company has not already invested in data center staff and equipment.

- ASP fees are negotiated according to levels of service, and can be more easily budgeted.

- If data center employees are difficult to find and keep, an ASP can offset this cost by providing development and maintenance services.

- ASPs sometimes specialize in certain applications, which can greatly reduce development and deployment time.

- If your business has extremely busy periods, an ASP may be able to host extra servers to temporarily increase capacity.

Before choosing an ASP, consider the following:

- For a larger company with an existing IT organization, an ASP may be more expensive. Analyze service level agreements, as well as fees for services above the negotiated level.

- A company that uses an ASP is not free from managing information. Customers, suppliers, or employees use the data, and the company is still responsible for that. The company also needs to manage the relationship with the ASP, including training the ASP on existing applications, negotiating terms of service, and evolving IT operations as they relate to business plans.

- Some companies are not comfortable with an ASP hosting critical or sensitive company data. However, ASPs are not an all-or-nothing choice. You may wish to outsource some applications and not others.

ASPs and Multiple Instances of SQL Server

SQL Server 2000 supports multiple instances of the relational database engine on the same server. This allows an ASP to more efficiently use resources. If a group of customer databases can run on one server, the ASP can install one default instance and multiple named instances on that one server, then define administrative privileges for each instance.

Summary

Running a data center is a complex task. However, with the proper facilities, a well-trained staff, and good operational procedures, a data center can provide the availability and reliability necessary for Internet and enterprise services.

The qualities of a well-planned data center include:

- Facilities that provide redundant support systems and enough space to properly host all people and equipment.

- A well trained staff that fills the roles necessary for planning, running, and supporting data center equipment and operations.

- Documented operational procedures that the staff uses to ensure maximum performance and system availability.

Not all companies want to, or can, run their own data center. For these companies, ASPs provide another option.

For more information about data center planning and operations, see http://www.microsoft.com/mof/.

High Availability Options

This chapter describes and recommends high availability alternatives for Microsoft® SQL Server™ 2000. Although many other sources detail the technical aspects of implementing high availability options, the unique value of this chapter is that it describes the strategic side of high availability, from SQL Server 2000 failover clustering to replication, and more. The details of this chapter concentrate on SQL Server solutions; however, most of the content will apply generically to any operations plan.

High availability is a phrase used to describe the continuous operation of a computer system. It is a complicated subject because it covers so many different areas within a company—from people, policies, and processes to hardware and software. There are two basic challenges in providing a highly available computer system. The first is to protect the primary server in the best manner possible. The second is to provide a remote copy of the database for the worst-case disaster. Each challenge has specific solutions, but a combination of solutions will yield the best results. The intent of this chapter is to better acquaint you with the high availability solutions available to you, describe optimal uses of each, and even suggest ways of combining solutions for maximum benefit.

The Importance of People, Policies, and Processes

Continuous computing is the ability of an organization to provide computerized application services all the time. You are likely familiar with other terms that describe the same fundamental principle: 24 x 7, uptime, and availability. Continuous computing is a difficult thing for organizations to maintain, and any organization should be aware that the cost and complexity of this undertaking rises the closer to 100 percent uptime a company attempts.

Are There Any 100 Percent Solutions?

No. Although there may be some instances of companies that have achieved a sustained record of 100 percent for some applications on some platforms over a defined period of time, these cases are rare. The majority of computer professionals are realistic and practical enough to attempt some form of 99.x percent solution, where x is some number of nines. The term "three nines" refers to 99.9 percent uptime, or about 8.76 hours of downtime per year. "Five nines" refers to 99.999 percent uptime, or approximately 5 minutes of downtime per year. For more information, see Chapter 16, "Five Nines: The Ultimate in High Availability."

Meeting High Uptime

Meeting high uptime is something that many companies face. The following section describes some things to consider when planning to meet these standards..

To plan for high uptime, consider doing the following:

- Increasing training budgets and making sure the right training and certifications are chosen.

- Increasing awareness of the problem at all levels of the company.

- Creating a technical operations plan.

Microsoft Readiness Framework can be used to assess the technology readiness of a company. A product called Microsoft Operations Framework can help guide the operations management and staff with setting policies, procedures, and skill sets.

Uptime Solutions and Risk Management

Investments in uptime solutions are nothing more than basic risk management—from the *proactive* side. How much are you willing to spend? To answer this, you first need to find out how much downtime costs your company. Do not try to be extremely precise; the calculation is complicated and an approximate figure is good enough. Factors such as payroll costs, lost revenue, overhead allocations, and support costs need to be considered. For example, if your server hosts data for an e-commerce application, the cost of even a small amount of downtime could be high. In that case, you might be willing to invest more in minimizing or eliminating downtime.

People: The Best Solution

Continuous operation is not just about technology. It is about people. Hiring the best people is crucial to a smooth running operation. Following closely in importance behind the role of staff are the roles of good policies and processes to help your people perform to their full potential. The role of technology is equally important and is related to the people, policies, and processes in your operation. For instance, the technology used in the company will dictate what skills you need to hire, what training plans you implement, and specific processes you define for managing that technology.

Roles of DBAs?

Database administrators (DBAs) have many roles in a data center. For example, they often handle support calls. Sometimes, the support calls come in with the message, "My database is broken." This is because the user sees messages that the database could not be contacted. Studies have shown 80 percent of downtime can be attributed to network outages, with the remainder of downtime caused by problems with applications, operating systems, or databases. So a DBA who gets such a the call needs to troubleshoot all these pieces.

Databases and directories are the primary storage for valuable company information. The other pieces in the process (network, operating systems, and applications) are just mechanisms for connecting to and working with the data. So, an important focus in a disaster recovery plan is the database, and the solutions are sometimes complex. The DBA needs to participate in creating, maintaining, and practicing disaster recovery to be well trained to handle the failover and failback situations.

Some DBAs must also be good at programming to participate in all phases of a development process, including the architecture, design, and development of an application, as well as its administration after the implementation is complete. Design and architecture work means training and experience in normalization and database design. Development participation includes knowing about application connectivity, connectivity constructs with the many different options available today (ADO, DAO, OLE-DB, ODBC, etc), Transact-SQL coding, version control, quality assurance techniques, and more.

The most difficult problem to solve in a high availability design is the database. The DBA is the one who must design, manage, and practice the recovery scenarios.

The Essentials of an Operations Plan

This chapter will not explain operations plans in depth, but since a good plan is critical to any discussion of high availability, it must be one of the first items mentioned. Recent products like Microsoft Operations Framework, coupled with the Microsoft Readiness Framework and the Microsoft Solutions Framework, are more helpful in formulating an operations plan, specifically tailored to IT staff and data centers using the Microsoft family of products. For more information about the Microsoft Operations Framework, documents on the subject of high availability project planning, and details about best practices and detailed project guidelines for disaster recovery and high availability, see http://www.microsoft.com/technet/.

Planning Redundancy

The key to high availability is redundancy. This includes people and processes as well as hardware, software, and data. For example, redundant power supplies are now standard—you should order redundant disk controllers and have at least one extra remote server to failover to. Unfortunately, this duplication of technical pieces increases the cost of uptime solutions.

Beyond hardware considerations, redundancy planning also includes personnel and training issues. What is your plan for when a night operator who calls in sick? Is someone else trained to cover those duties? Or, looking at redundancy from the process and policy point of view, can your sales staff take manual orders when the computer is down? What happens if you do need to fail over to a remote site? Is your plan in place for continuing the business?

For the redundant computers within the same room as the primary servers, here are more things to think about: Can you separate the servers onto a different public power grid? Do you need to do this if you have adequate UPS or generator capacity?

You can create redundant copies of your data in two ways. The first is the asynchronous method, which is sometimes implemented as a store and forward mechanism, and sometimes as a buffering or queuing mechanism. The basic premise is that the data is sent to the primary server and some other mechanism is used to eventually get the same exact data to another server. SQL Server replication and Microsoft Message Queuing use the asynchronous method. The second, or synchronous, method means that the application originally submitting the data must wait until the data is written to a primary server and a secondary server, or even multiple servers, before returning control to the application. Examples of the synchronous method are mirroring in hardware, and two-phase commit in software.

> **Note** Some companies use the word "synchronous" when the product is near real time. Other terms of "low latency" and "high keep-up rate" are near real time and not synchronous.

Segmenting Your Solutions

Redundancy is not the only part of the solution. Segmenting your solutions into different pieces can minimize the impact of downtime by relegating it to a particular section of the company. There are different kinds of segmentation. For example, putting the accounting application on a different server than the order entry server, which could be different than the warehouse server. Or segmentation by business division, where each division has its own server, most likely sharing data through some form of replication. In these scenarios, when one server or division has outages, the other segments are not affected.

Segmentation from a database perspective can mean different things. The first is to segment by usage by having a primary data collection server and a secondary read-only server for reporting. The next is to segment to multiple servers by application, for example, one server for accounting and another for manufacturing. Another way is to segment a very large database (VLDB) and distribute it over multiple servers with one acting as the primary, making it appear as one database through partitioned views.

Be aware that while segmenting your solutions can minimize downtime, it does complicate a disaster recovery plan because you now have to plan redundancy for each segment.

Manual Procedures

Backup plans extend beyond the technical arena. Manual procedures must be in place whenever possible to give some continuity of work in the event of a computer outage. For example, can the company still take orders on paper? This is an important point since every possibility of a computer recovery cannot be considered. At times, companies must fall back to manual procedures for keeping a business running.

Increased Corporate Awareness: The Importance of Communication

Creating redundancy with whatever mechanism you have chosen brings an increased complexity to any organization. Everyone involved, especially the upper levels of management, needs to be aware that with the added complexity comes a responsibility to create a support organization that knows how to deal with the solutions. This means planning larger training budgets, spending more time and money on disaster recovery plans, purchasing redundant hardware, and so on.

High Availability and Mobile and Disconnected Devices

Mobile and disconnected users provide special challenges for planning high availability solutions. Some of the data is stored locally on the device and some is stored centrally in a server. Redundancy can be built on the server side to protect the data, but what about the local data on the device? This is a special problem for corporations to solve. Each device will bring its own challenges. For example, local contact numbers might be stored in a cell phone, or hard disks in a laptop can hold valuable information. So, mobile and disconnected devices must be considered when defining high availability for a corporation.

The Technical Side of High Availability

From a technical point of view, high availability is generally considered in two parts: hardware and software alternatives. The best solution for availability is usually a combination of elements from each of these sections. As mentioned earlier, the key to high availability is redundancy, which is applicable not only to hardware and data, but also to software. Be sure to budget for the extra licensing costs of software copies.

Hardware Alternatives

Three basic problems must be solved in the technical arena for high availability. These are protection against physical hardware failures, logical failures, and failures causing the loss of a data center. Physical hardware failures can be at the component level—disk drives, memory, CPU, network, and so on. The most difficult problem to solve is the loss of an entire data center, so we will concentrate on this problem.

To begin, always do research before you make a hardware investment.

Create standard operational policies about who is authorized to install new hardware or work on a computer; even choose specific times of the day to schedule any hardware work. Always have support contracts for every piece of equipment used in a production environment.

To address the possibility of data center loss, organizations typically will create a remote data center to gain the security of redundancy. The uses of this remote data center add complexity to redundancy design. Most companies realize the data in the remote databases can still be used for important activities, such as read-only reporting. Many availability options, however, require exclusive use of the remote databases to keep them constantly synchronized with the production databases, and this prevents them from using the remote databases for reporting. Companies wanting to use the remote databases for reporting will choose an availability option that leaves the remote databases available for reports, at least during certain times during the day.

Disk Drives

Always buy the fastest hard disk drives. Most drives are measured by revolutions per minute (RPMs), seek time, and latency. The best recommendation for SQL Server is that multiple smaller drives are better than one large one. This goes for the disk arrays too—more smaller arrays are better than one big one. This creates a configuration that allows the distribution of various files onto other drives (including transaction log files, operating system files, database files, and even indexes).

RAID

Striping is the concept of using multiple disk drives to create a single logical disk. For example, your C:\ drive can be an array of multiple physical drives. RAID (redundant array of independent disks) is a technology used for striping disk drives. RAID comes in several different flavors, and special disk controllers are needed to implement them.

RAID 0 is pure striping (with no redundancy). Use this for best performance; it is frequently used, but does not by itself contribute to increased availability and redundancy. A minimum of two physical drives are needed to make one logical RAID 0 device.

RAID 1 is mirroring, meaning that every drive or drive array has another spare drive associated with it. When a block of data is written to the primary drive, the same block is also written to the corresponding mirror drive. Use hardware mirroring because hardware implementations have better performance and stability than software mirroring implementations, such as the software mirroring in Microsoft Windows® 2000.

RAID 2, 3, 4, and 6 are not typically used in the latest database environments.

RAID 5 is striping with parity. For every byte written across a striped set, an extra byte, called the parity byte, is written to another disk. The parity byte is similar to a checksum. RAID 5 takes a minimum of three physical disks to create a striped set. Most RAID 5 systems today are hot-swappable, meaning that while the system is running, one of the drives in the array can be removed and replaced with no interruption of service. RAID 5 is best used in a single server environment whether or not another redundancy solution is being used. RAID 5 is considered the simplest solution to manage and maintain; however, there is a performance penalty to pay by always writing to the parity drive. The bottom line is that larger databases that need the extra speed will opt for RAID 1+0 instead of RAID 5.

RAID 1+0 is a combination of striping (RAID 0) and mirroring (RAID 1). The idea is to have a corresponding mirror array for every primary array. This way you get the performance of striping and the redundancy protection of using mirrored drives. With the new technology, the mirrored set no longer has to be attached to the same server as the original drives. This is called distance mirroring and can be used to get an instantaneous backup of your database. This is one of the best solutions in a high availability scenario because it speeds up your primary goal of getting a redundant copy of your database.

SANS

System Area Networks, or SANs, are disk storage solutions delivered over high-speed networks, usually some type of fiber optic channel. The I/O requests from the applications go through the Windows operating system to the disk drive through network protocols.

For most applications, this is the easiest and most cost effective method of getting a redundant copy of your database. A high availability architecture calls for mirrored SAN drives. This gives you an instantaneous copy of the database in a failover situation, but the second copy of the database must be idle and cannot be used by another copy of SQL Server. This instantaneous copy is called a snapshot backup and is explained later in this chapter.

Some SANs technology is delivered through TCP/IP over regular network speeds. These are not as fast as a dedicated disk channel and are not used where the highest I/O performance is required. SANs are currently used in heterogeneous environments and for storing redundant copies of the database.

Disk Configuration

What does disk configuration have to do with high availability? Using multiple drive arrays gives you different choices for managing file groups, configuring mirrored redundancy, creating secondary servers, and so on. Added flexibility means additional complexity, especially if something goes wrong.

RAID Solutions

Most storage vendors offer high availability solutions. These solutions have redundant copies of everything—hardware, software, and data. A typical solution is two fibre channel–based disk arrays running RAID 1+0 for the largest databases, and a fibre channel–based disk array running RAID 5 for the smaller databases. Each fibre channel node has one hub, duplicate RAID controllers per server, and associated cabling. Each RAID array has two ports used to attach to the two fibre channels.

The RAID 5 solution is less expensive because it only adds one extra drive in the array to get the redundancy. For the RAID 1+0 solution, every drive purchased must have another drive for its mirror, so you are doubling your disk drive costs. Again, the tradeoff of using RAID 5 is slower performance.

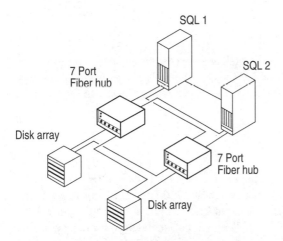

SQL Server with Windows Clustering and duplicate disks.

Full redundancy is added by using two or four node clustering in Windows Clustering, available in Windows 2000, Microsoft Cluster Service (MSCS), available in Windows NT® 4.0,, or by using Windows Network Load Balancing. Each of these is explained later in this chapter. Using this solution, you are protected against the following failures:

- **Server failure.** Clustering will automatically restart the application on another server in the cluster and the next time the users connect, they will be connected to the secondary server. If your applications are smart enough to detect a disconnect and attempt reconnection, the users may never know the primary server was down.

- **Fibre channel hub failure.** When a host adapter, hub, or part of the cabling fails, the Windows NT or Windows 2000 drivers will force all I/O requests to take the alternate path to the other fibre channel.

- **RAID controller failure.** If a controller fails, the MSCS software will detect this and redirect all I/O requests to the duplicate controller.

- **Disk Drive Failure.** The RAID 5 solutions will continue running if one drive fails. And by using hot-swappable drives, the replacement is inserted and automatically resynchronized to be come part of the array again. RAID 1 or RAID 1+0 solutions will fail over to the mirror. When the primary disks are fixed, the mirror is automatically resynchronized.

This configuration provides the best protection against failure from any component on one server, but it does not make a geographically remote copy of your database.

Fiber Distances

With the current technologies, creating geographically remote copies of databases is the fastest using fibre channel technologies. However, there are limits of 500 meters when using shortwave lasers using multimode optical fibers, and up to 10 kilometers using longwave lasers with at least two fabric switches.

Software Alternatives

Two major challenges must be faced to achieve high availability: protecting the servers and getting a redundant copy of the database. This section talks about the required bridge between the two challenges—namely, how to switch to the redundant server. Windows 2000 offers two primary methods for managing a failover, Windows Clustering and Network Load Balancing. These solutions are designed to protect against component, server, or application failure. They are not intended to protect against an entire data center loss, as in a fire.

Windows Clustering and SQL Server 2000 Failover Clustering

The Microsoft clustering solutions are a combination of hardware and software components. In a database environment, all servers share the same set of disk drives, so clustering in its simplest form does not protect against drive failures. The solution for protecting against disk drive failures is to have redundant hard disk sets. Work with your hardware vendor to set up one of the redundant disk solutions, like the duplicate fibre channels and disk sets described earlier.

Windows Clustering is designed to facilitate smooth software and hardware upgrades, because one of the computers in the cluster can be taken offline and upgraded while the others are still active.

For clustering, you will need to buy specific hardware on the Hardware Compatibility List (HCL). To find this list, search under "clusters" at the following Microsoft Web site: http://www.microsoft.com/hcl. It is best to purchase the entire server as a unit—do not substitute components. Work with a preferred vendor for assistance in setting up the clusters.

Decide what your service level expectations are on the secondary servers. Do you need 100 percent of the capacity of the original server after a failover? Perhaps you can have less horsepower and still give a high degree of service to the business users.

Windows 2000 Datacenter Server is designed to scale up with support for up to 32 processors and up to 64 GB of RAM. It is also designed to scale out with N+1 clustering. The Winsock direct support gives technology agnostic connections so you can upgrade to new technologies without having to rewrite applications. Operations management will like the Process Control tool, which takes advantage with the Job Object API. More important than the technology is the support and testing of the Windows 2000 Datacenter. The testing program to get on its HCL is very strict and the entire system is tested, not just the individual components. Part of the testing rules is a seven-day mandatory retest for firmware changes, software patches, and service packs. Joint support teams between Microsoft and the hardware OEM will give joint problem resolution and reproduction labs. Multiple parties will provide new value-added services for change control, on-site support, system evaluation, and so forth.

Advantages

Windows Clustering has a lot of features that make it very attractive for high availability solutions. The first is the flexibility of architecture and design choices, such as Active/Active or Active/Passive (or in a four-node cluster Active/Active/Active/Active or Active/Active/Active/Passive). The Passive computer can be designated as the failover computer for all the active servers. You can even plan for less excess capacity than if each computer were to have its own failover node. And the last node does not really have to be passive. It can be active and still be the designated failover computer for each of the other servers.

Service failures are protected on the primary computer, like SQL Server, SQL Agent, full-text search engine, Windows operating system failures or errors, and server hardware failures. For the database transactions, committed transactions are not lost as partially completed transactions are rolled back after the failover occurs. The typical SQL Server recovery rules apply during the failover. The log is read from the last checkpoint, committed transactions are reapplied, and uncommitted transactions are rolled back.

Clients do not have to know a failover occurred. Applications with retry logic written into them will simply reconnect to the same IP address or network name and will be connected to the new computer in the cluster. Those applications having short timeout settings may get a disconnect message because their request timed out. But, since most failovers can happen in less than one minute, and one minute is the default timeout for most connection APIs, the users may not experience a time-out error. However, recovery time depends upon database recovery times and possibly on network connectivity times to your DNS and/or WINS servers.

Considerations

When using Windows clustering in a SQL Server environment, consider the following:

- The disks are shared between all the computers in a cluster. Therefore, if any of the disk components fail, it does no good to switch to another server in the cluster, because it is using the same disks. The solution for this problem is to use redundant fibre channels and disk drives, as mentioned in the section in this chapter about disk drives.

Database corruption, either within the database (internal corruption) or introduced by the user (logical corruption), is not prevented by Windows Clustering or redundant disks. Logical corruption can be avoided by designing the application so that a user is prevented from corrupting the data.

- If you are using full-text search, you must make sure you have a replicated copy of the search indexes on the other computer in the cluster.

- A database can only be accessed by one SQL Server at a time. So, when a failure occurs on the primary server, the SQL Server on the secondary server is started during the failover process and must be given time to start. If the cause of the failure on the primary server is a corrupted database, then the failover to the secondary computer in the cluster is not going to work.

- In a cluster, the second server may be passive (Active/Passive), or may be used for other functions (Active/Active). If SQL Server is running on the second computer, it must be used by another application and linking to a different database than the primary server. In an Active/Active cluster, if one computer fails, another instance of SQL Server must be installed to manage the database from the primary server.

- Clustering is potentially expensive, especially when servers are separated by distance. The cluster computers must be on the same subnet, so the maximum distance is limited and depends upon your choice of networking components. Clustering can also be expensive in terms of the amount of increased knowledge the administrators must have to support the environment. The Active/Passive environments are easier to administer, but the Active/Active environments take a while to learn, and you should practice the administration taskscomputerTherefore, there is an additional cost of providing a lab setup similar to the production environment.

- You need to think about the software development, quality assurance, and staging environments. Perhaps the development SQL Servers do not need to be clustered, but in order for the quality assurance team to certify the application as ready for production, they must have a duplicate of the production environment. And the staging servers are almost always a duplicate of the production environment. So, when you are planning a clustering environment, you need to think about all the servers involved.

Cluster Option 1 – Shared Disk Backup

This is the easiest configuration supported in SQL Server 2000 and SQL Server version 7.0. In the illustration below, SQL Server is installed on each node in the cluster. Each node also has its own disk drives for its own databases. The shared disk is used for database backup files only. When a server in the cluster fails, SQL Server is started on another node and the backup copy of the database is used on the shared drive. This solution is better in SQL Server 2000 as another instance of SQL Server can be prepared on the other cluster nodes specifically for this purpose.

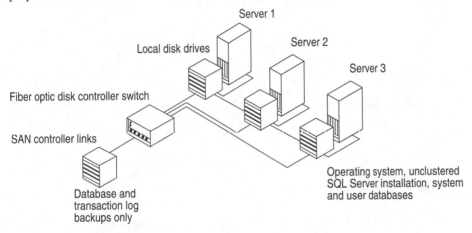

Cluster Option 2 – Snapshot Backup

A new feature of SQL Server 2000, snapshot backup is actually a hardware-assisted backup. The illustration below shows how this is implemented using mirrored disk volumes. When a backup is requested, writes on that server are suspended until the mirror is broken (usually a matter of milliseconds). Another copy of SQL Server on another server is started, linking to the previously mirrored disk drives. The second copy of the database can now be used for reporting, data base consistency checker (DBCC), volume testing, and/or backup to tape. At some later point, the drives are reattached to create a mirror again. The mirror gets synchronized again over a period of time, and the backup process can start over again.

As stated earlier, redundancy is the key. What happens if the server fails while the snapshot is occurring? Most companies choose to install two mirror sets to solve this problem. This way, an active hardware mirror is always on the server while the second mirror is involved in the snapshot backup.

Full and file backups are supported, but differential backups are not. The hardware vendors provide the hardware and software components to control this type of backup. The typical SQL Server backup and restore commands are not used.

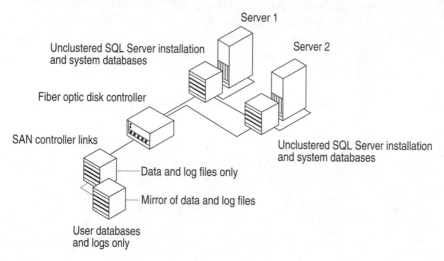

Option 3 – Failover Clustering

SQL Server 2000 is aware of clusters and SQL Server Setup automates the installation and configuration on all nodes in a cluster. Failover cluster nodes can now be easily added and removed and operating system upgrades can be upgraded without affecting the remaining nodes in the cluster. To accomplish this, all user and system databases are created on shared disk drives. See the illustration below to view a sample configuration.

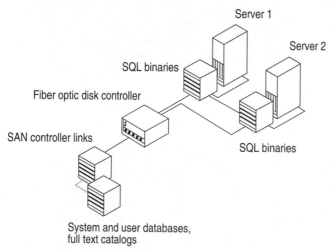

This option costs approximately 2.5 times that of a two node active/passive configuration. SQL Server upgrades will still require minimal downtime.

Detail Configuration Showing Database Placement

The illustration below shows where to place the different SQL Server databases in any of the above configurations.

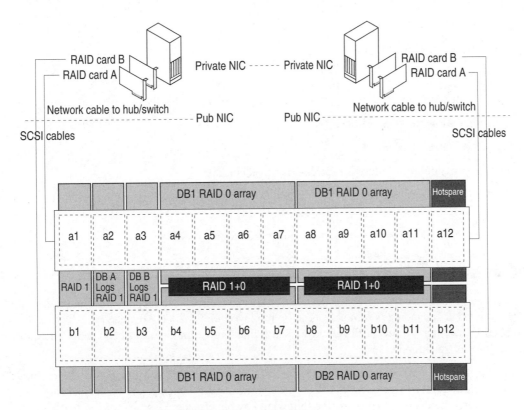

Windows 2000 / SQL Server 2000 Detail Clustering Solution

In this diagram you see the log disk for Server A, the log disk for Server B, the database disk for Server A, and the database disk for Server B across both RAID controllers and both RAID chassis.

By doing this you get the advantage of utilizing the bandwidth of the SCSI channels to their fullest extent, as well as having true redundancy for your hardware. This would work best if you have redundant processors, power supplies, and network interface cards (NICs). This is also assuming that the operating system is located on a RAID 1 set of drives housed within the server chassis, not the external disk storage chassis. Another set of RAID 1 mirrored disks can be installed in the chassis to hold the page file for Windows 2000. Both of these RAID Arrays can be driven from one of the RAID cards. These cards typically support two or three SCSI channels, so you should have a few extra SCSI channels left over.

The CD-ROM drive and the tape backup drive would be connected to a standard SCSI interface, not the RAID controllers. These are usually built into the motherboard of the server.

Many configurations start out with a single external chassis with several disk drives (12 total) as follows:

- 2 drives for Windows NT 4.0 and Windows 2000 (RAID 1)

- 2 drives for logs from database A (RAID 1)

- 2 drives for logs from database B (RAID 1)

- 3 drives for database A (RAID 5)

- 3 drives for database B (RAID 5)

- 0 drive for hot spare

This is a typical configuration, but one that in fact is not recommended, for the following reasons:

- Too much contention on the SCSI bus.

- Too much disk I/O contention.

- It becomes a single point of failure for the external disk chassis.

Make sure that database server performance is adequate when considering disk queuing and disk I/O contention.

Instead, configure the disk layout as shown in the illustration above.

Network Load Balancing

The Network Load Balancing technology is designed to spread the load between the different nodes of a cluster. Network Load Balancing is available as an option in Windows 2000 Advanced Server and Windows 2000 Datacenter Server. With Network Load Balancing, administrators can simply add another server to the node as traffic increases.

Network Load Balancing services TCP/IP services such as Web, Terminal Services, proxy, streaming media services, and virtual private networks (VPN). Network Load Balancing services in a cluster communicate among themselves to provide the following key benefits:

- **High availability:** A server failure is automatically detected by Network Load Balancing and traffic is routed among the remaining servers in the cluster within 10 seconds. However, any databases on the failed server are not immediately available to a SQL Server installation on the other servers. One of the remaining servers must start SQL Server to connect to the database.

- **Scalability:** Client requests are distributed across all servers in a cluster.

Network Load Balancing is used primarily as a performance enhancement to spread the requests between servers. One key point using Network Load Balancing is that it is only used in a non-clustered environment.

Network Load Balancing gives a virtual IP address for the multiple servers, allowing a potential failover. Like clustering, Network Load Balancing servers must be in the same subnet, which limits the geographic distance between the servers.

Network Load Balancing must be set up in a dual-NIC environment to work properly. The primary NIC is for Network Load Balancing, and the secondary NIC is for SQL Server on both computers to do the log shipping. Network Load Balancing is also good for load balancing on reporting databases. In this case, the dual-NIC setup is not required. In either scenario, the secondary NIC can boost overall network throughput.

Only the primary server is enabled for clients to log connect to. The failover is not instantaneous, especially if the clients do not have retry logic. OLE DB or ODBC clients without specifically written retry logic will have to be stopped and restarted to connect to the failover server. Microsoft Internet Information Services (IIS) is an example of a program that has built-in retry logic.

Here are some configuration tips to get this scenario to work. Network Load Balancing must be installed on only one NIC. TCP/IP should be the only protocol in existence for this adapter. Network Load Balancing and port rules must be identical on all the NIC cards, but the host parameters must be unique for each server. All port rules must be set for all ports used by the application. In this case, SQL Server is the application, and since its normal port is 1433, it must have a port rule of "1433 to 1433". Both a dedicated IP address and the virtual IP address must be entered, and the dedicated IP address must be listed first. Both IP addresses must be static, and Dynamic Host Configuration Protocol (DHCP) cannot be used.

In sum, you can use Network Load Balancing instead of clustering to provide failover capabilities in case of a server or component failure. Network Load Balancing has no provision for getting a redundant copy of the database to the other server, so another method, like log shipping or replication, must be used.

For more information on Network Load Balancing, see http://www.microsoft.com/windows2000/.

SQL Server Alternatives

This section discusses specific high availability solutions for SQL Server, and is written for DBAs and others who need to support the SQL Server portion of a data center. Up to this point we have discussed the best server protection methods with hardware redundancy, disk drive configurations, and managing the failover process with clustering or Network Load Balancing. The final step is to discuss methods of getting database copies to other servers.

Database Maintenance and Availability

Database systems need special attention from time to time. Although some of the new features in SQL Server 2000, such as online analysis and index maintenance, will help to diminish this need, a good operations plan will account for a certain amount of database maintenance.

Here is a list of maintenance tasks that need to be done occasionally, and that will either require some downtime or have some negative impact on performance:

- Rebuilding the index
- Running the DBCC
- Performing fragmentation analysis

For more information about the various features in SQL Server 2000 designed to minimize downtime, see SQL Server Books Online.

Backup and Restore

The most basic way to create a redundant copy of your server is to use the backup and restore solutions available through SQL Server and other backup software programs. The flexibility of the SQL Server backup solutions—including (but not limited to) full backups, filegroup backups, striped backups, differential backups, and transaction log backups—gives a solution for everyone.

One fundamental recommendation is to do SQL Server backups to disk, hopefully to a different disk drive/array than your database is residing on. Then, using another Windows backup program, copy the database backup files to tape.

More complex solutions may be preferable, as your database gets larger and larger. These solutions include striped backups and snapshot backups (both described earlier in this chapter, in "Hardware Alternatives").

Still greater complexity is added when your application has other dependent databases that need to also have synchronized backups and restores. This can happen, for example, between an order entry database, a warehouse database, and an accounting database. You cannot restore one without getting out of sync with the others. Additionally, adding replication to this scenario can introduce a cross-database dependency that will not occur with non-replicated deployments. The Publisher and Distributor databases should have synchronized backups. A new option in transactional replication in SQL Server 2000, **sync with backup**, ensures that the Log Reader Agent will not propagate any transactions to the distribution database that have not been backed up at the Publisher. For more information, see "Strategies for Backing Up and Restoring Transactional Replication" in SQL Server Books Online.

Finally, be aware that if you are using Active Directory™ as an additional data store, and you must restore to an older copy of the database, you will probably be out-of-sync with the Active Directory. So, make sure you consider this in your planning stages.

Another option is distance mirroring, which allows you to do almost instantaneous snapshot backups. This is where the data is collected with hardware mirroring and the mirrored disks actually exist in another location, attached to another server. Refer to the snapshot backup discussion earlier in this chapter in the hardware section. To perform a snapshot backup, the mirror link is disconnected from the primary server, a backup is taken from the mirrored files, and then the mirror link is reconnected. And to protect against failures during the time the mirror link is disconnected, a third set of disks is employed as another mirror. This way, the primary system always has at least one active mirror. For more information about this feature, see SQL Server Books Online.

Two-Phase Commit

Two-phase commit (2PC) is a term that describes a synchronous transaction: An application starts a distributed transaction, writes to the primary database, writes to the remote database, then commits both writes. If either part fails, the entire transaction fails. Using 2PC for creating a remote copy of a database is considered a form of front-end replication.

This is not recommended for most people, but the only 100 percent guarantee you have when designing a redundant database is to use 2PC. The only possible loss is the active transaction, which to most applications is an acceptable loss.

There are various ways to do a distributed transaction. The first is from the application, where the front-end program (or the ASP code in a web application) controls the links to both computers and controls the transaction. The second is for a middle-tier object to write to the different databases, in which case the transaction can be either explicitly controlled by the application or implicitly controlled using COM+ and Component Services, available in Windows 2000, in conjunction with the Microsoft Distributed Transaction Coordinator (MS DTC). The third way is to write to a single database and have a trigger send the data to another server. A fourth method is to use any of the forms of SQL Server replication that can employ 2PC. A fifth method is to use transacted message queues in the Microsoft Message Queuing (also known as MSMQ) product.

There can be more than one computer to handle the redundancy. You can send to a primary server, a redundant/backup server, and perhaps a reporting server, or as many other servers as you need. The performance of each transaction slows down with each server added.

Another potential problem with this method is that all computers maintaining copies of the data must be well connected at the time any INSERT, UPDATE, or DELETE operation occurs. If any of the computers participating in the distributed transaction are not connected, the transaction fails.

Replication

Replication is another option for many high availability solutions. Replication is extremely flexible, and offers multiple solutions that can be combined into many different scenarios. The following table shows different replication applications and their relative autonomy and connectivity requirements.

Replication Choices

Merge	Queued Updating Subscriber	Transaction Publish & Subscribe	Immediate Updating Subscriber	Microsoft Transaction Server
All databases can be updated	Subscriber queues transactions to be applied to Publisher at later time	Store and forward	One Subscriber updates Publisher. Other Subscribers are via transaction replication	Two-phase commit for all transactions
Full autonomy, low connectivity requirements	Full autonomy, low connectivity requirements	Full consistency, but with latency	Connections required during updates	Full consistency but little autonomy

Scenario 1: Reporting. If you intend to use your redundant copy of your database for reporting, then replication is your best bet since people can be running reports against the subscription database while replication is occurring. Most of the other solutions need exclusive access to the redundant copy/copies of your database, thereby locking out anyone wishing to do read-only reporting or other work. Consider the use of transactional replication when setting up a redundant copy of your database for reporting purposes. Transactional replication is well suited to deployments requiring read-only copies of data and can generally achieve replication of incremental changes with very low latency.

Scenario 2: Mobile users. Replication is a very strong solution for mobile/disconnected users. Use merge replication when providing mobile users the autonomy to make updates while offline is imperative. This solution automatically tracks changes to data on a laptop and merges it with the main database when the users are again connected to the network. So, disconnected users have a highly available application without being directly connected to the network.

Scenario 3: SQL farms. Although a slightly different concept than a Web farm using Network Load Balancing, a SQL farm is made possible by replicating the read-only (or low volatile) data from the primary database to database servers specifically assigned to certain IIS or middle-tier servers. In this scenario there is still usually one central data collection database and multiple read-only databases for lookup tables and other non-volatile or low-volatile data. Using transactional replication in this scenario will assist in giving higher availability to the Web application, but does not directly address the issue of getting geographically remote copies of your transactional data. This scenario is one form of scale-out architecture designed to improve aggregate read performance and to keep the volume on the central Publisher lower. In the illustration below, three Web servers work with one SQL Server to do all the data collection and modification. The read-only SQL Server on the left supports one Web server and the read-only SQL Server on the right supports two Web servers. This is just a sample layout showing one possible scenario. Of course, you will want to set up the read-only SQL Servers with Network Load Balancing so if one server fails, the other will take over.

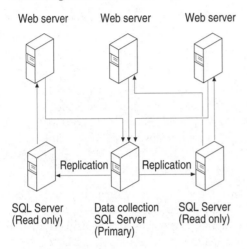

SQL Farm

Scenario 4: Many Publishers, centralized Subscriber. Autonomous divisions who need to do their own data collection and eventually copy it to a corporate office or to share with other divisions will use some form of replication. If one division experiences problems, the others are not affected, giving a slightly different view of high availability. This is sometimes called the roll-up scenario.

Scenario 5: Standby servers with replication. Creating a standby server with a redundant copy of the data could be done with replication, although there might be better solutions, like failover clustering or distance mirroring depending on your needs. Replication does not replicate code changes (views, triggers, and so on), security changes, **msdb** changes, or job changes (**msdb**). These and other issues are solvable problems if you want to use replication, but other solutions are easier for creating geographically remote copies of your server.

As with other forms of creating redundancy, when using replication, administrative overhead increases as soon as you make a copy of the data. Companies implementing replication should prepare to support the additional complexity. This usually means additional budget allocations for training, additional expenditures in personnel, cost and time to add to the disaster recovery plan, as well as additional time for each recovery practice session.

Be aware of some additional technical concerns with certain replication scenarios. For example, upgrading 100 Subscribers to the next version of SQL Server is a manually intensive process, even with the improvements in remote installation and upgrade options. The issue for high availability solutions using replication is the same for any asynchronous (store and forward) solution. In the worst-case scenario where the publication and the distribution servers are lost at the same time, transaction data could be lost. This is one reason for the recommendation to write your disaster recovery plan before installing replication and to include in that plan the possible loss of servers involved in replication.

Latency may not be a big problem for some applications using replication, but a large queue or store of waiting transactions can develop if the network is down. Or if a very large transaction is done, such as an update of 50,000 rows to fix a data problem, the replication transaction queue will grow until this abnormal transaction is complete, causing abnormal latency.

SQL Server replication offers both synchronous and asynchronous solutions. This is the most basic question to be answered when designing a copy of a database. Transactional replication is an asynchronous solution, using the store-and-forward methodology, where the potential loss of data comes when transactions are waiting to be distributed when a disaster occurs. Transactional replication with immediate updating allows synchronous updates to be made at Subscribers, using a 2PC method, where the only potential loss in an update made at the Subscriber is the current transaction

Merge replication is a low-cost way of having two synchronized, geographically separate servers. New features in SQL Server 2000 merge replication have made this type of replication easier to install and support. It can be more complex because of the need to learn about conflict resolution. And once again, you need to upgrade your disaster recovery plan before implementing merge replication. The best recommendation when considering merge replication is to include sufficient time for additional quality assurance tests.

The companies that have the best chance to succeed with replication will have:

- Increased the awareness of the difficulty of distribution to the highest levels of management.
- Written the additions to their disaster recovery plans before implementing replication.
- Increased the training budget for DBAs and operations/support staff.

Replication: Immediate Updating with Queued Updating as a Failover

The option immediate updating with queued updating as a failover can be used in transactional replication to synchronize the updates between a remote Subscriber and the Publisher. Immediate updating is where a 2PC transaction is done and both the Subscriber and Publisher are always synchronized. Using queued updating as a failover allows updates to continue at the Subscriber even if network connectivity between Publisher and Subscriber is lost.

Immediate updating typically requires a reliable connection because 2PC is the primary controller for the transaction on the Subscriber. Queued updating as a failover can be set to use SQL Server queues or Message Queuing to provide the ability to queue data modifications made at the Subscriber. The record modifications are saved in a local message queue and transmitted to the primary publishing server when the network is available again. Subscribers other than the originating one will receive the updates through the normal latent distribution method.

Applications must be made aware of a new error message that arises when a row version has been changed at the Publisher by another session. The error handling for this situation should be written to get the latest changes from the Publisher, and then have the user attempt the update again. For more information about immediate updating with queued updating as a failover, see SQL Server Books Online.

Log Shipping

Log shipping is another solution for creating redundant copies of databases on other servers. The basic premise is that the transaction logs are backed up on your primary server, copied across to another server, and restored. This is done using regular SQL Server backup and restore commands, with additional tables and stored procedures for tracking and administering the process.

In SQL Server 2000, log shipping is very robust due to new technology improvements in the backup/recovery features as well as the new recovery models. It is even incorporated into the Database Maintenance Plan Wizard for easy setup. The other improvements include easier administration through the Monitor features to track status, SQL Server Enterprise Manager additions to get to any server, and the ability to set up flexible actions and alerts. Additional features for flexible choices are the different frequencies for backup, copy, and restore—they do not have to be the same.

Log shipping for high availability solutions is attractive because it is inexpensive for most applications and is relatively easy to administer. This is the lowest cost method of creating remote databases. The basic problem of using log shipping is that your recoverability is only as good as your last backup. For example, if you are doing log shipping once per minute, how many potential transactions will you lose if you cannot recover that one last minute before a failover occurred? The second problem is that it needs exclusive use of the secondary database to do a restore.

If the time between restores is long enough, you can do DBCC commands to check the consistency of the database, and you can then do full backups of the data. Doing this removes these burdens from the primary server.

Log shipping may not be the best solution because it is a slower failover process than with Windows Clustering. The failover and recovery process on the second server may involve some manual processes. There are definitely manual processes if you need to get the last transaction log from the primary server. Most of the steps can be automated, but an administrator will want to run through a predefined checklist to validate the second server before allowing clients to access it.

Another problem with log shipping is that the full-text search will fail when the primary system fails. Another copy of the search indexes must be on the second server. As soon as the search service is restarted on the second computer, clients can use it again. This can be automated, but be aware that this is not an instantaneous failover.

Log shipping without Network Load Balancing means that the clients must either manually reconnect, or have connection retry logic built into the application.

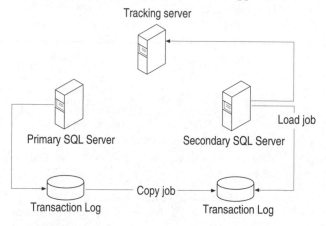

Log Shipping

Log shipping can be used together with replication, clustering, and hardware solutions to provide the ultimate in architecture and design choices. For more information about log shipping, see Chapter 13, "Log Shipping."

Message Queuing

Message Queuing (also known as MSMQ) actually has several intriguing reasons for consideration in architecting high availability solutions, especially using MSMQ version 3.0. It can exist as a guaranteed transport mechanism between the client computers and the database, it can exist between a middle tier layer and the database, or it can exist behind the database layer in a specific replication scenario. In any case, the primary reason for using it in high availability designs is to get a redundant copy of the database.

The basic premise switches from having a service like replication or log shipping create a redundant copy of the database after the initial write has been done, to having a service, like Message Queuing, that captures the input and sends it to two different servers.

Any time a message comes into the queue, there can be multiple Subscribers targeted to accept those messages. Using Message Queuing in the client layer, one Subscriber can be the primary database, and the other Subscribers can be your failover database or databases.

Message Queuing is primarily a store-and-forward strategy, similar to some forms of SQL Server replication. The latest version of Message Queuing has many features that make it an attractive consideration for creating a redundant copy of your data. For example, Message Queuing allows primary and backup queues. If the primary computer is lost, a failover occurs to a backup controller, with no loss of data.

The best solution for using Message Queuing in a high availability environment is to put the Primary Enterprise Controller (PEC) on a clustered computer and the Backup Site Controller (BSC) on another clustered computer in a remote location, and a very big pipeline connecting the two.

The downside is that applications must be written to use Message Queuing. This is not a solution for buying an off-the-shelf application, like an accounting system, and adding message queues to help solve your uptime problem. It takes design and development work to employ the Message Queuing technology.

Combining SQL Server Solutions

The above alternatives are meant to give you an overview of the different features of SQL Server and their strengths and weaknesses when used individually. This section combines different strategies, each solving the others weaknesses. Even in these combined solutions, remember that the first priority is to focus on the people, policies, and processes involved in your high availability solution.

All of these combined solutions assume that you are doing enough hardware protection on each database server, usually through RAID and/or fibre channel redundancy, as well as the usual redundant power supplies, disk controllers, and so on. This will protect you from a loss of individual components within a system or cluster.

There are several challenges to be solved. The first is to get a redundant copy of a database to at least one remote server, even if that database is always idle. The other is to get a read-only copy of the database to a remote server to remove reporting burdens from the primary server. What does creating a reporting server have to do with high availability? By shifting the reporting burden to a secondary server, it makes the primary server more available due to less locking conflicts.

The following is a step-by-step approach to designing a solution that will give your company the right mix of recoverability, failover, and reporting databases.

1. **Protect the individual components.**

   Solution: Hardware redundancy is the key. Purchase dual items of everything, from NIC cards to power supplies and disk drive sets. Every component must be duplicated.

2. **Protect the server.**

   Solution: Use failover clustering or Network Load Balancing. Different companies will assess the pros and cons of these methods differently, according to their particular applications.

3. **Create an idle copy of the database.**

   Solution: Backup and restore, replication, log shipping (per minute), Message Queuing, and hardware mirroring can be used.

4. **Create a read-only copy of the database (if needed).**

   Solution: Replication, log shipping (daily), and hardware mirroring.

Server Clusters, Hardware Mirroring, and Replication

Use server clusters, with all the redundant hardware, to give the ultimate protection for your primary server. Then, use hardware mirroring to make the failover copy of your database. And use replication to create a read-only reporting server. This is probably the best combination of all the technologies for the companies who can afford all the hardware and licenses, and who can afford the best-trained administrators.

Using this configuration assumes that there is one primary cluster for the database server and two secondary servers, one local and one geographically remote. This solution also assumes that a reporting server is required with 24 x 7 read-only access.

This solution protects against both logical and physical failures. Failover clustering is a good enterprise solution as long as the hardware in a cluster is in close physical proximity. And clustering solutions, combined with mirroring and dual fibre channel disk managers, offer a very good choice for instantaneous database failover. As discussed above in the clustering section of this chapter, it does not provide for a geographically remote failover server. Replication or periodic log shipping is good for that solution.

Log Shipping with Network Load Balancing

Network Load Balancing in conjunction with log shipping can be a good substitute for clustering. For a failover to be successful, there must be a current database on the other server. Log shipping will give you that other copy.

When Network Load Balancing and log shipping are used together, both servers are set to inactive at startup. The primary node is manually started. When Network Load Balancing is used for read-only reporting SQL Servers, all servers can be set in auto-start mode. In dual homed configurations, the NICs must be non-routable to each other. And although direct IP communication can be achieved, the preferred method is to use a WINS server entry, with LMHosts being another preferred alternative.

Here is a sample failure scenario and one possible recovery process. This is just a sample process and should be tailored for each application. As you can see, this is not an instantaneous failover.

1. Something happens to the primary server.

2. Attempt to recover the transaction log on the failed server. If it is accessible, copy it to the secondary server and do a final restore. This puts the secondary database in the latest state with no loss of transactions.

3. Start SQL Server on the secondary server and take the database out of standby mode.

4. Start Network Load Balancing on the secondary server allowing clients to log back on.

Variations to Account for Different Scenarios

The solutions above do not necessarily cover all environments. Other considerations can be made for different scenarios, especially if your systems are set up for the highest performance.

- **Scenario 1: VLDB with high number of active connections**

  Companies in this scenario like to have 24 x 7 coverage with very high availability requirements, usually five nines (99.999 percent), leaving only five minutes of outages allowed per year. The solution described here assumes the following for the largest database:

  One primary database for data collection, segmented over X number of databases on Y number of servers. Each server is a two node cluster (minimum), and each database is replicated to a standby server using SQL Server replication as the delivery mechanism.

  There is also one reporting server for read-only access, segmented over X number of databases on Y number of servers. This reporting server can be a data warehouse with or without the additional OLAP storage.

  The idea of segmenting your data collection servers into X number of databases (on the same server) is for increased performance and easier administration. Large databases are difficult to administer as they have long backup times, long DBCC times, and long index rebuild times. If you can split your application into multiple databases, it is easy to administer. The increased performance is achieved by putting the different databases in different file groups on different disk arrays. You can also split tables and indexes over different file groups and different disk arrays within the same database.

  If the databases are still too big for one computer to handle, SQL Server 2000 gives the option of spreading the database over Y number of servers. The added performance comes with additional administrative challenges by having to coordinate backups. This coordination may be minimized or avoided by architecting the split so one transaction never crosses a server boundary.

- **Scenario 1a: Very Large Database (VLDB) with high number of active connections**

  Instead of using replication to get a redundant copy of the database, use the new snapshot backup option. This was discussed before in an earlier section. And to solve the potential exposure problem of a disaster occurring while the mirror is broken, add a second mirror. This way, you always have a mirrored copy of the data on the primary server.

- **Scenario 2: Typical Web scenario**

  In this Web site scenario, everything is duplicated. Networks, SQL Server computers, and SMTP computers are all duplicated. Even the SQL Server disk arrays are duplicated, as are the fibre channel controllers for those disks.

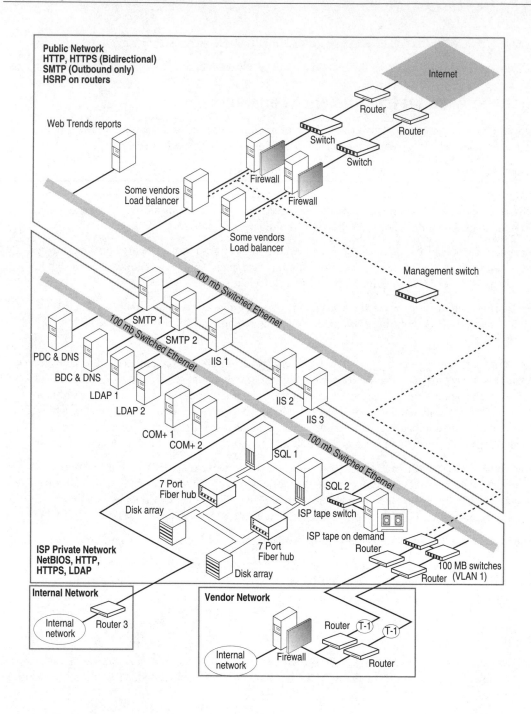

- **Scenario 3: Typical small/medium company (or department server)**

  The companies in this scenario will most like have a single server, with some form of RAID protection, usually RAID 5. The backup/restore strategy is the primary means of disaster recovery. In this scenario, off-site tape rotation is critical. Companies with this design most likely have another server that could be used as a spare, but it may not be configured for that use until a problem occurs. The requirements are usually for 8 x 5 or 12 x 5 instead of 24 x 7, giving plenty of opportunities for planned maintenance.

Conclusion

Achieving high availability is mostly accomplished by setting and following the best practices for your environment. This is achieved though the use of proper policies and procedures, as well as choosing the best redundancy option for your hardware, software, and application. Distributed data through log shipping is best when a geographically remote server is available that is not used for other usage. Distributed data through replication is best when your remote server needs to be accessed for reporting, analysis, and/or data entry. Hardware redundancy is required to give the best protection for a server in a specific location.

Five Nines: The Ultimate in High Availability

Achieving true 24 x 7 uptime (100 percent of the time) is virtually impossible, if for no other reason than that at certain times, an upgrade such as a service pack must be applied to a production server. This is where the concept of "nines" comes into play. The percentage of uptime all companies should strive for is some variation of 99.*x* percent, where *x* is a specified number of nines. Five nines is 99.999 percent uptime for your systems, which, to many, is considered to be the ultimate in availability. This may be difficult to achieve, since it means only about five total minutes of downtime in a calendar year. Three nines is a more practical number to shoot for. Three nines is just short of nine hours of downtime per year—a very respectable number for any production environment.

Creating redundancy for your databases and servers can help you get to five nines. If, for example, you use your production system only for production, and you perform database backups, health checks, and other tasks on other servers that have copies of the same data, your chances of getting to 99.999 percent uptime increase.

Keep in mind, however, that not all downtime is planned. You may encounter a disk controller failure, a power failure, or memory leaks in the application causing a failure. These events need to be taken into account when you develop a disaster recovery plan. Such a plan will mitigate the risk of a failure.

Mitigating the risk and the chance of an unplanned failure is the ultimate goal. In this chapter, you will learn more about the process of creating a highly available system, with a corresponding disaster recovery plan to protect from the worst-case scenario.

Determine Your Desired Level of Nines

There are 8,760 hours in a year (24 hours a day x 365 days a year). It is not uncommon for a business like an e-commerce Web site to schedule one night per month for a few hours of planned system maintenance. If eight hours a month are scheduled as planned downtime, that is 96 hours over the course of a year, which means that the company would have 98.9 percent uptime (or only one nine). If the maintenance window can be brought to two hours per month by doing such things having servers dedicated to checking database health and testing and timing upgrades, this might allow the company to reduce downtime to two hours per month, yielding an uptime percentage of 99.7. These examples demonstrate how difficult it is to achieve more than two nines, even with minimal planned downtime.

So how many nines can your organization realistically pursue? If you can make an educated guess as to the number of total hours down (planned and unplanned) you are likely to have, you can use these formulas (depending on whether you want to calculate your uptime for a year, a month, or a week):

```
% Uptime/year = (8760 - number of total hours down per year)/8760

% Uptime/month = ((24 * number of days in the month) - number of total hours down in
that calendar month)/(24 * number of days in the month)

% Uptime/week = (168 - number of total hours down in that week)/168
```

Achieving High Availability with SQL Server 2000

To achieve high availability, you must be aware of the various components involved and how they are used together to deliver best results.

Application Design

Before buying redundant hardware and coming up with failover and failback scenarios, consider the application itself—it is why you are striving for five nines in the first place, so it should really drive how you design your high availability solution. What is the architecture of the application? Does it lend itself to working in a high availability solution? Does it already have problems that may be magnified with a more complex hardware and/or software solution? Hardware or other software solutions (such as load 7balancer or disk mirroring tools) should not be used to solve problems with an application design.

Another issue to consider is data access (whether the access is needed by the application, a user, or a Web server). How is the database designed—does it sit all on one server, or is it partitioned over multiple servers? Any type of partitioned or distributed data, or the use of distributed partition views to create federated servers, complicates a five nines picture. An example of a federated server in a high availability solution will appear later in this chapter.

There are many other application design issues to consider as you try to achieve high availability. Here are some recommendations:

- Avoid anything that would cause blocking, especially in **tempdb** or system tables, since these conditions may cause long running transactions and, if left unattended, can potentially bring your SQL Server down.

- Do not hardcode server names, instance names, and IP addresses into the application. Instead, allow the connection to be made through a COM+ object, giving you not only a more flexible application, but also a more flexible disaster recovery plan.

- Since Microsoft® SQL Server™ 2000 can support collations at a more granular level, and not just at the server level, make sure the backup database plan takes into account the proper collation.

- If extended stored procedures are used, make sure the design is sound and will not accidentally consume additional system resources.

- If the application requires batch, scheduled, or other jobs run at various times—mainly in off hours—make sure that they will not interfere with other applications that may be part of the disaster recovery plan.

- Do not use the system or sample databases for the creation of application objects.

- When coding custom error messages, if the backup/failover server is going to host another application or database, make sure that one does not conflict with the other.

- Make sure application users are unique to prevent potential conflicts, because when certain high availability solutions may be implemented, conflicts may occur if two applications share the same username with different rights and responsibilities.

- Use integrated security. If special cases arise where other users would need access to the application (such as UNIX or Macintosh users), create logic in the COM layer to handle it. Using the standard SQL Server system administrator (SA) account in the application and its related tasks, packages, scripts, and so on, is not recommended.

- Do not code for a specific service pack or release level. If the backup scenario requires one server to host more than one application, and if the application is not compatible with a certain service pack, it will not be a highly available application.

- If you require that the backend servers be transparent to the client, and no client configuration can be done, that fact will dictate which technology or technologies can be used (such as clustering or log shipping). This type of consideration should be done at the design stage.

- Use Microsoft Message Queuing (also known as MSMQ) as a component in an application. It can sit between the application and database to store and forward transactions to one or more SQL Servers.

- Use XML to take advantage of a Web application and store the state of a transaction. SQL Server 2000 has built-in XML support. XML is an important part of Microsoft's .NET strategy.

- Use Component Services, available in Microsoft Windows® 2000, in conjunction with a COM+ object to achieve a two phase commit. Remember, however, that two phase commits may affect performance.

Underlying Hardware and Software

After ensuring the application will support a high availability solution, you can focus on the underlying technology, both from a hardware and software perspective.

Choosing the Right High Availability Technology for Your Environment

One of the toughest decisions is to choose which method of achieving high availability is the right one for your environment. Cost is often a factor.

The Options

The combination of SQL Server 2000 and your operating system can deliver a number of technologies designed to improve your availability solution. These technology options include:

- Failover clustering (SQL Server 2000 Enterprise Edition only)

- Log shipping (SQL Server 2000 Enterprise Edition only)

- Replication

- Backup and recovery

- Network Load Balancing (Windows® 2000 Advanced Server and Windows 2000 Datacenter Server)

Failover Clustering

Failover clustering is the most common way to create a highly available system. SQL Server 2000 failover clustering is built on top of industry standard hardware and software technologies and Microsoft Windows Clustering, available in Windows 2000 Advanced Server or Windows 2000 Datacenter Server , or Microsoft Cluster Services (MSCS), available in Windows NT® 4.0 Enterprise Edition. It allows up to four servers (with Windows 2000 Datacenter Server), or nodes, to be linked together through a private network and shared disk array to allow services such as a SQL Server instance to fail over from one server node to another in the event of a failure at the node of the owner, whether that failure is due to hardware or software. Failover clustering protects from logical and physical failures, but does not protect from denial of service attacks, corrupt data, or flawed software installations.

To an end user, application, Web server, or middle tier component such as Component Services, the connection would be broken in a failover, but a reconnect is all that is needed to reconnect once the failover is complete. This is one of the strengths of this technology—the failover is virtually transparent to users accessing the database. There may be a short loss of transactions in flux during the failover, but any committed transactions will be applied in the failover process. However, the servers must be located near each other physically unless hardware-assisted clustering is used.

For detailed information on SQL Server 2000 failover clustering, see Chapter 12, "Failover Clustering."

Log Shipping

Another popular and common option for creating a high availability solution is SQL Server 2000 log shipping. This is a method in which a warm standby server is created from an initial backup and restore from a primary server. After that, subsequent transaction logs are backed up, "shipped," and applied to this warm standby server. This creates a server that is only a small delta of time out of sync with the primary server. Like failover clustering, it can protect from logical and physical failures, but does not protect against things like viruses and logical data corruption. Although log shipping and failover clustering are similar, they differ in many ways. For a direct comparison of the two options, see the next section in this chapter.

Log shipping is basically a manual failover—an operator must initiate it, and transactions on the primary server may not be able to be applied before bringing the warm standby online. End users will potentially have to reconfigure their clients to talk to a new server to get to their data, or middle-tier application servers or applications must be redirected to the new database. The hardest part of the log shipping is the failback process to use the primary server again. Log shipping is easy to implement and administer, and does not saturate a network or server, making it an attractive option.

For detailed information on SQL Server 2000 log shipping, see Chapter 13, "Log Shipping."

Replication

Replication is a feature in all versions of SQL Server, although it is not specifically designed as a high availability solution like log shipping and failover clustering. It can create redundancy for data by creating duplicates of production databases, but a method would have to be devised to point an application, client, or Web server to the SQL Server, much like in log shipping. Moreover, there is a greater amount of administrative overhead and complexity involved in setting up and maintaining replication, especially if subscribers are allowed to update data. Using read-only replication options such as snapshot and transactional replication produces a better high availability solution.

Managing a large number of subscribers takes planning. If the version of SQL Server needs to be upgraded with a service pack, under most circumstances, upgrade the distributor first, then the publisher, and finally the subscribers. In some cases, you may need to roll all out at the same time, if the underlying application requires the upgrade. Certain replication methods may require making sure schema and security changes make it to the subscribers.

Another consideration for using replication as part of a high availability solution involves the size of the data being pushed out over the network. With log shipping, the size of the files should be relatively small, but replication may generate more traffic on your network. Finally, if the Distributor server goes down prior to an update, transactions may potentially be lost, which is not really an issue with another method—failover clustering—since all transactions in flux are rolled forward or back in failover clustering. The Distributor is the server that pushes the changes out to the subscribers. The Distributor and Publisher should be separate servers if possible. If the tail of the transaction log cannot be retrieved, replication may provide a more current solution than log shipping if replication fits your architecture. The replicated database can be available for reporting purposes without any special configuration or considerations.

Backup and Recovery

If you use backup and recovery as your disaster and recovery plan, consider the following::

- Your recovery plan is only as good as your last known good backups. If backups are being made, but not tested, there may be no way to recover, depending on the final high availability solution implemented, if the backups turn out to be invalid.

- You need to assess how long it will take to restore the backup. If it is going to take four hours to restore your very large database, and your e-commerce site is losing $50,000 an hour, you will want to consider this fact in your plan. Also consider that something may happen during the restore process that increases the restore time. Plus, if you are not using transaction marks in your database (commonly used with partitioned data), and you are restoring to restore due to data issues rather than hardware, then you will have to restore, check the data, restore, check the data, find the error, and then do it all over again.

- You need to consider how long it takes to roll any transaction logs forward.

- You should know where all backups of the database in question are stored, and when it was backed up. For more detail, see "Creating a Run Book" in this chapter.

SQL Server 2000 supports snapshot backups, which involves the mirroring of your disks, and then breaking a complete set of disks off the mirror and using them as a backup. This requires specialized hardware, but is fully supported within SQL Server. Snapshot backups may create higher availability.

If failover clustering is used, any third-party backup programs used must be cluster aware. Should the software not be cluster aware, it may result in unplanned downtime.

Network Load Balancing

While Network Load Balancing evenly distributes processing load among different servers, SQL Server 2000 itself cannot be load balanced. Network Load Balancing is intended for TCP/IP based services that either do not maintain state on each server or are designed to avoid storing state on the server, such as Internet Information Services (IIS) and Terminal Server. This option would work well as a high availability front end connected to a highly available clustered SQL Server 2000 back end (which may employ some of the technologies detailed here), since the load is balanced between servers, moves automatically in the event of failure, and renders SQL Server completely transparent to the end user.

The Choice

The choice of operating system and version of SQL Server affects which high availability options are available. If possible, use Windows 2000 Advanced Server and SQL Server 2000 Enterprise Edition. (As mentioned, failover clustering and log shipping both require SQL Server 2000 Enterprise Edition.) You may want to choose more than one high availability method.

When choosing a method, ask yourself the following questions:

1. How are we going to switch to the standby server, and do we have the infrastructure and people to accomplish the switch successfully?

2. How many transactions can we afford to lose?

3. How long can we afford to be down?

4. Does the backup server have enough capacity?

5. And if the backup server fails, do we have a backup for that server? How redundant does our environment need to be?

6. Is the application able to function if it is pointed to another database server?

In any high availability solution, the first option considered should be a failover cluster. This provides the quickest and most automatic failover and is virtually transparent to the end users. A potentially less expensive alternative would be log shipping, which gives a high level of protection, but not as much as failover clustering. This is due to the fact that in the event of an unplanned event, only failover clustering can guarantee that all completed transactions will not be lost. A tradeoff comes in if and when you need to flip the switch on the warm standby server.

The following table compares failover clustering and log shipping on several criteria.

Feature	Failover clustering	Log shipping
Failover	Fast and automatic; virtually transparent except for small disconnect	Slower and manual; involves changing of application, connectivity, or client. Also involves processes that must be run to bring warm standby online
Cost	More expensive	Potentially less expensive
Full-Text, DTS, Replication	Fails over cleanly	Does not work automatically in failover; needs manual intervention
Logins	Full server failover, so all transferred	Job must be created to synchronize users
Distance	Short unless using distance clustering	Can be geographically disperse
Secondary server	Failover node may have other active virtual servers, but is considered passive for the virtual server currently running on the designated primary.	Can use warm standby for other databases, and use the log-shipped database for maintenance tasks

continued on next page

Feature	Failover clustering	Log shipping
Transactions	All transactions are rolled forward if completed or rolled back in failover process.	If primary server is unavailable, last transactions cannot be retrieved, and warm standby will be a small delta of time out of sync.
Failing back to primary server	Automatic or manual, with minimal downtime	Manual, with unknown downtime

Many companies implement both failover clustering and log shipping to have a backup to the primary redundancy option, even though technically the other node(s) in a failover cluster solution are the backup plan.

If merge or transactional replication is a requirement of the overall application architecture, log shipping complements those technologies. For more information, see the topics "Strategies for Backing Up and Restoring Merge Replication" and "Transactional Replication and Log Shipping" in SQL Server Books Online.

Log shipping is also a good choice with Network Load Balancing. This scenario assumes that the SQL Server that the Network Load Balancing servers use is read-only, since it is best suited in a Web-based environment, like an e-commerce site that

uses catalog servers. Replication is a choice for replicating read-only data as well using transactional replication or snapshot replication, and, like log shipping, replication can be used with Network Load Balancing. Network Load Balancing can be used to mask a server name change.

Design either of these effective combinations:

- **Distance clustering with log shipping.** This solution may provide the ultimate in protection, since all nodes may be completely geographically dispersed, and the solution is built completely on enterprise class servers and software.

- **Failover clustering with hardware mirroring.** This solution will protect the primary instance with redundancy, and hardware mirroring can be used to create the failover/standby copy of the database if the failover cluster fails completely.

Other combinations and solutions are possible. The ones listed above are only some suggestions that could be implemented in your environment.

Designing Hardware for High Availability

After choosing the right SQL Server high availability method, you must choose reliable and scalable hardware to support it. The hardware must be fault tolerant, meaning the system can gracefully respond to an unexpected event. A few factors come into play when designing a highly available hardware solution:

- What is the current workload of the application or Web site, and what does it project to be six months, a year, or even two years from now?

Most people do not have this information prior to implementing a solution. Having benchmarks on how an application or site performs is critical in determining which operating system and what hardware to buy. The best way to benchmark an application prior to production is in a lab environment, but that is not always an option for some environments. Using tools such as System Monitor (Performance Monitor in Windows NT 4.0) can also establish performance trends. This method may not be as accurate as metrics obtained in a controlled lab environment, but would still serve as a baseline. Without a baseline, it will be hard to determine exactly what is needed. Also, any application issues affecting performance, either in current production versions or updates being planned, should be taken into account; SQL Server and its underlying hardware platform will only perform as well as the code that was written to access it.

- How much money is budgeted to the project?

In theory, organizations would all build the biggest and best boxes on every project. In reality, budget considerations often place some constraints on what you can do. A good rule of thumb is to plan for at least six months worth of capacity, but also take into account some amount of time, whether it is a year, two years, or more, in which the server being configured will still be employed and be expected to perform.

Processors

Depending on which operating system you choose, different numbers of processors would be available for use.

Operating system	Maximum number of processors
Windows NT 4.0 Enterprise Edition	8
Windows 2000 Advanced Server	8
Windows 2000 Datacenter Server	32

Testing the performance of an application in a lab or some sort of controlled environment should determine the basic processing power needed. Another way to do this is to analyze the growth overtime of your system by regularly recording pertinent statistics in order to make a graph displaying this information. This is an important step, since the configuration of a production server should take into account current workload as well as an increase over time. Failover clustering from an operating perspective requires either Windows 2000 Advanced or Datacenter servers. Windows 2000 Datacenter Server requires a Service Level Agreement and is specifically meant to be used for high availability. If the operating system is not listed above, it does not support more than four processors.

Note Windows 2000 Datacenter Server is part of the Windows Datacenter Program (WDP). For more information, see http://www.microsoft.com/windows2000/.

Memory

Depending on which operating system is employed, SQL Server can take advantage of different amounts of maximum memory. An installation of SQL Server 2000 Enterprise Edition supports up to 32 gigabytes (GB) of memory on Windows 2000 Datacenter Server (without AWE enabled). Below is a table detailing the maximum amount of memory available to SQL Server per operating system.

Operating system	Maximum
Windows NT 4.0 Enterprise Edition	3 GB
Windows 2000 Advanced Server	8 GB (with AWE enabled)
Windows 2000 Datacenter Server	64 GB (with AWE enabled)

Address Windowing Extensions Memory

Windows 2000 servers introduced the enhanced Address Windowing Extensions (AWE) API. AWE allows applications to access large amounts of physical memory. Due to limitations of 32-bit memory addressing, only up to 4 GB of physical memory can be used by Windows NT 4.0 and Windows 2000. By default, 2 GB of memory is dedicated to the operating system and 2 GB of memory to the application.

With a **/3GB** switch in the BOOT.INI used by the operating system, the application can access up to 3 GB of memory, and the operating system is reduced to 1 GB of memory. The difficulty presented by this design is that even if a server was configured with 8 GB of memory, anything past 4 GB was virtually unusable. This problem limited the amount of scalability of an application. AWE is the support built into the operating system for exposing extended memory to Win32-based applications.

With AWE, however, a memory-intensive application can now run much more efficiently under SQL Server 2000 to increase performance.

AWE requires an application to be coded specifically for AWE, like SQL Server 2000. AWE support within SQL Server 2000 must be configured using the **sp_configure** option **awe enabled**. This is set per instance. By default, **awe enabled** is set to 0, or off. Enabling AWE support in SQL Server 2000 also requires some additional operating system configuration. Consult SQL Server Books Online for more information. If enabling AWE memory, it is highly recommended that the configuration be tested prior to bringing the server(s) online in a production capacity.

There are considerations to take into account when implementing AWE memory:

- The SQL Server instance does not dynamically manage the size of the memory address space used.

  When AWE is enabled with SQL Server 2000, if the **max server memory** configuration parameter is not set, it will grab the total memory available (except 128 MB to allow the base operating system to function), potentially depriving the operating system and any other processes that would be running on the same server. For detailed information on configuring AWE in a SQL Server 2000 failover clustering environment, see Chapter 12, "Failover Clustering."

- Once initialized, AWE memory holds all the memory acquired at startup until it is shut down.

  If AWE is enabled and is taking too much memory, SQL Server would need to be shut down to reconfigure it, causing downtime (which makes a high availability option like failover clustering less available). Be sure to test for this scenario.

- Since the memory pages used by the SQL Server instance are taken from the nonpageable pool of Windows memory, none of the memory can be exchanged.

  This means that if the physical memory is filled up, it cannot use the page file set up on a physical disk to account for the surplus in memory usage. Planning how AWE is used is vital with any SQL Server instance.

For more information on configuring AWE memory on your server, see "Using AWE Memory on Windows 2000" in SQL Server Books Online.

Disk Storage

The heart of any database system is its storage—it contains the valuable data used and inserted by an application. For high availability, disks should be part of an external array and should be fault tolerant. The disks should be high speed for performance and support a large capacity.

The disks can be configured either with a small computer system interface (SCSI) or Fibre Channel. Fibre Channel is the preferred method of implementing. Historically, SCSI has been the popular method for implementing a disk array, but while it is generally cheaper, it does have a distance limitation. It also does not perform as well as Fibre Channel. Fibre Channel was specifically designed for high bandwidth and capacity. Storage Area Networks (SANs) are disk arrays that use networking protocols over Fibre to do all I/O. Use of SANs may be supported for use in conjunction with failover clustering as a Cluster/Multi-Cluster Device. SCSI is not supported for Windows 2000 Datacenter Server, so that is a consideration to take into account when deciding on hardware and the operating system.

When configuring the disks in the array, they should be configured as a redundant array of independent disks (RAID). There are different levels of RAID. The most popular and common options are:

- **RAID 0 – Striping**

  RAID Level 0 is striping data across multiple disk drives with no redundant information, making it not fault tolerant. Performance is maximized when data is striped over multiple controllers with one drive per controller and all the storage is available, but if one disk fails, the entire RAID array will become unavailable. RAID Level 0 requires a minimum of two drives to implement.

- **RAID 1 – Mirroring (Duplexing)**

  RAID Level 1 gives you the highest availability but can be expensive because it requires twice the desired disk space. With RAID 1, data is duplicated over separate disk drives (hence the mirroring). Reads may be even faster if the RAID array controller allows simultaneous reads from both of the mirrored pairs. . If the disks are on separate I/O buses, also known as duplexing, higher availability may be achieved. RAID Level 1 requires a minimum of two drives to implement.

- **RAID 5 – Striping And Parity**

  This is the most common, and affordable, RAID level. Availability is average. Parity and data is striped across a set of disks, so multiple read requests can be handled independently of each other providing high read performance. Since the parity information is used, a single disk can fail without losing access to the data. It requires a minimum of three disk drives to implement, with the third containing the parity information.

  The tradeoff comes in with writing. It is slower than other forms of RAID. Each write makes four independent disk accesses to finish (1. Old data and parity are read off separate disks; 2. New parity is calculated; and 3. New data and parity is written to separate disks). Some hardware vendors compensate by adding write caching into their hardware. However, because only one data disk of the set can be lost, and the parity disk cannot, this is not the best choice for high availability.

- **RAID 0+1 – Mirroring and Striping**

  This RAID level provides very high reliability combined with high performance. Essentially, it is a combination of Levels 0 and 1. One expense lies in the fact that you will use half of your physical disks for the mirror. Now that the standard disk sizes are larger than 18 GB, space should no longer be an issue for sites looking to invest in a scalable and available system. You can lose fully half the drives in the set without losing access to the data, provided no two are in the same mirror set. RAID 0+1 (sometimes called RAID 10) can read data from both the hot disk and the mirror as a performance boost, and it performs simultaneous writes to the hot disk and the mirror. This is the best solution for a database server requiring high performance and fault tolerance, but capacity may be an issue due to cost and the number of disks required. It requires a minimum of four disk drives to implement.

The RAID controller cards should have multiple channels, and can be internal to the server, or part of the RAID array itself. It is generally recommended to have these be part of the controller instead of in the server. The controller should have multiple channels, or independent buses, to allow different disks to essentially be configured to "talk" over different pipes in and out. This becomes important in the final configuration, because if the disks become a bottleneck because of contention, that could be a potential point of failure as well as a performance problem. If possible, use more than one disk controller card to split the I/O to the disks.

If failover clustering is used, make sure writeback caching is disabled if the RAID controller is internal to the server and not the disk array. The reason for this is that even with battery backup, once the resources fail over to another node, there could be items in the cache. If the services are failed back over to the node, corruption could occur because it will attempt to overwrite things on the disk. Always get a guarantee from the hardware vendor that data in the cache will be written to disk in the event of a failure.

For more information on hardware, see Chapter 33, "The Data Tier: An Approach to Database Optimization."

File Placement

Data and log devices, as well as **tempdb**, should be placed on separate disks. If possible, put them all on different channels. If your system is very large, or has hotspots, you may decide to use filegroups as a method of splitting up the disk I/O. Further segmenting this by putting filegroups on different disks and different channels can result in a performance boost. It is important to keep the file placement in mind when you are analyzing your high availability design. Performance issues caused by bottlenecks can be misinterpreted as availability problems.

Data should be configured with RAID 0+1 for high availability and performance, but RAID 5 is also acceptable (however RAID 5 may result in much slower restore times). Logs should be placed on RAID 1.

For more information on this subject, see Chapter 33, "The Data Tier: An Approach to Database Optimization."

Controller Configuration

Choose a card with enough channels to split the logical grouping of disks (for example, data and logs) to reduce I/O contention. If the Fibre Channel/RAID controller is internal to the server, and not in the shared disk array, writeback caching should be disabled. This is most important with failover clustering because, even with battery backup, once the resources fail over to another node, there could be items in the cache. If the services are failed back over to the node, corruption could occur because it will attempt to overwrite files on the disk. It would also cause data loss in a failover if transactions were in the cache but not yet processed.

Network Design

All high availability options require a reliable, highly performing network. Especially if options like log shipping and replication are involved, network latency looms largely in the picture. If the primary production SQL Server cannot connect to the server that may be the backup, there is no point in implementing the high availability solution until connectivity is reliable. Additionally, if there are connection problems between the clients and the SQL Server, this will be interpreted as an availability problem, and create the perception that you are not meeting your five nines service level agreement.

If larger bandwidth is required, SQL Server 2000 has support for higher bandwidth networking with Giganet or Compaq Servernet II technology on Compaq hardware. If used, these will create higher performance between multiple SQL Servers. Giganet support is built-in, and the update to enable Servernet II is located at http://www.microsoft.com/sql/.

Hardware Location

For the purposes of disaster recovery, the primary server and backup/warm/standby server(s) should never sit in the same location (with rare exceptions, such as some clustering solutions). A high availability solution works best by dispersing the parts of the puzzle in different places. This ensures that in the event of a catastrophe at the primary site, the backup plan does not go up in smoke with it. If all servers must sit in the same data center, make sure they are on completely separate power grids. That will at least provide some protection against one kind of disaster.

When placing the hardware in your data center, treat it as if you would a mainframe. Place it on a raised floor to protect the cabling. Make sure that an uninterrupted power supply (UPS) is attached to each server, and that the data center has proper backup generators in place should a disaster happen. Also ensure that the data center has the proper cooling facilities—causing failures due to system overheating is something that can be prevented.

For additional information about best practices for your data center, see Chapter 14, "Data Center Availability: Facilities, Staffing, and Operations."

Hardware Compatibility List

Before deciding on all final hardware, consult the Hardware Compatibility List (HCL). All hardware must appear on the HCL, or the cluster configuration will not be supported. Specific cluster categories are listed, including "Cluster." Only complete cluster solutions listed under the "Cluster" category are supported for use with SQL Server 2000 failover clustering.

The HCL can be found at http://www.microsoft.com/hcl/.

Service Level Agreements (SLA)

Make sure an equal level of protection is purchased for your hardware. In the event of a hardware problem, sometimes a 24-hour turnaround can be unacceptable on a mission-critical server. Any vendor selling a Windows 2000 Datacenter solution requires a SLA by default, and this is something to consider.

Creating a Disaster Recovery Plan

Along with the technical portion of your high availability solution, put a detailed disaster recovery plan in place as well. Proper planning will also aid in the ability to troubleshoot what went wrong so it can be corrected and prevented in the future. All problems and their resolutions, whether trivial or major, should be logged as they occur, since they may assist if the system goes down at a later date.

Preparing Your Environment

Operational excellence is a prerequisite to devising a disaster recovery plan. Below is a list of actions to take to ensure this operational excellence.

- Standardize your environment.

  - Standardize all server builds so all drives are the same and have the same purpose (for example, E:\ for backups, F:\ for logs, and G:\ for data).

  - Standardize how files and directories are accessed over your network, whether it is the same mapped drives or shares.

  - Use a well documented (and in some cases, the same) account to start and stop SQL Server services on all servers.

  - Use the same security model on all servers. If you have a large admin team, add each of their Windows logins to the **sysadmin** group, rather than have everyone log in as a universal **sa** user. Never use the **sa** login in any code; you should be able to change the **sa** password frequently, without notifying anyone or revising any code.

  - Never allow users to access a logical drive used by SQL Server for any reason, since that user may do something to reduce the availability of that disk.

- Perform database backups and maintenance.

  - Create a full backup of all databases on a regular basis, including the two main system databases: **msdb** and **master**. **msdb** is especially important to back up, since replication, distributed backups, data transformation services, and other system related information is stored in **msdb**.

  - If they are implemented, know where incremental or transaction log backups are stored for use and treat them the same as full backups.

  - Test the backups regularly by restoring them on another server to get timings and ensure that they can be restored with no errors.

  - Rotate backups to offsite tape storage, and make sure the destination uses data center principles and uses vault storage. Run test scenarios that involve retrieving offsite tapes.

  - Run DBCC statements and perform other maintenance tasks on the restored database (preferably on another server) to check the health of the database regularly. If the database shows signs of corruption, such as fragmented indexes or torn pages, immediately take the proper steps to correct the problem in a test environment to ensure that the fix works, and then apply it to the production environment.

  - Script out all users or have a list of all system and/or application users and passwords ready to restore in an emergency. Take security into account when undertaking this task. Document the process for informing the users and the help desk in the event of that you need to restore the logins from script (which would involve resetting passwords).

  - Store your DTS packages as files, to enable an easy restore or transfer.

  - Script out any custom error messages.

  - Script out and/or document any SQL Server jobs and tasks.

  - Script out and/or document any SQL Server linked servers.

- Monitor your environment.

  - Run System Monitor and capture System Monitor logs against your SQL Server 2000 instances. Establish baselines to know when things look abnormal.

  - Run SQL Profiler traces to establish a "normal" workload, and be able to identify abnormal SQL statements or logins.

  - Set up SQL Server and System Monitor alerts to warn of impending problems; it is always best to be proactive and not reactive.

- Regularly go through the Application, Event, and System logs on the server, as well as the SQL Server logs.

- Perform security audits for sensitive data access and administrative DDL and statements, and review the logs regularly. Monitor login failures.

- Establish change control.

  - Establish development, quality assurance (QA), and staging environments to allow easy transitions into production, and the people doing their respective jobs to be able to do them without impacting someone else's job. Never use your production environment as your test environment.

  - In the development environment, make sure all code, including schemas, scripts, stored procedures, and so on, is checked into a source control product such as Microsoft Visual SourceSafe™.

  - Make sure each script is "versioned" and can clearly be discerned from previous and future versions to ensure comparisons are easy to do. Make sure developers include comments to explain all changes.

  - When code is considered complete, and is accepted by QA, have a detailed step-by-step plan for rolling it out to the production environment, including time estimates and prerequisites like service pack levels.

  - Schedule the upgrade, and staff accordingly.

  - Back up the entire environment prior to installing the upgrade to make sure a rollback will be as smooth as possible.

  - Have a backout plan that is well documented and tested in QA or in a staging environment prior to the upgrade, and know when to make the go/no go call if the window of opportunity is tight.

- Make an investment in continued professional training and internal cross training of your current staff.

- Keep a record of all the contact people (including developers) for an application, with notes on what they typically can deal with.

- Keep a record of all related systems. For example, if this system fails over to a remote site, who would you need to notify? If there was a production change (say, a table changed), who would you need to notify so all related reports could be updated, so all data pushes could be adjusted, and so on?

- Make sure all support contracts are current and the numbers to call for support are documented along with any pertinent information and the justification process for placing a support call. This will ensure that the proper hardware and software support will be available at a moment's notice. This becomes more important if hardware fails and a component would need to be replaced.

- Treat your production boxes seriously.

  - Lock down security—make sure only the people who need to have to have access to the boxes can get to them. This means no blank **sa** passwords, obvious administrator passwords, and so on. If need be, only allow access to critical servers from certain known and trusted IP addresses.

  - Change control should also be applied here—any changes to the production environment such as a service pack should be held to the same standard as changes that come from development, and should be tested in a staging environment.

For more information, see Chapter 8, "Managing Database Change." For a full discussion of managing operational changes, visit http://www.microsoft.com/mof/.

The Failover Plan

By now, you have chosen the one or more technologies to build your high availability solution. Now the question is: How are you going to switch over to the designated backup server? If the solution is configured properly, tested, and the process documented, it should be an easy switch. Part of the plan, if applicable, is to ensure that no other users have access to the database or server while bringing it online. This may involve using single user mode. Another part of the plan is having a way to notify end users in the event of a failover, especially if it will take any length of time.

For detailed information on configuring failovers with failover clustering and log shipping, consult Chapter 12, "Failover Clustering" and Chapter 13, "Log Shipping," respectively.

The Failback Plan

Consider the following questions when you develop a disaster recovery plan: What do you do to get back to your original primary server? Do you do it immediately? On a scheduled basis? At a lull? Or do you go back at all? Have a hierarchy for recovery: If multiple failures happen at once, what gets the priority? Is one dependent on another?

If your servers are of equal hardware and capacity, you may have no reason to ever fail back to the original server, unless you have a business need or desire. Analyze the server to prevent failures from reoccurring. This can provide valuable information in the event that you decide to involve technical support. You may find that changes are driven back into the design or code of the system to make it more robust.

For detailed information on configuring a failback with failover clustering and log shipping, consult Chapter 12, "Failover Clustering" and Chapter 13, "Log Shipping," respectively.

Personnel

The most important aspect of any disaster recovery plan is the human one: choosing the right people to execute and staff the plan. Only trained employees should be entrusted with the responsibility of carrying out the final disaster recovery plan in the event of an emergency. A well-established shift rotation should be in place and documented, and contact information should be entered into the run book (described below) to ensure easy accessibility to that information.

Also be sure you have an up-to-date escalation structure, and/or clear chain of command, for dealing with disaster recovery. Assign specific tasks and roles to an individual, and ensure that person know what is expected of them. This will minimize any confusion. If you live in an area that has predictable disasters, make plans that accommodate this.

Creating a Run Book

Crucial to the success or failure of a disaster recovery plan is having a document or collection of documents that not only detail the steps of the plan, but any related documentation that would aid in the recovery and diagnosis of a disaster. Such a document is sometimes referred to as a "run book," and should be readily kept up-to-date and available to the whole team. It includes, but is not limited to:

- The failover plan.
- The failback plan.
- Backup file information and primary, secondary, and tertiary locations.

    In the event of a system failure, a backup would need to be restored.

- Location of software, including documented licensing keys and support numbers.

    In case of complete system failure, where everything would need to be reinstalled, the operating system and SQL Server 2000 software should be readily available with its corresponding licensing information.

- Contact information.

    This includes a list of all personnel and all relevant contact information for them. This should include everyone: administrators, developers, help desk employees, users, and also other related systems that depend on information in this system.

- Server configuration.

    If a software installation or hardware fails, the server itself may need to be rebuilt. You may choose to include the worksheets for log shipping and failover clustering, found in Chapter 12, "Failover Clustering" and Chapter 13, "Log Shipping," respectively. Other things that may be helpful:

    - Operating system version, with service pack level, and settings at the OS level

    - Registry settings (if applicable)

- Physical and logical disk configuration, including RAID levels and disk controller information (including write cache settings)

- Drivers and firmware

- SQL Server installation configuration, including the installation and service pack levels, and any hotfixes that were applied

- SQL Server instance names, IP addresses, ports, configuration options, database file locations, and so on

- File shares. Also note any shares, no matter whether they are mapped, reached by universal naming convention (UNC) names or through some special protocol, to which the service login must have permissions.

- Collations

   Prior to SQL Server 2000, collations were set only at the server level. With SQL Server 2000, collations can now also be set at the server and literal string level. This information is crucial for restoring a database properly.

- Database Schemas.

   These should also be saved out to script files for easy recreation.

- Jobs.

   A list of all automated SQL Server Agent jobs, what they do, their corresponding code, and what time(s) they are executed is necessary in case they need to be recreated. They could also be scripted out for possible recreation.

- Replication setup (if applicable).

- Log shipping setup (if applicable).

- Information related to distributed databases or partitions (if applicable): such as Data Dependent Routing Tables, distributed transaction marks, and so on.

- Linked server information and related security.

- Information on maintenance. For example if a remote server controls your maintenance.

- DTS packages, including associated login and password information, and any other custom-built code that runs on the server.

- Configuration information for any other software that runs on the same server. Make sure complete installation and configuration documentation is available, and/or that qualified support personnel are listed as contacts. Also list support numbers and Web sites for each piece of software.

- Any custom-made DBA objects that you depend on to maintain or administer the server.

- Any specialized configurations, such as XML support for IIS, Microsoft Active Directory™ support, and so on.

Other information can be in the run book as well, but the above is a helpful guideline to start with.

Testing the Plan

Last, but not least, test the disaster recovery plan. The business consequences of an untested plan can be very significant.

The following procedures will be useful as you conduct your "fire drill":

- Schedule a test.

  After the solution is put in place, testing of that solution should be done on a scheduled, regular basis. This is the only way to make sure that all personnel are trained and confident in what needs to be done. No testing should be done during a normal business day unless the servers involved have not been put into production yet. If the servers are not in production, testing is easier and can be done at any time prior to going live. If the servers are already in production, the testing should be done in off-peak hours so business activities are not adversely affected.

- Log the test.

  Using the aforementioned run book, log all tests of the disaster recovery plan. Note the day, start time, end time, whether or not it was a success, and, in the event of a failure, why it happened. It is crucial for tracking as well as diagnosing. No greater confidence can be gained than when you know the plan works and is documented to work. And if it fails, and the problem happened before, you know how to deal with the anomaly.

  At some point you may have to put your disaster recovery plan into action. If this occurs, make sure to document the entire process.

Diagnosing a Failure

In the event of a failure, you should try to determine the root cause, but this may be hard to attain depending on the failure itself. To assist in this effort, make sure the following measures are in place:

- Whatever was running on the server at the time of the failure should also be known. Whether this was just the application, or specific application tasks (such as daily processes), tasks, or anything that would make a possible suspect from the application/database angle. An effort should be made to document whether anyone in the operations staff or application administrators group was running a special process at the time, as well.

- Backup the database and save it off for analysis, and if possible, get a transaction log backup as well.

- Any error message present on the screen when the operator arrives should be carefully and completely documented.

- Make sure the Windows application, system, and event logs are available. They should be backed up from time to time to make sure that they can be used for historical research in the event of a failure.

- Similarly, SQL Server error logs should be backed up and archived for potential use to see what was going on at the SQL Server level at the time of the failure.

- If C2 auditing is enabled, make sure those logs are available and were part of a backup scheme. This will help to determine who or what may have caused the problem.

- The location of all log files should be standardized, well known and documented in the run book.

High Availability Scenarios

This section provides some typical scenarios for implementation of high availability solutions. All examples assume no deficiencies in application logic. The companies cited in the following scenarios are fictional.

Corporate Web Site with Dynamic Content, no E-Commerce

Background

A global recruiting company recently put up its official Web site. The site is an application that provides information about the company and its recruiters, and allows potential candidates to search for jobs and send in resumes. The company has offices in New York, Boston, Chicago, Los Angeles, Atlanta, London, Tokyo, Paris, Toronto, and elsewhere.

By default, the application defaults to the local database, but jobs can be searched from all over the world. Each location has its own single instance two node failover cluster, and that database is log shipped to a regional server sized to handle all databases (that is, all of the U.S. east coast, Europe, Southeast Asia, and so on). Log shipping sends the transaction logs to the warm standby server every 15 minutes, and the database name on the warm standby corresponds to the city name. Each virtual server is linked to the others around the world. Web users connect to a farm of web servers in each location that point to the proper database. The log shipped servers all employ snapshot backups to one server in the global headquarters in New York City as a last line of defense. While the Web site is not a strict 24 x 7 shop, it is expected to be up as many hours of the day as possible in the event of an emergency. Some losses in transactions are considered to be acceptable.

Technologies Used

- SQL Server 2000 Enterprise Edition

- Windows 2000 Advanced Server

- Network Load Balancing

- Internet Information Services

- Failover clustering

- Log shipping

- Snapshot backups

Scenario

The company:

Imagine that Tokyo experiences an earthquake. The data center powering the failover cluster loses all power—no connectivity whatsoever. The Global Operations Center (GOC) detects the failure, and uses Terminal Server to remotely access the Southeast Asia warm standby server. The GOC also puts up a special page on the site indicating that the Tokyo search database is temporarily offline, and will be up shortly. Since a proper disaster recovery scenario was in place, a job to bring the database online, with all of its proper steps, is started. The data source name (DSN) on all Web servers for the Tokyo database is redirected to the warm standby. The temporary Web page is removed.

The user:

Back in San Francisco, John goes to the site at the moment the earthquake happened. He looks for local jobs, but he is also considering a radical change. He decides to search for all QA jobs in Tokyo. Unfortunately, he receives the temporary offline notice on the site. Since this page notes that the database will be searchable again soon, he decides to surf the Web for a few minutes, and then return to the site. He goes to search for all jobs in Tokyo, and succeeds.

Failing Back

After 48 hours, all power is restored to the Tokyo data center. The health of the servers is deemed to be fine. The GOC puts the temporary Web page up again, and sets the database to single user mode to ensure that no errant connections can be made. A full database backup is made, copied to the Tokyo virtual server, and restored. The database is also restored to the warm standby server, except the database is put into standby mode. Log shipping is re-enabled. The GOC tests functionality to ensure all is well, redirects all Web servers to the primary database, turns off single user mode, and removes the temporary Web page.

E-Commerce Web Site

Background

A successful manufacturer of widgets has a Web site selling its products. The database grows rapidly each month, and currently consumes 15 GB of disk space. Microsoft Commerce Server 2000 handles the commerce piece. It accesses not only the shopping database, but also a series of LDAP membership databases spread out over three dedicated servers. A custom application sits on top of Commerce Server, and uses Component Services to queue transactions to be entered into the shopper database. The application also accesses three catalog servers, which are fed by a master catalog database. Daily changes, and not a whole copy of the catalog, are sent using transactional replication to all three catalog servers.

The following also are important features of the environment at the company:

- Catalog servers.

  These are protected with log shipping to another SQL Server daily at 1 AM, after changes are pushed to them.

- Main shopping database, which includes all transactions.

  This is set up as a two node single instance failover cluster, and is also log shipped to another server every 10 minutes.

- LDAP Membership Databases.

  This is set up as a two node single instance failover cluster, and is also log shipped to another server every 10 minutes.

The entire environment is mirrored with third-party hardware to a copy of the data center in another state, in case of a failure. Log shipping is also sent to these servers at the same time as log shipping to the other servers. This allows the database to be only a small delta of time out of sync with the main environment. No external connections can access these servers unless a DNS change is made. The catalogs are fronted by Network Load Balancing, and the Web servers also employ Network Load Balancing.

Because this is a site that is commerce based, every second that the site is down means lost revenue. Therefore, the site needs airtight backup plans, as well as redundancy from a data standpoint.

Technologies Used

- Windows NT Server 4.0, Enterprise Edition (for Site Server)

- Windows 2000 Advanced Server (for SQL Server)

- SQL Server 2000 Enterprise Edition

- Microsoft Commerce Server 2000

- Internet Information Services

- Network Load Balancing

- Component Services

- Log shipping

- Failover clustering

- Transactional replication

- Hardware server mirroring and disk mirroring

Scenario 1

The company:

Monday is a busy day for the company, especially from 11 AM to 4 PM. At 1 PM, the operations center notices ASP queuing starting to happen, and that no connections seem to be getting to the shopping database. Because it is protected with failover clustering, within a short time, the database comes back up and the ASP queuing lessens. An engineer starts to investigate why the primary node went down. Around 3 PM, the shopping database starts to exhibit dropped connections and fails before a final transaction log backup could be made. The company puts up a "store closed" page. Since the primary node is already unavailable, the company follows the instructions found in its run book for bringing the log shipped warm standby server online. After the warm standby is brought online and tested, the "store closed" page is removed.

The user:

Mary goes to the site at 1:03 PM and finds the site extremely slow. She decides to shop elsewhere. Even if a failover is happens cleanly, there is no guarantee of how a user will respond to online conditions.

At 3:05 PM, Ed needs to buy a widget. He goes to the site, only to find a store closed page that said the site will be back up soon. The page indicates that customers can use a special code to get 20 percent off their next order when they comes back. Ed goes back to work, and before he leaves his desk at 5:30, he goes back to the company Web site.

Failing Back Number 1

The problem on the clustered nodes is traced back to a faulty power circuit. It is repaired, and the servers are rebuilt from scratch the next day to ensure that the software installations were not damaged and will function properly, since they were not shut down cleanly and are well out of sync. Friday night during off hours is the scheduled time to bring the cluster back into service. At that time, the "store closed" page is put up and all site traffic to the back end is stopped. The current production shopping database—the log shipping server—is backed up. Then the files are copied to the cluster and restored to the virtual server. The backup is also restored to the log shipping server to put it into standby mode. Log shipping is enabled on the primary server, the site is tested, the "store closed" page is removed, and the store is back online again.

Scenario 2

The company:

At 12:03 AM on Tuesday, the main data center at the company loses all power. A call is made, and it is determined that the outage will last awhile. Because of the hardware mirroring and the log shipping of the main databases every 10 minutes, the backup environment is only three minutes out. The log shipped servers are brought online, and the catalog is pushed out from corporate headquarters to the catalog servers using a DTS package created specifically for this purpose. Then the site is tested, and the DNS change made to bring the backup environment completely live.

The user:

Susan cannot sleep, so she decides to browse the Web. She attempts to go to the company Web site at 12:10 AM, only to get a "page not found" error. She finds this odd, since she had browsed the site earlier in the evening, and decides to go back to bed. When she gets up in the morning, she checks the site for the widget she wanted more information on, and finds the site up.

Failing Back Number 2

In this case, a failback to the original environment would only happen in the event of a failure. If it was only one server to fail over, it would be easy, but moving a whole environment is quite difficult and time consuming. And especially where every second means revenue, going down to switch back when your alternate environment is working does not make sense.

Partitioned Database

Background

The Human Resources department of your company uses an in-house designed application that accesses SQL Server 2000. The SQL Server 2000 database is partitioned over three instances using a Distributed Partition View (DPV). These three instances are on a four node Datacenter cluster, with the fourth node being the passive failover node. This is the N+1 scenario described in Chapter 12, "Failover Clustering." Each instance is log shipped every 15 minutes to a single standalone server that has enough capacity to run all three databases, but the transaction logs are not applied because the database may need to be restored to a single point in time. The transaction log in each database is also marked with a known naming scheme every three minutes to make a restore to keep all three databases in sync.

Technologies Used

- SQL Server 2000 Enterprise Edition

- Windows 2000 Datacenter Server

- Marked transaction logs (for more information, see "Backup and Recovery of Related Databases" and "Recovering to a Named Transaction" in SQL Server Books Online, as well as Chapter 38, "Scaling Out on SQL Server.")

- Distributed Partition Views (federated servers)

- Failover clustering

Scenario

The company:

An air conditioning repairman accidentally pulls the plug out of the cluster when he walks through the wiring in the data center at 9:26 AM. The data center is three states away from the main operations center. Because the backup scheme for the DPVs is well known because it is in the run book, the operations team restores the databases to the last (and same) distributed mark point on the warm standby, redirects any ODBC data sources, and brings the databases online.

The user:

Moments after the failure is detected, Janet receives an e-mail from the corporate IT staff saying that the HR system is temporarily down. Fifteen minutes later she receives an e-mail saying the system is back up.

Failing Back

The power cord problem is corrected. Because the HR department is essentially a 9 to 5 shop, users are notified that the system will be shut down for maintenance that evening. At midnight, the operations staff puts the databases in single user mode to ensure no errant connections can be made, backups are made of the three databases, and those are copied and restored on their respective virtual servers. The databases are also restored on the log shipped server in standby mode. Log shipping is enabled, the ODBC data sources are redirected, and the application is tested to ensure functionality works.

Small Company

Background

A small accounting services business manages the books of 25 local businesses. Joe, the owner of the accounting business, uses a custom application. The data Joe works with *is* his business, but it is not volatile because it changes in small amounts every day. If a particular database has a large number of changes, he backs it up periodically during the day and copies it to the backup server. He manages his own servers since he is the owner and sole employee. He has two Windows 2000 Servers—one his primary, and one his backup. Both contain SQL Server 2000 Standard Edition instances. Joe could not afford to purchase SQL Server 2000 Enterprise Edition. Joe has a scheduled job that backs the primary database up every night onto both disk and tape, and that copies the backup files to the secondary server and automatically restores them. An external UPS protects each server. He also has a set of saved queries on each server so he can access the entries per day in each database to pull specific records out in the event of a failure.

Technologies Used

- SQL Server 2000 Standard Edition
- Windows 2000 Server

Scenario

The user and company:

Joe comes in one morning to find that his primary server will not boot up. In a panic, he sits down at the second server to see if the backup from the previous day completed, and was backed up and restored to the server. Unfortunately, the primary server went down before it had a chance to be backed up, so he is 24 hours out of sync. He goes through the business day and does his work on the secondary, deciding to deal with the failure in off hours.

Failing Back

After the office closes, he attempts to restore the primary server. He discovers that the power supply inside the system failed. He replaces it, and boots up the server. He runs DBCC statements and other diagnostics to see if the SQL Server has been damaged. The SQL Server checks out to be in good health. He then runs the query to get all new records out of the databases based on an **update_date** column in each table, and inserts them into temporary tables. He then proceeds to back up all databases on the secondary server and restore them on the primary. He then reinserts all the records from the temporary tables, runs queries to make sure the records were inserted with no problems, and drops the temporary tables.

Conclusion

A production environment is the lifeblood of any establishment that uses computers to power its day-to-day activities. Because the systems are vital, ensuring that they are up and running is paramount. This means that proper considerations must be taken into account to create a highly available SQL Server in conjunction with all other mission-critical systems. Attaining high availability does not happen merely by adding redundant hardware into the server mix. Hardware is only a part of the solution; it must be used in conjunction with other high availability concepts such as proper application design and disaster recovery planning. It is important to strive for the highest amount of uptime that is possible. Use this chapter as a guideline to assist in the development of designing highly available SQL Servers and the plans to support them.

Data Warehousing

Data Warehouse Design Considerations

Data warehouses support business decisions by collecting, consolidating, and organizing data for reporting and analysis with tools such as online analytical processing (OLAP) and data mining. Although data warehouses are built on relational database technology, the design of a data warehouse database differs substantially from the design of an online transaction processing system (OLTP) database.

The topics in this chapter address approaches and choices to be considered when designing and implementing a data warehouse. The chapter begins by contrasting data warehouse databases with OLTP databases and introducing OLAP and data mining, and then adds information about design issues to be considered when developing a data warehouse with Microsoft® SQL Server™ 2000.

Data Warehouses, OLTP, OLAP, and Data Mining

A relational database is designed for a specific purpose. Because the purpose of a data warehouse differs from that of an OLTP, the design characteristics of a relational database that supports a data warehouse differ from the design characteristics of an OLTP database.

Data warehouse database	OLTP database
Designed for analysis of business measures by categories and attributes	Designed for real-time business operations
Optimized for bulk loads and large, complex, unpredictable queries that access many rows per table	Optimized for a common set of transactions, usually adding or retrieving a single row at a time per table
Loaded with consistent, valid data; requires no real time validation	Optimized for validation of incoming data during transactions; uses validation data tables
Supports few concurrent users relative to OLTP	Supports thousands of concurrent users

A Data Warehouse Supports OLTP

A data warehouse supports an OLTP system by providing a place for the OLTP database to offload data as it accumulates, and by providing services that would complicate and degrade OLTP operations if they were performed in the OLTP database.

Without a data warehouse to hold historical information, data is archived to static media such as magnetic tape, or allowed to accumulate in the OLTP database.

If data is simply archived for preservation, it is not available or organized for use by analysts and decision makers. If data is allowed to accumulate in the OLTP so it can be used for analysis, the OLTP database continues to grow in size and requires more indexes to service analytical and report queries. These queries access and process large portions of the continually growing historical data and add a substantial load to the database. The large indexes needed to support these queries also tax the OLTP transactions with additional index maintenance. These queries can also be complicated to develop due to the typically complex OLTP database schema.

A data warehouse offloads the historical data from the OLTP, allowing the OLTP to operate at peak transaction efficiency. High volume analytical and reporting queries are handled by the data warehouse and do not load the OLTP, which does not need additional indexes for their support. As data is moved to the data warehouse, it is also reorganized and consolidated so that analytical queries are simpler and more efficient.

OLAP Is a Data Warehouse Tool

Online analytical processing (OLAP) is a technology designed to provide superior performance for ad hoc business intelligence queries. OLAP is designed to operate efficiently with data organized in accordance with the common dimensional model used in data warehouses.

A data warehouse provides a multidimensional view of data in an intuitive model designed to match the types of queries posed by analysts and decision makers. OLAP organizes data warehouse data into multidimensional cubes based on this dimensional model, and then preprocesses these cubes to provide maximum performance for queries that summarize data in various ways. For example, a query that requests the total sales income and quantity sold for a range of products in a specific geographical region for a specific time period can typically be answered in a few seconds or less regardless of how many hundreds of millions of rows of data are stored in the data warehouse database.

OLAP is not designed to store large volumes of text or binary data, nor is it designed to support high volume update transactions. The inherent stability and consistency of historical data in a data warehouse enables OLAP to provide its remarkable performance in rapidly summarizing information for analytical queries.

In SQL Server 2000, Analysis Services provides tools for developing OLAP applications and a server specifically designed to service OLAP queries.

Data Mining is a Data Warehouse Tool

Data mining is a technology that applies sophisticated and complex algorithms to analyze data and expose interesting information for analysis by decision makers. Whereas OLAP organizes data in a model suited for exploration by analysts, data mining performs analysis on data and provides the results to decision makers. Thus, OLAP supports model-driven analysis and data mining supports data-driven analysis.

Data mining has traditionally operated only on raw data in the data warehouse database or, more commonly, text files of data extracted from the data warehouse database. In SQL Server 2000, Analysis Services provides data mining technology that can analyze data in OLAP cubes, as well as data in the relational data warehouse database. In addition, data mining results can be incorporated into OLAP cubes to further enhance model-driven analysis by providing an additional dimensional viewpoint into the OLAP model. For example, data mining can be used to analyze sales data against customer attributes and create a new cube dimension to assist the analyst in the discovery of the information embedded in the cube data.

For more information and details about data mining in SQL Server 2000, see Chapter 24, "Effective Strategies for Data Mining."

Designing a Data Warehouse: Prerequisites

Before embarking on the design of a data warehouse, it is imperative that the architectural goals of the data warehouse be clear and well understood. Because the purpose of a data warehouse is to serve users, it is also critical to understand the various types of users, their needs, and the characteristics of their interactions with the data warehouse.

Data Warehouse Architecture Goals

A data warehouse exists to serve its users — analysts and decision makers. A data warehouse must be designed to satisfy the following requirements:

- Deliver a great user experience — user acceptance is the measure of success
- Function without interfering with OLTP systems
- Provide a central repository of consistent data
- Answer complex queries quickly
- Provide a variety of powerful analytical tools such as OLAP and data mining

Most successful data warehouses that meet these requirements have these common characteristics:

- Are based on a dimensional model

- Contain historical data

- Include both detailed and summarized data

- Consolidate disparate data from multiple sources while retaining consistency

- Focus on a single subject such as sales, inventory, or finance

Data warehouses are often quite large. However, size is not an architectural goal — it is a characteristic driven by the amount of data needed to serve the users.

Data Warehouse Users

The success of a data warehouse is measured solely by its acceptance by users. Without users, historical data might as well be archived to magnetic tape and stored in the basement. Successful data warehouse design starts with understanding the users and their needs.

Data warehouse users can be divided into four categories: Statisticians, Knowledge Workers, Information Consumers, and Executives. Each type makes up a portion of the user population as illustrated in this diagram.

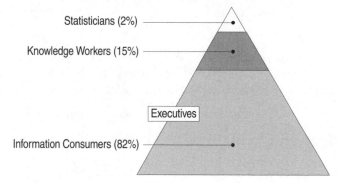

Statisticians: There are typically only a handful of statisticians and operations research types in any organization. Their work can contribute to closed loop systems that deeply influence the operations and profitability of the company.

Knowledge Workers: A relatively small number of analysts perform the bulk of new queries and analyses against the data warehouse. These are the users who get the Designer or Analyst versions of user access tools. They will figure out how to quantify a subject area. After a few iterations, their queries and reports typically get published for the benefit of the Information Consumers. Knowledge Workers are often deeply engaged with the data warehouse design and place the greatest demands on the ongoing data warehouse operations team for training and support.

Information Consumers: Most users of the data warehouse are Information Consumers; they will probably never compose a true ad hoc query. They use static or simple interactive reports that others have developed. They usually interact with the data warehouse only through the work product of others. This group includes a large number of people, and published reports are highly visible. Set up a great communication infrastructure for distributing information widely, and gather feedback from these users to improve the information sites over time.

Executives: Executives are a special case of the Information Consumers group.

How Users Query the Data Warehouse

Information for users can be extracted from the data warehouse relational database or from the output of analytical services such as OLAP or data mining. Direct queries to the data warehouse relational database should be limited to those that cannot be accomplished through existing tools, which are often more efficient than direct queries and impose less load on the relational database.

Reporting tools and custom applications often access the database directly. Statisticians frequently extract data for use by special analytical tools. Analysts may write complex queries to extract and compile specific information not readily accessible through existing tools. Information consumers do not interact directly with the relational database but may receive e-mail reports or access web pages that expose data from the relational database. Executives use standard reports or ask others to create specialized reports for them.

When using the Analysis Services tools in SQL Server 2000, Statisticians will often perform data mining, Analysts will write MDX queries against OLAP cubes and use data mining, and Information Consumers will use interactive reports designed by others.

Developing a Data Warehouse: Details

The phases of a data warehouse project listed below are similar to those of most database projects, starting with identifying requirements and ending with deploying the system:

- Identify and gather requirements
- Design the dimensional model

- Develop the architecture, including the Operational Data Store (ODS)
- Design the relational database and OLAP cubes
- Develop the data maintenance applications
- Develop analysis applications
- Test and deploy the system

Identify and Gather Requirements

Identify sponsors. A successful data warehouse project needs a sponsor in the business organization and usually a second sponsor in the Information Technology group. Sponsors must understand and support the business value of the project.

Understand the business before entering into discussions with users. Then interview and work with the users, not the data – learn the needs of the users and turn these needs into project requirements. Find out what information they need to be more successful at their jobs, not what data they think should be in the data warehouse; it is the data warehouse designer's job to determine what data is necessary to provide the information. Topics for discussion are the users' objectives and challenges and how they go about making business decisions. Business users should be closely tied to the design team during the logical design process; they are the people who understand the meaning of existing data. Many successful projects include several business users on the design team to act as data experts and sounding boards for design concepts. Whatever the structure of the team, it is important that business users feel ownership for the resulting system.

Interview data experts after interviewing several users. Find out from the experts what data exists and where it resides, but only after you understand the basic business needs of the end users. Information about available data is needed early in the process, before you complete the analysis of the business needs, but the physical design of existing data should not be allowed to have much influence on discussions about business needs.

Communicate with users often and thoroughly – continue discussions as requirements continue to solidify so that everyone participates in the progress of the requirements definition.

Design the Dimensional Model

User requirements and data realities drive the design of the dimensional model, which must address business needs, grain of detail, and what dimensions and facts to include.

The dimensional model must suit the requirements of the users and support ease of use for direct access. The model must also be designed so that it is easy to maintain and can adapt to future changes. The model design must result in a relational database that supports OLAP cubes to provide instantaneous query results for analysts.

An OLTP system requires a normalized structure to minimize redundancy, provide validation of input data, and support a high volume of fast transactions. A transaction usually involves a single business event, such as placing an order or posting an invoice payment. An OLTP model often looks like a spider web of hundreds or even thousands of related tables.

In contrast, a typical dimensional model uses a star or snowflake design that is easy to understand and relate to business needs, supports simplified business queries, and provides superior query performance by minimizing table joins.

For example, contrast the very simplified OLTP data model in the first diagram below with the data warehouse dimensional model in the second diagram. Which one better supports the ease of developing reports and simple, efficient summarization queries?

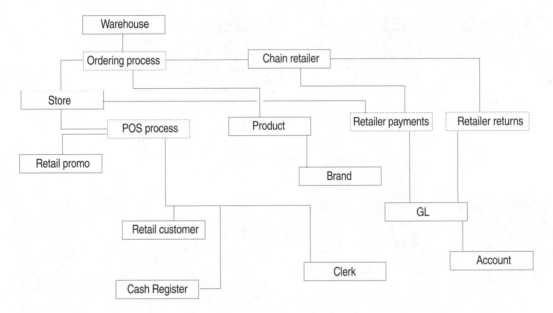

Dimensional Model Schemas

The principal characteristic of a dimensional model is a set of detailed business facts surrounded by multiple dimensions that describe those facts. When realized in a database, the schema for a dimensional model contains a central fact table and multiple dimension tables. A dimensional model may produce a *star schema* or a *snowflake schema*.

Star Schemas

A schema is called a *star schema* if all dimension tables can be joined directly to the fact table. The following diagram shows a classic star schema.

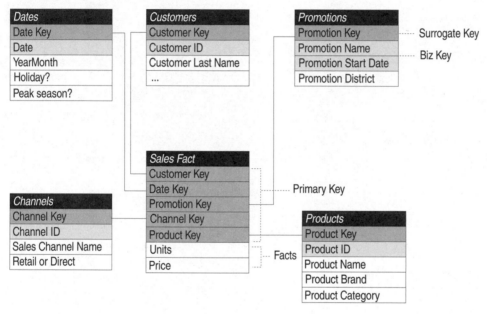

Classic star schema (sales)

The following diagram shows a clickstream star schema.

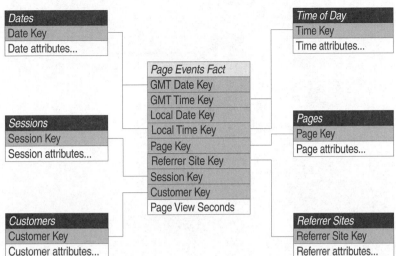

Clickstream star schema

Snowflake Schemas

A schema is called a *snowflake schema* if one or more dimension tables do not join directly to the fact table but must join through other dimension tables. For example, a dimension that describes products may be separated into three tables (snowflaked) as illustrated in the following diagram.

A snowflake schema with multiple heavily snowflaked dimensions is illustrated in the following diagram.

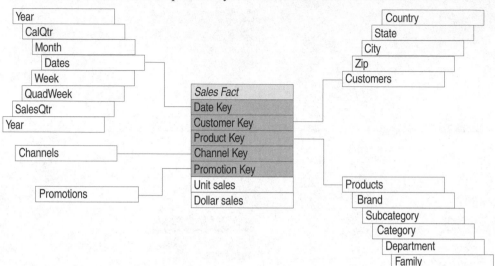

Star or Snowflake

Both star and snowflake schemas are dimensional models; the difference is in their physical implementations. Snowflake schemas support ease of dimension maintenance because they are more normalized. Star schemas are easier for direct user access and often support simpler and more efficient queries. The decision to model a dimension as a star or snowflake depends on the nature of the dimension itself, such as how frequently it changes and which of its elements change, and often involves evaluating tradeoffs between ease of use and ease of maintenance. It is often easiest to maintain a complex dimension by snowflaking the dimension. By pulling hierarchical levels into separate tables, referential integrity between the levels of the hierarchy is guaranteed. Analysis Services reads from a snowflaked dimension as well as, or better than, from a star dimension. However, it is important to present a simple and appealing user interface to business users who are developing ad hoc queries on the dimensional database. It may be better to create a star version of the snowflaked dimension for presentation to the users. Often, this is best accomplished by creating an indexed view across the snowflaked dimension, collapsing it to a virtual star.

Dimension Tables

Dimension tables encapsulate the attributes associated with facts and separate these attributes into logically distinct groupings, such as time, geography, products, customers, and so forth.

A dimension table may be used in multiple places if the data warehouse contains multiple fact tables or contributes data to data marts. For example, a product dimension may be used with a sales fact table and an inventory fact table in the data warehouse, and also in one or more departmental data marts. A dimension such as customer, time, or product that is used in multiple schemas is called a *conforming dimension* if all copies of the dimension are the same. Summarization data and reports will not correspond if different schemas use different versions of a dimension table. Using conforming dimensions is critical to successful data warehouse design.

User input and evaluation of existing business reports help define the dimensions to include in the data warehouse. A user who wants to see data by region and by product has just identified two dimensions (geography and product). Business reports that group sales by salesperson or sales by customer identify two more dimensions (salesforce and customer). Almost every data warehouse includes a time dimension.

In contrast to a fact table, dimension tables are usually small and change relatively slowly. Dimension tables are seldom keyed to date.

The records in a dimension table establish one-to-many relationships with the fact table. For example, there may be a number of sales to a single customer, or a number of sales of a single product. The dimension table contains attributes associated with the dimension entry; these attributes are rich and user-oriented textual details, such as product name or customer name and address. Attributes serve as report labels and query constraints. Attributes that are coded in an OLTP database should be decoded into descriptions. For example, product category may exist as a simple integer in the OLTP database, but the dimension table should contain the actual text for the category. The code may also be carried in the dimension table if needed for maintenance. This denormalization simplifies and improves the efficiency of queries and simplifies user query tools. However, if a dimension attribute changes frequently, maintenance may be easier if the attribute is assigned to its own table to create a snowflake dimension.

It is often useful to have a pre-established no such member or unknown member record in each dimension to which orphan fact records can be tied during the update process. Business needs and the reliability of consistent source data will drive the decision as to whether such placeholder dimension records are required.

Hierarchies

The data in a dimension is usually hierarchical in nature. Hierarchies are determined by the business need to group and summarize data into usable information. For example, a time dimension often contains the hierarchy elements: (all time), Year, Quarter, Month, Day, or (all time), Year Quarter, Week, Day. A dimension may contain multiple hierarchies – a time dimension often contains both calendar and fiscal year hierarchies. Geography is seldom a dimension of its own; it is usually a hierarchy that imposes a structure on sales points, customers, or other geographically distributed dimensions. An example geography hierarchy for sales points is: (all), Country, Region, State or Province, City, Store.

Note that each hierarchy example has an (all) entry such as (all time), (all stores), (all customers), and so forth. This top-level entry is an artificial category used for grouping the first-level categories of a dimension and permits summarization of fact data to a single number for a dimension. For example, if the first level of a product hierarchy includes product line categories for hardware, software, peripherals, and services, the question "What was the total amount for sales of all products last year?" is equivalent to "What was the total amount for the combined sales of hardware, software, peripherals, and services last year?" The concept of an (all) node at the top of each hierarchy helps reflect the way users want to phrase their questions. OLAP tools depend on hierarchies to categorize data – Analysis Services will create by default an (all) entry for a hierarchy used in a cube if none is specified.

A hierarchy may be balanced, unbalanced, ragged, or composed of parent-child relationships such as an organizational structure. For more information about hierarchies in OLAP cubes, see SQL Server Books Online.

Surrogate Keys

A critical part of data warehouse design is the creation and use of surrogate keys in dimension tables. A surrogate key is the primary key for a dimension table and is independent of any keys provided by source data systems. Surrogate keys are created and maintained in the data warehouse and should not encode any information about the contents of records; automatically increasing integers make good surrogate keys. The original key for each record is carried in the dimension table but is not used as the primary key. Surrogate keys provide the means to maintain data warehouse information when dimensions change. Special keys are used for date and time dimensions, but these keys differ from surrogate keys used for other dimension tables.

GUID and IDENTITY Keys

Avoid using GUIDs (globally unique identifiers) as keys in the data warehouse database. GUIDs may be used in data from distributed source systems, but they are difficult to use as table keys. GUIDs use a significant amount of storage (16 bytes each), cannot be efficiently sorted, and are difficult for humans to read. Indexes on GUID columns may be relatively slower than indexes on integer keys because GUIDs are four times larger. The Transact-SQL NEWID function can be used to create GUIDs for a column of

uniqueidentifier data type, and the ROWGUIDCOL property can be set for such a column to indicate that the GUID values in the column uniquely identify rows in the table, but uniqueness is not enforced.

Because a **uniqueidentifier** data type cannot be sorted, the GUID cannot be used in a GROUP BY statement, nor can the occurrences of the **uniqueidentifier** GUID be distinctly counted – both GROUP BY and COUNT DISTINCT operations are very common in data warehouses. The **uniqueidentifier** GUID cannot be used as a measure in an Analysis Services cube.

The IDENTITY property and IDENTITY function can be used to create identity columns in tables and to manage series of generated numeric keys. IDENTITY functionality is more useful in surrogate key management than **uniqueidentifier** GUIDs.

Date and Time Dimensions

Each event in a data warehouse occurs at a specific date and time; and data is often summarized by a specified time period for analysis. Although the date and time of a business fact is usually recorded in the source data, special date and time dimensions provide more effective and efficient mechanisms for time-oriented analysis than the raw event time stamp. Date and time dimensions are designed to meet the needs of the data warehouse users and are created within the data warehouse.

A date dimension often contains two hierarchies, one for calendar year and another for fiscal year.

Time Granularity

A date dimension with one record per day will suffice if users do not need time granularity finer than a single day. A date by day dimension table will contain 365 records per year (366 in leap years).

A separate time dimension table should be constructed if a fine time granularity, such as minute or second, is needed. A time dimension table of one-minute granularity will contain 1,440 rows for a day, and a table of seconds will contain 86,400 rows for a day. If exact event time is needed, it should be stored in the fact table.

When a separate time dimension is used, the fact table contains one foreign key for the date dimension and another for the time dimension. Separate date and time dimensions simplify many filtering operations. For example, summarizing data for a range of days requires joining only the date dimension table to the fact table. Analyzing cyclical data by time period within a day requires joining just the time dimension table. The date and time dimension tables can both be joined to the fact table when a specific time range is needed.

For hourly time granularity, the hour breakdown can be incorporated into the date dimension or placed in a separate dimension. Business needs influence this design decision. If the main use is to extract contiguous chunks of time that cross day boundaries (for example 11/24/2000 10 p.m. to 11/25/2000 6 a.m.), then it is easier if the hour and day are in the same dimension. However, it is easier to analyze cyclical and recurring daily events if they are in separate dimensions. Unless there is a clear reason to combine date and hour in a single dimension, it is generally better to keep them in separate dimensions.

Date and Time Dimension Attributes

It is often useful to maintain attribute columns in a date dimension to provide additional convenience or business information that supports analysis. For example, one or more columns in the time-by-hour dimension table can indicate peak periods in a daily cycle, such as meal times for a restaurant chain or heavy usage hours for an Internet service provider. Peak period columns may be Boolean, but it is better to decode the Boolean yes/no into a brief description, such as peak/ offpeak. In a report, the decoded values will be easier for business users to read than multiple columns of yes and no.

These are some possible attribute columns that may be used in a date table. Fiscal year versions are the same, although values such as quarter numbers may differ.

Column name	Data type	Format/Example	Comment
date_key	int	yyyymmdd	
day_date	smalldatetime		
day_of_week	char	Monday	
week_begin_date	smalldatetime		
week_num	tinyint	1 to 52 or 53	Week 1 defined by business rules
month_num	tinyint	1 to 12	
month_name	char	January	
month_short_name	char	Jan	
month_end_date	smalldatetime		Useful for days in the month
days_in_month	tinyint		Alternative for, or in addition to month_end_date
yearmo	int	yyyymm	
quarter_num	tinyint	1 to 4	
quarter_name	char	1Q2000	
year	smallint		
weekend_ind	bit		Indicates weekend
workday_ind	bit		Indicates work day
weekend_weekday	char	weekend	Alternative for **weekend_ind** and **weekday_ind**. Can be used to make reports more readable.

continued on next page

Column name	Data type	Format/Example	Comment
holiday_ind	bit		Indicates holiday
holiday_name	char	Thanksgiving	
peak_period_ind	bit		Meaning defined by business rules

Date and Time Dimension Keys

In contrast to surrogate keys used in other dimension tables, date and time dimension keys should be smart. A suggested key for a date dimension is of the form yyyymmdd. This format is easy for users to remember and incorporate into queries. It is also a recommended surrogate key format for fact tables that are partitioned into multiple tables by date.

Slowly Changing Dimensions

A characteristic of dimensions is that dimension data is relatively stable – data may be added as new products are released or customers are acquired, but data, such as the names of existing products and customers, changes infrequently. However, business events do occur that cause dimension attributes to change, and the effects of these changes on the data warehouse must be managed (in particular, the potential effect of a change to a dimension attribute on how historical data is tracked and summarized). Slowly changing dimensions is the customary term used for discussions of issues associated with the impact of changes to dimension attributes. Design approaches to dealing with the issues of slowly changing dimensions are commonly categorized into the following three change types:

- Type 1: Overwrite the dimension record.
- Type 2: Add a new dimension record.
- Type 3: Create new fields in the dimension record.

Type 1

Type 1 changes cause history to be rewritten, which may affect analysis results if an attribute is changed that is used to group data for summarization. Changes to a dimension attribute that is never used for analysis can be managed by simply changing the data to the new value. For example, if customer addresses are stored in the customer dimension table, a change to a customer's apartment number is unlikely to affect any summarized information, but a customer's move to a new city or state would affect summarization of data by customer location.

A Type 1 change is the easiest kind of slowly changing dimension to manage in the relational data warehouse. The maintenance procedure is simply to update an attribute column in the dimension table. However, the Type 1 slowly changing dimension presents complex management problems for aggregate tables and OLAP cubes. This is especially true if the updated attribute is a member of a hierarchy on which aggregates are pre-computed, either in the relational database or the OLAP store.

For business users, a Type 1 change can hide valuable information. By updating the attribute in the dimension table, the prior value history of the attribute's value is lost. Consider the example where a customer has upgraded from the Silver to the Gold level of service. If the dimension table simply updates the attribute value, business users will not easily be able to explore differences of behavior before, during, and after the change of service level. In many cases, these questions are of tremendous importance to the business.

Type 2

Type 2 changes cause history to be partitioned at the event that triggered the change. Data prior to the event continues to be summarized and analyzed as before; new data is summarized and analyzed in accordance with the new value of the data.

Consider this example: In a sales organization, salespeople receive commissions on their sales. These commissions influence the commissions of sales managers and executives, and are summarized by sales group in standard reports. When a salesperson transfers from one group in the organization to another group, the historical information about commission amounts must remain applicable to the original group and new commissions must apply to the salesperson's new group. In addition, the total lifetime commission history for the employee must remain available regardless of the number of groups in which the person worked. A type 1 change is not appropriate because it would move all of the salesperson's commission history to the new group.

The type 2 solution is to retain the existing salesperson's dimension record and add a new record for the salesperson that contains the new reporting information. The original record still associates historical commission data with the previous sales group and the new record associates new commission data with the new group. It is customary to include fields in the dimension table to document the change. The following are examples of some common fields that can be used to document the change event:

- Row Current, a Boolean field that identifies which record represents the current status

- Row Start, a date field that identifies the date the record was added

- Row Stop, a date field that identifies the date the record ceased to be current

Surrogate keys on the dimension table are required for type 2 solutions. The salesperson's employee number is most likely used as the record key in OLTP systems. Even if some other key is used, it is unlikely that OLTP systems will need to create a new record for this individual. A second record for this individual cannot be created in the dimension table unless a different value is used for its primary key – surrogate keys avoid this restriction. In addition, because the salesperson's employee number is carried in the dimension table as an attribute, a summarization of the entire employee's commission history is possible, regardless of the number of sales groups to which the person has belonged.

Some queries or reports may be affected by type 2 changes. In the salesperson example, existing reports that summarize by dimension records will now show two entries for the same salesperson. This may not be what is desired, and the report query will have to be modified to summarize by employee number instead of by the surrogate key.

Type 3

Type 3 solutions attempt to track changes horizontally in the dimension table by adding fields to contain the old data. Often only the original and current values are retained and intermediate values are discarded. The advantage of type 3 solutions is the avoidance of multiple dimension records for a single entity. However, the disadvantages are history perturbation and complexity of queries that need to access the additional fields. Type 2 solutions can address all situations where type 3 solutions can be used, and many more as well. If the data warehouse is designed to manage slowly changing dimensions using type 1 and 2 solutions, there is no need to add the maintenance and user complexity inherent in type 3 solutions.

Rapidly Changing Dimensions, or Large Slowly Changing Dimensions

A dimension is considered to be a rapidly changing dimension if one or more of its attributes changes frequently in many rows. For a rapidly changing dimension, the dimension table can grow very large from the application of numerous type 2 changes. The terms rapid and large are relative, of course. For example, a customer table with 50,000 rows and an average of 10 changes per customer per year will grow to about five million rows in 10 years, assuming the number of customers does not grow. This may be an acceptable growth rate. On the other hand, only one or two changes per customer per year for a ten million row customer table will cause it to grow to hundreds of millions of rows in ten years.

Tracking bands can be used to reduce the rate of change of many attributes that have continuously variable values such as age, size, weight, or income. For example, income can be categorized into ranges such as [0-14,999], [15,000-24,999], [25,000-39,999], and so on, which reduce the frequency of change to the attribute. Although type 2 change records should not be needed to track age, age bands are often used for other purposes, such as analytical grouping. Birth date can be used to calculate exact age when needed. Business needs will determine which continuously variable attributes are suitable for converting to bands.

Often, the correct solution for a dimension with rapidly changing attributes is to break the offending attributes out of the dimension and create one or more new dimensions. Consider the following example.

An important attribute for customers might be their account status (good, late, very late, in arrears, suspended), and the history of their account status. Over time many customers will move from one of these states to another. If this attribute is kept in the customer dimension table and a type 2 change is made each time a customer's status changes, an entire row is added only to track this one attribute. The solution is to create a separate account_status dimension with five members to represent the account states.

A foreign key in the customer table points to the record in the account_status dimension table that represents the current account status of that customer. A type 1 change is made to the customer record when the customer's account status changes. The fact table also contains a foreign key for the account_status dimension. When a new fact record is loaded into the fact table, the customer id in the incoming fact record is used to look up the current account_table key in the customer record and populate it into the fact record. This captures a customer's account history in the fact table.

In addition to the benefit of removing the rapidly changing item from the customer dimension, the separate account status dimension enables easy pivot analysis of customers by current account status in OLAP cubes. However, to see entire account history for a customer, the fact table must be joined to the customer table and the account_status table and then filtered on customer id, which is not very efficient for frequent queries for a customer's account history.

This scenario works reasonably well for a single rapidly changing attribute. What if there are ten or more rapidly changing attributes? Should there be a separate dimension for each attribute? Maybe, but the number of dimensions can rapidly get out of hand and the fact table can end up with a large number of foreign keys. One approach is to combine several of these mini-dimensions into a single physical dimension. This is the same technique used to create what is often called a junk dimension that contains unrelated attributes and flags to get them out of the fact table. However, it is still difficult to query these customer attributes well because the fact table must be involved to relate customers to their attributes. Unfortunately, business users are often very interested in this kind of historical information, such as the movement of a customer through the various account status values.

If business users frequently need to query a dimension that has been broken apart like this, the best solution is to create a factless schema that focuses on attribute changes. For example, consider a primary data warehouse schema that keeps track of customers' purchases. The Customer dimension has been developed as a Type 2 slowly changing dimension, and account status has been pulled out into a separate dimension. Create a new fact table, CustomerChanges, that tracks only the changes to the customer and account status. A sample schema is illustrated in the following figure.

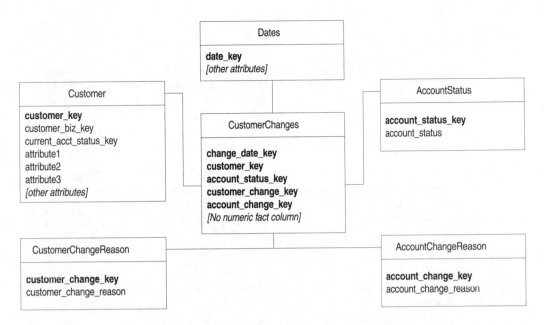

The fact table, CustomerChanges, receives a new row only when a change is made to the Customer table that includes information about the customer's current account status. The fact table has no numeric measure or fact; an entry in the table signifies that an interesting change has occurred to the customer. Optionally, the CustomerChanges schema can track the reason for the change in the CustomerChangeReason and AccountChangeReason dimension tables. Sample values for the account_change_reason might include Customer terminated account, Account closed for non-payment, and Outstanding balance paid in full.

Attribute history tables like this are neither dimension tables nor fact tables in the usual sense. The information in this kind of table is something like Quantity on Hand in an inventory fact table, which cannot be summarized by adding. However, unlike Quantity on Hand in an inventory table, these attributes do not change on a fixed periodic basis, so they cannot be numerically quantified and meaningfully averaged unless the average is weighted by the time between events.

Multi-Use Dimensions

Sometimes data warehouse design can be simplified by combining a number of small, unrelated dimensions into a single physical dimension, often called a junk dimension. This can greatly reduce the size of the fact table by reducing the number of foreign keys in fact table records. Often the combined dimension will be prepopulated with the Cartesian product of all dimension values. If the number of discrete values creates a very large table of all possible value combinations, the table can be populated with value combinations as they are encountered during the load or update process.

A common example of a multi-use dimension is a dimension that contains customer demographics selected for reporting standardization. Another multiuse dimension might contain useful textual comments that occur infrequently in the source data records; collecting these comments in a single dimension removes a sparse text field from the fact table and replaces it with a compact foreign key.

Fact Tables

A fact table must address the business problem, business process, and needs of the users. Without this information, a fact table design may overlook a critical piece of data or incorporate unused data that unnecessarily adds to complexity, storage space, and processing requirements.

Fact tables contain business event details for summarization. Fact tables are often very large, containing hundreds of millions of rows and consuming hundreds of gigabytes or multiple terabytes of storage. Because dimension tables contain records that describe facts, the fact table can be reduced to columns for dimension foreign keys and numeric fact values. Text, blobs, and denormalized data are typically not stored in the fact table.

Multiple Fact Tables

Multiple fact tables are used in data warehouses that address multiple business functions, such as sales, inventory, and finance. Each business function should have its own fact table and will probably have some unique dimension tables. Any dimensions that are common across the business functions must represent the dimension information in the same way, as discussed earlier in "Dimension Tables." Each business function will typically have its own schema that contains a fact table, several conforming dimension tables, and some dimension tables unique to the specific business function. Such business-specific schemas may be part of the central data warehouse or implemented as data marts.

Very large fact tables may be physically partitioned for implementation and maintenance design considerations. The partition divisions are almost always along a single dimension, and the time dimension is the most common one to use because of the historical nature of most data warehouse data. If fact tables are partitioned, OLAP cubes are usually partitioned to match the partitioned fact table segments for ease of maintenance. Partitioned fact tables can be viewed as one table with an SQL UNION query as long as the number of tables involved does not exceed the limit for a single query. For more information about partitioning fact tables and OLAP cubes, see Chapter 18, "Using Partitions in a SQL Server 2000 Data Warehouse."

Additive and Non-additive Measures

The values that quantify facts are usually numeric, and are often referred to as *measures*. Measures are typically additive along all dimensions, such as Quantity in a sales fact table. A sum of Quantity by customer, product, time, or any combination of these dimensions results in a meaningful value.

Some measures are not additive along one or more dimensions, such as Quantity-on-Hand in an inventory system or Price in a sales system. Some measures can be added along dimensions other than the time dimension; such measures are sometimes referred to as semiadditive. For example, Quantity-on-Hand can be added along the Warehouse dimension to achieve a meaningful total of the quantity of items on hand in all warehouses at a specific point in time. Along the time dimension, however, an aggregate function, such as Average, must be applied to provide meaningful information about the quantity of items on hand. Measures that cannot be added along any dimension are truly nonadditive. Queries, reports, and applications must evaluate measures properly according to their summarization constraints.

Nonadditive measures can often be combined with additive measures to create new additive measures. For example, Quantity times Price produces Extended Price or Sale Amount, an additive value.

Calculated Measures

A calculated measure is a measure that results from applying a function to one or more measures, for example, the computed Extended Price value resulting from multiplying Quantity times Price. Other calculated measures may be more complex, such as profit, contribution to margin, allocation of sales tax, and so forth.

Calculated measures may be precomputed during the load process and stored in the fact table, or they may be computed on the fly as they are used. Determination of which measures should be precomputed is a design consideration. There are other considerations in addition to the usual tradeoff between storage space and computational time. The ability of SQL to state complex relationships and expressions is not as powerful as that of MDX, so complex calculated measures are more likely to be candidates for precomputing if they are accessed using SQL than if they are accessed through Analysis Services using MDX.

Fact Table Keys

A fact table contains a foreign key column for the primary keys of each dimension. The combination of these foreign keys defines the primary key for the fact table. Physical design considerations, such as fact table partitioning, load performance, and query performance, may indicate a different structure for the fact table primary key than the composite key that is in the logical model. These considerations are discussed below in the section "Design the Relational Database and OLAP Cubes." For more information about partitioning fact tables, see Chapter 18, "Using Partitions in a SQL Server 2000 Data Warehouse."

The logical model for a fact table resolves many-to-many relationships between dimensions because dimension tables join through the fact table. For examples of fact tables, see the illustrations earlier in this chapter in "Dimensional Model Schemas."

Granularity

The grain of the fact table is determined after the fact content columns have been identified. Granularity is a measure of the level of detail addressed by an individual entry in the fact table. Examples of grain include "at the Transaction level", "at the Line Item level", "Sales to each customer, by product, by month". As you can see, the grain for a fact table is closely related to the dimensions to which it links. Including only summarized records of individual facts will reduce the grain and size of a fact table, but the resulting level of detail must remain sufficient for the business needs.

Business needs, rather than physical implementation considerations, must determine the minimum granularity of the fact table. However, it is better to keep the data as granular as possible, even if current business needs do not require it – the additional detail might be critical for tomorrow's business analysis. Analysis Services is designed to rapidly and efficiently summarize detailed facts into OLAP cubes so highly granular fact tables impose no performance burden on user response time. Alternatively, the OLAP cubes can be designed to include a higher level of aggregation than the relational database. Fine grained data allows the data mining functionality of Analysis Services to discover more interesting nuggets of information.

Do not mix granularities in the fact table. Do not add summary records to the fact table that include detail facts already in the fact table. Aggregation summary records, if used, must be stored in separate tables, one table for each level of granularity. Aggregation tables are automatically created by Analysis Services for OLAP cubes so there is no need to design, create, and manage them manually.

Care must also be taken to properly handle records from source systems that may contain summarized data, such as records for product orders, bills of lading, or invoices. An order typically contains totals of line items for products, shipping charges, taxes, and discounts. Line items are facts. Order totals are summarized facts – do not include both in the fact table. The order number should be carried as a field in the line item fact records to allow summarization by order, but a separate record for the order totals is not only unnecessary, including it will make the fact table almost unusable.

The most successful way to handle summary data like taxes and shipping charges is to get business users to define rules for allocating those amounts down to the detailed level. For taxes, the rule already exists and is easy to implement. By contrast, shipping charges may be allocated by weight, product value, or some more arcane formula. It is common for business users to resist providing an allocation scheme that they may view as arbitrary. It is important for the data warehouse designers to push on this point, as the resulting schema is generally much more useful and usable.

Business needs, rather than physical implementation considerations, must determine the minimum granularity of the fact table. However, it is better to keep the data as granular as possible, even if current business needs do not require it – the additional detail might be critical for tomorrow's business analysis. Analysis Services is designed to rapidly and efficiently summarize detailed facts into OLAP cubes so highly granular fact tables impose no performance burden on user response time. More detail also allows the data mining functionality of Analysis Services to discover more interesting nuggets of information.

Develop the Architecture

The data warehouse architecture reflects the dimensional model developed to meet the business requirements. Dimension design largely determines dimension table design, and fact definitions determine fact table design.

Whether to create a star or snowflake schema depends more on implementation and maintenance considerations than on business needs. Information can be presented to the user in the same way regardless of whether a dimension is snowflaked. Data warehouse schemas are quite simple and straightforward, in contrast to OLTP database schemas with their hundreds or thousands of tables and relationships. However, the quantity of data in data warehouses requires attention to performance and efficiency in their design.

Design for Update and Expansion

Data warehouse architectures must be designed to accommodate ongoing data updates, and to allow for future expansion with minimum impact on existing design. Fortunately, the dimensional model and its straightforward schemas simplify these activities. Records are added to the fact table in periodic batches, often with little effect on most dimensions. For example, a sale of an existing product to an existing customer at an existing store will not affect the product, customer, or store dimensions at all. If the customer is new, a new record is added to the customer dimension table when the fact record is added to the fact table. The historical nature of data warehouses means that records almost never have to be deleted from tables except to correct errors. Errors in source data are often detected in the extraction and transformation processes in the staging area and are corrected before the data is loaded into the data warehouse database.

The date and time dimensions are created and maintained in the data warehouse independent of the other dimension tables or fact tables – updating date and time dimensions may involve only a simple annual task to mechanically add the records for the next year.

The dimensional model also lends itself to easy expansion. New dimension attributes and new dimensions can be added, usually without affecting existing schemas other than by extension. Existing historical data should remain unchanged. Data warehouse maintenance applications will need to be extended, but well-designed user applications should still function although some may need to be updated to make use of the new information.

An entirely new schema can be added to a data warehouse without affecting existing functionality. A new business subject area can be added by designing and creating a fact table and any dimensions specific to the subject area. Existing dimensions can be reused without modification to maintain conformity throughout the entire warehouse. If a different, more aggregated, grain is used in a new subject area, dimensions may be reduced in size by eliminating fine-grained members, but the resulting dimension must still conform to the master dimension and must be maintained in conformance with it.

Analysis Services OLAP cubes can be extended to accommodate new dimensions by extending their schemas and reprocessing, or by creating new virtual cubes that contain the new dimensions and incorporate existing cubes without modification to them.

Design the Relational Database and OLAP Cubes

In this phase, the star or snowflake schema is created in the relational database, surrogate keys are defined, and primary and foreign key relationships are established. Views, indexes, and fact table partitions are also defined. OLAP cubes are designed that support the needs of the users.

Keys and Relationships

Tables are implemented in the relational database after surrogate keys for dimension tables have been defined and primary and foreign keys and their relationships have been identified. Primary/foreign key relationships should be established in the database schema. For an illustration of these relationships, see the sample star schema, Classic Sales, in "Dimension Model Schema," earlier in this chapter.

The composite primary key in the fact table is an expensive key to maintain:

*   The index alone is almost as large as the fact table.

*   The index on the primary key is often created as a clustered index. In many scenarios a clustered primary key provides excellent query performance. However, all other indexes on the fact table use the large clustered index key. All indexes on the fact table will be large, the system will require significant additional storage space, and query performance may degrade.

As a result, many star schemas are defined with an integer surrogate primary key, or no primary key at all. We recommend that the fact table be defined using the composite primary key. Also create an IDENTITY column in the fact table that could be used as a unique clustered index, should the database administrator determine this structure would provide better performance.

Indexes

Dimension tables must be indexed on their primary keys, which are the surrogate keys created for the data warehouse tables. The fact table must have a unique index on the primary key. There are scenarios where the primary key index should be clustered, and other scenarios where it should not. The larger the number of dimensions in the schema, the less beneficial it is to cluster the primary key index. With a large number of dimensions, it is usually more effective to create a unique clustered index on a meaningless IDENTITY column.

Elaborate initial design and development of index plans for end-user queries is not necessary with SQL Server 2000, which has sophisticated index techniques and an easy to use Index Tuning Wizard tool to tune indexes to the query workload.

The SQL Server 2000 Index Tuning Wizard allows you to select and create an optimal set of indexes and statistics for a database without requiring an expert understanding of the structure of the database, the workload, or the internals of SQL Server. The wizard analyzes a query workload captured in a SQL Profiler trace or provided by an SQL script, and recommends an index configuration to improve the performance of the database.

The Index Tuning Wizard provides the following features and functionality:

- It can use the query optimizer to analyze the queries in the provided workload and recommend the best combination of indexes to support the query mix in the workload.

- It analyzes the effects of the proposed changes, including index usage, distribution of queries among tables, and performance of queries in the workload.

- It can recommend ways to tune the database for a small set of problem queries.

- It allows you to customize its recommendations by specifying advanced options, such as disk space constraints.

A recommendation from the wizard consists of SQL statements that can be executed to create new, more effective indexes and, if wanted, drop existing indexes that are ineffective. Indexed views are recommended on platforms that support their use. After the Index Tuning Wizard has suggested a recommendation, it can then be implemented immediately, scheduled as a SQL Server job, or executed manually at a later time.

The empirical tuning approach provided by the Index Tuning Wizard can be used frequently when the data warehouse is first implemented to develop the initial index set, and then employed periodically during ongoing operation to maintain indexes in tune with the user query workload.

SQL Server Books Online provides detailed discussions of indexes and the Index Tuning Wizard, and procedures for using the wizard to tune database indexes.

Views

Views should be created for users who need direct access to data in the data warehouse relational database. Users can be granted access to views without having access to the underlying data. Indexed views can be used to improve performance of user queries that access data through views. Indexed views are discussed in depth in SQL Server Books Online.

View definitions should create column and table names that will make sense to business users. If Analysis Services will be the primary query engine to the data warehouse, it will be easier to create clear and consistent cubes from views with readable column names.

Design OLAP Cubes

OLAP cube design requirements will be a natural outcome of the dimensional model if the data warehouse is designed to support the way users want to query data. Effective cube design is addressed in depth in "Getting the Most Out of Analysis Services" in Chapter 22, "Cubes in the Real World."

Develop the Operational Data Store

Some business problems are best addressed by creating a database designed to support tactical decision-making. The Operational Data Store (ODS) is an operational construct that has elements of both data warehouse and a transaction system. Like a data warehouse, the ODS typically contains data consolidated from multiple systems and grouped by subject area. Like a transaction system, the ODS may be updated by business users, and contains relatively little historical data.

A classic business case for an operational data store is to support the Customer Call Center. Call center operators have little need for broad analytical queries that reveal trends in customer behavior. Rather, their needs are more immediate: the operator should have up-to-date information about all transactions involving the complaining customer. This data may come from multiple source systems, but should be presented to the call center operator in a simplified and consolidated way.

Implementations of the ODS vary widely depending on business requirements. There are no strict rules for how the ODS must be implemented. A successful ODS for one business problem may be a replicated mirror of the transaction system; for another business problem a star schema will be most effective. Most effective operational data stores fall between those two extremes, and include some level of transformation and integration of data. It is possible to architect the ODS so that it serves its primary operational need, and also functions as the proximate source for the data warehouse staging process.

A detailed discussion of operational data store design and its implications for data warehouse staging, is beyond the scope of this chapter.

Develop the Data Maintenance Applications

The data maintenance applications, including extraction, transformation, and loading processes, must be automated, often by specialized custom applications. Data Transformation Services (DTS) in SQL Server 2000 is a powerful tool for defining many transformations. Other tools are Transact-SQL and applications developed using Microsoft Visual Basic® Scripting Edition (VBScript) or languages such as Visual Basic.

An extensive discussion of the extraction, transformation, and loading (ETL) processes is provided in Chapter 19, "Data Extraction, Transformation, and Loading Techniques."

Develop Analysis Applications

The applications that support data analysis by the data warehouse users are constructed in this phase of data warehouse development.

OLAP cubes and data mining models are constructed using Analysis Services tools, and client access to analysis data is supported by the Analysis Server. Techniques for cube design, MDX, data mining, and client data access to Analysis Services data are covered in depth in the section "Getting the Most Out of Analysis Services."

Other analysis applications, such as Excel PivotTables®, predefined reports, Web sites, and digital dashboards, are also developed in this phase, as are natural language applications using English Query. Specialized third-party analysis tools are also acquired and implemented or installed. Details of these specialized applications are determined directly by user needs. Digital dashboards are discussed in Chapter 27, "Creating an Interactive Digital Dashboard," and Chapter 28, "A Digital Dashboard Browser for Analysis Services Meta Data."

Test and Deploy the System

It is important to involve users in the testing phase. After initial testing by development and test groups, users should load the system with queries and use it the way they intend to after the system is brought on line. Substantial user involvement in testing will provide a significant number of benefits. Among the benefits are:

- Discrepancies can be found and corrected.
- Users become familiar with the system.
- Index tuning can be performed.

It is important that users exercise the system during the test phase with the kinds of queries they will be using in production. This can enable a considerable amount of empirical index tuning to take place before the system comes online. Additional tuning needs to take place after deployment, but starting with satisfactory performance is a key to success. Users who have participated in the testing and have seen performance continually improve as the system is exercised will be inclined to be supportive during the initial deployment phase as early issues are discovered and addressed.

Conclusion

Businesses have collected operational data for years, and continue to accumulate ever-larger amounts of data at ever-increasing rates as transaction databases become more powerful, communication networks grow, and the flow of commerce expands. Data warehouses collect, consolidate, organize, and summarize this data so it can be used for business decisions.

Data warehouses have been used for years to support business decision makers. Data warehousing approaches and techniques are well established, widely adopted, successful, and not controversial. Dimensional modeling, the foundation of data warehouse design, is not an arcane art or science; it is a mature methodology that organizes data in a straightforward, simple, and intuitive representation of the way business decision makers want to view and analyze their data.

The key to data warehousing is data design. The business users know what data they need and how they want to use it. Focus on the users, determine what data is needed, locate sources for the data, and organize the data in a dimensional model that represents the business needs. The remaining tasks flow naturally from a well-designed model – extracting, transforming, and loading the data into the data warehouse, creating the OLAP and data mining analytical applications, developing or acquiring end-user tools, deploying the system, and tuning the system design as users gain experience.

Microsoft SQL Server 2000 provides a wide range of powerful and easy to use tools you can use to create a data warehouse and analyze the data it contains. The ability to design and create data warehouses is no longer isolated to experts working with primitive implements.

Using Partitions in a SQL Server 2000 Data Warehouse

This chapter discusses the role of partitioning data in the data warehouse. The relational data warehouse and Microsoft® SQL Server™ 2000 Analysis Services cubes both support the partitioning of data. The logical concept behind partitioning is the same in both engines of SQL Server: to horizontally partition data by a key such as date. In the relational database, partitioning is accomplished by creating separate physical tables — for example, one table for each month of data — and defining a union view over the member tables. Similarly, Analysis Services in SQL Server Enterprise Edition supports the explicit partitioning of cubes. In both the relational database and the online analytical processing (OLAP) engine, the complexity of the physical storage is hidden from the analytical user.

The benefits of partitioning a data warehouse are tremendous, substantially reducing query time, improving the load time and maintainability of the databases, and solving the data pruning problem associated with removing old data from the active database. The technique requires building a more complex data staging application than a non-partitioned system. This paper describes best practices for designing, implementing, and maintaining horizontally partitioned data warehouses.

Partitions are strongly recommended for large Analysis Services systems, because an effective partitioning plan will improve query performance substantially. Partitioning the relational data warehouse is not generally recommended, although it can be an effective and well performing solution to some specific warehouse maintenance issues, as discussed below. For a data warehouse that keeps a rolling window of data available (for example, 13 weeks or 37 months), partitions provide a clean mechanism for pruning old data.

> **Note** The code examples in this chapter are also available on the *SQL Server 2000 Resource Kit* CD-ROM in file, \Docs\ChapterCode\CH18Code.txt. For more information, see Chapter 39, "Tools, Samples, eBooks, and More."

Using Partitions in a SQL Server 2000 Relational Data Warehouse

A partitioned view joins horizontally partitioned data from a set of members, making the data appear as if from one table. SQL Server 2000 distinguishes between local and distributed partitioned views. In a local partitioned view, all participating tables and the view reside on the same instance of SQL Server. In a distributed partitioned view, at least one of the participating tables resides on a different (remote) server. Distributed partitioned views are not recommended for data warehouse applications.

Dimensional data warehouses are structured around facts and dimensions, and are usually physically instantiated as star schemas, snowflake schemas, and very occasionally as fully denormalized flat tables that combine both facts and dimensions. The discussion in this paper is focused on the use of partitions with a dimensional schema, as these schemas are the most common structure for a relational data warehouse. The recommendations herein are applicable to more general data warehousing schemas.

Advantages of Partitions

Data Pruning

Many data warehouse administrators choose to archive aged data after a certain time. For example, a clickstream data warehouse may keep only three to four months of detailed data online. Other common strategies keep 13 months, 37 months, or 10 years online, archiving and removing from the database the old data as it rolls past the active window. This rolling window structure is a common practice with large data warehouses.

Without partitioned tables, the process of removing aged data from the database requires a very large DELETE statement, for example:

```
DELETE FROM fact_table
WHERE date_key < 19990101
```

This statement is expensive to execute, and is likely to take more time than the load process into the same table. With partitioned tables, by contrast, the administrator redefines the UNION ALL view to exclude the oldest table, and drops that table from the database (presumably after ensuring it has been backed up) – a process that is virtually instantaneous.

As we discuss below, it is expensive to maintain partitioned tables. If data pruning is the only reason to consider partitioning, the designer should investigate a data nibbling approach to removing old data from an unpartitioned table. A script that deletes 1000 rows at a time (use the set rowcount 1000 command) could run continuously on a low-priority process, until all desired data are removed. This technique is used effectively on large systems, and is a more straightforward approach than building the necessary partition management system. Depending on load volumes and system utilization, this technique will be appropriate for some systems, and should be benchmarked on the system under consideration.

Load Speed

The fastest way to load data is into an empty table, or a table with no indexes. By loading into smaller partitioned tables the incremental load process can be significantly more efficient.

Maintainability

Once the data warehouse staging application has been built to support partitioning, the entire system becomes easier to maintain. Maintenance activities including loading data, and backing up and restoring tables, can execute in parallel, achieving dramatic increases in performance. The process of incrementally populating downstream cubes can be speeded up and simplified.

Query Speed

Query speed should not be considered a reason to partition the data warehouse relational database. Query performance is similar for partitioned and non-partitioned fact tables. When the partitioned database is properly designed, the relational engine will include in a query plan only the partition(s) necessary to resolve that query. For example, if the database is partitioned by month and a query is conditioned on Jan-2000, the query plan will include only the partition for Jan-2000. The resulting query will perform well against the partitioned table, about the same as against a properly indexed combined table with a clustered index on the partitioning key.

Disadvantages of Partitions

Complexity

The primary disadvantage of partitions is the requirement that the administrator build an application to manage the partitions. It would be inappropriate to move into production a data warehouse that uses horizontal partitions in the relational database, without first designing, testing, and rolling out an application to manage those partitions. One of the goals of this paper is to discuss the issues and design decisions underlying the partition management application.

Query Design Constraints

For the best query performance, all queries must place conditions on the filter key directly in the fact table. A query that places the constraint on a second table, such as a Dates dimension table, will include all partitions in the query.

Design Considerations

Dimensional data warehouses are structured around facts and dimensions, and are usually physically instantiated as star schemas, snowflake schemas, and very occasionally as fully denormalized flat tables that combine both facts and dimensions. The administrator of a dimensional data warehouse typically partitions only the fact tables; there would seldom be an advantage to partitioning a dimension table. In some circumstances, a very large dimension table containing more than 10 million members may benefit from partitioning. A non-dimensional relational data warehouse can also be partitioned, and the general remarks in this paper still apply.

An effective partitioning plan is developed in the context of the system architecture and design goals. Even with identical schema designs, a relational data warehouse that exists only to populate Analysis Services cubes may imply a different partitioning structure than one queried directly by analysts. A system with a rolling window will necessarily be partitioned by time; others may not.

If the data warehouse includes Analysis Services cubes, Microsoft recommends that the partitions in the relational data warehouse and Analysis Services databases be structured in parallel. The maintenance application is simplified: the application creates a new cube partition at the same time as it creates a new table in the relational database. Too, administrators need learn only one partitioning strategy. This is merely a simplifying recommendation, however. An application may have a compelling reason to partition the two databases differently, and the only downside would be the complexity of the maintenance application.

Overview of Partition Design

Partitioned tables in the SQL Server database can use updatable or queryable (nonupdatable) partitioned views. In both cases, the table partitions are created with CHECK constraints that each partition contains the correct data. An updatable partitioned view will support an INSERT (or UPDATE or DELETE) on the view, and push the operation to the correct underlying table. While this is a nice benefit, a data warehouse application typically needs to bulk load, which cannot be performed through the view. The table below summarizes the requirements, advantages, and disadvantages of updatable and queryable partitioned views.

Requirements	Advantages	Disadvantages
Updatable partitioned view		
• Partition key(s) enforced by CHECK constraint(s) • Partition key(s) part of the primary key • Partition key(s) part of no other database constraint • UNION ALL view defined over member tables	• *Query performance:* query plans include only those member tables necessary to resolve the query. • *Simplicity of maintenance application:* data can be loaded into the UNION ALL view and is inserted into the appropriate member table.	• *Load performance:* data loading through the view occurs too slowly for this approach to be viable for most data warehousing applications. • *Inflexibility:* database design may require additional constraints on the partition key.
Queryable partitioned view		
• Partition key(s) enforced by CHECK constraint(s) • UNION ALL view defined over member tables	• *Query performance:* query plans include only those member tables necessary to resolve the query. • *Load performance:* bulk load directly into the member tables with high performance. • *Storage:* Primary key index is not required for the partitioned view, although it is recommended practice to declare the primary key and create an index on it.	• View is limited to 256 member tables. • Maintenance application must be built to manage partitions and loads.

Microsoft's recommended practice is to design the fact table as a local (on a single server) partitioned union view with the primary key defined. In most cases this definition will result in the partitioned view also being updatable, but the data warehouse maintenance application should be designed to bulk load most data directly into the member tables rather than through the view.

Sample Syntax

The following code sample illustrates the syntax for defining the member tables and the union view, and for inserting data into the view:

```
-- Create the fact table for 1999
CREATE TABLE [dbo].[sales_fact_19990101] (
    [date_key] [int] NOT NULL
CHECK ([date_key] BETWEEN 19990101 AND 19991231),
    [product_key] [int] NOT NULL ,
    [customer_key] [int] NOT NULL ,
    [promotion_key] [int] NOT NULL ,
    [store_key] [int] NOT NULL ,
    [store_sales] [money] NULL ,
    [store_cost] [money] NULL ,
    [unit_sales] [float] NULL
)
ALTER TABLE [sales_fact_19990101]
ADD PRIMARY KEY (
[date_key], [product_key], [customer_key], [promotion_key], [store_key])

-- Create the fact table for 2000
CREATE TABLE [dbo].[sales_fact_20000101] (
    [date_key] [int] NOT NULL
CHECK ([date_key] BETWEEN 20000101 AND 20001231),
    [product_key] [int] NOT NULL ,
    [customer_key] [int] NOT NULL ,
    [promotion_key] [int] NOT NULL ,
    [store_key] [int] NOT NULL ,
    [store_sales] [money] NULL ,
    [store_cost] [money] NULL ,
    [unit_sales] [float] NULL
)
ALTER TABLE [sales_fact_20000101]
ADD PRIMARY KEY (
[date_key], [product_key], [customer_key], [promotion_key], [store_key])

--Create the UNION ALL view.
CREATE VIEW [dbo].[sales_fact]
AS
SELECT * FROM [dbo].[sales_fact_19990101]
UNION ALL
SELECT * FROM [dbo].[sales_fact_20000101]
```

```
--Now insert a few rows of data, for example:
INSERT INTO [sales_fact]
VALUES (19990125, 347, 8901, 0, 13, 5.3100, 1.8585, 3.0)

INSERT INTO [sales_fact]
VALUES (19990324, 576, 7203, 0, 13, 2.1000, 0.9450, 3.0)

INSERT INTO [sales_fact]
VALUES (19990604, 139, 7203, 0, 13, 5.3700, 2.2017, 3.0)

INSERT INTO [sales_fact]
VALUES (20000914, 396, 8814, 0, 13, 6.4800, 2.0736, 2.0)

INSERT INTO [sales_fact]
VALUES (20001113, 260, 8269, 0, 13, 5.5200, 2.4840, 3.0)
```

To verify that the partitioning is working correctly, use SQL Query Analyzer to show the query plan for a query such as:

```
SELECT TOP 2 * FROM sales_fact WHERE date_key = 19990324
```

You should see only the 1999 table included in the query plan. Compare this query plan with that generated by the same two tables with the primary key removed: the 2000 table is still excluded. Contrast these plans with the query plan generated against the schema with the constraint on date_key removed. With the constraint removed, both the 1999 and the 2000 tables are included in the query.

Note that in general, it is good practice to use the "TOP N" syntax when doing exploratory queries against large tables, as it returns results quickly with minimal server resources. When looking at partitioned table query plans, it's even more important, because the query plan generated by a "SELECT *" statement is difficult to parse. To the casual observer, it looks as if the query plan includes all the component tables of the UNION ALL view, although at query execution time only the appropriate tables are used in the query.

Apply Conditions Directly to the Fact Table

For the best query performance, all queries must place conditions on the filter key directly in the fact table. A query that places the constraint on a second table, such as a Dates dimension table, will include all partitions in the query. Standard star join queries into a UNION ALL fact table work well.

- Place conditions on the non-partitioned dimensions in those dimension tables, as is standard practice.

- Include attributes from the partitioning dimension (Dates).

- Design queries against a partitioned dimensional schema exactly as you would against a non-partitioned schema, with the exception that conditions on dates are most effective when placed directly on the date key in the fact table.

If each partition table has a clustered index with date as the first column in the index, the cost of going to all partitions to resolve an ad hoc query is relatively small. Predefined queries, such as those that generate standard reports or that incrementally update downstream databases, should be written as efficiently as possible.

Choice of Partition Key(s)

The fact table can be partitioned on multiple dimensions, but most practitioners will partition only date. As described previously, date partitioning enables easy "rolling window" management, and older partitions may even be located in a different place, or more lightly indexed, than fresher partitions. Too, most queries into the data warehouse filter on date.

For applications partitioned by date, the decision variables are:

- **How much data to keep online?** This decision should be driven largely from the business requirements, tempered by the cost-benefit ratio of keeping very large volumes of data online.

- **What should the date key look like?** It is a widely accepted data warehousing best practice to use surrogate keys for the dimension and fact tables. For fact tables partitioned by date, the recommended practice is to use "smart" integer surrogate keys of the form "yyyymmdd". As an integer, this key will use only 4 bytes, compared to the 8 bytes of a datetime key. Many data warehouses use a natural date key of type **datetime**.

- **How granular should the partitions be?** Although the example above uses annual partitions, most systems will choose a finer granularity such as month, week, or day. While it's mildly interesting to consider whether user queries tend to fall along month or week boundaries, by far the most important factor is the overall size and manageability of the system. Recall that any SQL query can reference at most 256 tables; for data warehouses that maintain more than a few months of data, a UNION ALL view over daily partitions will hit that limit. As a rule of thumb, a fact table that is partitioned only on date would most likely partition by week.

- **How are the partition ranges defined?** The BETWEEN syntax is most straightforward and human-readable, and performs efficiently. For example consider monthly partitions of the form:

```
date_key < 19990101
date_key BETWEEN 1990101 AND 19990131
date_key BETWEEN 19990201 AND 19990229
...
date_key BETWEEN 19991201 AND 19991231
date_key > 19991231
```

Note the first and last partitions above: it is a good practice to define these partitions even if you expect never to put data into them, in order to cover the universe of all possible date values. Note also that the February partition covers data through Feb-29, although 1999 is not a leap year. This structure removes the need to include leap year logic in the design of the application that creates partitions and constraints.

- **Are partitions merged together over time?** In order to minimize the number of active partitions, the database administrator may choose to build the partitioning application in such a way that daily partitions are merged into weeks or months. This approach is discussed in greater detail below, in the section on populating and maintaining partitions.

This detailed discussion of how to partition by date should illuminate the discussion of other prospective partition keys.

Data loading: If there is a strong tendency for incoming data to align by another dimension — for example, if data for each Store or Subsidiary are delivered by different systems — these are natural partition keys.

Data querying of cubes: Although there is no technical reason for the relational database and Analysis Services cubes to be partitioned in the same way, it is common practice to do so. The maintenance application is simpler if this assumption is made. Thus, even if the relational database exists only to populate Analysis Services cubes, consideration should be given to common query patterns when choosing partition keys.

Naming Conventions

The conventions for naming the member tables of a horizontally partitioned fact table should flow naturally from the partition design. For greatest generality, use the full partition start date in the title: [sales_fact_yyyymmdd] is preferred to [sales_fact_yyyy], even if the partitioning is annual.

If the database supports partitions at multiple granularities, the naming convention should reflect the time span held within each partition. For example, use sales_fact_20001101m for a monthly partition, and sales_fact_20001101d for a daily one.

The names of the member tables are hidden from end users, who access data through the view, so the member table names should be oriented to the maintenance application.

Partitioning for Downstream Cubes

If the only use of the relational data warehouse is to support Analysis Services cubes, it is not necessary to define the UNION ALL view. In this case, the 256-table limit would not apply to the application, but it is not a recommended practice to partition the relational data warehouse in such a way that a UNION ALL view could not be defined.

Managing the Partitioned Fact Table

The partitioned data warehouse should not be moved into production until the management of the partitions has been automated and tested. The partition management system is a simple application, and the general requirements of that system are outlined here.

The discussion below assumes that the partitioning will occur along date.

Meta Data

A robust partition management system is driven by meta data. That meta data can be stored anywhere, as long as the meta data is accessible programmatically. Most data warehouse systems use custom meta data tables defined on the data warehouse SQL Server, or SQL Server 2000 Meta Data Services.

Whatever the meta data storage mechanism, the contents of the meta data must include the following information on each partition:

- Partition name
- Date partition created
- Date ranges of data in partition
- Date partition moved online (included in UNION ALL view)
- Date partition moved offline (dropped from view)
- Date partition dropped

Other meta data tables that are part of the data warehouse's overall management system should track when and how much data are loaded into each partition.

Creating New Partitions

The first task of the partition management system is to create new partitions. A job should be scheduled to run periodically, to create a new table that will serve as the next partition.

There are many effective ways to perform this task. The recommended approach is to use SQL-DMO (SQL Distributed Management Objects) to create a new table with the same structure and indexes as the existing partitions, but with a new table name, index names, partition key constraint definitions, filegroups, and so on:.

- Get the template table definition (usually the most recent partition).
- Modify the table and index **Name** properties, check constraint **Text** property, and other properties.
- Use the ADD method to instantiate the table.

With intelligent naming conventions, the task can be accomplished with few lines of code.

As discussed later in this chapter, your application may use Analysis Services partitions for the data warehouse system's cubes. If so, the script or program that creates the partition tables in the RDBMS can go on to create the corresponding cube partition, using Decision Support Objects (DSO).

Populating the Partitions

As described above, data can be loaded into a UNION ALL view. In theory this is a great feature of the table partitioning structure, but in practice it is not recommended for data warehouse applications. Data loads into the UNION ALL view cannot be performed in bulk; the load process will be too slow for a data warehouse that is large enough to warrant partitioned tables.

Instead, the data warehouse loading application must be designed to fast load data for each period into the appropriate target table. If the data staging application is implemented in Data Transformation Services (DTS), the Dynamic Properties task can easily change the name of the target table of the Transform Data task or the Bulk Insert task.

As long as the new partition does not yet participate in the UNION ALL view, the data load requires no system downtime.

The data warehouse staging application should be designed to handle incoming data that does not belong in the current partition. This case could occur as an exception to normal events, if the data warehouse loading process did not occur one night. Other systems are faced with newly arrived old data on an ongoing basis. The system's design must consider the likelihood, frequency, and data volumes of these exceptions.

If old data arrives in sufficiently low volume, the simplest design would use the updatable UNION ALL view to load all data that doesn't belong to the current partition.

Defining the UNION ALL View

Once the incremental load has successfully finished, the UNION ALL view must be revised. SQL-DMO is again the recommended approach for this task: use the ALTER method to change the TEXT property of the VIEW object. The list of partitions to include in the view definition is best derived from the meta data table described above.

Merging Partitions

There are potential benefits in merging several partitions into a single larger partition. A data warehouse with large daily load volumes and a small load window may find significant gains in load performance by:

- Creating a text file with the data to be loaded, sorted in the order of the clustered index.
- Bulk-loading into empty daily partitions.
- Creating all nonclustered indexes.

- Bringing the new partition online by recreating the UNION ALL view.

- Weekly, creating and populating a new weekly partition by inserting from the daily partitions, rebuilding indexes, and recreating the UNION ALL view. The daily partitions could then be dropped.

  By moving to weekly or even monthly partitions as the data ages, more partitions can be kept online within the UNION ALL view.

Using Partitions in SQL Server 2000 Analysis Services

Analysis Services in SQL Server 2000 Enterprise Edition explicitly supports partitioned cubes that are analogous to partitioned tables in the relational database. For a cube of moderate to large size, partitions can greatly improve query performance, load performance, and ease of cube maintenance. Partitions can be designed along one or more dimensions, but cubes are often partitioned only along the Dates dimension. The incremental loading of a partitioned cube, including the creation of new partitions, should be performed by a custom application.

Partitions can be stored locally or distributed across multiple physical servers. Although very large systems can also benefit from distributing partitions among multiple servers, our tests indicate that distributed partition solutions provide the most benefit when cubes are in the multiterabyte size range. The current paper considers only locally partitioned cubes.

The incremental loading of a partitioned cube, including the creation of new partitions, should be performed by a custom application.

Advantages of Partitions

Query Performance

The performance of queries is substantially improved by partitioning the cube. Even moderate sized cubes, based on just 100 gigabytes (GB) of data from the relational database, will benefit from partitioning. The benefits of cube partitioning are particularly noticeable under multiuser loads.

The query performance improvement that each application will see varies by the structure of the cube, the usage patterns, and the partition design. A query that requests only one month of data from a cube partitioned by month, will access only one partition. In general, we expect that moving from a large cube in a single partition, to a well-designed local partitioning strategy, will result in average query performance improvement of 100 percent to 1,000 percent.

Pruning Old Data

As with the relational data warehouse, the Analysis Services system administrator may choose to keep only recent data in a cube. With a single partition, the only way to purge the old data is to re-process the cube. By partitioning along the Dates dimension, the administrator can drop old partitions without system downtime.

Maintenance

From an administrative point of view, partitions are independent data units that can be added and dropped without impacting other partitions. This helps with managing the lifecycle of data in the system. Each cube partition is stored in a separate set of files. Backup and restore operations of these data files are easier to manage with the smaller partition files. This is especially true if each partition file is under 2 GB in size. In this case the Archive and Restore utility will be effective. If a portion of the cube is corrupted or is discovered to contain incorrect or inconsistent data, that partition can be reprocessed much more quickly than the entire cube. In addition, it is possible to change the storage mode and aggregation design of older partitions to save space.

Different partitions can use different data sources. A single cube can combine data from multiple relational databases. For example, a corporate data warehouse may be constructed so that data from Europe and North America are hosted on different servers. If the cube is partitioned by geography, it can logically combine these disparate data sources. The relational schema must be virtually identical on the source servers for the single cube definition to work properly.

Load Performance

A partitioned cube can be loaded much more quickly than a non-partitioned cube, because multiple partitions can be loaded in parallel. As we discuss below, you must acquire a third part tool, or build a simple custom tool, in order to process partitions in parallel. On a multiprocessor computer, the performance benefits are significant. The parallel-processing tool should aim for 90 percent CPU utilization. This performance is typically achieved by simultaneously processing between one and two partitions for every two processors. For example, on a four-processor computer with all processors devoted to processing the cube, you will want to process between two and four partitions simultaneously. If you try to process more partitions than you have processors, performance will degrade significantly. One partition for each two processors is conservative; the ideal number depends on speed of data flow from the source databases, aggregation design, storage, and other factors.

Under some circumstances, it is more efficient to rebuild a partition than to incrementally process the partition. Of course, this is far less likely to be the case if the entire cube is held in a single partition.

Disadvantages of Partitions

Complexity

The primary disadvantage of partitions is the requirement that the administrator build an application to manage the partitions. It would be inappropriate to move a partitioned cube into production, without first designing, testing, and rolling out an application to manage those partitions. One of the goals of this chapter is to discuss the issues and design decisions underlying the partition management application.

Meta Data Operations

As the number of partitions increase, the performance of meta data operations such as browsing the cube definition, declines. This is a burden for the administrator rather than the end user, but an excessively partitioned cube will be difficult to administer.

Design Considerations

Overview of Partitions

An effective query plan balances multiple considerations:

- **Number of partitions:** Analysis Services imposes no practical limits on the number of partitions in a cube, but a cube with several thousand partitions will be challenging to manage. In addition, there is a point at which the cost of combining result sets from multiple partitions outweighs the query performance benefits of partition selectivity. It is difficult to provide a rule of thumb for where this point might be, as it depends on cube design, query patterns, and hardware, but it's probably safe to have one partition for every gigabyte of cube storage, or each ten million rows of fact data. In other words, a 100-GB cube (alternatively, 1 Billion facts) on hardware appropriate for that data volume, should easily support 100 partitions. If the partition design calls for significantly more partitions than that, test the performance of alternative partition plans.

- **Load and maintenance:** Data may naturally flow into the cube along certain dimensions such as time. In order to support the staging application to populate and incrementally refresh the cube, these dimensions may be natural partition slices. The Dates dimension, for example, is usually the first partition dimension. Other applications may receive data segmented by geographic region, customer segment, and so on. Because different partitions can use different data sources, the cube population program can efficiently load data from a distributed data warehouse or other source system.

- **Query performance:** An effective partition design relies on some knowledge of common user query patterns. An ideal partitioning dimension is very selective for most detailed user queries. For example, partitioning along Date often improves query performance, as many queries are focused on details in the most recent time periods. Similarly, perhaps many users focus queries along geographic or organizational lines. For maximum query performance improvement, you want queries touching as few partitions as possible.

It is easier to manage partitions along dimensions that are static or, like Date, change in a predictable way. For example, a partition along the "States in the US" is relatively static, as the application designers could expect to receive plenty of warning of a 51st state. By contrast, partitions along the Product dimension are likely to change over time, as new products are added relatively frequently. It may still be desirable to partition along a dynamic dimension, but the designer should note that the administrative system must necessarily be more complex. A dimension that is marked as "changing", then partitioning along that dimension is not permitted. In any case, it is recommended that you create an "all other" partition to hold data for unexpected dimension members.

Slices and Filters

Just as with relational partitions, Analysis Services partitions rely on the administrator to define the data to be found in each partition. The RDBMS uses the CHECK CONSTRAINT to perform this function; Analysis Services uses the slice. A slice is set to a single member in a dimension, such as [Dates].[1999] or [Dates].[1999].[Q1]. In the Analysis Manager Partition Wizard, the slice is set in the screen titled "Select the data slice (optional)". In DSO, the slice is accessed and set using the **SliceValue** property of the partition's dimension level object. Sample syntax is provided later in this document.

The definition of each partition also includes information about what source data flow into this partition. The partition meta data stores the information necessary to populate the partition. The administrator can set the data source and the fact table with the Partition Wizard, or programmatically with DSO. At the time a partition is processed, the settings of its **SliceValue** property are automatically transformed into a filter against the source. The partition definition optionally includes an additional filter, the **SourceTableFilter** property, that can be used to refine the query that will populate the partition. At the time the partition is processed, the WHERE clause of the query issued against the source data will include both the default conditions based on the slice definition, and any additional filter(s) defined by the **SourceTableFilter** property.

Slices and filters must both be properly defined in order for the partitions to work correctly. The role of the Slice is to improve query performance. The Analysis Services engine uses the information in the partition Slice definition to direct a query only to the partition(s) that contain the underlying data. Queries will resolve accurately on a partitioned cube without defined partition slices, but query performance will not be optimized because each query must examine all partitions in the absence of slice definitions.

The role of the filter and source meta data is to define the data that flow into the partition. These elements must be correctly defined, or the overall cube will have incorrect data. When a partition is processed, Analysis Services constrains the data stored in the cube to match the Slice. But no checks are performed to ensure the data are not also loaded into another partition.

For example, imagine that you've partitioned a cube by year, and you incorrectly set the Slice for the 1998 partition to [Dates].[Year].[*1997*], but constrained the filter to 1998. The partition, when processed, would contain zero rows: probably the desired result. By contrast, if you had an existing partition for 1998 and added a new partition for Dec-1998, it would be easy to load the Dec-1998 data twice, and you would receive no notification from Analysis Services that this event had occurred.

It is not difficult to keep partition slices and filters aligned, but it is imperative that the partition management system designer be aware of the issues.

Advanced Slices and Filters

Most partition strategies identify a dimension level to partition, and put the data for each member of that dimension in its own partition. For example, "partition by year" or "partition by state".

It is also common to define a partition plan that drills down on one part of the cube. For example, recent data may be partitioned by day or week; older data by month or year.

Depending on usage patterns and data cardinality, it may be desirable to design a more complex partition plan. For example, imagine that 80 percent of customers live in California, 10 percent in Oregon, and the remaining 10 percent are distributed evenly across the rest of the country. Further, most analysis is focused on local customers (California). In this case, the administrator may wish to create county-level partitions for California, a state-level partition for Oregon, and one partition for the rest of the United States.

The slices would be something like:

- California counties: [All USA].[CA].[Amador] ... [All USA].[CA].[Yolo]

- Oregon state: [All USA].[OR]

- Rest of the country: [All USA]

As discussed above, source data filters would have to be correctly defined to ensure that these partitions are populated correctly. Note that a query that needs to combine data from California and Oregon would also have to look at the "Rest of the country" partition. While it is not very expensive for Analysis Services to look at the map of the "Rest of the country" to learn there is no relevant data therein, query performance would have been better if the cube were partitioned uniformly by state with drilldown on CA. The application logic required to maintain uneven partitions is also more complex, and in general this partitioning approach is not recommended. However, with appropriate care in the design of the maintenance application, and understanding of the query performance tradeoffs, the technique may solve specific design problems.

Aligning Partitions

As the first half of this paper discusses partitions in the RDBMS, it is natural to ask whether Analysis Services partitions must be aligned with relational partitions. The two partition strategies do not need to be identical, but the partition management application is easier to design, build, and understand if the partitions are similar. A common strategy is to partition identically along date in both systems, with optionally a slice along a second or even third dimension in the cube.

The simplest strategy is to use the UNION ALL view as the source fact table for all cube partitions. If cube partitions are aligned with the relational partitions, each cube partition could point directly to its associated relational partition, circumventing the UNION ALL view. In this configuration the cube processing query that extracts data from the relational database will run fastest. The tradeoff for this performance improvement is that the maintenance application needs to ensure the source table is correctly associated with each partition.

If the relational database exists only to populate Analysis Services cubes and does not service any other queries, the system administrator may choose not to create and manage the UNION ALL view. Indexes on the relational tables would be designed to optimize the single query that loads data into the cube. In this case, the relational database is serving more as a staging area than a complete data warehouse.

Storage Modes and Aggregation Plans

Each partition can have its own storage and aggregation plan. Infrequently accessed data can be lightly aggregated, or stored as ROLAP or HOLAP rather than MOLAP, in both cases saving storage space. A cube that is incrementally loaded over time will not likely use this functionality along the time dimension of its partitions, as changing these parameters would require the partition to be reprocessed. The cost of processing time and system complexity would hardly seem to warrant the minimal space savings in most situations.

Partitions along other dimensions, by contrast, are likely to have different aggregation plans. The Usage-Based Optimization Wizard designs aggregations for each partition. The system administrator should focus the optimization wizard on the most recent partitions, and always base the aggregation design for each new set of partitions on the most current partitions, to keep the aggregation design as up-to-date as possible.

Managing the Partitioned Cube

The developer can use a variety of tools to build the management system for relational partitions. SQL-DMO is strongly recommended, but effective systems have been built using stored procedures, extended stored procedures, even Perl scripts that parse text files containing table definitions. The cube partition maintenance program, by contrast, must use DSO.

For system developers who come from a classic database background, the notion of using an object model to instantiate database objects may seem strange. The developer can use a familiar scripting language, such as Microsoft Visual Basic® Scripting Edition (VBScript), Microsoft JScript®, or Perl; or a development environment like Visual Basic (VB) or Microsoft Visual C++®, to develop the modules that use DMO and DSO. These modules can be scheduled from the operating system, from SQL Agent, or called from DTS packages. The requirement to use DSO to build the management system should not be viewed as a reason to forego the use of partitions, even if the developer has never used an object model before. A VBScript sample that illustrates how to use scripting to clone partitions is provided later in this chapter.

If the relational data warehouse uses partitions, the cube partition management system should be designed as part of the relational database partition management system. The cube partition management system must perform the following functions:

- Create new partitions as necessary, typically on a schedule related to the Dates dimension.

- Load data into the partitions.

- Drop old partitions (optional).

- Merge partitions (optional).

Create New Partitions

At the same time the partition management system creates a new date partition in the relational database, it should create all the necessary cube partitions corresponding to that date. It is good practice to incrementally update the cube's dimensions before creating new partitions, as a new dimension member may be added along one of the partition slices.

The simplest case is when the cube is partitioned only by date. The partition management system simply creates one new partition on the appropriate schedule (day, week, month, etc.).

If the cube is partitioned by another dimension in addition to the date, the partition management system will be adding many partitions at a time. For example, consider a cube that is partitioned by month and by state within the U.S. Each month the system will create 50 new state partitions. In this case, it is safe to create this month's partitions by cloning last month's partitions, editing the necessary attributes such as slice and source table name, and updating the partition definition in the cube.

However, consider a cube that is partitioned by month and product brand. Product brands are much more volatile than states or provinces; it is reasonable to expect that a new brand would be added to the product hierarchy during the life of the cube. The maintenance application must ensure that a partition is created to hold this new brand's data. The recommended practice is to:

- Process the dimensions before creating the new partitions.

- Clone existing partitions to ensure continuity in storage modes and aggregation plans.

- Search the processed dimension for new members, creating a partition for any new members of the partitioning level. The system would have to specify default storage mode and aggregation plan.

The partition management system must be carefully designed to ensure that partition slice and filter definitions are aligned and remain accurate over time. If the relational database is partitioned, and those partitions are periodically merged as described earlier in this paper, the partition management system should update the cube partition definitions to synchronize with the source data. The cube partition need not be reprocessed, but the definition should be changed in case reprocessing becomes necessary in the future.

Data Integrity

It is the job of the cube design and the partition management system to ensure that data are processed into one and only one partition. Analysis Services does not check that all rows from a fact table are instantiated in the cube, nor does it verify that a row is loaded into only one partition. If a fact row is inadvertently loaded into two partitions, Analysis Services will view them as different facts. Any aggregations will double-count that data, and queries will return incorrect results.

Processing Partitions

Processing a partition is fundamentally the same as processing a cube. The natural unit of work for a processing task is one partition. The Analysis Manager processing wizard provides the following three modes for processing a cube or partition.

- Incremental update adds new data to the existing cube or partition, and updates and adds aggregations affected by that new data.

- Refresh Data drops all data and aggregations in the cube or partition, and rebuilds the data in the cube or partition.

- Full Process completely rebuilds the structure of the cube or partition, and then refreshes the data and aggregations.

Incremental processing requires that the administrator define a filter condition on the source query, to identify the set of new data for the cube. Usually this filter is based on a date, either the event date or a processing date stored in the fact table.

Exactly this same functionality is available from the Analysis Services Processing task. Most systems use the Analysis Services Processing task to schedule the cube processing. Incrementally processed cubes use the Dynamic Properties task to change the source filter. This same functionality is available from custom coding in DSO as well, although the incremental update requires a few more lines of code than refreshing the data does.

When designing the partition management system, it's important to note that incremental cube or partition processing requires that the partition have been processed in the past. Do not use incremental processing on an unprocessed cube or partition.

A cube that is partitioned only along the Dates dimension has straightforward load management requirements. Typically there is a single partition to update for each load cycle; the only decision point is whether to incrementally update or refresh the data. Most Date-dimensioned cubes will be managed from a simple DTS package.

A cube that is partitioned along multiple dimensions has the following additional challenges and benefits:

- **Challenge:** Large number of partitions to process
- **Challenge:** Potentially changing number of partitions
- **Benefit:** Parallel loading of partitions
- **Benefit:** Greatly improved query performance on highly selective queries

Most applications that partition on multiple dimensions design the cube processing system to load partitions in parallel. A parallel loading system could launch multiple simultaneous DTS packages whose parameters have been updated with the Dynamic Properties task. While feasible, this structure is awkward, and many systems will choose instead to use native DSO code to update the partitions. A sample tool to process partitions in parallel is provided later in this chapter.

Merging Partitions

A cube that is partitioned along Date will see the number of its partitions grow over time. As discussed above, there is theoretically a point at which query performance degrades as the number of partitions increase. Our testing, including the development of a cube with over 500 partitions, has not reached this limit. The system administrators will probably rebel before that point is reached, as the other disadvantage of many partitions – slowness of meta data operations – will make it increasingly difficult to manage the database.

Analysis Services, both through DSO and the Analysis Manager, support the ability to merge partitions. When two partitions are merged, the data from one partition is incorporated into a second partition. Both partitions must have identical storage modes and aggregation plans. Upon completion of the merge, the first partition is dropped and the second partition contains the combined data. The merge processing takes place only on the cube data; the data source is not accessed during the merge process. The process of merging two partitions is very efficient.

If the system design includes merged partitions, the merging process should occur programmatically rather than through Analysis Manager. Merging partitions is straightforward, and like other DSO operations requires few lines of code. The partition merging system must take the responsibility for verifying that the final merged partition contains accurate meta data information for the source filter, to ensure that the partition could be reprocessed if necessary. The partition merge process correctly changes the slice definition, and combines Filter definitions as well as it can. But the merge process does not require that both partitions be populated from the same table or data source, so it is possible to merge two partitions that cannot be repopulated.

A second issue to consider is that the merged partition, like all partitions, cannot be renamed.

These problems can be avoided by using the following good system design practices:

- Use clear naming conventions.

- Follow a consistent partition merging plan.

- Take care to match up cube partitions with relational partitions, or do not partition the relational data warehouse.

For example, consider a Sales cube that partitions data by week. The current week is partitioned by day, and then merged at the end of the week. Our partitions are named Sales_yyyymmdd, where the date in the name is the first day of the data in the partition. In November 2000, we will have weekly partitions Sales_20001105, Sales_20001112, Sales_20001119, and Sales_20001126. During the next week, we create and process Sales_20001203, Sales_20001204, and so on through Sales_20001209. During the Sunday processing window, when there is little use of the system, we can merge 20001204 through 20001209 into Sales_20001203, leaving only the weekly partition. Alternatively, you could effectively rename a partition by creating a new empty partition with the desired name, and merging other partitions into it.

Rolling Off Old Partitions

Deleting old data in a cube partitioned by Date is as simple as dropping the oldest (set of) partitions. Like the other operations we have discussed, this process should be managed programmatically rather than on an ad hoc basis through Analysis Manager.

Conclusions

Using local partitions is recommended for medium to large Analysis Services cubes, containing more than 100 million fact rows. Query performance of the Analysis Services database improves with partitioning. It is easier to maintain partitioned cubes, especially if old data are dropped from the cube. However, partitioning a cube requires an application to manage those partitions.

Partitioning in the relational data warehouse database is similar in concept to partitioning in Analysis Services. As with Analysis Services, an application must be built to manage relational partitions. Partitioning addresses some maintenance problems such as pruning old data, but at the cost of system complexity. Query performance is not improved compared to a well-indexed single table.

Both Analysis Services and the SQL Server relational database support distributed partitions, wherein partitions are located on different servers. We do not recommend distributing relational partitions for a SQL Server 2000 data warehouse system that supports direct queries.

Partitioned cubes exhibit improved query performance with large numbers of partitions. The developer of a large cube should consider partitioning along several dimensions, to maximize the selectivity of user queries and improve processing performance by providing the opportunity for parallel processing.

Partitions are strongly recommended for large Analysis Services systems. Partitioning the relational data warehouse is not generally recommended, although it can be an effective and well-performing solution to some specific warehouse maintenance issues.

For More Information

SQL Server Books Online contains more information about partitions. For additional information, see the following resources.

- The Microsoft SQL Server Web site at http://www.microsoft.com/sql/.

- The Microsoft SQL Server Developer Center at http://msdn.microsoft.com/sqlserver/.

- *SQL Server Magazine* at http://www.sqlmag.com.

- The microsoft.public.sqlserver.server and microsoft.public.sqlserver.datawarehouse newsgroups at news://news.microsoft.com.

- The Microsoft Official Curriculum courses on SQL Server. For up-to-date course information, see http://www.microsoft.com/trainingandservices/.

VBScript Code Example for Cloning a Partition

Code Example 18.1

```
'/*********************************************************************
' File: ClonePart.vbs
'
' Desc: This sample script creates a new partition in the FoodMart 2000
'       Sales cube, based on the latest partition in the cube. The
'       purpose of the script is to show the kinds of DSO calls that
'       are used to clone a partition. The resulting partition is
'       processed, but adds no data to the cube.
'
```

```
'       Users of this script may want to delete the resulting partition
'       after running the script and exploring the results.
'
' Parameters: None
'*******************************************************************/


    Call ClonePart

Sub ClonePart()

    On Error Resume Next

    Dim intDimCounter, intErrNumber
    Dim strOlapDB, strCube, strDB, strAnalysisServer, strPartitionNew
    Dim dsoServer, dsoDB, dsoCube, dsoPartition, dsoPartitionNew

    ' Initialize server, database, and cube name variables.
    strAnalysisServer = "LocalHost"
    strOlapDB = "FoodMart 2000"
    strCube = "Sales"

    ' VBScript does not support direct use of enumerated constants.
    ' However, constants can be defined to supplant enumerations.
    Const stateFailed = 2
    Const olapEditionUnlimited = 0

    ' Connect to the Analysis server.
    Set dsoServer = CreateObject("DSO.Server")
    dsoServer.Connect strAnalysisServer

    ' If connection failed, then end the script.
    If dsoServer.State = stateFailed Then
        MsgBox "Error-Not able to connect to '" & strAnalysisServer _
            & "' Analysis server.", ,"ClonePart.vbs"
        Err.Clear
        Exit Sub
    End if

    ' Certain partition management features are available only
    ' in the Enterprise Edition and Developer Edition releases
    ' of Analysis Services.
```

```
   If dsoServer.Edition <> olapEditionUnlimited Then
      MsgBox "Error-This feature requires Enterprise or " & _
         "Developer Edition of SQL Server to " & _
         "manage partitions.", , "ClonePart.vbs"
      Exit Sub
   End If


   ' Ensure that a valid data source exists in the database.
   Set dsoDB = dsoServer.mdStores(strOlapDB)
   If dsoDB.Datasources.Count = 0 Then
      MsgBox "Error-No data sources found in '" & _
         strOlapDB & "' database.", , "ClonePart.vbs"
      Err.Clear
      Exit Sub
   End If


   ' Find the cube.
   If (dsoDB.mdStores.Find(strCube)) = 0 then
      MsgBox "Error-Cube '" & strCube & "' is missing.", , _
         "ClonePart.vbs"
      Err.Clear
      Exit Sub
   End If


   ' Set the dsoCube variable to the desired cube.
   Set dsoCube = dsoDB.MDStores(strCube)


   ' Find the partition
   If dsoCube.mdStores.Count = 0 Then
      MsgBox "Error-No partitions exist for cube '" & strCube & _
         "'.", , "ClonePart.vbs"
      Err.Clear
      Exit Sub
   End If


   ' Set the dsoPartition variable to the desired partition.
   Set dsoPartition = dsoCube.MDStores(dsoCube.MDStores.Count)
   MsgBox "New partition will be based on existing partition: " _
      & chr(13) & chr(10) & _
      dsoDB.Name & "." & dsoCube.Name & "." & _
      dsoPartition.Name, , "ClonePart.vbs"


   ' Get the quoting characters from the datasource, as
   ' different databases use different quoting characters.
   Dim sLQuote, sRQuote
   sLQuote = dsoPartition.DataSources(1).OpenQuoteChar
   sRQuote = dsoPartition.DataSources(1).CloseQuoteChar
```

```
'***********************************************************************
' Create the new partition based on the desired partition.
'***********************************************************************

    ' Create a new, temporary partition.
    strPartitionNew = "NewPartition" & dsoCube.MDStores.Count
    Set dsoPartitionNew = dsoCube.MDStores.AddNew("~temp")

    ' Clone the properties from the desired partition to the
    ' new partition.
    dsoPartition.Clone dsoPartitionNew

    ' Change the partition name from "~temp" to the
    ' name intended for the new partition.
    dsoPartitionNew.Name = strPartitionNew
    dsoPartitionNew.AggregationPrefix = strPartitionNew & "_"

    ' Set the fact table for the new partition.
    dsoPartitionNew.SourceTable = _
        sLQuote & "sales_fact_dec_1998" & sRQuote

    ' Set the FromClause and JoinClause properties of the new
    ' partition.
    dsoPartitionNew.FromClause = Replace(dsoPartition.FromClause, _
        dsoPartition.SourceTable, dsoPartitionNew.SourceTable)

    dsoPartitionNew.JoinClause = Replace(dsoPartition.JoinClause, _
        dsoPartition.SourceTable, dsoPartitionNew.SourceTable)

    ' Change the definition of the data slice used by the new
    ' partition, by changing the SliceValue properties of the
    ' affected levels and dimensions to the desired values.
    dsoPartitionNew.Dimensions("Time").Levels("Year").SliceValue = "1998"
    dsoPartitionNew.Dimensions("Time").Levels("Quarter").SliceValue = "Q4"
    dsoPartitionNew.Dimensions("Time").Levels("Month").SliceValue = "12"

    ' Estimate the rowcount.
    dsoPartitionNew.EstimatedRows = 18325

    ' Add another filter. The SourceTableFilter provides an additional
    ' opportunity to add a WHERE clause to the SQL query that will
    ' populate this partition. We're using this filter to ensure our new
    ' partition contains zero rows. For the purposes of this sample code
    ' we don't want to change the data in the FoodMart cube. Comment out
    ' this line if you want to see data in the new partition.
```

```
    dsoPartitionNew.SourceTableFilter = dsoPartitionNew.SourceTable _
        & "." & sLQuote & "time_id" & sRQuote & "=100"

    ' Save the partition definition in the metadata repository
    dsoPartitionNew.Update

    ' Check the validity of the new partition structure.
    IF NOT dsoPartitionNew.IsValid Then
        MsgBox "Error-New partition structure is invalid."
        Err.Clear
        Exit Sub
    End If

    MsgBox "New partition " & strPartitionNew & " has been created and " _
        & "processed. To see the new partition in Analysis Manager, you " _
        & "may need to refresh the list of partitions in the Sales cube " _
        & "of FoodMart 2000. The new partition contains no data.", , _
        "ClonePart.vbs"

    ' The next statement, which is commented out, would process the partition.
    ' In a real partition management system, this would likely be a separate
    ' process, perhaps managed via DTS.
    ' dsoPartitionNew.Process

    ' Clean up.
    Set dsoPartition = Nothing
    Set dsoPartitionNew = Nothing
    Set dsoCube = Nothing
    Set dsoDB = Nothing
    dsoServer.CloseServer
    Set dsoServer = Nothing


End Sub
```

Data Extraction, Transformation, and Loading Techniques

Chapter 17, "Data Warehouse Design Considerations," discussed the use of dimensional modeling to design databases for data warehousing. In contrast to the complex, highly normalized, entity-relationship schemas of online transaction processing (OLTP) databases, data warehouse schemas are simple and denormalized. Regardless of the specific design or technology used in a data warehouse, its implementation must include mechanisms to migrate data into the data warehouse database. This process of data migration is generally referred to as the extraction, transformation, and loading (ETL) process.

Some data warehouse experts add an additional term—management—to ETL, expanding it to ETLM. Others use the M to mean meta data. Both refer to the management of the data as it flows into the data warehouse and is used in the data warehouse. The information used to manage data consists of data about data, which is the definition of meta data.

The topics in this chapter describe the elements of the ETL process and provide examples of procedures that address common ETL issues such as managing surrogate keys, slowly changing dimensions, and meta data.

The code examples in this chapter are also available on the *SQL Server 2000 Resource Kit* CD-ROM, in the file \Docs\ChapterCode\CH19Code.txt. For more information, see Chapter 39, "Tools, Samples, eBooks, and More."

Introduction

During the ETL process, data is extracted from an OLTP database, transformed to match the data warehouse schema, and loaded into the data warehouse database. Many data warehouses also incorporate data from non-OLTP systems, such as text files, legacy systems, and spreadsheets; such data also requires extraction, transformation, and loading.

In its simplest form, ETL is the process of copying data from one database to another. This simplicity is rarely, if ever, found in data warehouse implementations; in reality, ETL is often a complex combination of process and technology that consumes a significant portion of the data warehouse development efforts and requires the skills of business analysts, database designers, and application developers.

When defining ETL for a data warehouse, it is important to think of ETL as a process, not a physical implementation. ETL systems vary from data warehouse to data warehouse and even between department data marts within a data warehouse. A monolithic application, regardless of whether it is implemented in Transact-SQL or a traditional programming language, does not provide the flexibility for change necessary in ETL systems. A mixture of tools and technologies should be used to develop applications that each perform a specific ETL task.

The ETL process is not a one-time event; new data is added to a data warehouse periodically. Typical periodicity may be monthly, weekly, daily, or even hourly, depending on the purpose of the data warehouse and the type of business it serves. Because ETL is an integral, ongoing, and recurring part of a data warehouse, ETL processes must be automated and operational procedures documented. ETL also changes and evolves as the data warehouse evolves, so ETL processes must be designed for ease of modification. A solid, well-designed, and documented ETL system is necessary for the success of a data warehouse project.

Data warehouses evolve to improve their service to the business and to adapt to changes in business processes and requirements. Business rules change as the business reacts to market influences—the data warehouse must respond in order to maintain its value as a tool for decision makers. The ETL implementation must adapt as the data warehouse evolves.

Microsoft® SQL Server™ 2000 provides significant enhancements to existing performance and capabilities, and introduces new features that make the development, deployment, and maintenance of ETL processes easier and simpler, and its performance faster.

ETL Functional Elements

Regardless of how they are implemented, all ETL systems have a common purpose: they move data from one database to another. Generally, ETL systems move data from OLTP systems to a data warehouse, but they can also be used to move data from one data warehouse to another. An ETL system consists of four distinct functional elements:

- Extraction
- Transformation
- Loading
- Meta data

Extraction

The ETL extraction element is responsible for extracting data from the source system. During extraction, data may be removed from the source system or a copy made and the original data retained in the source system. It is common to move historical data that accumulates in an operational OLTP system to a data warehouse to maintain OLTP performance and efficiency. Legacy systems may require too much effort to implement such offload processes, so legacy data is often copied into the data warehouse, leaving the original data in place. Extracted data is loaded into the data warehouse staging area (a relational database usually separate from the data warehouse database), for manipulation by the remaining ETL processes.

Data extraction is generally performed within the source system itself, especially if it is a relational database to which extraction procedures can easily be added. It is also possible for the extraction logic to exist in the data warehouse staging area and query the source system for data using ODBC, OLE DB, or other APIs. For legacy systems, the most common method of data extraction is for the legacy system to produce text files, although many newer systems offer direct query APIs or accommodate access through ODBC or OLE DB.

Data extraction processes can be implemented using Transact-SQL stored procedures, Data Transformation Services (DTS) tasks, or custom applications developed in programming or scripting languages.

Transformation

The ETL transformation element is responsible for data validation, data accuracy, data type conversion, and business rule application. It is the most complicated of the ETL elements. It may appear to be more efficient to perform some transformations as the data is being extracted (inline transformation); however, an ETL system that uses inline transformations during extraction is less robust and flexible than one that confines transformations to the transformation element. Transformations performed in the OLTP system impose a performance burden on the OLTP database. They also split the transformation logic between two ETL elements and add maintenance complexity when the ETL logic changes.

Tools used in the transformation element vary. Some data validation and data accuracy checking can be accomplished with straightforward Transact-SQL code. More complicated transformations can be implemented using DTS packages. The application of complex business rules often requires the development of sophisticated custom applications in various programming languages. You can use DTS packages to encapsulate multi-step transformations into a single task.

Listed below are some basic examples that illustrate the types of transformations performed by this element:

Data Validation
Check that all rows in the fact table match rows in dimension tables to enforce data integrity.

Data Accuracy
Ensure that fields contain appropriate values, such as only "off" or "on" in a status field.

Data Type Conversion
Ensure that all values for a specified field are stored the same way in the data warehouse regardless of how they were stored in the source system. For example, if one source system stores "off" or "on" in its status field and another source system stores "0" or "1" in its status field, then a data type conversion transformation converts the content of one or both of the fields to a specified common value such as "off" or "on".

Business Rule Application

Ensure that the rules of the business are enforced on the data stored in the warehouse. For example, check that all customer records contain values for both **FirstName** and **LastName** fields.

Loading

The ETL loading element is responsible for loading transformed data into the data warehouse database. Data warehouses are usually updated periodically rather than continuously, and large numbers of records are often loaded to multiple tables in a single data load. The data warehouse is often taken offline during update operations so that data can be loaded faster and SQL Server 2000 Analysis Services can update OLAP cubes to incorporate the new data. BULK INSERT, **bcp**, and the Bulk Copy API are the best tools for data loading operations. The design of the loading element should focus on efficiency and performance to minimize the data warehouse offline time. For more information and details about performance tuning, see Chapter 20, "RDBMS Performance Tuning Guide for Data Warehousing."

Meta Data

The ETL meta data functional element is responsible for maintaining information (meta data) about the movement and transformation of data, and the operation of the data warehouse. It also documents the data mappings used during the transformations. Meta data logging provides possibilities for automated administration, trend prediction, and code reuse.

Examples of data warehouse meta data that can be recorded and used to analyze the activity and performance of a data warehouse include:

- **Data Lineage**, such as the time that a particular set of records was loaded into the data warehouse.

- **Schema Changes**, such as changes to table definitions.

- **Data Type Usage**, such as identifying all tables that use the "Birthdate" user-defined data type.

- **Transformation Statistics**, such as the execution time of each stage of a transformation, the number of rows processed by the transformation, the last time the transformation was executed, and so on.

- **DTS Package Versioning**, which can be used to view, branch, or retrieve any historical version of a particular DTS package.

- **Data Warehouse Usage Statistics**, such as query times for reports.

ETL Design Considerations

Regardless of their implementation, a number of design considerations are common to all ETL systems:

Modularity

ETL systems should contain modular elements that perform discrete tasks. This encourages reuse and makes them easy to modify when implementing changes in response to business and data warehouse changes. Monolithic systems should be avoided.

Consistency

ETL systems should guarantee consistency of data when it is loaded into the data warehouse. An entire data load should be treated as a single logical transaction—either the entire data load is successful or the entire load is rolled back. In some systems, the load is a single physical transaction, whereas in others it is a series of transactions. Regardless of the physical implementation, the data load should be treated as a single logical transaction.

Flexibility

ETL systems should be developed to meet the needs of the data warehouse and to accommodate the source data environments. It may be appropriate to accomplish some transformations in text files and some on the source data system; others may require the development of custom applications. A variety of technologies and techniques can be applied, using the tool most appropriate to the individual task of each ETL functional element.

Speed

ETL systems should be as fast as possible. Ultimately, the time window available for ETL processing is governed by data warehouse and source system schedules. Some data warehouse elements may have a huge processing window (days), while others may have a very limited processing window (hours). Regardless of the time available, it is important that the ETL system execute as rapidly as possible.

Heterogeneity

ETL systems should be able to work with a wide variety of data in different formats. An ETL system that only works with a single type of source data is useless.

Meta Data Management

ETL systems are arguably the single most important source of meta data about both the data in the data warehouse and data in the source system. Finally, the ETL process itself generates useful meta data that should be retained and analyzed regularly. Meta data is discussed in greater detail later in this chapter.

ETL Architectures

Before discussing the physical implementation of ETL systems, it is important to understand the different ETL architectures and how they relate to each other. Essentially, ETL systems can be classified in two architectures: the homogenous architecture and the heterogeneous architecture.

Homogenous Architecture

A homogenous architecture for an ETL system is one that involves only a single source system and a single target system. Data flows from the single source of data through the ETL processes and is loaded into the data warehouse, as shown in the following diagram.

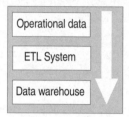

Operational data

ETL System

Data warehouse

Most homogenous ETL architectures have the following characteristics:

- Single data source: Data is extracted from a single source system, such as an OLTP system.

- Rapid development: The development effort required to extract the data is straightforward because there is only one data format for each record type.

- Light data transformation: No data transformations are required to achieve consistency among disparate data formats, and the incoming data is often in a format usable in the data warehouse. Transformations in this architecture typically involve replacing NULLs and other formatting transformations.

- Light structural transformation: Because the data comes from a single source, the amount of structural changes such as table alteration is also very light. The structural changes typically involve denormalization efforts to meet data warehouse schema requirements.

- Simple research requirements: The research efforts to locate data are generally simple: if the data is in the source system, it can be used. If it is not, it cannot.

The homogeneous ETL architecture is generally applicable to data marts, especially those focused on a single subject matter.

Heterogeneous Architecture

A heterogeneous architecture for an ETL system is one that extracts data from multiple sources, as shown in the following diagram. The complexity of this architecture arises from the fact that data from more than one source must be merged, rather than from the fact that data may be formatted differently in the different sources. However, significantly different storage formats and database schemas do provide additional complications.

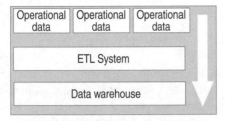

Most heterogeneous ETL architectures have the following characteristics:

- Multiple data sources.

- More complex development: The development effort required to extract the data is increased because there are multiple source data formats for each record type.

- Significant data transformation: Data transformations are required to achieve consistency among disparate data formats, and the incoming data is often not in a format usable in the data warehouse. Transformations in this architecture typically involve replacing NULLs, additional data formatting, data conversions, lookups, computations, and referential integrity verification. Precomputed calculations may require combining data from multiple sources, or data that has multiple degrees of granularity, such as allocating shipping costs to individual line items.

- Significant structural transformation: Because the data comes from multiple sources, the amount of structural changes, such as table alteration, is significant.

- Substantial research requirements to identify and match data elements.

Heterogeneous ETL architectures are found more often in data warehouses than in data marts.

ETL Development

ETL development consists of two general phases: identifying and mapping data, and developing functional element implementations. Both phases should be carefully documented and stored in a central, easily accessible location, preferably in electronic form.

Identify and Map Data

This phase of the development process identifies sources of data elements, the targets for those data elements in the data warehouse, and the transformations that must be applied to each data element as it is migrated from its source to its destination. High level data maps should be developed during the requirements gathering and data modeling phases of the data warehouse project. During the ETL system design and development process, these high level data maps are extended to thoroughly specify system details.

Identify Source Data

For some systems, identifying the source data may be as simple as identifying the server where the data is stored in an OLTP database and the storage type (SQL Server database, Microsoft Excel spreadsheet, or text file, among others). In other systems, identifying the source may mean preparing a detailed definition of the meaning of the data, such as a business rule, a definition of the data itself, such as decoding rules (O = On, for example), or even detailed documentation of a source system for which the system documentation has been lost or is not current.

Identify Target Data

Each data element is destined for a target in the data warehouse. A target for a data element may be an attribute in a dimension table, a numeric measure in a fact table, or a summarized total in an aggregation table. There may not be a one-to-one correspondence between a source data element and a data element in the data warehouse because the destination system may not contain the data at the same granularity as the source system. For example, a retail client may decide to roll data up to the SKU level by day rather than track individual line item data. The level of item detail that is stored in the fact table of the data warehouse is called the grain of the data. If the grain of the target does not match the grain of the source, the data must be summarized as it moves from the source to the target.

Map Source Data to Target Data

A data map defines the source fields of the data, the destination fields in the data warehouse and any data modifications that need to be accomplished to transform the data into the desired format for the data warehouse. Some transformations require aggregating the source data to a coarser granularity, such as summarizing individual item sales into daily sales by SKU. Other transformations involve altering the source data itself as it moves from the source to the target. Some transformations decode data into human readable form, such as replacing "1" with "on" and "0" with "off" in a status field. If two source systems encode data destined for the same target differently (for example, a second source system uses Yes and No for status), a separate transformation for each source system must be defined. Transformations must be documented and maintained in the data maps. The relationship between the source and target systems is maintained in a map that is referenced to execute the transformation of the data before it is loaded in the data warehouse.

Develop Functional Elements

Design and implementation of the four ETL functional elements, Extraction, Transformation, Loading, and meta data logging, vary from system to system. There will often be multiple versions of each functional element.

Each functional element contains steps that perform individual tasks, which may execute on one of several systems, such as the OLTP or legacy systems that contain the source data, the staging area database, or the data warehouse database. Various tools and techniques may be used to implement the steps in a single functional area, such as Transact-SQL, DTS packages, or custom applications developed in a programming language such as Microsoft Visual Basic®. Steps that are discrete in one functional element may be combined in another.

Extraction

The extraction element may have one version to extract data from one OLTP data source, a different version for a different OLTP data source, and multiple versions for legacy systems and other sources of data. This element may include tasks that execute SELECT queries from the ETL staging database against a source OLTP system, or it may execute some tasks on the source system directly and others in the staging database, as in the case of generating a flat file from a legacy system and then importing it into tables in the ETL database. Regardless of methods or number of steps, the extraction element is responsible for extracting the required data from the source system and making it available for processing by the next element.

Transformation

Frequently a number of different transformations, implemented with various tools or techniques, are required to prepare data for loading into the data warehouse. Some transformations may be performed as data is extracted, such as an application on a legacy system that collects data from various internal files as it produces a text file of data to be further transformed. However, transformations are best accomplished in the ETL staging database, where data from several data sources may require varying transformations specific to the incoming data organization and format.

Data from a single data source usually requires different transformations for different portions of the incoming data. Fact table data transformations may include summarization, and will always require surrogate dimension keys to be added to the fact records. Data destined for dimension tables in the data warehouse may require one process to accomplish one type of update to a changing dimension and a different process for another type of update.

Transformations may be implemented using Transact-SQL, as is demonstrated in the code examples later in this chapter, DTS packages, or custom applications.

Regardless of the number and variety of transformations and their implementations, the transformation element is responsible for preparing data for loading into the data warehouse.

Loading

The loading element typically has the least variety of task implementations. After the data from the various data sources has been extracted, transformed, and combined, the loading operation consists of inserting records into the various data warehouse database dimension and fact tables. Implementation may vary in the loading tasks, such as using BULK INSERT, **bcp**, or the Bulk Copy API. The loading element is responsible for loading data into the data warehouse database tables.

Meta Data Logging

Meta data is collected from a number of the ETL operations. The meta data logging implementation for a particular ETL task will depend on how the task is implemented. For a task implemented by using a custom application, the application code may produce the meta data. For tasks implemented by using Transact-SQL, meta data can be captured with Transact-SQL statements in the task processes. The meta data logging element is responsible for capturing and recording meta data that documents the operation of the ETL functional areas and tasks, which includes identification of data that moves through the ETL system as well as the efficiency of ETL tasks.

Common Tasks

Each ETL functional element should contain tasks that perform the following functions, in addition to tasks specific to the functional area itself:

Confirm Success or Failure. A confirmation should be generated on the success or failure of the execution of the ETL processes. Ideally, this mechanism should exist for each task so that rollback mechanisms can be implemented to allow for incremental responses to errors.

Scheduling. ETL tasks should include the ability to be scheduled for execution. Scheduling mechanisms reduce repetitive manual operations and allow for maximum use of system resources during recurring periods of low activity.

SQL Server 2000 ETL Components

SQL Server 2000 includes several components that aid in the development and maintenance of ETL systems:

- **Data Transformation Services (DTS)**: SQL Server 2000 DTS is a set of graphical tools and programmable objects that lets you extract, transform, and consolidate data from disparate sources into single or multiple destinations.

- **SQL Server Agent**: SQL Server Agent provides features that support the scheduling of periodic activities on SQL Server 2000, or the notification to system administrators of problems that have occurred with the server.

- **Stored Procedures and Views**: Stored procedures assist in achieving a consistent implementation of logic across applications. The Transact-SQL statements and logic needed to perform a commonly performed task can be designed, coded, and tested once in a stored procedure. A view can be thought of as either a virtual table or a stored query. The data accessible through a view is not stored in the database as a distinct object; only the SELECT statement for the view is stored in the database.

- **Transact SQL**: Transact-SQL is a superset of the SQL standard that provides powerful programming capabilities that include loops, variables, and other programming constructs.

- **OLE DB**: OLE DB is a low-level interface to data. It is an open specification designed to build on the success of ODBC by providing an open standard for accessing all kinds of data.

- **Meta Data Services**: SQL Server 2000 Meta Data Services provides a way to store and manage meta data about information systems and applications. This technology serves as a hub for data and component definitions, development and deployment models, reusable software components, and data warehousing descriptions.

The ETL Staging Database

In general, ETL operations should be performed on a relational database server separate from the source databases and the data warehouse database. A separate staging area database server creates a logical and physical separation between the source systems and the data warehouse, and minimizes the impact of the intense periodic ETL activity on source and data warehouse databases. If a separate database server is not available, a separate database on the data warehouse database server can be used for the ETL staging area. However, in this case it is essential to schedule periods of high ETL activity during times of low data warehouse user activity.

For small data warehouses with available excess performance and low user activity, it is possible to incorporate the ETL system into the data warehouse database. The advantage of this approach is that separate copies of data warehouse tables are not needed in the staging area. However, there is always some risk associated with performing transformations on live data, and ETL activities must be very carefully coordinated with data warehouse periods of minimum activity. When ETL is integrated into the data warehouse database, it is recommended that the data warehouse be taken offline when performing ETL transformations and loading.

Most systems can effectively stage data in a SQL Server 2000 database, as we describe in this chapter. An ETL system that needs to process extremely large volumes of data will need to use specialized tools and custom applications that operate on files rather than database tables. With extremely large volumes of data, it is not practical to load data into a staging database until it has been cleaned, aggregated, and stripped of meaningless information. Because it is much easier to build an ETL system using the standard tools and techniques that are described in this chapter, most experienced system designers will attempt to use a staging database, and move to custom tools only if data cannot be processed during the load window.

What does "extremely large" mean and when does it become infeasible to use standard DTS tasks and Transact-SQL scripts to process data from a staging database? The answer depends on the load window, the complexity of transformations, and the degree of data aggregation necessary to create the rows that are permanently stored in the data warehouse. As a conservative rule of thumb, if the transformation application needs to process more than 1 gigabyte of data in less than an hour, it may be necessary to consider specialized high performance techniques, which are outside the scope of this chapter.

This section provides general information about configuring the SQL Server 2000 database server and the database to support an ETL system staging area database with effective performance. ETL systems can vary greatly in their database server requirements; server configurations and performance option settings may differ significantly from one ETL system to another.

ETL data manipulation activities are similar in design and functionality to those of OLTP systems although ETL systems do not experience the constant activity associated with OLTP systems. Instead of constant activity, ETL systems have periods of high write activity followed by periods of little or no activity. Configuring a server and database to meet the needs of an ETL system is not as straightforward as configuring a server and database for an OLTP system.

For a detailed discussion of RAID and SQL Server 2000 performance tuning, see Chapter 20, "RDBMS Performance Tuning Guide for Data Warehousing."

Server Configuration

Disk storage system performance is one of the most critical factors in the performance of database systems. Server configuration options offer additional methods for adjusting server performance.

RAID

As with any OLTP system, the RAID level for the disk drives on the server can make a considerable performance difference. For maximum performance of an ETL database, the disk drives for the server computer should be configured with RAID 1 or RAID 10. Additionally, it is recommended that the transaction logs, databases, and **tempdb** be placed on separate physical drives. Finally, if the hardware controller supports write caching, it is recommended that write caching be enabled. However, be sure to use a caching controller that guarantees that the controller cache contents will be written to disk in case of a system failure.

Server Configuration Options (sp_configure)

No specific changes need to be made to the server configuration options in order to optimize performance for an ETL system. It is recommended that these options be left at their default settings unless there is a specific reason to modify them.

Database Configuration

In SQL Server 2000, database performance can be tuned by proper selection of settings for data file growth and adjusting database configuration options.

Data File Growth

When creating a database, an initial size for the data files for the database and transaction log must be specified. By default, SQL Server 2000 allows the data files to grow as much as necessary until disk space is exhausted. It is important to size the database appropriately before loading any data into it to avoid the I/O intensive operation of auto-growing data files. Failure to appropriately size the data files initially for the database means that SQL will be forced to frequently increase the size of the data files, which will degrade performance of the ETL processes.

Appropriate initial sizing of the data files can reduce the likelihood of SQL being forced to increase the size of the database, which eliminates an intensive I/O operation. If a data file is allowed to automatically grow, the file growth may be specified by a percentage or a set number value. The growth value can be specified in megabytes (MB), kilobytes (KB), or percent. If percent is specified, the increment size is the specified percentage of the file size at the time the increment occurs. If the data file is too small, the growth increments will be frequent. For example, if a data file is initially created at 10 MB and set to grow in 10 percent increments until it reaches 20 MB, SQL Server 2000 will perform eight auto-grow operations as the data file size increases to 20 MB. Therefore, it is recommended that a fixed MB value be chosen for data file growth increments.

Finally, if the server uses SCSI disks, special care should be paid to preventing disk space consumption from increasing beyond 85 percent of the capacity of the drive. Beyond 85 percent consumption, SCSI disk performance begins to degrade. Therefore, it is recommended that the data files for the database are set to grow automatically, but only to a predefined maximum size, which should be no more than 85 percent capacity of the drive.

Database Configuration Options

Several database options can be adjusted to enhance the performance of an ETL database. For a complete discussion of these options, see SQL Server Books Online. For more information about database performance tuning, see Chapter 20, "RDBMS Performance Tuning Guide for Data Warehousing."

The following table lists some database options and their setting that may be used to increase ETL performance.

Option name	Setting
AUTO_CREATE_STATISTICS	Off
AUTO_UPDATE_STATISTICS	On
AUTO_SHRINK	Off
CURSOR_DEFAULT	LOCAL
RECOVERY Option	Bulk_Loaded
TORN_PAGE_DETECTION	On

> **Caution** Different recovery model options introduce varying degrees of risk of data loss. It is imperative that the risks be thoroughly understood before choosing a recovery model.

Managing Surrogate Keys

Surrogate keys are critical to successful data warehouse design: they provide the means to maintain data warehouse information when dimensions change. For more information and details about surrogate keys, see Chapter 17, "Data Warehouse Design Considerations."

The following are some common characteristics of surrogate keys:

- Used as the primary key for each dimension table, instead of the original key used in the source data system. The original key for each record is carried in the table but is not used as the primary key.

- May be defined as the primary key for the fact table. In general, the fact table uses a composite primary key composed of the dimension foreign key columns, with no surrogate key. In schemas with many dimensions, load and query performance will improve substantially if a surrogate key is used. If the fact table is defined with a surrogate primary key and no unique index on the composite key, the ETL application must be careful to ensure row uniqueness outside the database. A third possibility for the fact table is to define no primary key at all. While there are systems for which this is the most effective approach, it is not good database practice and should be considered with caution.

- Contains no meaningful business information; its only purpose is to uniquely identify each row. There is one exception: the primary key for a time dimension table provides human-readable information in the format "yyyymmdd".

- Is a simple key on a single column, not a composite key.

- Should be numeric, preferably integer, and not text.

- Should never be a GUID.

The SQL Server 2000 **Identity** column provides an excellent surrogate key mechanism.

ETL Code Examples

Code examples in these sections use the **pubs** sample database included with SQL Server 2000 to demonstrate various activities performed in ETL systems. The examples illustrate techniques for loading dimension tables in the data warehouse; they do not take into consideration separate procedures that may be required to update OLAP cubes or aggregation tables.

The use of temporary and staging tables in the ETL database allows the data extraction and loading process to be broken up into smaller segments of work that can be individually recovered. The temporary tables allow the source data to be loaded and transformed without impacting the performance of the source system except for what is necessary to extract the data. The staging tables provide a mechanism for data validation and surrogate key generation before loading transformed data into the data warehouse. Transformation, validation, and surrogate key management tasks should never be performed directly on dimension tables in the data warehouse.

The code examples in this chapter are presented as Transact-SQL, in order to communicate to the widest audience. A production ETL system would use DTS to perform this work. A very simple system may use several Execute SQL tasks linked within a package. More complex systems divide units of work into separate packages, and call those subpackages from a master package. For a detailed explanation of how to use DTS to implement the functionality described in this chapter, please see SQL Server Books Online.

Tables for Code Examples

The examples use the **authors** table in the **pubs** database as the source of data. The following three tables are created for use by the code examples.

Table name	Purpose
Authors_Temp	Holds the data imported from the source system.
Authors_Staging	Holds the dimension data while it is being updated. The data for the authors will be updated in this table and then the data will be loaded into the data warehouse dimension table.
Authors_DW	Simulates the Authors dimension table in the data warehouse.

These are key points regarding the structures of these tables:

- There is no difference between the structure of the **authors** table in the **pubs** database and the **Authors_Temp** table in the staging area. This allows for straightforward extraction of data from the source system with minimum impact on source system performance.

- The **Author_Staging** table is used to generate the surrogate key (**Author_Key** column) that is used by the data warehouse. This table is also used to validate any data changes, convert data types, and perform any other transformations necessary to prepare the data for loading into the data warehouse.

- The structure of the **Author_Staging** table in the staging area is the same as that of the **Authors_DW** table in the data warehouse. This allows for straightforward loading of the dimension data from the staging database to the data warehouse. If the dimension table in the data warehouse is small enough, it can be truncated and replaced with data from the staging table. In many data warehouses, dimension tables are too large to be efficiently updated by dropping and reloading them in their entirety. In this case, the tables in both the staging area and data warehouse should contain a **datetime** column, which can be used to determine which records need to be updated, inserted, or deleted in the data warehouse table.

- The staging and data warehouse tables are identical after the data is loaded into the data warehouse. This fact can be considered for use in backup strategy planning.

Define Example Tables

The following three Transact-SQL statements create the **Authors_Temp** and **Authors_Staging** tables, and the **Authors_DW** table that simulates the Authors dimension table in the data warehouse:

Code Example 19.1

```
CREATE TABLE [Authors_Temp] (
   [au_id] [varchar] (11) PRIMARY KEY  CLUSTERED,
   [au_lname] [varchar] (40) DEFAULT ('Missing'),
   [au_fname] [varchar] (20) DEFAULT ('Missing'),
   [phone] [char] (12) DEFAULT ('000-000-0000'),
   [address] [varchar] (40) DEFAULT ('Missing'),
   [city] [varchar] (20) DEFAULT ('Missing'),
   [state] [char] (2) DEFAULT ('XX'),
   [zip] [char] (5) DEFAULT ('00000'),
   [contract] [bit] NOT NULL DEFAULT (0))
ON [PRIMARY]
GO

CREATE TABLE Authors_Staging (
   [Author_Key] int NOT NULL IDENTITY (1,1) PRIMARY KEY  CLUSTERED ,
   [au_id] varchar (11) NOT NULL ,
   [au_lname] varchar (40)  NOT NULL DEFAULT ('Missing'),
   [au_fname] varchar (20)  NOT NULL DEFAULT ('Missing'),
   [phone] char (12)  NOT NULL DEFAULT ('000-000-0000'),
   [address] varchar (40)  NULL DEFAULT ('Missing'),
   [city] varchar (20)  NOT NULL DEFAULT ('Missing'),
   [state] char (2)  NOT NULL DEFAULT ('XX') ,
   [zip] char (5)  NOT NULL DEFAULT ('00000') ,
   [contract] bit NOT NULL,
   [DateCreated] smalldatetime NOT NULL DEFAULT (getdate()),
   [DateUpdated] smalldatetime NOT NULL DEFAULT (getdate())
   )ON [PRIMARY]
GO

CREATE TABLE [Authors_DW] (
   [Author_Key] [int] NOT NULL PRIMARY KEY CLUSTERED,
   [au_id] [varchar] (11) NOT NULL,
   [au_lname] [varchar] (40) NOT NULL DEFAULT ('Missing'),
   [au_fname] [varchar] (20) NOT NULL DEFAULT ('Missing'),
   [phone] [char] (12) NOT NULL DEFAULT ('000-000-0000'),
```

```
  [address] [varchar] (40) NULL DEFAULT ('Missing'),
    [city] [varchar] (20) NOT NULL DEFAULT ('Missing'),
    [state] [char] (2) NOT NULL DEFAULT ('XX'),
    [zip] [char] (5) NOT NULL DEFAULT ('00000'),
    [contract] [bit] NOT NULL,
    [DateCreated] smalldatetime NOT NULL DEFAULT (getdate()),
    [DateUpdated] smalldatetime NOT NULL DEFAULT (getdate())
    ) ON [PRIMARY]
GO
```

Populate Example Tables

The following three Transact-SQL statements populate the temporary, staging, and data warehouse sample tables by loading all of the author records except the record for author Johnson White, which will be inserted later to illustrate a technique for adding records to the data warehouse dimension table:

Code Example 19.2

```
--Populate the Authors_Temp table with all author records except Johnson White's
INSERT INTO Authors_Temp
SELECT * FROM Authors
WHERE AU_ID <> '172-32-1176'
GO


--Populate the Authors_Staging table from Authors_Temp
INSERT INTO Authors_Staging (au_id, au_lname, au_fname, phone, address, city, state,
zip, contract)
SELECT au_id, au_lname, au_fname, phone, address, city, state, zip, contract
FROM Authors_Temp
GO


--Populate the simulated data warehouse dimension table, Authors_DW
INSERT INTO Authors_DW
SELECT * FROM Authors_Staging
GO
```

The contents of the three tables now simulate the state following the completion of all previous ETL processing before the author Johnson White is added to the source data table.

Inserting New Dimension Records

Loading new author records is a relatively simple task. If the extraction method is capable of generating a change set (a set of records that have been altered since the last data extraction) from the source system, we load the change set into the temporary table. If we cannot generate a change set from the source system, we will have to load the entire data set from the source system into the temporary table, even if only a single record has changed.

The following Transact-SQL code demonstrates a simple technique for loading new rows into the Authors dimension. This example assumes that there is a primary key on the source system that we can use and it assumes that we do not have a change set.

Code Example 19.3

```
--Truncate any data that currently exists in the Authors_Temp table
TRUNCATE TABLE Authors_Temp
GO


--Load all of the data from the source system into the Authors_Temp table
INSERT INTO Authors_Temp
SELECT * FROM Authors
GO


--Set a starting value for the Contract field for two records
-- for use by future examples
UPDATE Authors_Temp
SET Contract = 0
WHERE state = 'UT'
GO


--Locate all of the new records that have been added to the source system by
--comparing the new temp table contents to the existing staging table contents
--and add the new records to the staging table
INSERT INTO Authors_Staging (au_id, au_lname, au_fname, phone, address, city, state,
zip, contract)
SELECT T.au_id, T.au_lname, T.au_fname, T.phone, T.address, T.city, T.state, T.zip,
T.contract
FROM Authors_Temp T LEFT OUTER JOIN
    Authors_Staging S ON T.au_id = S.au_id
WHERE (S.au_id IS NULL)
GO
```

```
--Locate all of the new records that are to be added to the data warehouse
--and insert them into the data warehouse by comparing Authors_Staging to Authors_DW
INSERT INTO Authors_DW (Author_Key, au_id, au_lname, au_fname, phone, address, city,
state, zip, contract,
    DateCreated, DateUpdated)
SELECT S.Author_Key, S.au_id, S.au_lname, S.au_fname, S.phone, S.address, S.city,
S.state, S.zip, S.contract,
    S.DateCreated, S.DateUpdated
FROM Authors_Staging S LEFT OUTER JOIN
    Authors_DW D ON S.au_id = D.au_id
WHERE (D.au_id IS NULL)
GO
```

Managing Slowly Changing Dimensions

This section describes various techniques for managing slowly changing dimensions in the data warehouse. "Slowly changing dimensions" is the customary term used for dimensions that contain attributes that, when changed, may affect grouping or summarization of historical data. Design approaches to dealing with the issues of slowly changing dimensions are commonly categorized into the following three change types:

- **Type 1**: Overwrite the dimension record

- **Type 2**: Add a new dimension record

- **Type 3**: Create new fields in the dimension record

Type 1 and Type 2 dimension changes are discussed in this section. Type 3 changes are not recommended for most data warehouse applications and are not discussed here. For more information and details about slowly changing dimensions, see Chapter 17, "Data Warehouse Design Considerations."

Type 1 and Type 2 dimension change techniques are used when dimension attributes change in records that already exist in the data warehouse. The techniques for inserting new records into dimensions (discussed earlier in the section "Inserting New Dimension Records") apply to all dimensions regardless of whether changes to dimension attributes are incorporated using Type 1 or Type 2 change techniques.

The code examples in the following sections demonstrate techniques for managing Type 1 and Type 2 dimension changes. The examples have been kept simple to maintain clarity for technique illustration purposes—the examples assume that all changes for a dimension will be of the same type, whereas, in reality, most dimensions include some attributes that require Type 2 changes and other attributes that can be maintained using Type 1 changes. For example, a retailer may decide that a change in the marital status of a customer should be treated as a Type 2 change, whereas a change of street address for the same customer should be treated as a Type 1 change. Therefore, it is important to document all of the attributes in a dimension and, for each attribute, whether a value change should be applied as Type 1 or a Type 2 change.

Type 1: Overwrite the Dimension Record

A change to a dimension attribute that is never used for analysis can be managed by simply changing the data to the new value. This type of change is called a Type 1 change. For example, a change to a customer's street address is unlikely to affect any summarized information and the previous street address can be discarded without consequence.

Type 1 dimension changes are straightforward to implement. The following Transact-SQL code demonstrates a simple Type 1 technique for updating existing rows in the Authors dimension. For this example, we will change some data in the **Authors_Temp** table to simulate changed records received as a result of updates to the **authors** table in the source database. The value for the Contract field is assumed to be eligible for Type 1 changes in this example. In a later section, the Contract field will be updated using a Type 2 change. The following example assumes that there is a primary key on the source system that we can use and it assumes that we do not have a change set:

Code Example 19.4

```
--Change the Authors_Temp table to simulate updates received from the source system
UPDATE Authors_Temp
SET Contract = 0
WHERE state = 'UT'
GO


--Update the Authors_Staging table with the new values in Authors_Temp
UPDATE Authors_Staging
SET Contract = T.Contract,
   DateUpdated = getdate()
FROM Authors_Temp T INNER JOIN Authors_Staging S
   ON T.au_id = S.au_id
WHERE T.Contract <> S.Contract
GO


--Update the Author_DW with the new data in Authors_Staging
UPDATE Authors_DW
SET Contract = S.Contract,
   DateUpdated = getdate()
FROM Authors_Staging S INNER JOIN Authors_DW D
   ON S.Author_Key = D.Author_Key
WHERE S.Contract <> D.Contract
GO
```

Type 2: Add a New Dimension Record

Type 2 changes cause history to be partitioned at the event that triggered the change. Data prior to the event continues to be summarized and analyzed as before; new data is summarized and analyzed in accordance with the new value of the data. The technique for implementing a Type 2 change is to keep the existing dimension record and add a new record that contains the updated data for the attribute or attributes that have changed. Values are copied from the existing record to the new record for all fields that have not changed. A new surrogate key value is created for the new record and the record is added to the dimension table. Fact records that apply to events subsequent to the Type 2 change must be related to the new dimension record.

Although it is relatively straightforward to implement Type 2 change techniques in the ETL process to manage slowly changing dimensions, the data associated with a dimension member becomes fragmented as such changes are made. Data warehouse analysis and reporting tools must be capable of summarizing data correctly for dimensions that include Type 2 changes. To minimize unnecessary fragmentation, a Type 2 change should not be used if a Type 1 change is appropriate.

The techniques used to insert new records into a Type 2 dimension are the same as the ones used to insert new records into a Type 1 dimension. However, the techniques used to track updates to dimension records are different.

The following Transact-SQL code demonstrates a simple technique for applying Type 2 changes for existing rows in the Authors dimension. Unlike a Type 1 change, existing records are not updated in a Type 2 dimension. Instead, new records are added to the dimension to contain the changes to the source system records. In this example, the values of the contract field changed in the Type 1 example are changed to different values and we now assume the contract field is to be managed as a Type 2 change.

Notice that the Transact-SQL statement used to load updated records into the staging table is the same as the one used to insert new records into the staging table except that the predicate clause in the two statements differ. When loading new records, the WHERE clause uses the **auth_id** field to determine which records are new. When inserting records for Type 2 changes, the WHERE clause causes new records to be added when the value of the attribute of interest (contract) in the temporary table differs from the attribute value in the staging table.

Code Example 19.5

```
--Change the Authors_Temp table to simulate updates received from the source system
--This change reverses the change made in the Type 1 example by setting Contract to 1
UPDATE Authors_Temp
SET Contract = 1
WHERE state = 'UT'
GO
```

```
--For example purposes, make sure the staging table records have a different value
--for the contract field for the UT authors
UPDATE Authors_Staging
SET Contract = 0
WHERE state = 'UT'
GO


--Insert new records into the Staging Table for those records in the temp table
--that have a different value for the contract field
INSERT INTO Authors_Staging (au_id, au_lname, au_fname, phone, address, city, state,
zip, contract)
SELECT T.au_id, T.au_lname, T.au_fname, T.phone, T.address, T.city, T.state, T.zip,
T.contract
FROM Authors_Temp T
    LEFT OUTER JOIN Authors_Staging S ON T.au_id = S.au_id
WHERE T.Contract <> S.Contract
GO


--Insert the new records into the data warehouse Table
INSERT INTO Authors_DW (Author_Key, au_id, au_lname, au_fname, phone, address, city,
state, zip, contract,
    DateCreated, DateUpdated)
SELECT S.Author_Key, S.au_id, S.au_lname, S.au_fname, S.phone, S.address, S.city,
S.state, S.zip, S.contract,
    S.DateCreated, S.DateUpdated
FROM Authors_Staging S LEFT OUTER JOIN
    Authors_DW D ON S.Author_Key = D.Author_Key
WHERE (D.Author_Key IS NULL)
GO
```

Managing the Fact Table

After all dimension records have been loaded and updated, the fact table also must be loaded with new data. The fact table must be loaded after the dimension tables so the surrogate keys added to the dimension records during the ETL processes can be used as foreign keys in the fact table. This section demonstrates techniques for loading the fact table.

For purposes of these examples, a table (**Fact_Source**) is created that simulates a data table in a source system from which fact data can be extracted. The **Fact_Source** table data is a combination of data found in the **Sales** and **TitleAuthor** tables in the **pubs** database.

The following table lists definitions of the tables created for use with the examples that follow.

Table name	Purpose
Fact_Source	A simulated source data table that will be used in the example code. This table is a combination of **Sales** and **TitleAuthor** in the **pubs** database.
Fact_Temp	Receives data imported from the source system.
Fact_Staging	Holds the fact table data during transformation and surrogate key operations. Data is loaded to the data warehouse fact table after ETL operations are complete.
Fact_DW	The fact table in the data warehouse.
Titles_DW	A dimension table for Titles to demonstrate the use of surrogate keys in the fact table.
Store_DW	A dimension table for Stores to demonstrate the use of surrogate keys in the fact tables.

Several key points about the structures of these tables should be noted:

- There is no difference between the structures of the **Fact_Source** table and the **Fact_Temp** tables. This allows for the easiest method to extract data from the source system so that transformations on the data do not impact the source system.

- The **Fact_Staging** table is used to add the dimension surrogate keys to the fact table records. This table is also used to validate any data changes, convert any data types, and so on.

- The structures of the **Fact_Staging** and **Fact_DW** tables do not match. This is because the final fact table in the data warehouse does not store the original keys—just the surrogate keys.

- The fact table key is an identity column that is generated when the transformed data is loaded into the fact table. Since we will not be updating the records once they have been added to the **Fact_DW** table, there is no need to generate the key prior to the data load into the fact table. This is not how the key column is generated in dimension tables. As discussed above, the decision to use an identity key for a fact table depends on the complexity of the data warehouse schema and the performance of load and query operations; this example implements an identity key for the fact table.

The following Transact-SQL statements create the tables defined above:

Code Example 19.6

```
--Create the simulated source data table
CREATE TABLE [Fact_Source] (
    [stor_id] [char] (4) NOT NULL ,
    [ord_num] [varchar] (20) NOT NULL ,
    [ord_date] [datetime] NOT NULL ,
    [qty] [smallint] NOT NULL ,
```

```
   [payterms] [varchar] (12) NOT NULL ,
   [title_id] [tid] NOT NULL
) ON [PRIMARY]
GO

--Create the example temporary source data table used in the ETL database
CREATE TABLE [Fact_Temp] (
   [stor_id] [char] (4) NOT NULL ,
   [ord_num] [varchar] (20) NOT NULL ,
   [ord_date] [datetime] NOT NULL ,
   [qty] [smallint] NOT NULL ,
   [payterms] [varchar] (12) NOT NULL ,
   [title_id] [tid] NOT NULL
) ON [PRIMARY]
GO

--Create the example fact staging table
CREATE TABLE [Fact_Staging] (
   [stor_id] [char] (4) NOT NULL ,
   [ord_num] [varchar] (20) NOT NULL ,
   [ord_date] [datetime] NOT NULL ,
   [qty] [smallint] NOT NULL DEFAULT (0),
   [payterms] [varchar] (12) NOT NULL ,
   [title_id] [tid] NOT NULL,
   [Store_Key] [int] NOT NULL DEFAULT (0),
   [Title_Key] [int] NOT NULL DEFAULT (0)
) ON [PRIMARY]
GO

--Create the example data warehouse fact table
CREATE TABLE [Fact_DW] (
   [Store_Key] [int] NOT NULL DEFAULT (0),
   [Title_Key] [int] NOT NULL DEFAULT (0),
   [ord_num] [varchar] (20) NOT NULL ,
   [ord_date] [datetime] NOT NULL ,
   [qty] [smallint] NOT NULL DEFAULT (0),
   [payterms] [varchar] (12) NOT NULL ,
   [Fact_Key] [int] IDENTITY (1, 1) NOT NULL PRIMARY KEY CLUSTERED
) ON [PRIMARY]
GO

--Create the example titles dimension table
CREATE TABLE [Titles_DW] (
   [title_id] [tid] NOT NULL,
   [title] [varchar] (80) NOT NULL,
   [type] [char] (12) DEFAULT ('UNDECIDED'),
```

```
   [pub_id] [char] (4) NULL,
   [price] [money] NULL,
   [advance] [money] NULL,
   [royalty] [int] NULL,
   [ytd_sales] [int] NULL,
   [notes] [varchar] (200) NULL,
   [pubdate] [datetime] NOT NULL DEFAULT (getdate()),
   [Title_Key] [int] NOT NULL IDENTITY (1,1) PRIMARY KEY CLUSTERED
   ) ON [PRIMARY]
GO

--Create the example stores dimension table
CREATE TABLE [Stores_DW] (
   [stor_id] [char] (4) NOT NULL,
   [stor_name] [varchar] (40) NULL,
   [stor_address] [varchar] (40) NULL,
   [city] [varchar] (20) NULL,
   [state] [char] (2) NULL,
   [zip] [char] (5) NULL,
   [Store_Key] [int] IDENTITY (1,1) PRIMARY KEY CLUSTERED
   ) ON [PRIMARY]
GO
```

The following statements populate the sample fact and dimension tables and provide a base set of data for the remainder for the examples. The **Fact_Temp** and **Fact_Source** may appear to be redundant, but **Fact_Source** is only used to simulate a source table in an OLTP system.

Code Example 19.7

```
--Load the simulated Fact_Source table with example data
INSERT INTO Fact_Source
SELECT S.*
FROM titleauthor TA INNER JOIN sales S ON TA.title_id = S.title_id
GO

--Load the Fact_Temp table with data from the Fact_Source table
INSERT INTO Fact_Temp
SELECT *
FROM Fact_Source
GO
```

```
--Load the example dimension for Titles
INSERT INTO Titles_DW
SELECT *
FROM Titles
GO

--Load the example dimension for Stores
INSERT INTO Stores_DW
SELECT *
FROM Stores
GO
```

This completes the preparation of the sample data. The remaining examples demonstrate the tasks that prepare data for loading and load it into the data warehouse fact table.

The following code loads the **Fact_Staging** table. Notice that the **Store_Key** and **Title_Key** columns that are used for surrogate keys contain zeros when the data is first loaded into the staging table. This is because NULLs are not allowed in these columns. The prevention of NULLs allows for a very clean data load and it negates the need to do NULL logic checks in the ETL code or the reporting system. The zeros in the column also provide an easy mechanism for locating invalid data in the dimension and fact table data. If a zero appears in either column in the final fact table, then the ETL logic failed to handle a dimension attribute. It is good practice to always add a dimension record with zero key and assign it the description of "unknown." This helps preserve relational integrity in the data warehouse and allows reporting systems to display the invalid data, so that corrections can be made to the ETL logic or the source data.

Code Example 19.8

```
--Load the Fact_Staging table with data in the Fact_Temp table
INSERT INTO Fact_Staging (stor_id, ord_num, ord_date, qty, payterms, title_id,
Store_Key, Title_Key)
SELECT  stor_id, ord_num, ord_date, qty, payterms, title_id, 0, 0
FROM Fact_Temp
GO
```

Now that the **Fact_Staging** table is loaded, the surrogate keys can be updated. The techniques for updating the surrogate keys in the fact table will differ depending on whether the dimension contains Type 2 changes. The following technique can be used for Type 1 dimensions:

Code Example 19.9

```
--Update the Fact_Staging table with the surrogate key for Titles
--(Type 1 dimension)
UPDATE Fact_Staging
SET Title_Key = T.Title_Key
FROM Fact_Staging F INNER JOIN
    Titles_DW T ON F.title_id = T.title_id
GO


--Update the Fact_Staging table with the surrogate key for Store
--(Type 1 dimension)
UPDATE Fact_Staging
SET Store_Key = S.Store_Key
FROM Fact_Staging F INNER JOIN
    Stores_DW S ON F.Stor_id = S.Stor_id
GO
```

The technique above will not work for dimensions that contain Type 2 changes, however, because there may be more than one dimension record that contains the original source key. The following technique is appropriate for Type 2 dimensions:

Code Example 19.10

```
--Add a few new rows to the Stores_DW table to demonstrate technique
--Duplicate Store records are added that reflect changed store names
INSERT INTO Stores_DW (stor_id, stor_name, stor_address, city, state, zip)
SELECT stor_id, 'New ' + stor_name, stor_address, city, state, zip
FROM Stores_DW
WHERE state = 'WA'
GO


--Add some new rows to fact table to demonstrate technique
INSERT INTO Fact_Staging (stor_id, ord_num, ord_date, qty, payterms, title_id,
Store_Key, Title_Key)
SELECT  stor_id, ord_num, ord_date, qty, payterms, title_id, 0, 0
FROM Fact_Temp
GO


--Update the fact table. Use the maximum store key
--to relate the new fact data to the latest store record.
BEGIN TRANSACTION
    --get the maximum store_key for each stor_id
    SELECT MAX(STORE_KEY) AS Store_Key, stor_id
    INTO #Stores
```

```
    FROM Stores_DW
    GROUP BY stor_id
    ORDER BY stor_id

    --update the fact table
    UPDATE Fact_Staging
    SET Store_Key = S.Store_Key
    FROM Fact_Staging F INNER JOIN
        #Stores S ON F.stor_id = S.stor_id
    WHERE F.Store_Key = 0

    --drop the temporary table
    DROP TABLE #Stores
COMMIT TRANSACTION
GO
```

After the fact data has been successfully scrubbed and transformed, it needs to be loaded into the data warehouse. If the ETL database is not on the same server as the data warehouse database, then the data will need to be transferred using DTS, **bcp**, or another mechanism. An efficient approach is to use **bcp** to export the data from the ETL database, copy the data to the target server, and then use BULK INSERT to update the target database. However, if the databases are on the same server, a simple INSERT statement will load the new fact table rows:

Code Example 19.11

```
--Load the new fact table rows into the data warehouse
INSERT INTO Fact_DW  (ord_num, ord_date, qty, payterms, Store_Key, Title_Key)
SELECT ord_num, ord_date, qty, payterms, Store_Key, Title_Key
FROM Fact_Staging
GO
```

Finally, the following SELECT statement shows the data warehouse fact table, complete with Type 2 dimension for the stores dimension:

Code Example 19.12

```
--Demonstrate the success of the technique
SELECT S.stor_id, S.Store_Key, S.stor_name, F.ord_num, F.ord_date, F.qty, F.payterms
FROM Stores_DW S INNER JOIN
    Fact_DW F ON S.Store_Key = F.Store_Key
ORDER BY S.stor_id, S.Store_Key
GO
```

Advanced Techniques

While the sample techniques described above will work for small to medium-sized dimensions, they will not work for large dimensions. For large dimensions, variations of these techniques can provide greater efficiency. The code examples in this topic show some advanced techniques for Type 2 dimensions.

One of the key design decisions in the above techniques centers on the use of the staging tables. In the techniques illustrated above, the staging tables are exact copies of the final data warehouse dimension tables. However, the efficiency of the above techniques decreases as the number of rows in the dimension increase due to records added for Type 2 changes. For very large dimensions (millions of rows), the above technique will require massive amounts of processing power to complete. Therefore, for large dimensions, we need to introduce a variation of the above technique that will allow the system to scale with the data warehouse.

This variation involves creating a "current version" dimension table for use in the ETL process that contains only a single row for each of the dimension members. This record contains the current attributes of the dimension member. For example, if we have a Type 2 dimension for stores, and the data for the store Bookbeat has undergone three Type 2 changes, then the current version table would not contain all four records for the store. Instead, the table contains a single row for Bookbeat that contains all of the current information for it, including the current surrogate key value for the dimension member. This creates a smaller table with fewer rows that allows for faster access during the ETL process.

The following code incorporates a **Store_Current** table to demonstrate this technique for the Stores dimension. The table below describes each of the tables used in the example.

Table name	Purpose
AuthorsStores_Temp	Holds the data imported from the source system.
Stores_Staging	Holds the dimension data while it is being updated. The data for the stores will be updated in this table and then the data will be loaded into the data warehouse dimension table.
Stores_Current	Contains a single record for each store to track the current information for the store.
Stores_DW	Simulates the Stores dimension table in the data warehouse.

The following statements create the four tables:

Code Example 19.13

```
DROP TABLE Stores_DW
GO

CREATE TABLE [Stores_Temp] (
    [stor_id] [char] (4) NOT NULL,
    [stor_name] [varchar] (40) NULL,
```

```
    [stor_address] [varchar] (40) NULL,
    [city] [varchar] (20) NULL,
    [state] [char] (2) NULL,
    [zip] [char] (5) NULL
    ) ON [PRIMARY]
GO

CREATE TABLE [Stores_Staging] (
    [stor_id] [char] (4) NOT NULL,
    [stor_name] [varchar] (40) NULL,
    [stor_address] [varchar] (40) NULL,
    [city] [varchar] (20) NULL,
    [state] [char] (2) NULL,
    [zip] [char] (5) NULL,
    [DateCreated] smalldatetime NOT NULL DEFAULT (getdate()),
    [DateUpdated] smalldatetime NOT NULL DEFAULT (getdate()),
    [Store_Key] [int] IDENTITY (1,1) PRIMARY KEY CLUSTERED
    ) ON [PRIMARY]
GO

CREATE TABLE [Stores_Current] (
    [stor_id] [char] (4) NOT NULL,
    [stor_name] [varchar] (40) NULL,
    [stor_address] [varchar] (40) NULL,
    [city] [varchar] (20) NULL,
    [state] [char] (2) NULL,
    [zip] [char] (5) NULL,
    [DateCreated] smalldatetime NOT NULL DEFAULT (getdate()),
    [DateUpdated] smalldatetime NOT NULL DEFAULT (getdate()),
    [Store_Key] [int] PRIMARY KEY CLUSTERED
    ) ON [PRIMARY]
GO

CREATE TABLE [Stores_DW] (
    [stor_id] [char] (4) NOT NULL,
    [stor_name] [varchar] (40) NULL,
    [stor_address] [varchar] (40) NULL,
    [city] [varchar] (20) NULL,
    [state] [char] (2) NULL,
    [zip] [char] (5) NULL,
    [DateCreated] smalldatetime NOT NULL DEFAULT (getdate()),
    [DateUpdated] smalldatetime NOT NULL DEFAULT (getdate()),
    [Store_Key] [int] PRIMARY KEY CLUSTERED
    ) ON [PRIMARY]
GO
```

The following statements populate the **Stores_Temp**, **Stores_Staging**, and **Stores_Current** sample tables to provide a base set of data that will be used in the remainder of the example:

Code Example 19.14

```
--Load the Stores_Temp table with the default set of data
INSERT INTO Stores_Temp
SELECT * FROM Stores
GO


--Load the Stores_Staging table with the default set of data
INSERT INTO Stores_Staging (stor_id, stor_name, stor_address, city, state, zip,
DateCreated, DateUpdated)
SELECT stor_id, stor_name, stor_address, city, state, zip, getdate(), getdate()
FROM Stores_Temp
GO


--Load the Stores_Current table with the default set of data
INSERT INTO Stores_Current (stor_id, stor_name, stor_address, city, state, zip,
DateCreated, DateUpdated, store_key)
SELECT stor_id, stor_name, stor_address, city, state, zip, DateCreated, DateUpdated,
store_key
FROM Stores_Staging
GO
```

The following code adds some new records into the **Stores_Staging** table to simulate Type 2 changes to the Stores dimension. The new records reflect changes to existing store data; no new store records are added.

Code Example 19.15

```
--Insert some change records into Store_Staging to demonstrate the technique
--Duplicate records are added that reflect changes to store names for some stores
INSERT INTO Stores_Staging (stor_id, stor_name, stor_address, city, state, zip)
SELECT stor_id, stor_name + ' New', stor_address, city, state, zip
FROM Stores_staging
WHERE state <> 'ca'
GO
```

Records for new stores are loaded into **Stores_Current** before starting to process stores with change records. The following Transact-SQL code loads new stores in the **Stores_Staging** table into the **Stores_Current** table. This technique is the same as the one documented earlier in the chapter.

Code Example 19.16

```
--Insert any new stores in Stores_Staging into the Stores_Current table
--In this example there should not be any new stores
INSERT INTO Stores_Current (stor_id, stor_name, stor_address, city, state, zip,
DateCreated, DateUpdated)
SELECT S.stor_id, S.stor_name, S.stor_address, S.city, S.state, S.zip, S.DateCreated,
S.DateUpdated
FROM Stores_Staging S LEFT OUTER JOIN Stores_Current C ON S.stor_id = C.stor_id
WHERE (c.Store_Key IS NULL)
GO
```

The real change in this technique involves changing the way that dimension members are updated. The following Transact-SQL code demonstrates the alternative way to update the dimension members and load them into the data warehouse dimension. Once the new members of the dimension have been loaded, the next step is to check existing members for attributes changes that require Type 2 changes to the dimension. This example checks the stor_name attribute and updates the row in the **Stores_Current** table for every store that has had a name change (in this example, all stores that do not exist in CΛ).

Code Example 19.17

```
--Update Store_Current table for all stores that have had a name change
UPDATE Stores_Current
SET stor_name = S.stor_name,
    Store_key = S.Store_Key,
    DateUpdated = getdate()
FROM Stores_Staging S
    INNER JOIN Stores_Current C ON S.stor_id = C.stor_id
WHERE S.stor_name <> C.stor_name
GO
```

Now that all of the dimension records have been updated with the latest data, the surrogate keys can be updated for the fact table data with the following Transact-SQL statement. This technique is more efficient because a temporary table does not have to be created to determine the current value of the dimension table key.

Code Example 19.18

```
--generate some fact data rows that do not have a store_key
INSERT INTO Fact_Staging (stor_id, ord_num, ord_date, qty, payterms, title_id,
store_key, title_key)
SELECT stor_id, ord_num, getdate(), qty, payterms, title_id, 0, 0
FROM Fact_Staging
WHERE QTY < 20
GO
```

```
--Update the fact data using the Store_Key key from the Store_Current table
--to relate the new fact data to the latest store record
UPDATE Fact_Staging
SET Store_Key = C.Store_Key
FROM Fact_Staging F INNER JOIN
    Stores_Current C ON F.stor_id = C.stor_id
WHERE F.Store_Key = 0
GO
```

Meta Data Logging

A critical design element in successful ETL implementation is the capability to generate, store and review meta data. Data tables in a data warehouse store information about customers, items purchased, dates of purchase, and so on. Meta data tables store information about users, query execution times, number of rows retrieved in a report, etc. In ETL systems, meta data tables store information about transformation execution time, number of rows processed by a transformation, the last date and time a table was updated, failure of a transformation to complete, and so on. This information, if analyzed appropriately, can help predict what is likely to occur in future transformations by analyzing trends of what has already occurred.

In the code examples that follow, the terms "Job" and "Step" are used with the following meanings:

- A "Job" is an ETL element that is either executed manually or as a scheduled event. A Job contains one or more steps.

- A "Step" is an individual unit of work in a job such as an INSERT, UPDATE, or DELETE operation.

- A "Threshold" is a range of values defined by a minimum value and a maximum value. Any value that falls within the specified range is deemed acceptable. Any value that does not fall within the range is unacceptable. For example, a processing window is a type of threshold. If a job completes within the time allotted for the processing window, then it is acceptable. If it does not, then it is not acceptable.

Designing meta data storage requires careful planning and implementation. There are dependencies between tables and order of precedence constraints on records. However, the meta data information generated by ETL activities is critical to the success of the data warehouse. Following is a sample set of tables that can be used to track meta data for ETL activities.

Job Audit

ETL jobs produce data points that need to be collected. Most of these data points are aggregates of the data collected for the job steps and could theoretically be derived by querying the job step audit table. However, the meta data for the job itself is important enough to warrant storage in a separate table. Below are sample meta data tables that aid in tracking job information for each step in an ETL process.

tblAdmin_Job_Master

This table lists all of the jobs that are used to populate the data warehouse. These are the fields in **tblAdmin_Job_Master**:

Field	Definition
JobNumber	A unique identifier for the record, generally an identity column.
JobName	The name (description) for the job. For example, "Load new dimension data."
MinThreshRecords	The minimum acceptable number of records affected by the job.
MaxThreshRecords	The maximum acceptable number of records affected by the job.
MinThreshTime	The minimum acceptable execution time for the job.
MaxThreshTime	The maximum acceptable execution time for the job.
CreateDate	The date and time the record was created.

tblAdmin_Audit_Jobs

This table is used to track each specific execution of a job. It is related to the **tblAdmin_Job_Master** table using the **JobNumber** column. These are the fields in **tblAdmin_Audit_Jobs**:

Field	Definition
JobNumber	A unique identifier for the record, generally an identity column.
JobName	The name (description) for the job. For example, "Load new dimension data."
StartDate	The date and time the job was started.
EndDate	The date and time the job ended.
NumberRecords	The number of records affected by the job.
Successful	A flag-indicating if the execution of the job was successful.

This data definition language will generate the above audit tables:

Code Example 19.19

```
CREATE TABLE [dbo].[tblAdmin_Job_Master] (
   [JobNumber] [int] IDENTITY (1, 1) NOT NULL
      CONSTRAINT UPKCL_Job PRIMARY KEY CLUSTERED,
   [JobName] [varchar] (50) NULL DEFAULT ('Missing'),
   [MinThreshRecords] [int] NOT NULL DEFAULT (0),
   [MaxThreshRecords] [int] NOT NULL DEFAULT (0),
   [MinThreshTime] [int] NOT NULL DEFAULT (0),
   [MaxThreshTime] [int] NOT NULL DEFAULT (0)
GO
```

```
CREATE TABLE [dbo].[tblAdmin_Audit_Jobs] (
    [JobNumber] [int] IDENTITY (1, 1) NOT NULL
        CONSTRAINT UPKCL_Job PRIMARY KEY CLUSTERED,
    [JobName] [varchar] (50) NULL DEFAULT ('Missing'),
    [StartDate] [smalldatetime] NOT NULL DEFAULT (getdate()),
    [EndDate] [smalldatetime] NOT NULL DEFAULT  ('01/01/1900'),
    [NumberRecords] [int] NOT NULL DEFAULT (0),
    [Successful] [bit] NOT NULL DEFAULT (0),
GO
```

Step Audit

Many ETL jobs are multi-step, complicated transformations that involve INSERT, UPDATE, and DELETE statements with branching logic and an execution dependency. It is important to record meta data that tracks the successful completion of an operation, when it happened and how many rows it processed. This information should be stored for every step in an ETL job. Below are sample meta data tables that aid in tracking information for each step in an ETL job.

tblAdmin_Step_Master

This table lists all of the steps in a job. These are the fields in **tblAdmin_Step_Master**:

Field	Definition
JobNumber	The unique number of the job that this step is associated with.
StepSeqNumber	The step number within the object that executed the unit of work. Frequently, ETL jobs contain more than a single unit of work and storing the step number allows for easy debugging and specific reporting. If the object only has a single step, then the value of this field is "1".
StepDescription	A description of the step. For example, "Inserted records into tblA."
Object	The name of the object. For example, the name of a stored procedure or DTS package that accomplishes the step.
NumberRecords	The number of records affected by the step.
MinThreshRecords	The minimum "acceptable" number of records affected by the step.
MaxThreshRecords	The maximum "acceptable" number of records affected by the step.
MinThreshTime	The minimum "acceptable" execution time for the step.
MaxThreshTime	The maximum "acceptable" execution time for the step.
CreateDate	The date and time the record was created.
StepNumber	A unique value assigned to the record, generally an identity column.

tbl_Admin_Audit_Step

This table is used to track each specific execution of a job step. It is related to the **tblAdmin_Step_Master** table using the **StepNumber** column. These are the fields in **tblAdmin_Audit_Step**:

Field	Definition
RecordID	A unique value assigned to the record, generally an identity column.
JobAuditID	Used to tie the specific execution on a job step to the specific execution of a job.
StepNumber	The step number executed.
Parameters	Any parameters sent to the job step for the specific execution instance. These are the parameter values, not a list of the parameters.
NumberRecords	The number of records affected by the job step.
StartDate	The date and time the job step was started.
EndDate	The date and time the job step ended.
UserName	The name of the user that executed the job step.

Below is the data definition language that will generate the job step audit tables above.

Code Example 19.20

```
CREATE TABLE [dbo].[tblAdmin_Step_Master] (
[JobNumber] [int] NOT NULL DEFAULT (1),
    [StepSeqNumber] [int] NOT NULL DEFAULT (1),
    [StepDescription] [varchar] NOT NULL DEFAULT ('Missing'),
[Object] [varchar] (50) NULL DEFAULT ('Missing'),
    [MinThreshRecords] [int] NOT NULL DEFAULT (0),
    [MaxThreshRecords] [int] NOT NULL DEFAULT (0),
    [MinThreshTime] [int] NOT NULL DEFAULT (0),
    [MaxThreshTime] [int] NOT NULL DEFAULT (0),
[StartDate] [smalldatetime] NOT NULL DEFAULT (getdate()),
    [StepNumber] [int] IDENTITY (1, 1) NOT NULL
        CONSTRAINT UPKCL_PrimaryKey PRIMARY KEY CLUSTERED) ON [PRIMARY]
GO

CREATE TABLE [dbo].[tblAdmin_Audit_Step] (
    [RecordID] [int] IDENTITY (1, 1) NOT NULL
        CONSTRAINT UPKCL_PrimaryKey PRIMARY KEY CLUSTERED,
    [Object] [varchar] (50) NULL DEFAULT ('Missing'),
    [StepNumber] [tinyint] NOT NULL DEFAULT (1),
    [StepDescription] [varchar] NOT NULL DEFAULT ('Missing'),
```

```
    [Parameters] [varchar] (100) NULL,
    [NumberRecords] [int] NOT NULL DEFAULT (1),
    [StartDate] [smalldatetime] NOT NULL DEFAULT (getdate()),
    [EndDate] [smalldatetime] NOT NULL DEFAULT ('01/01/1900'),
    [UserName] [varchar] (20) NOT NULL DEFAULT ('Missing')) ON [PRIMARY]
GO
```

Error Tracking

Another important type of meta data about transformations is information that tracks what failed and why. ETL jobs produce errors. Just as tracking successful execution is important, tracking failures is equally important. Below is a sample meta data table that aids in tracking error information for each step in an ETL job. This table is designed to track SQL Server 2000 errors, although it could be modified to track OLE DB errors as well.

Note In SQL Server 2000, only the error number can be trapped, not the generated error message.

tblAdmin_Audit_Errors

This table lists all of the errors that are generated during a job step. These are the fields in **tblAdmin_Audit_Errors**:

Field	Definition
RecordID	A unique value assigned to the record, generally an identity column.
StepNumber	The step number executed that generated the error.
Parameters	Any parameters sent to the job step for the specific execution instance. These are the parameter values, not a list of the parameters.
ErrorNumber	The error number raised by SQL Server 2000 (generally the @@ERROR number).
RecordCount	The number of records affected by the job step.
UserName	The name of the user that executed the job step.
EndDate	The date and time the job step ended.

Code Sample: Job Audit

The following stored procedures demonstrate one method of logging job level meta data. The usp_Admin_Audit_Job_Start procedure indicates the start of an ETL job and should be the very first stored procedure executed in the ETL job:

Code Example 19.21

```
ALTER PROCEDURE usp_Admin_Audit_Job_Start
    @JobNumber int = 1    --The number of the job being executed (from the mast job table)
AS
SET NOCOUNT ON    --SET NoCount ON

--DECLARE variables
DECLARE @ErrorNumber int       --the number of the SQL error generated
DECLARE @ErrorRowCount int       --the number of rows in the unit of work affected by
error
DECLARE @Startdate smalldatetime    --the datetime the load job started
DECLARE @EndDate smalldatetime    --the datetime the load job ended

--INSERT the first record (start time) for the job into the tblAdmin_Audit_Jobs table
BEGIN TRANSACTION
    SET @StartDate = getdate()    --set a start date for the batch
    SET @EndDate = '01/01/1900'    --set a bogus endate for the batch
insert into tblAdmin_Audit_Jobs (JobNumber, StartDate, EndDate, NumberRecords,
Successful)
    values (@JobNumber, @StartDate, @EndDate, 0, 0)

SELECT @ErrorNumber = @@error, @ErrorRowCount = @@rowcount

    If @ErrorNumber <> 0
    BEGIN
        ROLLBACK TRANSACTION
        GOTO Err_Handler
    END
COMMIT TRANSACTION
RETURN (0)

Err_Handler:
    exec usp_AdminError @@ProcID, 'none', @ErrorNumber, @ErrorRowCount
    RETURN (1)
GO
```

The following stored procedure indicates the end of an ETL job and should be the last stored procedure executed in the ETL job. It is important to note that in addition to updating the **tblAdmin_Audit_Jobs** table, this stored procedure also updates the **tblAdmin_Audit_Step** table with the threshold information for each step. The threshold information is stored with each step in the table because over time, the acceptable thresholds for the step may change. If the threshold information is only stored in the master step table (a Type 1 dimension), any changes to the table affect meta data generated for historical steps.

Therefore, storing the threshold with the step (a Type 2 dimension) allows us to maintain historical execution records without affecting their integrity if the master step information is changed. For example, if a step initially loads 1,000 rows but over time the number of rows increases to 1 million, the acceptable threshold information for that step must be changed as well. If the threshold data is stored only in the **tblAdmin_Step_Master** table and not stored with each record, the context of the data will be lost, which can cause inaccuracies in reports built on the meta data information. For simplicity, to illustrate the technique, the sample code does not maintain threshold information automatically. In order to change the threshold information for a step, an administrator will need to modify the master step record manually. However, it would be possible to automate this process.

Code Example 19.22

```
CREATE PROCEDURE usp_Admin_Audit_Job_End
    @JobNumber int = 1,    --The number of the job (from the master job table) being
executed
    @Successful bit       --A flag indicating if the job was successful
AS

SET NOCOUNT ON           --SET NoCount ON

--DECLARE variables
DECLARE @ErrorNumber int       --the number of the SQL error generated
DECLARE @ErrorRowCount int        --the number of rows in the unit of work affected by
error
DECLARE @Startdate smalldatetime   --the datetime the load job started
DECLARE @EndDate smalldatetime   --the datetime the load job ended
DECLARE @JobAuditID int        --the # for the instance of the job
DECLARE @RowCount int       --the number of rows affected by the job

--UPDATE the job record (end time) in the Audit table
BEGIN TRANSACTION
    SET @EndDate = getdate()    --set the end date for the batch
    SET @JobAuditID = (SELECT MAX(JobAuditID) FROM tblAdmin_Audit_Jobs
where JobNumber = @JobNumber)    --get the job number
    SET @RowCount = (SELECT SUM(NumberRecords)     --get the total job record count
            FROM tblAdmin_Audit_Step WHERE JobAuditID = @JobAuditID)

    UPDATE tblAdmin_Audit_Jobs    --Update the Job record with the end time
    SET EndDate = @EndDate,
        NumberRecords = @RowCount,
        Successful = 1
    WHERE JobAuditID = @JobAuditID
```

```
    SELECT @ErrorNumber = @@error, @ErrorRowCount = @@rowcount
    UPDATE  tblAdmin_Audit_Step         --Update all steps for the job with the
    SET MinRecords = T.MinThreshRecords,    --threshold information for each step
       MaxRecords = T.MaxThreshRecords,
       MinTime = T.MinThreshTime,
       MaxTime = T.MaxThreshTime,
       TimeTarget =     CASE
WHEN DATEDIFF(mi, A.StartDate, A.EndDate) BETWEEN T.MinThreshTime AND T.MaxThreshTime
THEN 'On'
WHEN DATEDIFF(mi, A.StartDate, A.EndDate)< T.MinThreshTime THEN 'Under'
WHEN DATEDIFF(mi, A.StartDate, A.EndDate) > T.MaxThreshTime THEN 'Over'
         ELSE 'Unknown'
       END,
       RecordTarget = CASE
WHEN A.NumberRecords BETWEEN T.MinThreshRecords AND T.MaxThreshRecords THEN 'On'
         WHEN A.NumberRecords < T.MinThreshRecords THEN 'Under'
         WHEN A.NumberRecords > T.MaxThreshRecords THEN 'Over'
         ELSE 'Unknown'
       END
    FROM   tblAdmin_Step_Master T
       RIGHT OUTER JOIN tblAdmin_Audit_Step A ON T.StepNumber = A.StepNumber
    WHERE A.JobAuditID = @JobAuditID
    SELECT @ErrorNumber = @@error, @ErrorRowCount = @@rowcount
    If @ErrorNumber <> 0
    BEGIN
       ROLLBACK TRANSACTION
       GOTO Err_Handler
    END
COMMIT TRANSACTION
RETURN (0)
Err_Handler:
    exec usp_AdminError @@ProcID, 'none', @ErrorNumber, @ErrorRowCount
    RETURN (1)
GO
```

Code Sample: Step Audit

The following stored procedures demonstrate one method of logging step records from within ETL stored procedures. Notice that the @@**ProcID** is used to retrieve the object id of the executing stored procedure. Also note that the values of @@**error** and @@**rowcount** are retrieved immediately after the INSERT statement.

Code Example 19.23

```
ALTER PROCEDURE usp_Admin_Audit_Step
@StepNumber tinyint = 0,        --the uniue number of the step
@Parameters varchar(50) = 'none',   --any parameters used in the SP
@RecordCount int = 0,           --the number of records modified by the step
@StartDate smalldatetime,       --the date & time the step started
@EndDate smalldatetime      --the date & time the step ended
AS
SET NOCOUNT ON     --SET NoCount ON

--DECLARE variables
DECLARE @ErrorNumber int
DECLARE @ErrorRowCount int
DECLARE @JobAuditID int

BEGIN TRANSACTION   --INSERT the audit record into the tblAdmin_Audit_Step table
   SET @JobAuditID = (SELECT MAX(JobAuditID) FROM tblAdmin_Audit_Jobs)

INSERT INTO tblAdmin_Audit_Step ( JobAuditID, StepNumber, Parameters, NumberRecords,
      StartDate, EndDate, Username)
VALUES (@JobAuditID, @StepNumber, @Parameters, @RecordCount,
      @StartDate, @EndDate, user_name())

SELECT @ErrorNumber = @@error, @ErrorRowCount = @@RowCount

If @ErrorNumber <> 0
BEGIN
   ROLLBACK TRANSACTION
   GOTO Err_Handler
END
COMMIT TRANSACTION
RETURN (0)

Err_Handler:
exec usp_Admin_Log_Error @@ProcID, 1, 'none', @ErrorNumber, @ErrorRowCount
RETURN (1)
GO
```

The following stored procedure demonstrates the use of the auditing stored procedure detailed above:

Code Example 19.24

```
CREATE PROCEDURE usp_AuditSample
AS
SET NOCOUNT ON    --SET NoCount ON

--DECLARE variables
DECLARE @ErrorNumber int
DECLARE @RecordCount int
DECLARE @StartDate smalldatetime
DECLARE @EndDate smalldatetime

BEGIN TRANSACTION
   SET @StartDate = getdate()    --get the datetime the step started
   insert into tblTest
   select * from tblTest

   SELECT @ErrorNumber = @@error, @RecordCount = @@rowcount

   If @ErrorNumber <> 0     --error handler
   BEGIN
      ROLLBACK TRANSACTION
      GOTO Err_Handler
   END

   SET @EndDate = getdate()    --get the datetime the step finished

   --log the audit record into the tblAdmin_Audit_Step table
   exec usp_Admin_Audit_Step 1 , 'test from SP', @RecordCount, @StartDate, @EndDate
COMMIT TRANSACTION
RETURN (0)

Err_Handler:
   exec usp_Admin_Log_Error @@ProcID, 'none', @ErrorNumber, @RecordCount
   RETURN (1)
GO
```

Code Sample: Error Tracking

The following stored procedures demonstrate one possible method of logging errors in ETL stored procedures. Notice that the stored procedure uses the OBJECT_NAME function to retrieve the name of the object (table, view, stored procedure, and so on). This introduces a level of abstraction so that the code is only useful for stored procedures.

Code Example 19.25

```
CREATE PROCEDURE usp_Admin_Log_Error
    @ObjectID int,
    @StepNumber int,
    @Parameters varchar(50) = 'none',
    @ErrorNumber int = 0,
    @RecordCount int = 0
AS

--SET NoCount ON
SET NOCOUNT ON

--RETRIEVE the NAME of the object being audited
DECLARE @ObjectName varchar(50)
SET @ObjectName = OBJECT_NAME(@ObjectID)

--INSERT the audit record into the tblAdmin_Audit_Errors table
BEGIN TRANSACTION
    insert into tblAdmin_Audit_Errors (Object, StepNumber, Parameters, ErrorNumber,
RecordCount, UserName, RecordDate)
    values (@ObjectName, @StepNumber, @Parameters, @ErrorNumber, @RecordCount,
user_name(), getdate())
COMMIT TRANSACTION
GO
```

Once an error is generated and passed to the error logging stored procedure, it is logged to the **tblAdmin_Audit_Errors** table. Notice that the @@**ProcID** is used to retrieve the objected of the executing stored procedure. Also note that the values of @@**error** and @@**rowcount** are retrieved immediately after the INSERT statement. With the exception of modifying the value of @**Step**, this logic may be deployed with no other alterations to the code. The following stored procedure demonstrates how to deploy the error logging method detailed above:

Code Example 19.26

```
CREATE PROCEDURE usp_ErrorSample
AS
--SET NoCount ON
SET NOCOUNT ON

--DECLARE Variables
DECLARE @ObjectName varchar(50)
DECLARE @ErrorNumber int, @RecordCount int
DECLARE @Step  int
```

```
--INSERT the audit record into the Authors table
BEGIN TRANSACTION
    insert into Authors
    Select * from authors

    SELECT @ErrorNumber = @@error, @RecordCount = @@rowcount, @Step = 2

    If @ErrorNumber <> 0
    BEGIN
        ROLLBACK TRANSACTION
        GOTO Err_Handler
    END
COMMIT TRANSACTION
RETURN (0)

Err_Handler:
    exec usp_Admin_Log_Error @@ProcID, @Step, 'none', @ErrorNumber, @RecordCount
    RETURN (1)
GO
```

Conclusion

The ETL system efficiently extracts data from its sources, transforms and sometimes aggregates data to match the target data warehouse schema, and loads the transformed data into the data warehouse database. A well-designed ETL system supports automated operation that informs operators of errors with the appropriate level of warning. SQL Server 2000 Data Transformation Services can be used to manage the ETL operations, regardless of the techniques used to implement individual ETL tasks.

While it is tempting to perform some transformation on data as it is extracted from the source system, the best practice is to isolate transformations within the transformation modules. In general, the data extraction code should be designed to minimize the impact on the source system databases.

In most applications, the key to efficient transformation is to use a SQL Server 2000 database for staging. Once extracted data has been loaded into a staging database, the powerful SQL Server 2000 database engine is used to perform complex transformations.

The process of loading fact table data from the staging area into the target data warehouse should use bulk load techniques. Dimension table data is usually small in volume, which makes bulk loading less important for dimension table loading.

The ETL system is a primary source of meta data that can be used to track information about the operation and performance of the data warehouse as well as the ETL processes.

RDBMS Performance Tuning Guide for Data Warehousing

This performance tuning guide is designed to help database administrators and developers configure Microsoft® SQL Server™ 2000 for maximum performance and to assist in determining causes of poor performance of relational databases, including those used in data warehousing. It also provides guidelines and best practices for loading, indexing, and writing queries to access data stored in SQL Server. Various SQL Server tools that can be used to analyze performance characteristics are also discussed.

Introduction

Microsoft SQL Server 7.0 introduced a major enhancement: a database engine that is largely self-configuring, self-tuning, and self-managing. Before SQL Server 7.0, most database servers required a considerable amount of time and effort from the database administrator, who had to manually tune the server configuration to achieve optimal performance. In fact, a good many competitive database offerings still require administrators to manually configure and tune their database server. This is a key reason many customers are turning to SQL Server. SQL Server 2000 builds upon the solid foundation laid by SQL Server 7.0. The goal of SQL Server is to free DBAs from having to manually configure and constantly tune a database server by making the database engine self-tuning and allowing DBAs to automate administrative tasks.

While it is still possible to manually configure and adjust some **sp_configure** options, it is recommended that database administrators refrain from doing so and instead allow SQL Server to automatically configure and tune itself. SQL Server 7.0 has an established and proven track record for being able to make such adjustments; SQL Server 2000 significantly improves on this formula. Letting SQL Server self-tune allows the database server to dynamically adjust to changing conditions in your environment that could have an adverse effect on database performance.

Basic Principles of Performance Tuning

You can take a number of actions to manage the performance of your databases. SQL Server 2000 provides several tools to assist you in these tasks.

Managing Performance

- Let SQL Server do most of the tuning.

  SQL Server 2000 has been dramatically enhanced to create a largely auto-configuring and self-tuning database server. Take advantage of SQL Server's auto-tuning settings to help SQL Server run at peak performance even as user load and queries change over time.

- Manage RAM caching.

  RAM is a limited resource. A major part of any database server environment is the management of random access memory (RAM) buffer cache. Access to data in RAM cache is much faster than access to the same information from disk. But RAM is a limited resource. If database I/O (input/output operations to the physical disk subsystem) can be reduced to the minimal required set of data and index pages, these pages will stay in RAM longer. Too much unneeded data and index information flowing into buffer cache will quickly push out valuable pages. The primary goal of performance tuning is to reduce I/O so that buffer cache is best utilized.

- Create and maintain good indexes.

  A key factor in maintaining minimum I/O for all database queries is ensuring that good indexes are created and maintained.

- Partition large data sets and indexes.

  To reduce overall I/O contention and improve parallel operations, consider partitioning table data and indexes. Multiple techniques for achieving and managing partitions using SQL Server 2000 are addressed in this chapter.

- Monitor disk I/O subsystem performance.

  The physical disk subsystem must provide a database server with sufficient I/O processing power for the database server to run without disk queuing. Disk queuing results in bad performance. This document describes how to detect disk I/O problems and how to resolve them.

- Tune applications and queries.

  This becomes especially important when a database server will be servicing requests from hundreds or thousands of connections through a given application. Because applications typically determine the

SQL queries that will be executed on a database server, it is very important for application developers to understand SQL Server architectural basics and how to take full advantage of SQL Server indexes to minimize I/O.

- Optimize active data.

In many business intelligence databases, a significant majority of database activity involves data for the most recent month or quarter—as much as 80 percent of database activity may be due to the most recently loaded data. To maintain good overall database performance, make sure this data gets loaded, indexed, and partitioned in a way that provides optimal data access performance for it.

Take Advantage of SQL Server Performance Tools

- SQL Profiler and the Index Tuning Wizard

SQL Profiler can be used to monitor and log the workload of a SQL Server. This logged workload can then be submitted to the Index Tuning Wizard so index changes can be made to help performance if necessary. SQL Profiler and Index Tuning Wizard help administrators achieve optimal indexing. Using these tools periodically will keep SQL Server performing well, even if the query workload changes over time.

- SQL Query Analyzer and Graphical Execution Plan

In SQL Server 2000, SQL Query Analyzer provides Graphical Execution Plan, an easy method for analyzing problematic SQL queries. Statistics I/O is another important feature of SQL Query Analyzer described later in this chapter.

- System Monitor objects

SQL Server includes a set of System Monitor objects and counters to provide information for monitoring and analyzing the operations of SQL Server. This chapter describes key counters to watch.

Configuration Options That Impact Performance

max async IO

A manual configuration option in SQL Server 7.0, **max async IO** has been automated in SQL Server 2000. Previously, **max async IO** was used to specify the number of simultaneous disk I/O requests that SQL Server 7.0 could submit to Microsoft Windows NT® 4.0 and Windows® 2000 during a checkpoint operation. In turn, Windows submitted these requests to the physical disk subsystem. The automation of this configuration setting enables SQL Server 2000 to automatically and dynamically maintain optimal I/O throughput.

Note   Windows 98 does not support asynchronous I/O, so the **max async IO** option is not supported on this platform.

Database Recovery Models

SQL Server 2000 introduces the ability to configure how transactions are logged at a database level. The model chosen can have a dramatic impact on performance, especially during data loads. There are three recovery models: Full, Bulk-Logged, and Simple. The recovery model of a new database is inherited from the **model** database when the new database is created. The model for a database can be changed after the database has been created.

- Full Recovery provides the most flexibility for recovering databases to an earlier point in time.

- Bulk-Logged Recovery provides higher performance and lower log space consumption for certain large-scale operations (for example, create index or bulk copy). It does this at the expense of some flexibility of point-in-time recovery.

- Simple Recovery provides the highest performance and lowest log space consumption, but it does so with significant exposure to data loss in the event of a system failure. When using the Simple Recovery model, data is recoverable only to the last (most recent) full database or differential backup. Transaction log backups are not usable for recovering transactions because, in this model, the transactions are truncated from the log upon checkpoint. This creates the potential for data loss. After the log space is no longer needed for recovery from server failure (active transactions), it is truncated and reused.

Knowledgeable administrators can use this recovery model feature to significantly speed up data loads and bulk operations. However, the amount of exposure to data loss varies with the model chosen.

Important It is imperative that the risks be thoroughly understood before choosing a recovery model.

Each recovery model addresses a different need. Trade-offs are made depending on the model you chose. The trade-offs that occur pertain to performance, space utilization (disk or tape), and protection against data loss. When you choose a recovery model, you are deciding among the following business requirements:

- Performance of large-scale operations (for example, index creation or bulk loads)

- Data loss exposure (for example, the loss of committed transactions)

- Transaction log space consumption

- Simplicity of backup and recovery procedures

Depending on what operations you are performing, one model may be more appropriate than another. Before choosing a recovery model, consider the impact it will have. The following table provides helpful information.

Recovery model	Benefits	Work loss exposure	Recover to point in time?
Simple	Permits high-performance bulk copy operations. Reclaims log space to keep space requirements small.	Changes since the most recent database or differential backup must be redone	Can recover to the end of any backup. Then changes must be redone.
Full	No work is lost due to a lost or damaged data file. Can recover to an arbitrary point in time (for example, prior to application or user error).	Normally none. If the log is damaged, changes since the most recent log backup must be redone.	Can recover to any point in time.
Bulk-Logged	Permits high-performance bulk copy operations. Minimal log space is used by bulk operations.	If the log is damaged, or bulk operations occurred since the most recent log backup, changes since that last backup must be redone. Otherwise, no work is lost.	Can recover to the end of any backup. Then changes must be redone.

Multi-Instance Considerations

SQL Server 2000 also introduces the ability to run multiple instances of SQL Server on a single computer. By default, each instance of SQL Server dynamically acquires and frees memory to adjust for changes in the workload of the instance. Performance tuning can be complicated when multiple instances of SQL Server 2000 are each automatically and independently adjusting memory usage. This feature is not generally a consideration for most high-end business intelligence customers who typically install only a single instance of SQL Server on each computer. However, as individual computers become significantly larger (Windows 2000 Datacenter Server supports up to 64 gigabytes (GB) RAM and 32 CPUs), the desire for multiple instances may come into play even in some production environments. Special considerations apply to instances that utilize extended memory support.

Extended Memory Support

Generally speaking, because SQL Server 2000 dynamically acquires and frees memory as needed, it is not usually necessary for an administrator to specify how much memory should be allocated to SQL Server. However, SQL Server 2000 Enterprise Edition and SQL Server 2000 Developer Edition introduce support for using Microsoft Windows 2000 Address Windowing Extensions (AWE). This enables SQL Server 2000 to address significantly more memory (approximate maximum of 8 GB for Windows 2000 Advanced Server and 64 GB for Windows 2000 Datacenter Server). When extended memory is configured, each instance accessing the extended memory must be configured to statically allocate the memory it will use.

> **Note** This feature is available only if you are running Windows 2000 Advanced Server or Windows 2000 Datacenter Server.

Windows 2000 Usage Considerations

To take advantage of AWE memory, you must run the SQL Server 2000 database engine under a Windows 2000 account that has been assigned the Windows 2000 lock pages in memory privilege. SQL Server Setup will automatically grant the MSSQLServer service account permission to use the **Lock Page in Memory** option. If you are starting an instance of SQL Server 2000 from the command prompt using Sqlservr.exe, you must manually assign this permission to the interactive user's account using the Windows 2000 Group Policy utility (Gpedit.msc), or SQL Server will be unable to use AWE memory when not running as a service.

To enable the Lock Page in Memory option

1. On the **Start** menu, click **Run**, and then in the **Open** box, enter **gpedit.msc**.

2. In the **Group Policy** tree pane, expand **Computer Configuration**, and then expand **Windows Settings**.

3. Expand **Security Settings**, and then expand **Local Policies**.

4. Select the **Users Rights Assignment** folder.

5. The policies will be displayed in the details pane.

6. In the details pane, double-click **Lock pages in memory**.

7. In the **Local Security Policy Setting** dialog box, click **Add**.

8. In the **Select Users or Groups** dialog box, add an account with privileges to run **Sqlservr.exe**.

To enable Windows 2000 Advanced Server or Windows 2000 Datacenter Server to support more than 4 GB of physical memory, you must add the */pae* parameter to the Boot.ini file.

For computers with 16 GB or less you can use the *3gb* parameter in the Boot.ini file. This enables Windows 2000 Advanced Server and Windows 2000 Datacenter Server to allow user applications to address extended memory through the 3 GB of virtual memory, and it reserves 1 GB of virtual memory for the operating system itself.

If more than 16 GB of physical memory is available on a computer, the Windows 2000 operating system needs 2 GB of virtual memory address space for system purposes. Therefore, it can support only a 2 GB virtual address space for application usage. For systems with more than 16 GB of physical memory, be sure to use the *2gb* parameter in the Boot.ini file.

Note   If you accidentally use the *3gb* parameter, Windows 2000 will be unable to address any memory above 16 GB.

SQL Server 2000 Usage Considerations

To enable the use of AWE memory by an instance of SQL Server 2000, use **sp_configure** to set the **awe enabled** option. Next, restart SQL Server to activate AWE. Because AWE support is enabled during SQL Server startup and continues until SQL Server is shut down, SQL Server will notify users when AWE is in use by sending an "Address Windowing Extension enabled" message to the SQL Server error log.

When you enable AWE memory, instances of SQL Server 2000 do not dynamically manage the size of the address space. Therefore, when you enable AWE memory and start an instance of SQL Server 2000, one of the following occurs, depending on how you have set **max server memory**.

- If **max server memory** has been set and there are at least 3 GB of free memory available on the computer, the instance acquires the amount of memory specified in **max server memory**. If the amount of memory available on the computer is less than **max server memory** (but more than 3 GB), then the instance acquires almost all of the available memory and may leave only up to 128 MB of memory free.

- If **max server memory** has not been set and there is at least 3 GB of free memory available on the computer, the instance acquires almost all of the available memory and may leave only up to 128 MB of memory free.

- If there is less than 3 GB of free memory available on the computer, memory is dynamically allocated and, regardless of the parameter setting for **awe enabled**, SQL Server will run in nonAWE mode.

When allocating SQL Server AWE memory on a 32-GB system, Windows 2000 may require at least 1 GB of available memory to manage AWE. Therefore, when starting an instance of SQL Server with AWE enabled, it is recommend you do not use the default **max server memory** setting, but instead limit it to 31 GB or less.

Failover Clustering and Multi-Instance Considerations

If you are using SQL Server 2000 failover clustering or running multiple instances while using AWE memory, you must ensure that the summed value of the **max server memory** settings for all running SQL Server instances is less than the amount of physical RAM available. For failover, you have to take into consideration the lowest amount of physical RAM on any candidate surviving node. If a failover node has less physical memory than the original node, the instances of SQL Server 2000 may fail to start or may start with less memory than they had on the original node.

sp_configure Options

cost threshold for parallelism Option

Use the **cost threshold for parallelism** option to specify the threshold where SQL Server creates and executes parallel plans. SQL Server creates and executes a parallel plan for a query only when the estimated cost to execute a serial plan for the same query is higher than the value set in **cost threshold for parallelism**. The cost refers to an estimated elapsed time in seconds required to execute the serial plan on a specific hardware configuration. Only set **cost threshold for parallelism** on symmetric multiprocessors (SMP).

Longer queries usually benefit from parallel plans; the performance advantage negates the additional time required to initialize, synchronize, and terminate the plan. The **cost threshold for parallelism** option is actively used when a mix of short and longer queries is executed. The short queries execute serial plans while the longer queries use parallel plans. The value of **cost threshold for parallelism** determines which queries are considered short, thus executing only serial plans.

In certain cases, a parallel plan may be chosen even though the query's cost plan is less than the current **cost threshold for parallelism** value. This is because the decision to use a parallel or serial plan, with respect to **cost threshold for parallelism**, is based on a cost estimate provided before the full optimization is complete.

The **cost threshold for parallelism** option can be set to any value from 0 through 32767. The default value is 5 (measured in milliseconds). If your computer has only one processor, if only a single CPU is available to SQL Server because of the value of the **affinity mask** configuration option, or if the **max degree of parallelism** option is set to 1, SQL Server ignores **cost threshold for parallelism**.

max degree of parallelism Option

Use the **max degree of parallelism** option to limit the number of processors (a maximum of 32) to use in parallel plan execution. The default value is 0, which uses the actual number of available CPUs. Set the **max degree of parallelism** option to 1 to suppress parallel plan generation. Set the value to a number greater than 1 to restrict the maximum number of processors used by a single query execution. If a value greater than the number of available CPUs is specified, the actual number of available CPUs is used.

> **Note**   If the **affinity mask** option is not set to the default, the number of CPUs available to SQL Server on symmetric multiprocessor (SMP) systems may be restricted.

For servers running on an SMP computer, change **max degree of parallelism** rarely. If your computer has only one processor, the **max degree of parallelism** value is ignored.

priority boost Option

Use the **priority boost** option to specify whether SQL Server should run at a higher scheduling priority than other processes on the same computer. If you set this option to one, SQL Server runs at a priority base of 13 in the Windows scheduler. The default is 0, which is a priority base of seven. The **priority boost** option should be used only on a computer dedicated to SQL Server, and with an SMP configuration.

> **CAUTION**   Boosting the priority too high may drain resources from essential operating system and network functions, resulting in problems shutting down SQL Server or using other Windows tasks on the server.

In some circumstances, setting **priority boost** to anything other than the default can cause the following communication error to be logged in the SQL Server error log:

```
Error: 17824, Severity: 10, State: 0 Unable to write to ListenOn
connection '<servername>', loginname '<login ID>', hostname '<hostname>'
OS Error: 64, The specified network name is no longer available.
```

Error 17824 indicates that SQL Server encountered connection problems while attempting to write to a client. These communication problems may be caused by network problems, if the client has stopped responding, or if the client has been restarted. However, error 17824 does not necessarily indicate a network problem and may simply be a result of having the **priority boost** option set to on.

set working set size Option

Use the **set working set size** option to reserve physical memory space for SQL Server that is equal to the server memory setting. The server memory setting is configured automatically by SQL Server based on workload and available resources. It will vary dynamically between **min server memory** and **max server memory**. Setting **set working set size** means the operating system will not attempt to swap out SQL Server pages even if they can be used more readily by another process when SQL Server is idle.

Do not set **set working set size** if you are allowing SQL Server to use memory dynamically. Before setting **set working set size** to 1, set both **min server memory** and **max server memory** to the same value, the amount of memory you want SQL Server to use.

The options **lightweight pooling** and **affinity mask** are discussed in the section "Key Performance Counters to Watch" later in this chapter.

Optimizing Disk I/O Performance

When configuring a SQL Server that will contain only a few GB of data and not sustain heavy read or write activity, it is not as important to be concerned with the subject of disk I/O and balancing of SQL Server I/O activity across hard drives for maximum performance. But to build larger SQL Server databases that will contain hundreds of gigabytes or even terabytes of data and/or that can sustain heavy read/write activity, it is necessary to drive configuration around maximizing SQL Server disk I/O performance by load-balancing across multiple hard drives.

Optimizing Transfer Rates

One of the most important aspects of database performance tuning is I/O performance tuning. SQL Server is certainly no exception. Unless SQL Server is running on a computer with enough RAM to hold the entire database, I/O performance will be determined by how fast reads and writes of SQL Server data can be processed by the disk I/O subsystem.

Because transfer rates, I/O throughput, and other factors which may impact I/O performance are constantly improving, we will not provide specific numbers on what kinds of speed you should expect to see from your storage system. To better understand the capabilities you can expect, it is recommended that you work with your preferred hardware vendor to determine the optimum performance to expect.

What we do want to emphasize is the difference between sequential I/O operations (also commonly referred to as "serial" or "in disk order") in contrast to nonsequential I/O operations. We also want to draw attention to the dramatic effect read-ahead processing can have on I/O operations.

Sequential and Nonsequential Disk I/O Operations

It is worthwhile to explain what these terms mean in relation to a disk drive. Generally, a single hard drive consists of a set of drive platters. Each platter provides surfaces for read/write operations. A set of arms with read/write heads is used to move across the platters and read/write data from/to the platter surfaces. With respect to SQL Server, these are the two important points to remember about hard drives.

First, the read/write heads and associated disk arms need to move in order to locate and operate on the location of the hard drive platter that SQL Server requests. If the data is distributed around the hard drive platter in nonsequential locations, it takes significantly more time for the hard drive to move the disk arm (seek time) and to spin the read/write heads (rotational latency) to locate the data. This contrasts with the sequential case, in which all of the required data is co-located on one contiguous physical section of the hard drive platter, so the disk arm and read/write heads move a minimal amount to perform the necessary disk I/O.

The time difference between the nonsequential and the sequential case is significant: about 50 milliseconds for each nonsequential seek in contrast to approximately two to three milliseconds for sequential seeks. Note that these times are rough estimations and will vary based upon how far apart the nonsequential data is spread around on the disk, how fast the hard disk platters can spin (RPM), and other physical attributes of the hard drive. The main point is, sequential I/O is good for performance and nonsequential I/O is detrimental to performance.

Second, it is important to remember that it takes almost as much time to read or write 8 kilobytes (KB) as it does to read or write 64 KB. Within the range of 8 KB to about 64 KB it remains true that disk arm plus read/write head movement (seek time and rotational latency) account for the majority of the time spent for a single disk I/O transfer operation. So, mathematically speaking, it is beneficial to try to perform 64-KB disk transfers as often as possible when more than 64 KB of SQL Server data needs to be transferred, because a 64-KB transfer is essentially as fast as an 8-KB transfer and eight times the amount of SQL Server data is processed for each transfer. Remember that read-ahead manager does its disk operations in 64-KB chunks (referred to as a SQL Server extent). The log manager performs sequential writes in larger I/O sizes, as well. The main point to remember is that making good use of the read-ahead manager and separating SQL Server log files from other nonsequentially accessed files benefit SQL Server performance.

As a rule of thumb, most hard drives can deliver performance that is as much as 2 times better when processing sequential I/O operations as compared to processing nonsequential I/O operations. That is, operations that require nonsequential I/O take twice as long to carry out as sequential I/O operations. Therefore, if possible, avoid situations that may lead to random I/O occurring within your database. While it should always be the goal to perform I/O operations sequentially, situations like page splitting or out of sequence data do tend to cause nonsequential I/O to occur.

To encourage sequential I/O it is important to avoid situations that cause page splitting. It is also helpful to devise a well thought out data loading strategy. You can encourage data to be laid out sequentially on disk by employing a partitioning strategy that separates data and indexes. It is important that you set up jobs to periodically check for fragmentation in your data and indexes, and that you use utilities provided with SQL Server to resequence the data when it becomes too fragmented. More information about doing these operations appears later in this chapter.

Note Logs generally are not a major concern because transaction log data is always written sequentially to the log file in sizes ranging up to 32 KB.

RAID

RAID (redundant array of inexpensive disks) is a storage technology often used for databases larger than a few gigabytes. RAID can provide both performance and fault tolerance benefits. A variety of RAID controllers and disk configurations offer tradeoffs among cost, performance, and fault tolerance. This topic provides a basic introduction to using RAID technology with SQL Server databases and discusses various configurations and tradeoffs.

- **Performance.** Hardware RAID controllers divide read/writes of all data from Windows NT 4.0 and Windows 2000 and applications (like SQL Server) into slices (usually 16–128 KB) that are then spread across all disks participating in the RAID array. Splitting data across physical drives like this has the effect of distributing the read/write I/O workload evenly across all physical hard drives participating in the RAID array. This increases disk I/O performance because the hard disks participating in the RAID array, as a whole are kept equally busy, instead of some disks becoming a bottleneck due to uneven distribution of the I/O requests.

- **Fault tolerance.** RAID also provides protection from hard disk failure and accompanying data loss by using two methods: mirroring and parity.

Mirroring is implemented by writing information onto a second (mirrored) set of drives. If there is a drive loss with mirroring in place, the data for the lost drive can be rebuilt by replacing the failed drive and rebuilding the mirrorset. Most RAID controllers provide the ability to do this failed drive replacement and re-mirroring while Windows NT 4.0 and Windows 2000 and SQL Server are online. Such RAID systems are commonly referred to as "Hot Plug" capable drives.

One advantage of mirroring is that it offers the best performance among RAID options if fault tolerance is required. Bear in mind that each SQL Server write to the mirrorset results in two disk I/O operations, once to each side of the mirrorset. Another advantage is that mirroring provides more fault tolerance than parity RAID implementations. Mirroring can enable the system to survive at least one failed drive and may be able to support the system through failure of up to half of the drives in the mirrorset without forcing the system administrator to shut down the server and recover from the file backup.

The disadvantage of mirroring is cost. The disk cost of mirroring is one extra drive for each drive worth of data. This essentially doubles your storage cost, which, for a data warehouse, is often one of the most expensive components needed. Both RAID 1 and its hybrid, RAID 0+1 (sometimes referred to as RAID 10 or 0/1) are implemented through mirroring.

Parity is implemented by calculating recovery information about data written to disk and writing this parity information on the other drives that form the RAID array. If a drive should fail, a new drive is inserted into the RAID array and the data on that failed drive is recovered by taking the recovery information (parity) written on the other drives and using this information to regenerate the data from the failed drive. RAID 5 and its hybrids are implemented through parity.

The advantage of parity is cost. To protect any number of drives with RAID 5, only one additional drive is required. Parity information is evenly distributed among all drives participating in the RAID 5 array. The disadvantages of parity are performance and fault tolerance. Due to the additional costs associated with calculating and writing

parity, RAID 5 requires four disk I/O operations for each write, compared to two disk I/O operations for mirroring. Read I/O operation costs are the same for mirroring and parity. Read operations, however, are usually one failed drive before the array must be taken offline and recovery from backup media must be performed to restore data.

General Rule of Thumb: Be sure to stripe across as many disks as necessary to achieve solid disk I/O performance. System Monitor will indicate if there is a disk I/O bottleneck on a particular RAID array. Be ready to add disks and redistribute data across RAID arrays and/or small computer system interface (SCSI) channels as necessary to balance disk I/O and maximize performance.

Effect of On-Board Cache of Hardware RAID Controllers

Many hardware RAID controllers have some form of read and/or write caching. This available caching with SQL Server can significantly enhance the effective I/O handling capacity of the disk subsystem. The principle of these controller-based caching mechanisms is to gather smaller and potentially nonsequential I/O requests coming in from the host server (SQL Server) and try to batch them together with other I/O requests for a few milliseconds so that the batched I/Os can form larger (32–128 KB) and maybe sequential I/O requests to send to the hard drives.

In keeping with the principle that sequential and larger I/O is good for performance, this helps produce more disk I/O throughput given the fixed number of I/Os that hard disks are able to provide to the RAID controller. It is not that the RAID controller caching magically allows the hard disks to process more I/Os per second. Rather, the RAID controller cache is using some organization to arrange incoming I/O requests to make best possible use of the underlying hard disks' fixed amount of I/O processing ability.

These RAID controllers usually protect their caching mechanism with some form of backup power. This backup power can help preserve the data written in cache for some period of time (perhaps days) in case of a power outage. If the database server is also supported by an uninterruptible power supply (UPS), the RAID controller has more time and opportunity to flush data to disk in the event of power disruption. Although a UPS for the server does not directly affect performance, it does provide protection for the performance improvement supplied by RAID controller caching.

RAID Levels

As mentioned above, RAID 1 and RAID 0+1 offer the best data protection and best performance among RAID levels, but cost more in terms of disks required. When cost of hard disks is not a limiting factor, RAID 1 or RAID 0+1 are the best choices in terms of both performance and fault tolerance.

RAID 5 costs less than RAID 1 or RAID 0+1 but provides less fault tolerance and less write performance. The write performance of RAID 5 is only about half that of RAID 1 or RAID 0+1 because of the additional I/O needed to read and write parity information.

The best disk I/O performance is achieved with RAID 0 (disk striping with no fault tolerance protection). Because RAID 0 provides no fault tolerance protection, it should never be used in a production environment, and it is not recommended for development environments. RAID 0 is typically used only for benchmarking or testing.

Many RAID array controllers provide the option of RAID 0+1 (also referred to as RAID 1/0 and RAID 10) over physical hard drives. RAID 0+1 is a hybrid RAID solution. On the lower level, it mirrors all data just like normal RAID 1. On the upper level, the controller stripes data across all of the drives (like RAID 0). Thus, RAID 0+1 provides maximum protection (mirroring) with high performance (striping). These striping and mirroring operations are transparent to Windows and SQL Server because they are managed by the RAID controller. The difference between RAID 1 and RAID 0+1 is on the hardware controller level. RAID 1 and RAID 0+1 require the same number of drives for a given amount of storage. For more information on RAID 0+1 implementation of specific RAID controllers, contact the hardware vendor that produced the controller.

The illustration below shows differences between RAID 0, RAID 1, RAID 5, and RAID 0+1.

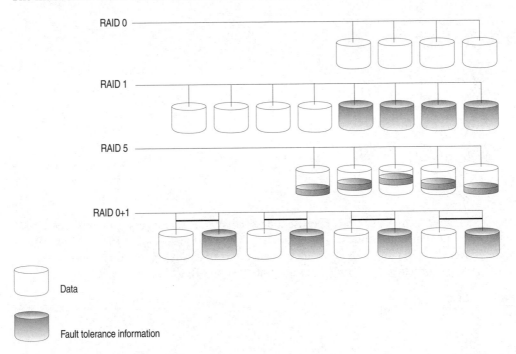

Note   In the illustration above, in order to hold four disks worth of data, RAID 1 (and RAID 0+1) need eight disks, whereas Raid 5 only requires five disks. Be sure to involve your storage vendor to learn more about their specific RAID implementation.

Level 0

This level is also known as disk striping because of its use of a disk file system called a stripe set. Data is divided into blocks and spread in a fixed order among all disks in an array. RAID 0 improves read/write performance by spreading operations across multiple disks, so that operations can be performed independently and simultaneously. RAID 0 is similar to RAID 5, except RAID 5 also provides fault tolerance.

The following illustration shows RAID 0.

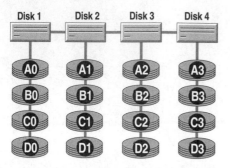

Level 1

This level is also known as disk mirroring because it uses a disk file system called a mirror set. Disk mirroring provides a redundant, identical copy of a selected disk. All data written to the primary disk is written to the mirror disk. RAID 1 provides fault tolerance and generally improves read performance (but may degrade write performance). The following illustration shows RAID 1.

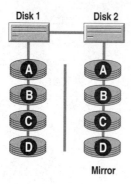

Level 2

This level adds redundancy by using an error correction method that spreads parity across all disks. It also employs a disk-striping strategy that breaks a file into bytes and spreads it across multiple disks. This strategy offers only a marginal improvement in disk utilization and read/write performance over mirroring (RAID 1). RAID 2 is not as efficient as other RAID levels and is not generally used.

Level 3

This level uses the same striping method as RAID 2, but the error correction method requires only one disk for parity data. Use of disk space varies with the number of data disks. RAID 3 provides some read/write performance improvement. RAID 3 also is rarely used.

Level 4

This level employs striped data in much larger blocks or segments than RAID 2 or RAID 3. Like RAID 3, the error correction method requires only one disk for parity data. It keeps user data separate from error-correction data. RAID 4 is not as efficient as other RAID levels and is not generally used.

Level 5

Also known as striping with parity, this level is the most popular strategy for new designs. It is similar to RAID 4 because it stripes the data in large blocks across the disks in an array. It differs in how it writes the parity across all the disks. Data redundancy is provided by the parity information. The data and parity information are arranged on the disk array so the two are always on different disks. Striping with parity offers better performance than disk mirroring (RAID 1). However, when a stripe member is missing, read performance degrades (for example, when a disk fails). RAID 5 is one of the most commonly used RAID configurations. The following illustration shows RAID 5.

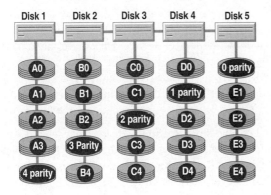

Level 10 (1+0)

This level is also known as mirroring with striping. This level uses a striped array of disks, which are then mirrored to another identical set of striped disks. For example, a striped array can be created using four disks. The striped array of disks is then mirrored using another set of four striped disks. RAID 10 provides the performance benefits of disk striping with the disk redundancy of mirroring. RAID 10 provides the highest read/write performance of any of the RAID levels at the expense of using twice as many disks. The following illustration shows RAID 10.

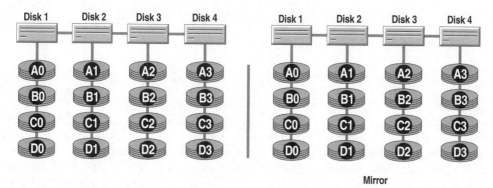

Mirror

Online RAID Expansion

This feature allows disks to be added dynamically to a physical RAID array while SQL Server remains online. Additional disk drives are automatically integrated into the RAID storage. Disk drives are added by installing them into physical positions called hot plug drive slots, or hot plug slots. Many hardware vendors offer hardware RAID controllers that are capable of providing this functionality. Data is automatically re-striped across all drives evenly, including the newly added drive, and there is no need to shut down SQL Server or Windows.

You can take advantage of this functionality by leaving hot plug slots free in the disk array cages. If SQL Server is regularly overtaxing a RAID array with I/O requests (this will be indicated by Disk Queue Length for the Windows logical drive letter associated with that RAID array), it is possible to install one or more new hard drives into the hot plug slots while SQL Server is still running. The RAID controller will move some existing SQL Server data to these new drives so data is evenly distributed across all drives in the RAID array. Then the I/O processing capacity of the new drives (75 nonsequential/150 sequential I/Os per second, for each drive) is added to the overall I/O processing capacity of the RAID array.

System Monitor and RAID

In System Monitor (Performance Monitor in Microsoft Windows NT® 4.0), information can be obtained for both logical and physical disk drives. The difference is that logical disks in System Monitor are associated with what Windows reads as a logical drive letter. Physical disks in System Monitor are associated with what Windows reads as a single physical hard disk.

In Windows NT 4.0, all disk counters for Performance Monitor were turned off by default because they could have a minor impact on performance. In Windows 2000 the physical disk counters are turned on by default and the logical disk counters are turned off by default. **Diskperf.exe** is the Windows command that controls the types of counters that can be viewed in System Monitor.

In Windows 2000, to obtain performance counter data for logical drives or storage volumes, you must type diskperf -yv at the command prompt, and then press ENTER. This causes the disk performance statistics driver used for collecting disk performance data to report data for logical drives or storage volumes. By default, the operating system uses the diskperf -yd command to obtain physical drive data.

The syntax for **Diskperf.exe** in Windows 2000 is as follows:

diskperf [-y[d|v] | -n[d|v]] [\\computername]

Parameters

(none)
　　Reports whether disk performance counters are enabled and identifies the counters enabled.

-y
　　Sets the system to start all disk performance counters when you restart the computer.

-yd
　　Enables the disk performance counters for physical drives when you restart the computer.

-yv
　　Enables the disk performance counters for logical drives or storage volumes when you restart the computer.

-n
　　Sets the system to disable all disk performance counters when you restart the computer.

-nd
　　Disables the disk performance counters for physical drives.

-nv
　　Disables the disk performance counters for logical drives.

\\computername
　　Specifies the computer you want to see or set disk performance counters to use.

With Windows NT 4.0 and earlier, `diskperf -y` was used for monitoring hard drives, or sets of hard drives and RAID controllers, that were not using Windows NT software RAID. When utilizing Windows software RAID, use `diskperf -ye` so that System Monitor will report physical counters across the Windows NT stripesets correctly. When `diskperf -ye` is used in conjunction with Windows NT stripesets, logical counters will not report correct information and should be disregarded. If logical disk counter information is required in conjunction with Windows NT stripesets, use `diskperf -y` instead.

With `diskperf -y`, logical disk counters will be reported correctly for Windows NT stripesets, but physical disk counters will not report correct information and should be disregarded.

> **Note** The effects of the diskperf command do not take effect until Windows has been restarted (both for Windows 2000 and Windows NT 4.0 and earlier).

Considerations for Monitoring Hardware RAID

Because RAID controllers present multiple physical hard drives as a single RAID mirrorset or stripeset to Windows, Windows reads the grouping as though it were a single physical disk. The resulting abstracted view of the actual underlying hard drive activity can cause performance counters to report information that can be misleading.

From a performance tuning perspective, it is very important to be aware of how many physical hard drives are associated with a RAID array. This information will be needed when determining the number of disk I/O requests that Windows and SQL Server are sending to each physical hard drive. Divide the number of disk I/O requests that System Monitor reports as being associated with a hard drive by the number of actual physical hard drives known to be in that RAID array.

To get a rough estimate of I/O activity for each hard drive in a RAID array, it is also important to multiply the number of disk write I/Os reported by System Monitor by either two (RAID 1 and 0+1) or four (RAID 5). This will give a more accurate account of the number of actual I/O requests being sent to the physical hard drives, because it is at this physical level that the I/O capacity numbers for hard drives apply. This method, however, will not calculate the hard drive I/O exactly, when the hardware RAID controller is using caching, because caching can significantly affect the direct I/O to the hard drives.

When monitoring disk activity, it is best to concentrate on disk queuing instead of on the actual I/O for each disk. Disk I/O speeds depend on the transfer rate capability of the drives, which cannot be adjusted. Because there is little you can do other than buy faster, or more, drives, there is little reason to be concerned with the amount of I/O that is actually occurring. However, you do want to avoid too much disk queuing. Significant disk queuing reveals that you have an I/O problem. Because Windows cannot read the number of physical drives in a RAID array, it is difficult to accurately assess disk queuing for each physical disk. A rough approximation can be determined by dividing the Disk Queue Length by the number of physical drives participating in the hardware RAID disk array for the logical drive being observed. It is optimal to attempt to keep the disk queue number below two for hard drives containing SQL Server files.

Software RAID

Windows 2000 supports software RAID to address fault tolerance by providing mirrorsets and stripesets (with or without fault tolerance) through the operating system when a hardware RAID controller is not used. You can set up RAID 0, RAID 1, or RAID 5 functionality using operating system procedures. Most large data warehouses use hardware RAID, but in the event that your installation is relatively small or you choose not to implement hardware RAID, software RAID can provide some data access and fault tolerance advantages.

Software RAID does utilize some CPU resources, because Windows has to manage the RAID operations that the hardware RAID controller would typically manage for you. Thus, performance with the same number of disk drives and Windows software RAID may be a few percent less than with hardware RAID, especially if the system processors are nearly 100 percent utilized for other purposes. By reducing the potential for I/O bottlenecks, Windows software RAID will generally help a set of drives service SQL Server I/O better than if the drives are used without software RAID. Software RAID should allow for better CPU utilization by SQL Server because the server will wait less often for I/O requests to complete.

Disk I/O Parallelism

An effective technique for improving the performance of large SQL Server databases that are stored on multiple disk drives is to create disk I/O parallelism, which is the simultaneous reading from and writing to multiple disk drives. RAID implements disk I/O parallelism through hardware and software. The next topic discusses using partitioning to organize SQL Server data to further increase disk I/O parallelism.

Partitioning for Performance

For SQL Server databases that are stored on multiple disk drives, performance can be improved by partitioning the data to increase the amount of disk I/O parallelism.

Partitioning can be done using a variety of techniques. Methods for creating and managing partitions include configuring your storage subsystem (disk, RAID partitioning) and applying various data configuration mechanisms in SQL Server such as files, filegroups, tables and views. While this section focuses on some of the partitioning capabilities as they relate to performance, Chapter 18, "Using Partitions in a SQL Server 2000 Data Warehouse," specifically addresses the subject of partitioning.

The simplest technique for creating disk I/O parallelism is to use hardware partitioning and create a single "pool of drives" that serves all SQL Server database files except transaction log files, which should always be stored on physically separate disk drives dedicated to log files only. The pool may be a single RAID array that is represented in Windows as a single physical drive. Larger pools may be set up using multiple RAID arrays and SQL Server files/filegroups. A SQL Server file can be associated with each RAID array and the files can be combined into a SQL Server filegroup. Then a database can be built on the filegroup so the data will be spread evenly across all of the drives and RAID controllers. The drive pool method depends on RAID to divide data across all physical drives to help ensure parallel access to that data during database server operations.

This drive pool method simplifies SQL Server I/O performance tuning because database administrators know there is only one physical location in which to create database objects. The single pool of drives can be watched for disk queuing and, if necessary, more hard drives can be added to the pool to prevent disk queuing. This method helps optimize for the common case, in which it is unknown what parts of databases may get the most usage. It is better not to have a portion of the total available I/O capacity

segregated on another disk partition just because five percent of the time SQL Server might be doing I/O to it. The "single pool of drives" method helps make all available I/O capacity "always" available for SQL Server operations. It also allows I/O operations to be spread across the maximum number of disks available.

SQL Server log files should *always* be physically separated onto different hard drives from all other SQL Server database files. For SQL Servers managing multiple busy databases that are very busy, the transaction log files for each database should be physically separated from each other to reduce contention.

Because transaction logging is primarily a sequential write I/O, the separation of log files tends to yield a tremendous I/O performance benefit. The disk drives containing the log files can very efficiently perform these sequential write operations if they are not interrupted by other I/O requests. At times, the transaction log will need to be read as part of SQL Server operations, such as replication, rollbacks, and deferred updates. Some implementations use replication as a front end to their data transformation utility as a means of loading new data into the data warehouse in near real time. Administrators of SQL Servers that participate in replication need to make sure that all disks used for transaction log files have sufficient I/O processing power to accommodate the reads that need to occur in addition to the normal log transaction writes.

Additional administration is required to physically segment files and filegroups. The additional effort may prove worthwhile when segmenting for the purposes of isolating and improving access to very active tables or indexes. Some of the benefits are listed below:

- More accurate assessments can be made of the I/O requirements for specific objects, which is not as easy to do when all database objects are placed within one big drive pool.

- Partitioning data and indexes using files and file groups can enhance the administrator's ability to create a more granular backup and restore strategy.

- File and filegroups may be used to maintain the sequential placement of data on disk, thus reducing or eliminating nonsequential I/O activity. This can be extremely important if your available window of time for loading data into the warehouse requires processing be performed in parallel to meet the deadline.

- Physically segmenting files and filegroups may be appropriate during database development and benchmarking so database I/O information can be gathered and applied to capacity planning for the production database server environment.

Objects For Partitioning Consideration

The following areas of SQL Server activity can be separated across different hard drives, RAID controllers, and PCI channels (or combinations of the three):

- Transaction log
- tempdb
- Database
- Tables
- Nonclustered indexes

> **Note** In SQL Server 2000, Microsoft introduced enhancements to distributed partitioned views that enable the creation of federated databases (commonly referred to as scale-out), which spread resource load and I/O activity across multiple servers. Federated databases are appropriate for some high-end online analytical processing (OLTP) applications, but this approach is not recommended for addressing the needs of a data warehouse.

The physical segregation of SQL Server I/O activity is quite easy to achieve using hardware RAID controllers, RAID hot plug drives, and online RAID expansion. The approach that provides the most flexibility is arranging RAID controllers so that separate RAID channels are associated with the different areas of activity mentioned above. Also, each RAID channel should be attached to a separate RAID hot plug cabinet to take full advantage of online RAID expansion (if available through the RAID controller). Windows logical drive letters are then associated to each RAID array and SQL Server files may be separated between distinct RAID arrays based on known I/O usage patterns.

With this configuration it is possible to relate disk queuing associated with each activity back to a distinct RAID channel and its drive cabinet. If a RAID controller and its drive array cabinet both support online RAID expansion and slots for hot plug hard drives are available in the cabinet, disk queuing issues on that RAID array can be resolved by simply adding more drives to the RAID array until System Monitor reports that disk queuing for that RAID array has reached an acceptable level (ideally less than two for SQL Server files). This can be done while SQL Server is online.

Segregating the Transaction Log

Transaction log files should be maintained on a storage device physically separate from devices that contain data files. Depending on your database recovery model setting, most update activity generates both data device activity and log activity. If both are set up to share the same device, the operations to be performed will compete for the same limited resources. Most installations benefit from separating these competing I/O activities.

Segregating tempdb

SQL Server creates a database, **tempdb**, on every server instance to be used by the server as a shared working area for various activities, including temporary tables, sorting, processing subqueries, building aggregates to support GROUP BY or ORDER BY clauses, queries using DISTINCT (temporary worktables have to be created to remove duplicate rows), cursors, and hash joins. By segmenting **tempdb** onto its own RAID channel, we enable **tempdb** I/O operations to occur in parallel with the I/O operations of their related transactions. Because **tempdb** is essentially a scratch area and very update intensive, RAID 5 is not as good a choice for **tempdb** – RAID 1 or 0+1 offer better performance. Raid 0, even though it does not provide fault tolerance, can be considered for **tempdb** because **tempdb** is rebuilt every time the database server is restarted. RAID 0 provides the best RAID performance for **tempdb** with the least number of physical drives, but the main concern about using RAID 0 for **tempdb** in a production environment is that SQL Server availability might be compromised if any physical drive failure were to occur, including the drive used for **tempdb**. This can be avoided if **tempdb** is placed on a RAID configuration that provides fault tolerance.

To move the **tempdb** database, use the ALTER DATABASE command to change the physical file location of the SQL Server logical file name associated with **tempdb**. For example, to move **tempdb** and its associated log to the new file locations E:\mssql7 and C:\temp, use the following commands:

```
alter database tempdb modify file (name='tempdev',filename=
'e:\mssql7\tempnew_location.mDF')
alter database tempdb modify file (name='templog',filename=
'c:\temp\tempnew_loglocation.mDF')
```

The master database, **msdb**, and model databases are not used much during production compared to user databases, so it is typically not necessary to consider them in I/O performance tuning considerations. The master database is usually used only for adding new logins, databases, devices, and other system objects.

Database Partitioning

Databases can be partitioned using files and/or filegroups. A filegroup is simply a named collection of individual files grouped together for administration purposes. A file cannot be a member of more than one filegroup. Tables, indexes, **text**, **ntext**, and **image** data can all be associated with a specific filegroup. This means that all their pages are allocated from the files in that filegroup. The three types of filegroups are described below.

Primary filegroup

This filegroup contains the primary data file and any other files not placed into another filegroup. All pages for the system tables are allocated from the primary filegroup.

User-defined filegroup

This filegroup is any filegroup specified using the FILEGROUP keyword in a CREATE DATABASE or ALTER DATABASE statement, or on the **Properties** dialog box within SQL Server Enterprise Manager.

Default filegroup

The default filegroup contains the pages for all tables and indexes that do not have a filegroup specified when they are created. In each database, only one filegroup at a time can be the default filegroup. If no default filegroup is specified, the default is the primary filegroup.

Files and filegroups are useful for controlling the placement of data and indexes and to eliminate device contention. Quite a few installations also leverage files and filegroups as a mechanism that is more granular than a database in order to exercise more control over their database backup/recovery strategy.

Horizontal Partitioning (Table)

Horizontal partitioning segments a table into multiple tables, each containing the same number of columns but fewer rows. Determining how to partition the tables horizontally depends on how data is analyzed. A general rule of thumb is to partition tables so queries reference as few tables as possible. Otherwise, excessive UNION queries, used to merge the tables logically at query time, can impair performance.

For example, assume business requirements dictate that we store a rolling ten years worth of transactional data in the central fact table of our data warehouse. Ten years of transactional data for our company represents more than one billion rows. A billion of anything is a challenge to manage. Now consider that every year we have to drop the tenth year of data and load the latest year.

A common approach administrators take is to create ten separate, but identically structured tables, each holding one year's worth of data. Then the administrator defines a single union view over top of the ten tables to provide end users with the appearance that all of the data is being housed in a single table. In fact, it is not. Any query posed against the view is optimized to search only the specified years (and corresponding tables). However, the administrator does gain manageability. The administrator can now granularly manage each year of data independently. Each year of data can be loaded, indexed, or maintained on its own. To add a new year is as simple as dropping the view, dropping the table with the tenth year of data, loading and indexing the new year of data, and then redefining the new view to include the new year of data.

When you partition data across multiple tables or multiple servers, queries accessing only a fraction of the data can run faster because there is less data to scan. If the tables are located on different servers, or on a computer with multiple processors, each table involved in the query can also be scanned in parallel, thereby improving query performance. Additionally, maintenance tasks, such as rebuilding indexes or backing up a table, can execute more quickly.

By using a partitioned view, the data still appears as a single table and can be queried as such without having to reference the correct underlying table manually. Partitioned views are updatable if either of the following conditions is met. For details about partitioned views and their restrictions, see SQL Server Books Online.

- An INSTEAD OF trigger is defined on the view with logic to support INSERT, UPDATE, and DELETE statements.

- The view and the INSERT, UPDATE, and DELETE statements follow the rules defined for updatable partitioned views.

Segregating Nonclustered Indexes

Indexes reside in B-tree structures, which can be separated from their related database tables (except for clustered indexes) by using the ALTER DATABASE command to set up a distinct filegroup. In the example below, the first ALTER DATABASE creates a filegroup. The second ALTER DATABASE adds a file to the newly created filegroup.

```
alter database testdb add filegroup testgroup1
alter database testdb add file (name = 'testfile',
   filename = 'e:\mssql7\test1.ndf') to filegroup testgroup1
```

After a filegroup and its associated files have been created, the filegroup can be used to store indexes by specifying the filegroup when the indexes are created.

```
create table test1(col1 char(8))
create index index1 on test1(col1) on testgroup1
```

SP_HELPFILE reports information back about files and filegroups in a given database. SP_HELP <tablename> has a section in its output, which provides information on a table's indexes and their filegroup relationships.

```
sp_helpfile
sp_help test1
```

Parallel Data Retrieval

SQL Server can perform parallel scans of data when running on a computer that has multiple processors. Multiple parallel scans can be executed for a single table if the table is in a filegroup that contains multiple files. Whenever a table is accessed sequentially, a separate thread is created to read each file in parallel. For example, a full scan of a table created on a filegroup that consists of four files will use four separate threads to read the data in parallel. Therefore, creating more files for each filegroup can help increase performance because a separate thread is used to scan each file in parallel. Similarly, when a query joins tables on different filegroups, each table can be read in parallel, thereby improving query performance.

Additionally, any **text**, **ntext**, or **image** columns within a table can be created on a filegroup other than the one that contains the base table.

Eventually, a saturation point is reached when there are too many files and therefore too many parallel threads causing bottlenecks in the disk I/O subsystem. These bottlenecks can be identified by using System Monitor to monitor the **PhysicalDisk** object and **Disk Queue Length** counter. If the **Disk Queue Length** counter is greater than three, consider reducing the number of files.

It is advantageous to get as much data spread across as many physical drives as possible in order to improve throughput through parallel data access using multiple files. To spread data evenly across all disks, first set up hardware-based disk striping, and then use filegroups to spread data across multiple hardware stripe sets if needed.

Parallel Query Recommendations

SQL Server can automatically execute queries in parallel. This optimizes the query execution in multiprocessor computers. Rather than using one operating system thread to execute one query, work is broken down into multiple threads (subject to the availability of threads and memory), and complex queries are completed faster and more efficiently.

The optimizer in SQL Server generates the plan for the query and determines when a query will be executed in parallel. The determination is made based on the following criteria:

- Does the computer have multiple processors?
- Is there enough memory available to execute the query in parallel?
- What is the CPU load on the server?
- What type of query is being run?

When allowing SQL Server to run parallel operations like DBCC and index creation in parallel, the server resources become stressed, and you might see warning messages when heavy parallel operations are occurring. If warning messages about insufficient resources appear frequently in the server error log, consider using System Monitor to investigate what resources are available, such as memory, CPU usage, and I/O usage.

Do not run heavy queries that are executed in parallel when there are active users on the server. Try executing maintenance jobs such as DBCC and INDEX creation during offload times. These jobs can be executed in parallel. Monitor the disk I/O performance. Observe the disk queue length in System Monitor (Performance Monitor in Windows NT 4.0) to make decisions about upgrading your hard disks or redistributing your databases onto different disks. Upgrade or add more processors if the CPU usage is very high.

The following server configuration options can affect parallel execution of the queries:

- **cost threshold for parallelism**
- **max degree of parallelism**

- **max worker threads**
- **query governor cost limit**

Optimizing Data Loads

There are multiple tips and techniques to keep in mind for accelerating your data loading activities. The techniques will likely vary based on whether you are doing initial data loads or incremental data loads. Incremental loads in general are more involved and restrictive. The techniques you choose might also be based on factors outside your control. Processing window requirements, your chosen storage configuration, limitations of your server hardware, and so on, can all impact the options available to you.

There are a number of common things to keep in mind when performing both initial data loads and incremental data loads. The following subjects will be discussed in detail below:

- Choosing an appropriate database recovery model
- Using **bcp**, BULK INSERT, or the bulk copy API
- Controlling the Locking behavior
- Loading data in parallel
- Miscellaneous, including:
  - Bypassing referential integrity checks (constraints & triggers)
  - Loading presorted data
  - Effects of removing indexes

Choosing an Appropriate Database Recovery Model

We discussed database recovery models in the section "Configuration Options That Impact Performance." It is important to remember that the recovery model you choose can have a significant impact on the amount of time needed to perform your data load. Basically, these recovery models control the amount of data that will be written out to the transaction log. This is important because performing write operations to the transaction log essentially doubles the workload.

Logged and Minimally Logged Bulk Copy Operations

When using the full recovery model, all row-insert operations performed by one of the bulk data load mechanisms (discussed below) are logged in the transaction log. For large data loads, this can cause the transaction log to fill rapidly. To help prevent the transaction log from running out of space you can perform minimally logged bulk copy operation. Whether a bulk copy is performed as logged or nonlogged is not specified as part of the bulk copy operation; it is dependent on the state of the database and the table involved in the bulk copy. A nonlogged bulk copy occurs if all the following conditions are met:

- The recovery model is Simple or Bulk-Logged or the database option **select into/bulkcopy** is set to true.

- The target table is not being replicated.

- The target table has no indexes, or if the table has indexes, it is empty when the bulk copy starts.

- The TABLOCK hint is specified using **bcp_control** with *eOption* set to BCPHINTS.

Any bulk copy into an instance of SQL Server that does not meet these conditions is fully logged.

On initial data loads you should always operate under the Bulk-Logged or Simple recovery model. For incremental data loads, consider using bulk-logged as long as the potential for data loss is low. Because many data warehouses are primarily read-only or have a minimal amount of transaction activity, setting the database recovery model to bulk-logged may pose no problem.

Using bcp, BULK INSERT, or the Bulk Copy APIs

Two mechanisms exist inside SQL Server to address the needs of bulk movement of data. The first mechanism is the **bcp** utility. The second is the BULK INSERT statement. **bcp** is a command prompt utility that copies data both into or out of SQL Server. With SQL Server 2000, the **bcp** utility was rewritten using the ODBC bulk copy application programming interface (API). Earlier versions of the **bcp** utility were written using the DB-Library bulk copy API.

BULK INSERT is a Transact-SQL statement included with SQL Server that can be executed from within the database environment. Unlike **bcp**, BULK INSERT can only pull data into SQL Server. It cannot push data out. An advantage to using BULK INSERT is that it can copy data into an instance of SQL Server using a Transact-SQL statement, rather than having to shell out to the command prompt.

A third option, which often appeals to programmers, is the bulk copy APIs. These APIs enable programmers to move data into or out of SQL Server using ODBC, OLE DB, SQL-DMO, or even DB-Library-based applications.

All of these options enable you to exercise control over the batch size. Unless you are working with small volumes of data, it is good to get in the habit of specifying a batch size for recoverability reasons. If none is specified, SQL Server commits all rows to be loaded as a single batch. For example, you attempt to load 1,000,000 rows of new data into a table. The server suddenly loses power just as it finishes processing row number 999,999. When the server recovers, those 999,999 rows will need to be rolled back out of the database before you attempt to reload the data. By specifying a batch size of 10,000 you could have saved yourself significant recovery time because you would have only had to rollback 9,999 rows instead of 999,999. This is because you would have already committed rows 1-990,000 to the database. Also, without a specified batch size, you would have to restart the load processing back at row 1 in order to reload the data. With the specified batch size of 10,000 rows, you could simply restart the load processing at row 990,001, effectively bypassing the 990,000 rows already committed.

Controlling the Locking Behavior

The **bcp** utility and BULK INSERT statement accept the **TABLOCK** hint, which allows the user to specify the locking behavior to be used. **TABLOCK** specifies that a bulk update table-level lock will be taken for the duration of the bulk copy operation. Using **TABLOCK** can improve performance of the bulk copy operation due to reduced lock contention on the table. This setting has significant implications when parallel loads are being processed against a single table (discussed in next section).

For example, to bulk copy data from the Authors.txt data file to the **authors2** table in the **pubs** database, specifying a table-level lock, execute from the command prompt:

```
bcp pubs..authors2 in authors.txt -c -t, -Sservername -Usa -Ppassword -h "TABLOCK"
```

Alternatively, you could use the BULK INSERT statement from a query tool, such as SQL Query Analyzer, to bulk copy data, as in this example:

```
BULK INSERT pubs..authors2 FROM 'c:\authors.txt'
WITH (
    DATAFILETYPE = 'char',
    FIELDTERMINATOR = ',',
    TABLOCK
)
```

If **TABLOCK** is not specified, the default locking uses row-level locks, unless the **table lock on bulk load** option is set to **on** for the table. Using the **table lock on bulk load** option with the **sp_tableoption** command is an alternative way to set the locking behavior for a table during a bulk load operation.

Table lock on bulk load	Table locking behavior
Off	Row-level locks used
On	Table-level lock used

Note If the **TABLOCK** hint is specified, it overrides the setting declared using the **sp_tableoption** for the duration of the bulk load.

Loading Data in Parallel

Parallel Load - Nonpartitioned Table

It is possible to perform parallel data loads into a single, nonpartitioned table using any of the bulk data load mechanisms in SQL Server. This is done by using running multiple data loads simultaneously. The data to be loaded in parallel needs to be split into separate files (data sources for the bulk insert API) prior to beginning the load. Then all the separate load operations can be initiated at the same time so that the data loads in parallel.

For example, assume you need to load a consolidation database for a service company that operates in four global regions, each reporting report hours billed to clients on a monthly basis. For a large service organization, this could represent a large amount of transactional data that needs to be consolidated. If each of the four reporting regions provided a separate file, it would be possible using the methodology described earlier to load all four files simultaneously into a single table.

Note   The number of parallel threads (loads) you process in parallel should not exceed the number of processors available to SQL Server.

The following illustration shows parallel loading on a nonpartitioned table.

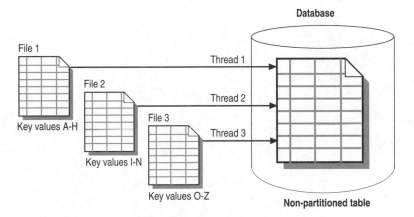

Parallel Load - Horizontal Partitioning (Table)

This section focuses on how horizontal partitioned tables can be used to improve the speed of your data loads. In a previous section, we discussed loading data from multiple files into a single (nonpartitioned) table. Horizontal partitioning of the table offers an opportunity to possibly improve the contiguousness of your data as well as speeding up the load process by reducing device contention. Though the above figure shows the data being loaded into different sections of the table, this may not be an accurate depiction. If all three threads in the above load were being processed simultaneously, the extents taken for the table would likely end up intermingled. The intermingling of the data could result in less than optimal performance when the data is retrieved. This is because the data was not stored in physically contiguous order, which could cause the system to access it using nonsequential I/O.

Building a clustered index over this table would solve the problem, because the data would be read in, sorted into the key order, and written back out in contiguous order. However, the reading, sorting, deletion of the old data, and writing back out of the newly sorted data can be a time consuming task (see loading presorted data below). To avoid this intermingling, consider using filegroups to reserve chunks of contiguous space where you can store large tables. Many installations also use filegroups to segregate index data away from table data.

To illustrate, assume a data warehouse that is allocated onto one large physical partition. Any load operations performed in parallel to that database are likely to cause the affected data/index pages to be stored in a noncontiguous (intermingled) state. What sort of operations? Any operation that modifies the data will cause the data to become noncontiguous. Initial data loads, incremental data loads, index creation, index maintenance, inserts, updates, deletes, and so on are all activities that one might be tempted to perform in parallel in order to meet processing window requirements.

The following illustration shows partitioning a table across multiple filegroups.

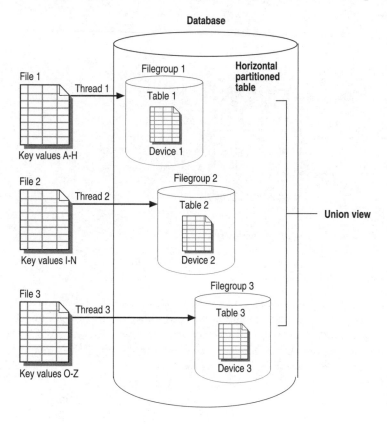

Loading Pre-Sorted Data

Earlier versions of SQL Server included an option that allowed you to specify a SORTED_DATA option when creating an index. This has been eliminated in SQL Server 2000. The reason for specifying this option as part of your CREATE INDEX statement in earlier versions is that it enabled you to avoid a sort step in the index creation process. By default in SQL Server, when creating a clustered index, the data in the table is sorted during the processing. To get the same effect with SQL Server 2000, consider creating the clustered index before bulk loading the data. Bulk operations in SQL Server 2000 use enhanced index maintenance strategies to improve the performance of data importation on tables having a preexisting clustered index, and to eliminate the need for resorting data after the import.

Impact of FILLFACTOR and PAD_INDEX on Data Loads

FILLFACTOR and PAD_INDEX are explained more fully under the section titled "Indexes and Index Maintenance." The key thing to remember about both FILLFACTOR and PAD_INDEX is that leaving them set to default, when creating an index, may cause SQL Server to perform more writes and read I/O operations than are needed to store the data. This is especially true of data warehouses having very little write activity going on in them, but high amounts of read activity. To get SQL Server to write more data to a single page of the data or index pages, you can specify a particular FILLFACTOR when creating the index. It is a good idea to specify the PAD_INDEX when providing an overriding FILLFACTOR value.

General Guidelines for Initial Data Loads

While Loading Data

- Remove indexes (one exception might be in loading pre-sorted data – see above)
- Use BULK INSERT, **bcp** or bulk copy API
- Parallel load using partitioned data files into partitioned tables
- Run one load stream for each available CPU
- Set Bulk-Logged or Simple Recovery model
- Use the TABLOCK option

After Loading Data

- Create indexes
- Switch to the appropriate recovery model
- Perform backups

General Guidelines for Incremental Data Loads

- Load data with indexes in place.

- Performance and concurrency requirements should determine locking granularity (**sp_indexoption**).

- Change from Full to Bulk-Logged Recovery model unless there is an overriding need to preserve point-in-time recovery, such as online users modifying the database during bulk loads. Read operations should not affect bulk loads.

Indexes and Index Maintenance

I/O characteristics of the hardware devices on the server have been discussed. Now the discussion will move to how SQL Server data and index structures are physically placed on disk drives. Index placement is likely to be the single biggest influence you can have over your data warehouse to improve performance once your design is set.

Types of Indexes in SQL Server

Although SQL Server 2000 introduced several new types of indexes, all of them are based on two core forms. The two core forms are a clustered index or a nonclustered index format. The two primary types of indexes available to database designers in SQL Server are:

- Clustered indexes.

- Nonclustered indexes.

Additional variations of the two primary types include:

- Unique indexes.

- Indexes on computed columns.

- Indexed views.

- Full text indexes.

Each index type mentioned above will be described in detail in the following sections below except for Full text indexes. Full text indexing is a special case unlike other database indexes and is not covered in this chapter. An indexed view is a new type of index introduced in SQL Server 2000 that should prove to be of particular interest to the data warehousing audience. Another new feature introduced in SQL Server 2000 is the ability to create indexes in either ascending or descending order.

How Indexes Work

Indexes in databases are similar to indexes in books. In a book, an index allows you to find information quickly without reading the entire book. In a database, an index allows the database program to find data in a table without scanning the entire table. An index in a book is a list of words with the page numbers that contain each word. An index in a database is a list of values in a table with the storage locations of rows in the table that contain each value.

Indexes can be created on either a single column or a combination of columns in a table and are implemented in the form of B-trees. An index contains an entry with one or more columns (the search key) from each row in a table. A B-tree is stored in sorted order on the search key in either ascending or descending order (depending on the option chosen when the index is created), and can be searched efficiently on any leading subset of that search key. For example, an index on columns **A**, **B**, **C** can be searched efficiently on **A**, on **A**, **B**, and **A**, **B**, **C**.

When you create a database and tune it for performance, you should create indexes for the columns used in queries to find data. In the **pubs** sample database provided with SQL Server, the **employee** table has an index on the **emp_id** column. When someone executes a statement to find data in the **employee** table based on a specified **emp_id** value, SQL Server query processor recognizes the index for the emp_id column and uses the index to find the data. The following illustration shows how the index stores each **emp_id** value and points to the rows of data in the table with the corresponding value.

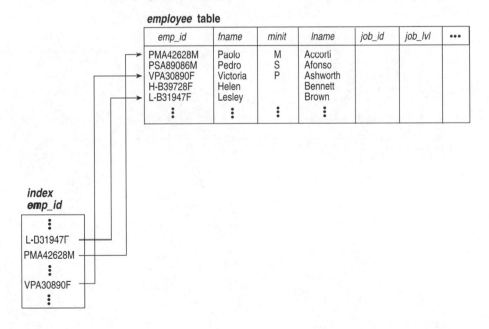

However, tables with indexes require more storage space in the database. Also, commands that insert, update, or delete data can take longer and require more processing time to maintain the indexes. When you design and create indexes, ensure that the performance benefits outweigh the extra cost in storage space and processing resources.

Index Intersection

A unique feature found inside the SQL Server query processor is the ability to perform index intersection. This is a special form of index covering, which we explain in detail later, but index intersection bears mentioning now for two reasons. First, it is a technique that may influence your index design strategy.

Second, this technique can possibly reduce the number of indexes you need, which can save significant disk space for very large databases.

Index intersection allows the query processor to use multiple indexes to solve a query. Most database query processors use only one index when attempting to resolve a query. SQL Server can combine multiple indexes from a given table or view, build a hash table based on those multiple indexes, and utilize the hash table to reduce I/O for a given query. The hash table that results from the index intersection becomes, in essence, a covering index and provides the same I/O performance benefits that covering indexes do. Index intersection provides greater flexibility for database user environments in which it is difficult to predetermine all of the queries that will be run against the database. A good strategy in this case is to define single-column, nonclustered indexes on all the columns that will be frequently queried and let index intersection handle situations where a covered index is needed.

The following example makes use of index intersection:

```
Create index Indexname1 on Table1(col2)
Create index Indexname2 on Table1(col3)
Select col3 from table1 where col2 = 'value'
```

When the previous query is performed, the indexes can be combined to quickly and efficiently resolve the query.

Index Architecture In SQL Server

All indexes in SQL Server are physically built upon a B-tree index structures, which are stored on 8-KB index pages. Each index page has a page header followed by the index rows. Each index row contains a key value and a pointer to either a lower-level index page or an actual data row. Each page in an index is also referred to as an index node. The top node of the B-tree is called the root node. The bottom layer of nodes in an index are called the leaf nodes. Any index levels between the root and the leaves are collectively known as intermediate levels or nodes. Pages in each level of the index are linked together in a doubly-linked list.

SQL Server data and index pages are both 8 KB in size. SQL Server data pages contain all of the data associated with a row of a table, with the possible exception of text and image data. In the case of text and image data the SQL Server data page that contains the row associated with the text or image column will contain, by default, a pointer to a binary tree (or B-tree) structure of one or more 8-KB pages that contain the text or image data. A new feature in SQL Server 2000 is the ability to store small text and image values in-row, which means that small text or image columns will be stored on the data page. This feature can reduce I/O because the additional I/O required to fetch corresponding image or text data can be avoided. For information about how to set a table to store text or images in row, see SQL Server Books Online.

Clustered Indexes

Clustered indexes are very useful for retrieving ranges of data values from a table. Nonclustered indexes are ideally suited for targeting specific rows for retrieval, whereas clustered indexes are ideally suited for retrieving a range of rows. However, adhering to this simple logic for determining which type of index to create is not always successful. This is because only one clustered index is allowed for each table. There is a simple physical reason for this. While the upper parts (nonleaf levels) of the clustered index B-tree structure are organized just like their nonclustered counterparts, the bottom level of a clustered index is made of the actual 8-KB data pages from the table. An exception to this is when a clustered index is created over the top of a view. Because indexed views will be explained below, we will discuss clustered indexes being created on actual tables. When a clustered index is created on a table, the data associated with that table is read, sorted, and physically stored back to the database in the same order as the index search key. Because data for the table can only be persisted to storage in one order without causing duplication, the restriction of one clustered index applies.

The following diagram depicts the storage for a clustered index.

Clustered index

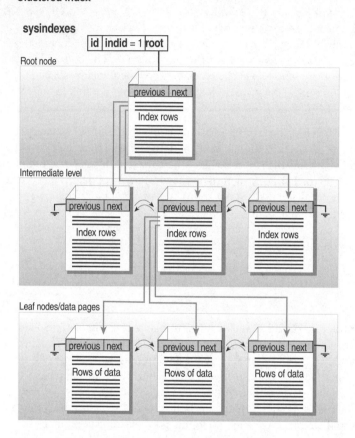

Clustered Indexes and Performance

There are some inherent characteristics of clustered indexes that affect performance.

Retrieval of SQL Server data based on key search with a clustered index requires no pointer jump (involving a likely nonsequential change of location on the hard disk) in order to retrieve the associated data page. This is because the leaf level of the clustered index is, in fact, the associated data page.

As mentioned previously, the leaf level (and consequentially the data for the table or indexed view) is physically sorted and stored in the same order as the search key. Because the leaf level of the clustered index contains the actual 8-KB data pages of the table, the row data of the entire table is physically arranged on the disk drive in the order determined by the clustered index. This provides a potential I/O performance advantage when fetching a significant number of rows from this table (at least greater than 64 KB) based on the value of the clustered index, because sequential disk I/O is being used (unless page splitting is occurring on this table, which will be discussed elsewhere in the section titled "FILLFACTOR and PAD_INDEX"). That is why it is important to pick the clustered index on a table based on a column that will be used to perform range scans to retrieve a large number of rows.

The fact that the rows for table associate with a clustered index have to be sorted and stored in the same order as the index search key has the following implications:

- When you create a clustered index, the table is copied, the data in the table is sorted, and then the original table is deleted. Therefore, enough empty space must exist in the database to hold a copy of the data.

- By default, the data in the table is sorted when the index is created. However, if the data is already sorted in the correct order, the sort operation is automatically skipped. This can have a dramatic effect in speeding up the index creation process.

- Whenever possible, you should load your data into the table in the same order as the search key you intend to use to build the clustered index. On large tables, like those that often characterize data warehouses, this approach will dramatically speed up your index creation, allowing you to reduce the amount of time needed to process initial data load(s). This same approach can be taken when dropping and rebuilding a clustered index, as long as the rows of the table remain in sorted order during the time that the clustered index is not in place. If any rows are not correctly sorted, the operation cancels, an appropriate error message will be given, and the index will not be created.

- Also, building clustered indexes on sorted data requires much less I/O. This is because the data does not have to be copied, sorted, stored back to the database, then the old table data deleted. Instead, the data is left in the extents where it was originally allocated. Index extents are simply added to the database to store top and intermediate nodes.

    Note   The preferred way to build indexes on large tables is to start with the clustered index and then build the nonclustered indexes. In this way, no nonclustered indexes will need to be rebuilt due to the data moving. When dropping all indexes, drop the nonclustered indexes first and the clustered index last. That way, no indexes need to be rebuilt.

Nonclustered Indexes

Nonclustered indexes are most useful for fetching few rows with good selectivity from large SQL Server tables based on a specific key value. As mentioned previously, nonclustered indexes are binary trees formed out of 8-KB index pages. The bottom, or leaf level, of the binary tree of index pages contains all the data from the columns that comprised that index. When a nonclustered index is used to retrieve information from a table based on a match with the key value, the index B-tree is traversed until a key match is found at the leaf level of the index. A pointer jump is made if columns from the table are needed that did not form part of the index. This pointer jump will likely require a nonsequential I/O operation on the disk. It might even require the data to be read from another disk, especially if the table and its accompanying index B-trees are large in size. If multiple pointers lead to the same 8-KB data page, less of an I/O performance penalty will be paid because it is only necessary to read the page into data cache once. For each row returned for an SQL query that involves searching with a nonclustered index, at least one pointer jump is required.

Note The overhead associated with each pointer jump is the reason that nonclustered indexes are better suited for processing queries that return only one or a few rows from a table. Queries that require a range of rows are better served with a clustered index.

The following diagram shows the storage for a nonclustered index. Notice the added leaf level that points to the corresponding data pages. That is where the added pointer jump takes place when using a nonclustered index to access table data as opposed to using a clustered index. For more information on nonclustered indexes, see SQL Server Books Online.

Nonclustered index

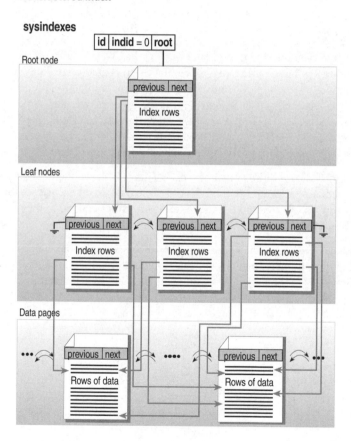

Unique Indexes

Both clustered and nonclustered indexes can be used to enforce uniqueness within a table by specifying the UNIQUE keyword when creating an index on an existing table. Using a UNIQUE constraint is another way to ensure uniqueness within a table. UNIQUE constraints, like unique indexes, enforce the uniqueness of the values in a set of columns. In fact, the assignment of a UNIQUE constraint automatically creates an underlying unique index to facilitate the enforcement of the constraint. Because the uniqueness can be defined and documented as part of the CREATE TABLE statement, a UNIQUE constraint is often preferred over the creation of a separate unique index.

Indexes on Computed Columns

SQL Server 2000 introduced the capability to create indexes on computed columns. This is a handy feature for situations where queries are commonly submitted and computed columns are routinely provided, but the administrator would prefer not to persist the data into an actual column of a table simply to allow the creation of an index. In this case, computed columns can be referenced to create an index as long as the computed column satisfies all conditions required for indexing. Among other restrictions, the computed column expression must be deterministic, precise, and must not evaluate to **text**, **ntext**, or **image** data types.

Deterministic

A nondeterministic user-defined function cannot be invoked by either a view or computed column if you want to create an index on the view or computed column. All functions are deterministic or nondeterministic:

- Deterministic functions always return the same result any time they are called with a specific set of input values.

- Nondeterministic functions may return different results each time they are called with a specific set of input values.

For example, the DATEADD built-in function is deterministic because it always returns a predictable result for a given set of argument values passed in via its three input parameters. GETDATE is not deterministic. While it is always invoked with the same argument value, the value it returns changes each time executed.

Precise

A computed column expression is precise if:

- It is not an expression of the **float** data type.

- It does not use in its definition a float data type. For example, in the following statement, column **y** is **int** and deterministic, but not precise.

```
CREATE TABLE t2 (a int, b int, c int, x float,
    y AS CASE x
            WHEN 0 THEN a
            WHEN 1 THEN b
            ELSE c
END)
```

The **IsPrecise** property of the COLUMNPROPERTY function reports whether a **computed_column_expression** is precise.

> **Note** Any **float** expression is considered nonprecise and cannot be a key of an index; a **float** expression can be used in an indexed view but not as a key. This is true also for computed columns. Any function, expression, user-defined function, or view definition is considered nondeterministic if it contains any **float** expressions, including logical ones (comparisons).

Creation of an index on a computed column or view may cause the failure of an INSERT or UPDATE operation that previously operated correctly. Such a failure may take place when the computed column results in an arithmetic error. For example, although computed column c in the following table will result in an arithmetic error, the INSERT statement will work:

```
CREATE TABLE t1 (a int, b int, c AS a/b)
GO
INSERT INTO t1 VALUES ('1', '0')
GO
```

If, instead, after creating the table, you create an index on computed column **c**, the same INSERT statement now will fail.

```
CREATE TABLE t1 (a int, b int, c AS a/b)
GO
CREATE UNIQUE CLUSTERED INDEX Idx1 ON t1.c
GO
INSERT INTO t1 VALUES ('1', '0')
GO
```

Indexed Views

Indexed views are views whose results are persisted in the database and indexed for fast access. As with any other views, indexed views depend on base tables for their data. Such dependency means that if you change a base table contributing to an indexed view, the indexed view might become invalid. For example, renaming a column that contributes to a view invalidates the view. To prevent such problems, SQL Server supports creating views with schema binding. Schema binding prohibits any table or column modification that would invalidate the view. Any indexed view you create with the View Designer automatically gets schema binding, because SQL Server requires that indexed views have schema binding. Schema binding does not mean you cannot modify the view; it means you cannot modify the underlying tables or views in ways that would change the view's result set. Also, indexed views, like indexes on computed columns, must be deterministic, precise, and must not contain **text**, **ntext**, or **image** columns.

Indexed views work best when the underlying data is infrequently updated. The maintenance of an indexed view can be higher than the cost of maintaining a table index. If the underlying data is updated frequently, then the cost of maintaining the indexed view data may outweigh the performance benefits of using the indexed view.

Indexed views improve the performance of these types of queries:

- Joins and aggregations that process many rows.

- Join and aggregation operations that are frequently performed by many queries.

  For example, in an OLTP database that is recording inventories, many queries would be expected to join the **Parts**, **PartSupplier**, and **Suppliers** tables. Although each query that performs this join may not process many rows, the overall join processing of hundreds of thousands of such queries can be significant. Because these relationships are not likely to be updated frequently, the overall performance of the entire system could be improved by defining an indexed view that stores the joined results.

- Decision support workloads.

- Analysis systems are characterized by storing summarized, aggregated data that is infrequently updated. Further aggregating the data and joining many rows characterizes many decision support queries.

Indexed views usually do not improve the performance of these types of queries:

- OLTP systems with many writes.

- Databases with many updates.

- Queries that do not involve aggregations or joins.

- Aggregations of data with a high degree of cardinality for the key. A high degree of cardinality means the key contains many different values. A unique key has the highest possible degree of cardinality because every key has a different value. Indexed views improve performance by reducing the number of rows a query has to access. If the view result set has almost as many rows as the base table, then there is little performance benefit from using the view. For example, consider this query on a table that has 1,000 rows:

```
SELECT PriKey, SUM(SalesCol)
FROM ExampleTable
GROUP BY PriKey
```

  If the cardinality of the table key is 100, an indexed view built using the result of this query would have only 100 rows. Queries using the view would, on average, need one tenth of the reads needed against the base table. If the key is a unique key, the cardinality of the key is 1000 and the view result set returns 1000 rows. A query has no performance gain from using this indexed view instead of directly reading the base table.

- Expanding joins, which are views whose result sets are larger than the original data in the base tables.

Design your indexed views to satisfy multiple operations. Because the optimizer can use an indexed view even when the view itself is not specified in the FROM clause, a well-designed indexed view can speed the processing of many queries. For example, consider creating an index on this view:

```
CREATE VIEW ExampleView (PriKey, SumColx, CountColx)
AS
SELECT PriKey, SUM(Colx), COUNT_BIG(Colx)
FROM MyTable
GROUP BY PriKey
```

Not only does this view satisfy queries that directly reference the view columns, it can also be used to satisfy queries that query the underlying base table and contain expressions such as SUM(Colx), COUNT_BIG(Colx), COUNT(Colx), and AVG(Colx). All such queries will be faster because they only have to retrieve the small number of rows in the view rather than reading the full number of rows from the base tables.

The first index created on a view must be a unique clustered index. After the unique clustered index has been created, you can create additional nonclustered indexes. The naming conventions for indexes on views are the same as for indexes on tables. The only difference is that the table name is replaced with a view name.

All indexes on a view are dropped if the view is dropped. All nonclustered indexes on the view are dropped if the clustered index is dropped. Nonclustered indexes can be dropped individually. Dropping the clustered index on the view removes the stored result set, and the optimizer returns to processing the view like a standard view.

Although only the columns that make up the clustered index key are specified in the CREATE UNIQUE CLUSTERED INDEX statement, the complete result set of the view is stored in the database. As in a clustered index on a base table, the B-tree structure of the clustered index contains only the key columns, but the data rows contain all of the columns in the view result set.

Note   Indexed views can be created in any edition of SQL Server 2000. In SQL Server 2000 Enterprise Edition, the indexed view will be automatically considered by the query optimizer. To use an indexed view in all other editions, the NOEXPAND hint must be used.

Covering Indexes

A covering index is a nonclustered index that is built upon all of the columns required to satisfy an SQL query, both in the selection criteria and the WHERE predicate. Covering indexes can save a huge amount of I/O, and hence bring a lot of performance to a query. But it is necessary to balance the costs of creating a new index (with its associated B-tree index structure maintenance) against of the I/O performance gain the covering index will bring. If a covering index will greatly benefit a query or set of queries that will be run very often on SQL Server, the creation of that covering index may be worth it.

The following example demonstrates use of a covering index intersection:

```
Create index indexname1 on table1(col2,col1,col3)
Select col3 from table1 where col2 = 'value'
```

When the above query is performed, the values needed from the underlying table could be retrieved quickly by just reading the smaller index pages and the query would be resolve quite efficiently. In general, if the covering index is small, in terms of the number of bytes from all the columns in the index compared to the number of bytes in a single row of that table, and it is certain that the query taking advantage of the covered index will be executed frequently, it may make sense to use a covering index.

Index Selection

The choice of indexes significantly affects the amount of disk I/O generated and, subsequently, performance. Nonclustered indexes are good for retrieval of a small number of rows and clustered indexes are good for range-scans. The following guidelines can be helpful in choosing what type of index to use:

- Try to keep indexes as compact (fewest number of columns and bytes) as possible. This is especially true for clustered indexes because nonclustered indexes will use the clustered index as its method for locating row data.

- In the case of nonclustered indexes, selectivity is important. If a nonclustered index is created on a large table with only a few unique values, use of that nonclustered index will not save much I/O during data retrieval. In fact, using the index will likely cause much more I/O than simply performing a sequential table scan. Good candidates for a nonclustered index include invoice numbers, unique customer numbers, social security numbers, and telephone numbers.

- Clustered indexes perform better than nonclustered indexes for queries that involve range scans or when a column is frequently used to join with other tables. The reason is because the clustered index physically orders the table data, allowing for sequential 64-KB I/O on the key values. Some possible candidates for a clustered index include states, company branches, date of sale, zip codes, and customer district.

  Only one clustered index can be created for a table; if a table contains a column from which typical queries frequently fetch large sequential ranges and columns of unique values, use the clustered index on the first column and nonclustered indexes on the columns of unique values. The key question to ask when trying to choose the best column on each table to create the clustered index on is, "Will there be a lot of queries that need to fetch a large number of rows based on the order of this column?" The answer is very specific to each user environment. One company may do a lot of queries based on ranges of dates, whereas another company may do a lot of queries based on ranges of bank branches.

Index Creation and Parallel Operations

The query plans built for the creation of indexes allow parallel, multi-threaded index create operations on computers with multiple microprocessors in the SQL Server 2000 Enterprise and Developer editions.

SQL Server uses the same algorithms to determine the degree of parallelism (the total number of separate threads to run) for create index operations as it does for other Transact-SQL statements. The only difference is that the CREATE INDEX, CREATE TABLE, or ALTER TABLE statements that create indexes do not support the MAXDOP query hint. The maximum degree of parallelism for an index creation is subject to the **max degree of parallelism** server configuration option, but you cannot set a different MAXDOP value for individual index creation operations.

When SQL Server builds a create index query plan, the number of parallel operations is set to the lowest value of:

- The number of microprocessors, or CPUs in the computer.

- The number specified in the **max degree of parallelism** server configuration option.

- The number of CPUs not already over a threshold of work performed for SQL Server threads.

For example, on a computer with eight CPUs, but where the **max degree of parallelism** option is set to 6, no more than six parallel threads are generated for an index creation. If five of the CPUs in the computer exceed the threshold of SQL Server work when an index creation execution plan is built, the execution plan specifies only three parallel threads.

The main phases of parallel index creation include:

- A coordinating thread quickly and randomly scans the table to estimate the distribution of the index keys. The coordinating thread establishes the key boundaries that will create a number of key ranges equal to the degree of parallel operations, where each key range is estimated to cover similar numbers of rows. For example, if there are four million rows in the table, and the **max degree of parallelism** option is set to 4, the coordinating thread will determine the key values that delimit four sets of rows with one million rows in each set.

- The coordinating thread dispatches a number of threads equal to the degree of parallel operations, and waits for these threads to complete their work. Each thread scans the base table using a filter that retrieves only rows with key values within the range assigned to the thread. Each thread builds an index structure for the rows in its key range.

After all the parallel threads have completed, the coordinating thread connects the index subunits into a single index. Individual CREATE TABLE or ALTER TABLE statements can have multiple constraints that require the creation of an index. These multiple index creation operations are performed in series, although each individual index creation operation may be performed as a parallel operation on a computer with multiple CPUs.

Index Maintenance

When you create an index in the database, the index information used by queries is stored in index pages. The sequential index pages are chained together by pointers from one page to the next. When changes are made to the data that affect the index, the information in the index can become scattered in the database. Rebuilding an index reorganizes the storage of the index data (and table data in the case of a clustered index) to remove fragmentation. This can improve disk performance by reducing the number of page reads required to obtain the requested data.

Fragmentation occurs when large amounts of insert activity or updates, which modify the search key value of the clustered index, are performed. For this reason, it is important to try to maintain open space on index and data pages to prevent pages from splitting. Page splitting occurs when an index page or data page can no longer hold any new rows and a row needs to be inserted into the page because of the logical ordering of data defined in that page. When this occurs, SQL Server needs to divide up the data on the full page and move approximately half of the data to a new page so that both pages will have some open space. Because this consumes system resources and time, doing it frequently is not recommended.

When indexes are initially built, SQL Server attempts to place the index B-tree structures on pages that are physically contiguous; this allows for optimal I/O performance when scanning the index pages using sequential I/O. When page splitting occurs and new pages need to be inserted into the logical B-tree structure of the index, SQL Server must allocate new 8-KB index pages. If this occurs somewhere else on the hard drive, it breaks up the physically sequential nature of the index pages. This can cause I/O operations to switch from being performed sequentially to nonsequentially. It can also dramatically reduce performance. Excessive amounts of page splitting should be resolved by rebuilding your index or indexes to restore the physically sequential order of the index pages. This same behavior can be encountered on the leaf level of the clustered index, thereby affecting the data pages of the table.

In System Monitor, pay particular attention to "SQL Server: Access Methods – **Page Splits/sec**." Nonzero values for this counter indicate that page splitting is occurring and that further analysis should be done with DBCC SHOWCONTIG.

The **DBCC SHOWCONTIG** command can also be used to reveal whether excessive page splitting has occurred on a table. Scan Density is the key indicator that **DBCC SHOWCONTIG** provides. It is good for this value to be as close to 100 percent as possible. If this value is significantly below 100 percent, consider running maintenance on the problem indexes.

DBCC INDEXDEFRAG

One index maintenance option is to use a new statement (DBCC INDEXDEFRAG), which was introduced in SQL Server 2000. DBCC INDEXDEFRAG can defragment clustered and nonclustered indexes on tables and views. DBCC INDEXDEFRAG defragments the leaf level of an index so the physical order of the pages matches the left-to-right logical order of the leaf nodes, thus improving index-scanning performance.

DBCC INDEXDEFRAG also compacts the pages of an index, taking into account the FILLFACTOR specified when the index was created. Any empty pages created as a result of this compaction will be removed.

If an index spans more than one file, DBCC INDEXDEFRAG defragments one file at a time. Pages do not migrate between files. Every five minutes, DBCC INDEXDEFRAG will report to the user an estimated percentage completed. DBCC INDEXDEFRAG can be terminated at any point in the process, and any completed work is retained.

Unlike DBCC DBREINDEX (or the index building operation in general), DBCC INDEXDEFRAG is an online operation. It does not hold locks long term and thus will not block running queries or updates. A relatively unfragmented index can be defragmented faster than a new index can be built because the time to defragment is related to the amount of fragmentation. A very fragmented index might take considerably longer to defragment than to rebuild. In addition, the defragmentation is always fully logged, regardless of the database recovery model setting (see ALTER DATABASE). The defragmentation of a very fragmented index can generate more log than even a fully logged index creation. The defragmentation, however, is performed as a series of short transactions and thus does not require a large log if log backups are taken frequently or if the recovery model setting is SIMPLE.

Also, DBCC INDEXDEFRAG will not help if two indexes are interleaved on the disk because INDEXDEFRAG shuffles the pages in place. To improve the clustering of pages, rebuild the index. DBCC INDEXDEFRAG cannot correct page splits for the same reason. It essentially reorders index pages already allocated into sequential order reflective of the search key. Index pages may get out of order for a variety of reasons, such as unordered data loads, excessive insert, update, delete activity, etc.

SQL Server Books Online includes a piece of sample code that you can use to automate a variety of index maintenance tasks with a few modifications. The example shows a simple way to defragment all indexes in a database that have fragmented above a declared threshold. For more information, see the topic "DBCC SHOWCONTIG" in SQL Server Books Online.

DBCC DBREINDEX

DBCC DBREINDEX can rebuild just a single specified index for a table or all indexes for a table depending on the syntax used. Similar in the approach taken to dropping and re-creating individual indexes, the DBCC DBREINDEX statement has the advantage of being able to rebuild all of the indexes for a table in one statement. This is easier than coding individual DROP INDEX and CREATE INDEX statements and a table's index or indexes can be rebuilt without knowledge of the table structure or any assigned constraints. Also, the DBCC REINDEX statement is inherently atomic. To achieve the equivalent atomicity when coding separate DROP INDEX and CREATE INDEX statements, you would have to wrap the multiple separate commands within a transaction.

DBCC DBREINDEX automatically takes advantage of more optimizations than individual DROP INDEX and CREATE INDEX statements do, especially if multiple nonclustered indexes reference a table that has a clustered index. DBCC DBREINDEX is also useful to rebuild indexes enforcing PRIMARY KEY or UNIQUE constraints without having to delete and re-create the constraints (because an index created to enforce a PRIMARY KEY or UNIQUE constraint cannot be deleted without deleting the constraint first). For example, you may want to rebuild an index on a PRIMARY KEY constraint to reestablish a given fill factor for the index.

DROP_EXISTING

Another way to rebuild or defragment an index is to drop and recreate it. Rebuilding a clustered index by deleting the old index and then re-creating the same index again is expensive because all the secondary indexes depend upon the clustering key that points to the data rows. If you simply delete the clustered index and re-create it, you may inadvertently cause all referencing nonclustered indexes to be deleted and re-created twice. The first drop/recreate occurs when you drop the clustered index. A second drop/recreate will occur when you go to re-create the clustered index.

To avoid this expense, the DROP_EXISTING clause of CREATE_INDEX allows this re-create to be performed in one step. Re creating the index in a single step tells SQL Server that you are reorganizing an existing index and avoids the unnecessary work of deleting and re-creating the associated nonclustered indexes. This method also offers the significant advantage of using the presorted data from the existing index, thus avoiding the need to perform a sort of the data. This can significantly reduce the time and cost of re-creating the clustered index.

DROP INDEX / CREATE INDEX

The final way to perform index maintenance is simply to drop the index and then re-create it. This option is still widely practiced and might be preferable to people who are familiar with it and who have the processing window to accommodate full re-creates of all indexes on a table. The drawback to using this approach is that you must manually control events so they happen in proper sequence. When manually dropping and re-creating indexes, be sure to drop all nonclustered indexes before dropping and recreating the clustered index. Otherwise, all nonclustered indexes will automatically be recreated when you go to create the clustered index.

One advantage to manually creating nonclustered indexes is that individual nonclustered indexes can be recreated in parallel. However, your partitioning strategy may affect the resulting physical layout of the indexes. If two nonclustered indexes are rebuilt at the same time on the same file (filegroup), the pages from both indexes might be interwoven together on disk. This may cause your data to be stored in a nonsequential order. If you have multiple files (filegroups) located on different disks, you can specify separate files (filegroup) to hold the index upon creation, thus maintaining sequential contiguousness of the index pages.

The same issues mentioned above about building indexes on pre-sorted data apply here. Clustered indexes built on sorted data do not have to perform an additional sort step, which can significantly reduce the time and processing resources needed to build the index.

FILLFACTOR and PAD_INDEX

The FILLFACTOR option provides a way to specify the percentage of open space to leave on index and data pages. The PAD_INDEX option for CREATE INDEX applies what has been specified for FILLFACTOR on the nonleaf level index pages. Without the PAD_INDEX option, FILLFACTOR affects mainly the leaf level index pages of the clustered index. It is a good idea to use the PAD_INDEX option with FILLFACTOR.

PAD_INDEX and FILLFACTOR are used to control page splitting. The optimal value to specify for FILLFACTOR depends on how much new data will be inserted within a given time frame into an 8-KB index and data page. It is important to keep in mind that SQL Server index pages typically contain many more rows than data pages because index pages contain only the data for columns associated with that index, whereas data pages hold the data for the entire row.

Also, bear in mind how often there will be a maintenance window that will permit the rebuilding of indexes to correct page splits, which are bound to occur. Try to rebuild the indexes only when the majority of the index and data pages have become filled with data. If a clustered index is properly selected for a table, the need to rebuild indexes will be infrequent. If the clustered index distributes data evenly so new row inserts into the table happen across all of the data pages associated with the table, the data pages will fill evenly. Overall, this provides more time before page splitting starts to occur and rebuilding the clustered index becomes necessary.

Determining the proper values to use for PAD_INDEX and FILLFACTOR requires you to make a judgment call. Your decision should be based on the performance tradeoffs between leaving a lot of open space on pages, on the one hand, and the amount of page splitting that might occur, on the other. If a small percentage for FILLFACTOR is specified, it will leave large open spaces on the index and data pages, causing SQL Server to read large numbers of partially filled pages in order to answer queries. For large read operations, SQL Server will obviously perform faster if more data is compressed onto the index and data pages. Specifying too high a FILLFACTOR may leave too little open space on pages and allow pages to overflow too quickly, causing page splitting.

Before arriving at a FILLFACTOR or PAD_INDEX value, remember that reads tend to far outnumber writes in many data warehousing environments. Periodic data loads, however, may invalidate the above statement. Many data warehouse administrators attempt to partition and structure tables/indexes to accommodate the periodic data loads they anticipate.

As a general rule of thumb, if writes are anticipated to be a substantial fraction of reads, the best approach is to specify as high a FILLFACTOR as feasible, while still leaving enough free space in each 8-KB page to avoid frequent page splitting, at least until SQL Server can reach the next available window of time needed to re-create indexes. This strategy balances I/O performance (keeping the pages as full as possible) and avoids page splitting (not letting pages overflow). If there will be no write activity into the SQL Server database, FILLFACTOR should be set at 100 percent so that all index and data pages are filled completely for maximum I/O performance.

SQL Server Tools for Analysis and Tuning

This section provides sample code to load a table with data, which is then used to illustrate the use of SQL Profiler and SQL Query Analyzer for analyzing and tuning performance.

Sample Data and Workload

To illustrate using the SQL Server performance tools, use the following example. First, the following table is constructed:

```
create table testtable
   (nkey1 int identity,
   col2 char(300) default 'abc',
   ckey1 char(1))
```

Next, the table is loaded with 20,000 rows of test data. The data being loaded into column nkey1 lends itself to a nonclustered index. The data in column ckey1 lends itself to a clustered index and the data in col2 is merely filler to increase the size of each row by 300 bytes.

```
declare @counter int
set @counter = 1
while (@counter <= 4000)
begin
   insert testtable (ckey1) values ('a')
   insert testtable (ckey1) values ('b')
   insert testtable (ckey1) values ('c')
   insert testtable (ckey1) values ('d')
   insert testtable (ckey1) values ('e')
   set @counter = @counter + 1
end
```

The following queries make up the database server workload:

```
select ckey1 from testtable where ckey1 = 'a'
select nkey1 from testtable where nkey1 = 5000
select ckey1,col2 from testtable where ckey1 = 'a'
select nkey1,col2 from testtable where nkey1 = 5000
```

SQL Profiler

A common approach to performance tuning is often called *mark and measure*. To verify that changes made to improve performance actually do improve performance, you first need to establish a baseline or *mark* of the existing bad performance situation. *Measure* refers to establishing quantifiable ways to demonstrate that performance is improving.

SQL Profiler is a tool for marking and measuring. Not only can it capture activity that is taking place within your server for performance analysis; it can also playback that activity again at a later time. The playback capabilities in SQL Server provide a useful regression-testing tool. Using playback, you can conveniently determine whether actions being taken to improve performance are having the desired effect.

The playback capabilities can also simulate load or stress testing. Multiple profiler client sessions can be set up to play back simultaneously. This capability allows the administrator to easily capture activity from five concurrent users, for example, and then start ten simultaneous playbacks to emulate what the system performance might look like if there were 50 concurrent users. You can also take traces of database activity and play that activity back against a database modification under development or against a new hardware configuration being tested.

The thing to remember is that SQL Profiler allows you to record activity that is occurring on your SQL Server databases. SQL Profiler can be configured to watch and record one or many users executing queries against SQL Server. In addition to the SQL statements, a wide and varied amount of performance information is available for capture using the tool. Some of the performance information available for recording using SQL Profiler includes items such as I/O statistics, CPU statistics, locking requests, Transact-SQL and RPC statistics, index and table scans, warnings and errors raised, database object create/drop, connection connect/disconnects, stored procedure operations, cursor operation, and more.

Capturing Profiler Information to Use with the Index Tuning Wizard

When used together, SQL Profiler and the Index Tuning Wizard provide a very powerful tool combination to help database administrators ensure that proper indexes are placed on tables and views. SQL Profiler records the resource consumption for queries into one of three places. Output can be directed to the .trc file, to a SQL Server table, or to the monitor. The Index Tuning Wizard can then read the captured data from either the .trc file or the SQL Server table. The Index Tuning Wizard analyzes information from the captured workload and information about the table structures, and then presents recommendations about what indexes should be created to improve performance. The Index Tuning

Wizard provides a choice of automatically creating the proper indexes for the database, scheduling the index creation for a later time, or generating a Transact-SQL script that can be reviewed and executed manually.

The following steps are required for analyzing a query load:

Set up SQL Profiler

9. Start SQL Profiler from SQL Server Enterprise Manager by selecting **SQL Profiler** on the **Tools** menu.

10. Press CTRL+N to create a new SQL Profiler trace. In the **Connect to SQL Server** dialog box, select the server you want to connect to.

11. Select the **SQLProfilerTuning** template from the dropdown list box.

12. Select either the **Save to file** or **Save to table** checkbox. The **Save to table** option opens the **Connection** dialog box, where you can save trace information to a server other than the server profiling the query. Both checkboxes can be selected if you would like to save traced activity to both. Point to a valid directory and file name if you want to save as a .trc file. Point to an existing trace table if you have already run the trace and are running it again; you can also provide a new table name if this is the first time you have captured trace activity to the table. Click OK.

13. Click Run.

Run the workload several (3-4) times

1. Start SQL Query Analyzer, either from SQL Server Enterprise Manager or from the **Start** menu.

2. Connect to SQL Server and set the current database to the database where you created the test table.

3. Enter the following queries into the query window of SQL Query Analyzer:

```
select ckey1 from testtable where ckey1 = 'a'
select nkey1 from testtable where nkey1 = 5000
select ckey1,col2 from testtable where ckey1 = 'a'
select nkey1,col2 from testtable where nkey1 = 5000
```

4. Press CTRL+E to execute the queries. Do this three or four times to generate a sample workload.

Stop SQL Profiler

- In the SQL Profiler window, click the red square to stop the Profiler trace.

Load the trace file or table into Index Tuning Wizard

1. In SQL Profiler, start the Index Tuning Wizard by selecting **Index Tuning Wizard** on the **Tools** menu. Click **Next**.

2. Select the database to be analyzed. Click **Next**.

3. Choose options of whether or not to keep existing indexes, or add indexed views.

4. Choose one of the tuning modes (**Fast**, **Medium**, or **Thorough**). Index Tuning Wizard requires less time to perform the analysis for Fast tuning mode but does a less thorough analysis—Thorough mode produces the most thorough analysis but takes the most time.

5. To locate the trace file/table that was created with SQL Profiler, select **My workload file** or the **SQL Server Trace Table**. Click **Next**.

6. In the **Select Tables to Tune** dialog box, select the tables you want to analyze and then click **Next**.

7. **Index Tuning Wizard** will analyze the traced workload and table structures to determine the proper indexes to create in the **Index Recommendations** dialog box. Click **Next**.

8. The wizard provides the choice of creating the indexes immediately, scheduling the index creation (an automated task for later execution), or creating a Transact-SQL script containing the commands to create the indexes. Select the preferred option and then click **Next**.

9. Click **Finish**.

Transact-SQL Generated by Index Tuning Wizard for the Sample Database and Workload

```
/* Created by: Index Tuning Wizard    */
/* Date: 9/6/2000         */
/* Time: 4:44:34 PM         */
/* Server Name: JHMILLER-AS2         */
/* Database Name: TraceDB        */
/* Workload File Name: C:\Documents and Settings\jhmiller\My Documents\trace.trc */
USE [TraceDB]
go
SET QUOTED_IDENTIFIER ON
SET ARITHABORT ON
SET CONCAT_NULL_YIELDS_NULL ON
SET ANSI_NULLS ON
SET ANSI_PADDING ON
SET ANSI_WARNINGS ON
SET NUMERIC_ROUNDABORT OFF
go
DECLARE @bErrors as bit

BEGIN TRANSACTION
SET @bErrors = 0

CREATE CLUSTERED INDEX [testtable1] ON [dbo].[testtable] ([ckey1] ASC )
IF( @@error <> 0 ) SET @bErrors = 1
```

```
CREATE NONCLUSTERED INDEX [testtable2] ON [dbo].[testtable] ([nkey1] ASC )
IF( @@error <> 0 ) SET @bErrors = 1

IF( @bErrors = 0 )
  COMMIT TRANSACTION
ELSE
  ROLLBACK TRANSACTION
```

The indexes recommended by Index Tuning Wizard for the sample table and data are what we would expect – a clustered index on ckey1 and a nonclustered index on nkey1. There are only five unique values for ckey1 and 4000 rows of each value. Given that one of the sample queries (select ckey1, col2 from testtable where ckey1 = 'a') requires retrieval from the table based on one of the values in ckey1, it makes sense to create a clustered index on the ckey1 column. The second query (select nkey1, col2 from testtable where nkey1 = 5000) fetches one row based on the value of the column nkey1. Because nkey1 is unique and there are 20,000 rows, it makes sense to create a nonclustered index on this column.

The combination of SQL Profiler and the Index Tuning Wizard becomes very powerful in real database server environments, where many tables are used and many queries are processed. Use SQL Profiler to record a .trc file or trace table while the database server is experiencing a representative set of queries. Then load the trace into the Index Tuning Wizard to determine the proper indexes to build. Follow the prompts in the Index Tuning Wizard to automatically generate and schedule index creation jobs to run at off-peak times. You may want to run the combination of SQL Profiler and the Index Tuning Wizard regularly (perhaps weekly or monthly) to see if queries being executed on the database server have changed significantly, thus possibly requiring different indexes. Regular use of SQL Profiler and the Index Tuning Wizard together helps database administrators keep SQL Server running in top form as query workloads change and database size increase over time.

Analyzing the Information Recorded in Profiler with SQL Query Analyzer

After the information is recorded into the SQL Server table, SQL Query Analyzer can be used to determine which queries on the system are consuming the most resources. In this way, database administrators can concentrate on improving the queries that require the most help. Storing the trace data to a table enables you to easily select from and filter out subsets of trace data in order to identify the poorest performing queries for tuning purposes. For instance, in the example above, the column **Duration**, which is captured automatically when you use the **SQLProfiler Tuning** template, can be used to identify queries that required the greatest number of milliseconds to execute. To find the top ten percent of the longest running queries you can run a query like the following:

```
SELECT TOP 10 PERCENT *
FROM [TraceDB].[dbo].[Trace]
ORDER BY Duration DESC
```

To find the top five longest running queries you can run a query like the following:

```
SELECT TOP 5 *
FROM [TraceDB].[dbo].[Trace]
ORDER BY Duration DESC
```

To place only the rows you want to use for tuning into a separate table, consider using the following SELECT/INTO statement:

```
SELECT TOP 10 PERCENT *
INTO TuningTable
FROM [TraceDB].[dbo].[Trace]
ORDER BY Duration DESC
```

The **SQLProfiler Tuning** template, mentioned above, is simply a suggested set of preselected columns and filter settings recommended for tuning purposes. You may find that you want to capture more information. It is certainly possible for you to create your own custom tuning templates by simply opening one of the presupplied templates and saving it under a different name. Many events can be captured, including I/O statistics, locking information, and much more.

SQL Query Analyzer

You can use SQL Query Analyzer to tune queries. This tool provides a number of mechanisms such as Statistics I/O and the execution plans you can use to troubleshoot problem queries.

Statistics I/O

SQL Query Analyzer provides an option that you can use to obtain information about the I/O consumption for a query that you execute in SQL Query Analyzer. To set this option, in SQL Query Analyzer, select **Current Connection Properties** on the **Query** menu to display the **Current Connection Properties** dialog box. Select the **Set statistics** I/O checkbox and close the dialog box. Next, execute a query and select the **Message** tab in the results pane to see the I/O statistics.

For example, the following query on the sample data created earlier in the SQL Profiler section returns the following I/O information on the messages tab when the **Set statistics IO** option is selected:

```
select ckey1, col2 from testtable where ckey1 = 'a'
Table 'testtable'. Scan count 1, logical reads 800, physical reads 62, read-ahead reads
760.
```

Using statistics I/O is a great way to monitor the effect of query tuning. For example, create the indexes that Index Tuning Wizard suggested for the sample data and then run the query again.

```
select ckey1, col2 from testtable where ckey1 = 'a'
Table 'testtable'. Scan count 1, logical reads 164, physical reads 4, read-ahead reads
162.
```

Notice that the number of logical and physical reads is significantly lower when an index is available.

Execution Plan

Graphical execution plans can be used to focus attention on problematic SQL queries by displaying detailed information on what the query optimizer is doing.

An estimated execution plan for a query can be displayed in the Results pane of SQL Query Analyzer by executing an SQL query with CTRL+L or by selecting **Display Estimated Execution Plan** on the **Query** menu. Icons indicate the operations that the query optimizer would have performed if it had executed the query. Arrows indicate the direction of data flow for the query. Details about each operation can be displayed by hovering the mouse pointer over the operation icon. The approximate cost of each step of the operation is also noted beneath each operation icon. This label allows you to quickly zero in on which operation is most expensive in the query.

You can also see the actual execution plan for a query by selecting **Show Execution Plan** on the **Query** menu and then executing the query. In contrast to the **Display Estimated Execution Plan** option, **Show Execution plan** executes the query before displaying the actual execution plan used for the query.

A text version of an execution plan can be created by selecting **Current Connection Properties** on the **Query** menu and then checking the **Set showplan_text** option in the dialog box. The execution plan will be displayed as text in the results tab when the query is executed.

Execution plan options can also be set within the query by executing either of the following commands:

```
set showplan_all on
go
set showplan_text on
go
```

SET SHOWPLAN_ALL is intended to be used by applications designed to read its output. Use SET SHOWPLAN_TEXT to return readable output for Microsoft MS-DOS® applications, such as the **osql** utility.

SET SHOWPLAN_TEXT and SET SHOWPLAN_ALL return information as a set of textual rows that form a hierarchical tree representing the steps taken by the SQL Server query processor as it executes each statement. Each statement reflected in the output contains a single row with the text of the statement, followed by several rows with the details of the execution steps.

Examples of Execution Plan Output

Using the example queries defined earlier and "set showplan_text on" executed in SQL Query Analyzer provides these results.

Query 1

```
select ckey1,col2 from testtable where ckey1 = 'a'
```

Text-based execution plan output

```
|--Clustered Index Seek (OBJECT:([TraceDB].[dbo].[testtable].[testtable1]),
SEEK:([testtable].[ckey1]='a') ORDERED FORWARD)
```

Equivalent graphical execution plan output

The following illustration shows the graphical execution plan for query 1.

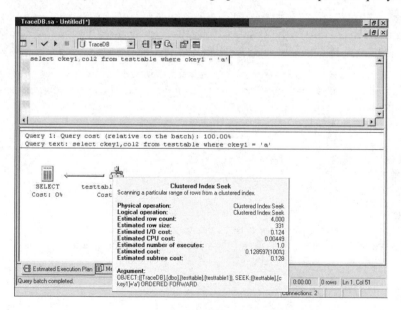

The execution plan takes advantage of the clustered index on column ckey1 to resolve the query, as indicated by **Clustered Index Seek**.

If the clustered index is removed from the table and the same query is executed again, the query reverts to using a table scan. The following graphical execution plan indicates the change in behavior.

Text-based execution plan output

```
|--Table Scan(OBJECT:([TraceDB].[dbo].[testtable]), WHERE:([testtable].[ckey1]=[@1]))
```

Equivalent graphical execution plan output

The following illustration shows the graphical execution plan for query 1.

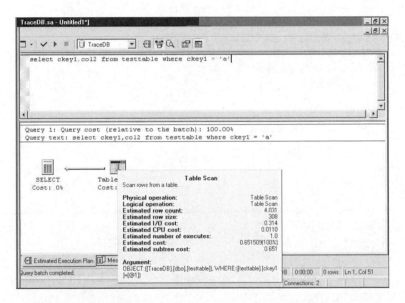

This execution plan uses a table scan to resolve query 1. Table scans are the most efficient way to retrieve information from small tables. But on larger tables, table scans indicated by an execution plan are a warning that the table may need better indexes or that the existing indexes need to have their statistics updated. Statistics can be updated on a table or an index using the UPDATE STATISTICS command. SQL Server automatically updates indexes if the heuristic pages get too far out of synch with the underlying index values. An example would be if you deleted all the rows containing a ckey1 value = "b" from your testtable and then ran queries without first updating the statistics. It is a good idea to allow SQL Server to automatically maintain index statistics because it helps guarantee that queries will always have good index statistics to work with. SQL Server will not auto update statistics if you set the AUTO_UPDATE_STATISTICS database options to OFF using the ALTER DATABASE statement.

Query 2

```
select nkey1,col2 from testtable where nkey1 = 5000
```

Text-based execution plan output

```
--Bookmark Lookup(BOOKMARK:([Bmk1000]),
OBJECT:([TraceDB].[dbo].[testtable]))
       |--Index Seek(OBJECT:([TraceDB].[dbo].[testtable].[testtable2]),
 SEEK:([testtable].[nkey1]=Convert([@1])) ORDERED FORWARD)
```

Equivalent graphical execution plan output

The following two illustrations show the graphical execution plan for query 2.

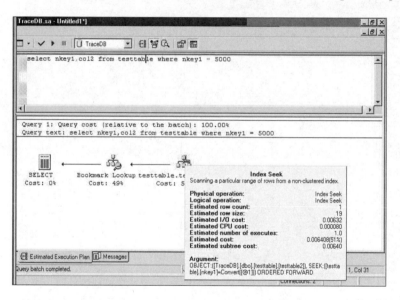

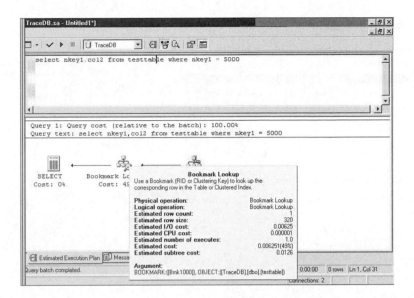

The execution plan for query 2 uses the nonclustered index on the column nkey1. This is indicated by the Index Seek operation on the column nkey1. The Bookmark Lookup operation indicates that SQL Server needed to perform a pointer jump from the index page to the data page of the table to retrieve the requested data. The pointer jump was required because the query asked for the column col2, which was not a column contained within the nonclustered index.

Query 3

```
select nkey1 from testtable where nkey1 = 5000
```

Text-based execution plan output

```
|--Index Seek(OBJECT:([TraceDB].[dbo].[testtable].[testtable2]),
SEEK:([testtable].[nkey1]=Convert([@1])) ORDERED FORWARD)
```

Equivalent graphical execution plan output

The following illustration shows the graphical execution plan for query 3.

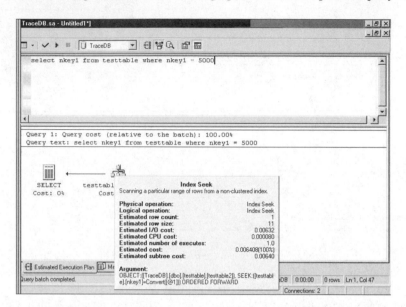

The execution plan for query 3 uses the nonclustered index on nkey1 as a covering index. Note that no Bookmark Lookup operation was needed for this query. This is because all of the information required for the query (both SELECT and WHERE clauses) is provided by the nonclustered index. This means that no pointer jumps to the data pages are required from the nonclustered index pages. I/O is reduced in comparison to the case where a bookmark lookup was required.

System Monitoring

System Monitor provides a wealth of information about what Windows and SQL Server operations are taking place during database server execution.

In System Monitor graph mode, take note of the **Max** and **Min** values. Because heavily polarized data points can distort the average, be careful of overemphasizing the average. Study the graph shape and compare to **Min** and **Max** to get an accurate understanding of the behavior. Use the BACKSPACE key to highlight counters with a white line.

It is possible to use System Monitor to log all available Windows and SQL Server system monitor objects/counters in a log file, while at the same time looking at System Monitor interactively (chart mode). The setting of sampling interval determines how quickly the logfile grows in size. Log files can get very large, very fast (for example, 100 megabytes in one hour with all counters turned on and a sampling interval of 15 seconds). It is hoped that the test server has enough free gigabytes to store these types of files. If conserving space is important, however, try running with a large log interval so System Monitor does not sample the system as often. Try 30 or 60 seconds. This way all of the counters are resampled with reasonable frequency but a smaller log file size is maintained.

System Monitor also consumes a small amount of CPU and disk I/O resources. If a system does not have much disk I/O and/or CPU to spare, consider running System Monitor from another computer to monitor SQL Server over the network. When monitoring over the network, use graph mode only—it tends to be more efficient to log performance monitoring information locally on the SQL Server instead of sending the information across a local area network. If you must log over the network, reduce the logging to only the most critical counters.

It is a good practice to log all counters available during performance test runs into a file for later analysis. That way any counter can be examined further at a later time. Configure System Monitor to log all counters into a log file and at the same time monitor the most interesting counters in one of the other modes, like graph mode. This way, all of the information is recorded but the most interesting counters are presented in an uncluttered System Monitor graph while the performance run is taking place.

Setting up a System Monitor Session to be Logged

1. From the Windows 2000 **Start** menu point to **Programs**, point to **Administrative Tools**, and then click **Performance** to open System Monitor.

2. Double-click **Performance Logs and Alerts**, and then click **Counter Logs**.

3. Any existing logs will be listed in the details pane. A green icon indicates that a log is running; a red icon indicates that a log has been stopped.

4. Right-click a blank area of the details pane, and click **New Log Settings**.

5. In **Name**, type the name of the log, and then click **OK**.

6. On the **General** tab, click **Add**. Select the counters you want to log. This is where you decide which SQL Server counters to monitor during the session.

7. If you want to change the default file, make the changes on the **Log Files** tab.

8. Logged sessions can be set to run automatically for predefined time periods. To do this, you modify the schedule information on the **Schedule** tab.

   Note To save the counter settings for a log file, right-click the file in the details pane and click **Save Settings As**. You can then specify an .htm file in which to save the settings. To reuse the saved settings for a new log, right-click the details pane, and then click **New Log Settings From**.

Starting a Logged Monitoring Session

1. From the Windows 2000 **Start** menu, point to **Programs**, point to **Administrative Tools**, and then select **Performance** to open System Monitor.

2. Double-click **Performance Logs and Alerts**, and then click **Counter Logs**.

3. Right-click the **Counter Log** to be run and select start.

4. Any existing logs will be listed in the details pane. A green icon indicates that a log is running; a red icon indicates that a log has been stopped.

Stopping a Logged Monitoring Session

1. From the Windows 2000 **Start** menu point to **Programs**, point to **Administrative Tools**, and then select **Performance** to open System Monitor.

2. Double-click **Performance Logs and Alerts**, and then click **Counter Logs**.

3. Right-click the **Counter Log** to be run and select stop.

Loading data from a Logged Monitoring Session into System Monitor for analyzing

1. From the Windows 2000 **Start** menu point to **Programs**, point to **Administrative Tools**, and then select **Performance** to open System Monitor.

2. Click **System Monitor**.

3. Right-click the System Monitor details pane and click **Properties**.

4. Click the **Source** tab.

5. Under **Data Source**, click **Log File**, and type the path to the file or click **Browse** to browse for the log file you want.

6. Click **Time Range**. To specify the time range in the log file that you want to view, drag the bar or its handles for the appropriate starting and ending times.

7. Click the **Data** tab and click **Add** to open the **Add Counters** dialog box. The counters you selected during log configuration are shown. You can include all or some of these in your graph.

How to relate System Monitor logged events back to a point in time

- From within the System Monitor session, right-click the System Monitor details pane and click **Properties**. A time range and a slider bar lets you position the begin, current, and end times to be viewed in your graph.

Key Performance Counters to Watch

Several performance counters provide information about the following areas of interest: memory, paging, processors, I/O, and disk activity.

Monitoring Memory

By default, SQL Server changes its memory requirements dynamically, based on available system resources. If SQL Server needs more memory, it queries the operating system to determine whether free physical memory is available and uses the available memory. If SQL Server does not need the memory currently allocated to it, it releases the memory to the operating system. However, the option to dynamically use memory can be overridden using the **min server memory**, **max server memory**, and **set working set size** server configuration options. For more information, see SQL Server Books Online.

To monitor the amount of memory being used by SQL Server, examine the following performance counters:

- **Process: Working Set**
- **SQL Server: Buffer Manager: Buffer Cache Hit Ratio**
- **SQL Server: Buffer Manager: Total Pages**
- **SQL Server: Memory Manager: Total Server Memory (KB)**

The **Working Set** counter shows the amount of memory used by a process. If this number is consistently below the amount of memory SQL Server is configured to use (set by the **min server memory** and **max server memory** server options), SQL Server is configured for more memory than it needs. Otherwise, adjust the size of the working set using the **set working set size** server option.

The **Buffer Cache Hit Ratio** counter is application specific; however, a rate of 90 percent or higher is desirable. Add more memory until the value is consistently greater than 90 percent, indicating that more than 90 percent of all requests for data were satisfied from the data cache.

If the **Total Server Memory (KB)** counter is consistently high compared to the amount of physical memory in the computer, more memory may be required.

Hard Paging

If **Memory: Pages/sec** is greater than zero or **Memory: Page Reads/sec** is greater than five, Windows is using disk to resolve memory references (hard page fault). This costs disk I/O + CPU resources. **Memory: Pages/sec** is a good indicator of the amount of paging that Windows is performing and the adequacy of the database server's current RAM configuration. A subset of the hard paging information in System Monitor is the number of times per second Windows had to read from the paging file to resolve memory references, which is represented by **Memory: Pages Reads/sec**. If **Memory: Pages Reads/sec** > 5, this is bad for performance.

Automatic SQL Server memory tuning will try to adjust SQL Server memory utilization dynamically in order to avoid paging. A small number of pages read per second is normal, but excessive paging requires corrective action.

If SQL Server is automatically tuning memory, adding more RAM or removing other applications from the database server are two options to help bring **Memory: Pages/sec** to a reasonable level.

If SQL Server memory is manually configured on the database server, it may be necessary to reduce memory given to SQL Server, remove other applications from the database server, or add more RAM to the database server.

Keeping **Memory: Pages/sec** at or close to zero helps database server performance. It means Windows and all its applications (this includes SQL Server) are not going to the paging file to satisfy any data in memory requests, so the amount of RAM on the server is sufficient. If **Pages/sec** is greater than zero by a small amount, this is acceptable, but remember that a relatively high performance penalty (disk I/O) is paid every time data is retrieved from the paging file rather than RAM.

It is useful to compare **Memory: Pages Input/sec** to **Logical Disk: Disk Reads/sec** across all drives associated with the Windows paging file, and **Memory: Page Output/sec** to **Logical Disk: Disk Writes/sec** across all drives associated with the Windows paging file, because they provide a measure of how much disk I/O is strictly related to paging rather than other applications (that is, SQL Server). Another easy way to isolate paging file I/O activity is to make sure that the paging file is located on a separate set of drives from all other SQL Server files. Separating the paging file away from the SQL Server files can also help disk I/O performance because it allows disk I/O associated with paging to be performed in parallel to disk I/O associated with SQL Server.

Soft Paging

If **Memory: Pages Faults/sec** is greater than zero, Windows is paging, but includes both hard and soft paging within the counter. In the previous section, we discussed hard paging. Soft paging means that application(s) on the database server are requesting memory pages still inside RAM but outside of Windows **Working Set**. **Memory: Page Faults/sec** is helpful for deriving the amount of soft paging that is occurring. There is no counter called Soft Faults per second. Instead, use this computation to calculate the number of soft faults happening per second: **Memory: Pages Faults/sec** - **Memory: Pages Input/sec** = **Soft Page Fault/sec**

To determine if SQL Server, rather than another process, is causing excessive paging, monitor the **Process: Page Faults/sec** counter for the SQL Server process and note whether the number of page faults per second for the Sqlservr.exe instance in question is similar to the number of **Memory: Pages/sec**.

Soft faults generally are not as bad as hard faults for performance because they consume CPU resources. Hard faults consume disk I/O resources. The best environment for performance is to have no faulting of any kind.

Note   When SQL Server accesses all of its data cache pages for the first time, the first access to each page will cause a soft fault. Do not be concerned with initial soft faulting occurring when SQL Server first starts up and the data cache is first being exercised.

Monitoring processors

Your goal should be to keep all of the processors that are allocated to the server busy enough to maximize performance, but not so busy that processor bottlenecks occur. The performance tuning challenge is that if CPU is not the bottleneck, something else is (a primary candidate is the disk subsystem), so CPU capacity is being wasted. CPU is usually the hardest resource to expand (above some configuration specific level, such as four or eight on many current systems), so it should be seen as a good sign that CPU utilization is more than 95 percent on busy systems. At the same time, the response time of transactions should be monitored to ensure they are within reason; if not, CPU usage greater than 95 percent may simply mean that the workload is too much for the available CPU resources and either CPU resources have to be increased or workload has to be reduced or tuned.

Look at the System Monitor counter **Processor: % Processor Time** to make sure all processors are consistently below 95 percent utilization on each CPU. **System:Processor Queue Length** is the processor queue for all CPUs on a Windows system. If **System: Processor Queue Length** is greater than two for each CPU, it indicates a CPU bottleneck. When a CPU bottleneck is detected, it is necessary to either add processors to the server or reduce the workload on the system. Reducing workload can be accomplished by query tuning or improving indexes to reduce I/O and, subsequently, CPU usage.

Another System Monitor counter to watch when a CPU bottleneck is suspected is **System: Context Switches/sec** because it indicates the number of times per second that Windows and SQL Server had to change from executing on one thread to executing on another. This costs CPU resources. Context switching is a normal component of a multithreaded, multiprocessor environment, but excessive context switching can degrade system performance. The approach to take is to only worry about context switching if there is processor queuing.

If processor queuing is observed, use the level of context switching as a gauge when performance tuning SQL Server. If context switching seems to be a contributor, there are two approaches you might want to consider: using the **affinity mask** option, and using fiber-based scheduling.

Use the **affinity mask** option to increase performance on symmetric multiprocessor (SMP) systems (with more than four microprocessors) operating under heavy load. You can associate a thread with a specific processor and specify which processors SQL Server will use. You can also exclude SQL Server activity from using certain processors using an **affinity mask** option setting. Before you change the setting of **affinity mask**, keep in mind that Windows assigns deferred process call (DPC) activity associated with NICs to the highest numbered processor in the system. In systems with more than one NIC installed and active, each additional card's activity is assigned to the next highest numbered processor. For example, an eight-processor system with two NICs has DPCs for each NIC assigned to processor 7 and to processor 6 (0-based counting is used). When using the **lightweight pooling** option, SQL Server switches to a fiber-based scheduling model rather than the default thread-based scheduling model. You can think of fibers as essentially lightweight threads. Use the command sp_configure 'lightweight pooling',1 to enable fiber-based scheduling.

Watch processor queuing and context switching to monitor the effect of setting values for both **affinity mask** and **lightweight pooling**. In some situations, these settings can make performance worse instead of better. Also, they generally do not yield much benefit unless your system has four or more processors. DBCC SQLPERF (THREADS) provides more information about I/O, memory, and CPU usage mapped back to spids. Execute the following SQL query to take a survey of current top consumers of CPU time:

```
select * from master.sysprocesses order by cpu desc
```

Monitoring Processor Queue Length

If **System: Processor Queue Length** is greater than two, this means the server's processors are receiving more work requests than they can handle as a collective group. Therefore, Windows needs to place these requests in a queue.

Some processor queuing is an indicator of good overall SQL Server I/O performance. If there is no processor queuing and if CPU utilization is low, it may be an indication that there is a performance bottleneck somewhere else in the system, the most likely candidate being the disk subsystem. Having a reasonable amount of work in the processor queue means that the CPUs are not idle and the rest of the system is keeping pace with the CPUs.

A general rule of thumb for a good processor queue number is to multiply the number of CPUs on the database server by two.

Processor queuing significantly above this calculation needs to be investigated and may indicate that your server is experiencing a CPU bottleneck. Excessive processor queuing costs query execution time. Several different activities could be contributing to processor queuing. Eliminating hard and soft paging will help save CPU resources. Other methodologies that help reduce processor queuing include SQL query tuning, picking better indexes to reduce disk I/O (and, hence, CPU), or adding more CPUs (processors) to the system.

Monitoring I/O

Disk Write Bytes/sec and **Disk Read Bytes/sec** counters provide an idea of the data throughput in terms of bytes per second per logical or physical drive. Weigh these numbers carefully along with **Disk Reads/sec** and **Disk Writes/sec**. Do not let a low amount of bytes per second lead you to believe that the disk I/O subsystem is not busy.

Monitor the **Disk Queue Length** for all drives associated with SQL Server files and determine which files are associated with excessive disk queuing.

If System Monitor indicates that some drives are not as busy as others, there is the opportunity to move SQL Server files from drives that are bottlenecking to drives that are not as busy. This will help spread disk I/O activity more evenly across hard drives. If one large drive pool is being used for SQL Server files, the resolution to disk queuing is to make the I/O capacity of the pool bigger by adding more physical drives to the pool.

Disk queuing may be an indication that one SCSI channel is being saturated with I/O requests. System Monitor cannot directly determine if this is the case. Storage vendors generally offer additional tools to help monitor the amount of I/O being serviced by a RAID controller and whether the controller is queuing I/O requests. This is more likely to occur if many disk drives (ten or more) are attached to the SCSI channel and they are all performing I/O at full speed. In this case, the solution is to connect half of the disk drives to another SCSI channel or RAID controller to balance that I/O. Typically, rebalancing drives across SCSI channels requires a rebuild of the RAID arrays and full backup/restore of the SQL Server database files.

Percent Disk Time

In System Monitor, the **PhysicalDisk: % Disk Time** and **LogicalDisk: % Disk Time** counters monitor the percentage of time that the disk is busy with read/write activity. If the **% Disk Time** counter is high (more than 90 percent), check the **Current Disk Queue Length** counter to see how many system requests are waiting for disk access. The number of waiting I/O requests should be sustained at no more than 1.5 to 2 times the number of spindles making up the physical disk. Most disks have one spindle, although redundant array of inexpensive disks (RAID) devices usually have more. A hardware RAID device appears as one physical disk in System Monitor; RAID devices created through software appear as multiple instances.

Disk Queue Length

It is important to monitor for excessively long disk queues.

To monitor disk queue length, you will need to observe several System Monitor disk counters. To enable these counters, run the command `diskperf -y` from the Windows 2000 or Windows NT command window and restart the computer.

Physical hard drives that are experiencing disk queuing will hold back disk I/O requests while they catch up on I/O processing. SQL Server response time will be degraded for these drives. This costs query execution time.

If you use RAID, it is necessary to know how many physical hard drives are associated with each drive array that Windows sees as a single physical drive, in order to calculate disk queuing for each physical drive. Ask a hardware expert to explain the SCSI channel and physical drive distribution in order to understand how SQL Server data is held by each physical drive and how much SQL Server data is distributed on each SCSI channel.

There are several choices for looking at disk queuing through System Monitor. Logical disk counters are associated with the logical drive letters assigned through Disk Administrator, whereas physical disk counters are associated with what Disk Administrator sees as a single physical disk device. Note that what appears to Disk Administrator as a single physical device may either be a single hard drive or a RAID array, which consists of several hard drives. **Current Disk Queue Length** is an instantaneous measure of disk queuing whereas **Average Disk Queue Length** averages the disk queuing measurement over the sampling period. Take note if one of the following conditions is indicated:

- **Logical Disk: Avg. Disk Queue Length** > 2

- **Physical Disk: Avg. Disk Queue Length** > 2

- **Logical Disk: Current Disk Queue Length** > 2

- **Physical Disk: Current Disk Queue Length** > 2

These recommended measurements are for each physical hard drive. If a RAID array is associated with a disk queue measurement, the measurement needs to be divided by the number of physical hard drives in the RAID array to determine the disk queuing per physical hard drive.

Note On physical hard drives or RAID arrays that hold SQL Server log files, disk queuing is not a useful measure because the log manager does not queue more than a single I/O request to SQL Server logfile(s).

Understanding SQL Server Internals

Understanding some of the internals of SQL Server 2000 can assist you in managing the performance of your databases.

Worker Threads

SQL Server maintains of pool of Windows threads that are used to service batches of SQL Server commands being submitted to the database server. The total number of these threads (referred to in SQL Server terminology as worker threads) available to service all incoming command batches is dictated by the setting for the **sp_configure** option **max worker threads**. If the number of connections actively submitting batches is greater than the number specified for **max worker threads**, worker threads will be shared among connections actively submitting batches. The default of 255 will work well for many installations. Note that the majority of connections spend most of their time waiting for batches to be received from the client.

Worker threads take on most of the responsibility of writing out dirty 8-KB pages from the SQL Server buffer cache. Worker threads schedule their I/O operations asynchronously for maximum performance.

Lazy Writer

The lazy writer is a SQL Server system process that functions within the buffer manager. The lazy writer flushes out batches of dirty, aged buffers (buffers containing changes that must be written back to disk before the buffer can be reused for a different page) and makes them available to user processes. This activity helps to produce and maintain available free buffers, which are 8-KB data cache pages empty of data and available for reuse. As the lazy writer flushes each 8-KB cache buffer to disk, the identity of the cache page is initialized so other data may be written into the free buffer. The lazy writer minimizes the impact of this activity on other SQL Server operations by working during periods of low disk I/O.

SQL Server automatically configures and manages the level of free buffers. The performance counter **SQL Server: Buffer Manager: Lazy Writes/sec** indicates the number of 8-KB pages being physically written out to disk. Monitor **SQL Server: Buffer Manager: Free Pages** to see if this value dips. Optimally, the lazy writer keeps this counter level throughout SQL Server operations, which means the lazy writer is keeping up with the user demand for free buffers. If the value of System Monitor object **SQL Server: Buffer Manager: Free Pages** reaches zero, there were times when the user load demanded a higher level of free buffers than the lazy writer was able to provide.

If the lazy writer is having problems keeping the free buffer steady, or at least above zero, it could mean the disk subsystem is not able to provide sufficient disk I/O performance. Compare drops in free buffer level to disk queuing to confirm this. The solution is to add more physical disk drives to the database server disk subsystem in order to provide more disk I/O processing power.

Monitor the current level of disk queuing in System Monitor by looking at the performance counters **Average Disk Queue Length** or **Current Disk Queue Length** for logical or physical disks, and ensure the disk queue is less than 2 for each physical drive associated with any SQL Server activity. For database servers that employ hardware RAID controllers and disk arrays, remember to divide the number reported by Logical/Physical Disk counters by the number of actual hard drives associated with that logical drive letter or physical hard drive number (as reported by Disk Administrator), because Windows and SQL Server are unaware of the actual number of physical hard drives attached to a RAID controller. It is important to be aware of the number of drives associated with the RAID array controller in order to properly interpret the disk queue numbers that System Monitor is reporting.

For more information, see SQL Server Books Online.

Checkpoint

Periodically, each instance of SQL Server ensures that all dirty log and data pages are flushed to disk. This is called a checkpoint. Checkpoints reduce the time and resources needed to recover from a failure when an instance of SQL Server is restarted. During a checkpoint, dirty pages (buffer cache pages that have been modified since being brought into the buffer cache) are written to the SQL Server data files. A buffer written to disk at a checkpoint still contains the page and users can read or update it without rereading it from disk, which is not the case for free buffers created by the lazy writer.

Checkpoint logic attempts to let worker threads and the lazy writer do the majority of the work writing out dirty pages. Checkpoint logic does this by trying an extra checkpoint wait before writing out a dirty page if possible. This provides the worker threads and the lazy writer more time to write out the dirty pages. The conditions under which this extra wait time for a dirty page occurs is detailed in SQL Server Books Online in the topic "Checkpoints and the Active Portion of the Log." The main idea to remember is that checkpoint logic attempts to even out SQL Server disk I/O activity over a longer time period with this extra checkpoint wait.

For more efficient checkpoint operations when there are a large number of pages to flush out of cache, SQL Server sorts the data pages to be flushed in the order the pages appear on disk. This helps to minimize disk arm movement during cache flush and takes advantage of sequential disk I/O where possible. The checkpoint process also submits 8-KB disk I/O requests asynchronously to the disk subsystem. This allows SQL Server to finish submitting required disk I/O requests faster because the checkpoint process doesn't wait for the disk subsystem to report back that the data has been actually written to disk.

It is important to watch disk queuing on hard drives associated with SQL Server data files to determine if SQL Server is sending more disk I/O requests than the disk(s) can handle; if this is true, more disk I/O capacity must be added to the disk subsystem so it can handle the load.

Log Manager

Like all other major RDBMS products, SQL Server ensures that all write activity (insert, update, and delete) performed on the database will not be lost if something were to interrupt SQL Server's online status, such as power failure, disk drive failure, fire in the data center, and so on. The SQL Server logging process helps guarantee recoverability. Before any implicit (single SQL query) or explicit transaction (defined transaction that issues a BEGIN TRAN/COMMIT, or ROLLBACK command sequence) can be completed, the log manager must receive a signal from the disk subsystem that all data changes associated with that transaction have been written successfully to the associated log file. This rule guarantees that if SQL Server is abruptly shut down for whatever reason and the transactions written into the data cache are not yet flushed to the data files by the checkpoint and lazy writer, the transaction log can be read and reapplied in SQL Server upon startup. Reading the transaction log and applying the transactions to SQL Server data after a server stoppage is referred to as recovery.

Because SQL Server must wait for the disk subsystem to complete I/O to SQL Server log files as each transaction is completed, it is important that the disks containing SQL Server log files have sufficient disk I/O handling capacity for the anticipated transaction load.

The method of watching out for disk queuing associated with SQL Server log files is different from SQL Server database files. Use the System Monitor counters **SQL Server: Databases <database instance>: Log Flush Waits Times** and **SQL Server: Databases <database instance>: Log Flush Waits/sec** to see if there are log writer requests waiting on the disk subsystem for completion.

A caching controller provides the highest performance, but should not be used for disks that contain log files unless the controller guarantees that data entrusted to it will be written to disk eventually, even if the power fails. For more information on caching controllers, refer to the section in this chapter titled "Effect of On-Board Cache of Hardware RAID Controllers."

Read-Ahead Management

SQL Server 2000 provides automatic management for reading large sequential reads for activities such as table scans. Read-ahead management is completely self-configuring and self-tuning, and is tightly

integrated with the operations of the SQL Server query processor. Read-ahead management is used for large table scans, large index range scans, probes into clustered and nonclustered index binary trees, and other situations. This is because read-aheads occur with 64-KB I/Os, which provide higher disk throughput potential for the disk subsystem than do 8-KB I/Os. When it is necessary to retrieve a large amount of data, SQL Server uses read-ahead to maximize throughput.

SQL Server uses a simple and efficient Index Allocation Map (IAM) storage structure that supports read-ahead management. The IAM is the SQL Server mechanism for recording the location of extents – each 64 KB extent contains eight pages of data or index information. Each IAM page is an 8-KB page that contains tightly packed (bitmapped) information about which extents contain required data. The compact nature of IAM pages makes them fast to read, and more regularly used IAM pages can be maintained in buffer cache.

Read-ahead management can construct multiple sequential read requests by combining query information from the query processor with information about the location of all extents that need to be read from the IAM page(s). Sequential 64-KB disk reads provide extremely good disk I/O performance. The **SQL Server: Buffer Manager: Read-Ahead Pages/sec** performance counter provides information about the effectiveness and efficiency of read-ahead management.

SQL Server 2000 Enterprise Edition dynamically adjusts the maximum number of read ahead pages based on the amount of memory present. For all other editions of SQL Server 2000 the value is fixed. Another advance in SQL Server 2000 Enterprise Edition is commonly called merry-go-round scan, which allows multiple tasks to share full table scans. If the execution plan of an SQL statement calls for a scan of the data pages in a table, and if the relational database engine detects that the table is already being scanned for another execution plan, the database engine joins the second scan to the first at the current location of the second scan. The database engine reads each page once and passes the rows from each page to both execution plans. This continues until the end of the table is reached. At that point, the first execution plan has the complete results of a scan, but the second execution plan must still retrieve the data pages that occur before the point at which it joined the in-progress scan. The scan for second execution plan then wraps back to the first data page of the table and scans forward to the point at which it joined the first scan. Any number of scans can be combined in this way; the database engine will keep looping through the data pages until it has completed all the scans.

One caveat about read-ahead management is that too much read-ahead can be detrimental overall to performance because it can fill cache with unneeded pages, using I/O and CPU that could have been used for other purposes. The solution is a general performance tuning goal to tune all SQL queries so a minimal number of pages are brought into buffer cache. This includes making sure you have the right indexes in place and are using them. Use clustered indexes for efficient range scanning and define nonclustered indexes to help quickly locate single rows or smaller rowsets. For example, if you plan to have only one index in a table and that index is for the purposes of fetching single rows or smaller rowsets, you should make the index clustered. Clustered indexes are nominally faster than nonclustered indexes.

Miscellaneous Performance Topics

Database Design Using Star and Snowflake Schemas

Data warehouses use dimensional modeling to organize data for the purpose of analysis. Dimensional modeling produces star and snowflake schemas, which also provide performance efficiency for the massive data read operations that are frequently performed in data warehousing. High-volume data (often hundreds of millions of rows) is stored in a fact table that has very short rows, which minimizes storage requirements and query time. Attributes of business facts are denormalized into dimension tables to minimize the number of table joins when retrieving data.

For a discussion of database design for data warehouses, see Chapter 17, "Data Warehouse Design Considerations."

Use Equality Operators in Transact-SQL Queries

Using inequality operators in SQL queries will force databases to use table scans to evaluate the inequalities. This generates high I/O if these queries regularly run against very large tables. WHERE clauses that contain the "NOT" operators (!=, <>, !<, !>), such as `WHERE <column_name> != some_value` will generate high I/O.

If these types of queries need to be run, try to restructure the queries to eliminate the NOT keyword. For example:

Instead of:

```
select * from tableA where col1 != "value"
```

Try using:

```
select * from tableA where col1 <  "value" and col1 > "value"
```

Reduce Rowset Size and Communications Overhead

Database programmers who work in SQL work with easy-to-use interfaces like the Microsoft ActiveX® Data Objects (ADO), Remote Data Objects (RDO) and Data Access Objects (DAO) database APIs need to consider the result sets they are building.

ADO, RDO, and DAO provide programmers with great database development interfaces that allow rich SQL rowset functionality without requiring a lot of SQL programming experience. Programmers can avoid performance problems if they carefully consider the amount of data their application is returning to the client, and keep track of where the SQL Server indexes are placed and how the SQL Server data is arranged. SQL Profiler, the Index Tuning Wizard, and graphical execution plans are very helpful tools for pinpointing and fixing these problem queries.

When using cursor logic, choose the cursor that is appropriate for the type of processing you intend to do. Different types of cursors come with varying costs. You should understand what types of operations you intend to perform (read-only, forward processing only, and so forth) and then choose your cursor type accordingly.

Look for opportunities to reduce the size of the result set being returned by eliminating columns in the select list that do not need to be returned, or by returning only the required rows. This helps reduce I/O and CPU consumption.

Using Multiple Statements

You can reduce the size of your resultset and avoid unnecessary network communications between the client and your database server by performing the processing on the database. To perform processes that cannot be done using a single Transact-SQL statement, SQL Server allows you to group Transact-SQL statements together in the following ways.

Grouping method	Description
Batches	A batch is a group of one or more Transact-SQL statements sent from an application to the server as one unit. SQL Server executes each batch as a single executable unit.
Stored procedures	A stored procedure is a group of Transact-SQL statements that has been predefined and precompiled on the server. The stored procedure can accept parameters, and can return result sets, return codes, and output parameters to the calling application.
Triggers	A trigger is a special type of stored procedure. It is not called directly by applications. It is instead executed whenever a user performs a specified modification (INSERT, UPDATE, or DELETE) to a table.
Scripts	A script is a series of Transact-SQL statements stored in a file. The file can be used as input to the **osql** utility or SQL Query Analyzer. The utilities then execute the Transact-SQL statements stored in the file.

The following SQL Server features allow you control the use of multiple Transact-SQL statements at a time.

Feature	Description
Control-of-flow statements	Allow you to include conditional logic. For example, if the country is Canada, perform one series of Transact-SQL statements. If the country is U.K., do a different series of Transact-SQL statements.
Variables	Allow you to store data for use as input in a later Transact-SQL statement. For example, you can code a query that needs different data values specified in the WHERE clause each time the query is executed. You can write the query to use variables in the WHERE clause, and code logic to fill the variables with the proper data. The parameters of stored procedures are a special class of variables.
Error handling	Lets you customize the way SQL Server responds to problems. You can specify appropriate actions to take when errors occur, or display customized error messages that are more informative to a user than a generic SQL Server error.

Reusing Execution Plans

Performance gains can be realized when SQL Server is able to leverage an existing execution plan from a prior query. There are a number of things the developer can do to encourage SQL Server to reuse execution plans. Transact-SQL statements should be written according to the following guidelines.

- Use fully qualified names of objects, such as tables and views.

    For example, do not code this SELECT:

    ```
    SELECT * FROM Shippers WHERE ShipperID = 3
    ```

    Instead, using ODBC as an example, use the **SQLBindParameter** ODBC function:

    ```
    SELECT * FROM Northwind.dbo.Shippers WHERE ShipperID = 3
    ```

- Use parameterized queries, and supply the parameter values instead of specifying stored procedure parameter values or the values in search condition predicates directly. Use either the parameter substitution in **sp_executesql** or the parameter binding of the ADO, OLE DB, ODBC, and DB-Library APIs.

  For example, do not code this SELECT:

  ```
  SELECT * FROM Northwind.dbo.Shippers WHERE ShipperID = 3
  ```

  Instead, using ODBC as an example, use the **SQLBindParameter** ODBC function to bind the parameter marker (?) to a program variable and code the SELECT statement as:

  ```
  SELECT * FROM Northwind.dbo.Shippers WHERE ShipperID = ?
  ```

- In a Transact-SQL script, stored procedure, or trigger, use **sp_executesql** to execute the SELECT statement:

  ```
  DECLARE @IntVariable INT
  DECLARE @SQLString NVARCHAR(500)
  DECLARE @ParmDefinition NVARCHAR(500)
  /* Build the SQL string. */
  SET @SQLString =
      N'SELECT * FROM Northwind.dbo.Shippers WHERE ShipperID = @ShipID'
  /* Specify the parameter format once. */
  SET @ParmDefinition = N'@ShipID int'
  /* Execute the string. */
  SET @IntVariable = 3
  EXECUTE sp_executesql @SQLString, @ParmDefinition,
                        @ShipID = @IntVariable
  ```

  sp_executesql is a good alternative when you do not want the overhead of creating and maintaining a separate stored procedures.

Reusing Execution Plans for Batches

If multiple concurrent applications will execute the same batch with a known set of parameters, implement the batch as a stored procedure that will be called by the applications.

When an ADO, OLE DB, or ODBC application will be executing the same batch multiple times, use the PREPARE/EXECUTE model of executing the batch. Use parameter markers bound to program variables to supply all needed input values, such as the expressions used in an UPDATE VALUES clause or in the predicates in a search condition.

Maintaining Statistics on Columns

SQL Server allows statistical information regarding the distribution of values in a column to be created even if the column is not part of an index. This statistical information can be used by the query processor to determine the optimal strategy for evaluating a query. When you create an index, SQL Server automatically stores statistical information regarding the distribution of values in the indexed column(s). In addition to indexed columns, if the AUTO_CREATE_STATISTICS database option is set to ON (which it is by default), SQL Server automatically creates statistics for columns that get used in a predicate even if the columns are not in indexes.

As the data in a column changes, index and column statistics can become outdated and cause the query optimizer to make less-than-optimal decisions about how to process a query. Periodically, SQL Server automatically updates this statistical information as the data in a table changes. The sampling is random across data pages, and taken from the table or the smallest nonclustered index on the columns needed by the statistics. After a data page has been read from disk, all the rows on the data page are used to update the statistical information. The frequency at which the statistical information is updated is determined by the volume of data in the column or index and the amount of changing data.

For example, the statistics for a table containing 10,000 rows may need to be updated after 1,000 index values have changed because 1,000 values may represent a significant percentage of the table. However, for a table containing 10 million index entries, 1,000 changing index values is less significant, and so the statistics may not be automatically updated. SQL Server, however, always ensures that a minimum number of rows are sampled; tables that are smaller than 8 MB are always fully scanned to gather statistics.

> **Note** Outdated or missing statistics are indicated as warnings (table name in red text) when the execution plan of a query is graphically displayed using SQL Query Analyzer. Additionally, monitoring the **Missing Column Statistics** event class using SQL Profiler indicates when statistics are missing.

Statistics can easily be created on all eligible columns in all user tables in the current database in a single statement by using the **sp_createstats** system stored procedure. Columns not eligible for statistics include nondeterministic or nonprecise computed columns, or columns of **image**, **text**, and **ntext** data types.

Creating statistics manually allows you to create statistics that contain multiple column densities (average number of duplicates for the combination of columns). For example, a query contains the following clause:

```
WHERE a = 7 and b = 9
```

Creating manual statistics on both columns together (**a**, **b**) can allow SQL Server to make a better estimate for the query because the statistics also contain the average number of distinct values for the combination of columns **a** and **b**. This allows SQL Server to make use of the index (preferably clustered in this case), if it is built on col1 rather than needing to resort to a table scan. For information on how to create column statistics, see the topic "CREATE STATISTICS" in SQL Server Books Online.

Finding More Information

- SQL Server Books Online provides information on SQL Server architecture and database tuning along with complete documentation on command syntax and administration. SQL Server Books Online can be installed from the SQL Server installation media on any SQL Server client or server computer.

- For the latest information on Microsoft SQL Server, including technical papers on SQL Server, visit the Microsoft SQL Server Web sites at:

  - http://www.microsoft.com/sql/

  - http://www.microsoft.com/technet/sql/

  - http://msdn.microsoft.com/sqlserver/

- An external resource that provides information in the form of a periodical can be found on http://www.sqlmag.com. You will find many optimization and tuning hints, code samples, and insightful articles outlining the internal workings of SQL Server and other valuable information.

- Delaney, Kalen & Soukup, Ron. *Inside Microsoft SQL Server 2000*, Microsoft Press, 2001

  This book updates the previous version (*Inside Microsoft SQL Server 7.0*) with information for SQL Server 2000. This book delves into many of the internal concepts of SQL Server.

- Kimball, Ralph. *The Data Warehouse Lifecycle Toolkit*, John Wiley and Sons, 1998.

  This book provides insight into data warehouse database design and explains dimensional modeling concepts.

Monitoring the DTS Multiphase Data Pump in Visual Basic

The purpose of this chapter is to illustrate a technique for monitoring the phases of the Data Transformation Services (DTS) data pump process from an application external to the DTS package. This chapter may aid in both the understanding of multiphase data pump behavior and in troubleshooting. It includes a sample solution that graphically depicts phase activity and allows you to set phase breakpoints during the execution of a package that contains a Transform Data task or a Data Driven Query task. This solution uses a COM+ event class to communicate to a Microsoft® Visual Basic® application.

This chapter assumes that you have some experience setting up Microsoft ActiveX® script transformations for multiphase data pump processes. This chapter also assumes that the multiphase data pump has been exposed from within SQL Server Enterprise Manager. If necessary, please review SQL Server Books Online before proceeding further.

Exposing the Multiphase Data Pump

To understand the architecture of the sample solution presented in this chapter, it is important to understand what multiphase data pump programming interfaces are available, the context in which a DTS package executes, and some rationale for developing the sample solution.

Programming Interfaces

The custom transform interface that allows access to each phase of the data pump is only exposed natively through COM in Microsoft Visual C++®. But a full automation interface to the data pump is available to Visual Basic.

Elements of the multiphase data pump are exposed within the ActiveX script transformation. A data structure that indicates phase information (for example, transform status, source and destination row counts, and error information) is passed into each of these phases.

Package Execution Context

DTS packages are always run as a client-side process. The context of the running package depends on the calling application. If a user called the package through an application such as DTS Designer or DTS Run, the package runs in the context of that user account. If a user schedules a package as part of a SQL Server Agent job, then the package runs in the context of the SQLServerAgent service account or the designated non-**sysadmin** job step proxy account. For more information, search for Knowledge Base article Q266663 at http://support.microsoft.com/directory/.

Because DTS is free threaded, any COM object that is called by a step or a task must support this threading model. If an object does not support this threading model, then the step utilizing it must be set to execute on the main thread. Custom tasks written in Visual Basic are forced by DTS to execute on the main package thread. Although packages that are free threaded can be created and executed in Visual Basic, any package created in Visual Basic that supports events must return those events to the main thread. Tasks, ActiveX scripts, and any objects instantiated within ActiveX script are usually executed as in-process objects within the DTS package.

Troubleshooting the Data Pump

By default, the data pump runs until it is complete or until a maximum number of errors are encountered. Identify what happened during package execution by examining error logs, error files, and exception files.

Because the progress indicator does not provide complete information about the state of the multiphase data pump, you may find it helpful to expose that information and set breakpoints for each phase, to step through each phase, and to monitor state and error information through a user interface.

> **Note** You can expose a user interface while executing a package. For example, when a package is run from SQL Server Enterprise Manager, the **Executing DTS Package** dialog box displays the progress of package execution. However, it is not recommended that you embed a user interface into the package if your package will be run in an environment that does not support a user interface. For example, if you embed a user interface into a package that has been scheduled through SQL Server Agent, the package may stop responding.

Multiphase Data Pump Review

This section does not go into great detail about multiphase data pump functionality. Rather, it is provided as a review and as context for subsequent code examples. For more information about multiphase data pump functionality, see SQL Server Books Online.

Basic Multiphase Data Pump Process

When copying a row of data from source to destination, the data pump follows this basic process: individual rows of data are read from a data source into a batch buffer, transformed on a row-by-row basis, and written to a data destination. The different phases that the process goes through are controlled by the data pump architecture and the status and result of each phase, unless you override this behavior programmatically.

Transformation Status

The data pump goes through many different phases, and each phase is meaningful only if you understand how the data pump arrived at that phase and what it will do after it leaves a phase. All this information is controlled by a combination of the transformation status and the phase status.

There are many variations on the status of a given row transformation phase. Status codes can be strictly informative, or they can be used to control the data pump. For more information on how these types of status codes can be combined, see "DTSTransformStatus" in SQL Server Books Online.

Success/Failure

Default conversions (if any) or phase has succeeded or failed.

Call Error Sink

Instruct the data pump to call the error sink handler. It is possible to keep processing phases in spite of errors if the appropriate status code is set.

Skip Fetch

Variations of this status code instruct the data pump not to retrieve the next source row.

Skip Insert

Variations of this status code instruct the data pump not to forward the row on to the destination data source.

Multiphase Data Pump Phases

The following diagram depicts a flow chart of the defined data pump phases, along with two additional implied phases. Directional lines show the possible flow between each phase, based on processing paths and transformation status.

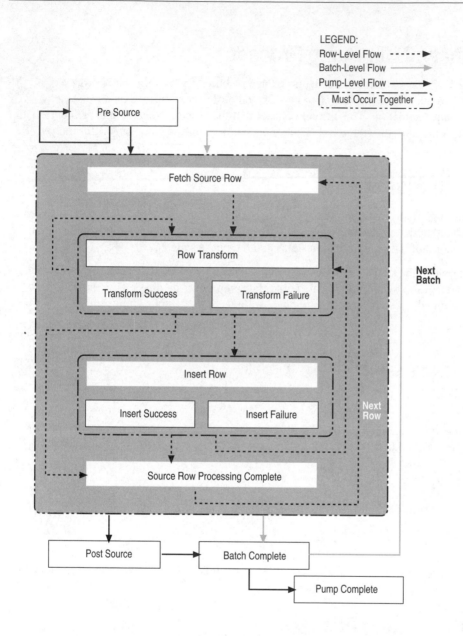

The data pump does not have access to the data source and destination at all times. Source data operations are available in all phases from the Fetch Row phase until the Post Source phase. Destination data operations are not available during the Insert Success and Insert Failure phases. No data operations are available during the Pump Complete phase.

Pre Source

The Pre Source phase is executed before source data is fetched. A skip fetch status can be returned here to create a loop to be used for initialization or the polling of a data source.

You can add a pre-source data pump function to read or write information to a file, or to initialize objects, connections, and memory so they can be used during subsequent phases.

Fetch Source Row (Implied)

Although there is not an explicit phase defined for fetching a row, there is an implied event. This implied event can be seen by the branching paths that a data pump process can follow.

Row Transform

This is the only phase that is available in DTS Designer without your activating the multiphase data pump feature.

> **Note** To activate this feature, select the **Show multi-phase pump in DTS Designer** check box. In this phase, a single row of source data is transformed and mapped to a destination. The transformation status returned from this phase influences subsequent branching.

Transform Failure

This phase occurs when the Row Transform phase returns a status that is a variation on an error or exception status. The status returned from this phase controls subsequent branching.

This phase is referred to in SQL Server Books Online as a subphase of the Post Row Transform phase. The Post Row Transform phase is not a real phase, but rather a conceptual grouping of the phases that occur after each Row Transform phase. On the diagram, the Post Row Transform phase includes the boxes for Transform Success, Transform Failure, Insert Row, Insert Success, and Insert Failure.

Transform Success (Implied)

Although there is not an explicit phase defined to indicate a successful transformation, there is an implied event whenever the Transform Failure phase did not occur for a given row. It is listed on the flow chart for illustrative purposes only.

Insert Row (Implied)

Although there is not an explicit phase defined to indicate when a row is inserted, there is an implied event, which is seen by the branching paths that a data pump process can follow. This implied event would be skipped if the Row Transform status were set appropriately.

In the case of a Data Driven Query task, this event indicates the execution of a particular query, which is not necessarily an insert operation.

Insert Success

This phase signifies the success of an Insert operation, or the success of any query if the transformation is part of a Data Driven Query task. You cannot specify any destination operations in the returned status.

Insert Failure

This phase signifies the failure of an Insert operation, or the failure of any query if the transformation is part of a Data Driven Query task. You cannot specify any destination operations in the returned status.

Source Row Processing Complete (Implied)

This event indicates that a single row has been completely processed and that the next row, if there is one, should be fetched.

Batch Complete

This phase will occur at least once during the data pump process. If the destination connection is using the SQL Server OLE DB driver, if the **Use Fast Load** property is enabled, and if the **Insert Batch Size** property is set to anything besides zero, this phase will occur every time a batch of rows is flushed out to the destination data source. Otherwise, it occurs only at the end of the data transfer.

Post Source

This phase occurs after all source data has been retrieved, transformed, and inserted, but before a final Batch Complete phase.

> **Note** In the **ActiveX Script Transformation Properties** dialog box, under **Entry Functions**, the phases are listed out of order. Also, if you click **AutoGen.**, the last two phases are listed out of order from their typical execution sequence. However, this will not affect the execution of these phases.

Pump Complete

This is the last phase to occur. Neither source nor destination data is available. It is generally used for cleanup operations.

Properties that Impact Phases

The following properties, which can be manipulated either programmatically or graphically through DTS Designer, establish parameters for the data pump process. For more information, see SQL Server Books Online.

Use Fast Load

This property specifies that the data pump should use high-speed bulk-load processing. Batches are processed by the destination as a group instead of row by row. This property is only available on the Transform Data task.

Insert Batch Size

This property controls the number of destination records that are committed as a single batch. Note: If a record fails, it is not counted as a member of the batch. This property only applies when the destination connection is using the Microsoft OLE DB Provider for SQL Server, and the Use Fast Load property has been set. This property is only available on the Transform Data task.

Max Error Count

This property sets a limit on the number of unhandled errors that can occur within the data pump process before the task terminates. It is possible to intercept different types of transformation errors and incorporate custom error handling, thereby avoiding the limit set by this property.

Sample Monitoring Solution

The following sample solution enables you to monitor the phases of the data pump from an external client application while the package is running.

The sample code for this solution is divided into a COM+ Event Class, a Visual Basic Project for publishing events, a Visual Basic Project for subscribing to events, and a DTS package. The sample code is located on the *Microsoft SQL Server 2000 Resource Kit* CD-ROM in the folder, \ToolsAndSamples\MonitorDTS. For the code to work, the appropriate DLLs and EXE need to be copied and registered. A batch file is included in the sample code folder which registers the DLLs, but the Component Services registration needs to be done manually, as specified below.

The sample solution was developed on the Microsoft Windows® 2000 platform, using SQL Server® 2000, and Visual Basic 6.0 (SP4).

Solution Architecture

The monitoring solution is based on the following ideas:

View Phases as Events

For the purpose of this application, the occurrence of and the circumstances leading into each phase can be thought of as an explicit event. Phases are actually handled programmatically as events in Visual C++.

ActiveX Scripting Calls

It is possible to create your own Visual Basic COM object and reference it from within the ActiveX scripting environment. Within an ActiveX script transformation, you can create scripting functions that are called at the end of each data pump phase. Each event function that is called from within the ActiveX script could in turn call the object and pass its state and status information to that object.

COM+ Managed Events

The crux of the monitoring problem revolves around handling communication and synchronization between client-side DTS packages and out-of-process monitoring applications. The sample solution will use Windows 2000 Component Services to forward and receive COM+ events for interprocess communications.

A COM+ event class will be created as an ActiveX DLL and registered with Component Services. That event class can then be referenced by other applications, making it possible for applications, with minimal code, to send and receive COM+ events through Component Services.

Visual Basic Publish and Subscribe Applications

Two applications, each of which interface with the COM+ event class, are needed. One application will relay information from the ActiveX scripting environment as a COM+ event. The other will listen for and implement the COM+ events through Component Services.

COM+ Event Class: MonitorDTSEvents.DLL

The sample Visual Basic project used to create the MonitorDTSEvents.DLL event class is located on the *SQL Server 2000 Resource Kit* CD-ROM in the folder, \ToolsAndSamples\MonitorDTS\EventClass.

DTSTransformPhaseInfo Data Structure

The information relating to phase state and status is contained in a data structure called DTSTransformPhaseInfo. This includes the number of rows read, the number of rows successfully passed through to the destination, the number of errors encountered, the current phase, and the last transformation error status.

Creating the Event Class DLL

The COM+ event class is created as an ActiveX DLL called MonitorDTSEvents, with a description of "Monitor DTS Events." It is set for unattended execution and retained in memory.

Each event is a separate class and is only a placeholder function that defines the interface to the event. All parameters must be passed by value, as they will be copied to multiple applications by COM+.

For this application, a single event class called MPDPEvent is defined that accepts a user-defined parameter called MonitorID, the individual DTSTransformPhaseInfo fields as required parameters, and an optional variant field that will be used to pass an array of phase counters. The event class is defined as follows:

```
Public Sub MPDPEvent( _
    ByVal MonitorID As Integer, _
    ByVal CurrentPhase As Integer, _
    ByVal CurrentSourceRow As Long, _
    ByVal DestinationRowsComplete As Long, _
    ByVal ErrorCode As Long, _
    ByVal ErrorRows As Long, _
    ByVal TransformStatus As Long, _
    Optional ByVal PhaseOrdinal As Integer, _
    Optional ByVal PhaseCounters As Variant)
End Sub
```

Registering the DLL

The precompiled MonitorDTSEvents DLL can be registered by issuing the following command in the MonitorDTS\EventClass folder: **regsvr32 MonitorDTSEvents.DLL**. A batch file is provided in the sample code folder to do this. If you used the Visual Basic project to create the DLL, no further steps are necessary.

Registering the COM+ Component

The event class must be properly registered as part of a COM+ application within Component Services.

To register the newly created event class

1. Bring up the Component Services MMC console and navigate to the COM+ Applications folder

2. Right-click **COM+ Application**, point to **New**, and then click **Application**.

3. In the **Welcome to the COM Application Install Wizard** screen, click **Next**, and then click **Create an empty application**.

4. In the **Create Empty Application** screen, type **MonitorDTS** in the name box and then click **Library Application**.

5. Open the MonitorDTS application, right-click **Components**, point to **New**, and then click **Component**.

6. In the **Import or Install Component Screen**, click **Install new event class(es)**.

7. In the **Select Files to Install** screen, find and open MonitorDTSEvents.dll.

8. In the **Install new event class** screen, select the **Find MonitorDTSEvents.dll** check box.

9. Right-click **MonitorDTSEvents.MPDP Event**, click **Properties**, click the **Advanced** tab, and then click **Fire in parallel**.

   Selecting this check box permits multiple applications to access each event independently of one another.

Publisher Application: MonitorDTS.DLL

The sample Visual Basic project used to create the publisher application MonitorDTS.DLL is located on the *SQL Server 2000 Resource Kit* CD-ROM in the folder, \ToolsAndSamples\MonitorDTS\Publisher.

A method called **PhaseRelay** in the publisher application will be called by ActiveX script. The publisher needs to identify which phase the data pump is in, manage an array of phase counters, and only process events with the same MonitorID that was first used with a given instance of the publisher. If appropriate, it will fire a COM+ event.

You can step through this process, or you can access the provided code samples. The publisher application is structured in the following way.

Creating the Publisher Application

The publisher application is created as an ActiveX DLL called MonitorDTS, with a description of "Monitor DTS Publisher." This application has its project properties set for unattended execution, and is retained in memory. A project reference to the Monitor DTS Event object library (MonitorDTSEvents.dll) is enabled.

The publisher application is implemented entirely within a class called PhaseRelay. This class processes the method call from the ActiveX script, and in turn fires the MPDPEvent COM+ event.

Registering the DLL

The precompiled MonitorDTS DLL can be registered by issuing the following command in the MonitorDTS\Publisher folder: **regsvr32 MonitorDTS.DLL**. A batch file is provided in the sample code folder to do this. If the reader used the Visual Basic project to create the DLL, then no further steps are necessary.

Initializing the PhaseRelay Class

The MonitorID for a given instance is not defined until the first time the PhaseRelay method is called.

An array called mPhaseArray is defined which contains the expected allowable return values for CurrentPhase. The ordinal position of each value in the array will later be used to reference the phase.

An array is defined that contains counters for each observable phase. The mPhaseArray array will be used to look up the ordinal position that correlates to the position of the counter for a given phase. Each value in the counter array is set initially at zero.

An instance of the MPDPEvent COM+ event class called objDTSMonitor is created when the PhaseRelay class is instantiated. No other coding is required, as Component Services handles all of the communications.

Identifying the Phase

The MonitorID parameter value for a given event is checked against the value used when the object was instantiated. If the values do not match, no further handling is done for the event.

Maintaining Counters

The array is searched for a value that matches the CurrentPhase value for a given phase, and the ordinal position within the array is used to identify that phase.

If the phase value indicates a completed batch, then the counters for the Row Transform and Transform Failure phases are reset to zero for each batch.

Phase counters are maintained within the publisher application to record how many times the event was fired. They are not maintained in the subscriber application since the subscriber may not observe all of the posted events, depending upon when subscriber was launched.

Firing the Event

The MPDPEvent COM+ event is fired, relaying the information sent from the ActiveX script, with the addition of the optional phase counter array and ordinal position.

Component Services relies on applications to register and deregister themselves properly. If an application does not do this properly, then an error will be propagated back to the publishing applications that are sending events. An error handler is put in place that generically detects any error encountered during the event call and attempts to remedy the error by simply disconnecting and reconnecting to the COM+ event.

Cleanup

Setting the objDTSMonitor object to **nothing** cleanly shuts down the publisher application's Component Services event handling.

Subscriber Application: MonitorDTSWatch.EXE

The sample Visual Basic project used to create the subscriber application MonitorDTSWatch.EXE is located on the *SQL Server 2000 Resource Kit* CD-ROM in the folder, \ToolsAndSamples\MonitorDTS\Subscriber.

The Visual Basic ActiveX executable application will register itself at run-time with Component Services, and implement the MPDPEvent COM+ events that are fired by the publisher application. It will display the information relayed by the COM+ events on a form as the DTS package runs in the background.

You can step through this process, or you can access the provided code samples. The subscriber application is structured in the following way.

Creating the Subscriber Application

The subscriber application is created as an ActiveX executable called MonitorDTSWatch, with a description of "Monitor DTS Watcher". This application has its project properties set for unattended execution, for is retained in memory. Its startup object is set to Sub Main, and its start mode is set to standalone.

A project reference to the Monitor DTS Event object library (MonitorDTSEvents.dll) is enabled, as well as one to the COM+ 1.0 Admin Type Library (comadmin.dll).

Application Initialization

Initialize the global array containing verbose phase information. The ordinal position of each phase in the array correlates to the ordinal position determined for the phase counters in the publishing application. The actual CurrentPhase values are in the array in ascending order.

Initialize the global array containing the verbose transformation status information. The actual TransformationStatus values are in the array in ascending order.

Declare a public constant that contains the Component Services event class ID GUID for the registered phase info COM+ event class. This value needs to be copied and pasted from the properties of the event with Component Services.

Initializing the Subscriber Class

Upon form load, create a transient subscription with Component Services as an implementer of the MPDPEvent COM+ event, using the event class ID GUID defined earlier. For more information about this technique, see Knowledge Base article #Q250292 at http://support.microsoft.com/directory/.

Handling Events

Receive the MPDPEvent COM+ event, and discard the message if it contains a MonitorID different than the one intended for the form. This prevents double counting of events from different publishers.

Pass the parameters received from the COM+ event to a form subroutine that posts the information to a form.

MonitorDTSWatch GUI

The MonitorDTSWatch main form graphically contains a flow chart of the defined data pump phases, along with two additional implied phases. Directional lines show the possible flow between each phase.

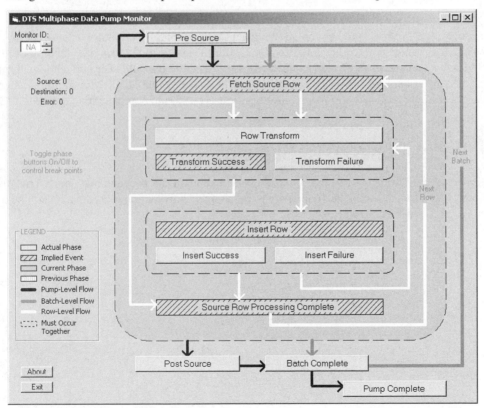

The phases themselves are represented by an array of CheckBox controls displayed in graphical style. The ordinal position of each button in the control array corresponds to the ordinal position in the global array containing verbose phase information.

The caption of each CheckBox control is updated with the name of the phase, appended by the current counter value for that respective phase.

The color of the CheckBox control representing the current phase is set to green. The color of the control representing the previous phase is set to orange. You should be able to discern what happened in between each phase by tracing the path of the directional lines between the last phase and the current phase.

Phase breakpoint functionality is built into the form. If the value of a given CheckBox control is set to checked (depressed), then the application will pause the next time it receives an event for that CheckBox's phase. It will then display a separate modeless form detailing the transform phase information at that point in time, and temporarily halt the data pump. While this information is displayed, it is possible to go back to the main form and check or uncheck any of the CheckBox controls. The important implication here is that the event handling is blocking, meaning that the data pump cannot proceed until the posting subroutine completes.

Cleanup

It is necessary to deregister the subscriber application from Component Services before shutting down. This is essentially the reverse of the procedure used to register the application during the loading of the main form. Because a COM+ related error handler was incorporated in the publisher application, abruptly shutting down the subscriber will not affect the publisher. The COM+ event handler for the subscriber application will eventually time out, but as a matter of practice you should deregister the application in an orderly fashion.

DTS Package: MonitorDTS Sample.DTS

To illustrate how the monitoring code works, we will create a simple DTS package that uses a Transform Data task and the Publisher Visual Basic application to relay phase information to a Subscriber Visual Basic application by way of COM+ events.

You can step through this process, or you can access the provided code samples.

Creating the DTS Package

Open and review the sample DTS package called 'MonitorDTS Sample.dts', which is located on the *SQL Server 2000 Resource Kit* CD-ROM in the folder, \ToolsAndSamples\MonitorDTS\DTS Package. Alternatively, to set up the DTS package:

1. Activate the multiphase data pump in DTS Designer. For detailed instructions, see SQL Server Books Online.

2. Create a simple DTS package that consists of a SQL Server connection to the **Northwind** database and a SQL Server connection to the **tempdb** database and a transformation between the two. The source table for the transformation should be the **Northwind.dbo.Orders** table.

3. Set the destination to create an identical table structure called **Orders2**.

4. Delete all existing transformations, select all fields, and create a single new ActiveX script transformation.

5. Set the Insert Batch Size to 250 records.

6. Save the script, task, and package.

Setting up the ActiveX Script Transformation

1. Copy and paste the sample ActiveX script transformation, which implements the multiphase functions. The file that contains this script is called 'MPDP Transform.txt' and is located on the *SQL Server 2000 Resource Kit* CD-ROM in the folder, \ToolsAndSamples\MonitorDTS\DTS Package. Alternatively, to set up the data pump script: Go into the properties of the new transformation to edit its ActiveX script.

2. Click the **Phases** tab, and select the check boxes for all eight phases that are shown.

3. Click **AutoGenerate** to create Visual Basic script placeholder event functions for each phase. Alternatively, copy a version of the completed transformation script from the file called 'MPDP Transform.txt', which is located on the *SQL Server 2000 Resource Kit* CD-ROM in the above mentioned folder.

4. At the top of the script, outside of any of the functions, add the following code. This code creates a global function called **PhaseRelay**. The **PhaseRelay** function accepts a parameter that is to be used as a user-defined monitor ID. The script should look like:

```
Dim oMonitor
Function PhaseRelay( MonitorID )

'Set Status Info within Monitor object & process the event
oMonitor.PhaseRelay MonitorID _
    ,DTSTransformPhaseInfo.CurrentPhase _
    ,DTSTransformPhaseInfo.CurrentSourceRow _
    ,DTSTransformPhaseInfo.DestinationRowsComplete _
    ,DTSTransformPhaseInfo.ErrorCode _
    ,DTSTransformPhaseInfo.ErrorRows _
    ,DTSTransformPhaseInfo.TransformStatus
End Function
```

5. Inside of the Pre Source phase entry function, create a new instance of the DTSMonitor.DLL publisher application, set the phase status to OK, and call the PhaseRelay function:

```
Function PreSourceMain()
'Create the monitor
set oMonitor = CreateObject("MonitorDTS.PhaseRelay")

PreSourceMain = DTSTransformStat_OK
PhaseRelay(1)
End Function
```

6. Inside of the Pump Complete phase entry function, relay the phase information passed into the function, preserve the transform status, and clean up and shut down the Publisher application:

```
Function PumpCompleteMain()
PhaseRelay(1)

'Pass on the TransformStatus
PumpCompleteMain = DTSTransformPhaseInfo.TransformStatus

'Release the monitor object
set oMonitor = nothing
End Function
```

7. At the end of the Row Transform phase entry function, just before the function ends, call the PhaseRelay function to report the row transform status that the script determined for that phase:

```
Function RowTransformMain()
...
   RowTransformMain = DTSTransformStat_OK
   PhaseRelay(1)
End Function
```

8. Inside of the Insert Success and Insert Failure phase entry functions, relay the phase information at the beginning of the function, and set the phase status to OK:

```
Function InsertFailureMain()
PhaseRelay(1)
InsertFailureMain = DTSTransformStat_OK
End Function


'----------------------------------------------------------


Function BatchCompleteMain()
PhaseRelay(1)

'Pass on the TransformStatus
BatchCompleteMain = DTSTransformPhaseInfo.TransformStatus
End Function
```

9. Inside of the other phase entry functions, relay the phase information passed into each function, and preserve the transform status:

```
Function TransFailureMain()
PhaseRelay(1)

'Pass on the TransformStatus
TransFailureMain = DTSTransformPhaseInfo.TransformStatus
End Function


'----------------------------------------------------------


Function BatchCompleteMain()
PhaseRelay(1)
```

```
'Pass on the TransformStatus
BatchCompleteMain = DTSTransformPhaseInfo.TransformStatus
End Function


'-----------------------------------------------------------

Function PostSourceMain()
PhaseRelay(1)

'Pass on the TransformStatus
PostSourceMain = DTSTransformPhaseInfo.TransformStatus
End Function
```

Executing the Solution

To step through the solution presented above, follow these steps:

1. Execute the DTS package and verify that it completes and processes 830 rows without error.

2. Start up the subscriber application by executing MonitorDTSWatch.exe. The form with the flow diagram should come up with no activity. Select the phases for which you would like to set initial breakpoints.

3. Execute the DTS package and monitor the activity using MonitorDTSWatch.exe. Use the breakpoints to examine phase information and transformation status. Trace the process flow lines between the current phase, which is green, and the previous phase, which is orange.

4. Start another instance of the subscriber application. Notice how multiple subscribers can monitor and implement COM+ event calls from a single publisher.

Suggested Enhancements

There are many opportunities for enhancing this solution. For example:

- Create other COM+ events. The architecture now in place can easily support different types of events. Consider creating separate events or handlers for different transformation status or error codes.

- Record the phase information to a journal file or database table for later examination. Incorporate that feedback into a new event handler that replays a data pump process.

- Push data fields out across events or selected rows. Recycle the data out-of-process from DTS.

- Create a centralized monitor that could easily receive events from multiple monitors.

- Incorporate Microsoft Messaging Queuing into the publisher and subscriber applications to enable asynchronous monitoring.

Analysis Services

Cubes in the Real World

Microsoft® SQL Server™ 2000 Analysis Services offers myriad options for creating cubes, and the flexibility and power to support almost any business case. This chapter presents practical guidelines for designing cubes and dimensions, design fundamentals, and other considerations.

Design Fundamentals

When using any online analytical processing (OLAP) product, including Analysis Services, several common fundamental design considerations arise. Typically, OLAP products are used to present aggregation data efficiently, while lessening the load that large queries and on-the-fly aggregation put on data warehouse and online transaction processing (OLTP) data sources. Calculating and storing aggregation data in a separate area for later retrieval by the OLAP product allows users to retrieve a large amount of information while it reduces the amount of data to be processed. This functionality, while it relieves data warehouses of the potentially large workload of aggregating and responding to such queries by users, presents its own special set of issues.

Two of the most common issues, *data explosion* and *sparsity*, are caused by OLAP products' need to establish and access aggregation storage. Although Analysis Services efficiently handles both issues, understanding them can improve your cube design and performance.

Data Explosion

The term *data explosion* applies to the tendency of cube structures to grow exponentially due to excessive aggregation. In other words, data explosion occurs when, in the interests of improving performance, too many pre-calculated aggregations are generated and stored for a cube. In theory, every non-leaf member in a cube can be pre-calculated such that every aggregation in a cube can be read from disk storage instead of being calculated at run time, increasing query performance. In reality, aggregation storage can increase exponentially, easily outstripping the storage requirements of the fact table upon which the cube is based.

Analysis Manager provides two effective mechanisms, the Storage Design Wizard and the Usage-Based Optimization Wizard, to intelligently manage aggregation storage. The Storage Design Wizard uses mathematical simulations to determine the optimal aggregation storage pattern based on a uniform query distribution, and can modify the simulation to limit either storage requirements or performance gain. The Storage Design Wizard is based on a uniform simulation of usage patterns for a given cube. Consequently, the performance increase is not as much as it would be if the actual usage patterns for a cube were analyzed. The Usage-Based Optimization Wizard can analyze actual usage patterns from a variety of viewpoints and generate aggregations tailored to the actual usage patterns of the cube. By using both the Storage Design Wizard and the Usage-Based Optimization Wizard when designing aggregations, you can minimize data explosion and tailor cube performance to the particular needs of your users.

For more information about aggregation design and impact, see "Aggregations" later in this chapter.

Sparsity

Sparsity is a measurement of the density of data within a cube or dimension. The more empty cells found in a cube, the sparser the cube data. Ideally, a cube should contain few or no empty cells; realistically, cubes will contain empty cells based on the dimensions from which the cube is organized.

Dimension sparsity, similarly, is a measurement of empty members (members with no data associated to them in any fact table) within a dimension. The more empty members found in a dimension, the more likely the dimension is to introduce cube sparsity when employed in a cube.

In traditional OLAP systems, disk storage is allocated for every intersection of members across dimensions in a cube, even if the resulting cell is empty (in other words, it contains no data). In other OLAP products, creating a sparse cube means that disk storage is wasted because of a lack of cube data. Because Analysis Services does not allocate storage for empty cells, disk storage is effectively handled for sparse cubes; in terms of storage, all cubes are completely dense. However, a sparse cube can also indicate a flawed cube design.

The primary cause of cube sparsity is the use of dimensions with sparse or unrelated data. This may seem obvious, but the combination of even marginally sparse dimensions can exponentially increase the sparsity of a cube.

For example, the following diagram indicates three dimension hierarchies used to construct a cube for tracking orders. Each is based on a dimension table that contains the definitions for the members of each dimension. Not all the members of all the dimensions contain data, however; not all the customers in the Customers dimension, for instance, have purchased a given product in the Product dimension, nor have all customers purchased a given product for every member in the Time dimension. For this example, each dimension has five members, three of which have data completely associated with the other dimensions.

For example, Customer 1 in the Customers dimension has purchased Product 2 in the Products dimension, during the period indicated by the Time 1 member in the Time dimension.

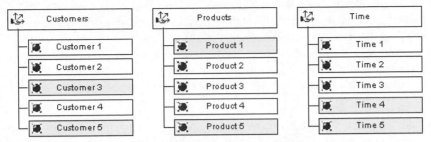

By themselves, the dimensions do not appear overly sparse; each dimension has members with relevant fact table data. If these dimensions are used together in a cube, however, the sparsity of the cube increases exponentially with each dimension, because the introduction of each dimension exponentially increases the number of cells within the cube. The following diagram indicates which cells actually contain data.

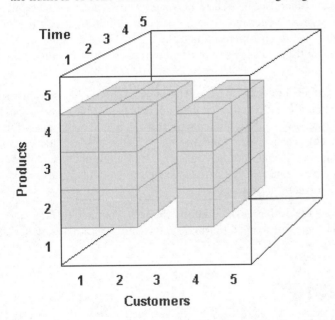

Although three out of five members of each dimension have relevant data, out of a possible total of 125 cells (five times five times five) in the constructed cube (not counting aggregate members), only 27 cells (three times three times three) are actually populated. The other cells represent intersections of empty members, creating empty cells in the cube.

This cube is a theoretical example; in reality, many dimensions are much more sparse than those indicated in the previous diagrams. The previous diagram, for example, assumes that all members with data in each dimension are completely cross-linked. Customer 1 in the Customers dimension has purchased all three Products dimension members in all three periods indicated by the members in the Time dimension. Even this level of density is rare in real-world situations. Unfortunately, sparse dimensions are often unavoidable; dimension structures are a tradeoff between density and granularity. In order to increase granularity, density is reduced as more potentially empty members are added. In order to increase data density, granularity is reduced, as members are often pre-aggregated into the underlying dimension table.

Dimensions with unrelated data can also greatly increase cube sparsity, especially if the dimensions are included as part of an associative relationship. For example, a business case is designed to compare the sales from retail customers with the sales from vendors, so a cube with three dimensions representing sales, customers, and vendors is created. The Customers dimension organizes retail customers by location, the Vendors dimension organizes vendors by sales region and vendor type, and the Orders dimension organizes order quantities by date. Both the Customers and Vendors dimension share elements with the Orders dimension, but not with each other. Because customers and vendors do not directly relate, from the viewpoint of the underlying data source, the result is a very sparse cube. In this case, it is easier to construct two cubes, one for vendors and one for customers, which share the Orders dimension. A number of techniques can be used to correlate the data across two (or more) cubes without requiring that a very sparse cube be created.

Query performance can also be adversely affected by cube sparsity. However, Analysis Services manages the storage and access to multidimensional data so efficiently that the impact is negligible. For example, a very sparse cube can take slightly longer to resolve calculated members and calculated cells, and MDX functions involving empty cells, such as **CoalesceEmpty** or **NonEmptyCrossjoin**, take slightly longer to process because of the large volume of empty cells that must be considered by such functions. Only very sparse, very large cubes will be affected on performance – for all practical purposes, cube sparsity provides a negligible performance impact in Analysis Services.

The best way to prevent sparsity is to review the design of shared dimensions, and ensure that the appropriate balance of density and granularity is maintained. For more information on dimension design, see "Designing Dimensions" later in this chapter.

Designing Dimensions

The design of dimensions in Analysis Services is central to cube design; after all, a cube is a representation of aggregated fact table data organized along dimensions.

The key influence on the design of dimensions is the structure of the underlying dimension data. Companies that employ an OLTP strategy complex enough to require an OLAP solution often have an established data warehouse, whose fact and dimension tables can be used to create dimensions and cubes in Analysis Services. Although it is possible to derive the required dimension design and the resulting underlying dimension and fact table structure by starting with the end result of the desired cube and working backwards, is not recommended for companies that have established data warehouses. This approach is better suited to solutions tailored to a small but specific set of business requirements, or used as part of a comprehensive data warehousing strategy, to better identify data warehouse business requirements.

Initial Design Questions

Two questions must be asked when designing dimensions; the answers directly influence the rest of the dimension design. Should a star schema or a snowflake schema be used, and, should dimensions be shared or private?

Star Schema or Snowflake Schema?

When designing a dimension, the first major decision is based not on the requirements of the dimension, but on the structure of the underlying dimension tables from which the dimension is to be based. OLTP data sources typically use an entity-relationship (E-R) schema technique for modeling transactional data, because OLTP transactions usually involve a large number of transactions of small amounts of data. Data warehouses, on the other hand, usually involve fewer transactions of very large amounts of data, so E-R schema technique is not as efficient. Instead, data warehouses generally employ one of two approaches towards schema design, referred to as star schema or snowflake schema.

The following features characterize a star schema.

- One or more dimension tables, each with a generated primary key, which contain one or more descriptive fields used to determine level attributes for each dimension.

- A single fact table, containing additive and numeric fields, that employs a compound primary key. This key is constructed from the generated key of each dimension used by the fact table.

One table is used for each dimension, and that table contains all of the information needed to define a particular dimension. Most data warehouses are constructed from multiple, overlapping star schemas.

The following diagram illustrates a typical star schema.

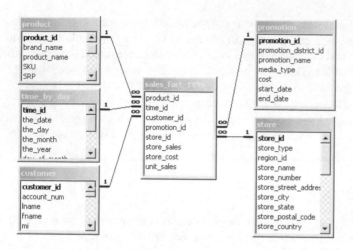

The following features characterize a snowflake schema:

- One or more dimension tables, each with a generated primary key, which contain one or more descriptive fields used to determine some level attributes for each dimension. In addition, a dimension table may contain a join to one or more other tables that supply additional level attributes for each dimension.

- A single fact table, containing additive and numeric fields, that employs a compound primary key. This key is constructed from the generated key of each dimension used by the fact table.

In a snowflake schema, more than one table is required to completely define the relationship of a dimension to a fact table. For example, the Product table uses the Product_Class table in the **FoodMart 2000** sample database to provide additional level attribute information, such as product department and product subcategory, about the Product dimension. The Product dimension employs a snowflake schema, because more than one table is required in order to completely describe the dimension.

The following diagram illustrates a typical snowflake schema:

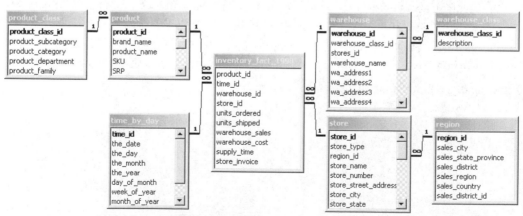

The most common reason for using a snowflake schema is to reduce storage requirements for large dimension tables. Low cardinality fields are removed from a dimension table, stored in a separate table with a primary key, and joined back to the dimension table. This can considerably reduce storage for a dimension table that includes members, but can also introduce complexity.

Another reason for using a snowflake schema is to supply information, not about the level attributes of a dimension, but the secondary attributes of a level. For example, the County table contains basic demographic information, such as name, state, region, and so on, for a given county, as well as sales and marketing aggregation data for that county. The Customers table has a join to the County table, but the information supplied by that join is not needed directly to describe a customer. However, it can provide additional information, in the form of member properties, to the County level or, in the form of additional levels, to the Customers dimension. While the County table is not required to describe the Customers dimension completely, using a snowflake schema allows additional information to be added to the Customers dimension that would otherwise require a separate dimension.

Data warehouses and other data sources suitable for OLAP are usually constructed by using overlapping star or snowflake schemas. For example, because the Customers dimension table would serve for the Orders fact table and the Returns fact table, the star schema representing orders and the star schema representing returns would both contain the Customers dimension. Other forms of database modeling, such as E-R modeling, can also be used, but are not recommended. Although it is possible to create dimensions and cubes directly from OLTP data sources, for better performance, using a separate data source derived from the OLTP data source is recommended. Because of the high transactional demand placed on OLTP databases, OLTP database systems are aggressively optimized for a very high number of insert/update transactions. Data warehouses, on the other hand, are usually bulk-loaded during off hours and optimized with an emphasis on retrieval speed and efficiency. Analysis Services can load an OLTP database system with requests that require high volumes of data, especially during cube and dimension processing.

Dimensions in Analysis Services can be optimized based on the type of schema used for the underlying dimension tables. In general, snowflake schemas should be used only when necessary, as the additional joins impact query performance, especially with ROLAP dimensions or dimensions that store few or no aggregations.

For more information about using star and snowflake schemas in an overall data warehousing strategy, including performance tuning and schema optimization, see Chapter 20, "RDBMS Performance Tuning Guide for Data Warehousing."

Shared or Private?

The next decision to make when designing a dimension is whether to share it for use in multiple cubes. Typically, you will create shared dimensions to deal with almost every business case — the more conformed the dimension, the more useful it is, and therefore the more likely you will use it in multiple cubes. In rare situations, though, private dimensions are quite useful when dealing with certain business cases.

The purpose behind using a private dimension is to restrict its usage in other cubes. Unlike shared dimensions, private dimensions cannot be used in multiple cubes, nor can a private dimension be the source for creating a virtual dimension. Although usage restrictions can be accomplished with dimension security, you may want to restrict the use of a dimension because of its specificity or sparsity. For example, a dimension that relates specifically to a small subset of inventory may not be suitable for general use, but is appropriate for providing reporting for a specific client or vendor. In this business case, a private dimension may be more appropriate than a shared dimension.

Private dimensions offer an advantage in terms of administration: private dimensions are always processed when the cube they reside in is processed.

In addition, private dimensions offer a hard level of security for sensitive data; because private dimensions cannot be used in other cubes, correlating sensitive data can be controlled. Although dimension and cell security features can be utilized to enforce security, a private dimension provides a straightforward and solid barrier against unauthorized usage of data.

Shared dimensions offer a performance advantage because shared dimensions make more efficient use of memory; the members of a shared dimension are loaded once, then cached. This allows for faster response times from queries that involve shared dimensions.

You should consider the question of making shared or private dimensions carefully. Although a previously shared dimension can be made private, the reverse is not true; once a dimension becomes private, it can never be shared. Unless your business requirements indicate that a dimension should not be used in multiple cubes, shared dimensions are usually recommended.

Design Guidelines

- Treat a dimension as an object interface.

    Approach the design of dimensions in a manner similar to the design of objects in an object-oriented programming language. A dimension can be thought of as an interface to a cube, with the structure of the dimension used to provide attributes to a cube.

    Shared dimensions are intended for use in more than one cube; the decision to include levels, members, member properties, and so on can be approached in the same way that the decision to include attributes in an object interface is approached. As with any other interface, polymorphism is inversely proportional to the specificity of its attributes - the more numerous and specific the attributes of an interface, the fewer the number of objects that can use it. Abstraction mechanisms, such as virtual dimensions and dimension hierarchies, can exploit a well-designed regular dimension to provide additional complexity as required.

    You should design shared dimensions independently of the design of a specific cube, for reasons similar to those used when designing an interface implemented by more than one object. A private dimension, on the other hand, acts as a private interface, and as such should be designed for a specific cube.

Dimension Varieties

The power and flexibility of dimensions has been greatly expanded in Microsoft® SQL Server™ 2000 Analysis Services, to provide support for complex OLAP applications. Many of the new dimension varieties and characteristics are interrelated; cube performance can be affected not just by a dimension variety, but also by the combination of characteristics used in a dimension.

SQL Server Books Online details the combinations of dimension characteristics that can be used within each dimension variety. Practical application of dimension varieties and characteristics depends, however, almost entirely on the business requirements for the dimension and the cubes for which the dimension is created.

Changing Dimensions

Changing dimensions are dimensions optimized for frequent changes to either data or structure. Unlike other dimensions, changing dimensions do not need to be fully processed when certain types of changes are made to the underlying dimension data or dimension structure. Because fully processing a dimension also requires fully processing the cubes to which the dimension is associated, changing dimensions can increase the availability of cubes whose data changes frequently.

Changing dimensions can also take advantage of lazy processing in cubes, further increasing the availability of data for users accessing cubes that include the dimension.

Changing dimensions should be used when immediate user availability to aggregated data is needed or when member and hierarchy flexibility is required. Although changing dimensions do allow a great deal of flexibility in terms of both data and structure, the tradeoff is performance. Typically, queries involving changing dimensions take much longer than queries involving regular dimensions.

Design Guidelines

- Use sparingly, and only where appropriate.

  Changing dimensions are best used for medium-latency to low-latency OLAP data. Most dimensions contain high-latency OLAP data, in which the time taken to reflect changes in underlying dimension data can be measured in days, weeks or months. At the other end of the scale, real-time OLAP demonstrates low-latency OLAP data, in which immediate changes to underlying dimension data are reflected as they happen. Changing dimensions occupy the middle to low end of this scale, including real-time OLAP.

  Changing dimensions, by definition, reflect frequent unpredictable changes to the data and structure of a dimension. However, not all changes to the underlying dimension data need to be quickly reflected to users - consider the business requirements of such data first. If changes do not need to be made available to users quickly, avoid using a changing dimension.

A good rule to use is:

- If the granularity of changes to a dimension is finer than the granularity of processing for a dimension or for the cubes that include the dimension, and the data needs to be reflected in cubes that include the dimension, consider a changing dimension.

For example, if you plan on processing the entire database once each week, but you expect daily hierarchical changes to a particular dimension that should be shown to users, a changing dimension may be appropriate. Conversely, you may want to increase your processing frequency for this particular dimension to once each day and avoid using a changing dimension, increasing query performance and decreasing latency for your users.

Virtual Dimensions

A virtual dimension is a type of changing dimension that allows you to use an existing regular dimension to obtain additional information. For example, a virtual dimension based on the member properties of a regular dimension can provide a different view on existing dimension data without the cost of additional disk storage.

Virtual dimensions are fully indexed, improving query performance over previous versions of Analysis Services. However, because virtual dimensions do not store source data or aggregations, queries involving virtual dimensions may not perform as well as queries against regular dimensions.

By using virtual dimensions based on member properties you can fully exploit the benefits of member properties. In terms of overall design, it is more efficient to use virtual dimensions that are based on regular dimensions but are specifically targeted for a subset of dimension data represented by member properties, than it is to use multiple regular dimensions based on the same underlying dimension data.

Design Guidelines

- Use to exploit additional data offered by regular dimensions.

  The greatest value of virtual dimensions is the ability to expose existing additional regular dimension data, such as member properties, in a different hierarchical framework; this is especially useful when used with regular dimensions that represent multiple yet similar business entities.

- Do not use as a replacement for dimension hierarchies.

  Avoid using virtual dimensions just to represent a regular dimension with a different hierarchy; better performance and easier administration is gained by using multiple hierarchies for a dimension. Dimension hierarchies are basically regular dimensions with aggregation and data shared with a base regular dimension, organized into a different hierarchical structure. Virtual dimensions can be used for this purpose, but they do not perform as well. For more information on the use of multiple hierarchies, see "Dimension Hierarchies" later in this chapter.

Parent-Child Dimensions

A parent-child dimension is a special dimension designed to support self-referencing dimension tables in data warehouses. In regular dimensions, the level structure of the hierarchy depends on the number of columns chosen from the underlying dimension tables and the number of columns that are mapped to a level in the dimension. Each column used for a regular dimension represents a single business entity in a dimension; for example, the members of a Country level in a geographic dimension can represent countries.

This is not true of parent-child dimensions. In such a dimension, two columns from the underlying dimension table define relationships among the members of the dimension. One column supplies the unique identifier of the referenced member, and the other column supplies the unique identifier of the parent for a referenced member.

By its very nature, such a self-referencing dimension table can produce an unbalanced hierarchy. For example, the following table lists the employees of an organization.

Employee ID	Name	Parent Employee ID
1	Bill	
2	Ralph	1
3	Jane	2
4	Tom	3
5	Beth	4
6	Elaine	5

In this example, not all records have a parent employee ID – one record must be at the top. Analysis Services supports four ways to determine a topmost member, or root member, through the **Root Member If** property of a dimension. For more information on the settings for the **Root Member If** property, see SQL Server Books Online.

A parent-child dimension can also support ragged hierarchies. To do this, the **Skipped Levels Column** property must contain the name of a column in the dimension table that stores the number of skipped levels between the referenced member and its parent member.

There are other benefits to parent-child dimensions, such as the ability to write-enable a parent-child dimension. Virtual dimensions and regular dimensions based on ROLAP partitions are also considered changing dimensions, but that encompasses the possibility of changes to underlying dimension data by other mechanisms. Write-enabling a parent-child dimension allows you to change the hierarchy or properties of members in the dimension directly, using Analysis Services as the primary mechanism, instead of indirectly changing the dimension hierarchy by changing the underlying dimension table data, using the relational database server as the primary mechanism. Unlike write-enabled cubes, which use a special table to maintain changes to the cube, parent-child dimensions write directly to the underlying dimension table. This feature is useful in rapid development scenarios or when an established data warehouse does not exist.

Parent-child dimensions have some limitations. Parent-child dimensions cannot support huge dimensions (ten million members or more), because parent-child dimensions require MOLAP storage. Because of this storage requirement, parent-child dimensions cannot support real-time OLAP.

Design Guidelines

- Use only where absolutely necessary.

    Parent-child dimensions offer some very powerful features, but at a high cost in performance and ease of administration. A parent-child dimension is used only for business scenarios that demand an unbalanced hierarchy; avoid using them in any other situation.

Dimension Characteristics

Dimension characteristics help determine the behavior and organization of a dimension by supplying additional functionality to each variety of dimension. Multiple hierarchies, member properties, even storage and processing options influence the performance of an individual dimension and the performance of the cubes to which the dimension is associated. Because of this potential effect on cubes, understanding the complex interaction of dimension characteristics and varieties should be a priority when designing cubes.

Dimension Hierarchies

Using hierarchies within dimensions properly can greatly increase dimension performance and allow you to represent business data more efficiently. A dimension can represent three types of hierarchies: balanced, unbalanced, and ragged.

Typically, the underlying dimension data and table structure will determine the hierarchy used by a given dimension. If a specific hierarchy is desired, the underlying dimension data can be represented by a database view.

Balanced Hierarchies

A balanced hierarchy contains no skipped or empty levels. All branches of the dimension hierarchy tree descend through all existing levels, and each level has at least one member. All members at a given level have the same number of ancestors. This type of hierarchy is usually represented in time dimensions or in highly conformed dimensions that represent a specific business entity, such as a product or an order. Most dimensions employ a balanced hierarchy.

Unbalanced Hierarchies

An unbalanced hierarchy, in contrast to a balanced hierarchy, can contain skipped or empty levels, and levels that contain no members can exist. Similarly, members at a given level may have different numbers of ancestors. Branches of an unbalanced hierarchy may not descend through all existing levels.

Unbalanced hierarchies can be used in dimensions that represent organizational or accounting data, or for dimensions with unclear level demarcation. Because of the inferential nature of unbalanced hierarchies, only parent-child dimensions can support unbalanced hierarchies.

Ragged Hierarchies

The only conceptual difference between a ragged and an unbalanced hierarchy is the fact that branches of a ragged hierarchy descend through all existing levels, even levels that do not contain data. Unlike an unbalanced hierarchy, a placeholder member is automatically created to support the subordinate levels for levels without data, ensuring that all branches descend through all levels. The placeholder also ensures that all members at a given level have the same number of ancestors. The representation of placeholder members is managed through the use of the **Hide Member If** property in the Dimension Editor. For more information about placeholders and the **Hide Member If** property, see SQL Server Books Online.

Geography-based dimensions, especially those that use international data, or dimensions that represent multiple yet similar business entities are excellent candidates for ragged hierarchies.

Multiple Hierarchies In A Single Dimension

You can provide different views of existing dimension data by creating multiple hierarchies for a single dimension. Analysis Services can create aggregations that are optimized on the common members and levels of all the hierarchies for a given dimension. The benefit to this is that all of the hierarchies of a given dimension use the same source data for aggregation purposes and use as much of the aggregated data as possible. This can save disk storage, especially in the case of very large and huge dimensions, as well as increase performance more than creating separate regular dimensions with a different hierarchy in each one.

Adding a dimension hierarchy to a dimension is not unlike creating a view for a table in a relational database. While the table contains the source data, the view offers a different way of examining the source data. Although at first glance this functionality appears to overlap with the functionality of virtual dimensions, there are differences. Unlike a virtual dimension, a dimension hierarchy can store aggregations as needed, providing additional performance gain when querying a cube. Also, most client tools understand the concept of dimensions with multiple hierarchies, and can use this functionality to full effect.

Dimensions that store highly conformed business information are likely candidates for the use of multiple hierarchies, such as customer or order information, to prevent duplicate aggregations. Time dimensions are also excellent candidates for the use of multiple hierarchies, especially for financial applications.

Design Guidelines

*   Know your dimension data.

    Understanding how the underlying dimension data is structured and stored will all but determine the hierarchical structures needed by the dimension, as well as the dimension type itself. For example, if your dimension data is used to illustrate the management organization of a particular company, you will most likely need to employ an unbalanced hierarchy, which also means you will need to construct a parent-child dimension, which in turn determines the value of several other properties in a dimension.

    If the properties of a particular dimension type are desired, you may need to construct a view to base the dimension on, in order to confirm the underlying dimension data to an appropriate hierarchy.

*   Use multiple hierarchies instead of many levels.

    Rather than constructing a regular dimension with ten levels and a dozen or so member properties to organize business entities, such as products, with many different categorization attributes, use multiple hierarchies to group such business entities in different, but related, views of aggregation. Time dimensions are also prime candidates for this approach; create different hierarchies to represent different views of time periods, such as fiscal year and calendar year, of the same dimension data, instead of attempting to combine both views into a single hierarchy.

    This approach should be balanced with the use of virtual dimensions to supply additional views of aggregation. For more information about the use of virtual dimensions, see "Virtual Dimensions" later in this chapter.

Levels and Members

The layout and data associated with members directly influences the processing performance, query performance, and resources needed for a dimension.

Member Keys

The member key is the most important property of a member when it comes to processing performance. During dimension processing the server checks each member against the index of the dimension. If the member key does not exist in the index, the server inserts the new member key into the index for the dimension, which is also sorted by the member key.

Based on the cardinality of the dimension, hierarchies in which the count of members for a given parent in a level varies widely may be slower to process than hierarchies in which the count of members for each parent is more balanced. When the dimension is queried, groups of members are sent to the client based on parentage. A large number of members for a single parent, then, can degrade performance, as large blocks of data must be transferred to the client.

Design Guidelines

- Include as few levels as possible.

  Reducing complexity is one of the primary reasons OLAP technology is used. When you design dimensions, your view should be on balancing complexity and ease of use. Too many levels in a dimension can make it too complex to easily reference in an MDX query, and it can impact performance and increase data explosion because each level above the last level contains aggregate members. Instead, if an alternate view on dimension data is needed, consider using a different hierarchy or a virtual dimension for the dimension in question.

- Avoid data type coercion for member keys.

  The size and data type of the member key value itself can affect processing and query performance. Avoid creating member keys with a data type different from that of the value actually stored in the underlying dimension table; coercion of data types takes time during processing. If data type coercion is necessary, create a view or table on the relational database that converts the data type as needed.

- Try to use integer member key values.

  When you choose a data type for a member key, remember that a numeric type (such as a 32-bit long integer) performs much better than a string, especially if the string for the member key is different than the member name. If a string is necessary, use a string with a data length as small as possible. A 4-byte numeric, such as a long integer, performs much better than an 8-byte numeric, such as a double precision number.

  If a string must be used as a member key to satisfy business requirements, one method to improve performance is to change the compare mode of the server. Binary comparison performs best, followed by case sensitive comparison and case insensitive comparison. Before you consider this, though, first try all other options; changing the compare mode of the server affects all string comparisons, and so may affect query performance in unexpected ways.

- Use unique member keys and names wherever possible.

  Unique member keys allow the Analysis server to use the identifier supplied by the underlying relational database, increasing query and processing performance. For more information about the performance benefits of unique member keys, see "Dimension Storage and Processing" later in this chapter.

  Similarly, unique member names in a given dimension allow for faster addressing when MDX queries are run against the Analysis server where the cube with that dimension resides.

Member Properties

Initially, member properties in Analysis Services seem like an interesting, useful idea because they supply a useful mechanism for storing additional attributes of members in a given level of a dimension.

However, these extra attributes also allow you to create a virtual dimension with a hierarchy completely different from that of the regular dimension on which it is based, yet still take advantage of shared aggregations and storage. Member properties can also provide an easy mechanism for custom rollups, specialized calculations, and multiple language implementations, without the difficulties associated with pre-aggregation or data transformation on the relational database.

Design Guidelines

- Include as few as possible, as high in the hierarchy as possible.

  Because member properties are cached along with other dimension data, retrieving member properties can be extremely fast. Conversely, because member properties place additional load on the server-side cache, they should be used only as needed if performance is a priority. A good approach to using member properties is to include only the minimum needed at the highest level possible to satisfy business requirements. For example, in a geographical dimension with levels based on Country, State, County, and Postal Code, a member property for sales regions can be created on either the County or Postal Code level. Creating it on the County level will save disk storage and cache space, which increases query performance.

Real-time OLAP

Any dimension that is based on a Microsoft® SQL Server™ 2000 data source and that uses ROLAP storage can take advantage of real-time OLAP, also referred to as real-time updates. Real-time OLAP is on-the-fly aggregation taken one step further: the underlying data source provides notification of changes to the fact table of a dimension. This allows the dimension to aggregate in real-time. SQL Server indexed views are used as the underlying dimension and fact tables to support real-time OLAP, to take advantage of the aggregation storage and performance benefits offered by indexed views.

For more information about real-time OLAP, see "Real-Time Cubes" later in this chapter.

Design Guidelines

- Use this feature sparingly.

  Although real-time OLAP is a powerful and exciting new feature for Analysis Services, most business scenarios do not require real-time OLAP. Real-time OLAP places real-time load on both the Analysis server and the underlying relational database, and should be used only if there is a very strong business requirement for low-latency OLAP data.

- Design the dimension around real-time OLAP, not with it.

  The decision to use real-time OLAP should be a central issue in designing a dimension; do not design a dimension and then later decide to include real-time OLAP. The structure and use of a dimension is heavily influenced by the decision to use real-time OLAP, which affects dimension processing, dimension data latency, dimension storage requirements, and other factors. If real-time OLAP is needed, consider the ramifications and make your decision early in the design process of the dimension.

- Familiarize yourself with indexed views.

  A new feature of SQL Server 2000, indexed views provide the speed and power of indexes with the abstraction, flexibility, and performance benefits of views. The requirements of an indexed view, however, should be considered when using real-time OLAP. Some data warehouses may not be able to exploit indexed views; query time increases because aggregations cannot be stored.

Dimension Security

Dimension security should be not considered as a final step, applied to a fully designed dimension after construction. Instead, dimension security should be considered an integral part of the overall design process for a dimension; dimension security alters the way a dimension is employed and viewed by users.

Design Guidelines

When designing dimension security, keep these considerations in mind.

- Enable visual totals for all visible parent levels.

  By default, visual totals are disabled for all visible parent levels. This means that, although you may have hidden several levels and members, the aggregate value for visible parent levels still includes the hidden data; users may be able to deduce secure information from the visible parent levels. Enabling visual totals allows you to display to the user the aggregate values of visible parent levels computed with only the subordinate levels and members visible to the user.

- Use a layered approach to roles.

  Dimension security is directly attached to roles. A user can be assigned to multiple roles, as is common in business scenarios, with a layered approach to various permissions. Therefore, dimension security should have a layered approach to various permissions. Avoid using the All Users role as a blanket security tool; creating very specific, encapsulated roles that provide access to specific layers of dimension data will help, not only in the security of a particular dimension, but in all of the cubes that use that dimension. It will also ease administration, as there are typically users that do not fit into a single, job-oriented role; using multiple roles to encapsulate specific business requirements allows you, as an administrator, the ability to match roles to specific job actions, not just to the job.

Dimension Storage and Processing

Dimension Storage

The storage mode used by a dimension directly affects not just the query and processing performance of the dimension, but also the results obtained by querying the dimension.

Typically, MOLAP is the recommended storage mode for dimensions. Although ROLAP may reduce disk storage size, it places additional load on the underlying relational database, and can provide misleading information if the underlying dimension data changes even infrequently.

Dimension Processing

The design of a dimension influences processing performance. The impact on processing speed, query performance, and storage increases as the number of levels and members within a dimension increase. More disk storage is allocated not only for the data, but also for the index files needed by the dimension, and this affects not just the dimension, but also any cube that uses the dimension.

When designing dimensions, do not include members or levels that are not needed. As dimension information is cached on both server and client, this design change can noticeably improve not only server response, but also client application speed.

While unique members minimally affect processing performance for dimensions, the proper (or improper) use of unique members can greatly affect the processing and query performance of cubes a dimension is associated with, especially based on the storage mode of the partition involved. For more information about the effect of unique members on cube processing and querying, see "Cube Storage and Processing" later in this chapter.

Design Guidelines

- Use MOLAP for dimension storage as often as possible.

  MOLAP dimensions use a multidimensional storage area separate from the underlying dimension data, while ROLAP dimensions directly use the underlying dimension data. Hence, if a change to the underlying dimension data is made, a ROLAP dimension may provide inconsistent information. ROLAP is only necessary for dimensions with ten million or more members, or for dimensions that support real-time OLAP. Avoid using ROLAP unless your dimension fits these criteria.

- Use unique member keys whenever possible.

  The proper use of unique members, especially at the lowest level of the dimension, helps in removing unneeded joins when processing a dimension, or for processing a partition using the dimension in a cube. A shared dimension, for example, that meets the following requirements for the members of the lowest level of the dimension does not require a join to be made when processing a partition that uses the dimension:

  - The values in the member key column are unique.

  - A one-to-one relationship exists between the member key column and the member name column.

  - There is only one join between the underlying fact table for the partition and the dimension tables of the dimension, based on the member key column.

- Ensure that all columns involved in joining the underlying dimension table with fact tables are indexed.

  If joins are required to process a dimension, especially after the dimension has been added to a cube, indexing all involved columns will speed the access and retrieval time from the underlying dimension table.

Designing Cubes

The design of a cube, as indicated in the previous section, is heavily influenced by the design of its constituent dimensions. However, there is more to cube design in Analysis Services than dimension design and implementation. In Analysis Services, cubes can use calculated members, calculated cells, named sets, actions, custom rollup formulas, and other features to make a cube more than the sum of its dimensions. Special cube varieties, such as virtual or linked cubes, can be created to take advantage of existing regular cubes, allowing an atomic approach to designing regular cubes.

Your cube design should take into account the effects of cube sparsity and data explosion.

Design Guidelines

- Treat cubes as objects.

  When designing regular cubes, approach the design process as if you were designing an object in an object-oriented programming language. Dimensions serve as interfaces to a cube, providing attributes that the cube can exploit to reveal fact table data. Encapsulate cubes the same way you would encapsulate any other object, ensuring that it reveals only the data pertinent to the purpose of the object. A cube for inventory information, for example, should not contain order information. If correlation between inventory and order information is required, build two cubes and join them across one or more common dimensions in a virtual cube, with the common dimensions serving as a pseudo-polymorphic interface between the two cubes.

- Use well-designed dimensions.

  Construct dimensions with the business purpose for the dimension as the focus; very often, dimensions are constructed that mirror exactly the underlying dimension table structure of an existing data source. While this is generally a good practice, it can be advantageous to pair similar dimensions together into parent-child dimensions in order to decrease dimension sparsity.

  Remember, too, that Analysis Services is a multidimensional presentation tool, used to solve business problems. Traditional E-R modeling techniques typically used for online transaction processing (OLTP) databases may not produce well-designed dimensions. Other techniques, such as dimensional modeling, should be employed to ensure low dimension sparsity.

- Use sparse and unrelated dimensions cautiously.

  Sparse dimensions are common and sometimes required in order to satisfy a specific business requirement. Too many sparse dimensions included in the same cube can degrade performance when using complex MDX queries. As a rule, if you have included five or more sparse dimensions in your cube, you can probably redesign the cube into two smaller cubes with at least one shared dimension. A virtual cube can later be used if correlation between the two cubes is required.

Cube Varieties

In contrast to dimensions, the basic functionality of cubes does not vary as much among cube varieties. For example, the primary difference between a regular cube and a distributed partitioned cube has nothing to do with the direct functionality of the cube, but the retrieval of the underlying data for the cube. Similarly, virtual cubes and linked cubes are views of regular cubes, whereas real-time cubes are regular cubes using ROLAP partitions that support real-time OLAP.

Regular Cubes

The best way to define a regular cube is by exclusion. SQL Server Books Online describes a regular cube as ". . . a cube that is not a linked cube, virtual cube, or local cube." Most business requirements are satisfied with regular cubes, and will be the most commonly created cube type in SQL Server 2000 Analysis Services. Indeed, virtual cubes and linked cubes require underlying regular cubes, while write-enabled cubes, real-time cubes, and distributed partitioned cubes are regular cubes with special storage support.

When designing enterprise solutions that include Analysis Services, keep in mind that regular cubes form the basis of all Analysis Services applications. Design regular cubes first, before you plan other cubes, and approach the design process in a fashion similar to the approach used to develop objects and interfaces in an object-oriented programming language. Cubes should be designed to satisfy a specific business purpose, and should only include information relevant to that business purpose. While the temptation of creating a few super-cubes to satisfy every business requirement is strong, performance and maintainability will suffer as a result. Other cube varieties, such as virtual cubes, become more effective when cubes are designed to satisfy single business purposes.

Design Guidelines

- Always design cubes with a specific and encapsulated business focus in mind.

  Use the minimum number of dimensions required when constructing a cube designed to resolve a specific business case. When considering cube sparsity, it is often easier to construct two smaller, dense cubes and use a virtual cube or other mechanism to correlate data than to build one large, sparse cube. A good guideline to follow is the assumption that the disk storage of a fully aggregated cube will at least double with each added dimension, provided the density of data for each dimension is about the same.

Virtual Cubes

One of the most powerful features in Analysis Services is the ability to create virtual cubes - a single cube based on one or more regular cubes that share at least one common dimension. A good way to look at a virtual cube is as a view to a table in a relational database. A virtual cube gives you the ability to construct cubes in an atomic fashion, constructing individual regular cubes for specific business purposes, and then using virtual cubes to correlate data across business purposes. For example, the **FoodMart 2000** database uses the Sales cube to encapsulate aggregations relating to sales orders, while the Warehouse cube is used to encapsulate aggregations relating to inventory. The Sales and Warehouse virtual cube is then used to correlate incoming inventory against outgoing sales orders, eliminating duplication of aggregates across common dimensions and providing additional business intelligence.

However, virtual cubes are at their most effective only when at least two or three common dimensions exist in the underlying regular cubes. Because all dimensions used by all source cubes are included in the virtual cube, cube sparsity can become an issue if dissimilar cubes are used to create a virtual cube. For example, a cube with five dimensions and a cube with four dimensions, which both share only a single dimension, are used as the underlying cubes for a virtual cube. Assuming the other dimensions used in both cubes are dissimilar (that is, they share no underlying data in dimension or fact tables), the resulting virtual cube now has eight dimensions (since both cubes share a dimension), seven of which have little intersecting data. This is an extremely sparse cube by any measurement. Although Analysis Services minimizes performance issues when dealing with sparse cubes, this design is not the most efficient use of resources, and querying it could take longer than necessary due to the sheer volume of empty cells that need to be negotiated.

If you are considering constructing a virtual cube to resolve a single member or process a single MDX formula, other approaches may be more useful and require less maintenance. For example, you can meet these needs by using the MDX **LookupCube** function to create a calculated member in one of the regular cubes that uses the **LookupCube** function to retrieve information from a different regular cube.

In general, virtual cubes should be used when correlating many values across two or more congruent dimensions is required, or when most of the values along a single congruent dimension are needed, while the **LookupCube** function should be employed when a specific subset of values or members from another cube are required.

Linked Cubes

Linked cubes are an easy way for you to alias cubes from remote servers on a local server. The local server contains the meta data for the linked cube, while the remote server maintains the actual data and underlying fact table and dimension table data for the underlying regular cube. For example, a server in the central office of a health care corporation can link to cubes created at individual health care sites, and then a set of virtual cubes can be created that are based on these linked cubes to correlate data across regions.

From a business perspective, linked cubes remove the repetition of regional data and can allow access to non-conformed data sets without the construction of additional regular cubes. Another benefit is the ability to create marketable OLAP data, as access to a cube can be fully controlled.

Because both local and remote server caches are used when retrieving data from a linked cube, query performance involving linked cubes is increased in comparison to a user directly accessing a cube on a remote server, depending on network latency. Virtual cubes created from multiple regular and linked cubes allow for distribution of load across multiple servers, also improving performance.

Distributed Partitioned Cubes

The term distributed partitioned cube refers to any cube for which at least one of its partitions resides on a server other than the server used to store the meta data for the cube. For example, although server \\SERVER1 stores the Budget cube and the partition that represents the data slice for the current year, a remote partition on server SERVER2 also exists for this cube that stores the data slices for the previous five years. A third server, SERVER3, provides storage for a remote partition that stores the data slices for older data.

The primary benefit of distributed partitioned cubes is the ability to leverage mass storage servers on an existing network. In the previous example, the server \\SERVER1 is optimized for performance, not storage, but \\SERVER2 and \\SERVER3 may access RAID arrays that can support the high storage requirements of the historical data stored by the Budget cube. Because all meta data for distributed partitions resides on the server that stores the cube definition, remote management of servers that support distributed partitions is unnecessary. Synchronization of the distributed partition structure is propagated to other servers automatically.

Also, most of the processing and query performance is delegated to the server that stores the remote partition. Because of this feature, you can distribute the process and query load of a large cube across multiple servers, improving performance. The handling of this distribution is transparent; Analysis Services handles all of the details involved with synchronization, latency, and so on.

The primary drawback of distributed partitioned cubes is that remote partitions cannot be processed in parallel, nor can a remote partition be archived or restored.

Real-Time Cubes

Unlike dimensions, cubes have to satisfy more requirements in order to use real-time OLAP. Because of the notification mechanism used by Analysis Services, the underlying data for a cube must be based on a SQL Server 2000 relational database. The cube must use ROLAP partitions; however, only those partitions that require real-time OLAP need to use ROLAP storage. The ROLAP partition must either contain no aggregations, so that all aggregations are calculated on the fly, or must use a SQL Server 2000 indexed view to supply the underlying fact table data.

Both options supply the same basic functionality. Although using a ROLAP partition with no aggregations forces Analysis Services to compute and cache necessary aggregations from the fact table, using a SQL Server 2000 indexed view allows pre-computed aggregations to be stored in the index of the view, reducing computations during query time. For more information about the general performance increase provided by indexed views, refer to the white paper, "Improving Performance with SQL Server 2000 Indexed Views," available in the MSDN® Library. You should use partitions based on indexed views in preference to partitions without stored aggregations, as performance is somewhat better.

Because remote partitions cannot be used to support real-time OLAP for cubes, during the design phase you need to consider the physical architecture of the Analysis server. Typically, real-time OLAP is used for Internet and intranet-based applications desiring live information, although any client application needing low-latency OLAP data can use real-time OLAP. Real-time OLAP is not recommended as a convenient way to circumvent the implementation of a data warehouse; the necessary query load can impact the performance of an OLTP data source.

Real-time OLAP for cubes is best used when predictable latency periods can be enforced. For example, an online financial application can replicate data from an OLTP database to a data mart for a specific business purpose at set times—every 20 minutes or so. The notification mechanism for real-time OLAP handles the rest, triggering the indexing and aggregation process and refreshing the server cache.

Offline Cubes

Microsoft PivotTable™ Service provides the ability to create offline cubes (also referred to as local cubes). An offline cube is a cube constructed on the client workstation, as opposed to a cube constructed on an Analysis server.

Caching and Cubes

While many traditional OLAP products offer server-side caching of frequently accessed multidimensional data, Analysis Services also offers client-side caching. The client-side cache is managed by an algorithm that uses the frequency of access for a given query to determine which query datasets are replaced.

The client-side cache can be a benefit for cubes that use well structured and highly utilized shared dimensions. If the client-side cache can provide all of the data needed to handle a request, no network activity takes place; consequently, the response speed is much faster. The server-side cache is available to all users of a given Analysis server, so fulfilling queries that involve such shared dimensions, even if the dimension is used in different cubes queried by different users, is also much faster. The server-side cache can respond and populate the client-side cache, all without requiring direct retrieval from the cube or dimension.

Cube Characteristics

Although described as separate objects in SQL Server Books Online, cube characteristics such as partitions, aggregations, and measures can add functionality to the cube varieties discussed earlier in this chapter. Used properly, such cube characteristics can dramatically increase the performance and flexibility of cubes.

Partitions

The organization and storage method of partitions for a cube can greatly influence the query and processing performance of the cube. The use of multiple partitions greatly speeds query and processing performance for cubes, provided that the partitions are properly organized and use an appropriate storage mechanism.

Partition Organization

The first decision about using multiple partitions is typically based on the organization of the underlying fact table and dimension table data associated with a cube.

For example, underlying fact table data that is infrequently accessed (closed accounts, obsolete product lines, and so on) can be partitioned in such a way as to take advantage of storage optimizations, while frequently accessed fact table data for the same cube can be partitioned to take advantage of performance optimizations.

Creating such data slices, however, requires forethought. Because queries can retrieve data in parallel from multiple partitions, data slices should be created from commonly used delineations. Determine such delineations by separating data that will not be queried as a whole or combined in order to fulfill a query. For example, a financial cube containing accounting information is organized on a Time dimension that uses Year, Quarter, and Week levels. Most queries against this cube analyze data across weeks and quarters, but rarely across years. This cube can then be organized with a single partition for each year to improve query speed.

When processing a cube with multiple partitions, the server can also optimize processing by creating segment map and data files that involve only those dimensions and levels relevant to a particular partition, generating smaller and more efficient partitions.

Partition Storage

Although partition data can be organized as needed to satisfy business requirements, there are restrictions on which storage formats can be used based on other features used by the cube or associated dimensions.

Each partition storage mode influences the processing performance, query performance, and storage requirements of a partition. If performance is required, MOLAP or HOLAP storage modes are recommended. When queried, MOLAP performs better than HOLAP; when processed, both storage modes perform equally well. If storage is the primary concern, HOLAP partitions are recommended because, unlike MOLAP, HOLAP does not duplicate fact table data. ROLAP partitions must be used to support specific functionality such as real-time OLAP, but in all other cases ROLAP partitions are recommended only if resources are unavailable to support the other storage modes, or functionality specific to the underlying RDBMS is necessary for management purposes.

Record Size

Cube processing and query performance is directly affected by the record size of the partitions for the cube. When processing a cube, the record size impacts file size and load times, while retrieval and transfer speeds are directly affected when querying a cube.

You can estimate the size of a record by using the following calculation[1]

$$Size = (2*levels*C_{path})+(4*measures4*C_{data4})+(8*measures8*C_{data8})$$

The elements of the formula are explained below:

- levels – For fact data, the total number of levels in the cube (excluding the All level). For aggregation data, the total number of levels used in the aggregation (also excluding the All level).

- C_{path} – The coefficient of compression for paths in the cube. The value for this variable can range from 0.11 to 1.0, but is typically close to 0.25.

- measures4 – The number of 4 byte measures in the cube.

- C_{data4} – The coefficient of compression for 4 byte data in the cube. The value for this variable typically ranges from 0.6 to 0.8.

- measures8 – The number of 8 byte measures in the cube.

- C_{data8} – The coefficient of compression for 8 byte data in the cube. The value for this variable typically ranges from 0.4 to 0.5.

Minimizing record size has a direct impact on the performance of large cubes. Record size can be reduced, for example, by the use of 4-byte measures, such as long integers. Less raw disk storage is needed, and the compression coefficient for 4-byte measures is typically better than that of 8-byte measures.

---

[1]Alexander Berger and Ashvini Sharma, *OLAP Services: Performance Implications of the Architecture*. (Microsoft Corporation, June 1999)

Partition Processing

The processing performance of a partition depends not just on the optimization of the partition design, but the optimization of data retrieval from the underlying fact and dimension tables used by a partition.

Aggregations

Designing aggregation storage is essentially a tradeoff between disk storage and CPU time; more aggregations reduce CPU time, but increase disk storage requirements. Due to the nature of multidimensional structures, the disk storage can increase exponentially. For example, using the Storage Design Wizard on the **FoodMart 2000** database to increase the performance of the MOLAP partition for the Sales cube by 50 percent adds 91 aggregations, involving a total disk storage of approximately 68.987 megabytes (MB). By comparison, increasing the performance gain to 100 percent adds 1036 aggregations, involving total disk storage of approximately 1290.089 MB. In other words, if the approximate size of the data stored in the fact table used by the Sales cube is 3.64 MB (44 bytes per record, 86837 records), then the first option provides a data explosion factor of 2.06, while the second option causes a data explosion factor of 354.42.

The percentage used in deciding performance gain represents the percentage of queries that can be answered from pre-calculated aggregation data, rather than by calculations performed on underlying fact table data (also referred to as on-the-fly aggregations).

The performance gains provided by the increase in pre-calculated aggregations, however, can offset the additional resource demand for disk storage. For example, a sample query which takes approximately 3.9 seconds when run against the Sales cube after the partition has been optimized for 50 percent performance gain, takes only 2.2 seconds after the partition has been optimized for 100 percent performance gain.

Administration of a cube with a high number of pre-calculated aggregations can be adversely affected, however, because the processing time needed to refresh a cube increases with the number of aggregations. Most cubes become unavailable during processing, so increased number of pre-calculated aggregations could mean increased unavailability to users. Scheduling cube processing with Data Transformation Services (DTS) during off hours is one way to deal with this problem, however, and this is typically approached as an administrative task rather than a design issue.

There is also a point at which using pre-calculated aggregations can actually slow query performance, because it takes longer to retrieve the aggregations from disk storage than it does to calculate them on the fly from the underlying fact table data. A number of factors, such as the disk storage retrieval speed, processor speed, number of aggregations, density of data in the cube, influences the point at which the number of pre-calculated aggregations slow performance. Case-by-case experimentation can determine the optimum performance gain. Typically, the curve of performance gain and disk storage tends to flatten out after a performance gain of 70 to 80 percent. For example, reducing the performance gain on the Sales cube to 90 percent reduces the number of aggregations to 262, requiring only 319.477 MB of disk storage, and the sample query used earlier takes about 3.0 seconds to complete execution.

The storage mode of the partition the aggregation is associated with can also affect aggregation design and performance. Analysis Services compresses multidimensional storage, so aggregations stored in MOLAP or HOLAP partitions typically require less disk storage than ROLAP partitions, and ROLAP partitions are generally slower in retrieving aggregations than MOLAP partitions. Because ROLAP partitions do not store a copy of the source data, they should be used when archival storage is required to deal with historical queries, or if real-time OLAP is required. For more information about cube storage, see "Cube Storage" later in this chapter.

Design Guidelines

A balance between disk storage and processing time can be achieved with a few storage design guidelines.

- Know who uses the cube and why they use it.

  Knowing the intended users and business requirements of a cube can help you determine the right balance of stored and on-the-fly aggregations. For example, if the intended users of a given cube are limited to a specific group and the cube is tailored to resolve a specific business case, then initial storage design should involve usage-based optimization. Design the cube without designing storage, so all aggregations are calculated on the fly, and allow your user base to access the cube for a predetermined period; at least a week is advised. Then use the Usage-Based Optimization Wizard to design storage based on the queries of the previous week.

  If, on the other hand, the intended group of users is more open, or if the business requirements for the cube are loosely defined, the Storage Design Wizard can be used to set a low number of initial aggregations, typically using a 20 percent to 25 percent performance gain, then the Usage-Based Optimization Wizard can be used later to raise the number of stored aggregations as needed.

- Know what data is used when.

  Limit the number of pre-calculated aggregations stored for infrequently used dimensions. This is especially true for data in ROLAP partitions, because of the relatively large amount of disk storage required for such partitions.

Measures

From an administrative point of view, cube measures provide instruction to the cube about how to aggregate fact table data. A new method of aggregation, DISTINCT COUNT, has been added to cube measures.

Distinct count measures, a new feature for Analysis Services, allow users to analyze many-to-many relationships between business entities. You should use distinct count measures with care, however; improper use can be disastrous for a cube.

When a distinct count measure is added to a cube, the entire cube is treated as if all measures are non-additive. This means that there is no way to directly infer the value of an aggregate member from the values of immediately subordinate lower level members. For example, a music store has 100 customers, some of whom buy more than one type of product, such as cassettes, albums, and compact discs. The following MDX query represents a typical query executed against a cube with a Customers and a Products dimension, with unit sales for each product and customer represented as a SUM aggregated measure and the distinct count of customers purchasing a particular product represented as a DISTINCT COUNT measure.

```
SELECT
{ [Unit Sales], [Distinct Customers] } ON COLUMNS,
[Products].MEMBERS ON ROWS
FROM SalesCube
```

The following table represents the results returned by such an MDX query.

Product Type	Unit Sales	Distinct Customers
All products	33025	100
Audio and video equipment	30900	90
CD players	6700	60
Cassette players	1100	40
DVD players	17500	55
VHS players	5600	50
Audio and video media	2125	50
CDs	600	45
DVDs	600	30
Cassettes	175	12
VHS videotapes	750	61

The **Unit Sales** column correctly aggregates from level to level; the *All Products* level is the sum of its two subordinate levels, *Audio and video equipment* and *Audio and video media*. Each of the subordinate levels, in turn, accurately represents the aggregate of their subordinate levels.

The **Distinct Customers** column, however, does not correctly aggregate from level to level, because customers can purchase more than one product. A single customer, for example, may have purchased both a CD player and a DVD player, which means that a single customer is represented in both the CD players and DVD players level. Hence, the subordinate levels cannot be added up to represent a distinct count of customers at higher levels. The *All products* level, for example, would usually add up to 140 if its two subordinate levels were added together, a clearly incorrect total as only 100 customers actually exist in the cube.

This example represents the root of the problem for cubes that depend upon aggregation of immediately subordinate members to supply information. For this reason, SQL Server Books Online recommends that each required distinct count measure be housed in its own cube. Virtual cubes can be used to link such non-additive cubes to regular cubes for correlation.

Certain features cannot be supported for cubes that use distinct count measures. Any functionality that requires a dynamically created member will fail, returning an error value for each affected cell. The features that are affected are:

- Visual totals, including the **VisualTotals** MDX function

- Custom unary operators

- Custom rollup formulas

Design Guidelines

- Use the smallest data type possible for measures

    Cubes perform best with measures that use 4-byte values, such as long integers. While measures support larger values, disk storage and retrieval performance is affected. Similarly, more memory is required in both server-side and client-side caches for 8-byte members, such as double precision numbers.

Calculated Cells

Although calculated members are extremely powerful, they have a significant limitation. Calculated members must work on all members of a given level in the dimension in which they are created. There are elaborate, and unwieldy, ways of working around this, but they suffer from the requirement of data knowledge – the formula needs specifics about the data in order to function correctly.

Another limitation is that calculated members are not recursive; a calculated member can only be calculated once, and all calculated members are handled on the same calculation pass, based on their solve order.

Calculated cells, however, can handle specific subsets of cells within a cube, referred to as subcubes, and can be calculated iteratively in multiple calculation passes. Calculated cells can also be calculated after all calculated members are calculated, and can be applied selectively based on role security.

Design Guidelines

- Use only where absolutely necessary.

    Calculated cells can duplicate other types of functionality in Analysis Services, such as calculated members or custom unary operators. Calculated cells, however, do not perform as well as these other features, because although the calculation condition is processed whenever the cube is processed, the calculation formula is calculated only when the cube is queried.

You should use calculated cells only if the desired results cannot be efficiently achieved through the use of other features in Analysis Services.

Actions

Actions provide a way to extend client applications by supplying standardized functionality, such as execution of supplemental programs or the display of HTML pages, without having to change a client application to supply such functionality.

This feature is specifically for client applications – the Analysis server simply makes actions available to client applications, but does not actually perform such actions. Hence, actions are useful only if a client application supports their display and execution. For example, the Cube Browser in Analysis Services fully supports the display and execution of actions, and can be used to test actions before release. The statement stored by the action is parsed by the MDX parser, so that dynamically constructed actions based on cube information can be created; the action type determines the behavior the client should perform using the parsed action statement.

Actions can be used in a variety of ways within client applications. For example, the underlying SQL Server 2000 dimension table for a dimension that represents retail items contains a column that stores the picture of the retail item. Instead of including the large binary column in the dimension as a member property, forcing a large amount of data into the server-side cache and significantly impacting performance, you can construct an action that, if selected from the client application, calls a dynamically constructed URL, using SQL-DMO, to access the picture. Not only does this prevent the server-side cache from filling up with picture data, but the action limits network impact by loading only picture information for the item on demand.

Design Guidelines

* Be aware of security interaction.

  The availability of actions depends directly on the availability of the target to which the action is attached. For example, if an action is targeted for a level in a dimension that is secured through dimension security, only those users who can view the level will be able to use the action. Combined with dimension and cell security, actions can change the functionality of a client application for groups of users, an excellent way of handling multi-level functionality.

* Be aware of safety implications.

  It is possible to create potentially damaging actions, especially for client applications that take advantage of general actions, such as command execution of HTML display. As an Analysis Services administrator, you should never create actions that execute unsafe or unknown applications, nor should you create URL actions to external Web pages unless you can verify the content of the Web page as safe.

Named Sets

Named sets are a convenient way to construct subsets from a cube based on business requirements. Rather than having to copy the same large set expression in each MDX query that uses it, the set can be constructed once, named, and referred to directly in MDX queries. There is no appreciable impact on performance when using named sets.

One benefit of using named sets in MDX queries is the ability to provide an abstract reference to a specified set. The set itself can be changed to reflect changes in the structure of the cube, without necessarily having to change MDX queries that use the named set. This level of abstraction can be used for a variety of business requirements, such as sets of products or inventory, groups of accounts, and so on.

Design Guidelines

- Use wherever possible.

  The use of named sets to replace lengthy, commonly used set expressions is highly recommended. There is no appreciable performance impact one way or another, and this feature makes administration of Analysis servers easier by providing a useful level of abstraction for client applications and MDX queries in general.

Cell Security

Cell security is designed to complement dimension security as it applies to a cube. While dimension security is extremely flexible, the granularity stops at a single member. In a cube, that can affect quite a few cells. The granularity for cell security, on the other hand, stops at a single cell; you have very fine control over who sees what in a given cube.

The different cell security permissions can be difficult to understand and effectively implement, though. An excellent discussion on cell security can be found in the white paper, "Microsoft SQL Server OLAP Services Cell-Level Security," posted on the MSDN® Online Library. You should become familiar not just with cell security, but the interaction of dimension security and cell security. In particular, focus on the order of evaluation of both dimension and cell security, as it can be the primary cause for confusion when using client applications to access secured cubes and dimensions.

Design Guidelines

- Do not use as a replacement for dimension security.

  You should regard dimension security as a broad brush: General security requirements can be enforced as part of a blanket security policy for all cubes. Cell security should be viewed as a fine brush that provides you with an additional mechanism to fine-tune security for a particular cube, and is designed to complement dimension security. Because of all of the steps needed to check cell security, query performance is adversely affected. You should use dimension security in preference to cell security, and use cell security only where appropriate.

Cube Storage and Processing

Unlike dimensions, the storage and processing requirements for cubes are influenced by a number of factors.

Cube Storage

Cube storage is handled by the partitions associated with a cube, which store the aggregations associated with a cube. Fore information about partition design and processing, and about aggregations, see "Partitions" and "Aggregations" earlier in this chapter.

Cube Processing

Several additional factors can affect the processing speed of cubes. Measure size, for example, can make a difference in very large cubes.

Schema Optimization

When a cube is processed, a number of SQL queries are executed against the underlying relational data to retrieve fact and dimension data. These queries are automatically constructed using basic rules stored in the meta data of the cube.

The cube uses the dimension table information, such as the **Source Table** and **Member Key Column** properties, to construct joins between the fact table and involved dimension tables. While this information practically guarantees that the safest query possible will be executed to retrieve the appropriate fact table data, it does not guarantee that the fastest query possible will be constructed.

For example, the SQL SELECT statement constructed by Analysis Services for the first partition of the Warehouse cube in the **FoodMart 2000** database resembles the following:

```
SELECT
    store.store_id,
    time_by_day.quarter,
    time_by_day.month_of_year,
    warehouse.warehouse_id,
    product.product_id,
    inventory_fact_1997.store_invoice,
    inventory_fact_1997.supply_time,
    inventory_fact_1997.warehouse_cost,
    inventory_fact_1997.warehouse_sales,
    inventory_fact_1997.units_shipped,
```

```
    inventory_fact_1997.units_ordered,
    inventory_fact_1997.warehouse_sales-inventory_fact_1997.warehouse_Cost
FROM
    inventory_fact_1997,
    time_by_day,
    store,
    warehouse,
    product
WHERE
    (time_by_day.the_year=?) AND
    (inventory_fact_1997.time_id=time_by_day.time_id) AND
    (inventory_fact_1997.store_id=store.store_id) AND
    (inventory_fact_1997.warehouse_id=warehouse.warehouse_id) AND
    (inventory_fact_1997.product_id=product.product_id)
```

While this SQL accurately represents the data used by the first partition of the Warehouse cube, it is not necessarily the most efficient way of retrieving such data. The Cube Editor offers a menu option for schema optimization, **Optimize Schema**, for dimensions that meet the following criteria:

- The values in the member key column for the dimension are unique.

- A one-to-one relationship exists between the member key column and the member name column.

- There is only one join between the underlying fact table for the partition and the dimension tables of the dimension, based on the member key column.

Of the four dimensions represented in the WHERE clause, Time, Store, Product, and Customer, the last three dimensions meet the criteria needed to optimize the schema. The joins to those three dimension tables are unnecessary, because the information needed to identify the member key columns is contained within the fact table.

If the Optimize Schema command is executed on the Warehouse cube in **FoodMart 2000**, the following message appears.

```
The following MemberKeyColumn properties have been updated:
Level: Store Name: "store"."store_id" -> "inventory_fact_1997"."store_id"
Level: Product Name: "product"."product_id"->"inventory_fact_1997"."product_id"
Level: Warehouse Name: "warehouse"."warehouse_id"-> "inventory_fact_1997"."customer_id"
```

The Optimize Schema command replaced the references from the original member key columns in the last three dimensions to the corresponding foreign key columns in the fact table. When the Warehouse cube is processed, the SQL SELECT statement used to retrieve fact table data for the first partition now resembles the following:

```
SELECT
    inventory_fact_1997.store_id,
    time_by_day.quarter,
    time_by_day.month_of_year,
    inventory_fact_1997.warehouse_id,
    inventory_fact_1997.product_id,
    inventory_fact_1997.store_invoice,
    inventory_fact_1997.supply_time,
    inventory_fact_1997.warehouse_cost,
    inventory_fact_1997.warehouse_sales,
    inventory_fact_1997.units_shipped,
    inventory_fact_1997.units_ordered,
    inventory_fact_1997.warehouse_sales-inventory_fact_1997.warehouse_Cost
FROM
    inventory_fact_1997,
    time_by_day
WHERE
    (time_by_day.the_year=?) AND
    (inventory_fact_1997.time_id=time_by_day.time_id)
```

The resulting SQL SELECT statement now contains only one join in the WHERE clause, offering a significant performance increase without disturbing the information retrieved from the underlying fact table.

When designing cubes optimized for processing performance, remember that private and virtual dimensions cannot be optimized. While this does not greatly affect the performance of virtual dimensions, private dimensions should be used only if necessary to satisfy a business requirement for a particular cube. For more information on private dimensions, see "Designing Dimensions" earlier in this chapter.

Measure Size

The data size of cube measures has a direct impact on cube processing. Use the smallest possible data type to represent a cube measure. The server does not check for overflow when coercing data types, however, so check the underlying fact table data before attempting to coerce measures to a smaller data type.

Design Guidelines

- Use Optimize Schema whenever possible.

    As mentioned earlier, schema optimization can give a great performance boost when querying and processing a cube. The **Optimize Schema** menu item in the **Tools** menu of the Cube Editor handles the schema analysis process automatically, once selected, but you must initiate the process for it to happen.

To take advantage of schema optimization, dimensions must meet certain requirements, most of which are based on the uniqueness of member keys. For more information on the requirements of schema optimization, see "Schema Optimization" earlier in this chapter.

- Use only the processing option needed to get the job done.

Full processing of cubes is not always required; be aware of the differences in processing options, and use only the appropriate processing option. Full processing takes much more time, and renders the cube unavailable longer, than other processing options, so use it only when necessary.

Business Case Solutions Using MDX

The purpose of the Multidimensional Expressions (MDX) language is to make access to multidimensional data more concise and efficient. However, because MDX reflects the natural complexity of multidimensional data structures, simple business questions may sometimes require complex MDX solutions.

This chapter draws from a variety of sources to provide solid solutions to some of the more common MDX questions asked by both business and development users alike, presenting and explaining ready-to-run MDX examples for each question.

The code examples in this chapter are also available on the *SQL Server 2000 Resource Kit* CD-ROM in the file, \Docs\ChapterCode\CH23Code.txt. For more information, see Chapter 39, "Tools, Samples, eBooks, and More."

Syntax Conventions

The syntax presented in each example is formatted to provide a better understanding of how the MDX query functions by highlighting the use of each MDX function. All MDX functions and keywords are in uppercase, while all other elements, such as member and set names, are in a case appropriate to the element.

To better illustrate the use of MDX functions and keywords within the query examples, the query is indented similarly to the way C programming language is indented.

The formatting of MDX syntax within the examples may not be consistent; the syntax convention is used to make potentially difficult MDX syntax clearer and easier to understand, and the syntax convention rules may be broken to facilitate such clarity and ease of understanding as needed.

General Questions

The questions in this section pertain to understanding general MDX concepts and their application in common business scenarios.

How Can I Retrieve Results from Different Cubes?

One of the most useful functions in MDX for an enterprise-level Microsoft® SQL Server™ 2000 Analysis Services solution is the **LookupCube** MDX function. Basically, the **LookupCube** function can evaluate a single MDX statement against a cube other than the cube currently indicated by query context to retrieve a single string or numeric result.

For example, the Budget cube in the **FoodMart 2000** database contains budget information that can be displayed by store. The Sales cube in the **FoodMart 2000** database contains sales information that can be displayed by store. Since no virtual cube exists in the **FoodMart 2000** database that joins the Sales and Budget cubes together, comparing the two sets of figures would be difficult at best.

> **Note** In many situations a virtual cube can be used to integrate data from multiple cubes, which will often provide a simpler and more efficient solution than the **LookupCube** function. This example uses the **LookupCube** function for purposes of illustration.

The following MDX query, however, uses the **LookupCube** function to retrieve unit sales information for each store from the Sales cube, presenting it side by side with the budget information from the Budget cube.

Code Example 23.1

```
WITH MEMBER
    Measures.[Store Unit Sales]
AS
    'LookupCube(
      "Sales",
      "(" + MemberToStr(Store.CurrentMember) + ", Measures.[Unit Sales])"
    )'

SELECT
    {Measures.Amount, Measures.[Store Unit Sales]} ON COLUMNS,
    Store.CA.CHILDREN ON ROWS
FROM
    Budget
```

The **LookupCube** function takes a string expression; additional MDX functions can be used to concatenate the string sent to the referenced cube as demonstrated in the previous MDX query. The results returned by the previous MDX query resemble the following table.

	Amount	Store Unit Sales
Alameda	($56,520.00)	
Beverly Hills	$36,183.84	21,333.00
Los Angeles	$44,563.20	25,663.00
San Diego	$44,159.14	25,635.00
San Francisco	$3,593.98	2,117.00

How Can I Perform Basic Basket Analysis?

Basket analysis is a topic better suited to data mining discussions, but some basic forms of basket analysis can be handled through the use of MDX queries.

For example, one method of basket analysis groups customers based on qualification. In the following example, a qualified customer is one who has more than $10,000 in store sales or more than 10 unit sales. The following table illustrates such a report, run against the Sales cube in **FoodMart 2000** with qualified customers grouped by the Country and State Province levels of the Customers dimension. The count and store sales total of qualified customers is represented by the **Qualified Count** and **Qualified Sales** columns, respectively.

	Qualified Count	Qualified Sales
All Customers	4719	$553,587.77
Canada	0	
BC	0	
Mexico	0	
DF	0	
...		
USA	4719	$553.587.77
CA	2149	$151,509.69
OR	1008	$141,889.84
WA	1562	$260,178,24

To accomplish this basic form of basket analysis, the following MDX query constructs two calculated members. The first calculated member uses the MDX **Count**, **Filter**, and **Descendants** functions to create the **Qualified Count** column, while the second calculated member uses the MDX **Sum**, **Filter**, and **Descendants** functions to create the **Qualified Sales** column.

The key to this MDX query is the use of **Filter** and **Descendants** together to screen out non-qualified customers. Once screened out, the **Sum** and **Count** MDX functions can then be used to provide aggregation data only on qualified customers.

Code Example 23.2

```
WITH
MEMBER
   [Measures].[Qualified Count]
AS
   'COUNT(
      FILTER(
         DESCENDANTS(
            Customers.CURRENTMEMBER,
            [Customers].[Name]
         ), ([Measures].[Store Sales]) > 10000 OR
         ([Measures].[Unit Sales]) > 10
      )
   )'
MEMBER
   [Measures].[Qualified Sales]
AS
   'SUM(
      FILTER(
         DESCENDANTS(
            Customers.CURRENTMEMBER,
            [Customers].[Name]
         ), ([Measures].[Store Sales]) > 10000 OR
         ([Measures].[Unit Sales]) > 10
      ), ([Measures].[Store Sales])
   )'
SELECT
   {[Measures].[Qualified Count], [Measures].[Qualified Sales]}
ON COLUMNS,
   DESCENDANTS(
      [Customers].[All Customers],
      [State Province],
      SELF_AND_BEFORE)
ON ROWS
FROM
   Sales
```

This technique works for a wide variety of business scenarios, and can be expanded on to provide more types of basket analysis.

How Can I Perform Complex String Comparisons?

MDX can handle basic string comparisons, but does not include complex string comparison and manipulation functions, for example, for finding substrings in strings or for supporting case-insensitive string comparisons. However, since MDX can take advantage of external function libraries, this question is easily resolved using string manipulation and comparison functions from the Microsoft Visual Basic® for Applications (VBA) external function library.

For example, you want to report the unit sales of all fruit-based products—not only the sales of fruit, but canned fruit, fruit snacks, fruit juices, and so on. By using the **LCase** and **InStr** VBA functions, the following results are easily accomplished in a single MDX query, without complex set construction or explicit member names within the query.

	Unit Sales
Applause Canned Mixed Fruit	205.00
Big City Canned Mixed Fruit	204.00
...	...
Nationeel Raspberry Fruit Roll	167.00
Nationeel Strawberry Fruit Roll	138.00

The following MDX query demonstrates how to achieve the results displayed in the previous table. For each member in the Product dimension, the name of the member is converted to lowercase using the **LCase** VBA function. Then, the **InStr** VBA function is used to discover whether or not the name contains the word "fruit". This information is used to then construct a set, using the **Filter** MDX function, from only those members from the Product dimension that contain the substring "fruit" in their names.

Code Example 23.3

```
SELECT
    {Measures.[Unit Sales]} ON COLUMNS,
    FILTER(
        [Product].[Product Name].MEMBERS,
        INSTR(
            LCASE([Product].CURRENTMEMBER.NAME),
            "fruit"
        ) <> 0
    )
ON ROWS
FROM
    Sales
```

A wide variety of string manipulation functions are available in the VBA function library. For more information about available VBA string functions, see "Visual Basic For Applications Functions" in SQL Server Books Online.

How Can I Show Percentages as Measures?

Another common business question easily answered through MDX is the display of percent values created as available measures.

For example, the Sales cube in the **FoodMart 2000** database contains unit sales for each store in a given city, state, and country, organized along the Sales dimension. A report is requested to show, for California, the percentage of total unit sales attained by each city with a store. The results are illustrated in the following table.

	Unit Sales	Unit Sales Percent
Alameda		
San Francisco	2,117.00	2.83
Beverly Hills	21,333.00	28.54
San Diego	25,635.00	34.30
Los Angeles	25,663.00	34.33

Because the parent of a member is typically another, aggregated member in a regular dimension, this is easily achieved by the construction of a calculated member, as demonstrated in the following MDX query, using the **CurrentMember** and **Parent** MDX functions.

Code Example 23.4

```
WITH
   MEMBER
      Measures.[Unit Sales Percent] AS
         '((Store.CURRENTMEMBER, Measures.[Unit Sales])/
         (Store.CURRENTMEMBER.PARENT, Measures.[Unit Sales])) ',
         FORMAT_STRING = 'Percent'
SELECT
   {Measures.[Unit Sales], Measures.[Unit Sales Percent]}
ON COLUMNS,
   ORDER(
      DESCENDANTS(
         Store. CA,
         Store.[Store City],
         SELF
      ),
```

```
      [Measures].[Unit Sales],
      ASC
   )
ON ROWS
FROM
   Sales
```

The MDX query simply takes the unit sales value for each of the members in the Store dimension and divides it by the value of the parent member, then multiplies it by 100 to obtain a percent value. The **Order** and **Descendants** MDX functions are used to rank the cities from least to most significant, in terms of unit sales, in California.

How Can I Show Cumulative Sums as Measures?

Another common business request, cumulative sums, is useful for business reporting purposes. However, since aggregations are handled in a hierarchical fashion, cumulative sums present some unique challenges in Analysis Services.

The best way to create a cumulative sum is as a calculated measure in MDX, using the **Rank**, **Head**, **Order**, and **Sum** MDX functions together.

For example, the following table illustrates a report that shows two views of employee count in all stores and cities in California, sorted by employee count. The first column shows the aggregated counts for each store and city, while the second column shows aggregated counts for each store, but cumulative counts for each city.

	Number of Employees	Cumulative Number of Employees
Los Angeles	62	62
Store 7	62	62
San Diego	62	124
Store 24	62	62
Beverly Hills	48	172
Store 6	48	48
Alameda	17	189
HQ	17	17
San Francisco	4	193
Store 14	4	4

The cumulative number of employees for San Diego represents the value of both Los Angeles and San Diego, the value for Beverly Hills represents the cumulative total of Los Angeles, San Diego, and Beverly Hills, and so on.

Since the members within the state of California have been ordered from highest to lowest number of employees, this form of cumulative sum measure provides a form of pareto analysis within each state.

To support this, the **Order** function is first used to reorder members accordingly for both the **Rank** and **Head** functions. Once reordered, the **Rank** function is used to supply the ranking of each tuple within the reordered set of members, progressing as each member in the Store dimension is examined. The value is then used to determine the number of tuples to retrieve from the set of reordered members using the **Head** function. Finally, the retrieved members are then added together using the **Sum** function to obtain a cumulative sum. The following MDX query demonstrates how all of this works in concert to provide cumulative sums.

Code Example 23.5

```
WITH
    MEMBER
        Measures.[Cumulative No of Employees]
    AS
        'SUM(
          HEAD(
            ORDER(
                {[Store].Siblings},
                [Measures].[Number of Employees],
                BDESC
            ) AS OrderedSiblings,
            RANK(
                [Store],
                OrderedSiblings
            )
          ),
          [Measures].[Number of Employees]
        )'
SELECT
    {[Measures].[Number of Employees],
    [Measures].[Cumulative No of Employees]}
ON COLUMNS,
    ORDER(
        DESCENDANTS(
            Store.CA,
            [Store State],
            AFTER
        ),
```

```
        [Measures].[Number of Employees],
        BDESC
    )
ON ROWS
FROM
    HR
```

As an aside, a named set cannot be used in this situation to replace the duplicate **Order** function calls. Named sets are evaluated once, when a query is parsed—since the set can change based on the fact that the set can be different for each store member because the set is evaluated for the children of multiple parents, the set does not change with respect to its use in the **Sum** function. Since the named set is only evaluated once, it would not satisfy the needs of this query.

How Can I Implement a Logical AND or OR Condition in a WHERE Clause?

For SQL users, the use of AND and OR logical operators in the WHERE clause of a SQL statement is an essential tool for constructing business queries. However, the WHERE clause of an MDX statement serves a slightly different purpose, and understanding how the WHERE clause is used in MDX can assist in constructing such business queries.

The WHERE clause in MDX is used to further restrict the results of an MDX query, in effect providing another dimension on which the results of the query are further sliced. As such, only expressions that resolve to a single tuple are allowed. The WHERE clause implicitly supports a logical AND operation involving members across different dimensions, by including the members as part of a tuple. To support logical AND operations involving members within a single dimensions, as well as logical OR operations, a calculated member needs to be defined in addition to the use of the WHERE clause.

For example, the following MDX query illustrates the use of a calculated member to support a logical OR. The query returns unit sales by quarter and year for all food and drink related products sold in 1997, run against the Sales cube in the **FoodMart 2000** database.

Code Example 23.6

```
WITH
MEMBER
    [Product].[Food OR Drink]
AS
    '([Product].[Food], Measures.[Unit Sales]) + ([Product].[Drink], Measures.[Unit
Sales])'
SELECT
    {Measures.[Unit Sales]}
ON COLUMNS,
    DESCENDANTS(Time.[1997], [Quarter], SELF_AND_BEFORE)
```

```
ON ROWS
FROM
    Sales
WHERE
    [Product].[Food OR Drink]
```

The calculated member simply adds the values of the Unit Sales measure for the Food and the Drink levels of the Product dimension together. The WHERE clause is then used to restrict return of information only to the calculated member, effectively implementing a logical OR to return information for all time periods that contain unit sales values for either food, drink, or both types of products.

You can use the **Aggregate** function in similar situations where all measures are not aggregated by summing. To return the same results in the above example using the **Aggregate** function, replace the definition for the calculated member with this definition:

```
'Aggregate({[Product].[Food], [Product].[Drink]})'
```

A logical AND, by contrast, can be supported by using two different techniques. If the members used to construct the logical AND reside on different dimensions, all that is required is a WHERE clause that uses a tuple representing all involved members. The following MDX query uses a WHERE clause that effectively restricts the query to retrieve unit sales for drink products in the USA, shown by quarter and year for 1997.

Code Example 23.7

```
SELECT
    {Measures.[Unit Sales]}
ON COLUMNS,
    DESCENDANTS([Time].[1997], [Quarter], SELF_AND_BEFORE)
ON ROWS
FROM
    Sales
WHERE
    ([Product].[Drink], [Store].USA)
```

The WHERE clause in the previous MDX query effectively provides a logical AND operator, in which all unit sales for 1997 are returned only for drink products and only for those sold in stores in the USA.

If the members used to construct the logical AND condition reside on the same dimension, you can use a calculated member or a named set to filter out the unwanted members, as demonstrated in the following MDX query.

Code Example 23.8

```
WITH
SET
    [Good AND Pearl Stores]
AS
    'FILTER(
        Store.Members,
        ([Product].[Good], Measures.[Unit Sales]) > 0 AND
        ([Product].[Pearl], Measures.[Unit Sales]) > 0
    )'
SELECT
    DESCENDANTS([Time].[1997], [Quarter], SELF_AND_BEFORE)
ON COLUMNS,
    [Good AND Pearl Stores]
ON ROWS
FROM
    Sales
```

The named set, [Good AND Pearl Stores], restricts the displayed unit sales totals only to those stores that have sold both Good products and Pearl products.

How Can I Use Custom Member Properties in MDX?

Member properties are a good way of adding secondary business information to members in a dimension. However, getting that information out can be confusing—member properties are not readily apparent in a typical MDX query.

Member properties can be retrieved in one of two ways. The easiest and most used method of retrieving member properties is to use the DIMENSION PROPERTIES MDX statement when constructing an axis in an MDX query.

For example, a member property in the Store dimension in the **FoodMart 2000** database details the total square feet for each store. The following MDX query can retrieve this member property as part of the returned cellset.

Code Example 23.9

```
SELECT
    {[Measures].[Units Shipped], [Measures].[Units Ordered]}
ON COLUMNS,
    NON EMPTY  [Store].[Store Name].MEMBERS
    DIMENSION PROPERTIES  [Store].[Store Name].[Store Sqft]
ON ROWS
FROM
    Warehouse
```

The drawback to using the DIMENSION PROPERTIES statement is that, for most client applications, the member property is not readily apparent. If the previous MDX query is executed in the MDX sample application shipped with SQL Server 2000 Analysis Services, for example, you must double-click the name of the member in the grid to open the **Member Properties** dialog box, which displays all of the member properties shipped as part of the cellset, including the [Store].[Store Name].[Store Sqft] member property.

The other method of retrieving member properties involves the creation of a calculated member based on the member property. The following MDX query brings back the total square feet for each store as a measure, included in the COLUMNS axis.

Code Example 23.10

```
WITH
    MEMBER
        Measures.[Store SqFt]
    AS
        '[Store].CURRENTMEMBER.PROPERTIES("Store SQFT")'
SELECT
    { [Measures].[Store SQFT], [Measures].[Units Shipped], [Measures].[Units Ordered] }
ON COLUMNS,
    [Store].[Store Name].MEMBERS
ON ROWS
FROM
    Warehouse
```

The [Store SqFt] measure is constructed with the **Properties** MDX function to retrieve the [Store SQFT] member property for each member in the Store dimension. The benefit to this technique is that the calculated member is readily apparent and easily accessible in client applications that do not support member properties.

Navigation Questions

All of the questions in this section deal specifically with the ability to navigate dimension hierarchies within an MDX query. Drilling up, down, and through multidimensional data is an essential part of user interfaces designed to show query data, but can be difficult to understand and successfully implement using MDX queries. Likewise, the ability to exploit MDX hierarchy navigation functions to compare and contrast values across hierarchical organizations within a dimension is key to the effective use of dimensions within a cube.

How Can I Drill Down More Than One Level Deep, or Skip Levels When Drilling Down?

Drilling down is an essential ability for most OLAP products, and Analysis Services is no exception. Several functions exist that support drilling up and down the hierarchy of dimensions within a cube. Typically, drilling up and down the hierarchy is done one level at a time; think of this functionality as a zoom feature for OLAP data.

There are times, though, when the need to drill down more than one level at the same time, or even skip levels when displaying information about multiple levels, exists for a business scenario.

For example, you would like to show report results from a query of the Sales cube in the **FoodMart 2000** sample database showing sales totals for individual cities and the subtotals for each country, as shown in the following table.

	Unit Sales
Canada	
Burnaby	
Cliffside	
...	...
USA	266,773.00
Altadena	2,574.00
Arcadia	2,440.00
...	...

The Customers dimension, however, has Country, State Province, and City levels. In order to show the above report, you would have to show the Country level and then drill down two levels to show the City level, skipping the State Province level entirely.

However, the MDX **ToggleDrillState** and **DrillDownMember** functions provide drill down functionality only one level below a specified set. To drill down more than one level below a specified set, you need to use a combination of MDX functions, including **Descendants**, **Generate**, and **Except**. This technique essentially constructs a large set that includes all levels between both upper and lower desired levels, then uses a smaller set representing the undesired level or levels to remove the appropriate members from the larger set.

The following MDX query provides the results as shown in the previous example.

Code Example 23.11

```
SELECT
    {[Measures].[Unit Sales]}
ON COLUMNS,
    EXCEPT(
        GENERATE(
            [Customers].[Country].MEMBERS,
            {DESCENDANTS(
                [Customers].CURRENTMEMBER,
                [Customers].[City], SELF_AND_BEFORE)
            }
        ),
        {[Customers].[State Province].MEMBERS}
    )
ON ROWS
FROM
    Sales
```

The MDX **Descendants** function is used to construct a set consisting of the descendants of each member in the Customers dimension. The descendants are determined using the MDX **Descendants** function, with the descendants of the City level and the level above, the State Province level, for each member of the Customers dimension being added to the set.

The MDX **Generate** function now creates a set consisting of all members at the Country level as well as the members of the set generated by the MDX **Descendants** function. Then, the MDX **Except** function is used to exclude all members at the State Province level, so the returned set contains members at the Country and City levels.

Note, however, that the previous MDX query will still order the members according to their hierarchy. Although the returned set contains members at the Country and City levels, the Country, State Province, and City levels determine the order of the members.

How Do I Get the Topmost Members of a Level Broken Out by an Ancestor Level?

This type of MDX query is common when only the facts for the lowest level of a dimension within a cube are needed, but information about other levels within the same dimension may also be required to satisfy a specific business scenario.

For example, a report that shows the unit sales for the store with the highest unit sales from each country is needed for marketing purposes. The following table provides an example of this report, run against the Sales cube in the **FoodMart 2000** sample database.

	Store Country	Unit Sales
Store 19	Canada	
Store 9	Mexico	
Store 13	USA	41,580.00

This looks simple enough, but the **Country Name** column provides unexpected difficulty. The values for the **Store Country** column are taken from the Store Country level of the Store dimension, so the **Store Country** column is constructed as a calculated member as part of the MDX query, using the MDX **Ancestor** and **Name** functions to return the country names for each store.

A combination of the MDX **Generate**, **TopCount**, and **Descendants** functions are used to create a set containing the top stores in unit sales for each country.

The following MDX query provides the results as shown in the previous example.

Code Example 23.12

```
WITH MEMBER
    Measures.[Country Name]
AS
    'Ancestor(Store.CurrentMember, [Store Country]).Name'
SELECT
    {Measures.[Country Name], Measures.[Unit Sales]}
ON COLUMNS,
    GENERATE(
        [Store Country].MEMBERS,
        TOPCOUNT(
            DESCENDANTS(
                [Store].CURRENTMEMBER,
                [Store].[Store Name]
            ),1,[Measures].[Unit Sales]
        )
    )
ON ROWS
FROM
    Sales
```

The MDX **Descendants** function is used to construct a set consisting of only those members at the Store Name level in the Store dimension. Then, the MDX **TopCount** function is used to return only the topmost store based on the Unit Sales measure. The MDX **Generate** function then constructs a set based on the topmost stores, following the hierarchy of the Store dimension.

Alternate techniques, such as using the MDX **Crossjoin** function, may not provide the desired results because non-related joins can occur. Since the **Store Country** and **Store Name** levels are within the same dimension, they cannot be cross-joined. Another dimension that provides the same regional hierarchy structure, such as the Customers dimension, can be employed with the **Crossjoin** function. But, using this technique can cause non-related joins and return unexpected results.

For example, the following MDX query uses the **Crossjoin** function to attempt to return the same desired results.

Code Example 23.13

```
SELECT
    {Measures.[Unit Sales]}
ON COLUMNS,
    CROSSJOIN(
        Customers.CHILDREN,
        TOPCOUNT(
            DESCENDANTS(
                [Store].CURRENTMEMBER,
                [Store].[Store Name]
            ),1,[Measures].[Unit Sales]
        )
    )
ON ROWS
FROM
    Sales
```

However, some unexpected surprises occur because the topmost member in the Store dimension is cross-joined with all of the children of the Customers dimension, as shown in the following table.

		Unit Sales
Canada	Store 13	
Mexico	Store 13	
USA	Store 13	41,580.00

In this instance, the use of a calculated member to provide store country names is easier to understand and debug than attempting to cross-join across unrelated members.

Manipulation Questions

The questions addressed in this section deal with the manipulation of dimension hierarchies within MDX queries. Some of the most difficult MDX questions lie within the scope of this section–almost half of the functions in MDX are devoted to the manipulation hierarchies, sets, tuples, and members.

How Can I Rank or Reorder Members?

One of the issues commonly encountered in business scenarios is the need to rank the members of a dimension according to their corresponding measure values. The **Order** MDX function allows you to order a set based on a string or numeric expression evaluated against the members of a set. Combined with other MDX functions, the **Order** function can support several different types of ranking.

For example, the Sales cube in the **FoodMart 2000** database can be used to show unit sales for each store. However, the business scenario requires a report that ranks the stores from highest to lowest unit sales, individually, of nonconsumable products.

The following table illustrates the desired report results.

	Unit Sales
Store 13	7,940.00
Store 17	6,712.00
Store 11	5,076.00
...	...
HQ	

Because of the requirement that stores be sorted individually, the hierarchy must be broken (in other words, ignored) for the purpose of ranking the stores. The **Order** function is capable of sorting within the hierarchy, based on the topmost level represented in the set to be sorted, or, by breaking the hierarchy, sorting all of the members of the set as if they existed on the same level, with the same parent.

The following MDX query illustrates the use of the **Order** function to rank the members according to unit sales.

Code Example 23.14

```
SELECT
   {[Measures].[Unit Sales]}
ON COLUMNS,
   ORDER(
      [Store].[Store Name].MEMBERS, (Measures.[Unit Sales])
      ,BDESC
   )
```

```
ON ROWS
FROM
  Sales
WHERE
  [Product].[Non-Consumable]
```

The BDESC flag in the **Order** function instructs the function to sort the members in descending order, breaking the hierarchy to do so. By comparison, the following table represents the results obtained by the above query if the DESC flag, which sorts the members in descending order while following the hierarchy, was used instead.

	Unit Sales
Store 17	6,712.00
Store 15	4,639.00
Store 3	4,479.00
...	...
Store 18	

The change in output is caused by the fact that the stores are sorted according to the hierarchy. Store 17, for example, is not the highest-ranked store across all stores in the Store dimension, as shown in the first example. However, in this example, it is the highest ranked store of the [Tacoma] member in the [Store City] level, which is the highest ranked city of the [WA] member in the [Store State] level, which is the highest ranked state of the [USA] member in the [Store Country] level. According to the hierarchy, the members of the [Store Country] level are sorted first, then the members of the [Store City] level for each member in the [Store Country] level, and so on until all members have been sorted. The ranking in the above example reflects this hierarchical sorting behavior.

How Can I Use Different Calculations for Different Levels in a Dimension?

This type of MDX query frequently occurs when different aggregations are needed at different levels in a dimension. One easy way to support such functionality is through the use of a calculated measure, created as part of the query, which uses the MDX **Descendants** function in conjunction with one of the MDX aggregation functions to provide results.

For example, the Warehouse cube in the **FoodMart 2000** database supplies the [Units Ordered] measure, aggregated through the Sum function. But, you would also like to see the average number of units ordered per store. The following table demonstrates the desired results.

	Units Ordered	Average Units Ordered
BC		
DF		
Guerrero		
Jalisco		
Veracruz		
Yucatan		
Zacatecas		
CA	66,307	16,577
OR	44,906	22,453
WA	116,025	16,575

By using the following MDX query, the desired results can be achieved. The calculated measure, [Average Units Ordered], supplies the average number of ordered units per store by using the **Avg**, **CurrentMember**, and **Descendants** MDX functions.

Code Example 23.15

```
WITH
MEMBER
    Measures.[Average Units Ordered]
AS
    'AVG(DESCENDANTS([Store].CURRENTMEMBER, [Store].[Store Name]), [Measures].[Units
Ordered])'
SELECT
    {[Measures].[Units ordered], Measures.[Average Units Ordered]}
ON COLUMNS,
    [Store].[Store State].MEMBERS
ON ROWS
FROM
    Warehouse
```

This calculated measure is more powerful than it seems; if, for example, you then want to see the average number of units ordered for beer products in all of the stores in the California area, the following MDX query can be executed with the same calculated measure.

Code Example 23.16

```
WITH
MEMBER
    Measures.[Average Units Ordered]
AS
    'AVG(DESCENDANTS([Store].CURRENTMEMBER, [Store].[Store Name]), [Measures].[Units
Ordered])'
SELECT
    {[Measures].[Units ordered], Measures.[Average Units Ordered]}
ON COLUMNS,
    [Product].[Beer].CHILDREN
ON ROWS
FROM
    Warehouse
WHERE
    [Store].CA
```

This MDX query, once executed, provides results similar to those in the following table.

	Units Ordered	Average Units Ordered
Good		
Pearl	151	76
Portsmouth	95	95
Top Measure		
Walrus	211	106

The same calculated measure could also be used, if the MDX query were narrowed to but a single store, to determine the average number of products ordered by that store. Using calculated measures in this manner can provide a great deal of information with relatively little effort in terms of MDX query formulation.

How Can I Use Different Calculations for Different Dimensions?

Each measure in a cube uses the same aggregation function across all dimensions. However, there are times where a different aggregation function may be needed to represent a measure for reporting purposes. Two basic cases involve aggregating a single dimension using a different aggregation function than the one used for other dimensions.

- Aggregating minimums, maximums, or averages along a time dimension

- Aggregating opening and closing period values along a time dimension

The first case involves some knowledge of the behavior of the time dimension specified in the cube. For instance, to create a calculated measure that contains the average, along a time dimension, of measures aggregated as sums along other dimensions, the average of the aggregated measures must be taken over the set of averaging time periods, constructed through the use of the **Descendants** MDX function. Minimum and maximum values are more easily calculated through the use of the **Min** and **Max** MDX functions, also combined with the **Descendants** function.

For example, the Warehouse cube in the **FoodMart 2000** database contains information on ordered and shipped inventory; from it, a report is requested to show the average number of units shipped, by product, to each store. Information on units shipped is added on a monthly basis, so the aggregated measure [Units Shipped] is divided by the count of descendants, at the Month level, of the current member in the Time dimension. This calculation provides a measure representing the average number of units shipped per month, as demonstrated in the following MDX query.

Code Example 23.17

```
WITH
    MEMBER
        [Measures].[Avg Units Shipped]
    AS
        '[Measures].[Units Shipped] /
        COUNT(
            DESCENDANTS(
                [Time].CURRENTMEMBER,
                [Time].[Month],
                SELF
            )
        )'
SELECT
    {Measures.[Units Shipped], Measures.[Avg Units Shipped]}
ON COLUMNS,
```

```
NONEMPTYCROSSJOIN(
    Store.CA.Children,
    Product.MEMBERS
    )
ON ROWS
FROM
    Warehouse
```

The **NonEmptyCrossjoin** MDX function is used to remove stores and products without values, significantly improving the performance of the query.

The second case is easier to resolve, because MDX provides the **OpeningPeriod** and **ClosingPeriod** MDX functions specifically to support opening and closing period values.

For example, the Warehouse cube in the **FoodMart 2000** database contains information on ordered and shipped inventory; from it, a report is requested to show on-hand inventory at the end of every month. Because the inventory on hand should equal ordered inventory minus shipped inventory, the **ClosingPeriod** MDX function can be used to create a calculated measure to supply the value of inventory on hand, as demonstrated in the following MDX query.

Code Example 23.18

```
WITH
    MEMBER
        Measures.[Closing Balance]
    AS
      '(
          [Measures].[Units Ordered],
          CLOSINGPERIOD(
              [Time].[Month],
              [Time].CURRENTMEMBER
          )
      ) -
      (
          [Measures].[Units Shipped],
          CLOSINGPERIOD(
              [Time].[Month],
              [Time].CURRENTMEMBER
          )
      )'
SELECT
    {[Measures].[Closing Balance]} ON COLUMNS,
    Product.MEMBERS ON ROWS
FROM
    Warehouse
```

Date and Time Questions

Date and time business questions tend to fall into two groups in MDX. The first group involves the use of the various period MDX functions to compare and contrast information across periods. The second group involves the use of both MDX and external functions to establish absolute date and time information for a variety of purposes. Both groups involve both navigation and manipulation MDX functions, and this section contains the most commonly asked questions from both groups.

How Can I Use Date Ranges in MDX?

Date ranges are a frequently encountered problem. Business questions use ranges of dates, but OLAP objects provide aggregated information in date levels.

Using the technique described here, you can establish date ranges in MDX queries at the level of granularity provided by a time dimension. Date ranges cannot be established below the granularity of the dimension without additional information. For example, if the lowest level of a time dimension represents months, you will not be able to establish a two-week date range without other information. Member properties can be added to supply specific dates for members; using such member properties, you can take advantage of the date and time functions provided by VBA and Excel external function libraries to establish date ranges.

The easiest way to specify a static date range is by using the colon (:) operator. This operator creates a naturally ordered set, using the members specified on either side of the operator as the endpoints for the ordered set. For example, to specify the first six months of 1998 from the Time dimension in **FoodMart 2000**, the MDX syntax would resemble:

```
[Time].[1998].[1]:[Time].[1998].[6]
```

For example, the Sales cube uses a time dimension that supports Year, Quarter, and Month levels. To add a six-month and nine-month total, two calculated members are created in the following MDX query.

Code Example 23.19

```
WITH
MEMBER
    [Time].[1997].[Six Month]
AS
    'SUM([Time].[1]:[Time].[6])'
MEMBER
    [Time].[1997].[Nine Month]
AS
    'SUM([Time].[1]:[Time].[9])'
SELECT
    AddCalculatedMembers([Time].[1997].Children)
```

```
ON COLUMNS,
   [Product].Children
ON ROWS
FROM
   Sales
```

This is by far the easiest way to supply static date ranges for MDX queries. There are many other methods, such as using member properties for better granularity, but this is the simplest method of handling static date ranges.

Handling rolling date ranges can be much more complex, and involve the use of external function libraries to supply date information. For more information on handling rolling date ranges, see "How Can I Use Rolling Date Ranges in MDX?" in this chapter.

How Can I Use Rolling Date Ranges in MDX?

There are several techniques that can be used in MDX to support rolling date ranges. All of these techniques tend to fall into two groups. The first group involves the use of relative hierarchical functions to construct named sets or calculated members, and the second group involves the use of absolute date functions from external function libraries to construct named sets or calculated members. Both groups are applicable in different business scenarios.

In the first group of techniques, typically a named set is constructed which contains a number of periods from a time dimension. For example, the following table illustrates a 12-month rolling period, in which the figures for unit sales of the previous 12 months are shown.

	Unit Sales
1	21,628.00
2	20,957.00
...	...
11	25,270.00
12	26,796.00

The following MDX query accomplishes this by using a number of MDX functions, including **LastPeriods**, **Tail**, **Filter**, **Members**, and **Item**, to construct a named set containing only those members across all other dimensions that share data with the time dimension at the Month level. The example assumes that there is at least one measure, such as [Unit Sales], with a value greater than zero in the current period. The Filter function creates a set of months with unit sales greater than zero, while the Tail function returns the last month in this set, the current month. The **LastPeriods** function, finally, is then used to retrieve the last 12 periods at this level, including the current period.

Code Example 23.20

```
WITH
   SET
      Rolling12
   AS
      'LASTPERIODS(
          12,
          TAIL(
             FILTER(
                [Time].[Month].MEMBERS,
                ([Customers].[All Customers],
                [Education Level].[All Education Level],
                [Gender].[All Gender],
                [Marital Status].[All Marital Status],
                [Product].[All Products],
                [Promotion Media].[All Media],
                [Promotions].[All Promotions],
                [Store].[All Stores],
                [Store Size in SQFT].[All Store Size in SQFT],
                [Store Type].[All Store Type],
                [Yearly Income].[All Yearly Income],
                Measures.[Unit Sales])
             >0),
          1).ITEM(0).ITEM(0)
       )'
SELECT
   {[Measures].[Unit Sales]}
   ON COLUMNS,
   Rolling12
   ON ROWS
FROM
   Sales
```

To ensure proper calculation, the [All] levels of every dimension in the cube are added to the set—if those dimensions are not explicitly mentioned, the **CurrentMember** function is used.

MDX also supports the use of external function libraries, and already provides the functions supported in the VBA and Excel function libraries for your use. Creating a rolling date range is more difficult than creating a static date range, and using external VBA functions makes the task easier to manage. Unlike static date ranges, which can dictate the starting and ending points explicitly within the query, the starting and ending points of a rolling date range must be determined dynamically. While MDX supports a number of period-related functions for you to use, all of them have one thing in common—they need an explicit frame of reference. If no frame of reference, in the form of a member or set expression, is provided, time period functions in MDX also use the **CurrentMember** function to provide an explicit frame of reference.

How Can I Use Different Calculations for Different Time Periods?

A few techniques can be used, depending on the structure of the cube being queried, to support different calculations for members depending on the time period. The following example includes the MDX **IIf** function, and is easy to use but difficult to maintain. This example works well for ad hoc queries, but is not the ideal technique for client applications in a production environment.

For example, the following table illustrates a standard and dynamic forecast of warehouse sales, from the Warehouse cube in the **FoodMart 2000** database, for drink products. The standard forecast is double the warehouse sales of the previous year, while the dynamic forecast varies from month to month—the forecast for January is 120 percent of previous sales, while the forecast for July is 260 percent of previous sales.

	1	2	3	...
Drink	881.85	579.05	476.29	...
Food	8,383.45	4,851.41	5,353.19	...
Non-Consumable	2,040.40	1,269.82	1,460.69	...
Drink Forecast - Standard	1,763.69	1,158.10	952.58	...
Drink Forecast - Dynamic	1,058.22	752.77	666.81	...

The most flexible way of handling this type of report is the use of nested MDX **IIf** functions to return a multiplier to be used on the members of the Products dimension, at the Drinks level. The following MDX query demonstrates this technique.

Code Example 23.21

```
WITH
MEMBER
   [Product].[Drink Forecast - Standard]
AS
   '[Product].[All Products].[Drink] * 2'
MEMBER
   [Product].[Drink Forecast - Dynamic]
AS
   '[Product].[All Products].[Drink] *
   IIF([Time].CurrentMember.Name = "1", 1.2,
      IIF([Time].CurrentMember.Name = "2", 1.3,
```

```
            IIF([Time].CurrentMember.Name = "3", 1.4,
              IIF([Time].CurrentMember.Name = "4", 1.6,
                IIF([Time].CurrentMember.Name = "5", 2.1,
                  IIF([Time].CurrentMember.Name = "6", 2.4,
                    IIF([Time].CurrentMember.Name = "7", 2.6,
                      IIF([Time].CurrentMember.Name = "8", 2.3,
                        IIF([Time].CurrentMember.Name = "9", 1.9,
                          IIF([Time].CurrentMember.Name = "10", 1.5,
                            IIF([Time].CurrentMember.Name = "11", 1.4,
                              IIF([Time].CurrentMember.Name = "12", 1.2, 1.0)
                              )
                            )
                          )
                        )
                      )
                    )
                  )
                )
              )
            )
          )'

SELECT
    DESCENDANTS(Time.[1997], [Month], SELF)
ON COLUMNS,
    {[Product].CHILDREN, [Drink Forecast - Standard], [Drink Forecast - Dynamic]}
ON ROWS
FROM
    Warehouse
```

This technique allows the most flexibility for a user performing speculative analysis involving time series business questions; the multipliers can be changed within the query. The MDX query is not efficient, however, as it potentially needs to perform 12 nested functions to resolve the calculated member representing the dynamic forecast.

Other techniques, such as the addition of member properties to the Time or Product dimensions to support such calculations, are not as flexible but are much more efficient. The primary drawback to using such techniques is that the calculations are not easily altered for speculative analysis purposes. For client applications, however, where the calculations are static or slowly changing, using a member property is an excellent way of supplying such functionality to clients while keeping maintenance of calculation variables at the server level. The same MDX query, for example, could be rewritten to use a member property named [Dynamic Forecast Multiplier] as shown in the following MDX query.

Code Example 23.22

```
WITH
MEMBER
    [Product].[Drink Forecast - Standard]
AS
    '[Product].[All Products].[Drink] * 2'
MEMBER
    [Product].[Drink Forecast - Dynamic]
AS
    '[Product].[All Products].[Drink] *
    [Time].CURRENTMEMBER.PROPERTIES("Dynamic Forecast Multiplier")'

SELECT
    DESCENDANTS(Time.[1997], [Month], SELF)
ON COLUMNS,
    {[Product].CHILDREN, [Drink Forecast - Standard], [Drink Forecast - Dynamic]}
ON ROWS
FROM
    Warehouse
```

How Can I Compare Time Periods in MDX?

To answer such a common business question, MDX provides a number of functions specifically designed to navigate and aggregate information across time periods. For example, year-to-date (YTD) totals are directly supported through the **YTD** function in MDX. In combination with the MDX **ParallelPeriod** function, you can create calculated members to support direct comparison of totals across time periods.

For example, the following table represents a comparison of YTD unit sales between 1997 and 1998, run against the Sales cube in the **FoodMart 2000** database.

	1998
YTD Unit Sales	0
Previous YTD Unit Sales	266,773.00
YTD Growth	-266,773.00

The following MDX query uses three calculated members to illustrate how to use the **YTD** and **ParallelPeriod** functions in combination to compare time periods.

Code Example 23.23

```
WITH
MEMBER
   [Measures].[YTD Unit Sales]
AS
   'COALESCEEMPTY(
      SUM(
         YTD(),
         [Measures].[Unit Sales]
      ), 0
   )'
MEMBER [Measures].[Previous YTD Unit Sales]
AS
   '(Measures.[YTD Unit Sales], PARALLELPERIOD([Time].[Year]))'
MEMBER
   [Measures].[YTD Growth]
AS
   '[Measures].[YTD Unit Sales] - ([Measures].[Previous YTD Unit Sales])'
SELECT
   {[Time].[1998]}
ON COLUMNS,
   {[Measures].[YTD Unit Sales],
   [Measures].[Previous YTD Unit Sales],
   [Measures].[YTD Growth]}
ON ROWS
FROM
   Sales
```

The current year is established by the use of the [Time].[1998] member in the Columns axis. The first calculated member uses the **YTD** function to provide the unit sales for the current year-to-date period and also uses the **CoalesceEmpty** function to set empty cells equal to zero for display purposes. The second calculated member uses the first calculated member to create the same totals for the previous year-to-date period, obtained by using the **ParallelPeriod** function to obtain the member representing the previous year. The third calculated member subtracts the second calculated member from the first calculated member, deriving the absolute YTD growth in unit sales between the current and previous years.

Effective Strategies for Data Mining

Data mining is an effective set of analysis tools and techniques used in the decision support process. However, misconceptions about the role that data mining plays in decision support solutions can lead to confusion about and misuse of these tools and techniques.

Introduction

Databases were developed with an emphasis on obtaining data; more data meant more information. Professionals trained in decision support analysis analyzed such data and discovered information in the form of patterns and rules hidden in the relationships between its various attributes. This assisted in the business decision process by providing feedback on past business actions and helped to guide future decisions. The volume of captured data has grown to the extent that there is too much data from which to discover information easily. For example, sampling, a technique designed to reduce the total amount of data to be analyzed for meaningful information, fails because even a marginally statistical sample of data can mean millions of records.

In the business world, the current emphasis on data warehouses and online analytical processing (OLAP) registers this need to convert huge volumes of data into meaningful information. This information can then be converted into meaningful business actions, which provide more data to be converted into more information, and so on in a cyclical manner, creating a "closed loop" in the decision support process. Ideally, this "closed loop" behavior is the key behind such decision support strategies, recursively improving the efficacy of business decisions.

Unfortunately, because most businesses implement only the data warehouse and OLAP portions of this closed loop, they fail to secure true decision support. For example, obtaining customer demographic data and account data from an online transaction processing (OLTP) database, cleaning and transforming the data, translating the prepared data into a data warehouse, constructing and aggregating the data warehouse data into OLAP cubes for presentation, and then making such data available through data marts still does not provide such necessary insight as to why certain customers close their accounts or why certain accounts purchase certain services or products. Without this information, the business actions that attempt to reduce the number of closed accounts or improve sales of certain services or products can be ineffectual or even cause more harm than good.

It is frustrating to know that the information you want is available but only if the right questions are asked of the data warehouse or OLAP cube. The data mining tools in Microsoft® SQL Server™ 2000 Analysis Services provide a way for you to ask the right questions about data and, used with the right techniques, give you the tools needed to convert the hidden patterns and rules in such data into meaningful information.

Another use for data mining is supplying operational decision support. Unlike the closed loop decision support approach, in which the time between the discovery of information and the business decision resulting from the information can take weeks or months and is typically used to provide long-term business decision support, operational decision support can happen in minutes and is used to provide short-term or immediate decision support on a very small set of cases, or even on a single case.

For example, a financial client application can provide real-time analysis for customer support representatives in a banking call center. The client application, by using a data mining model to analyze the demographic information of a prospective customer, can determine the best list of products to cross-sell to the customer. This form of data mining is becoming more and more common as standardized tools, such as Analysis Services, become more accessible to users.

What Is Data Mining?

Simply put, data mining is the process of exploring large quantities of data in order to discover meaningful information about the data, in the form of patterns and rules. In this process, various forms of analysis can be used to discern such patterns and rules in historical data for a given business scenario, and the information can then be stored as an abstract mathematical model of the historical data, referred to as a data mining model. After a data mining model is created, new data can be examined through the model to see if it fits a desired pattern or rule. From this information, actions can be taken to improve results in the given business scenario.

Data mining is not a "black box" process in which the data miner simply builds a data mining model and watches as meaningful information appears. Although Analysis Services removes much of the mystery and complexity of the data mining process by providing data mining tools for creating and examining data mining models, these tools work best on well-prepared data to answer well-researched business scenarios—the GIGO (garbage in, garbage out) law applies more to data mining than to any other area in Analysis Services. Quite a bit of work, including research, selection, cleaning, enrichment, and transformation of data, must be performed first if data mining is to truly supply meaningful information.

Data mining and data warehouses complement each other. Well-designed data warehouses have handled the data selection, cleaning, enrichment, and transformation steps that are also typically associated with data mining. Similarly, the process of data warehousing improves as, through data mining, it becomes apparent which data elements are considered more meaningful than others in terms of decision support and, in turn, improves the data cleaning and transformation steps that are so crucial to good data warehousing practices.

Data mining does not guarantee the behavior of future data through the analysis of historical data. Instead, data mining is a guidance tool, used to provide insight into the trends inherent in historical information.

For example, a data warehouse, without OLAP or data mining, can easily answer the question, "How many products have been sold this year?" An OLAP cube using data warehouse data can answer the question, "What has been the difference in volume of gross sales for products for the last five years, broken down by product line and sales region?" more efficiently than the data warehouse itself. Both products can deliver a solid, discrete answer based on historical data. However, questions such as "Which sales regions should be targeted for telemarketing instead of direct mail?" or "How likely is it that a particular product line would sell well, and in which sales regions?" are not easily answered through data warehouses or OLAP. These questions attempt to provide an educated guess about future trends. Data mining provides educated guesses, not answers, towards such questions through analysis of existing historical data.

The difficulty typically encountered when using a data mining tool such as Analysis Services to create a data mining model is that too much emphasis is placed on obtaining a data mining model; very often, the model itself is treated as the end product. Although you can peruse the structure of a data mining model to understand more about the patterns and rules that constitute your historical data, the real power of data mining comes from using it as a predictive vehicle with current data. You can use the data mining model as a lens through which to view current data, with the ability to apply the patterns and rules stored in the model to predict trends in such data. The revealed information can then be used to perform educated business decisions. Furthermore, the feedback from such decisions can then be compared against the predicted result of the data mining model to further improve the patterns and rules stored in the model itself, which can then be used to more accurately predict trends in new data, and so on.

A data mining model is not static; it is an opinion about data, and as with any opinion, its viewpoint can be altered as new, known data is introduced. Part of the "closed loop" approach to decision support is that all of the steps within the loop can be increasingly improved as more information is known, and that includes data mining models. Data mining models can be retrained with more and better data as it becomes available, further increasing the performance of such a model.

Closed Loop Data Mining

Closed loop data mining is used to support long-term business decision support by analyzing historical data to provide guidance not just on the immediate needs of business intelligence, but also to improve the entire decision support process.

The following diagram illustrates the analysis flow used in closed loop data mining.

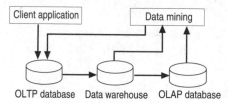

In closed loop data mining, the analysis improves the overall quality of data within the decision support process, as well as improves the quality of long-term business decisions. Input for the data mining model is taken primarily from the data warehouse; Analysis Services also supports input from multidimensional data stores. The information gained from employing the data mining model is then used, either directly by improving data quality or indirectly by altering the business scenarios which supply data, to impact incoming data from the OLTP data store.

For example, one action involving closed loop data mining is the grooming and correction of data based on the patterns and rules discovered within data mining feedback. As mentioned earlier, many of the processes used to prepare data for data mining are also used by data warehousing solutions. Consequently, problems found in data during data mining generally reflect problems in the data in the data warehouse, and the feedback provided by data mining can improve data cleaning and transformation for the whole decision support process, including data warehousing and OLAP.

Closed loop data mining can take either a continuous view, in which data is continually analyzed against a data mining model to provide constant feedback on the decision support process, or a one-time view, in which a one-time result is generated and recommended actions are performed based on the provided feedback. Decisions involving closed loop data mining can take time, and time can affect the reliability of data mining model feedback. When constructing a data mining model for closed loop data mining, you should consider the time needed to act on information. Discovered information can become stale if acted on months after such information is reported.

Also, the one-time result process can be performed periodically, with predictive results stored for later analysis. This is one method of discovering significant attributes in data; if the predictive results differ widely from actual results over a certain period of time, the attributes used to construct the data mining model may be in question and can themselves be analyzed to discover relevance to actual data.

Closed loop data mining can also supply the starting point for operational data mining; the same models used for closed loop data mining can also be used to support operational data mining.

Operational Data Mining

Operational data mining is the next step for many enterprise decision support solutions. Once closed loop data mining has progressed to the point where a consistent, reliable set of data mining models can be used to provide positive guidance to business decisions, this set of data mining models can now be used to provide immediate business decision support feedback in client applications.

The following diagram highlights the analysis flow of operational data mining.

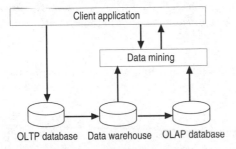

As with closed loop data mining, input for the data mining model is taken from data warehousing and OLTP data stores. However, the data mining model is then used to perform immediate analysis on data entered by client applications. Either the user of the client application or the client application itself then acts upon the analysis information, with the resulting data being sent to the OLTP data store.

For example, financial applications may screen potential credit line customers by running the demographic information of a single customer, received by a customer service representative over the telephone, against a data mining model. If this is an existing customer, the model could be used to determine the likelihood of the customer purchasing other products the financial institution offers (a process known as cross-selling), or indicate the likelihood of a new customer being a bad credit risk.

Operational data mining differs from the more conventional closed loop data mining approach because it does not necessarily act on data already gathered by a data warehousing or other archival storage system. Operational data mining can occur on a real-time basis, and can be supported as part of a custom client application to complement the decision support gathered through closed loop data mining.

Client-based data mining models, duplicated from server-based data mining models and trained using a standardized training case set, are an excellent approach for supporting operational data mining. For more information about how to construct client-based data mining models, see "Creating Data Mining Models" in this chapter.

The Data Mining Process

Analysis Services provides a set of easy-to-use, robust data mining tools. To make the best use of these tools, you should follow a consistent data mining process, such as the one outlined below:

- Data Selection

  The process of locating and identifying data for data mining purposes.

- Data Cleaning

  The process of inspecting data for physical inconsistencies, such as orphan records or required fields set to null, and logical inconsistencies, such as accounts with closing dates earlier than starting dates.

- Data Enrichment

  The process of adding information to data, such as creating calculated fields or adding external data for data mining purposes.

- Data Transformation

  The process of transforming data physically, such as changing the data types of fields, and logically, such as increasing or decreasing granularity, for data mining purposes.

- Training Case Set Preparation

  The process of preparing a case set for data mining. This may include secondary transformation and extract query design.

- Data Mining Model Construction

  The process of choosing a data mining model algorithm and tuning its parameters, then running the algorithm against the training case set to construct a data mining model.

- Data Mining Model Evaluation

  The process of evaluating the created data mining model against a case set of test data, in which a second training data set, also called a holdout set, is viewed through the data mining model and the resulting predictive analysis is then compared against the actual results of the second training set to determine predictive accuracy.

- Data Mining Model Feedback

  After the data mining model has been evaluated, the data mining model can be used to provide analysis of unknown data. The resulting analysis can be used to supply either operational or closed loop decision support.

If you are modeling data from a well-designed data warehouse, the first four steps are generally done for you as part of the process used to populate the data warehouse. However, even data warehousing data may need additional cleaning, enrichment, and transformation, because the data mining process takes a slightly different view of data than either data warehousing or OLAP processes.

Data Selection

There are two parts to selecting data for data mining. The first part, locating data, tends to be more mechanical in nature than the second part, identifying data, which requires significant input by a domain expert for the data. (A *domain expert* is someone who is intimately familiar with the business purposes and aspects, or *domain*, of the data to be examined.)

Locating Data

Data mining can be performed on almost every database, but several general database types are typically supported in business environments. Not all of these database types are suitable for data mining.

The recommended database types for data mining are listed below:

- Enterprise Data Warehouse

  For a number of reasons, a data warehouse maintained at the enterprise level is ideal for data mining. The processes used to select, clean, enrich, and transform data that will be used for data mining purposes are nearly identical to the processes used on data that will be used for data warehousing purposes. The enterprise data warehouse is optimized for high-volume queries and is usually designed to represent business entities in a dimensional format, making it easier to identify and isolate specific business scenarios. By contrast, OLTP databases are generally optimized for high-volume updates and typically represent an entity-relation (E-R) format.

- Data Mart

  A data mart is a subset of the enterprise data warehouse, encapsulated for specific business purposes. For example, a sales and marketing data mart would contain a copy of the dimensional tables and fact tables kept in the enterprise data warehouse that pertain to sales and marketing business purposes. The tables in such a data mart would contain only the data necessary to satisfy sales and marketing research.

Because data marts are aggregated according to the needs of business users, most data marts are not suitable for data mining. However, a data mart designed specifically for data mining can be constructed, giving you the power of data mining in an enterprise data warehouse with the flexibility of additional selection, cleaning, enrichment, and transformation specifically for data mining purposes. Data marts designed for this purpose are known by other terms, but serve the same purpose.

OLAP databases are often modeled as a data mart. Because their functionality and use are similar to other types of data marts, OLAP databases fit into this category neatly. OLAP databases are also aggregated according to the needs of business users, so the same issues apply.

Overaggregation can also cause problems when mining OLAP data. OLAP databases are heavily aggregated; indeed, the point of such data is to reduce the granularity of the typical OLTP or data warehouse database to an understandable level. This involves a great deal of summarization and "blurring" when it comes to viewing detailed information, including the removal of attributes unnecessary to the aggregation process. If there is too much summarization, there will not be enough attributes left to mine for meaningful information. This overaggregation can start well before the data reaches Analysis Services, as data warehouses typically aggregate fact table data. You should carefully review the incoming relational and OLAP data first before deciding to mine OLAP data.

Conversely, you should not mine data in the database types listed below.

- OLTP database

   OLTP databases, also known as operational databases, are not optimized for the kind of wholesale retrieval that data mining needs; marked performance impacts in access and transaction speed can occur on other applications that depend on the high-volume update optimization of such databases. Lack of pre-aggregation can also impact the time needed to train data mining models based on OLTP databases, because of the many joins and high record counts inherent in bulk retrieval queries executed on OLTP databases.

- Operational data store (ODS) database

   The operational data store (ODS) database has come into popular use to process and consolidate the large volumes of data typically handled by OLTP databases. The business definition of an ODS database is fluid, but ODS databases are typically used as a "buffer zone" between raw OLTP data and applications that require access to such high-granularity data for functionality, but need to be isolated from the OLTP database for query performance reasons.

   While data mining ODS databases may be useful, ODS databases are known for rapid changes; such databases mirror OLTP data with low latency between updates. The data mining model then becomes a lens on a rapidly moving target, and the user is never sure that the data mining model accurately reflects the true historical view of the data.

Data mining is a search for experience in data, not a search for intelligence in data. Because developing this experience requires a broad, open view of historical data, most volatile transactional databases should be avoided.

When locating data for data mining, ideally you should use well-documented, easily accessible historical data; many of the steps involved in the data mining process involve free and direct access to data. Security issues, interdepartmental communications, physical network limitations, and so on can restrict free access to historical data. All of the issues that can potentially restrict such free access should be reviewed as part of the design process for implementing a data mining solution.

Identifying Data

This step is one of the most important of all steps in the data mining process. The quality of selected data ultimately determines the quality of the data mining models based on the selected data. The process of identifying data for use in data mining roughly parallels the process used for selecting data for data warehousing.

When identifying data for data mining, you should ask the following three questions:

1. Does this data meet the requirements for the proposed business scenario?

    The data should not only match the purpose of the business scenario, but also its granularity. For example, attempting to model product performance information requires the product data to represent individual products, because each product becomes a case in a set of cases.

2. Is this data complete?

    The data should have all of the attributes needed to accurately describe the business scenario. Remember that a lack of data is itself information; in the abovementioned product performance scenario, lack of performance information about a particular product could indicate a positive performance trend for a family of products; the product may perform so well that no customer has reported any performance issues with the product.

3. Does this data contain the desired outcome attributes?

    When performing predictive modeling, the data used to construct the data mining model must contain the known desired outcome. Sometimes, to satisfy this requirement, a temporary attribute is constructed to provide a discrete outcome value for each case; this can be done in the data enrichment and data transformation steps.

Data that can immediately satisfy these questions is a good place to start for data mining, but you are not limited to such data. The data enrichment and data transformation steps allow you to massage data into a more useful format for data mining, and marginally acceptable data can be made useful through this manipulation.

Data Cleaning

Data cleaning is the process of ensuring that, for data mining purposes, the data is uniform in terms of key and attribute usage. Identifying and correcting missing required information, cleaning up "orphan" records and broken keys, and so on are all aspects of data cleaning.

Data cleaning is separate from data enrichment and data transformation because data cleaning attempts to correct misused or incorrect attributes in existing data. Data enrichment, by contrast, adds new attributes to existing data, while data transformation changes the form or structure of attributes in existing data to meet specific data mining requirements.

Typically, most data mining is performed on data already that has been processed for data warehousing purposes. However, some general guidelines for data cleaning are useful for situations in which a well-designed data warehouse is not available, and for applications in which business requirements require cleaning of such data.

When cleaning data for data warehouses, the best place to start is at home; that is, clean data in the OLTP database first, rather than import bad data into a data warehouse and clean it afterward. This rule also applies to data mining, especially if you intend to construct a data mart for data mining purposes. Always try to clean data at the source, rather than try to model unsatisfactory data. Part of the "closed loop" in the decision support process should include data quality improvements, such as data entry guidelines and optimization of validation rules for OLTP data, and the data cleaning effort provides the information needed to enact such improvements.

Ideally, a temporary storage area can be used to handle the data cleaning, data enrichment, and data transformation steps. This allows you the flexibility to not only change the data itself, but also the meta data that frames the data. Data enrichment and transformation in particular, especially for the construction of new keys and relationships or conversion of data types, can benefit from this approach.

Cleaning data for data mining purposes usually requires the following steps:

1. Key consistency verification

   Check that key values are consistent across all pertinent data. They will most likely be used to identify cases or important attributes.

2. Relationship verification

   Check that relationships between cases conform to defined business rules. Relationships that do not support defined business rules can skew the results of a data mining model, misleading the model into constructing patterns and rules that may not apply to a defined business scenario.

3. Attribute usage and scope verification

    Generally, the quality and accuracy of a data attribute is in direct proportion to the importance of the data to the business. Inventory information, for a manufacturing business that creates parts and products for the aerospace industry, is crucial to the successful operation of the business, and will generally be more accurate and of higher quality than the contact information of the vendors that supply the inventory.

    Check that the attributes used are being used as intended in the database, and that the scope or domain of selected attributes has meaning to the business scenario to be modeled.

4. Attribute data analysis

    Check that the values stored in attributes reasonably conform to defined business rules. As with attribute usage and scope verification, the data for less business-critical attributes typically requires more cleaning than attributes vital to the successful operation of the business.

    You should always be cautious about excluding or substituting values for empty attributes or missing data. Missing data does not always qualify as missing information. The lack of data for a specific cluster in a business scenario can reveal much information when asking the right questions. Consequently, you should be cautious when excluding attributes or data elements from a training case set.

Data cleaning efforts directly contribute to the overall success or failure of the data mining process. This step should never be skipped, no matter the cost in time or resources. Although Analysis Services works well with all forms of data, it works best when data is consistent and uniform.

Data Enrichment

Data enrichment is the process of adding new attributes, such as calculated fields or data from external sources, to existing data.

Most references on data mining tend to combine this step with data transformation. Data transformation involves the manipulation of data, but data enrichment involves adding information to existing data. This can include combining internal data with external data, obtained from either different departments or companies or vendors that sell standardized industry-relevant data.

Data enrichment is an important step if you are attempting to mine marginally acceptable data. You can add information to such data from standardized external industry sources to make the data mining process more successful and reliable, or provide additional derived attributes for a better understanding of indirect relationships. For example, data warehouses frequently provide preaggregation across business lines that share common attributes for cross-selling analysis purposes.

As with data cleaning and data transformation, this step is best handled in a temporary storage area. Data enrichment, in particular the combination of external data sources with data to be mined, can require a number of updates to both data and meta data, and such updates are generally not acceptable in an established data warehouse.

Data Transformation

Data transformation, in terms of data mining, is the process of changing the form or structure of existing attributes. Data transformation is separate from data cleansing and data enrichment for data mining purposes because it does not correct existing attribute data or add new attributes, but instead grooms existing attributes for data mining purposes.

The guidelines for data transformation are similar to both data mining and data warehousing, and a large amount of reference material exists for data transformation in data warehousing environments. For more information about data transformation guidelines in data warehousing, see Chapter 19, "Data Extraction, Transformation, and Loading Techniques."

One of the most common forms of data transformation used in data mining is the conversion of continuous attributes into discrete attributes, referred to as *discretization*. Many data mining algorithms perform better when working with a small number of discrete attributes, such as salary ranges, rather than continuous attributes, such as actual salaries. This step, as with other data transformation steps, does not add information to the data, nor does it clean the data; instead, it makes data easier to model. Some data mining algorithm providers can discretize data automatically, using a variety of algorithms designed to create discrete ranges based on the distribution of data within a continuous attribute. If you intend to take advantage of such automatic discretization, ensure that your training case set has enough cases for the data mining algorithm to adequately determine representative discrete ranges.

Too many discrete values within a single attribute can overwhelm some data mining algorithms. For example, using postal codes from customer addresses to categorize customers by region is an excellent technique if you plan to examine a small region. If, by contrast, you plan on examining the customer patterns for the entire country, using postal codes can lead to 50,000 or more discrete values within a single attribute; you should use an attribute with a wider scope, such as the city or state information supplied by the address.

Training Case Set Preparation

The training case set is used to construct the initial set of rules and patterns that serve as the basis of a data mining model. Preparing a training case set is essential to the success of the data mining process. Generally, several different data mining models will be constructed from the same training case set, as part of the data mining model construction process. There are several basic guidelines used when selecting cases for the preparation of a training case set, but the usefulness of the selection is almost entirely based on the domain of the data itself.

Sampling and Oversampling

Typically, you want to select as many training cases as possible when creating a data mining model, ensuring that the training case set closely represents the density and distribution of the production case set. Select the largest possible training case set you can, to smooth the distribution of training case attributes. The process of creating such a representative set of data, called *sampling*, is best handled by selecting records completely at random. In theory, such random sampling should provide a truly unbiased view of data.

However, random sampling does not always provide for specific business scenarios, and a large training case set may not always be best. For example, if you are attempting to model a rare situation within your data, you want to ensure that the frequency of occurrences for the desired situation is statistically high enough to provide trend information.

This technique of increasing the density of rare occurrences in a sample, called *oversampling*, influences the statistical information conveyed by the training case set. Such influence can be of great benefit when attempting to model very rare cases, sensitive cases in which positive confirmation of the existence of a case must first be made, or when the cases to be modeled occur within a very short period of time. For example, "no card" credit card fraud, in which a fraudulent credit card transaction occurs without the use of a credit card, represents about 0.001 percent of all credit card transactions stored in a particular data set. Sampling would theoretically return 1 fraud case per 100,000 transaction cases—while accurate, the model would overwhelmingly provide information on successful transactions, because the standard deviation for fraud cases would be unacceptably high for modeling purposes. The data mining model would be 99.999 percent accurate, but would also be completely useless for the intended business scenario—finding patterns in no-card fraud transactions.

Instead, oversampling would be used to provide a larger number of fraudulent cases within the training case set. A higher number of fraudulent cases can provide better insight into the patterns behind fraudulent transactions. There are a few drawbacks with oversampling, though, so use this technique carefully. Evaluation of a data mining model created with oversampled data must be handled differently because of the change in ratios between rare and common occurrences in the training case set. For example, the above credit card fraud training set is constructed from five years of transaction data, or approximately 50 million records. This means that, out of the entire data set to be mined, only 500 fraudulent records exist. If random sampling was used to construct a training case set with 1 million records (a 2 percent representative sample), only 10 desired cases would be included. So, the training case set was instead oversampled, so that the fraudulent cases would represent 10 percent of the total number of training cases. We extract all 500 fraudulent cases, so an additional 4,500 cases are randomly selected to construct a training case set with 5,000 cases, of which 10 percent are fraudulent transactions. When creating a data mining model involving the probability of two likely outcomes, the training case set should have a ratio of rare outcomes to common outcomes at approximately 10 to 40 percent, with 20 to 30 percent considered ideal. This ratio can be achieved through oversampling, providing a better statistical sample focusing on the desired rare outcome.

The difficulty with this training case set is that one non-fraudulent case, in essence, represents 11,111 cases in the original data set. Evaluating a data mining model using this oversampled training case set means taking this ratio into account when computing, for example, the amount of lift provided by the data mining model when evaluating fraudulent transactions.

For more information on how to evaluate an oversampled data mining model, see "Data Mining Model Evaluation" later in this chapter.

Selecting Training Cases

When preparing a training case set, you should select data that is as unambiguous as possible in representing the expected outcome to be modeled. The ambiguousness of the selected training cases should be in direct proportion to the breadth of focus for the business scenario to be predicted. For example, if you are attempting to cluster products that failed to discover possible failure patterns, selecting all products that failed is appropriate to your training set. By contrast, if you are trying to predict product failure for specific products due to environmental conditions, you should select only those cases where the specific product directly failed as a result of environmental conditions, not simply all failed products.

This may seem like adding bias to the training case set, but one of the primary reasons for wide variances between predicted and actual results when working with data mining models is due to the fact that the patterns stored in the data mining model are not relevant to prediction of the desired business scenario, and irrelevant patterns are introduced in part by ambiguous training cases.

One of the difficulties encountered when selecting cases is the definition of a business scenario and desired outcome. For example, a common business scenario involves grouping cases according to a set of known attributes to discover hidden patterns. The clustering algorithm is used in just this way to discover hidden attributes; the clustering of cases based on exposed attributes can be used to reveal a hidden attribute, the key to the clustering behavior. So, the desired outcome may not have anything to do with the clusters themselves, but the hidden attribute discovered by the clustering behavior. Before you select cases, be sure you understand both the business scenario used to create the data mining model and the information produced by the created data mining model.

The training case set is not the only source of stored pattern and rule information for the data mining model. The data mining model evaluation step of the data mining process can allow you to refine this stored information with the use of additional case sets. The data mining model, through refinement, can unlearn irrelevant patterns and improve its prediction accuracy. But, the data mining model uses the training case set as its first step towards learning information from data, so your model will benefit through careful selection of training cases.

Data Mining Model Construction

The construction of a data mining model consists of selecting a data mining algorithm provider that matches the desired data mining approach, setting its parameters as desired, and executing the algorithm provider against a training case set. This, in turn, generates a set of values that reflects one or more statistical views on the behavior of the training case set. This statistical view is later used to provide insights into similar case sets with unknown outcomes.

This may sound simple, but the act of constructing a data mining model is much more than mere mechanical execution. The approach you use can decide the difference between an accurate but useless data mining model and a somewhat accurate but very useful data mining model.

Your domain expert, the business person who provides guidance into the data you are modeling, should be able to give you enough information to decide on an approach to data mining. The approach, in turn, assist in deciding the algorithm and cases to be modeled.

You should view the data mining model construction process as a process of exploration and discovery. There is no one formula for constructing a data mining model; experimentation and evaluation are key steps in the construction process, and a data mining process for a specific business scenario can go through several iterations before an effective data mining model is constructed.

Model-Driven and Data-Driven Data Mining

The two schools of thought on decision support techniques serve as the endpoints of a spectrum, with many decision support techniques incorporating principles from both schools. Data warehousing, OLAP, and data mining break down into multiple components. Depending on the methodology and purpose of the component, each has a place in this spectrum.

This section focuses on the various methods and purposes of data mining. The following diagram illustrates some of these components and their approximate place in this spectrum.

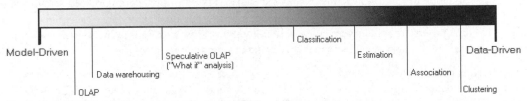

After data has been selected, actual data mining is usually broken down into the following tasks:

- Classification

  Classification is the process of using the attributes of a case to assign it to a predefined class. For example, customers can be classified at various risk levels for mortgage loan applications. Classification is best used when a finite set of classes can be defined—classes defined as high risk, medium risk, or low risk can be used to classify all customers in the previous example.

- Estimation

  While classification is used to answer questions from a finite set of classes, estimation is best used when the answer lies within an unknown, continuous set of answers. For example, using census tract information to predict household incomes. Classification and estimation techniques are often combined within a data mining model.

- Association

  Association is the process of determining the affinity of cases within a case set, based on similarity of attributes. Simply put, association determines which cases belong together in a case set. Association can be used to determine which products should be grouped together on store shelves, or which services are most useful to package for cross-selling opportunities.

- Clustering

  Clustering is the process of finding groups in scattered cases, breaking a single, diverse set of cases into several subsets of similar cases based on the similarity of attributes. Clustering is similar to classification, except that clustering does not require a finite set of predefined classes; clustering simply groups data according to the patterns and rules inherent in the data based on the similarity of its attributes.

Each of these tasks will be discussed in detail later in this chapter. Classification and estimation are typically represented as model-driven tasks, while association and clustering are associated more often with data-driven tasks. Visualization, the process of viewing data mining results in a meaningful and understandable manner, is used for all data mining techniques, and is discussed in a later section.

Model-Driven Data Mining

Model-driven data mining, also known as directed data mining, is the use of classification and estimation techniques to derive a model from data with a known outcome, which is then used to fulfill a specific business scenario. The model is then compared against data with an unknown outcome to determine the likelihood of such data to satisfy the same business scenario. For example, a common illustration of directed data mining is account "churning," the tendency of users to change or cancel accounts. Generally speaking, the data mining model drives the process in model-driven data mining. Classification and estimation are typically categorized as model-driven data mining techniques.

This approach is best employed when a clear business scenario can be employed against a large body of known historical data to construct a predictive data mining model. This tends to be the "I know what I don't know" approach: you have a good idea of the business scenarios to be modeled, and have solid data illustrating such scenarios, but are not sure about the outcome itself or the relationships that lead to this outcome. Model-driven data mining is treated as a "black box" operation, in which the user cares less about the model and more about the predictive results that can be obtained by viewing data through the model.

Data-Driven Data Mining

Data-driven data mining is used to discover the relationships between attributes in unknown data, with or without known data with which to compare the outcome. There may or may not be a specific business scenario. Clustering and association, for example, are primarily data-driven data mining techniques. In data-driven data mining, the data itself drives the data mining process.

This approach is best employed in situations in which true data discovery is needed to uncover rules and patterns in unknown data. This tends to be the "I don't know what I don't know" approach: you can discover significant attributes and patterns in a diverse set of data without using training data or a predefined business scenario. Data-driven data mining is treated as a "white box" operation, in which the user is concerned about both the process used by the data mining algorithm to create the model and the results generated by viewing data through the model.

Which One Is Better?

Asking this question is akin to asking whether a hammer is better than a wrench; the answer depends on the job. Data mining depends on both data-driven and model-driven data mining techniques to be truly effective, depending on what questions are asked and what data is analyzed. For example, a data-driven approach may be used on fraudulent credit card transactions to isolate clusters of similar transactions. Clustering uses a self-comparison approach to find significant groups, or clusters, of data elements. The attributes of each data element are matched across the attributes of all the other data elements in the same set, and are grouped with records that are most similar to the sampled data element. After they are discovered, these individual clusters of data can be modeled using a model-driven data mining technique to construct a data mining model of fraudulent credit card transactions that fit a certain set of attributes. The model can then be used as part of an estimation process, also model-driven, to predict the possibility of fraud in other, unknown credit card transactions.

The various tasks are not completely locked into either model-driven or data-driven data mining. For example, a decision tree data mining model can be used for either model-driven data mining, to predict unknown data from known data, or data-driven data mining, to discover new patterns relating to a specific data attribute.

Data-driven and model-driven data mining can be employed separately or together, in varying amounts, depending on your business requirements. There is no set formula for mining data; each data set has its own patterns and rules.

Data Mining Algorithm Provider Selection

In Analysis Services, a data mining model is a flexible structure that is designed to support the nearly infinite number of ways data can be modeled. The data mining algorithm gives the data mining model shape, form, and behavior.

The two algorithms included in Analysis Services, Microsoft® Decision Trees and Microsoft Clustering, are very different in behavior and produce very different models, as described below.

Both algorithms can be used together to select and model data for business scenarios. For more information on using both algorithms in concert, see "Model-Driven and Data-Driven Data Mining" earlier in this chapter.

Microsoft Decision Trees

The Microsoft Decision Trees algorithm is typically employed in classification and estimation tasks, because it focuses on providing histogram information for paths of rules and patterns within data. One of the benefits of this algorithm is the generation of easily understandable rules. By following the nodes along a single series of branches, a rule can be constructed to derive a single classification of cases.

One of the criteria used for evaluating the success of a data mining algorithm is referred to as *fit*. Fit is typically represented as a value between 0 and 1, and is calculated by taking the covariance between the predicted and actual values of evaluated cases and dividing by the standard deviations of the same predicted and actual values. This measurement, also referred to as *r-squared*, is returned—0 means that the model provides no predictive value at all, because none of the predicted values were even close to the actual values, while 1 means the model is a perfect fit, because the predicted values completely match the actual values of evaluated cases.

However, a perfect fit is not as desirable as it sounds. One of the difficulties encountered with data mining algorithms in general is this tendency to perfectly classify every single case in a training case set, referred to as *overfitting*. The goal of a data mining model, generally speaking, is to build a statistical model of the business scenario that generates the data, not to build an exact representation of the training data itself. Such a data mining model performs well when evaluating training data extracted from a particular data set, but performs poorly when evaluating other cases from the same data set. Even well-prepared training case sets can fall victim to overfitting, because of the nature of random selection.

For example, the following table illustrates a training case set with five cases, representing customers with cancelled accounts, extracted from a larger domain containing thousands of cases.

Customer Name	Gender	Age	Account Months
Beth	Female	28	6
Dennis	Male	45	12
Elaine	Female	45	24
Michelle	Female	47	18
John	Male	37	36

The following diagram illustrates a highly overfitted decision tree, generated from the training case set, created by a data mining model.

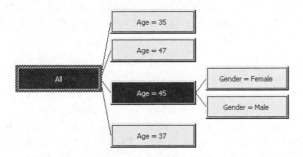

The decision tree perfectly describes the training data set, with a single leaf node per customer. Because the Age and Gender columns were used for input and the Account Months column was used as output, it correctly predicted for this training data set that every female customer with an age of 45 would close their account in 24 months, while every male customer with an age of 45 will close their account in 12 months. This model would be practically useless for predictive analysis—the training set has too few cases to model effectively, and the decision tree generated for this training set has far too many branches for the data.

There are two sets of techniques used to prevent such superfluous branches in a data mining model while maintaining a good fit for the model. The first set of techniques, referred to as *pruning* techniques, allows the decision tree to completely overfit the model and then removes branches within the decision tree to make the model more generalized. This set of techniques is knowledge-intensive, typically requiring both a data mining analyst and a domain expert to properly perform pruning techniques.

The second set of techniques, referred to as *bonsai* or *stunting* techniques, are used to stunt the growth of the tree by applying tests at each node to determine if a split is statistically significant. The Microsoft Decision Trees data mining algorithm automatically employs stunting techniques on data mining models, guided by adjustable data mining parameters, and prevents overfitting training case sets in data mining models that use the algorithm.

There are two data mining parameters that can be adjusted to fine tune the stunting techniques used by the Microsoft Decision Trees algorithm. The first, MINIMUM_LEAF_CASES, determines how many leaf cases are needed to generate a new split in the decision tree. To generate the data mining model in the above example, this parameter was set to 1, so that each case could be represented as a leaf node in the decision tree. Running the same training case set against the same data mining model, but with the MINIMUM_LEAF_CASES parameter set to 2, provides the following decision tree.

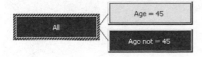

The above decision tree diagram is less overfitted; one leaf node is used to predict two cases, while the other leaf node is used to predict the other three cases in the training data set. The algorithm was instructed not to make a decision unless two or more leaf cases would result from the decision. This is a "brute force" way of ensuring that not every case ends up a leaf case in a data mining model, in that it has obvious and easily understood effects on a data mining model.

Using the second parameter, COMPLEXITY_PENALTY, involves more experimentation. The COMPLEXITY_PENALTY parameter adds cumulative weight to each decision made at a specific level in a decision tree, making it more difficult to continue to make decisions as the tree grows. The smaller the value provided to the COMPLEXITY_PENALTY parameter, the easier it is for the data mining algorithm to generate a decision. For example, the data mining model examples used to demonstrate the MINIMUM_LEAF_CASES parameter were created using a COMPLEXITY_PENALTY value of just 0.000001, to encourage a highly complex model with such a few number of cases. By setting the value to 0.50, the default used for data mining models with between 1 and 10 attributes, the complexity penalty is greatly increased. The following decision tree represents this penalization of mode complexity.

Because the individual cases do not differ significantly, based on the total number of cases included in the training case set, the complexity penalty prevents the algorithm from creating splits. Therefore, the data mining algorithm provider can supply only a single node to represent the training case set; the data mining model is now too generalized. The value used for COMPLEXITY_PENALTY differs from data mining model to data mining model, because of individuality of the data being modeled. The default values provided in the SQL Server Books Online are based on the total number of attributes being modeled, and provide a good basis on which to experiment.

When using data mining parameters to alter the process of generating data mining models, you should create several versions of the same model, each time changing the data mining parameters and observing the reaction in the data mining model. This iterative approach will provide a better understanding of the effects of the data mining parameters on training a data mining model when using the Microsoft Decision Trees algorithm.

The Microsoft Decision Trees algorithm works best with business scenarios involving the classification of cases or the prediction of specific outcomes based on a set of cases encompassing a few broad categories.

Microsoft Clustering

The Microsoft Clustering algorithm provider is typically employed in association and clustering tasks, because it focuses on providing distribution information for subsets of cases within data.

The Microsoft Clustering algorithm provider uses an expectation-maximization (EM) algorithm to segment data into clusters based on the similarity of attributes within cases.

The algorithm iteratively reviews the attributes of each case with respect to the attributes of all other cases, using weighted computation to determine the logical boundaries of each cluster. The algorithm continues this process until all cases belong to one (and only one) cluster, and each cluster is represented as a single node within the data mining model structure.

The Microsoft Clustering algorithm provider is best used in situations where possible natural groupings of cases may exist, but are not readily apparent. This algorithm is often used to identify and separate multiple patterns within large data sets for further data mining; clusters are self-defining, in that the variations of attributes within the domain of the case set determine the clusters themselves. No external data or pattern is applied to discover the clusters internal to the domain.

Creating Data Mining Models

Data mining models can be created a number of ways in Analysis Services, depending on the location of the data mining model. Data mining models created on the Analysis server can only be created through the Decision Support Objects (DSO) library. Analysis Manager uses DSO, through the Mining Model Wizard, used to create new relational or OLAP data mining models. Custom client applications can also use DSO to create relational or OLAP data mining models on the server.

Relational data mining models can be also created on the client through the use of PivotTable Service and the CREATE MINING MODEL statement. For example, the following statement can be used to recreate the Member Card RDBMS data mining model from the **FoodMart 2000** database on the client.

```
CREATE MINING MODEL
    [Member Card RDBMS]
    ([customer id] LONG KEY,
    [gender] TEXT DISCRETE,
    [marital status] TEXT DISCRETE,
    [num children at home] LONG CONTINUOUS,
    [total children] LONG DISCRETE,
    [yearly income] TEXT DISCRETE,
    [education] TEXT DISCRETE,
    [member card] TEXT DISCRETE PREDICT)
USING
    Microsoft_Decision_Trees
```

This statement can be used to create a temporary data mining model, created at the session level, as well as to create a permanent data mining model, stored on the client. To create a permanent data mining model on the client, the **Mining Location** PivotTable Service property is used to specify the directory in which the data mining model will be stored. The same property is also used to locate existing permanent data mining models for reference.

The Data Mining Sample Application, provided with the SQL Server 2000 Resource Kit, is a great tool for prototyping data mining models. You can test each data mining model at session scope; once a data mining model is approved, the same query can be used to construct it locally.

The CREATE MINING MODEL statement can be issued as an action query through any data access technology capable of supporting PivotTable Service, such as Microsoft ActiveX® Data Objects (ADO). The USING clause is used to assign a data mining algorithm provider to the data mining model.

For more information on the syntax and usage of the CREATE MINING MODEL statement, see PivotTable Service Programmer's Reference in SQL Server Books Online. For more information regarding the details of data mining column definition, see the OLE DB for Data Mining specification in the MSDN® Online Library.

Training Data Mining Models

Once a data mining model is created, the training case set is then supplied to the data mining model through the use of a *training query*.

Training case sets can be constructed either by physically separating the desired training data from the larger data set into a different data structure used as a staging area and then retrieving all of the training records with a training query, or by constructing a training query to extract only the desired training data from the larger data set, querying the larger data set directly. The first approach is recommended for performance reasons, and because the training query used for the data mining model does not need to be changed if the training case set changes – you can instead place alternate training data into the physically separated staging area. However, this approach can be impractical if the volume of data to be transferred is extremely large or sensitive, or if the original data set does not reside in an enterprise data warehouse. In such cases, the second approach is more suitable for data mining purposes.

Once the records are extracted, the data mining model is trained by the use of an INSERT INTO query executed against the data mining model, which instructs the data mining algorithm provider to analyze the extracted records and provide statistical data for the data mining model.

In Analysis Services, the training query of a data mining model is typically constructed automatically, using the first approach. The information used to supply input and predictable columns to the data mining model is also used to construct the training query, and the schema used to construct the data mining model is used to supply the training data as well.

For example, the training query used for the Member Card RDBMS relational data mining model in the **FoodMart 2000** database is shown below.

```
INSERT INTO
    [Member Card RDBMS'S]
    (SKIP,
    [gender],
    [marital status],
    [num children at home],
    [total children],
    [yearly income],
    [education],
    [member card])
```

```
OPENROWSET
    ('MSDASQL.1', 'Provider=MSDASQL.1;Persist Security Info=False;Data Source=FoodMart
2000',
    'SELECT DISTINCT
    "Customer"."customer_id" AS 'customer id',
    "Customer"."gender" AS 'gender',
    "Customer"."marital_status" AS 'marital status',
    "Customer"."num_children_at_home" AS 'num children at home',
    "Customer"."total_children" AS 'total children',
    "Customer"."yearly_income" AS 'yearly income',
    "Customer"."education" AS 'education',
    "Customer"."member_card" AS 'member card'
FROM
    "Customer"')
```

The MDX INSERT INTO statement is used to insert the data retrieved by the OPENROWSET command into the data mining model. The data mining model assumes that all records in the **Customer** table, which was used to define the data mining model, are to be used as the training case set for the data mining model.

The second approach, the construction of a custom training query, is more difficult to perform in Analysis Services. The property used to supply custom training queries is not directly available through the Analysis Manager or either of the data mining model editors.

There are two methods used to support the second approach. The first method involves the use of the Decision Support Objects (DSO) library in a custom application to change the training query used by the data mining model. The DSO **MiningModel** object provides the **TrainingQuery** property specifically for this purpose. If the default training query is used for a data mining model, this property is set to an empty string (" "); otherwise, you can supply an alternate training query for use with the mining model.

The second method involves the use of another data access technology, such as ADO, to directly supply a training query to a data mining model. In this case, the training query can be directly executed against the data mining model.

The following statement example is a custom training query for the Member Card RDBMS data mining model that selects only those customers who own houses for analysis. A WHERE clause is used in the OPENROWSET statement to restrict the selection of records from the **Customer** table.

```
INSERT INTO
    [Member Card RDBMS'S]
    (SKIP,
    [gender],
    [marital status],
    [num children at home],
    [total children],
    [yearly income],
    [education],
    [member card])
```

```
OPENROWSET
   ('MSDASQL.1', 'Provider=MSDASQL.1;Persist Security Info=False;Data Source=FoodMart
2000',
   'SELECT DISTINCT
   "Customer"."customer_id" AS 'customer id',
   "Customer"."gender" AS 'gender',
   "Customer"."marital_status" AS 'marital status',
   "Customer"."num_children_at_home" AS 'num children at home',
   "Customer"."total_children" AS 'total children',
   "Customer"."yearly_income" AS 'yearly income',
   "Customer"."education" AS 'education',
   "Customer"."member_card" AS 'member card'
FROM
   "Customer"
WHERE
   "Customer"."houseowner" = "Y"')
```

The resulting data mining model provides analysis on the same attributes, but with a different training case set. By using custom training queries, the same data mining model structure can be used to provide different outlooks on data without the need to completely redevelop a data mining model.

The Microsoft OLE DB for Data Mining provider supports a number of options in the INSERT INTO statement for selecting training data. The OPENROWSET statement, shown in the previous example, is the most common method used, but other methods are supported. For more information about the various supported options, see the OLE DB for Data Mining specification in the MSDN Online Library.

Also, the Data Mining Sample Application, shipped with the *SQL Server 2000 Resource Kit*, can be used to construct and examine a wide variety of training queries quickly and effectively.

Data Mining Model Evaluation

After the data mining model has been processed against the training data set, you should have a useful view of historical data. But how accurate is it?

The easiest way to evaluate a newly created data mining model is to perform a predictive analysis against an evaluation case set. This case set is constructed in a manner similar to that of the construction of a training case set—a set of data with a known outcome. The data used for the evaluation case set should be different from that used in the training case set; otherwise you will find it difficult to confirm the predictive accuracy of the data mining model; evaluation case sets are often referred to as holdout case sets, and are typically created when a training case set is created in order to use the same random sampling process.

Remove or isolate the outcome attributes from the evaluation case set, then analyze the case set by performing prediction queries against the data mining model, using the evaluation case set. After the analysis is completed, you should have a set of predicted outcomes for the evaluation case set that can be compared directly against the known outcomes for the same set to produce an estimate of prediction accuracy for the known outcomes. This comparison, misleadingly referred to as a *confusion matrix*, is a very simple way of communicating the benefits of a data mining model to business users. Conversely, the confusion matrix can also reveal problems with a data mining model if the comparison is unfavorable. Because a confusion matrix works with both actual and predicted outcomes on a case by case basis, using a confusion matrix will give you the ability to exactly pinpoint inaccuracies within a data mining model.

This step can be divided into two different steps, depending on the needs of the data mining model. Before evaluating the data mining model, additional training data can be applied to the model to improve its accuracy. This process, called refinement, uses another training case set, called a test case set, to reinforce similar patterns and dilute the interference of irrelevant patterns. Refinement is particularly effective when using neural network or other genetic algorithms to improve the efficacy of a data mining model. The evaluation case set can then be used to determine the amount of improvement provided by the refinement.

For more information on how to issue prediction queries against a data mining model in Analysis Services, see "Data Mining Model Feedback" later in this chapter.

Calculating Effectiveness

There are several different ways of calculating the effectiveness of a data mining model, based on analysis of the resulting prediction data as compared with actual data. Several of the most common forms of measurement are described in the following section.

- Accuracy

  A brute-force measurement, accuracy is the percentage of total predictions that were correct. "Correct," in this case, means either that, for discrete prediction attributes, the correct value was returned, or, for continuous prediction attributes, a value was returned within a pre-defined threshold established as a criterion for accuracy. For example, predicting the total amount of store sales within a $5,000 threshold could be considered an accurate prediction.

- Error Rate

  Another brute-force measurement, this measures the total predictions that were wrong. Typically calculated at 100—(accuracy in percent), error rates are often used when accuracy rates are too high to be viewed meaningfully. For instance, if the total amount of store sales was correctly calculated 98 percent of the time for the previous year, but calculated correctly 99 percent of the time for the current year, this measurement of accuracy does not have as much impact as being able to say that the error rate was reduced by 50 percent, although both measurements are true.

- Mean-Squared Error

  A special form of error rate for prediction involving continuous, ordered attributes, the mean-squared error is the measurement of variation between the predicted value and the actual value. Subtracting the two values and squaring the result provides the rate of squared error. Then, this value is averaged over all predictions for the same attribute to provide an estimate of variation for a given prediction. The reason this number is squared is to ensure that all errors are positive and can be added together when the average is taken, as well as to more severely weight widely varying prediction values. For example, if the prediction for unit sales (in thousands) for one store is 50 and the actual unit sales (in thousands) for the store was 65, the mean squared error would be 65 - 50, or 15, raised to the power of 2, or 225. Mean-squared error can be used in an iterative manner to consistently establish the accuracy threshold of continuous ordered attributes.

- Lift

  Simply put, lift is a measurement of how much better (or worse) the data mining model predicted results for a given case set over what would be achieved through random selection. Lift is typically calculated by dividing the percentage of expected response predicted by the data mining model by the percentage of expected response predicted by a random selection. For example, if the normal density of response to a direct mail campaign for a given case set was 10 percent, but by focusing in on the top quartile of the case set predicted to respond to the campaign by the data mining model the density of response increases to 30 percent, lift would be calculated at 3, or 30/10.

- Profit

  While the best measurement of any business scenario, profit or returns on investment (ROI) is also the most subjective to calculate, because the variables used to calculated this measurement are different for each business scenario. Many business scenarios involving marketing or sales often have a calculation of ROI included; used in combination with lift, a comparison of ROI between the predicted values of the data mining model and the predicted values of random sampling will simplify any guess as to which subset of cases should be used for lift calculation.

Evaluating an Oversampled Model

The primary drawback of oversampling as a technique for selecting training cases is that the resulting data mining model does not directly correspond to the original data set. It instead provides an exaggerated view of the data, so the exaggerated prediction results must be scaled back to match the actual probability of the original data set. For example, the original data set for credit card transactions, in which 0.001 percent of transactions represent "no card" fraudulent transactions, contains 50 million cases. Statistically speaking, this means only 500 transactions within the original data set are fraudulent. So, a training case set is constructed with 100,000 transactions, in which all 500 fraudulent transactions are placed. The density of the fraudulent data has gone up from 0.001 percent to 0.5 percent – still too low, though, for our purposes. So, the training case set is pared down to just 5,000 transactions, raising the density of fraudulent transactions to 10 percent. The training case set now has a different ratio of representation for the non-fraudulent and fraudulent cases. The fraudulent cases still have a one to one relationship with the original data set, but now each case in the training data set represents 10,000 cases in the original data set. This ratio of cases must be reflected in the sampling of cases from a case set for lift calculation.

For example, the above credit card fraud training case set assumes a binary outcome—either fraudulent or non-fraudulent. We have increased the density of fraudulent cases from 0.001 percent to 10 percent, so this ratio should be taken into account when computing lift. If a selected segment consisting of the top 1 percent of cases within the case set represents a predicted density of 90 percent of fraudulent cases, with a data density of 10 percent for fraudulent cases in the training case set, then the lift for the top 1 percent of total cases, based on the oversampled training case set, is calculated as 9. Since the original data set had an actual data density of 0.001 percent for fraudulent cases, however, the ratio of oversampling, defined earlier as 1 to 10,000 cases, is multiplied by the percent of non-fraudulent cases in the top 1 percent of cases, or 10, added to the percent of fraudulent cases, and is then divided into the predicted density to establish a calculated predicted density of about 0.892 percent for this selected 1 percent of cases. This calculation is illustrated below, with the answer rounded to 10 decimal places.

```
90 /(90 + (10 * (0.001 / 10)) = 0.0089197225
```

Once this calculation is performed, you can then calculate the corresponding lift of the original data set by dividing the calculated density by the density of the original set. Since the density of fraudulent cases for the original data set is 0.001 percent, the lift for this selected 1 percent of cases jumps from 9 to about 892.

The calculated lift value for this selected segment of cases seems abnormally high. However, the selected percentage of cases also changes based on the same ratio of densities. Since the 90 percent predicted response rate occurs for the top 1 percent, then the size of this segment decreases because of the ratio of cases between the training case set and the original data set.

A similar calculation is performed to obtain the new size of the selected segment. The density of the fraudulent cases for the segment, 90 percent, is added to the density of the non-fraudulent cases, or 10 percent, multiplied by the ratio of cases between the training case set and the original case set, or 10000. The product is then divided by the same ratio, 10000, and is then multiplied by the actual size of the segment to get the new relative segment size. This calculation is illustrated below.

```
.01 * ((90 + (10 * 10000))) / 10000) = 0.10009
```

So, the lift figure of 892 only applies to the top 0.10009 percent, or 50,045 cases, of the original case set of 50 million cases, representing a very narrow band of cases at the high end of the lift curve.

As you can see, oversampling is very useful for obtaining information about rare occurrences within large data sets, but providing accurate figures can be quite difficult. Oversampling should only be used in specific situations to model extremely rare cases, but is an essential tool for modeling such situations.

Visualizing Data Mining Models

The visualization tools supplied with Analysis Services are ideal for the evaluation of data mining models. The Data Mining Model Browser and Dependency Network Browser both display the statistical information contained within a data mining model in an understandable graphic format.

The Data Mining Model Browser is used to inspect the structure of a generated data mining model from the viewpoint of a single predictable attribute, to provide insight into the effects input variables have in predicting output variables. Because the most significant input variables appear early within decision tree data mining models, for example, generating a decision tree model and then viewing the structure can provide insight into the most significant input variables to be used in other data mining models.

For example, using the Data Mining Model Browser to view the Member Card RDBMS data mining model presents the following decision tree.

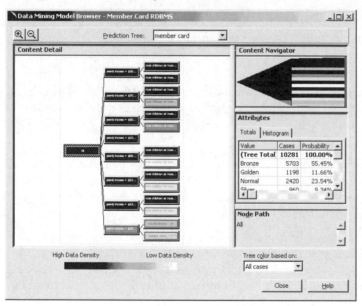

The decision tree is shown from left to right, or from most significant split to least significant split. Just from looking at this decision tree, you should be able to determine that, when predicting the member card attribute, the most significant attribute is yearly income. However, the next most significant attribute varies slightly, depending on the value of the yearly income attribute. For those customers who make more than $150,000 for yearly income, the next most significant attribute is marital status. For all others, the next most significant attribute is num children at home.

The Dependency Network Browser, by contrast, constructs a network-like depiction of the relationships within a data mining model from the viewpoints of all predictable attributes, providing a better understanding of the relationships between attribute values within the domain of cases depicted by the data mining model. The Dependency Network Browser not only shows the relationships between attributes, but ranks the relationships according to the level of significance to a given attribute. The browser can be adjusted to display relationships of a specified significance level across the domain of the data mining model, allowing an informal exploration of the domain itself.

For example, using the Dependency Network Browser to view the Member Card RDBMS data mining model presents the following network of nodes.

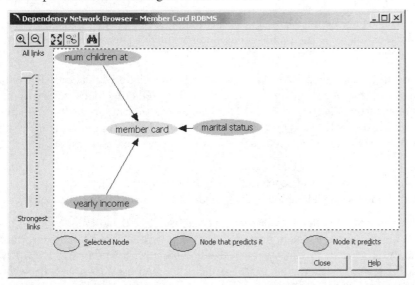

All other attributes tend to predict the member card attribute, indicated by the direction of the arrows between nodes. The slider in the Dependency Network Browser can be used to determine which attributes most influence the member card attribute. Once examined in this fashion, you can determine that the member card attribute is most strongly influenced by the yearly income attribute, then by the num children at home attribute, then finally by the marital status attribute. Note, too, that this coincides with the previously presented view provided by the Data Mining Model Browser, in which the decision tree used to predict the member card attribute illustrates this same significance of attributes

The network represented in the previous example is based on only a single predictable attribute. The Dependency Network Browser is best used with very complex data mining models involving multiple predictable attributes to better understand the domain represented by the model. You can use the Dependency Network Browser to focus on a single predictable attribute, study its relationship to other attributes within the domain, then explore the decision tree used to predict the selected attribute and related attributes using the Data Mining Model browser.

Used in concert, both tools can provide valuable insight into the rules and patterns stored in a data mining model, allowing you to tune the data mining model to the specific needs of the data set to be modeled.

Data Mining Model Feedback

The true purpose of data mining is to provide information for decision support and, ultimately, for making business decisions based on the provided information. Although data mining is an excellent way to discover information in data, information without action invalidates the purpose of data mining. When designing a data mining model, remember that the goal of the model is to provide insight or predictions for a business scenario.

The use of data mining models to provide information generally falls into two different areas. The most common form of data mining, closed loop data mining, is used to provide long-term business decision support.

There are other business uses for data mining feedback, especially in financial organizations. The process of operational data mining, in which unknown data is viewed through a predictive model to determine the likelihood of a single discrete outcome, is commonly used for loan and credit card applications. In this case, feedback can be reduced to a simple "yes or no" answer. Operational data mining is unique in this respect—it occurs in a real-time situation, often on data that may or may not be first committed to a database.

These actions, however, fall outside the typical scope of the data mining analyst. The goal of the data mining analyst is to make data mining model feedback easily understandable to the business user.

Visualization plays an important role in both the evaluation and feedback of a data mining model—if you cannot relate the information gained from a data mining model to the people who need it, the information might as well not exist. Analysis Services supplies two visualization tools, Data Mining Model Browser and Dependency Network Browser, for data mining model visualization purposes. However, these tools may be incomprehensible to a typical business user, and are more suited for the data mining analyst. There are numerous visualization tools available from third-party vendors, and can provide views on data mining model feedback that are meaningful to the business user. For more information about understanding the information presented in the Data Mining Model Browser and Dependency Network Browser, see "Visualizing Data Mining Models" in this chapter.

Custom client applications developed for data mining visualization have an advantage over external visualization tools in that the method of visualization can be tailored specifically for the intended business audience. For more information about developing custom client applications, see Chapter 25, "Getting Data to the Client."

Predicting with Data Mining Models

The true purpose of a data mining model is to use it as a tool through which data with unknown outcomes can be viewed for the purposes of decision support. Once a data mining model has been constructed and evaluated, a special type of query, known as a *prediction query*, can be run against it to provide statistical information for unknown data.

However, the process of construction prediction queries is the least understood step of the data mining process in Analysis Services. The Data Mining Sample Application, shipped with SQL Server 2000 Resource Kit, is an invaluable tool for constructing and examining prediction queries. You can also use it as an educational tool, as the sample provides access to all of the syntax used for data mining.

Basically, the syntax for a prediction query is similar to that of a standard SQL SELECT query in that the data mining model is queried, from a syntactical point of view, as if it were a typical database view. There are, however, two main differences in the syntax used for a prediction query.

The first difference is the PREDICTION JOIN keyword. A data mining model can only predict on data if data is first supplied to it, and this keyword provides the mechanism used to join unknown data with a data mining model. The SELECT statement performs analysis on the data supplied by the prediction join and returns the results in the form of a recordset. Prediction joins can be used in a variety of ways to support both operational and closed loop data mining.

For example, the following prediction query uses the PREDICTION JOIN keyword to join a rowset, created by the OPENROWSET function from the **Customer** table in the **FoodMart 2000** database, to predict the customers most likely to select a Golden member card.

```
SELECT
    [MemberData].[customer_id] AS [Customer ID],
    [MemberData].[education] AS [Education],
    [MemberData].[gender] AS [Gender],
    [MemberData].[marital_status] AS [Marital Status],
    [MemberData].[num_children_at_home] AS [Children At Home],
    [MemberData].[total_children] AS [Total Children],
    [MemberData].[yearly_income] AS [Yearly Income]
FROM
    [Member Card RDBMS]
PREDICTION JOIN
    OPENROWSET
        ('Microsoft.Jet.OLEDB.4.0',
        'Provider=Microsoft.Jet.OLEDB.4.0;
        Data Source=C:\Program Files\Microsoft Analysis Services\samples\FoodMart
2000.mdb;
        Persist Security Info=False',
        'SELECT
            [customer_id],
            [education],
            [gender],
            [marital_status],
            [num_children_at_home],
            [total_children],
            [yearly_income]
        FROM
            [customer]')
```

```
AS
    [MemberData]
ON
    [Member Card RDBMS].[gender] = [MemberData].[gender] AND
    [Member Card RDBMS].[marital status] = [MemberData].[marital_status] AND
    [Member Card RDBMS].[num children at home] = [MemberData].[num_children_at_home] AND
    [Member Card RDBMS].[total children] = [MemberData].[total_children] AND
    [Member Card RDBMS].[yearly income] = [MemberData].[yearly_income] AND
    [Member Card RDBMS].[education] = [MemberData].[education]
WHERE
    [Member Card RDBMS].[member card] = 'Golden' AND
    PREDICTPROBABILITY([Member Card RDBMS].[member card])> 0.8
```

The ON keyword links columns from the rowset specified in the PREDICTION JOIN clause to the input attributes defined in the data mining model, in effect instructing the data mining model to use the joined columns as input attributes for the prediction process, while the WHERE clause is used to restrict the returned cases. In this prediction query, only those cases that are most likely to select the Golden member card are returned. The **PredictProbability** data mining function is used to establish a probability of correct prediction, also known as the confidence of the prediction, and further restrict the returned cases only to those whose confidence level is equal to or higher than 80 percent.

The following table represents the results returned from the previous prediction query. The cases represented by the table are the cases most likely to choose the Golden member card, with a confidence level of 80 percent or greater.

Customer ID	Education	Gender	Marital Status	Children At Home	Total Children	Yearly Income
105	Bachelor's Degree	M	M	3	3	$150K+
136	Bachelor's Degree	M	M	3	3	$150K+
317	High School Degree	M	M	0	0	$150K+
340	Bachelor's Degree	F	M	0	2	$150K+
343	Bachelor's Degree	F	M	1	2	$150K+
...	...	...	...	...	...	...

This prediction query is a typical example of closed loop data mining. The cases returned by the prediction query can be targeted, for example, for direct promotion of the Golden member card. Or, the actual results of the selected cases can be compared against the predicted results to determine if the data mining model is indeed achieving an 80 percent or better confidence level of prediction. This provides information that can be used to evaluate the effectiveness of this particular data mining model, by constructing a confusion matrix or by computing the fit of the data mining model against this particular case set. The business decisions to be taken by the review of this data affect not just a single case, but a subset of a larger case set, and the effects of such business decisions may take weeks or months to manifest in terms of additional incoming data.

Data mining models can take data from a variety of sources, provided that the data structure of incoming cases is similar to the data structure of expected cases for the data mining model.

For example, the following prediction query uses the PREDICTION JOIN keyword to link a singleton query (a query that retrieves only one row), with both column and value information explicitly defined within the query, to the Member Card RDBMS data mining model in the **FoodMart 2000** database, to predict the type of member card most likely to be selected by a specific customer, as well as the confidence of the prediction.

```
SELECT
    [Member Card RDBMS].[member card] AS [Member Card],
    (100 * PREDICTPROBABILITY([Member Card RDBMS].[member card])) AS [Confidence Percent]
FROM
    [Member Card RDBMS]
PREDICTION JOIN
    (SELECT 'F' as Gender, 'M' as [Marital Status], 3 as [num children at home],
    '$130K - $150K' as [yearly income], 'Bachelors Degree' as education ) AS singleton
ON
    [Member Card RDBMS].[gender]=[singleton].[gender] AND
    [Member Card RDBMS].[marital status] = [singleton].[marital status] AND
    [Member Card RDBMS].[num children at home] = [singleton].[num children at home] AND
    [Member Card RDBMS].[yearly income] = [singleton].[yearly income] AND
    [Member Card RDBMS].[education] = [singleton].[education]
```

The following table illustrates the returned resultset from the previous prediction query. From the analysis provided by the data mining model on the case defined in the singleton query, the customer is most likely to choose a Golden member card, and the likelihood of that choice is about 63 percent.

Member Card	Confidence Percent
Golden	62.666666666666671

This prediction query is an excellent example of applied prediction in an operational data mining scenario. The case information supplied by the singleton query used in the PREDICTION JOIN clause of the prediction query is not supplied directly from a database; all columns and values are constructed within the singleton query. This information could just have easily been supplied from the user interface of a client application as from a single database record, and the immediate response of the data mining model allows the client application to respond to this information in real time, immediately affecting incoming data.

Using Data Mining Functions

In both of the prediction query examples presented earlier, the **PredictProbability** data mining function is used to provide confidence information on the predictions made by the queries. Other data mining functions are also available, which can be used to provide additional statistical information, such as variance or standard deviation, for cases analyzed through the data mining model.

For example, the previous query can instead use the **PredictHistogram** function to supply several common statistical measurements about the single case being examined, as demonstrated in the following query.

```
SELECT
    [Member Card RDBMS].[member card] AS [Predicted Member Card],
    PredictHistogram([Member Card RDBMS].[member card])
FROM
    [Member Card RDBMS]
PREDICTION JOIN
    (SELECT 'F' as Gender, 'M' as [Marital Status], 3 as [num children at home],
    '$130K - $150K' as [yearly income], 'Bachelors Degree' as education ) AS singleton
ON
    [Member Card RDBMS].[gender]=[singleton].[gender] AND
    [Member Card RDBMS].[marital status] = [singleton].[marital status] AND
    [Member Card RDBMS].[num children at home] = [singleton].[num children at home] AND
    [Member Card RDBMS].[yearly income] = [singleton].[yearly income] AND
    [Member Card RDBMS].[education] = [singleton].[education]
```

This prediction query returns a recordset that contains the predicted member card, all of the possible member card choices, and the statistical information behind each choice, or histogram, as shown in the following table. The $ADJUSTEDPROBABILITY, $VARIANCE and $STDEV columns, representing the adjusted probability, variance and standard deviation values of the various member card choices, have not been shown in the table due to space limitations.

Predicted Member Card	member card	$SUPPORT	$PROBABILITY	...
Golden	Golden	46	0.62666666666666671	
	Silver	14	0.20000000000000001	
	Bronze	7	0.10666666666666667	
	Normal	3	$5.3333333333333337E-2$	
		0	$1.3333333333333334E-2$	

Histogram information can be useful in both operational and data mining. For example, the previous prediction query indicates that this customer is more than three times as likely to choose the Golden member card instead of the Silver member card, but is twice as likely to select the Silver member card over the Bronze member card and about four times as likely to select the Silver member card over the Normal member card. The customer service representative, using a client application employing operational data mining, would then be able to rank the various member cards and offer each in turn to the customer based on this histogram information.

For more information about the use and availability of data mining functions, see SQL Server Books Online.

Getting Data to the Client

Microsoft® SQL Server™ 2000 Analysis Services supplies a robust server engine for online analytical processing (OLAP) and data mining. The server components, however, are useful only if the data managed by the server can be retrieved by and displayed to the user.

In this chapter, both data and meta data retrieval are discussed in relation to the data access technologies available for use with Analysis Services. Basic overviews and usage guidelines for each data access technology are provided, as well as samples illustrating the use of each technology.

Developing Analysis Services Client Applications

Analysis Services provides access to data and meta data through its implementation of the OLE DB for OLAP specification, Microsoft PivotTable® Service. Other OLE DB-compatible data access services, such as Microsoft ActiveX® Data Objects (ADO), can be used to supply a common, standard data access technology to client applications.

In conjunction with Microsoft Internet Information Services (IIS), PivotTable Service can also send and receive data and meta data across the Internet. For more information about using the Internet, see "Using The Internet With Analysis Services" in this chapter.

In addition to the above technologies, meta data on Analysis servers can also be accessed through Decision Support Objects (DSO), a powerful object model specifically designed to support Analysis Services. For more information about meta data access with DSO, see "Meta Data and Decision Support Objects" in this chapter.

Local Data and Meta Data

PivotTable Service also provides the ability to create offline, or local, cubes and data mining models. Client applications can connect to offline cubes and data mining models transparently, allowing client applications to copy and cache commonly-used OLAP and data mining objects from the server to the client and reduce network and resource usage. PivotTable Service supports a basic data definition language (DDL) useable only for offline OLAP and data mining objects.

Using offline OLAP and data mining objects allows for a third type of client architecture, in which the client application connects periodically and unpredictably to a server to synchronize its offline information. This architecture is prevalent in client applications designed for portable workstation and personal digital assistant clients.

Working with Data

One of the challenges with online analytical processing (OLAP) is the basic issue of multidimensional retrieval. The OLE DB for OLAP specification resolves this issue, detailing a complete solution, based on OLE DB, but capable of supporting the intricacies of multidimensional data access.

PivotTable Service is the Microsoft implementation of the OLE DB for OLAP specification, an OLE DB provider that can be used either with OLE DB directly, or with OLE DB in conjunction with other standardized data access technologies, such as ADO.

Data and PivotTable Service

PivotTable Service is an OLE DB provider, designed for Analysis Services, which implements the OLE DB for OLAP specification. It is used by other OLE DB compliant data access technologies, such as ADO and ADO MD to work with Analysis Services and relational database data.

However, PivotTable Service can be a complicated provider to use. The PivotTable Service provider is configured through the use of properties, usually set either through the connection string used to connect the PivotTable Service OLE DB provider to a data source, or through the collection of properties exposed, after a connection is made to an Analysis server.

Properties

PivotTable Service properties are accessible by other data access technologies, typically by the connection string used to connect the provider to the server or by registry settings stored on the client. The following properties are of particular interest when you develop client applications:

- **Auto Synch Period**

  The interval specified in this property determines how often the client cache synchronizes with the Analysis server during the course of a session. This property should be set depending on the current usage context of the session; for example, if the client application is accessing only historical data, the **Auto Synch Period** parameter can be set to zero, because nothing is likely to change between queries. Other applications may require automatic synchronization, and a useful value for this setting may change from usage context to usage context within a single session. One effective method of performance tuning is to allow this value to be set by the user or administrator as needed, as a tunable property available through the client application.

  If the parameter is set to zero, automatic synchronization is disabled. The client cache synchronizes with the server cache only when a query is executed against the server. While this setting is useful in certain situations, this value is not recommended for most client applications.

For more information about managing the client-side cache, see Chapter 26, "Performance Tuning Analysis Services."

- **Client Cache Size**

  The default value for this parameter is 25, or 25 percent of available virtual memory, but it can be changed during a session. Setting this parameter to zero can be problematic, because the client cache can quickly use most of the resources available to a client. Setting this value to a percentage of virtual memory can be imprecise if a client application is installed on a wide variety of machines; setting this value to a fixed amount of kilobytes can also be problematic for the same reason.

  As with the **Auto Synch Period** property, supplying access to this property as a tunable property available through the client application can improve performance and reduce resource overload.

  For more information about managing the client-side cache, see Chapter 26, "Performance Tuning Analysis Services."

- **CompareCaseNonSensitiveStringFlags** and **CompareCaseSensitiveStringFlags**

  Both of these settings can be set by a client application either through the connection string or through the use of registry keys. Both keys are kept in \HKEY_LOCAL_MACHINE\SOFTWARE\Microsoft\ OLAP Server\CurrentVersion, and are stored as bitmapped long integers. The settings for both properties affect all sessions made by a specific client, and the values for subsequent connections are determined by the values used for the first connection in a given process thread. After they are set, they cannot be changed for a given session.

  Typically, these keys do not require changes. The default value for the **CompareCaseSensitiveStringFlags** property is set to NORM_IGNOREWIDTH, NORM_IGNOREKANATYPE, and NORM_IGNORECASE, while the default value for **CompareCaseNonSensitiveStringFlags** property is set to zero (in other words, no settings are applied.)

- **Connect Timeout**

  This property maps directly to the DBPROP_INIT_TIMEOUT property supported by OLE DB, and the default setting for this property is 15 seconds. If the connection timeout period elapses before a connection can be completed to an Analysis server, the error &H80004005, "OLAP server error: The operation requested failed due to network problems", will be raised.

  This value may need to be changed depending on network latency issues and how busy the OLAP Server is. We recommend not setting this value lower than the default value, but if the client application generates timeout errors, you may want to raise it to 30 seconds or higher.

- **Data Source**

  PivotTable Service can connect to Analysis servers in two ways, using either TCP/IP or HTTP. If you are connecting to the Analysis server in the same domain, the data source is the computer name for the Analysis server. If you are connecting using HTTP or HTTPS, you can specify either an IP address or URL in order to establish a connection to the Analysis server.

- **Default GUID Dialect**

Depending on the client application, queries can be processed slightly faster if the appropriate default dialect is selected. The default setting assumes that the SQL parser will be first used to parse submitted queries, which means that Multidimensional Expressions (MDX) queries will always be parsed twice—once by the SQL parser, which fails, and then by the MDX parser. A similar behavior exists for data mining queries. This can also prevent analysis of errors from the MDX or data mining parser, because the error message from the default parser is returned to the client application.

If your client application is used primarily for MDX, set this property to MDGUID_MDX. Otherwise, the default setting should be sufficient.

- **Execution Location** and **Mining Execution Location**

The default value allows PivotTable Service to determine whether a query will be executed on the client computer or on the server. However, in certain situations, setting this property so that queries are executed on the server can improve performance. Two separate properties are used to separate OLAP and data mining queries.

- **Initial Catalog**

This property determines the database context used by the connection. You must use this property to correctly establish this context for a specific database. If you do not specify this, the first database stored in Analysis Services is used as the database context. This property is especially necessary for handling meta data.

- **Log File**

This property is extremely useful for debugging client applications; it functions in much the same way as an ODBC trace log, storing the process ID, date and time, query type, and query text for each query issued through the PivotTable Service OLE DB provider. However, using the log file affects performance because of increased file activity on the client, and should be used only in debugging situations.

- **MDX Compatibility**

This property affects how ragged and unbalanced hierarchies are viewed. If your client application can handle the display of ragged hierarchies as managed in Analysis Services, this property should be set to 2. Note that this property affects only placeholder members with data or with subordinate nonplaceholder members within the hierarchy. If the placeholder has no data and has no subordinate nonplaceholder members, it is always hidden regardless of the value of this property.

- **Mining Location**

This property must be set in order to create permanent local data mining models on the client. Not setting this property is one of the common reasons that local data mining models are not properly persisted to the client.

- **Mining Persistence Format**

  Although the default setting for this property causes PivotTable Service to store data mining models in binary format, you can change this property to store data mining models as Extensible Markup Language (XML) to make the information portable with only a slight decrease in performance as a tradeoff.

- **Safety Options**

  This setting should be changed cautiously. The setting can be relaxed to allow external function libraries with potentially unsafe functions to be loaded for a given session, but this should never be done for function libraries with unknown contents. Corruption or data loss, or worse, can potentially result from using unsafe function libraries.

- **Secured Cell Value**

  A valuable property when used properly, **Secured Cell Value** formats the contents of a secured cell (in other words, a cell whose contents the client application cannot view due to lack of security rights) into a variety of settings. This can be very effective when using numeric calculations of cell data in client applications, as the default value sets secured cells to a string. This can interfere with most client-side calculations; if so, set this property to either three, which will return a NULL, or four, which will return a zero for secured cells.

- **SSPI**

  This property is important if the Analysis server is on a domain that supports multiple security packages, such as Kerberos. Typically, this property needs to be changed from its default only if security measures for a given domain require such a change.

- **Writeback Timeout**

  This property can be tuned if a client application experiences timeouts due to network latency issues or if the client application hangs due to server-side difficulties with writebacks. This property must be set in the connection string, because it cannot be changed for a session once set. If not set, the default setting for this property is Null; writebacks never time out by default.

Data and ActiveX Data Objects

ActiveX Data Objects (ADO) is an OLE DB-compliant data access technology, designed to handle relational and, to a limited extent, multidimensional data. Although best used in conjunction with ADO MD, this data access technology can support access to Analysis Services data and meta data directly.

Because ADO encapsulates OLE DB, which in turn uses PivotTable Service when connected to an Analysis server, most of the functionality available to OLE DB is available to the ADO library and, consequently, to the client application. Most client applications can use ADO and ADO MD without having to directly call or reference the OLE DB library. This is the preferred route for applications that support COM interfaces, such as Microsoft Visual Basic®.

ADO can be used to retrieve the data from the Analysis server in a tabular form (a flattened view of multidimensional data). You can use this approach for accessing multidimensional cubes if your client application is designed to retrieve data from relational sources, and you want to start querying relational and multidimensional sources without changing your code. The ADO **Connection** object has an open schema method that enables you to retrieve all meta data about cubes, dimensions, and other objects on the Analysis server in the form of schema rowsets. Later in this chapter we show that using ADO MD provides a much richer object model for easier exploration when accessing data and meta data.

The MDX Sample Application, shipped with SQL Server 2000 Analysis Services as a sample, provides an excellent example of using both ADO and ADO MD to view multidimensional data.

Usage Guidelines

The following basic guidelines will allow you to make better use of ADO in Analysis Services client applications:

- Use the **ConnectionString** property to your advantage.

   The **ConnectionString** property, used by the ADO **Connection** object when connecting to a database, is used to pass information to the PivotTable Service OLE DB provider. The connection string information, however, can do much more than simply provide the data source and initial catalog used by ADO. The connection string can also configure the PivotTable Service OLE DB provider and, to a limited extent, perform offline operations. Each property used by PivotTable Service serves as a connection string parameter when using ADO or ADO MD.

   For more information on individual connection string parameters, see "Data and PivotTable Service" in this chapter.

- Take advantage of actions in Analysis Services.

   In Analysis Services, actions are context-sensitive commands, stored on the Analysis server and defined as part of the structure of a cube. Actions are available to all client applications that access the cell, subject to the security defined for the action. Client applications can review the action type, which defines the general intended behavior of an action, and perform an application step based on the statement returned with the action. Because actions are typically provided as part of the retrieval of cube data, user interfaces tend to support actions within a display of cube data. For example, Cube Browser in Analysis Services supports actions as part of the pop-up menu available from the grid used to display cell data.

Actions can be retrieved from the SCHEMA_ROWSET_ACTIONS schema rowset through the **OpenSchema** method of an ADO **Connection** object or through the **Commands** collection of a cube in the DSO library.

Actions allow you to provide shared business functionality across multiple client applications without the maintenance issues typically associated with such shared functionality.

Data and ActiveX Data Objects (Multidimensional)

The ActiveX Data Objects (Multidimensional) library (ADO MD) is an extension library for ADO. ADO MD provides access to multidimensional data through an object model designed to access online analytical processing (OLAP) structures, and serves as an automation layer above PivotTable Service, the OLE DB provider that implements the OLE DB for OLAP specification. ADO MD can be used from any programming language that supports COM interfaces, such as Visual Basic, Microsoft Visual C++®, Microsoft Visual Basic Scripting Edition (VBScript), and Microsoft JScript®.

ADO MD takes advantage of the common features provided by the ADO library when connecting to an Analysis server. ADO MD uses an ADO **Connection** object, and supports the ability to pass a variety of commands through the **ConnectionString** property for PivotTable Service property support.

Using MDX, the ADO MD **Cellset** object provides a multidimensional representation of dimension and cell information retrieved from Analysis Services cubes. The cell data is provided on demand; the **Cellset** does not retrieve cell information until the cells are referenced.

One of the benefits of using the ADO MD **Cellset** object is the ability to handle speculative, or what if, analysis on retrieved multidimensional data. Analysis Services supports writing information back to a cube for a single cell or a set of cells, as a distribution, and ADO MD can take advantage of this feature. ADO MD supports either temporary writeback, which lasts only for the lifetime of a connection and can be used to perform speculative analysis without harm to underlying data, or permanent writeback, which allows the results of such analysis to be committed to a special table maintained by the Analysis server.

You should use ADO MD in conjunction with ADO to provide the best possible support for interactive client applications. For example, the MDX **DrillThrough** command allows you to drill through to underlying relational data, and retrieves the data in an ADO **Recordset** object. Drilling through becomes more complex in cubes with multiple partitions, as multiple resultsets are potentially returned (one resultset per partition). ADO and ADO MD complement each other in this manner, and can use the full range of functionality provided by Analysis Services when implemented together in a client application.

The MDX Sample Application, shipped with SQL Server 2000 Analysis Services as a sample, provides an excellent example of using both ADO and ADO MD to view multidimensional data.

Usage Guidelines

The following recommendations should help in employing ADO MD to access data from Analysis Services:

- Take advantage of actions in Analysis Services.

  In Analysis Services, actions are context-sensitive commands, stored on the Analysis server and defined as part of the structure of a cube. Actions are available to all client applications that access the cell, subject to the security defined for the action. Actions allow you to provide shared business functionality across multiple client applications without the maintenance issues typically associated with such shared functionality.

  For more information about using actions, see "Data and ActiveX Data Objects" in this chapter.

- Use the **Axes** and **Positions** collections for determining the hierarchy of a member.

  A common issue when displaying multidimensional data in a two-dimensional format is the need to flatten the data retrieved by an ADO MD **Cellset** object. One method commonly employed is the parsing of the unique member name to determine the ancestry of a particular cell or member—this is not a recommended technique. Instead, you should take advantage of the **LevelDepth** property, as well as the **Axes** and **Positions** collections, supplied by the ADO MD **Cellset** to determine the ancestry of a specific cell. The unique member name should instead be viewed as an arbitrarily generated unique key, lacking information for the purposes of client application development.

- Take advantage of MDX functionality for user interface support.

  MDX provides a number of functions designed for user interface support, such as drilling up and down on members or formatting individual cells based on member properties. For more information about using MDX to provide user interface support, see Chapter 23, "Business Case Solutions Using MDX."

- Take care with resource usage in user interfaces.

  Multidimensional data, in general, is overwhelmingly large. ADO MD, by definition, supports an exponential growth of referenced data; each dimension supported in an ADO MD **Cellset** object increases the potential number of retrieved cells by an order of magnitude. When designing user interfaces to support ADO MD data, you should be conscious of the resources required to display such data. For example, an ADO MD **Cellset** object accessing a cube with five dimensions, each with just 50 members per dimension, can potentially return 312,500,000 (50 x 50 x 50 x 50 x 50) cells. ADO MD refers to such data on demand, because of this potential for very large multidimensional cell sets. The client application, as well, should take advantage of an on demand methodology for showing large cell sets, such as using hierarchical grids and other limited-view techniques for displaying large amounts of information in a controlled manner.

Working with Meta Data

Meta data is a term used to describe the information about the schema and structure of data, such as the schema for a database. Meta data is simply data about the structure and organization of data—tables, columns, relationships, indexes, and so on.

For most client applications, meta data is used for informative purposes. Filling list boxes with available cubes, selecting a data mining model from a dropdown list, and so on, are common uses for meta data in client applications. Administrative client applications, however, make extensive use of meta data to create, delete, change, and manage all aspects of Analysis Services. Analysis Manager, for example, is an administrative client application, designed as a Microsoft Management Console (MMC) add-in with supplemental ActiveX DLL libraries.

In Analysis Services, access to meta data can be almost as important as access to data for client applications, due to the inherent complexity of multidimensional storage. Several technologies, listed below, support meta data access:

- DSO

- OLE DB with PivotTable Service

- ADO with PivotTable Service

- ADO MD with PivotTable Service

DSO does not require PivotTable Service to function, because it works directly with proprietary interfaces supported by Analysis Services.

Meta Data and Decision Support Objects

The Decision Support Objects (DSO) library consists of an object model that mirrors the object hierarchy of Analysis Services exactly. Unlike other data access methods for working with meta data, DSO works directly with the Analysis server, bypassing PivotTable Service as a provider. Using DSO for working with Analysis Services meta data is preferred over other methods discussed in this chapter for the following reasons:

- Safety

  The DSO library gives you power and flexibility without sacrificing the safety and stability of the Analysis server; the hierarchical nature of meta data in Analysis Services is directly represented and enforced by the DSO object model.

- Ease of Use

  The strictly enforced hierarchy of the DSO library makes it easier to work with potentially complex meta data in the right place at the right time.

- Flexibility

  DSO can be used in any programming language that supports COM interfaces, including scripting languages and languages that can handle only late-bound COM objects.

- Power

  The DSO library is designed specifically to handle the meta data needs of Analysis Services, including access to features like calculated cells, actions, and data mining models.

The following diagram illustrates the object model of the DSO library.

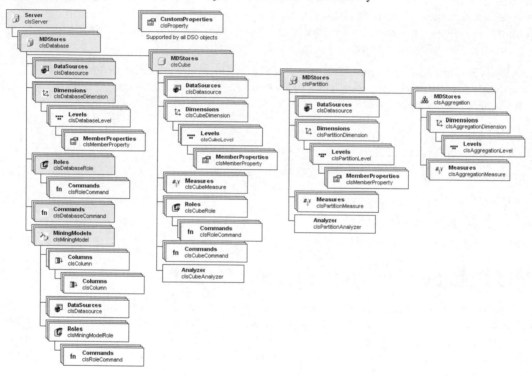

The DSO library handles only meta data. To access the data stored in OLAP and data mining objects, you need to use another library, such as ADO MD. DSO is ideally suited for administrative applications that specialize in handling meta data, such as installation or remote maintenance applications, or for Analysis Services add-ins.

DSO cannot be used to handle offline cubes or data mining models, because the DSO object model works directly with the Analysis server.

DSO is highly recommended for administrative client applications and for client applications that need to work with Analysis Services meta data on a read-write basis. For client applications that need meta data for informative purposes only, another data access technology is recommended, such as ADO MD.

Usage Guidelines

The following basic recommendations are useful if you plan to use DSO in an Analysis Services client application. For more information on the effective use of DSO in client applications, see the white paper "Developing Effective Decision Support Objects (DSO) Solutions with Microsoft SQL Server 2000 Analysis Services" at http://msdn.microsoft.com/sqlserver/.

- Use only documented interfaces.

   DSO objects implement a variety of interfaces, and many similar objects in DSO use one of several common interfaces. Use only the interfaces documented in SQL Server Books Online. Other interfaces, such as **ICommon**, are intended for internal use only, and can have unpredictable results on your meta data. The only exception to this rule is the **Database** interface, which must be used instead of the **MDStore** interface if you intend to trap database events in your client application.

- Know the difference between major and minor objects.

   In DSO, minor objects cannot commit their own changes. All minor objects belong to a major object; the major object commits changes not just for itself, but for its minor objects as well. If you do not use the major object to commit changes to the minor object, unpredictable results can occur.

- Know the order of precedence.

   Because DSO enforces the hierarchy of objects in Analysis Services, some objects must be created before other objects. The technical paper, "Developing Effective Decision Support Objects Solutions with Microsoft SQL Server 2000 Analysis Services," provides detailed information about the order of precedence for DSO objects. For more information about this white paper, see http://msdn.microsoft.com/sqlserver/.

- Lock DSO objects when changing meta data.

   DSO allows object locking while working with meta data, to prevent other users from reading, writing, or processing locked objects in Analysis Services. Use locks when changing meta data to prevent user confusion and lost changes.

Sample Application—Meta Data Scripter

The Meta Data Scripter sample provides an excellent way to exploit the features of DSO. The Meta Data Scripter (**MetaDataScripter**) is available on the *SQL Server 2000 Resource Kit* CD-ROM in the folder, \ToolsAndSamples\MetaDataScripter.

The Meta Data Scripter sample consists of a Visual Basic® 6.0 ActiveX DLL project used to construct an Analysis Services add-in, as well as two VBScript template files. The add-in enables you to script the meta data of any object, including dependent objects that can be selected in Analysis Manager. The add-in generates a VBScript file that uses DSO to recreate the scripted objects.

The routines that use DSO to recreate the scripted objects are contained in the Footer.vbs template file included with the sample. The global variables used by the generated VBScript file are contained in the Header.vbs template file, also supplied with the sample. The Analysis Services add-in copies both files into the generated VBScript file. The generated VBScript script file can be executed either from the command line on any Analysis server with the Microsoft Windows® Script Host or in any environment that can support the VBScript scripting language.

Installation Instructions

The Meta Data Scripter is supplied as Visual Basic 6.0 source code and supporting files. Because this sample is an Analysis Services add-in, additional steps are required to register the add-in with Analysis Services.

1. Copy the MetaDataScripter files from the ToolsAndSamples folder of the *SQL Server Resource Kit* CD-ROM to a folder on your local hard drive.

2. Open the Metadatascripter.vbp project file using Visual Basic 6.0.

3. To register the Analysis Services add-in, execute the RegisterAddIn subroutine from the **Immediate** window. This routine writes the registry keys needed by Analysis Services to recognize the add-in.

4. Either compile the add-in into an ActiveX DLL or execute the Meta Data Scripter project from Visual Basic 6.0. If Analysis Manager is already running, close it first.

Usage Instructions

The Meta Data Scripter sample can script any object in the DSO hierarchy (including objects not directly viewable through the Analysis Manager). Follow these instructions to script an object in Analysis Manager.

1. Start Analysis Manager.

2. In the tree pane of Analysis Manager, expand the **Analysis Servers** folder.

3. Expand the server containing the database you want to use.

   If the server does not appear, right-click the **Analysis Servers** folder and click **Register Server**.

4. Right-click the server or any object under it for which you want to create a meta data script.

5. Point to **All Tasks,** and then click **Create meta data script**.

Meta Data and PivotTable Service

As with any other OLE DB provider, PivotTable Service is not meant to be used directly, but in concert with OLE DB or an OLE DB compliant data access technology, such as ADO and ADO MD, to retrieve meta data.

Usage Guidelines

Although more information about using other data access technologies with PivotTable Service can be found in other sections of this chapter, there are a few things to know about using the PivotTable Service provider with other data access technologies:

- Know your schema rowsets.

  The PivotTable Service provider does not support many of the expected OLE DB schema rowsets. ADO and ADO MD do not support the **GetSchemas** method provided by the **IDBSchemaRowset** interface in OLE DB; this can make discovering which schemas are supported difficult.

- Know your properties.

  The PivotTable Service provider supports over 40 different properties, most of which are accessible by connection string parameters and the **Properties** collection in ADO and ADO MD. For more information about using specific PivotTable Service properties, see "Data and PivotTable Service" earlier in this chapter.

Meta Data and OLE DB

OLE DB serves as the underpinning to ADO and ADO MD, and works in concert with PivotTable Service to retrieve meta data from Analysis servers.

PivotTable Service is the Microsoft implementation of the OLE DB for OLAP specification. Other data access technologies, such as ADO and ADO MD, also serve as a layer above both OLE DB and PivotTable Service.

OLE DB is usually not directly employed in client applications. Instead, other data access technologies such as ADO and ADO MD are used to access meta data. As with ADO, the easiest way to retrieve meta data in OLE DB is through schema rowsets. The **IDBSchemaRowset** interface provides access to schema rowsets, with the **GetSchemas** method allowing enumeration of supported schema rowsets and the **GetRowset** method allowing retrieval of a specific schema rowset.

Schema rowsets can be retrieved in OLE DB only by using the GUID to identify the desired schema rowset. Not all schema rowsets are required to be supported by OLE DB providers.

Usage Guidelines

The following general guidelines are essential for successful meta data retrieval from Analysis Services:

- Use both **GetSchemas** and **GetRowset** methods in **IDBSchemaRowset**.

  The **GetRowset** method does not perform type checking of restriction values in the array supplied to the *rgRestrictions* parameter and does not validate the number of restrictions supplied to the *cRestrictions* parameter; you can inadvertently supply too few or too many restrictions in the array, or supply the wrong data type for restriction values.

  If you are unsure of the number and data type of restrictions supported by a schema rowset, or even if the OLE DB provider supports the schema rowset, use the **GetSchemas** method first to retrieve all supported schema rowset GUIDs and their restrictions. Use this information to correctly construct a VARIANT array of restrictions to supply to the **GetRowset** method.

Meta Data and ActiveX Data Objects

Using ADO with ADO MD gives you the ability to manipulate both data and meta data for any multidimensional data provider (MDP), including Analysis Services.

Because ADO encapsulates OLE DB, which in turn uses PivotTable Service when connected to an Analysis server, most of the functionality available to OLE DB is available to the ADO library and, consequently, to the client application. Most client applications can use ADO and ADO MD without having to directly call or reference the OLE DB library. This is the preferred route for applications that support COM interfaces, such as Visual Basic.

One way to retrieve all forms of meta data is to use ADO to retrieve the schema rowsets for Analysis Services objects.

The **OpenSchema** method of the ADO **Connection** object makes the meta data of Analysis Services available as schema rowsets, returning an ADO **Recordset** object for a specified schema rowset. There are two techniques for using the **OpenSchema** method: either use an enumeration constant for the desired schema rowset or directly use the GUID for a desired schema rowset. The **SchemaEnum** enumeration included in the ADO DB library supplies the constants used for the first technique. If you intend to work with both OLAP and data mining meta data, the second technique is preferred; no constants are supplied with ADO for retrieving data mining schema rowsets. If you intend to work only with OLAP data, the first technique is preferable, because you do not need to make the GUID information for OLAP schema rowsets available for the client application.

Usage Guidelines

ADO is an excellent tool for retrieving meta data from Analysis Services. The following guidelines will help you do so efficiently:

- Know your restrictions.

  The **OpenSchema** method of the ADO Connection object effectively encapsulates the **IDBSchemaRowset** interface of OLE DB, specifically the **GetRowset** method of the interface. The *cRestrictions* and *rgRestrictions* parameters for the **IDBSchemaRowset::GetRowset** method in OLE DB are based on the array supplied to the *Restrictions* parameter of the **OpenSchema** method in ADO. There is no type checking of individual restriction values or of the appropriate count of restrictions for a specified schema rowset; it is very easy to supply an incorrect number of restrictions or the wrong data type for a specific restriction value.

  However, unlike in OLE DB, there is no corresponding method in ADO to retrieve a list of supported schema rowsets.

Sample Application—Schema Rowset Explorer

The Schema Rowset Explorer (**SchemaRowsetExplorer**) is available on the *SQL Server 2000 Resource Kit* CD-ROM in the folder, \ToolsAndSamples\SchemaRowsetExplorer.

This sample illustrates the direct use of the OLAP and data mining schema rowset GUIDs to retrieve schema rowsets. Written in Visual Basic 6.0, the sample also illustrates the use of restriction columns, which allow you to retrieve only the desired meta data from the schema rowset. The information provided in the *Restrictions* parameter of the **OpenSchema** method is used to construct a SQL WHERE clause when querying the schema rowset.

The sample application uses a resource file to store the GUID and restrictions information for each schema rowset. When a schema rowset is selected, the restrictions information is retrieved and used to configure the application form, allowing you to enter restrictions for the selected schema rowset.

When the Load Schema Rowset button is clicked, the GUID for the selected schema rowset is retrieved. The values supplied for the restrictions, if any, are stored in a Variant array. Both the array and the GUID are supplied to the ADO **OpenSchema** method, returning an ADO **Recordset** object. The column layout and data from the ADO **Recordset** object is then loaded into the **MSFlexGrid** control on the application form for display.

Installation Instructions

The Schema Rowset Explorer is supplied as Visual Basic 6.0 source code and supporting files.

- Copy the SchemaRowsetExplorer files from the ToolsAndSamples folder of the *SQL Server Resource Kit* CD-ROM to a folder on your local hard drive.

Usage Instructions

The Schema Rowset Explorer sample can view any schema rowset supported by the PivotTable Service OLE DB provider. Follow these instructions to start the application and view a schema rowset.

1. Start the Schema Rowset Explorer to display the **Schema Rowset Explorer** dialog box.

2. Enter a valid Analysis server and schema rowset into the **Server Name** and **Schema Rowset** fields, respectively.

3. Optionally, enter valid restriction values in the text boxes provided for the restriction columns in the **Restrictions** frame.

4. Click **Load Schema Rowset** to load the schema rowset.

Meta Data and ActiveX Data Objects (Multidimensional)

The ActiveX Data Objects (Multidimensional) library (ADO MD) is an extension library for ADO. ADO MD provides access to multidimensional meta data through an object model designed to access OLAP data. If you intend to use data mining meta data in your client application, you should use either DSO for read-write access or ADO for read-only access, because ADO MD does not support data mining models. ADO MD is best used in client applications that need to support multiple heterogeneous multidimensional data sources, or with ADO in client applications that access both relational and OLAP meta data. As with ADO, ADO MD encapsulates OLE DB, so most of the functionality available through OLE DB and PivotTable Service is available to client applications that use ADO MD.

ADO MD is specifically designed to handle multidimensional data access. ADO uses flattened recordsets when retrieving multidimensional information from Analysis Services cubes, but ADO MD preserves the multidimensional nature of such data by returning ADO MD **Cellset** objects from queries performed against Analysis Services cubes. While this is useful when working with data, it is not necessary when dealing with meta data.

One of the benefits of using ADO MD is the ability to consistently use the same data access technology for both data and meta data retrieval. The object model used by ADO MD compares roughly to that of DSO, although the ADO MD object model is designed to work with meta data from any MDP supporting the OLE DB for OLAP specification, while DSO is specifically designed to handle the intricacies of Analysis Services meta data. As such, ADO MD does not support access to some of the more specialized features of Analysis Services, such as calculated cells and actions, as meta data. Combined with ADO, complete support of relational, OLAP, and data mining data can be easily handled within a client application.

One drawback, however, is that the topmost object in the ADO MD hierarchy, the **Catalog** object, represents a database in Analysis Services. ADO MD, as with ADO, supports the concept of a default database; you must specify a database when you connect to the Analysis server, using the *Initial Catalog* parameter in the connection string to set the initially selected database. In other words, you cannot connect to an Analysis server and enumerate the available databases using the ADO MD object model. For non-administrative client applications, this is not much of a problem; most client applications of this nature use a specific database for their data access requirements.

Usage Guidelines

- Know your catalog.

   This guideline is very important for ADO MD because of the way the initial catalog is established through the connection string used to connect to the Analysis server. There is no direct way, at the time of this writing, to retrieve a schema rowset in ADO MD containing the databases on a specific Analysis server; another technology, such as ADO or DSO, must instead be used to retrieve a list of databases on an Analysis server.

Sample Application—Analysis Server Catalog Explorer

The Analysis Server Catalog Explorer (**CatalogExplorer**) sample application is available on the *SQL Server 2000 Resource Kit* CD-ROM in the folder, \ToolsAndSamples\CatalogExplorer. This sample application illustrates using ADO and ADO MD to retrieve the meta data relating to OLAP objects, such as cubes and dimensions, from an Analysis server. Given a valid server name and catalog name, an ADODB **Connection** object is connected to the Analysis server, and then used for the **ActiveConnection** property of an ADO MD **Catalog** object.

The **Catalog** object, in turn, retrieves the entire available object model when the **Retrieve catalog from Analysis server button** is clicked. The subordinate objects of the **Catalog** object are then loaded into a **TreeView** control for perusal.

Installation Instructions

The Analysis Server Catalog Explorer is supplied as Visual Basic 6.0 source code and supporting files.

- Copy the CatalogExplorer files from the CatalogExplorer folder of the *SQL Server Resource Kit* CD-ROM to a folder on your local hard drive.

Usage Instructions

The Analysis Server Catalog Explorer sample can view any database that can be selected from the Analysis Manager tree view. Follow these instructions to start the application and view the meta data for a database using ADO MD.

1. Start Catalog Explorer to view the **Catalog Explorer** dialog box.

2. For **Server Name**, type the computer name for a valid Analysis server.

   For the local computer, use "LocalHost".

3. For **Catalog Name**, type the name of a database on the server.

4. Click **Retrieve catalog from Analysis Server** to load the database meta data into the tree view.

Using the Internet with Analysis Services

Analysis Services offers the ability to access multidimensional data across the Internet or intranet from servers running IIS, using HTTP or HTTPS to transfer data. A special Active Server Page (ASP), msolap.asp, and an ActiveX DLL, msmdpump.dll, are used on the server to support data transfer.

To use this functionality, the Uniform Resource Locator (URL) of the IIS server should be specified for the **Data Source** parameter used in the connection string sent to PivotTable Service on the client. PivotTable Service automatically and transparently handles the transfer of data across the Internet; most thick client applications can support Internet access directly, with no coding changes.

Usage Guidelines

Most of the guidelines presented below refer more to administration issues, rather than development issues, with Analysis Services.

- Use HTTPS whenever possible.

  The nature of OLAP information is typically sensitive and proprietary; information-rich aggregated business data. You should take advantage of security features in IIS, such as the use of secure data transfer with HTTPS, to protect your OLAP data. Ideally, the virtual web site used to support msolap.asp should be separate from other web sites managed by the IIS server, to further isolate any additional required security.

- Be aware of IIS security issues.

  For example, one of the most common security issues encountered when accessing Analysis Services from IIS is that many Analysis Services objects, such as cubes, are not available to Internet or intranet users.

  IIS uses a default user account, typically named **IUSER_<Server Name>**, when accessing external applications. This user account is not included as part of the All Users database role in Analysis Services; most Analysis Services administrators forget about this user account when planning access. If you plan on using Analysis Services across the Internet, this user account should be included in database, cube, and mining model roles where appropriate.

Performance Tuning
Analysis Services

Microsoft® SQL Server™ 2000 Analysis Services provides a complete server solution for online analytical processing (OLAP) and data mining business needs, while simplifying the typically complex tasks involved with the design and maintenance of OLAP servers. One of the benefits of Analysis Services is the ability to tune the performance of the Analysis server to meet specific business requirements. This chapter presents a discussion of performance tuning for increased overall, querying, and processing performance, including detailed information about Analysis Services architecture. For information about tuning the performance of the SQL Server 2000 relational database that manages data used by Analysis Services, see Chapter 20, "RDBMS Performance Tuning Guide for Data Warehousing."

Introduction

OLAP products are becoming an essential part of decision support systems because of the flexibility and performance offered by the presentation of large amounts of information in an easily accessible form. Analysis Services allows the high resource demand needed for such information extraction to be managed at the server level, providing an additional presentation layer while simultaneously decreasing the ad hoc query load on data warehouses.

This chapter assumes the reader has a basic knowledge of SQL Server 2000 Analysis Services and a familiarity with basic data warehousing concepts.

Why Use OLAP?

When attempting to query information in a multidimensional fashion, Analysis Services offers two very important advantages over relational databases—flexibility and speed.

Analysis Services provides MDX, a robust query language specifically designed for working with multidimensional information. Typically, data warehouses are implemented in a relational database system, such as SQL Server 2000, designed to support two-dimensional queries using Structured Query Language (SQL) as the query language of choice.

Consider, for example, the following two queries. The first query, written in SQL, retrieves the average economic income per household, grouped by product, from a relational database:

```
CREATE TABLE
    #qry1_temp1
    (product_id INT, households INT, total_ei MONEY)
INSERT INTO
    #qry1_temp
    (product_id, households, total_ei)
    SELECT
        product_id, COUNT(DISTINCT household-id), SUM(economic_income)
    FROM
        VLDBMart.dbo.Account_prof_fact
    GROUP BY
        product_id
SELECT
    a.prod_name, b.total_ei / b.households
FROM
    VLDBMart.dbo.ProductDim a, #qry1_temp1 b
WHERE
    a.product_id = b.product_id
```

By contrast, this query is written in MDX and uses a multidimensional database to retrieve the same information:

```
WITH MEMBER
    [Measures].[Average Economic Income]
AS
    'SUM({[Measures].[Economic Income]}) / ([Measures].[Distinct Household Count])'
SELECT
    {[Measures].[Average Economic Income]}
    ON COLUMNS,
    {[ProductDim].[Product ID].MEMBERS}
    ON ROWS
FROM
    AccountProfitabilityH0
```

The first and most apparent difference between these two queries is the amount and complexity of the code needed to perform them. While the SQL query needs temporary table storage to construct a single attribute and multiple database actions to retrieve aggregated results, the MDX query needs a single attribute of information, created in memory, and a single database action to retrieve the same results.

The other difference between these two queries is processing speed. Both queries were executed on the same hardware platform. The first query took approximately 88 seconds to complete; the second query took only four seconds—in other words, the first query was 2200 percent slower than the second query. Because Analysis Services stores and manages aggregations in a multidimensional structure, access to aggregated data is considerably faster.

In a data warehousing solution, available resources are typically at a premium; such resources should be allocated as little and as late as possible, and should be released as early as possible. Analysis Services allows the full range of data warehousing information to be made available in an aggregated form while minimizing the data warehousing resources typically required to support such availability.

As impressive as this is, Analysis Services can supply even better querying and processing performance. With the proper adjustment and design consideration, querying and processing performance can be improved through the judicial application of techniques discussed in this chapter.

Architecture

The performance tuning of Analysis Services can be a complex series of tasks, involving many elements within both server and client components. An overview of Analysis Services architecture clarifies how the server and client components interact with each other and helps in identifying bottlenecks in querying and processing performance.

Overview

The following diagram details the architecture of Analysis Services in terms of data and meta data access.

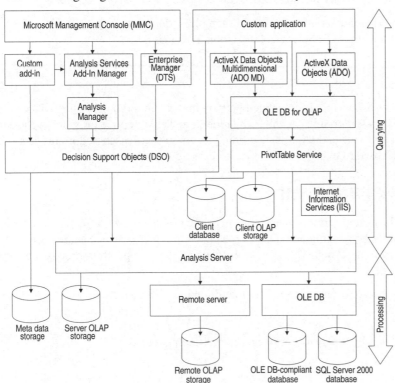

Administration of Analysis Services is performed with Analysis Manager, a user interface for the Decision Support Objects (DSO) library. The DSO library consists of a robust object model constructed from COM interfaces, easily accessible by any programming language capable of handling early or late bound COM objects. This includes languages such as Microsoft Visual Basic®, Visual C++®, Microsoft Visual Basic Scripting Edition (VBScript), and Microsoft JScript®.

Access to Analysis Services data is supported through PivotTable® Service, an OLE DB provider that implements the OLE DB for OLAP specification. PivotTable Service is not directly accessed by client applications; other data access technologies, such as OLE DB, ActiveX® Data Objects (ADO), and ActiveX Data Objects Multidimensional (ADO MD), use PivotTable Service as a data provider. PivotTable Service also provides a mechanism for disconnected usage. Portions of cubes defined and accessed from an Analysis server can be saved on the client for later use when disconnected from the network. Also, users can create cubes and OLAP and data mining models locally, accessing information from data sources through OLE DB providers.

Internet and intranet access to Analysis Services data is also supported, through the use of a special Active Server Page (ASP), Msolap.asp, and companion library, Msmdpump.dll, which can be used through Microsoft Internet Information Services (IIS) to supply secure data transfer between a client application using PivotTable Service and a remote Analysis server. A variety of deployment scenarios is also possible for access to analysis data using Web pages hosted on IIS. In these scenarios, PivotTable Service runs on the IIS server, effectively making the IIS server a client to Analysis Services.

Analysis Services can access relational data from OLE DB compliant databases, even flat files. However, real-time OLAP is supported only by SQL Server 2000 relational databases.

Memory Management

Memory management in Analysis Services is conducted both on the server and on the client. The Analysis server directly manages server-side caching, while the PivotTable Service provider caches data on the client, as well. Both server-side and client-side caching techniques are discussed in this section, including the economic model used to manage server-side processing memory.

Server Memory Management

Analysis Services uses a sophisticated form of memory management on the server, effectively balancing memory conservation against the processing and querying load. Several memory cache areas are allocated for specific purposes on the Analysis server, with an emphasis on separating processing and querying operations, in terms of memory.

Memory usage for an Analysis server is broken out into the following areas:

- Read-ahead buffer

  The read-ahead buffer is used by Analysis Services when retrieving data.

- Dimension memory

  Used to cache dimension members and member properties, dimension memory is allocated at startup and retained at all times, subject to dynamic size changes when processing dimensions. With the exception of very large or huge dimensions, all dimension members are loaded into memory when the MSSQLServerOLAPService service is started or a new dimension is added, and occupy part of the virtual address space of the process.

  The total size of data for all members and member properties in all dimensions is used to calculate the space required to support dimensions in memory. A guideline for estimating this value is approximately 125 bytes per member, plus the size of data for member properties.

  A special tool, the Very Large Dimension Manager (VLDM), is used to support very large and huge dimensions. A dimension whose size exceeds the VLDM Threshold will be stored in a separate process address space. For large dimensions this frees virtual address space in the main Analysis Services process for other uses, at a small cost in the speed of accessing dimension members. This is handled transparently; no administrative action is necessary to use the VLDM.

  ROLAP dimensions can be used if a dimension is so large (approximately 20 million members or more) that the members cannot be stored in the address space of a process. In this case, the members are not read into memory; they are retrieved as needed from the relational data source. However, a ROLAP dimension may be used only in a ROLAP cube, and this type of storage has a substantial performance impact. ROLAP dimensions are recommended only when dimensions are so large that they cannot be handled in any other way.

- Shadow dimension memory

  Before processing a dimension, a copy (shadow dimension) is made of the original dimension contents to allow users to continue to access cubes that contain the dimension while the dimension is being updated. Queries are directed to the shadow dimension during processing. When processing is completed, queries are redirected to the updated dimension and the shadow dimension memory is deallocated.

- Process buffer

  The process buffer is used to store temporary indexing and aggregation data while processing cubes and dimensions on the Analysis server. Process buffers are used during explicitly initiated cube processing and also during lazy processing as a result of alterations to a changing dimension. One process buffer is allocated for each partition being processed at any given time. Because of the potentially high usage of process buffers, an economic model strategy, discussed later in this chapter, is used to handle allocation of process buffer memory. The process buffer is not used during querying operations.

  If the set of aggregations computed for a partition can be fully contained in the process buffer, aggregations can be computed in memory without access to disk. If there is insufficient memory to contain the full set of aggregations, aggregations must be partially computed, stored to disk, and re-read to merge with new partial aggregations. Because of the disk I/O and merging operations, this repeated read-merge-write cycle slows processing considerably.

- Query results cache

  The query results cache is used to cache cell data for cubes and partitions queried by client applications, and is not used during processing operations. Cube data cached within the query results cache is versioned to maintain synchronization with client applications. An expiration scheme is used to dispose of stale data.

  The query results cache is allocated dynamically, and is allowed to fill the available space remaining after subtracting the size of all other memory uses from the value of the **HighMemoryLimit** registry setting.

Server memory is allocated in the following order:

1. Read-ahead buffer

2. Dimension memory

3. Shadow dimension memory (when processing dimensions)

4. Process buffer (when processing)

5. Query results cache

Economic Model Management

The process buffer, in order to provide a consistent memory management structure, uses an economic model to manage the allocation of process buffer memory to memory-intensive processing operations.

Borrowing from the basic set of rules that govern supply and demand, process buffer memory is bought and sold in 64K segments by processing operations. The Analysis Server memory manager establishes the value of memory and the amount of credit to be extended to processing operations, and in effect, serves as a broker for process buffer memory.

The following process steps are used when an operation request needs process buffer memory:

1. When the MSSQLServerOLAPService service is started, the segments of memory represented by the process buffer are given a purchase price, set at a very low value.

2. Each operation request that would require an allocation of process buffer memory registers with the Analysis Services memory manager.

3. The Analysis Services memory manager lends the operation request an amount of credit based on the type and potential complexity of the operation request.

4. The operation request first attempts to purchase memory, providing its minimum and maximum memory requirements and the amount of credit available to it. Most operation requests cannot establish a maximum memory requirement, and will request additional memory as the operation request requires it.

5. Based on the amount of credit offered, Analysis Manager will allocate process buffer memory for the first request. If the minimum memory requirement cannot be satisfied with the amount of credit available to the operation request, the needed amount is still allocated.

6. Because the number of available segments drops after this allocation, the purchase price for memory correspondingly rises.

7. Operation requests, during execution, continue to keep this memory by paying rent on it. As each operation request completes an amount of work, the Analysis Services memory manager pays it an amount of credit, which can be used to pay rent and purchase additional memory. If the operation request cannot afford to pay rent on its allocated memory, the Analysis Services memory manager revokes allocated memory; however, the amount of memory allocated to the operation request will not drop below its minimum required amount.

8. If the operation request needs additional memory, it can pay an additional amount of credit to purchase more memory from the Analysis Services memory manager. As memory is allocated, and the cost for memory rises, this mechanism keeps the allocation of memory for large operation requests under control by making it prohibitively expensive to purchase inordinate amounts of memory.

9. As the operation request releases segments of memory no longer required, the memory is placed back into the pool of available segments. This deallocation of memory has two effects on the economic model. The first effect is to reduce the purchase price of memory, as demand has decreased and supply has increased. The second effect is to reduce the amount of rent required from existing operation requests, making more credit available to each existing operation request to purchase more memory as needed.

The Analysis Services memory manager supports two basic types of operation requests: dynamic and static. Dynamic operation requests require memory to perform a series of operations, and then release memory as each operation is processed. Static operation requests, by contrast, require memory and remain resident. Dynamic requests earn credit by completing their series of operations, while static operation requests earn credit by providing information to other requests.

As with any economic model, situations arise in which there is too much demand without enough supply. In Analysis Services, this occurs primarily when too many operation requests are initiated; since all operation requests are allocated their minimum required amounts of memory, memory becomes prohibitively expensive.

The Analysis Services memory manager can take a number of steps to relieve such an "economic crisis" situation. The Analysis Services memory manager can terminate any operation request as needed, and can revoke memory as required. Processing operations can easily exhaust both physical and virtual memory, so additional steps, discussed later in this chapter, are taken to conserve memory.

Server Settings

The following registry entries are used to control various aspects of server cache management. All of the following registry values are located at \HKEY_LOCAL_MACHINE\Software\Microsoft\OLAP Server\CurrentVersion.

Registry value	Purpose	Default value
HighMemoryLimit	The maximum size, in bytes, of the Analysis Services process virtual memory space. If allocated memory meets or exceeds this value, memory conservation techniques are initiated.	Total amount of physical memory
HugeLevelThreshold	The minimum number of members used to indicate a large level. Large levels are loaded incrementally, to conserve dimension memory.	0x000003e8 (1000)
LowMemoryLimit	The minimum size, in bytes, of process memory space.	Half of physical memory
ProcessReadAheadSize	The size, in bytes, of the read-ahead buffer.	0x00400000 (4194304)
ProcessReadSegmentSize	The size, in bytes, of the process buffer.	0x00400000 (4194304)
ProcessRecordsReportGranularity	The number of records read at one time into the process buffer. Also specifies granularity of processing progress updates for user interface.	0x000003e8 (100)
TempDirectory	The directory path used to store temporary files during processing operations.	\Microsoft Analysis Services\Data subdirectory

Certain settings can be changed directly through Analysis Manager, using the **Properties** dialog box. For more information about how to access the **Properties** dialog box, see SQL Server Books Online.

The following table details the tab and option in the **Properties** dialog box, as well as the corresponding registry value, used to change a specific registry setting.

Properties tab	Option	Registry value
Environment	Minimum allocated memory	**LowMemoryLimit**
	Memory conservation threshold	**HighMemoryLimit**
Processing	Read-ahead buffer size	**ProcessReadAheadSize**
	Process buffer size	**ProcessReadSegmentSize**

Client Cache Management

PivotTable Service also provides caching services on the client, but the caching provided on the client roughly corresponds to the query results cache maintained by the server. The client cache uses a background thread to manage data, with a version-numbering algorithm to synchronize data on the client with data on the server. Whenever PivotTable Service discovers that the client cache version number is different from the server cache version number, PivotTable Service discards the data stored in the client cache. The client cache data is also discarded when the current database is changed.

When PivotTable Service receives a query, it parses the query and may break it up into several query requests. Each query request is first checked against the client cache; if it can be answered with data from the client cache, and the data is recent, no round trip to the server is required for that particular query request.

Client Settings

The connection string used to connect the PivotTable Service provider to an Analysis server is also used to pass values for various properties to the provider. The following properties are used specifically to control the behavior of the client-side cache.

Property name	Purpose	Default value
Client Cache Size	The size in percent or bytes of the maximum amount of memory that can be allocated to the cache. If the value of this property is 99 or less, the value is interpreted as the percentage of total available (physical and virtual) memory. If the value of this property is 100 or more, the value is interpreted as the number of kilobytes of total available memory.	25

Thread Management

Analysis Services is designed to handle complex multiuser, multiprocess interaction. Both server and client interactions involve multiple thread usage, coordinated to ensure optimized data transfer when used in concert with server and client cache management techniques.

Server Thread Management

The Analysis server uses the following five types of threads to support server operations:

- Listener thread

  The listener thread waits for new connection requests and is responsible for creating server connections as needed. The listener thread also manages the worker thread pool, assigning worker threads to requests, initiating worker threads if there are not enough active worker threads in the pool, and ending idle worker threads as needed.

  The Analysis server uses the **BackgroundInterval** registry setting to determine how often the listener thread should perform these tasks.

- Worker threads

  Worker threads serve as the first line of response for requests. Worker threads are responsible for checking the server cache for data pertinent to a request, and for allocating process threads to retrieve data from storage.

- Process threads

  Process threads retrieve data from storage, asynchronously querying and retrieving stored data in parallel. Different process threads can concurrently retrieve data from different partitions. The size of this thread pool determines how much concurrent activity is being performed in the system.

- Log thread

  The log thread logs query requests to a query log database maintained by the Analysis server. Logged queries can then be used for usage pattern analysis, which is crucial to the effective design of aggregations and partitions.

- Cleaner thread

  The results obtained by process threads are stored in the query result cache for later retrieval. Because data that is cached for queries, but infrequently accessed by other queries, can accumulate, the cleaner thread iteratively removes the least recently used cache data. Usually, this thread is set to a below-normal priority, to prevent resource drain from active tasks. However, if allocated cache memory meets or exceeds the halfway point (determined by subtracting the **LowMemoryLimit** registry value from the **HighMemoryLimit** registry setting and dividing the result by two), the cleaner thread flushes the cache whenever possible.

If the allocated cache memory meets or exceeds the **HighMemoryLimit** registry setting, the priority of the cleaner thread is set to normal and the cache is cleaned again. If this step does not reduce allocated cache memory back to the half-way point, the priority of the cleaner thread is set to above normal and the server cache is cleaned again.

The Analysis server uses the **BackgroundInterval** registry setting to determine how often the cleaner thread should perform these tasks.

Worker and Process Thread Interaction

The following diagram shows how, through the efficient management of threads, such complex interaction is supported.

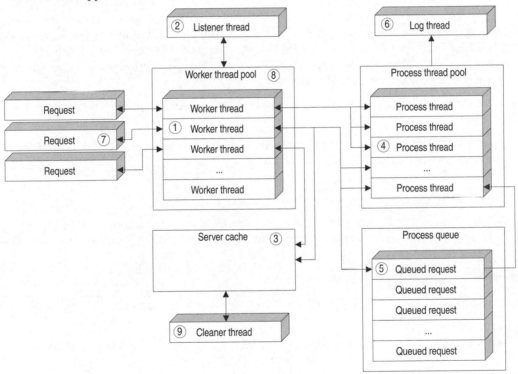

The numbers in the previous diagram match the steps needed to resolve a request, as outlined below:

1. All requests, whether initiated by Analysis Services or by a client application, are submitted to the Analysis server.

2. The listener thread, which manages the worker thread pool, matches idle worker threads to requests. If there are not enough idle worker threads in the pool to handle requests, the listener thread starts up additional worker threads. If the pool is at the maximum number of worker threads, and no worker thread is idle, a worker thread cannot be allocated and the listener thread sends an error to the request.

3. Each worker thread then evaluates the request against the server cache. If some or all of the data slices needed to fulfill a request reside in the server cache, the worker thread directly retrieves and fulfills as much of the request as possible from the server cache.

4. If the worker thread cannot complete the request from the server cache, it requests the needed number of process threads from the process thread pool.

5. If a worker thread cannot allocate enough process threads to support its requirements, additional process thread requests will be queued until process threads are available.

6. If query logging is enabled, the log thread records every nth query request, determined by the value of the **QueryLogSampling** registry setting, in a database for later reference.

7. As each process thread returns its result, the worker thread stores the information. When the last process thread concludes its process, the worker thread then returns the results of the request to the initiating application. Because the worker thread cannot return until all of its process requests have been concluded, the worker thread waits until all queued requests have been assigned to and processed by an available process thread. Queued processes are given priority over other incoming process requests until the process queue is empty.

8. If a worker thread is idle for a specified period of time, the listener thread can terminate it to conserve resources.

9. After a certain period of time or in memory conservation situations, the cleaner thread cleans unused and expired data from the server cache.

Server Settings

The following table describes the registry settings used to control thread management in Analysis Services. All of the settings reside in the registry at \HKEY_LOCAL_MACHINE\Software\Microsoft\OLAP Server\CurrentVersion.

Registry value	Purpose	Default value
BackgroundInterval	The number of seconds between background processing periods	0x0000001e (30)
InitWorkerThreads	The number of worker threads initially started by the listener thread	0x00000004 (4)
PoolProcessThreads	The maximum number of process threads maintained by the process thread pool	0x00000028 (40)
PoolWorkerThreads	The maximum number of worker threads maintained by the worker thread pool	0x0000001e (30)

continued on next page

Registry value	Purpose	Default value
ProcessThreads	The number of process threads that can simultaneously use the processors available on the Analysis server	2 per processor
QueryLogConnectionString	The connection string used by the log thread to connect to the query log database	Varies
QueryLogSampling	The number of queries used by the log thread to determine the sampling interval	0x0000000a (10)
WorkerThreads	The number of worker threads that can simultaneously use the processors available on the Analysis server	2 per processor

Typically, the value of the **PoolProcessThreads** registry setting should be set to 125 percent of the value of the **PoolWorkerThreads** registry setting, because each worker thread can allocate more than one process thread to complete a request. If the Analysis server consistently handles numerous and complex requests, raising the value of the **PoolProcessThreads** registry setting to 150 percent or more of the **PoolWorkerThreads** value will reduce queuing and improve perceived performance. If the Analysis server consistently returns errors during peak usage periods, increasing the value of the **PoolWorkerThreads** and **PoolProcessThreads** registry settings will provide more available worker threads and reduce the rate of errors related to non-available worker threads.

Only one setting can be directly changed through Analysis Manager, using the **Properties** dialog box. For more information about how to access the **Properties** dialog box, see SQL Server Books Online.

The following table details the tab and option in the **Properties** dialog box, as well as the corresponding registry value, used to change a specific registry setting.

Properties tab	Option	Registry value
Environment	Maximum number of threads	**WorkerThreads**

Client Thread Management

Client thread management is much less complex than server thread management. PivotTable Service uses only two threads to interact with an Analysis server:

- Ping thread

  The ping thread is a background thread used to support the synchronization process between the server data cache and the client data cache. After a set number of milliseconds, determined by the **Auto Synch Period** property discussed earlier, the version stamp for the data and meta data stored in the client cache is compared against the version stamp for the data and meta data stored in the server data cache. If the versions differ, the information in the client data cache is synchronized with the information in the server data cache.

- Query thread

  The query thread is a foreground thread used to support query requests between the client application and the Analysis server. When a query request is made, the query thread is used to first scan the client cache for data pertinent to the query request. If the data does not reside in the client cache, it then submits a query request to the Analysis server to retrieve and cache the desired data.

If the ping thread is turned off (by setting the **Auto Synch Period** property to zero), the query thread can still support caching and synchronization, but the process is no longer automatic; the latency period of stale data in the client cache is dependent on the elapsed time between submitted query requests.

Client Settings

The following properties can be used with PivotTable Service to control the behavior of client thread management.

Property name	Purpose	Default value
Auto Synch Period	The interval in milliseconds of synchronization between the client cache and the server cache by the ping thread	250

Processing Interaction

The act of processing a cube or dimension in Analysis Services requires a lot of interaction between the Analysis server and underlying relational databases. Processing cubes and dimensions in Analysis Services involves at least two of three phases. The first phase, or base phase, retrieves data from underlying data sources. The second phase, or indexing phase, constructs indexes for the retrieved data to speed data transfer. The last phase, or aggregating phase, scans the indexed data for aggregation, creating aggregations in memory and writing them to storage.

Whenever a dimension is processed, the following steps are performed:

1. Analysis Services queries the underlying relational database for unique members. The volume of data to be processed depends on the processing option selected and the state of the existing dimension.

2. The data is then resorted in memory for multidimensional access.

3. Dimension indexes, used to optimize member access from the dimension, are then created.

4. Both members and dimension indexes are then stored in memory (for shared dimensions) and in disk storage.

Whenever a partition is processed, the following steps are performed. (Every cube contains at least one partition, so processing a cube requires processing one or more partitions.)

1. Each dimension, shared and private, in an inconsistent state, is first processed following the previous set of steps for dimension processing.

2. Analysis Services reads the fact table for the partition, sorts the data in memory for multidimensional access, and stores the data on disk in segments of 64K rows each.

3. The data segments are read back and indexes are generated. In the same pass, aggregations are created in memory. A temporary file is used to swap aggregations into and out of memory if process buffer memory is insufficient to store all aggregations.

4. The fact table is then scanned, and aggregations are created in memory on a per partition basis. If process buffer memory is exhausted while storing aggregations, a temporary file is used to swap aggregations in and out of memory.

5. Indexes and aggregations are then stored on disk.

Processing does not always have to complete before users can access processed cube data. With the use of lazy optimization in Analysis Services, the indexing and aggregating phases can be made to return cube data as it is aggregated. More information about how to use this form of process optimization, and its ramifications, is discussed later.

Two types of process threads are allocated during processing. Both threads work in parallel, so Analysis Services can use multiple-processor server configurations more effectively:

- Reader threads

  Reader threads populate the process buffer with records retrieved from the underlying data source. Reader threads are used to read in records a block at a time, with the number of records per block specified in the **ProcessRecordsReportGranularity** registry setting, until a single segment of data is retrieved. Once retrieved, the segment is written to the partition file.

  For more information about the **ProcessRecordsReportGranularity** registry setting, see "Memory Management" in this chapter.

- Aggregation threads

  Once a segment is available in the partition file, multiple aggregation threads aggregate the data and cache the aggregations in memory. If the processing operation can no longer afford memory, the aggregations are then written to alternating temporary files. As one segment is processed, the aggregations for that segment are written to the first temporary file. When the second segment is processed, the aggregations in memory for the second segment are merged with the aggregations in the first temporary file, and are written to the second temporary file. When a third segment is processed, the aggregations in memory from the third segment are merged with the aggregations in the second temporary file, and are written to the first temporary file. This process repeats until the last segment is aggregated, at which point all of the aggregations stored in the last-used temporary file are compressed and stored for use.

Because of the amount of data handled during processing, several factors can affect processing performance:

- Hardware configuration
- Cube and dimension design

- Storage mode
- Aggregation design
- Schema optimization
- Partition strategy
- Processing option
- Memory management

Querying Interaction

When a query is issued by a client application to Analysis Services, a lot of action happens in the background. The following steps are used to resolve a query from a client application.

The numbers in the previous diagram correspond to the steps detailed below:

1. PivotTable Service parses the query and, if the query references multiple data slices, the query is then broken apart into individual query requests.

2. The query processor parses the query requests and then retrieves dimension information from dimension memory to determine the levels and members needed to resolve the query requests.

3. PivotTable Service then checks the client cache to determine if query requests can be answered by cached results. Individual query requests that cannot be fulfilled from the client cache are sent to the Analysis server.

4. The query processor then retrieves as much data as possible from the query result cache for each query request that can be answered from the cached data.

5. For the query requests that cannot be answered from the query result cache, the query processor then retrieves the data for each query request from the appropriate partition. If applicable, the retrieved cube data is also placed in the query result cache.

6. PivotTable Service receives the returned data for all of the individual query requests and post-processes the data, if needed, to fulfill the original query.

Because of this multi-step process, several factors can affect querying performance:

- Hardware configuration
- Cube and dimension design
- Storage mode
- Memory management, including the relevance of query result cache and dimension cache content
- Aggregation design, including the involvement of usage analysis
- Partition strategy

Improving Overall Performance

The information in this section outlines the techniques common to improving both processing and querying performance. Several factors affect overall performance:

- Hardware configuration
- Dimension and cube design
- Storage mode selection
- Aggregation design
- Schema optimization
- Partition strategy

Hardware Configuration

When you choose a server configuration to support Analysis Services, you should follow several general guidelines. Three main factors—processors, memory, and disk storage—affect the overall performance of an Analysis server. Each is discussed separately, in detail, and recommendations are provided for improving overall performance.

Processors

Scaling up to multiprocessor servers allows for much greater Analysis server performance. Scaling up, however, does not necessarily provide a linear increase in performance. Other factors, such as physical memory or disk storage, can affect the increase provided by scaling up an Analysis server. Using a symmetrical multiprocessor (SMP) server, however, can significantly increase the performance of an Analysis Services solution at an acceptable relative cost.

An alternate way to distribute load through Analysis Services is to use distributed partitioned cubes and linked cubes. Linked cubes allow you, in essence, to alias cubes from other Analysis servers, while distributed partitioned cubes allow you to distribute partitions for a single locally administered cube across multiple Analysis servers. Both options provide a limited form of load distribution, but they significantly increase administration complexity and should not be used as a substitute for scaling up the Analysis server. Other scale out solutions can also be considered such as creating specialized data marts, each with its own Analysis server.

Memory

There are two items to consider regarding memory: the virtual address space of the Analysis Services process and the physical memory that backs that virtual space.

Microsoft Windows® 2000 and Windows NT generally limit a process to a 2GB virtual address space. This space can be extended to 3GB using the **/3GB** boot setting. This is recommended if Analysis Services is the primary use of the server machine and if large dimensions are involved. Within the address space, the service allocates memory for all uses: dimension storage, process buffers, and the query result cache, as described above. However, if any dimension exceeds the VLDM Threshold, it will be migrated to a separate process and will occupy a different virtual address space.

Note When the **/3GB** switch is used, the upper bound on memory must be set using the **HighMemoryLimit** registry setting, because the Memory conservation threshold property cannot be set greater than 2GB when using Analysis Manager.

System performance will be improved if the entire virtual address space can be backed by physical memory. This enables the system to avoid paging, the great time waster. Because the Analysis Services processes cannot use more than 3GB of address space, however, the only time a system would benefit from more than about 4GB of memory (3GB for Analysis Services + 1GB for the operating system and file system cache) is:

- When VLDM is involved.

- To support other applications.

Disk Storage

Disk storage planning is important for Analysis Services solutions, because even mid-range implementations of Analysis Services can involve large amounts of disk storage and disk access. Combined with the high performance and fault tolerance generally required for decision support solutions, a RAID (Redundant Array of Inexpensive Disks) array is an excellent choice for improving disk storage performance.

One of the most common methods of ensuring reliable and fast disk storage, RAID uses an array of disk storage devices, treating them as one disk storage device in terms of disk access. RAID can be implemented as a hardware solution, in the form of a RAID controller, or a software solution, such as the form of the Windows 2000 software RAID solution involving dynamic disks. RAID provides two benefits to overall server performance:

- Fault tolerance

  RAID protects against data loss due to disk storage device failure by distributing information across multiple disk storage devices, including information needed to recreate a disk storage device if it should fail.

- Performance increase

  Most RAID controllers divide data I/O operations evenly across all disk storage devices in the RAID array, effectively providing parallel I/O and increasing perceived performance.

For information about RAID, see Chapter 20, "RDBMS Performance Tuning Guide for Data Warehousing."

Recommendations

- Scale up, and then scale out.

  Analysis Services is designed to support multiple processors, assigning worker and process threads as needed to distribute processor load within a single server. A single multiprocessor Analysis server can support all but the most demanding enterprise-level implementations. Scaling out can be more difficult and adds significant administrative complexity; for Analysis Services, scaling up is generally more useful than scaling out.

- Allocate physical memory as appropriate.

  Overall Analysis Services performance can be greatly improved with a small increase in physical memory. This is especially true for processing operations, which can be quite memory-intensive. Avoid setting the **HighMemoryLimit** registry setting higher than the amount of available physical memory, to enforce the use of physical memory, and reduce the number of other active applications on the Analysis server. Ideally, to prevent crowding of Windows 2000, the **HighMemoryLimit** registry setting should be set to no more than approximately 90 percent of available physical memory; this is especially true for installations with 64 MB or less total physical memory.

  Although 64 MB of physical memory is recommended, it is not unreasonable to install gigabytes of memory on a server. This enables the system to avoid paging, use large process buffers to avoid I/O in creating aggregations, and allocate a large query result cache so more queries can be answered directly from cache.

- Use hardware or software RAID solutions to achieve the storage volume, disk speed, and redundancy needed.

Dimension and Cube Design

Designing dimensions and cubes to increase performance can be a highly subjective process; cubes and dimensions should be defined primarily by the requirements of underlying data and business scenarios.

A detailed discussion of dimension and cube design is beyond the scope of this chapter. For more detailed information about dimension and cube design, including a discussion of new features in Analysis Services, see Chapter 22, "Cubes in the Real World."

Storage Mode Selection

The storage mode selected for partitions and dimensions can greatly affect both processing and querying performance.

Multidimensional OLAP (MOLAP)

MOLAP storage stores both the underlying data used to create the cube and the aggregations created for the cube in a multidimensional structure maintained on the Analysis Server. Because Analysis Services can answer all queries directly from this multidimensional structure, this storage mode presents the best overall querying performance of all three storage modes.

Because the underlying data used to create the cube is copied from the relational database to this multidimensional structure, the storage requirements needed to support MOLAP can be the largest of the three storage modes. However, for MOLAP storage Analysis Services compresses the data to about 20 to 30 percent of its original storage requirements in the source database tables (excluding relational database indexes, which are not copied to MOLAP storage). Thus, the storage penalty for MOLAP is not as severe as might be expected and becomes a factor only when very large amounts of data are processed.

Relational OLAP (ROLAP)

On the other end of the spectrum, ROLAP stores the aggregations created for the cube in the same relational database that provides the underlying data for the cube. This involves the construction of aggregation tables in the relational database, as well as large table joins to reference fact and dimension tables stored in the database.

Because Analysis Services must query the relational database to retrieve all data for a partition or dimension that uses ROLAP, this storage mode provides the slowest querying performance of the three storage modes in Analysis Services. ROLAP can also have significantly slower processing performance than the other storage modes because new tables and numerous table joins must be created in order to store aggregations in the relational database. ROLAP also incurs a significantly higher load on the relational database than the other two storage modes because of the potentially immense joins between the fact and dimension tables from which the aggregation tables are generated.

ROLAP typically uses less additional storage than MOLAP, but more than HOLAP; although underlying data is not copied, the aggregations stored in the relational database are not compressed.

ROLAP, however, has some features that make it useful as a storage mode. ROLAP storage allows for very large or huge dimensions, because dimension size is not limited by memory address space. Also, when used with SQL Server 2000 relational databases, ROLAP allows real-time OLAP for Analysis Services, because indexed views can be constructed for ROLAP dimensions and partitions on the relational database and used as underlying data, and the relational database can notify Analysis Services when data changes.

Hybrid OLAP (HOLAP)

HOLAP combines elements from both MOLAP and ROLAP storage modes. As with MOLAP, aggregations are stored on the Analysis server in multidimensional storage. However, the underlying data for a cube is not also copied into multidimensional storage. Similar to ROLAP, underlying data is accessed from the relational database.

Because underlying data does not need to be copied to the Analysis server, HOLAP often provides the best processing performance and uses the least additional storage. Query performance is typically better than ROLAP but not as good as MOLAP, depending on aggregation design. Queries that can be answered with data from aggregations will perform as well in HOLAP as MOLAP because access to relational tables is not required. On the other hand, queries that require access to data stored in the relational database to retrieve individual facts or to create on-demand aggregations can be as slow in HOLAP as in ROLAP.

Recommendations

- Use MOLAP before HOLAP, HOLAP before ROLAP.

  You should use MOLAP wherever feasible, unless business or data requirements dictate otherwise.

  HOLAP is best used wherever MOLAP is recommended but is prohibited due to storage requirements.

  ROLAP should only be used to support dimensions that are too large for other storage modes, or if real-time OLAP is needed.

Aggregation Design

Designing aggregation storage involves tradeoffs between processing time, disk storage, and query response time. Processing time and disk storage increase as more aggregations are designed, but more aggregations increase the probability that queries can be answered from precalculated aggregations. Also, due to the nature of multidimensional structures, the disk storage for aggregations can increase exponentially as more aggregations are designed. For more information on how aggregation affects disk storage, see Chapter 22, "Cubes in the Real World."

In general, minimal aggregations should be designed initially and additional aggregations created in response to analysis of typical user queries. For very large and complex cubes that contain numerous dimensions with many levels, initial aggregation design will take a long time, consume large amounts of disk space, and will be less likely to provide a mix of aggregations that can be used by many queries. A more effective approach in this case is to design zero aggregations and then iteratively use the Usage Optimization wizard to create aggregations based on several sessions of typical user activity.

Partition strategy also complements overall aggregation design. For information on how partition strategy affects aggregation design, see "Partition Strategy" later in this chapter.

Recommendations

A balance between disk storage and processing time can be achieved with a few storage design guidelines:

- Start at 25 percent performance gain, and then optimize aggregations based on usage.

  The Storage Design Wizard can be used to initially design aggregations based on a mathematical model of uniform usage. Use the Storage Design Wizard to design aggregations based on an anticipated 25 percent performance gain. Allow users to access the cube for a specified period of time, and then use the Usage-Based Optimization Wizard to perform usage-based analysis and redesign aggregations based on real world data. For very large and complex cubes that contain numerous dimensions with many levels, start with zero aggregations.

Schema Optimization

Analysis Services uses solid, dependable techniques to ensure that the cubes and dimensions you design are stable and reliable. However, this also means that Analysis Services automatically takes the safest possible path when designing the queries used to populate cube and dimension data from underlying data sources. After the design of a cube has become stable, you can use schema optimization to reduce the number of joins required when processing.

For more information about the effects of schema optimization, including examples, see Chapter 22, "Cubes in the Real World."

Partition Strategy

The organization of files used to store cube data, referred to as partitions, can make a great deal of difference in the performance and maintainability of cubes in Analysis Services. Cubes can use either a single partition, in which all fact table and aggregation data are stored in a single file, or multiple partitions, in which fact table and aggregation data can be logically and physically divided into multiple files.

Within a cube, different partitions can have different data sources, source tables, aggregation designs, and even storage modes. This allows a great deal of flexibility when managing large cubes. Using multiple partitions offers the following performance and maintenance benefits:

- Historical data management

  The technique for managing historical data using partitions in Analysis Services is no different, in theory, than the technique used for managing historical data using partitioned tables in data warehousing. The rolling window technique can be used to keep a set number of partitions, storing data slices based on a time dimension, to maintain a set number of time periods. After a time period expires, the old partition can be removed and a new partition can be added to maintain the rolling window.

- Querying performance

Queries executed against a cube are separated into individual query requests, each representing a data slice. If the data for the cube is divided into multiple partitions, less I/O is potentially required to retrieve data from the cube.

For example, a financial cube contains 13 partitions, each representing a monthly data slice derived from a time dimension. If a user issues a query requesting all of the sales figures for a particular department for a single month, the retrieval process does not need to scan all 13 partitions; because the data slice resides in a single month, only a single partition needs to be scanned. If the cube stored all 13 months of data in a single partition, the entire partition would need to be scanned.

Aggregation designs can be different for different partitions. If you have a cube with both current and historical data, and the current data represents 80 percent of total query interaction, you can use a much more aggressive aggregation design on the partitions that contain current data as compared to the partitions that contain historical data. This concept also applies to storage modes—for example, you can use MOLAP for the partitions that contain current data, and HOLAP or even ROLAP for the partitions that contain historical data, conserving disk storage on the Analysis server.

Partition support, for querying purposes, is transparent. The user is not aware of the underlying partition model while querying the cube.

- Processing performance

Partitions can be processed individually, allowing for better selective processing and reducing the total amount of time needed to process a cube. For example, a financial cube with 13 partitions, each representing a month of financial data, does not need full processing for all 13 partitions—only one partition needs to be fully processed every month.

Also, the ability to tailor aggregation design and storage modes for each partition allows you to manage disk storage and server usage more effectively. Data that is infrequently accessed can be relegated to HOLAP or ROLAP storage with few or no stored aggregations, minimizing disk storage. Frequently accessed data, by comparison, can use MOLAP or HOLAP storage and contain a large number of stored aggregations, increasing performance and decreasing server usage by reducing the number of aggregations computed at query time.

The techniques used to construct and maintain cube partitions are similar to the techniques used to construct and maintain partition tables in a data warehouse.

For more information about partition strategy in a data warehouse environment, see Chapter 18, "Using Partitions in a SQL Server 2000 Data Warehouse."

Recommendations

- Slice your data based on business requirements.

  Maximum querying performance is obtained by constructing partitions with data slices that mirror the data slices that are required for business support. For example, a financial cube typically tracks data as a time series and most queries will retrieve data based on time period, so partitioning the cube by time period provides the most performance benefit.

  The business requirements for the data represented by the cube will generally dictate the structure and data slice for each partition.

Improving Processing Performance

Processing performance is almost entirely dependent on memory availability, but it is also affected by CPU speed and disk storage speed. There are additional considerations that affect processing performance above the considerations that affect overall performance.

Processing Options

You do not have to fully process cubes and dimensions in Analysis Services every time underlying data changes. Several different options are available to you when processing, and using the right processing option can mean measuring the time needed to process a cube in minutes, rather than hours or days.

Most shared dimensions seldom require full processing. Full processing involves the complete reconstruction of a dimension, and should occur only if the hierarchy of a dimension changes in some way, such as the addition or deletion of a level. Adding new members or changing existing members does not alter the hierarchy. Private dimensions require full processing more often, because their structure is inextricably linked to the structure of their cube.

Correspondingly, most cubes do not require full processing once operational. As with dimensions, cubes should only be fully processed if the structure of the cube changes. Adding or removing dimensions or measures, changing partitions or aggregations, and so on require full processing of the cube. Additions to underlying fact table data, by contrast, only require an incremental update of cube data.

Recommendations

- Use selective processing.

  Use the incremental update option when processing dimensions and cubes, unless structural changes have occurred. Use full processing only when absolutely necessary.

- Incrementally update dimensions when updating cubes.

  Take advantage of this option when processing cubes—you can streamline the maintenance of most Analysis Services solutions in this manner.

- Take advantage of lazy processing where appropriate.

  Lazy processing essentially turns the indexing and aggregating processing phases into background operations, allowing users to continue accessing the cube while these phases are completed. This option is not appropriate in all circumstances, because queries will run slower until the background processing is completed, but it can increase cube availability for users.

- Ensure enough disk storage for shadow copies and temporary files.

  During the indexing and aggregating phases, shadow copies and temporary files are often needed to maintain aggregation data during processing. Processing can fail if there is not enough disk storage for temporary files and aggregation data.

Memory Requirements

The memory requirements for processing are different than those for querying. Processing cubes and dimensions, especially large cubes and dimensions, can easily become overwhelming in terms of physical and virtual memory if no restrictions are placed on memory allocation.

Process buffer memory, as discussed earlier, is allocated at a finite limit; no matter how many processing operations there are, the process buffer allocation cannot exceed the limit established by the **ProcessReadSegmentSize** registry setting. A set of economic model algorithms, discussed earlier, are used to manage the process buffer, ensuring that those processing operations that require priority receive an optimized amount of process buffer memory automatically.

Process buffer size is central not just to the raw available capacity during processing, but also to the resultant overall performance of the partition once processed. During the indexing phase, the process buffer is used to sort fact table data and construct indexes based on the results of the sort. As such, partition access may be adversely affected if the process buffer is unable to efficiently sort the fact table data.

Recommendations

- Set the **ProcessReadSegmentSize** registry setting based on available physical memory.

  This value should be set according to the needs of your Analysis server. A good rule of thumb is to set this value to between 70 and 80 percent of the total physical memory available to the server. Avoid the temptation to set it higher than 80 percent, because this may force memory to be paged to disk. Setting it to 100 percent or higher will definitely cause forced memory paging, and will most likely cause your Analysis server to thrash, or spend more time in swapping memory to and from disk than in executing applications.

- Increase the memory available to Analysis Services.

  Use the Windows **/3GB** boot setting and adjust the Analysis Services **HighMemoryLimit** registry setting.

Storage Requirements

Disk storage issues can adversely affect processing performance in Analysis Services. Disk storage is used not only to store data and meta data for Analysis Services objects, but also for temporary files used during processing.

Recommendations

- Remember the effects of data explosion.

  Data explosion can dramatically increase the amount of disk storage needed for storing aggregations. Compression helps conserve disk storage, but minimizing aggregations to save disk storage penalizes users by increasing query response time.

- Plan disk storage space for shadow copies and temporary files.

  Ensure that enough free storage space is available to completely copy the largest single partition stored on an Analysis server, and add enough available storage to maintain two complete copies of aggregation data for the largest single partition stored on the server.

- Err on the side of caution.

  Provide as much storage as possible to permit growth—new cubes or additional partitions for existing cubes are not uncommon as an Analysis Services solution matures. Having too much disk is far preferable to having too little.

Improving Querying Performance

While improving processing performance directly benefits administrators, this is only half of achieving optimal performance. Good performance while querying the Analysis server is also crucial to the success of any Analysis Services solution, and directly benefits clients.

Memory Requirements

Query performance depends heavily on whether data relevant to the query already resides in the query result cache maintained by the Analysis server, or in the client cache maintained by PivotTable Service.

Ideally, the best possible performance for a specific query is obtained by having all data needed to fulfill the query cached on the client. No round trip to the server is needed; PivotTable Service is fully capable of analyzing a query against the client cache to determine if server data is needed.

Realistically, memory and usage limitations typically prevent this from happening. Instead, a combination of client cache retrieval, server cache retrieval, and disk storage retrieval is usually needed to fulfill a stream of queries, in differing proportions based on the state of both the client cache and the server cache.

The most striking effect on query speed is the comparison between a cold cache and a warm cache. A cold cache occurs when the Analysis server first starts up; because no queries have yet been processed, no data is cached. After enough queries execute to build up a common set of cached data, a warm cache can provide significantly faster performance; no storage interaction is needed for cached data.

One of the easiest steps to take to reduce the effects of a cold cache is to create a simple application, executed every time the MSSQLServerOLAPService service is started, to execute the most commonly used MDX queries against the Analysis server. This, in essence, preheats the server cache with the most commonly used data. To obtain the most commonly used MDX queries, the Properties dialog box from Analysis Manager can be used to change the logging habits of the Analysis server. From the query log information, suitable MDX queries can be constructed.

Preheating the cache can also be useful on the client in certain situations. By executing the same commonly used MDX queries from the client application as well, the client cache is populated with commonly used cube data. Camouflaged during the startup sequence of a typical custom client application, this technique can significantly increase the perceived performance of the client application without extensive coding.

Maximum memory allocation for the server query result cache can be determined by subtracting the memory allocated for all other buffers from the **HighMemoryLimit** registry value. This information can then be used to determine if allocation levels for the other buffers can be altered to balance querying and processing performance.

For more information about the various registry settings used to improve querying performance, see "Memory Management" and "Thread Management," in this chapter.

Usage Analysis and Aggregation Design

The Storage Design Wizard allows for basic aggregation design, based on a mathematical model that assumes that one query request is as likely as another query request in terms of usage. This uniform model allows for quick construction of aggregation, but does not always produce the optimum aggregation design.

Realistically, the only way to accurately optimize the aggregation design for a cube is to allow users to access the cube, gathering historical data on query requests, and then use the historical data to model the actual usage patterns for the cube. Once the usage patterns are determined, aggregations can be constructed to more exactly match business needs.

The Usage-Based Optimization Wizard automates the process of usage pattern analysis. Usage-based optimization can be performed for a variety of query patterns. Queries can be analyzed by date, frequency, user, and data storage access, or any combination of these criteria, to determine an optimal aggregation design for a specific set of query requests.

The criteria used will also be determined by business requirements. For frequently used cubes available to a wide audience, usage patterns based on frequency, the most commonly executed query requests, are most often analyzed. For infrequently used cubes, usage patterns based on time may be more applicable. Cubes designed for a specific group of users may benefit as much from a user based usage pattern analysis as from a frequency based usage pattern analysis.

Ultimately, the best way to determine the optimal usage pattern analysis is through experimentation. Initially, design aggregations using the Storage Design Wizard, allowing for 25 percent performance gain, and then expose the cube to your audience. (For very large and complex cubes, start with zero aggregations.) Collect usage information, and then analyze it based on your understanding of the business behavior of your audience.

Recommendations

- Allow sufficient time to record usage pattern information.

    As with any other pattern analysis, more data typically provides better analysis. Attempting to model usage patterns from a few days of usage data will probably not produce an optimum solution. For example, cubes used by financial applications will typically see uniform usage patterns during the middle of a financial period, slightly wider usage patterns during the beginning of a financial period, and much wider usage patterns near the end of a financial period. Allowing for at least one month of usage data to be accumulated for such cubes will provide a better insight into the actual usage patterns of the cube, producing a better aggregation design.

    Allow your business requirements to dictate the time needed to record usage before usage-based optimization is performed.

- Remember that usage-based optimization is on a per partition basis.

    Not all partitions need to have the same aggregation design. When you perform usage-based optimization, the recommended changes are executed only for a single partition, not on all of the partitions across the cube. For cubes with multiple partitions, the Usage-Based Optimization Wizard should be executed for each partition to model an effective aggregation design for the entire cube.

Evaluating Performance

While a discussion on improving performance is useful, and providing recommendations is also useful, implementing such recommendations without the tools necessary to evaluate their relative success is, at best, a process of educated guesses.

The Windows 2000 System Monitor, part of the Windows 2000 Performance Tool, is an excellent utility for examining the performance of an Analysis server, either by obtaining a snapshot of current performance or by reviewing historical performance. To this end, Analysis Services provides several performance objects, each representing several performance counters, to track the minutiae of Analysis server activities. Combined with the performance counters provided to track system performance, the Windows 2000 System Monitor can be used to assist in fine-tuning overall Analysis Services performance on a server-by-server basis.

Analysis Services Performance Counters

Analysis Services provides over 140 of performance counters, measuring almost every possible metric within the Analysis server. Each of the performance counters belongs to one of three separate groups:

- Current

  All of the counters in this group provide a current view of performance information. The latency of the information provided by the counters in this group is subject to system conditions, such as server load or network latency, and should be viewed as a snapshot of the current system behavior.

- Total

  All of the counters in this group provide a total of performance information, accumulated from the start of the MSSQLServerOLAPService service.

- Ratio

  All of the counters in this group provide a ratio of performance information, typically over time. For many ratio counters, this information is constructed by averaging the values of total counters over the time elapsed from the start of the MSSQLServerOLAPService service.

Although all of the performance counters are useful, many are difficult to directly relate to system performance. This section focuses on performance counters that can be directly related to system performance, including performance counters that demonstrate the impact various registry settings can have on the Analysis server.

Each performance counter in Analysis Services belongs to a specific performance object; to access a specific performance counter, you must first select its performance object in the Windows 2000 System Monitor.

For more information on how to use the Windows 2000 System Monitor, see "System Monitor" in Windows 2000 documentation, or "Windows 2000 System Monitor" in the Platform SDK section of the MSDN® Online Library.

Analysis Server:Agg Cache

The performance counters contained in this performance object monitor the server query result cache, examining such metrics as size and throughput. The following counters are best used to examine cache performance:

- **Current bytes**

  The current number of bytes also allows you to examine memory usage for the server data cache. Monitored over a period of time, this value can indicate whether or not you have additional available memory for expanding other buffers, such as the process buffer or the read-ahead buffer, to increase processing performance.

- **Direct hits/sec**

  The number of data slices that are fully completed by the server cache. The higher this number is, the better the perceived performance.

- **Filter hits/sec**

  The number of data slices that are partially completed by the server cache. This number should be much higher than the **Misses/sec** performance counter, but not as high as the **Direct hits/sec** performance counter.

- **Lookups/sec**

  The total number of query requests that are reviewed by the server cache. This number should represent the combined total of the **Direct hits/sec**, **Filter hits/sec**, and **Misses/sec** performance counters.

- **Misses/sec**

  The number of data slices that are not completed by the server cache, requiring retrieval from disk storage. This number should be as low as possible.

The last four performance counters describe how effective the cache is in responding to query requests. A high number of direct hits and lookups per second, as well as a low number of filter hits and misses per second, indicates that the cache is being well-utilized. The concept of a preheated cache works well here, increasing the **Direct hits/sec** and **Filter hits/sec** values and reducing the **Misses/sec** value by making more cached data immediately available on server startup.

Analysis Server:Connection

The **Connection** object essentially measures the performance of the listener and worker threads. The following counters are best used to examine connection performance:

- **Current connections**

  Each connection has a worker thread assigned to it, so this performance counter is an excellent metric for observing current worker thread allocations.

- **Failures/sec**

  This performance counter represents the number of failed connection requests, for whatever reason, made to the listener thread. One of the reasons a connection request can fail is the lack of available worker threads, so this performance counter can be an indication, if consistently high, of a too-small worker thread pool.

- **Requests/sec**

  A basic performance counter, this indicates the total number of connection requests made to the Analysis server per second. This counter is generally useful as a basic measure of work performed by the Analysis server.

Analysis Server:Last Query

The **Last Query** performance object is best used to observe bottlenecks in the steps used to answer a single query.

- **Data bytes**

  The number of bytes read from the data file, used to store aggregation data for a cube. If this number is inordinately high when the query request is executed against a warm cache, this can indicate less than optimal cache management.

- **Data reads**

  The number of read operations needed to read data from the data file. As with the **Data bytes** performance counter, inordinately high values for this performance counter can indicate less than optimal cache management.

- **DSN requested**

  The data set name, represented as the ordinal number of each level needed from each dimension in a cube requested to satisfy a query request. This information is also used during the usage analysis process in aggregation design.

- **DSN used**

  The data set name, represented as the ordinal number of each level needed from each dimension in a cube actually used to satisfy a query request. This information is also used during the usage analysis process in aggregation design.

- **Index bytes**

  The number of bytes read from the index file, used to locate members within dimensions.

- **Index reads**

  The number of read operations needed to retrieve index information.

- **Map bytes**

  The number of bytes read from the map file, used to locate cells within the cube.

- **Map reads**

  The number of read operations needed to read data from the map file.

- **Rows created**

  The number of rows created in memory to answer a query request. Combined with the **Rows read** performance counter, this can be used to measure the effectiveness of aggregation design for a given cube.

- **Rows read**

  The number of rows read from the data file to answer a query request. Combined with the **Rows created** performance counter, this can also be used to measure aggregation design effectiveness.

- **Time (ms)**

  A useful metric from any viewpoint, this performance counter measures the total elapsed time, in milliseconds, to answer a query request. For this performance counter, lower is definitely better.

Analysis Server:Locks

The **Locks** performance object tracks the number and performance of read and write locks managed by the Analysis server. Although this can be useful, for example, in determining deadlocking behavior, this performance object is generally not needed for reviewing overall Analysis server performance.

Analysis Server:Proc

The **Proc** performance object monitors the base phase of processing, providing detailed information for reviewing processing performance.

- **File bytes written/sec**

  This counter represents the number of bytes written to multidimensional storage.

- **File rows written/sec**

  This counter, similar to the **File bytes written/sec** performance counter, represents the number of rows written to multidimensional storage. Used together, they can assist in locating bottlenecks caused by disk storage on the Analysis server.

- **Memory size bytes**

  This counter represents the size of memory, in bytes, needed to contain the rows currently being resorted in memory during the base phase.

- **Memory size rows**

  This counter represents the estimated number of rows in memory currently being resorted during the base phase. Combined with the **Memory size bytes** performance counter, this counter can assist in determining process buffer utilization during the base phase.

- **Rows created/sec**

  This counter represents the rate of aggregated rows created in multidimensional storage. Although this counter should be close to the **Rows read/sec** counter, it may be lower because of duplication in incoming rows.

- **Rows merged/sec**

  This performance counter shows the rate of rows merged from the underlying data source into multidimensional storage. This figure should be as close as possible to the **Rows read/sec** performance counter for optimal performance.

- **Rows read/sec**

  This performance counter shows the rate of rows read from the underlying data source by the reader thread during the base phase. Combined with the **Rows created/sec** and **Rows merged/sec** counters, this can indicate if bottlenecks occur at the relational database or at the Analysis server during processing.

Analysis Server:Proc Aggs

The **Proc Aggs** performance object monitors the aggregating phase of processing, providing detailed information for reviewing processing performance.

- **Memory size bytes**

  This counter represents the size of memory, in bytes, used to contain aggregations being created in memory.

- **Memory size rows**

  This counter represents the estimated number of aggregations in memory currently being created. Combined with the **Memory size bytes** performance counter, this counter can assist in determining process buffer utilization during the aggregating phase.

- **Rows created/sec**

  This counter represents the rate of aggregated rows created in multidimensional storage. Although this counter should be close to the Rows read/sec counter, it may be lower because of duplication in incoming rows.

- **Rows merged/sec**

  This performance counter shows the rate of aggregation rows merged from the fact table into multidimensional storage. This figure should be as close as possible to the **Rows read/sec** performance counter for optimal performance.

- **Temp file bytes written/sec**

  This counter represents the number of bytes written, per second, to temporary files used to hold aggregations during the aggregating phase. Ideally, this counter should have a value of zero—all aggregations should take place in memory. Processing performance significantly degrades if temporary files are required, so this performance counter is an excellent metric for determining if additional process buffer memory is needed.

Analysis Server:Proc Indexes

The **Proc Indexes** performance object monitors the indexing phase of processing, also providing detailed information for reviewing processing performance. The indexing phase is not as memory-intensive as the base and aggregating phases, however.

- **Rows/sec**

  This performance counter shows the rate of rows read from multidimensional storage by the reader thread during the indexing phase. A low rate can indicate a problem with disk storage on the Analysis server.

Analysis Server:Query

The **Query** performance object represents overall Analysis server querying performance. The following counters can assist in determining issues in querying interaction, with a focus on thread management.

Remember, however, that a query request on the Analysis server does not necessarily correspond on a one-to-one basis with MDX queries issued by client applications. Each query request represents a request to retrieve data for a single data slice, and an MDX query can represent many data slices.

- **Avg time/query**

  A basic performance counter, this indicates the average elapsed time, in milliseconds, per query request. Used in conjunction with the Time (ms) performance counter in the **Last Query** performance object, relative query performance can be quantified for very complex queries.

- **Current process thread pool**

  This counter represents the current number of process threads, both active and idle, in the process thread pool.

- **Current process thread queue length**

  This counter represents the current number of queued process requests. Ideally, this counter should be zero—there should always be enough process threads in the process thread pool to handle process requests. Realistically, this number should be as low as possible; consistently high numbers in this counter indicate that the number of threads allocated for the process thread pool is too low.

- **Current process threads active**

    This counter represents the number of active threads in the process thread pool. Subtract the value of this counter from the value of the **Current process thread pool** counter to determine the number of idle process threads; if this number is consistently high, too many process threads may be allocated.

- **Current threads**

    This performance counter represents the total number of both worker and process threads actively working on query requests.

- **Current worker thread pool**

    This counter represents the current number of worker threads, both active and idle, in the worker thread pool.

- **Current worker threads active**

    This counter shows the number of active threads in the worker thread pool. Ideally, this number should never be equal to the number of threads allocated to the worker thread pool; if all worker threads are active, there are none available to answer new query requests, causing errors to be returned by the listener thread to client applications. Realistically, this number should be between 50 to 75 percent of the total number of worker threads allocated for the worker thread pool, evaluated over time. If this number is consistently over 75 percent, or if it hits 100 percent, you may need to allocate more worker threads. If this number is consistently less than 50 percent, you may be able to reduce the number of allocated worker threads.

Analysis Server:Query Dims

The **Query Dims** performance object tracks the particulars of dimension data retrieval. Typically, the performance counters maintained by this performance object are not as useful for tracking overall performance, but a few of the counters can provide clues to dimension cache behavior and possible querying and processing performance bottlenecks:

- **Requests/sec**

    This performance counter tracks the number of requests made for members or member properties per second. This performance counter is directly related to the **HugeLevelThreshold** registry setting; if the setting is set too low, this counter will be correspondingly high. Increasing the value of the **HugeLevelThreshold** registry setting will decrease the value of this performance counter, at a corresponding cost in dimension cache memory.

- **VLDM requests/sec**

   This performance counter tracks the number of requests made for members or member properties, per second, to the Very Large Dimension Manager (VLDM). Since very large and huge dimensions are not cached in the same way that other dimensions are cached, using very large and huge dimensions can slow performance. This performance counter can assist in quantifying the effect of very large and huge dimensions on overall performance.

Analysis Server:Startup

Although all of the performance counters in the **Startup** performance object are interesting, only one is useful for quantifying server performance:

- **Server uptime**

   This performance counter represents the elapsed time since the MSSQLServerOLAPService service was started, and is used as the time over which total counters are averaged to construct ratio counters.

System Performance Counters

In order for Analysis Services performance counters to prove useful, they should be compared not only with each other for relative Analysis server performance, but also with overall system performance counters to determine how well Analysis Services is utilizing system resources. The most relevant system performance objects and counters are discussed in this section.

Memory

Although all of the counters in the **Memory** performance object are useful, two stand out when measuring Analysis Services overall performance:

- **Pages/sec**

   This performance counter indicates the number of I/O operations needed to support virtual memory. Ideally, this number should be as low as possible; a high number demonstrates too little available physical memory. Increasing available physical memory should reduce the number of page faults, and therefore reduce the amount of virtual memory used to support active processes such as Analysis Services.

- **Available bytes**

   This performance counter indicates the amount, in bytes, of available physical memory. Combined with the **Pages/sec system** counter, this counter can be used to further quantify the amount of available physical memory.

Network Interface

The **Network Interface** performance object monitors network traffic, tracking a number of metrics for performance evaluation. One counter, in particular, can be used to isolate possible bottlenecks in processing and querying performance:

- **Bytes Total/sec**

  In order to use this counter, you must select a network interface for monitoring purposes. This counter represents the total number of bytes that are sent and received, per second, for a given network interface.

  The best use of this performance counter is to compare it with the various ratio counters, maintained in the **Analysis Server:Proc**, **Analysis Server:Proc Indexes**, and **Analysis Server:Proc Aggs** performance objects, used to track data transfer, such as the **Rows read/sec** counter in the **Analysis Server:Proc** performance object. For underlying data sources that are not resident on the Analysis server, if this counter matches the fluctuations of the ratio counters during poor processing performance, the network may be the cause of processing performance impact.

PhysicalDisk

Disk storage performance is central to Analysis Services performance. The following counters can be compared directly with various performance counters maintained by the Analysis Services performance objects to determine if disk storage represents querying or processing performance impact.

A common cause of poor disk storage performance is the performance of other applications running on the system. Disk storage supports all applications running on a given system; active applications draw resources away from Analysis Services. These performance counters can provide a better picture of absolute querying and processing performance by comparing all of the disk storage activity on the system with the disk storage activity tracked by Analysis Services.

- **Avg. Disk Bytes/Read**

  This represents the average number of bytes transferred from disk storage during a single read operation.

- **Current Disk Queue Length**

  This counter represents the current number of queued disk operations. If this number spikes during poor processing performance, especially during the base or aggregating phases, then the current disk storage solution may not be adequate to support the needs of Analysis Services. Ideally, the value of this performance counter should be as low as possible at any given time.

The following performance counters are especially useful for determining total disk storage system performance, to be compared with the relative performance information tracked by Analysis Services:

- **Disk Bytes/sec**
- **Disk Reads/sec**
- **Disk Transfers/sec**
- **Disk Writes/sec**

For example, the **Disk Writes/sec** can be compared with the **File Rows Written/sec** performance counter from the **Analysis Server:Proc** performance object to determine the percentage of disk writes established during the base phase of processing, compared to other applications on the server.

Process

To examine system performance for Analysis Services, you must first select the correct instance. For Analysis Services, the msmdsrv instance represents the MSSQLServerOLAPService service process. Once selected, you can view Analysis Services overall performance from the viewpoint of the operating system.

The following performance counters can be used to generally review Analysis Services performance:

- **% Privileged Time**
- **% Processor Time**
- **% User Time**
- **IO Data Bytes/sec**
- **IO Data Operations/sec**
- **IO Other Bytes/sec**
- **IO Other Operations/sec**
- **IO Read Bytes/sec**
- **IO Read Operations/sec**
- **IO Write Bytes/sec**
- **IO Write Operations/sec**
- **Thread Count**
- **Virtual Bytes**
- **Working Set**

The **Thread Count** performance counter, for example, can be compared against the various thread performance counters in the **Analysis Server:Query** performance object to determine thread behavior for additional threads in the Analysis server.

Processor

The performance counters represented by the **Processor** performance object track performance at the processor level, but typically at too low a level to be directly relevant. However, one performance counter can be used in a general fashion to determine overall performance:

- **% Processor Time**

    This performance counter represents the percentage of time spent processing non-idle threads, either for the entire system or on a processor-by-processor basis. A general indicator of processor usage, this can be compared against other Analysis Services performance counters to determine processor impact. Additionally, a consistently high processor usage may indicate a bottleneck in calculating aggregations.

System

The System performance object contains general system performance counters. Several performance counters can be used, when compared with Analysis Services performance counters for a relative viewpoint of overall performance:

- **Context Switches/sec**

    This counter indirectly indicates the efficiency of thread allocation for all processors, per second, for Analysis Services. Compared against the various thread performance counters in the **Analysis Server:Query** performance object, a view on overall system thread management can be established.

- **File Control Operations/sec**

    This counter tracks the number of non-read, non-write I/O operations performed by the disk storage system per second, and directly indicates the efficiency of the disk storage system. Compared against the various counters used to track disk storage I/O in Analysis Services, this counter can be used to reveal bottlenecks involving disk storage.

- **Processor Queue Length**

    This counter tracks the number of queued threads waiting for processor time. Compared against the various active thread performance counters in Analysis Services, this counter can be used to examine thread management efficiency.

- **System Calls/sec**

    Another basic performance counter, this counter tracks the number of Windows NT system service routines called per second. This counter is generally useful, when compared against the various performance counters in Analysis Services, to isolate possible operating system bottlenecks.

Digital Dashboards

Creating an Interactive Digital Dashboard

Introduction

A digital dashboard is a portal composed of Web components (called Web Parts) that can be combined and customized to meet the needs of individual users. Web Parts are reusable components that wrap Web-based content such as XML, HTML, and scripts with a standard property schema that controls how Web Parts are rendered in a digital dashboard.

This chapter explains how to build a digital dashboard that contains interactive Web Parts that respond to events generated by other parts in the same dashboard. (This chapter assumes you are familiar with Microsoft® SQL Server™ 2000, XML, scripting, and Web application development.) Dashboards support part integration through a set of services provided by the Digital Dashboard Services Component (DDSC). The DDSC includes Part Discovery, Part Notification, Session State Management, and Item Retrieval. There is an underlying object model that you can use to program the services into your code.

When building an integrated or interactive dashboard, Part Notification provides the most relevant service. Part Notification service refers to event notification and a corresponding response. Understanding how this service works is key to building interactive Web Parts. This chapter describes how to deploy this service in the context of building a simple dashboard.

A dashboard can be an arbitrary container for unrelated parts (for example, a collection of your favorite Web sites or applications arranged into a personal dashboard for easy access), or it can be a container of parts that work together by sharing, summarizing, or filtering the same data set. In the later case, the dashboard operates more like an application, with features and functionality distributed across multiple parts. This chapter describes the basic techniques you need to build exactly this kind of dashboard.

The objective of this chapter is to show you the process of creating an interactive dashboard and how to retrieve sample data from the **Northwind** database using the XML features in SQL Server 2000. Specifically, this chapter teaches you how to:

- Create parts that get and transform XML-based data from SQL Server.

- Reference an HTC file that defines HTML behaviors in your dashboard.

- Use the Digital Dashboard Service Component (DDSC) to raise and respond to events occurring at the part level.

- Create isolated frames that enable DDSC events to occur on the client, eliminating round trips to the server and improving security.

To illustrate these points, a Customer Information dashboard that contains two parts is created. The first Web Part presents a list of customers retrieved from **Northwind**. The second Web Part is a bar chart that shows order volume by year for a specific customer that you select. When the user clicks a value in the customer list in the first part, the DDSC raises an event that causes the second part to get and display summarized order data about that customer.

The actual dashboard and Web Part definitions will be created by you. The code samples included with this chapter provide the Web-based content that you use to create the Web Parts. Code for this chapter is provided on the *SQL Server 2000 Resource Kit* CD-ROM. Each step of the process is explained, and the tools and software you need to perform each step are identified.

To follow the steps in this chapter, you must have SQL Server 2000 running on Microsoft Windows® 2000, and the Digital Dashboard Resource Kit (DDRK) 2.01. From the DDRK, you must also install the SQL Server sample Administration digital dashboard. The sample dashboard provides a way to create dashboards and parts. The sample Administration dashboard is used to define the dashboard and parts described in this chapter.

In the process of creating the dashboard, you will need to do the following:

- Ensure that your SQL Server 2000 installation supports SQL Server authentication.

- Install the DDRK 2.01.

- Install the SQL Server sample Administration dashboard from the DDRK.

- Create virtual and physical directories to store the code sample files.

- Copy the files to the directories you created in the previous step.

- Edit the files to correct server name and path information.

- Define a dashboard using the sample Administration digital dashboard.

- Define a Customer List Web Part.

- Define a Customer Order Chart Web Part.

About the Code Samples

Code samples provide the content of the Web Parts you will create. Web Part content can be XML, HTML, or scripts that get and transform data or that define events and behaviors. You can put the content in separate files that you reference or you can type it directly into the Web Part definition. For this exercise, the content is provided in files. Note that a single Web Part can use multiple files to supply functionality.

Code samples provided with this chapter include the following:

- Customerlist.htm (provides content for the Customer List Web Part).

- Customerlist.xml (contains an XML-based SQL Server query. This query gets a list of company names from the Customers table in **Northwind**).

- Customerlist.xsl (transforms the company names in the Customer List Web Part).

- Customerlist.htc (defines **mouseover**, **mouseout**, and **click** events for the Customer List Web Part).

- Orderchart.htm (provides content for the Order Chart Web Part).

- Orderchart.xsl (transforms order data for a specific customer).

The code sample files are commented to help you interpret the purpose and intent of the code. Snippets from these files appear in this chapter to illustrate key points.

> **Note**   Code samples require editing before you can use them. Many of the files contain placeholder values for your Microsoft Internet Information Services (IIS) server and virtual directories. Where indicated in the instructions, you need to replace the placeholder values with values that are valid for your computer.

Required Software

This chapter requires Microsoft SQL Server 2000, Microsoft Windows 2000, Internet Explorer 5.0 or later, and the Digital Dashboard Resource Kit (DDRK) 2.01.

SQL Server 2000

SQL Server 2000 is required because it includes XML support for exposing relational data as XML. In the sample dashboard you create, you access **Northwind** as XML from your Web browser by way of a virtual directory. SQL Server 2000 provides a tool for configuring a virtual directory for the **Northwind** database. Instructions for configuring this directory are covered later in this chapter.

If you install the DDRK on the same computer as SQL Server, your SQL Server installation needs to support SQL Server authentication. Hosting a dashboard and a SQL Server on the same computer means that the Web server (IIS) and SQL Server need to talk to each other. Having both the Web Server and SQL Server use the same integrated authentication mode results in a security violation; the Web server will be prevented from issuing a query to a SQL query when both servers reside on the same computer. To be able to query **Northwind** from your development computer, you need to use SQL Server authentication. Note that if SQL Server authentication is not enabled, you may need to reinstall SQL Server, selecting SQL Server authentication during the install process.

If SQL Server and the DDRK are installed on different computers, you can use whatever authentication mode you like. For more information about supported platforms and installation, see SQL Server Books Online.

Windows 2000

For this chapter, Windows 2000 and IIS 5.0 are required on the server hosting the digital dashboard. This means that the computer on which you install the DDRK must be running some edition of Windows 2000 server.

Clients do not require Windows 2000. Client platforms include any edition of Windows 2000, Windows NT®, and Windows 98.

Internet Explorer 5.X

Viewing the dashboard and processing the underlying XML requires Internet Explorer 5.0 or 5.5.

Digital Dashboard Resource Kit (DDRK)

Dashboard development starts with the DDRK, which provides the design-time framework and run-time components you need to deploy dashboards and parts. The DDRK 2.01 provides information and development resources. To learn about dashboards, you can read white papers, reference material, and overviews. Development resources include sample Administration digital dashboards that you can analyze to further your understanding of dashboard functionality.

More important, the sample Administration digital dashboards offer real functional value—installing a sample dashboard simultaneously installs digital dashboard components, such as the dashboard factory, the DDSC, and dashboard storage support. The sample Administration digital dashboards also provide a user interface for creating new and modifying existing dashboards and parts, as well as the ability to set properties that control access and presentation.

The DDRK contains several sample Administration digital dashboards. For this chapter, we assume you are using the SQL Server Sample Administration Digital Dashboard. You will use this dashboard to create your own dashboard as well as define the Customer List and Order Chart parts.

Downloading and Installing the DDRK and SQL Server Sample Digital Dashboard

You can download and install the DDRK 2.01 from http://www.microsoft.com/business/DigitalDashboard/.

To install the SQL Server Sample Digital Dashboard, open the DDRK and go to **Building Digital Dashboards**. Choose **Install the Microsoft SQL Server 7.0 Sample Digital Dashboard** (note that this sample dashboard is fully compatible with SQL Server 2000).

During installation, you will be asked to create a new SQL Server database to store the dashboards and parts you create. When defining the login to this database, use **sa** for the user name and leave the password blank.

After installation completes, the **Welcome** page of the SQL Server Sample Administration Digital Dashboard appears (note the HTTP address for future reference). Click **Administration** to open the Administration page. This is the page you will use later to define a new dashboard and Web Parts.

Setting Up

This section explains how to get files into the right places and configure virtual directories.

Download the Code Samples

The code samples for this chapter are available on the *SQL Server 2000 Resource Kit* CD-ROM in the folder, \ToolsAndSamples\DigitalDashboard. There are six files altogether.

In the next several steps, we will tell you where to place the files and which files need editing.

Create Physical and Virtual Directories for Your HTM and HTC Files

Use Windows Explorer to create a physical directory in your Default Web Site directory. By default, the path is C:\Inetpub\Wwwroot. To this path, you can add a subdirectory named Tutorial, resulting in this path: C:\Inetpub\Wwwroot\Tutorial.

Into this directory, copy the following code sample files:

- Customerlist.htm
- Customerlist.htc
- Orderchart.htm.

Use Internet Services Manager to create a new virtual directory under Default Web Site for your HTM and HTC files. In Windows 2000, this tool is located in the Administrative Tools program group. To create a virtual directory, right-click **Default Web Site**, and then click **New Virtual Directory**. To match the path names used in the code samples, name your virtual directory Tutorial.

Create Physical and Virtual Directories for Your XML and XSL Files

To issue an SQL query through HTTP, you need to configure **Northwind** as a virtual directory. To do this, you use the **Configure SQL XML Support in IIS** tool, located in the Microsoft SQL Server program group. Instructions that describe this process in detail are provided in the topic "Creating the **nwind** Virtual Directory" in SQL Server Books Online. You should follow the instructions exactly. When you are finished, you should have the following physical directories:

- \Inetpub\Wwwroot\nwind

- \Inetpub\Wwwroot\nwind\schema

- \Inetpub\Wwwroot\nwind\template

For each physical directory, you should have a corresponding virtual directory of the same name.

Into the \Inetpub\Wwwroot\nwind\template directory, copy the following code sample files:

- Customerlist.xml

- Customerlist.xsl

- Orderchart.xsl

   Note   The **nwind** virtual directory is accessed by SQL Server when it retrieves data. The application virtual directory that you use to store the HTM and HTC files is accessed by the dashboard. This is why you need separate directories for each group of files.

Copy and Edit the HTM and HTC Files

After you copy all the files, you can adjust the server name and paths in the code sample files. In all cases, replace *<your server name>* with the name of your IIS server, correcting the virtual path names if necessary. Use the proper name rather than localhost for the server name. Using localhost results in permission denied errors when you add Web Parts later in the tutorial.

1. Open Customerlist.htm from the Tutorial folder using an HTML or text editor.

2. Edit the path in the **IFRAME** element: <IFRAME ID="CustFrame" SRC="http://*<your server name>*/nwind/template/customerlist.xml".

3. Save and close the file.

4. Open Orderchart.htm from the Tutorial folder using an HTML or text editor.

5. Edit the path in the SRC property of the ChartFrame object: document.all.ChartFrame.src = "http://*<your server name>*/Nwind?xsl=…".

6. Save and close the file.

7. Open Customerlist.xsl from the Template folder using an HTML or text editor.

8. Edit the path in td style element: td {behavior:url(http://*<your server name>*/tutorial/customerlist.htc)}.

9. Save and close the file.

Building the Dashboard

This section tells you how to use the Administration sample dashboard to define a new dashboard and the parts that go in it.

Defining the Dashboard

A dashboard is a container for Web Parts. It is defined by a schema and supports properties that determine dashboard appearance and behavior. To create the Customer Information dashboard, you start by defining a new dashboard.

1. In your browser, open the Administration page of the SQL Server Sample Digital Dashboard. The default address is http://*<your server name>*/Dashboard/Dashboard.asp?DashboardID=http://*<your server name>*/Sqlwbcat/Welcome/Administration.

2. In the Dashboard View pane, select **Sqlwbcat**, and then click **New** to define a new dashboard. **Sqlwbcat** is the default name of both the SQL Server database and IIS extension that manages dashboard and part storage. The dashboard that you define will be stored and managed by **Sqlwbcat**.

3. In the Dashboard Properties pane, replace the default name **NewDashboard1** with **CustomerInfo**, and then replace the default title **New Dashboard** with **Customer Information Dashboard**.

4. If you wish, choose a different predefined stylesheet.

5. Click **Save**. The **CustomerInfo** dashboard is added to the list of dashboards for **Sqlwbcat**.

To test your progress so far, open your browser and paste this Address: http://*<your server name>*/Dashboard/Dashboard.asp?DashboardID=http://*<your server name>*/Sqlwbcat/CustomerInfo. You should see an empty dashboard, correctly titled and styled, with the **Content**, **Layout**, and **Settings** items in the top right corner.

Save this URL in your Favorites list so that you can view the changes as you add each part.

Defining the Customer List Web Part

The Customer List Web Part contains a list of customers, identified by Company Name. The content for this Web Part is an HTM file.

1. In your browser, open the Administration page of the SQL Server Sample Digital Dashboard. In the Dashboard View pane, select the **CustomerInfo** dashboard.

2. Scroll down to the Web Part List pane, and then click **New** to define a new part.

3. In the **General** tab of Web Part Properties, do the following four things:

   1. Replace the default name **NewPart1** with **CustomerList.**

   2. Replace the default title **NewPart1** with **Customer List.**

   3. Select **Left Column** for the position on the page.

   4. Set **Fixed Size** to a fixed height of 500 pixels. This shows more rows in the **Customer List**.

4. Click the **Advanced** tab.

5. Choose **HTML** for the Content Type.

6. In Content Link, type the following: http://<*your server name*>/tutorial/customerlist.htm

7. Click **Save**.

Note that if you subsequently change any properties (for example, to adjust the part position or change the title), the values you entered for fixed height will migrate to the fixed width fields. This bug will be fixed in a subsequent release. The workaround for now is to redo the fixed height, and then click no to disable the fixed width.

To test your progress so far, open or refresh the Customer Information dashboard in your browser. The Customer List Web Part should appear in the dashboard.

Defining the Order Chart Web Part

The Order Chart Web Part is an HTML file that contains summarized order data for the customer selected in the Customer List Web Part.

1. In your browser, open the Administration page of the SQL Server Sample Digital Dashboard, then select the **CustomerInfo** dashboard.

2. Scroll down to the Web Part List pane, and then click **New** to define a new part.

3. In the **General** tab of Web Part Properties, do the following four things:

   1. Replace the default name **NewPart1** with **OrderChart**.

   2. Replace the default title **NewPart1** with **Order Chart**.

   3. Select **Right Column** for the position on the page.

   4. Set Fixed Size to a fixed height of 350 pixels to give the part more room.

4. Click the **Advanced** tab.

5. Choose **HTML** for the **Content Type**.

6. In Content Link, type the following: http://*<your server name>*/tutorial/orderchart.htm

7. Click **Save**.

Testing the Dashboard

After you add the two parts, the dashboard is ready to use. Open the Customer Information dashboard in your browser. Click a Company Name in the Customer List Web Part. The Order Chart Web Part responds by querying **Northwind** for order information about the customer, and then aggregating that information into a set of values that can be represented by a bar chart. The name of the customer you select appears above the chart. The following sections detail the events and actions occurring behind the scenes that create the appearance and behavior you see in this dashboard.

Reviewing the Code Samples

This section highlights the more interesting aspects of the code samples. Each file is discussed separately. The following table describes the role of each file.

File	Description
Customerlist.htm	Creates a structure for the part.
Customerlist.xml	Gets customer data.
Customerlist.xsl	Transforms data by selecting it and applying HTML.
Customerlist.htc	Adds dynamic HTML behaviors, including definitions for the **onclick** event used to raise an event notification. This notification is received by the Order Chart Web Part.
Orderchart.htm	Creates a basic structure for the part, gets data by building a query that includes a Company Name passed through the **onclick** event defined in Customerlist.htc.
Orderchart.xsl	Transforms the data by selecting it and applying HTML. The bars in the bar chart are dynamically sized based on the amount of annual orders. Two functions different functions are used to calculate these values.

Customerlist.htm

This HTML file provides the content for the Customer List Web Part. It contains a reference to the Customerlist.xml file, which in turn contains a reference to Customerlist.xsl, which references the Customerlist.htc file.

The Customerlist.htm file defines an isolated frame to contain Customer data from **Northwind**. Although you can isolate Web Parts in the Web Part definition, using this approach (that is, manually creating IFRAME elements) offers more security and allows you to invoke the DDSC at the part level.

Invoking the DDSC at the part level means that you can control other Web Parts (in this case, the Order Chart Web Part) from script inside an IFRAME. To do this, you create a variable named DDSC in the IFRAME content and then set its value equal to the DDSC that exists outside of the frame (that is, the DDSC instance for the dashboard). You can then use the DDSC variable to communicate with other parts.

In this example, a DDSC variable is declared in the source for the IFRAME (that is, in the Customerlist.xsl file, which in turn is referenced by the Customerlist.xml file, which provides the content to the IFRAME element).

This approach works because a parent can access an IFRAME (note that the reverse case of IFRAMEs accessing parents is not true). In this case, the DDSC instance at the dashboard level can access the IFRAME content you define and participate in the script that you associate with a given IFRAME element.

In the code snippet below, the IFRAME ID attribute is defined so that you can reference the frame in script.

Next, the IFRAME SRC attribute specifies the XML template file containing the **Northwind** query. This file is used to populate the frame with a scrollable list of Company Names. The names are retrieved from **Northwind** when the dashboard loads. Note that UTF-16 encoding is needed to accurately display foreign language characters in the data.

Finally, the IFRAME HEIGHT and WIDTH attributes expand the frame so that it occupies all of the available space of the Web Part.

```
<IFRAME ID="CustFrame"
SRC="http://<server>/nwind/template/customerlist.xml?contenttype=text/html&outputencodin
g=UTF-16" HEIGHT="100%" WIDTH="100%">
</IFRAME>
```

Further on in this file, you find a script block that instantiates a DDSC instance at the frame level, using the value of the IFRAME ID. The DDSC is one of the objects used to implement the Part Notification service. It exposes methods that both raise and respond to event notifications.

```
CustFrame.ddsc= DDSC;
```

Customerlist.xml

This XML template file issues an SQL SELECT statement through IIS using the **nwind** virtual directory you configured earlier. Specifying the **nwind** virtual directory is equivalent to specifying the **Northwind** database (recall that this specification is part the value for the IFRAME SRC attribute in Customerlist.htm).

The root element defines a namespace and the XSL file used to transform the result set. The query statement is a child of the root element.

```
<root xmlns:sql='run:schemas-microsoft-com:xml-sql' sql:xsl='customerlist.xsl'>
<sql:query>
SELECT CompanyName FROM Customers FOR XML AUTO
</sql:query>
</root>
```

Customerlist.xsl

This XSL file transforms the XML result set so that it appears in the page. It defines a template pattern that finds all Customer nodes and gets the value of the Company Name. The Company Name is inserted into a TD element in the order returned by the query.

In the code snippet below, the STYLE element defines CSS styles for TH and TD elements.

The STYLE TH element is styled with a gray background color.

The STYLE TD element calls an HTC file that combines style attributes with script to produce dynamic HTML for the content in each **TD** element.

```
<STYLE>
TH {background-color:#CCCCCC}
TD {behavior:url(http://<server>tutorial/customerlist.htc)}
</STYLE>
```

This file also declares a variable for DDSC. This variable is used in the Customerlist.htm file to invoke the DDSC object for an IFRAME element. Note that this declaration was discussed previously, in the Customerlist.htm section.

```
<script language="JScript">
var DDSC;
</script>
```

Customerlist.htc

The Customer List Web Part is programmed for three events: **onmouseover**, **onmouseout**, **onclick**.

Onmouseover and **onmouseout** define rollover behavior.

Through the Click function, the **onclick** event instantiates the DDSC object at the part level. Clicking a company name raises an event (that is, broadcasts an event notification to other parts in the same dashboard). The **RaiseEvent** method is a method of the DDSC object.

```
function Click() {
ddsc.RaiseEvent("URN:Customer", "SelectCustomer", this.innerHTML);
}
```

The *URN:Customer* parameter is a user-defined namespace that you can create to provide a context for the event. For example, in any given application you may have multiple Click functions. Using a namespace provides a way to distinguish between click events that occur in an Employee form, a Customer list, or an Order bar chart.

The *SelectCustomer* parameter is an event name. This is a user-defined name that identifies the event to other Web Parts that respond to this event. Script attached to the responding Web Part (that is, the Order Chart) refers to the same event name when registering for the event.

The *this.innerHTML* parameter is an event object. This is the object upon which the function operates. In this case, it is a specific Company Name that the user clicks on. This value is passed as part of the event notification, making it available to other parts that want to use it.

Orderchart.htm

This file provides the content for the Order Chart Web Part. The file contains an SQL SELECT statement issued through IIS using the **nwind** virtual directory you configured earlier. The query is multipart, using a combination of fixed strings and a Company Name value that is passed in as a parameter. The data that is returned is total order volume for a single customer, grouped by year. Clicking a different customer in the Customer List issues another query against the database, using new values that correspond to the selected customer. The return values are used to update the contents of the Order Chart.

The code that relates the Order Chart to the Customer List Web Part is the following:

```
DDSC.RegisterForEvent("URN:Customer", "SelectCustomer", this.innerHTML);
```

The *SelectCustomer* parameter is the event name, and *this.innerHTML* is the event object.

As with the Customer List, an isolated frame is used to contain the data. The IFRAME element is defined as follows:

```
<IFRAME ID="ChartFrame" WIDTH="100%" FRAMEBORDER="0" NORESIZE SCROLLING="auto"></IFRAME>
```

The **onSelectCustomer** function provides the code that creates the multipart query. (Note that the first several lines of this function are used to search and replace special characters like ampersands and apostrophes to XML or HTTP equivalents). The query is specified through the *SRC* parameter of the IFRAME element by way of the document object model.

```
document.all.ChartFrame.src =
"http://<server>/nwind?xsl=template/orderchart.xsl&contenttype=text/html&outputencoding=
UTF-
16&sql=Select+datepart(year,%20Orders.OrderDate)+as+Year,Sum([order%20details].UnitPrice
*[order%20details].Quantity)+as+OrderTotal+from+[order
details]+inner+join+Orders+on+[order%20details].OrderID=Orders.OrderID+inner+join+Custom
ers+on+Orders.CustomerID=Customers.CustomerID+where+customers.companyname='"
+customerName +"'+group+by+datepart(year,%20Orders.OrderDate)+FOR+XML+RAW&root=root";
```

In this query, an XSL file and encoding attribute are specified before the SELECT statement.

The SELECT statement itself is articulated in HTTP syntax. Because the query contains a dynamic element (CustomerName, which is the value passed in as "this.innerHTML" and it varies each time the user clicks a Company Name), a static XML template file could not be used. Passing the SQL query as a string provides a way to combine static and dynamic elements together.

Orderchart.xsl

This file transforms the XML result set returned for the Order Chart, creating the bar chart and displaying customer information based on an SQL query. This file is referenced in the HTTP statement for the *SRC* parameter.

The bar chart is simple HTML (in this case, TD elements in a table) and it shows differences among annual order volumes for a specific customer. To get differences in bar color and size, different attributes on the TD element are set. These attributes are BACKGROUND-COLOR and WIDTH. WIDTH is an XSL attribute (name=style) that is attached to the TD element. The value of WIDTH is calculated through script.

Color coding is based on the year (year values are detected through XSL). Because there are only three years worth of data in the **Northwind** database, we get by with XSL test cases that detect 1996, 1997, and 1998.

```
<xsl:attribute name="style">width:<xsl:eval>getOrderPercent(this)</xsl:eval>;
    <xsl:choose>
        <xsl:when test=".[@Year='1996']">background-color:red</xsl:when>
        <xsl:when test=".[@Year='1997']">background-color:blue</xsl:when>
        <xsl:otherwise>background-color:purple;</xsl:otherwise>
    </xsl:choose>
```

Sizing is based on order volume. In **Northwind** data, order volumes vary from two-digit to five-digit values. The wide range makes it difficult to scale the bars using fixed values (a bar chart based on pixels would need to accommodate bars that are 42 pixels long and 64,234 pixels long). To work around this, we use percentages. Percentage values show relative rather than absolute differences in the order volumes. For a specific customer, each annual volume (for 1996, 1997, or 1998) is some percentage of the combined three-year volume. To get the three different WIDTH values needed for the three bars in the bar chart, we use two functions.

The **getOrderPercent** function calculates the value of the TD WIDTH attribute by dividing an Order Total by the sum of all Order Totals. This function is called from an xsl:eval element (as shown in the first line of the previous code snippet).

The **getOrderTotal** function sums the Order Totals into one lump sum. This sum becomes the denominator in the **getOrderPercent** function.

Both functions are reproduced here in their entirety:

```
var nTotal = 0;
function getOrderPercent(nNode)  {
    var nPercent;
    if (nTotal == 0)
        nTotal=getOrderTotal(nNode.ParentNode);
    nPercent=Math.round((nNode.getAttribute("OrderTotal") / nTotal) * 100) + '%';
    return nPercent;
    }

function getOrderTotal(nNode)  {
    var sum=0;
        var rows=nNode.selectNodes("row");
        for (var i = rows.nextNode(); i; i = rows.nextNode())
        sum += parseInt(i.getAttribute("OrderTotal"));
        return sum;
    }
```

A Digital Dashboard Browser for Analysis Services Meta Data

Introduction

This chapter steps through creating a digital dashboard browser to view Microsoft® SQL Server™ 2000 Analysis Services meta data. Using interactive digital dashboard concepts, the components are created using Active Server Pages (ASP), Microsoft Visual Basic® Scripting Edition (VBScript), and Decision Support Objects (DSO). The completed dashboard will allow the user to connect to a selected analysis server, choose a database, and view meta data about cubes, dimensions, roles, and other objects made available by the DSO object model.

Digital dashboards are a means of assembling various pieces of HTML and scripts, called Web Parts, into a single Web interface. Web Parts are reusable components that may contain pieces of HTML, XML, or full Web pages. In this example, individual ASP files, which could function as stand-alone pages, combine into a single Web application using the dashboard as a wrapper. The Web Parts provide a means of coordinating the data within each of the pages using the Digital Dashboard Service Component (DDSC) to register for and/or raise events in each part.

In this chapter, you will learn how to:

- Access DSO using ASP and VBScript.

- Create a dashboard, incorporating the ASP pages.

- Use DDSC in VBScript to update each part as other parts change.

The dashboard created in this chapter displays simple top-level meta data on the Analysis server. It can easily be modified to display multiple levels of meta data and data from Microsoft SQL Server™ and Analysis Services. The Digital Dashboard Browser for Analysis Services Meta Data (**MetaDataDashboard**) sample files discussed in this chapter are available on the *SQL Server 2000 Resource Kit* CD-ROM in the folder, \ToolsAndSamples\MetaDataDashboard.

Requirements

The server used for this chapter will need Microsoft Windows® 2000 Server, SQL Server 2000 with Analysis Services and Digital Dashboard Resource Kit 2.01. Individual clients and the development computer require only Internet Explorer 5.5 on any supported operating system.

Windows 2000 Server

The Digital Dashboard Resource Kit 2.0 requires a Windows 2000 server running Internet Information Services (IIS) 5.0 as the Web server. Any of the Windows Server family may be used: Windows 2000 Server, Advanced Server, or Datacenter Server.

SQL Server 2000 with Analysis Services

This example uses a SQL Server Digital Dashboard, which stores dashboard definitions in a SQL Server database. Analysis Services is also required because the dashboard will be accessing meta data from the Analysis Server. It is recommended that the SQL and Analysis server installation exist on the same computer as the Web server. If a separate installation is desired, DSO must be installed on the Web server. For information on how to install DSO without installing Analysis Services, see "Redistributing Decision Support Objects" in SQL Server Books Online.

Digital Dashboard Resource Kit (DDRK) 2.01

In this chapter, you will be using a digital dashboard as the front end for viewing Analysis Services meta data. The Digital Dashboard Resource Kit (DDRK) is available for download at http://www.microsoft.com/business/DigitalDashboard/. After the DDRK is downloaded and installed, open it on the computer running Windows 2000 and IIS 5.0. Select **Building Digital Dashboards** then choose **Install the Microsoft SQL Server 7.0 Digital Dashboard** to begin installation.

Part of the installation will set up a new database on SQL Server. You will need administrator rights on your SQL Server in order to complete this step.

When installation is complete, the DDRK will automatically open the **Welcome** page in Internet Explorer. Select **Administration** to view the **Administration** page, where you will be creating your dashboards. You may want to bookmark this page for future reference. Alternately, you can access your dashboard's **Welcome** page through the http://SERVERNAME/Dashboard, where SERVERNAME is the name of your Web server.

Internet Explorer 5.5

While the DDRK requires Internet Explorer 5.0 and later, certain Web Parts in this dashboard will only function on Internet Explorer 5.5.

DDSC Versions

When you open a DDRK page for the first time on a client computer, the Microsoft Digital Dashboard Service Component (DDSC) will be installed. It is important that the correct version of the DDSC be installed; an incorrect version can cause various problems. One version in particular raises display issues with embedded content in Web Part Properties.

If the DDSC is installed while opening your new dashboard page (from DDRK 2.01), you should have the correct version. However, if you need to check the version of DDSC, open \WINNT\Downloaded Program Files, right-click on the DDSC Class file, and choose **Properties**. On the **Version** tab, under **Version**, you should see **2000,0,176,0**, the version shipped with 2.01. If you have another version, and wish to replace it, right-click on the DDSC Class file again and click **Remove**. Then, open your dashboard page again. The correct version will then be installed.

Setup

Before creating your dashboard, you will need to update the Web server with the appropriate settings and files.

Copy Files

The Digital Dashboard Browser for Analysis Services Meta Data (**MetaDataDashboard**) sample files discussed in this chapter are available on the *SQL Server 2000 Resource Kit* CD-ROM, in the folder \ToolsAndSamples\MetaDataDashboard. This procedure places the included files into the appropriate directories:

1. Copy the five .txt files (1_serverconnect.txt, 2_dbselect.txt, 3_collselect.txt, 4_memberselect.txt, and 5_metadata.txt) to a temporary directory.

2. Create a directory on the Web server. This directory will become a virtual directory in IIS.

3. Copy the five .asp files (Serverconnect.asp, Dbselect.asp, Collselect.asp, Memberselect.asp, and Metadata.asp) to the directory created in the previous step.

Set Up an IIS Virtual Directory

The previously copied files now need to be accessible by IIS. To do this, set up a virtual directory:

1. Open Internet Services Manager.

2. Right-click on **Default Web Site** and select **New – Virtual Directory**.

3. When prompted for **Alias**, type **AnalysisMetaData**. For **Directory**, type the directory you created in Step 2 of "Copy Files" above, and for **Access Permissions**, leave the defaults (**Read, Run scripts**).

4. Close Internet Services Manager.

Grant Permissions

In order for IIS to access Analysis Server data, the IIS anonymous login must be a member of the OLAP Administrators group.

1. In **Control Panel**, in **Administrative Tools**, open **Computer Management**.

2. Expand **Local Users and Groups** and select **Users**. Make a note of the user name for the Internet Guest Account (typically **IUSR_SERVERNAME**, where SERVERNAME is the name of the IIS computer).

3. Under **Local Users and Groups**, select **Groups**, and open **OLAP Administrators**. Select **Add** to add a new user to the group.

4. Enter the name of the Internet Guest Account.

You may also need to stop and restart the Web server and the Analysis server for the new security settings to take effect. To do so:

1. In **Control Panel**, in **Administrative Tools**, open **Computer Management**.

2. Expand **Services and Applications**, and select **Services**.

3. Right-click **World Wide Publishing Service** and click **Restart**.

4. Right-click **MSSQLServerOLAPService** and click **Restart**.

There may be security concerns regarding the use of the anonymous login within the OLAP Administrators group. It is possible to set up IIS so your digital dashboard uses a different anonymous login, or requires Windows Authentication. See your Windows 2000 documentation for more information.

Creating the Digital Dashboard

This section outlines setting up the digital dashboard and incorporating various Web Parts. The text files referred to in this section are the files you copied to your temporary directory earlier in this chapter.

Set Up the Dashboard

The first phase in creating your digital dashboard is defining the dashboard itself. To accomplish this, follow these steps:

1. Open the DDRK Administration screen using the bookmark you saved earlier. (The URL should look something like this: http://SERVERNAME/dashboard/dashboard.asp?DashboardID=http://SERVERNAME/Sqlwbcat/Welcome/Administration/.)

2. Select **Sqlwbcat** under **Dashboard View** and click **New**.

3. Select the new dashboard (for example, **NewDashboard1**).

4. Under **Dashboard Properties**, enter a name of **AnalysisMetaData** and a title of **Analysis Meta Data**.

5. Leave the defaults for the remaining properties and choose **Save**.

Create the ServerConnect Web Part

This procedure adds the first Web Part, called **ServerConnect**:

1. Under **Web Part List**, click **New**.

2. Enter the following information inthe **General** section **of Web Part Properties**:

    Name: ServerConnect

    Title: Connect to Server

    Position on the Page: Left column

    Position within the Column: 1

    Fixed Size: No for both width and height (other parts will use fixed height).

3. In the **Advanced** section of **Web Part Properties**, copy the contents of 1_serverconnect.txt into the **Embedded Content** text box, replacing the string "SERVERNAME" with the name of the Web server.

4. Turn off (uncheck) **Allow users to remove this Web Part from the dashboard** and **Allow users to minimize this Web Part on the dashboard**.

5. Click **Save** to save the Web Part.

Create the DBSelect Web Part

This procedure adds the second Web Part, called **DBSelect**:

1. Under **Web Part List**, click **New**.

2. Enter the following information in the **General** section of **Web Part Properties**:

   Name: DBSelect

   Title: Select Database

   Position on the Page: Left column

   Position within the Column: 2

   Fixed Size: fixed height of 85 pixels

3. In the **Advanced** section of **Web Part Properties**, copy the contents of 2_dbselect.txt into the **Embedded Content** text box, replacing the string "SERVERNAME" with the name of the Web server.

4. Turn off (uncheck) **Allow users to remove this Web Part from the dashboard** and **Allow users to minimize this Web Part on the dashboard.**

5. Click **Save** to save the Web Part.

Create the CollSelect Web Part

This procedure adds the third Web Part, called **CollSelect**:

1. Under **Web Part List**, click **New**.

2. Enter the following information in the **General** section of **Web Part Properties**:

   Name: CollSelect

   Title: Select Collection

   Position on the Page: Left column

   Position within the Column: 3

   Fixed Size: fixed height of 85 pixels

3. In the **Advanced** section of **Web Part Properties**, copy the contents of 3_collselect.txt into the **Embedded Content** text box, replacing the string "SERVERNAME" with the name of the Web server.

4. Turn off (uncheck) **Allow users to remove this Web Part from the dashboard** and **Allow users to minimize this Web Part on the dashboard**.

5. Click **Save** to save the Web Part.

Create the MemberSelect Web Part

This procedure adds the fourth Web Part, called **MemberSelect**:

1. Under **Web Part List**, click **New**.

2. Enter the following information in the **General** section of **Web Part Properties**:

   Name: MemberSelect

   Title: Select Collection Member

   Position on the Page: Left column

   Position within the Column: 4

   Fixed Size: fixed height of 85 pixels

3. In the **Advanced** section of **Web Part Properties**, copy the contents of 4_memberselect.txt into the **Embedded Content** text box, replacing the string "SERVERNAME" with the name of the Web server.

4. Turn off (uncheck) **Allow users to remove this Web Part from the dashboard** and **Allow users to minimize this Web Part on the dashboard**.

5. Click **Save** to save the Web Part.

Create the MetaData Web Part

This procedure adds the fifth and final Web Part, called **MetaData**:

1. Under **Web Part List**, click **New**.

2. Enter the following information in the **General** section of **Web Part Properties**:

   Name: MetaData

   Title: Meta Data

   Position on the Page: Right column

   Position within the Column: 1

   Fixed Size: fixed height of 485 pixels

3. In the **Advanced** section of **Web Part Properties**, copy the contents of 5_metadata.txt into the **Embedded Content** text box, replacing the string "SERVERNAME" with the name of the Web server.

4. Turn off (uncheck) **Allow users to remove this Web Part from the dashboard** and **Allow users to minimize this Web Part on the dashboard**.

5. Click **Save** to save the Web Part.

Test the Dashboard

Open your new digital dashboard (the URL should look something like this: http://SERVERNAME /Dashboard/dashboard.asp?DashboardID=http://SERVERNAME/Sqlwbcat/AnalysisMetaData). All five ASP files should load in their separate Web Parts. If they do not, verify that you have replaced the string "SERVERNAME" with the name of your Web server in the embedded content of each of your Web Parts, and that the virtual directory AnalysisMetaData is set up and available.

Note There is an issue with the height and width properties of Web Parts that may affect your dashboard. For more information see "Sizing of Web Parts" in the "Known Issues" section below.

Using the Dashboard

Initially, only the first Web Part, titled "Connect to Server," is available when you first open the page. This is because you must log in before you can perform any other tasks. To log in to Analysis Services using the dashboard, enter the name of the Analysis server into that first Web Part. Your Web server will then log in and display connection status. If there is a problem with the analysis server or the name given, an error message will appear, giving you the opportunity to fix the problem and try again.

The remaining Web Parts become available as you progress down each Web Part. The database selection part becomes available after you log in. The collection part becomes available after you select a database, and the collection member part displays after you have chosen a collection. The meta data itself will appear only after you have made selections in all the other Web Parts.

Sample Files

Sample code has been provided to assist you in creating a digital dashboard to access your analysis server. Each ASP file is placed in a single Web Part to perform a specific function. The first connects to the analysis server, and the second retrieves the databases available on that server. The third displays the available collections (data sources, cubes, etc.) while the fourth retrieves the members of the selected collection. The fifth and final page displays the meta data itself, based on the information chosen in the previous four pages. All five parts are displayed in a single digital dashboard. The DDSC coordinates the five parts so a change in one part refreshes the other parts as required. This refresh ensures that each part (specifically, the ASP file within each part) is updated with the most recent information.

Text Files (Embedded Content)

Each text file contains HTML and VBScript code that displays the ASP file and sets up DDSC to refresh the page as individual parts change. The first portion of each file includes HTML that places an individual ASP file in an IFRAME. This is an example from the serverconnect.txt file:

```
<IFRAME ID="ConnectFrame_WPQ_"
SRC="http://SERVERNAME/AnalysisMetaData/serverconnect.asp" HEIGHT="100%" WIDTH="100%"
NAME="ConnectFrame"></IFRAME>
```

The **ID** attribute identifies the frame to the DDSC. The _WPQ_ (Web Part Qualifier) suffix on the ID allows for unique identification of the frame within the Web Part; _WPQ_ becomes a unique number for the part assigned by the DDSC. This is useful if there are multiple parts with identical object or variable names: **ConnectFrame_WPQ_** becomes **ConnectFrameWPQ1** in one part, and if it is repeated in another part, it could become **ConnectFrameWPQ2** for that part. This helps avoid confusion when there are many parts with many objects included in a single dashboard Web page.

The **HEIGHT** and **WIDTH** attributes tell the frame how much of the page or part to take up. In this example, they are both 100 percent; however in some of the other files the height is reduced to 85 percent. This, combined with the height property on the dashboard administration page, helps fit all of the Web Parts onto a single screen.

The second portion of each text file contains script that sets up a raise event for the DDSC:

```
<SCRIPT FOR="ConnectFrame_WPQ_" LANGUAGE="VBScript" EVENT="onreadystatechange">
    Dim strConnected
    strConnected =
document.frames("ConnectFrame_WPQ_").document.forms("frmConnect").item("txtConnected").v
alue
    If strConnected = "Yes" Then
        DDSC.RaiseEvent "urn:Change", "onUpdate"
    End If
</SCRIPT>
```

Any time the frame raises the **onreadystatechange** event (for instance, the user submits a form within the ASP file) the script raises another event using DDSC.RaiseEvent. In this case, it raises the event **onUpdate**. Any part registered for the **onUpdate** event would then trigger any code written for that event. All text files except metadata.txt contain this script (the MetaData part cannot be modified by the user, so it will never raise an event).

The third portion of the file contains script that registers for a DDSC event:

```vbscript
<SCRIPT language="VBScript">
    Sub RefreshPage_WPQ_ (ByVal param)
        location.reload(True)
    End Sub
    DDSC.RegisterForEvent "urn:Change", "onUpdate", GetRef ("RefreshPage_WPQ_")
</SCRIPT>
```

This sets the part up to "listen" for an event. When any part raises the onUpdate event, this part will run a subroutine defined within the script (for example, **RefreshPage_WPQ_**). For this dashboard, only the **ServerConnect** part registers. This is because the subroutine refreshes the entire page, including all parts. If separate effects were desired for individual parts, then each part could use DDSC.RegisterForEvent.

Note the use of the *ByVal param* parameter when declaring the **RefreshPage_WPQ_** function, and the use of **GetRef** in DDSC.RegisterForEvent when calling that function. Both of these are required in VBScript in order for RegisterForEvent to work (unlike JavaScript, which does not require this syntax).

ASP Files

Each of the five included ASP files has a specific function within the meta data browser application. Separate ASP files are used in this example to illustrate how each can be incorporated into individual Web parts and still work together. Each part assesses the state of other parts using ASP session variables and displays its own content as appropriate. For example, the Memberselect.asp file contains code that displays grayed-out text until a certain condition is met; that is, when the user selects a collection in the Select Collection part. When the user does this, Collselect.asp stores the collection type in an ASP session variable. Upon refresh, Memberselect.asp detects this variable and displays a list of collection members for the user to select.

Each ASP file is discussed below, and each is written using VBScript. The code, with full comments, can be viewed by opening the files in any text editor. For information about the DSO object model used in these ASP files, see "Decision Support Objects" in SQL Server Books Online.

Serverconnect.asp

This file contains code that logs into the analysis server. A form with a single text box and button is displayed, allowing the user to enter an analysis server name. If the name is blank, or an error occurs when trying to connect, the user is alerted and the form is displayed again. At this point, a value of "No" is stored in the ASP session variable **strConnected**. As long as this value is "No," Serverconnect.asp will continue to display the server form.

Only when a successful connection is made will the server name be stored in an ASP session variable named **dsoServer**. At this time, a value of "Yes" is stored in ASP session variable **strConnected**, and three new variables (**strSelectDB**, **strSelectColl**, and **strSelectMbr**) are initialized for use by other parts.

Because "Yes" is now stored in **strConnected**, serverconnect.asp displays a connection status message instead of the server connect form. This message will continue to display as long as the session is active.

Dbselect.asp

The code on this page is designed to display a read-only page with a gray Database message until it detects a value of "Yes" in the ASP session variable **strConnected**, as set by the Serverconnect.asp file. When it does detect a connection has been made through this variable, dbselect.asp uses the connection stored in the ASP session variable **dsoServer** to retrieve a list of available databases. This list is then displayed in a combo box within a form.

When the user selects a database from this combo box, Dbselect.asp stores the name of the database in the ASP session variable **strSelectDB**. Since the user can select a database at any time, even after other selections have been made, the ASP session variable resets the value in **strSelectMbr** to prevent Metadata.asp from erroneously retrieving data from a member not belonging to the selected database. (It essentially resets the **Select Member** and **Meta Data** parts so the user has to select the member again after changing the database.)

Collselect.asp

This ASP file, like Dbselect.asp, displays a read-only page with a gray View message until it detects a value from an ASP session variable, this time from **strSelectDB** (as stored by dbselect.asp). Unlike the others, however, it does not retrieve or store information about the analysis server or any of its objects once this variable is detected. It simply displays a fixed list of collection types in a combo box: **Data Source, Cube, Shared Dimension, Mining Model** and **Database Role**. When the user chooses a collection type, Collselect.asp stores the selected collection type in another session variable, **strSelectColl**.

Memberselect.asp

This ASP file also displays a read-only page with a gray View message until it detects a value in the ASP session variable **strSelectColl**. When it detects a value, Memberselect.asp retrieves a list of collection members based on the values selected in previous parts, and displays these members in another combo box. When the user selects a member, this member name (for example, Sales from the Cubes collection) is stored in the ASP session variable **strSelectMbr**.

Metadata.asp

The Metadata.asp file is where all the previously selected information comes together. This code displays a gray no data message until a value from the final part, Memberselect.asp, is stored in the **strSelectMbr** ASP session variable. When it detects this variable, it displays the meta data for the selected member. It uses all the variables stored by Serverconnect.asp, Dbselect.asp, Collselect.asp, and Memberselect.asp to retrieve the appropriate information about the selections.

For example, the user may have entered *DDTest* as the server, *FoodMart 2000* as the database, *Cube* as the collection, and *Sales* as the collection member. Using all this information, Metadata.asp displays meta data for the Sales cube in the **FoodMart 2000** database of the DDTest server.

To display this information, Metadata.asp code uses the various DSO object properties to create a string. The composition of this string is based on the selected collection type, since the available meta data can differ between collection types. For example, the **EstimatedSize** property can apply to cubes, but not data sources, so the string built for data sources cannot include this property. There are a few properties that are only valid if another property contains the appropriate value; for instance, a cube's **LastProcessed** property is not available if the cube's **State** property is 0 (never processed). If you attempt to access **LastProcessed** for a cube that has not been processed, an error will be generated. It is important to understand the DSO object model in order to avoid these situations.

Another factor to be aware of is that VBScript does not support the use of enumerations and constants available from the DSO object model. This means that the integer values stored in some properties must be translated within the code itself. For example, the **SubClassType** property is used often throughout Metadata.asp. In a language like Visual Basic, you could use the constants like **sbclsRegular** and **sbclsVirtual** to help read the DSO properties. However, since VBScript does not support these constants, you must use the integer values directly (for example, 0 for **sbclsRegular** and 1 for **sbclsVirtual**).

Known Issues

Unable to Connect to the Registry

IIS may have difficulty accessing the Analysis Server if IIS is controlling the anonymous login password. In this case, the following error may occur:

DSO (0x80040031)
Unable to connect to the registry on the server (SERVERNAME), or you are not a member of the OLAP Administrators group on this server.

This error occurs because the Internet Guest Account used by IIS cannot access the Analysis Server hidden share or registry settings. The most likely cause is lack of permissions or logon failure by IIS.

To avoid the error, ensure that the Internet Guest Account (a logon typically beginning with "IUSR_") on the IIS server is a member of the **OLAP Administrators** group. Turn off the **Password Synchronization** or **Allow IIS to Control Password** option for the account used for anonymous access. For more information on this issue, see KnowledgeBase article Q216828: "Password Synchronization/Allow IIS to Control Password May Cause Problems" at http://search.support.microsoft.com/kb/.

Sizing of Web Parts

There is an issue in version 2.01 of the DDRK where the value of the height property of the Web Part may be saved erroneously to the width property. This results in an incorrectly sized Web Part. If this occurs, open the Web Part in the dashboard Administration page, reset the width property to **No,** and enter the correct size again into the height property. Save the Web Part, then reload the dashboard page to view the change to your Web Part.

Replication

Common Questions in Replication

This chapter provides answers to some common questions that may arise when you plan for Microsoft® SQL Server™ 2000 replication. These questions are by no means all of the issues that need be considered when planning or implementing replication. For more information about replication, see SQL Server Books Online.

Types of Replication and Replication Options

- What Type of Replication Should I Use?
- What Is the Difference Between Merge Replication and Updatable Subscriptions?
- Should I Use SQL Server Queues or Microsoft Message Queuing Services When Using Transactional Replication and Queued Updating?

Implementing Replication

- What Is the Difference Between a Local Distributor and a Remote Distributor?
- What Type of Subscription Should I Use: Push or Pull?
- If I Am Using Pull Subscriptions, When Should I Specify Them as Anonymous?
- What Are the Advantages of Scripting Replication?
- Should I Apply the Snapshot Manually or Apply It Automatically?
- Can I Replicate Data Between SQL Server and Heterogeneous Databases?
- If I Am Using SQL Server 6.5 or SQL Server 7.0 Subscribers, Can I Use the New Features in SQL Server 2000?
- Can Microsoft SQL Server Desktop Edition Participate in Replication?
- When Upgrading to SQL Server 2000, Do I Need to Upgrade All Servers in Replication at the Same Time?

Replication and Warm Standby Server Recovery Options

- Should I Use Replication, Log Shipping, or Clustering as a Failover Solution?
- Does Replication Work on a Cluster?

Types of Replication and Replication Options

When designing a replication topology, it is critical that you understand the types of replication and the options available. This will enable you to design a replication topology that will be appropriate for your business needs and environment.

What Type of Replication Should I Use?

The types of replication are transactional replication and merge replication. With any type, you need to determine if data modifications are going to occur and at which sites they are going to occur.

Use transactional replication when:

- Most changes for a given data set are made at one site (for example, the Publisher). With transactional replication, there is an owner with any given data, where most of the data modifications are made. With transactional replication options, data can be modified at other locations, but there is always one, primary owner of the data.

- You want data modifications made at the Publisher to be propagated to Subscribers, often within seconds of when they occur.

- Transactions meet the requirements of full ACID properties.

- Your application will not tolerate high latency for Subscribers receiving changes.

- When it makes more sense, or it is more practical, to replicate the whole data set, rather than incremental changes (for example, a lot of changes at one time); consider using snapshot replication. Snapshot replication is best used when: a small, whole set of data needs to be replicated; a large set of data where most of the data has been changed needs to be replicated; and when data is very static.

Use merge replication when:

- Data modifications need to be made at multiple Subscribers at various times.

- Subscribers need to receive data, make changes offline, and synchronize changes later with the Publisher and other Subscribers.

- Site autonomy is important.

- You expect data modifications to occur at multiple sites and, therefore, conflicts to occur. Default and custom choices for conflict resolution are available with merge replication.

- You want to use join filters to maintain referential integrity between two tables. Join filters allow cross-table relationships to be used in merge replication filters when the filter of one table is based on another table in the publication.

- You want to use dynamic filters that allow you to filter data from the publishing table that is providing different partitions of data to different Subscribers. Using dynamic filters allows for fewer publications to be stored at the Publisher. In addition, using dynamic filters enables you to filter criteria by using system or user-defined functions. The Subscriber receives only the information needed because the data is filtered based on the connection properties of the Merge Agent for the subscription.

What Is the Difference Between Merge Replication and Updatable Subscriptions?

With merge replication...	With snapshot replication and transactional replication with queued updating...
The replicated data is read and updated at either the Publisher or Subscriber.	The replicated data is mostly read-only at the Subscriber.
The Subscriber and Publisher may only be connected occasionally.	The Subscriber, Distributor, and Publisher may be connected most of the time or may only be connected occasionally, when data needs to be dequeued.
Conflicts caused by multiple updates to the same data are automatically handled and resolved.	Conflicts caused by multiple updates to the same data are infrequent but are resolved according to predetermined conflict resolution.
You need updates to be propagated on a row-by-row basis, and conflicts to be evaluated and resolved at the row level or according to a set of business rules, or with default or customized conflict resolution applications.	You need updates to be propagated on a transaction basis, and conflicts to be evaluated and resolved on a transaction basis (the entire transaction is either committed or rolled back).

Should I Use SQL Server Queues or Microsoft Message Queuing Services When Using Transactional Replication and Queued Updating?

Use SQL Server 2000 queues when:

- You need to work with SQL Server on various Microsoft Windows® platforms (Windows 98, Windows NT 4.0, and Windows 2000).

- No additional components need to be installed.

Use Microsoft Message Queuing when:

- You are already working with Microsoft Message Queuing.

- You are working only with the Windows 2000 operating system.

- You intend to have a large number of queued updating subscriptions. Using Microsoft Message Queuing is more scalable than SQL Server queues.

- You need additional routing and centralized monitoring and centralized queue administration (beyond what is available with SQL Server queues).

- You need offline capabilities, such as propagating offline changes to the queue at the Distributor without SQL Server running on the Subscriber (but Microsoft Message Queuing must be running).

- You do not require availability of the Publisher when the Subscriber reconnects to the network after updating published data.

Implementing Replication

Implementing replication includes configuring publishing and distribution, creating publications and subscriptions, and applying the initial snapshot of data at the Subscriber.

What Is the Difference Between a Local Distributor and a Remote Distributor?

A local Distributor is a computer that is configured to be both a Publisher and a Distributor of replication. A remote Distributor is a computer that is physically separate from the Publisher and is configured as a Distributor of replication.

Use a local Distributor when:

- The computer running the Publisher has the capacity to also absorb the workload of the Distributor residing on the same computer.

- Typically, merge replication topologies use a local Distributor because the distribution database has a limited role and does not grow large. With merge replication, the Distributor stores history information but it does not store transactions that are propagated during replication. For transactional replication, the transactions are stored temporarily in the distribution database, which requires more processing overhead on the server where the distribution database resides.

Use a remote Distributor when:

- You want to offload processing to another computer because of a decrease in performance, either due to an increase in the replication activity or due to constraints on the server or network resources.

- Remote Distributors are used more often in transactional replication because of the processing and storage requirements of the distribution database. In transactional replication, the distribution database temporarily stores transactions that are being propagated to other servers.

What Type of Subscription Should I Use: Push or Pull?

Use push subscriptions when:

- You want easier administration from a centralized location (the Distributor).

- When Subscribers are always or almost always connected on the network.

- Data needs to be updated at the Subscribers whenever any changes are made at the Publisher.

Use pull subscriptions when:

- Administration of the subscription will take place at the Subscriber.

- The publication has a large number of Subscribers (for example, Subscribers using the Internet), and when it would be too resource-intensive to run all the agents at one site or all at the Distributor. You can also use push subscriptions with remote agent activation to offload processing from the Distributor to the Subscriber.

- Subscribers are autonomous, disconnected, and/or mobile. Subscribers will determine when they will connect to the Publisher/Distributor and synchronize changes.

If I am Using Pull Subscriptions, When Should I Specify Them as Anonymous?

Specify a pull subscription as anonymous when:

- Applications have a large number of Subscribers.

- You do not want the overhead of maintaining extra information at the Publisher or Distributor.

- Subscribers use the Internet to access data and you do not want to track information about these Subscribers. The necessary privileges and security are still in place and Subscribers are using anonymous subscriptions to have the appropriate permissions.

If you specify that anonymous subscriptions be allowed, SQL Server will generate new snapshots on a regular basis, which can be kept available for new Subscribers. This may be a consideration if generating the snapshot is resource intensive.

What are the Advantages of Scripting Replication?

You can script commonly performed replication functions, such as configuring publishing and distribution, and creating or deleting publications and subscriptions. After you configure or create a replication component, you can automate the creation of a script by using SQL Server Enterprise Manager.

The script contains the Transact-SQL system stored procedures necessary to implement the replication component. Composed primarily of a series of stored procedures, you can view, execute, and/or modify and run the script using SQL Query Analyzer or the **osql** utility.

You can choose to script the creation or deletion of one or a combination of the following:

- Distributor properties
- Publications and push subscriptions
- Pull subscriptions

If you need to delete multiple push subscriptions or a mix of push and pull subscriptions, you can automate the process by creating a script to delete the publication. All subscriptions to the publication will be deleted with the publication. If you are deleting pull subscriptions, you can generate a script that deletes one or more pull subscriptions without deleting the publication.

The number of Subscribers and the number of subscriptions needed at each Subscriber determine whether to script replication or implement replication using SQL Server Enterprise Manager.

Additionally, scripting can aid in recovery from a failure, and it can be used to clone the replication environment.

Should I Apply the Snapshot Manually or Apply It Automatically?

Applying the snapshot automatically saves time because SQL Server propagates the necessary data and schema files to the Subscriber. Apply the snapshot automatically if:

- You have a reliable and fast network connection.
- The publication and the articles within it are of reasonable size.
- You want the convenience of SQL Server automatically applying the snapshot.

Applying the snapshot manually involves saving the snapshot to removable media or to an accessible network location and transferring it to Subscribers. Apply the snapshot manually if:

- The publication is large. It may be more efficient to load the snapshot manually from a compact disc, or other storage device.

- You are transferring a large amount of data over the network, or if you have a slow link.

- The data already exists at the Subscriber.

When you apply the snapshot manually for transactional publications, custom stored procedures for each article must be created at the Subscriber.

Another way to apply the snapshot manually at Subscribers is to use attachable subscription databases. The attachable subscription databases feature allows you to transfer a database with published data and subscriptions from one Subscriber to another. After the database is attached to the new Subscriber, the database at the new Subscriber will automatically receive its own pull subscriptions to the publications at those Publishers.

For additional considerations when applying the snapshot manually, see "Applying the Initial Snapshot" and "Using Custom Stored Procedures in Articles" in SQL Server Books Online.

Can I Replicate Data Between SQL Server and Heterogeneous Databases?

Methods for implementing snapshot replication or transactional replication published by heterogeneous data sources to your SQL Server 2000 applications are:

- Building applications with SQL-DMO and the Replication Distributor Interface

- Using third-party tools

Microsoft SQL Server 2000 provides a programming framework that enables heterogeneous data sources to become Publishers of snapshot and transactional publications within the SQL Server 2000 replication framework. You can use the Replication Distributor Interface with programmable SQL-DMO objects and third-party tools to publish data incrementally from heterogeneous Publishers.

Several vendors, including BMC and DataMirror, have developed products that support the replication distribution interface included with SQL Server 2000. Using these third-party tools, it is possible to propagate data directly from Oracle or DB2 into a SQL Server distribution database. The Replication Distributor Interface is a public interface that allows the development of custom applications that write transactions and commands to a SQL Server distribution database from virtually any other data source, and then take advantage of SQL Server replication distribution services including the replication monitor in SQL Server Enterprise Manager.

To view a programming sample using the Replication Distributor Interface, see "Programming Snapshot or Transactional Replication from Heterogeneous Data Sources" in SQL Server Books Online.

There is no method within SQL Server 2000 for heterogeneous data sources to publish merge replication data to SQL Server; however, you can use third-party solutions for this type of replication.

If I Am Using SQL Server 6.5 or SQL Server 7.0 Subscribers, Can I Use the New Features in SQL Server 2000?

Features available in SQL Server 2000 are not supported with Subscribers running SQL Server version 7.0 or earlier; however, backward compatibility is assured when you replicate with earlier versions of SQL Server.

For example, if a merge publication contains features valid only in SQL Server 2000, and you use a push subscription to a Subscriber running SQL Server 7.0, backward compatibility is checked, and the Merge Agent will fail and display an error message indicating that the Subscriber does not meet the compatibility level.

If a transactional publication contains features valid only in SQL Server 2000, and you use a push subscription to a Subscriber running SQL Server 7.0, backward compatibility is not checked, and the Distribution Agent may fail with an error message not related to backward compatibility, or the Distribution Agent may succeed, but transactional processing will fail at another point.

If you upgrade a Distributor to an instance of SQL Server 2000, but you have a Publisher running an instance of SQL Server version 7.0, and a Subscriber running an instance of SQL Server version 6.5, you are limited to the replication functionality of SQL Server 6.5 and unable to use features introduced in SQL Server 7.0 or SQL Server 2000. To use the new functionality, upgrade all servers used for replication to SQL Server 2000.

If a publication has active subscriptions to Subscribers running SQL Server version 7.0 or earlier, and you add a feature to the publication that is valid only for SQL Server 2000, the Merge Agents or Distribution Agents for the SQL Server 7.0 subscriptions will fail. Even if the SQL Server 2000 feature is installed, the agents will not run successfully. You must delete the subscription and re-create the publication and subscription.

Can Microsoft SQL Server Desktop Engine Participate in Replication?

Yes, Microsoft SQL Server Desktop Engine can participate in replication. A Desktop Engine installation can be a Subscriber to any type of publication: snapshot , transactional, or merge. An instance of the Desktop Engine can also be a Publisher for snapshot replication or merge replication, but not for transactional replication. A Desktop Engine installation that is a Publisher must use a local Distributor (the Publisher must also be the Distributor and host the distribution database for any publications it creates).

When Upgrading to SQL Server 2000, Do I Need to Upgrade All Servers in Replication at the Same Time?

When upgrading to SQL Server 2000, you can upgrade servers in your organization one at a time; however, when servers are used for replication, you must upgrade the Distributor first, the Publisher second, and then Subscribers. Upgrading servers one at a time following this sequence is recommended when a large number of Publishers and Subscribers exist because you can continue to replicate data even though servers are running different versions of SQL Server. You can create new publications and subscriptions with servers running instances of SQL Server 2000, and still maintain subscriptions created in SQL Server 6.5 or SQL Server 7.0.

When using transactional replication, you can upgrade Subscribers before the Publisher. If you are using immediate updating with snapshot replication or transactional replication, there are additional upgrade recommendations in "Upgrading and Immediate Updating" in this chapter.

You can upgrade replication servers running SQL Server 6.5 or SQL Server 7.0 to SQL Server 2000. If the server is running SQL Server 6.5, you do not need to upgrade it to SQL Server 7.0 before upgrading to SQL Server 2000.

For more information, see "Replication and Upgrading" in SQL Server Books Online.

Replication and Warm Standby Server Recovery Options

Although replication is not an out-of-the-box solution as a warm standby server, it can play a role in the need for a warm standby server. If you want to make replication part of a disaster recovery solution, account for the following:

- Retarget applications to the subscription database in the event of a Publisher failure.

- Remember that only data is replicated. Actions such as schema changes (beyond add/drop column) and security changes are not replicated.

- Have a solution to failback from the Subscriber to the Publisher when the Publisher comes back online.

SQL Server 2000 transactional replication can be configured to work with log shipping as a warm standby server recovery option if the Publisher fails.

SQL Server 2000 merge replication can be configured to work with log shipping to provide a warm standby server recovery option if the Publisher fails. Merge replication also allows Subscribers to synchronize with an alternate Publisher in the event the Publisher at which their subscriptions originated is unavailable.

For more information about using transactional replication or merge replication with log shipping, see SQL Server Books Online.

Should I Use Replication, Log Shipping, or Clustering as a Failover Solution?

- Use SQL Server clustering when you want a hot, standby, failover support. Clustering offers automatic detection of server failure and automatic failover between nodes participating in the cluster. Client application connections can automatically be redirected to the current active server instance and application data requests will be serviced with little or no interruption.

- Use log shipping when you want a warm standby solution. Log shipping transfers database dumps and logs from the primary server to the secondary server. As with any warm standby solution, failure detection and failover processing is not automated. When log shipping is employed, the standby database cannot be used for data access. The standby database is unavailable throughout the continual process of loading database and transaction log dumps from the primary server. Because log shipping transfers complete database logs, all logged schema and data changes are transferred from the primary to secondary node. When log shipping is employed, it is not possible to partition the data or transfer only a subset of the objects from the database.

- Use replication when you want a warm standby solution, and when simultaneous data access on the secondary node (scale out for read) or object or data partitioning is a requirement.

Clustering is a shared disk, hardware solution protecting against computer failure. The cluster computers are usually in close proximity to one another. Log shipping and replication provide geographically disparate copies of the database. A combination of these solutions can be used to provide protection against different types of failure.

Does Replication Work on a Cluster?

Yes, all types of SQL Server replication work on a cluster server running Microsoft SQL Server 2000 Enterprise Edition. For information about setting up clusters, see "Failover Clustering" in SQL Server Books Online. For more information about configuring replication, see SQL Server Books Online.

Creating Merge Replication Custom Conflict Resolvers Using Visual Basic

Microsoft® SQL Server™ 2000 includes several merge replication conflict resolution options, such as a merge text conflict resolver, an averaging conflict resolver, several DATETIME conflict resolvers, and other commonly used conflict resolvers. In the majority of merge replication conflicts, one of these built-in solutions will resolve the conflicts that may occur as part of merge replication. However, when a unique business need requires customized logic to determine the final merged data at Publisher and Subscriber sites, you can write an application that resolves the conflict according to specified business rules.

When writing custom conflict resolver applications, you will need to:

- Define the conditions you want to handle with the application logic.

- Determine the type of change condition that is currently being handled.

- Initialize the source and destination information.

- Gather column information as to which column has changed if any special resolver tracker has been implemented, such as column tracking.

- Determine what phase the merge process is in: upload or download.

- Determine what data should be the winning data in a change.

- Propagate the data to the matching table on the other server and overwrite the losing data.

To help you accomplish these steps, this chapter includes sections on using the Microsoft SQL Replication Conflict Resolver Library, learning to register a custom conflict resolver, and examining some merge replication custom conflict resolver samples.

The merge replication conflict resolvers discussed in this chapter are written in Microsoft Visual Basic®. An intermediate-level understanding of Visual Basic, as well as a beginning understanding of Component Object Model (COM) and Interface Definition Language (IDL), is assumed.

Using the Microsoft SQL Replication Conflict Resolver Library

To write a merge replication custom conflict resolver, use the Microsoft SQL Replication Conflict Resolver Library. It is a DLL file that is installed as part of SQL Server 2000. This library of methods enables your application to respond as changes are applied during synchronization.

The Microsoft SQL Replication Conflict Resolver Library contains methods available to retrieve data and commit data between servers. To use the library in your merge replication custom conflict resolver applications, you need to:

- Include the Microsoft SQL Replication Conflict Resolver Library in a Visual Basic application.

- Implement the IVBCustomResolver interface.

- Understand the methods in the IReplRowChange interface.

- Understand the methods in the IConnectionInfo interface.

- Understand the enumerated constants in the library.

The Microsoft SQL Replication Conflict Resolver Library file is **replrec.dll**. It provides methods to return information from SQL Server to the application, including information about changes, details on how the rows are affected, details on which columns differ, and connection information about the Publisher and Subscriber.

It also contains methods that perform actions, such as evaluating a change to a table, determining winning data and placing it into a table, or removing data from a table.

The following diagram shows a COM representation of the Microsoft SQL Replication Conflict Resolver Library object and its three interfaces: IVBCustomResolver, IReplRowChange, and IConnectionInfo.

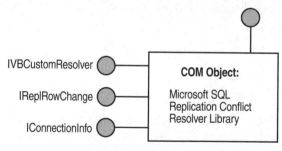

Adding the Microsoft SQL Replication Conflict Resolver Library to Visual Basic

To include the Microsoft SQL Replication Conflict Resolver Library in a Visual Basic application, your application must be a project of type ActiveX® DLL, and you must add the SQL Merge Conflict Resolver component to your project.

If you install SQL Server 2000 to the default location, the SQL Merge Conflict Resolver component will be in C:\Program Files\Microsoft SQL Server\80\COM\. To add the component to your project, click the **Project | References** menu. In the **References** dialog box, click **Microsoft SQL Replication Conflict Resolver Library**.

Component	Reference	Library
SQL Merge Conflict Resolver	Microsoft SQL Replication Conflict Resolver Library	Replrec.dll

To get detailed information about the component once it has been added to the project in Visual Basic, inspect its type library in the Object Browser. In the **Library** menu, select the **SQLResolver** library. In the **Classes** pane, the SQL Resolver shows the three interfaces, **IVBCustomResolver, IConnectionInfo**, and **IReplRowChange**, as well as several predefined constants.

IVBCustomResolver Interface

The **IVBCustomResolver** interface, used in a new class module by using the **Implements** keyword, contains two methods that must be coded by the developer in the application: the **GetHandledStates** method and the **Reconcile** method.

GetHandledStates Method

Method Syntax

```
GetHandledStates(ResolverBm As Long)
```

This method enables you to list the conditions that the resolver will handle. The REPOLE_CHANGE_TYPE enumerations listed become a logical **OR** of the change types the resolver supports. The **GetHandledStates** method is invoked once when the table is loaded by the merge process. Then, for every change that needs to be propagated, the custom resolver is invoked if the change is a state that is handled by the resolver.

Although this process is commonly referred to as a conflict resolver, the changes that can be handled include non-conflict changes, such as new rows inserted at the Subscriber. All the available conflict and non-conflict changes that can be handled are listed in the REPOLE_CHANGE_TYPE enumeration. For a complete list of change types available, see the Constants topic in this chapter.

Reconcile Method

Method Syntax

```
Sub Reconcile(pRowChange As IReplRowChange, dwFlags As Long, pvReserved As
IReplRowChange)
```

Use the **Reconcile** method to define the business logic that determines what data is applied to the losing table.

The important parameter for the **Reconcile** method is a reference to an **IReplRowChange** object, shown as the variable **pRowChange** in the method syntax. **IReplRowChange** is defined in an include file, **sqlres.h**. Through the supporting methods available in **IReplRowChange**, you can determine the columns in conflict, examine the conflicting data, and update the appropriate table with the winning data based on the criteria established in your **Reconcile** method code.

For best results when using the **Reconcile** method, it is important to understand the different stages of the merge process. The first stage that occurs is the upload of changes from the Subscriber to the Publisher. The second stage is a download of changes from the Publisher to the Subscriber. During the upload, the Subscriber is considered as the source of the change, and the Publisher is the destination. During the download, the Publisher is considered the source and the Subscriber is the destination. This means the variables that designate source and destination change depending on the stage of the merge process.

When a custom resolver is a Visual Basic application, conflicts are resolved immediately after the application executes the appropriate resolution action. If the user wishes to review the changes before implementation, and then either accept the resolution or resubmit the changes, it is possible to do so. The option is available to write the losing row to a conflict table named **conflict_<PublicationName>_<ArticleName>_usertablename**, and to apply the winning row to the appropriate table. The custom resolver logs a special message to the conflict table that provides context information, which the user can evaluate before making a final decision about accepting the changes.

During coding in the Reconcile method, you will usually use some of the enumerations that are available as constants defined in the SQL Merge Conflict Resolver library component. It is recommended you use symbols for these enumerations whenever possible, instead of using hard-coded constants.

IReplRowChange and IConnectionInfo Interfaces

The **IReplRowChange** and **IConnectionInfo** interfaces provide methods that can be called during use of your merge replication custom conflict resolver application. The methods provide three functions:

- Getting table, column, and connection information for the Publisher and Subscriber.
- Getting conflict information.
- Performing resolution actions.

Here you will find a description of what each method does, as well as the Visual Basic signature and the IDL semantics for each method. The IDL semantics are provided as a quick reference for parameter direction.

IReplRowChange Interface and Methods

The IReplRowChange interface contains methods that deliver core replication functionality, such as the ability to query column values and to copy rows from source database to destination database. The methods available in this interface are called from the custom resolver application to return data used in decision-making logic, or to gather information about the database and tables and about the column in conflict.

Many of the methods use a **ColumnID** parameter. The **ColumnID** contains a number that represents the position of the column in the table, ranging from 1 to <number of columns>. This number is used as a parameter to methods instead of the column name.

If the table is vertically partitioned, a column position in the table at the Subscriber does not necessarily match what the column position value would be in the publishing table at the Publisher. For example, if a table contains five columns, but column 3 is not published, ColumnID=4 corresponds to the last column of the table. The following sections give the Visual Basic and IDL signatures of the methods.

Summary of Methods in IReplRowChange

Method	Description
CopyColumnFromSource	Sets the destination column to contain the same value as the respective source column.
CopyRowFromSource	Sets the destination row to contain the same data as is contained in the source row.
DeleteRow	Deletes the destination row.
DoDummyUpdate	Updates source or destination row meta data . This allows a subsequent merge process to pick up a change as a new change.

continued on next page

Method	Description
ForceRememberChange	Called before invoking **IReplRowChange** operations that alter the destination row.
GetChangeType	Returns information regarding the type of change that occurred.
GetColumnAttributes	Returns a bitmap indicating if column is an identity column and/or updatable.
GetColumnDatatype	Returns the column type.
GetColumnName	Returns the column name.
GetColumnStatus	Returns the column status.
GetDestinationColumnValue	Returns the value of the column from the destination table.
GetDestinationConnectionInfo	Returns connection information about the destination.
GetDestinationOwnerName	Returns the owner name of the destination table.
GetErrorInfo	Returns a detailed error code and description if the resolver has been invoked to handle an error situation.
GetExtendedError	Returns additional information about the error, such as whether the error was a duplicate key or a unique index violation.
GetNumColumns	Returns the number of columns in the base table.
GetPriorityWinner	Returns a value indicating which one has the higher priority, the source or the destination.
GetResolverProcedureName	Returns the resolver-specific information (for example, a column name).
GetRowGuidColName	Returns the name of the column in the base table that is the **uniqueidentifier** column used in merge replication.
GetRowIdentifier	Returns the **uniqueidentifier** for the row in conflict.
GetSourceColumnValue	Returns the value of the column from the source table.
GetSourceConnectionInfo	Returns connection information about the source.
GetTableName	Returns the name of the table in conflict.
GetTableOwnerName	Returns the owner name of the table.
InsertRow	Inserts the row at the destination.
LogConflict	Indicates whether the conflict should be logged, where, and what message to include.
LogError	Logs the error and an optional description.
UpdateRow	Updates the destination row.

Methods in the IReplRowChange Interface

CopyColumnFromSource(
ColumnId As Long)

Invoke this method if the corresponding destination column should be set to the same value contained in the source column referenced by the input parameter **ColumnID**.

IDL Semantics

```
HRESULT CopyColumnFromSource (INTEGERTYPE ColumnId)
```

CopyRowFromSource()

Invoke this method if the source is the conflict winner. The row at the destination will then be set to the same values as the source row.

IDL Semantics

```
HRESULT CopyRowFromSource ()
```

DeleteRow()

Invoke this method to delete the row at the destination. This method does not automatically delete the row at the source. It is used if a delete at the source conflicts with an update at the destination, and the delete is the winner.

IDL Semantics

```
HRESULT DeleteRow ()
```

DoDummyUpdate(
fUpLineage As REPOLE_BOOL,
fAtPublisher As REPOLE_BOOL)

Updates the row meta data at either the source or the destination. Invoke this method at one of the two nodes to make sure the resulting row is propagated back to the originating node. The parameter **fAtPublisher** is used to determine whether the meta data to be updated is at the Publisher or the Subscriber. Set to TRUE to update at the Publisher. Set to FALSE to update at the Subscriber.

Consider, for example, the scenario of a merge replication conflict in which the destination is the conflict winner. Calling **DoDummyUpdate** on the destination (having **fAtPublisher**=TRUE in the upload phase, FALSE otherwise) ensures the losing source row gets the values of the winning destination row as soon as it becomes the destination itself. Thus, if the Subscriber loses during upload, the **DoDummyUpdate** method guarantees the Publisher's row will be downloaded to the Subscriber during the next phase.

Calling the method on the source can be used in error situations, when a resend should be forced. You might need to resend, for example, when you are using a Subscriber-always-wins resolver, but the upload of the Subscriber change has failed because the Publisher inserted a row with the same primary key. The download of the inserted row from the Publisher will fail due to the same reason, leading to the deletion of the inserted row at the Publisher. Therefore, the subsequent upload of the row that originated at the Subscriber will succeed when resending is forced.

Set **fUpLineage** to TRUE to keep version information about the changed row. If you are unsure what value to use for the parameter, use TRUE.

IDL Semantics

```
HRESULT DoDummyUpdate (
                    [in] BOOLTYPE fUpLineage,
                    [in] BOOLTYPE fAtPublisher)
```

ForceRememberChange()

Call this method before invoking **IReplRowChange** operations that alter the destination row, such as CopyRowFromSource(), CopyColumnFromSource(), or DeleteRow(), if the conflict resolver allows an update/insert/delete at a Subscriber to win over an update/insert/delete at either the Publisher or another Subscriber which has since then already merged with the Publisher.

IDL Semantics

```
HRESULT ForceRememberChange()
```

GetChangeType(
pChangeType As REPOLE_CHANGE_TYPE)

Returns what type of change occurred. The value returned is one of the enumerated constants from REPOLE_CHANGE_TYPE.

IDL Semantics

```
HRESULT _stdcall GetChangeType([out] REPOLE_CHANGE_TYPE* pChangeType)
```

GetColumnAttributes(
ColumnId As Long,

PlColumnAttributes As REPOLE_COLUMN_ATTRIBUTES)

Returns a bitmap of the enumerated constants from REPOLE_COLUMN_ATTRIBUTES into **plColumnAttributes**, for the column being referenced by the input parameter **ColumnID**. The bitmap indicates whether the referenced column is an identity column and/or an updatable column. It can be both. Check the results with *plColumnAttributes & REPOLEColumnAttribute_Updatable, or *plColumnAttributes & REPOLEColumnAttribute_Identity, respectively.

IDL Semantics

```
HRESULT _stdcall GetColumnAttributes(
             long ColumnId,
             [out] REPOLE_COLUMN_ATTRIBUTES* plColumnAttributes)
```

GetColumnDatatype(
ColumnId As Long,
plDataType As REPOLE_SQL_DATATYPE)

Returns a value in **plDataType** that indicates what type of column is being referenced by the input **ColumnID** parameter. The type of column returned is one of the enumerated constants from REPOLE_SQL_DATATYPE.

IDL Semantics

```
HRESULT _stdcall GetColumnDatatype(
             long ColumnId,
             [out] REPOLE_SQL_DATATYPE* plDataType)
```

GetColumnName(
ColumnId As Long,
pColumnName As String,
cbColumnName As Long)

Returns the name of the column being referenced by the input parameter **ColumnID,** into **pColumnName**. The input parameter **cbColumnName** gives a buffer size for **pColumnName**. HRESULT returns an error if the buffer is too small.

IDL Semantics

```
HRESULT _stdcall GetColumnName(
             long ColumnId,
             [out] LPWSTR pColumnName,
             long cbColumnName)
```

GetColumnStatus(
ColumnId As Long,
pColStatus As REPOLE_COLSTATUS_TYPE)

Returns a value into **pColStatus** that indicates the status of the column being referenced by the input **ColumnID** parameter. The status of the column returned is one of the enumerated constants from REPOLE_COLSTATUS_TYPE.

IDL Semantics

```
HRESULT _stdcall GetColumnStatus(
             long ColumnId,
             [out] REPOLE_COLSTATUS_TYPE* pColStatus)
```

GetDestinationColumnValue(
ColumnId As Long,
pvBuffer,
cbBufferMax As Long,
pcbBufferActual As Long)

Returns the value of the column, referenced by the **ColumnID** parameter, into **pvBuffer**. The column value returned is the value of the column at the destination table. The output parameter **pcbBufferActual** returns the number of bytes that the column value uses. The input parameter **cbBufferMax** indicates the size of **pvBuffer**. HRESULT returns an error if the buffer is too small.

IDL Semantics

```
HRESULT _stdcall GetDestinationColumnValue(
                    long ColumnId,
                    [out] VARIANT* pvBuffer,
                    [in] long cbBufferMax,
                    [out] long* pcbBufferActual)
```

GetDestinationConnectionInfo(
ppDestinationConnectionInfo As IConnectionInfo,
pfIsPublisher As REPOLE_BOOL)

Returns a pointer to the object that contains all the connection information about the destination in the **ppDestinationConnectionInfo** parameter. This variable can then be used to make all the calls in the **IConnectionInfo** object. For example, this is the line of code that initializes the **IConnectionInfo** variable from the AdditiveResolver sample:

```
Call rrc.GetDestinationConnectionInfo(DestConnectionInfo, DestIsPublisher)
```

Once initialized, the **DestConnectionInfo** variable can be used as the qualifier to all the methods available in the **IConnectionInfo** object, by using:

```
Call DestConnectionInfo.GetServerName(stSubscriber, Len(stSubscriber))
```

The **GetDestinationConnectionInfo** method also returns a Boolean, into **pfIsPublisher,** that indicates whether or not the Publisher is the destination. TRUE indicates that the system is in the upload phase and the Publisher is the destination, not the source. FALSE indicates that the system is in the download phase and the Publisher is the source, not the destination.

IDL Semantics

```
HRESULT _stdcall GetDestinationConnectionInfo(
                [out] IConnectionInfo** ppDestinationConnectionInfo,
                [out] REPOLE_BOOL* pfIsPublisher)
```

GetDestinationOwnerName(

pDestOwnerName As String,
cbDestName As Long)

Returns the name of the owner of the destination table into **pDestOwnerName**. The input parameter **cbDestName** indicates the size of **pDestOwnerName**. HRESULT returns an error if the buffer is too small.

IDL Semantics

```
HRESULT _stdcall GetDestinationOwnerName(
                 [out] LPWSTR pDestOwnerName,
                 long cbDestName)
```

GetErrorInfo(

pErrCode As Long,
pErrText As String)

Returns the error code into **pErrCode** and the string description of the error into **pErrText**.

IDL Semantics

```
HRESULT _stdcall GetErrorInfo(
                 [out] long* pErrCode,
                 LPWSTR pErrText)
```

GetExtendedError(

pExtError As REPOLE_EXTENDEDERROR_TYPE)

Returns additional information about the error, such as whether the error was a duplicate key or a unique index violation. The value returned is one of the enumerated constants from REPOLE_EXTENDEDERROR_TYPE.

IDL Semantics

```
HRESULT GetExtendedError ([out] REPOLE_EXTENDEDERROR_TYPE* pExtError)
```

GetNumColumns(

pdwColumnCount As Long)

Finds the number of columns in the base table. If there is a vertical partition, the number of columns in the table may not match the number of columns in the underlying table. For example, if a table contains five columns, but column 3 is not published, ColumnID=4 corresponds to the last column of the table.

IDL Semantics

```
HRESULT _stdcall GetNumColumns([out] long* pdwColumnCount)
```

GetPriorityWinner(
pPriorityWinner As REPOLE_PRIORITY_TYPE)

Returns a value indicating if the source or destination has the higher priority, using one of the enumerated constants from REPOLE_PRIORITY_TYPE. This method always returns the source or the destination as the winner. With equal priorities, the default winner is the Publisher. The value REPOLE_Priority_Equal is not used.

IDL Semantics

```
HRESULT _stdcall GetPriorityWinner(
                    [out] REPOLE_PRIORITY_TYPE*
                    pPriorityWinner)
```

GetResolverProcedureName(
pResolverProcedureName As String,
cbResolverProcedureName As Long)

Retrieves resolver-specific information into **pResolverProcedureName**. For example, if the merge conflict process is focused on a particular column that has been specified in the **Resolver** tab of the table properties, this method returns that column name. **cbResolverProcedureName** indicates the size of the buffer. HRESULT returns an error if the buffer is too small.

IDL Semantics

```
HRESULT _stdcall GetResolverProcedureName(
                    [out] LPWSTR pResolverProcedureName,
                    long cbResolverProcedureName)
```

GetRowGuidColName(
pRowGuidColName As String,
cbRowGuidColName As Long)

Retrieves the name of the column in the base table, which is the **uniqueidentifier** column used in merge replication. The input parameter **cbRowGuidColName** indicates the size of the buffer. HRESULT returns an error if the buffer is too small.

IDL Semantics

```
HRESULT _stdcall GetRowGuidColName(
                    [out] LPWSTR pRowGuidColName,
                    long cbRowGuidColName)
```

GetRowIdentifier(
pRowGuid As REPLGUID)

Returns the row **uniqueidentifier,** which is used to uniquely identify the row.

IDL Semantics

```
HRESULT _stdcall GetRowIdentifier([out] REPLGUID* pRowGuid)
```

GetSourceColumnValue(
ColumnId As Long,
pvBuffer,
cbBufferMax As Long,
pcbBufferActual As Long)

Returns the value of the column, referenced by the **ColumnID** parameter, into **pvBuffer**. The column value returned is the value of the column at the source table. The parameter **pcbBufferActual** returns the number of bytes the column value uses. The input parameter **cbBufferMax** indicates the size of pvBuffer. HRESULT returns an error if the buffer is too small.

IDL Semantics

```
HRESULT _stdcall GetSourceColumnValue(
                    long ColumnId,
                    [out] VARIANT* pvBuffer,
                    [in] long cbBufferMax,
                    [out] long* pcbBufferActual)
```

GetSourceConnectionInfo(
ppSourceConnectionInfo As IConnectionInfo,
pfIsPublisher As REPOLE_BOOL)

Returns a pointer to the object that contains all the connection information about the source in the **ppSourceConnectionInfo** parameter. This variable can then be used to make all the calls in the **IConnectionInfo** object. For example, this is the line of code that initializes the **IConnectionInfo** variable from the AdditiveResolver sample:

```
Call rrc.GetSourceConnectionInfo(SrcConnectionInfo, SrcIsPublisher)
```

Once initialized, the **SrcConnectionInfo** can be used as the class identifier to call all the methods available in the **IConnectionInfo** object, by using:

```
Call SrcConnectionInfo.GetServerName(stPublisher, en(stPublisher))
```

The **GetSourceConnectionInfo** method also returns a Boolean that indicates whether or not the Publisher is the source. TRUE indicates that the system is in the download phase and the Publisher is the source, not the destination. FALSE indicates that the system is in the upload phase and the Publisher is the destination, not the source.

IDL Semantics

```
HRESULT _stdcall GetSourceConnectionInfo(
                    [out] IConnectionInfo** ppSourceConnectionInfo,
                    [out] REPOLE_BOOL* pfIsPublisher)
```

GetTableName(
pTableName As String,
cbTableName As Long)

Returns the name of the table, against which the conflict is occurring, into **pTableName**. The parameter **cbTableName** is an input parameter that gives a buffer size for **pTableName**. HRESULT returns an error if the buffer is too small.

IDL Semantics

```
HRESULT _stdcall GetTableName(
                   [out] LPWSTR pTableName,
                   long cbTableName)
```

GetTableOwnerName(
pOwnerName As String,
cbOwnerName As Long)

Returns the name of the table owner into **pOwnerName**. The input parameter **cbOwnerName** gives a buffer size for **pOwnerName**. HRESULT returns an error if the buffer is too small.

IDL Semantics

```
HRESULT _stdcall GetTableOwnerName(
                   [out] LPWSTR pOwnerName,
                   long cbOwnerName)
```

InsertRow()

Inserts the row at the destination.

IDL Semantics

```
HRESULT InsertRow ()
```

LogConflict(
bLogSourceConflict As REPOLE_BOOL,
ConflictType As REPOLE_CONFLICT_TYPE,
bOnlyLogIfUpdater As REPOLE_BOOL,
[pszConflictMessage As String],
[bLogConflictOnUpload As REPOLE_BOOL])

Takes input parameters that indicate whether the conflict should be logged, specifications on what message to log, and where the log is kept.

The first parameter, **bLogSourceConflict**, is a Boolean indicating whether or not to log the conflict at the source.

If **bOnlyLogIfUpdater** is set to TRUE, a conflict is logged only if the database that has the losing version actually created that version. Thus, if a Publisher propagates a change to multiple Subscribers and then receives a change that causes a conflict and makes the version at all of those Subscribers lose, a conflict will not be logged for each of those Subscribers, because they would not have made the losing change. They merely would have received it from the Publisher, due to a change from some other Subscriber.

If **bOnlyLogIfUpdater** is FALSE, the losing version is logged regardless of whether the replica made the losing update.

The input parameter **ConflictType** is the message to log. The optional input parameter **pszConflictMessage** can be used as additional text to the conflict message being logged. This allows the conflict message to be customized with additional information.

The optional input parameter **bLogConflictOnUpload** does not need to be used. It is a default parameter that is not used by a custom resolver.

IDL Semantics

```
HRESULT _stdcall LogConflict(
    [in] REPOLE_BOOL bLogSourceConflict,
    [in] REPOLE_CONFLICT_TYPE ConflictType,
    [in] REPOLE_BOOL bOnlyLogIfUpdater,
    [in, optional, defaultvalue("")] BSTR pszConflictMessage,
    [in, optional, defaultvalue(0)] REPOLE_BOOL bLogConflictOnUpload)
```

LogError(
ChangeType As REPOLE_CHANGE_TYPE,
[pszErrorMessage As String])

Logs an error, such as a duplicate primary key error. It logs the input parameter **ChangeType** and the text in the optional input parameter **pszErrorMessage** string, as the description.

IDL Semantics

```
HRESULT LogError ([in] REPOLE_CHANGE_TYPE ChangeType,
      [in, optional, defaultvalue("")] BSTR pszErrorMessage)
```

UpdateRow()

Updates the row at the destination.

IDL Semantics

```
HRESULT UpdateRow ()
```

IConnectionInfo Interface and Methods

The methods available in **IConnectionInfo** are called from the merge replication custom conflict resolver application to return information about the database and tables. The **IConnectionInfo** interface is also used when a resolver needs to access a stored procedure. A limitation of the **IConnectionInfo** interface is that only the GET methods are accessible to user-implemented resolvers. Although the Object Browser shows many SET methods, only the GET methods are documented.

Many of the methods use a ColumnID parameter. The **ColumnID** contains a number that represents the position of the column in the table, ranging from 1 to <number of columns>. This number is used as a parameter to methods instead of the column name.

If the table is vertically partitioned, a column position in the table at the Subscriber does not necessarily match what the column position value would be in the underlying table at the Publisher. For example, if a table contains five columns, but column 3 is not published, ColumnID=4 corresponds to the last column of the table.

Qualification of Method Calls

The methods in **IConnectionInfo** return information about the databases and tables involved in the merge process. The methods can return information about the source or the destination. To specify which one you want information about, qualify the procedure call with a variable. For example, this code returns information about the destination:

```
Call DestConnectionInfo.GetServerName(stPublisher, Len(stPublisher))
```
This code returns information about the source:

```
Call SrcConnectionInfo.GetServerName(stPublisher, Len(stPublisher))
```
Although the same method is called (**GetServerName**), the distinction regarding what it returns is specified in the qualifier.

To initialize the qualifiers, use the **GetDestinationConnectionInfo** in the **IReplRowChange** interface to initialize the DestConnectionInfo variable. Use the **GetSourceConnectionInfo** method in the **IReplRowChange** interface to initialize the SrcConnectionInfo variable.

Summary of Methods in IConnectionInfo

Method	Description
GetApplicationName	Returns the name of the application using the connection.
GetBcpBatchSize	Returns a value that indicates the setting of the batch size of commit.
GetCatalog	Returns the name of the catalog.
GetCodePage	Returns the current CodePage setting for the server.

Continued on next page

Method	Description
GetComparisonStyle	Returns a value that indicates the SQL collation.
GetConnectName	Returns the connection name.
GetDatabase	Returns the database name.
GetDatabaseStatus	Returns the database status.
GetDatasource	Returns the data source name.
GetDatasourcePath	Returns the path to the **.mdb** file.
GetDataSourceType	Returns the type of data source.
GetDBCreatedThisSession	Returns a value that indicates whether or not the database has been created in this session.
GetHostName	Returns the host name being used in the **IConnectionInfo** object.
GetInternetAddress	Returns the Internet address.
GetInternetNetwork	Returns the NetLibrary to use when connecting.
GetLCID	Returns the preferred locale ID value.
GetLogin	Returns into Login the login currently in use if using SQL Server Authentication. If using Windows Authentication, the value returned to the Login parameter is an empty string.
GetLoginTimeout	Returns the number of seconds the system will wait before returning from a failed login attempt.
GetMajorVersion	Returns the product major version number.
GetMinorVersion	Returns the product minor version number.
GetPacketSize	Returns the packet size, in bytes.
GetPassword	Returns the current **IConnectionInfo** object password.
GetProviderName	Returns the OLE DB provider name.
GetProviderString	Returns the OLE DB property provider string.
GetQueryTimeout	Returns the number of seconds of the time-out value for queries against a server.
GetSecurityMode	Returns the security mode being employed to connect to SQL Server by the Windows user or group of users.
GetServerName	Returns the server name.
GetServerRole	Returns a string that indicates whether the server role is as a Subscriber, Distributor, or Publisher.
GetUseInprocLoader	Returns a value indicating whether or not the agent is using inproc loader (BULK INSERT statement) to load the data from bcp files into tables.

Methods in the IConnectionInfo Interface

GetApplicationName(
ApplicationName As String,
cbApplicationName As Long)

Returns the name of the application that uses this connection into **ApplicationName** (for example, "Merge Agent"). The input parameter **cbApplicationName** indicates the buffer size. HRESULT returns an error if the buffer is too small.

IDL Semantics

```
HRESULT _stdcall GetApplicationName(
                  [out] LPWSTR ApplicationName,
                  long cbApplicationName)
```

GetBcpBatchSize(
plBcpBatchSize As Long)

Returns into **plBcpBatchSize** a long that indicates the setting of the batch size of commit.

IDL Semantics

```
HRESULT _stdcall GetBcpBatchSize(
                  [out] long* plBcpBatchSize)
```

GetCatalog(
Catalog As String,
cbCatalog As Long)

Returns into **Catalog** the name of the catalog. The input parameter **cbCatalog** indicates the buffer size. HRESULT returns an error if the buffer is too small.

IDL Semantics

```
HRESULT _stdcall GetCatalog(
                  [out] LPWSTR Catalog,
                  long cbCatalog)
```

GetCodePage(
plCodePage As Long)

Returns into **plCodePage** the current CodePage setting for the server. For more information on CodePage, see "Collations" in SQL Server Books Online.

IDL Semantics

```
HRESULT _stdcall GetCodePage(
                  [out] long* plCodePage)
```

GetComparisonStyle(
plComparisonStyle As Long)

Returns into **plComparisonStyle** an integer that indicates the SQL collation. For more information on collation, see "SQL Server Collation Fundamentals" in SQL Server Books Online.

IDL Semantics

```
HRESULT _stdcall GetComparisonStyle(
                    [out] long* plComparisonStyle)
```

GetConnectName(
ConnectName As String,
cbConnectName As Long)

Returns the connection name into **ConnectName**. The input parameter **cbConnectName** indicates the buffer size. HRESULT returns an error if the buffer is too small.

IDL Semantics

```
HRESULT _stdcall GetConnectName(
                    [out] LPWSTR ConnectName,
                    long cbConnectName)
```

GetDatabase(
Database As String,
cbDatabase As Long)

Returns into **Database** the name of the database. The input parameter **cbDatabase** indicates the buffer size. HRESULT returns an error if the buffer is too small.

IDL Semantics

```
HRESULT _stdcall GetDatabase(
                    [out] LPWSTR Database,
                    long cbDatabase)
```

GetDatabaseStatus(
plDatabaseStatus As Long)

Returns a value into **plDatabaseStatus** that is one of the enumerated constants from REPOLE_DBAddoption.

IDL Semantics

```
HRESULT _stdcall GetDatabaseStatus(
                    [out] long* plDatabaseStatus)
```

GetDatasource(
Datasource As String,
cbDatasource As Long)

Returns into **Datasource** the name of the data source. The input parameter, **cbDatasource**, indicates the buffer size. HRESULT returns an error if the buffer is too small.

IDL Semantics

```
HRESULT _stdcall GetDatasource(
                    [out] LPWSTR Datasource,
                    long cbDatasource)
```

GetDatasourcePath(
DatasourcePath As String,
cbDatasourcePath As Long)

If the data source is a Jet database, this method returns the path to the **.mdb** file into **DatasourcePath**. This is the same data stored in the **Datasource_path** column, which you can see by running the stored procedure **sysmergesubscriptions**. The input parameter, **cbDatasourcePath**, indicates the buffer size. HRESULT returns an error if the buffer is too small.

IDL Semantics

```
HRESULT _stdcall GetDatasourcePath(
                    [out] LPWSTR DatasourcePath,
                    long cbDatasourcePath)
```

GetDataSourceType(
pRetValue As REPOLE_DATASOURCE_TYPE)

Returns the type of data source into **pRetValue**. The value returned is one of the enumerated constants from REPOLE_DATASOURCE_TYPE.

IDL Semantics

```
HRESULT _stdcall GetDataSourceType(
                    [out] REPOLE_DATASOURCE_TYPE* pRetValue)
```

GetDBCreatedThisSession(
pbDBCreatedThisSession As Long)

Returns into **pbDBCreatedThisSession** a value that indicates whether the database has been created in this session. A value of 0 indicates FALSE, or not created this session, while a value of 1 indicates TRUE, the database was created this session.

IDL Semantics

```
HRESULT _stdcall GetDBCreatedThisSession(
                    [out] long* pbDBCreatedThisSession)
```

GetHostName(

HostName As String,
cbHostName As Long)

Returns the host name being used in the **IConnectionInfo** object into **HostName**. The input parameter **cbHostName** indicates the buffer size. HRESULT returns an error if the buffer is too small.

IDL Semantics

```
HRESULT _stdcall GetHostName(
                 [out] LPWSTR HostName,
                 long cbHostName)
```

GetInternetAddress(

InternetAddress As String,
cbInternetAddress As Long)

Returns the Internet address as a string into **InternetAddress**. The input parameter **cbInternetAddress** indicates the buffer size. HRESULT returns an error if the buffer is too small.

IDL Semantics

```
HRESULT _stdcall GetInternetAddress(
                 [out] LPWSTR InternetAddress,
                 long cbInternetAddress)
```

GetInternetNetwork(

InternetNetwork As String,
cbInternetNetwork As Long)

Returns into **InternetNetwork** the NetLibrary to use when connecting. The NetLibrary string does not contain the **.dll** extension. This option is useful when configuring the Merge Agent to connect over the Internet. The input parameter **cbInternetNetwork** indicates the buffer size. HRESULT returns an error if the buffer is too small.

IDL Semantics

```
HRESULT _stdcall GetInternetNetwork(
                 [out] LPWSTR InternetNetwork,
                 long cbInternetNetwork)
```

GetLCID(

plLCID As Long)

Returns a value into **plLCID** that indicates the preferred locale ID.

IDL Semantics

```
HRESULT _stdcall GetLCID(
                 [out] long* plLCID)
```

GetLogin(
Login As String,
cbLogin As Long)

Returns into **Login** the login currently in use if you are using SQL Server Authentication. If you are using Windows Authentication, the value returned to the **Login** parameter is an empty string. The input parameter **cbLogin** indicates the buffer size. HRESULT returns an error if the buffer is too small.

IDL Semantics

```
HRESULT _stdcall GetLogin(
                [out] LPWSTR Login,
                long cbLogin)
```

GetLoginTimeout(
plLoginTimeout As Long)

Returns the number of seconds the system will wait before returning from a failed login attempt.

IDL Semantics

```
HRESULT _stdcall GetLoginTimeout(
                [out] long* plLoginTimeout)
```

GetMajorVersion(
plMajorVersion As Long)

Returns the major version number of the product into **plMajorVersion**. The value returned is one of the enumerated constants from REPOLE_SERVER_VERSION.

IDL Semantics

```
HRESULT _stdcall GetMajorVersion(
                long* plMajorVersion)
```

GetMinorVersion(
plMinorVersion As Long)

Returns the minor version number of the product into **plMinorVersion**. The value returned is one of the enumerated constants from REPOLE_SERVER_MINOR_VERSION.

IDL Semantics

```
HRESULT _stdcall GetMinorVersion(
                long* plMinorVersion)
```

GetPacketSize(
pusPacketSize As Long)

Returns the packet size, in bytes, into **pusPacketSize**. The default is 4096 bytes. For more information, see "network packet size Option" in SQL Server Books Online.

IDL Semantics

```
HRESULT _stdcall GetPacketSize(
                        [out] unsigned long* pusPacketSize)
```

GetPassword(
Password As String,
cbPassword As Long)

Returns the password currently being used in the **IConnectionInfo** object into **Password**. The input parameter **cbPassword** indicates the buffer size. HRESULT returns an error if the buffer is too small.

IDL Semantics

```
HRESULT _stdcall GetPassword(
                        [out] LPWSTR Password,
                        long cbPassword)
```

GetProviderName(
ProviderName As String,
cbProviderName As Long)

Returns the OLE DB provider name into **ProviderName**. The input parameter **cbProviderName** indicates the buffer size. HRESULT returns an error if the buffer is too small.

IDL Semantics

```
HRESULT _stdcall GetProviderName(
                        [out] LPWSTR ProviderName,
                        long cbProviderName)
```

GetProviderString(
ProviderString As String,
cbProviderString As Long)

Returns the OLE DB provider string into **ProviderString**. The **ProviderString** property specifies the OLE DB provider-specific connection data required to implement a connection to the referenced OLE DB data source. The input parameter **cbProviderString** indicates the buffer size. HRESULT returns an error if the buffer is too small.

IDL Semantics

```
HRESULT _stdcall GetProviderString(
                        [out] LPWSTR ProviderString,
                        long cbProviderString)
```

GetQueryTimeout(
plQueryTimeout As Long)

Returns the number of seconds of the time-out value for queries against a server into **plQUeryTimeout**.

IDL Semantics

```
HRESULT _stdcall GetQueryTimeout(
                    [out] long* plQueryTimeout)
```

GetSecurityMode(
pRetValue As REPOLE_SECURITY_TYPE)

Returns into **pRetValue** the security mode being employed to connect to SQL Server by the Windows user or group of users. The value returned is one of the enumerated constants from REPOLE_SECURITY_TYPE.

IDL Semantics

```
HRESULT _stdcall GetSecurityMode(
                    [out] REPOLE_SECURITY_TYPE* pRetValue)
```

GetServerName(
ServerName As String,
cbServerName As Long)

Returns into **ServerName** the name of the server. The input parameter, **cbServerName**, indicates the buffer size. HRESULT returns an error if the buffer is too small.

IDL Semantics

```
HRESULT _stdcall GetServerName(
                    [out] LPWSTR ServerName,
                    long cbServerName)
```

GetServerRole(
ServerRole As String,
cbServerRole As Long)

Returns a string into **ServerRole** that indicates which server role is being used, Subscriber, Distributor, or Publisher. The input parameter **cbServerRole** indicates the buffer size. HRESULT returns an error if the buffer is too small.

IDL Semantics

```
HRESULT _stdcall GetServerRole(
                    [out] LPWSTR ServerRole,
                    long cbServerRole)
```

GetUseInprocLoader(
pbUseInprocLoader As Long)

Returns a value into **pbUseInprocLoader** indicating whether or not the agent is using inproc loader (BULK INSERT statement) to load the data from bcp files into tables. It returns FALSE if the agent is using ODBC BCP to load data from bcp files into the tables.

IDL Semantics

```
HRESULT _stdcall GetUseInprocLoader(
                      [out] long* pbUseInprocLoader)
```

Constants

This section provides detail on the enumerated data types that are defined in the SQL Replication Conflict Resolver Library, and are used as parameters and return values to the methods in the SQL Merge Conflict Resolver component.

REPLGUID

The **REPLGUID** constants provide a class identifier that is a properly formatted GUID.

Constant	Description
Data1	Long
Data2	Short
Data3	Short
Data4	Unsigned char(8)

REPOLE_BOOL

The **REPOLE_BOOL** constants specify values that indicate true or false.

Constant	Value	Description
REPOLEBool_FALSE	0	Value is false.
REPOLEBool_TRUE	1	Value is true.

REPOLE_CHANGE_TYPE

The **REPOLE_CHANGE_TYPE** constants specify what the database operation (update, insert, delete) is, whether or not there is a conflict, and whether or not column tracking is active.

Constant	Value	Description
REPOLEChange_SubscriberInsert	0x00000001	Subscriber is inserting new row in upload phase.
REPOLEChange_PublisherInsert	0x00010000	Publisher is inserting new row in download phase.
REPOLEChange_SubscriberDelete_ NoConflict	0x00000002	Subscriber is deleting a row. No conflict detected.
REPOLEChange_PublisherDelete_ NoConflict	0x00020000	Publisher is deleting a row. No conflict detected.
REPOLEChange_SubscriberSystem Delete	0x00000004	Subscriber is deleting the row due to reasons like primary key violations.
REPOLEChange_PublisherSystemDelete	0x00040000	Publisher is deleting the row due to reasons like primary key violations.
REPOLEChange_SubscriberDelete_ Conflict	0x00000008	Subscriber is deleting a row. Conflict detected.
REPOLEChange_PublisherDelete_ Conflict	0x00080000	Publisher is deleting a row. Conflict detected.
REPOLEChange_SubscriberRemove FromPartial	0x00000010	Not used.
REPOLEChange_PublisherRemove FromPartial	0x00100000	The publisher tells the subscriber to delete the row, because it is no longer in the partition.
REPOLEChange_SubscriberUpdate_ NoConflict	0x00000020	Subscriber is updating a row. No conflict detected.
REPOLEChange_PublisherUpdate_ NoConflict	0x00200000	Publisher is updating a row. No conflict detected.
REPOLEChange_SubscriberUpdate_ Conflict WithDelete	0x00000040	Subscriber is updating a row and has a conflict with a delete coming from the Publisher.
REPOLEChange_PublisherUpdate_ ConflictWith Delete	0x00400000	Publisher is updating a row and has a conflict with a delete coming from the Subscriber.

continued on next page

Constant	Value	Description
REPOLEChange_SubscriberUpdate_ConflictColTrack	0x00000080	Subscriber is updating a specific column, column tracking is in effect, and the update has a conflict with a change coming from the Publisher.
REPOLEChange_PublisherUpdate_ConflictColTrack	0x00800000	Publisher is updating a specific column, column tracking is in effect, and the update has a conflict with a change coming from the Subscriber.
REPOLEChange_SubscriberUpdate_ConflictNoColTrack	0x00000100	Subscriber is updating a specific column, column tracking is not in effect, and the update has a conflict with a change coming from the Publisher.
REPOLEChange_PublisherUpdate_ConflictNoColTrack	0x01000000	Publisher is updating a specific column, column tracking is not in effect, and the update has a conflict with a change coming from the Subscriber.
REPOLEChange_UploadInsertFailed	0x00000200	A row was inserted at the Subscriber, but the subsequent insertion at the Publisher failed.
REPOLEChange_DownloadInsertFailed	0x02000000	A row was inserted at the Publisher, but the subsequent insertion at the Subscriber failed.
REPOLEChange_UploadDeleteFailed	0x00000400	A row was deleted at the Subscriber, but the subsequent deletion at the Publisher failed.
REPOLEChange_DownloadDeleteFailed	0x04000000	A row was deleted at the Publisher, but the subsequent deletion at the Subscriber failed.
REPOLEChange_UploadUpdateFailed	0x00000800	A row was updated at the Subscriber, but the subsequent update at the Publisher failed.
REPOLEChange_DownloadUpdateFailed	0x08000000	A row was updated at the Publisher, but the subsequent update at the Subscriber failed.

continued on next page

Constant	Value	Description
REPOLEUpdateConflicts		The combination of:
		(REPOLEChange_SubscriberUpdate_ConflictColTrack |
		REPOLEChange_PublisherUpdate_ConflictColTrack |
		REPOLEChange_SubscriberUpdate_ConflictNoColTrack |
		REPOLEChange_PublisherUpdate_ConflictNoColTrack)
REPOLEAllConflicts		The combination of:
		(REPOLEChange_SubscriberDelete_Conflict |
		REPOLEChange_PublisherDelete_Conflict |
		REPOLEChange_SubscriberUpdate_ConflictWithDelete |
		REPOLEChange_PublisherUpdate_ConflictWithDelete |
		REPOLEUpdateConflicts)
REPOLEAllErrors		The combination of:
		(REPOLEChange_UploadInsertFailed |
		REPOLEChange_DownloadInsertFailed |
		REPOLEChange_UploadDeleteFailed |
		REPOLEChange_DownloadDeleteFailed |
		REPOLEChange_UploadUpdateFailed |
		REPOLEChange_DownloadUpdateFailed)

continued on next page

Constant	Value	Description
REPOLEAllNonConflicts		The combination of:
		(REPOLEChange_SubscriberInsert |
		REPOLEChange_PublisherInsert |
		REPOLEChange_SubscriberDelete_ NoConflict |
		REPOLEChange_PublisherDelete_ NoConflict|
		REPOLEChange_SubscriberSystemDelete |
		REPOLEChange_PublisherSystemDelete |
		REPOLEChange_SubscriberRemoveFrom Partial |
		REPOLEChange_SubscriberUpdate_ NoConflict |
		REPOLEChange_PublisherUpdate_ NoConflict)
REPOLEAllChanges		The combination of:
		(REPOLEAllConflicts | REPOLEAllErrors |
		REPOLEAllNonConflicts)

REPOLE_COLSTATUS_TYPE

The **REPOLE_COLSTATUS_TYPE** constants specify the status of an individual column.

Constant	Value	Description
REPOLEColumn_NotUpdated	0x0001	No updates to column, or data values match.
REPOLEColumn_UpdatedNoConflict	0x0002	Column updated at source, no column-level conflict.
REPOLEColumn_UpdatedWithConflict	0x0003	Column updated at source, conflicts with change at destination.
REPOLEColumn_DifferNoTrack	0x0004	No column tracking information; data values are different.

REPOLE_COLUMN_ATTRIBUTES

The **REPOLE_COLUMN_ATTRIBUTES** constants specify whether the column is updatable, an identity column, or both.

Constant	Value	Description
REPOLEColumnAttribute_Updatable	0x0001	This column is updatable.
REPOLEColumnAttribute_Identity	0x0002	This column is an identity column.

Remarks

The values returned from methods that use this constant return a bitmap of the values, and because a column can be both updatable and an identity column, check the results with ***plColumnAttributes & REPOLEColumnAttribute_Updatable**, or ***plColumnAttributes & REPOLEColumnAttribute_Identity**, respectively.

REPOLE_CONFLICT_TYPE

The **REPOLE_CONFLICT_TYPE** constants specify a value that describes the type of conflict that occurred and if the failure occurred during the upload or download phase.

Constant	Value	Description
REPOLEConflict_Min	1	For internal use only.
REPOLEConflict_UpdateConflict	1	The two replicas made conflicting updates to the same row.
REPOLEConflict_ColumnUpdateConflict	2	The two replicas made conflicting updates to the same column of the same row.
REPOLEConflict_UpdateDeleteWinsConflict	3	An update conflicted with a delete, and the delete won.
REPOLEConflict_UpdateWinsDeleteConflict	4	An update conflicted with a delete, and the update won.
REPOLEConflict_UploadInsertFailed	5	Corresponds to the respective REPOLE_CHANGE_TYPE.
REPOLEConflict_DownloadInsertFailed	6	Corresponds to the respective REPOLE_CHANGE_TYPE.
REPOLEConflict_UploadDeleteFailed	7	Corresponds to the respective REPOLE_CHANGE_TYPE.

continued on next page

Constant	Value	Description
REPOLEConflict_DownloadDeleteFailed	8	Corresponds to the respective REPOLE_CHANGE_TYPE.
REPOLEConflict_UploadUpdateFailed	9	Corresponds to the respective REPOLE_CHANGE_TYPE.
REPOLEConflict_DownloadUpdateFailed	10	Corresponds to the respective REPOLE_CHANGE_TYPE.
REPOLEConflict_ResolutionDone	11	For internal use only.
REPOLEConflict_Max	11	For internal use only.

REPOLE_DATASOURCE_TYPE

Because SQL Server 2000 offers the ability to replicate data to any heterogeneous data source that provides a 32-bit ODBC or OLE DB driver on either Microsoft Windows® 2000, Microsoft Windows NT® Server 4.0, or Windows 98 operating systems, the **REPOLE_DATASOURCE_TYPE** constants provide data source type values for the application. For more information, see "DATASOURCE_TYPE" in SQL Server Books Online.

Constant	Value	Description
REPOLEDataSource_Native	0x0000	Microsoft SQL Server Subscriber data source.
REPOLEDataSource_Jet	0x0002	Microsoft Jet 4.0 database.

The object browser shows more constants for this enumeration. They are not valid, however, in a Visual Basic merge replication conflict resolver application, and therefore are not listed here.

REPOLE_DBADDOPTION

The **REPOLE_DBADDOPTION** constants specify if the Subscriber database exists or if it must be created or attached, or if the subscription must be attached.

Constant	Value	Description
REPOLEExisting_Database	0x0000	Uses an existing Subscriber database.
REPOLECreate_Database	0x0001	Creates the Subscriber database (SQL Server Subscribers only).

continued on next page

Constant	Value	Description
REPOLEAttach_Database	0x0002	Attaches a Subscriber database file, typically an .mdf (SQL Server Subscribers only).
REPOLEAttach_Subscription	0x0003	Attaches a subscription file, typically an .msf (Microsoft Subscription File).

REPOLE_EXTENDEDERROR_TYPE

The **REPOLE_EXTENDEDERROR_TYPE** constants return additional error information.

Constant	Value	Description
REPOLEExtErrorNoneOrNotSpecified	0x00000000	All errors not specifically addressed.
REPOLEExtErrorDupKey	0x00000001	SQL Server error 2627: Violation of %ls constraint '%.*ls'. Cannot insert duplicate key in object '%.*ls'.
REPOLEExtErrorDupUniqueIndex	0x00000002	SQL Server error 2601: Cannot insert duplicate key row in object '%.*ls' with unique index '%.*ls'.

REPOLE_PRIORITY_TYPE

The REPOLE_PRIORITY_TYPE constants return the assigned priority. For more information, see "Subscriber Types and Conflicts" in SQL Server Books Online.

Constant	Value	Description
REPOLEPriority_Source	0x0001	The source has the higher priority.
REPOLEPriority_Destination	0x0002	The destination has the higher priority.
REPOLEPriority_Equal	0x0003	The source and destination have equal priority.

Note   If priorities are equal, you will receive **REPOLEPriority_Source** during download or **REPOLEPriority_Destination** during upload, instead of **REPOLEPriority_Equal**.

REPOLE_SECURITY_TYPE

These constants specify what kind of security is used when connecting to SQL Server.

Constant	Value	Description
REPOLESecurity_Min	0	For internal use only.
REPOLESecurity_Normal	0	Specifies SQL Server Authentication mode.
REPOLESecurity_Integrated	1	Specifies Windows Authentication mode.
REPOLESecurity_Mixed	2	Specifies Windows Authentication or SQL Server Authentication. SQL Server Authentication is provided for backward compatibility.
REPOLESecurity_Max	2	For internal use only.
REPOLESecurity_Invalid	-1	Indicates that the security mode is not specified. Security mode is retrieved from the Publisher.

Remarks

The terminology used in several of these constants contains some references for backward compatibility to SQL Server version 6.5. The terms, Windows Authentication and Mixed Mode, replace integrated security and mixed security, respectively. Standard security has no equivalent. For more information, see "Authentication Modes" in SQL Server Books Online.

REPOLE_SERVER_VERSION

This is an enumeration that describes what version of SQL Server is running.

Constant	Value	Description
REPOLEVersion_Invalid	-1	Unknown or not set.
REPOLEVersion_70RTM	10	SQL Server 7.0.
REPOLEVersion_70SP1	20	SQL Server 7.0 with Service Pack 1.
REPOLEVersion_70SP2	30	SQL Server 7.0 with Service Pack 2.
REPOLEVersion_70SP3	35	SQL Server 7.0 with Service Pack 3.
REPOLEVersion_80	40	SQL Server 2000.

REPOLE_SERVER_MINOR_VERSION

This is an enumeration that indicates the minor version number that is running.

Constant	Value	Description
REPOLEMinorVersion_Invalid	-1	Unknown or not set.
REPOLEMinorVersion_80Beta2	10	SQL Server 2000, Beta 2.
REPOLEMinorVersion_80EAP6	20	SQL Server 2000, Early Adopter Program 6.
REPOLEMinorVersion_80RTM	30	SQL Server 2000 Retail.

REPOLE_SQL_DATATYPE

This is an enumeration of the ODBC data types. For more information on the default ODBC data types and their descriptions, see the topic, SQL Data Types, in the Microsoft Open Database Connectivity (ODBC) section of the Microsoft Data Access Components (MDAC) SDK (available on the MSDN Library CD). Additionally, the ODBC SDK can also be downloaded from http://www.microsoft.com/data/, and is available in Microsoft ODBC 3.0 Software Development Kit and Programmer's Reference from Microsoft Press®.

Constant	Value
REPOLEType_SQL_UNKNOWN_TYPE	0
REPOLEType_SQL_CHAR	1
REPOLEType_SQL_NUMERIC	2
REPOLEType_SQL_DECIMAL	3
REPOLEType_SQL_INTEGER	4
REPOLEType_SQL_SMALLINT	5
REPOLEType_SQL_FLOAT	6
REPOLEType_SQL_REAL	7
REPOLEType_SQL_DOUBLE	8
REPOLEType_SQL_DATETIME	9
REPOLEType_SQL_DATE	9
REPOLEType_SQL_INTERVAL	10

continued on next page

Constant	Value
REPOLEType_SQL_TIME	10
REPOLEType_SQL_TIMESTAMP	11
REPOLEType_SQL_VARCHAR	12
REPOLEType_SQL_LONGVARCHAR	-1
REPOLEType_SQL_BINARY	-2
REPOLEType_SQL_VARBINARY	-3
REPOLEType_SQL_LONGVARBINARY	-4
REPOLEType_SQL_BIGINT	-5
REPOLEType_SQL_TINYINT	-6
REPOLEType_SQL_BIT	-7
REPOLEType_SQL_GUID	-11

Remarks

For any of the datetime and interval data types, this field returns the verbose data type: SQL_DATETIME or SQL_INTERVAL. The developer is responsible for knowing the concise data type, as there is no **REPOLE_SQL_DATATYPE** enumeration that maps directly to the individual ODBC data types.

Registering a Custom Conflict Resolver

The merge replication custom conflict resolver must be registered in order to be recognized by SQL Server.

To Register a Merge Replication Custom Conflict Resolver

In Visual Basic, go to the **File** menu and click **Make <yourproject>.DLL**. This will compile and register the application on the current computer. If the .DLL needs to be registered on a different computer, run **REGSVR32 <yourproject>.DLL** from the command prompt. The .DLL must be registered on the computer that is invoking the merge agent. If you are using this application with a push subscription, the resolver must be registered at the Distributor that is invoking the merge agent. Similarly, for pull subscriptions, the resolver must be registered at the Subscriber that is invoking the merge agent. To ensure the resolver is registered properly, run **sp_enumcustomresolvers** on the computer on which it is registered. If the application name is returned in the result set, it is registered properly.

Registering Custom Resolvers on a Cluster

When using custom conflict resolvers with merge replication on a failover cluster, register the custom resolver on all nodes of the failover cluster. This ensures the custom resolver will be able to load the resolver properly after a failover. Merge replication conflict resolvers that come with SQL Server are automatically registered.

Merge Replication Custom Conflict Resolver Samples

The Merge Replication Custom Conflict Resolver (SampleResolver) sample is available on the SQL Server 2000 Resource Kit CD-ROM in the folder, \ToolsAndSamples\SampleResolver. The samples demonstrate the implementation of the SQL Replication Conflict Resolver Library in merge replication custom conflict resolver applications. Samples included are:

- Additive Resolver

- Minimum Resolver

The samples contain a SQL Script that will register the custom conflict resolvers.

Additive Resolver

The Additive Resolver is designed to handle several types of UPDATE conflicts. The Additive Resolver chooses the sum of the column values from the Publisher and Subscriber as the winning column value in an UPDATE conflict.

When a custom application is used to resolve conflicts on a particular column, the user is required to enter the name of the column when creating the publication using the Create Publication Wizard, or using the **@resolver_info** parameter of the **sp_addmergearticle** system stored procedure. For more information, see "Specifying a Custom Resolver" in SQL Server Books Online.

The IVBCustomResolver_Reconcile Method

The **IVBCustomResolver_Reconcile** method is where the conflict logic is coded. It is necessary to gather all the data needed (the order in which the data is gathered is not critical) before invoking the resolve code. The resolve code is in the **IVBCustomResolver_ComputeAdditiveValues** method in the AdditiveResolver sample.

To gather the necessary data, the first task done in the **Reconcile** method is to determine what kind of change occurred. The type of change can be found by calling the method **GetChangeType** and passing to it a variable of type SQLResolver.REPOLE_CHANGE_TYPE. The value returned will be one of the REPOLE_CHANGE_TYPE variables.

The next task, which you will see in the sample, is to retrieve the data connection information. This is done by calling the **GetSourceConnectionInfo** and **GetDestinationConnectionInfo** methods. These two methods take, as their parameters, a variable declared as **IConnectionInfo**, as well as a variable defined as a Boolean (REPOLE_BOOL). The application then uses the **GetRowIdentifier** method to get the GUID of the row in the table. It then determines whether the merge process is being done in the upload phase or the download phase.

When a custom application is used to resolve conflicts on a particular column, the code retrieves the column name the user has entered by calling the **GetResolverProcedureName** method of **IReplRowChange**. The name of this function is somewhat of a misnomer, as it does not get a procedure name, but a column name. When that application has the column name, it needs to convert the name to a value that indicates the position of the column in the table. The application loops through all the columns in the table, comparing the retrieved column name to each column name in the table. When it finds a match, the application calls the **IVBCustomResolver_ComputeAdditiveValues** method, which determines the new column value.

The IVBCustomResolver_ComputeAdditiveValues Method

The application first determines the status of the column in question by calling **GetColumnStatus**. This gives the following status options:

REPOLEColumn_DifferNoTrack

REPOLEColumn_NotUpdated

REPOLEColumn_UpdatedNoConflict

REPOLEColumn_UpdatedWithConflict

Depending on the state of the column, the application can then make a decision on how to proceed. In the sample, if the column has been updated at both source and destination, retrieve the value from both computers using calls to **GetSourceColumnValue** and **GetDestinationColumnValue**. The application then adds them together.

To put the desired value back into the table column, the application uses the **SetColumn** function. The **SetColumn** function does not commit the value. To commit the value to the table, the **UpdateRow** function must be called and changes to the entire row are committed.

For columns that have been updated without changes, the application copies the column data by using **CopyColumnFromSource**. Again, to commit the value to the table, call the **UpdateRow** function.

MinimumResolver

The MiminumResolver handles several types of conflicts. When an UPDATE conflict occurs, it determines the minimum value between the source and destination column values, and sets the minimum value as the winning value. If the column values match, then the winning data is based on priorities. For more information on assigning priorities in conflicts, see "Subscriber Types and Conflicts" in SQL Server Books Online.

The IVBCustomResolver_Reconcile Method

The **IVBCustomResolver_Reconcile** method is where the conflict logic is coded. It is necessary to gather all the data needed (the order in which the data is gathered is not critical) before invoking the resolve code. The resolve code in this sample is in the **IVBCustomResolver_ComputeMinimumValue** method.

To gather the necessary data, the first task done in the **Reconcile** method is to determine what kind of change occurred. The type of change can be found by calling the method **GetChangeType** and passing to it a variable of type SQLResolver.REPOLE_CHANGE_TYPE. The value returned will be one of the REPOLE_CHANGE_TYPE variables.

The next task, which you will see in the sample, is to retrieve the data connection information. This is done by calling the **GetSourceConnectionInfo** and **GetDestinationConnectionInfo** methods. These two methods take, as their parameters, a variable declared as **IConnectionInfo**, as well as a variable defined as a Boolean (REPOLE_BOOL). The application then uses the **GetRowIdentifier** method to get the GUID of the row in the table. It then determines whether the merge process is being done in the upload phase or the download phase.

Since this application is designed to resolve conflicts in a particular column, the code retrieves the column name the user has entered by calling the **GetResolverProcedureName** method of **IReplRowChange**. The name of this function is somewhat of a misnomer, as it does not get a procedure name, but a column name. Now that the application has the column name, it must convert the name to a value that indicates the position of the column in the table. The application loops through all the columns in the table, comparing the retrieved column name to each column name in the table. When it finds a match, the application calls the **IVBCustomResolver_ComputeMinimumValue** method, which determines the new column value.

The IVBCustomResolver_ComputeMinimumValue Method

The application first retrieves the values of the column from the source and the destination. Then IF/ELSE logic is used to determine which value is less than the other, or if they are equal. If they are equal, the application calls **GetPriorityWinner** to determine the winner.

To put the desired value back into the table column, the application uses the **SetColumn** function. The **SetColumn** function does not commit the value. To commit the value to the table, the **UpdateRow** function must be called and changes to the entire row are committed.

The application copies the column data by using **CopyColumnFromSource**, and uses the **UpdateRow** method to commit the value to the table.

To Run the Samples

1. In SQL Query Analyzer, open \ToolsAndSamples\SampleResolver**vbresolver_1.sql.** This script registers both sample resolvers, and creates a publication and subscription. The script:

   - Registers the Sample Additive Resolver using the CLSID of SampleCustomResolver.AdditiveResolver component.

   - Registers the Sample Minimum Values Resolver using the CLSID of SampleCustomResolver.MinumumResolver component.

   - Creates the SampleNorthwind publication.

   - Creates the Orders article and sets the Sample Minimum Values Resolver as the resolver, with the resolver column OrderDate as the resolver_info property.

   - Creates the Products article and sets the Sample Additive Resolver as the resolver, with the resolver column UnitsOnOrder as the resolver_info property.

   - Creates subscription database SampleNorthwindSubscription, and sets up an anonymous subscription to SampleNorthwind that can be synchronized using the Windows Synchronization Manager.

   - Runs the snapshot agent for the publication.

2. When the script in **vbresolver_1.sql** is finished, merge the data using Windows Synchronization Manager. From the Windows **Start** menu, click **Start**, select **Programs**, select **Accessories**, and then click **Synchronize**.

3. After the Subscription has been synchronized using the Merge Agent, use SQL Query Analyzer to open the file \ToolsAndSamples\SampleResolver**vbresolver_2.sql**. When the script in **vbresolver_2.sql** is run, it will create an update conflict, which will then demonstrate the custom resolvers.

Web Programming

Exposing SQL Server Data to the Web with XML

Extensible Markup Language (XML) is a meta-markup language that provides a format for describing structured data. Unlike HTML, XML does not handle the presentation of data. Instead, the tags used to encompass the data are used to describe the data. This allows for a simplified passing of data between two programs. Microsoft® SQL Server™ 2000 introduces a set of features that enable XML support. This chapter introduces some of the XML features of SQL Server 2000, demonstrating the speed and ease of configuring SQL Server for XML support.

For information about the latest updates relating to XML support, see the XML Developer Center at http://msdn.microsoft.com/xml/.

Generating XML with the SELECT Statement

It is possible to retrieve XML formatted results using the Transact-SQL SELECT statement and the FOR XML clause. The modes within the FOR XML clause are:

- **FOR XML RAW**. Returns each row of the query result set in a generic row element with each non-null column as an attribute.

- **FOR XML AUTO**. Returns the query results as nested elements corresponding to the tables in the FROM clause of the select statement. By default, the AUTO mode maps the selected table columns as attributes of the element; however if the ELEMENTS option is enabled, the selected table columns become sub-elements of the table element.

- **FOR XML EXPLICIT**. Allows the query more control over the formatting of the returned XML result set. The query is designed to explicitly define the XML document returned; therefore, the author of the query becomes responsible for creating a well-formed XML document. This option allows for the most control over the query result set.

To generate an XML formatted result set

1. Start SQL Query Analyzer, and then connect to the **Northwind** database.

2. Execute the following query:

```
SELECT * from CUSTOMERS FOR XML RAW
```

SQL Server returns the result set in a single column named in part with a Globally Unique Identifier (GUID). Unlike the XML Technology preview, the results are not wrapped in the <root></root> tags that are needed for a properly formatted XML document. This allows multiple queries to produce one XML document.

Generating XML over the Internet

To exploit the full functionality of SQL Server XML support over the Internet, download and install the latest Web Release for SQL Server 2000 XML support from the Developer Center on MSDN. For more information, see http://msdn.microsoft.com/xml/.

Before accessing SQL Server over the Internet, a virtual directory must be set up on the computer running Internet Information Services (IIS) specifically for the XML queries.

To enable IIS for SQL Server XML support

1. On the **Start** menu, point to **Program Files**, click **Microsoft SQL Server**, and then click **Configure SQL XML Support in IIS**.

2. Expand your server, right-click the **Default Web Site** folder, select **New**, and then select **Virtual Directory**.

3. On the **General** tab of the properties page, type **XMLTest** for the virtual directory name.

4. For **Local Path**, type **C:\ reskit\xmltest**.

5. On the **Security** tab, enter a user name and password with administrative permissions in the **Northwind** database.

6. On the **Datasource** tab, enter the database server name, and then enter **Northwind** as the **Database name**.

7. On the **Settings** tab, select **Virtual URL Queries and Template Queries**.

8. On the **Virtual Names** tab, click **New**, and then add a new virtual name of queries with a type of template and a path to C:\reskit\xmltest.

9. Click **OK** to save your settings, and then close the Virtual Directory Management Tool.

Retrieving XML Formatted Data from SQL Server

You can query SQL Server 2000 and retrieve an XML formatted document in any of the following ways:

- Send SQL Server a query string in the HTTP request (this can be either a Transact-SQL SELECT statement or an X-Path query).

  Important security considerations should be considered when exposing your database to queries through the browser. Any user can execute a query within the user context of the username specified in the virtual root. If you choose to allow this type of access, make sure that you apply the appropriate permissions within the database for this user.

- Create template files that contain Transact-SQL or X-Path queries and attach XML Template (.xsl) files to format the XML document that is returned. (This is generally easier and more secure than sending a query string.)

To Retrieve XML using a Transact-SQL statement in a URL

1. In the Microsoft Internet Explorer address bar, type the following query, ensuring that the query is entered without any line breaks.

   ```
   http://localhost/xmltest?sql=SELECT+contactname,+phone+FROM+Customers+FOR+XML+
   raw&root=root
   ```

2. With your cursor still in the address bar, press ENTER to execute the query.

These results have been truncated for readability.

```
<root>
<row contactname="Maria Anders" phone="030-0074321" />
<row contactname="Ana Trujillo" phone="(5) 555-4729" />
<row contactname="Antonio Moreno" phone="(5) 555-3932" />
<row contactname="Thomas Hardy" phone="(171) 555-7788" />
<row contactname="Christina Berglund" phone="0921-12 34 65" />
<row contactname="Hanna Moos" phone="0621-08460" />
...
</root>
```

The **contactname** and **phone** columns named in the query are attributes of the row element. By using a JOIN and the FOR XML AUTO clause, the results appear as XML elements to form a more hierarchical structure.

To execute a query that generates AUTO formatted XML results

1. In Microsoft Internet Explorer, copy the following query into the address bar, ensuring that the query is entered without any line breaks.

   ```
   http://localhost/xmltest?sql=SELECT+customers.CustomerID,OrderID,OrderDate+FROM+Custo
   mers+INNER+JOIN+Orders+ON+customers.CustomerID=orders.CustomerID+ORDER+BY+customers.C
   ustomerID,OrderID+FOR+XML+AUTO&root=root
   ```

2. With your cursor still in the address bar, press ENTER to execute the query.

These results have been truncated for readability.

```
- <root>
- <Customers CustomerID="ALFKI">
<Orders OrderID="10643" OrderDate="1997-08-25T00:00:00" />
<Orders OrderID="10692" OrderDate="1997-10-03T00:00:00" />
<Orders OrderID="10702" OrderDate="1997-10-13T00:00:00" />
<Orders OrderID="10835" OrderDate="1998-01-15T00:00:00" />
<Orders OrderID="10952" OrderDate="1998-03-16T00:00:00" />
<Orders OrderID="11011" OrderDate="1998-04-09T00:00:00" />
</Customers>
- <Customers CustomerID="ANATR">
<Orders OrderID="10308" OrderDate="1996-09-18T00:00:00" />
<Orders OrderID="10625" OrderDate="1997-08-08T00:00:00" />
<Orders OrderID="10759" OrderDate="1997-11-28T00:00:00" />
<Orders OrderID="10926" OrderDate="1998-03-04T00:00:00" />
</Customers>
...
</root>
```

You can expand or collapse customer information to view the **Orders** elements of a particular customer.

Reserved Characters

There is a set of reserved characters for both URLs and XML documents. The following table lists each special character, its function, and the hexadecimal value that can be used to replace the character. Queries in a URL must replace the special characters that are used in URLs with their Hex Values.

Special Characters in URLs

Character	Use	Hex value
+	Indicates a space	%20
/	Separates directories and subdirectories	%2f
?	Separates the URL and the parameters	%3f
%	Specifies special characters	%25
#	Indicates bookmarks	%23
&	Separator between URL parameters	%26

Queries in XML Template documents must properly encode the special characters used in XML with the values listed in the following table.

Special Characters in XML

Special character	User	Entity encoding
<	Begins a tag	&gt;
>	Ends a tag	&lt;
"	Quotation mark	&quot;
'	Apostrophe	&apos;
&	Ampersand	&amp;

To execute an XML generating Transact-SQL query with special characters

1. In Microsoft Internet Explorer, enter the following query into the address bar, ensuring that the query is entered without any line breaks.

   ```
   http://localhost/xmltest?sql=SELECT+'<ROOT>';SELECT+DISTINCT+ContactTitle+FROM+Custom
   ers+WHERE+ContactTitle+LIKE+'Sa%25'+ORDER+BY+ContactTitle+FOR+XML+AUTO;SELECT+'</ROOT
   >'
   ```

2. With your cursor still in the address bar, press ENTER to execute the query.

In addition to the use of special characters, this query also manually generated the <ROOT></ROOT> tags by explicitly naming them.

Stored procedures can also be executed from the URL. They can be called either with the Transact-SQL syntax EXECUTE **sp_name** or with the ODBC syntax {call sp_name}. The following example shows how a stored procedure is created to dynamically publish the **Northwind** product catalog to third parties.

To execute a stored procedure using Internet Explorer

1. Start SQL Query Analyzer, and then connect to your server.

2. Ensure that the current **Query** window is pointing to the **Northwind** database, and then execute the following:

   ```
   CREATE PROCEDURE sp_rk_xmlCatalog
   as
   SELECT
       Category.CategoryName as 'Category',
   product.productName as 'Product',
   Product.UnitPrice as 'Price'
   FROM
   ```

```
Categories Category
INNER JOIN Products Product
ON Category.CategoryID = Product.CategoryID
Order by
Category.CategoryName,
Product.ProductName
FOR XML AUTO
```

3. In Microsoft Internet Explorer, enter the following query into the address bar, ensuring that the query is entered without any line breaks.

```
http://localhost/xmltest?sql=EXECUTE+sp_rk_XMLCatalog&root=root
```

4. With your cursor still in the address bar, press ENTER to execute the query.

A list of products in the **Northwind** database will appear, sorted by category. These results are truncated to enhance readability

```
<?xml version="1.0" encoding="utf-8" ?>
- <root>
- <Category Category="Beverages">
<Product Product="Chai" Price="80" />
<Product Product="Chang" Price="19" />
<Product Product="Chartreuse verte" Price="80" />
<Product Product="Côte de Blaye" Price="263.5" />
<Product Product="Guaraná Fantástica" Price="4.5" />
<Product Product="Ipoh Coffee" Price="46" />
<Product Product="Lakkalikööri" Price="80" />
<Product Product="Laughing Lumberjack Lager" Price="14" />
<Product Product="Outback Lager" Price="15" />
<Product Product="Rhönbräu Klosterbier" Price="7.75" />
<Product Product="Sasquatch Ale" Price="14" />
<Product Product="Steeleye Stout" Price="80" />
</Category>
   - <Category>
   ...
   </Category>
   ...
</root>
```

This stored procedure can be modified to take a parameter to allow for queries against the database for specific categories. A default parameter can be added to the stored procedure defined above, **sp_rk_xmlCatalog**. Next, the procedure can be called from Internet Explorer.

1. Execute the following code in SQL Query Analyzer.

```
ALTER PROCEDURE sp_rk_xmlCatalog
@CategoryName nvarchar(30) = '%'
as
```

```
SELECT
    Category.CategoryName as 'Category',
product.productName as 'Product',
Product.UnitPrice as 'Price'
FROM
Categories Category
INNER JOIN Products Product
ON Category.CategoryID = Product.CategoryID
WHERE
Category.CategoryName like @CategoryName
Order by
Category.CategoryName,
Product.ProductName
FOR XML AUTO
```

2. In Microsoft Internet Explorer, enter the following query into the address bar, and then press ENTER.

```
http://localhost/xmltest/?sql=EXECUTE+sp_rk_xmlCatalog+@CategoryName="Confections"&ro
ot=root
```

Only the products in the **Confections** category should be listed.

```
- <root>
- <Category Category="Confections">
      <Product Product="Chocolade" Price="12.75" />
      <Product Product="Gumbär Gummibärchen" Price="31.23" />
      <Product Product="Maxilaku" Price="20" />
      <Product Product="NuNuCa Nuß-Nougat-Creme" Price="14" />
      <Product Product="Pavlova" Price="17.45" />
      <Product Product="Schoggi Schokolade" Price="43.9" />
      <Product Product="Scottish Longbreads" Price="12.5" />
      <Product Product="Sir Rodney's Marmalade" Price="81" />
      <Product Product="Sir Rodney's Scones" Price="10" />
<Product Product="Tarte au sucre" Price="49.3" />
<Product Product="Teatime Chocolate Biscuits" Price="9.2" />
<Product Product="Valkoinen suklaa" Price="16.25" />
<Product Product="Zaanse koeken" Price="9.5" />
  </Category>
</root>
```

XML Templates

As queries grow in complexity, it becomes impractical to send them through URLs. Furthermore, you might not want to expose the queries in the address bar of the browser where they can be edited by third parties. Instead, queries can be stored in XML templates. Templates are well-formed XML documents that contain one or more SQL statements or X-Path queries. The XML virtual root for IIS must be specifically configured to use templates before they will work on your system.

To enable the XML virtual root within IIS to use templates, create a virtual name within the Virtual Directory that is enabled for XML templates.

To allow IIS virtual roots to use template files

1. On the **Start** menu, point to **Programs**, click **Microsoft SQL Server**, and then click **Configure SQL XML Support in IIS**.

2. Expand your server, and then click **Default Web Site**.

3. Right-click the XMLTest virtual directory, and then click **Properties**.

4. On the **Settings** tab, ensure that **Allow template queries** is selected.

5. On the **Virtual Names** tab, click **New** to add a virtual name for the templates folder.

   Use a virtual name for templates that is type **Template**, and then set the path to **C:\reskit\xmltest**.

6. Click **Save**, and then close the IIS Virtual Directory Manager for SQL Server.

The following steps show you how to create a simple XML template and access the result set using Internet Explorer.

To create an XML template that executes a simple Transact-SQL query

1. Paste the following code into your text editor:

```
<ROOT xmlns:sql="urn:schemas-microsoft-com:xml-sql">
<sql:query>
SELECT
SupplierID,
CompanyName,
ContactName,
Phone
FROM
suppliers
ORDER BY
CompanyName
FOR XML AUTO
</sql:query>
</ROOT>
```

2. Save the file as **C:\xmltest\suppliers.xml**.

3. In Microsoft Internet Explorer, enter the following query into the address bar, and then press ENTER.

```
http://localhost/xmltest/templates/suppliers.xml
```

The URL includes the \templates directory even though the template is stored directly in the xmltest directory. This is because it is mapped to the suppliers.xml template through the templates virtual name that was created earlier.

Using EXPLICIT Mode

EXPLICIT mode brings an additional level of complexity to a query, but allows for much more control over the XML document that is generated by the query. EXPLICIT mode requires that the query produce a result set in the universal table format. The universal table fully describes the resulting XML document.

The following table demonstrates the logical structuring of the data within a query that returns Products, Categories, and Product Details such as Price and Supplier.

Tag	Parent	Category!1 !name	Product!2 !Name	Product!2 !Supplier!Element	Product!2 !Price!Element
1	NULL	Beverages	NULL	NULL	NULL
2	1	NULL	Chai	Exotic Liquids	80
2	1	NULL	Chang	Exotic Liquids	19
1	NULL	Condiments	NULL	NULL	NULL
2	1	NULL	Aniseed Syrup	Exotic Liquids	10

The column names are encoded using XML generic identifiers and attribute names. These names are specified as:

ElementName!TagNumber!AttributeName!Directive

To learn more about this syntax and the EXPLICIT mode, see SQL Server Books Online.

To return the Northwind store catalog using EXPLICIT mode

1. Paste the following code into your text editor:

```
SELECT
1       as 'Tag',
null       as 'Parent',
Category.CategoryName as 'Category!1!Name',
null       as 'Product!2!Name',
null       as 'ProductDetail!3!Supplier',
null       as 'ProductDetail!3!Price',
null       as 'ProductDetail!3!NumberSold'
FROM
categories Category

UNION ALL
SELECT
2,
1,
Category.CategoryName,
```

```
Product.ProductName,
null,
null,
null
FROM
categories Category
INNER JOIN products Product
on Category.CategoryID = Product.CategoryID

UNION ALL
SELECT
3,
2,
Category.CategoryName,
Product.ProductName,
null,
Product.UnitPrice,
null
FROM
categories Category
INNER JOIN products Product
on Category.CategoryID = Product.CategoryID
INNER JOIN suppliers s
on product.supplierid = s.supplierid

UNION ALL
SELECT
3,
2,
Category.CategoryName,
Product.ProductName,
s.CompanyName,
null,
null
FROM
categories Category
INNER JOIN products Product
on Category.CategoryID = Product.CategoryID
INNER JOIN suppliers s
on product.supplierid = s.supplierid

UNION ALL
SELECT
3,
2,
```

```
Category.CategoryName,
Product.ProductName,
null,
null,
sum(quantity)
FROM
categories Category
INNER JOIN products Product
on Category.CategoryID = Product.CategoryID
INNER JOIN suppliers s
on product.supplierid = s.supplierid
LEFT JOIN [order details] od
ON product.productid = od.productid
group by category.categoryname,product.productname,s.companyname
ORDER BY
'Category!1!Name',
'Product!2!Name',
'ProductDetail!3!Supplier',
'ProductDetail!3!Price',
'ProductDetail!3!NumberSold'
FOR XML EXPLICIT
```

2. Save the file as **Catalog.xml**.

3. In Microsoft Internet Explorer, enter the following query into the address bar, and then press ENTER.

```
http://localhost/xmltest/templates/catalog.xml
```

The results are hierarchical; each piece of information is stored as an XML element instead of an attribute to an element. Elements on the same level, such as those owned by the Product Element, can have different attributes, such as Price and Supplier.

```
- <ROOT xmlns:sql="urn:schemas-microsoft-com:xml-sql">
- <Category Name="Beverages">
- <Product Name="Chai">
        <ProductDetail Price="80" />
        <ProductDetail Supplier="Exotic Liquids" />
    </Product>
- <Product Name="Chang">
        <ProductDetail Price="19" />
        <ProductDetail Supplier="Exotic Liquids" />
    </Product>
    ...
  </Category>
  ...
</root>
```

XSL Style Sheets

If the XML formatted information will be displayed directly to the user, you can use XSL Style Sheets (XSL) to format the information. You can also use XSL to filter the XML document so that only certain information is displayed.

For example, if you are publishing a list of all of your employees, you might want to display their phone numbers internally and not externally to the public. The following example creates an XML template that returns employee information and two XSL style sheets, one to format information for external use and another for internal use.

Save the following XML template as **EmpList.xml**.

```
<?xml version ='1.0' encoding='UTF-8'?>
 <root xmlns:sql='urn:schemas-microsoft-com:xml-sql'>
   <sql:query>
      SELECT FirstName, LastName, Extension 'Extension' FROM Employees FOR XML AUTO
   </sql:query>
</root>
```

View the data from the XML template in Internet Explorer by loading http://localhost/xmltest/templates/emplist.xml. The attributes in the Employee Element are: FirstName, LastName, and Extension.

The next example creates a style sheet to format the results into an HTML document. The style sheet performs recursion on the returned XML document for all Employee elements and creates a new row in an HTML table to store the attributes.

Save the following XSL style sheet in your XMLtest directory as **empInternal.xsl**.

```
<?xml version='1.0' encoding='UTF-8'?>
 <xsl:stylesheet xmlns:xsl="http://www.w3.org/1999/XSL/Transform" version="1.0">

    <xsl:template match = '*'>
       <xsl:apply-templates />
    </xsl:template>
    <xsl:template match = 'Employees'>
      <TR>
        <TD><xsl:value-of select = '@FirstName' /></TD>
        <TD><B><xsl:value-of select = '@LastName' /></B></TD>
        <TD><xsl:value-of select = '@Extension' /></TD>
      </TR>
    </xsl:template>
    <xsl:template match = '/'>
      <HTML>
        <HEAD>
           <STYLE>th { background-color: #CCCCCC }</STYLE>
        </HEAD>
        <BODY>
```

```
    <TABLE border='1' style='width:300;'>
      <TR><TH colspan='3'>Employees</TH></TR>
      <TR><TH >First name</TH><TH>Last name</TH><TH>Extension</TH></TR>
      <xsl:apply-templates select = 'root' />
    </TABLE>
   </BODY>
  </HTML>
 </xsl:template>
</xsl:stylesheet>
```

View the formatted results of the XML template in Internet Explorer by loading
http://localhost/xmltest/templates/emplist.xml?xsl=empInternal.xsl. The style sheet is applied to the XML
template from the URL. Different versions of this Web page can be displayed to different types of users
by applying different style sheets to the same XML.

The next example creates an XSL Style Sheet to post employee names externally, and without the phone
numbers.

Save the following style sheet as **EmpInternal.xsl**.

```
<?xml version='1.0' encoding='UTF-8'?>
 <xsl:stylesheet xmlns:xsl="http://www.w3.org/1999/XSL/Transform" version="1.0">

    <xsl:template match = '*'>
        <xsl:apply-templates />
    </xsl:template>
    <xsl:template match = 'Employees'>
      <TR>
        <TD><xsl:value-of select = '@FirstName' /></TD>
        <TD><B><xsl:value-of select = '@LastName' /></B></TD>
      </TR>
    </xsl:template>
    <xsl:template match = '/'>
      <HTML>
        <HEAD>
           <STYLE>th { background-color: #CCCCCC }</STYLE>
        </HEAD>
        <BODY>
         <TABLE border='1' style='width:300;'>
           <TR><TH colspan='3'>Employees</TH></TR>
           <TR><TH >First name</TH><TH>Last name</TH></TR>
           <xsl:apply-templates select = 'root' />
         </TABLE>
        </BODY>
      </HTML>
    </xsl:template>
</xsl:stylesheet>
```

View the new results in Internet Explorer by loading
http://localhost/xmltest/templates/emplist.xml?xsl=empExternal.xsl.

Although the same XML file was used in this example, the results do not show the extension column.

For more information about XML and SQL Server see the following:

- "XML and Internet Support" in SQL Server Books Online

- http://msdn.microsoft.com/xml/

- http://msdn.microsoft.com/sqlserver/

English Query Best Practices

English Query is a set of tools that database administrators, application developers, and Web professionals can use to develop a natural-language interface to a database. Using English Query applications, users can perform ad hoc database queries using English questions or statements.

English Query provides a robust environment for developing an English Query model. However, because databases tend to be unique and users ask unique questions, creating a model that answers users' questions can be a complex process.

This chapter provides best practices for starting, expanding, and deploying an English Query application using the tools provided with Microsoft® SQL Server™ 2000.

An Overview of English Query

English Query works by receiving a question or statement in English and translating the English into Transact-SQL. For example, a user might submit, "Count the customers." English Query translates the statement into Transact-SQL, such as:

```
SELECT count(*) as "count"
FROM dbo.Customers
```

Note The exact Transact-SQL generated depends on the English Query model.

In an application that includes English Query, the English Query engine performs the translation. The engine uses a domain file (.eqd), which contains a model of the database. The model contains information specific to the database being queried by the application, including the database schema, a semantic abstraction layer that is built over the schema, and the mapping between them.

In the model, tables and fields are represented by **entities** and the joins are represented by **relationships**. The entities and relationships defined in a model allow English Query to translate English into Transact-SQL.

The English Query Project Wizard can automatically define some entities and relationships based on database structure. Developers define other entities and relationships by using the English Query development environment. A complete and well-designed model will allow an English Query application to do a better job of translating questions into queries.

A Simple Example

The following illustration shows a simple database, which is based on the **Northwind** sample database. The database contains three user-defined tables: **customers**, **orders**, and **products**. Both the **customers** and **products** tables are joined to the **orders** table.

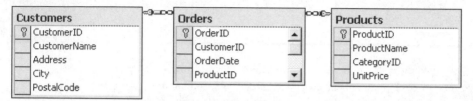

Using an English Query project wizard called the SQL Project Wizard is the easiest way to start an SQL-based project. For this simple database, the SQL Project Wizard initializes the English Query model with the set of entities and relationships shown in the following table.

Entities	Relationships
customer	*customers_have_customer_addresses*
customer_address	*customers_have_customer_cities*
customer_city	*customers_have_customer_ids*
customer_id	*customer_names_are_the_names_of_customers*
customer_name	*customers_have_customer_postal_codes*
customer_postal_code	*customers_have_products*
order	*orders_have_order_dates*
order_date	*order_ids_are_the_unique_ids_of_orders*
order_id	*orders_have_customers*
product	*orders_have_products*
product_id	*products_have_product_ids*
product_name	*product_names_are_the_names_of_products*
product_unit_price	*products_have_product_unit_prices*

Note When using the SQL Project Wizard with a complete database, the wizard creates many other entities and relationships.

Notice that there are relationships between each table entity (such as **customer**) and the columns within that table (such as **customer_id**). A **customer_id** is a trait of a **customer**, so the relationship is phrased as *customers have customer_ids*. Also note there are relationships between table entities when a join exists between them: *orders have customers*, *orders have products,* and *customers have products*. One of the relationships, *customers have products*, must be modified to be useful. A more useful phrasing for this relationship is *customers buy products*.

Here are two sample questions that can be answered by this simple model:

- "List the customers."

- "Which orders have the product Chai?"

However, the model cannot answer the following variations of these questions:

- "List the customers and their IDs."

  The word "ID" is not defined in the model.

- "Which orders contain Chai?"

  The verb "contain" is not associated with any entity or relationship.

Refining entity and relationship definitions, as well as creating additional relationships and phrasings, will allow this model to answer these questions and many more.

Before You Begin

To become familiar with English Query, work through the tutorials that are provided when English Query is installed. The tutorials introduce the English Query development environment and show how to start a project, how to create entity relationships, and how to deploy the solution to the Web.

English Query provides four tutorials:

- Creating a Basic SQL Model

- Creating a Complex Model

- Creating an OLAP Model

- Deploying the Application

To access the tutorials

- On the **Start** menu, point to **Programs/Microsoft SQL Server/English Query**, and then click **English Query Tutorials**.

Starting a Basic Model

Once you are familiar with the English Query development environment, starting a basic model is easy if you prepare your database and follow a few guidelines. The following best practices will help you successfully start an English Query model.

Prepare Your Database

When you start an English Query project, your most important consideration is to ensure that your database is well designed and ready to be imported into the English Query environment. If your database is designed well, the English Query wizards can do much of the preliminary development work for you. If your database is poorly designed, getting the expected results can be difficult.

- Normalize the database.

    Applying normalization rules to a database ensures each table represents a single entity, each column defines one unique attribute, and each row represents one instance of the entity. English Query can best translate English into Transact-SQL when a database is normalized, and results generated from a normalized database will be more accurate.

    If you do not own the database or cannot normalize the database for other reasons, consider using views to solve some normalization problems. For example, if an **orders** table exists for each financial quarter, create a view from a UNION of all **orders** tables, and then define relationships using the entity for the view.

    For more information about how the normalization rules apply to English Query and how to use views to solve normalization problems, see "SQL Database Normalization Rules" in SQL Server Books Online.

- Define primary and foreign keys.

    English Query recognizes joins based on primary and foreign keys, and establishes relationships for these joins with the wizards. You can define joins in the English Query environment, but defining the keys and joins in the database before starting a project helps keep the database and model synchronized.

- Use meaningful names.

    The Project Wizard creates entity names based on the table and column names. Often these names are abbreviations. To make developing and using the model easier, it is good practice either to use meaningful names in the database or to rename all entities with meaningful names. For example, "**EEs** work in **ETs**" is not as meaningful as "**Employees** work in **EmployeeTerritories**". You can also provide synonyms for the entity names at the same time.

Start with the SQL Project Wizard

After you have prepared the database, use the SQL Project Wizard to start a SQL project. The wizard makes project setup and initial development easy. You simply follow the wizard's screens, selecting which server, database, and tables to use, and the wizard builds the model based on the database structure.

Edit Entity Properties

Review all entities that are created by the SQL Project Wizard. The wizard will guess each entity's properties where it can, and leave others blank by default. For this reason, you should verify all the entities' properties in your English Query model and, at the same time, further define the entities. For descriptions of the fields on each tab and dialog box, click **Help**.

Formulate and Test Typical Questions

After you have edited entity properties, the basic model created with the wizard should answer many questions, especially those regarding a single table or simple join. However, this simple model cannot answer all questions.

To discover the questions that the model will answer, generate a list of typical questions. If multiple groups use the database (such as executives, sales managers, production staff, and human resources staff), devise questions that each of those groups might ask.

Once you have a list of questions, you can test individual questions using the Model Test tool, which automatically appears after each project build. Click **View Results** to see query results. Click the **Analysis** tab to view the entities and relationships used to answer the question.

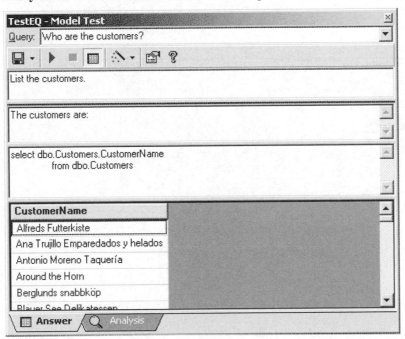

Click **Save** to save the current question and its results to a regression file (.eqr). This regression file can be used to retest the question, and can be used as the source of sample questions in your final English Query application.

Use the Suggestion Wizard

To answer questions that are not answered during testing, you will have to continue to improve your model by adding or modifying relationships. An easy way to build relationships that answer specific questions is to use the Suggestion Wizard provided in the Model Test tool.

When a question is not answered, click **Suggestion Wizard** on the Model Test toolbar. The Suggestion Wizard will direct you to provide information for the question.

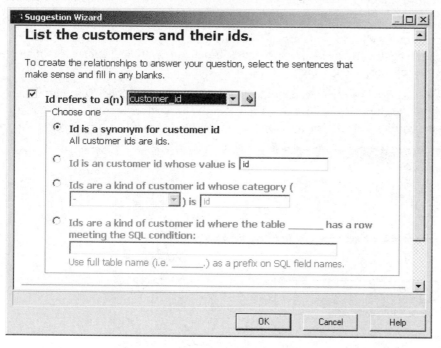

After English Query modifies the model, test the question again to ensure the results are what you expect.

Add Help Text

Each entity and relationship in an English Query model can contain help text. Users can access the text to learn about the model, or to obtain any kind of helper information you want to provide.

To add help text, open the **Entity** dialog box by double-clicking an entity.

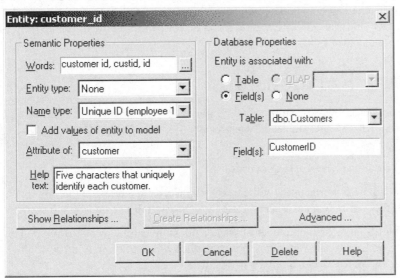

In the illustration, the help text "Five characters that uniquely identify each customer" describes the **customer_id** entity. If a user submits the question, "What is a customer id?" English Query will return the help text.

Expanding a Model

An English Query application created using the SQL Project Wizard and the Suggestion Wizard can answer many user questions. However, to create a comprehensive solution that answers a broad range of user questions, even those that you do not plan for, you must go beyond what the wizards offer. You must develop a comprehensive set of relationships that fully describes the database model and how the database objects are related.

As with basic models, creating a comprehensive set of relationships requires knowledge of the database and of questions people will ask. Forming entity relationships that answer specific questions or a wide range of questions requires at least two more skills:

- Knowledge of English language semantics

  If it has been a long time since you diagrammed a sentence, brush up on the basics, including subjects, verbs, adjectives, prepositional phrases, and direct objects.

- Knowledge of the English Query development environment

  For information about the dialog box options, click **Help** on each dialog box. SQL Server Books Online contains information that can help you decide when to use each option, and often provides examples. The English Query tutorials also are a good resource for learning how to use the English Query development environment.

Create Good Entity Relationships

An English Query model is only as good as its entities and relationships. To create good relationships for a model, think about how users will ask questions and what results the users expect. Good entity relationships:

- Contain words that people will use when asking questions.

  Try to define the relationship with words users will enter. If the words in a question are not recognized in the model, the user may receive a response like "Sorry, I didn't understand that."

  Defining synonyms for words increase the number of ways a question can be asked. Both the **Entities** and **Relationships** dialog boxes support synonyms. You can click a word box to add your own synonyms, or click the **...** button to select synonyms from a list.

- Avoid ambiguity.

  Ambiguous relationships decrease the chance that users will get consistent results. Ambiguity is often introduced when multiple relationships serve similar purposes. For example, if a **customer** table contains **city**, **state**, and **region** columns, the following relationships introduce ambiguity:

  - *Customers live in cities*

  - *Customers live in states*

  - *Customers live in regions*

  When a user asks, "Where does customer 10101 live?" what will the answer be? If the desired answer is the city, try the following relationships:

  - *Customers live in cities*

  - *Cities are in states*

  - *States are in regions*

- Help users obtain the desired result set.

  Most databases contain more information than a user wants to see at one time. If a user enters "List the orders" into an English Query application, does the user really want to see all orders or just the orders for today, this week, or this year? Once you define what information should be provided to the user by default, you can add these defaults to the English Query model.

  If the desired result set for orders contains only today's orders, you can easily specify a default date for questions about orders. For a relationship such as *orders have order_dates*, open the **Relationship** dialog box, select **order_date** in the **When** box, and then select **Today** in the **Default Date** box.

  If users really want to see all the orders, they can ask the question more specifically. The statement "List all the orders" will show all orders, regardless of the default setting.

First Create Broad Relationships, and Then Work on Specific Questions

When you create a model, you probably know how several database objects relate to each other. For example, you might know that *customers buy products*, *suppliers sell products*, and *some products are discontinued*. Creating these types of broad relationships, as well as fully defining entities, will allow the model to translate many questions that can be answered by the database.

After the broad relationships have been defined, test the model to see what questions it does and does not answer. For the questions the model does not answer, work on modifying entities and relationships to answer these questions, creating new entities and relationships if necessary.

When modifying the model to answer specific questions, try simple adjustments first. Create synonyms, define default conditions, or add lookup table data to the model before making several complex changes.

Retest Questions

The process of building a model can change the results of question. To find these changes, make use of the regression file in the Model Test tool. When a question works, save it. Both the question and the results are saved to the regression file.

After you have saved questions to the regression file, periodically retest the questions. In the Project Explorer, right-click the .eqr file and click **Run Regression**. When the regression test is finished, right-click the .eqr file, and click **View Differences**. Any differences in answers will appear in a Regression Differences window.

For "Free-Form" Text Searches, Enable Full-Text Search

Many databases contain description or comment text fields. These fields may contain just about anything, and querying these fields using Transact-SQL may not generate the desired results. Full-text search provides a solution to this problem. Advantages of full-text search include:

- Searches may work much faster than SQL table scans because they can take advantage of full-text indexes.

- Searches can retrieve more information because the full-text searches support alternate tenses, singular and plural forms, phrases, and words near each other (proximity searches).

- Results are ordered by relevance.

A full-text index is not the same as an SQL index. Each table can have only one full-text index. The index can be administered through the database but is stored in a file system. For more information, see "Full-Text Indexes" in SQL Server Books Online.

To enable full-text search for an English Query application

1. In SQL Server Enterprise Manager or using Transact-SQL, enable full-text indexing for the database.

2. In SQL Server Enterprise Manager or using Transact-SQL, enable full-text indexing for the table. During this step, choose the columns to include in the index.

3. In the English Query development environment, enable full-text searching for each full-text column using the **SQL** tab.

For more information about using full-text search with English Query, see "Enabling Full-Text Search for an English Query Model" in SQL Server Books Online.

For Data Analysis Questions, Create an OLAP Model

While creating an English Query model, you may find that not all of the questions are answered using the current database. Some questions require data analysis. For example, a question such as "What region sells the most Chai?" may be a data analysis question, not the type of question easily answered by a basic model. The user may really want aggregated data, possibly for multiple regions.

SQL Server Analysis Services (previously called OLAP) is a solution for organizing and aggregating data for quick analysis. Data is organized into multidimensional cubes. For example, a sales cube may provide aggregated data for sales by customer, city, and region, separating data into total sales and sales by product or category. For more information about Analysis Services, see "Analysis Services Overview" in SQL Server Books Online.

An Analysis Services database contains cubes, dimension tables, and fact tables, and is separate from the database that contains the original data. Therefore, in an English Query OLAP model, relationships are between cubes and the cube's dimension and fact tables.

To create an OLAP model

1. Create and test the Analysis Services database. For more information, see "Administering Analysis Services" in SQL Server Books Online.

2. Use the OLAP Wizard to create an English Query model for the database. Instead of selecting tables for the model, you select OLAP cubes.

3. Formulate typical questions and test the OLAP model.

4. Expand the model by modifying entities and relationships and then creating new relationships.

A mixed English Query model supports access to both the original database and the Analysis Services database. Using mixed models, you can ask questions that can be answered by either model, which can speed up the retrieval for questions that do not require aggregation of data.

For more information about using Analysis Services with English Query, see "Analysis Services in English Query" in SQL Server Books Online.

Deploying an English Query Solution

You can deploy an English Query application in several ways, including within a Microsoft Visual Basic® or Microsoft Visual C++® application and on a Web page running on Microsoft Internet Information Service (IIS). On the Web, the interface to English Query is provided by a set of Microsoft Active Server Pages (ASP).

Note If you have built an English Query solution for earlier versions of SQL Server and you want to use the solution with a SQL Server 2000 database, the English Query domain files must be rebuilt.

Use the Sample Applications

When you install English Query, you have the option of installing several sample applications and client interface examples. These examples are very useful when deploying an application. By borrowing source code from these examples, you can save hours or days of development work. Sample applications for Microsoft C++, Microsoft Visual Basic, and Active Server Pages (ASP) are installed to the \Program Files\Microsoft English Query\Samples directory.

If you are deploying a Web solution, the easiest way to deploy your application is to use the **Deploy to Web** command on the **Project** menu. When you deploy your project to the Web, several files are copied to the Web server. By developing an interface using these files, you can customize the English Query application and update the English Query model from the English Query development environment.

Note If you are deploying an English Query solution to the Web, you must install the full version of Microsoft Visual InterDev® before you can deploy the project. Also, the server you deploy the Web files to must be running Microsoft IIS 4.0 or later, and must have Microsoft FrontPage® extensions installed.

Provide Sample Questions for Users

When you deploy your English Query application, give users sample questions. If you simply have a box labeled "Ask a Question", users might not know how to get started. Sample questions will help users learn what they can do with your English Query application.

When you test a model using the Model Test tool, you can save sample questions to the regression file (.eqr). When you deploy the application to the Web, the questions in this file appear on the application's Web page.

Provide Question Builder

The sample applications contain Question Builder, a Microsoft ActiveX® control that exposes the English Query model. When Question Builder is integrated into an application, the interface allows users to explore what information is available to them, and to build questions based on the model.

To use Question Builder, users select a combination of entities and relationships. English Query then displays a list of questions that can be asked about that combination. Users can submit a questions as-is, or can modify the question before submitting it to the English Query engine.

In both Web and Microsoft Windows® applications, the user is presented with a multi-pane interface, as shown in the following illustration.

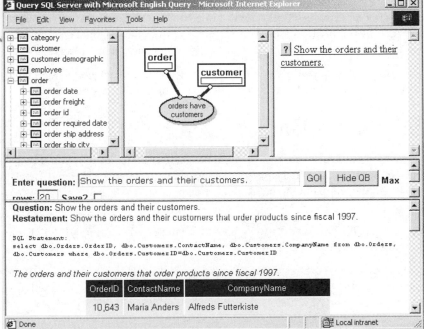

At the top of the screen, the first pane provides the schema for the English Query model. The second pane is a workspace in which users can drag entities and form questions. The third pane provides a list of questions users can ask about objects selected in the second pane. The lower panes provide the question and results interface.

The sample applications contain Question Builder, so you can see how Question Builder works and use the source code to integrate Question Builder into your applications. For more information, see "Adding Question Builder to an English Query Application" in SQL Server Books Online.

Maintaining and Improving a Model

When a database schema is modified, English Query applications must be updated as well. The English Query application depends greatly on the database schema. If the English Query model and the database schema are not the same, questions may not be answered correctly or may not be answered at all.

After you deploy your English Query application, you may discover it does not answer enough questions. By tracking which questions are not answered, you can improve your model to meet user demands.

Keep the Model Up-To-Date

When you initially create an English Query model, you might not include all tables. Or, you might want to add views or new tables to the model at a later time. In either case, you can add tables and views to your model with the **Import Table** command on the **Model** menu.

When you modify a table in the database, such as adding columns, the changes are not automatically reflected in the English Query model. The easiest way to update the table is from the **SQL** tab. Right-click the modified table, and then click **Refresh Table**.

After you add a table or view, or after you refresh a table, you can use the wizard to create new entities and relationships. Right-click the table or view and click **Create Relationships**. The wizard will display entities and relationships for the table or view and its columns. Click **OK** to add the entities and relationships to the model.

Use Logs to Improve Results

English Query may provide good answers to all the questions you ask. But how do you know if user questions are being answered? To find out, you will need to build some functionality into your application for reporting and finding problems:

- For standard applications, provide a way for a user to send feedback, such as an e-mail address or Web form in which users can enter problem reports.

- For Web applications, a user-driven solution is built into each application deployed using the English Query **Deploy to Web** tools. When you deploy the application, a log file named Problems.txt is copied to the Web server. When English Query cannot generate a Transact-SQL query, a "Report as Problem Question" link appears on the Web page. When a user clicks this link, the question is added to Problems.txt.

- Another solution that is built into Web applications is the ability to log all questions to a table in the database. The first time a question is asked in the deployed Web solution, a table is created called **EQLog**. The first question and all subsequent questions asked using the Web-deployed application are logged in this table along with a response type, which indicates if the question was successfully answered or not. Periodically review the data in this table and improve the model to answer the questions that failed.

   Note   The **EQLog** table is owned by the run-time Web application user account. The first time a question is asked, the Web user account needs permission to create a table in the database. After the table is created, remove the permission to create a table and give the Web user account INSERT permission for the **EQLog** table.

Troubleshooting

During your testing phase or after the application is finished, you may discover that specific questions are not being answered correctly. Because database designs and ad hoc questions are unique, it is impossible to give instructions on how to fix specific problems. Here is one troubleshooting methodology:

- On the **Analysis** tab of the **Model Test** Window, look at the relationships being used by English Query. A setting in one of those entities or relationships may be causing the problem. Or, you may need to create another relationship.

- Look at the Transact-SQL generated by English Query. The Transact-SQL can show you how English Query is generating results. For example, if a question returns the necessary data along with unwanted data, the problem may an outer join. You can disable outer joins for individual joins on the **SQL** tab, or for the entire model in the **Project Properties** dialog box.

- Look at how English Query has rephrased the question. If the rephrased question is very different from the original question, the phrasing of the question may be the problem. You may need to define synonyms, or there may be ambiguous relationships in the model.

- Ask the question another way. If a question is answered when asked one way, but not another, the difference can give you hints about what is going wrong. For example, you may need to add synonyms for key words.

Designing for Peformance and Scalability

The Data Tier: An Approach to Database Optimization

This chapter describes a basic approach to optimizing the *data tier*, a concept that is based on the distributed Web-based architecture for the .NET Enterprise Servers (which includes Microsoft® SQL Server™ 2000). The data tier encompasses the database server as a whole, a system comprised of several interrelated layers: the SQL code, the database design, the data storage components on the physical disk, and the server configuration. Given this broad definition, the data tier brings into play three activities that had previously be treated as separate concerns: design, performance tuning, and hardware sizing (capacity planning). In this chapter, you will learn how all three activities can be brought together into one approach. The particular aspects of optimizing the data tier that are described in this chapter are understanding the cycle of optimization, evaluating system performance, and making strategic hardware choices.

A New Approach

Optimization of any system obeys the Pareto Principle, which states that only a vital few factors are responsible for producing most of the problems. This is also known as the 80/20 Rule, meaning that most of the problems in a system result from just a few causes. Specifically, the biggest optimizations will be effected at the business process end of a system, then the application code, the database schema, and physical data storage, and the server configuration.

In a business environment that does not yet have a unified approach to solving business problems by combining business process with technology, the system administrators would tend to apply optimization to the parts of the system that were within reach. In fact, prior to the architectural enhancements made in SQL Server version 7.0 and SQL Server 2000, this was the standard approach. The logical approach seemed to be building on the server as a foundation, then the database configuration parameters, and then working upward to the parts that were less easy to reach because they involve a larger group of people for the changes required. This approach was heavily weighted toward the server, as shown here:

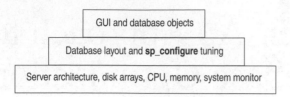

However, applying the Pareto Principle reveals that this approach is not going to produce the best resolution to the problem, in part because SQL Server has become a more advanced product. As SQL Server has changed over time, the central focus of optimization has shifted toward application tuning. The database administrator (DBA) can focus on areas that will have more impact (database and application design), without needing to spend so much time on areas that have less effect long term (server hardware and configuration).

The following diagram illustrates the data tier elements, and an approach in optimization moving from left to right:

The Data Tier

1. Data components	2. Code components	3. Storage components	4. Server components
Physical structure	Layer of abstraction:	Filegroups	sp_configure
Indexes	Stored procedures	Disk storage	
Tables	Functions		
Indexed views	Standard views		

————————— **Order of optimization** —————————▶

Ideally, all four columns must be addressed, or the application will not be tuned optimally. In cases where tuning must be approached sequentially, then the order of effort becomes extremely significant. The elements on the left are the most difficult, but they also give the largest rewards in terms of performance. For example, while some gains in performance may be achieved by tuning the environmental settings (**sp_configure**), this approach will not reach the same level of performance that could be reached by tuning the code elements. Only large systems, in terms of concurrency or transaction volume, need to worry about elements three and four, the storage components and server components. The new approach is more focused on optimization as a cycle.

Optimization Cycle

Optimizing the data tier is a process with defined steps. It is important to remember that a system changes over time due to gradual shifts in usage patterns, transaction load, application or optimization changes, and hardware upgrades. Optimization is a cycle. To stay on top of it, keep a schedule. Optimization or maintenance updates can be included in the regular release cycle, or can be implemented separately. It is better to have a scheduled plan, rather than waiting for a production issue to require one

The first step in optimizing your system is an obvious one, but bears mentioning: Look at what you have. Observe and make records of the following information in relation to the server, so you will have a very clear picture of your environment before you begin to make changes to it.

- What is the formal service level agreement (SLA), if any, for this system (everything from hardware to software)? An SLA should include at a minimum the required uptime and usage hours of the system as a whole, the transaction load that must be supported, and the response time windows for emergency situations. Once you have located (or created) an SLA, observe if the current system performance falls within its bounds—you might save yourself wasted work by focusing on what the users believe to be important.

- What applications touch the data? There may be several using the same tables, or separate tables within the same database. What other things rely on the data? For example, is the data exported nightly to a data mart? Does some data get transferred to other application systems? Also, find out if this is a third-party application or custom-built. This will tell you how much you can change in the database.

- What is the basic design of the system and how is database interaction handled? Do they use ADO or OLE DB? Do they maintain open connections or get a connection each time (as from a Web page)? Do they directly access the tables to run pass-through queries? Do they use stored procedures for all or some of the queries? How is security controlled?

- Open the database you are going to be focusing on. Note how many of each object the database has.

- How many and how large are the databases (and tables/indexes) on the server? How many users are there, and how many of them are online?

- Check **sp_configure** for any discrepancies from the defaults. Make a note of each and the reasons for the change. For more information, see "Setting Configuration Options" in SQL Server Books Online.

- Where are the data files located? Transaction log files? **tempdb**?

- How many spindles (disks) do you have? How are they laid out, and what is the RAID level? If you have external storage, note the cache settings, and which channels are associated with which drives.

- Where are the results of running the **sqldiag** tool stored for easy access? A great deal of information about the server can be obtained by scheduling **sqldiag** on a regular basis. Save the output to compare server changes over time with other issues that arise on the system. The output from **sqldiag** is also usually required if you need to call in a support issue. For more information, see "sqldiag Utility" in SQL Server Books Online.

- What other server software running along with SQL Server? How many instances of SQL Server are using the same server resources?

- What version, service pack, and hotfixes are you running, for both the operating system and SQL Server?

- Check the drivers for all of your hardware, to make sure that you are using the most recent version.

Compile this information for each of your applications in advance. Store it to a standard place across for every server. For example, you might make a standard directory (C:\SQLAdmin) on all servers and store all of the database administration report output there. This information could be collected onto one server by a later process, and imported into a SQL Server database for trend analysis. For ease of administration, make the data available on a Web site for the database administration team. The point is that the material should be easily accessible.

In a crisis situation, you may rely on this information to help you make a decision on what to fix. Do not try to troubleshoot as your record; just make notes for now. For items that may require involving other staff in other groups, make a note that you are awaiting the information and move on. Do not spend an excessive amount of time on this; the object of this stage is simply for you to get a clear idea of the bigger picture. Simply keep all this information in mind, and move on to the next step.

For information about tracking server and application information, search for "Configuration Management" and "Process Model for Operations" at http://www.microsoft.com/TechNet/.

Evaluating the Situation

In any situation, you must collect as much data as is feasible given your resources and the time you have. Once you have the data, analyze it for potential opportunities to correct problems or to optimize based on usage patterns. It is best to collect performance statistics over time, so you can analyze the system patterns, and make well-informed decisions on changes to be made. The pattern of statistics over time is called a baseline. The process of collecting baseline data can be started at any point, regardless of your current state of optimization (or lack thereof). The point is that the data becomes useful for analysis over time, meaning as aggregate data.

In addition to collecting system statistics, and configuration information, remember to talk to the users of the system. Often, they can easily identify which parts of the system are slow, and whether they are slow at certain times. This helps in two ways. First it helps you focus on problem areas more quickly, and it also helps you fix the problems that are having the most impact.

- After you have collected information on all the parts of the data tier, you are in a better position to judge what settings to use in monitoring for optimization opportunities. Several performance monitoring tools are discussed later in this chapter.

Unless your system is completely new, you should collect data on the production system first. Then, if possible, test potential changes on a test system. Create a script (either an SQL script, or a list of steps to perform) and use this to test the implementation process of your proposed changes on the test server. Using the same settings used to monitor production, monitor the same scenarios on the test server.

After confirming that your proposed changes look good, schedule the production implementation. It is important to note that even in a crisis situation, you should observe this step. In a crisis, your "implementation schedule" might simply consist of notifying your change control department and your help desk of the impending change and what issues you expect to occur during the change process (for example, downtime, or slow connections).

After implementation, you should promptly follow up by repeating the same monitoring processes you used to observe the problem. This will confirm (or refute) that your performance or problem-solving changes have had the desired effect, or that any changes made for the sake of administrative purposes have not caused a problem. Keep in mind during this confirmation period that, even with the best planning, you may find that another problem has arisen, either as a result of your changes, or because a secondary underlying issue is now made clearer in the absence of the first issue. Optimization is an ongoing process.

Performance Monitoring Tools

The following tools can help in locating problems during production hours:

- SQL Profiler
- System Stored Procedures (**sp_lock**, **sp_who2**, and so on)
- System Monitor in Microsoft Windows® 2000 (known also as Performance Monitor)

The primary benefit of using these tools to monitor performance is to learn from the data you collect over time. Therefore, it is essential to import the data into SQL tables, create aggregate tables to focus on specific details, and then analyze the information for patterns. One good way to do this is to use SQL Server Analysis Services. When you are able to see performance on a larger scale, then you will be able to identify which parts of the system you can apply the Pareto Principle to. In other words, you will easily be able to identify where you can make changes that will have the largest effect on the system.

SQL Profiler

SQL Profiler is useful for observing events in a SQL Server environment. It can be scoped to many levels of detail, ranging from every transaction in an instance all the way down to a specific event for a specific session. Use SQL Profiler to:

- Monitor the performance of an instance of SQL Server.
- Identify slow-executing queries.
- Test and debug SQL statements and stored procedures in the development phase of a project by stepping through statements to confirm that the code works as expected.
- Troubleshoot problems in SQL Server by capturing events on a production system and replaying them on a test system.

- Replay manually created SQL test scripts.

- Audit and review activity that occurred on an instance of SQL Server.

When you set up a new session in SQL Profiler, you can specify what events to capture and to what level of detail. You can also specify the set of circumstances in which to capture the events, and you can choose to capture event data to either a file or a table for later analysis. A stored trace can be replayed against an instance of SQL Server, effectively re-executing the saved events as they occurred originally. You can also create your own SQL scripts and use SQL Profiler to replay these. In a testing scenario, the replay option is the real value of SQL Profiler. For information specific to creating traces to be replayed, see "Replaying Traces" in SQL Server Books Online.

A very useful feature of SQL Profiler is the ability to create templates. These can be created and reused for specific monitoring situations. SQL Profiler comes with a set of common templates that you can use to make this process easier, especially if you are new to the tool. This way you can develop particular views of your system that will help you track specific performance issues.

To run a template against your system, open SQL Profiler, point to the **File** menu, select **New**, and then click **Trace**. A connection menu will appear so you can connect to the appropriate instance of SQL Server. In the next screen, you can select the template to use, and whether to save the trace to a file or a table. It is very important to record information traced for future analysis. The best way to do this is to store the trace to a file (but not on a drive used by SQL Server), and then copy the data from the file into a table for analysis.

System Stored Procedures

Monitoring can be performed through the use of system stored procedures and functions as well:

Command	Description
sp_who and **sp_who2**	The **sp_who** procedure will provide information such as system process id, status, associated login, host name, blocking processes, database name, and command type. The other (undocumented) version of it, **sp_who2**, provides the same information, plus: usage of CPU, Disk and Memory, and also the calling Program Name for that **spid**.
sp_lock and OBJECT_NAME()	Use these to help track down issues regarding improper data access design, or to find ways to balance and optimize locking required by business needs versus isolation level settings. These are especially useful in tracking down blocking issues. You can also use Trace Flag 1204, which returns the type of locks participating in the deadlock and the current command affected.
fn_virtualfilestats(db_id, file_id)	Returns I/O statistics for database files, including log files.

continued on next page

Command	Description
fn_trace_geteventinfo(trace_id)	Returns information about the events traced.
fn_trace_getinfo(trace_id)	Returns information about a specified trace or existing traces.
sp_trace_create	Creates a trace definition. The new trace will be in a stopped state.
sp_trace_generateevent	Creates a user-defined event.
sp_trace_setevent	Adds or removes an event or event column to a trace.
sp_trace_setstatus	Modifies the current state of the specified trace: Start, Stop, or Close.
fn_trace_getfilterinfo(trace_id)	Returns information about the filters applied to a specified trace.
sp_trace_setfilter	Applies a filter to a trace.
fn_trace_gettable(filename, number_of_files)	Returns trace file information in a table format.

For more information, see "Monitoring with SQL Server Enterprise Manager" in SQL Server Books Online.

Also, while the SQL Profiler interface is most commonly used, some system procedures correlate to the SQL Profiler actions and allow you to control profiling from within SQL Server, such as from within a procedure or job. It is worth noting that these have all changed in SQL Server 2000.

For simplicity, you can use the Profiler interface to set up a trace, and then script the trace settings to SQL Server (on the **File** menu, click **Script**). A good use for a scripted trace is to coordinate simultaneous monitoring with different tools. Another practical use is to capture events occurring at a specific time, so you do not have to be there to do it manually. By running the scripted trace from a scheduled job, you can make this the first step in a process that will also import the trace data and transform it into a set of report tables, so it is ready for your viewing. For more information, see "Creating and Managing Traces and Templates" in SQL Server Books Online.

System Monitor

System Monitor (formerly called Performance Monitor in Windows NT® 4.0) provides detailed data about the resources used by specific components of the operating system and by server programs that have been designed to collect performance data. You can use the data you gather to:

- Understand your workload and the corresponding effect on system resources.

- Observe changes and trends in workloads and resource usage so you can plan for future upgrades.

- Test configuration changes or other tuning efforts by monitoring the results.

- Diagnose problems and target components or processes for optimization.

System monitor data is collected as counter logs, which store data collected for the specified counters at regular intervals, or in trace logs, which record data when certain activities such as a disk I/O operation or a page fault occur. A parsing tool is required to interpret the trace log output. Developers can create such a tool using APIs provided on http://msdn.microsoft.com/.

The performance data is typically displayed in a graph form, whether you are running the monitoring tool "live" or whether you are viewing previously saved counter logs. You can also create alerts to notify you when a counter value reaches, rises above, or falls below a defined threshold. Some sample templates to help you isolate specific types of problems, and also to give you some ideas for ways to use this tool, are available on the *SQL Server 2000 Resource Kit* CD-ROM in the folder, \ToolsAndSamples\DBManagement.

One feature of System Monitor is that it is a Microsoft ActiveX® object. This means that you can easily incorporate a view of a log into a document or a Web page. This can be useful for both issue and trend analysis. It would also be useful to centralize administration if you have a team Web site.

You can use SQL Profiler and System Monitor simultaneously on the same system to gather more detailed time-related information on the interaction between hardware and software. For more information about System Monitor counters and interpreting them, see the System Monitor online help. Also consult the Microsoft Developers Network (MSDN) at http://msdn.microsoft.com/.

Staging a Test

You can use these tools against a production system to monitor real-time performance, or you can stage a test of the system on a test server. To do this, you should ideally have a server available which closely matches the production configuration. Make notes on the differences between the systems, as these differences may affect the level of accuracy in the test results. For example, if your production system has an external array of disks, and your test server does not, you will not be able to get a completely accurate picture of disk usage on the test server. On an application level, however, you can gather a lot of very useful information on the performance of a system.

On a basic level, you can test a small set of queries for performance comparisons to the production system. In this case, you would simply turn on SQL Profiler (selecting the appropriate events or using a template), and run the queries in SQL Query Analyzer (with "Show Execution Plan") to get a basic feel for how it is working. However, for a large test you will need to analyze usage patterns on your production server, or create simulations based on the test environment, and then create scripts that can be replayed to simulate many users working concurrently.

Two levels to testing a system are interrelated: the application and the data tier. Testing either one alone will not provide a complete picture of the scalability or performance of a system. Testing the front end to learn what transaction load it can support involves creating a recording (or script) of actions performed on the front end or Web page. These are replayed by testing software, and provide feedback on how much of a load the application can support. This type of testing, performed for the purpose of scalability and reliability, is known as stress testing, and is an important part of ensuring the success of a system prior to production implementation. Many full-featured third party tools are available to test your application. Microsoft provides a free tool for basic Web testing: the Web Application Stress Tool. For more information, see http://msdn.microsoft.com/library/ and search for "Web application stress tool."

Some data tier information can be gathered during these tests, but you will achieve more thorough results if you test the database as well. Be aware that the way the application works will necessarily have an effect on database performance. For example, if your application connects to the database from Internet Information Services (IIS), and it has data caching turned on, then some queries which look like "frequent use" queries may be used only once: when the cache is refreshed. This might be the case for a re-pricing function for all "sale items" on an e-commerce site. If this function dynamically prices each item every time the Web page is called, this looks like it would be a huge problem. If data caching is turned on, however, then this is no longer an issue because the pricing function will only run when the cache is refreshed (a time increment you should be aware of). This function would still be on your list of performance issues, but the usage of it would lower the priority to the bottom of your list.

The contents of the cache during a test have a significant impact on the results. A cold cache is when nothing is in memory, and all data is read from the disk; a warm cache is when the system has been running and most data and stored procedures are loaded and compiled (for example, all the lookup tables); and a hot cache is when the entire data set required is in memory.

A performance test that does not take caching into account can lack repeatability, and therefore have less value. It is best to clear the cache prior to starting each test by stopping and restarting SQL services or by running DBCC DROPCLEANBUFFERS and DBCC FREEPROCCACHE. Or, you can start recording the test results after a suitable warm-up period, or design some hot cache code to get things loaded into cache. To do this, simply make a script that runs the necessary stored procedures, DBCC PINTABLE, or queries tables in such a way that you would get the required table or index scans.

For information about testing, search for "Testing Process," at http://msdn.microsoft.com/library/.

Monitoring and Optimizing

The previous section covered the basics regarding the tools and the general process; this section provides examples of how you would use SQL Profiler, system stored procedures, and System Monitor to approach a specific problem: slowness of response time. Lack of speed is one of the most common complaints about applications, particularly when that application has outgrown its original design, or was inefficiently designed from the start. A close examination of this problem will reveal more about how proper design and configuration can free the server to scale to whatever level you require. Because a full explanation of all possible scenarios is outside the scope of this chapter, the examples will be limited to the following scenario.

Sample Scenario: Suppose you have accepted a new job managing the database systems of a mid-sized company. They are growing, and now need someone to optimize their flow of data. Clearly, you need to define and document the servers you are now responsible for. In the course of exploring the data environment, you learn from the company help desk that two of the systems are getting complaints of slow response time.

In addition to showing the steps to follow for our example, these general guidelines can be applied in any testing, tuning, or troubleshooting situation.

Monitoring a System

Before starting an optimization project, you should have already gathered as much information about the system as possible, paying special attention to how the application works and how it is used.

In terms of the previous scenario, assume that this is a custom built application, and that the two applications running on the database are the order system of the company and a trend analysis reporting application. These two systems access data in very different ways, and to be fully optimized, the systems will be different from the hardware level up. Assume that due to a business need, the design of these systems was less than optimal. The reporting application is made of an interface that queries a set of report and parameter definition tables, and then runs stored procedures or embedded SQL based on user input. In addition, reports are run during peak hours. If reports were instead run during off-peak hours, or once every week or month, performance issues regarding reporting would be improved.

Knowing how the application is used, and what is important to the users at what times, should help you understand what should be improved first, and may also give you some clues on what issues you might expect to find in the data tier. The application information will save you a lot of time in the long run, and focus your tuning efforts to make them more effective.

For the purposes of the example, looking at the overall problem and the application information, you choose to go through some basic steps, and then focus in on the possibility of problems with the indexes and the stored procedure code.

Address Operating System and SQL Server Errors

Before beginning work on optimization, you should make sure you are starting with a clean server. Check the Event Viewer system and application logs on the server. Do not check just SQL Server messages— skim through all of the messages. Then, check the SQL Server error logs.

For example, if you were investigating slow or failed connections to the server, and you open Event Viewer to find an error indicating that the SQL Server cannot reach the primary domain controller, then you should have that error resolved first. Before proceeding with any further investigation, verify the status with the users reporting the original problem. This way you do not spend time on a problem that was not database related.

For more information about how to troubleshoot errors, see SQL Server Books Online. For more information about a specific problem, search the Knowledge Base at http://support.microsoft.com/, or see the online newsgroup at microsoft.public.sqlserver.server.

Monitor to Identify Areas for Improvement

When you are not sure what you are looking for, it is best to use several tools on some general settings in order to capture a broader range of data.

Depending on the situation, you may choose to monitor the server locally or remotely (meaning that you are either running the tools on the same server that you are monitoring, or you are running them from a different server). Here are some things to keep in mind:

- Local monitoring can exploit a shared memory connection and avoid network I/O for large amounts of trace information. Choose local if you are regularly monitoring most of your servers, simultaneously or with a large number of counters.

- Remote monitoring may be best if you have eliminated network problems from your list of potential suspects, and if you are monitoring a few computers at a time. Ensure that your network can easily support remote monitoring, and that latency is low so you get accurate results.

When setting up System Monitor, it is a good idea set the sample interval to between one and three minutes. The default value is every one second, which has an impact on the server under observation. Setting the value too low generates a lot of data without providing much more valuable information. A larger interval also allows for a more steady reading; and is better for initial analysis. Keep in mind that the more counters you monitor, the more overhead you will incur, the larger a saved log file will become, and the more data you will have to import and analyze later on.

You should establish a baseline set of counters that you monitor regularly, and this may be a separate process from optimization monitoring, depending on your baseline/optimization goals. To run a baseline, run the System Monitor for a brief period on a regular basis, so you can report on trends over time. Consider importing the counter log data into a SQL Server table, so you can use either stored procedure reports or Analysis Services to show trends. Here is a good sample set of counters you could use for baseline monitoring:

```
\Memory\Available MBytes
\Memory\Pages/sec
\Memory\Cache Faults/sec
\Memory\Page Faults/sec
\Processor(_Total)\% Processor Time
\Processor(_Total)\Interrupts/sec
\Process(sqlmangr)\% Processor Time
\Process(sqlservr)\% Processor Time
\System\Processor Queue Length
\System\Context Switches/sec
\Processor(_Total)\% Privileged Time
```

```
\Processor(_Total)\% User Time
\PhysicalDisk(_Total)\% Disk Time
\PhysicalDisk(_Total)\% Idle Time
\PhysicalDisk(_Total)\Avg. Disk Queue Length
\PhysicalDisk(_Total)\Current Disk Queue Length
\PhysicalDisk(_Total)\Disk Reads/sec
\PhysicalDisk(_Total)\Disk Writes/sec
\PhysicalDisk(_Total)\Avg. Disk sec/Read
\PhysicalDisk(_Total)\Avg. Disk sec/Write
\SQLServer:Buffer Manager\Buffer cache hit ratio
\SQLServer:Databases(_Total)\Transactions/sec
\SQLServer:General Statistics\User Connections
\SQLServer:Locks(_Total)\Lock Requests/sec
\SQLServer:Locks(_Total)\Lock Timeouts/sec
\SQLServer:Locks(_Total)\Number of Deadlocks/sec
```

There is a sample "Baseline.htm" located on the *SQL Server 2000 Resource Kit* CD-ROM in the folder, \ToolsAndSamples\DBManagement. And for some useful tips on monitoring, see "Setting up a monitoring configuration" in System Monitor online help.

Wherever feasible, you should first record a trace and play it back on a similar server (such as the standby server or a test server). By doing this you can search for errors using all available counters, with no impact on production. Running on a test server, you can also experiment with changes more easily. If you use a standby server for this, make sure you do not change anything that might disrupt any disaster recovery plans. Obviously you will only be able to get some measurements on the production system. However, as a standard practice, always minimize the impact to production.

If you know exactly what type of problem you have, you can narrow down to just the monitoring that applies to that issue. By running several tools in coordination, you get a time slice of the data that reveals a total picture of all activity related to your research. When using multiple tools, it is vital to run them simultaneously if you want a clear picture of everything happening on the server. All of the SQL Server tools discussed in this chapter can be scheduled and run from a job for the same period of time.

- System stored procedures, such as those for current activity and locking, can be scheduled like any other procedure, and the output redirected to a file and later imported to a table for ease of analysis.

- SQL Profiler: If you wish to schedule a trace, you need to use the trace-related set of system stored procedures (such as **sp_trace_setstatus**), and schedule them as SQL Server Agent jobs. To make things easier, you can set up a trace in SQL Profiler; then go to the **File** menu and click **Script Trace** to create Transact-SQL for your trace. For more information, see "Creating and Managing Traces and Templates" in SQL Server Books Online. Also, scripts of all the default SQL Profiler traces are located on the *SQL Server 2000 Resource Kit* CD-ROM in the folder, \ToolsAndSamples\DBManagement.

- System Monitor: To schedule a counter log from a SQL Server job, simply create an alert on the SQL Server:User Settable(User Counter 1)\Query counter (10 of these are available), and have it respond to a counter value above 0. Then, in SQL Server, create a job with the following code:

```
EXEC sp_user_counter1 1
```

> **Note**   Your job should later set the value back to 0, to avoid setting off the alert accidentally.

Setting the counter to 1 will set off the counter log for the defined interval. An example of how to set this up is located on the SQL Server 2000 Resource Kit CD-ROM in the folder, \ToolsAndSamples\DBManagement.

If you are trying to capture an elusive error condition, try to identify something that happens when the error occurs, or just before it, and use that event to generate an alert that starts the monitoring process job. Also, consider tracing a single user who is experiencing a particular problem, rather than profiling everything on the system. This generates a cleaner representation of the data for analysis.

Monitoring SQL Server in General

When you approach a database system for the purpose of optimization, or in fact for capacity planning or trend analysis, you want to assess system performance as a whole. The purpose of this is twofold. First, you want to get a baseline on how the server is performing. This helps you understand what is normal for your system; it also helps you understand developing trends, which can be an important part of being prepared for the future. Secondly, the overall view of the system will allow you to put the symptoms you have observed (slowness, for example), together with the behavior you can observe through the monitoring tools.

Returning to the scenario mentioned previously, assume that you set up your monitoring tools on your own desktop, and schedule system stored procedures on the server, so you will get a complete time slice.

System Monitor will not provide all the answers you need, simply because not everything can usefully be reported in the form of a counter. You should also examine your system using SQL Profiler or a trace running from a system stored procedure.

You may choose to monitor for each focus area in a separate trace file, where the information will be already grouped in a meaningful fashion (depending on how you set it up). Or, you may choose to monitor in general, store the trace to an SQL table, and do your own reporting from there. You should set standards for monitoring a database server. Store all your templates and scripts in a central repository somewhere so they are backed up, protected, and readily available to your group. This gets especially important the larger your team is and the more database servers you have.

Once you have a clear general idea of what is happening on the server, you can begin to focus on the issues that warrant your attention.

In the case of a complaint of slow response time against one of the major systems of your new company, you already know that you can have a much larger impact on the server by improving the application and the database design. Because you are tasked with improving performance without changing the front-end application, you focus immediately on database design.

You choose to monitor for slow queries, blocking issues, and indexing issues, figuring that if you turn up anything these give you a good start on optimizing your system. Because you want everything to run simultaneously, you schedule all of your tools. Because the problem is so urgent that your management has authorized daytime monitoring, you choose a time of moderate activity (based on input from the network administrators and user contacts). You decide to run a full half-hour test this time, although normally you would elect to run two 15-minute periods within an hour.

To monitor for database or application design issues, you decide to set up System Monitor with the following counters:

```
\SQLServer:Access Methods\Full Scans/sec
\SQLServer:Access Methods\Index Searches/sec
\SQLServer:SQL Statistics\SQL Re-Compilations/sec
\SQLServer:Locks(_Total)\Average Wait Time (ms)
\SQLServer:Locks(_Total)\Lock Waits/sec
\SQLServer:Locks(_Total)\Number of Deadlocks/sec
\SQLServer:Cache Manager(Prepared Sql Plans)\Cache Hit Ratio
```

Then, you set up a job to run **sp_who2** and **sp_lock** periodically throughout the monitoring period, saving the output to a file. These two procedures can be customized to provide information in a format you find most useful.

Now run two traces, one for the Duration template and one for the Replay template. The Duration template generates a list of Transact-SQL statements, and the duration of time they took to complete. The Replay template could be used for the Index Tuning Wizard.

Analyzing the Results: Database and Code Level

When you are starting this process, a seemingly endless number of things could be wrong, and you have many different ways to observe these problems. The key is to choose valid monitoring parameters that you understand well, and then to focus your priorities on the areas where you can have the greatest impact.

First, look at the data and code levels, knowing that this is the best way to get a performance increase. Technically, the biggest gain is to be found in optimizing the application and the code it rests on.It is also worthwhile to examine the indexing, however. Very often, indexing originally done for the application may not have been sufficiently tested; in addition, the usage of the application usually shifts over time, especially as enhancements are introduced and the volume of users and transactions increases.

You may find that your initial monitoring efforts uncover a number of problems to which you can turn your attention. However, to be most effective, it is best to choose a few and concentrate on those, saving the other discovered issues for the next optimization cycle. The idea here is that every time you do any tuning, the system is altered, so you want to get a new monitoring report before making a decision on what the next priority should be.

Blocking Based on Database Design

Looking in SQL Profiler at the trace file you created through **sp_trace_create**, you convert the **Duration** value from milliseconds to seconds, and discover that you have several queries that run for over one minute. One of them appears many times on your list; the other appears only once, but it takes far longer. You should select the most frequently used, longest-running queries for your first optimization pass on the code. This will have the greatest impact on the system. The other query, although it takes longer to run, is used very infrequently, and should be left as the lowest optimization priority.

This is an important distinction to make. The user who is running the very slow query may very well call in to complain of the slowness. Meanwhile, all of the users may be suffering because of general system slowness caused by the queries that run very frequently (such as those which populate the main screens). The important distinction to make here is that the complaint of general slowness is very difficult to handle from a help desk perspective. The single user with a complaint on an easily identifiable report is much easier to address.

Since you already suspect locking in the sample scenario, you look at the data you collected with **sp_who2** and **sp_lock**. Sure enough, the procedure you chose from the trace is listed often in **sp_lock**, and the same SPIDs are also blocked processes listed in the **BlkBy** column of **sp_who2**.

> **Note** Trace Flag 1204 can be used to get more information on the type of locks participating in the deadlock and the current command affected.

Studying **sp_lock**, you see the following results as representative of the pattern that is common for many of the spids listed:

spid	dbid	ObjId	IndId	Type	Resource	Mode	Status
76	20	usp_productbytype	0	TAB		Sch-S	GRANT
76	20	usp_priceit	0	TAB	[COMPILE]	X	GRANT
76	20	usp_priceit _	0	TAB		Sch-S	GRANT
76	20	usp_productpromote	0	TAB		Sch-S	GRANT
76	20	usp_priceit	0	TAB	[COMPILE]	X	WAIT
76	20	usp_priceit	0	TAB		Sch-S	GRANT
77	20	usp_productpromote	0	TAB		Sch-S	GRANT
77	20	usp_priceit _	0	TAB		Sch-S	GRANT
77	20	usp_priceit	0	TAB	[COMPILE]	X	GRANT

Comparing this to the data from **sp_who2**, you focus in on the spids 76 and 77. (Note that this sample is missing a few columns for purposes of display.)

SPID	HostName	BlkBy	Command	CPUTime	DiskIO
62	WRKSTN07	64	EXECUTE	25797	273
63	WRKSTN08	.	AWAITING COMMAND	15531	310
64	WRKSTN08	89	EXECUTE	2563	324
65	WRKSTN08	64	INSERT	8344	461
69	WRKSTN07	64	EXECUTE	17188	531
70	WRKSTN08	64	EXECUTE	103281	141
71	WRKSTN07	64	INSERT	13438	76
72	WRKSTN08	.	AWAITING COMMAND	46469	6
73	WRKSTN08	.	AWAITING COMMAND	14281	270
74	WRKSTN08	64	EXECUTE	13109	305
75	WRKSTN07	.	AWAITING COMMAND	25375	232
76	WRKSTN07	64	EXECUTE	68094	367
77	WRKSTN07	64	INSERT	14328	419

Comparing this to information gathered in System Monitor, you see:

Counter	Condition
\SQLServer:SQL Statistics\SQL Re-Compilations/sec	This is more than 1,000. You make a note to investigate other stored procedure code and look for embedded or ad hoc SQL queries, once the current optimization effort is complete.
\SQLServer:Locks(_Total)\Average Wait Time (ms)	The average wait time is substantially more than 30 seconds.
\SQLServer:Locks(_Total)\Lock Waits/sec	This number is high, but this is consistent with the blocking.
\SQLServer:Locks(_Total)\Number of Deadlocks/sec	This is very low in proportion to the other lock counters. Fortunately, although a blocking issue exists, it looks as though the tables are processed in a consistent sequence.

Open the code and trace through the logic. For this example, assume that you find a stored procedure, which creates a temporary table of items to price, populates it, and then executes a nested stored procedure to individually update the price of each item in the temporary table. This type of design would cause numerous recompiles, which would in turn cause the blocking issue.

The first step in fixing this is asking what went into choosing the design. As a DBA, your first instinct would be to get rid of the temporary table and consolidate the code into one procedure. However, you must understand the reason behind the design, the system requirements, before you begin. For the example,assume you learn the following: 1) The nested procedure was created to simplify maintenance, since the same pricing routine is used in numerous other procedures; and 2) the pricing is done dynamically because prices are changed during the day.

Both of these are valid reasons for the design. But there is often more than one way to provide a solution, and in this case you can meet the requirements and still provide some optimization. In the end, all of performance tuning is an act of balancing needs: Speed, ease of administration, and cost are all factors that must be balanced, meaning that if you go for an extreme in one area, you must be willing to make some sacrifices in another.

In this case, to fix the problem, you could look for a way to eliminate the nested procedure, and price the items without the temporary table. This would mean that the same pricing routine must be incorporated into all the calling procedures. It simplifies the procedure, and eliminates blocking issues. How do you keep the goal of simplifying code maintenance? With documentation. Put a block of comments in every procedure to explain that the code fragment is scattered throughout the database. Use a code scanning procedure for this. An example of **sp_searchcode** is available on the *SQL Server 2000 Resource Kit* CD-ROM in the folder, \ToolsAndSamples\DBManagement.

Another alternative is to look for a way to avoid pricing the items dynamically. Perhaps the price column could be added to the product table, and any re-pricing would simply include a process that updated this column. This design would offer far better performance, especially given the fact that the process that should have priority is the one that queries the data repeatedly. Even if the items are re-priced frequently during the day, the frequency of sessions doing pricing will never reach the frequency of sessions searching for items will. So, you add speed by denormalizing in the area of high reads. In this case you add speed by adding the extended prices to each item, rather than calculating the various extended or discounted prices. You keep the functionality for changing price, but the process of changing the price will be a bit slower because now it will include updating the product table as well. If that slowness is also an issue, you could consider queuing the requests to change prices. Once the real business priorities become clear (in this case that the customer should not wait), then you can more accurately choose a design which fulfills your needs.

For more information on blocking issues, see "Understanding and Avoiding Blocking" in SQL Server Books Online.

Slowness Due to Indexing Schema

Sometimes a problem has multiple causes. In this case, a lack of proper indexes could possibly cause blocking issues. Indexes help the database select data for the result sets; no indexes are used by the query, a user query must wait if someone has a row locked on a table where a full scan is initiated.

You should give regular attention to your indexing schema. In the area of database maintenance, poor indexing is the most common cause of slow queries, and it is also the easiest to fix. Correcting the indexes for a query can have a near-magical effect on increasing query speed.

The most obvious symptom that indexes are in the wrong place is slow response to frequently used queries. Other things, of course, can cause this, but the lack of proper indexes should be a prime suspect. On the contrary, if you are getting slow response on inserts and updates, take a look at how many and how wide (in columns) the indexes are on the target table. Too many indexes can slow data changes. For this reason, you will also want to eliminate indexes that are never or rarely used by queries, or which are only used for minor benefit to queries that are infrequently run.

Note If you have a system where you would like to index most of the columns, because you feel they will all be used, you should use the **auto create statistics** and **auto update statistics** database options. The query processor can use this statistical information to determine the optimal strategy for evaluating a query. For more information, see "Statistical Information" in SQL Server Books Online.

For the sample scenario, assume that you have the following counter values, indicating that you should check the index placement:

Counter	Condition
\SQLServer:Access Methods\Full Scans/sec	This database has many full scans; a rate of 3 is recorded as the average.
\SQLServer:Access Methods\Index Searches/sec	There are fewer of these, but you may suspect that the blocking issue may artificially lower this.

How do you determine the proper index placement? The Indexing Tuning Wizard included with SQL Server can give you immediate feedback on your indexing schema, based on some fairly complex analysis of the data volume, distribution, and usage. This tool, which can also be opened from the command line with **itwiz**, should be a regular part of the optimization cycle, run on a standby server with a trace from the production server.

As your system changes over time, you should run the Index Tuning Wizard to evaluate how current usage has changed the best indexing schema. This can be run on one query, in Query Analyzer, or on a trace script (use SQL Profiler template SQLProfilerTSQL_Replay.tdf, provided in Transact-SQL form on the *SQL Server 2000 Resource Kit* CD-ROM in the folder, \ToolsAndSamples\DBManagement).

For some complex types of queries or design requirements, you may find that you still want to do some indexing analysis without the tool. For example, if you have a distributed process that you want to control, or if you have some queries which for some reason must be the most optimal even if they will not appear so in a trace. If you have cases like this, run the wizard to get feedback so you have additional automated recommendations. For information about indexes and their options, see "Create Index" and "Index Tuning Wizard" in SQL Server Books Online, and the MSDN white paper "Index Tuning Wizard for Microsoft SQL Server 2000" at http://msdn.microsoft.com/library.

Data Storage Component Issues

It is also important to address data storage issues, including both the data file layout and the hardware configuration. This section will focus on problems that can be caused by inappropriate disk layout. For information on filegroup layouts, see "Optimizing the Storage Components" in this chapter.

If you examine the server and discover that you have poor throughput even on a reasonably large server, you should look at some System Monitor counters to get more information. For this example, we have already found several issues that require fixing. At the server layer,assume that the **sp_configure** settings on the server were default settings, and therefore should not be examined first. Instead, we should check the hardware to make sure it is being used optimally before taking any action on the server configuration.

Assume that you go up our example server, armed with all the information you have gathered, and you run the some counters related to page faults and observe the following.

Counter	Condition
\Memory\Pages/sec	A large amount of hard paging is taking place. The average value is more than 70.
\Memory\Page Faults/sec	A large amount of soft paging is indicated; the average value is more than 250.
\SQLServer:Cache Manager()\Cache Hit Ratio	The average amount is 65 for Prepared SQL Plans, Procedure Plans, and Adhoc SQL Plans.

The Performance Monitor log shows that the page faults per second is very high. In addition, the SQL Server cache hit ratio is proportionally very low. This indicates a need for more memory. Memory\Pages/sec should be as close to 0 as possible; the higher the value, the more hard paging is taking place. Hard paging is when the operating system goes to disk to resolve memory references. The operating system will incur some paging, because this is how it handles memory. But when excessive paging takes places, this process uses disk I/O and CPU resources, which can intensify slowness in the database. Because soft faults consume CPU resources, soft faults are generally not as bad on performance as hard faults. Hard faults consume disk I/O resources. The combination of these can intensify a variety of other performance problems.

To be thorough, you should go ahead and look at all the server resources on a general level, to get a better picture for what is going on.

Counter	Condition
\Processor(_Total)\% Processor Time	The processors are being well utilized, but there are frequent spikes over 80 percent.

In this case, you can see a significant amount of processor utilization. Spikes appear above 80 percent, so an extra processor might be in order. The application should be tuned first, however, and the paging problem investigated as well.

Counter	Condition
\PhysicalDisk(_Total)\Current Disk Queue Length	A significant amount of queuing is taking place; the amount frequently spikes to a value of 21.

In this example, the amount of disk queuing is a bit high for the system. Five physical disks are configured into a RAID 5 array, so with a total of four disks utilized, queuing should never be higher than 8. Here it spikes to 21.

You have several choices for looking at disk queuing in System Monitor. Logical disk counters are associated with the logical drive letters assigned by Disk Administrator, whereas physical disk counters are associated with what Disk Administrator sees as a single physical disk device. What looks like a single physical device to Disk Administrator may be either a single hard disk drive, or a RAID array, which consists of several hard disk drives.

The difference between the physical and logical disk layout is important. Understanding exactly which disks you mean when you say "Drive E" is absolutely crucial to being effective in monitoring the storage components of a database server. Equally important is understanding which database-related files are on which drive. In the case of the example, the operating system is on the C drive, the data is on the D drive, and the log is on the E drive. However, each of these three are logical drives configured on one physical disk array (also called a partition). So, while these three drives (C, D, and E) appear to be separate, the fact is that all of the files—paging file, data files, and log files—are all on the same physical disk.

A good practice is to always use the physical disk counters. These are already on by default on Windows 2000 systems. By relying on the physical counters only, you also save some driver overhead by not collecting the logical disk statistics. Plus, using the physical disk counters will help make it clearer how the drives are physically laid out.

In this real world example, many different problems are found in the same system, and they combine and make each other worse. In this case, the disk queuing is likely to be worse because frequent writes are made to the order system (random I/O) in addition to reporting queries (sequential I/O). Plus, this system

seems to need more memory, so data is flowing through the cache before it can be reused. However, you have already identified coding problems and indexing problems that could also be aggravating hardware utilization problems. It is far more efficient to optimize the application first, and then adjust the hardware. If you always do it the other way around, you will soon find yourself in the same bind, because the design problems will continue to grow in magnitude as the system grows in volume.

For our example server, you can see that you might get some gain from reconfiguring the system in RAID 0+1, so you reduce some of the I/O. If the amount of memory on this server were less than 512 MB, then you might also look at purchasing memory as well. Other than these minor adjustments to the storage component level, you are much better served by turning your attention immediately back to the design issues.

For information on identifying hardware problems, see "Identifying Bottlenecks" in SQL Server Books Online.

Other Issues for Optimization

Regarding the example scenario, it would be a good idea to move the reporting application onto a different server. Decision Support Systems (DSS) and Online Transaction Processing (OLTP) systems make dissimilar use of system resources such as CPU, memory, and disk. A DSS system generally accesses data by retrieving large numbers of rows for the purpose of analyzing the data. This involves sequential I/O. An OLTP system, on the other hand, usually hits one or just a few rows from a single table, a random I/O process. The two types of I/O have different and sometimes opposing optimization goals and tactics. They do not belong on the same disk. Some reads are natural to OLTP. Very few systems are pure data entry; many of them involve selecting items from a list, or viewing minor reports (not DSS scale). In a larger (higher volume) system, you might consider separating out the data into different filegroups on different disks by access pattern. However, if the DSS system and the OLTP system are both heavily used during the same hours, the strain on the resources will necessitate separating the systems onto different resources; the easiest way to do this is to put them on different servers.

Moving the reporting system off to another server to reduce the strain of reporting demands on the ordering system would be easy to justify, since looking at how well the business is doing should not have an impact on how well it does. You could estimate the performance gains by doing a trace for Replay on the OLTP application, and running that script against a test server of similar hardware configuration. The performance numbers you could get by monitoring this test environment (one without reporting interference) would tell you whether your plan would be worthwhile. System Monitor graphs could be included in a brief report, along with an estimate for the tasks involved in making the change.

Looking for table scans in the monitoring tools is a good idea, and it will often lead you to problems that can be corrected by appropriate indexing. However, you should also keep in mind that the query processor chooses the best plan possible. If you have a very small table of very few rows, reading the whole table is going to be faster than using an index; in fact, putting an index on such a small table would be detrimental. Also, if you are going to be reading a large number of rows from the table, or if the index column only has a couple of unique values, a table scan will be more efficient. It is important to understand how SQL Server works behind the scenes, if your optimization efforts are to be effective.

> **Note** If you do not feel that you have sufficient evidence to support a change you think needs to be made, or if you are having difficulty isolating a problem, consider returning to your general monitoring, but with all counters being recorded. Be very careful of the performance considerations of running such a large number of counters, especially if you choose a short update interval. This is sometimes the only way to find a relevant pattern in the performance data, however.

Finally, remember that the database server does not exist in isolation, and can be subject to problems that are not SQL Server related. A good example of this is network issues. For more information on network issues that relate to SQL Server, see the chapter, "Configuring Microsoft SQL Server on the Network" in *Microsoft SQL Server 2000 Administrator's Companion*. Also see "Monitoring Network Activity" in System Monitor online help.

Managing the Changes

It is important to be careful in fixing the issues that appear to be the cause of performance degradation. Fix one thing at a time and observe the system again, so you will know the effect of your change. This is useful for documentation purposes if your fix works. If, however, your change causes a larger or a different problem, it would be better to know exactly what you changed. That way, you could remove the specific change, rather than having to remove a large set of changes to see what caused the new problem. Another advantage is that you could make small changes more frequently, and thus see a continuous gain in performance. This is the goal of the optimization cycle described in this chapter.

Optimizing the Data Components

Logical modeling often does not translate into a physical model, because the physical model must also be influenced by the usage of the set of tables. You must find a balance between normalized and denormalized so the database structure provides the required functionality, while meeting requirements of performance and scalability.

Stored procedures and functions assist in a single implementation of logic across your application—they are designed and coded once—and provide a layer of abstraction which allows you to better manage the underlying data. For added administrative flexibility, you can build your stored procedures on top of views of the tables. This is especially useful in any system which is likely to grow or change over time, or where you would like to have control over the physical database structure for future optimization or enhancement opportunities.

The needs at the structural level will almost always change over time. The more levels of abstraction (views, procedures) you have between the front-end and the physical tables, the more flexibility you will have in adapting the physical design to meet performance goals. The ability to manage the flow of data through the physical structures is crucial to adaptive administration of the database, and should be a design priority on larger systems.

Probably the greatest benefit of using views from a performance perspective is that it allows you to alter the underlying table structure without altering the front-end application. Using simple views provides you with the option to do that if you wish, so you can migrate your system from one design to another with minimal impact. However, your ultimate goal should still be to have a good table layout, as you cannot fix a bad one exclusively by using views.

The usage of the system will change the indexing schema requirements as well. It is a good idea to develop a plan for your indexes, including fillfactor settings, policies on placement of indexes, and a standardization of names. Here are some tips on good indexing:

- Try to use narrow indexes (on just one column). This provides the most efficient indexing scheme.

- Base indexes on WHERE clauses, joins, and GROUP BY statements, in that order of priority.

- Choose a non-clustered index for values where there are many unique values in that column (for example, an identity column, or a name column).

- Consider using indexed views as a means of instantiating alternate clustered indexes on a table.

- The best way to find the optimal indexing schema for your database is by using the Index Tuning Wizard with a sample workload. You can collect the workload information by using the replay template in SQL Profiler. Do this regularly to adapt the database to changes in usage.

You should also develop a plan for maintaining indexes. Several utilities are available for maintaining and analyzing indexes. Also make sure you also update statistics. It is a good idea to use the database options for **auto create statistics** and **auto update statistics**. For information on index utilities and statistics, see SQL Server Books Online.

Optimizing the Code Components

To get the best design, you need to do some performance analysis. Usage changes everything. Design is an iterative process. Your design should be able to adapt to changes in the system, just as your configuration does. Clearly, changes to the database objects can involve change to the front-end code as well, so these adjustments should be planned carefully.

It is also important to establish priorities when choosing which parts of the design to alter first. Some of these are not so obvious; for example when you are tuning stored procedures, you should be aware that shaving one second off of a two second procedure that runs hundreds of times per second is a much better use of your time than shaving 30 minutes off a one hour procedure that runs once a week.

Here are some tips that can give you an idea of what to be aware of in considering the best design.

- Always use stored procedures and user-defined functions for data access if at all possible. Because these objects are compiled on the server, they can provide in the range of 40 percent higher throughput on the system as a whole. Using stored procedures and functions for the purpose of scalability, you also can add in much of the business logic to stored procedures to prevent additional unnecessary roundtrips over the network. The main consideration here is that you want to reduce network traffic, but you must also keep the transactions as atomic as possible.

- The best security plan is to use application roles, and grant them execute permissions on the stored procedures. The users and application should never have access directly to the underlying views and tables. This is crucial for good security, and will protect your data from being accessed through query tools other than the application front-end. This approach also has other benefits: You can rely on stored procedures to enforce business rules and you also protect your ability to manage the physical structures as needed without fear of damaging any unauthorized, yet mission critical, ad hoc reports.

- An easy way to collect meta data on stored procedure usage is to add a little piece of audit code to each of them. This can simplify trend analysis, and at the same time make it far more accurate because you will have all the data, not just a small sample of it. Examples for this are available on the *SQL Server 2000 Resource Kit* CD-ROM in the folder, \ToolsAndSamples\DBManagement.

If you think of stored procedures and function objects as groups of SQL statements compiled into a single execution plan, then you will have the right perspective to optimize them. Design code maximizes the effectiveness of the caching mechanisms for execution plans by following these tips:

- Ensure all users execute with the same environmental settings. The environment is determined by server settings (**sp_configure**), database settings (**sp_dboption**), and connection settings (SET option). Don't change SET or database settings in the middle of an application or connection.

- Ensure batches and procedures do not require implicit resolution. The best way to do this is to use complete, explicit four-part names for all objects referenced in code: For instance, rather than selecting from "authors", select from "server1.pubs.dbo.authors". This will avoid unnecessary recompilations to resolve the name of the object.

- As an extra measure for optimizing the use of stored plans, study the effect of different parameter values on the stored procedure. Base a stored procedure on a range of data rather than just one ID or value. For example, use this code:

```
select * from tablename where value1 is between @x and @y
```

You will get a different optimal execution plan if @x and @y are very close in value (needing an index lookup) than if they are widely separate (requiring a full scan). There is a trick to storing more than one execution plan for the same query:

```
sp_executesql ('select * from T where c >= @p1 AND c <= @p2
--the index lookup plan','@p1 int @p2 int',5,10)

sp_executesql ('select * from T where c >= @p1 AND c <= @p2
--the tablescan plan','@p1 int @p2 int',5,95)
```

The comment at the end of the query (for example, "--the index lookup plan...") will cause SQL Server to store a separate plan for each of these queries, even though the query itself is the same.

- Too many recompiles can seriously degrade processing performance, even with a large server. You should make sure that you generate a recompile only when one is necessary for optimal execution. When you are examining options such as WITH RECOMPILE or the use of EXEC, look at the negative effect these have in relation to the total system. Excessive recompilations are far more expensive than an occasional poor execution plan for a rarely requested query.

- In general, you should always use **sp_executesql** rather than EXEC to run a dynamically created query. The reason for this is that **sp_executesql** has a greater possibility of reusing a cached execution plan; EXEC will cause a recompile every time. So for example, if you are calling such a procedure in a loop, the use of EXEC will cause one recompile per loop, whereas **sp_executesql** will not. On a large scale, recompiles can seriously degrade performance. For more information see "Using **sp_executesql**" in SQL Server Books Online.

- Instead of using dynamically built queries, consider writing multiple procedures to cover the scenarios that require different execution plans.

- Avoid using temporary tables if you can use a table variable instead. Table variables can be more efficient. In any case, avoid sharing a temporary table with a nested stored procedure in any procedure that is called frequently by the system.

For more information see "Transact-SQL Tips" and "Query Tuning" in SQL Server Books Online.

Optimizing the Storage Components

In SQL Server, the way that data files/filegroups and log files are laid out on disk contributes to database performance. Data and log files should always be separated onto different physical disks. **tempdb**, which has changed in SQL Server 2000, will provide better performance when placed on a large array of disks. Both the transaction log and **tempdb** benefit from being placed on fast drives.

Database File Placement

Here are a few tips and best practices regarding the placement of your database files:

- The most important considerations in determining where to place your files on the server are the number of disks (spindles) available to a particular drive and the speed of the drives involved. For this reason, it is good to design the server layout with your database needs in mind.

- If you have a set of tables that is used together frequently, you should consider putting these tables on separate filegroups on separate physical drives, to balance I/O between them. In a larger, more heavily used system, this could be a significant difference.

- Consider putting non-clustered indexes in a separate filegroup, in order to split I/O between filegroups.

- Group your tables based on usage, to generate as many simultaneous reads to different filegroups (and therefore disks) as possible. Grouping tables into filegroups based on a maintenance need for convenient backup plans will not generate as much performance as separating the tables and indexes by usage.

- For smaller systems, use autogrow for your database files, but keep in mind that when a "grow" is initiated, transactions must wait while the database grows. In a small database or lightly queried system this is not a big issue, but if you have a 100 GB OLTP database set to grow in 10 percent increments, and it runs out of space during peak times, the online users will be held up while the 10 GB is allocated.

- For a larger system the best practice is to anticipate database growth, and manually increase the database at a scheduled time. Or, choose a reasonable amount to grow by that is neither too cumbersome nor so small that it will initiate expansion too frequently.

- If you have multiple files in your filegroup, you will need to expand them in order to reestablish proportional fill.

For more information see "Using Files and Filegroups" in SQL Server Books Online.

Log File Placement

Here are a few tips and best practices regarding the placement of your log files:

- Create the transaction log on a physically separate disk or RAID array. The transaction log file is written sequentially; therefore, using a separate, dedicated disk allows the disk heads to stay in place for the next write operation. For this reason, smaller systems will do well by using a single mirrored disk for the transaction log. A single mirrored physical disk should support up to approximately 1,000 transactions per second, depending on the speed of the disk itself. Systems requiring more than that should stripe the transaction log across a RAID 0+1 array for maximum performance. For highest bandwidth, the RAID controller on this array should have a (battery backed) write-back cache to speed log writes.

- Set your transaction log to autogrow, but try to size it so it should not need to grow. The optimal size should be based on your recovery model, the level of logged activity in the database, and the interval of time between backups. Set the growth increment to a reasonable percentage, but try to anticipate when the log should be resized. If the transaction log expands too frequently or takes a long time to expand, performance can be affected.

- The size of the log should be based on your current recovery model and your application design. If you find that you need to shrink the log periodically, you should further investigate what is causing the log to fill up, in order to fix the problem at the root rather than simply fixing the symptom.

tempdb File Placement

Here are a few tips and best practices regarding the placement of your **tempdb** files:

- Place the **tempdb** database on a fast I/O subsystem to ensure good performance. Stripe the **tempdb** database across multiple disks for better performance. Move the **tempdb** database to disks different from those used by user databases.

- The **tempdb** database can be located with the data in most situations. Larger systems that make heavy use of **tempdb** should consider putting **tempdb** on a set of disks by itself, for purposes of extra performance. It is not a good idea to co-locate any database files with the page file of the operating system.

Other File Placement

Here are some tips and best practices regarding the placement of other files:

- The operating system should be created on a single mirrored disk (RAID 1). The page file performs well on the operating system drive, and may be left there for a database server. If you must move the page file, make sure that you do not locate it on any drive that contains a data file or log file, or **tempdb**. This provides resilience to disk failure (but have a boot disk ready to boot off the mirror).

- If you are storing your backups on the same server with your data, make sure not to store them on the same disks with your data files or log files.

Optimizing the Server Configuration

SQL Server 2000 has been enhanced so performance tuning is handled dynamically. This means that all those settings that were formerly based on usage are now based on an algorithm that monitors the server and dynamically adjusts the settings. This automatic process keeps the configuration settings constantly within 10 percent of the optimal setting based on system usage. Settings which relate to system resources can still be adjusted, and once adjusted will function dynamically within the bounds set by the DBA.

It is very important not to adjust anything in **sp_configure** unless you have overwhelming evidence (documentation) that your server issue cannot be resolved by fixing the code or by adjusting your storage deployment. Use the default settings. If you examine your server and find that some settings are not the default value, leave the settings at the current values, whether default or not. The reason for this is that some custom adjustments may have already been made. Carefully document this, and investigate why they were changed.

Apart from dynamic performance tuning and the important caution about **sp_configure**, though, an examination of your server settings may be required at times. For instance, if you are supporting third-party software that you cannot adjust, and you have already adjusted the hardware to the highest level, server configuration would be a logical area to look at.

Here are some general tips on adjusting the server configuration:

- Before you begin, research the issue thoroughly both online and in relevant books. You will also need to run System Monitor at intervals over a period of time (a month is a good general rule). Save your results to a file, but do not create that file on the same drive with your data or log files. Also, although you want the recording interval to be frequent enough to capture problems, if you run it continually and you have more than a couple of counters turned on, you could very well cause a performance issue, thus skewing your results. Do not collect more detail than you need You can always run another test at a finer granularity if you discover a problem that requires closer analysis.

- Before changing any server setting, always note the original value and the time that you made the change. Always monitor the server after making changes, to see whether you have had the desired effect, or an unexpected one. Do not change too many settings at once.

Exploiting the Hardware

Another consideration when tuning a database server is the tuning of stored procedures, function code, indexes, and the data model. With capacity planning, for example, you can find out how much hardware you need to support a specific load, but it is unusual for a site to reach the hardware capacity right away, because the limiting factor is usually the application or database design or layout. Certainly as your system grows, you may need to do some capacity planning to decide what new hardware would be of most benefit. But you should not do this in a vacuum. Indeed, other than actual hardware errors, and a first cursory look at what you have, your focus in performance tuning should mostly be on application design and database objects. That being said, you should still make sure you are getting the most out of your server, including everything from disk arrays and data file placement to the CPU and memory.

Maximizing Performance

You will find any number of books that tell you how to maximize performance on your system by extensive monitoring, tweaking a few settings in **sp_configure**, and continually upgrading the hardware. Beyond a correct configuration for your system usage, you cannot do much more. Any of the steps you take to compensate for application performance, are just that: compensation. They should be viewed as temporary measures. Do not spend an excessive amount of time monitoring your system for opportunities to improve hardware when you could spend that time optimizing code instead.

The primary risk in concentrating on hardware rather than design is money. Here is a common scenario: A growing company has an application that was designed for a small user base. The company is very successful, and now it has many more users on its system. Managers make a decision to upgrade their hardware to a four-way processor server with external storage, to speed up the application. Fortunately, this works nicely.

As they continue to grow, they need still more performance: Because upgrading hardware worked before, they do the same thing again, this time upgrading to an eight-way processor server with a System Area Network (SAN). Performance increases, although not as much as before. Now the budget comes in for an application enhancement project, but it is a much higher estimate than it was before. Now application data is spread throughout the company, used in many reports, and exported to other systems as well. Redesigning the core application will mean redesigning each interface as well. Additionally, many more users will be affected by the application change; rolling out changes to desktops and laptops is now a significant part of the project. Analysis also reveals that the system now requires more extensive maintenance to accommodate the original design, and that the practical limitations of the design limit the disaster recovery options and also the service level agreement (SLA).

The application cannot be linearly upsized to the next largest server without incurring a much larger expense, and preliminary investigation into scaling out, rather than up, has shown that the expense is not only higher for hardware, but also would require more maintenance cost, and the addition of support staff. The users, on the other hand, are incurring lost time waiting for system response. Because the correct approach was delayed for too long, the business is now incurring risk based on a database design.

Capacity Planning

Capacity planning does not need to be a complicated process, although it can be if your system is very large or complex. Traditional capacity planning will tell you how much hardware you need to support a specific load on the server (assuming that the application takes full advantage of the hardware). As your system grows you may need to do this evaluative process more than once, and as you gain experience with it, you will undoubtedly refine and enhance the process for your individual system.

For a smaller system, the level of detail in a thorough capacity planning process may seem like overkill. It is still a good idea to go through the steps of capacity planning, as the process itself reveals much about your system. Collecting data for the plan is an iterative process: It must be repeated to accurately reflect the changes in usage over time. Detailed plans that involve careful collection and analysis of data generally are of immediate practical use in two situations: when you are planning for the purchase of hardware for a large system, or when your system has outgrown its current hardware and you must justify the purchase of additional hardware.

However, the best practice for capacity planning is to monitor your system periodically, making certain that you communicate the disparity between what the server is capable of and what the application can support..

For detailed coverage of capacity planning techniques, see the *Microsoft SQL Server 2000 Administrator's Companion*.

General Hardware Recommendations

CPU Planning

Processor planning is fairly straightforward. Monitor your current CPU utilization (\Processor(_Total)\% Processor Time). If the average is over 75 percent, if you have frequent peak usage periods where the current CPU utilization spikes over 90 percent, or if you have a situation in which the usage spikes and stays up for a while, then you should consider adding either additional processor(s) or faster processors.

In general, the processors you choose should be able to deliver the speed implied in your other system purchases. If your system is highly specialized and filled with processor intensive activities, you will become aware of that as you observe the system over time. Examples of such activities include extensive or frequent usage of Data Transformation Services, or anything involving a lot of calculations (science, accounting, and so on). SQL Server is a CPU-intensive application, so look for processors with a large high-speed cache.

If you have a dedicated SQL Server computer, use all of the processors for SQL Server. If your system is running applications in addition to SQL Server (such as Microsoft Commerce Server), then consider restricting SQL Server from using one or more processors. Otherwise, allow SQL Server and the operating system to balance across all processors.

Memory Planning

While the sum of all hardware together dictates the capacity of a system, memory is mainly focused on data access optimization. SQL Server uses memory to store execution plans, data pages between uses, and so on. Without enough memory, you will incur more disk I/O in reading data. If your system does many reads, you might reduce disk I/O by significantly increasing your memory, because the data will then remain in cache. Insufficient memory, or over-allocation of memory, can result in paging. Memory plays an important role in SQL Server, and is a resource you should carefully monitor.

For systems where reads are the highest priority (DSS), more memory is better. Memory can be used to compensate for disk I/O, and large amounts of memory can significantly decrease the number of disk (spindles) you will need to achieve high performance.

For systems where writes are the highest priority (OLTP), memory is still an important part of the system, but you may benefit more from the addition of disk spindles and controller channels, rather than memory. To be sure, you will need to monitor your system carefully to see which resources are in highest demand.

Disk Planning

The important point to remember about data storage is that the number of disks is far more important than the total storage size of the disks. One big physical disk may hold all your data, but it still has only one disk arm to execute each data request. More disk arms result in better performance.. So, when you size for new disks, check to be sure this is enough drive space; but spend more time on analyzing how many spindles you really need. For example, if your system does a lot of transactions, you will enhance performance by adding more spindles (provided there is sufficient memory and CPU to support the system as well).

When you are ordering your hardware, request a specific number of disks, rather than a specific amount of disk space. You want to have many smaller disks rather than fewer larger disks. If you have external storage, purchase the fastest array controller card and one that has multiple channels. Look at this card as a potential bottleneck: If you have many spindles, you need to make the investment in the card to support them. How much performance you get will be directly proportional to the quality of the controller, and the type of I/O your system produces.

In OLTP, you can have more disks per controller card, the disk spends more time looking for the data, and the controller channel will not become so saturated.

In DSS, where more of the queries are apt to be sequential reads, you will need more controller channels for a smaller set of disk drives. Also remember that memory is a good way to increase I/O in a DSS system.

Important   Using software RAID on a server running SQL Server will increase your CPU usage. Using file compression is not recommended because it will also increase your CPU usage.

For more information on all of these topics, please see SQL Server Books Online. Also see *Inside SQL Server 2000* and *Microsoft SQL Server 2000 Administrator's Companion*.

Working with Existing Hardware

If you are working with hardware you already own, you should be sure that you are getting the most out of it. At the outset, you must observe a few things about your system to configure the hardware for it correctly.

What kind of system is it? Is it DSS or OLTP? Any kind of reporting system, or any system that is query oriented and does not support transactions falls into the DSS category. OLTP includes any system doing work that consists of altering data: e-commerce, order processing, accounting, and so on. These two basic high-level categories are the starting point for system configuration. The differences between them begin at a hardware level.

Is the application mission critical? If the success of your company depends on the application, if the cost per hour of system downtime is high, or if an entire department simply goes home if they cannot log in, then those are signs that this may be mission critical.

Is the system 24 x 7? If it has to be available all day every day, and it is mission critical, you will need to investigate high availability systems. For more information about high availability, see Chapter 16, "Five Nines: The Ultimate in High Availability."

If it is not a 24 x 7 system, define the hours of required uptime. This will not only help you on the hardware side, it will also let you know how to support the system. If you do not already have a SLA, collecting this information will help you create one.

How many concurrent sessions do you need to support? How many transactions (selects, inserts, updates, and deletes) will each user do per minute?

How much space do you need (in MB) for data and indexes? How big is the log and **tempdb**? If there are multiple databases, you will need estimates for each.

Storage Subsystem Design

When you are ready to configure the disks, you should make a diagram of the hardware to help you decide how to configure the hardware in accordance with the data file layout strategy you need. You should be aware of a few concepts. Except for the amount of total disk space you need, you should give less attention to the size of the hard drives than you give to the number of hard drives in a set. This was important in ordering the hardware, and it is important now as you layout the data files.

Before you diagram your subsystem layout, there are some things to consider beyond the data storage components: channel, RAID level, and Read/Write cache settings.

Standardize Your Configuration

Although this is vital in an environment with many servers, standardizing configurations across servers is useful in any environment. To do this, create a list of all available settings on the server that you are not leaving at the default value, and document them. This would be labeled as the standard configuration for every new computer. Obviously, many of your systems may need to deviate from the standard settings. To handle this, document the difference for that computer between the set standard and the server in question. These documents, stored as read-only files in an easily accessible area (such as a Web repository), can help you better support a large number of servers.

For the storage subsystem, standardizing drive letters is very helpful. For example.

Logical drive letter	Description
C	Operating system, SQL executables
D	Usually a CD-ROM drive
E	Reserve for another system drive, if needed
F through H	**Tempdb**
I through P	Data files
Q	Quorum drive
R, S	SQL executables and system databases
T through V	Transaction log files
X, Y, Z	Backups, or imported data for bulk loading
\SQLAdmin	A standard admin directory to store reports such as logs, trace results, **sqldiag** output, and so on

For network drives, consider using Universal Naming Conventions (UNC) to allow maximum portability of code relying on these network drives.

RAID

For a database server, you should choose hardware level RAID rather than software RAID. Software RAID uses CPU cycles, and this prevents SQL Server from performing at the maximum level. Two core RAID levels are of value for a database server: striping with parity (RAID 5) and striped mirror (RAID 0+1). The best overall option is to choose RAID 0+1 (also called RAID 01 or "striped mirror"). RAID 5 can be used in certain circumstances, but is generally more expensive in the long run, and less reliable.

Data is protected by keeping redundant copies of it on different physical disks, so if one disk is lost through hardware failure, enough information exists on the remaining disks to reconstruct the original data. In RAID 5, each time data is written to disk, it actually takes four I/O operations in order to create the read data and parity blocks, and the write data and parity blocks. This is slow for two reasons: First, each process is consecutive, so they must wait on each other; second, this operation occurs while many other transactions are vying for the disk resources. RAID 0+1 writes to the primary disk and the mirror in one operation. Although you do have to wait for the write to complete on both drives, both writes are simultaneous.

The hidden cost of RAID 5 is in the lower write performance rate, a limiting factor on the amount of records that can be entered, orders that can be processed, and data requests that can be returned. When deciding to use RAID 5, which seems more economical at first glance, you are actually balancing a few thousand dollars in hard drives against system productivity.

The advantage of RAID 5 is that it gives you more storage space. So, the question to ask is: Do you need to store a lot of data on as little hardware as possible (but still have some fault tolerance), or do you need fast access and higher fault tolerance? Take a look at the size of your data files before making this decision, even on a small server with internal-only drives.

Given the same number of physical disks, RAID 0+1 will be faster than RAID 5. An increase in the number of drives in RAID 0+1 provides a linear increase in I/O capacity. A read can be obtained from either the primary drive or its mirror, so as I/O increases, the drives will become faster as a set because they can perform multiple reads simultaneously.

You should understand how choosing a RAID option affects the result to your server of losing a RAID drive. Although the loss of a RAID drive can sometimes affect the operation of a server, you can recover the data by restoring a backup of the database. In RAID 5, if any two disks fail, the database will stop (unless you have a hot standby disk that has had time to be synched within the chain, but even then, you cannot lose more than one disk from the whole working set). RAID 0+1 will stop the database only if a disk fails in both sides of a mirrored set the same time, and the odds of that occurring based on random factors are about 5.3 percent. RAID 5 imposes a significant penalty for losing even one disk. When one drive is lost on a RAID 5 system, the read performance of the system immediately decreases. Every read or write request to the failed drive initiates a verification process against all other drives in the parity group. This performance degradation will exist until the drive is replaced and completely rebuilt by the system. During the rebuild process, the system will be more sensitive to system load due to the considerably heavier I/O requirements of the failed system as described previously. This can be a critical consideration.

RAID 0+1 will see minimal loss of performance in a failed state where the hardware allows reads from both disks in a set. In this case read performance would be slightly reduced, but only for data stored on that particular set. RAID 0+1 can actually read simultaneously from both drives in a mirrored set. This is not a simultaneous read for the same I/O operation, but for different ones. So when you have multiple read requests for the same physical disk, the I/O operations are spread over the two disks in the mirrored set.

Changing the Subsystem

After a RAID level is selected, it can be changed only by complete reconfiguration at the hardware level. This will destroy all the data on that drive, so if you decide to change your RAID level, make sure that you have verified backups of the system, and that you also either have a sufficient window of agreed-upon downtime to rebuild it, or have a standby server to take over during the implementation. Before you begin to reconfigure the storage subsystem, carefully plan exactly how you want your data files laid out. Then, according to those requirements, determine which array each disk will be allocated to, how the arrays will be configured, and how the logical drives will be formatted and laid out.

Disk Controllers

Cache

Not all write caching is safe for use by a database server. You should make sure that your disk controller has features such as: safeguards to avoid uncontrolled reset of the caching controller, on-board battery backup, and mirrored or ERC (error checking and correcting) memory. Check with your hardware vendor to ensure that the write cache includes these and any other features necessary to avoid data loss. Do not implement write caching unless the hardware vendor guarantees that their write cache includes these features and any others required to prevent data loss.

Array accelerator cache settings can be left at the default value, which is typically 50:50 Read:Write. These settings can also be adjusted to favor reads or writes if you know which your system requires. Note that if you are using a Write setting above 0 here, you have enabled write caching.

For more information on SQL Server and caching controllers, see Knowledge Base article Q86903 at http://search.support.microsoft.com/kb/.

Channels

If your array configuration controller supports using more than one channel, make sure you take advantage of it. The only way to check this is to open the configuration tool provided by your controller manufacturer and look at the settings. Use caution when doing this, because if you press OK or Save at any point while viewing the controller settings, you may inadvertently reconfigure your array (which would result in immediate loss of any data stored on that drive).

Windows NT File System (NTFS) Allocation Unit

When you format the new drives in Disk Administrator, you should choose an allocation unit, or block size, which will provide optimal performance. Significant performance gains may be obtained by sizing this to a larger value in order to reduce disk I/Os; however, the default value is based on the size of the physical disk. The best practice for SQL Server is to choose 64 KB because this reduces the likelihood of I/Os that span distinct NTFS allocations, which then might result in split I/Os.

For more information on planning and configuring hardware, see *Inside SQL Server 2000*. For specific information on your hardware, refer to the customer service site of your hardware manufacturer.

Sample Server Configurations

The following section shows examples of various storage component plans, categorized by system type and size. It is not possible for this chapter to address all pf the various situations appropriate to each application, but these examples are based on commercially available servers and standard applications designed by Microsoft customers. Assume for each of these configurations that they are dedicated SQL Servers. If you are using these guidelines, and have other applications or services running on the computer, such as IIS, adjust the memory levels as needed. For clarity, standardized drive letters are used throughout these examples.

Small Entry-Level System Layout

These are characteristic of small servers. The key consideration on a system this small is to make sure your application is designed for the growth that you anticipate. To get maximum value out of your hardware investment, you should do optimization cycles as described in this chapter, even on this smaller, growing system.

The primary goal at this level is separating the operating system, page file, data, and transaction logs.

- Number of processors: two

- Memory: 512 MB; 384 MB dedicated to SQL Server

- Disk configuration: three internal high speed drives

  - Internal 1: 18 GB—contains the OS, page file, SQL executables, and system databases

  - Internal 2: 18 GB—contains the data files, including **tempdb**

  - Internal 3: 18 GB—contains the transaction log for SQL Server

This server is very simple compared to the later examples. Using RAID in this type of system is generally unnecessary, unless it is a high availability requirement or cost is no issue. If the application uses **tempdb** often, some disk I/O contention may take place since the rest of the data is also on the same disk. This server will not scale to support an enterprise system, and is a better fit for a departmental server or a company server that sees minimal use. If this server is supporting an application that is crucial to the company and has substantial activity, you definitely need to consider a larger server. To help the server scale along with the business, log the baseline monitoring counters (described earlier) on a regular basis, perhaps monthly. Document values of key counters, perhaps using a spreadsheet, so you have a permanent record to use for planning. These can be presented in report format, with a simple line graph showing the rise of specific counters as they change over time. A more sophisticated method of reporting system growth is detailed earlier in the chapter.

This server may function as either a transaction processing or reporting system, but not as both at once, unless the usage for either system is very low. The difference in disk access patterns between the two types of systems would cause an excessive amount of disk queuing and paging. You can still run simple reports on an OLTP system, and you can also run DSS style queries during off hours or build OLAP cubes during off hours. However, large analytical queries akin to those in a data mart would cause unnecessary slowness for the users of an OLTP system on the same server, provided they were both running during standard work hours.

A database server should never be used as a file server. This additional and random pattern of disk access would be even more of a problem than DSS reporting. Fileshare use on a database server also may introduce some security risks, and even worse, allows the possibility that a vital drive will fill with user files even if it is controlled at the operating system level by imposing quotas.

Expanding Capacity

As system usage grows, application performance may begin to suffer. After analyzing the system, you may decide to increase the capacity of the server by adding an external RAID array for the SQL Server data and log. SQL Server is reconfigured to use the existing files in their new locations. The new configuration might look like this:

- Number of processors: two

- Memory: 2 GB; 1.5 GB dedicated to SQL Server

- Disk configuration: two internal high speed drives, one SCSI RAID controller with two channels, external 12 disk bay array with eight drives. All drives are configured as RAID 0+1.

	GB	RAID partition	Total disks	Files
Drive C	18	N/A	2 internal	OS, page file, SQL executables, and system databases
Drive I	54	A	6 external	Data files and **tempdb**
Drive T	18	B	2 external	Transaction log

A common assumption is that with more capacity, running DSS on the same system would now be acceptable. Disk access is only part of the issue, because even if you were to separate the disk pairs to completely separate I/O for the DSS system, you would still be sharing the processors and memory. It should be worth a slightly higher investment to purchase two smaller servers. This would be most beneficial in cases where DSS users are allowed to access tables ad hoc.

This system will be noticeably faster. It has an additional CPU, more memory, and more spindles. Additionally, the transaction log has been split onto another RAID channel, which will result in some performance gain by itself. The data is now spread over four disks (two usable disks and two mirror disks). This number of spindles will provide good performance, provided the system has been properly optimized at the code and database level. The transaction log has only one usable disk, but this can support up to 1,000 transactions per second, and since these are all sequential writes, this configuration should be more than adequate for most growing systems.

If your system performs a lot of replication activity (for example, transactional replication frequently during business hours), you will want to leave the Read:Write cache at the default of 50:50, and consider adding an extra pair of disks to the transaction log (if replication is very heavy). The reason for this is that the log always writes and moves forward, except in two situations: in replication and in rollbacks.

OLTP System Server Layout

For this type of system, the transaction log for the application is split over multiple drives, so the site can support a larger number of transactions per second. For safety, backups are stored on a separate disk, which can also be used to hold data to be imported into a table. Memory is set to dynamically adjust itself.

- Number of processors: four (up to 32)
- Memory: 4 GB (up to 64 GB)
- Disk Configuration: 12 internal drives, one SCSI RAID controller with two channels, external 12 disk bay array with 12 drives. All drives are RAID 0+1.

	GB	Raid partition	Total disks	Files
Drive C	18	A	2 internal	Operating system, page file, SQL executables, and system databases
Drive T	54	B	4 internal	Transaction log
Drive Z	18	C	2 internal	Backups/Imported data files
Drive I	126	D	14 external	Data files **tempdb**

Note that this server is designed to support one heavily used application, or several lightly used applications. The difference lies in the isolation of resources. If you support multiple systems on the same server, and you wish to isolate resources a bit further, you would consider making more than one transaction log raid array. Because data is written to the transaction log sequentially, you might get better performance per application, depending on usage, by splitting the Array B in this table into two or three arrays, one for each application transaction log. A system that supports replication or performs many rollbacks, in addition to transaction volume, will need more disks (spindles) than one that does not have any such random I/O on the transaction log drive.

The data and **tempdb** remain striped across as many spindles as possible. Only on a very large system, one with both heavy usage and many disks available, would you consider separating the data files onto separate sets of physical disks. The only exception to this would be if multiple channels are available on your array controller. If so, then make full use of them. Using channels increases the amount of disk I/O you can support.

DSS System Server Layout

DSS focuses more on **tempdb** than on transaction log use. It also makes different use of CPU and memory because of the different type of data access. Memory is set to dynamically adjust itself. Here is a sample layout for a DSS system.

- Number of processors: eight (up to 32)

- Memory: 12 GB (up to 64 GB)

- Disk configuration: 12 internal drives, two SCSI RAID controllers with two channels, two external 12 disk bay array with 12 drives. All disks RAID 0+1.

	GB	RAID partition	Controller	Total disks	Files
Drive C	18	A	1	2 internal	OS, page file, SQL executables, and system databases
Drive T	54	B	1	6 internal	Transaction log
Drive Z	36	C	1	4 internal	Backups/Imported data files
Drive I	72	D	1	8 external	Data files
Drive F	36	E	2	4 external	**tempdb**, possibly some data files
Drive J	90	F	2	10 external	Data files
Drive T	54	G	2	6 external	Data files, possibly indexes

Multi-Instance N+1 Failover Cluster Configuration: SQL Server 2000 on Windows 2000 Datacenter Server

In this scenario, you have four servers of similar internal disk configuration, which share an external fibre channel SAN. Three SQL Server instances are active in the failover cluster. The requirements for CPU and RAM will vary depending on what role the server plays role in the cluster. Three of the cluster nodes are exactly the same, and own one instance apiece. The fourth node is the designated failover node, and will require a larger capacity in the event all three instances fail. AWE memory will be used. A failover cluster requires a well thought-out and certified hardware solution. For more information on failover clusters, AWE memory, and the N+1 configuration, see Chapter 12, "Failover Clustering."

Three active instances: These three servers should be exactly the same.

- Number of processors: eight

- Memory: 6 GB, SQL Server limited to 4 GB

- Disk configuration: 2 to 4 internal drives. RAID 1.

One failover: The failover node must have enough memory and CPU to support all three active instances, in case of failover.

- Number of processors: 32

- Memory: 16 GB

- Disk configuration: 2 to 4 internal drives. RAID 1.

SAN with fibre, 84 drives total

	GB	Total Disks (external)	Files
Drive Q	18	2	Quorum Drive
Drive T	36	4	Instance 1: Transaction Log
Drive U	36	4	Instance 2: Transaction Log
Drive V	18	2	Instance 3: Transaction Log
Drive I	90	10	Instance 1: Data files Instance 1: TempDB
Drive J	108	12	Instance 2: Data Files Instance 2: TempDB
Drive K	162	18	Instance 3: Data Files
Drive L	72	8	Instance 1: Data Files, possibly indexes
Drive M	72	8	Instance 2: Data Files, possibly indexes
Drive N	72	8	Instance 3: TempDB
Drive Z	36	4	Backups/Imported Data Files

It is important to keep in mind the separation of the internal disks from the external arrays on a cluster. The internal drive configuration will be similar on each server, and nothing that needs to be accessible to the failover instance should be stored on any internal drive.

Due to the way failover clustering works, each instance owns specific logical drives, which cannot be used by other instances. However, the logical drives can still be part of a single RAID partition, which is made up of many physical disks, as shown here. For this example, Instance 1 and 2 are OLTP applications of similar access patterns. Instance 3 is an example of a DSS type system that uses **tempdb** heavily enough that you would want to move it to a different drive. Note that, correspondingly, Instance 3 has the smaller transaction log drive (only two disks).

Conclusion

The architectural advances inside SQL Server mean that the DBA now focuses attention in a slightly different way. SQL Server is a flexible product, with many different levels. If your system is simple, then it may be simple from an administrative perspective as well.

The concepts and processes here are not new. This unified approach involves a simple shift in the focus of the job of a DBA, based on advances in SQL Server 2000, to accommodate the new complexities of managing a database system. The data tier is not a disparate collection of systems to be analyzed in isolation, but instead a complex synthesis of all database system components

Identifying Common Administrative Issues

This chapter describes user-defined stored procedures that can be used to identify server and database configurations that are outside the recommended configuration parameters for Microsoft® SQL Server™ 2000. The stored procedures are:

- **sp_rk_audit_configure**

  Checks server configuration for potential improvements.

- **sp_rk_audit_db_options**

  Checks the configuration of each database for potential improvements.

- **sp_rk_blocker_blockee**

  Returns information about all blocking and blocked processes.

These stored procedures can be used "as is" or modified by a database administrator to fit the specific needs of an enterprise. The stored procedures are available on the *SQL Server 2000 Resource Kit* CD-ROM in folder, \ToolsAndSamples\AdminStoredProcedures. The code examples in this chapter are also available on the *SQL Server 2000 Resource Kit* CD-ROM in file, \Docs\ChapterCode\CH34Code.txt. For more information, see Chapter 39, "Tools, Samples, eBooks, and More."

> **WARNING** Do not use the stored procedures described in this chapter on a production server without fully understanding how they work and what they do. It is strongly recommended that the techniques described in this chapter be tested on a development computer.

Installing the Stored Procedures

This installation procedure assumes that the instance of SQL Server on which these stored procedures are being installed allows trusted connections, and that the installation script is run by someone with **sysadmin** privileges. If you are unfamiliar with terms used in this chapter, see SQL Server Books Online.

To install the stored procedures

1. On the *SQL Server 2000 Resource Kit* CD-ROM, in the \ToolsAndSamples\AdminStoredProcedures folder, copy the .sql files to the hard drive of your computer.

2. Start SQL Query Analyzer, and on the **File** menu, click **Open**.

3. Navigate to the folder in which the SQL scripts are stored, and then double-click **sp_rk_create_audit_sp_in_master.sql**. This loads the master setup stored procedure.

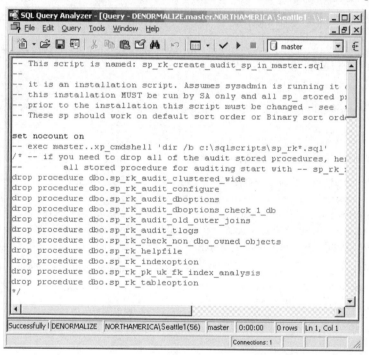

1. In the script, locate the comment "--Begin Customer changes here." Following this comment, there are three parameters whose values must be changed:

   - **@srcdir**

     The location of the SQL scripts that were installed on the computer.

   - **@lisdir**

     The location of where the output files generated by this installation script are to be stored.

   - **@srv**

     The name of the instance of SQL Server on which the stored procedures are to be installed.

2. On the **Query** menu, click **Results in Text**, and then execute the procedure. This installs the stored procedures in the **master** database.

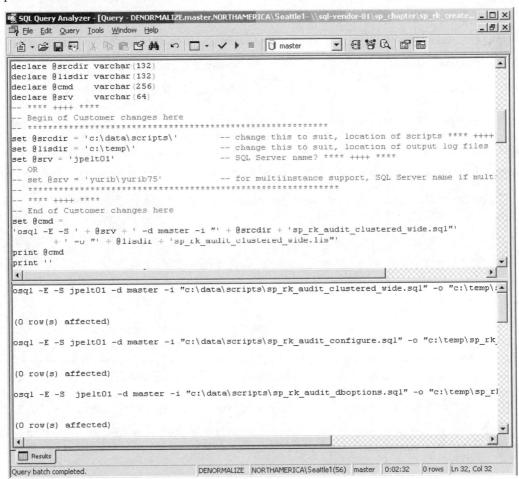

As shown in the preceding illustration, the **sp_rk_create_audit_sp_in_master.sql** script dynamically generates a command prompt call to the **osql** utility, and then runs it in the **xp_cmdshell** extended stored procedure. The **–E** flag means that **osql** is using trusted connections. If **osql** is not using trusted connections, each command line must be modified to use the **–U** *username* and **–P** *password* flags.

Very little data is returned to the SQL Query Analyzer results pane because the work is shelled out to the command line; however, the **osql** calls generate log files that are stored in C:\Temp by default.

In SQL Query Analyzer, in **Object Browser**, click **master**, and then click **Stored Procedures**. The following stored procedures should be listed:

dbo.sp_rk_audit_clustered_wide	**dbo.sp_rk_audit_clustered_wide**
dbo.sp_rk_audit_configure	**dbo.sp_rk_audit_configure**
dbo.sp_rk_audit_dboptions	**dbo.sp_rk_audit_dboptions**
dbo.sp_rk_audit_dboptions_check_1_db	**dbo.sp_rk_audit_dboptions_check_1_db**
dbo.sp_rk_audit_old_outer_joins	**dbo.sp_rk_audit_old_outer_joins**
dbo.sp_rk_audit_tlogs	**dbo.sp_rk_audit_tlogs**
dbo.sp_rk_blocker_blockee	**dbo.sp_rk_blocker_blockee**

If the stored procedures are not listed and there are no error messages in the results pane, check the log files generated by the **osql** calls. You will not see any error messages if, for example, the procedures are run against a server that does not exist, or with an account that does not have the appropriate permissions.

To view the log files in their default directory

1. On the **Start** menu, click **Run**, and then type **c:\temp** (or, if you changed this default, type the directory where the log files are stored).

2. Select one of the sp_rk*.lis files.

3. On the **File** menu, click **Open With**, and then select **Notepad**.

After the stored procedures have been installed, they can be run immediately with their default set of checks.

SQL Server 2000 can adjust many of its configuration parameters automatically at run time. For this reason, database administrators are advised to leave these parameters set at their default values. Some options, for example, **max worker threads**, can be adjusted manually to improve performance. The **max worker threads** option can be used to configure the number of worker threads available to SQL Server processes. The stored procedures described in this chapter can help determine which, if any, server configurations are outside the Microsoft recommendations for a database application.

> **Note** Some of the **sp_configure** parameters apply only to SQL Server version 7.0 and have been removed in SQL Server 2000, for example, **max async IO**.

Check Server Configuration (sp_rk_audit_configure)

The **sp_rk_audit_configure** stored procedure is a stand-alone stored procedure. **sp_rk_audit_configure** checks the server configuration options. The default ranges for these server configuration options are hard-coded into the stored procedure based on Microsoft recommendations. Changing these ranges and adding a new option to check are covered in "Modifying sp_rk_audit_configure" in this chapter. **sp_rk_audit_configure** has no required parameters.

Configuration Options that Are Checked

The **sp_rk_audit_configure** stored procedure checks whether or not TCP/IP Sockets is installed and whether the **tempdb** or **msdb** databases have grown since the last time SQL Server was started.

The following table shows the configuration options that **sp_rk_audit_configure** checks and the recommended values.

Configuration option	Recommended value
affinity mask	= 0
allow updates	= 0
fill factor (%)	Not between 1 and 49
lightweight pooling	= 0
locks	Not between 1 and 9999
max async IO	>= 32 (SQL Server 7.0 only)
max server memory (MB)	> 32 or > (Total RAM – 48 megabytes (MB))
min memory per query (KB)	>= 1024
network packet size (B)	Between 4096 and 16384
open objects	= 0
priority boost	= 0
query governor cost limit	= 0
query wait (s)	= -1
recovery interval (min)	= 0 or between 5 and 30
resource timeout (s)	= 10
set working set size	= 0
spin counter	= 0
time slice (ms)	Between 100 and 300

Running sp_rk_audit_configure

sp_rk_audit_configure gathers information about the server configuration by running stored procedures, such as **sp_configure** and **xp_msver,** and then storing their results in temporary tables.

To run sp_rk_audit_configure

1. In SQL Query Analyzer, in the query window, type **sp_rk_audit_configure**.

2. On the **Query** menu, click **Results in Text,** and then execute the stored procedure.

    As shown in the following illustration, the Results pane lists server configuration options that are less than optimal, as well as the number of possible problems to investigate.

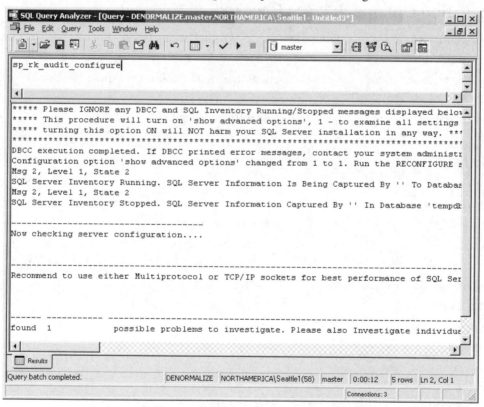

How sp_rk_audit_configure Works

This section describes some of the important sections of code in the **sp_rk_audit_configure** stored procedure.

The **#t** temporary table stores results from the **sp_configure** system stored procedure:

```
create table #t (
    [name] varchar(128),
    minimum int,
    maximum int,
    config_value int,
    run_value int
)
```

The **#t_serverinfo** temporary table stores results from the **xp_msver** stored procedure:

```
create table #t_serverinfo(
    [Index] int,
    [Name] varchar(255),
    Internal_Value int,
    Character_Value varchar(255)
)
```

To see all possible configuration settings in **sp_configure**, the **sp_rk_audit_configure** stored procedure sets the **show advanced options** parameter to 1:

```
execute sp_configure 'show advanced options', 1
reconfigure with override
reconfigure
```

sp_configure and **xp_msver** are run and the results from these stored procedures are inserted into their respective temporary tables:

```
insert into #t ([name], minimum, maximum, config_value, run_value)
execute sp_configure
insert into #t_serverinfo( [Index] , [Name] , Internal_Value ,
Character_Value )
exec master..xp_msver
```

Most of the remaining code in **sp_rk_audit_configure** compares the entries in the **#t** temporary table created by **sp_configure** to the hard-coded values. For example, the following code checks to see whether an affinity mask is in place. For more information about using an affinity mask in a multiprocessor environment, see SQL Server Books Online.

```
if exists (select 1 from #t where [name] = 'affinity mask' and
                        (config_value <> 0 or run_value <> 0))
begin
  select 'Recommend value to be set to 0 for ', *
  from #t
  where name = 'affinity mask'
  set @nr = @nr + 1
end
```

Finally, **sp_rk_audit_configure** checks to see whether the **tempdb** or **msdb** databases have expanded since SQL Server was started. If these databases have expanded, the **sp_rk_audit_configure** stored procedure recommends that the databases be resized. The stored procedure does this by exploiting the different times at which SQL Server updates its system tables when a database file expands. The **sysfiles** system table in the local database always has current information about the size of the database files; however, the **sysaltfiles** system table in the **master** database is updated only when the server is restarted.

```
select *
from   master.dbo.sysaltfiles a
       inner join tempdb.dbo.sysfiles f
       on a.fileid = f.fileid
where dbid = db_id('tempdb') and
       a.size <> f.size
```

Modifying sp_rk_audit_configure

The **sp_rk_audit_configure** stored procedure can be customized to:

- Check for nested triggers.

- Check for product version information.

- Increase **max async IO** (SQL Server 7.0 only).

For example, if the servers are high performance servers with intelligent disk subsystems, the amount of asynchronous IO requests can be changed from 32 to 64.

To increase the max async IO

1. In SQL Query Analyzer, in **Object Browser**, expand the **master** database.

2. In **Stored Procedures**, right-click **sp_rk_audit_configure**, and then click **Edit**.

   This loads the stored procedure in a new query window.

   Instead of being in a CREATE PROCEDURE statement, **sp_rk_audit-configure** is now in an ALTER PROCEDURE statement. Thus, all existing permissions and dependencies will not be lost. For more information, see "ALTER PROCEDURE" in SQL Server Books Online.

3. Locate the following code:

   ```
   if exists (select 1 from #t where [name] = 'max async IO' and
                   (config_value < 32 or run_value < 32))
   begin
   select 'Recommend value to be set to 32 or more for ', * from #t where
                   name = 'max async IO'
   set @nr = @nr + 1
   end
   ```

4. In the code in Step 3, replace the value 32 with 64:

5. Recompile the stored procedure.

To see whether nested triggers are enabled

1. In SQL Query Analyzer, in **Object Browser**, expand the **master** database.

2. In **Stored Procedures**, right-click **sp_rk_audit_configure**, and then click **Edit**. This loads the stored procedure in a new query window.

3. Locate the following code:

   ```
   -- conclusions
       if @nr > 0
       begin
       select 'found ', @nr, ' possible problems to investigate. Please also Investigate
   individual databases. End of Report.'
       end
       else
       begin
       select 'found nothing to investigate server wide. Please Investigate individual
   databases. End of Report.'
       end

       return 0
   ```

4. Paste the following code into the stored procedure just before the "--conclusions" comment shown in Step 3.

Code Example 34.1

```
if exists (select 1 from #t where [name] = 'nested triggers' and
                 (config_value = 0))
begin
select 'Nested Triggers are currently disabled!'
set @nr = @nr + 1
end
```

5. Recompile the stored procedure.

To check the version of SQL Server you are running

To check whether the server is running SQL Server 2000, look at the product version information returned from **xp_msver**, which is called by **sp_rk_audit_dboptions_check_1_db**. You can also check for any release of SQL Server, including service packs, by adjusting the major and the minor release numbers in the **character_value** string.

1. In SQL Query Analyzer, in **Object Browser**, expand the **master** database.

2. In **Stored Procedures**, right-click **sp_rk_audit_configure**, and then click **Edit**. This loads the stored procedure in a new query window.

3. Locate the following line of code:

```
from #t_serverinfo where [Name] = 'ProductVersion'
```

4. Paste the following code into the stored procedure immediately after the line of code in Step 3.

Code Example 34.2

```
If Exists (select 1 from #t_serverinfo where [Name] = 'ProductVersion'
                      and Character_Value = '8.00.100')
Begin
Select 'This server is running SQL 2000 .'
End
```

5. Recompile the stored procedure.

Check Database Configuration (sp_rk_audit_dboptions)

The **sp_rk_audit_dboptions** stored procedure is the entry point to a suite of stored procedures that will check a number of database-specific parameters for one or all of the databases on the server. This section contains a short description of each of these stored procedures.

Important   The **sp_rk_audit_dboptions** stored procedure must be run first because it creates all the temporary tables that are referenced by the other stored procedures described in this section.

sp_rk_audit_dboptions_check_1_db

Checks the following database options. It also checks all databases for database and transaction log backups within the last month and makes sure that log and database files are on separate disks.

Database option	Value
auto update statistics	OFF
auto create statistics	OFF
autoclose	ON
autoshrink	ON
dbo use only	ON
Offline	ON

If the database is not a system database, the following options and values are also reported.

Database option	Value
select into/bulkcopy	ON
trunc. log on chkpt.	ON

sp_rk_check_non_dbo_owned_objects

Checks the database for objects not owned by **dbo**.

sp_rk_indexoption

Looks for indexes with option values. For more information, see "sp_indexoption" in SQL Server Books Online.

sp_rk_tableoption

Looks for tables with option values. For more information, see "sp_tableoption" in SQL Server Books Online.

sp_rk_pk_uk_fk_index_analysis

Checks each table for at least one PRIMARY KEY, FOREIGN KEY, or UNIQUE constraint. It also lists any table without an index.

sp_rk_audit_old_outer_joins

Checks for all user-defined stored procedures in the database with old (non–SQL-92 standard) joins (*= or =*).

sp_rk_audit_clustered_wide

Looks for wide clustered keys with secondary indexes.

For more information about SQL Server performance tuning, see the topics "Optimizing Database Performance" and "Setting Database Options" in SQL Server Books Online.

Running sp_rk_audit_dboptions

The **sp_rk_audit_dboptions** stored procedure creates temporary tables that will store information about the environment of each database.

To run sp_rk_audit_dboptions

1. In SQL Query Analyzer, in the query window, type **sp_rk_audit_dboptions**.

2. On the **Query** menu, select **Results in Text**, and then execute the stored procedure.

   The following illustration shows a section of the results.

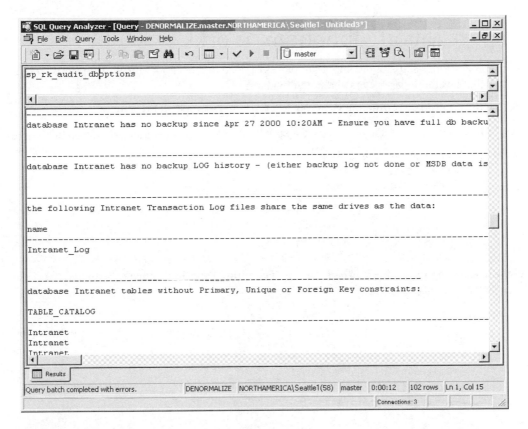

sp_rk_audit_dboptions discovered the following:

- A database called **intranet** has not been backed up in more than a week.

- The transaction log for this database has never been backed up.

- The log and database files share the same drive, which is not recommended.

- Some tables do not have PRIMARY KEY, UNIQUE, or FOREIGN KEY constraints.

How sp_rk_audit_dboptions Works

This section describes some of the important pieces of code in the **sp_rk_audit_dboptions** stored procedure that has these parameters and default values:

sp_rk_audit_dboptions(@dbname sysname = NULL, @DebugFlag int = 0)

The **#t_indexes** temporary table is used by the **sp_rk_pk_uk_fk_index_analysis** stored procedure:

```
create table #t_indexes(
        tablename varchar(255),
        indexname varchar(255),
        indid int,
        indextype varchar(15),
        objectowner varchar(80)
)
```

The **#t_dbfiles** temporary table is used by the **sp_rk_audit_dboptions_check_1_db** and the **sp_rk_helpfile** stored procedures:

```
create table #t_dbfiles(
        [name] varchar(256),
        fileid int,
        [filename] varchar(1024),
        [filegroup] varchar(256),
        [size] decimal(15,0),
        maxsize decimal(15,0),
        growth decimal(15,0),
        usage char(12),
        growth_type char(1) -- '%' percent, 'K' Kb
)
```

The **#t_serverversioninfo** temporary table is used by the **sp_rk_audit_dboptions** stored procedure:

```
create table #t_ serverversioninfo (
    [Index] int,
        [Name] varchar(255),
        Internal_Value int,
        Character_Value varchar(255)
)
```

The **#t_sp** temporary table is used by the **sp_rk_audit_dboptions** and the **sp_rk_audit_old_outer_joins** stored procedures:

```
create table #t_sp([text] varchar(8000) )
```

The **#t_logs80** temporary table is used by the **sp_rk_audit_dboptions** and the **sp_rk_audit_tlogs** stored procedures:

```
create table #t_logs80(
    FileID int,
    FileSize int,
    StartOffset int,
    FSeqNo int,
    Status int,
    Parity int,
    CreateLSN varbinary(48)
)
```

The **#t** temporary table is used by the **sp_rk_audit_dboptions** and the **sp_rk_audit_dboptions_check_1_db** stored procedures:

```
    create table #t (
        [name] varchar(128),
        dbname varchar(256) default null
    )
```

If the **sp_rk_audit_dboptions** stored procedure is called without any parameters, it will call **sp_rk_audit_dboptions_check_1_db** for each database. Otherwise, it will call the **sp_rk_audit_dboptions_check_1_db** stored procedure for the specified database only.

```
sp_rk_audit_dboptions_check_1_db(
@dbname sysname- NULL,
@SQLServerVersion int = 70,
@DebugFlag int = 0)
```

Most of the code in the **sp_rk_audit_dboptions_check_1_db** stored procedure examines the result set from **sp_dboption**, including:

auto update statistics	**dbo use only**
auto create statistics	**offline**
autoclose	**select into/bulkcopy**
autoshrink	**trunc. log on chkpt.**

sp_dboption *database name* will list all of the database options that are set to ON for a database. The **#t** temporary table created by **sp_rk_audit_dboptions** stores the list of all options that are set to ON for each database. To check whether a database has an option set to ON, the code must check the **#t** temporary table. For example, the following code checks to see whether a database has the **auto update statistics** option set to ON.

```
if not exists (select 1 from #t where dbname = @dbname and [name] =
                        'auto update statistics')
begin
    select 'database ' + @dbname + ' disables: auto update statistics' +
                        ' - not recommended'
end
```

After checking for a variety of options in the **#t** temporary table, **sp_rk_audit_dboptions_check_1_db** checks the database and log backup history stored in **msdb.dbo.backupset**.

sp_rk_audit_dboptions_check_1_db first checks to see whether the database has been backed up. Then, it stores the **backup_finish_date** in **@db_backup_finish_date**. If this value is NULL, the database has never been backed up.

```
select top 1 @db_backup_finish_date = backup_finish_date
from msdb.dbo.backupset
where database_name = @dbname and type = 'D' -- Database
order by backup_finish_date desc

if (@db_backup_finish_date is NULL)
begin
    select 'database ' + @dbname + ' has no backup history (either backup not done or
msdb data is lost). Ensure you have full db backup!'
end
```

If the value is not NULL, the stored procedure checks to see whether the database has been backed up in the last seven days:

```
else if (DATEDIFF(day, @db_backup_finish_date, getdate()) > 7) -
                recommend backup at least on weekly basis
begin
    select 'database ' + @dbname + ' has no backup since ' +
                convert(varchar(30),@db_backup_finish_date,100) + ' -
                Ensure you have full db backup.'
End
```

The stored procedure then checks to see whether the transaction log has been backed up:

```
select top 1 @tlog_backup_finish_date = backup_finish_date
from msdb.dbo.backupset
```

```
where database_name = @dbname and type = 'L' -- Log file (Transactional)
order by backup_finish_date desc
if (@tlog_backup_finish_date is NULL)
begin
   select 'database ' + @dbname + ' has no backup LOG history (either
                       backup log not done or msdb data is lost). Ensure
                       you have T-LOG backup!'
end
```

If the transaction log has been backed up, then the stored procedure checks to see whether it has been backed up within the last day:

```
else if (DATEDIFF(day, @tlog_backup_finish_date, getdate()) > 1) -
                 recommend backup at least on daily basis
begin
   select 'database ' + @dbname + ' has no T-LOG backup since ' +
                  convert(varchar(30),@tlog_backup_finish_date,100) + ' -
                  Ensure you have periodic T-LOG backup.'
End
```

The stored procedure then checks the table to ensure that the database and transaction log files are stored on separate logical drives.

Other Stored Procedures Called by sp_rk_audit_dboptions_check_1_db

sp_rk_audit_dboptions_check_1_db then calls a series of other stored procedures:

sp_rk_check_non_dbo_owned_objects
Checks the **uid** (user ID) column of **sysobjects** for objects owned by users other than **dbo** or **INFORMATION_SCHEMA**.

sp_rk_indexoption
Checks the **lockflags** column of **sysindexes**. This indicates whether locking constraints have been set on any indexes.

sp_rk_tableoption
Checks **sysobjects** for any table options.

sp_rk_pk_uk_fk_index_analysis
Finds tables that do not have a PRIMARY KEY, FOREIGN KEY, or UNIQUE constraint. It also looks for tables on which no indexes are defined.

sp_rk_audit_old_outer_joins
Checks the text of all stored procedures stored in the text column of the **syscomments** table to find any procedures that are using the old syntax for outer joins (*= or =*).

sp_rk_audit_clustered_wide

Finds tables that have wide clustered and other indexes present.

sp_rk_audit_tlogs

Checks the amount of virtual log files (30+) and growth factor (<10%) of transaction logs.

Modifying sp_rk_audit_dboptions_check_1_db to Look at Different Values

The **sp_rk_audit_dboptions_check_1_db** stored procedure checks all of the database options by looking at the result set of the **sp_dboption** stored procedure, which is stored in the **#t** temporary table. By default, **sp_rk_audit_dboptions_check_1_db** does not check all of the configurable database options that are queried by **sp_dboption**. One such option is **recursive triggers**. If your application uses recursive triggers, which are disabled by default, you can use **sp_rk_audit_dboptions_check_1_db** to check this option.

To modify sp_rk_audit_dboptions_check_1_db to look at different values

1. In SQL Query Analyzer, in **Object Browser**, expand the **master** database, and then click the **Stored Procedures** folder.

2. Right-click **sp_rk_audit_dboptions_check_1_db**, and then select **Edit**.

   This loads the stored procedure into a new query window.

   Instead of being in a CREATE PROCEDURE statement, the stored procedure is now in an ALTER PROCEDURE statement. Thus, all existing permissions and dependencies will not be lost.

3. Find the section of the stored procedure that begins to look at the **sp_dboption** information (stored in **#t**). The first part of the code looks like this:

Code Example 34.3

```
if not exists (select 1 from #t where dbname = @dbname and [name] =
                'auto update statistics')
begin
    select 'database ' + @dbname + ' disables: auto update
                statistics' + ' - not recommended'
    set @nr = @nr + 1
end
```

4. Copy the preceding code and paste it directly above the first IF statement.

   Note   This code checks the **auto update statistics** option. To check the **recursive triggers** option, replace the **auto update statistics** with **recursive triggers**.

```
if not exists (select 1 from #t where dbname = @dbname and [name] =
              'recursive triggers')
begin
    select 'database ' + @dbname + ' disables: recursive triggers' +
              ' - not recommended'
    set @nr = @nr + 1
end
```

5. On the **Query** menu, select **Execute**. The screen should look like the following illustration.

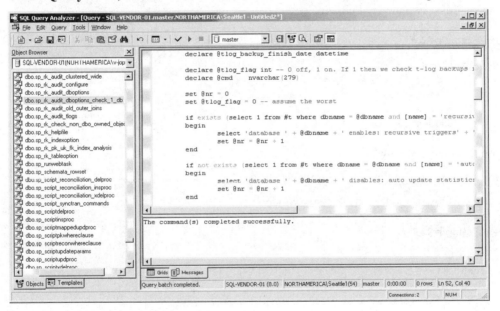

Application Troubleshooting

Blocking is one of the common issues a database administrator encounters. The **sp_rk_blocker_blockee** stored procedure, another stand-alone procedure, lists all of the blocking server process identifiers (SPIDs), their input buffers, the SPIDs that they are blocking, their wait time, and input buffers. The data returned from this stored procedure makes it easy to identify the causes of blocking.

Running sp_rk_blocker_blockee

sp_rk_blocker_blockee has no parameters.

After this stored procedure is installed, it can be run immediately.

In SQL Query Analyzer, in the query window, type **sp_rk_blocker_blockee**. You will not see any results unless blocking is in progress.

To test the stored procedure with simulated blocking

1. In SQL Query Analyzer, in the database drop-down list, select **pubs**, and then open a new query window.

2. Paste, and then execute the following code:

Code Example 34.4

```
Create table a(
Col1 int
)
GO
insert a values(1)
```

3. Close the query window.

4. Open a new query window for the **pubs** database.

5. Paste the following code into the query window:

Code Example 34.5

```
Begin tran
-- Execute this first!
Update a set Col1 = 1 where Col1 = 1
-- this will keep this transaction opened for 1 minute
Waitfor delay '000:01:00'
Commit tran
```

6. Open another new query window for the **pubs** database.

7. Paste the following code into the query window:

Code Example 34.6

```
Begin Tran
-- Execute this second!
Update a set Col1 = 5 - 4 where Col1 = 1
Commit tran
```

8. Open one more new query window.

   Select any database from the database drop-down list.

9. In the query window, type **sp_rk_blocker_blockee**, but do not execute the stored procedure immediately.

10. In SQL Query Analyzer, click **Window**, and then select **Tile Vertically** so the three query windows are displayed.

11. Execute the code from Step 5, and then execute the code from Step 7.

12. Within one minute of executing the code from Step 5, execute the **sp_rk_blocker_blockee** stored procedure from Step 9. The Results pane should look like the following illustration.

```
--------- -----------
Blocker:  59

EventType       Parameters EventInfo
------------- ---------- ---------------------------------------------------------------
Language Event 0         Begin tran
        -- Execute this first!
        Update a set col1 = 1 where col1 = 1
        -- this will keep this transaction opened for 1 minute
        Waitfor delay '000:01:00'
Commit tran


DBCC execution completed. If DBCC printed error messages, contact your system administrator.

-------------------- ----------- -----------
Blockee:    Waittime: 60        3225

EventType       Parameters EventInfo
------------- ---------- ---------------------------------------------------------------
Language Event 0         Begin Tran
        -- Execute this second!
        Update a set col1 = 5 - 4 where col1 = 1
Commit tran

DBCC execution completed. If DBCC printed error messages, contact your system administrator.
```

How sp_rk_blocker_blockee Works

sp_rk_blocker_blockee queries the **master.dbo.sysprocesses** system table. This table is dynamically generated and holds information about the processes that are running on SQL Server. For more information about **sysprocesses** and the other system tables, see SQL Server Books Online.

Examine the following columns of the **sysprocesses** table:

- **spid**

  Holds the server process ID for the process.

- **blocked**

  Is either 0 or holds the SPID of a blocking process.

- **waittime**

  Indicates the amount of time that the process has been blocked.

sp_rk_blocker_blockee stores the information it retrieves from the **sysprocesses** table in two cursors: **blocker_cursor** and **blockee_cursor**.

blocker_cursor holds all of the SPIDs that appear at the head of the blocking chains:

```
DECLARE blocker_cursor CURSOR for
    SELECT spid from master.dbo.sysprocess WHERE spid IN (SELECT blocked
FROM master.dbo.sysprocesses) AND blocked = 0
```

blockee_cursor holds all blocked processes:

```
Declare blockee_cursor CURSOR for
SELECT spid, blocked, waittime FROM master.dbo.sysprocesses WHERE
            blocked > 0
```

sp_rk_blocker_blockee then loops through the **blocker_cursor**, each time finding the SPIDs in the **blockee_cursor** whose blocked columns match the blocker SPID. For each SPID it finds, **sp_rk_blocker_blockee** lists the wait time and input buffer. To find the input buffer of a process, run DBCC INPUTBUFFER(*spid*). For more information about the DBCC commands, including DBCC INPUTBUFFER, see SQL Server Books Online.

Modifying sp_rk_blocker_blockee

The code for **sp_rk_blocker_blockee** does not need much modification. When checking for blocking problems, you must be careful not to add complex logic because this will only make the problem worse. However, if catching the blocking is a problem, use the SQL Server Agent to run **sp_rk_blocker_blockee** at specified intervals automatically. The SQL Server Agent can be modified to log its results to a table instead of printing them on the screen. For more information about the SQL Server Agent, see "Automating Administrative Tasks" in SQL Server Books Online.

Using Visual Basic to Remotely Manage SQL Server 2000

In a world where data must be available 24 hours a day, 7 days a week, database administrators (DBAs) are in demand. It is not always possible to staff data operation centers with fully-qualified SQL DBAs. This chapter shows you how to construct such a tool using SQL Database Management Objects (SQL-DMO) and SQL Namespace (SQL-NS) objects with Microsoft® Visual Basic®.

SQL-DMO and SQL-NS are COM interfaces you can access from Visual Basic or any other COM-speaking language. SQL-DMO is a collection of objects that encapsulate SQL Server's database, scheduling, and replication management. SQL-NS is a collection of objects, accessed slightly differently, that encapsulate the functionality in SQL Server Enterprise Manager.

One advantage of passing SQL Server management tasks through a COM interface is the extra layer of protection it provides. For example, if several people in your organization need remote SQL Server administrative capability, but you want to maintain specific control of what they can do or access after they are inside the system, SQL-DMO can provide a solution. This chapter demonstrates a sample Visual Basic application, the SQL Junior Administrator, that provides administrative capability without granting total access.

As mentioned, SQL-DMO exposes SQL Server as a series of objects in collections. The **Application** object contains all the SQL Server objects, each of which contains a collection of **Database** objects. Each **Database** object holds a group of collections, such as **Tables**, each of which is made up of a series of objects, such as **Column** objects, each of which has a series of properties. There are different building blocks for each of the collections but they share the same general architecture. SQL-DMO allows programmatic access to every layer.

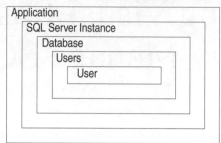

Using SQL-DMO and SQL-NS, you can perform almost any administrative or management task through simple dot notation coding. The major difference between SQL-DMO and SQL-NS is in the way they allow access to the server objects. SQL-DMO uses a collection of collections, and SQL-NS uses a tree-and-node model. Although you can manipulate SQL Server through either one, most of this chapter will focus on SQL-DMO. For more information about SQL-DMO and SQL-NS, see SQL Server Books Online.

The sample application discussed in this chapter uses only a few of the ways that you can manipulate a SQL Server database using SQL-DMO. In fact, almost every property of every object in the database can be manipulated including logins, indexes, relationships, foreign keys, and triggers.

Inside the SQL Junior Administrator Application

The SQL Junior Administrator sample application is provided on the accompanying CD. The code is immediately usable, and it can be easily modified or upgraded for more secure or thorough functionality.

User Interface

The application provides a simple graphical user interface, through which users can log in, view existing data objects, create new data objects, and access a subset of the SQL Server tools.

Log In

Open SQLDMO.exe on the accompanying CD. The drop-down box displays any SQL Server instances available on your network or local computer and allows for login.

Note   This sample application contains only basic error handling functionality.

Setting Permissions

Successful login brings you to the main screen. You can create and view server logins without selecting a database, but if you want to perform database-specific actions involving tables or stored procedures, you must select a database.

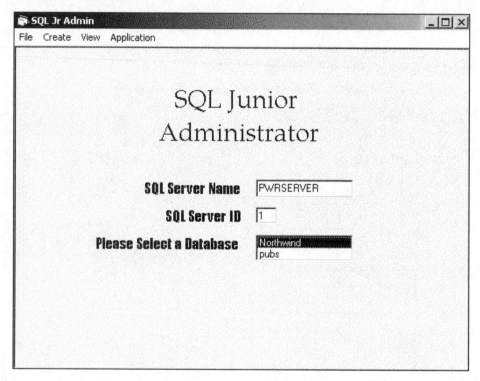

To create a login, on the **Create** menu click **Login**.

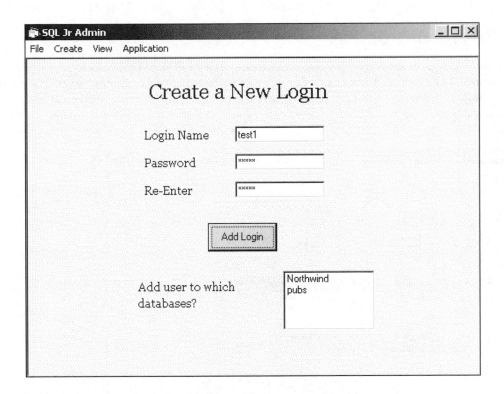

After you enter the login information, a list box appears, displaying the names of the databases found on that server instance. To add user permissions to an individual database, select the database in that list and then confirm the choice in the dialog box that appears.

The application automatically adds DB_DDLADMIN and DB_DATAWRITER permissions to the chosen database. These permissions allow users to create and modify new tables as well as view and edit data in existing tables.

To view existing logins, click **Logins** on the **View** menu. To delete a login, select it in the list box, and then confirm your choice.

Viewing Existing Data Objects

After the user has been given the correct permissions, existing tables and stored procedures within that database are available through the **View** menu. The stored procedures themselves cannot be modified, but the columns within a chosen table can be seen and added to (although the properties of existing fields cannot be changed from this application). For example, to view existing data objects, click **Table** on the **View** menu.

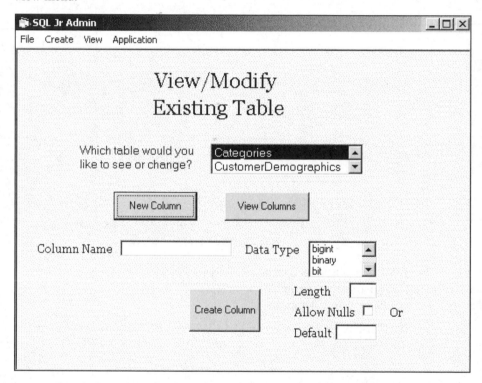

After you select a table, two buttons appear, offering a choice to add a new column or to view existing columns. Clicking **Add Column** causes several fields to appear on the form in which the basic properties of a new column can be set. (Only the properties required for the creation of a new column are present here, though every column property can be set programmatically.) To create the new column, set the property values and then click **Add Column**. Clicking **View Columns** produces a list box showing all available columns. After you select a column, fields appear, containing the existing column properties.

Note It is not possible to modify existing column properties using this application.

Creating New Data Objects

You can also create new data objects from this interface. For example, to create a new table in a database, click **Table** on the **Create** menu and then fill in the form fields. After you enter the name for the new table, you can use the controls that appear to enter property information for new columns. (The **TableName_ID** column, which is an ID column, is created automatically.)

Using SQL Server Tools

The **Application** tab provides access to the administrative functionality, such as wizards and backup, you can use through SQL-DMO.

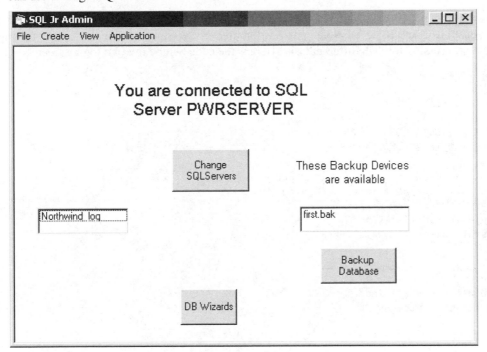

The list box on the left shows all existing logs in that instance of SQL Server, the list box on the right shows all existing backup devices, and the **Change SQLServers** button opens the main form and allows you to log into a different SQL Server database.

This form only allows you to view existing objects, such as backup devices. If you want to add functionality to create new objects, follow this sample application's model for creating tables and columns. You just need to provide the code to set or access the correct properties within the appropriate collection. SQL-DMO docs the rest.

Note that frmApp provides a higher level of access than other parts of this application. The **DB Wizards** button allows direct access to the SQL Server Enterprise Manager wizards. These wizards allow the user to implement a wide variety of administrative tasks. Clicking this button opens the master wizard, from which any of the other wizards can be selected and put into action. The full functionality of these wizards is too extensive to be covered here, but it includes all of the individual processes shown on frmApp. For more information about the SQL Server Enterprise Manager wizards, see SQL Server Books Online

> **Note** The SQL Server Enterprise Manager wizards are accessed through SQL-NS, not SQL-DMO. For more information, see "Application Tasks" in this chapter.

Visual Basic Code

By exploring the code behind the user interface, you can learn more about using SQL-DMO and SQL-NS to implement custom Visual Basic solutions. This section follows the path a user might follow, starting with login and progressing through different tasks. Here is the code behind the first login screen:

```
Private Sub Form_Load()

On Error GoTo ErrorHandler

    Dim SQL7 As New SQLDMO.Application
    Dim NameList As SQLDMO.NameList

    Set NameList = SQL7.ListAvailableSQLServers
      ' Show all available servers running SQL Server
    Dim x As Integer
    For x = 0 To NameList.Count
      Me.lstSrvrs.AddItem NameList(x)
    Next

    ' Clean up
    Set SQLInstance = Nothing
    Set NameList = Nothing

    Exit Sub

ErrorHandler:

  MsgBox "Unable to get list of servers."

End Sub
```

This subroutine uses the **ListAvailableSQLServers** method of the **Application** object to populate the **NameList** DMO object when the form loads. The **NameList** object is a collection object, which the code iterates through to produce a list box that contains all the instances of SQL Server that are available to that computer.

The following subroutine records the user-entered information and attempts to log in to the selected instance of SQL Server through the **Connect** property of the instance. Each required layer of the SQL-DMO nest must be instantiated.

```
Private Sub btnGo_Click()

On Error GoTo ErrorHandler

        ' Set application variables for login
    Dim SQL7 As New SQLDMO.Application
    Dim SQLInstance As SQLDMO.SQLServer
    Set SQLInstance = New SQLDMO.SQLServer
      ' Log in
    SQLInstance.Connect Me.lstSrvrs.Text, Me.txtLogin.Text, Me.txtPassword.Text

      ' If OK then
    Set SQLInstance = Nothing
    Set SQL7 = Nothing
      ' Set global variables
    ServerName = Me.lstSrvrs.Text
    User = Me.txtLogin.Text
    Password = Me.txtPassword.Text
      ' Open the body of the program
    Load frmMain
    Me.Hide
    frmMain.Show

    Call HideOthers("frmMain")

    Exit Sub

ErrorHandler:

  MsgBox "Unable to log you in to " & ServerName & "."

End Sub
```

The final, one-line subroutine sets the cursor into the login box automatically after a SQL Server instance is selected:

```
Private Sub lstSrvrs_Click()

  Me.txtLogin.SetFocus

End Sub
```

> **Note** Global variables, as set in the btnGo_Click subroutine after the successful login, are rarely the best way to store user information. On the other hand, the global module may be the perfect place to initialize application and server instances, which are required for every task in SQL-DMO, although those initializations are included in every subroutine here. This particular application has been written to be immediately usable and at the same time easily modified or upgraded for more secure or thorough functionality.

The **HideOthers** function called from the btnGo_Click subroutine can be found in the global module. It takes the name of one form (the one the user has selected to see) as a parameter and hides the rest, with the exception of the MDI parent form in which most of the application windows live:

```
Public Sub HideOthers(ByVal FormName As String)

    Dim Form As Form
    For Each Form In Forms

        If Form.Name <> FormName And Form.Name <> "frmMDIMain" Then Form.Hide

    Next

End Sub
```

Main

The MDI parent (frmMDIMain) opens after successful login, and it initially contains the Main form (frmMain) with the database list box discussed earlier in this chapter. The MDI form has some code behind it, but it only refers to the menu controls present on the form, such as the **On_Load** event that disables some of them initially:

```
Private Sub MDIForm_Load()

    Me.cmdTable.Enabled = False
    Me.cmdViewTable.Enabled = False
    Me.cmdViewSP.Enabled = False
    mnuApp.Enabled = False

End Sub
```

The same menu provides basic program functionality, such as exiting the application:

```
Private Sub cmdClose_Click()

      'Exit the program
Dim Form As Form
For Each Form In Forms
     Unload Me
Next

End Sub
```

The following code provides one example of program navigation, coded similarly throughout the application (only the menu choice name and the form name change):

```
Private Sub cmdViewTable_Click()

    Load frmViewTable
    frmViewTable.Show

    Call HideOthers("frmViewTable")

End Sub
```

The Main form is straightforward. The two read-only text boxes display the server name and **ConnectionID** value, which is the value SQL-DMO uses to attach you to the correct SQL Server instance. A list box shows each of the databases on that SQL Server in much the same way as the **SQLServers** collection was generated on the login screen.

The only thing your code must do is instantiate a SQL-DMO object for each layer of the nest you want to access. In this case, the user will access one layer deeper than from the login screen; the list box here will show the databases inside the previously selected server instance.

> **Note** The base index value for collections in SQL-DMO is 1 instead of 0 (which is the usual index value of the first object in a Visual Basic collection or array). Because of this, any counter variables must be initialized.

```
Public Sub GetDBList()

                'This subroutine retrieves a list of databases
                'that reside on the server specified by name
                'in the Connect property of the instance of SQL Server
```

```
On Error GoTo ErrorHandler

        ' Create a SQL-DMO application and SQL Server 2000 instance
    Dim SQL2000 As New SQLDMO.Application
    Dim SQLInstance As SQLDMO.SQLServer
    Dim DB As SQLDMO.Database

        ' Instance variables
    Dim SQLSrvrID As Long

    Set SQLInstance = New SQLDMO.SQLServer
        ' Connect to the server by name (from global variable)
    SQLInstance.Connect ServerName, User, Password
        ' Set the instance to that server ID
    SQLSrvrID = SQLInstance.ConnectionID
    Set SQLInstance = SQL2000.SQLServers.ItemByID(SQLSrvrID)

        ' Display the available databases in a list box
        Dim x As Integer

        x = 1

        For Each DB In SQLInstance.Databases

                'Do not add system databases to the list
            If Not SQLInstance.Databases(x).SystemObject Then
                Me.lstDBs.AddItem (SQLInstance.Databases(x).Name)
            End If

        x = x + 1

        Next

        ' Show the connection ID
        Me.txtCnxnID = SQLSrvrID

        ' Clean up
    Set SQLInstance = Nothing
    Set SQL2000 = Nothing

        Exit Sub

ErrorHandler:

    MsgBox "Unable to get database list."

End Sub
```

The **ConnectionID** value is also the value required to execute the **ItemByID** method of the **SQLServers** collection in the **Application** object:

```
SQLSrvrID = SQLInstance.ConnectionID
Set SQLInstance = SQL2000.SQLServers.ItemByID(SQLSrvrID)
```

These two lines assure connection to the instance of SQL Server while you work with the database objects inside.

In the For Each loop that produces the list box of databases, take note of this line:

```
If Not SQLInstance.Databases(x).SystemObject Then
```

The **SystemObject** property (which holds a Boolean value) of each database within the **Databases** collection allows you to display only the available non-system databases. This is an example of the additional security that SQL-DMO can provide while still allowing some administrative tasks on the server to be accomplished.

The final subroutine in the form enables the balance of those tasks after a database has been selected:

```
Private Sub lstDBs_Click()

    frmMDIMain.cmdTable.Enabled = True
    frmMDIMain.cmdViewTable.Enabled = True
    frmMDIMain.cmdViewSP.Enabled = True
    frmMDIMain.mnuApp.Enabled = True

End Sub
```

Create Login

Adding permissions for someone to work within that instance of SQL Server is a two-step process. In this application, both processes are taken care of in the same form (frmCreateLogin). The first step is to create a login to the server itself. To do this, add a **Login** to the **Logins** collection of the server instance and then assign the correct server permissions to that login:

```
Private Sub CreateLogin(ByVal NewLoginID As String, ByVal NewPassword As String)

On Error GoTo ErrorHandler

        Dim SQL2000 As New SQLDMO.Application
        Dim SQLInstance As SQLDMO.SQLServer
        Dim SQLSrvrID As Long
        Dim Login As SQLDMO.Login

            ' User objects
        Dim NewLogin As SQLDMO.Login
        Dim ServerRole As SQLDMO.ServerRole
```

```
        Dim ServerRole2 As SQLDMO.ServerRole

        Set SQLInstance = New SQLDMO.SQLServer
            ' Connect to the server by name (from global variables)
        SQLInstance.Connect ServerName, User, Password
        SQLSrvrID = CLng(frmMain.txtCnxnID)
        Set SQLInstance = SQL2000.SQLServers.ItemByID(SQLSrvrID)

          ' Create the login
        Set NewLogin = CreateObject("SQLDMO.Login")
          ' Server roles for the login
        Set ServerRole = SQLInstance.ServerRoles("dbcreator")
        Set ServerRole2 = SQLInstance.ServerRoles("diskadmin")

     ' Check to see if that login already exists
        Dim x As Integer
        For Each Login In SQLInstance.Logins
          If Login.Name = NewLoginID Then
              MsgBox "That login already exists in " & ServerName & "."
              Exit Sub
          End If
        Next

          ' If not then assign login values
        NewLogin.Type = SQLDMOLogin_Standard
        NewLogin.SetPassword "", NewPassword
        NewLogin.Name = NewLoginID

          ' Add the new login to the correct roles
        SQLInstance.Logins.Add NewLogin
        ServerRole.AddMember (NewLoginID)
        ServerRole2.AddMember (NewLoginID)

        MsgBox "New login added to " & ServerName & "."
          ' Show database user fields
        Me.lblDB.Visible = True
        Me.lstDBs.Visible = True
        Exit Sub

            ' Clean up
        Set SQLInstance = Nothing
        Set SQL2000 = Nothing
        Set ServerRole = Nothing
```

```
        Set ServerRole2 = Nothing
        Set Login = Nothing
        Set NewLogin = Nothing
        Exit Sub

ErrorHandler:

    MsgBox "Unable to add login successfully."

End Sub
```

After all of the objects and variables have been initialized, the login is checked against all of the existing logins in the **Logins** collection using this code:

```
        Dim x As Integer
        For Each Login In SQLInstance.Logins
            If Login.Name = NewLoginID Then
                MsgBox "That login already exists in " & ServerName & "."
                Exit Sub
            End If
        Next
```

Then the **Login** object itself is created and assigned values for the required properties:

```
        Set NewLogin = CreateObject("SQLDMO.Login")
        NewLogin.Type = SQLDMOLogin_Standard
        NewLogin.SetPassword "", NewPassword
        NewLogin.Name = NewLoginID
```

The first argument contains an empty string because there is no previous password for this login. You can also use the **SetPassword** method to change existing passwords.

Permissions must also be set for new logins. In SQL Server, permissions are often granted through server roles. The SQL Junior Administrator application creates two server roles, DBCREATOR and DISKADMIN:

```
        Set ServerRole = SQLInstance.ServerRoles("dbcreator")
        Set ServerRole2 = SQLInstance.ServerRoles("diskadmin")
```

ServerRoles is a collection contained in each SQL Server instance. For more information about security, see Chapter 10, "Implementing Security," and SQL Server Books Online.

After the roles are created, use the following code to add the new login to members of the **Logins** collection of the server instance:

```
        SQLInstance.Logins.Add NewLogin
        ServerRole.AddMember (NewLoginID)
        ServerRole2.AddMember (NewLoginID)
```

Next, grant users access to individual databases. Creating these permissions is similar to adding logins to a server instance. Instead of adding a login to the **Logins** collection of the server instance, add a user to the **Users** collection of each database and assign that user the appropriate database roles:

```
Private Sub CreateDBUser(ByVal DBName As String, ByVal NewLoginID As String, ByVal
NewPassword As String)

    On Error GoTo ErrorHandler

    Dim SQL2000 As New SQLDMO.Application
    Dim SQLInstance As SQLDMO.SQLServer
    Dim SQLSrvrID As Long
    Dim DB As SQLDMO.Database

        ' User objects
    Dim DBUser As SQLDMO.User
    Dim Role As SQLDMO.DatabaseRole
    Dim Role2 As SQLDMO.DatabaseRole

    Set SQLInstance = New SQLDMO.SQLServer
        ' Connect to the server by name (from global variables)
    SQLInstance.Connect ServerName, User, Password
    SQLSrvrID = CLng(frmMain.txtCnxnID)
    Set SQLInstance = SQL2000.SQLServers.ItemByID(SQLSrvrID)

    ' Add the login as a user to the database
    ' with the appropriate permissions
    Set DBUser = CreateObject("SQLDMO.User")
    DBUser.Name = NewLoginID
    DBUser.Login = NewPassword

    Set DB = SQLInstance.Databases(DBName)
    Set Role = DB.DatabaseRoles("DB_DDLADMIN")
    Set Role2 = DB.DatabaseRoles("DB_DATAWRITER")

    DB.Users.Add DBUser
    Role.AddMember NewLoginID
    Role2.AddMember NewLoginID

    MsgBox "New user permissions to create database objects and to read and write
data " & vbCrLf _
        & "have been added to " & DBName & "."

        ' Clean up
    Set SQLInstance = Nothing
    Set SQL2000 = Nothing
    Set DB = Nothing
```

```
        Set DBUser = Nothing
        Set Role = Nothing
        Set Role2 = Nothing
        Exit Sub

ErrorHandler:

    MsgBox "Unable to add database user."

End Sub
```

The newly created login now has permissions in the selected databases to create and modify tables and to read and write data.

Create Table

Creating a table is similar to creating a user; both are objects (and members of collections) within a database. Only the collection references and required property settings change.

```
Private Sub AddTable(ByVal DBName As String, ByVal TableName As String)

On Error GoTo ErrorHandler

        Dim SQL2000 As New SQLDMO.Application
        Dim SQLInstance As SQLDMO.SQLServer
        Dim CnxnID
            ' Database objects
        Dim DB As SQLDMO.Database
            ' Table objects
        Dim NewTable As SQLDMO.Table
        Dim NewColumn As SQLDMO.Column

        Set SQLInstance = New SQLDMO.SQLServer
            ' Connect to the server by name (from global variable)
        SQLInstance.Connect ServerName, User, Password
        CnxnID = frmMain.txtCnxnID
        Set SQLInstance = SQL2000.SQLServers.ItemByID(CnxnID)

        ' Create table and column
        Set NewTable = CreateObject("SQLDMO.Table")
        Set NewColumn = CreateObject("SQLDMO.Column")

          ' Name the table and give ownership to the dbo
        NewTable.Name = TableName
        NewTable.Owner = "dbo"
```

```
        ' Add the first column as identity -
        ' at least one column must be present before you add a table
        NewColumn.Name = TableName & "_ID"
        NewColumn.Datatype = "int"
        NewColumn.Identity = True
        NewColumn.IdentitySeed = 0
        NewColumn.IdentityIncrement = 1

        'Add it to the Columns collection
        NewTable.Columns.Add NewColumn

        'Add the whole thing to the Tables collection
        Set DB = SQLInstance.Databases(DBName)
        DB.tables.Add NewTable

        MsgBox "table added to " & DBName

            ' Show the column controls
        Me.lblAddColumns.Visible = True
        Me.lblColName.Visible = True
        Me.lblDataType.Visible = True
        Me.lblOr.Visible = True
        Me.lblDefault.Visible = True
        Me.lblNulls.Visible = True
        Me.lblLength.Visible = True

        Me.txtColName.Visible = True
        Me.lstDT.Visible = True
        Me.chkNulls.Visible = True
        Me.txtDefault.Visible = True
        Me.txtLength.Visible = True
        Me.btnCreateColumn.Visible = True

        Exit Sub

ErrorHandler:

    MsgBox "Unable to add table."

End Sub
```

Note The previous subroutine contains code to make certain controls appear only after the table creation process has actually begun. This is not required; it is there to keep the form uncluttered.

The only difference between creating a table object and creating a user object is the addition of the first **Column** object in the table. This is required by the **Add** method of the **Tables** collection. The previous code defines the first column it creates as an identity column. (Only one identity column is allowed in each table.)

```
NewColumn.Name = TableName & "_ID"
NewColumn.Datatype = "int"
NewColumn.Identity = True
NewColumn.IdentitySeed = 0
NewColumn.IdentityIncrement = 1
```

The following line of code sets the owner of the table:

```
NewTable.Owner = "dbo"
```

Here, ownership rights have been given to the database owner. If your code does not do this, the **Owner** property of the object is automatically mapped to the current login. This can create problems if you try to remove that login from the system.

To add columns, access the **Columns** collection in the table and add a column to it:

```
Private Sub AddColumn(ByVal DBName As String, ByVal TableName As String, ByVal
ColumnName As String)

On Error GoTo ErrorHandler

        Dim SQL2000 As New SQLDMO.Application
        Dim SQLInstance As SQLDMO.SQLServer
        Dim CnxnID As Long
            ' Database object
        Dim DB As SQLDMO.Database
            ' Table objects
        Dim table As SQLDMO.table
        Dim NewColumn As SQLDMO.Column

        Set SQLInstance = New SQLDMO.SQLServer
            ' Connect to the server by name (from global variable)
        SQLInstance.Connect ServerName, User, Password
        CnxnID = CLng(frmMain.txtCnxnID)
        Set SQLInstance = SQL2000.SQLServers.ItemByID(CnxnID)
        Set DB = SQLInstance.Databases(DBName)

         ' Get the table
        Set table = DB.Tables(TableName)
         ' Create the column
        Set NewColumn = CreateObject("SQLDMO.Column")
```

```
      ' Add the column with basic properties
      NewColumn.Name = ColumnName
      NewColumn.Datatype = Me.lstDT.Text
      NewColumn.Length = Me.txtLength.Text
      If Me.chkNulls.Value = 1 Then NewColumn.AllowNulls = True
      NewColumn.Default = Me.txtDefault.Text

      'Add it to the Columns collection
      table.Columns.Add NewColumn

      MsgBox "Column " & ColumnName & " added to " & TableName & "."

        ' Reset the form
      Me.txtColName = ""
      Me.txtDefault = ""
      Me.txtLength = ""
      Me.chkNulls.Value = 0
      Me.txtColName.SetFocus

      Exit Sub

ErrorHandler:

    MsgBox "Unable to add column."

End Sub
```

As shown in the two previous subroutines, certain properties of the column must be set for the **Add** method of the **Columns** collection to work. For example, the **Datatype** property must be set, so that all of the existing data types are listed in a list box on frmCreateTable. To do this, loop through each member of the **SystemDataTypes** collection of the database (using a variant to hold each value).

```
Private Sub GetDataTypes()

On Error GoTo ErrorHandler

      Dim SQL2000 As New SQLDMO.Application
      Dim SQLInstance As SQLDMO.SQLServer
      Dim CnxnID
          ' Database objects
```

```
Dim DB As SQLDMO.Database
        Dim DBName As String

        Set SQLInstance = New SQLDMO.SQLServer
            ' Connect to the server by name
        SQLInstance.Connect ServerName, User, Password
        CnxnID = frmMain.txtCnxnID
        Set SQLInstance = SQL2000.SQLServers.ItemByID(CnxnID)

            ' Get the database by name
        DBName = frmMain.lstDBs.Text
        Set DB = SQLInstance.Databases(DBName)

        Dim dt
        Dim x As Integer

        x = 1

        For Each dt In DB.SystemDatatypes

            Me.lstDT.AddItem DB.SystemDatatypes.Item(x).Name
            x = x + 1

        Next

            ' Clean up
        Set DB = Nothing
        Set SQLInstance = Nothing
        Set SQL2000 = Nothing
        Exit Sub

ErrorHandler:

    MsgBox "Unable to get list of data types."

End Sub
```

This application sets only the properties required to make the called method work correctly. However, you can use SQL-DMO to manipulate all column properties, just as if you were within SQL Server Enterprise Manager.

Note   You do not have to memorize all of the properties and methods, because the standard dot notation statement completion works with SQL-DMO. When you dot any correctly instantiated object, a list of available properties and methods appears.

View Table

Retrieving the existing columns for any tables in the database is a simple two-step process that begins with iterating through the **Tables** collection added to in the previous example. In the GetTableList subroutine shown here, the results of the loop are again placed in a list box:

```
Private Sub GetTableList(ByVal SQLSrvrID As Long, ByVal DBName As String)


        ' Application objects
    Dim SQL2000 As New SQLDMO.Application
    Dim SQLInstance As SQLDMO.SQLServer
        ' Database object
    Dim DB As SQLDMO.Database
        ' Table and column objects
    Dim table As SQLDMO.Table
    Dim NewColumn As SQLDMO.Column

    Set SQLInstance = New SQLDMO.SQLServer
        ' Connect to the server by name (from global variable)
    SQLInstance.Connect ServerName, User, Password
    Set SQLInstance = SQL2000.SQLServers.ItemByID(SQLSrvrID)
    Set DB = SQLInstance.Databases(DBName)

     ' Show the tables one at a time
    Dim x As Integer
    For x = 1 To DB.Tables.Count
        ' But do not show system tables
      If Not DB.Tables(x).SystemObject Then
          Me.lstTables.AddItem DB.Tables(x).Name
      End If
        x = x + 1
    Next

End Sub
```

The second part of the operation, the listing of the columns themselves, can be completed after the table has been selected:

```
Private Sub GetFieldList(ByVal SQLSrvrID As Long, ByVal DBName As String, ByVal
TableName As String)


        ' Application objects
    Dim SQL2000 As New SQLDMO.Application
```

```
    Dim SQLInstance As SQLDMO.SQLServer
            ' Database object
    Dim DB As SQLDMO.Database
            ' Table and column objects
    Dim table As SQLDMO.table
    Dim Column As SQLDMO.Column

    Set SQLInstance = New SQLDMO.SQLServer
            ' Connect to the server by name (from global variable)
    SQLInstance.Connect ServerName, User, Password
    Set SQLInstance = SQL2000.SQLServers.ItemByID(SQLSrvrID)
    Set DB = SQLInstance.Databases(DBName)
    Set table = DB.Tables(TableName)

     ' Show the columns one at a time
    Dim x As Integer

    x = 1
    For x = 1 To table.Columns.Count
            Me.lstFields.AddItem table.Columns(x).Name
            x = x + 1
    Next

End Sub
```

In this application, the capability to add a column to an existing table is present in the same form (frmViewTable).

View Login

The process for seeing existing logins for a server is similar to the process for seeing databases on the server. To view existing logins, use the **Logins** collection. (This is the same collection used to add a new login and to loop through to see if a login already exists by accessing the **Name** property.) The following code adds logins to a list box:

```
Sub GetLogins(ByVal SQLSrvrID As Long)

On Error GoTo ErrorHandler

    Dim SQL2000 As New SQLDMO.Application
    Dim SQLInstance As SQLDMO.SQLServer
            ' User objects
    Dim Login As SQLDMO.Login
```

```
                Set SQLInstance = New SQLDMO.SQLServer
                    ' Connect to the server by name (from global variable)
                SQLInstance.Connect ServerName, User, Password
                Set SQLInstance = SQL2000.SQLServers.ItemByID(SQLSrvrID)

                    ' Fill the list box
                Dim x
                x = 1
                For Each Login In SQLInstance.Logins
                    Me.lstLogins.AddItem SQLInstance.Logins(x).Name
                x = x + 1
                Next

                  ' Clean up
                Set SQLInstance = Nothing
                Set SQL2000 = Nothing

                Exit Sub

        ErrorHandler:

            MsgBox "Unable to get login list."

        End Sub
```

A common reason for retrieving a list of logins is so you can delete someone's login. This is a two-step process that is the reverse of adding a login. You must remove the login as a user from all appropriate databases before you remove it as a server login. You can accomplish this in one procedure, using the **Remove** method of the **Users** and **Logins** collections:

```
Sub DeleteLogin(ByVal SQLSrvrID As Long, ByVal Login As String)

On Error GoTo ErrorHandler

            Dim SQL2000 As New SQLDMO.Application
            Dim SQLInstance As SQLDMO.SQLServer
            Dim DB As SQLDMO.Database

            Set SQLInstance = New SQLDMO.SQLServer
                ' Connect to the server by name (from global variable)
            SQLInstance.Connect ServerName, User, Password
            Set SQLInstance = SQL2000.SQLServers.ItemByID(SQLSrvrID)

                ' Remove the user from all databases
```

```
For Each DB In SQLInstance.Databases
    If DB.IsUser(Login) Then DB.Users.Remove (Login)
Next

    ' Remove the user from the server
SQLInstance.Logins.Remove (Login)

    ' Show confirmation
MsgBox Login & " has been removed from " & ServerName

    ' Fill the list box again
Dim x As Integer
x = 1
Dim UserName As SQLDMO.Login

Me.lstLogins.Clear
For Each UserName In SQLInstance.Logins
    Me.lstLogins.AddItem SQLInstance.Logins(x).Name
x = x + 1
Next

    ' Clean up
Set UserName = Nothing
Set SQLInstance = Nothing
Set SQL2000 = Nothing
Set DB = Nothing

    Exit Sub
ErrorHandler:

    MsgBox "Unable to delete login."

End Sub
```

The **IsUser** method removes the user from the **Users** collection in only the appropriate databases in the **Database** object:

```
For Each DB In SQLInstance.Databases
    If DB.IsUser(Login) Then DB.Users.Remove (Login)
Next
```

Failing to use this method results in an error for any database if the chosen login is not currently shown as a member of that database's **Users** collection. The previous procedure also automatically refills the logins list box once the login is removed from the system.

Changing permissions for an existing login or user requires only slight modification of the previous procedures.

View Stored Procedures

The viewing of stored procedures is functionality added to the SQL Junior Administrator with Visual Basic and Active Server Pages (ASP) developers in mind. You must usually know the exact names of the stored procedures you want to execute programmatically. Getting all of the existing stored procedures in a database by name and displaying them conveniently is easy in SQL-DMO:

```
Private Sub GetSPList(ByVal SQLSrvrID As Long, ByVal DBName As String)

On Error GoTo ErrorHandler

        ' Application objects
    Dim SQL2000 As New SQLDMO.Application
    Dim SQLInstance As SQLDMO.SQLServer
        ' database object
    Dim DB As SQLDMO.Database

    Set SQLInstance = New SQLDMO.SQLServer
        ' Connect to the server by name (from global variable)
    SQLInstance.Connect ServerName, User, Password
    Set SQLInstance = SQL2000.SQLServers.ItemByID(SQLSrvrID)
    Set DB = SQLInstance.Databases(DBName)

     ' Show the stored procedures one at a time
    Dim x As Integer
    For x = 1 To DB.StoredProcedures.Count
            Me.lstSPs.AddItem DB.StoredProcedures(x).Name
    Next

    Set SQL2000 = Nothing
    Set SQLInstance = Nothing
    Set DB = Nothing
    Exit Sub

ErrorHandler:

    MsgBox "Unable to retrieve stored procedures."

End Sub
```

> **Note** Because SQL syntax checking is not provided, you cannot use this application to view and edit the actual SQL code within the stored procedure.

Application Tasks

You can begin to explore the full functionality of SQL-DMO by using this sample application to retrieve (but not modify) two other collections in SQL Server. These collections, **Backup Devices** and **Database Logs**, are geared more directly toward actual administrative tasks and represent only a small subset of the accessible collections.

You can use similar code to complete both retrieval tasks. This code shows how to retrieve the logs:

```
Sub GetLogs(ByVal SQLSrvrID As Long, ByVal DBName As String)

        ' Application objects
    Dim SQL7 As New SQLDMO.Application
    Dim SQLInstance As SQLDMO.SQLServer
        ' Database object
    Dim DB As SQLDMO.Database

    Set SQLInstance = New SQLDMO.SQLServer
        ' Connect to the server by name (from global variable)
    SQLInstance.Connect ServerName, User, Password
    Set SQLInstance = SQL7.SQLServers.ItemByID(SQLSrvrID)
    Set DB = SQLInstance.Databases(DBName)

      ' Show the log files one at a time
    Dim x As Integer
    For x = 1 To DB.TransactionLog.LogFiles.Count
       Me.lstLog.AddItem DB.TransactionLog.LogFiles(x).Name
       x = x + 1
    Next

       ' Clean up
    Set DB = Nothing
    Set SQLInstance = Nothing
    Set SQL7 = Nothing

End Sub
```

This code shows how to retrieve the list of backup devices:

```
Sub GetBackupDvcs(ByVal SQLSrvrID As Long)

        ' Application objects
    Dim SQL7 As New SQLDMO.Application
    Dim SQLInstance As SQLDMO.SQLServer
        ' Database object
    Dim DB As SQLDMO.Database
```

```
        Set SQLInstance = New SQLDMO.SQLServer
            ' Connect to the server by name (from global variable)
        SQLInstance.Connect ServerName, User, Password
        Set SQLInstance = SQL7.SQLServers.ItemByID(SQLSrvrID)

        Dim x As Integer
        If SQLInstance.BackupDevices.Count = 0 Then
            Me.lstBUDvc.AddItem "No Backup Devices"

        Else
          ' Show the log files one at a time
            For x = 1 To SQLInstance.BackupDevices.Count
                Me.lstBUDvc.AddItem SQLInstance.BackupDevices(x).Name
                x = x + 1
            Next

        End If

          ' Clean up
        Set DB = Nothing
        Set SQLInstance = Nothing
        Set SQL7 = Nothing

End Sub
```

You will probably use SQL-DMO to construct applications to offer only limited capability to manage administrative tasks in SQL Server. However, if you want to offer a more robust interface to SQL Server, SQL-NS may be the better solution. Although the overall capabilities of SQL-DMO and SQL-NS are similar, SQL-NS allows you to access the SQL Server Enterprise Manager wizards. The SQL Server Enterprise Manager wizards provideremote administrative capabilities.

The **DB Wizards** button invokes SQL-NS to call the various wizards in SQL Server Enterprise Manager. You can use SQL-NS to allow full remote administrative access to the database. Every wizard is accessible through this simple piece of code:

```
Private Sub GetWiz()

    Dim NS As SQLNS.SQLNamespace
    Dim NSO As SQLNS.SQLNamespaceObject
    Dim Srvr As Long
    Dim strCnxn As Variant
```

```
Set NS = CreateObject("SQLNS.SQLNamespace")

    strCnxn = String(255, 0)
    strCnxn = "Server="
    strCnxn = strCnxn & ServerName & ";"
    strCnxn = strCnxn & "UID=" & User & ";"
    strCnxn = strCnxn & "pwd=" & Password & ";"

    MsgBox "Your connection string is:" & vbCrLf & strCnxn
    NS.Initialize "SQLDMO", SQLNSRootType_Server, strCnxn, frmMDIMain.hWnd

  Srvr = NS.GetRootItem
  If Srvr <> 0 Then
      Set NSO = NS.GetSQLNamespaceObject(Srvr)
      NSO.ExecuteCommandByID (SQLNS_CmdID_WIZARDS)
  Else
      MsgBox "No server"
  End If

End Sub
```

When you use SQL-NS, objects are instantiated to create a node-and-tree object structure (as opposed to collections as in SQL-DMO):

```
Dim NS As SQLNS.SQLNamespace
Dim NSO As SQLNS.SQLNamespaceObject
```

Connections are also created differently, although the server name, user ID, and password are all still required. For example, a specific cast is required instead of simple string variable creation before the connection string is assembled.

```
Dim strCnxn As Variant
strCnxn = String(255, 0)
strCnxn = "Server="
strCnxn = strCnxn & ServerName & ";"
strCnxn = strCnxn & "UID=" & User & ";"
strCnxn = strCnxn & "pwd=" & Password & ";"
```

The connection is then established through the **Initialization** property (not the **Connect** property) of the **NameSpace** object:

```
NS.Initialize "SQLDMO", SQLNSRootType_Server, strCnxn, frmMDIMain.hWnd
```

In the previous line of code, the first argument is the requesting application, the second is the root type, the third is the connection string, and the last is the handle of the requesting MDI form within the application that was passed in the first parameter.

Finally, object references are also different in SQL-NS and SQL-DMO. In SQL-NS, server objects are accessed through the appropriate root node:

```
Srvr = NS.GetRootItem
If Srvr <> 0 Then
     Set NSO = NS.GetSQLNamespaceObject(Srvr)
     NSO.ExecuteCommandByID (SQLNS_CmdID_WIZARDS)
  Else
     MsgBox "No server"
  End If
```

This is the line of code that retrieves the wizard:

```
NSO.ExecuteCommandByID (SQLNS_CmdID_WIZARDS)
```

In this case, the constant that shows all of the other wizards (SQLNS_CmdID_WIZARDS) was selected, but each of the following wizards is available by passing the appropriate CommandID constant.

Command	Constant
Create Database Wizard	SQLNS_CmdID_WIZARD_CREATEDB
Create Index Wizard	SQLNS_CmdID_WIZARD_CREATEINDEX
Data Import/Export Wizard	SQLNS_CmdID_WIZARD_DTSIMPORT
Data Import/Export Wizard	SQLNS_CmdID_WIZARD_DTSEXPORT
Create Job Wizard	SQLNS_CmdID_WIZARD_CREATEJOB
Security Wizard	SQLNS_CmdID_WIZARD_SECURITY
Create Stored Procedure Wizard	SQLNS_CmdID_WIZARD_SP
Create View Wizard	SQLNS_CmdID_WIZARD_VIEW
Index Tuning Wizard	SQLNS_CmdID_WIZARD_INDEXTUNING
Create Alert Wizard	SQLNS_CmdID_WIZARD_ALERT
Database Maintenance Plan Wizard	SQLNS_CmdID_WIZARD_MAINTPLAN
Web Assistant Wizard	SQLNS_CmdID_WIZARD_WEBASST
Create Database Backup Wizard	SQLNS_CmdID_WIZARD_BACKUP
Create Trace Wizard	SQLNS_CmdID_WIZARD_CREATETRACE

For more information, see SQL Server Books Online.

Summary

The SQL Junior Administrator sample application demonstrates the use of SQL-DMO. It provides access to the various collections within SQL Server and manipulates those collections and the objects contained in them. The sample also takes advantage of the power and convenience of SQL-NS, which can allow programmatic access to the SQL Server Enterprise Manager wizards.

Using Views with a View on Performance

Microsoft® SQL Server™ 2000 supports the ability to create virtual tables known as views. Views provide a useful mechanism for restricting users to certain subsets of data and allowing users to access customized logical aspects of the data. Views usually contain multiple base-table joins and complex aggregations or return large result sets; therefore, without the aid of an index, views frequently suffer from poor performance.

In SQL Server 2000, the functionality of SQL Server views is expanded to provide system performance benefits through the use of indexed views. Creating a unique clustered index on a view, as well as nonclustered indexes, can improve data-access performance on the most complex queries.

> **Note** Indexed views can be created in any edition of SQL Server 2000. In SQL Server 2000 Enterprise Edition, the indexed view will be automatically considered by the query optimizer. To use an indexed view in all other editions, the NOEXPAND hint must be used.

What Is an Indexed View?

An indexed view is any view that has a unique clustered index. At the time a CREATE INDEX statement is executed on a view, the result set for the view is materialized (expanded) and stored in the database with the same structure as a table that has a clustered index. The indexed view automatically reflects modifications made to the data in the base tables after the index is created, the same way an index created on a base table does. The requirement that the view's clustered index be unique improves the efficiency with which SQL Server can find the rows in the index that are affected by any data modification.

When a standard view is created, the meta data (or description of the data) is defined by encapsulating a SELECT statement that defines a result set to be represented as a virtual table. When a view is referenced in the FROM clause of another query, this meta data is retrieved from the system catalog and materialized in place of the reference to the view. After the view is expanded, the query optimizer compiles a single execution plan for the executing query.

When you use a nonindexed view, the result set of a view is materialized at run time. Any computations, such as joins or aggregations, are performed during query execution for each query that references the view. (The view does not always need to be fully materialized. The query can contain additional predicates, joins, or aggregations that can be applied to the tables and views referenced in the view, eliminating the need for full materialization.) When you use a unique clustered index that is created on the view, the result set of the view is materialized immediately and persisted in physical storage in the database, saving the overhead of performing this costly operation at execution time.

Performance Gains from Indexed Views

Using indexed views provides additional performance benefits that cannot be achieved using standard indexes. Indexed views can increase query performance in the following ways:

- Aggregations can be precomputed and stored in the index to minimize expensive computations during query execution.

- Tables can be prejoined and the resulting data set stored.

- Combinations of joins or aggregations can be stored.

The following illustration shows the typical performance increases that can be achieved when the query optimizer uses an indexed view. The represented queries varied in complexity (for example, the number of aggregate calculations, the number of tables used, or the number of predicates) and included large multimillion-row tables from a real production environment.

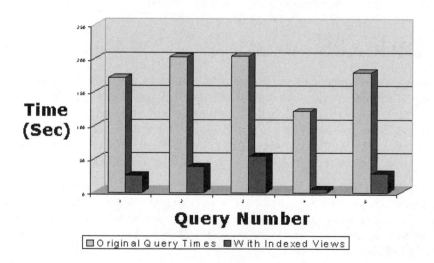

Using Secondary Indexes on Views

Secondary, nonclustered indexes on views can provide additional query performance. Similar to secondary indexes on tables, secondary indexes on views may provide more options for the query optimizer to choose from during the compilation process. For example, if the query includes columns that are not covered by the clustered index, the optimizer can choose one or more secondary indexes in the plan to avoid a time-consuming full scan of the indexed view or base tables.

Adding indexes to the schema increases the overhead on the database because the indexes will require ongoing maintenance. Careful consideration should be given to finding the right balance of indexes and maintenance overhead.

Getting the Most from Indexed Views

Similar to ordinary indexes, if the indexed views are not used, there is no benefit. In this case, not only are performance gains not realized but the additional cost of disk space, maintenance, and optimization is incurred. When indexed views are used, however, they can provide significant improvements (by orders of magnitude) in data access. This is because the query optimizer uses the precomputed results stored in the indexed view, which substantially reduces the cost of the query execution.

It is important to analyze your database workload before implementing indexed views. Not all queries will benefit from indexed views. Use your knowledge of the queries as well as various tools (for example SQL Profiler) to identify the queries that can benefit from indexed views. Frequently occurring aggregations and joins are the best candidates for indexed views.

The query optimizer considers indexed views only for queries with nontrivial cost. This avoids situations in which trying to match various indexed views during the query optimization costs more than the savings achieved by using indexed views. Indexed views are rarely used in queries with a cost of less than 1 unit of execution time.

Applications that benefit from using indexed views include:

- Decision support workloads

- Data marts

- Online analytical processing (OLAP) stores and sources

- Data mining workloads

Benefiting applications can be characterized as those that contain these, or a combination of these, query types and patterns:

- Joins and aggregations of large tables

- Repeated patterns of queries

- Repeated aggregations on the same or overlapping sets of columns

- Repeated joins of the same tables on the same keys

    Note Online transaction processing (OLTP) systems with many writes, or databases with frequent updates, may not be able to take advantage of the indexed views because of the increased maintenance cost associated with updating both the view and underlying base tables.

How the Query Optimizer Uses Indexed Views

The indexed view can be used in a query execution in these ways:

- The query can reference the indexed view directly in the FROM clause of the SELECT statement.

- The query optimizer can select the view if it determines that the view can be substituted for some or all of the query and it is the low-cost query plan.

In the latter case, the indexed view is used instead of the underlying tables and their ordinary indexes. The view does not need to be referenced in the query for the query optimizer to use it during query execution. This allows existing applications to benefit from the newly created indexed views without changing those applications.

Optimizer Considerations

The query optimizer considers several conditions to determine whether an indexed view can cover a portion or the entire query. These conditions correspond to a single FROM clause in the query and consist of the following:

- The tables in the FROM clause of the query must be a superset of the tables in the FROM clause of the indexed view.

- The join conditions in the query must be a superset of the join conditions in the view.

- The aggregation columns in the query must be a subset of the aggregation columns in the view.

- All expressions in the query select list must be derivable from the view select list or from the tables that are not included in the view definition.

- The query search condition predicates must be a superset of the search condition predicates in the view definition. Each component in the view search predicate must appear in the same form as a conjunct in the query search predicate.

- All columns in the query search condition predicates that belong to tables in the view definition must appear in one or more of the following:

- The same predicate in the view definition.

- A GROUP BY list in the view definition.

- The view select list if there is no GROUP BY clause.

If the query contains more than one FROM clause (subqueries, derived tables, or UNION), the optimizer may select several indexed views to manage a query with multiple FROM clauses.

Note There are exceptional situations when the optimizer may collapse two FROM clauses into one (a subquery to join, or derived table to join transformation). If that happens, the indexed view substitution may cover more than one FROM clause in the original query.

Example queries demonstrating these conditions are presented at the end of this document. Allowing the query optimizer to determine which indexes, if any, to use in the query execution plan is recommended.

Using the NOEXPAND Option

The NOEXPAND option forces the query optimizer to treat the view like an ordinary table with a clustered index. In this case, the indexed view must be referenced directly in the FROM clause. For example:

```
SELECT Column1, Column2, ... FROM Table1, View1 WITH (NOEXPAND)WHERE ...
```

Using the EXPAND VIEWS Options

Alternatively, you can explicitly exclude indexed views from consideration by using the EXPAND VIEWS option at the end of the query. For example:

```
SELECT Column1, Column2, ... FROM Table1, View1 WHERE ...OPTION (EXPAND VIEWS)
```

When you use this option, the query optimizer ignores all view indexes when estimating the low-cost method of covering the columns referenced in the query.

Designing Indexed Views

Identifying an appropriate set of indexes for a database system can be complex. Numerous possibilities should be considered when designing ordinary indexes; adding indexed views to the schema dramatically increases the complexity of the design and the potential results. For example, indexed views can be used on:

- Any subset of tables referenced in the query.

- Any subset of the conditions in the query for that subset of tables.

- Grouping columns.

- Aggregate functions (for example, SUM).

Indexes on tables and indexed views should be designed concurrently to get the best results from each construct. Because both indexes and indexed views may be useful for a given query, designing them separately can lead to redundant recommendations that incur high storage and maintenance overhead. Tuning the physical design of a database creates trade-offs between the performance requirements of a diverse set of queries and updates that the database system must support. Identifying an appropriate physical design for indexed views is a challenging task, and the Index Tuning Wizard should be used whenever it is possible.

Query optimization cost may increase substantially if the query optimizer must consider many indexed views. A query optimizer may consider all indexed views that are defined on any subset of tables in the query. It must parse and investigate each view for the potential substitution before it is rejected. This may take same time, especially if a given query has hundreds of such views.

A view must meet several requirements before you can create a unique clustered index on it. During the design phase, consider these requirements:

- The view, and all tables referenced in the view, must be in the same database and have the same owner.

- The indexed view does not need to contain all the tables referenced in the query to be used by the optimizer.

- A unique clustered index must be created before any other indexes can be created on the view.

- Certain SET options (see "Using SET Options to Obtain Consistent Results" later in this chapter) must be set correctly when the base tables, view, and index are created, and whenever data in the base tables and view are modified.

    Note The query optimizer will not consider the indexed view unless these SET options are correct.

- The view must be created using schema binding and any user-defined functions referenced in the view must also be created with the SCHEMABINDING option.

- Additional disk space will be required to hold the data defined by the indexed view.

Guidelines for Designing Indexed Views

Consider these guidelines when you design indexed views:

- Design indexed views that can be used by several queries or multiple operations.

  For example, an indexed view that contains the SUM of a column and the COUNT_BIG of a column can be used by queries that contain the functions SUM, COUNT, COUNT_BIG, or AVG. The queries will be faster because only a small number of rows from the view need to be retrieved, rather than the full number of rows from the base tables, and a portion of the computations required for performing the AVG function have already been done.

- Keep the index compact.

  By using the fewest number of columns and bytes as possible, the optimizer gains maximum efficiency in locating the row data. Conversely, if a large clustered index key is defined, any secondary, nonclustered indexes defined on the view will be significantly larger because the nonclustered index entries will contain the clustering key in addition to the columns defined by the index.

- Consider the size of the resulting indexed view.

  In the case of pure aggregation, the indexed view may not provide any significant performance gains if its size is similar to the size of the original table.

- Design multiple smaller indexed views that accelerate parts of the process.

  You may not always be able to design an indexed view that addresses the entire query. Should that situation occur, consider creating several indexed views, each performing a portion of the query.

  Consider these examples:

  - A frequently executed query aggregates data in one database, aggregates data in another database, and then joins the results. Because an indexed view cannot reference tables from more than one database, you cannot design a single view to perform the entire process. However, you can create an indexed view in each database that does the aggregation for that database. If the optimizer can match the indexed views against existing queries, at least the aggregation processing will be faster without the need to recode existing queries. Although the join processing is not faster, the overall query is faster because it uses the aggregations stored in the indexed views.

- A frequently executed query aggregates data from several tables, and then uses UNION to combine the results. UNION is not allowed in an indexed view. You can design views to perform each of the individual aggregation operations. The optimizer can then select the indexed views to speed up queries with no need to recode the queries. Although the processing for UNION is not improved, the individual aggregation processes are improved.

Using the Index Tuning Wizard

The Index Tuning Wizard recommends indexed views in addition to indexes on base tables. Using the wizard enhances an administrator's ability to determine the combination of indexes and indexed views that optimize the performance of the typical mix of queries executed against a database.

Because the Index Tuning Wizard forces all the required SET options (to ensure the result set is correct), the wizard successfully creates the indexed views. Your application may not be able to take advantage of the views, however, if its option settings are not set as required. The inserts, updates, or deletes may fail on tables that participate in the indexed view definitions.

Maintaining Indexed Views

SQL Server automatically maintains indexed views similar to any other index. In the case of ordinary indexes, each index relates directly to a single table. After each insert, update, or delete operation performed on the underlying table, the index is updated accordingly, so that the values stored in the index are always consistent with the table.

Indexed views are similarly maintained; however, if the view references several tables, updating any of them may require updating the indexed view. Unlike ordinary indexes, a single-row insert into any of the participating tables may cause multiple-row inserts into the indexed view. The same is true for updates and deletes. Consequently, the maintenance of an indexed view may be more expensive than maintaining an index on the table.

In SQL Server 2000, some views can be updated. When a view is updatable, the underlying base tables are modified directly through the view using INSERT, UPDATE, and DELETE statements. Creating an index on a view does not prevent the view from being updatable. For more information about updatable views, see "Modifying Data Through a View" in SQL Server Books Online.

Maintenance Cost Considerations

When you design indexed views, consider these points:

- Additional storage is required in the database for the indexed view. The result set of an indexed view is physically persisted in the database in a manner similar to that of typical table storage.

- SQL Server maintains views automatically, so any changes to a base table on which a view is defined may initiate one or more changes in the view indexes. Thus, additional maintenance overhead is incurred.

The net performance improvement achieved by a view is the difference of the total query execution savings offered by the view and the cost to store and maintain the view.

Approximating the required storage the view will consume is relatively easy. To evaluate the SELECT statement encapsulated by the view definition, in SQL Query Analyzer, on the **Query** menu, click **Display Estimated Execution Plan**. This will yield an approximation of the number of rows returned by the query and the size of the row. By multiplying these two values together, it is possible to approximate the potential size of the view. This is only an approximation, however. The actual size of the index on the view can be accurately determined only by creating the index on the view.

From the standpoint of automated maintenance considerations performed by SQL Server, the **Display Estimated Execution Plan** command functionality may give some insight on the impact of this overhead. If a statement that modifies the view (UPDATE on the view, INSERT into a base table) is evaluated with SQL Query Analyzer, the showplan will include the maintenance operation for that statement. Taking this cost into consideration along with an idea of how many times this operation will occur in the production environment may indicate the potential cost of view maintenance.

Creating Indexed Views

The following steps are required to create an indexed view and are critical to the successful implementation of the view:

1. Verify the SET options are correct for all existing tables that will be referenced in the view.

2. Verify that the SET options for your session are set correctly before creating any new tables and the view.

3. Verify the view definition is deterministic.

4. Create the view using the WITH SCHEMABINDING option.

5. Create the unique clustered index on the view.

Using SET Options to Obtain Consistent Results

Evaluating the same expression can produce different results in SQL Server if different SET options are active when the query is executed. For example, after the SET option CONCAT_NULL_YIELDS_NULL is set to ON, the expression 'abc' + NULL returns the value NULL. But after CONCAT_NULL_YIEDS_NULL is set to OFF, the same expression produces 'abc'. Indexed views require fixed values for several SET options to ensure that the views can be maintained correctly and return consistent results.

The SET options in the following table must be set to the values shown in the **Required Value** column whenever these conditions occur:

- The indexed view is created.

- Any insert, update, or delete operation is performed on any table participating in the indexed view.

- The indexed view is used by the query optimizer to produce the query plan.

SET options	Required value	Default server value	OLE DB and ODBC value	DB Library value
ANSI_NULLS	ON	OFF	ON	OFF
ANSI_PADDING	ON	ON	ON	OFF
ANSI_WARNING	ON	OFF	ON	OFF
ARITHABORT	ON	OFF	OFF	OFF
CONCAT_NULL_YIELDS_NULL	ON	OFF	ON	OFF
NUMERIC_ROUNDABORT	OFF	OFF	OFF	OFF
QUOTED_IDENTIFIER	ON	OFF	ON	OFF

If you are using an OLE DB or ODBC server connection, the only value that must be modified is the ARITHABORT setting. All DB-Library values must be set correctly either at the server level using **sp_configure** or from the application using the SET command. For more information about SET options, see "Using Options in SQL Server" in SQL Server Books Online.

Using Deterministic Functions

The definition of an indexed view must be deterministic. A view is deterministic if all expressions referenced in the view's select list, WHERE, and GROUP BY clauses are deterministic. Deterministic expressions always return the same result any time they are evaluated with a specific set of input values. Therefore, only deterministic functions may participate in deterministic expressions. For example, the DATEADD function is deterministic because it always returns the same result for any given set of argument values for its three parameters. GETDATE is not deterministic because it is always invoked with the same argument, yet the value it returns changes each time it is executed. For more information, see "Deterministic and Nondeterministic Functions" in SQL Server Books Online.

Even if an expression is deterministic, if it contains **float** expressions, the exact result may depend on the processor architecture, the version of processor microcode, or SQL Server algorithms for evaluating floating-point expressions. To ensure data integrity in SQL Server 2000, such expressions can participate only as nonkey columns of indexed views. Deterministic expressions that do not contain **float** expressions are called precise. Only precise deterministic expressions may participate in key columns and WHERE or GROUP BY clauses of indexed views.

Use the COLUMNPROPERTY function and **IsDeterministic** property to determine whether a view column is deterministic. Use the COLUMNPROPERTY function and **IsPrecise** property to determine whether a deterministic column in a view WITH SCHEMABINDING is precise. COLUMNPROPERTY returns 1 if TRUE, 0 if FALSE, and NULL for invalid input (the column is not deterministic). For example:

```
SELECT COLUMNPROPERTY(Object_Id('Vdiscount1'),'SumDiscountPrice','IsPrecise')
```

This query returns 0 because the **SumDiscountPrice** column references **float** column **Discount** from the table **Order Details**. Alternatively, the column **SumPrice** in the same view is both deterministic and precise.

> **Note** The view that this SELECT statement is based on can be found in "View 1: Including Aggregations in the View" in "Indexed Views Examples" later in this chapter.

Additional Requirements for Indexed Views

In addition to the design requirements for creating indexed views presented previously in this chapter, the following requirements must be met.

Base Table Requirements

- Base tables must have the correct SET options set at the time the table is created or it cannot be referenced by the view WITH SCHEMABINDING.

- Tables must be referenced by two-part names (**owner.tablename**) in the view definition.

Function Requirements

- User-defined functions must be created using the WITH SCHEMABINDING option.

- User-defined functions must be referenced by two-part names (owner.function).

View Requirements

- The view must be created using the WITH SCHEMABINDING option.

- The view must reference only base tables in the same database, not other views.

- The view must be indexable.

  Note Use the **IsIndexable** property of OBJECTPROPERTY to verify the index capability of the view. For example:

  ```
  SELECT OBJECTPROPERTY(object_id('View Name'),'IsIndexable')
  ```

  This statement will return the value 1 if the view can be indexed, or 0 if the view cannot be indexed. This statement may consume significant computer resources because the evaluation of the **IsIndexable** property requires the parsing of the view definition, normalization, and partial optimization.

Syntax Restrictions

The syntax of a view definition has several restrictions. The following table lists the items that a view definition must not contain.

COUNT(*)	ROWSET function
Derived table	Self-join
DISTINCT	STDEV, VARIANCE, or AVG
float[*], **text**, **ntext**, or **image** columns	Subquery
Full-text predicates (CONTAIN or FREETEXT)	SUM on nullable expression
MIN or MAX	TOP
OUTER join	UNION

* The indexed view may contain **float** columns; however, such columns cannot be included in the clustered index key.

GROUP BY Restrictions

If GROUP BY is not used, expressions cannot be used in the select list.

If GROUP BY is present, the VIEW definition must:

- Contain COUNT_BIG(*).
- Not contain HAVING, CUBE, or ROLLUP.

These restrictions are applicable only to the indexed view definition. A query can use an indexed view in its execution plan even if it does not satisfy these GROUP BY restrictions.

Index Requirements

- The user executing the CREATE INDEX statement must be the view owner.
- If the view definition contains a GROUP BY clause, the key of the unique clustered index can reference only the columns specified in the GROUP BY clause.

Indexed View Examples

This section provides examples to show the use of indexed views with two major groups of queries: aggregations and joins. These examples also demonstrate the conditions used by the query optimizer when determining whether an indexed view is applicable. For information about query optimizer conditions, see "How the Query Optimizer Uses Indexed Views" earlier in this chapter.

The queries are based on tables in the **Northwind** sample database in SQL Server 2000, and can be executed as written. To view the plans selected by the query optimizer before and after the views are created in SQL Query Analyzer, on the **Query** menu, click **Show Execution Plan**. Although the examples demonstrate how the optimizer chooses the low cost execution plan, the **Northwind** sample database is too small to show performance gains. These code examples are also available on the *SQL Server 2000 Resource Kit* CD-ROM in file, \Docs\ChapterCode\CH36Code.txt. For more information, see Chapter 39, "Tools, Samples, eBooks, and More."

The following queries show two methods to return the five products with the largest total discount from the **Order Details** table.

Query 1: Using Aggregate Functions (Method 1)

Code Example 36.1

```
SELECT TOP 5 ProductID, SUM(UnitPrice*Quantity) - SUM(UnitPrice*Quantity*(1.00-
Discount))AS Rebate
FROM [Order Details]
GROUP BY ProductID
ORDER BY Rebate DESC
```

Query 2: Using Aggregate Functions (Method 2)

Code Example 36.2

```
SELECT TOP 5 ProductID, SUM(UnitPrice*Quantity*Discount)AS Rebate
FROM [Order Details]
GROUP BY ProductID
ORDER BY Rebate DESC
```

The execution plan selected by the query optimizer for both queries contains:

- A Clustered Index Scan on the **Order Details** table with a row estimate of 2,155 rows.

- A Hash Match/Aggregate operator that puts the selected rows into a hash table based on the column in the GROUP BY clause and computes the SUM aggregation for each row.

- A TOP 5 sort operator based on the ORDER BY clause.

View 1: Including Aggregations in the View

Adding an indexed view that includes the aggregations required for the **Rebate** column will change the query execution plan for Query 1. On a large table (multimillion rows), the performance of the query would also improve significantly.

Code Example 36.3

```
CREATE VIEW Vdiscount1 WITH SCHEMABINDING
ASSELECT SUM(UnitPrice*Quantity)AS SumPrice, SUM(UnitPrice*Quantity*(1.00-Discount))AS
SumDiscountPrice, COUNT_BIG(*) AS Count, ProductID FROM dbo.[Order Details]GROUP BY
ProductIDGO
CREATE UNIQUE CLUSTERED INDEX VDiscountInd ON Vdiscount1 (ProductID)
```

The execution plan for the first query shows that the optimizer uses the **Vdiscount1** view. However, the view will not be used by the second query because it does not contain the SUM(UnitPrice*Quantity*Discount) aggregation. Another indexed view can be created that will address both queries.

View 2: Expanding View 1 Functionality

Code Example 36.4

```
CREATE VIEW Vdiscount2 WITH SCHEMABINDING
AS
SELECT SUM(UnitPrice*Quantity)AS SumPrice, SUM(UnitPrice*Quantity*(1.00-Discount))AS
SumDiscountPrice, SUM(UnitPrice*Quantity*Discount)AS SumDiscountPrice2, COUNT_BIG(*) AS
Count, ProductID
FROM dbo.[Order Details]
GROUP BY ProductID
GO
CREATE UNIQUE CLUSTERED INDEX VDiscountInd ON Vdiscount2 (ProductID)
```

With this indexed view, the query execution plan for both queries now contains:

- A Clustered Index Scan on the **Vdiscount2** view with a row estimate of 77 rows

- A TOP 5 sort function based on the ORDER BY clause

The query optimizer selects the view because it provides the lowest execution cost although it was not referenced in either query.

Query 3: Including Columns from Other Tables

Query 3 is similar to the previous queries, except **ProductID** is replaced by the **OrderID** column, which is not included in the view definition. This violates the condition that all expressions in the query select list must derive from the view select list or from tables not included in the view definition.

Code Example 36.5

```
SELECT TOP 3 OrderID, SUM(UnitPrice*Quantity*Discount) OrderRebate
FROM dbo.[Order Details]GROUP BY OrderID
ORDER BY OrderRebate desc
```

A separate indexed view is required to address this query. The view **Vdiscount2** can be modified to include **OrderID**; however, the resulting view contains as many rows as the original table and does not provide a performance improvement over using the base table.

Query 4: Using Complex Aggregations

Query 4 produces the average price for each product by using the complex AVG aggregate function.

Code Example 36.6

```
SELECT ProductName, od.ProductID, AVG(od.UnitPrice*(1.00-Discount)) AS AvgPrice,
SUM(od.Quantity) AS Units FROM [Order Details] od, Products p WHERE
od.ProductID=p.ProductID GROUP BY ProductName, od.ProductID
```

Complex aggregate functions (for example, STDEV, VARIANCE, or AVG) cannot be included in the definition of an index view. However, indexed views can be used to execute a query containing an AVG by including the simple aggregate functions that, when combined, perform the complex aggregation.

View 3: Using Simple Aggregate Functions to Create Complex Functions

This indexed view contains the simple aggregate functions needed to perform an AVG function. When Query 4 is executed after the creation of View 3, the execution plan shows the view being used. The optimizer can derive the AVG expression from the view's simple aggregation columns **Price** and **Count**.

Code Example 36.7

```
CREATE VIEW View3 WITH SCHEMABINDING
AS
SELECT ProductID, SUM(UnitPrice*(1.00-Discount))AS Price, COUNT_BIG(*)AS Count,
SUM(Quantity)AS Units FROM dbo.[Order Details] GROUP BY ProductID GoCREATE UNIQUE
CLUSTERED INDEX iv3 ON View3 (ProductID)
```

Query 5: Adding Search Condition Columns from Other Tables

This query is the same as Query 4, but includes one additional search condition. View 3 works for this query, although the additional search condition references only columns from a table that is not included in the view definition.

Code Example 36.8

```
SELECT ProductName, od.ProductID, AVG(od.UnitPrice*(1.00-Discount))AS AvgPrice,
SUM(od.Quantity)AS Units FROM [Order Details] AS od, Products AS p WHERE
od.ProductID=p.ProductID AND p.ProductName like '%Tofu%'
GROUP BY ProductName, od.ProductID
```

Query 6: Adding Search Condition Columns Without a GROUP BY Clause

The query optimizer cannot use View 3 for this query. The added search condition **od.UnitPrice>10** contains a column from the table in the view definition, but the column does not appear in the GROUP BY list nor does the search predicate appear in the view definition.

Code Example 36.9

```
SELECT ProductName, od.ProductID, AVG(od.UnitPrice*(1.00-Discount)) AS AvgPrice,
SUM(od.Quantity) AS Units FROM [Order Details] od, Products p WHERE od.ProductID =
p.ProductID AND od.UnitPrice > 10
GROUP BY ProductName, od.ProductID
```

Query 7: Using a GROUP BY Clause

In contrast to Query 6, the query optimizer can use View 3 for Query 7, because the column defined in the new search condition **od.ProductID in (1,2,13,41)** is included in the GROUP BY clause in the view definition.

Code Example 36.10

```
SELECT ProductName, od.ProductID, AVG(od.UnitPrice*(1.00-Discount)) AS AvgPrice,
SUM(od.Quantity) AS UnitsFROM [Order Details] AS od, Products AS pWHERE od.ProductID =
p.ProductIDAND od.ProductID in (1,2,13,41)
GROUP BY ProductName, od.ProductID
```

View 4: Adding Search Condition Columns to the View

This view satisfies the conditions for Query 6 by including the column **od.Discount** in the view definition.

Code Example 36.11

```
CREATE VIEW View4 WITH SCHEMABINDING
AS
SELECT ProductName, od.ProductID, SUM(od.UnitPrice*(1.00-Discount)) AS AvgPrice,
SUM(od.Quantity) AS Units, COUNT_BIG(*) AS Count FROM dbo.[Order Details] AS od,
dbo.Products AS p WHERE od.ProductID = p.ProductID AND od.UnitPrice > 10GROUP BY
ProductName, od.ProductID
GO
CREATE UNIQUE CLUSTERED INDEX VdiscountInd on View4 (ProductName, ProductID)
```

Query 8: Using Table Joins

The same index on View 4 is also used for a query where a join to the **Orders** table is added. This query meets the condition that the tables listed in the query FROM clause are a superset of the tables in the FROM clause of the indexed view.

Code Example 36.12

```
SELECT ProductName, od.ProductID, AVG(od.UnitPrice*(1.00-Discount)) AS AvgPrice,
SUM(od.Quantity) AS Units FROM dbo.[Order Details] AS od, dbo.Products AS p, dbo.Orders
AS o WHERE od.ProductID = p.ProductID and o.OrderID = od.OrderID AND od.UnitPrice > 10
GROUP BY ProductName, od.ProductID
```

The final two queries are modifications of Query 8. Each modification violates one of the optimizer conditions and, unlike Query 8, cannot use View 4.

Query 8a: Search Condition Mismatches

This query cannot use the indexed view because of the mismatch between the WHERE clause **UnitPrice > 10** in the view definition and **UnitPrice > 25** in the query. The query search condition predicate must be a superset of the search condition predicates in the view definition.

Code Example 36.13

```
SELECT ProductName, od.ProductID, AVG(od.UnitPrice*(1.00-Discount)) AvgPrice,
SUM(od.Quantity) AS Units FROM dbo.[Order Details] AS od, dbo.Products AS p, dbo.Orders
AS o WHERE od.ProductID = p.ProductID and o.OrderID = od.OrderID AND od.UnitPrice > 25
GROUP BY ProductName, od.ProductID
```

Query 8b: Adding a Search Predicate on a Joined Table

In this query, the **Orders** table does not participate in the indexed view definition in View 4. Nevertheless, adding a predicate on this table disallows using the indexed view, because the added predicate may eliminate additional rows participating in the aggregations as it is shown in Query 8b.

Code Example 36.14

```
SELECT ProductName, od.ProductID, AVG(od.UnitPrice*(1.00-Discount)) AS AvgPrice,
SUM(od.Quantity) AS Units FROM dbo.[Order Details] AS od, dbo.Products AS p, dbo.Orders
AS o WHERE od.ProductID = p.ProductID and o.OrderID = od.OrderID AND od.UnitPrice > 10
AND o.OrderDate > '01/01/1998'
GROUP BY ProductName, od.ProductID
```

Extending Triggers with INSTEAD OF

In Microsoft® SQL Server™ 2000, the data manipulation and data-integrity features of tables and views have been significantly enhanced with the introduction of INSTEAD OF triggers. Using INSTEAD OF triggers, you can enforce new business rules by extending or replacing the normal triggering actions of an INSERT, UPDATE, or DELETE statement. Using INSTEAD OF triggers in views, you can:

- Update multiple tables through a single view.

- Enforce more complex restrictions on columns than CHECK constraints allow.

- Evaluate the state of a table before and after modifying data and performing additional actions, such as modifying other tables or displaying a customized error message.

- Allow parts of a batch to be rejected while allowing other parts of the batch to succeed.

This chapter presents code examples illustrating the use of INSTEAD OF triggers, design guidelines, and optimization recommendations. The code examples are also available on the *SQL Server 2000 Resource Kit* CD-ROM in file, \Docs\ChapterCode\CH37Code.txt. For more information, see Chapter 39, "Tools, Samples, eBooks, and More," in this book.

What Are INSTEAD OF Triggers?

Similar to AFTER triggers (FOR triggers in earlier versions of SQL Server), INSTEAD OF triggers are special stored procedures that perform user-defined actions and are activated by INSERT, UPDATE, or DELETE statements. Triggers fire (execute) each time an INSERT, UPDATE, or DELETE statement executes on a specified table or view. A single trigger can apply to one specific triggering action (for example, INSTEAD OF UPDATE) or to multiple actions (INSTEAD OF INSERT, UPDATE, DELETE) in which the same trigger is applied to all the actions listed. As with the AFTER trigger, the INSTEAD OF trigger uses the logical **inserted** and **deleted** tables to store the modified records while the trigger is active. Each column in these tables maps directly to a column in the base table referenced in the trigger. For example, if table **T1** contains the columns **C1**, **C2**, **C3**, and **C4**, the **inserted** and **deleted** tables will contain the values for all four columns, even if the trigger only modifies columns **C1** and **C3**. SQL Server automatically creates and manages the **inserted** and **deleted** tables as memory-resident objects.

An INSTEAD OF trigger differs from an AFTER trigger by when the trigger is fired, what actions are performed, and what objects the trigger can be created on. The actions defined in the AFTER trigger code are supplemental to the triggering action and occur only after constraint processing has been applied and the transaction created by the triggering action has been committed. For example, an AFTER trigger attached to an **Order Detail** table may update an **Order Summary** table whenever the **Order Detail** table is modified. In contrast with the AFTER trigger, the INSTEAD OF trigger fires before constraint processing and replaces the normal triggering action with the actions defined in the trigger. For example, an INSTEAD OF trigger attached to a view of historical sales data can prevent the data from being modified by replacing the insert, update, and delete triggering actions with a customized error message. Because the INSTEAD OF trigger supersedes the triggering action, the data modification that caused the trigger to execute in this example is never executed. The INSTEAD OF trigger code must include the appropriate INSERT, UPDATE, or DELETE statements if those actions are required. Executing the INSERT, UPDATE, or DELETE statement from inside the INSTEAD OF trigger code will not fire the same trigger again; instead, the insert, update, or delete action is performed.

Customizing Error Messages with INSTEAD OF Triggers

You can customize error messages and perform complex error handling such as validating columns in the **inserted** or **deleted** tables with columns in other tables with INSTEAD OF triggers. Because the INSTEAD OF trigger fires before constraints are applied, you can perform error checking prior to the data changes and either continue with the triggering action if there are no errors, or perform other actions such as displaying an error message and inserting the erroneous data into an error log table. From within the INSTEAD OF trigger, different actions can be performed for different inserted, updated, or deleted records.

In the following example, the **T_ProtectSalaryUpdate** INSTEAD OF trigger:

- Checks individual updated rows, allowing those that meet the trigger criteria to succeed and others to fail.

- Produces customized messages.

- Enforces complex rules that cannot be enforced using simple constraints.

The trigger is based on a new **Salary** table. Code Example 37.1 creates this table in the **Northwind** sample database. The table contains the columns **EmployeeID**, **SalaryClass**, and **Salary**. The **EmployeeID** uses a reference to the **EmployeeID** column in the table **Employees** to ensure that the value entered refers to a valid employee. **SalaryClass** holds the payment frequency (for example, monthly or weekly), and **Salary** contains the current salary amount. The trigger, as shown in Code Example 37.2, ensures that modifications to the **Salary** table are not performed on the first day of any month, because this could interfere with the processing of monthly salaries. Modifications made on the first of the month are rejected, and a customized error message is displayed. Although rowset-based logic is recommended, this example uses a cursor to allow batch updates to the table.

Code Example 37.1

```
-- ==============================================================================
-- Create the Salary table for use with the T_ProtectSalaryUpdate trigger.
-- ==============================================================================
CREATE TABLE Salary (EmployeeID int References Employees (EmployeeID),
SalaryClass int not null,
Salary int not NULL)
```

Code Example 37.2

```
-- ==================================================
-- This INSTEAD OF trigger shows how the INSTEAD OF trigger may be used to:
--    Check individual updated rows, allowing those that meet the trigger criteria
--       to succeed and others to fail.
-- Produce customized messages.
-- Enforce complex rules that cannot be enforced using simple constraints.


-- ==================================================
CREATE TRIGGER T_ProtectSalaryUpdateTwo ON Salary
INSTEAD OF Update
AS
BEGIN
  DECLARE @EmployeeID int, @SalaryClass int, @Salary int, @OldSalary int
  DECLARE OneChange CURSOR LOCAL READ_ONLY FORWARD_ONLY STATIC
    FOR SELECT [EmployeeID], [SalaryClass], [Salary] FROM inserted
  OPEN OneChange
  FETCH NEXT FROM OneChange INTO @EmployeeID, @SalaryClass, @Salary
  WHILE (@@FETCH_STATUS=0)
    BEGIN
      SELECT @OldSalary=Salary
      FROM Salary
      WHERE EmployeeID=@EmployeeID
      IF ((DATEPART(day,getdate())= 1) AND (@OldSalary <> @Salary))
         PRINT 'Error. Salary change for employee '+ Cast(@EmployeeID as varchar(10))+ '
cannot be changed on the first day of the month.'
      ELSE
         UPDATE Salary SET Salary=@Salary, SalaryClass=@SalaryClass where
EmployeeID=@EmployeeID
      FETCH NEXT FROM OneChange INTO @EmployeeID, @SalaryClass, @Salary
    END
END
```

Code Example 37.3 inserts test data into the **Salary** table and tests the triggering action. You may want to temporarily reset your system date to the first of the month to see the trigger results when an updated row fails.

Code Example 37.3

```
-- ======================================================================
-- Test the T_ProtectSalaryUpdate INSTEAD OF TRIGGER.
-- These modifications should fail and produce the custom error message.
-- ======================================================================
USE Northwind
GO
-- Add test data to the Salary table for later testing.
INSERT INTO Salary
VALUES (1,1, 3500)
INSERT INTO Salary
VALUES (2,1, 5000)
INSERT INTO Salary
VALUES (3,4,1000)
GO
--This UPDATE statement will fail if the current date is the first of the month.
UPDATE Salary
SET "Salary" = 3750
WHERE "EmployeeID" = 1
GO
-- This UPDATE statement will succeed because only the SalaryClass column is being
updated.
UPDATE Salary
SET "SalaryClass" = 4
WHERE "EmployeeID" = 3
GO
```

When UPDATE statements are executed, the **inserted** table contains the new values supplied in the UPDATE statement, and the **deleted** table contains the current values for each column in the database. This allows you to compare the existing data with the updated values before the transaction is committed to the database.

To force the UPDATE statement to fail, temporarily set your system date to the first day of the month and execute this UPDATE statement:

```
UPDATE Salary
SET "SalaryClass" = 4000
WHERE "EmployeeID" = 1
GO
```

Additional triggers would need to be applied to the table to cover the insert and delete triggering actions.

Creating Updatable Views with INSTEAD OF Triggers

In earlier versions of SQL Server, views could only modify data in a single base table. In SQL Server 2000, using INSTEAD OF triggers, you can modify multiple base tables from the view and manage the complexities associated with multiple table updates.

In the following example, the INSTEAD OF trigger **T_InsertInvoice** demonstrates:

- Inserting data into multiple base tables.

- Resolving foreign key constraints between tables.

- Excluding columns not requiring modification.

- Handling columns containing system generated data.

When you update base tables through a view, it is important to understand the relationships among the base tables, how the view will be used, and other database features, such as data types or constraints that may affect the actions required of the trigger. Permissions granted on the view and underlying base tables must also be considered. If the same user owns both the view and the base table, user permissions to read or update has to be granted only on the view. When the view owner does not own a base table, their respective owners must grant user permissions separately for both the view and the base table.

In the following example, the INSTEAD OF INSERT trigger is attached to the **Invoices** view (part of the **Northwind** sample database) and modifies columns in the **Orders** and **Order Details** tables. The **Invoice** view would probably be used in a Point of Sale (POS) application or as the basis for a data entry form developed in a product, such as Microsoft Access. The **Invoice** view references the **Orders**, **Order Details**, **Shippers**, **Employees**, and **Products** tables; however, only columns in the **Orders** and **Order Details** tables require modification. The **Shippers**, **Employee**, and **Products** tables are used to verify existing information.

A FOREIGN KEY constraint on the **OrderID** column keeps the **Orders** and **Order Details** tables synchronized, which must be enforced in the trigger. The **OrderID** column in the **Orders** table uses the IDENTITY property to determine the **OrderID** value, and this data must be passed to the **Order Details** table. In addition, the **Invoices** view references the **EmployeeName** and the shipper's **CompanyName** columns, but the **Orders** table records the **Employee ID** and the **Shipper ID** columns. To insert the correct data into the **Orders** table, the SELECT statement in the trigger must reference the **Shipper** and **Employees** tables to extract the corresponding ID data. The example assumes that a single row is being inserted. The example is not designed to handle multiple row INSERT statements.

Code Example 37.4

```
-- ================================================
-- Create INSTEAD OF INSERT trigger to insert new
-- records through the Invoices view to
-- multiple base tables Orders and Order Details.
-- ================================================
USE Northwind
GO
IF EXISTS (SELECT name FROM   sysobjects
           WHERE  name = 'T_InsertInvoice'
           AND    type = 'TR')
  DROP TRIGGER T_InsertInvoice
GO
CREATE TRIGGER T_InsertInvoice ON Invoices INSTEAD OF INSERT
AS
  BEGIN
-- Insert the Invoices information into the Orders table from the inserted table.
-- Get the EmployeeID and ShipperID information from the Employees and Shippers tables.
    INSERT INTO Orders (CustomerID, EmployeeID, OrderDate, RequiredDate, ShippedDate,
                        Freight, ShipVia, ShipName, ShipAddress, ShipCity, ShipRegion,
                        ShipPostalCode, ShipCountry)
      SELECT

inserted.CustomerID,Employees.EmployeeID,inserted.OrderDate,inserted.RequiredDate,
           inserted.ShippedDate,inserted.Freight,Shippers.ShipperID,inserted.ShipName,
           inserted.ShipAddress, inserted.ShipCity, inserted.ShipRegion,
           inserted.ShipPostalCode, inserted.ShipCountry
      FROM Employees, inserted, Shippers
      WHERE  inserted.Salesperson = (Employees.FirstName + ' ' + Employees.LastName)
                                and inserted.ShipperName = Shippers.CompanyName
-- Insert the Invoices information into the Order Details table.
-- Get the current OrderID from the inserted table.
    INSERT INTO "Order Details"
      SELECT SCOPE_IDENTITY() AS OrderID,ProductID,UnitPrice,Quantity,Discount
      FROM inserted
    COMMIT TRANSACTION
  END
```

To test the trigger, execute the sample data in Code Example 37.5.

Code Example 37.5

```
INSERT INTO Invoices (CustomerID,OrderDate, RequiredDate, ShippedDate,ShipperName,
                      Freight,ShipName,ShipAddress, ShipCity, ShipRegion,
ShipPostalCode,
                      ShipCountry,ProductID,UnitPrice,Quantity,Discount,
                      CustomerName,Salesperson,OrderID,ProductName)
VALUES ('SAVEA',
GETDATE(),
GETDATE() + 10,
GETDATE() + 3,
'Speedy Express',
214.27,
'Save-a-lot Markets',
'187 Suffolk Ln.',
'Boise',
'ID',
'83720',
'USA',
16,
13.9000,
21,
0.15000001,
'Save-a-lot Markets',
'Anne Dodsworth',
IDENT_CURRENT('Orders')+ 1,
'Pavlova'
)
```

Handling NOT NULL Values and Computed Columns in Updatable Views with INSTEAD OF Triggers

When you use INSTEAD OF triggers to modify base tables through a view, certain rules apply to INSERT and UPDATE statements referencing base-table columns that are defined with one of these attributes:

- NOT NULL

- NOT NULL with a DEFAULT definition

- Columns for which input values are not allowed, but may be treated by SQL Server as not nullable:

  - Computed columns

  - IDENTITY columns for which IDENTITY INSERT is set to OFF

  - Columns with the **timestamp** data type

Columns with one of these NOT NULL definitions are treated differently in the column list of an INSERT or UPDATE statement, depending on whether the statement references the updatable view or is embedded in the INSTEAD OF trigger code. INSERT and UPDATE statements referencing the view must supply values for every base table column defined with the NOT NULL attributes listed above. This is required to satisfy the NOT NULL requirement for those columns. However, when the INSERT or UPDATE statements are part of the INSTEAD OF trigger logic, the treatment of these columns varies. Modified columns explicitly defined as NOT NULL or NOT NULL with a DEFAULT value must be included in the column list of the INSERT or UPDATE statement. However, the computed IDENTITY or **timestamp** data type columns must not be included in column list of these statements. When these columns are not listed, the INSTEAD OF trigger ignores the values passed by the INSERT statement referencing the view, and the correct values are set by SQL Server.

Columns that are defined as nullable can be included or excluded in the column list of INSERT or UPDATE statements under both conditions.

This table summarizes the treatment of NOT NULL columns, system-generated columns, and nullable columns in the column list of INSERT and UPDATE statements.

If the INSERT or UPDATE statement	And the column is defined as	Column must be included in the column list	Column must be excluded in the column list
References a view updatable through an INSTEAD OF Trigger	Explicitly declared NOT NULL	●	
	NOT NULL with a DEFAULT value	●	
	Computed, IDENTITY, or **timestamp**	●	
	NULL	Optional	
	Nullable and system generated	Optional	
In the INSTEAD OF trigger code	Explicitly declared NOT NULL	●	
	NOT NULL with a DEFAULT value		●
	Computed, IDENTITY, or **timestamp**		●
	NULL	Optional	
	Nullable and system generated	Optional	

To meet the NOT NULL requirement for these columns, the INSERT or UPDATE statement referencing the view may pass dummy values for those columns that are system generated. For example, a view **CurrentInventory** references the base table **Inventory**, which contains the computed column **TotalQuantity** defined as **QtyOnOrder + QtyInStock**. A value must be passed for the **TotalQuantity** column, but that value does not need to represent the actual computed value. In the following example, zero (0) is passed as the dummy value for this column; however, SQL Server generates the actual value inserted into the database.

Code Example 37.6

```
-- ==================================================
-- Create the Inventory table
-- with a computed column TotalQuantity.
-- ==================================================
USE Northwind
GO
CREATE TABLE Inventory
(PartNumber char(10) NOT NULL,
Description varchar(30) NOT NULL DEFAULT 'Unknown',
QtyOnOrder  smallint,
QtyInStock smallint,
TotalQuantity AS (QtyOnOrder + QtyInStock),
LastModified datetime NULL DEFAULT GETDATE())
GO


-- ==================================================
-- Create the CurrentInventory view
-- selecting all columns from the Inventory table.
-- ==================================================
IF EXISTS (SELECT TABLE_NAME
            FROM INFORMATION_SCHEMA.VIEWS
            WHERE TABLE_NAME = N'CurrentInventory')
    DROP VIEW CurrentInventory
GO
CREATE VIEW CurrentInventory
AS
    SELECT PartNumber, Description, QtyOnOrder, QtyInStock, TotalQuantity, LastModified
    FROM Inventory
GO
```

Bypassing the Computed Column in the INSTEAD OF Trigger

The INSERT statement in the INSTEAD OF INSERT trigger lists **QtyOnOrder** and **QtyInStock**, but not the computed column **TotalQuantity**.

Code Example 37.7

```
CREATE TRIGGER T_InsertInventory ON CurrentInventory
INSTEAD OF INSERT AS
BEGIN
  INSERT INTO Inventory (PartNumber, Description, QtyOnOrder, QtyInStock)
    SELECT PartNumber, Description, QtyOnOrder, QtyInStock
    FROM inserted
END
```

Including the Computed Column when Referencing the View

The INSERT statement referencing the **CurrentInventory** view in the following example will succeed. Because the INSTEAD OF trigger code does not include the **TotalQuantity** column, the value 0 is ignored and the column is computed correctly.

Code Example 37.8

```
INSERT INTO CurrentInventory (PartNumber,Description, QtyOnOrder,
QtyInStock,TotalQuantity)
VALUES ('LA-61-4679', 'Unknown', 100,25,0)
```

Executing a SELECT statement on the **CurrentInventory** view would return a result set similar to that shown in the table.

Part Number	Description	QtyOnOrder	QtyInStock	TotalQuantity	LastModified
LA-61-4679	Unknown	200	10	210	2000-12-07 14:28:51.853

INSTEAD OF Triggers on Partitioned Views

Tables that have been spread across one or more databases or servers can be updated by using a partitioned view. However, several restrictions are associated with partitioned views that may prevent their use. You can use INSTEAD OF triggers to replace the actions of the partitioned view command. For more information about partitioned views, see Chapter 38, "Scaling Out on SQL Server," in this book.

Guidelines for Designing INSTEAD OF Triggers

INSTEAD OF triggers are often used to enforce specific business rules or apply application logic and error handling. They can add flexibility by providing cross-table or cross-database referential integrity, and they work no matter what caused the data modification: a data entry form, a report calculation, or a user interface application. This section provides several guidelines to consider when you design tables and updatable views.

Restrictions of INSTEAD OF Triggers

When you design INSTEAD OF triggers, consider these restrictions:

- INSTEAD OF triggers are not allowed on updatable views WITH CHECK OPTION.

- Only one INSTEAD OF trigger per INSERT, UPDATE, or DELETE statement can be defined on a table or view.

- The CREATE TRIGGER statement must be the first statement in the batch. All other statements that follow in that batch are interpreted as part of the definition of the CREATE TRIGGER statement.

- Permission to create triggers defaults to the table owner, who cannot transfer it to other users.

- Triggers are database objects, and their names must follow the rules for identifiers.

- You can create a trigger only in the current database, although a trigger can reference objects outside of the current database.

- A trigger cannot be created on a temporary or system table, although triggers can reference temporary tables. System tables should not be referenced; use the information schema views instead.

- The WRITETEXT statement does not cause the INSERT or UPDATE triggers to fire.

Constraints vs. Triggers

You should use constraints rather than triggers to enforce rules or default values whenever possible. Constraints usually perform the same task faster than triggers. Entity integrity should always be enforced at the lowest level by indexes that are part of PRIMARY KEY and UNIQUE constraints. Domain integrity should be enforced by CHECK constraints, and referential integrity enforced through FOREIGN KEY constraints.

Triggers are most useful when the features supported by constraints cannot meet the needs of the application, for example:

- A CHECK constraint can validate a column value only against a logical expression or another column in the same table. If your application requires that a column value be validated against a column in another table, you must use a trigger.

- Constraints can only display standardized system error messages. Customized error messages and more complex error handling require the use of triggers.

- Constraints are checked at the statement level, but INSTEAD OF triggers can be programmed to perform checks selectively and to allow some of the modifications to succeed and others not.

If constraints exist on the trigger table, they are checked after the INSTEAD OF trigger execution. If the constraints are violated, the INSTEAD OF trigger actions are rolled back.

Using the bcp Utility and BULK INSERT with INSTEAD OF Triggers

All bulk copy operations (the BULK INSERT statement, the **bcp** utility, and the bulk copy API) support a bulk copy hint, FIRE_TRIGGERS. If FIRE_TRIGGERS is specified on a bulk copy operation that is copying rows into a table, INSERT and INSTEAD OF triggers defined on the destination table are executed once for all rows inserted by the bulk copy operation. By default, bulk copy operations do not execute triggers.

These considerations apply to bulk copy operations that specify FIRE_TRIGGERS:

- Bulk copy operations that would usually be minimally logged are fully logged.

- Triggers are fired once for each batch in the bulk copy operation. The **inserted** table passed to the trigger contains all of the rows inserted by the batch. Specify FIRE_TRIGGERS only when bulk copying into a table with INSERT and INSTEAD OF triggers that support multiple-row inserts.

- No result sets generated by the insert triggers are returned to the client performing the bulk copy operation.

Order of Trigger Execution

It is important to understand the order of event execution when using an INSTEAD OF trigger to modify data through a view. INSTEAD OF triggers are invoked after the **inserted** and **deleted** tables are created. If the UPDATE statement in the trigger references the same view as the trigger, the trigger is not called recursively. Rather, the UPDATE statement is applied directly to the base tables. Each UPDATE statement must reference a single table and begins the chain of applying all constraints and AFTER triggers defined on the base tables.

Performance Guidelines for INSTEAD OF Triggers

The overhead for trigger performance is usually very low. The time involved in running a trigger is spent mostly in referencing other tables, which may be in memory or on the disk. The **deleted** and **inserted** tables are always in memory because they are logical tables. The location of the other tables referenced by the trigger determines the amount of time the operations requires.

Consider these optimization guidelines:

- Minimize the number of tables referenced to reduce time spent referencing tables on disk.

- Minimize the number of rows affected by the trigger.

- Avoid **text**, **ntext**, and **image** columns with INSTEAD OF triggers because the query is built on the fly. The **insert** and **delete** virtual tables will contain the data for those columns and may result in slow processing of the trigger.

- Take these actions to optimize SELECT statements in the trigger:

  - Include appropriate indexes.

  - Minimize the number of referenced tables.

  - Minimize the result set affected by the query.

- Avoid the use of cursors in triggers. Cursors can result in poor performance and are not recommended. Use rowset-based logic rather than cursors for triggers affecting multiple rows.

Scaling Out on SQL Server

This chapter addresses the different types of partitioned data in respect to partitioned views, distributed partitioned views and data dependent routing, and provides some guidelines for determining whether and how to use this technology for your application.

An application's level of throughput has a direct impact on productivity and revenue. Performance and throughput are a not only a measure of the underlying hardware platform, but a measure of the design of the application itself. After the application and the database have been carefully optimized, there are two main methods of increasing throughput: scaling up and scaling out. Scaling up is maximizing the capabilities of an existing server by adding more memory, storage capacity, and processors or replacing these existing components with newer, faster versions. The best approach is to explore all options for scaling up to see how they can be best utilized for your particular system.

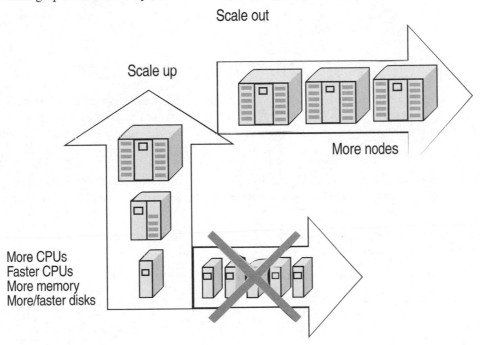

Scaling out is adding additional servers can provide increased scalability. When the server for a particular application is at its maximum potential, and is no longer able to meet user demands, you should consider scaling out. In Microsoft® SQL Server™ 2000, scaling out is both a hardware solution and a data storage solution; the data itself is partitioned over multiple servers. New features in SQL Server 2000 simplify administration of partitioned data.

The servers containing the partitioned data are sometimes known as a federation, if certain distributed data techniques are used. Each server in the scale-out scenario is administered independently, but share part of the processing load. This chapter details different types of data partitioning and how and when to implement it. This high-end architecture is intended for customers who need to implement very high volume OLTP workloads. For more information, see "Designing Applications to Use Federated Database Servers" in SQL Server Books Online.

SQL Server 2000 delivers impressive performance when the application is optimized and the hardware is scaled up to the appropriate level. But, in situations where a fully optimized database and application support a database load beyond the reasonable expectations of a single server, scaling out can help. By scaling out using SQL Server 2000, you can support the tremendous processing loads and growth requirements of the largest Web or enterprise systems.

Readiness Checklists

This section provides some checklists to help you ensure you have considered the important issues involved in choosing to scale out your system.

Are You Ready to Scale Out on SQL Server?

The following checklist will help you determine whether scaling out is a viable approach for your application. All of the following questions, which are focused on an existing application, should be resolved before you begin to design a scaled-out enterprise:

- Are the queries optimized and tuned?

- Does each table have indexes that are appropriately designed and maintained, to optimize performance? Are **auto create statistics** and **auto update statistics** options turned on to keep up with changing usage patterns in the database?

- Is the schema appropriate? Is the level of normalization adjusted for the usage of the table (normalized for writes, denormalized for reads)?

- Have all stored procedures and functions been optimized?

- Has application logic been streamlined? Have all blocking issues been eliminated?

- Is the hardware scaled appropriately for the application? If the hardware is already being pushed to the limit, have processors, memory, or disk storage (spindles) been added?

- Is the physical layout (that is, where the database files are placed) of the database storage components optimal?

These are the things you should consider when you design a new application. The advantage with a new system is that it is easier to start out designing for partitioning than it is to design a partitioned/distributed solution for an existing application. But in either case, care should be taken to make the application take maximum advantage of good design principles to obtain the best performance and scalability. Be sure to consider how you will maintain the system, with an eye toward high availability and ease of administration considerations.

For more information, see Chapter 16, "Five Nines: The Ultimate in High Availability," and Chapter 33, "The Data Tier: An Approach to Database Optimization."

Scaling up is the first approach you should consider. For most applications, scaling up provides higher performance for the same cost than scaling out on the same level of hardware. There are some unusual cases; for example, some applications are naturally partitionable based on application requirements, and so might benefit from the inclusion of the scale-out design concepts. With the understanding that there are very few exceptions, scaling out should be the final consideration. Scaling out provides scalability for a system where throughput is a higher requirement than providing the highest speed for each individual transaction.

Scaling out provides the best value on larger servers; there is little advantage in scaling out on small servers. Because distributed database management requires much higher administrative overhead, the smaller benefits of running on a higher number of smaller computers may not be worth the administrative cost. Because the primary focus of throughput for scaling out is based on processing power (CPU), smaller servers do not provide much gain. It is better to reserve this design for systems that need it (for example, for geographical considerations), and for shops that are willing to commit to the extra expense in higher-level hardware and administration for the purpose of scalability.

Design Considerations

After you have fully optimized your application, database design, and layout, and you have scaled up to the largest feasible server configuration, you may determine that your scalability requirements can be met by scaling up rather than by scaling out. If you decide that your application is a good candidate for scaling out, here are some more things to consider.

Designing a scale-out solution of any type requires analysis and careful planning. There are several techniques that can be applied to designing for scale out:

- Distributed partitioned views

- Data-dependent routing

- Replication

- Message Queuing

- A combination of these

Although these techniques can be combined in many different ways, depending on your requirements, the classic federated server scenario combines the use of distributed partitioned views with data-dependent routing, usually with some form of replication. This solution is the focus of this chapter.

The following list provides some initial design considerations, which can also be used to determine how much your system might benefit from scaling out, whether it is a current system, a new one, or one being migrated from another database platform.

- Are you trying to support a high volume of concurrent transactions? The decision to scale out is most often driven by the need to support a database load that exceeds the capacity of a large multiprocessor server. The transaction volume is not directly the issue, but rather the overall load on the DBMS.

  Concurrency issues are frequently based on application design problems, but can also be based on disk I/O limitations, a problem that can be addressed by adding more physical disks, by using filegroups, or by significantly increasing the amount of memory to reduce physical I/O with a larger cache. Because applying standard solutions can increase concurrency, this issue alone does not make your system a candidate for a federated scenario.

  The key factor is the processing capacity requirements. The primary reason for scaling out is that your requirement exceeds the processor capacity of the largest SMP hardware available.

- Is transaction throughput more important than the precise speed of each individual query? This question will become important if your application frequently requires data from a partition on a remote server. How often do you need to retrieve remote data? The fewer calls that must be made to remote servers to accumulate all the data to satisfy the request, the better performance will be.

  The more frequently you collect remote data for the total result set, the more of a performance issue this will become. This is less of a concern; however, for a query that is used occasionally, or in cases where the query can be directed to the server containing the majority of the data related to that result set. For example, if a set of information is frequently queried, you should try to organize the data and queries so the queries run on the same node as the data.

- Can you store related partitioned data together on one server in the federation (known as *collocating* the data), and then direct the incoming query to the server that has that data? A key consideration for scaling out is considering how the data will be organized, and how data access will occur, along slices of the database.

  The locality of the data, which is the measure of how much of a query can be completed with local data rather than remote data, is a performance consideration. If you have a high degree of data locality, you will get better performance. How much data needs to move between servers?

  The amount of data being exchanged between servers should also be considered (you can get this number by multiplying bytes per row by number of rows). If you frequently transfer a large amount of data, approaching thousands of kilobytes per rowset, this performance consideration should influence your design. In this case, look for a more optimal way of partitioning your data, or a better way to handle data access.

Like everything else in the database, it all depends on usage. For queries that are used frequently, examine the data involved and do some quick calculations on how often these are executed compared to how much data is requested. If you cannot collocate related data, calculate the amount of data you expect to be requested from remote servers. If the rowsets involved are large, approaching thousands of kilobytes, and the frequency of the requests is high, consider organizing the data differently. If the rowsets are large, but the query will only be run occasionally, then this might also provide acceptable performance for the system as a whole.

- How large is the data involved? It is easy to assume you should simply partition your largest tables. Companies considering this scenario often have large tables: for example, more than one billion narrow rows or more than 20 million wide rows (more than 5 KB). However, if you are using partitioning as part of a scale-out solution, you should partition based on data access patterns rather than just choosing the largest tables (even if they are in the terabyte range). Some partitionable tables are apt to grow large, but size alone should not be the deciding factor.

Data size also relates to the amount of data exchanged between servers. While large volumes could become an issue in extreme cases, the linked server connection can easily support exchanges of hundreds or thousands of rows per transaction, depending on the byte size of the rows in question. The exchange of large volumes of data becomes a problem only if the volume of remote traffic degrades response time to an unacceptable level.

Understanding the Federation

Distributed partitioned views in SQL Server 2000 are only a first step toward the shared-nothing clustering used in clustered business services environments. When considering partitioned views for your environment, make sure you understand what you are undertaking:

- By using distributed partitioning correctly, with an eye to maintenance, administration and usage, for an application that is a good candidate for this solution, you can achieve a linear increase in scalability. This is something to consider if you have scaled up completely on one server to the maximum feasible capacity (that is, a maximized 8-way). The trade off in this scenario is that you are increasing the maximum throughput your system can accommodate, and the price is that each individual transaction will take a little longer to complete.

- The idea with scale-out is not that response time improves for each individual query (in fact, it typically goes down), but rather that you can ultimately perform more transactions because of more total hardware capacity. For example, imagine that a single 8-way symmetric multiprocessing (SMP) server can perform 100 transactions per second on a particular workload. With distributed partitioned views, the rate might drop to 50 transactions per second, but you would be able to add more and more hardware. Four servers could do 200 transactions per second, which is twice the capacity of the original SMP. It is easy to see how this could scale to meet a large workload: Scaling out provides you with a way to apply more processing power to meet your system requirements.

- All servers in a given distributed partitioned view must be available for that distributed partitioned view to be usable. There is no built-in failure tolerance. If one server is down, the view cannot access data from any of the member tables even if the queries do not need data from the unavailable node. Therefore, you should consider using a failover cluster, grouping servers in sets of four for maximum hardware advantage. This will minimize the amount of time that the system is unavailable in the event of a hardware failure.

- SQL Server 2000 does not support the process load balancing available through Microsoft Windows 2000 COM+ components. When distributed partitioned views are used across a group of servers, each server operates autonomously with separate operational rules supporting independent processes and data.

- You will need at least three servers in your federation to see a benefit in increased throughput versus the reduced response time. It is possible to have fewer than three servers, but the cost will outweigh the benefits. Distributed servers work best with a Storage Area Network between servers.

- Each server must be maintained independently. There are currently no management tools to allow unified administration of the federated servers or to automate repartitioning of views. There is no easy way to repartition the data without interrupting service of the distributed partitioned view (note that data-dependent routing might still work while the distributed partitioned view is unavailable, provided you have planned your design with that in mind).

- You must plan ahead for how you will support a scale-out solution. Partitioned views add significant operational and administrative overhead, even where maintenance is automated.

- Disaster recovery plans are far more complex where partitioned data is involved. For more information, see "Disaster Recovery and Partitioning" in this chapter.

Data Partitioning Components

Now that you have examined your application for the possibility of optimization and scale-up, and you have looked at the design considerations, you should know how good a candidate your system is for scaling out. Most scaled-out systems rely on some form of data partitioning, so your next step is to begin planning your partitions from a design and administrative perspective.

SQL Server uses partitioned views to facilitate access to partitioned data. A federation is created when data is partitioned and distributed across servers by using a distributed partitioned view. This feature involves creating a view across multiple tables of identical physical structure in order to treat all of them as one entity. There are several different ways to partition data. Some common uses of application data partitioning include dividing data by geographical region or by time perspective on the data. This is a natural type of partitioning. Data partitions similar to this have been used for many years in application design. The advent of distributed partitioned view technology in SQL Server facilitates dividing data by usage, in addition to other reasons for partitioning. For example, you could divide a **Customer** table into sections to balance out the number of hits to each section. If you are approaching this from the server only, a simple distributed partitioned view functions exactly like the original table, so that the front-end application code does not need to be changed. If you are designing (or redesigning) an application, you can optimize by using data-dependent routing in addition to distributed partitioned views.

The best situation is when you can partition the data symmetrically. This means that, in addition to having a distributed partitioned view and a member table on each server in the federation, you also have a related set of tables containing only data related to the primary partition. When a query comes in from the application, you can use data-dependent routing to send this query to the server containing most of the data for that result set. A good test of whether this can be achieved is to see whether the partition allows all rows to be placed on the same member server as all their referencing foreign key rows. Database designs that support this goal are the best candidates for partitioning.

It would be an unusual application that contained only tables that could be partitioned easily. Most applications have look-up tables, which do not need to be, and often cannot be, usefully partitioned. These can be copied (using replication or INSTEAD OF triggers) between servers.

Partitioned views can be either read-only or updatable. A read-only partitioned view is similar to a copy of the member tables and is useful when accessing historical or other data that is read only, such as catalog information for an e-commerce site. An updatable partitioned view can exhibit all the capabilities of a single table.

Partitioned views are further categorized as either local or distributed. Local partitioning is geared toward midsize systems; distributed partitioning is for enterprise-level systems. A local partitioned view resides with the member tables on a single instance of SQL Server on a single server. Within that instance, member tables can reside in a single database or multiple databases. In the case of multiple databases, the partitioned view resides in each database. In the following illustration, the partitioned view and tables are implemented in a single server.

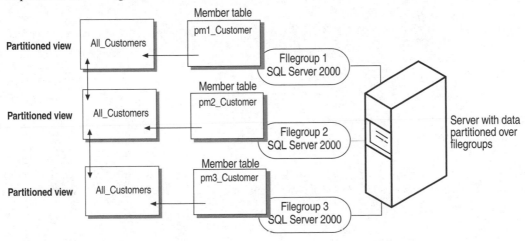

The typical use for partitioning within the same database include facilitating occasional querying of data divided into historical or other natural partitions. The benefits to doing this are mainly administrative. For example, running maintenance or optimization procedures against each partition table simultaneously reduces the amount of time these procedures will take to run. However, this adds a layer of complexity to administration, and this complexity will increase if you partition over filegroups or databases. If you are interested in using partitioned views for this purpose, give careful consideration to how much usage each member table will receive, as well as maintenance issues that may become relevant.

If you are attempting to alleviate disk contention, the best approach is to solve this as a standard disk I/O problem. Partitioning data on the same server does not provide noticeable performance gains, and most likely you would be better served to use a single table with good indexes that contain all the data.

A distributed partitioned view has several implementation options. The standard implementation is to use every server in the federation in the same manner. This involves partitioning data across all the servers and putting a distributed partitioned view on each server, so each server can be queried by the application, and provide the same result. You would not partition every table in your database, just those whose usage is appropriate for partitioning.

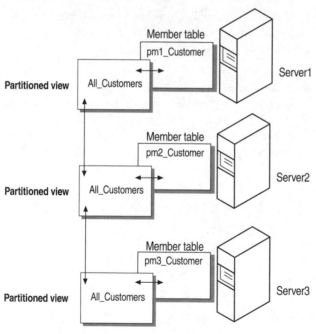

When you are designing partitioned views for a distributed environment, carefully consider how the data will be routed to the member tables. The most important goal is to minimize the processing done on each server to return the requested data, ensuring reasonable performance in such a system. You should be able to collocate related data on the same member server, and then route each SQL statement to a member server that contains most, if not all, of the data required to process the statement. Examining the WHERE clause of the queries is also a good way of determining what data should be collocated.

For example, you may find that all the sales, customer, sales representative, and inventory tables in a database can be partitioned by sales region, and that most SQL statements only reference data in a single region. You can then create member servers where each server has the horizontally partitioned data for one or more regions. The partitioned view will submit any generated SQL statement only to the member server containing the data for that region. The only SQL statements that will generate distributed queries are those that reference data from multiple regions.

Careful design of the partitioned data is the most time consuming element in creating partitioned views. It is important to remember that distributed partitioning is all related to data usage. The steps to create the member tables and partitioned views are straightforward:

1. Create and populate the member tables on the appropriate member servers.

2. Add linked server definitions on each member server (for distributed partitions only).

3. Set the lazy schema validation option on each member server (for distributed partitions only).

4. Create the distributed partitioned view on each member server.

How Partitioned Views Work

SQL Server has enhancements to optimize support of distributed partitioned views. Improvements to the query processor to better use OLE DB between linked servers significantly increases access speed to remote data. As queries are run against each partition for the first time, execution plans related to each partition are stored for reuse. If the execution plans remain in the cache and there have been no schema changes, the optimized plans will be reused to eliminate needless trips to remote servers. In addition, if lazy schema validation is enabled, schema validation for remote partitions occurs only when there is a need to access them.

Another enhancement, function shipping, is an improvement to the way the SQL Server works. Function shipping allows requests to be passed to the remote servers, so the function is shipped, rather than the data. The goal with function shipping is that fewer rows are shipped over the wire. It is not specific to distributed partitioned views, although it benefits queries of partitioned data. Function shipping minimizes the amount of data transferred between the remote servers. This effect cannot be planned, but it is intrinsic to the way the engines work. Certain queries will still invoke data shipping, which is slower; mainly this would be queries that require that all the data be on the calling server before the result set can be processed to provide the answer the user wanted. The result of this is that it will minimize the amount of distributed data that is transferred between servers, while the partition-aware execution plans allow a larger set of queries to benefit from the improved performance gains of partitioned views.

Creating Partitioned Views

Partitioned views are created by horizontally dividing a table into many smaller member tables and then overlaying those smaller tables with a partitioned view that merges all the data so the table divisions are transparent to the end user or application. Whether the view is really made up of one or ten tables, it looks and acts like one entity. Each member table must have an identical schema, with one difference: A CHECK constraint on the partitioning column limits the range of the data for that particular member table. When you are creating partitioned views, consider the following:

- The servers participating in a distributed partitioned view must all use SQL Server 2000. The reason for this is the schema validation. The table structures must be identical in every way (including collation) except for the check constraint on the partitioning column.

- You can modify data through a partitioned view only if it runs under SQL Server 2000 Enterprise Edition or SQL Server 2000 Developer Edition.

- Member tables updated through the partitioned view must not contain triggers or cascading actions.

For example, this illustration shows a **Customer** table segmented into three member tables using the **CustomerID** column as the partitioning column.

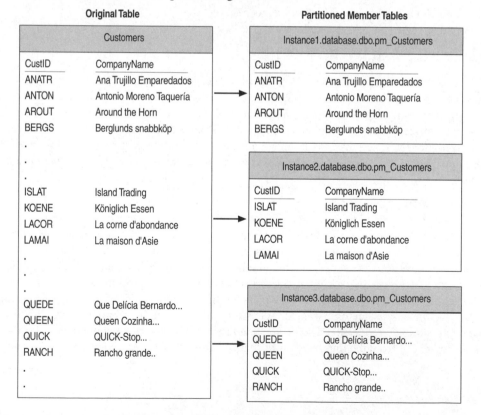

The following Transact-SQL example creates the member table for all customers with a customer ID between 'AAAAA' and 'HZZZZ'. The constraint on the **CustomerID** column identifies it as the partitioning column. In our examples here, the prefix 'pm' stands for partition member. Avoid naming your partitions after the range of data they contain. Because partition members in a distributed partitioned view are located on different computers, in most cases you should avoid numbering your partition member tables. Consistently using standard four-part naming will make your code more portable; the table names would be the same everywhere, distinguished by their explicit four-part name: server.database.owner.table.

```
CREATE TABLE pm_Customers (
CustomerID   char(05)PRIMARY KEY NOT NULL
CONSTRAINT CustRange1 CHECK (CustomerID BETWEEN 'AAAAA' AND 'HZZZZ'),
-- This constraint creates the partitioning column
CompanyName varchar(40) NOT NULL,
Address   varchar(60),
City   varchar(15),
Region varchar(15),
PostalCode   varchar(10),
Country   varchar(15) )
```

Regardless of the physical placement of the member tables in data storage, the partitioned view provides seamless integration of data access to all the member tables. The syntax for creating the view uses the UNION ALL operator to combine the member tables, as shown in the following example:

```
CREATE VIEW Customers AS
SELECT * FROM LinkedServer1.Northwind.dbo.pm_Customers
UNION ALL
SELECT * FROM LinkedServer2.Northwind.dbo.pm_Customers
UNION ALL
SELECT * FROM LinkedServer3.Northwind.dbo.pm_Customers
```

For more information about setting up partitioned views, see "Creating a Partitioned View" in SQL Server Books Online.

Partitioned Query Plans

Based on the query and the constraints, redundant partitions are discarded at compile time if possible or at run time with a mechanism called *startup filters* or *dynamic filters*. A startup filter is a condition on the parameters in the query that indicates if the partition needs to be accessed. The cost of evaluating a startup filter locally is dramatically lower than going to a remote server, executing a query and then discovering that no rows qualify.

To see your partitioned query running, examine a showplan output showing startup filter plans. You will see that all the partitions are acknowledged in the plan, but the startup filter registers the range of values that are available per partition. You can use **set statistics io on** and **set statistics showplan on** for more complete information.

```
CREATE TABLE T1(I INT PRIMARY KEY CHECK (I < 0))
CREATE TABLE T2(I INT PRIMARY KEY CHECK (I >= 0))

CREATE VIEW V AS
   SELECT * FROM T1
   UNION ALL
   SELECT * FROM T2

CREATE PROC P @P INT = NULL AS SELECT * FROM V WHERE I = @P
```

When you query the table, you get the showplan output below. When the query runs, the startup expressions prune redundant partitions dynamically. When the key values are not known at the time the plan is built, SQL Server builds an execution plan with conditional logic to control which member tables is accessed. This execution plan that has startup filters: conditional logic that controls which member table is accessed based on the input parameter value. You will see in the graphical query analyzer view that all of the remote partitions are acknowledged in the display. At runtime, the unnecessary partitions will be pruned from the execution plan, based on the parameter supplied, and in the statistics profile you will see that only one partition is actually queried.

```
SET STATISTICS IO ON
SET STATISTICS PROFILE ON

EXEC P
```

STATISTICS IO shows that neither table was scanned, as no parameter was supplied:

```
Table 't2'. Scan count 0, logical reads 0, physical reads 0, read-ahead reads 0.
Table 't1'. Scan count 0, logical reads 0, physical reads 0, read-ahead reads 0.
```

STATISTICS PROFILE shows the same, with more detail. Notice the Startup Expr on the filter:

Executes	StmtText
1	select * from v where i = @p
1	|--Concatenation
1	|--Filter(WHERE:(STARTUP EXPR([@p]<0)))
0 <	| |--Clustered Index Seek(OBJECT:([t1].[PK1]), SEEK:([t1].[i]=[@p]) ORDERED FORWARD)
1	|--Filter(WHERE:(STARTUP EXPR([@p]>=0)))
0 <	|--Clustered Index Seek(OBJECT:([t2].[PK2]), SEEK:([t2].[i]=[@p]) ORDERED FORWARD)

```
EXEC P 1
```

STATISTICS IO shows that table **t2** was scanned, based on the parameter supplied, this was the correct partition for it to scan.

```
Table 't2'. Scan count 1, logical reads 0, physical reads 0, read-ahead reads 0.
Table 't1'. Scan count 0, logical reads 0, physical reads 0, read-ahead reads 0.
```

Statistics profile now shows that table **t2** had an execute performed against it.

Executes	StmtText
1	select * from v where i = @p
1	|--Concatenation
1	|--Filter(WHERE:(STARTUP EXPR([@p]<0)))
0 <	| |--Clustered Index Seek(OBJECT:([t1].[PK1]), SEEK:([t1].[i]=[@p]) ORDERED FORWARD)
1	|--Filter(WHERE:(STARTUP EXPR([@p]>=0)))
1 <	|--Clustered Index Seek(OBJECT:([t2].[PK2]), SEEK:([t2].[i]=[@p]) ORDERED FORWARD

An important part of preparing to partition data involves analyzing the queries and execution plans. A good practice would be to add some audit code to your queries, or run SQL Profiler to establish baseline information on the specific queries used, the data they access and how often. This information will provide valuable insights on the best possibilities for distributing your data.

Data-Dependent Routing

There are two main ways to access partitioned data. One is by partitioned views. Another method, which can be used instead of partitioned views or in combination with them, is data-dependent routing. This method uses code to determine where the target data is located, and routes connections to the appropriate server.

The goal of partitioning is to distribute the workload among physical resources: disks or servers. As with any other type of system, application design is the most influential part of performance. To optimize performance, simplify and reduce distributed processing; eliminate all unnecessary round trips to remote servers.

Data-dependent routing is an application-based approach. How the data is laid out is no different than with distributed partitioned view. In data-dependent routing, which can be used for more situations than just federated servers, the information on how to go after the data is made available to the application. Data-dependent routing does not use the linked server connections, instead sending the data requests directly to the appropriate server. For this to be most effective, the databases containing the partitioned table should be identical in terms of name and structure.

The standard federated server design uses both distributed partitioned views and data-dependent routing, in order to take full advantage of all possible performance opportunities. A simple way to do this is to create a routing table that contains the information on which server has the data the application is requesting. Deciding where to put the routing table is important. For ease of administration, you can put the table in SQL Server. In SQL Server, it can be updated easily and as often as it needs to be. However, you should not query this table every time you indicate which partition has the data you need in it. The data should be cached in the application layer using a method such as data caching on Microsoft Internet Information Services (IIS).

Putting the table in a COM+ object within the code is another possibility, but the tradeoff comes in when it needs to be updated. Updating the table requires the code itself to be updated and recompiled. You can also store the table in a registry setting or text file. Instead of using a routing table, you could choose to use a custom hashing algorithm based on the partitioning column to send the data to the correct partition or server. This facilitates repartitioning because you can alter the algorithm to change the number of partitions. Determine which method will allow you to manage the data partitions, which is done by moving the data around to balance usage..

An example of a data-dependent routing solution is included on the *SQL Server 2000 Resource Kit* CD-ROM, in the folder \ToolsAndSamples\FederatedToolKitSamples.

Other Options

The following other options can be used, as part of a standard federated configuration, to achieve partitioning with SQL Server.

Replication

If data is read-only, replication may be a strong candidate. This is especially helpful in an environment such as an e-commerce Web site, where it could be used for catalog information or environments that report or use the same data, but have network latency (for example, Tokyo accessing a New York server).

Adding a Unique Column

Instead of looking to partition the data to other servers, or even to multiple databases in one instance of SQL Server, you can add a column with a unique value that could be queried on. This may also require minimal code changes to the application. An example is adding a **state_id** column to a sales receipt table. This would allow an application to grab the right state data easily. Later, if the table gets too large, this modification will make true partitioning easy.

INSTEAD OF Trigger

If a view is not a partitioned view (one that does not follow the guidelines outlined in this chapter), it can be made updatable by using an INSTEAD OF trigger. The query optimizer may not always be able to build execution plans for a view utilizing an INSTEAD OF trigger that are as efficient as the plans for a true partitioned view.

Administration Considerations

Partition Maintenance

Successfully partitioning a large existing system usually requires a series of iterative improvements. The tables chosen for partitioning in each step are usually those that will give the highest performance gain at that time. Data usage shifts over time, so in order to remain effective, partitions will occasionally need to be adjusted.

Balancing the load among the tables, or repartitioning, can be challenging. Currently, there is not an automated method to do this. If you have made a miscalculation in planning your partitions, you may decide to repartition an entire table. For example, if you partition your order table by a sequential order number, you will find that the last partition in the group not only grows largest, but also is queried most frequently. If instead you partition by geographical region, you still may find that one area grows faster or is queried much more frequently. In either case, you will need to rebalance the load by moving some of this data around. This will be less disruptive if you do it more frequently, moving smaller amounts of data.

The most straightforward way to do this is to disable the relevant constraint temporarily while you shift the data between partitions, and then re-create the constraint when you are finished. If your application is able to use data-dependent routing exclusively, at least for the duration of the partition adjustment, you may not have much downtime. You should shift the data around first, update your routing table, update any data-dependent routing-related or COM objects that contain partition-specific information, refresh any caching of the data-dependent routing information, and finally, delete the rows that should no longer be in a particular partition because they have been moved to a better location.

If you add a new partition, you will have much the same type of work to perform, in addition to altering any distributed partitioned view or other SQL procedures, functions, or tasks (especially backup tasks) that need to be aware of the new partition.

Other than the maintenance of the partition, it is good to keep in mind that partitioned tables are just like any other table. Each server and database in a federation must be separately maintained. They still need index maintenance, and they still need to be backed up. Occasionally, you may want to run DBCC checks in order to be as thorough with maintenance as possible. One advantage to maintenance in a federation is that because each partition is an independent database and maintenance is run separately on each, you can run maintenance on all partitions at the same time. Each partition would also benefit from parallel processing during DBCC and index builds, a feature of SQL Server 2000 Enterprise Edition.

Disaster Recovery and Partitioning

The following sections provide tips on creating an optimal backup and restore strategy for partitioned databases.

Backing Up and Restoring Partitioned Databases

SQL Server 2000 does not require you to coordinate backups across member servers. If you do not require transactional consistency between member servers, backups can be taken of each database independently, without regard for the state of the other member databases. With this method, overhead for synchronization is minimized, so it has the lowest possible effect on transaction processing. Another option is to attempt to back up all databases simultaneously; however, this option is not recommended.

If transactional consistency – making sure all partitions are able to be backed up to the same point – is a requirement, you can achieve this in SQL Server 2000 by using named marks in the transaction log. This special mark allows the restore of a database to a named point, and with partitioned views, they enable all databases with member tables to be synchronized to the same point. This requires that the recovery mode be set to Full for each database that is part of the partition.

During backup and restore operations, distributed partitioned views and data-dependent routing partitioned databases must remain synchronized. Because data-dependent routing is essentially code-controlled partitioning, you can employ methods such as marked backups. To stay transactionally current and avoid transaction loss, you can use coding or middle-tier technology.

Data-dependent routing can also take advantage of log marks. However, unlike partitioned views, data can get out of synchronization because each server is independent from each other from a partitioned standpoint. This means that each server is theoretically only linked in the application code, even if the servers are linked to put the mark in the transaction log.

To restore a partitioned database that uses data-dependent routing, roll each database back to the damaged server's last known good mark to ensure that all servers are synchronized. Rolling back can result in lost transactions. This may be handled with another technology, such as Message Queuing or Microsoft Component Services, or with code that uses XML to store the transaction state. If you choose one of these technologies, test carefully before relying on it to recover lost data.

For more information about marking transactions, see the topics "Backup and Recovery of Related Databases" and "Recovering to a Named Transaction" in SQL Server Books Online.

High Availability

Your data is now partitioned, but what happens if one server goes down? If you are using partitioned views, the entire view will become unavailable if the execution plan is not in the cache.

If you are using data-dependent routing, only the data on that one server will become unavailable. This also presents other challenges: If one server fails, and the other servers that are part of the partition are up and being added to, the data set gets out of sync, especially if the data on each server is necessary. For example, if a database partitioned over three servers is accessed only by data-dependent routing, these are essentially three separate databases. If the application inserts records into B and C, but not matching records into A, the application needs to be aware that A has gone down, and account for that. In a partitioned view, this is not as much of a concern.

There are two high-availability methods that compliment partitioning: failover clustering and log shipping. For the first option, each server would need to be part of a failover cluster. If your database is partitioned across three virtual servers, the best solution would be a minimum of four servers to create the N+1 scenario using Windows 2000 Datacenter, which is described in Chapter 12, "Failover Clustering." Another option would be to have each instance be a separate virtual server on a dedicated SQL Server failover cluster. So if you have three database partitions, you would need six servers to make three independent failover clusters.

In conjunction with or in place of failover clustering, you can use log shipping to create a warm standby server. This can be one server to host all the partitioned databases (unless your databases do not have unique names), or a 1:1 ratio for partitioned server to log shipped server.

For more information about creating a highly available server, consult Chapter 16, "Five Nines: The Ultimate in High Availability." For more information about optimizing the database as a whole, see Chapter 33, "The Data Tier: An Approach to Database Optimization."

CD-ROM Content

Tools, Samples, eBooks, and More

This chapter describes the contents of the CD that accompanies the *Microsoft SQL Server 2000 Resource Kit*, which includes an electronic version of the printed book, several files of information in eBook format, an electronic version of the popular Microsoft SQL Server 2000 System Tables Map, and a number of tools and samples.

Electronic Version of the Resource Kit Book

An electronic version of the *Microsoft SQL Server 2000 Resource Kit* printed book is available on the CD in the file Sqlrk.chm, located in the \Docs folder. You can view this file by double-clicking the file name.

eBooks

Six files available on the CD have been prepared in eBook format for viewing on a personal or laptop computer, or a Pocket PC device using Microsoft® Reader with ClearType™ technology. Microsoft Reader for personal computers and laptops can be downloaded from http://www.microsoft.com/reader/. Microsoft Reader is available on Pocket PC devices manufactured by Hewlett-Packard, Casio, and Compaq. The eBook files are located in the \Docs\eBooks folder on the CD, and contain information from this resource kit and from SQL Server Books Online.

These are the eBook files and their contents:

File	Contents
Whatsnew.lit	The "What's New in SQL Server 2000" section of SQL Server Books Online
Architec.lit	The "SQL Server Architecture" section of SQL Server Books Online
Replsql.lit	The "SQL Server Replication" section of SQL Server Books Online
Security.lit	The "Managing SQL Server Security" section of SQL Server Books Online
Dwdesign.lit	The "Data Warehouse Design Considerations" chapter in this Resource Kit
Indxview.lit	The "Using Views with a View on Performance" chapter in this Resource Kit

For more information about installing and using these files, see Readme.txt on the CD.

Content in the eBook files differs from how it appears in SQL Server Books Online and the *Microsoft SQL Server 2000 Resource Kit* due to limitations in the Reader format for the handheld devices. The limitations are:

- Link functionality is not available in eBook format. Therefore, in the eBook files that contain sections from SQL Server Books Online, all See Also links have been removed. In addition, remaining links in these files may not be available, as some links reference sections of SQL Server Books Online that are not included on this CD. To view these links, see SQL Server Books Online.

  Note You can access URLs in both SQL Server Books Online and the online version of the *Microsoft SQL Server 2000 Resource Kit.*

- All tables have been converted to lists.

- All of the illustrations have been removed. To view illustrations, see SQL Server Books Online or the print or electronic version of the *Microsoft SQL Server 2000 Resource Kit.*

System Table Map

The printed SQL Server 2000 System Table Map has been a very popular tool for database administrators, programmers, and other professionals working with SQL Server 2000. The Online System Table Map incorporates the benefits of the visual representation of table relationships from the printed version of the map with the same level of technical detail found in the system table topics in the Transact-SQL Reference.

The Online System Table Map supplies a visual representation of the relationships between tables, similar to that found in the printed version of the map. Selecting a specific table in the online map displays a topic with all of the information from the Transact-SQL Reference topic documenting the table. The See Also section in each topic has links to all tables related to the table you are currently viewing, allowing you to easily move between related tables. The Online System Table Map file, Systbl.chm, is located in the \Docs folder on the CD. You can view this file by double-clicking the file name.

The SQL Server 2000 System Table Map is 27 inches by 34 inches and printed in color. You can order the SQL Server 2000 SystemTable Map at http://mssqlserver.e-storefront.com/.

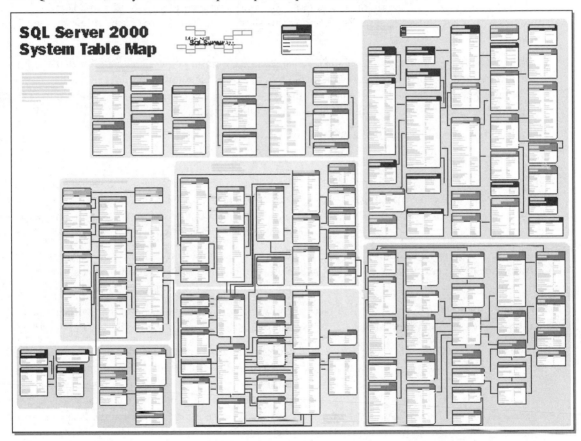

Tools and Samples

The tools and samples listed below are available on the CD to help you more effectively use, manage, and develop applications for Microsoft SQL Server™ 2000.

Detailed information about these items can be found in the file Sqlrktls.chm in the \ToolsAndSamples folder on the CD. (An additional copy of this file also located in the \Docs folder on the CD.)

Tools and samples are located on the CD in the ToolsAndSamples folder. A short name is provided in parentheses for each tool or sample listed below; this short name is the name of the folder on the CD that contains the item.

> **Note** If a chapter in the book contains extensive code example listings, the code for that chapter is also contained in a text file, located on the CD, in the Docs\ChapterCode folder in a file named CHnnCode.txt, where *nn* is the number of the chapter. You can copy and paste chapter code examples from the text file without having to enter them from the keyboard.

The following tools and samples can be found on the CD:

Tool Name	Description
Microsoft Access 2000 Upgrade for SQL Server 2000 (**AccessUpsizing**)	Provides two fixes for Access 2000 so that Access 2000 can upsize an Access database (.mdb) to SQL Server 2000, and use an Access project (.adp) to create new databases against SQL Server 2000.
Administration Stored Procedures (**AdminStoredProcedures**)	User-defined stored procedures that identify SQL Server 2000 configurations with parameter settings outside of the recommended configuration.
Analysis Services Thin Web Client Browser (**AnalysisServicesThinWebClient**)	Browses an Analysis Services cube with Microsoft Internet Explorer using Active Server Pages (ASP).
Bulk Image Insert (**BII**)	Copies data between an instance of SQL Server 2000 and a data file. This utility behaves much like the **bcp** utility packaged with SQL Server 2000, except that when the input is the name of a locatable file and the destination is an image field, then the **bii** utility inserts the contents of the file into the image field.
Binary Large Objects (**BLOB**)	Demonstrates ways to read, retrieve, and save binary large objects (BLOBs) in the **Northwind** sample database using Microsoft ActiveX® Data Objects (ADO) (Microsoft Visual Basic®), OLE DB (Microsoft Visual C++®), and ODBC (Visual C++).

Continued on next page

Tool Name	Description
Catalog Explorer (**CatalogExplorer**)	Retrieves meta data relating to OLAP objects, such as cubes and dimensions, from an Analysis server using ADO and Microsoft ActiveX Data Objects (Multidimensional) (ADO MD).
Database Hammer (**DatabaseHammer**)	A customizable tool for testing your database server with various loads.
Data Mining Visual ToolKit (**DataMiningVisualToolKit**)	Displays data mining operations of the Microsoft ActiveX Data Objects Library (ADODB). Includes three ActiveX controls: the Decision Tree Viewer, the Segment Viewer (for Cluster Analysis), and the Life Chart.
Database Generator (**DBGen**)	Populates tables in databases with dummy information. You can specify the distribution of the data for each column.
Database Management (**DBManagement**)	Tools and samples for administering SQL Server databases, including Web pages to display system information, trace procedures, development procedures, administration procedures, and a customizable MMC console for managing SQL Server.
Digital Dashboard (**DigitalDashboard**)	A sample interactive digital dashboard that displays data in a SQL Server database.
Federated Toolkit Samples (**FederatedToolkitSamples**)	Demonstrates distributed partitioned views using a sample ordering application that emulates an online store with multiple worldwide ordering locations.
MetaData Dashboard (**MetaDataDashboard**)	A digital dashboard that displays Analysis Services meta data.
Meta Data Scripter (**MetaDataScripter**)	Scripts the meta data of Analysis Services objects, generating a Microsoft Visual Basic Scripting Edition (VBScript) file that uses Decision Support Objects (DSO) to re-create the objects.
Multiphase Data Pump (**MonitorDTS**)	Monitors a Data Transformation Services (DTS) Multiphase Data Pump in Visual Basic.
Desktop SQL Server Configuration Tool (**MSDEAdministrationTool**)	An administration and configuration tool that demonstrates how Access 2000 can be used to programmatically connect to and manage a SQL Server.

Continued on next page

Tool Name	Description
Northwind Cube (**NorthwindCube**)	Demonstrates the efficiency of a query that utilizes a star schema rather than a normalized OLTP schema.
OLE Database Data Mining Query (**OLEDBDMQuery**)	Demonstrates how to execute OLE DB for Data Mining queries against an Analysis Services server.
Parallel Process (**ParallelProcess**)	Processes Analysis Services cubes and partitions in parallel.
Partition Manager (**PartitionManager**)	Manages Analysis Services cube partitions.
Sample Resolver (**SampleResolver**)	Shows how an application can be used against specific events called by SQL Server and how to use methods in a DLL provided by the SQL Server Library.
Schema Rowset Explorer (**SchemaRowsetExplorer**)	Retrieves Analysis Services schema rowsets and meta data and displays the column layout and data for ADO Recordset objects.
Set Certificate (**SetCert**)	Allows you to specify which Microsoft Windows security certificate SQL Server 2000 will use to perform encryption.
Simple Log Shipper (**SimpleLogShipper**)	A simplified log-shipping tool that provides basic log-shipping functionality.
SQL DMO (**SQLDMO**)	Demonstrates how to manipulate SQL Distributed Management Objects (SQL-DMO) objects.
Stored Procedure Builder (**StoredProcBuilder**)	Manages and controls the building of SQL Server stored procedures maintained in Microsoft Visual SourceSafe™.
Transact-SQL Quick Reference (**TSQLQuickReference**)	An online quick reference of syntax differences between Transact-SQL in SQL Server 7.0 and SQL Server 2000, and of core-level syntax differences between SQL standard (SQL:1999) and SQL Server 2000.
UDF MixCase (**UDF_MixCase**)	An SQL function that converts all uppercase or lowercase strings to title case (first letter capitalized).
USP Shutdown Database (**USP_ShutdownDB**)	A procedure that terminates all open user connections to a specified SQL Server database, and optionally executes a command after it terminates the connections.

About the Authors

Dave Browning is the documentation manager for data warehousing, data analysis, and meta data technologies.

Jim Carroll is a senior consultant for Microsoft Consulting Services and specializes in data warehousing and application development with SQL Server.

Cathan Cook is a consultant for Microsoft Consulting Services in the Gulf States District and focuses on database system scalability, availability, and large-scale management.

Kevin Cox is a principal consultant for Microsoft Consulting Services in the Rocky Mountain District.

Gail Erickson is a technical writer for the SQL Server user education team.

Pete Fenton is a programmer/writer for the SQL Server user education team.

Andrea Fox is a programmer/writer for the .NET XML Framework user education team.

Allan Hirt is a consultant for Microsoft Consulting Services in the New England District. He has been working with enterprise-class database systems since the early 1990s.

Ninia Ingram is a programmer/writer for the SQL Server user education team.

Dennis Kennedy is a programmer/writer for the SQL Server user education team.

Charlie Kindschi is the documentation manager for data access and XML technologies, both COM-based (MDAC) and those managed by the .NET Framework. He is co-author of *"Building Interactive Entertainment and E-Commerce Content for Microsoft TV"* from Microsoft Press.

Michelle Larez is a technical writer for the SQL Server user education team.

Diane Larsen is a technical writer for the SQL Server user education team.

Kami LeMonds is a lead technical writer for the SQL Server user education team.

Tom Mathews is a programmer/writer for the SQL Server user education team.

John H. Miller is a product manager for SQL Server on the data warehousing and analysis practices team.

Joy Mundy is a program manager for the SQL Server data warehouse and analysis practices team.

Seth Paul is a programmer/writer for the SQL Server user education team.

Jeff Ressler is a product manager responsible for SQL Server product management and planning.

Heidi Steen is a lead technical writer for the SQL Server user education team.

LeRoy Tuttle, Jr. is a program manager for database management training for Microsoft Training and Certification.

Index

% Disk Time counter 406, 643
% Free Space counter 406
% Privileged Time counter 836
% Processor Time counter 407, 641, 836, 837
% User Time counter 836
24x7 *See high availability*
2PC *See two-phase commit*
64-GB memory support 16
80/20 Rule 953
99.*x* uptime 443

A

Access *See migrating Access databases*
accounts
    administrator account for clustering 343
    domain user accounts 296
    guest accounts 301
    guest login accounts 115
    local system accounts 295
    local user accounts 295
    login accounts 115
    Oracle migration 115
    renaming 282, 286
    service accounts 294
actions 27, 705, 783, 785
Active Server Pages 795, 863
active servers 61
ActiveX Data Objects
    Access migration 80
    Analysis Services data 801
    BLOBs 327
    meta data 791
    overview 782
ActiveX Data Objects (Multidimensional)
    Analysis Services data 801
    meta data 793
    overview 784
ActiveX scripting 663, 670
ad hoc queries 477, 510, 935
Add method 1035

adding
    attributes to data 751
    constraints 137
    dimension record 491
    fields in dimension record 492
    help text 942
    items to English Query model 949
    nodes 371
    servers for scalability 1085
    SQL Replication Conflict Resolver Library 882
    TCP/IP addresses 370
    users to server roles 265
additive measures 496
Additive Resolver 915
Address Windowing Extensions 16, 350, 453, 580
administrative tasks *See stored procedures for administrative issues*
administrator account for clustering 343
ADO
    Access migration 80
    Analysis Services data 801
    BLOBs 327
    meta data 791
    overview 782
ADO MD
    Analysis Services data 801
    meta data 793
    overview 784
affinity mask option 641, 999
AFTER triggers 14, 147, 1069
aged buffers 645
Agg Cache object 827
Aggregate function 720
aggregate functions 172, 1063
aggregation threads 812
aggregations 519, 675, 701, 728, 818, 1015
algorithm provider 754, 757–761
aliasing 293
allocated writeback 32
allocations 988
allow updates option 999
ALTER DATABASE 251

G

END-USER LICENSE AGREEMENT FOR MICROSOFT SOFTWARE

Book Companion CD

MICROSOFT SQL SERVER 2000 RESOURCE KIT

IMPORTANT-READ CAREFULLY: This Microsoft End-User License Agreement ("EULA") is a legal agreement between you (either an individual or a single entity) and Microsoft Corporation for the Microsoft software identified above, which includes computer software and may include associated media, printed materials, additional computer software applications, and "online" or electronic documentation ("SOFTWARE"). By downloading, installing, copying, or otherwise using the SOFTWARE, you agree to be bound by the terms of this EULA. If you do not agree to the terms of this EULA, do not install or use the SOFTWARE.

SOFTWARE LICENSE

The SOFTWARE is protected by copyright laws and international copyright treaties, as well as other intellectual property laws and treaties. **The SOFTWARE is licensed, not sold.**

1. **GRANT OF LICENSE.** This EULA grants you the following rights:

   a. **SOFTWARE.** Except as otherwise provided herein, you, as an individual, may install and use copies of the SOFTWARE for internal use to design, develop and test your application(s) ("Application(s)") on any number of computers, including workstations, terminals or other digital electronic devices ("COMPUTERS"), provided that you are the only individual using the SOFTWARE. If you are an entity, you may designate one individual within your organization to have the right to use the SOFTWARE in the manner provided above. The SOFTWARE is in "use" on a COMPUTER when it is loaded into temporary memory (i.e., RAM) or installed into permanent memory (e.g., hard disk, CD-ROM, or other storage device) of that COMPUTER. Microsoft further grants you, solely with respect to the file labeled "setcert.exe," a personal, non-exclusive license to make, use, and install copies of such setcert.exe file on any number of computers that are running validly licensed copies of Microsoft SQL Server 2000 for general business purposes.

   b. **General.** The SOFTWARE may comprise certain third party products licensed to Microsoft or additional Microsoft products subject to their own EULA (each, a "COMPONENT PRODUCT"). A COMPONENT PRODUCT may contain its own license agreement (each, a "COMPONENT LICENSE AGREEMENT"). In the event of inconsistencies between this EULA and any COMPONENT LICENSE AGREEMENT, the terms of the COMPONENT LICENSE AGREEMENT shall control with respect to use of the specific COMPONENT PRODUCT.

   c. **Sample Code. SOLELY WITH RESPECT TO YOUR APPLICATIONS THAT WORK IN CONJUNCTION WITH MICROSOFT SQL SERVER:** You may modify the portions of the SOFTWARE designated as "Sample Code" to design, develop and test such Applications and reproduce and distribute the Sample Code in object code form along with any modifications you make to the Sample Code, provided that you comply with the Distribution Requirements described below. For purposes of this EULA, (i) "Sample Code" means source code and related documentation and (ii) "modifications" means enhancements to the functionality of the Sample Code.

   d. **Electronic Documentation.** Except as otherwise specifically provided in connection with documentation related to Sample Code as provided in Paragraph (c) above, with respect to electronic and other documentation, you may make an unlimited number of copies (either in hard copy or electronic form) provided that such copies shall be used only for internal purposes and are not republished or distributed beyond the user's premises.

   e. **Distribution Requirements.** You may copy and redistribute the Sample Code in conjunction with Applications that work in conjunction with Microsoft SQL Server 2000 as described above, provided that you agree:

      (i) to distribute the Sample Code in object code form and only in conjunction with and as part of your Applications that adds significant and primary functionality to the Sample Code;

      (ii) to not use Microsoft's name, logo or trademarks to market your Application;

      (iii) to include a valid copyright notice in your name on your Application;

      (iv) to indemnify, hold harmless and defend Microsoft from and against any claims or lawsuits, including attorneys fees, that arise or result from the use or distribution of the your Application; and

      (v) to not permit further distribution of the Sample Code by your end users.

   f. **Reservation of Rights.** Microsoft reserves all rights not expressly granted herein.

2. **DESCRIPTION OF OTHER RIGHTS AND LIMITATIONS.**

   a. **Limitations on Reverse Engineering, Decompilation, and Disassembly.** You may not reverse engineer, decompile, or disassemble the SOFTWARE, except and only to the extent that such activity is expressly permitted by applicable law notwithstanding this limitation.

b. **Rental.** You may not rent, lease, or lend the SOFTWARE.

c. **Support Services.** Microsoft does not support the SOFTWARE, <u>however, in the event Microsoft does provide you with support services related to the SOFTWARE ("Support Services")</u>, use of <u>such</u> Support Services is governed by the Microsoft policies and programs described in the user manual, in "online" documentation, and/or in other Microsoft-provided materials. Any supplemental software code provided to you as part of the Support Services shall be considered part of the SOFTWARE and subject to the terms and conditions of this EULA. With respect to technical information you provide to Microsoft as part of the Support Services, Microsoft may use such information for its business purposes, including for product support and development. Microsoft will not utilize such technical information in a form that personally identifies you.

d. **Software Transfer.** You may permanently transfer of all of your rights under this EULA, provided you retain no copies, you transfer all of the SOFTWARE (including all component parts, the media and printed materials, any upgrades, this EULA, and, if applicable, the Certificate of Authenticity), **and** the recipient agrees to the terms of this EULA. If the SOFTWARE is an upgrade, any transfer must include all prior versions of the SOFTWARE.

e. **Termination.** Without prejudice to any other rights, Microsoft may terminate this EULA if you fail to comply with the terms and conditions of this EULA. In such event, you must destroy all copies of the SOFTWARE and all of its component parts.

3. **UPGRADES.** If the SOFTWARE is labeled as an upgrade, you must be properly licensed to use a product identified by Microsoft as being eligible for the upgrade in order to use the SOFTWARE. SOFTWARE labeled as an upgrade replaces and/or supplements the product that formed the basis for your eligibility for the upgrade. You may use the resulting upgraded product only in accordance with the terms of this EULA. If the SOFTWARE is an upgrade of a component of a package of software programs that you licensed as a single product, the SOFTWARE may be used and transferred only as part of that single product package and may not be separated for use on more than one computer.

4. **INTELLECTUAL PROPERTY RIGHTS.** All title and intellectual property rights in and to the SOFTWARE (including but not limited to any images, photographs, animations, video, audio, music, text and "applets" incorporated into the SOFTWARE), and any copies you are permitted to make herein are owned by Microsoft or its suppliers. All title and intellectual property rights in and to the content which may be accessed through use of the SOFTWARE is the property of the respective content owner and may be protected by applicable copyright or other intellectual property laws and treaties. This EULA grants you no rights to use such content. If this SOFTWARE contains documentation which is provided only in electronic form, you may print one copy of such electronic documentation. You may not copy the printed materials accompanying the SOFTWARE.

5. **U.S. GOVERNMENT LICENSE RIGHTS.** SOFTWARE provided to the U.S. Government pursuant to solicitations issued on or after December 1, 1995 is provided with the commercial license rights and restrictions described elsewhere herein. SOFTWARE provided to the U.S. Government pursuant to solicitations issued prior to December 1, 1995 is provided with "Restricted Rights" as provided for in FAR, 48 CFR 52.227-14 (JUNE 1987) or DFAR, 48 CFR 252.227-7013 (OCT 1988), as applicable.

6. **EXPORT RESTRICTIONS.** You agree that the SOFTWARE is subject to U.S. export jurisdiction. You agree to comply with all applicable international and national laws that apply to the SOFTWARE including the U.S. Export Administration Regulations, as well as end-user, end use and destination restrictions issued by the U.S. and other governments. For additional information see http://www.microsoft.com/exporting/.

7. **DISCLAIMER OF WARRANTIES. To the maximum extent permitted by applicable law, Microsoft and its suppliers provide the SOFTWARE and any (if any) Support Services *AS IS AND WITH ALL FAULTS*, and hereby disclaim all warranties and conditions, either express, implied or statutory, including, but not limited to, any (if any) implied warranties or conditions of merchantability, of fitness for a particular purpose, of lack of viruses, of accuracy or completeness of responses, of results, and of lack of negligence or lack of workmanlike effort, all with regard to the SOFTWARE, and the provision of or failure to provide Support Services. ALSO, THERE IS NO WARRANTY OR CONDITION OF TITLE, QUIET ENJOYMENT, QUIET POSSESSION, CORRESPONDENCE TO DESCRIPTION OR NON-INFRINGEMENT, WITH REGARD TO THE SOFTWARE. THE ENTIRE RISK AS TO THE QUALITY OF OR ARISING OUT OF USE OR PERFORMANCE OF THE SOFTWARE AND SUPPORT SERVICES, IF ANY, REMAINS WITH YOU.**

8. **EXCLUSION OF INCIDENTAL, CONSEQUENTIAL AND CERTAIN OTHER DAMAGES. TO THE MAXIMUM EXTENT PERMITTED BY APPLICABLE LAW, IN NO EVENT SHALL MICROSOFT OR ITS SUPPLIERS BE LIABLE FOR ANY SPECIAL, INCIDENTAL, INDIRECT, OR CONSEQUENTIAL DAMAGES WHATSOEVER (INCLUDING, BUT NOT LIMITED TO, DAMAGES FOR LOSS OF PROFITS OR CONFIDENTIAL OR OTHER INFORMATION, FOR BUSINESS INTERRUPTION, FOR PERSONAL INJURY, FOR LOSS OF PRIVACY, FOR FAILURE TO MEET ANY DUTY INCLUDING OF GOOD FAITH OR OF REASONABLE CARE, FOR NEGLIGENCE, AND FOR ANY OTHER PECUNIARY OR OTHER LOSS WHATSOEVER) ARISING OUT OF OR IN ANY WAY RELATED TO THE USE OF OR INABILITY TO USE THE SOFTWARE, THE PROVISION OF OR FAILURE TO PROVIDE SUPPORT SERVICES, OR OTHERWISE UNDER OR IN CONNECTION WITH ANY PROVISION OF THIS EULA, EVEN IN THE EVENT OF THE FAULT, TORT (INCLUDING NEGLIGENCE), STRICT LIABILITY, BREACH OF CONTRACT OR BREACH OF WARRANTY OF MICROSOFT OR ANY**

SUPPLIER, AND EVEN IF MICROSOFT OR ANY SUPPLIER HAS BEEN ADVISED OF THE POSSIBILITY OF SUCH DAMAGES.

9. **LIMITATION OF LIABILITY AND REMEDIES. Notwithstanding any damages that you might incur for any reason whatsoever (including, without limitation, all damages referenced above and all direct or general damages), the entire liability of Microsoft and any of its suppliers under any provision of this EULA and your exclusive remedy for all of the foregoing shall be limited to the greater of the amount actually paid by you for the SOFTWARE or U.S.$5.00. The foregoing limitations, exclusions and disclaimers shall apply to the maximum extent permitted by applicable law, even if any remedy fails its essential purpose.**

10. **NOTE ON JAVA SUPPORT.** THE SOFTWARE MAY CONTAIN SUPPORT FOR PROGRAMS WRITTEN IN JAVA. JAVA TECHNOLOGY IS NOT FAULT TOLERANT AND IS NOT DESIGNED, MANUFACTURED, OR INTENDED FOR USE OR RESALE AS ONLINE CONTROL EQUIPMENT IN HAZARDOUS ENVIRONMENTS REQUIRING FAIL-SAFE PERFORMANCE, SUCH AS IN THE OPERATION OF NUCLEAR FACILITIES, AIRCRAFT NAVIGATION OR COMMUNICATION SYSTEMS, AIR TRAFFIC CONTROL, DIRECT LIFE SUPPORT MACHINES, OR WEAPONS SYSTEMS, IN WHICH THE FAILURE OF JAVA TECHNOLOGY COULD LEAD DIRECTLY TO DEATH, PERSONAL INJURY, OR SEVERE PHYSICAL OR ENVIRONMENTAL DAMAGE. Sun Microsystems, Inc. has contractually obligated Microsoft to make this disclaimer.

11. **APPLICABLE LAW.** If you acquired this SOFTWARE in the United States, this EULA is governed by the laws of the State of Washington. If you acquired this SOFTWARE in Canada, unless expressly prohibited by local law, this EULA is governed by the laws in force in the Province of Ontario, Canada; and, in respect of any dispute which may arise hereunder, you consent to the jurisdiction of the federal and provincial courts sitting in Toronto, Ontario. If this SOFTWARE was acquired outside the United States, then local law may apply.

12. **ENTIRE AGREEMENT. This EULA (including any addendum or amendment to this EULA which is included with the SOFTWARE) is the entire agreement between you and Microsoft relating to the SOFTWARE and the Support Services (if any) and it supersedes all prior or contemporaneous oral or written communications, proposals and representations with respect to the SOFTWARE or any other subject matter covered by this EULA. To the extent the terms of any Microsoft policies or programs for Support Services conflict with the terms of this EULA, the terms of this EULA shall control.**

13. **QUESTIONS?** Should you have any questions concerning this EULA, or if you desire to contact Microsoft for any reason, please contact the Microsoft subsidiary serving your country, or write: Microsoft Sales Information Center, One Microsoft Way, Redmond, WA 98052-6399.

SI VOUS AVEZ ACQUIS VOTRE PRODUIT MICROSOFT AU CANADA, LA GARANTIE LIMITÉE SUIVANTE VOUS CONCERNE :

RENONCIATION AUX GARANTIES. Dans toute la mesure permise par la législation en vigueur, Microsoft et ses fournisseurs fournissent le PRODUIT LOGICIEL et tous (selon le cas) Services d'assistance TELS QUELS ET AVEC TOUS LEURS DÉFAUTS, et par les présentes excluent toute garantie ou condition, expresse ou implicite, légale ou conventionnelle, écrite ou verbale, y compris, mais sans limitation, toute (selon le cas) garantie ou condition implicite ou légale de qualité marchande, de conformité à un usage particulier, d'absence de virus, d'exactitude et d'intégralité des réponses, de résultats, d'efforts techniques et professionnels et d'absence de négligence, le tout relativement au PRODUIT LOGICIEL et à la prestation ou à la non-prestation des Services d'assistance. DE PLUS, IL N'Y A AUCUNE GARANTIE ET CONDITION DE TITRE, DE JOUISSANCE PAISIBLE, DE POSSESSION PAISIBLE, DE SIMILARITÉ À LA DESCRIPTION ET D'ABSENCE DE CONTREFAÇON RELATIVEMENT AU PRODUIT LOGICIEL. Vous supportez tous les risques découlant de l'utilisation et de la performance du PRODUIT LOGICIEL et ceux découlant des Services d'assistance (s'il y a lieu).

EXCLUSION DES DOMMAGES INDIRECTS, ACCESSOIRES ET AUTRES. Dans toute la mesure permise par la législation en vigueur, Microsoft et ses fournisseurs ne sont en aucun cas responsables de tout dommage spécial, indirect, accessoire, moral ou exemplaire quel qu'il soit (y compris, mais sans limitation, les dommages entraînés par la perte de bénéfices ou la perte d'information confidentielle ou autre, l'interruption des affaires, les préjudices corporels, la perte de confidentialité, le défaut de remplir toute obligation y compris les obligations de bonne foi et de diligence raisonnable, la négligence et toute autre perte pécuniaire ou autre perte de quelque nature que ce soit) découlant de, ou de toute autre manière lié à, l'utilisation ou l'impossibilité d'utiliser le PRODUIT LOGICIEL, la prestation ou la non-prestation des Services d'assistance ou autrement en vertu de ou relativement à toute disposition de cette convention, que ce soit en cas de faute, de délit (y compris la négligence), de responsabilité stricte, de manquement à un contrat ou de manquement à une garantie de Microsoft ou de l'un de ses fournisseurs, et ce, même si Microsoft ou l'un de ses fournisseurs a été avisé de la possibilité de tels dommages.

LIMITATION DE RESPONSABILITÉ ET RECOURS. Malgré tout dommage que vous pourriez encourir pour quelque raison que ce soit (y compris, mais sans limitation, tous les dommages mentionnés ci-dessus et tous les dommages directs et généraux), la seule responsabilité de Microsoft et de ses fournisseurs en vertu de toute disposition de cette convention et votre unique recours en regard de tout ce qui précède sont limités au plus élevé des montants suivants: soit (a) le montant que vous avez payé pour le PRODUIT LOGICIEL, soit (b) un montant équivalant à cinq dollars U.S. (5,00 $ U.S.). Les limitations, exclusions et renonciations ci-dessus s'appliquent dans toute la mesure permise par la législation en vigueur, et ce même si leur application a pour effet de priver un recours de son essence.

LÉGISLATION APPLICABLE. Sauf lorsqu'expressément prohibé par la législation locale, la présente convention est régie par les lois en vigueur dans la province d'Ontario, Canada. Pour tout différend qui pourrait découler des présentes, vous acceptez la compétence des tribunaux fédéraux et provinciaux siégeant à Toronto, Ontario.

Si vous avez des questions concernant cette convention ou si vous désirez communiquer avec Microsoft pour quelque raison que ce soit, veuillez contacter la succursale Microsoft desservant votre pays, ou écrire à: Microsoft Sales Information Center, One Microsoft Way, Redmond, Washington 98052-6399.

System Requirements

Microsoft SQL Server 2000 Evaluation Edition CD. To use the evaluation edition of the Microsoft SQL Server 2000 Enterprise Edition software included with this book, you need a computer equipped with the following minimum configuration:

- PC with an Intel Pentium or compatible 166-megahertz (MHz) or higher processor.

- Microsoft Windows 2000 Professional, Server, Advanced Server, or Datacenter operating system, or Microsoft Windows NT 4.0 Workstation, Server, or Enterprise Edition with Service Pack 5 (SP5) or later.

- 64 MB of RAM; 128 MB recommended. Additional memory may be required, depending on operating system requirements.

- 95–270 MB of hard disk space for server; 250 MB for typical installation. 50 MB for minimum installation of Analysis Services; 130 MB for typical installation. Hard disk requirements vary based on your system configuration and the applications and features you install.

- CD-ROM drive.

- VGA or higher-resolution monitor.

- Microsoft Internet Explorer 5.0 or later.

- Networking support. Windows 2000 and Windows NT 4.0 have built-in network software. Additional network software is required if you are using Banyan VINES or AppleTalk ADSP. Novell NetWare IPX/SPX client support is provided by the NWLink protocol or Windows-based networking.

- Client support. Microsoft Windows 95 is supported for client connectivity only. Windows 98, Windows Me, Windows NT Workstation 4.0, and Windows 2000 Professional have client support. UNIX, Apple Macintosh, and OS/2 require Open Database Connectivity (ODBC) client software from a third-party vendor.

Tools, Utilities, Sample Code and Electronic Books CD. To use the items on the CD:

- HTML Help (.chm) files. The viewer is built in to Windows 2000, and installed on Windows NT 4.0 by SQL Server 2000.

- eBook (.lit) files require Microsoft Reader for personal computers and laptops, which can be downloaded from http://www.microsoft.com/reader/. Pocket PC devices manufactured by Hewlett-Packard, Casio, and Compaq contain the required viewer.

- Most items in the ToolsAndSamples folder on the CD are designed for use with SQL Server 2000 Standard Edition. Some items use features available only in SQL Server 2000 Enterprise, Evaluation, or Developer Editions — the enclosed SQL Server 2000 Evaluation Edition CD can be used to examine these items if an appropriate SQL Server 2000 edition is not otherwise available. Some sample items require Microsoft Visual Basic 6.0 with SP3 or later, or Microsoft Visual C++ 6.0 with SP3 or later. Some items, such as digital dashboards and Web clients, require Microsoft Internet Information Services (IIS) and other related technologies. Detailed system requirements for each item are listed in the Tools and Samples documentation, accessible from the CD Start menu (Autorun.exe), or by opening the file \Docs\Sqlrktls.chm.

- Total disk storage requirement to install all the items from the CD is 60 MB.